Juniper SRX Series

Brad Woodberg and Rob Cameron

Beijing • Cambridge • Farnham • Köln • Sebastopol • Tokyo

Juniper SRX Series

by Brad Woodberg and Rob Cameron

Printed in the United States of America.

Published by O'Reilly Media, Inc., 1005 Gravenstein Highway North, Sebastopol, CA 95472.

O'Reilly books may be purchased for educational, business, or sales promotional use. Online editions are also available for most titles (*http://my.safaribooksonline.com*). For more information, contact our corporate/institutional sales department: 800-998-9938 or *corporate@oreilly.com*.

Editors: Mike Loukides and Meghan Blanchette
Production Editor: Rachel Steely
Copyeditor: Teresa Horton
Development Editor: Patrick Ames
Proofreader: BIM, Inc.
Indexer: Bob Pfahler
Cover Designer: Randy Comer
Interior Designer: David Futato
Illustrator: Rebecca Demarest

June 2013: First Edition

Revision History for the First Edition:

2013-06-06: First release

See *http://oreilly.com/catalog/errata.csp?isbn=9781449338961* for release details.

ISBN: 978-1-449-33896-1

[LSI]

Table of Contents

Foreword

My career in networking and system administration took me from a hobbyist and self-proclaimed accidental tourist in the field of security to someone with a focused, passionate, and all-consuming obsession. It all started with a little thing called the firewall.

Back in the late 1980s and into the early 1990s, the commercial Internet boom began and organizations rushed to connect their computing resources directly to the burgeoning collective that would ultimately become known as the World Wide Web.

As the computing assets under my watch became more exposed and interconnected—and thus potentially ubiquitously accessed—I found myself spending a lot of quality time evaluating the various emerging network firewalls of the period as a way of reducing the scope of the things I had to protect.

These firewalls came in all shapes, sizes, speeds, and architectural designs. They evolved from primitive stateless access control lists in Internet-connected routers to full-fledged proxies, circuit-level gateways, and stateful packet filters that provided more robust protocol and services support, logging, and Network Address Translation capabilities.

Each firewall platform promised a dizzying array of benefits, but given the myriad of designs, each one often forced a trade-off among isolation, usability, manageability, scalability, performance, features, and efficacy.

After a startup or two and deploying many of these firewalls, I found myself in the employ of a large networking service provider that charged me with the creation of a global managed service providing secure Internet ingress and egress to thousands of the largest companies worldwide.

The demand for expanded security services from customers was eclipsed only by the availability of Internet-connected computing resources, the proliferation of easy-to-use "security" tools, and the emergence of skilled and curious "security enthusiasts" to use them.

New classes of threats appeared, and as with any successful economic enterprise, new adversaries, tactics, and motivations emerged also. Keeping up with the velocity, variety, and volume of services, and the creative attacks that followed against the infrastructure providing them, became a challenge.

New operating systems took hold and new programming languages were invented and pressed into service quickly, as were rapidly deployed application frameworks and service delivery platforms, most of which presented a dizzying set of new attack surfaces, vulnerabilities, and risks.

The Internet arms race was officially on . . . and it's been running strong for the 20 plus years that have followed.

Ironically, if instead of 20 years ago, I began this timeline only five years ago, one would recognize much of it as the present!

The challenges we have in keeping pace with the innovation of attackers, the broad attack surface against which attacks can be launched, the availability of technology, and the skill sets and motivations of the adversaries who seek to do us harm, make it clear that our choice of security solutions is that much more important.

This book describes how to operate, deploy, and optimize a world-class security platform with capabilities that allow security professionals to more effectively defend the assets they are charged to protect.

You might have already made that choice and invested in a Juniper Networks SRX Series security solution, or perhaps you are considering doing so, possibly for some of the scenarios just I described. In either case, you will find this book absolutely invaluable.

The SRX is an instrument of supreme precision, born from the networking heritage of a company long steeped in solving the toughest problems thrown its way. It is designed as a hyperscalable and extensible security services platform that provides next-generation security capabilities as you need them.

While attacks against infrastructure continue at a ferocious pace and with dazzling effectiveness, so will we witness even more surgically targeted and extremely sophisticated application-level attacks in complement.

Designed to be as supremely competent in securing Level 2 and Level 3 connectivity, the SRX also enables intelligent application-aware capabilities for Levels 4 through 7, leveraging features such as intrusion protection services, Unified Threat Management, and the AppSecure suite for application identification, classification, enforcement, control, and protection.

The SRX is a platform that enables the best and brightest engineers to design and implement security solutions that are as capable in their networking capabilities as they are in providing airtight security with the explicit capability to provide a user experience that can bridge the gap between these two disciplines. It's a security engineer's best friend and a solution that any networking professional can easily find comfort in using.

Speaking of engineers, I have had the privilege of working with and befriending the two amazing gentlemen who have written this book. Like myself, they, too, have focused their passion, knowledge, and expertise to deliver the best security solutions money can buy, and this book will help you get the most out of your investment.

I am thrilled that Brad and Rob were kind enough to ask me to write the foreword for this invaluable resource, because were there ever a way I could thank them for the endless advice and amazing depth and breadth of knowledge regarding the capabilities of the SRX, doing so publicly and at the beginning of such an excellent resource is one of the best ways I can think of.

Thank you, Brad and Rob, for all you have done to both help create an amazing security solution for our customers and also make it easier to use. What a perfect guide to accompany an amazing security platform.

—Christofer Hoff
Chief Security Architect
Security Business Unit
Juniper Networks

Preface

Security is one of the fastest moving segments within the realm of technology. Whereas most technology is created to offer new services or products, security is created to prevent the abuse of these new products and or services. In today's world, where we are always connected in ways that have never been available to us before, the need to secure this connectivity is greater than ever.

Most of the world's pockets hold smart phones. These tiny devices contain more computing power than what was used to land people on the moon; the pocket GPS device that assists you in navigating your day is more advanced than the technology used on the *Apollo* spacecraft. That same smart phone can photograph a paper check and instantly deposit its funds to your bank account. These types of technologies were always dreamed about but now are available to almost everyone.

In this same vein, there is a humongous generation of data that is currently being created every minute of every day. More data was created within 2012 than all the other years before combined. For example, 60 hours of video are uploaded to YouTube every minute of the day. This means that there is more content uploaded to one website than you could watch within your lifetime, even if you did nothing but watch YouTube. And that's just one website and one type of media. The rapid expanse of information and data and media puts security needs at an all-time high, not only to provide security, but to provide it at higher scales and performance levels.

This scaling has happened at extremely fast rates due to the amount and the diversity of network-based applications. In the past, simple packet filters could limit the few network protocols that were being used. Only a few open ports were needed at the time. From packet filters on simple routers evolved proxy-based firewalls. These firewalls offered some of the most secure methods of securing transit data by literally controlling both sides of the transaction between the client and servers. They were able to inspect all parts of the traffic flows. However, as Internet circuits increased with available bandwidth, the maximum performance of these devices was being exceeded and a new technology was needed.

Then came the rise of stateful firewalls. Stateful firewalls were able to maintain the state of the connection and were able to allow and deny network traffic dynamically on the network. These firewalls did not need to proxy or broker the connections between the client and the servers. The stateful firewall could partially inspect the traffic and very well control which Internet Protocol (IP) addresses could contact other IPs. This is the primary technology that was used when the NetScreen ScreenOS platforms were created, and stateful monitoring could happen very effectively within these devices. However, as protocols evolved and became streamlined, more and more importance was put onto the application side of the traffic. This meant that simply inspecting the IP addresses and ports was not enough, and an additional depth of inspection was needed.

Learning from how stateful firewalls and proxy firewalls operated, a new technology called intrusion prevention systems (IPS) was created. This merged together the passive monitoring concepts from intrusion detection and the active blocking from stateful firewalls. It offered similar properties to what a proxy could do without the need to proxy all of the connections, allowing for deeper inspection of the applications but without the performance overhead of terminating two connections per session.

But all these technologies were typically done across several different types of devices. Each device had different management paradigms, different operating systems, and new behaviors for their administrators to learn. On the networking side of things, Juniper Networks had been producing the Junos operating system for more than 10 years before the SRX project. The goal was to provide the robustness of Junos and integrate these various security technologies into the platform. Juniper took its high-end custom ASICs and rock solid OS, and merged them with a new generation of high-speed network-focused processors to create the SRX. The SRX was designed to incorporate packet filtering, IPS, stateful firewalling, and future-focused hardware into a single device all running the Junos operating system. This idea was always dreamed of and called the "god box," but after 2008, you could simply call it the SRX.

Since the SRX product line was launched, new technologies have been developed, such as application firewalling that allows you to block traffic based on what protocols are being used within the connection and not just on the ports that are utilized. Because the design of the SRX was so forward thinking, it has been trivial for Juniper to add this and other new features to the SRX. Now we're at the point where the next generation of SRX hardware and features have launched to not only combat the security issues that we see today, but to ensure that the new hardware can last for at least five years. That's a herculean task in our data-filled world, but for Juniper Networks and the amazing engineering minds there, it is not so much a task; instead, it is simply what the company does.

In its first four years, the SRX has quickly become one of the most deployed products that Juniper has ever made. We have personally deployed hundreds, from retail locations to data centers. Although the hardware platforms have been stable for some time, we are now starting to see some of the first new hardware refreshes, starting with the big-iron SRX5000 Series devices, and the entire product line will soon have new hardware revisions. Again, Juniper takes a different approach by starting with extremely robust hardware and then continually adding new features to it over its life cycle, including both throughput and capacity increases within the same hardware. An example of this was the largest SRX launched with 4 million maximum sessions, and yet using the same hardware, it can now handle up to 20 million concurrent sessions. With the next generation of hardware, Juniper is starting with 60 million sessions and plans to continually increase to hundreds of millions over time.

We believe, and have witnessed, that learning the SRX is an investment that pays off for any networking professional. There are so many aspects to the capabilities of the SRX and Junos that taking the time to learn them can only benefit you—even the smallest SRX can offer IPS, application security, UTM, stateful firewalling, packet filtering, and attack screening—and each of these offers a lot of depth. Then on the networking side, even the smallest SRX offers MPLS, VPLS, OSPF, BGP, switching, and well, almost every modern networking protocol in one device. So, if your future takes you toward more of a networking focus, the SRX can help guide you down that path, too. But that is not all. There's Junos.

Junos is a FreeBSD-based operating system that contains all the familiar facilities that one would find within a Unix-like environment, including raw device control over the BSD side of the device. Junos also allows scripting tasks, so you can utilize automation all the way up to, and including, creating your own processes that can run on the platform. No matter where you want to start with Junos, it can be your best friend on a journey of learning that spans many different technologies within the Junos ecosphere. What you learn in this book can be applied to other Junos devices and other network segments.

The discussions for writing this book started in 2012, and by completion it will have taken the effort of nearly a dozen people at least a year. We wrote this book not only because we care, but also because both of us have been there. We have experienced those late-night cutovers where nothing goes right. Both of us have been placed onsite with a new product that we have never used and we had no idea how to use it. We understand your pain and what you have been through; we know what it is like to be tasked with the impossible knowing that perfection is the only acceptable outcome. We are very thankful for every copy we sell, but most important, we are thankful for every person that we help.

So how does this book differ from the previous published *Junos Security* book? Well, we took what we learned from talking to our readers and various customers after the publication of *Junos Security* and respun the book to better fit your needs. In that first book, our goal was to be hyperdetailed about all possible aspects of the SRX. Most of the focus was around the data center devices, as those had been out for the longest time.

This time around we want the book to be focused on best practices and what matters with the products in the field. Finally, *Junos Security* was written with five authors, and that's just too many cooks. This book is tightly focused because we have had the opportunity to keep a consistent tone and reading experience throughout the book.

Note that much of the content in *Junos Security* was considered too advanced, or about a feature set that is simply not commonly used, and we removed it from this book. This allows the *Junos Security* book to stand on its own for its depth and breadth, but also to be complementary to this, the newer book.

We have worked with hundreds of customers and thousands of design scenarios since *Junos Security* was published, and we have spent countless hours going into the bowels of the SRX. Now, we have come back to talk about it. This book is focused around how to get the most out of your SRX and the best ways to accomplish that: it is literally field-tested and battle hardened.

This book is focused on two aspects of the SRX: Junos and security. A good friend of ours once said that the problem with security books is that security often starts too late into the book. With that in mind, each chapter was either rewritten or retooled to focus on security. Even in cases where Junos is the topic, the goal of those sections is not only how Junos works, but how to secure it.

We also took out a lot of topics that focused only on networking. Although the SRX is an extremely capable networking device, we wanted to focus purely on security. This was one of the biggest bits of feedback that we received on the previous book. There are many other books in the Juniper Networks Technical Library from O'Reilly Media that more deeply define the networking capabilities of Junos. Throughout this book we will point you to those books, or other guides that can help out in this area, as they do much more justice on the topics than we can put into this book.

We think we have been truthful to our initial goals: update the topic, improve the focus, include the new features and capabilities, and try to answer the questions we constantly get from the field. We hope you like it.

How to Use This Book

How can you get the most out of this book? We are assuming that you have some basic networking knowledge. If you don't, that's okay, because we made an effort to write in a "fireside chat" method as if we were walking each reader personally though the material. The various configuration examples were written as if we were typing them with you in the same room. We used variations in the examples to highlight different tips and tricks for how to utilize the CLI. This should also keep the reading interesting as you go through the book. Each example has a bit of variation in it, so do look for that.

We do not expect you to have any prior firewall or SRX experience. We wrote the first five chapters so they could be read at any level. This means that even if you have no idea what an IP is, you can still follow along. Often we talk to customers who just want to learn more about the SRX but really have no interest in ever getting "hands-on" with the products, so these initial chapters are open for anyone to read. But these chapters are also valuable to the experienced administrator, as we incorporated best practices from our experiences in the field. So, although the first chapter is a very basic explanation of what the SRX is, and how it can work, it also shows the SRXs in ways in which they are actually deployed in real customer networks. This should keep the book interesting for both the novice and the advanced reader alike.

If you are not familiar with networking or Junos, here are some basic terms and concepts that you should know before you start on these pages.

OSI model
: The Open Systems Interconnection (OSI) model defines seven different layers of technology: physical, data link, network, transport, session, presentation, and application. This model allows network engineers and network vendors to easily discuss and apply technology to a specific OSI level. This segmentation lets engineers divide the overall problem of getting one application to talk to another into discrete parts and more manageable sections. Each level has certain attributes that describe it and each level interacts with its neighboring levels in a very well-defined manner. Knowledge of the layers above Layer 7 is not mandatory, but understanding that interoperability is not always about electrons and photons will help.

Switches
: These devices operate at Layer 2 of the OSI model and use logical local addressing to move frames across a network. Devices in this category include Ethernet in all it variations, VLANs, aggregates, and redundant.

Routers
: These devices operate at Layer 3 of the OSI model and connect IP subnets to each other. Routers move packets across a network in a hop-by-hop fashion.

Ethernet
: These broadcast domains connect multiple hosts together on a common infrastructure. Hosts communicate with each other using Layer 2 media access control (MAC) addresses.

IP addressing and subnetting
: Hosts using IP to communicate with each other use 32-bit addresses. Humans often use a dotted decimal format to represent this address. This address notation includes a network portion and a host portion, which is normally displayed as 192.168.1.1/24.

TCP and UDP
: These Layer 4 protocols define methods for communicating between hosts. The Transmission Control Protocol (TCP) provides for connection-oriented communications, whereas the User Datagram Protocol (UDP) uses a connectionless paradigm. Other benefits of using TCP include flow control, windowing/buffering, and explicit acknowledgments.

ICMP
: Network engineers use this protocol to troubleshoot and operate a network, as it is the core protocol used (on some platforms) by the ping and traceroute programs. In addition, the Internet Control Message Protocol (ICMP) is used to signal error and other messages between hosts in an IP-based network.

Junos CLI
: Juniper Networks routers use the Junos command-line interface (CLI), which is the primary method for configuring, managing, and troubleshooting the router. Junos documentation covers the CLI in detail, and it is freely available on the Juniper Networks website (*http://www.juniper.net*). The Juniper Day One Library (*http://www.juniper.net/books*) offers free PDF books that explore the Junos CLI step by step.

Supported Features
: Because there are many variations of platforms and releases, it would be too extensive to compile into a book. The best option is to refer to the pathfinder tool, which documents up-to-date releases with what features are supported. To view pathfinder please go to *http://pathfinder.juniper.net*. This requires a customer portal login. In pathfinder you will want to use the feature explorer to review feature limitations for transparent mode as well as any other feature support that is listed here.

What's in This Book?

This book is presented in 14 chapters. The first four chapters are designed to get you started using the SRX. If you are an advanced user, don't skip these chapters, as they include some best practices about Junos and the SRX when it comes to the initial setup.

The remaining chapters were ordered by the popularity of the features. Chapters 5 through 9 are features that are used in almost every SRX deployment. Because of this, we wrote them in a manner that assumes the reader would read them sequentially. They will stand on their own, of course, but if you read them in order you'll notice more about the concepts that we are building on. Chapters 10 through 14 are all standalone chapters. These also are the deeper chapters in terms of complexity, as they focus on some of the more compelling and complex features of the SRX, including AppSecure, IPS, UTM, and more.

Get comprehensive coverage of the SRX Series by using the following chapters:

Chapter 1, Welcome to the SRX
: This chapter explains what the SRX is and how it can be best utilized. The content covers the various deployment scenarios for the SRX and the history of the SRX. This chapter is a great read for anyone who wants to know more about the SRX. No technical background is required for this chapter.

Chapter 2, SRX Series Product Lines
: Moving on from how the SRXs are deployed, we focus on the hardware itself. We take a look at the components and platforms that make up the SRX product line. The content of this chapter is great for anyone who needs to deploy, select, or understand the products that make up the SRX Series.

Chapter 3, SRX GUI Management
: Although Junos is primarily a CLI-focused platform, it does have several different tools to manage both the devices and your Juniper Security infrastructure. This chapter takes a look at the on-box Junos GUI management tools as well as the centralized management tools available. This chapter offers an overview of the tools more so than an in-depth look at them. GUI tools are the ones that most rapidly evolve within the Junos ecosphere. Because of this, we focused on teaching you how to use the tools rather than the specifics of the tools. This chapter is the one that is most likely to lose relevance over the lifetime of the book, so it was written to best provide value over the long haul.

Chapter 4, SRX Networking Basics
: The SRX contains an extreme amount of networking features. This chapter focuses on the most core networking features of the SRX and the best practices in configuring them.

Chapter 5, System Services
: Junos has the option of not only providing traffic processing capabilities, but it also has many different services it can offer the network. These include both services such as DHCP, NTP, DNS, JFlow, and Logging and system management services such as Secure Shell and others. This chapter reviews how to both configure and secure the most important services on an SRX.

Chapter 6, Transparent Mode
: Typically, an SRX is deployed much like a traditional router with IP addresses on the interfaces, but there are times when security is still needed and the traditional

deployment model is unacceptable. Because of this, the SRX can act in a transparent mode or as a bump in the wire. This chapter reviews this function in its entirety and how you can use this mode to your advantage.

Chapter 7, High Availability
Around 90 percent of all SRX deployments are done in a highly available configuration. In today's "always connected" world, service failures are simply not an option. This chapter works to take the hard work out of high availability and show you the best practices to configure, troubleshoot, and deploy your SRXs in a highly available manner.

Chapter 8, Security Policies
The fundamental value proposition of the SRX is to restrict and to protect access to hosts on the network. This chapter reviews how to configure and implement security policies on the SRX. This is the cornerstone for all security that the SRX provides.

Chapter 9, Network Address Translation
Manipulating the IP address in a packet or network address translation (NAT) is a key feature that almost all SRX devices use. This chapter covers the most common types of NAT and how to optimally configure them for use in your network. Both IPv4 and IPv6 are covered within the chapter. Although the popularity of IPv6 is steadily growing, most enterprises do not tend to use it. But within this chapter, and the rest of the book, IPv6 is treated as a first-class citizen, as it is commonly used within Junos implementations.

Chapter 10, IPsec VPN
Securely connecting networks together is a staple for any firewall. The SRX offers a host of IPsec features that allow you to securely transport your information anywhere in the world. This chapter details the best practices for configuring and securing the transport of your critical data.

Chapter 11, Screens and Flow Options
Screening is a very basic but fundamental method to protect your network and the SRX itself. A screen is a simple policy that defines how the SRX should respond to potential Layer 3 and Layer 4 attacks. These attacks can cripple almost any network or firewall. This is why the configuration of screens is so critical. An SRX without the correct screens configured can be attacked by anyone on the network. But by enabling a few screens, the SRX and its connected network are secured from these otherwise devastating attacks.

Chapter 12, AppSecure Basics
AppSecure is a suite of features that allow you to provide security past the IP address and port. It gives you the power to block individual users from using specific applications. It also offers statistical analysis on what protocols are being used on your

network. This chapter covers most of what makes up a next-generation firewall. This is one of the hottest and most interesting features that has come to the SRX.

Chapter 13, Intrusion Prevention
: AppSecure provides deeper inspection into the applications on your network, but IPS offers extreme depth and security. IPS is able to detect individual attacks that are often buried deep within a protocol and stop them before they hit critical hosts. This chapter covers the overview of IPS as well as the best ways to take advantage of the technology to secure your infrastructure.

Chapter 14, Unified Threat Management
: Unified Threat Management (UTM) is a suite of tools that are used to provide protection for specific kinds of threats. These include but are not limited to antivirus and antispam. These types of tools are used typically within branch office locations, but they can also be scaled to protect larger enterprises. This chapter covers the configuration and best methodologies on how to use these features to protect your network.

Conventions Used in This Book

The following typographical conventions are used in this book:

Italic
: Indicates new terms, URLs, email addresses, filenames, file extensions, pathnames, directories, and Unix utilities

`Constant width`
: Indicates commands, options, switches, variables, attributes, keys, functions, types, classes, namespaces, methods, modules, properties, parameters, values, objects, events, event handlers, XML tags, HTML tags, macros, the contents of files, and the output from commands

`Constant width bold`
: Shows commands and other text that should be typed literally by the user, as well as important lines of code

`Constant width italic`
: Shows text that should be replaced with user-supplied values

This icon signifies a tip, suggestion, or general note.

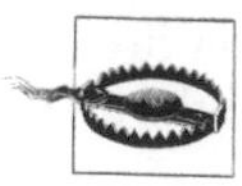

This icon indicates a warning or caution.

Using Code Examples

This book is here to help you get your job done. In general, if this book includes code examples, you may use the code in this book in your own configuration and documentation. You do not need to contact us for permission unless you're reproducing a significant portion of the material. For example, deploying a network based on actual configurations from this book does not require permission. Selling or distributing a CD-ROM of examples from this book does require permission. Answering a question by citing this book and quoting example code does not require permission. Incorporating a significant amount of sample configurations or operational output from this book into your product's documentation does require permission.

We appreciate, but do not require, attribution. An attribution usually includes the title, author, publisher, and ISBN, for example: "*Juniper SRX Series*, by Brad Woodberg and Rob Cameron. Copyright 2013 Brad Woodberg and Rob Cameron, 978-1-449-33896-1."

If you feel your use of code examples falls outside fair use or the permission given here, feel free to contact us at *permissions@oreilly.com*.

Safari® Books Online

Safari Books Online (*www.safaribooksonline.com*) is an on-demand digital library that delivers expert content in both book and video form from the world's leading authors in technology and business.

Technology professionals, software developers, web designers, and business and creative professionals use Safari Books Online as their primary resource for research, problem solving, learning, and certification training.

Safari Books Online offers a range of product mixes and pricing programs for organizations, government agencies, and individuals. Subscribers have access to thousands of books, training videos, and prepublication manuscripts in one fully searchable database from publishers like O'Reilly Media, Prentice Hall Professional, Addison-Wesley Professional, Microsoft Press, Sams, Que, Peachpit Press, Focal Press, Cisco Press, John Wiley & Sons, Syngress, Morgan Kaufmann, IBM Redbooks, Packt, Adobe Press, FT Press, Apress, Manning, New Riders, McGraw-Hill, Jones & Bartlett, Course Technology, and dozens more. For more information about Safari Books Online, please visit us online.

How to Contact Us

Please address comments and questions concerning this book to the publisher:

> O'Reilly Media, Inc.
> 1005 Gravenstein Highway North
> Sebastopol, CA 95472
> 800-998-9938 (in the United States or Canada)
> 707-829-0515 (international or local)
> 707-829-0104 (fax)

We have a web page for this book, where we list errata, examples, and any additional information. You can access this page at *http://oreil.ly/Juniper_SRX*.

To comment or ask technical questions about this book, send email to *bookquestions@oreilly.com*.

For more information about our books, courses, conferences, and news, see our website at *http://www.oreilly.com*.

Find us on Facebook: *http://facebook.com/oreilly*

Follow us on Twitter: *http://twitter.com/oreillymedia*

Watch us on YouTube: *http://www.youtube.com/oreillymedia*

Acknowledgments

From Brad Woodberg: I would like to dedicate this book to several important people in my life. First and foremost, my wife Tarah, for her infinite patience and support in undertaking yet another book project, and as if patience wasn't enough, for helping to bring the most wonderful blessing I've ever known, our daughter Lydia Claire Woodberg, who was born shortly after starting this project. Next, I would like to thank all of the mentors who have generously shared their knowledge and experience: Chuck Morgan, Dr. Jonathan Shapiro, Bryan Burns, and Kevin Kennedy. My accomplishments would also not be possible without the support of those past and present, including Alex Waterman, Mike Stailey, Steve Fuller, Krishna Narayanaswamy, and perhaps one of the most amazing friends I've ever known, Rob Cameron. Finally, I would like to dedicate this book to everyone who loves security and networking technologies, is passionate, and shares their knowledge and experience with the community at large.

From Rob Cameron: I would like to first thank my wife Katie for her support during the writing of this book. Any project like this takes away precious hours from your family, and I truly appreciate her patience and encouragement through this process. If it weren't for her, I wouldn't have had the strength to complete this project. Second, I would like to thank Brad for working on this project with me. I had no intentions of working on an update for the *Junos Security* book, but Brad helped me immensely with encouragement and support through the process and during the most difficult time of my life.

At the end of this book, I made the decision to leave Juniper and pursue other interests. I would like to thank my old PLE team at Juniper, as the four plus years we worked together was the best time I have had in my professional life. You each touched me and helped me grow, so to Chris, Aditi, Nikhil, Kamakshi, Bill, Brad, Galina, Patricio, and Stefan, I deeply thank all of you for letting me be your leader. It was truly a profound time and I will never forget it. I also want to thank Patrick Ames for being so helpful through the publishing process. You made the tough parts easy for me and let me focus on the content. Working with you was awesome, and I hope to continue to work on projects with you in the future.

Last, I want to thank the readers of this book. I have spent much of the last eight years of my life at Juniper working to make Junos and the SRX a better product for you. If it weren't for your excitement and enthusiasm, I couldn't have gone through it. For every night that you toil working on a Junos issue, for every crash, and for every confusing CLI command, I understand your feelings and I hope this book helps you get through those times. And may you always have an "I heart Junos" or "I wish this ran Junos" sticker on your laptop covers.

CHAPTER 1

Welcome to the SRX

Firewalls are an important part of almost every network in the world. The firewall protects nearly every network-based transaction that occurs, and even the end user understands its metaphoric name, meant to imply keeping out the bad stuff. Despite what some competitive marketing campaigns have said, the is not dead, and it is every bit as necessary today as it was yesterday. But firewalls have had to change. Whether it's the growth of networks or the growth of network usage, they have had to move beyond the simple devices that only require protection from inbound connections. A firewall now has to transcend its own title, the one end users are so familiar with, into a whole new type of device and service. This new class of device is a *services gateway*. And it needs to provide much more than just a firewall—it needs to look deeper into the packet and use the contained data in new ways that are advantageous to the network for which it is deployed. Can you tell if an egg is good or not by just looking at its shell? Once you break it open, isn't it best to use all of its contents? *Deep packet inspection* from a services gateway is the new firewall of the future.

Deep packet inspection isn't a new concept, nor is it something that Juniper Networks invented. What Juniper did do, however, is start from the ground up to solve the technical problems of peering deeply. With the Juniper Networks SRX Series Services Gateways, Juniper built a new platform to answer today's problems while scaling the platform's features to solve the anticipated problems of tomorrow. It's a huge challenge, especially with the rapid growth of enterprise networks. How do you not only solve the needs of your network today, but also anticipate the needs for tomorrow?

Juniper expended an enormous amount of effort to create a platform that can grow over time. The scalability is built into the features, performance, and multifunction capability of the SRX Series. This chapter introduces the solutions the SRX Series can provide for your organization today, while detailing its architecture to help you anticipate and solve your problems of tomorrow.

Evolving into the SRX

The predecessors to the SRX Series products are the legacy ScreenOS products. They really raised the bar when they were introduced to the market, first by NetScreen and then by Juniper Networks. Many features might be remembered as notable, but the most important was the migration of a split firewall software and operating system (OS) model. Firewalls at the time of their introduction consisted of a base OS and then firewall software loaded on top. This was flexible for the organization, because it could choose the underlying OS it was comfortable with, but when any sort of troubleshooting occurred, it led to all sorts of finger-pointing among vendors. ScreenOS provided an appliance-based approach by combining the underling OS and the features it provided.

The integrated approach of ScreenOS transformed the market. Today, most vendors have migrated to an appliance-based firewall model, but it has been more than 10 years since the founding of NetScreen Technologies and its ScreenOS approach. So, when Juniper began to plan for a totally new approach to firewall products, it did not have to look far to see its next-generation choice for an operating system: Junos became the base for the new product line called the SRX Series.

ScreenOS to Junos

Juniper Networks' flagship OS is Junos. The has been a mainstay of Juniper and it runs on the majority of its products. Junos was created in the mid-1990s as an offshoot of the FreeBSD Unix-like operating system. The goal was to provide a robust core OS that could control the underlying chassis hardware. At that time, FreeBSD was a great choice on which to base Junos, because it provided all of the important components, including storage support, a memory controller, a kernel, and a task scheduler. The BSD license also allowed anyone to modify the source code without having to return the new code. This allowed Juniper to modify the code as it saw fit.

Junos has evolved greatly from its initial days as a spin-off of BSD. It contains millions of lines of code and an extremely strong feature set.

The aged gracefully over time, but it hit some important limits that prevented it from being the choice for the next-generation SRX Series products. First, ScreenOS cannot separate the running of tasks from the kernel. All processes effectively run with the same privileges. Because of this, if any part of ScreenOS were to crash or fail, the entire OS would end up crashing or failing. Second, the modular architecture of Junos allows for the addition of new services, because this was the initial intention of Junos and the history of its release train. ScreenOS could not compare.

Over time, solutions to yesterday's problems age and become less relevant to today's needs. Because of this, the functionality that is needed to solve today's problems is greatly focused on deep packet inspection. This is a problem that ScreenOS was never designed to solve. With its ASIC-focused architecture, it allowed for amazing performance for stateful firewalling but poor performance deeper in the packet. Although ScreenOS could be further evolved into this market, Junos already had the necessary underpinnings to allow for deeper inspection.

Inherited ScreenOS features

Although the next-generation SRX Series devices were destined to use the well-developed and long-running Junos operating system, that didn't mean the familiar features of ScreenOS were going away. For example, ScreenOS introduced the concept of *zones* to the firewall world. A zone is a logical entity that interfaces are bound to, and zones are used in security policy creation, allowing the specification of an ingress and egress zone in the security policy. Creating ingress and egress zones means the specified traffic can only pass in a specific direction. It also increases the overall speed of policy lookup, and because multiple zones are always used in a firewall, it separates the overall firewall rulebase into many subsets of zone groupings. We cover zones further in Chapter 3.

The virtual router (VR) is an example of another important feature developed in ScreenOS and embraced by the new generation of SRX Series products. A VR allows for **substitute** command the creation of multiple routing tables inside the same device, providing the administrator with the ability to segregate traffic and virtualize the firewall.

Table 1-1 elaborates on the list of popular ScreenOS features that were added to Junos for the SRX Series. Although some of the features do not have a one-to-one naming parity, the functionality of these features is generally replicated on the Junos platform.

Table 1-1. ScreenOS-to-Junos major feature comparisons

Feature	ScreenOS	Junos
Zones	Yes	Yes
Virtual routers (VRs)	VRs	Yes as routing instances
Screens	Yes	Yes
Deep packet inspection	Yes	Yes as full intrusion prevention
Network Address Translation (NAT)	Yes as NAT objects	Yes as NAT policies
Unified Threat Management (UTM)	Yes	Yes
IPsec virtual private network (VPN)	Yes	Yes
Dynamic routing	Yes	Yes
High availability (HA)	NetScreen Redundancy Protocol (NSRP)	Chassis cluster
Virtual firewalls	Virtual Systems (VSYS)	Logical Systems (LSYS)

Device management

Junos has evolved since it was first deployed in service provider networks. Over the years, many lessons were learned regarding how to best use the device running the OS. These practices have been integrated into the SRX Series and are shared throughout this book, specifically in how to use the command-line interface (CLI).

For the most part, Junos users traditionally tend to utilize the CLI for managing the platform. As strange as it may sound, even very large organizations use the CLI to manage their devices. The CLI was designed to be easy to utilize and navigate through, and once you are familiar with it, even large configurations are completely manageable through a simple terminal window. Throughout this book, we will show you various ways to navigate and configure the SRX Series products using the CLI.

In Junos, the CLI extends beyond just a simple set of commands. The CLI is actually implemented as an Extensible Markup Language (XML) interface to the operating system. This XML interface is called Junoscript and is even implemented as an open standard called NETCONF. Third-party applications can integrate with Junoscript or a user may even use it on the device. Juniper Networks provides extensive training and documentation covering this feature; an example is its Day One Automation Series (*http://www.juniper.net/dayone*).

Sometimes, getting started with such a rich platform is a daunting task, if only because thousands of commands can be used in the Junos operating system. To ease this task and help users get started quickly, the SRX Series of products provides a web interface called J-Web. The J-Web tool is automatically installed on the SRX Series (on some other Junos platforms it is an optional package), and it is enabled by default. The interface is intuitive and covers most of the important tasks for configuring a device.

For large networks with many devices, we all know mass efficiency is required. It may be feasible to use the CLI, but it's hard to beat a policy-driven management system. Juniper provides two tools for efficient management. The first tool is called Network and Security Manager (NSM). This is the legacy tool that you can use to manage networks. It was originally designed to manage ScreenOS products, and, over time, it evolved to manage most of Juniper's products. However, the architecture of the product is getting old, and it's becoming difficult to implement new features. Although it is still a viable platform for management, just like the evolution of ScreenOS to Junos, a newly architected platform is available.

This new platform is called Junos Space, and it is designed from the ground up to be a modular platform that can integrate easily with a multitude of devices, and even other management systems. The goal for Junos Space is to allow for the simplified provisioning of a network.

To provide this simplified provisioning, three important things must be accomplished:

- Integrate with a heterogeneous network environment.
- Integrate with many different types of management platforms.
- Provide this within an easy-to-use web interface.

By accomplishing these tasks, Junos Space will take network management to a new level of productivity and efficiency for an organization. Junos Space is an application platform, meaning that you can load applications on it to provide additional functions. The most important to SRX users is Security Design (SD). This application focuses on the policy management of the SRX. It makes managing one or thousands of firewalls a breeze. The intuitive UI makes even the most complex policies simple to manage. It not only provides the traditional management that firewall administrators crave, but it has new paradigms that drive management efficacy in a whole new direction.

The SRX Series Platform

The SRX Series hardware platform is a next-generation departure from the previous ScreenOS platforms, built from the ground up to provide scalable services. Now, the question that begs to be answered is this: What exactly is a service?

A *service* is an action or actions that are applied to the network traffic passing through the SRX Series of products. Two examples of services are stateful firewalling and intrusion prevention.

The ScreenOS products were designed primarily to provide three services: stateful firewalling, NAT, and virtual private networking (VPN). When ScreenOS was originally designed, these were the core value propositions for a firewall in a network. In today's network, these services are still important, but they need to be provided on a larger scale because the number of Internet Protocol (IP) devices in a network has grown significantly, and each of them relies on the Internet for access to information they need to run. Because the SRX is going to be processing this traffic, it is critical that it provides as many services as possible on the traffic in one single pass.

Built for Services

So, the SRX provides services on the passing traffic, but it must also provide *scalable services*. This is an important concept to review. *Scale* is the ability to provide the appropriate level of processing based on the required workload, and it's a concept that is often lost when judging firewalls because you have to think about the actual processing capability of a device and how it works. Although all devices have a maximum compute capability, or the maximum level at which they can process information, it's very important to understand how a firewall processes this load. This allows the administrator to better judge how the device scales under such load.

Scaling under load is based on the services a device is attempting to provide and the scale it needs to achieve. The traditional device required to do all this is either a branch device or the new, high-end data center firewall. A *branch firewall* needs to provide a plethora of services at a performance level typical of the available wide area network (WAN) speeds. These services include the traditional stateful firewall, VPN, and NAT, as well as more security-focused services such as UTM and intrusion prevention.

A *data center firewall*, on the other hand, needs to provide highly scalable performance. When a firewall is placed in the core of a data center, it cannot impede the performance of the entire network. Each transaction in the data center contains a considerable amount of value to the organization, and any packet loss or delay can cause financial implications. A data center firewall requires extreme stateful firewall speeds, a high session capacity, and very fast new sessions per second.

In response to these varied requirements, Juniper Networks created two product lines: the branch SRX Series and the data center SRX Series. Each is targeted at its specific market segments and the network needs of the device in those segments.

SRX Series Common Features: Junos

No matter which SRX Series platform you use, or plan to use, each has a common shared codebase.

One of the most powerful aspects of the Junos operating system is that a single source base, or pool of source code, is used to build a release of the network software. This provides great efficiency when it comes to integrating features and providing quality assurance testing. As new products such as those in the SRX Series are created, it is easier to take previous features, such as the Junos implementation of routing, and bring them to the new platform.

The same idea is implemented across the SRX Series. Where it makes sense, common features and code are shared. There are challenges to this mantra, such as the implementation of features in what is known as the Packet Forwarding Engine (PFE). That's because this is the location that actually processes the packets and provides services on the network traffic. The PFE in each SRX Series platform typically contains different components, creating the largest barrier for feature parity across the platforms. But as stated before, the products are designed to meet the needs of the deployment, using Junos to provide commonality.

Deployment Solutions

Networking products are created to solve problems and increase efficiencies. Before diving into the products that comprise the SRX Series, let's look at some of the problems these products solve in the two central locations in which they are deployed:

- The *branch SRX Series* are designed for small to large office locations consisting of anywhere from a few individuals to hundreds of employees, representing either a small, single device requirement or a reasonably sized infrastructure. In these locations, the firewall is typically deployed at the edge of the network, separating the users from the Internet.
- The *data center SRX Series products* are Juniper's flagship high-end firewalls. These products are targeted at the data center and the service provider. They are designed to provide services to scale. Data center and service provider deployments are as differentiated as branch locations.

Let's look at examples of various deployments and what type of services the SRX Series products provide. We will look at the small branch first, then larger branches, data centers, service providers, and mobile carriers, and finally all the way up (literally) to cloud networks.

Small Branch

A small branch location is defined as a network with no more than a dozen hosts. Typically, a small branch has a few servers or, most often, connects to a larger office. The requirements for a firewall device are to provide not only connectivity to an Internet source, or larger office connection, but also connectivity to all of the devices in the office. The branch firewall also needs to provide switching and, in some cases, wireless connectivity, to the network.

Figure 1-1 depicts a small branch location. Here a Juniper Networks SRX100 or SRX210 Services Gateway can be utilized. If WAN interfaces are not required, then the SRX100 is ideal. The SRX210 series is the same horsepower as the SRX100, but includes the ability to include WAN interfaces. The SRX220 can do dual WAN interfaces for ISP redundancy. Several hosts can connect to an upstream device that provides Internet connectivity. In this deployment, the device consolidates a firewall, Digital Subscriber Line (DSL) modem, and switch.

The small-location deployment keeps the footprint to one small device and keeps branch management to one device—if the device were to fail, it's simple to replace and get the branch up and running using a backup of the current configuration. Finally, you should note that all of the network hosts are directly connected to the branch.

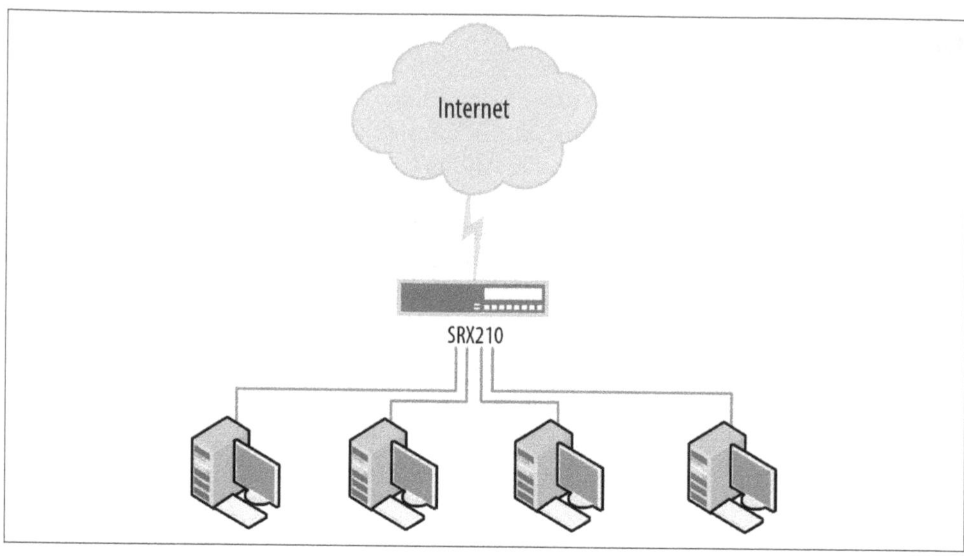

Figure 1-1. An example of a small branch network

Medium Branch

In medium to large branch offices, the network has to provide more to the location because there are 20 or more users—our network example contains about 50 client devices—so here the solution is the Juniper Networks SRX200 Series Services Gateway branch device. Figure 1-2 shows the deployment of the SRX240 placed at the Internet edge. It utilizes a WAN port to connect directly to the Internet service provider (ISP).

Note that the servers are connected directly to the SRX240 to provide maximum performance and security. Because this branch provides email and web-hosting services to the Internet, security must be provided. Not only can the SRX240 provide stateful firewalling, but it can also offer intrusion protection services (IPS) for the Web and email services, including antivirus services for email.

Juniper has also introduced the SRX550, which is about twice as powerful as the SRX240. It also provides more interface density and gives more headroom for future expansion, so it is also a good consideration for the medium branch deployments.

Because of the size of the branch, the network can never go down. Using chassis cluster or ensures that if one device were to fail, the other will keep the network up and running. The servers have also been given dual network interface cards (NICs) to have an interface on each SRX. Because the SRX can offer HA switching, it allows the servers to stay up in the event of a single device failure.

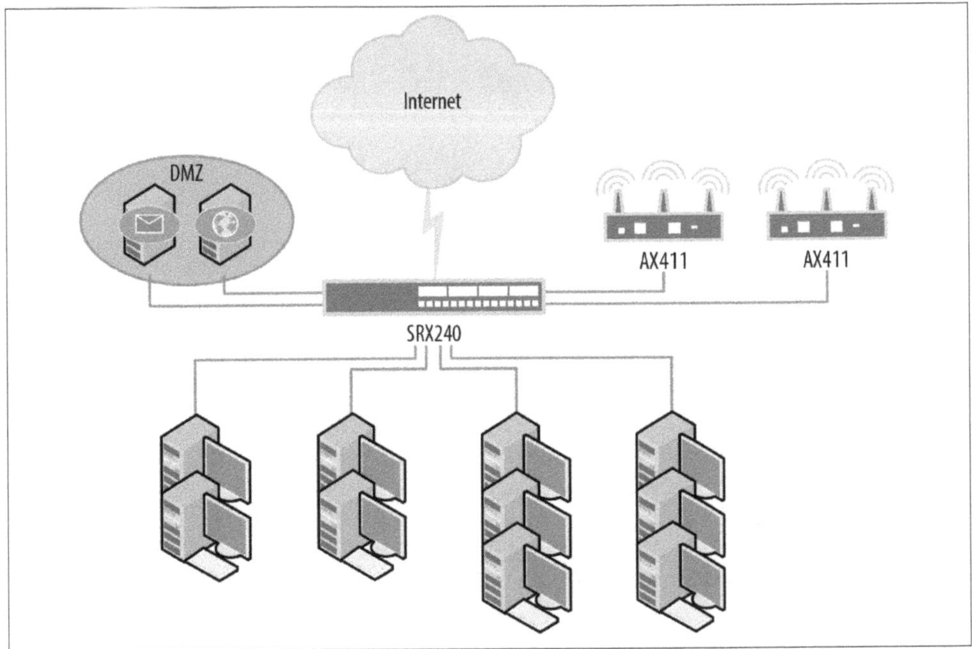

Figure 1-2. An example of a medium branch network

Large Branch

The last branch deployment to review is the large branch. For our example, the large branch has 250 clients. This network requires significantly more equipment than was used in the preceding branch examples. Note that for this network, the Juniper Networks EX Series Ethernet Switches were reutilized to provide client access to the network. Figure 1-3 depicts our large branch topology.

Our example branch network needs to provide Ethernet access for 250 clients, so to realistically depict this, six groupings of two EX4200 switches are deployed. Each switch provides 48 tri-speed Ethernet ports. To simplify management, all of the switches are connected using Juniper's virtual chassis technology.

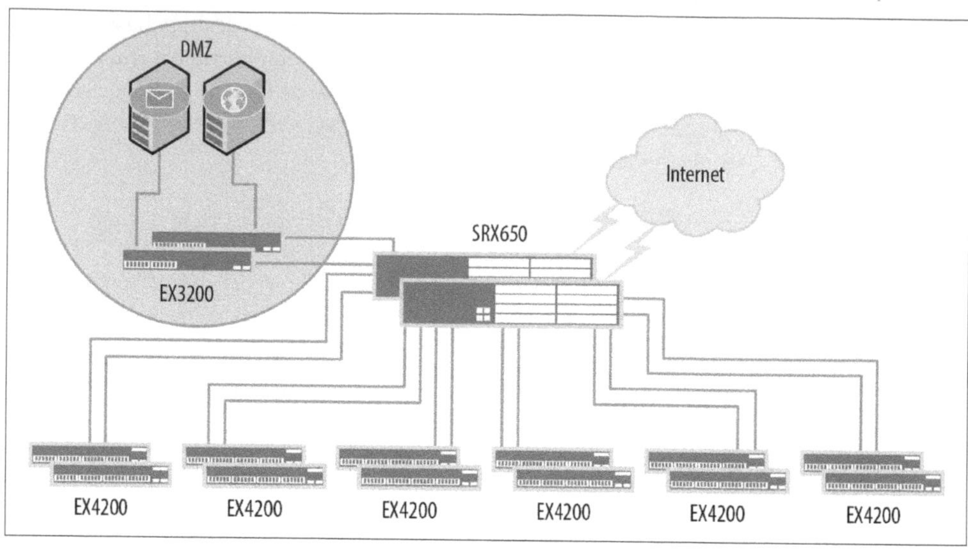

Figure 1-3. An example of a large branch network

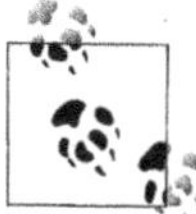

For more details on how the EX Series switches and the virtual chassis technology operates, as well as how the EX switches can be deployed and serve various enterprise networks, see *JUNOS Enterprise Switching (http://oreilly.com/catalog/9780596153984/)* by Harry Reynolds and Doug Marschke (O'Reilly).

The SRX Series platform of choice for the large branch is the Juniper Networks SRX 550 or SRX650 Services Gateway. The SRX550 is ideal if you do not need additional headroom for your deployment. The SRX650 is the largest of the branch SRX Series products; its performance capabilities actually exceed those of the branch, allowing for future adoption of features in the branch. Just as was done in the previous deployment, the local servers will sit off of an arm of the SRX650, but note that in this deployment, HA was utilized, so the servers must sit off of their own switch (here the Juniper Networks EX3200 switch).

Also because the SRX is a next-generation firewall, it's possible to have user-based dynamic firewalling. Each individual user can get authenticated for services using AppSecure. This is further discussed in the AppSecure chapter later in the book. The HA deployment of the SRX650 products means two devices are used, allowing the second SRX650 to take over in the event of a failure on the primary device. The SRX650 HA model provides an extreme amount of flexibility for deploying a firewall, and we detail its capabilities in Chapter 7.

Data Center

What truly is a data center has blurred in recent times. The traditional concept of a data center is a physical location that contains servers that provide services to clients. The data center does not contain client hosts (a few machines here and there to administer the servers don't count) or clear bounds of ingress and egress to the network. Ingress points may be Internet or WAN connections, but each type of ingress point requires different levels of security.

The new data center of today seems to be any network that contains services, and these networks could even span multiple physical locations. In the past, a data center and its tiers were limited to a single physical location because there were some underlying technologies that were hard to stretch. But today, it's much easier to provide the same Layer 2 network across two or more physical locations, thus expanding the possibilities of creating a data center. With the popularization of multiprotocol label switching (MPLS) and virtual private LAN service (VPLS) technologies, data centers can be built in new and creative ways.

The traditional data center design consists of a two- or three-tier switching model. Figure 1-4 shows both a two-tier and a three-tier switching design. Both are fundamentally the same, except that between the two is the addition of the aggregation switching tier. The aggregation tier compensates for the lack of port density at the core (only in the largest switched networks should a distribution tier be required).

Note that the edge tier is unchanged in both models. This is where the servers connect into the network, and the number of edge switches (and their configuration) is driven by the density of the servers. Most progressively designed data centers are using virtualization technologies that allow multiple servers to run on the same bit of hardware, reducing the overall footprint, energy consumption, and rack space.

Neither this book nor this chapter is designed to be a comprehensive primer on data centers. Design considerations for a data center are enormous and can easily fill up several volumes. The point here is to give a little familiarity to the next few deployment scenarios and to show how the various SRX Series platforms scale to the needs of those deployments.

Data Center Edge

As discussed in the previous section, a data center needs to have an ingress point to allow clients to access the data center's services. The most common service is ingress Internet traffic, and as you can imagine, the ingress point is a very important area to secure. This area needs to allow access to the servers, yet in a limited and secure fashion, and because the data center services are typically high profile, they could be the target of denial-of-service (DoS), distributed denial-of-service (DDoS), and botnet attacks. It

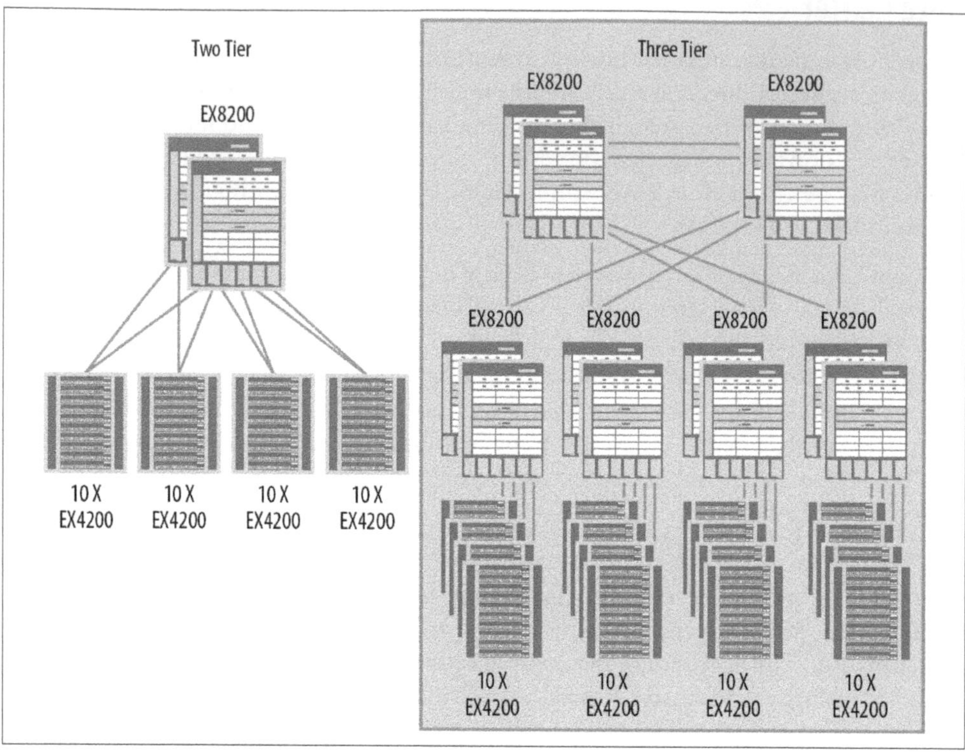

Figure 1-4. Two- and three-tier switching design

is a fact of network life that must be taken into consideration when building a data center network.

An SRX Series product deployed at the edge of the network must handle all of these tasks, as well as handle the transactional load of the servers. Most connections into applications for a data center are quick to be created and torn down, and during the connection, only a small amount of data is sent. An example of this is accessing a web application. Many small components are actually delivered to the web browser on the client, and most of them are delivered asynchronously, so the components might not be returned in the order they were accessed. This leads to many small data exchanges or transactions, which differs greatly from the model of large continual streams of data transfer.

Figure 1-5 illustrates where the SRX Series would be deployed in our example topology. The products of choice are the Juniper Networks SRX1400 and SRX3000 line, because they can meet the needs identified in the preceding paragraph. Figure 1-5 might look familiar to you, as it is part of what we discussed regarding the data center tier in Figure 1-4. The data center is modeled after that two-tier design, with the edge being placed at the top of the diagram. The SRX1400 and SRX3000 line of products do not have WAN interfaces, so upstream routers are used. The WAN routers consolidate the various network connections and then connect to the SRX1400 and SRX3000 products. For connecting into the data center itself, the SRX1400 and SRX3000 line uses its 10-gigabit Ethernet to connect to the data center core and WAN routers.

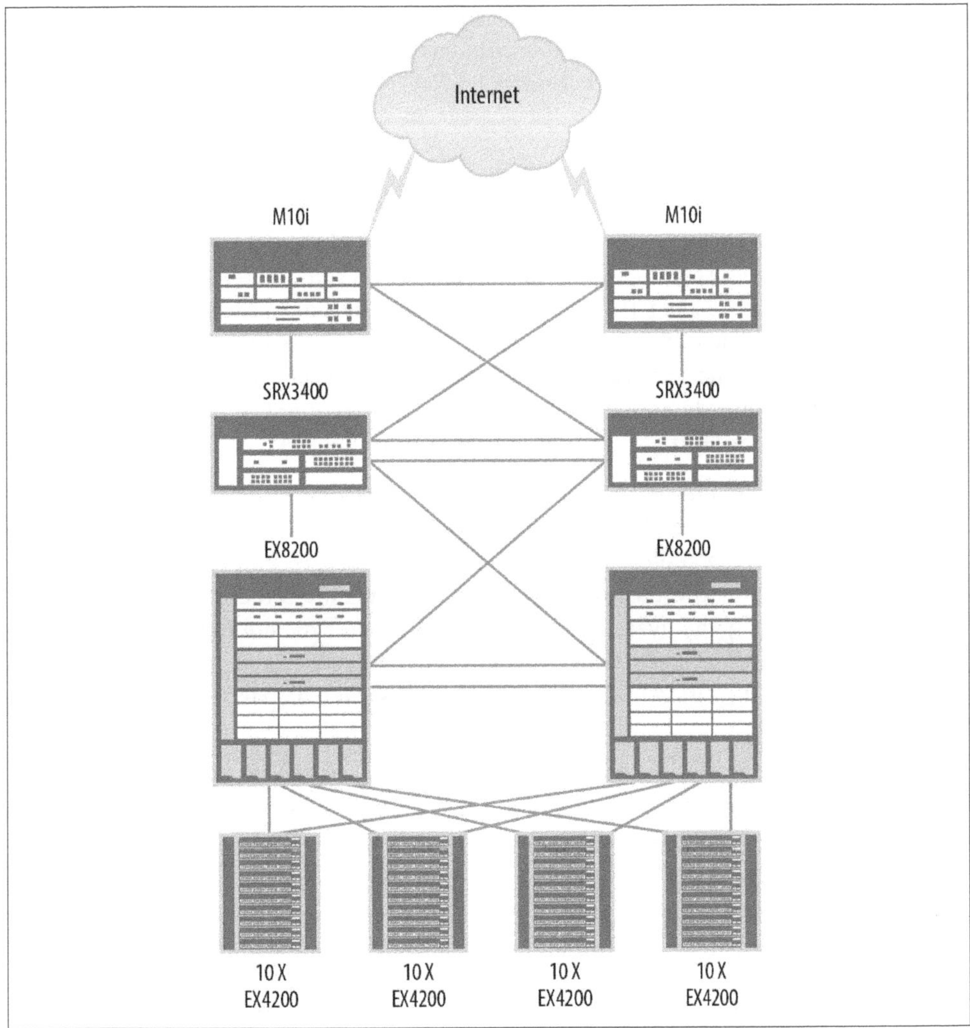

Figure 1-5. The data center edge with the SRX3000 line

A data center relies on availability—all systems must be deployed to ensure that there is no single point of failure. This includes the SRX Series. The SRX3000 line provides a robust set of HA features. In Figure 1-5, both SRX3000 line products are deployed in what is traditionally called an *active/active* deployment. This means both firewalls can pass traffic simultaneously. When a product in the SRX3000 line operates in a cluster, the two boxes operate as though they are one unit. This simplifies HA deployment because management operations are reduced. Also, traffic can enter and exit any port on either chassis. This model is flexible compared to the traditional model of forcing traffic to only go through an active member.

Data Center Services Tier

The data center core is the network's epicenter for all server communications, and most connections in a data center flow through it. A firewall at the data center core needs to maintain many concurrent sessions. Although servers may maintain long-lived connections, they are more likely to have connectivity bursts that last a short period of time. This, coupled with the density of running systems, increases the required number of concurrent connections, but at the rate of new connections per second. If a firewall fails to create sessions quickly enough, or falls behind in allowing the creation of new sessions, transactions are lost.

For this example, the Juniper Networks SRX5800 Services Gateway is a platform that can meet these needs. The SRX5800 is the largest member of the SRX5000 line, and is well suited for the data center environment. It can meet the scaling needs of today as well as those of tomorrow. Placing a firewall inside the data center core is always challenging, and typically the overall needs of the data center dictate the placement of the firewall. However, there is a perfect location for the deployment of our SRX5800, as shown in Figure 1-6, which builds on the example shown as part of the two-tier data center in Figure 1-4.

This location in the data center network is called the *services tier*, and it is where services are provided to the data center servers on the network traffic. This includes services provided by the SRX5800, such as stateful firewalling, IPS, Application Denial of Service (AppDoS) prevention, and server load balancing. This allows the creation of a pool of resources that can be shared among the various servers. It is also possible to deploy multiple firewalls and distribute the load across all of them, but that increases complexity and management costs. The trend over the past five years has been to move toward consolidation for all the financial and managerial reasons you can imagine.

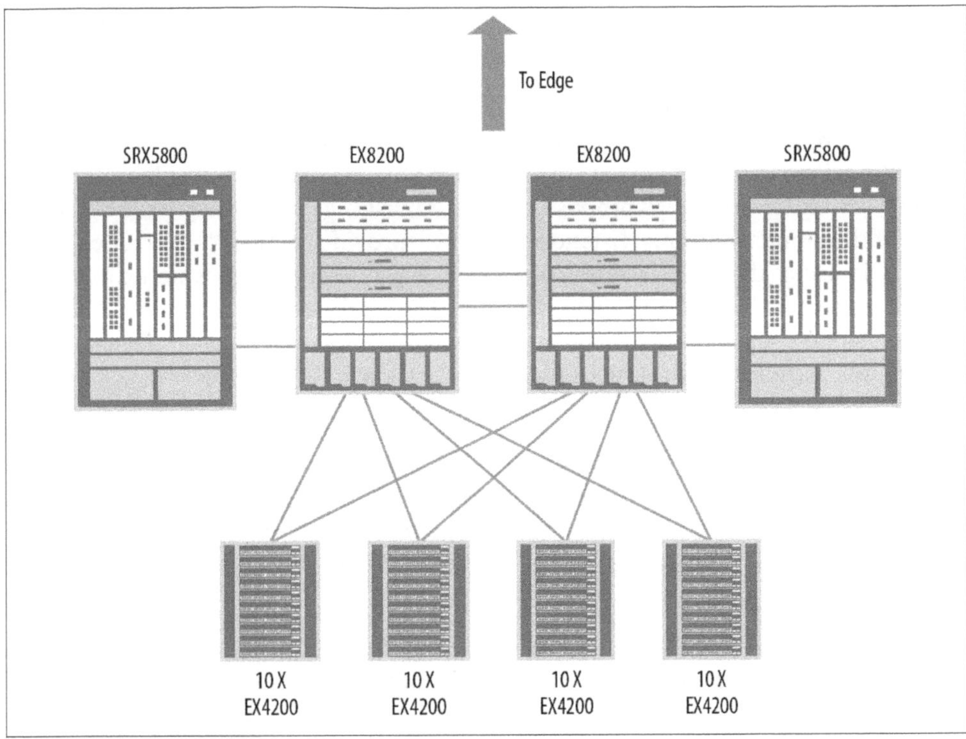

Figure 1-6. An SRX5800 in the data center core

In the data center core, AppSecure and IPS are two key services to include in the data center services tier design. The AppSecure feature allows the SRX5800 to look for attack patterns, unlike other security products. AppSecure can perform actions like application firewalling, application Quality of Service (QoS), and advanced application usage reporting.

A separate SRX Series specialty is IPS. The IPS feature differs from AppSecure as it looks for specific attacks through the streams of data. When an attack is identified, it's possible to block, log, or ignore the threat. Because all of the connections to the critical servers will pass through the SRX5800, adding the additional protection of the IPS technology provides a great deal of value, not to mention additional security for the services tier.

Service Provider

Although most administrators are more likely to use the services of a service provider than they are to run one, looking at the use case of a service provider can be quite interesting. Providing connectivity to millions of hosts in a highly available and scalable method is an extremely tough proposition. Accomplishing this task requires a herculean effort of thousands of people. Extending a service provider network to include stateful security is just as difficult. Traditionally, a service provider processes traffic in a *stateless* manner, meaning that each packet is treated independently of any other. Although scaling stateless packet processing isn't inexpensive, or simple by any means, it does require less computing power than *stateful* processing.

In a stateful processing device, each packet is matched as part of a new or existing flow. Each packet must be processed to ensure that it is part of an existing session, or a new session must be created. All of the fields of each packet must be validated to ensure that they correctly match the values of the existing flow. For example, in TCP, this would include TCP sequencing numbers and TCP session state. Scaling a device to do this is extremely challenging.

A firewall can be placed in many locations in a service provider's network. Here we'll discuss two specific examples: in the first, the firewall provides a managed service, and in the second, the service provider protects its own services.

Starting with the managed service provider (MSP) environment, Figure 1-7 shows a common MSP deployment. On the left, several customers are shown, and depending on the service provider environment, this could be several dozen to several thousand (for the purposes of explanation, only a handful are needed). The connections from these customers are aggregated to a Layer 2 and Layer 3 routing switch, in this case a Juniper Networks MX960 3D Universal Edge Router. Then the MX Series router connects to an SRX5800. The SRX5800 is logically broken down into smaller firewalls for each customer so that each customer gains the services of a firewall while the provider consolidates all of these "devices" into a single hardware unit. The service provider can minimize its operational costs and maximize the density of customers on a single device.

Our second scenario for service providers involves protecting the services that they provide. Although a service provider provides access to other networks, such as the Internet, it also has its own hosted services. These include, but are not limited to, Domain Name System (DNS), email, and web hosting. Because these services are public, it's important for the service provider to ensure their availability, as any lack of availability can become a front-page story or at least cause a flurry of angry customers. For these services, firewalls are typically deployed, as shown in our example topology in Figure 1-8.

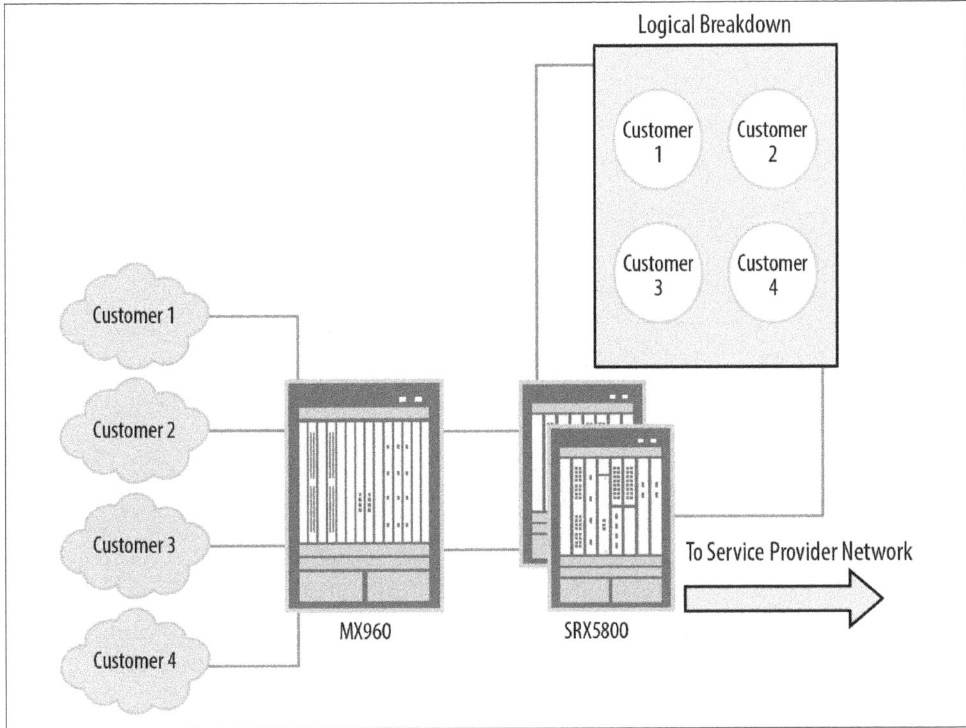

Figure 1-7. MSP SRX5800 deployment

Several attack vectors are available to service providers' public services, including DoS, DDoS, and service exploits. They are all the critical types of attacks that the provider needs to be aware of and defend. The data center SRX products can protect against both DDoS and the traditional DoS attack. In the case of a traditional DoS attack, the *screen* feature can be utilized.

A screen is a mechanism that is used to stop more simplistic attacks such as SYN and UDP floods (note that although these types of attacks are "simple" in nature, they can quickly overrun a server or even a firewall). Screens allow the administrator of an SRX Series product to set up specific thresholds for TCP and UDP sessions. Once these

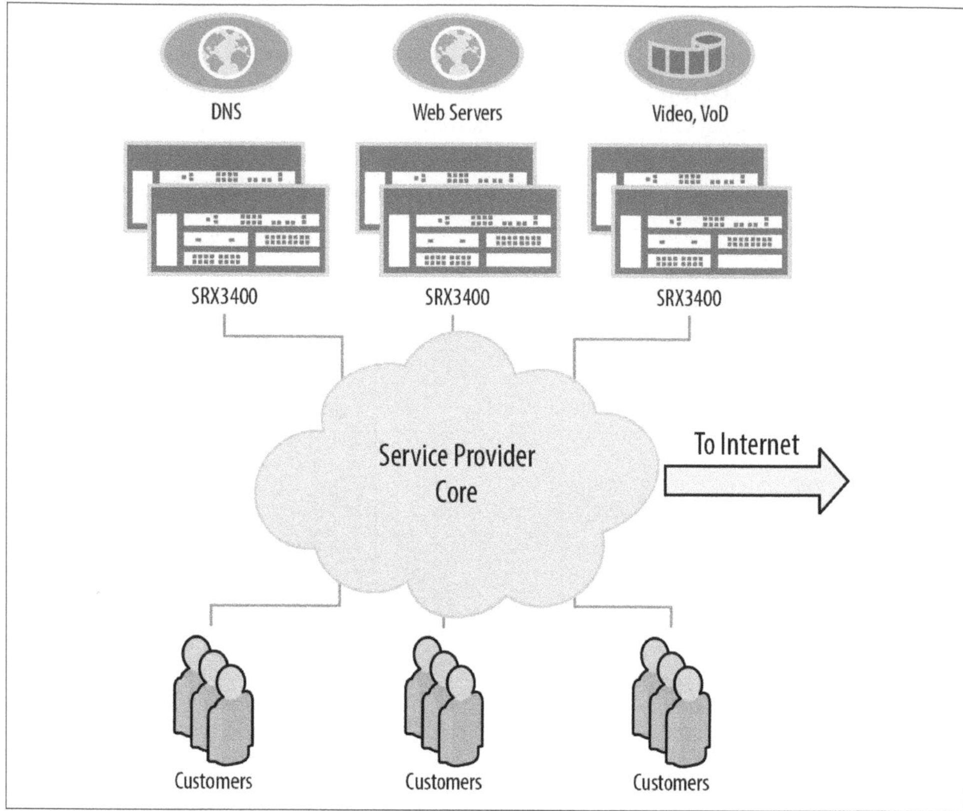

Figure 1-8. Service provider public services

thresholds have been exceeded, protection mechanisms are enacted to minimize the threat of these attacks. We discuss the screen feature in detail in Chapter 11.

Mobile Carriers

The phones of today are more than the computers of yesterday; they are fully fledged modern computers in a hand-held format, and almost all of a person's daily tasks can be performed through them. Although a small screen doesn't lend itself to managing 1,000-line spreadsheets, the devices can easily handle the job of sharing information through email or web browsing. More and more people who would typically not use the Internet are now accessing the Internet through these mobile devices, which means that access to the public network is advancing in staggering demographic numbers.

This explosion of usage has brought a new challenge to mobile operators: how to provide a resilient data network to every person in the world. Such a mobile network, when broken down into smaller, easy-to-manage areas, provides a perfect example of how an SRX Series firewall can be utilized to secure such a network.

For mobile carrier networks, an SRX5800 is the right choice for a few specific reasons: its high session capacity and its high connections-per-second rate. In the network locations where this device is placed, connection rates can quickly vary from a few thousand to several hundred thousand. A quick flood of new emails or everyone scrambling to see a breaking news event can strain any well-designed network. And as mentioned in the preceding service provider example, it's difficult to provide firewall services in a carrier network.

Figure 1-9 shows a simplified example of a mobile operator network. It's simplified to focus more on the firewalls and less on the many layers of the wireless carrier's network. For the purposes of this discussion, the way in which IP traffic is tunneled to the firewalls isn't relevant.

In Figure 1-9, the handsets are depicted on the far left, and their radio connections, or cell connections, are terminated into the provider's network. Then, at the edge of the provider's network, when the actual data requests are terminated, the IP-based packet is ready for transport to the Internet or to the provider's services.

An SRX5800 at the location depicted in Figure 1-9 is designed to protect the carrier's network, ensuring that its infrastructure is secure. By protecting the network, it ensures that its availability and the service that customers spend money on each month continues. If the protection of the handsets is the responsibility of the handset provider in conjunction with the carrier, the same goes for the cellular or 3G Internet services that can be utilized by consumers using cellular or 3G modems. These devices allow users to access the Internet directly from anywhere in a carrier's wireless coverage network—these computers need to employ personal firewalls for the best possible protection.

For any service provider, mobile carriers included, the provided services need to be available to the consumers. As shown in Figure 1-9, the SRX5800 devices are deployed in a highly available design. If one SRX5800 experiences a hardware failure, the second SRX5800 can completely take over for the primary. Of course, this failover is transparent to the end user for uninterrupted service and network uptime that reaches to the five, six, or even seven 9s, or 99.99999 percent of the time. As competitive as the mobile market is these days, the mobile carrier's networks need to be a competitive advantage.

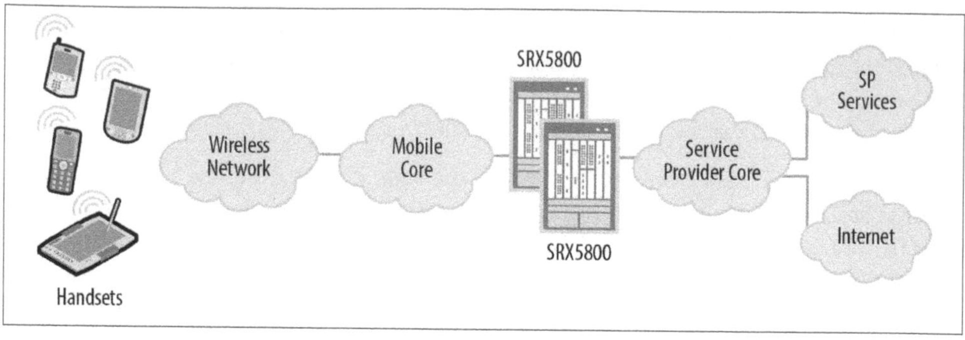

Figure 1-9. The SRX5800 in a mobile carrier network

Cloud Networks

It seems like cloud computing is on everyone's mind today. The idea of providing any service to anyone at any time to any scale with complete resilience is a dream that is becoming a reality for many organizations. Both cloud computing vendors and large enterprises are providing their own private clouds.

Although each cloud network has its own specific design needs, the SRX Series can and should play an important role.

That's because a cloud network must scale in many directions to really be a cloud. It must scale in the number of running operating systems it can provide. It must scale in the number of physical servers that can run these operating systems. And it must scale in the available number of networking ports that the network provides to the servers. The SRX Series must be able to scale to secure all of this traffic, and in some cases, it must be able to be bypassed for other services. Figure 1-10 depicts this scale in a sample cloud network that is meant to merely show the various components and how they might scale.

The logical items are easier to scale than the physical items, meaning it's easy to make 10 copies of an operating system run congruently, because they are easily instantiated, but the challenge is in ensuring that enough processing power can be provided by the servers, as they are a physical entity and it takes time to get more of them installed. The same goes for the network. A network in a cloud environment will be divided into many virtual LANs (VLANs) and many routing domains. It is simple to provide more VLANs in the network, but it is hard to ensure that the network has the capacity to handle the needs of the servers. The same goes for the SRX Series firewalls.

For the SRX Series in particular, the needs of the cloud computing environment must be well planned. As we discussed in regard to service providers, the demands of a stateful device are enormous when processing large amounts of traffic. Because the SRX Series device is one of the few stateful devices in the cloud network, it needs to be deployed to scale. As Figure 1-10 shows, the SRX5800 is chosen for this environment because it can

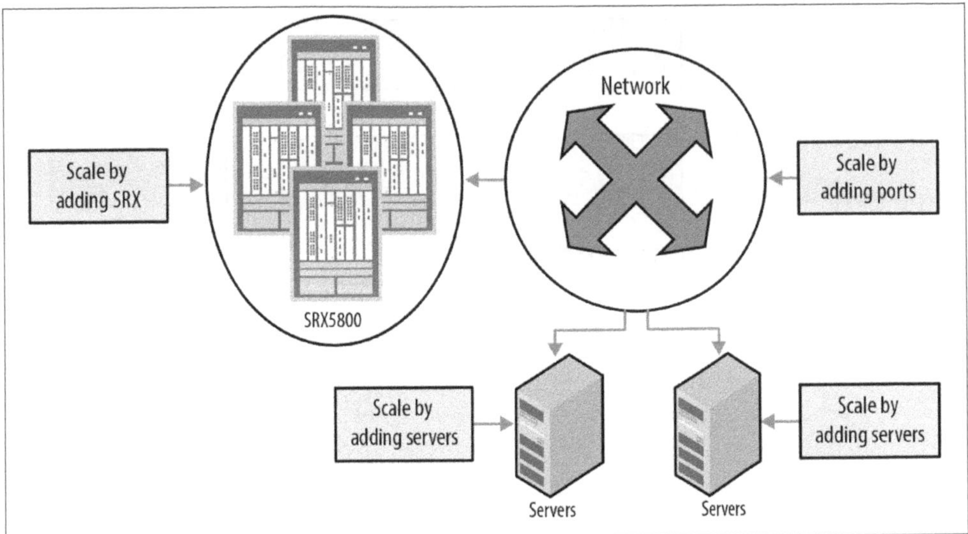

Figure 1-10. Cloud computing scaling

be deployed in many different configurations based on the needs of the deployment. The capabilities of the SRX5800 are discussed in Chapter 2.

Because of the dynamic nature of cloud computing, infrastructure provisioning of services must be done seamlessly. This goes for every component in the network, including the servers, the network, and the firewalls. Juniper Networks provides several options for managing all of its devices, as shown in Figure 1-11, which illustrates the management paradigm for the devices.

Just as the provisioning model scales for the needs of any organization, so does the cloud computing model. On the far left in Figure 1-11, direct hands-on or user device management is shown. This is the device management done by an administrator through the CLI or web management system (J-Web). The next example is the command of the device by way of its native application programming interface (API; either Junos automation or NETCONF, both of which we discuss in Chapter 2), where either a client or a script would need to act as the controller that would use the API to provision the device.

The remaining management examples are similar to the first two examples of the provisioning model, except they utilize a central management console provided by Juniper Networks. Model three shows a user interacting with the default client provided by the Juniper Networks NSM or Junos Space. In this case, the NSM uses the native API to talk to the devices.

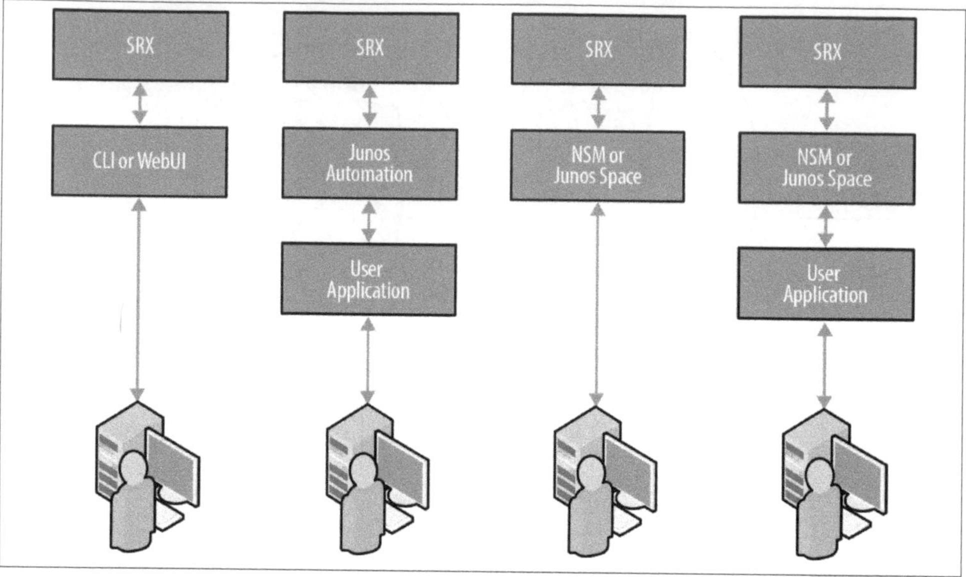

Figure 1-11. Juniper Networks management paradigm

Lastly, management option six is the most layered and scalable approach. It shows a custom-written application controlling the NSM directly with its own API, and then controlling the devices with its own API.

Although this approach seems highly layered, it provides many advantages in an environment where scaling is required. First, it allows for the creation of a custom application to provide network-wide provisioning in a case where a single management product is not available to manage all of the devices on the network. Second, the native Juniper application is developed specifically around the Juniper devices, thus taking advantage of the inherent health checks and services without having to integrate them.

The Junos Enterprise Services Reference Network

To simplify the SRX Series learning process, this book consistently uses a single topology that contains a number of SRX Series devices and covers all of the scenarios, many of the tutorials, and all of the case studies in the book. A single reference network allows the reader to follow along and only have to reference one network map.

This book's reference network is primarily focused on branch topologies because the majority of readers have access to those units. For readers who are interested in or are using the data center SRX products, these are discussed as well, but the larger devices are not the focus for most of the scenarios. Where differences exist, they will be noted.

Figure 1-12 shows this book's reference network. The network consists of three branch deployments, two data center firewall deployments, and remote VPN users. Five of the topologies represent HA clusters with only a single location that specifies a non-HA deployment. The Internet is the network that provides connectivity among all of the SRX Series deployments. Although the reference network is not the perfect "real-world" network, it does provide the perfect topology to cover all of the features in the SRX Series.

Although three of the locations are called *branches*, they could also represent standalone offices without a relationship to any other location.

The first location to review is the South Branch location. The South Branch location is a typical small branch, using a single SRX100 device. This device is a small, low-cost appliance that can provide a wide range of features for a location with 2 to 10 users and perhaps a wireless access point, as shown in the close-up view in Figure 1-13. The remote users at this location can access both the Internet and other locations over an IPsec VPN connection. Security is provided by using a combination of stateful firewalling, IPS, and UTM.

The West Branch, shown in Figure 1-14, is a larger remote branch location. The West Branch location uses two SRX240 firewalls. These firewalls are larger in capacity than the SRX210 devices in terms of ports, throughput, and concurrent sessions. They are designed for a network with more than 10 users or where greater throughputs are needed. Because this branch has more local users, HA is required to prevent loss of productivity due to loss of access to the Internet or the corporate network.

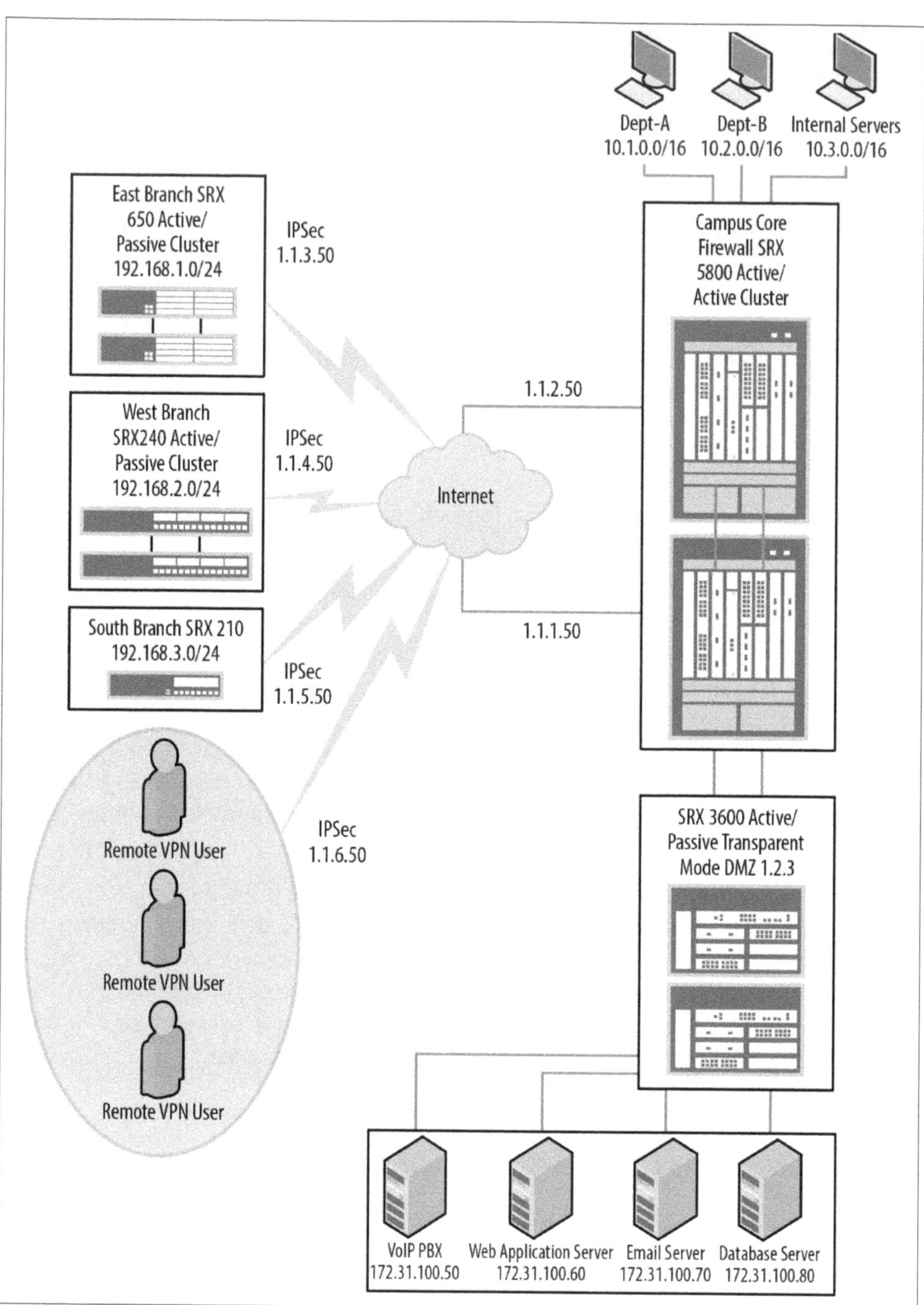

Figure 1-12. Reference network

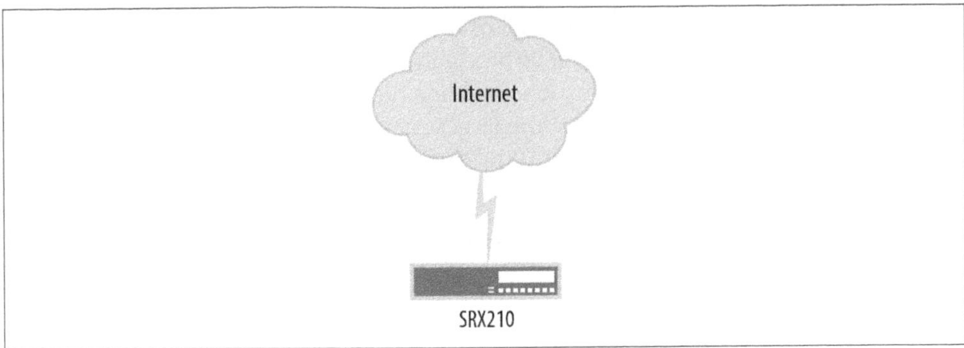

Figure 1-13. South Branch reference network

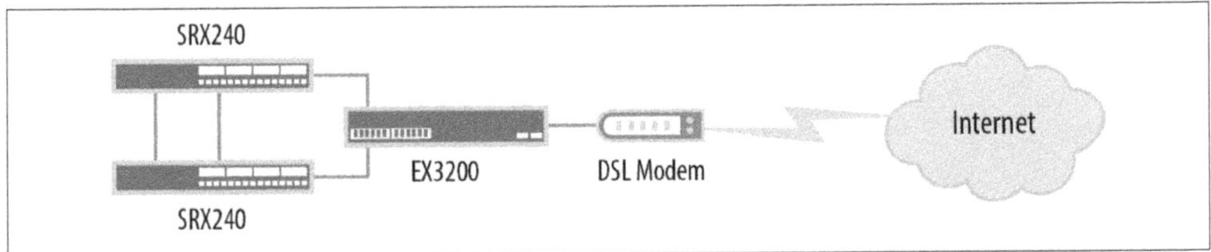

Figure 1-14. West Branch reference network

The East Branch location uses the largest branch firewall, the SRX650. This deployment represents both a large branch and a typical office environment where support for hundreds of users and several gigabits per second of throughput is needed. The detailed view of the East Branch is shown in Figure 1-15. This deployment, much like that of the West Branch, utilizes HA. Just as with the other branch SRX Series devices, the SRX650 devices can also use IPS, UTM, stateful firewalling, NAT, and many other security features. The SRX650 provides the highest possible throughput for these features compared to any other *branch* product line.

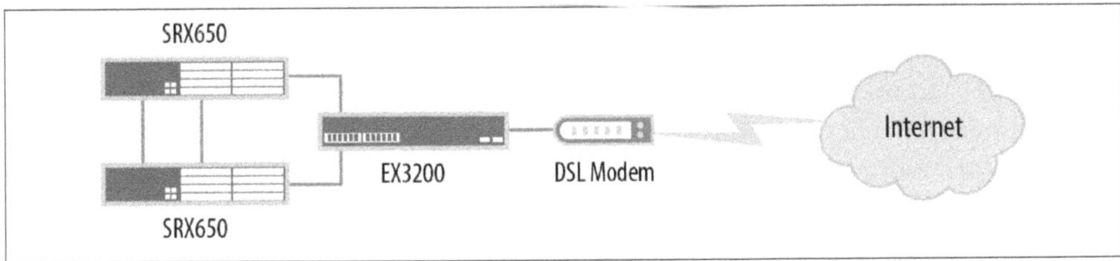

Figure 1-15. East Branch reference network

Deployment of the campus core firewalls of our reference network will be our first exploration into the high-end or data center SRX Series devices. These are the largest firewalls of the Juniper Networks firewall product line (at the time of this book's publication). The deployment uses SRX5800 products, and more than 98 percent of the data center SRX Series firewalls sold are deployed in a highly available deployment, as represented here. These firewalls secure the largest network in the reference design, and Figure 1-16 illustrates a detailed view of the campus core.

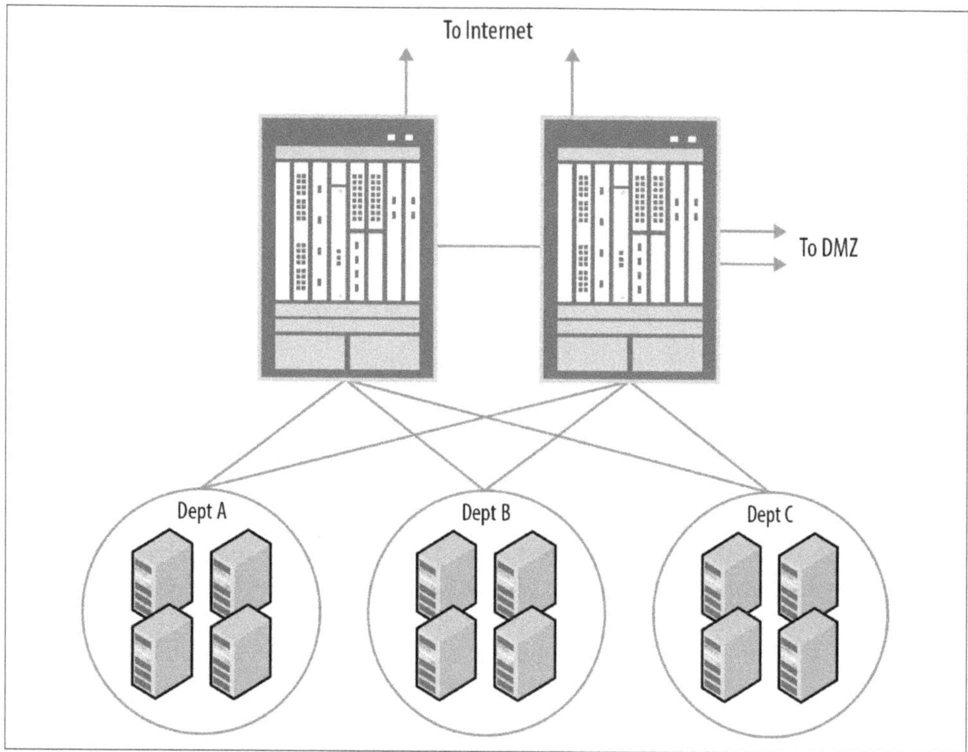

Figure 1-16. Campus core detailed view

Our campus core example network shows three networks; in a "real-world" deployment this could be hundreds or thousands of networks, but to show the fundamentals of the design and to fit on the printed page, only three are used: Department-A, Department-B, and the Internal Servers networks. These are separated by the SRX5800 HA cluster. Each network has a simple switch to allow multiple hosts to talk to each other. Off the campus core firewalls is a demilitarized zone (DMZ) SRX Series firewall cluster, as shown in Figure 1-17.

The DMZ SRX Series devices' firewall deployment uses an SRX3600 firewall cluster. The SRX3600 firewalls are perfect for providing interface density with high capacity and performance. In the DMZ network, several important servers are deployed. These servers provide critical services to the network and need to be secured to ensure service continuity.

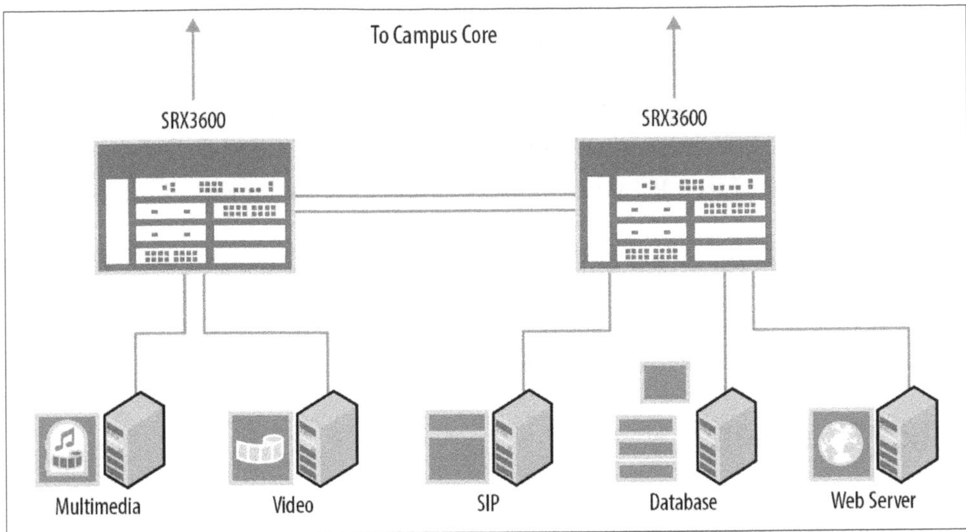

Figure 1-17. DMZ firewalls detailed view

This DMZ deployment is unique compared to the other network deployments because it is the only one that highlights *transparent mode* deployment, which allows the firewall to act as a bridge. Instead of routing packets like a Layer 3 firewall would, it routes packets to a destination host using its media access control (MAC) address. This allows the firewall to act as a transparent device, hence the term.

Finally, you might note that the remote VPN users are an example use case of two different types of IPsec access to the SRX Series firewalls. The first is the Dynamic VPN client, which is a dynamically downloaded client that allows client VPN access into the branch networks. The second client type highlighted is a third-party client, which is not provided by Juniper but is recommended when a customer wants to utilize a standalone software client. We will cover both use cases in Chapter 10. Last, customers often deploy a MAG Pulse appliance. This allows for Secure Sockets Layer (SSL) VPN termination.

The reference network contains the most common deployments for the SRX Series products, allowing you to see the full breadth of topologies within which the SRX Series is deployed. The depicted topologies show all the features of the SRX Series in ways in which actual customers use the products. We intend for real administrators to sit down and understand how the SRX Series is used and learn how to configure it. We have seen the majority of SRX Series deployments in the world and boiled them down to our reference network.

Summary

This chapter covered the most common deployment options for an SRX. This by no means covers all of the possible types of configurations. The new types of designs that customers use to solve complex network issues always impress us at Juniper Networks. By harnessing the power of Junos and a bit of creativity, the SRX can solve most network deployments. This speaks volumes about the capabilities of the SRX. Often we are tapping into new possible deployment models to solve complex problems.

The development of the SRX tends to focus on the use cases covered in this book. It ensures that the SRX can offer optimal solutions for the most desired use cases. These specific scenarios are covered in various test beds ensuring the best possible stability and features to solve these common problems. Without a specific direction, the SRX would become a mismatch of features that wouldn't solve anyone's problems without expending a great amount of configuration effort.

Study Questions

Questions

1. What is the importance of deep packet inspection?
2. What was the name of the OS that the SRX evolved from?
3. What security concept did the SRX inherit from its predecessor that simplified policy creation?
4. What application is used in Junos Space to manage SRX policies?
5. What is the core design change that SRX brought over the NetScreen devices?
6. What are the two classes or types of SRX devices?

Answers

1. Deep packet inspection allows looking inside of the application layer of a packet. This technology is used in IPS, AppSecure, UTM, and other features to determine what the traffic contains.
2. ScreenOS was the OS that SRX used as a starting point for the products' evolution.
3. This concept is called zones. It allows for a simpler abstract to use when creating policies. It also reduces the lookup tables for policies, providing faster lookups for matches.

4. Security Design is the application that simplifies policy management for the SRX devices.
5. The SRX is focused on providing services, whereas the NetScreen devices were focused on stateful inspection.
6. The two SRX device classes are branch and data center. The data center devices are also often called high-end firewalls.

CHAPTER 2

SRX Series Product Lines

In Chapter 1, we focused on SRX Series examples and concepts more than anything, and hopefully this approach has allowed you to readily identify the SRX Series products and their typical uses. In this chapter, we take a deep dive into the products so that you can link the specific features of each to a realistic view of its capabilities. We begin with what is common to the entire SRX Series, and then, as before, we divide the product line into branch and data center categories.

Before the deep dive into each SRX Series product, we must note that each SRX Series platform has a core set of features that are shared across the other platforms. Some of the platforms have different features that are not shared. This might lead to some confusion, because feature parity is not the same across all of the platforms, but the two product lines were designed with different purposes and the underlying architectures vary between the branch and the data center.

The branch SRX Series was designed for small and wide needs, meaning that the devices offer a wide set of features that can solve a variety of problems. This does not mean performance is poor, but rather that the products provide a lot of features.

The data center SRX Series was designed for scale and speed. This means these firewalls can scale from a smaller deployment up to huge performance numbers, all while keeping performance metrics to scale linearly. So, when configuring the modular data center SRX Series device, the designer is able to easily determine how much hardware is required.

Branch SRX Series

The majority of SRX Series firewalls sold and deployed are from within the branch SRX Series, designed primarily for average firewall deployment. Its three-digit product number can identify a branch SRX Series product. The first digit represents the series and the last two digits specify the specific model number. The number is used simply to identify the product; it doesn't represent performance, the number of ports, or have another special meaning.

When a branch product is deployed in a small office, as either a remote office location or a company's main firewall, it needs to provide many different features to secure the network and its users. This means it has to be a jack-of-all-trades, and in many cases, it is an organization's sole source of security.

Branch-Specific Features

Minimizing the number of pieces of network equipment is important in a remote or small office location, as that reduces the need to maintain several different types of equipment, their troubleshooting, and of course, their cost. One key to all of this consolidation is the network switch, and all of the branch SRX Series products provide full switching support. This includes support for spanning tree and line rate blind switching. Table 2-1 is a matrix of the possible number of supported interfaces per platform.

Table 2-1. Branch port matrix

	SRX100	SRX110	SRX210	SRX220	SRX240	SRX550	SRX650
10/100	8	8	6	0	0	0	0
10/100/1000	0	0	2	8	20	46	52
PoE	0	0	4	8	16	40	48
Fixed WAN	0	1	0	0	0	0	0
SFP	0	0	0	0	0	4	0

As of Junos 12.1X45, the data center SRX Series firewalls do not support blind switching. Although the goal is to provide this feature in the future, it is more cost-effective to utilize a Juniper Networks EX Series Ethernet Switch to provide line rate switching and then create an aggregate link back to a data center SRX Series product to provide secure routing between VLANs. In the future, Juniper may add this feature to its data center SRX Series products.

In most branch locations, SRX Series products are deployed as the only source of security. Because of this, some of the services that are typically distributed can be consolidated into the SRX, such as antivirus. Antivirus is a feature that the branch SRX Series can offer to its local network when applied to the following protocols: Simple Mail Transfer Protocol (SMTP), Post Office Protocol 3 (POP3), Internet Message Access Protocol (IMAP), Hyper Text Transfer Protocol (HTTP), and File Transfer Protocol (FTP). The SRX Series scans for viruses silently as the data is passed through the network, allowing it to stop viruses on the protocols where viruses are most commonly found.

The data center SRX Series does not support the antivirus feature as of Junos 12.1X45. In organizations that deploy a data center SRX Series product, the antivirus feature set is typically decentralized for increased security as well as enabling antivirus scanning while maintaining the required performance for a data center. A bigger focus for security is utilizing IPS to secure connections into servers in a data center. This is a more common requirement than antivirus. The IPS feature is supported on both the high-end and branch SRX Series product lines.

Antispam is another UTM feature set that aids in consolidation of services on the branch SRX Series. Today, it's reported that almost 95 percent of the email in the world is spam. And this affects productivity. In addition, although some messages are harmless, offering general-use products, others contain vulgar images, sexual overtures, or illicit offers. These messages can be offensive, a general nuisance, and a distraction.

The antispam technology included on the SRX Series can prevent such spam from being received, and it removes the need to use antispam software on another server.

Much like antivirus, the data center SRX Series does not provide antispam services. In data center locations where mail services are intended for thousands of users, a larger solution is needed that is distributed on mail proxies or on the mail servers.

Controlling access to what a user can or can't see on the Internet is called *universal resource locator* (URL) *filtering*. URL filtering allows the administrator to limit what categories of websites can be accessed. Sites that contain pornographic material might seem like the most logical to block, but other types of sites are common too, such as social networking sites that can be time sinks for employees. There is also a class of sites that company policy blocks or temporarily allows access to—for instance, during lunch hour. In any case, all of this is possible on the branch SRX Series products.

For the data center SRX Series product line, URL filtering is not currently integrated. In many large data centers where servers are protected, URL filtering is not needed or is delegated to other products.

Because *branch* tends to mean small locations all over the world, these branches typically require access to the local LAN for desktop maintenance or to securely access other resources. To provide a low-cost and effective solution, Juniper has introduced the *Dynamic VPN client*. This IPsec client allows for dynamic access to the branch without any preinstalled software on the client station, a very helpful feature to have in the branch so that remote access is simple to set up and requires very little maintenance.

Dynamic VPN is not available on the data center SRX devices. Juniper Networks recommends the use of its SA Series SSL VPN Appliances, allowing for the scaling of tens of thousands of users while providing a rich set of features that go beyond just network access.

When the need for cost-saving consolidation is strong in certain branch scenarios, adding wireless, both cellular and WiFi, can provide interesting challenges. Part of the challenge concerns consolidating these capabilities into a device while not providing radio frequency (RF) interference; the other part concerns providing a device that can be centrally placed and still receive or send enough wireless power to provide value.

All electronic devices give off some sort of RF interference, and all electronic devices state this clearly on their packaging or labels. Although this might be minor interference in the greater scheme of things, it can also be extremely detrimental to wireless technologies such as cellular Internet access or WiFi—therefore, extreme care is required when integrating these features into any product. Some of the branch SRX Series products have the capability to attach a cellular Internet card or USB dongle directly to them, which can make sense in some small branch locations because, typically, cellular signals are fairly strong throughout most buildings.

But what if the device is placed in the basement where it's not very effective at receiving these cellular signals? Because of this and other office scenarios, Juniper Networks provides a product that can be placed anywhere and is both powered and managed by the SRX Series: the Juniper Networks CX111 Cellular Broadband Data.

The same challenge carries over for WiFi. If an SRX Series product is placed in a back room or basement, an integrated WiFi access point might not be very relevant, so Juniper took the same approach and provides an external access point (AP) called the AX411 Wireless LAN Access Point. This AP is managed and powered by any of the branch SRX Series products.

As you might guess, although the wireless features are very compelling for the branch, they aren't very useful in a data center. Juniper has abstained from bringing wireless features to the data center SRX Series products. Instead Juniper recommends deploying the Juniper Wireless LAN solutions based on the Trapeze acquisition.

The first Junos products for the enterprise market were the Juniper Networks J Series Services Routers, and the first iteration of the J Series was a packet-based device. This means the device acts on each packet individually without any concern for the next packet—typical of how a traditional router operates. Over time, Juniper moved the J Series products toward the capabilities of a flow-based device, and this is where the SRX Series devices evolved from.

Although a flow-based device has many merits, it's unwise to move away from being able to provide packet services, so the SRX Series can run in packet mode as well as flow. It's even possible to run both modes simultaneously! This allows the SRX Series to act as traditional packet-based routers and to run advanced services such as MPLS.

MPLS as a technology is not new—carrier networks have been using it for years. Many enterprise networks have used MPLS, but typically it has been done transparently to the enterprise. Now, with the SRX Series, the enterprise has a low-cost solution, so it can create its own MPLS network, bringing the power back to the enterprise from the service providers and saving money on MPLS as a managed service. On the flip side, it allows the service providers to offer a low-cost service that can provide security and MPLS in a single platform. MPLS and its family of protocols is fairly complex and is outside of the scope of this book. Please refer to *Junos Enterprise Routing* for an in-depth look at the subject.

The last feature common to the branch SRX Series products is their ability to utilize many types of WAN interfaces. We will detail these interface types as we drill down into each SRX Series platform.

The data center SRX Series products only utilize Ethernet interfaces. These are the most common interfaces used in the locations where these products are deployed, and where a data center SRX Series product is deployed, they are typically paired with a Juniper Networks MX Series 3D Universal Edge Router, which can provide WAN interfaces.

SRX100 Series

The SRX100 series, as of Junos 12.1X45, has two products in the line (if you remember from the SRX numbering scheme, the 1 is the series number and the 00 is the product number inside that series). The SRX100 Services Gateway is shown in Figure 2-1, and it is a fixed form factor, meaning no additional modules or changes can be made to the product after it is purchased. As you can see in Figure 2-1, the SRX100 has a total of eight 10/100 Ethernet ports, and perhaps more difficult to see, but clearly onboard, are a serial console port and a USB port.

Figure 2-1. The SRX100

The eight Ethernet ports can be configured in many different ways. They could be configured in the traditional manner, in which each port has a single IP address, or they can be configured in any combination as an Ethernet switch. The same switching capabilities of the EX Series switches have been combined into the SRX100 so that the SRX100 not only supports line rate blind switching but also supports several variants of the spanning tree protocols; therefore, if the network is expanded in the future, an errant configuration won't lead to a network loop. The SRX100 can also provide a default gateway on its local switch by using a VLAN interface, as well as a Dynamic Host Configuration Protocol (DHCP) server.

Although the SRX100 is a small, desktop-sized device, it's also a high-performing platform. It certainly stands out by providing up to 650 Mbps of throughput. This might seem like an exorbitant amount of throughput for a branch platform, but it's warranted where security is needed between two local network devices. For such a WAN connection, 650 Mbps is far more than what would be needed in a location that would use this type of device, but small offices have a way of growing.

Speaking of performance, the SRX100 supports high rates of VPN, IPS, and antivirus as well if the need to use these features arises in locations where the SRX100 is deployed. The SRX100 also supports a session ramp-up rate of 2,000 new connections per second (CPS), or the number of new TCP-based sessions that can be created per second. UDP sessions are also supported, but this new-session-per-second metric is rated with TCP because it takes three times the number of packets per second to process than it would UDP to set up a session (see Table 2-2).

Table 2-2. SRX100 capacities

Type	Capacity
CPS	1,800
Maximum firewall throughput	700 Mbps
Maximum IPS throughput	75 Mbps
Maximum AppSecure throughout	90 Mpbs
Maximum VPN throughput	65 Mbps

Type	Capacity	
Maximum antivirus throughput (Sophos AV)	25 Mbps	
Maximum concurrent sessions	16K (512 MB of RAM)	32K (1 GB of RAM)
Maximum firewall policies	384	
Maximum concurrent users	Unlimited	

Although 1,800 new connections per second seems like overkill, it isn't. Many applications today are written in such a way that they might attempt to grab 100 or more data streams simultaneously. If the local firewall device is unable to handle this rate of new connections, these applications could fail to complete their transactions, leading to user complaints and, ultimately, the cost or loss of time in troubleshooting the network.

Also, because users might require many concurrent sessions, the SRX100 can support up to 32,000 sessions. A *session* is a current connection that is monitored between two peers, and can be of the more common protocols of TCP and UDP or of other protocols such as Encapsulating Security Payload (ESP) or Generic Routing Encapsulation (GRE).

The SRX100 has two separate memory options: low-memory and high-memory versions. They don't require a change of hardware, but simply the addition of a license key to activate access to the additional memory. The base memory version uses 512 MB of memory and the high-memory version uses 1 GB of memory. When the license key is added, and after a reboot, the new SRX Series flow daemon is brought online. The new flow daemon is designed to access the entire 1 GB of memory.

Activating the 1 GB of memory does more than just enable twice the number of sessions; it is required to utilize UTM. If any of the UTM features are activated, the total number of sessions is cut back to the number of low-memory sessions. Reducing the number of sessions allows the UTM processes to run. The administrator can choose whether sessions or the UTM features are the more important option.

The SRX100 series has also added a new model: the SRX110. There are two differences between the SRX110 and the SRX100, a built-in VDSL/ADSL2+ port being the biggest difference. This allows for the small device to deliver an integrated WAN port, removing the need to go to a larger device if you need a DSL port. The second difference is the SRX110 only comes in a high-memory model. It is the only SRX that comes with a fixed WAN interface. Figure 2-2 shows off the SRX110.

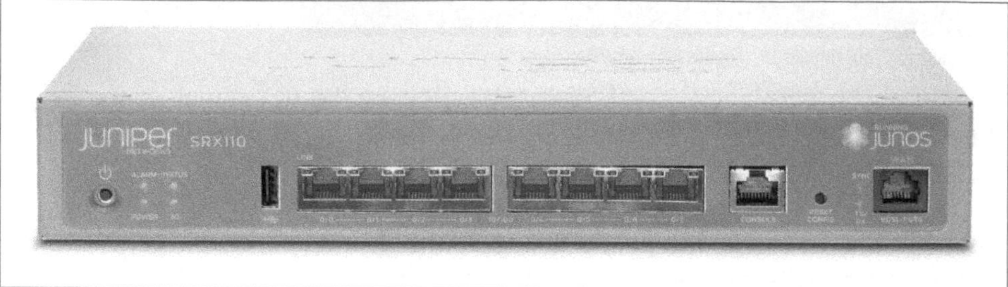

Figure 2-2. The SRX110

The SRX100 can be placed in one of four different options. The default placement is on any flat surface. The other three require additional hardware to be ordered: vertically on a desktop, in a network equipment rack, or mounted on a wall. The wall mount kit can accommodate a single SRX100, and the rack mount kit can accommodate up to two SRX100 units in a single rack unit.

SRX200 Series

The SRX200 line is the next step up in the branch SRX Series. The goal of the SRX200 line is to provide modular solutions to branch environments. This modularity comes through the use of various interface modules that allow the SRX200 line to connect to a variety of media types such as T1. Furthermore, the modules can be shared among all of the devices in the line.

The first device in the line is the SRX210. It is similar to the SRX100, except that it has additional expansion capabilities and extended throughput. The SRX210 has eight Ethernet ports, like the SRX100 does, but it also includes two 10/100/100 tri-speed Ethernet ports, allowing high-speed devices such as switches or servers to be connected. In addition, the SRX210 can be optionally ordered with built-in Power over Ethernet (PoE) ports. If this option is selected, the first four ports on the device can provide up to 15.4W of power to devices, be they Voice over Internet Protocol (VoIP) phones or Juniper's AX and CX wireless devices.

Figure 2-3 shows the SRX210. Note in the top right the large slot where the mini-PIM is inserted. The front panel includes the eight Ethernet ports. Similar to the SRX100, the SRX210 includes a serial console port and, in this case, two USB ports. The eight Ethernet ports can be used (just like the SRX100) to provide line rate blind switching, a traditional Layer 3 interface, or both.

The rear of the box contains a surprise. In the rear left, as depicted in Figure 2-4, an ExpressCard slot is shown. This ExpressCard slot can utilize 3G or cellular modem cards to provide access to the Internet, which is useful for dial backup or the new concept of a *zero-day branch*. In the past, when an organization wanted to roll out branches rapidly, it required the provisioning of a private circuit or a form of Internet access. It might take weeks or months to get this service installed. With the use of a 3G card, a branch can be installed the same day, allowing organizations and operations to move quickly to reach new markets or emergency locations. Once a permanent circuit is deployed, the 3G card can be used for dial backup or moved to a new location.

Figure 2-3. The front of the SRX210

Figure 2-4. The back of the SRX210

The performance of the SRX210 is within the range of the SRX100, but it is a higher level of performance than the SRX100 across all of its various capabilities. As you can see in Table 2-3, the overall throughput increased from 650 Mbps on the SRX100 to 750 Mbps on the SRX210. The same goes for the IPS, VPN, and antivirus throughputs. They each increased by about 10 percent over the SRX100. A significant change is the fact that the total number of sessions doubles, for both the low-memory and high-memory versions. That is a significant advantage in addition to the modularity of the platform. In 2012 the SRX210 platform was silently upgraded, giving newer devices increased throughput over the original edition. The new SRX210 is called the enhanced version, but the name is interchangeable.

Table 2-3. SRX210 capacities

Type	Capacity	
CPS	2,200	
Maximum firewall throughput	850 Mbps	
Maximum IPS throughput	65 Mbps	
Maximum AppSecure throughput	250 Mbps	
Maximum VPN throughput	85 Mbps	
Maximum antivirus throughput (Sophos AV)	30 Mbps	
Maximum concurrent sessions	32K (512 MB of RAM)	64K (1 GB of RAM)
Maximum firewall policies	512	
Maximum concurrent users	Unlimited	

The SRX210 consists of three hardware models: the base memory model, the high-memory model, and the PoE with high-memory model (it isn't possible to purchase a base memory model and PoE). Unlike the SRX100, the memory models are actually fixed and cannot be upgraded with a license key. So when planning for a rollout with the SRX210, it's best to plan ahead in terms of what you think the device will need. The SRX210 also has a few hardware accessories: it can be ordered with a desktop stand, a rack mount kit, or a wall mount kit. The rack mount kit can accommodate one SRX210 in a single rack unit.

The SRX220 fits cleanly between the SRX210 and SRX240. The SRX220 is characterized by having 8x10/100/1000 ports and two mini-PIM slots. The SRX220 does not have an ExpressCard slot, but it can use its onboard USB port to connect 3G modems (see Figure 2-5 and Figure 2-6). The SRX220 is a great choice for a branch network where you require additional mini-PIM slots and up to eight tri-speed Ethernet ports. All eight Ethernet ports also offer Power over Ethernet.

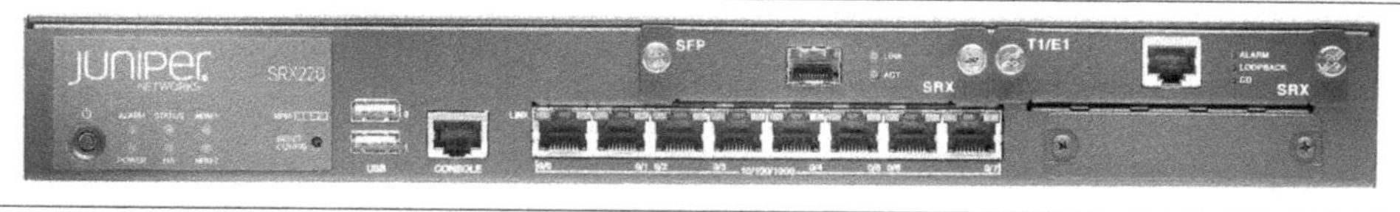

Figure 2-5. The front of the SRX220

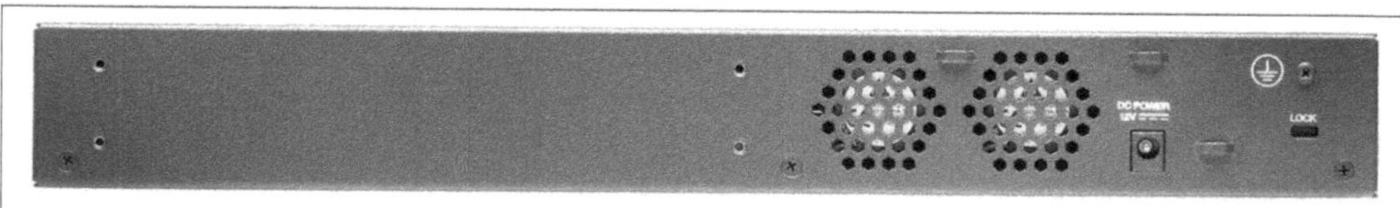

Figure 2-6. The back of the SRX220

As expected, the performance of the SRX220 does fit cleanly between the SRX240 and SRX210 (see Table 2-4). The SRX220 offers a marginal performance boost over the SRX210 but only offers about half the performance of the SRX240. The SRX220 is a good fit into a network when more connectivity than the SRX210 is needed but the pricing of the SRX240 is too much.

Table 2-4. SRX220 capacities

Type	Capacity
CPS	2,800
Maximum firewall throughput	950 Mbps
Maximum IPS throughput	80 Mbps
Maximum AppSecure throughput	300 Mbps
Maximum VPN throughput	100 Mbps
Maximum antivirus throughput (Sophos AV)	35 Mbps
Maximum concurrent sessions	96K
Maximum firewall policies	2048
Maximum concurrent users	Unlimited

The SRX240 is the first departure from the small desktop form factor, as it is designed to be mounted in a single rack unit. It also can be placed on the top of a desk and is about the size of a pizza box. The SRX240, unlike the other members of the SRX200 line, includes sixteen 10/100/1000 Ethernet ports, but like the other two platforms, line rate switching can be achieved between all of the ports that are configured in the same VLAN. It's also possible to configure interfaces as a standard Layer 3 interface, and each interface can also contain multiple subinterfaces. Each subinterface is on its own separate VLAN. This is a capability that is shared across all of the SRX product lines, but it's typically used on the SRX240 because the SRX240 is deployed on larger networks.

Figure 2-7 shows the SRX240, and you should be able to see the sixteen 10/100/1000 Ethernet ports across the bottom front of the device. There's the standard fare of one serial console port and two USB ports, and on the top of the front panel of the SRX240 are the four mini-PIM slots. These slots can be used for any combination of supported mini-PIM cards.

The performance of the SRX240 is double that of the other platforms. It's designed for midrange to large branch locations and can handle more than eight times the connections per second, for up to 9,000 CPS. Not only is this good for outbound traffic, but it is also great for hosting small- to medium-size services behind the device—including web, DNS, and email services, which are typical services for a branch network. The throughput for the device is enough for a small network, as it can secure more than 1 gigabit per second of traffic. This actually allows several servers to sit behind it and for the traffic to them from both the internal and external networks to be secured. The

Figure 2-7. The SRX240

device can also provide for some high IPS throughput, which is great for inspecting traffic as it goes through the device from untrusted hosts.

Again, Table 2-5 shows that the total number of sessions on the device has doubled from the lower models. The maximum rate of 128,000 sessions is considerably large for most networks. Just as you saw on the SRX210, the SRX240 provides three different hardware models: the base memory model that includes 512 MB of memory (it's unable to run UTM and runs with half the number of sessions); the high-memory version, which has twice the amount of memory on the device (it's able to run UTM with an additional license); and the high-memory with PoE model that can provide PoE to all 16 of its built-in Ethernet ports. In 2012, the SRX240 was silently bumped up to what is known as the enhanced model. This model offers up to 2 GB of RAM, which boosts the overall capacity of the device. Also the CPU was slightly increased to offer some additional throughput. The SRX240 enhanced and the SRX240 model names are used interchangeably. The only real restriction is that the older and newer SRX240s cannot be clustered together.

Table 2-5. SRX240 capacities

Type	Capacity	
CPS	8,500	
Maximum firewall throughput	1.8 Gbps	
Maximum IPS throughput	230 Mbps	
Maximum VPN throughput	300 Mbps	
Maximum antivirus throughput	85 Mbps	
Maximum concurrent sessions	128K (1 GB of RAM)	256K (2 GB of RAM)
Maximum firewall policies	4,096	
Maximum concurrent users	Unlimited	

Interface modules for the SRX200 line

The SRX200 Series Services Gateways currently support six different types of mini-PIMs, as shown in Table 2-6. On the SRX240 these can be mixed and matched to support any combination that the administrator chooses, offering great flexibility if there is a need to have several different types of WAN interfaces. The administrator can also add up to a total of four Small Form-Factor Pluggable Interface Modules (SFP) mini-PIM modules on the SRX240, giving it a total of 20 gigabit Ethernet ports. The SFP ports can be either a fiber optic connection or a copper twisted pair link. The SRX210 can only accept one card at a time, so there isn't a capability to mix and match cards, although, as stated, the SRX210 can accept any of the cards. Although the SRX210 is not capable of inspecting gigabit speeds of traffic, a fiber connection might be required in the event that a long haul fiber is used to connect the SRX210 to the network.

Table 2-6. Mini-PIMs

Type	Description
ADSL	1-port ADSL2+ mini-PIM supporting ADSL/ADSL2/ADSL2+ Annex A
ADSL	1-port ADSL2+ mini-PIM supporting ADSL/ADSL2/ADSL2+ Annex B
G.SHDSL	8-wire (4-pair) G.SHDSL mini-PIM
Serial	1-port Sync Serial mini-PIM
SFP	1-port SFP mini-PIM
T1/E1	1-port T1/E1 mini-PIM
DOCIS 3.0 Cable Model	1-port 75 OHM coaxial cable

The ADSL cards support all of the modern standards for DSL and work with most major carriers. The G.SHDSL standard is much newer than the older ADSL, and it is a higher speed version of DSL that is provided over traditional twisted pair lines. Among the three types of cards, all common forms of ADSL are available to the SRX200 line.

New to the mini-PIM line is the DOCSIS 3.0 card. This card allows an SRX200 Series device to act as a cable modem. This is quite desirable as cable modems are both stable and fast enough for most businesses today.

The SRX200 line also supports the use of the tried-and-true serial port connection. This allows for connection to an external serial port and is the least commonly used interface card. A more commonly used interface card is the T1/E1 card, which is typical for WAN connection to the SRX200 line. Although a T1/E1 connection might be slow by today's standards, compared to the average home broadband connection, it is still commonly used in remote branch offices.

SRX500 Series

The SRX500 line is a device that sits between the SRX240 and the SRX650. It is designed to offer cost-effective, high-performing security to the branch market. It offers G-PIM, X-PIM, and mini-PIM support for both WAN and LAN interfaces. This is the largest device that offers mini-PIM support. This series of devices was created when customers craved the performance of an SRX650 but wanted mini-PIM support in a more cost-effective package. There is currently only one product in this series, the SRX550 (see Figure 2-8).

Figure 2-8. The SRX550

The performance of the SRX550 (see Table 2-7) is a bit more than double that of the SRX240 and about 30 percent less than that of the SRX650. Its performance is very strong for its price point in the SRX line. It includes 10 fixed ports, 6 of which are tri-speed copper Ethernet ports and the other 4 of which are SFPs. The SRX550 supports dual power supplies, and the base power supplies include the capability to provide partial Power over Ethernet support. To provide full PoE powering, two power supplies are required. When enabling UTM on the SRX550, the maximum session capacity is cut in half to allow for the additional UTM processing. At a base of 375,000 concurrent sessions, even with UTM enabled, there still should be a significant amount of session capacity available for most environments.

Table 2-7. SRX550 capacities

Type	Capacity
CPS	27,000
Maximum firewall throughput	5.5 Gbps
Maximum IPS throughput	800 Mbps
Maximum VPN throughput	1 Gbps
Maximum antivirus throughput	300 Mbps
Maximum concurrent sessions	375K
Maximum firewall policies	7,256
Maximum concurrent users	Unlimited

SRX600 Series

The SRX600 line is the most different from the others in the branch SRX Series. This line is extremely modular and offers very high performance for a device that is categorized as a branch solution.

The only model in the SRX600 line (at the time of this writing) is the SRX650. The SRX650 comes with four onboard 10/100/1000 ports. All the remaining components are modules. The base system comes with the chassis and a component called the *Services and Routing Engine* (SRE). The SRE provides the processing and management capabilities for the platform. It has the same architecture as the other branch platforms, but this time the component for processing is modular.

Figure 2-9 shows the front of the SRX650 chassis, and the four onboard 10/100/1000 ports are found on the front left. The other items to notice are the eight modular slots, which are different here than in the other SRX platforms. Here the eight slots are called *G-PIM slots*, but it is also possible to utilize another card type called an *X-PIM*, which utilizes multiple G-PIM slots.

On the back of the SRX650 is where the SRE is placed. There are two slots that fit the SRE into the chassis, but note that as of the Junos 13.1 release, only the bottom slot can be used. In the future, the SRX650 might support a new double-height SRE, or even multiple SREs. On the SRE, there are several ports: first, the standard serial console port, and then a secondary serial auxiliary port, shown in the product illustration in Figure 2-10. Also, the SRE has two USB ports.

Figure 2-9. The front of the SRX650

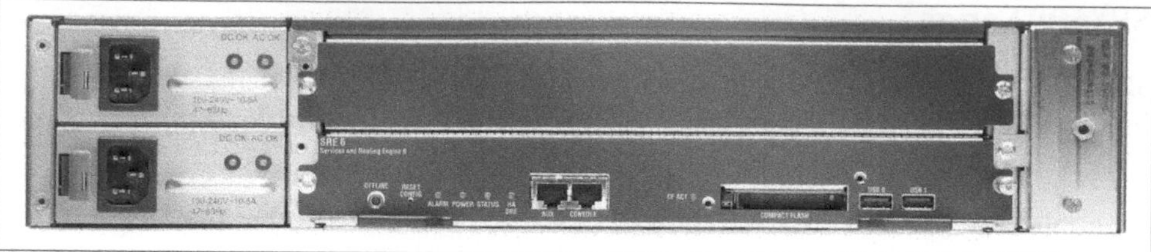

Figure 2-10. The back of the SRX650

New to this model is the inclusion of a secondary compact flash port. This port allows for expanded storage for logs or software images. The SRX650 also supports up to two power supplies for redundancy.

The crowning feature of the SRX650 is its performance capabilities. The SRX650 is more than enough for most branch office locations, allowing for growth in the branch office. As shown in Table 2-8, it can provide up to 30,000 new CPS, which is ample for a fair bit of servers that can be hosted behind the firewall. It also accounts for a large number of users that can be hosted behind the SRX. The total number of concurrent sessions is four times higher than on the SRX240, with a maximum of 500,000 sessions. Only 250,000 sessions are available when UTM is enabled; the other available memory is shifted for the UTM features to utilize.

Table 2-8. SRX650 capacities

Type	Capacity
CPS	30,000
Maximum firewall throughput	7 Gbps
Maximum IPS throughput	1.5 Gbps
Maximum VPN throughput	1.5 Gbps
Maximum antivirus throughput	350 Mbps
Maximum concurrent sessions	512K (2 GB of RAM)
Maximum firewall policies	8,192
Maximum concurrent users	Unlimited

The SRX650 can provide more than enough throughput on the device, and it can provide local switching as well. The maximum total throughput is 7 gigabits per second. This represents a fair bit of secure inspection of traffic in this platform. Also, for the available UTM services it provides, it is extremely fast. IPS performance exceeds 1 gigabit as well as VPN. The lowest performing value is the inline antivirus, and although 350 Mbps is far lower than the maximum throughput, it is very fast considering the amount of inspection that is needed to scan files for viruses.

Interface modules for the SRX600 line

The SRX650 has lots of different interface options that are not available on any other platform today. This makes the SRX650 fairly unique as a platform compared to the rest of the branch SRX Series. The SRX650 can use two different types of modules: the G-PIM and the X-PIM. The G-PIM occupies only one of the possible eight slots, whereas an X-PIM takes a minimum of two slots, and some X-PIMs take a maximum of four slots. Table 2-9 lists the different interface cards.

Table 2-9. SRX600 interface matrix

Type	Description	Slots
Dual T1/E1	Dual T1/E1, two ports with integrated CSU/DSU – G-PIM. Single G-PIM slot.	1
Quad T1/E1	Quad T1/E1, four ports with integrated CSU/DSU – G-PIM. Single G-PIM slot.	1
16-port 10/100/1000	Ethernet switch 16-port 10/100/1000-baseT X-PIM.	2
16-port 10/100/1000 PoE	Ethernet switch 16-port 10/100/1000-baseT X-PIM with PoE.	2
24-port 10/100/1000 plus four SFP ports	Ethernet switch 24-port 10/100/1000-baseT X-PIM. Includes four SFP slots.	4
24-port 10/100/1000 PoE plus four SFP ports	PoE Ethernet switch 24-port 10/100/1000-baseT X-PIM. Includes four SFP slots.	4

Two different types of G-PIM cards provide T1/E1 ports. One provides two T1/E1 ports and the other provides a total of four ports. These cards can go in any of the slots on the SRX650 chassis, up to the maximum of eight slots.

The next type of card is the dual-slot X-PIM. These cards provide sixteen 10/100/1000 ports and come in the PoE or non-PoE variety. Using this card takes up two of the eight slots. They can only be installed in the right side of the chassis, with a maximum of two cards in the chassis.

The third type of card is the quad-slot X-PIM. This card has 24 10/100/1000 ports and 4 SFP ports and comes in a PoE and non-PoE version. The SFP ports can use either fiber or twisted pair SFP transceivers. Figure 2-11 shows the possible locations of each type of card.

Local switching can be achieved at line rate for ports on the same card, meaning that on each card, switching must be done on that card to achieve line rate. It is not possible to configure switching across cards. All traffic that passes between cards must be inspected by the firewall, and the throughput is limited to the firewall's maximum inspection. Administrators who deploy the SRX should be aware of this limitation.

JunosV Firefly (Virtual Junos)

Today, buying computing power is cheap. For a few thousand dollars, one can buy a server with 12 or more processing cores and hundreds of gigabytes of memory. Because of this, the shift to virtualization has been occurring over the last several years. Today,

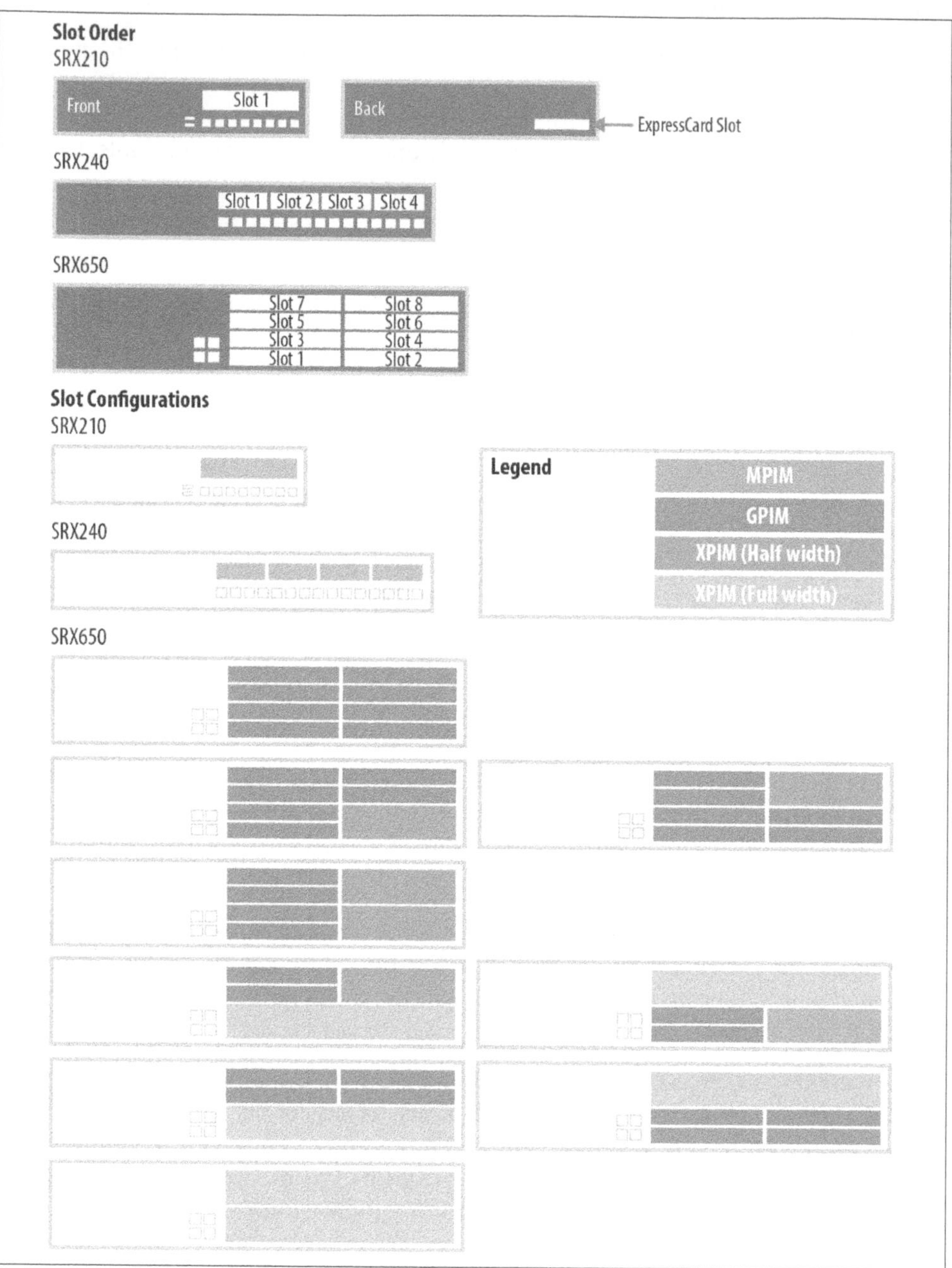

Figure 2-11. SRX650 PIM card diagram

you can contain what used to be an entire data center on just a few servers, so the virtualizing networking is a necessity. Originally, just switching was virtualized as part of the hypervisor (the software that provides an abstraction layer between the hardware and the virtual OS), but it is common to have entire networks exist within a server. Every network needs a border, and for servers, that would be a firewall.

The most popular hypervisor for virtualization is made by VMware. Because of this, the initial release of the product supports only VMware. In the future, Firefly will support other hypervisors such as Xen and KVM. As of early 2013, JunosV Firefly is in controlled availability, but it will be openly available soon.

AX411

The AX411 Wireless LAN Access Point is not an SRX device, but more of an accessory to the branch SRX Series product line. The AX411 cannot operate on its own without an SRX Series appliance. To use the AX411 device, simply plug it into an SRX device that has DHCP enabled and an AX411 license installed. The AP will get an IP address from the SRX and register with the device, and the configuration for the AX411 will be pushed down from the SRX to the AX411. Then queries can be sent from the SRX to the AX411 to get status on the device and its associated clients. Firmware updates and remote reboots are also handled by the SRX product.

The AX411 is designed to be placed wherever it's needed: on a desktop, mounted on a wall, or inside a drop ceiling. As shown in Figure 2-12, the AX411 has three antennas and one Ethernet port. It also has a console port, which is not user-accessible.

The AX411 has impressive wireless capabilities, as it supports 802.11a/b/g/n wireless networking. The three antennas provide multiple input–multiple output (MIMO) for maximum throughput. The device features two separate radios, one at the 2.4 GHz range and the other at the 5 GHz range. For the small branch, it meets all of the requirements of an AP. The AX411 is not meant to provide wireless access for a large campus network, so administrators should not expect to be able to deploy dozens of AX411 products in conjunction; the AX411 is not designed for this purpose.

Each SRX device in the branch SRX Series is only capable of managing a limited number of AX411 appliances, and Table 2-10 shows the number of APs per platform that can be managed. The SRX100 can manage up to two AX411 devices. From there, each platform doubles the total number of APs that can be managed, going all the way up to 16 APs on the SRX650.

Table 2-10. Access points per platform

Platform	Number of access points
SRX100	2
SRX210	4
SRX240	8
SRX650	16

Figure 2-12. The AX411 WLAN Access Point

CX111

The CX111 Cellular Broadband Data Bridge (see Figure 2-13) can be used in conjunction with the branch SRX Series products. The CX111 is designed to accept a 3G (or cellular) modem and then provide access to the Internet via a wireless carrier. The CX111 supports about 40 different manufacturers of these wireless cards and up to 3 USB wireless cards and 1 ExpressCard. Access to the various wireless providers can be always-on or dial-on-demand.

There aren't any specific hooks between the CX111 bridge and the SRX products. The CX111 can be utilized in combination with any branch product to act as a wireless bridge. The biggest benefit is that the CX111 can be placed anywhere that a wireless signal can be best reached, so the CX111 can be powered by using PoE or a separate power supply. This way, the SRX device can be placed in a back closet or under a counter, and the CX111 can be placed by a window.

Figure 2-13. The CX111

Branch SRX Series Hardware Overview

Although the branch SRX Series varies greatly in terms of form factors and capabilities, the underlying hardware architecture remains the same. Figure 2-14 is highly simplified, but it is meant to illustrate how the platforms have a common architecture. It also provides a certain clarity to how the data center SRX Series looks when compared to the branch SRX Series.

In the center of Figure 2-14 is the shared computer resource or processor. This processor is specifically designed for processing network traffic and is intended for scaling and to provide parallel processing. With parallel processing, more than one task can be executed at a time. In this case, parallel processing is achieved by having multiple hardware cores running separate threads of execution. See the sidebar "Parallel Processing".

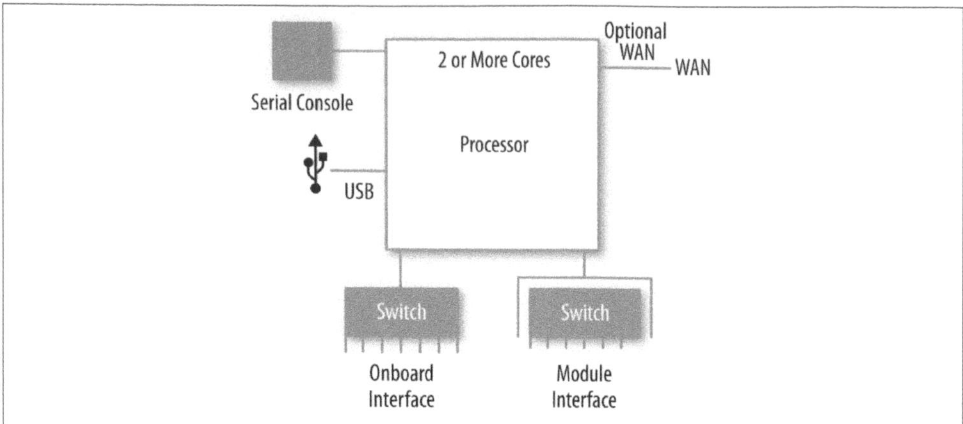

Figure 2-14. Branch SRX Series hardware overview

Connected off of this processor are the serial console and the USB ports. This allows the user to access the running system directly off of the serial console and any attached storage off of the USB ports.

Finally, in the overview are the interfaces. The interfaces connect off of the processor, and all of the onboard ports from each platform are connected as a local Ethernet switch. This is the same for all of the SRX products. Each WAN card is treated as a separate link back to the processor, and in the case of the SRX650, each Ethernet card is its own switch and then connects back to the processor. Although oversimplified, this should provide a simple understanding of what is happening inside the sheet metal.

Parallel Processing

The majority of the SRX products utilize dense processors. These processors have multiple cores, or the capability to run multiple simultaneous threads. Because there are many terms floating around, a little cleanup is in order. A *process* is an instance of a running program. It has its own memory space. On a CPU, only a single process can run at any given time.

A process can contain one or more *threads of execution*. A thread is a series of tasks that are being run in the CPU. To scale processing, tasks are broken up into individual threads. Much like when a user uses a GUI, all of the elements seem to work simultaneously, even though the computer might run only one at a time.

To use all of the processor capabilities, a process would need to run multiple *threads* or *spawn off* child processes. When a process spawns off a child process, the child process is born and receives a copy of the parent's process memory. At this point, if the parent process adds or removes anything from its memory, only the parent process is aware of it. The child process is running as its own atomic unit. If the parent process wants to notify the child process of a change, it has to use inter-process communication to send data.

Sending data across processes is slow in terms of processing. Scaling this level of communication and messaging can also be difficult. There are many good use cases for this, such as scaling a web server. A web server can run many processes to serve multiple clients. The processes might need to communicate, but the speed at which they communicate could be within several milliseconds. This is completely reasonable, as other processes, such as running a script or serving an image, will be slower.

In a firewall, the inter-process communication model is best avoided because adding several milliseconds to process traffic might not be acceptable. Of course, it depends on the device. Although in a branch device several additional milliseconds of latency might be fine, in the data center this must be avoided at all costs.

The SRX Series utilizes the thread methods for processing firewall flow data. The thread model uses a single process but utilizes multiple threads. Each thread is run on a processor core or individual hardware thread. All of the threads can execute simultaneously and process network traffic very quickly. By being part of a process, they can all share the same memory space. This allows threads to work on the same streams of information without having to pass information between them. This reduces latency and increases traffic processing efficiency.

Although this might seem like the best thing since sliced bread, it's very difficult to do. The application must be programmed to be *thread-safe*. Because all of the memory is shared, several conditions can occur where the process will crash, lock, or run infinitely without processing data. Avoiding these conditions has been one of the biggest challenges in programming over the past 40 years, and although there are several ways to solve the problem, it requires a huge amount of planning and expertise.

Licensing

The branch SRX Series supports numerous built-in features, including firewalling, routing, VPN, and NAT. However, some of the features require licensing to activate. This section is meant to clarify the licensing portion of the SRX products. Table 2-11 breaks out all of the possible licenses by vendor, description, and terms.

In regard to Table 2-11, note the following:

- You can purchase a single license for all of the UTM features, including the antivirus, antispam, intrusion protection, and web filtering features.
- Dynamic VPN is sold as a per-seat license, which counts the number of active users utilizing the features. This feature is only supported on the SRX100, SRX210, and SRX240.

- The SRX650 and SRX550 can support the ability to act as a Border Gateway Protocol (BGP) route reflector. This is effectively a route server that can share routes to other BGP hosts. This is licensed as a separate feature and is only applicable to the SRX650 and SRX550.
- To manage an AX411 AP, a license is required. Two licenses are included with the purchase of the AX411; additional licenses can be purchased separately.

Table 2-11. Licensing options

Type	Vendor	Description	Terms
Antivirus	Juniper-Kaspersky/ Juniper-Express/ Juniper-Sophos	Antivirus updates	1-, 3-, or 5-year
Antispam	Juniper-Sophos	Antispam updates	1-, 3-, or 5-year
Intrusion protection	Juniper	Attack updates	1-, 3-, or 5-year
Web filtering	Websense	Category updates	1-, 3-, or 5-year
AppSecure	Juniper	Attack and IPS updates	1-, 3-, or 5-year
Combined set	All of the above	All of the above	1-, 3-, or 5-year
Dynamic VPN client	Juniper	Concurrent users for Dynamic VPN, SRX100, SRX210, and SRX240 only	5, 10, 25, 50, 250, or 500 users, permanent
BGP router reflector	Juniper	Route reflector capability, SRX650 or SRX550 only	Permanent
AX411 access point	Juniper	License to run AX411	Included with access point

Branch Summary

The branch SRX Series product line is extremely well rounded. In fact, it is the most fully featured, lowest-cost Junos platform that Juniper Networks offers. (This is great news for anyone who wants to learn how to use Junos and build a small lab.)

The branch SRX Series has both flow and packet modes, allowing anyone to test flow-based firewalling and packet-based routing. It features the same routing protocol support as all Junos-based devices, from BGP to Intermediate System-to-Intermediate System (IS-IS). It has the majority of the EX Series switching features with the same configuration set. Most important for study, it also supports MPLS and VPLS. No other router platform supports these features at such an attractive price point.

In terms of the hardware in the branch SRX Series, the underlying device is fairly simple. It does not utilize any of the routing application-specific integrated circuits (ASICs) from the high-end routers or data center SRX Series products. Some behaviors on these features might vary across platforms, so it is not feasible to try to make a sub-$1,000 platform and have the exact same silicon as a million-dollar device. Those behaviors are noted in the documentation and throughout this book where applicable.

The branch SRX Series product line is the most accessible platform for a majority of this book's readers. And because of its lower cost, there will be many more branch SRX Series products in the field.

Where differences exist between these SRX platforms, they will be noted so that you can learn these discrepancies and take them to the field, but note that many features are shared, so there will not be large differences across platforms. Zones and firewall policies remain the same across platforms, so you will see few differences when this book delves into this material.

Data Center SRX Series

The data center SRX Series product line is designed to be scalable and fast for data center environments where high performance is required. Unlike the branch products, the data center SRX Series devices are highly modular—a case in point is the base chassis for any of the products, which does not provide any processing power to process traffic because the devices are designed to scale in performance as cards are added. (It also reduces the total amount of investment that is required for an initial deployment.)

There are three lines of products in the data center SRX Series: the SRX1000, SRX3000, and the SRX5000 line. Each uses almost identical components, which is great because any testing done on one platform can carry over to the other. It's also easier to have feature parity between the two product lines because the data center SRX Series has specific ASICs and processors that cannot be shared unless they exist on both platforms. Where differences do exist, trust that they will be noted.

The SRX1000 line is the smallest of the three, designed for small- to medium-size data centers and Internet edge applications. A step up from the SRX1000 line is the SRX3000 series. This series offers a more configurable midsized device. The SRX5000 line is the largest services gateway that Juniper offers. It is designed for medium to very large data centers and it can scale from a moderate to an extreme performance level.

All three platforms are open for flexible configuration, allowing the network architect to essentially create a device for her own needs. Because processing and interfaces are both modular, it's possible to create a customized device, such as one with more IPS with high inspection and lower throughput. Here, the administrator would add fewer interface cards but more processing cards, allowing only a relatively small amount of traffic to enter the device but providing an extreme amount of inspection. Alternatively, the administrator can create a data center SRX with many physical interfaces but limited processors for inspection. All of this is possible with the data center SRX Series.

Data Center SRX-Specific Features

The data center SRX Series products are built to meet the specific needs of today's data centers. They share certain features that require the same underlying hardware to work as well as the need for such features—it's important to be focused on meeting the needs of the platform.

In the data center, IPS is extremely important in securing services, and the data center SRX Series devices have several features for IPS that are currently not available for the branch SRX Series devices. *Inline tap mode* is one such feature for the data-center-specific SRX platform, allowing the SRX to copy any off sessions as they go through the device. The SRX will continue to process the traffic in Intrusion Detection and Prevention (IDP), as well as passing the traffic out of the SRX, but now it will alert (or log) when an attack is detected, reducing the risk of encountering a false positive and dropping legitimate traffic.

Another specific feature that is common to the data center SRX Series is that they can be configured in what is known as *dedicated mode*. The data center SRX Series firewalls have dense and powerful processors, allowing flexibility in terms of how they can be configured. And much like adding additional processing cards, the SRX processors themselves can be tuned. Dedicated mode allows the SRX processing to be focused on IDP, and the overall throughput for IDP increases, as do the maximum session counts.

Because the branch SRX Series products utilize different processors, it is not possible to tune them for dedicated mode.

We cover many of these features, and others, throughout this book in various chapters and sections. Use the index at the end of the book as a useful cross-reference to these and other data center SRX Series features.

SPC

The element that provides all of the processing on the SRX Series is called the *Services Processing Card* (SPC). An SPC contains one or more *Services Processing Units* (SPUs). The SPU is the processor that handles all of the services on the data center SRX Series firewalls, from firewalling, NAT, and VPN to session setup and anything else the firewall does. There are two generations of the SPC. The first generation SPC is simply called the SPC. For most of this section we cover that version of the SPC. Later in the SRX5000 series section we discuss the NG-SPC, which is only available for the platform. The largest difference between the two is that the NG-SPC offers two times the number of processors and the processors offer more advanced performance.

Each SPU provides extreme multiprocessing and can run 32 parallel tasks simultaneously. A task is run as a separate hardware thread (see the sidebar "Parallel Processing" on page 52 earlier in this chapter for an explanation of hardware threads). This equates to an extreme amount of parallelism. An SPC can operate in four modes: full central point, small central point, half central point, and full flow. SPUs that operate in both central point and flow mode are said to be in *combo mode*. Based on the mode, the number of hardware threads will be divided differently.

The SPU can operate in up to four different distributions of threads, which breaks down to two different functions that it can provide: the central point and the flow processor. The central point (CP) is designed as the master session controller. The CP maintains a table for all of the sessions that are active on the SRX—if a packet is ever received on the SRX that is not matched as part of an existing session, it is sent to the CP. The CP can then check against its session table and see if there is an existing session that matches it. (We discuss the new session setup process in more detail shortly, once all of the required components are explained.)

The CP has three different settings so that users can scale the SRX appropriately. The CP is used as part of the new session setup process or new CPS. The process is distributed across multiple components in the system. It would not make sense to dedicate a processor to provide maximum CPS if there were not enough of the other components to provide this. So, to provide a balanced performance, the CP is automatically tuned to provide CPS capabilities to the rest of the platform. The extra hardware threads that are remaining go back into processing network traffic. At any one time, only one processor is acting as the CP, hence the term *central point*.

The remaining SPUs in the SRX are dedicated to process traffic for services. These processors are distributed to traffic as part of the new session setup process. Because each SPU eventually reaches a finite amount of processing, as does any computing device, an SPU will share any available computing power it has among the services. If additional processing power is required, more SPUs can be added. Adding more SPUs provides near-linear scaling for performance, so if a feature is turned on that cuts the required performance in half, simply adding another SPU will bring performance back to where it was.

The SPU's linear scaling makes it easier to plan a network. If needed, a minimal number of SPUs can be purchased up front, and then, over time, additional SPUs can be added to grow with the needs of the data center. To give you an indication of the processing capabilities per SPU, Table 2-12 shows off the horsepower available.

Table 2-12. SPU processing capacities

Item	Capacity
Packets per second	1,100,000
New CPS	50,000
Firewall throughput	10 Gbps
IPS throughput	2.5 Gbps
VPN throughput	2.5 Gbps

Each SPC in the SRX5000 line has two SPUs, and each SPC in the SRX1000/SRX3000 lines has a single SPU. As more processing cards are added, the SRX gains the additional capabilities listed in Table 2-12, so when additional services such as logging and NAT are turned on and the capacity per processor decreases slightly, additional processors can be added to offset the performance lost by adding new services.

NPU

The Network Processing Unit (NPU) is similar in concept to the SPU, whereby the NPU resides on either an input/output card (IOC) or its own Network Processing Card (NPC) based on the SRX platform type (in the SRX5000 line, the NPU sits on the IOC; in the SRX1000/3000 lines, it is on a separate card).

When traffic enters an interface card, it has to pass through an NPU before it can be sent on for processing. The physical interfaces and NPCs sit on the same interface card, so each interface or interface module has its own NPU. In the SRX3000 line, each interface card is bound to one of the NPUs in the chassis, so when the SRX3000 line appliances boot, each interface is bound to an NPU in a round-robin fashion until each interface has an NPU. It is also possible to manually bind the interfaces to the NPUs through this configuration.

The biggest difference in the design of the SRX1000/3000 and SRX5000 lines' usage of NPUs concerns providing a lower cost platform to the customer. Separating the physical interfaces from the NPU reduces the overall cost of the cards. Optionally, the SRX now offers a 10 GB Ethernet card that has an integrated IOC + NPC. This is described in more detail later. This allows users to utilize the low latency firewall (LLFW) features.

The NPU is used as a part of the session setup process to balance packets as they enter the system. The NPU takes each packet and balances it to the correct SPU that is handling that session. In the event that there is not a matching session on the NPU, it forwards the packet to the CP to figure out what to do with it.

Each NPU can process about 6.5 million packets per second inbound and about 16 million packets outbound. This applies across the entire data center SRX Series platform. The method the NPU uses to match a packet to a session is based on matching the packet to its wing table; a *wing* is half of a session and one part of the bidirectional flow. Figure 2-15 depicts an explanation of a wing in relation to a flow.

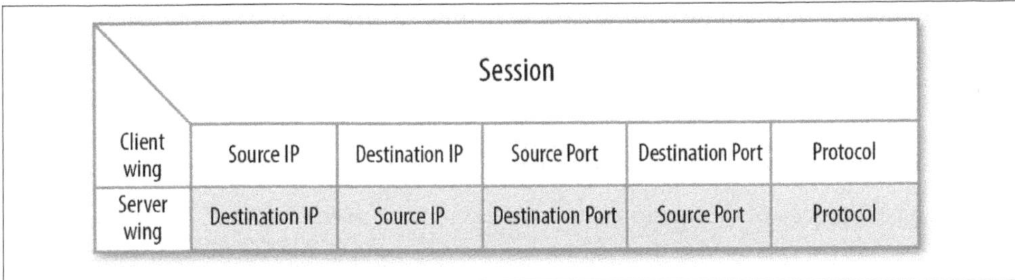

Figure 2-15. Sessions and wings

The card to which the NPU is assigned determines how much memory it will have to store wings (some cards have more memory, as there are fewer components on them). Table 2-13 lists the number of wings per NPU. Each wing has a five-minute keepalive. If five minutes pass and a packet matching the wing hasn't passed, the wing is deleted.

Table 2-13. Number of wings per NPU

Card type	NPUs per card	Wings per NPU
4x10G SRX5000	4	3 million
40x1G SRX5000	4	3 million
Flex I/O SRX5000	2	6 million
NPC SRX1000/3000	1	6 million
NP-IOC	1	6 million

It is possible that the wing table on a single SPU can fill up, and it is a possibility in the SRX5000 line because the total number of sessions exceeds the total number of possible wings on a single NPU. To get around this, Juniper introduced a feature called *NPU bundling* in Junos 9.6, allowing two or more NPUs to be bundled together. The first NPU is used as a load balancer to balance packets to the other NPUs, and then the remaining NPUs in the bundle are able to process packets. This benefits not only the total number of wings, but also the maximum number of ingress packets per second. NPUs can be bundled on or across cards with up to 16 NPUs to be used in a single bundle, and up to 8 different bundles can be created. You can also use link aggregation to balance traffic across all of the NPUs in a link bundle. Generally, filling up wings on NPUs are not a problem for customers. Only in extreme cases is this ever an issue, so for most customers this will never be a problem.

Additionally, in 12.1X44, an alternate mechanism was added to balance the traffic to the SPUs. This offers a more robust way to prevent the central point from being overwhelmed.

The NPU also provides other functions, such as a majority of the screening functions. A screen is an intrusion detection function. These functions typically relate to single packet matching or counting specific packet types. Examples of this are matching land attacks or counting the rate of TCP SYN packets. The NPU also provides some QoS functions.

Data Center SRX Series Session Setup

We discussed pieces of the session setup process in the preceding two sections, so here let's put the entire puzzle together. It's an important topic to discuss, because it is key to how the SRX balances traffic across its chassis. Figure 2-16 shows the setup we use for our explanation.

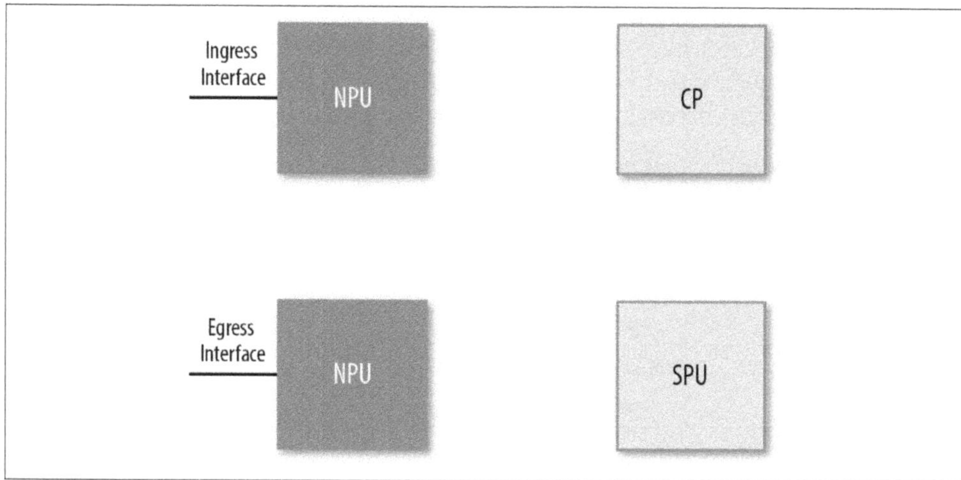

Figure 2-16. Hardware setup

Figure 2-16 depicts two NPUs: one for ingress traffic and the other for egress traffic. It also shows the CP. For this example, the processor handling the CP function will be dedicated to that purpose. The last component shown is the flow SPU, which is used to process the traffic flow.

Figure 2-17 shows the initial packet coming into the SRX. For this explanation, a TCP session will be created. This packet is first sent to the ingress NPU, where the ingress NPU checks against its existing wings. Because there are no existing wings, the NPU then must forward the packet to the CP, where the CP checks against its master session table to see if the packet matches an existing flow. Because this is the first packet into the SRX, and no sessions exist, the CP recognizes this as a potential new session.

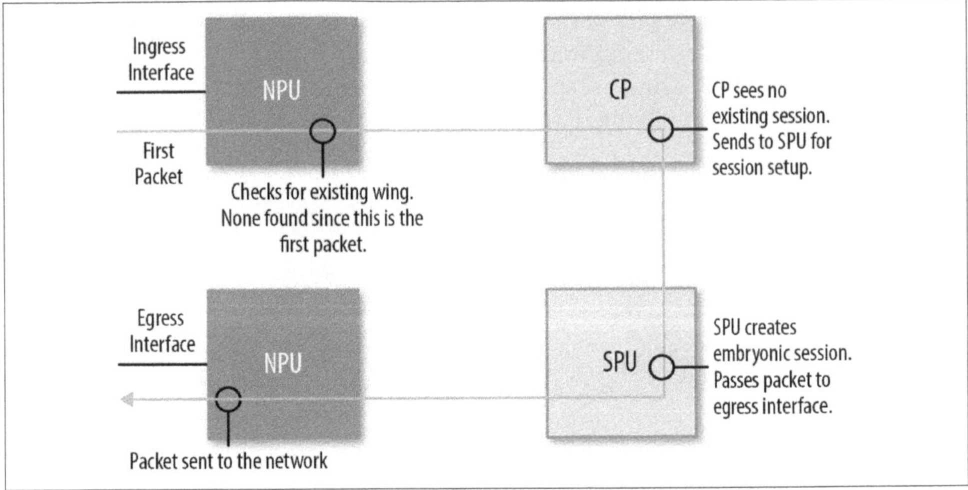

Figure 2-17. The first packet

The packet is then sent to one of the flow SPUs in the system using the weighted round-robin algorithm.

Each SPU is weighted. A full SPU is given a weight of 100, a combo-mode SPU is given a weight of 60 if it's a majority flow and a small CP, and a half-CP and half-flow SPU is given a weight of 50. This way, when the CP is distributing new sessions, the sessions are evenly distributed across the processors.

In Figure 2-17, there is only a single SPU, so the packet is sent there.

The SPU does a basic sanity check on the packet and then sets up an embryonic session, which lasts for up to 20 seconds. The CP is notified of this embryonic session. The remaining SYN-ACK and ACK packets must be received before the session will be fully established. Before the session is completely established, the NPUs will forward the SYN-ACK and ACK packets to the CP and the CP then must forward them to the correct SPU, which it does here because the SPU has the embryonic session in its session table.

In Figure 2-18, the session has been established. The three steps in the three-way handshake have completed. Once the SPU has seen the final ACK packet, it completes the session establishment in the box, first sending a message to the CP to turn the embryonic session into a complete session, and then starting the session timer at the full timeout for the protocol. Next, the SPU notifies the ingress NPU. Once the ingress NPU receives a message, it installs a wing. This wing identifies this session and then specifies which SPU is responsible for the session. When the ACK packet that validated the establishment of the session is sent out of the SRX, a message is tacked onto it. The egress NPU interprets this message and then installs the wing into its local cache, which is similar to the ingress wing except that some elements are reversed. This wing is matching the destination talking to the source (see Figure 2-15 for a representation of the wing).

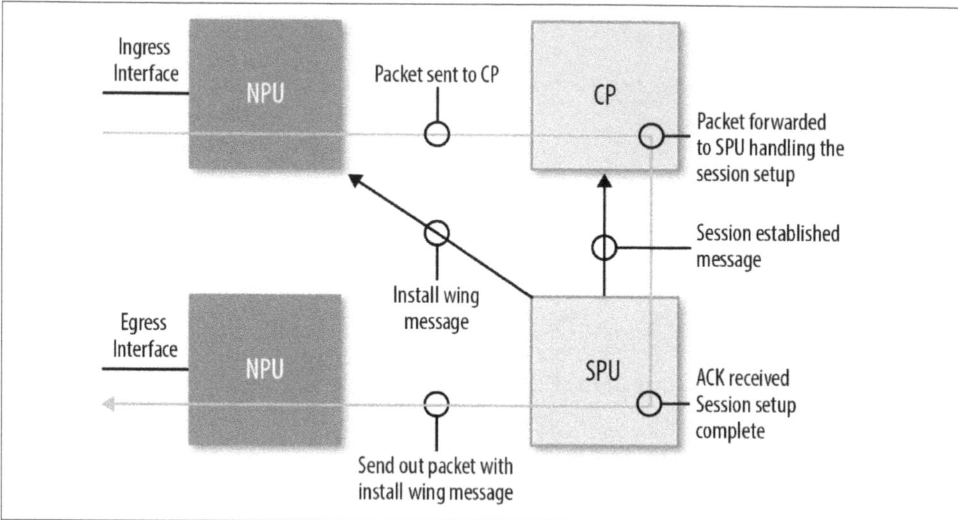

Figure 2-18. Session established

Now that the session is established, the data portion of the session begins, as shown in Figure 2-19 where a data packet is sent and received by the NPU. The NPU checks its local wing table and sees that it has a match and then forwards the packet to the SPU. The SPU then validates the packet, matching the packet against the session table to ensure that it is the next expected packet in the data flow. The SPU then forwards the packet out the egress NPU. (The egress NPU does not check the packet against its wing table; a packet is only checked upon ingress to the NPU.) When the egress NPU receives a return packet, it is being sent from the destination back to the source. This packet is matched against its local wing table and then processed through the system as was just done for the first data packet.

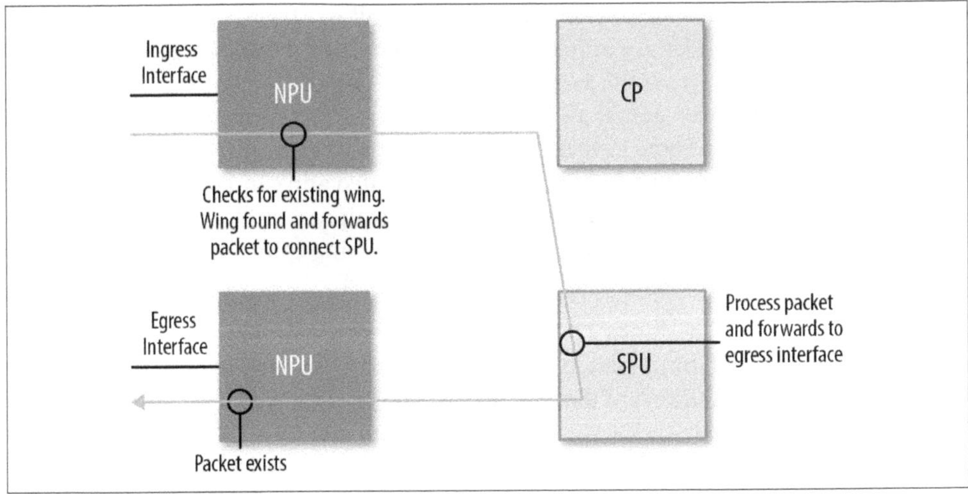

Figure 2-19. Existing session

Last, when the session has completed its purpose, the client will start to end the session. In this case, a four-way FIN close is used. The sender starts the process, and the four closing packets are treated the same as packets for the existing session. What happens next is important, as shown in Figure 2-20. Once the SPU has processed the closing process, it shuts down the session on the SRX, sending a message to the ingress and egress NPUs to delete their wings. The SPU also sends a close message to the CP. The CP and SPU wait about eight seconds to complete the session close to ensure that everything was closed properly.

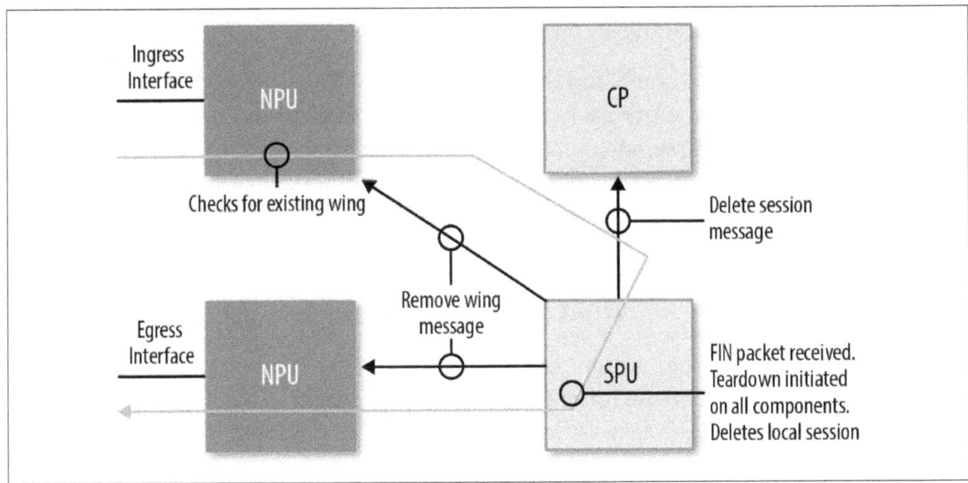

Figure 2-20. Session teardown

Although this seems like a complex process, it also allows the SRX to scale. As more and more SPUs and NPUs are added into the system, this defined process allows the SRX to balance traffic across the available resources. Over time, session distribution is almost always nearly even across all of the processors, a fact proven across many SRX customer deployments. Some have had concerns that a single processor would be overwhelmed by all of the sessions, but that has not happened and cannot happen using this balancing mechanism. In the future, if needed, Juniper could implement a least-connections model or least-utilization model for balancing traffic, but it has not had to as of Junos 10.2.

As mentioned earlier, the Junos 12.1X44 release offers a new way to increase session scale. This feature is off by default, but once enabled, it prevents the central point from being overwhelmed in the event that the NPU cache is exhausted.

Data Center SRX Series Hardware Overview

So far we've talked about the components of the data center SRX Series, so let's start putting the components into the chassis. The data center SRX Series consists of two different lines and four different products. Although they all use the same fundamental components, they are designed to scale performance for where they are going to be deployed, and that isn't easy. The challenge is that a single processor can only be so fast and it can only have so many simultaneous threads of execution. To truly scale to increased performance within a single device, a series of processors and balancing mechanisms must be utilized.

Because the initial design goal of the SRX was to do all of this scaling in a single product, and allow customers to choose how they wanted (and how much) to scale the device, it should be clear that the SPUs and the NPUs are the points to scale (especially if you just finished reading the preceding section).

The NPUs allow traffic to come into the SRX, and the SPUs allow for traffic processing. Adding NPUs allows for more packets to get into the device, and adding SPUs allows for linear scaling. Of course, each platform needs to get packets into the device, which is done by using interface cards, and each section on the data center SRX Series will discuss the interface modules available per platform.

What Is Performance?

A very hot firewall topic centers on performance. Is performance the maximum throughput? Is it based on the Internet Mix (IMIX) standard? What does performance really mean? Although the answers to these questions vary among people and organizations, let's find some common ground.

The first item to examine is the throughput of the firewall. At first, it would seem like an equitable item by which to compare devices, but there is no standard regarding what packet size should be used when testing a firewall. Throughput is the result of the packet rate multiplied by the packet size. When a vendor typically tests, it does so with the maximum-sized frame for an Ethernet network, typically 1,514 bytes. If the vendor tests with packets, it is doing the testing without the Ethernet header, but it only makes sense to count the Ethernet header as it has to go into the device so that the packet can ride on top of it.

There is a 20-byte gap between packets, consisting of an 8-byte preamble and a minimum of 12 bytes of packet gap. So, when testing a firewall, this is added to the overall throughput. This additional 20 bytes is not a matter of cheating, but it has to be counted because it takes up space on the wire. Add these 20 bytes to the 1,514-byte packet and it becomes 1,534 bytes. At the end of the packet is a 4-byte CRC, making the packet 1,538 bytes.

Now, again, this might seem insignificant, but it is often overlooked when a customer looks at the performance of a firewall. It's often thought that if 1 Gbps of data is being transferred on the wire, that is actually 1 gigabit of data per second. In fact, for every 1,538 bytes on the wire frame, only 1,460 bytes of it can be data.

Let's also consider performance definitions when using TCP. For TCP to be a reliable protocol, it has to send acknowledgments after it receives a certain amount of data. By default, this is one ACK packet for every four full data packets. So, if the data rate is at millions of packets per second, that's lots of empty packets that the device has to process. So, when thinking about throughput with TCP, there is a greater chance to get less-than-expected throughput.

Sometimes using large packets is good because it shows the maximum possible throughput of the device, and it's good to know the total capacity of the device. But then this question comes up: How will the device perform in a real-world network? The best way to determine the average packet size on a network is to use analysis tools or look at switch-packet counters. One number that is often thrown around is the *IMIX* number. The IMIX average packet size is 386 bytes, which was determined based on the average packet size on the Internet back in 2001. A lot has changed since then, but it is still common for vendors and customers to refer to this number.

At the root of all of these performance numbers is the actual packet rate that can go through a device, which is the maximum number of packets per second that a device can handle. To test this, an engineer would generate 64-byte packets, being the smallest possible valid packet size, and then, based on the determined packet rate multiplied by the maximum packet size, the total maximum throughput could be calculated. So, it's always best to ask a firewall vendor how to achieve the maximum possible rates on its device.

This is so important because any network device can only process so many packets per second. Think of this as the number of workloads per second that the device can compute. Any network device is nothing more than a computer, and for each packet that it receives, it needs to execute a series of tasks on it. The longer it takes to execute these tasks, the higher the latency. The more operations it has to process, the fewer packets it can process. A firewall has to validate that it has the correct attributes and that the packet is in state, and if it matches an existing session, it has to name a few of those operations it has to perform. To put that in simple terms, this is how a firewall device operates. So, firewall customers should come to the purchasing table with all of the correct data from their network and then work with the vendor to best determine the capabilities of the vendor's platform.

Before leaving this sidebar, in regard to throughput testing let's talk briefly about the concept of the *jumbo frame*. A jumbo frame is a frame that is larger than the standard 1,514-byte frame, typically around 9,000 bytes. It is used more commonly in supercomputer environments and not on a common LAN, but it's actually good for a vendor to test using jumbo frames. It allows the vendor to demonstrate the maximum throughput of the device by reducing the number of packets the device has to process by nearly a factor of six and just focus on the maximum throughput. One point to be aware of is when vendors state that throughput is tested with jumbo frames, which could hint at a limitation in terms of its packet rate.

CPS is another topic that is often discussed, because for each new TCP connection created, three packets must be processed. This is just to establish the session, which is magnitudes more difficult than passing packets from an existing session, because a firewall has many more things to check when establishing a session. When looking at a firewall and its maximum CPS rate, think about that rate and multiply it by three. That is the maximum number of packets the device can process for establishing sessions.

And the other side of the new session CPS is the *sustained* CPS rate, or how many sessions can be opened and closed per second. This metric isn't often discussed, perhaps because it is much more intensive. It requires the processing of up to nine packets per session per second. Three packets are required to open the session, another for the data, another for acknowledgment of the data, and then up to four packets to close the session. That is a total of nine packets times the total sustained CPS. It's a tough number for a product to sustain.

A network architect who can think about a firewall device like this holds a lot of powerful questions when talking to the vendor. These are the core concepts when talking about performance on a flow-based device. It's information that will be helpful for the rest of chapter as we look individually at the capabilities of the data center SRX Series firewalls.

SRX1000 Series

The SRX1000 line is the smallest of the three data center SRX Series lines. It is designed for the Internet edge or small data center environments. The SRX1400 product, the only product currently available in the SRX1000 line, offers some modularity but is the least flexible of the data center SRXs. The base chassis comes with a route engine (RE), a system I/O (SYSIO), and one power supply.

The RE is a computer that runs the management functions for the chassis, controlling and activating the other components in the device. All configuration management is also done from the RE. The reason it is called a *route engine* is because it runs the routing protocols, and on other Junos device platforms such as the M Series, T Series, and MX Series, the RE is, of course, a major part of the device. However, although SRX devices do have excellent routing support, most customers do not use this feature extensively.

The SYSIO contains several important components for the system: the data plane fabric, the control plane Ethernet network, and built-in Ethernet data ports. The SYSIO has six 10/100/1000 ports and six SFPs. There is also a second version of the SYSIO port that has nine 10/100/1000 Ethernet ports and three SFP+ ports that allow for either 1G or 10G ports. This option must be ordered from the factory.

The SRX1400 has a special card called an NSPC. This card is double-wide and fits into a single slot. It offers a lower cost card that combines both one NPC and one SPC on a single card. Alternatively, you can buy a carrier tray that lets you use a single NPC and SPC module in the chassis. This is a good option if you have other SRXs with which you want to interchange cards.

The four types of cards that the SRX1400 can use are interface cards, NPCs, and SPCs, and Table 2-14 lists the minimum and maximum number of cards per chassis by type.

Table 2-14. SRX3400 FPC numbers

Type	Minimum	Maximum	Install location
I/O card	0	1	Front slots
SPC	0	2	Any
NPC	0	1	Top right slot
NSPC	0	1	Top double-wide slot

The SRX1400 is 3 rack units high and only 14 inches deep. You could potentially put two SRX1400s back to back in a four-post rack. Figure 2-21 shows the SRX1400. As of Junos 12.1X44, you can use up to two SPCs on this SRX. The SPC can be added to the slot on the bottom left. Alternatively, you could use an I/O card in that slot. The SRX1400 is actually the rear end of an SRX3400. Effectively, that chassis was cut in half and only the rear of the device was used.

Figure 2-21. The SRX1400

The performance of the SRX1400 is enough for most Internet edge or small data center applications. It offers up to 20 Gbps of firewall throughput if two SPCs are utilized. However, most customers use a single SPC to reduce the overall cost of the platform. The ability to add a second SPC offers a little room for growth.

As shown in Table 2-15, the SRX1400 can also offer both IPS and VPN up to 4 Gbps of throughput. Each number is mutually exclusive (each SPU has a limited amount of computing power). The SRX1400 can use the same interface modules as the SRX3000 series. These modules are listed in the next section.

Table 2-15. SRX1400 capacities

Type	Capacity
CPS	90,000
Maximum firewall throughput	20 Gbps
Maximum IPS throughput	4 Gbps
Maximum VPN throughput	4 Gbps
Maximum concurrent sessions	1.5 million
Maximum firewall policies	40,000
Maximum concurrent users	Unlimited

SRX3000 Series

The SRX3000 line is the middle line of the three data center SRX Series lines. It is designed for the Internet edge or large data centers. The SRX3000 products are extremely modular. The base chassis comes with an RE, a switch fabric board (SFB), and the minimum required power supplies. The RE is a computer that runs the management functions for the chassis, controlling and activating the other components in the device.

The SFB contains several important components for the system: the data plane fabric, the control plane Ethernet network, and built-in Ethernet data ports. The SFB has eight 10/100/1000 ports and four SFPs. It also has a USB port that connects into the RE and a serial console port. All products in the SRX3000 line contain the SFB. The SFB also contains an out-of-band network management port, which is not connected to the data plane, the preferred way to manage the SRX3000 line.

The SRX3400 is the base product in the SRX3000 line. It has seven FPC or *flexible PIC concentrator* slots (a PIC is a *physical interface card*, with four slots in the front of the chassis and three in the rear). The slots enable network architects to mix and match the cards, allowing them to decide how the firewall is to be configured. The three types of cards that the SRX3400 can use are interface cards, NPCs, and SPCs, and Table 2-16 lists the minimum and maximum number of cards per chassis by type.

Table 2-16. SRX3400 FPC numbers

Type	Minimum	Maximum	Install location
I/O card	0	4	Front slots
SPC	1	4	Any
NPC	1	2	Rear three

The SRX3400 is 3 rack units high and a full 25.5 inches deep. That's the full depth of a standard four-post rack. Figure 2-22 shows the front and back of the SRX3400, in which the SFB can be seen as the wide card that is in the top front of the chassis on the left, the FPC slots in both the front and rear of the chassis, and the two slots in the rear of the chassis for the REs. You can add a CRM module in the second slot, which offers dual control ports.

Figure 2-22. The front and back of the SRX3400

Performance on the SRX3400 is impressive, and Table 2-17 lists the maximum performance. The SRX3400 is a modular platform that includes the use of four SPCs, two NPCs, and one IOC. It's no wonder, therefore, that the SRX3400 can provide up to 175,000 new CPS, even though this is a huge number and might dwarf the performance of the branch series. The average customer might not need such rates on a continuous basis, but it's great to have the horsepower in the event that traffic begins to flood through the device.

The SRX3400 offers an optional mode, called extreme mode, where the CPS are increased to 300,000. This converts the partial central point into a full central point, increasing the new CPS rate. Originally, this was a paid-for license, but now the feature is free.

The SRX3400 can pass a maximum of 20 Gbps of firewall throughput. This limitation comes from two components: the maximum number of NPCs, and interfaces, which limits the overall throughout. As discussed before, each NPC can take a maximum number of 6.5 million packets per second inbound, and in the maximum throughput configuration, one interface card and the onboard interfaces are used. With a total of 20 Gbps ingress, it isn't possible to get more traffic into the box.

Table 2-17. SRX3400 capacities

Type	Capacity
CPS	180,000-300,000 (with extreme mode)
Maximum firewall throughput	20 Gbps
Maximum IPS throughput	6 Gbps
Maximum VPN throughput	6 Gbps
Maximum concurrent sessions	2.25/3 million
Maximum firewall policies	40,000
Maximum concurrent users	Unlimited

As shown in Table 2-17, the SRX3400 can also provide several other services, such as both IPS and VPN up to 6 Gbps. Each number is mutually exclusive (each SPU has a limited amount of computing power). The SRX3400 can also have a maximum of 2.25 million sessions. In today's growing environment, a single host can demand dozens of sessions at a time, so 2.25 million sessions might not be a high enough number, especially for larger scale environments. By installing an extreme license you can boost the capacity up to 3 million sessions. The license is available free of charge.

If more performance is required, it's common to move up to the SRX3600. This platform is nearly identical to the SRX3400, except that it adds more capacity by increasing the total number of FPC slots in the chassis. The SRX3600 has a total of 14 FPC slots, doubling the capacity of the SRX3400. This does increase the chassis height to five rack units (the depth remains the same). Table 2-18 lists the minimum and maximum number of cards by type per chassis.

Table 2-18. SRX3600 FPC numbers

Type	Minimum	Maximum	Install location
I/O card	0	6	Front slots
SPC	1	7	Any
NPC	1	3	Last rear three

As mentioned, the SRX3600 chassis is nearly identical to the SRX3400, except for the additional FPC slots. But two other items are different between the two chassis, as you can see in Figure 2-23, where the SRX3600 has an additional card slot above the SFB. Although it currently does not provide any additional functionality, a double-height SFB could be placed in that location in the future. In the rear of the chassis, the number of power supplies has doubled to four, to support the additional power needs. A minimum of two power supplies are required to power the chassis, but to provide full redundancy, all four should be utilized.

Figure 2-23. The SRX3600

Table 2-19 lists the maximum performance of the SRX3600. These numbers are tested with a configuration of two 10G I/O cards, three NPCs, and seven SPCs. This configuration provides additional throughput. The firewall capabilities rise to a maximum of 30 Gbps, primarily because of the inclusion of an additional interface module and NPC.

The VPN and IPS numbers also rise to 10 Gbps, whereas the CPS and session maximums remain the same. The SRX3000 line utilizes a combo-mode CP processor, where half of the processor is dedicated to processing traffic and the other to set up sessions. The SRX5000 line has the capability of providing a full CP processor.

Table 2-19. SRX3600 capacities

Type	Capacity
CPS	180,000/300,000
Maximum firewall throughput	30 Gbps
Maximum IPS throughput	10 Gbps
Maximum AppSecure throughput	25 Gbps
Maximum VPN throughput	10 Gbps
Maximum concurrent sessions	2.25/6 million
Maximum firewall policies	40,000
Maximum concurrent users	Unlimited

IOC modules

In addition to the built-in SFP interface ports, you can use three additional types of interface modules with the SRX3000 line, and Table 2-20 lists them by type. Each interface module is oversubscribed, with the goal of providing port density rather than line rate cards. The capacity and oversubscription ratings are also listed.

Table 2-20. SRX3000 I/O module summary

Type	Description
10/100/1000 copper	16-port 10/100/1000 copper with 1.6:1 oversubscription
1G SFP	16-port SPF with 1.6:1 oversubscription
10G XFP	2 × 10G XFP with 2:1 oversubscription
10G XFP+ with NPC	2 × 10G SFP+ with 2:1 oversubscription

Table 2-20 lists two types of 1G interface card, and both contain 16 1G interface slots. The media type is the only difference between the modules, and one has 16 1G 10/100/1000 copper interfaces and the other contains 16 SFP ports. The benefit of the 16 SFP interfaces is that a mix of fiber and copper interfaces can be used as opposed to the fixed-copper-only card. Both of the cards are oversubscribed to a ratio of 1.6:1.

The 2 × 10G XFP or 10 Gigabit Small Form Factor Pluggable card provides two 10G interfaces and is oversubscribed by a ratio of 2:1. Although the card is oversubscribed by two times, the port density is its greatest value because providing more ports allows for additional connectivity into the network. Most customers will not require all of the ports on the device to operate at line rate speeds, and if more are required, the SRX5000 line can provide these capabilities.

The remaining card listed in Table 2-20 is a 2 × 10G SPF+ card. This card offers not only two 10G, ports but it also includes a dedicated NPC. This is used in conjunction with the LLFW or services offload. It offers low latency stateful firewall performance. This is excellent for environments where low latency is required.

Each module has a 10G full duplex connection into the fabric. This means 10 gigabits of traffic per second can enter and exit the module simultaneously, providing a total of 20 gigabits of traffic per second that could traverse the card at the same time.

SRX5000 Series

The SRX5000 line of firewalls are the largest devices in the SRX Series, both in size and capacity. The SRX5000 line provides maximum modularity in the number of interface cards and SPCs the device can utilize, for a "build your own services gateway" approach, while allowing for expansion over time.

The SRX5000 line currently includes two different models: the SRX5600 and the SRX5800. Fundamentally, both platforms are the same. They share the same major components, except for the chassis and how many slots are available, dictating the performance of these two platforms.

The first device to review is the SRX5600. This chassis is the smaller of the two, containing a total of eight slots. The bottom two slots are for the switch control boards (SCBs), an important component in the SRX5000 line, as they contain three key items: a slot to place the RE; the switch fabric for the device; and one of the control plane networks.

The RE in the SRX5000 line is the same concept as in the SRX3000 line, providing all of the chassis and configuration management functions. It also runs the processes that run the routing protocols (if the user chooses to configure them). The RE is required to run the chassis and it has a serial port, an auxiliary console port, a USB port, and an out-of-band management Ethernet port. The USB port can be used for loading new firmware on the device, and the out-of-band Ethernet port is the suggested port for managing the SRX.

The switch fabric is used to connect the interface cards and the SPCs together, and all traffic that passes through the switch fabric is considered to be part of the data plane. The control plane network provides the connectivity between all of the components in the chassis. This gigabit Ethernet network is used for the RE to talk to all of the line cards. It also allows for management traffic to come back to the RE from the data plane. And if the RE was to send traffic, it goes from the control plane and is inserted into the data plane.

Only one SCB is required to run the SRX5600; a second SCB can be used for redundancy. (Note that if just one SCB is utilized, unfortunately the remaining slot cannot be used for an interface card or an SPC.) The SRX5600 can utilize up to two REs, one to manage the SRX and the other to create dual control links in HA.

On the front of the SRX5600, as shown in Figure 2-24, is what is called a *craft port*. This is the series of buttons that are labeled on the top front of the chassis, allowing you to enable and disable the individual cards. The SRX5600, unlike the SRX5800, can use 120v power, which could be beneficial in environments where 220v power is not available, or without any need to rewire electrical feeds. The SRX5600 is eight rack units tall and 23.8 inches deep.

Figure 2-24. The SRX5600

The SRX5000 line is quite flexible in its configuration, with each chassis requiring a minimum of one interface module and one SPC. Traffic must be able to enter the device and be processed; hence, these two cards are required. The remaining slots in the chassis are the network administrator's choice. This offers several important options.

The SRX5000 line has a relatively low barrier of entry because just a chassis and a few interface cards are required. In fact, choosing between the SRX5600 and the SRX5800 comes down to space, power, and long-term expansion.

For space considerations, the SRX5600 is physically half the size of the SRX5800, a significant fact considering that these devices are often deployed in pairs, and that two SRX5800s take up two thirds of a physical rack. In terms of power, the SRX5600 can run on 110v, whereas the SRX5800 needs 220v.

The last significant difference between the SRX5600 and the SRX5800 data center devices is their long-term expansion capabilities. Table 2-21 lists the FPC slot capacities of the SRX5600. As stated, the minimum is two cards, one interface card and one SPC, leaving four slots that can be mixed and matched among cards. Because of the high-end fabric in the SRX5600, placement of the cards versus their performance is irrelevant. This means the cards can be placed in any slots and the throughput is the same, which is important to note because in some vendors' products, maximum throughput will drop when attempting to go across the back plane.

Table 2-21. SRX5600 FPC numbers

Type	Minimum	Maximum	Install location
FPC slots used	1 (SCB)	8	All slots are FPCs
I/O card	1	5	Any
SPC	1	5	Any
SCB	1	2	Bottom slots

In the SRX5800, the requirements are similar. One interface card and one SPC are required for the minimum configuration, and the ten remaining slots can be used for any additional combination of cards. Even if the initial deployment only requires the minimum number of cards, it still makes sense to look at the SRX5800 chassis. It's always a great idea to get investment protection out of the purchase. Table 2-22 lists the FPC capacity numbers for the SRX5800.

Table 2-22. SRX5800 FPC numbers

Type	Minimum	Maximum	Install location
FPC slots used	2 (SCBs)	14	All slots are FPCs
I/O card	1	11	Any
SPC	1	11	Any
SCB	2	3	Center slots

The SRX5800 has a total of 14 slots, and in this chassis, the 2 center slots must contain SCBs, which doubles the capacity of the chassis. Because it has twice the number of slots, it needs two times the fabric. Even though two fabric cards are utilized, there isn't a performance limitation for going between any of the ports or cards on the fabric (this is important to remember, as some chassis-based products do have this limitation). Optionally, a third SCB can be used, allowing for redundancy in case one of the other two SCBs fails.

Figure 2-25 illustrates the SRX5800. The chassis is similar to the SRX5600, except the cards are positioned perpendicular to the ground, which allows for front-to-back cooling and a higher density of cards within a 19-inch rack. At the top of the chassis, the same craft interface can be seen. The two fan trays for the chassis are front-accessible above and below the FPCs.

In the rear of the chassis there are four power supply slots. In an AC electrical deployment, three power supplies are required, with the fourth for redundancy. In a DC power deployment, the redundancy is 2 + 2, or two active supplies and two supplies for redundancy. Check with the latest hardware manuals for the most up-to-date information.

Optionally, you can use the NG-PSU or next-generation power supply units. These units offer 2 + 2 redundancy as they provide more power per power supply.

The performance metrics for the SRX5000 line are very impressive, as listed in Table 2-23. The CPS rate maxes out at 350,000, which is the maximum number of packets per second that can be processed by the central point processor. This is three per CPS multiplied by 350,000, or 1.05 million packets per second, and subsequently is about the maximum number of packets per second per SPU. Although this many connections per second is not required for most environments, at a mobile services provider, a large data center, or a full cloud network—or any environment where there are tens of thousands of servers and hundreds of thousands of inbound clients—this rate of CPS might be just right.

Table 2-23. SRX5000 line capacities for original SPC

Type	SRX5600 capacity	SRX5800 capacity
CPS	380,000	380,000
Maximum firewall throughput	70 Gbps	150 Gbps
Maximum IPS throughput	12 Gbps	26 Gbps
Maximum VPN throughput	15 Gbps	30 Gbps
Maximum concurrent sessions	9 million	12.5/20 million
Maximum firewall policies	80,000	80,000
Maximum concurrent users	Unlimited	Unlimited

For the various throughput numbers shown in Table 2-23, each metric is doubled from the SRX5600 to the SRX5800, so the maximum firewall throughput number is 70 Gbps on the SRX5600 and 150 Gbps on the SRX5800. This number is achieved using HTTP large gets to create large stateful packet transfers; the number could be larger if UDP streams are used, but that is less valuable to customers, so the stateful HTTP numbers are utilized. The IPS and VPN throughputs follow the same patterns. These numbers

Figure 2-25. The SRX5800

are 15 Gbps and 30 Gbps for each of these service types on the SRX5600 and SRX5800, respectively.

It is possible to increase the session capacity on the SRX5800 from 12.5 million sessions up to 20 million sessions. This requires eight SPCs and then enabling the max sessions knob in the CLI.

The IPS throughput numbers are achieved using the older NSS 4.2.1 testing standard. Note that this is not the same test that is used to test the maximum firewall throughput. The NSS test accounts for about half of the possible throughput of the large HTTP transfers, so if a similar test were done with IPS, about double the amount of throughput would be achieved.

These performance numbers were achieved using two interface cards and four SPCs on the SRX5600. On the SRX5800, four interface cards and eight SPCs were used. As discussed throughout this section, it's possible to mix and match modules on the SRX platforms, so if additional processing is required, more SPCs can be added. Table 2-24 lists several examples of this "more is merrier" theme.

Table 2-24. Example SRX5800 line configurations

Example network	IOCs	SPCs	Goal
Mobile provider	1	6	Max sessions and CPS
Financial network	2	10	Max PPS
Data center IPS	1	11	Maximum IPS inspection
Maximum connectivity	8 flex IOCs	4	64 10G interfaces for customer connectivity

A full matrix and example use cases for the modular data center SRX Series could fill an entire chapter in a how-to data center book. Table 2-24 highlights only a few, the first for a mobile provider. A mobile provider needs to have the highest number of sessions and the highest possible CPS, which could be achieved with six SPCs. In most environments, the total throughput for a mobile provider is low, so a single IOC should provide enough throughput.

In a financial network, the packets-per-second (PPS) rate is the most important metric. To provide these rates, two SPCs are used, each configured using NPU bundling to allow for 10 Gbps ingress of small 64-byte packets. The 10 SPCs are used to provide packet processing and security for these small packets.

In a data center environment, an SRX can be deployed for IPS capabilities only, so here the SRX would need only one IOC to have traffic come into the SRX. The remaining 11 slots would be used to provide IPS processing, allowing for a total of 45 Gbps IPS inspection in a single SRX. That is an incredible amount of inspection in a single chassis.

The last example in Table 2-24 is for maximum connectivity. This example offers sixty-four 10G Ethernet ports. These ports are oversubscribed at a ratio of 4:1, but again the idea here is connectivity. The remaining four slots are dedicated to SPCs. Although the number of SPCs is low, this configuration still provides up to 70 Gbps of firewall throughput. Each 10G port could use 1.1 Gbps of throughput simultaneously.

NG-SPC

Because the needs for service providers and high-end data centers are always growing, Juniper focuses on innovating new products for the future. The most important area of growth is the SPC as it is the largest bottleneck in the SRX. The Next Generation SPC (NG-SPC) is a new product that is being launched for the SRX in early 2013. This card provides an extreme boost to the performance of the SRX5000 series. Unlike the original SPC, it contains four SPUs, and each SPU is a new processor that is a newer generation of chip than the one used on the original SPC.

The projected performance at launch of the NG-SPC is a considerable boost over the existing cards. They are projected to do a minimum of 5 Mpps for firewall versus 2 Mpps on the existing cards. On new CPS, one NG-SPC card is capable of doing 240,000 new CPS. This is a 100 percent improvement over the existing cards as well. On the services side, IPsec boosts up to 16 Gbps and IPS gets bested to between 11 Gbps and 5 Gbps. These numbers are all preliminary for the new card, as this is based on the 12.1X44 release of software. Expect these things to increase over time, and look for official up-to-date numbers on Juniper's website.

Due to the additional processor capabilities, an existing SRX5000 series chassis will need a slight upgrade to support these new cards. The fans and power supplies are needed to provide additional cooling and power for these high compute capable cards. Currently, these processors are only for the SRX5000, but expect them to trickle through to the other data center SRX products over time.

IOC modules

The SRX5000 line has three types of IOCs, two of which provide line rate throughput while the remaining is oversubscribed. Figure 2-26 illustrates an example of the interface complex of the SRX5000 line. The image on the left is the PHY, or physical chip, that handles the physical media. Next is the NPU or network processor. The last component is the fabric chip. Together, these components make up the interface complex. Each complex can provide 10 Gbps in both ingress and egress directions, representing 20 Gbps full duplex of throughput.

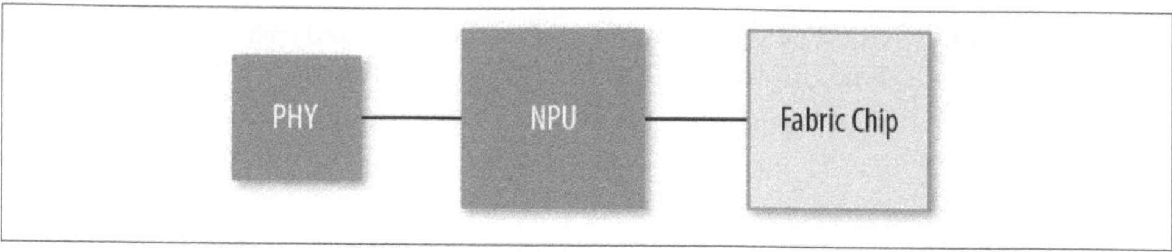

Figure 2-26. Interface complex of the SRX5000 line

Each type of card has a different number of interface complexes on it, with Table 2-25 listing the number of interface complexes per I/O type. Each complex is directly connected to the fabric, meaning there's no benefit to passing traffic between the complexes on the same card. It's a huge advantage of the SRX product line because you can place any cards you add anywhere you want in the chassis.

Table 2-25. Complexes per line card type

Type	Complexes
4 × 10G	4
40 × 1G	4
Flex IOC	2
NG-IOC	4

The most popular IOC for the SRX is the four-port 10 gigabit card. The 10 gigabit ports utilize the XFP optical transceivers. Each 10G port has its own complex providing 20 Gbps full duplex of throughput, which puts the maximum ingress on a 4 × 10G IOC at 40 Gbps and the maximum egress at 40 Gbps.

The second card listed in Table 2-25 is the 41 gigabit SFP IOC. This blade has four complexes, just as the four-port 10 gigabit card has, but instead of four 10G ports, it has ten 1G ports. The blade offers the same 40 Gbps ingress and 40 Gbps egress metrics of the four-port 10 gigabit card, but this card also supports the ability to mix both copper and fiber SFPs.

The Flex IOC card has two complexes on it, with each complex connected to a modular slot. The modular slot can utilize one of three different cards:

- The first card is a 16-port 10/100/1000 card. It has 16 tri-speed copper Ethernet ports. Because it has sixteen 1G ports and the complex it is connected to can only pass 10 Gbps in either direction, this card is oversubscribed by a ratio of 1.6:1.
- Similar to the first card is the 16-port SFP card. The difference here is that instead of copper ports, the ports utilize SFPs and the SFPs allow the use of either fiber or copper transceivers. This card is ideal for environments that need a mix of fiber and copper 1G ports.

- The last card is the dense four-port 10G card. It has four 10-gigabit ports. Each port is still an XFP port. This card is oversubscribed by a ratio of 4:1 and is ideal for environments where connectivity is more important than line rate throughput.

Summary

Juniper Networks' SRX Series Services Gateways are the company's next-generation firewall offerings. Juniper brings the Junos OS onto the SRX, enabling carrier-class reliability. This chapter introduced a multitude of platforms, features, and concepts; the rest of the book will complete your knowledge in all of the areas that have been introduced here. The majority of the features are shared across the platforms, so as you read through the rest of the book, you will be learning a skill set that you can apply to small hand-sized firewalls as well as larger devices. Your journey through the material might seem great, but the reward will be great as well. The concepts in this book apply not only to the SRX, but to all of the products in the Junos product line.

Study Questions

Questions

1. Which of the SRX platforms can use WAN interfaces?
2. What are the Ethernet switching restrictions on the branch SRX Series?
3. What is the true cutoff limit for using a branch device in a branch and not using it in a larger environment such as a data center?
4. The SRX5000 line seems to have "too much" performance. Is such a device needed?
5. What is the biggest differentiator between the branch SRX Series and data center SRX Series platforms?
6. Which SRX platforms support the UTM feature set?
7. Why can't the data center SRX Series manage the AX411 Wireless LAN Access Point?
8. For how long a term can you purchase a license for a Junos feature?
9. What does a Services Processing Card do?
10. What is the benefit of the distributed processing model on the data center SRX Series?

Answers

1. The SRX210, SRX220, SRX240, SRX550, and SRX650 can use WAN interfaces. These are part of the branch SRX Series. As they are placed in a branch, they

are more likely to be exposed to non-Ethernet interfaces and need to accommodate various media types.

2. Ethernet switching can only be done across the same card. It is not possible to switch across multiple line cards. The branch SRX Series devices use a switching chip on each of their interface modules. Switched traffic must stay local to the card. It is possible to go across cards, but that traffic will be processed by the firewall.

3. It's possible to place a branch device in any location. The biggest cutoff typically is the number of concurrent sessions. When you are unable to create new sessions, there isn't much the firewall can do with new traffic besides drop it. The second biggest limit is throughput. If the firewall can create the session but not push the traffic, it doesn't do any good. If a branch SRX Series product can meet both of these needs, it might be the right solution for you.

4. The SRX5800 can provide an unprecedented amount of throughput and interface density. Although this device might seem like overkill, in many networks it's barely enough. Mobile carriers constantly drive for additional session capacity. In data center networks, customers want more throughput. It's not the correct device for everyone, but in the correct network, it's just what is needed.

5. The data center SRX Series devices allow the administrator to increase performance by adding more processing. All of the branch devices have fixed processing.

6. Only the branch SRX Series devices support UTM. The focus was for a single small device to handle all of the security features for the branch. As of the writing of this book, the UTM feature set is in beta for the high-end or data center devices.

7. It doesn't make sense for the data center SRX Series to manage the AX411 because of the typical deployment location for the product. Although it is technically possible, it is not a feature that many people would want to use, and hence Juniper didn't enable this.

8. The maximum length a Juniper license can be purchased for is five years.

9. A Services Processing Card on the data center SRX Series enables the processing of traffic for all services. All of the services available on the SRX, such as IDP, VPN, and NAT, are processed by the same card. There is no need to add additional cards for each type of service.

10. The distributed processing model of the data center SRX Series allows the device to scale to an unprecedented degree. Each component in the processing of a flow optimizes the processing capabilities to allow you to add more than a dozen processors to the chassis, with equal distribution of sessions across all of the cards.

CHAPTER 3

SRX GUI Management

In the beginning, there was the command line. At the time, the small single line of text that was printed out on a Teletype was the greatest evolution in human–computer interaction. If you showed this to the average six-year-old, she might play with the paper and laugh. However, give that same child one of today's smart phones and she will cruise the Internet on it as an expert. This small story tells us that the user interfaces for the world around us have changed dramatically over the last 50 years. Today, the focus on usability and the design of an interface is truly an art form. Unfortunately, the SRX does not have a user interface that is so easy a six-year-old can use it. It does, however, have a series of tools that do simplify many of the management tasks.

The SRX has several different GUI tools that administrators can use to maximize the effectiveness of their management. The SRX has an on-box web management console called J-Web. J-Web originated with the J-Series router back in late 2004. From there it has been molded and developed into the tool it is today. Because managing each device individually would be impossible, Juniper also offers several solutions to simplify the management of dozens of devices.

In this chapter, we review all of the available options for managing an SRX using a GUI. We take a look at the various management platforms and the best practices for using them. Because each platform has lots of depth to it, this chapter is meant as an overview to the various platforms and not a complete guide.

Finally, an important item to note about GUIs is that they are always evolving to meet the needs of the future. Because of this, screens that are shown in this chapter might be drastically different by the time you see this book.

J-Web: Your On-Box Assistant

For most of your Junos adventure, you will be working with or handling the results of the CLI. However, whereas the command line is a great tool to look at a device from the 10-foot view, often enough you need to see the bigger picture from a bit farther out. This is where our journey begins. J-Web is the on-device GUI management tool available on the SRX. Unlike the M/MX/T Series, which require a separate package and license, the SRX software installation includes the J-Web tool. By default, J-Web is enabled on most SRX devices. To learn how to enable the GUI tool on the SRX, please review Chapter 5.

The goal of J-Web is to reduce the administrator's effort spent performing various tasks. That sounds like basic information, but it is important to keep this in mind when using J-Web. It is not meant to solve all of your potential management issues, but it is a tool in the fight toward a better configuration.

To get started with J-Web, you must log in. The best practice is to always use an HTTPS or SSL secured connection. This will protect your login credentials as well as any communication to the SRX. If attackers were able to gain access to your session, they could potentially make unauthorized changes to your device.

Logging in is straightforward, as you only need to input your username and password. Depending on the device, the login process can take up to a minute, so be patient as you are waiting for the J-Web application to load. For best performance, it is suggested you use a modern version of Google Chrome, Firefox, or Internet Explorer 10. Although J-Web does not officially support all of these versions, it should work well. Figure 3-1 is a screenshot of what you should see when connecting to J-Web.

Dashboard

After logging in to J-Web for the first time, you will be directed to the dashboard. This is a great tool to use to instantly see the state of the device. The last section you were at within J-Web is stored as a cookie within your browser. Because of this, subsequent logins might not take you directly back to the dashboard.

Getting started, let's take a look at the initial dashboard in Figure 3-2. The initial dashboard offers some important information at a quick glace. It gives you basic inventory stats as well as a chassis view. All of the panels in the dashboard can be dragged and dropped around to customize the view to your liking.

Chassis view

The view of the chassis is much more than just a boring picture. It allows you to see the status lights on the chassis as well as the physical status of ports. Many of the elements

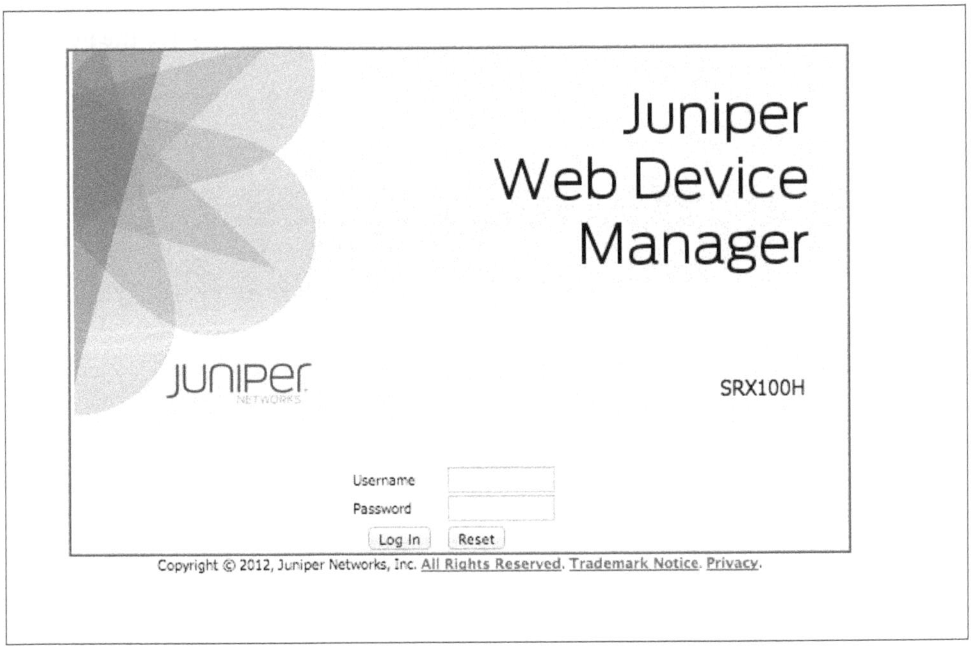

Juniper
Web Device
Manager

JUNIPER
NETWORKS

SRX100H

Username
Password
Log In Reset

Figure 3-1. J-Web login screen

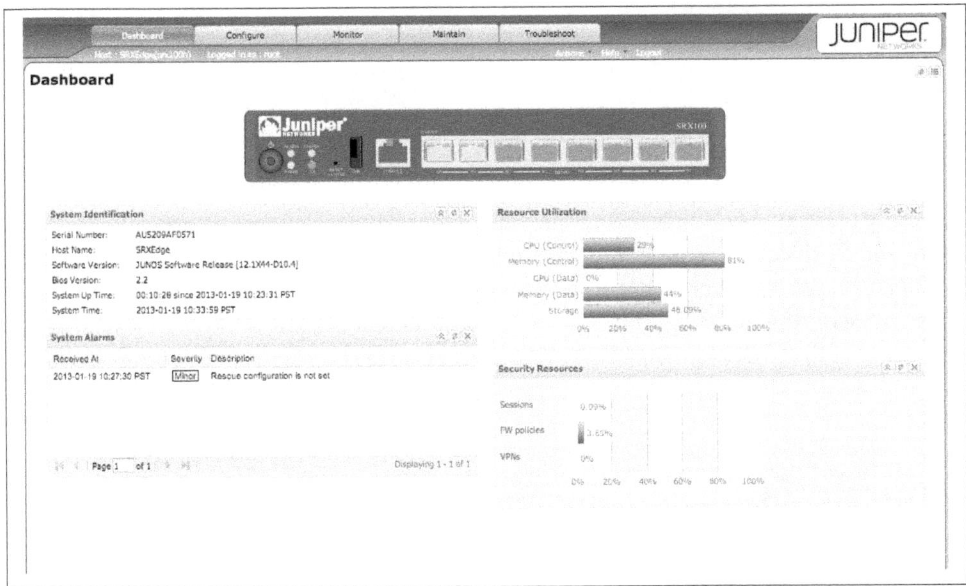

Figure 3-2. The initial dashboard

can be hovered over, and it allows you to see more detail about each element's status. In Figure 3-3, you can see an example of this as the mouse hovers over one of the Ethernet ports.

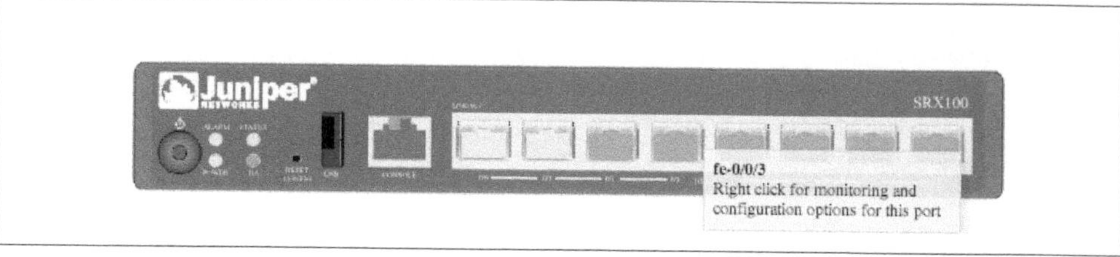

Figure 3-3. Port detail on the dashboard

Because devices are more than just a front panel, there is the ability to right-click the chassis and access a shortcut menu. This menu allows you to flip the view to the back of the chassis as well as see additional details about the chassis by taking you to the monitoring page. In Figure 3-4, you can see an example of the shortcut menu.

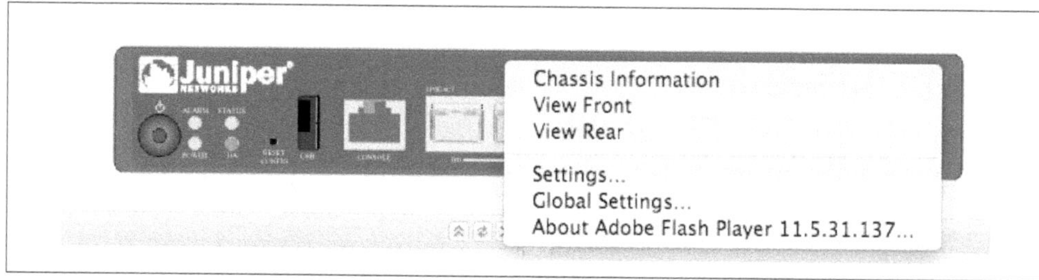

Figure 3-4. Shortcut menu

Selecting the rear view will bring up the back of the chassis. Depending on your platform, there will be different amounts of available information. Here on our example device, an SRX100, we have very little information available to us. This feature provides the most value on the SRX3000 series, as they have rear-facing ports. Figure 3-5 shows the rear view of the SRX100.

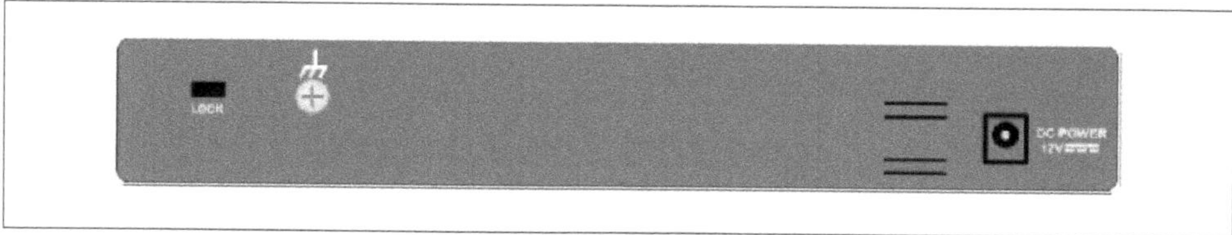

Figure 3-5. Rear view

Finally, you can select the Chassis Information view from the menu. This will take you to the detailed chassis information page in the monitoring section of the UI, depicted in Figure 3-6. This allows you to review all of the detailed information for the hardware components on the device. An administrator can cycle through the various tabs and combo boxes to select all the various components in the chassis.

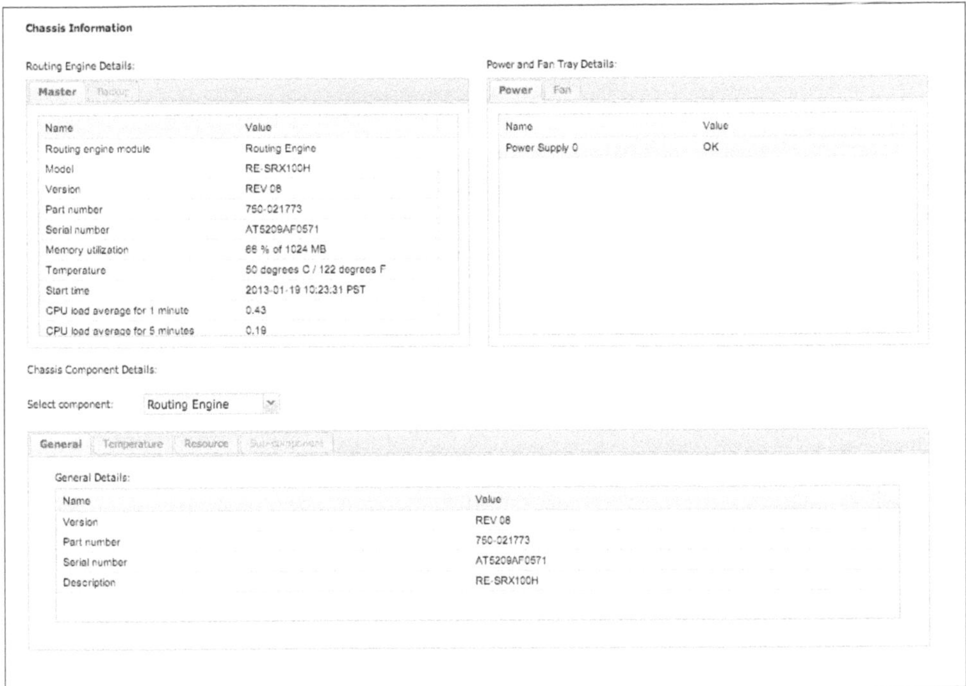

Figure 3-6. Chassis information details

Informational panels

There are other various informational panels available within the dashboard. The displayed data can be either informational or status oriented.

The first panel to discuss is the System Identification panel, depicted in Figure 3-7. This shows the device basics such as uptime, time, software version, and serial number.

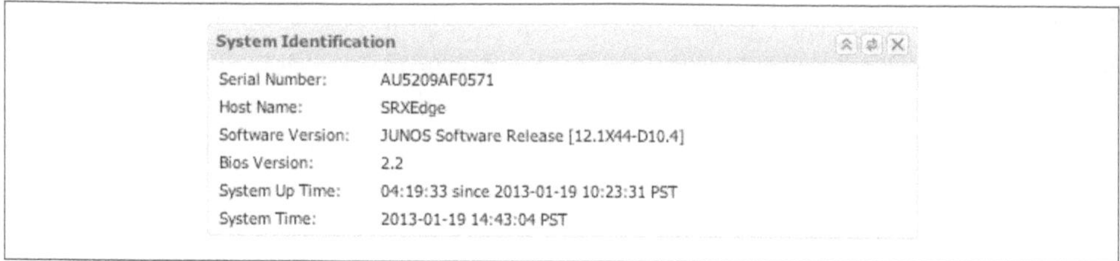

Figure 3-7. System Identification panel

The most popular and arguably the most valuable panel is the Resource Utilization panel, shown in Figure 3-8. This shows the memory, CPU for both the control and data plane, and available system storage. This will periodically update (once per two minutes by default, but this setting is customizable) with current information. It is important to note the CPU on the smaller devices might seem to always have high utilization on the control plane. Driving the various web UI tasks can be quite resource intensive. Because of this, the CPU utilization might seem high.

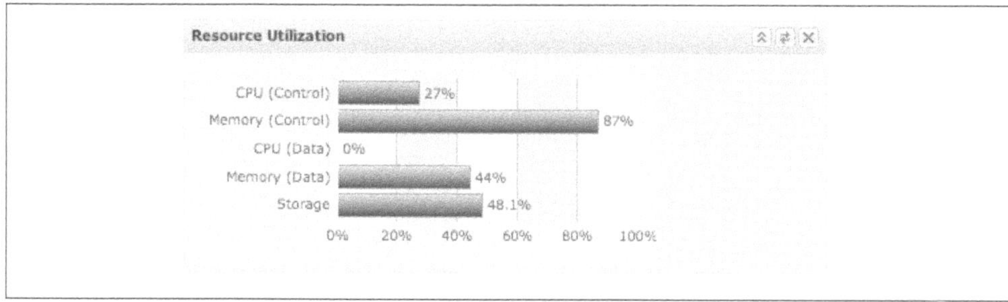

Figure 3-8. Resource Utilization panel

If there are any outstanding alarms on the device, the System Alarms panel, shown in Figure 3-9, displays them. This is helpful to show any hardware faults or other important alarms.

System Alarms

Received At	Severity	Description
2013-01-19 10:27:30 PST	Minor	Rescue configuration is not set

Page 1 of 1 Displaying 1 - 1 of 1

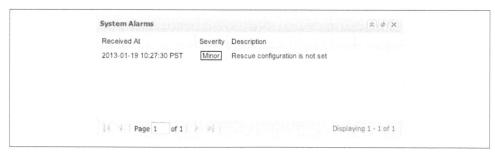

Figure 3-9. System Alarms panel

The second most useful panel is the Security Resources panel, depicted in Figure 3-10. This panel displays the percentage of resources that have been allocated. Because each platform can only have so many active sessions, this is a great tool to see how close your device is to session exhaustion.

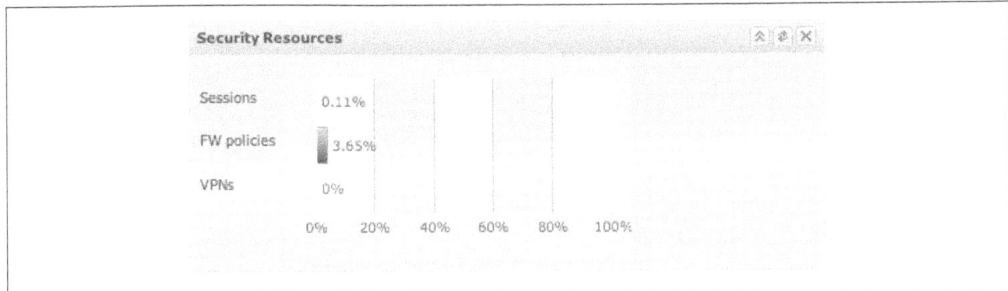

Figure 3-10. Security Resources panel

One thing you never want to have happen is to fill up your firewall's disk. This can cause the device to seize or lose logging data. The File Usage panel, shown in Figure 3-11, displays how much of the disk is being utilized. It also offers a quick link to solve the problem if the disk is full. Because the branch devices typically have anemic storage, this is an important thing to monitor.

File Usage

Log Files:	62M
Temporary Files:	66K
Crash (Core) Files:	8.0K
Database Files:	102M

Maintain >

Figure 3-11. File Usage panel

It is important to make sure that unauthorized users are not accessing your firewall. The Login Sessions panel, displayed in Figure 3-12, displays any users logged into the device. It shows both CLI and web UI users.

Because the SRX has a great amount of security features packed into the device, it is important to monitor the efficacy of its policies. The Threats Activity panel, shown in Figure 3-13, shows the threats that have been detected across UTM and IPS. It also offers a quick link to the more detailed reporting.

The Chassis Status panel, shown in Figure 3-14, displays a quick view of hardware status. It is not really useful on the branch devices, because if any of these states were alarmed, then the device is most likely to go down. On the larger devices this can offer more value.

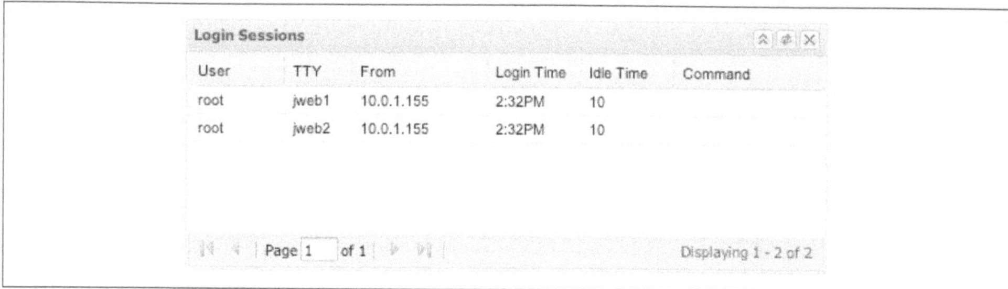

Figure 3-12. Login Sessions panel

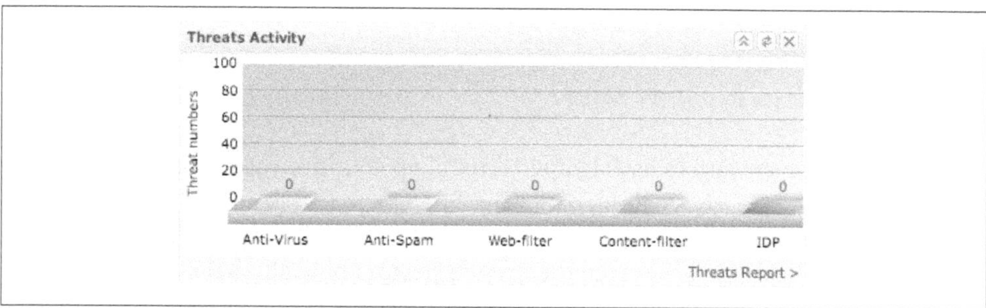

Figure 3-13. Threats Activity panel

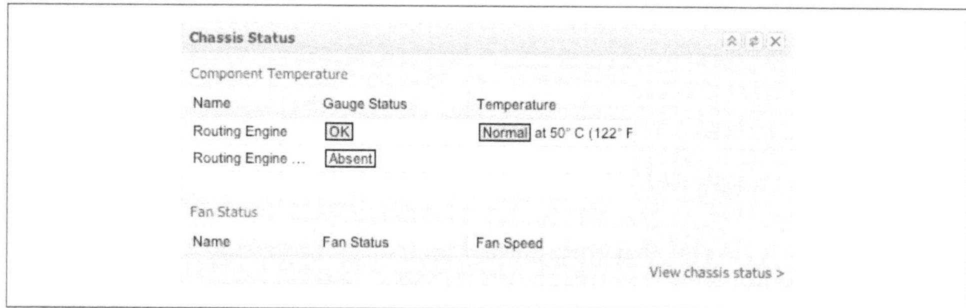

Figure 3-14. Chassis Status panel

The last panel is the Storage Usage panel, pictured in Figure 3-15. It provides details around how much of the disk is utilized.

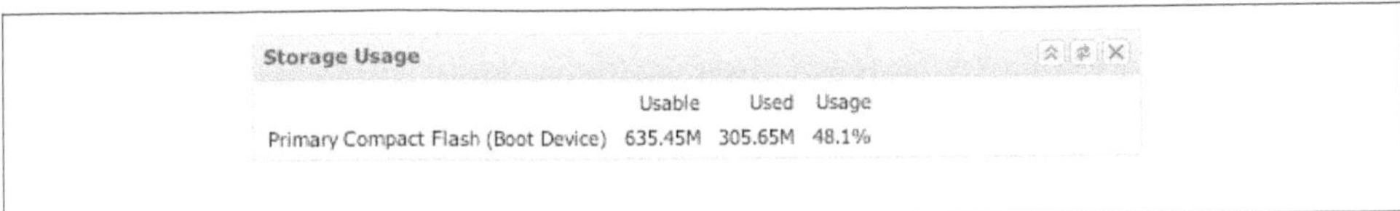

Figure 3-15. Storage Usage panel

Customizing the dashboard allows you to select and remove panels that are not important to you. It is easy to do this by selecting the preferences dialog button in the upper-right corner of the dashboard (see arrow in Figure 3-16). From here, the various panels can be selected and the refresh time can be changed.

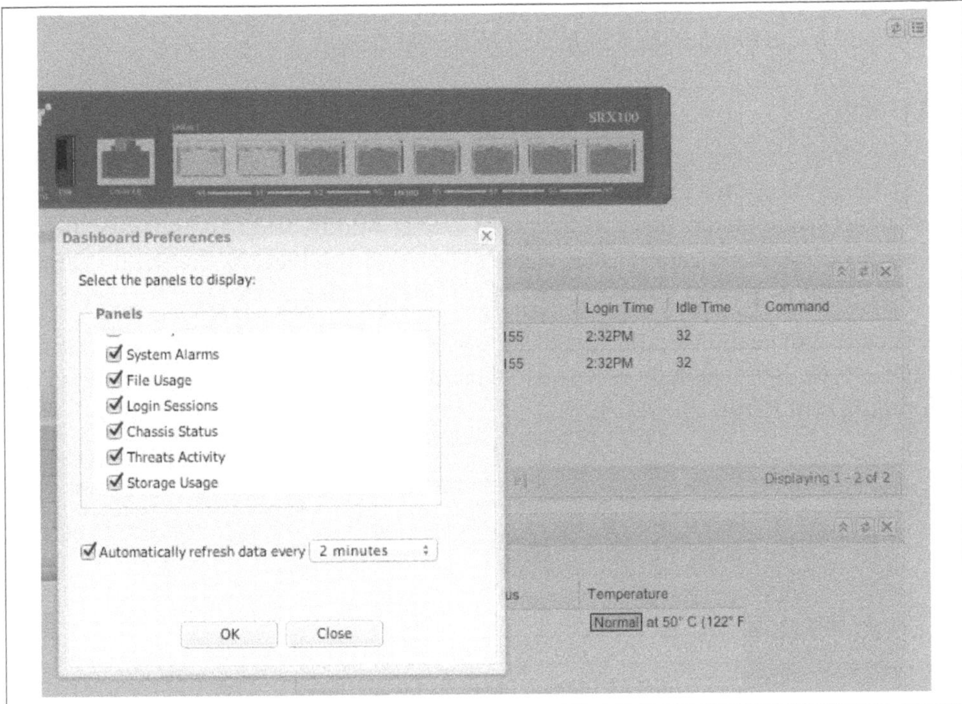

Figure 3-16. Dashboard Preferences dialog box

Device Configuration

The configuration options available within J-Web are extremely detailed. Often, web management tools are slimmed down and many configuration options are not made available. This is a double-edged sword when it comes to managing your device. The good news is that almost every possible option is available within J-Web. The downside is finding what you want to do can be daunting at times. Generally, J-Web follows the flow of the CLI. If you know the CLI, then J-Web will follow a logical flow. Alternatively, if you don't know the CLI, J-Web will assist you in learning its structure.

This section does not go over every possible feature, nor does it go into any specific feature in detail. It focuses on how to navigate some of the more important and popular features of the configuration in J-Web. As already discussed, GUIs are constantly evolving, so it is quite possible that even between minor releases there will be major UI changes. To navigate to the configuration section of J-Web, select the Configure tab, highlighted in Figure 3-17.

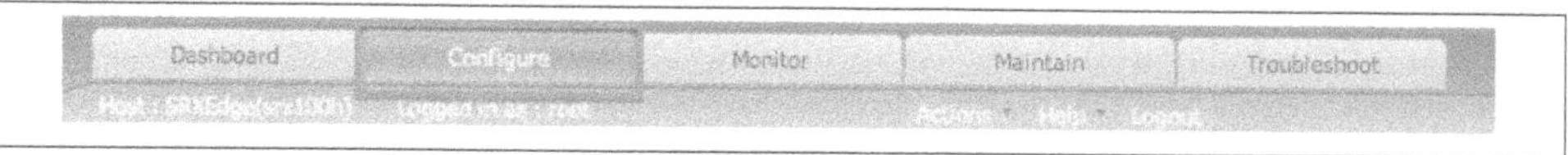

Figure 3-17. How to select the Configure tab for the device

Task wizards

When we look to solve a problem where we do not know an answer, we tend to look at product experts. When one isn't available, you can always call on the J-Web wizards. Wizards receive mixed reviews, as they tend to oversimplify tasks and not give the user the results they would expect. This is not the case with J-Web, as the wizards are extremely useful to get you started.

The wizards can be found in the upper-left corner of the configuration screen, as shown in Figure 3-18. If you look for the word "Wizards" this might be a bit confusing, so it is helpful to point it out.

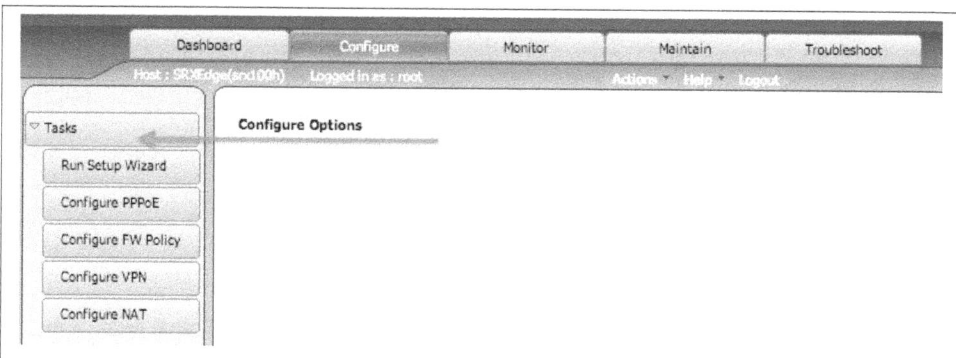

Figure 3-18. Wizards are located under the Tasks menu

The most helpful wizard is the Setup wizard. It not only can perform an initial setup, but it also helps modify the device's configuration. If you want to configure your SRX but you don't know how to get started, best practice is to use this wizard. In Figure 3-19, it is easy to see how the wizard will take you down a path.

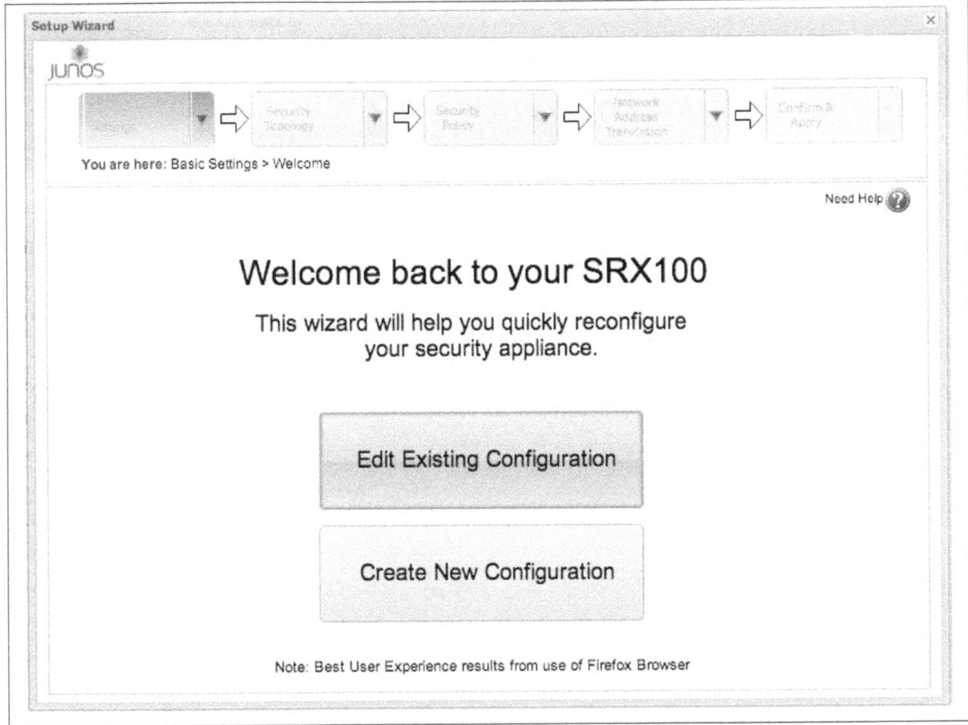

Figure 3-19. Getting started with the Startup wizard

If you choose to create a new configuration through the wizard, you will have the option to select the default setup that will preconfigure many of the best practices for you (see Figure 3-20). Alternatively, you can walk through the guided setup that will take you through all of the same configuration steps. Taking the guided tour is suggested for all new users. This shows you the most common elements that need to be configured and what is important from an SRX configuration standpoint. This is an excellent primer for any new user.

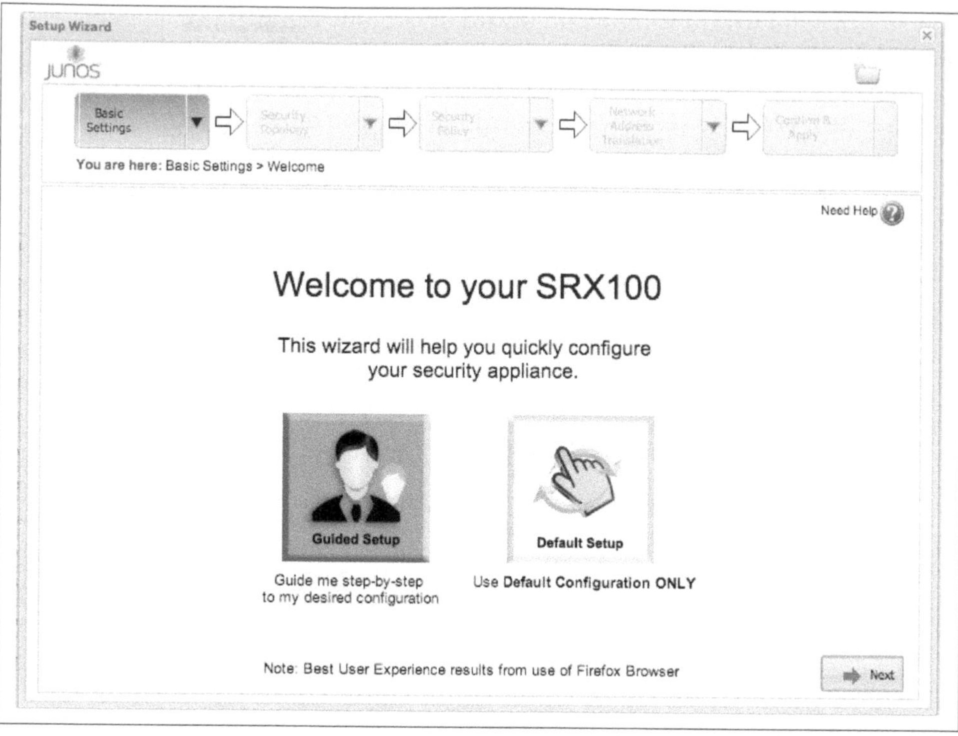

Figure 3-20. Choose your path wisely

If you select the guided setup, the wizard will ask you to select your level of expertise, as shown in Figure 3-21. Selecting the basic path will take you through only the required set of options. If you select expert, you will be taken through a more advanced set of options. You should stick to the basic path if this is your first adventure in the SRX. If you have an understanding of zones, policies, and system services, please veer onto the expert path, as it will open up some newer options for you.

The wizard contains more than 120 screens, so we won't review all of them. However, the first step for device information is important to call out. On any new Junos device you are always required to set the root password on authentication. Second, you always want to define a hostname, as once you access the device it is easy to forget which device you are on. This first step of the wizard makes you set up both. The example in Figure 3-22 shows you that it will walk you through the same process that an experienced Junos expert would take setting up the device from the CLI. After running through the wizard, you will know just what steps you would want to take if you were to set the device up through the CLI manually.

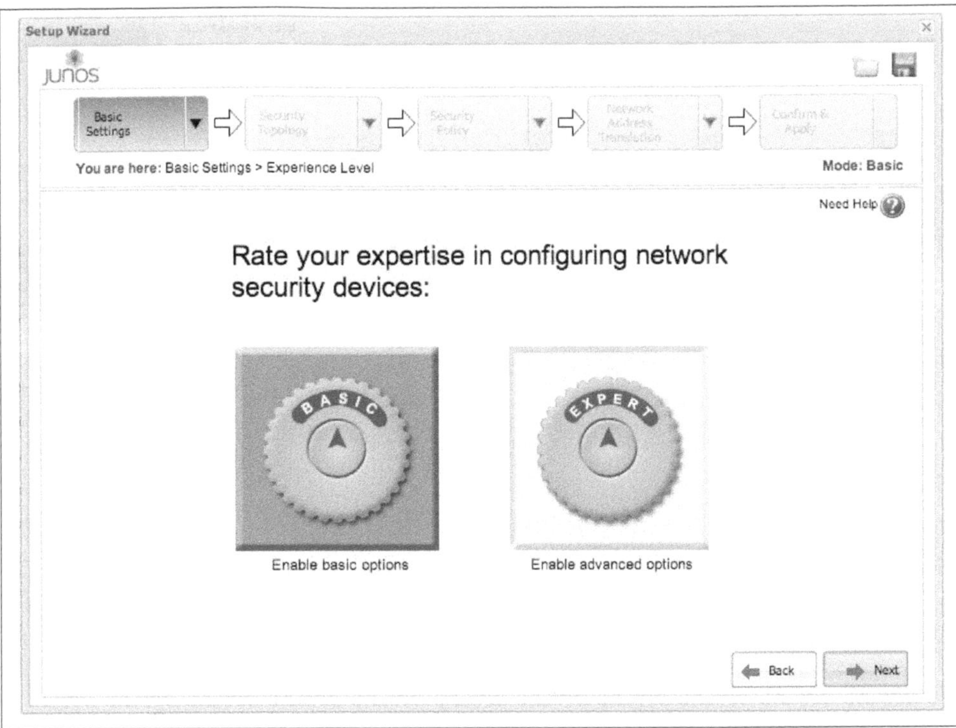

Figure 3-21. Are you an expert?

Committing the configuration

Originally, J-Web required you to commit each and every change that was made in J-Web. This was a really slow process, and frankly it ruined the experience of a GUI. Juniper listened to customers and created the ability to batch commit the configuration. It is important to understand how this works so you ensure that you apply the configuration changes that you make. The first time you make a configuration change you will see the informational pop-up box shown in Figure 3-23. It will let you know that you need to commit the configuration.

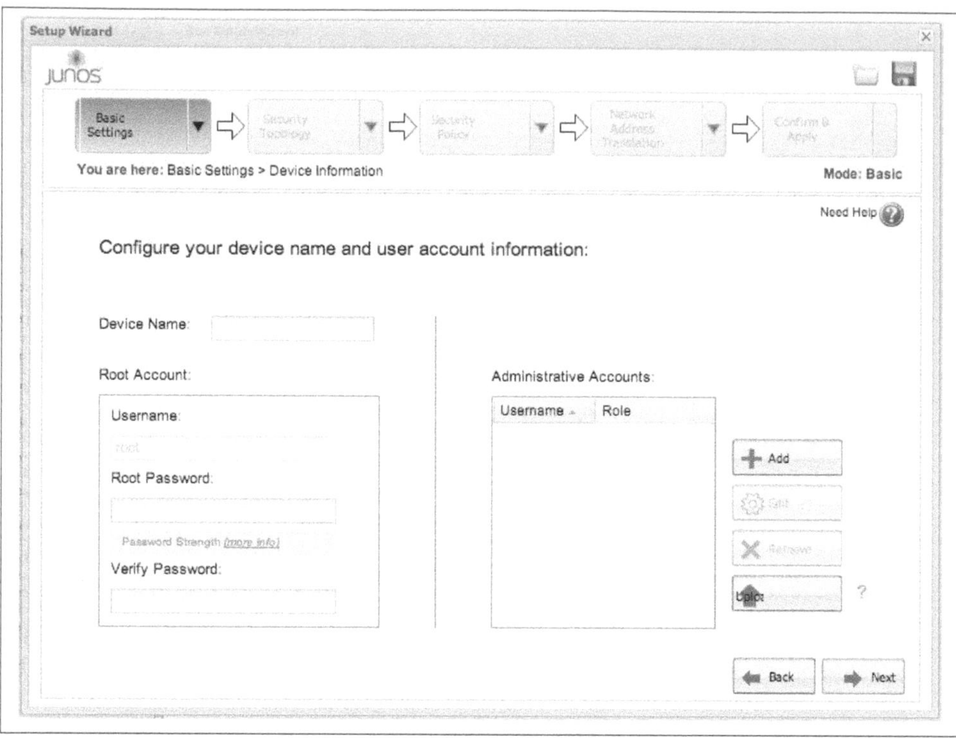

Figure 3-22. First things first: root authentication

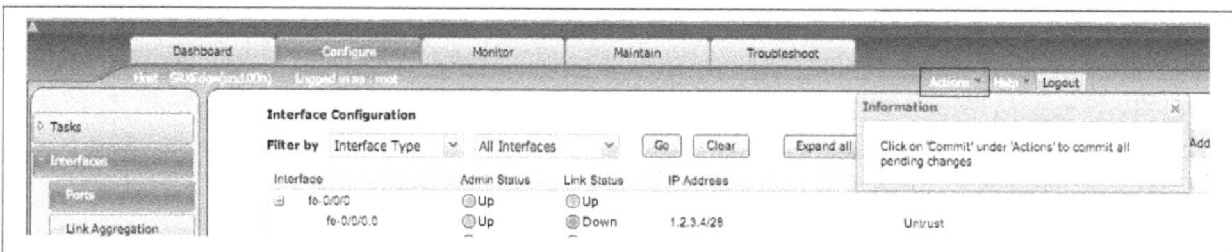

Figure 3-23. The need to commit changes is shown through an informational pop-up box

After you select to commit the changes, the configuration is first verified. This is exactly how a commit works through the CLI. This makes sense, as underneath J-Web is effectively the CLI. If the validation fails, it will instruct you on what to go back and change. If the validation succeeds, as shown in Figure 3-24, the committing of the configuration begins.

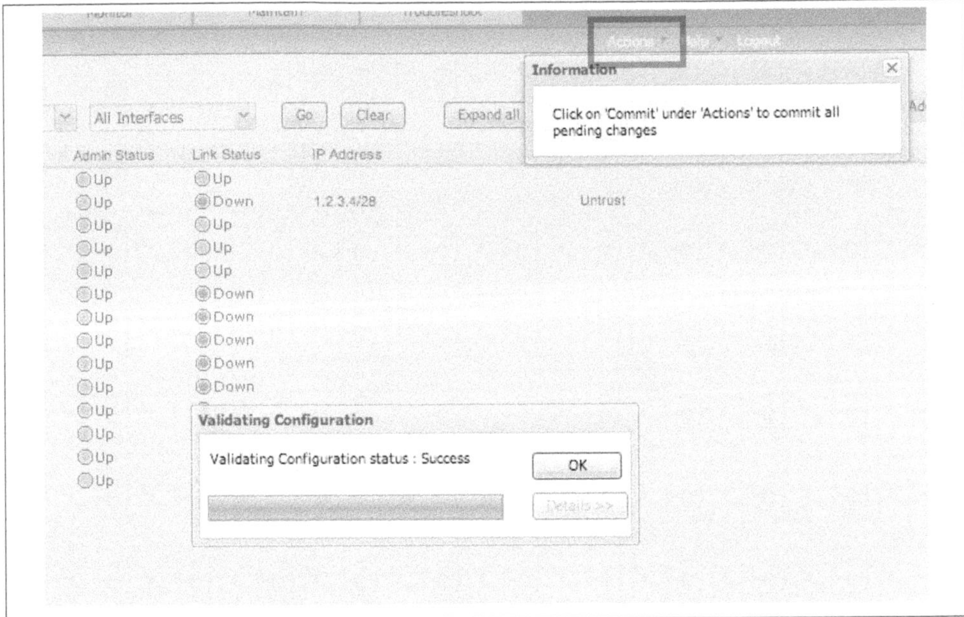

Figure 3-24. Validation success

The time it takes to deliver the configuration and apply it will depend on what platform you are using and how big the configuration is. J-Web will generally move more slowly to commit a configuration than if you were to do the same task from the CLI. Be patient, therefore, as you are committing the configuration. Let the configuration commit, as displayed in Figure 3-25, and do not attempt to reload the page or close any windows.

Interfaces

One of the two most common tasks performed through J-Web is interface management. Often, new subinterfaces will need to be created or IP addresses added. J-Web does an excellent job of dealing with interfaces and managing them. The interfaces selection is the first item under the Tasks menu among the selections found on the left side of the J-Web interface. Once selected, a list of interfaces will appear in a tree format in the main panel. There will be lots of strange interface names, such as lt-0/0/0. These are virtual interfaces that are used for various protocols and packet encapsulations. Most of the time, you will be dealing with Ethernet interfaces, so let's take a look at one of those in Figure 3-26.

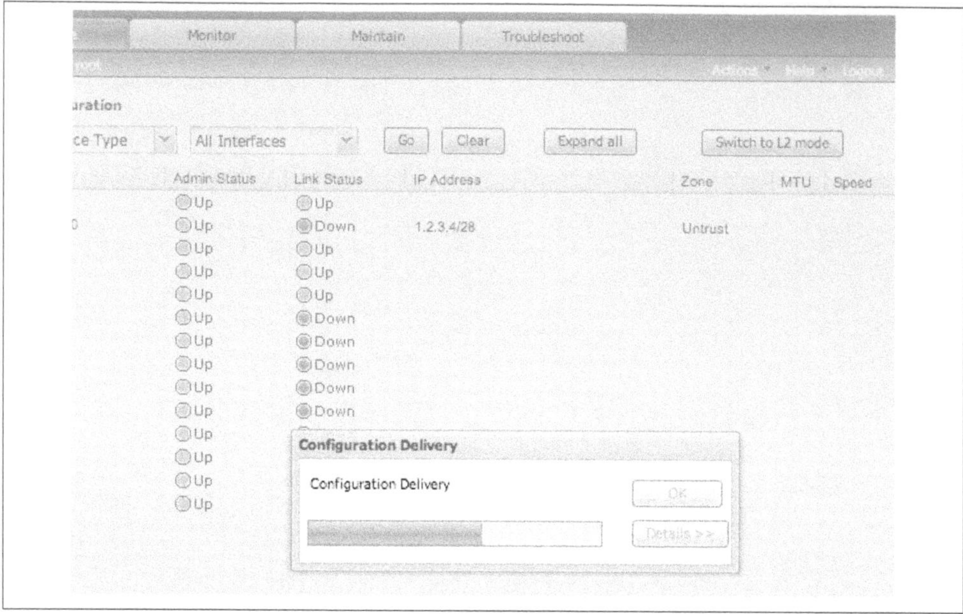

Figure 3-25. Delivery of the configuration

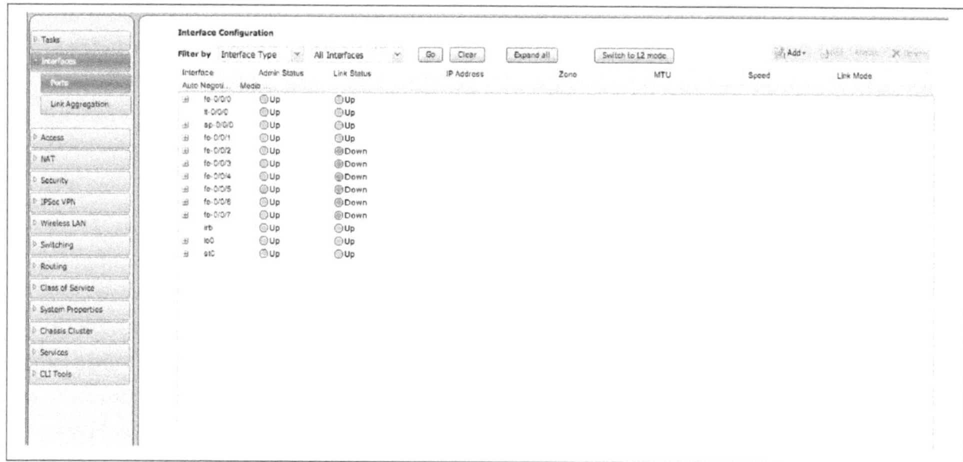

Figure 3-26. Interface listing in J-Web

From this page, it is also possible to get more details on the units of interfaces that are configured. Within the tree of interfaces, you can click on the small plus sign to expand all the units under an interface (see Figure 3-27). This is helpful to show the IP addresses that are configured on an interface.

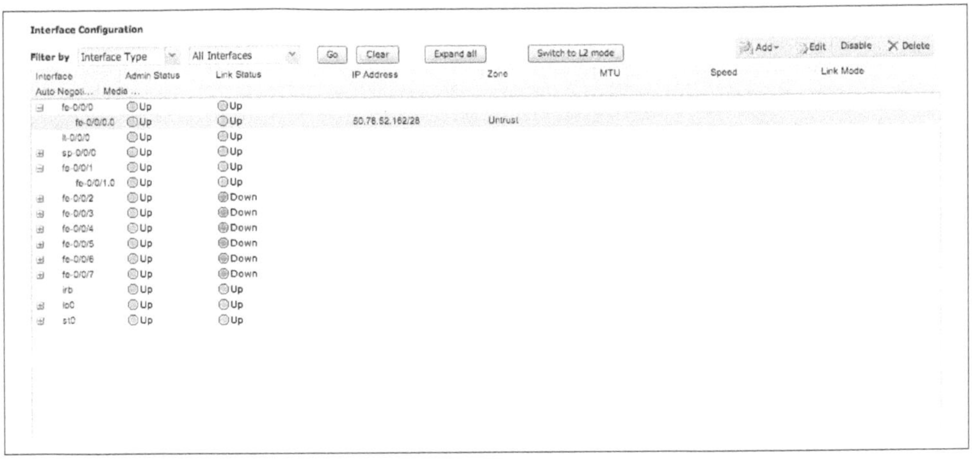

Figure 3-27. Interface unit detail

To edit an interface in detail, right-click the interface or select Edit from the upper-right corner. Once you open the interface, shown in Figure 3-28, the most common configuration options are available to you. The three most important elements for the interface are zone, IP, and VLAN ID, all of which can be created from within this screen. Both IPv4 and IPv6 addressing are supported. The configuration of the interface is different from the web UI compared to the CLI. In the CLI, the zone configuration would be in a completely different area of the configuration outside of the interface, thus showing the effectiveness of J-Web.

Firewall policies

The most common task of any firewall is to manage policies. For most firewalls, this is a daily task. Because of this, any firewall management tool needs to be extremely strong when it comes to this task. J-Web is such a tool, as its policy management capabilities are very strong. A point to note is that if you plan on managing hundreds or thousands of policies on a device, you will want to move to the Space platform, which is optimized for such tasks.

The SRX has many different types of firewall policies. These range from NAT and IPS to stateful firewall. The most commonly used type is the stateful firewall polices. Getting into the policies is a bit confusing in J-Web. To access the policies through the web UI, select Security→Policy→Apply Policy. This strange naming convention comes through a legacy configuration in J-Web. It is preserved to keep those who are familiar with J-Web in logical territory.

Figure 3-29 shows what a standard firewall policy looks like. It is a traditional tabular design containing one policy per row. Each column represents a different element of

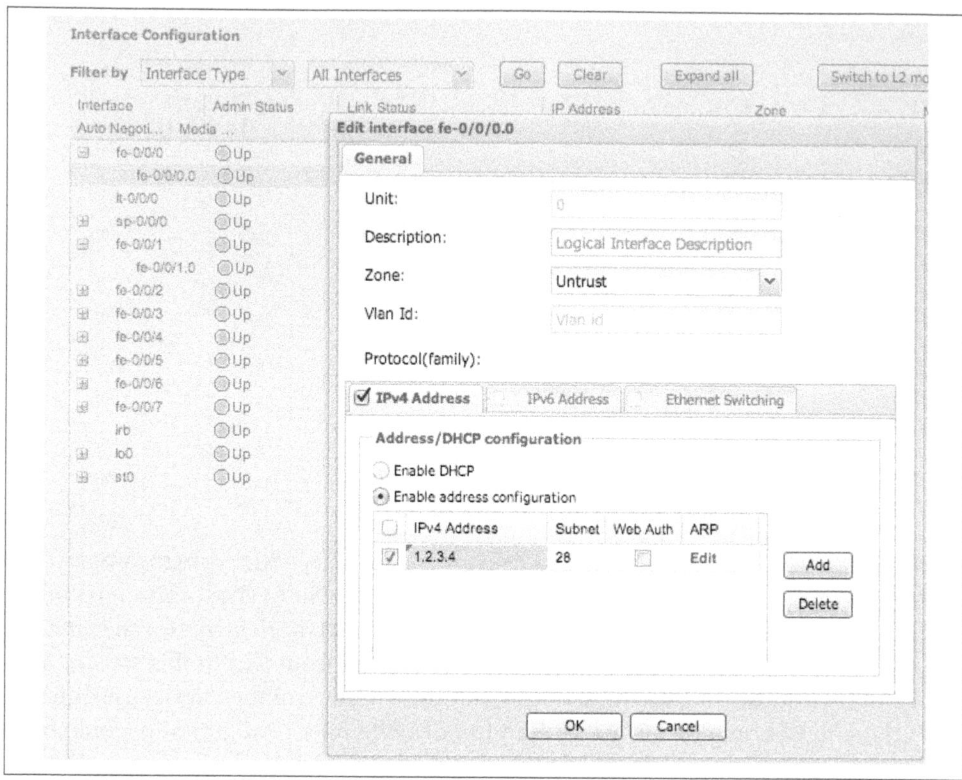

Figure 3-28. Editing interface details

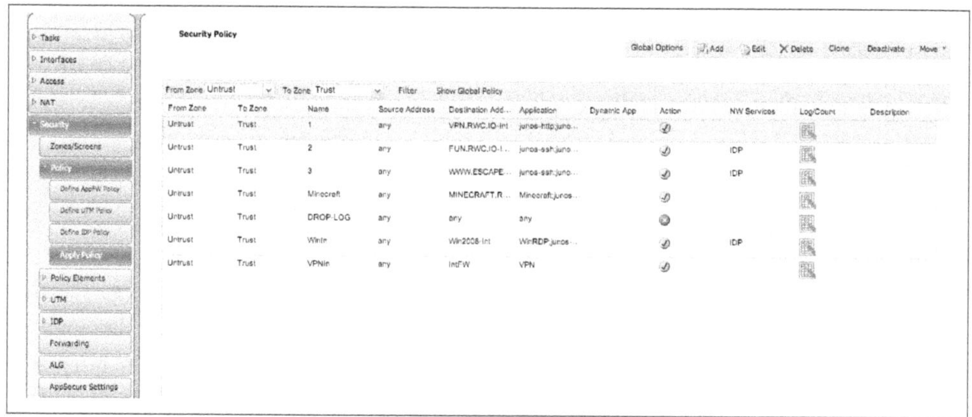

Figure 3-29. Stateful firewall policy management

the policy. Because the SRX utilizes a zone-based design, it is possible to filter the displayed policies by zones in the menu bar above the policy table. Those of you with a NetScreen background might notice that the icons used in the policies are the same from ScreenOS.

If you right-click a policy or click Edit in the upper,right corner, the details window will open, allowing you to configure all of the elements of the firewall policy (see Figure 3-30).

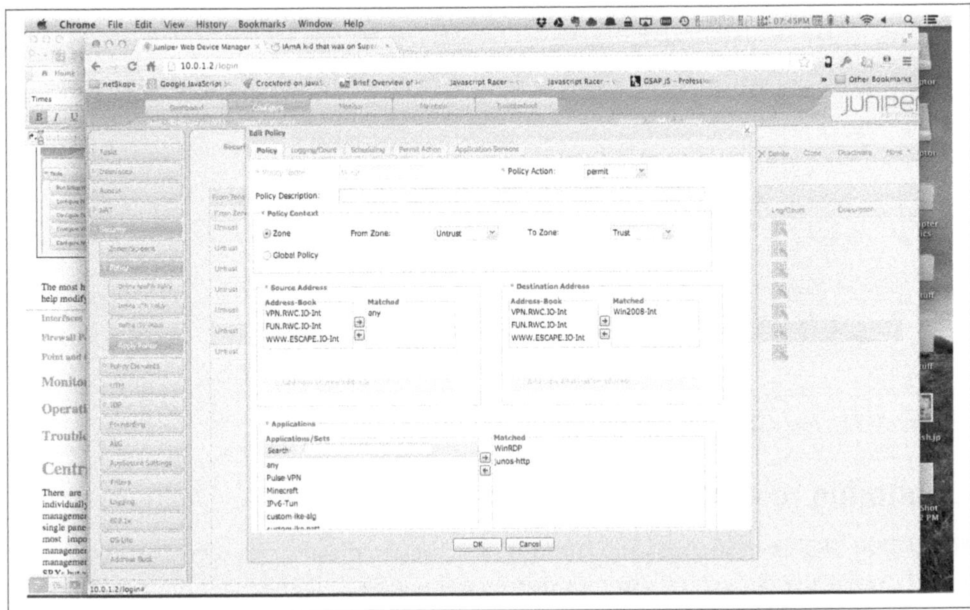

Figure 3-30. Firewall policy details

Point and click CLI

When all else fails, you can bring back the original J-Web design from 2005 and utilize the point and click CLI, shown in Figure 3-31. This is a literal interpretation of the CLI represented as a GUI. It is nice to use, as you can better understand how the hierarchy of the command line works. Sometimes you might know how to configure an element of the configuration only from the CLI, but you are unable to find it in the GUI. This tool will help bridge the gap between the web UI and the CLI, unifying both interfaces into one.

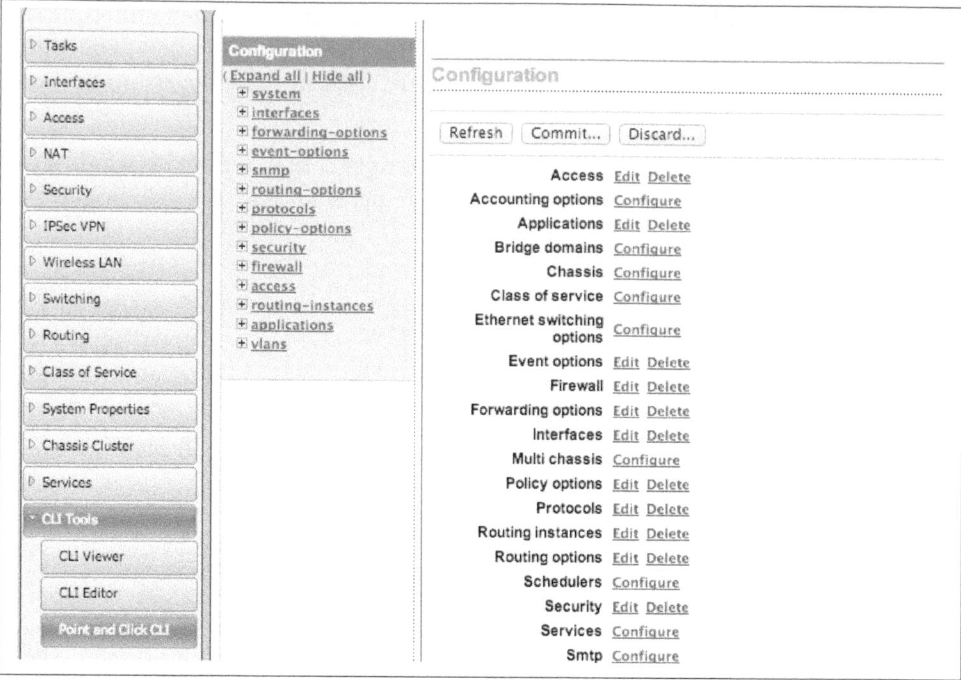

Figure 3-31. The GUI of last resort

Monitoring Your SRX

Once your SRX is configured and running, it is time to monitor your environment. The J-Web tool is the perfect tool for monitoring a single SRX. It gives you many of the stats that you need to know about. Because the SRX has so many features, the monitoring capabilities vary per platform and release. In this section, we review the most important elements to monitor from J-Web.

Interface monitoring

Following the progression of our configuration section, first we look at how to monitor interfaces. Start by selecting the Monitor tab at the top of the page and then Interfaces on the left. This opens a table for all of the interfaces. In Figure 3-32, we have selected an interface, which brings up two traffic graphs, one for the input stats and the other for the output stats. These stats will show you how much traffic is going through the interface.

Figure 3-32. Interface monitoring for throughput

More important, if you scroll down on the same page, you can review both the error and packet counters. If you notice a significant amount of errors, something could be wrong with the cable, interface, or the remote node. In Figure 3-33, you can see these charts.

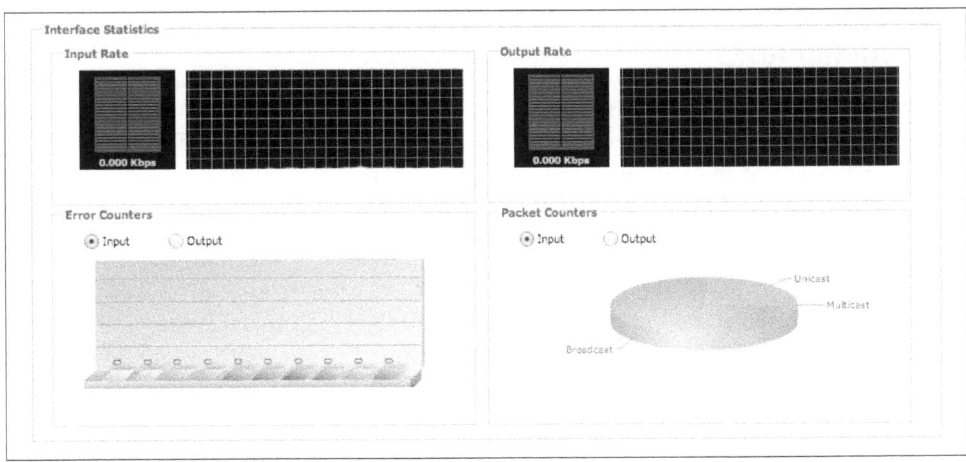

Figure 3-33. Full interface statistics

Traffic reports

The interface stats are excellent, but those are only counters for packets. To drill down further into the protocol stack, you can access the traffic reports under the Reports → Traffic menu on the left side. In Figure 3-34, you can see the breakdown of the traffic data. The flows are broken up by L3/L4 protocols of TCP, UDP, and ICMP. Then on the right side you can see the recently closed traffic sessions. This shows how much traffic has passed through the various sessions. You can customize how often these stats are refreshed automatically through the Refresh Interval drop-down box.

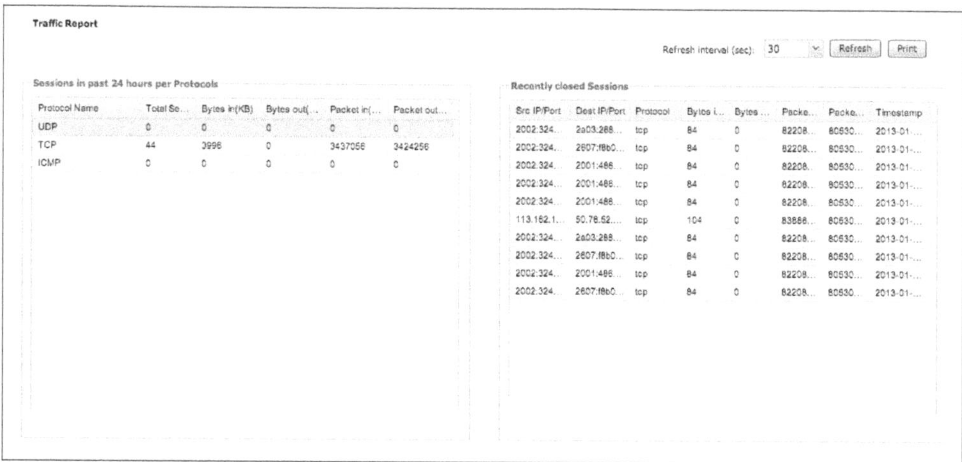

Figure 3-34. Traffic reporting

Operational Tasks

To maintain your SRX and prevent service outages, you must periodically perform operational tasks. There are a few important tasks that we review here. The best practice is to review each of these important tasks, so when the time comes to perform them, you will be ready to do so.

Software management

The Junos OS is developed under rigorous standards. Fresh releases are often packed with new features and bug fixes. Because of this, updating your SRX might be required several times per year, so it is good to be familiar with the SRX upgrade process. Most users choose to do the upgrade process from the CLI, but that can be complex. J-Web offers some simple ways to manage the software lifetime of your device.

To update your software, you must first upload an image. This is done through the Software → Upload Package menu. Updating is easy to do. Simply choose the file you want to upload from your computer, then select a few options (see Figure 3-35). You will always have to reboot. If you are able to reboot at that time, select the Reboot If Required checkbox. The "Do not save backup" option prevents the upgrade device from saving a backup copy of the image. Select this on the smaller branch devices, as they do not have enough disk storage to hold image backups. Once you have selected the options, click Upload and Install Package. This might take a while to complete, so be patient. Once the image is uploaded, a message will notify you that the process is complete. Do not close your browser before that, as it will interrupt the process.

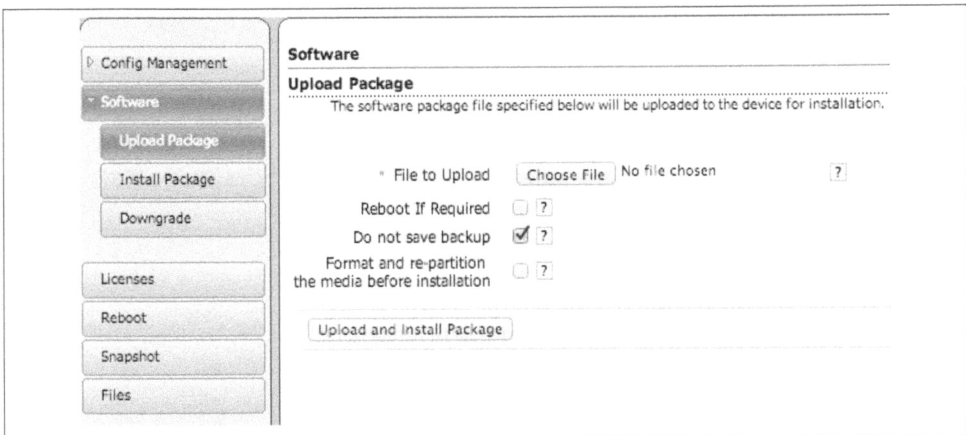

Figure 3-35. Uploading software images

Instead of having to push a package to the SRX, you can alternatively pull the image. This is great if you have a central repository of software for your data center. The location is required to specify where to pull the image from. You can use FTP, TFTP, HTTP, and SCP. Optionally, you can input a username and password for the package retrieval. The other options are the same as we reviewed before (see Figure 3-36).

Junos always keeps the last version of installed software available on the device. In the event you are experiencing unexpected behavior and need to roll back to the last installed release, you can simply go to the downgrade page shown in Figure 3-37 and click the Downgrade button. This will roll back to the previously installed release, but it will take some time and require the device to reboot. Once this process is started, you cannot stop it, so please be cautious in beginning the downgrade process.

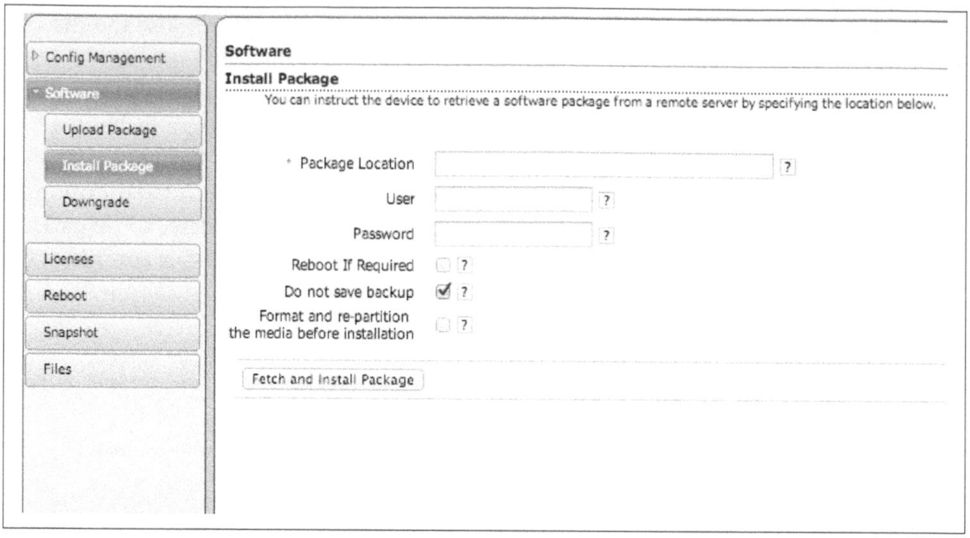

Config Management
Software
Upload Package
Install Package
Downgrade
Licenses
Reboot
Snapshot
Files

Software

Install Package

You can instruct the device to retrieve a software package from a remote server by specifying the location below.

* Package Location

User

Password

Reboot If Required

Do not save backup

Format and re-partition the media before installation

Fetch and Install Package

Figure 3-36. Software installation via retrieval

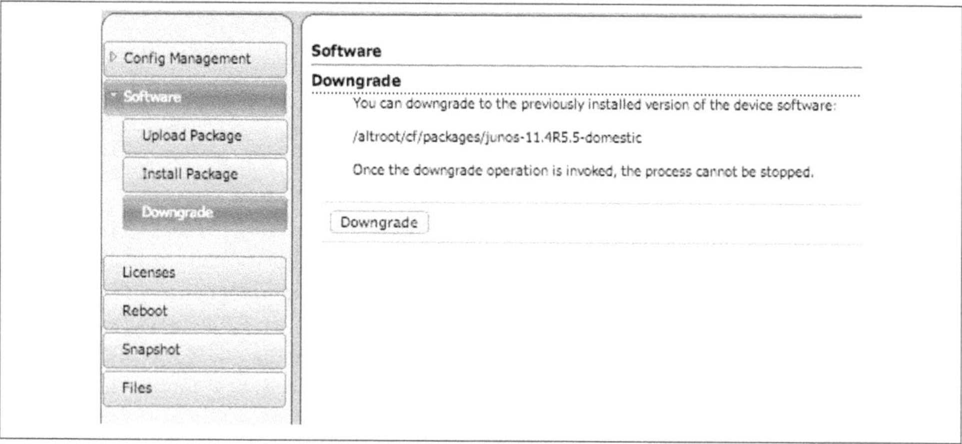

Figure 3-37. Software downgrades

Configuration management

Each time a configuration change is made, J-Web takes a snapshot of the configuration. Each device stores from between 5 and 50 different versions of the configuration. On the Config Management → History page, displayed in Figure 3-38, you can download, compare, and optionally roll back to an older version of the configuration. You might want to roll back your configuration if a change that you made did not work out as intended. Also you can see which user made the configuration change to determine who made the bad change.

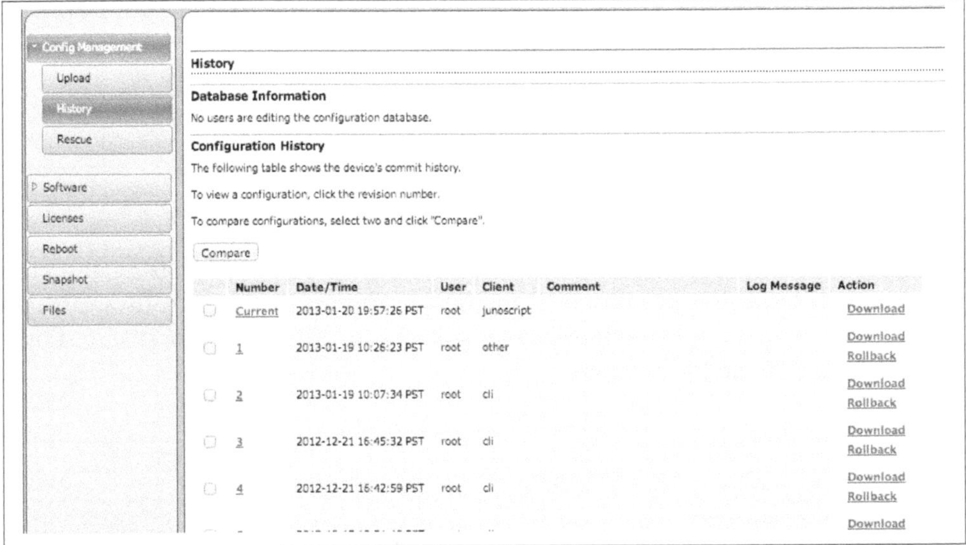

Figure 3-38. Reviewing the device's configuration history

Rebooting

Whether after a software upgrade or doing operational tasks, you will need to reboot your SRX from time to time. The Reboot screen, shown in Figure 3-39, allows you to reboot or halt the device. Halting the device will stop the OS. It is best to do that if you have console access so you can complete the reboot. The other options are to reboot immediately, reboot in X minutes, or schedule the reboot for a specific time. Optionally, you can display and log a message about why the reboot was needed.

Disk management

Junos offers very verbose monitoring and has a large software image that gets installed. Because of this, the disk often gets cluttered with many files. Potentially, your device's disk could get filled and cause it to lose data or, even worse, it could crash. Using the options on the Files menu, you can manually run a cleanup process to delete unneeded

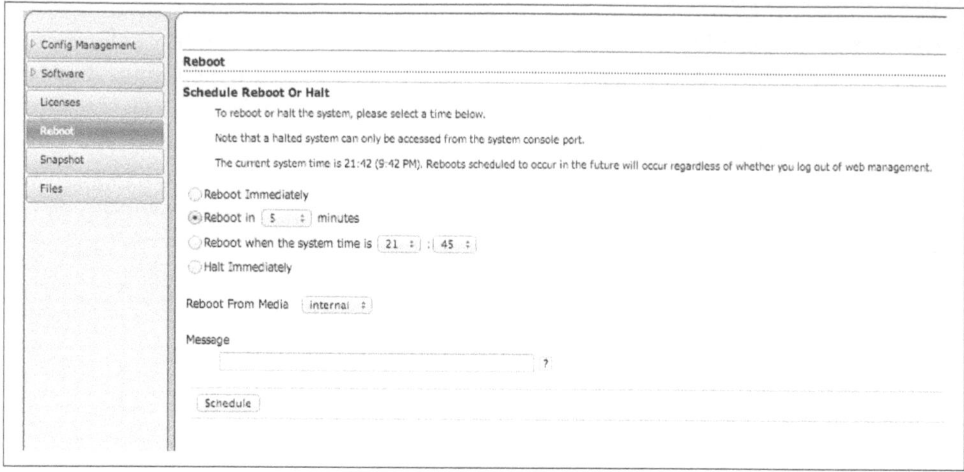

Figure 3-39. Options for rebooting

files (see Figure 3-40). Alternately, if you click any of the links, you can manually delete or download files. This is great for collecting any core dumps, logfiles, or software images on your device, and it is helpful for grabbing diagnostic information or just to simply view a logfile through the browser.

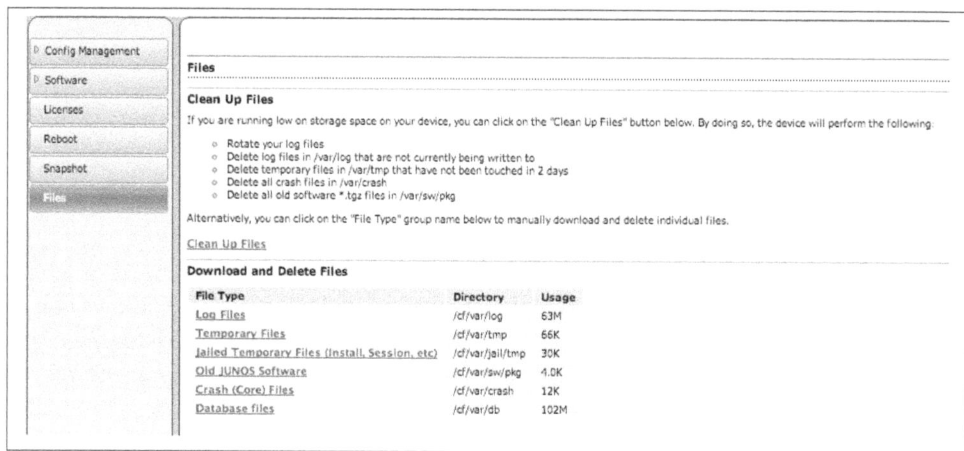

Figure 3-40. File management options

Troubleshooting from J-Web

Occasionally, things will go bad on your network. This is what makes being a network engineer so fun. Once things go wrong, though, it is time to right them. Several common tasks can be handled through J-Web. Ultimately, deep debugging will need to be done through the command line, but the two most common tasks are available through the web interface as well.

Packet capture

For many troubleshooting issues, you need to perform a packet capture on traffic (see Figure 3-41). This will allow you to analyze flows and see where traffic is potentially going wrong. Packet capture support will vary per release, platform, and potentially hardware card. Please check with the latest documentation to see if your platform is supported. It is simple to configure the options. You should select which interface you want to collect packets from.

To select the entire packet that is on the wire, you must enter *0* into the Packet Size field. You can also add various filters to specify the IP, protocol, and ports that the traffic will use.

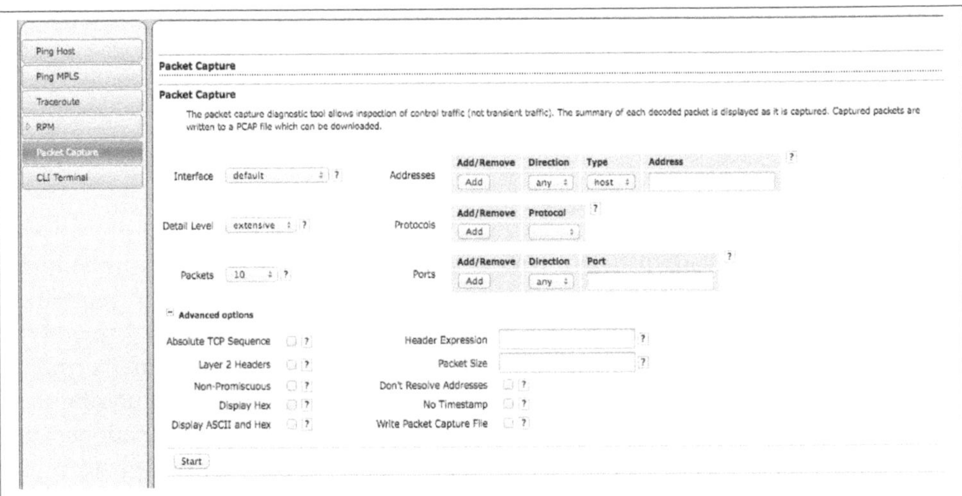

Figure 3-41. Packet capture

Network connectivity

Mike Muus changed the world one fine day in 1983. He created a utility called ping, named after sonar pings. Today, this tool is used as a basic network connectivity tester and as a starting point for almost any network troubleshooting. You can harness this tool through J-Web. By selecting the Ping option, you can send ICMP packets to remote hosts. You simply need to enter the IP address or hostname to send the packet. There are several other options that can be selected when sending pings, as shown in Figure 3-42.

The most important thing to note is the routing instance. This will be needed to change from the default to the specific routing instance that you would like to use to generate the ping. Second, you might want to select which interface to source the packet from as well.

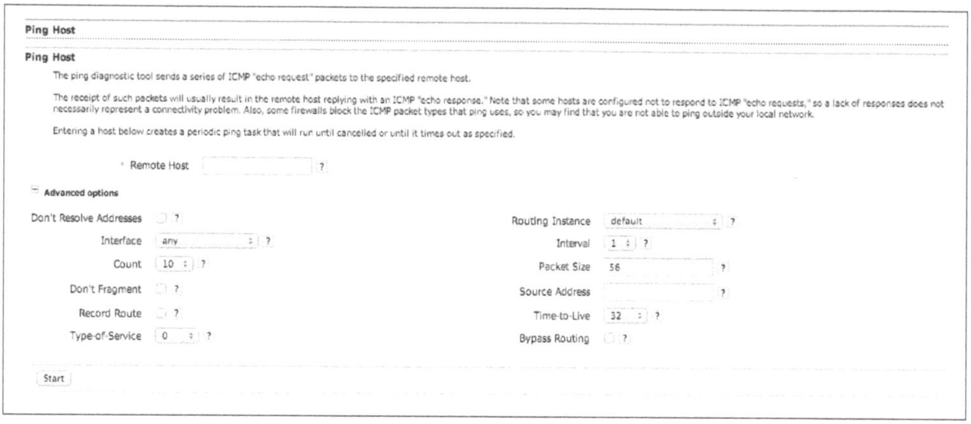

Figure 3-42. Ping host

Centralized Management

There are times when you will have too many devices to effectively manage individually. When this event occurs is to the decision of an individual administrator. A centralized management tool can simplify the management of your infrastructure and provide you a single pane of glass through which see your infrastructure and report on its activity. These are the two most important tasks of centralized management. Juniper offers several different management solutions that can provide you with these functions. Currently, from a management perspective, Junos Space is the premier platform for managing not only SRXs, but also all Junos devices.

To complement Junos Space, Juniper Networks utilizes the Statistical Report Manager software (STRM). The STRM platform not only collects logs, but also provides detailed analytics for then. And because security is not only provided by firewalls in a network, the STRM platform can accept logs from almost any device. The goal of this book is to focus on the individual devices themselves and not on the entire Junos ecosphere. Because of this, the centralized management section is a review of what is available and is not meant to be an exhaustive resource for these platforms.

Finally, in this section, we provide a brief review of the legacy management platform NSM. NSM has been around for more than seven years, and although its design is starting to show its age, it still is a very popular management platform for both legacy and new products alike.

Space: The Final Frontier of Management

Junos Space is more than a management console; it is a platform on which management is run. Back in 2007, once NSM was remade to include Junos, revolutionary thinking was going on about how management needed to be performed. NSM was an amazing security management tool, but it was not as flexible is Juniper would have liked to add new services on. Because of this, Juniper knew it was time to start investing in a platform that was extensible to meet all of its management needs for the next 10 years. Based on this need, Junos Space was created.

As new products were created and as new needs were to arise, Junos Space needed to be designed to meet this challenge. In Figure 3-43, we take a look at the platform and the basics of its design.

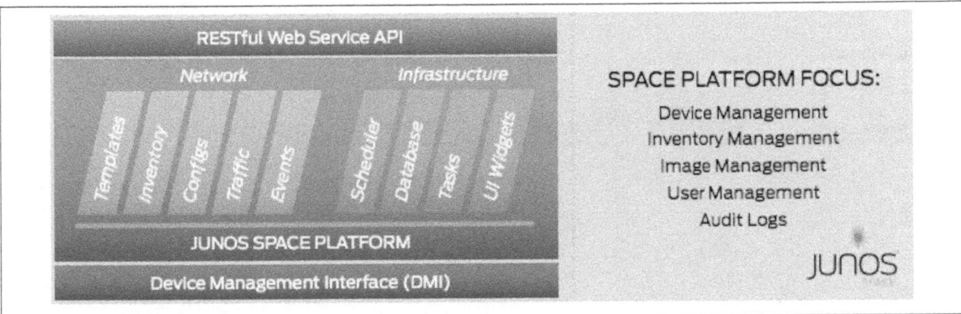

Figure 3-43. The Junos Space platform design

The Space platform utilizes Device Management Interface (DMI) to communicate with Junos devices. This is also known as a superset of the NetConf protocol that was defined originally in RFC 4741 as an XML-RPC-like protocol to provide configuration management of devices. The platform uses various technologies such as templates, inventory management, and event aggregation to store and manage device configurations. All of these elements are accessible via a Representational State Transfer (REST) HTTP protocol. This API is available to all users of the Space platform as well as its applications. The power of Space truly is in its RESTful API architecture. All of the Junos Space applications utilize a central API that is available to all users of Space. This way the platform is designed to be the underpinnings of the applications and gives each application designer the freedom to focus on the apps and not worry about how to connect to the devices.

The Junos Space ecosphere

Applications are the heart of where users spend their time when floating through Junos Space. Each application (see Figure 3-44) provides the specific tools that are needed to solve a problem from within your network. Applications like Security Director are built to manage your security infrastructure, whereas Service Now provides automated troubleshooting and reporting of any open issues that might arise on your network. Service Now can also automatically publish your issues to Juniper's customer support to ensure that an engineer will be working on your issue before you even notice a problem occurred.

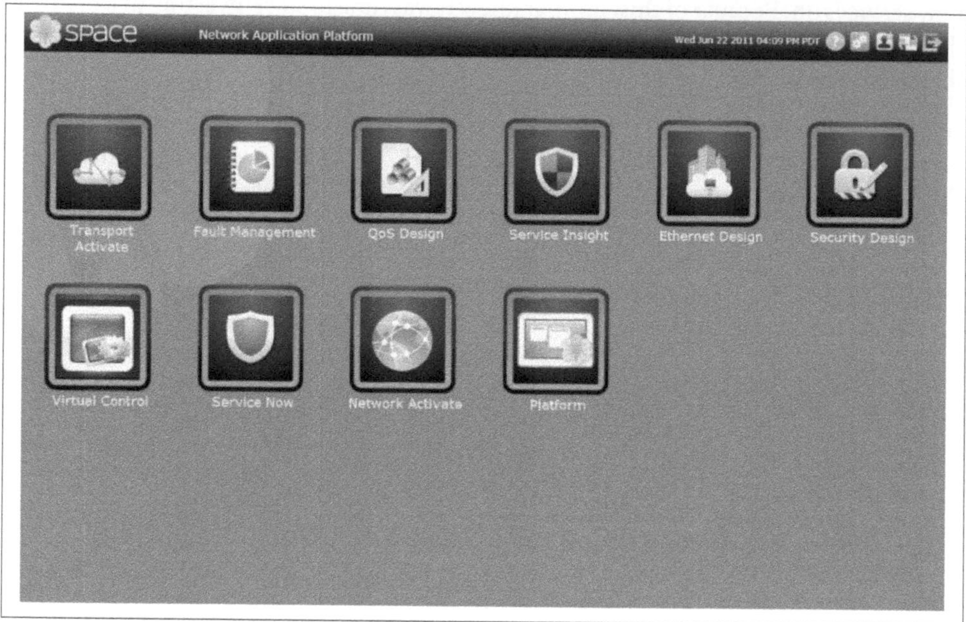

Figure 3-44. Junos Space application dashboard

Security Director

To manage your security needs, the Security Director application takes this type of management to new levels. It not only provides you with a GUI to manage policies, but it can assist in managing the complete ecosystem of your security needs. Each new release of Security Director offers newer features to simplify policy management and increase the overall security efficacy of your network. Due to the advanced development and rapid releases, it is difficult to cover this product within a book that contains static content on publication. It is suggested that you view the publically available documentation to see all of the current features of the Security Director application (see Figure 3-45).

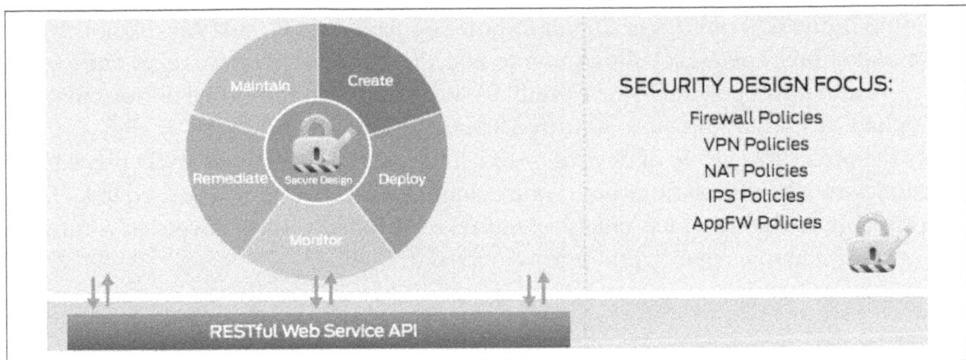

Figure 3-45. Security Director architecture

Firewall policy management

The top task to use Security Director for is firewall policy management. Security Director brings in many tools that advanced administrators are looking for. It allows you to create multiple policy templates, which you can use to automatically merge them into a single policy that is pushed down to a device. This eases administration as opposed to having to create these complex policies by hand. The policy UI, shown in Figure 3-46, is also more fluid and advanced than what is available from the J-Web interface.

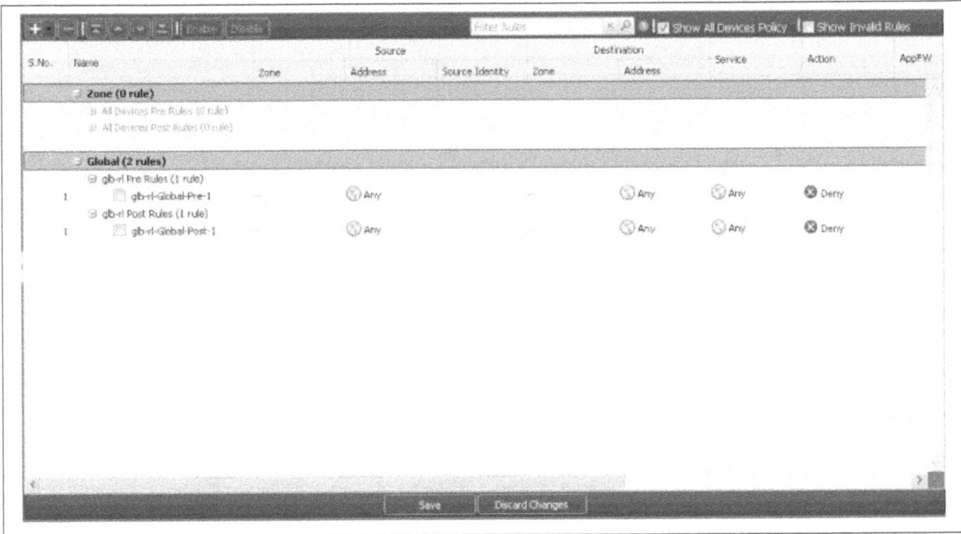

Figure 3-46. Policy management through Space

Defining individual policies is similar to how you would do it on J-Web. A policy creation dialog box opens and allows you to add the standard elements that you would expect to add into a policy. However, unlike J-Web, there are additional options that can be applied to a policy. Because Security Director is centrally managed, it allows you to apply the policy to a group of devices or to a single device. It also can apply precedence to a policy so when the various policies are compiled before they are pushed to an SRX, you are able to define which policy would take precedence in the event of a conflict. These central management options are depicted in Figure 3-47.

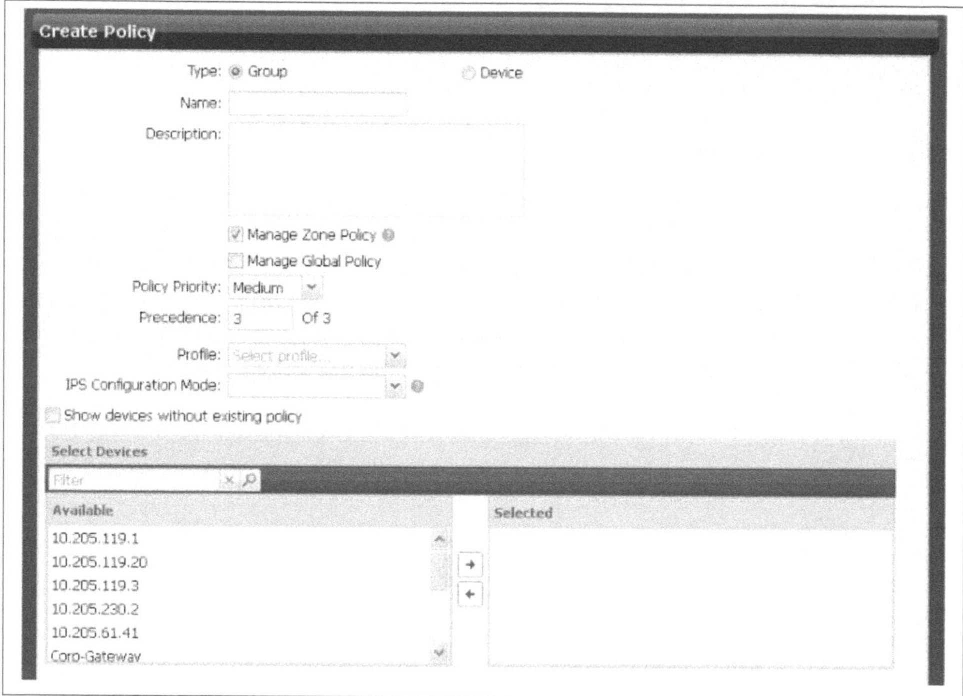

Figure 3-47. Detailed policy creation options

Log Management with STRM

Configuring policies is only one side of the equation of managing a security infrastructure. The other half is looking at the efficacy of these policies. This is best done using the STRM platform from Juniper Networks. Although the focus of this discussion is the SRX, it should not be overlooked that the STRM platform can take in logs from almost any device. This includes other Junos platforms but also things such as Microsoft Active Directory and even Cisco products. The goal of the platform is to not just collect logs, but to use data aggregation to take those logs and make them into valuable reports.

Reporting with STRM

The heart of STRM is its reporting infrastructure. There are many built-in reports for STRM, but an administrator can also create predefined reports. These reports can correlate logs from various sources into a dashboard that defines the exact activities of your network.

Reporting on what applications are being used within your network is a popular task for STRM. Figure 3-48 is a depiction of this report. It takes logs from the AppSecure or AppID that come from the SRX and provides reporting for it. It reports on the top applications as well as the top application source IP addresses.

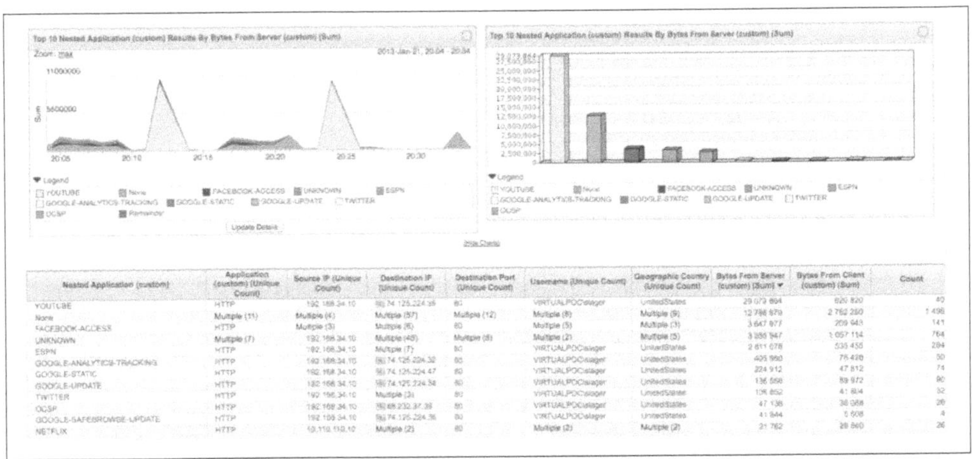

Figure 3-48. Application reporting

IP addresses are typically sourced by geographic location. This is an interesting point to report on for many reasons. If you are hosting a website, you might want to see where your potential clients are coming from. In the case of security, you want to see where specific attacks are starting. Is China your biggest threat or is it Detroit, Michigan? STRM has built-in reporting to be able to correlate country data to the IP address (see Figure 3-49).

Reporting by IP addressing is great, but determining the actual user who is accessing data is even better. It is possible to tie STRM into your user authentication infrastructure (see Figure 3-50) to be able to correlate this information. Through this, you can see if Darren has been spending too much time on YouTube or if Charlie has had his productivity reduced by reading home improvement articles. This is a more human approach to seeing the activity on your network. It has been proven in the US courts that an IP address does not directly show what activities a user has performed. Because of this, being able to correlate the activities of users is invaluable to any enterprise.

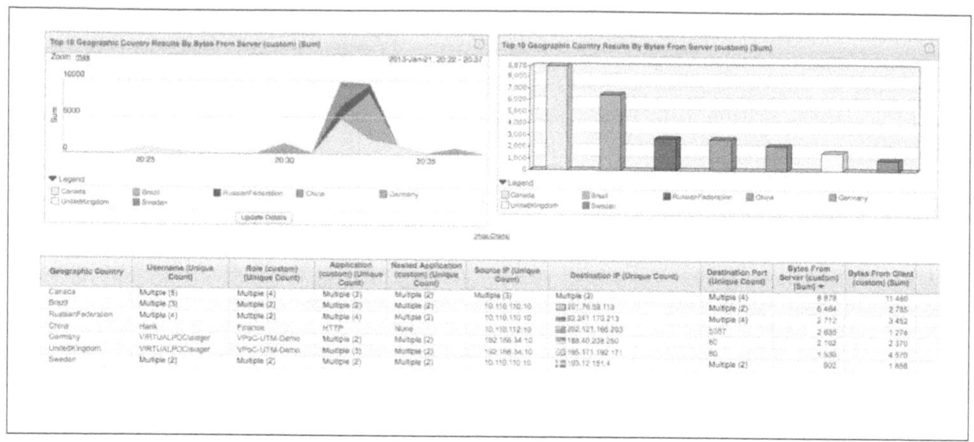

Figure 3-49. Traffic by country report

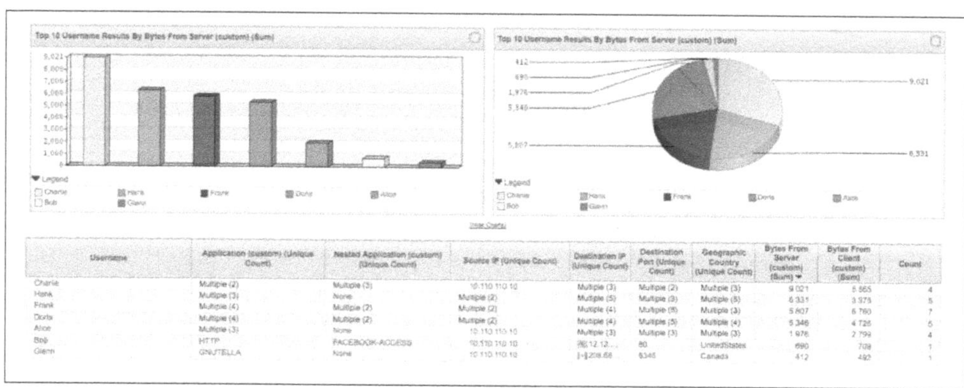

Figure 3-50. Top applications by user

Legacy Security Management

162_Ma Before the SRX, and before Juniper even acquired NetScreen, the world had NetScreen Security Manager. This platform was the successor to Global Pro to manage the ScreenOS platforms. For its time, the platform was a revolution in management for the security industry. However, over time, as Juniper was in need for managing Junos in the enterprise, it worked to move this product to support Junos. Network and Security Manager became the product's name, retaining the NSM acronym.

As of this writing, the NSM platform has been put into maintenance mode. This means that no new features will be put into the platform but all subsequent releases will be to patch the existing platform. NSM is not suggested for new deployments unless ScreenOS or IDP standalone support is needed. Both of these legacy platforms are only supported through NSM, so if centralized management is required for them, NSM must be used. Because NSM is no longer being developed, it will not be able to support new features in future versions of Junos. It will be able to manage newer releases through schema updates, but if a new feature requires a custom screen to configure it, that will not be created.

Using NSM

The NSM management tool follows a bit more traditional paradigms of management than Junos Space. It offers a similar dashboard, shown in Figure 3-51, to select which tasks you want to undertake. Because NSM is focused on network and security management, its capabilities are a bit more limited than what is found within Junos Space.

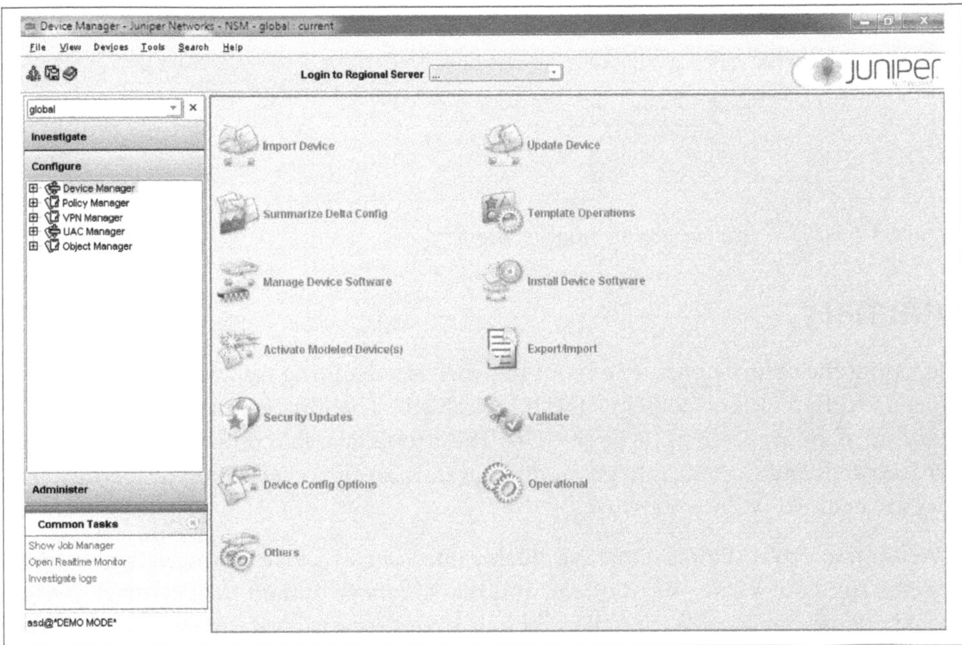

Figure 3-51. NSM dashboard

Policy management is still the most common task that is handled within NSM. It offers the traditional style of policy management that we have seen throughout this chapter. It also has some of the same policy template features that we have seen in Security Director (see Figure 3-52). In fact many of the features that you find in Junos Space are present within NSM.

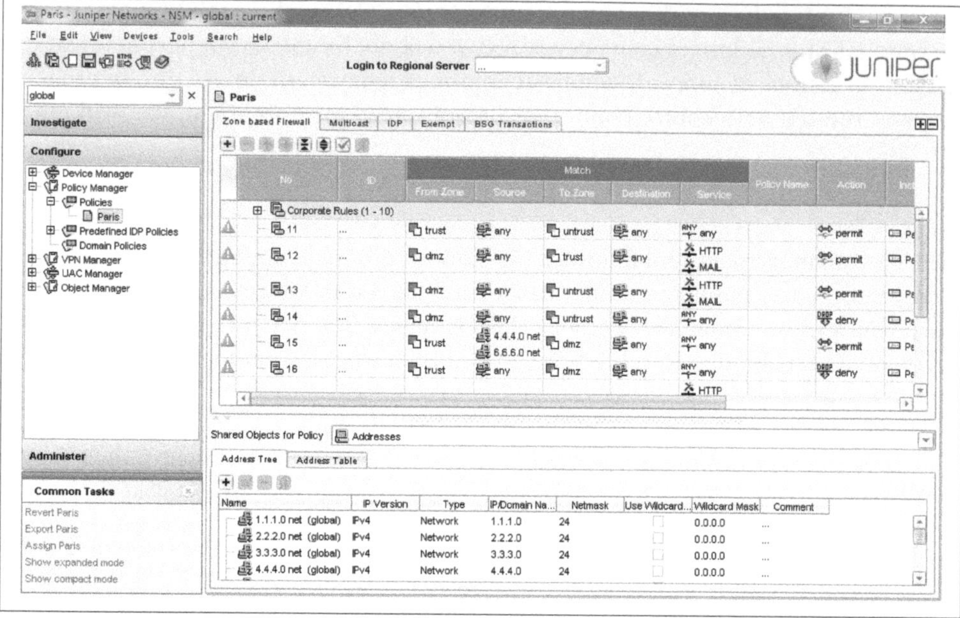

Figure 3-52. NSM firewall policy management

Summary

Managing the security posture of your network is a daunting task. Different organizations use different tools to help solve this problem. The most common way to handle this kind of management is through GUIs. These tools take the complex nature of policy management and simplify it to give administrators an enhanced vision over which policies are enabled on their network.

J-Web offers a robust toolset that is available on every SRX system and also most Junos systems right out of the box. It offers tools that are more limited than central management systems, but capable enough to provide simplified on-device management. J-Web is constantly evolving to meet the needs of today's customers. Throughout this chapter we have looked at many features of J-Web. Due to the advanced methodology and rapid software release cycle of Junos, new features and enhancements are popping up all the time. For the latest capabilities and features of Junos, please refer to the documentation of the current release of Junos that your device is running.

Although Junos Space has only been out for a few years, it has made herculean progress in its capabilities. The future of the Space platform, as well as Security Design, is bright. There most certainly will be more amazing features coming right around the corner to increase the efficacy of your network security policies.

Study Questions

Questions

1. What management platform supports the legacy ScreenOS and standalone IDP?
2. When did J-Web originate?
3. What is the defining component of Junos Space?
4. What is the most common task for GUI management of security devices?
5. What is the alternate name for wizards that is used in J-Web?
6. Is it possible to manage your device's software image through J-Web?
7. What is the name of the legacy security management platform for the SRX?
8. What tool does Juniper make to handle log management?

Answers

1. NSM is the only platform that supports the ScreenOS and standalone IDP. It also supports most Junos platforms, including the SRX.
2. J-Web was originally created in 2005 and has had significant development around its feature set since it was launched.
3. Junos Space is a platform and not just a management tool. It allows applications to use a common API to control and access information about the devices connected to it. Through this, new applications and services can be rapidly built on the solid Space platform.
4. Policy management is the most common task done for security devices through a GUI. Being able to see all of the policies and how they interact through a single window is critical for any security administrator.
5. J-Web also defines its wizards as tasks.
6. J-Web offers complete device management, including software installation and rollbacks.
7. NSM is the legacy management platform. All new installations should focus on utilizing Junos Space.
8. Statistical Reports Manager (STRM) is the ideal tool for log management and reporting. STRM is not limited to Junos devices only; it can accept logs from nearly any device.

CHAPTER 4

SRX Networking Basics

The Junos OS has support for the majority of the available networking protocols. A small device such as an SRX100 supports MPLS, VPLS, switching, IS-IS, BGP, and dozens of other protocols. It is quite amazing to have such a wide variety of technologies available in one device. The SRX is a versatile device. Being able to offer so much protocol support and also offering security features is wonderful. As SRX experts, both my coauthor and myself have discussed hundreds of use cases and deployment models with customers. The majority of these deployments use only the minimal amount of networking features. Around 25 percent of SRX deployments use the more advanced networking features of the SRX. These specific deployments would not be possible if the SRX was unable to support these advanced features. However, when deciding on how to best cover networking on the SRX, we chose to keep the networking section focused on best practices rather than covering the corner case deployments. We want to guide you to supported, commonly used designs that we consider best practices.

The majority of the book is focused on the security aspects of the SRX. In this chapter, we review the basics of getting the SRX onto your network and how to deploy the SRX in what we consider a standard best practice. Because the networking side of Junos is so robust, we often see customers attempting to be overly creative with their networking designs. There is nothing wrong with this. It is fun to deploy a dozen routing instances and multiple routing protocols. Often it is needed, but for the majority of SRX deployments it is not. When dealing with a network deployment, it is best to focus on the minimal requirements for a working design. Each additional component that is added can cause an unexpected level of difficulty. Our suggestion is to keep your designs simple and focus on keeping the design minimalistic. This will ensure a successful deployment and ease troubleshooting in the event that trouble occurs.

Interfaces

To get our networking device to apply security to traffic, we must first integrate it into our network. To do so, we must start by configuring its interfaces. This is a very basic and essential step to any deployment, but it is typically where an installation starts. The majority of the administration time on an SRX is spent on policy tuning and reviewing the security logs. For a security device, this is where you want to spend your time, sharpening your security policy.

The deployment capabilities are quite diverse when it comes to an SRX. The majority of the SRX deployments use Ethernet interfaces. Although the branch SRX devices do offer dozens of WAN interfaces, the configuration is essentially the same outside of the physical configuration for the interface. We suggest you check the latest Junos documentation on the WAN interfaces as this changes quite often with newer drivers in current versions of Junos. Also we have made a decision to treat IPv6 as a first-class citizen. Throughout this chapter we show how to configure both IPv4 and IPv6. If you have not had a chance, please do take some time to learn IPv6. It is relatively simple once you start using it (128-bit IP addresses do take some getting used to). If you are not familiar with IPv6, I suggest Silvia Hagen's *IPv6 Essentials* (O'Reilly). This is where I started a number of years ago, and I highly recommend it.

Physical Interfaces

A networking device without interfaces isn't much of a networking device. Because a Junos device is always in the network, and most of the time it is in the path of the network, it is critical to understand interface configuration.

Some Junos interface concepts might seem foreign to administrators who are migrating from other OSs. Remember that the Junos CLI is designed to be extensible and scalable, and once an element is added to the configuration hierarchy after a software release is made, it is not changed. Because of this, creating an interface and modifying its parameters might seem overly complex, but it is done for a good reason: to ensure that 10 years from now the general structure of creating an interface is backward compatible.

A physical interface is an actual device that someone can touch and a cable of some sort goes into it. A logical interface is an entity that has a protocol and a network address assigned to it. A physical interface can also be called an *IFD*, and a logical interface is called an *IFL*, terms sometimes sprinkled around in the documentation or in various Junos material.168

An interface is named in a common format, and the format is shared regardless of the interface type. The first part of an interface name is the media type. Table 4-1 lists a few of the common media types and their abbreviations.

Table 4-1. Interface media types

Name	Media type
fe	Fast Ethernet 10/100
ge	Gigabit Ethernet 1000
xe	10 gigabit Ethernet
t1	T1 interface
vlan	Virtual interface that resides in a virtual LAN (VLAN)

There are many different types of interfaces, and only a handful are represented in Table 4-1. For more information on the various interface types, refer to the Junos documentation set (*http://www.juniper.net/techpubs*).

Interface names also include the location in which they are found in the chassis. This portion of the interface name consists of three numbers: the FPC number, the PIC number, and the port number.

FPC, or flexible PIC concentrator, is simply a slot in a chassis. The differentiation of FPCs typically determines how the FPC plugs into the back plane of the device. A PIC represents a physical or pluggable (both terms are seen and sometimes used interchangeably) interface card on which interfaces or ports reside. The numbering for an interface is represented in an *X*/*Y*/*Z* pattern, with *X* being the FPC, *Y* being the PIC, and *Z* being the port. An example of a complete interface name is "ge-0/0/0".

A few interface types do not fit into this format. One of these is fxp0, which is used as a management port. You can configure it with most of the options that an interface can use, such as IP addresses, but this interface cannot route traffic because it is not a transient interface. We discuss the fxp0 interface in the next section.

Each physical interface has some physical properties that you can configure, such as speed, duplex, and auto-negotiation; these properties vary based on interface type. Because of all the variations that are possible, it's best to check the latest Junos documentation to get the most up-to-date configuration options. In most cases, though, the command-line help, using ?, will give you what you need. Typically, on an Ethernet interface, you will not need to configure the specific properties.

For physical interfaces, the physical configuration properties are under the "ether-options" hierarchy. The configuration specifics and name of this "options" section will vary based on the type of interface, the Junos platform, or both. Under the ether-options, as we will call it from now on, you can specify the duplex as well as the speed. These are the most common settings that someone would configure under the physical interfaces properties. The most common would be disabling the physical interface. In this next configuration example, we look at both.

```
root@SRXEdge# set fastether-options ?
Possible completions:
> 802.3ad                IEEE 802.3ad
+ apply-groups              Groups from which to inherit configuration data
+ apply-groups-except       Don't inherit configuration data from these groups
  auto-negotiation          Enable auto-negotiation
  ignore-l3-incompletes     Ignore L3 incomplete errors
  ingress-rate-limit        Ingress rate at port (1..100 megabits per second)
  loopback                  Enable loopback
> mpls                   MPLS options
  no-auto-negotiation       Don't enable auto-negotiation
  no-loopback               Don't enable loopback
> redundant-parent       Parent of this interface
> source-address-filter  Source address filters
[edit interfaces fe-0/0/0]
root@SRXEdge#
```

As we can see here, these are the configuration options under a fast Ethernet interface on an SRX100. It doesn't offer much in the customization for physical properties as these options are found under the interface itself. Because the underlying hardware is different on each platform the options might vary a bit.

```
[edit interfaces fe-0/0/0]
root@SRXEdge# set ?
Possible completions:
  accounting-profile     Accounting profile name
+ apply-groups           Groups from which to inherit configuration data
+ apply-groups-except    Don't inherit configuration data from these groups
  description            Text description of interface
  disable                Disable this interface
  encapsulation          Physical link-layer encapsulation
> fastether-options    Fast Ethernet interface-specific options
  flexible-vlan-tagging  Support for no tagging, or single and double
                             802.1q VLAN tagging
  gratuitous-arp-reply   Enable gratuitous ARP reply
> hold-time              Hold time for link up and link down
  link-mode              Link operational mode
  mac                    Hardware MAC address
  mtu                    Maximum transmit packet size (256..9192)
  native-vlan-id         Virtual LAN identifier for untagged frames (0..4094)
  no-gratuitous-arp-reply    Don't enable gratuitous ARP reply
  no-gratuitous-arp-request  Ignore gratuitous ARP request
  no-per-unit-scheduler      Don't enable subunit queuing on Frame Relay or
                                 VLAN IQ interface
  no-traps                   Don't enable SNMP notifications on state changes
  passive-monitor-mode       Use interface to tap packets from another router
  per-unit-scheduler         Enable subunit queuing on Frame Relay or VLAN IQ
                                 interface
  speed                      Link speed
```

```
> traceoptions          Interface trace options
  traps                       Enable SNMP notifications on state changes
> unit                  Logical interface
  vlan-tagging                802.1q VLAN tagging support
[edit interfaces fe-0/0/0]
root@SRXEdge#
```

Here we can see that both speed and duplex can be set under the interface itself.

```
[edit interfaces fe-0/0/0]
root@SRXEdge# show
speed 100m;
link-mode full-duplex;

[edit interfaces fe-0/0/0]
root@SRXEdge#
```

They can also be set as shown with the set commands instead of the Junos hierarchy.

```
[edit interfaces fe-0/0/0]
root@SRXEdge# show | display set
set interfaces fe-0/0/0 speed 100m
set interfaces fe-0/0/0 link-mode full-duplex

[edit interfaces fe-0/0/0]
root@SRXEdge#
```

Here is an example from an SRX3600 displaying the gigabit Ethernet options as well as the rest of the physical options at the root hierarchy under the interface itself. Both speed and link mode are in bold.

```
root@srx3600n0# set gigether-options ?
Possible completions:
> 802.3ad               IEEE 802.3ad
+ apply-groups          Groups from which to inherit configuration data
+ apply-groups-except   Don't inherit configuration data from these groups
> auto-negotiation      Enable auto-negotiation
  flow-control          Enable flow control
  ignore-l3-incompletes  Ignore L3 incomplete errors
  loopback              Enable loopback
  no-auto-negotiation   Disable auto-negotiation
  no-flow-control       Don't enable flow control
  no-loopback           Don't enable loopback
> redundant-parent      Parent of this interface
[edit interfaces ge-0/0/0]
root@srx3600n0# set ?
Possible completions:
  accounting-profile    Accounting profile name
+ apply-groups          Groups from which to inherit configuration data
+ apply-groups-except   Don't inherit configuration data from these groups
  description           Text description of interface
  disable               Disable this interface
  encapsulation         Physical link-layer encapsulation
> gigether-options      Gigabit Ethernet interface-specific options
```

```
    gratuitous-arp-reply  Enable gratuitous ARP reply
  > hierarchical-scheduler  Enable hierarchical scheduling
  > hold-time            Hold time for link up and link down
    link-mode            Link operational mode
    mac                  Hardware MAC address
    mtu                  Maximum transmit packet size (256..9192)
    native-vlan-id       Virtual LAN identifier for untagged frames (0..4094)
    no-gratuitous-arp-reply  Don't enable gratuitous ARP reply
    no-gratuitous-arp-request  Ignore gratuitous ARP request
    no-per-unit-scheduler  Don't enable subunit queuing on Frame Relay or VLAN
                             IQ interface
    no-traps             Don't enable SNMP notifications on state changes
  > optics-options       Optics options
  > otn-options          Optical Transmission Network interface-specific options
    per-unit-scheduler   Enable subunit queuing on Frame Relay or VLAN IQ inter-
face
    port-mirror-instance  Port-mirror the packet to specified instance
    promiscuous-mode     Enable promiscuous mode for L3 interface
    speed                Link speed
  > traceoptions         Interface trace options
    traps                Enable SNMP notifications on state changes
  > unit                 Logical interface
    vlan-tagging         802.1q VLAN tagging support
[edit interfaces ge-0/0/0]
root@srx3600n0#
```

Finally, disabling an interface is easy to do and it can be done as one command. It is common to disable interfaces during testing or troubleshooting.

```
[edit interfaces fe-0/0/0]
root@SRXEdge# show
disable;

[edit interfaces fe-0/0/0]
root@SRXEdge# show | display set
set interfaces fe-0/0/0 disable

[edit interfaces fe-0/0/0]
root@SRXEdge#
```

Either way, configuring the options is straightforward. Depending on the version of Junos and the underlying hardware, the options can vary. It is best to check the latest Junos documentation to see how to configure the specific options that you are looking for. By default, Junos interfaces do not have to be shown in the configuration. This is great, as you can preconfigure interfaces before you even have the hardware, but it is also confusing to first-time users, as you might wonder what interfaces you have available. It is easy to see what hardware you have installed in your device. This can be done a few different ways. Most commonly, you would use the `show interfaces terse` command. This would display what interfaces are in the system, their physical status (up or down), and if there are any logical interfaces configured.

```
[edit interfaces fe-0/0/0]
root@SRXEdge# run show interfaces terse
Interface               Admin Link Proto    Local                 Remote
fe-0/0/0                up    up
fe-0/0/0.0              up    up   inet     11.12.13.14/28
gr-0/0/0                up    up
ip-0/0/0                up    up
lt-0/0/0                up    up
mt-0/0/0                up    up
sp-0/0/0                up    up
sp-0/0/0.0              up    up   inet
sp-0/0/0.16383          up    up   inet     10.0.0.1            --> 10.0.0.16
                                            10.0.0.6            --> 0/0
                                            128.0.0.1           --> 128.0.1.16
                                            128.0.0.6           --> 0/0
fe-0/0/1                up    up
fe-0/0/1.0              up    up   eth-switch
fe-0/0/2                up    up
fe-0/0/2.0              up    up   eth-switch
fe-0/0/3                up    up
fe-0/0/3.0              up    up   eth-switch
fe-0/0/4                up    down
fe-0/0/4.0              up    down eth-switch
fe-0/0/5                up    down
fe-0/0/5.0              up    down eth-switch
fe-0/0/6                up    down
fe-0/0/6.0              up    down eth-switch
fe-0/0/7                up    down
fe-0/0/7.0              up    down eth-switch
gre                     up    up
ipip                    up    up
irb                     up    up
lo0                     up    up
lo0.16384               up    up   inet     127.0.0.1           --> 0/0
lo0.16385               up    up   inet     10.0.0.1            --> 0/0
                                            10.0.0.16           --> 0/0
                                            128.0.0.1           --> 0/0
                                            128.0.0.4           --> 0/0
                                            128.0.1.16          --> 0/0
lo0.32768               up    up
lsi                     up    up
mtun                    up    up
pimd                    up    up
pime                    up    up
pp0                     up    up
ppd0                    up    up
ppe0                    up    up
st0                     up    up
st0.0                   up    up   inet     10.250.0.1/30
tap                     up    up
```

```
[edit interfaces fe-0/0/0]
root@SRXEdge#
```

There certainly is a lot to take in from that one command. You will be able to see all of the physical, virtual, and logical interfaces in the system with that one command. The part that we want to focus on in this section is finding the physical interfaces. In the preceding display all of the physical interfaces are shown in bold. We can verify that these are physical interfaces in two ways. First, we can see that they display the media type, fe for fast Ethernet, and they use the **X/Y/Z** naming to show where they are located in the chassis. It is possible to use the `show chassis hardware` command to also see what cards are physically installed in the chassis.

```
root@SRXEdge> show chassis hardware
Hardware inventory:
Item             Version  Part number  Serial number     Description
Chassis                                AU5209AF0571      SRX100H
Routing Engine   REV 08   750-021773   AT5209AF0571      RE-SRX100H
FPC 0                                                    FPC
  PIC 0                                                  8x FE Base PIC
Power Supply 0

root@SRXEdge>
```

In this, we can see that there is one 8xFE (eight fast Ethernet port) PIC installed. These interfaces are built into the chassis. A more complex example can be seen next from an SRX3600 chassis. Because the SRX3600 is a modular platform, the administrator installs the majority of its components. The physical interfaces are displayed in bold in the following example:

```
root@srx3600n0> show chassis hardware
Hardware inventory:
Item          Version  Part number  Serial number  Description
Chassis                             AB3009AA0002   SRX 3600
Midplane      REV 07   710-020310   AAAR9529       SRX 3600 Midplane
PEM 0         rev 10   740-027644   I262GR008F10P  DC Power Supply
PEM 1         rev 10   740-027644   I262GR00CC10P  DC Power Supply
CB 0          REV 16   750-021914   AAAZ3985       SRX3k RE-12-10
  Routing Engine       BUILTIN      BUILTIN        Routing Engine
  CPP                  BUILTIN      BUILTIN        Central PFE Processor
  Mezz        REV 08   710-021035   AAAT1432       SRX HD Mezzanine Card
FPC 0         REV 12   750-021882   AAAK9268       SRX3k SFB 12GE
  PIC 0                BUILTIN      BUILTIN        8x 1GE-TX 4x 1GE-SFP
FPC 1         REV 16   750-020321   AABV2891       SRX3k 2x10GE XFP
  PIC 0                BUILTIN      BUILTIN        2x 10GE-XFP
    Xcvr 0    REV 01   740-014289   C745XU00K      XFP-10G-SR
    Xcvr 1    REV 01   740-014289   T08A15927      XFP-10G-SR
FPC 2         REV 13   750-016077   AACV7526       SRX3k SPC
FPC 3         REV 13   750-016077   AACV7484       SRX3k SPC
  PIC 0                BUILTIN      BUILTIN        SPU Cp-Flow
FPC 4         REV 05   750-016077   TV3939         SRX3k SPC
  PIC 0                BUILTIN      BUILTIN        SPU Flow
```

```
FPC 5          REV 13  750-016077   AABS4961        SRX3k SPC
  PIC 0                BUILTIN      BUILTIN         SPU Flow
FPC 6          REV 13  750-016077   AACY8034        SRX3k SPC
  PIC 0                BUILTIN      BUILTIN         SPU Flow
FPC 7          REV 11  750-016077   AAAK0085        SRX3k SPC
  PIC 0                BUILTIN      BUILTIN         SPU Flow
FPC 8          REV 13  750-016077   AACV5262        SRX3k SPC
  PIC 0                BUILTIN      BUILTIN         SPU Flow
FPC 9          REV 13  750-016077   AACW2994        SRX3k SPC
  PIC 0                BUILTIN      BUILTIN         SPU Flow
FPC 10         REV 13  750-017866   AAAK8644        SRX3k NPC
  PIC 0                BUILTIN      BUILTIN         NPC PIC
FPC 11         REV 12  750-017866   AAAF7971        SRX3k NPC
  PIC 0                BUILTIN      BUILTIN         NPC PIC
FPC 12         REV 15  750-017866   AACY0754        SRX3k NPC
  PIC 0                BUILTIN      BUILTIN         NPC PIC
Fan Tray 0     REV 06  750-021599   VR9733          SRX 3600 Fan Tray

root@srx3600n0>
```

Management Interfaces

One of the most controversial interfaces in a Junos platform is the dedicated management port, also known as fxp0. All data center SRX devices come with a built-in physically dedicated fxp0 port. On the branch devices, the fxp0 interface is only created on entering cluster mode (discussed in Chapter 7). The original design of the fxp0 interface was to provide a dedicated physical interface that is directly connected to the route engine, the idea being that even if the data plane would be completely utilized, you would still have direct access to the route engine for management.

In a typical service provider network, there is a dedicated segment to just device management. This way, all of the devices could be reachable no matter the state of the transit network, and no management protocols would need to be turned on where customer's traffic passes. This is an excellent idea, and we consider this to be an ideal best practice. If possible, please do create an out-of-band network and use it as your sole method of management.

Now the reality is that most enterprise customers do not follow this as a best practice. Typically, in an enterprise, management is done in-band or on traffic passing ports. In a service provider, you have nontrusted third-party data transiting your network. In no way would you want to trust any management traffic that is intermixed with this traffic. In an enterprise, the situation is very different. An enterprise typically has trusted or partially trusted traffic transiting their networks. Because of this, in-band management is logical and it saves the enterprise from building another dedicated network. I use the term enterprise loosely, as here I use it as any non-service-provider network.

With that said, let's talk about the challenges that are currently presented with the fxp0 interface. This interface is stuck in the main or often referred to as the master routing instance or table (routing instances are discussed later in the chapter). This creates a bit of a dilemma, as most enterprises would want to keep their network simple and utilize a single routing table. However, it seems strange to have this other management interface inside the same routing table. Let's break down the various concerns for this scenario in the remainder of this section.

First, routes that are associated with fxp0 are never pushed into the data plane's forwarding table. This means that those routes are not in a place that would impact transit traffic. To show this further, let's take a look at the routing table from the perspective of the CLI and what the data plane can see. In our example, the only default route that we have configured is via fxp0.

```
root@srx3600n0> show configuration routing-options
rib inet6.0 {
    static {
        route 2003::0/120 next-hop 2001::fe;
        route 2004::0/120 next-hop 2005::fe;
    }
}
static {
    route 0.0.0.0/0 next-hop 172.19.100.1;
    route 10.102.5.0/24 next-hop 10.102.1.254;
    route 10.102.6.0/24 next-hop 10.102.2.254;
}

root@srx3600n0> show route

inet.0: 16 destinations, 16 routes (16 active, 0 holddown, 0 hidden)
+ = Active Route, - = Last Active, * = Both

0.0.0.0/0          *[Static/5] 1w1d 23:50:11
                    > to 172.19.100.1 via fxp0.0
10.102.1.0/24      *[Direct/0] 1w1d 23:49:26
                    > via xe-1/0/0.0
10.102.1.1/32      *[Local/0] 5w1d 23:08:37
                      Local via xe-1/0/0.0
10.102.2.0/24      *[Direct/0] 1w1d 23:49:25
                    > via xe-1/0/1.0
10.102.2.1/32      *[Local/0] 5w1d 23:08:37
                      Local via xe-1/0/1.0
10.102.3.0/24      *[Direct/0] 1w1d 23:49:26
-- truncated ---

root@srx3600n0> show route forwarding-table
Routing table: default.inet
Internet:
Destination        Type RtRef Next hop           Type Index NhRef Netif
default            user     2 0:1b:c0:56:a0:0 ucst   357     5 fxp0.0
default            perm     0                    rjct    36     1
0.0.0.0/32         perm     0                    dscd    34     1
10.102.1.0/24      intf     0                    rslv   569     1 xe-1/0/0.0
```

```
10.102.1.0/32      dest     0 10.102.1.0      recv   567      1 xe-1/0/0.0
10.102.1.1/32      intf     0 10.102.1.1      locl   568      2
10.102.1.1/32      dest     0 10.102.1.1      locl   568      2
10.102.1.254/32    dest     0 10.102.1.254    hold   602      3 xe-1/0/0.0
10.102.1.255/32    dest     0 10.102.1.255    bcst   566      1 xe-1/0/0.0
10.102.2.0/24      intf     0                 rslv   585      1 xe-1/0/1.0
10.102.2.0/32      dest     0 10.102.2.0      recv   583      1 xe-1/0/1.0
10.102.2.1/32      intf     0 10.102.2.1      locl   584      2
10.102.2.1/32      dest     0 10.102.2.1      locl   584      2
10.102.2.254/32    dest     0 10.102.2.254    hold   604      3 xe-1/0/1.0
10.102.2.255/32    dest     0 10.102.2.255    bcst   582      1 xe-1/0/1.0
10.102.3.0/24      intf     0                 rslv   573      1 xe-1/0/0.0
-- truncated ---
```

At this point, if you look, you can see the default route in all of the preceding commands. This would look as if the fxp0 route is present in the data plane. However, if we go into the data plane directly (don't try this at home!), we can see that the route is not installed on the data plane.

```
[flowd]FPC3.PIC0(vty)# show route ip

IPv4 Route Table 0, default.0, 0x0:
Destination    NH IP Addr       Type     NH ID Interface
------------   --------------- -------- ----- ---------
default                         Reject     36 RT-ifl 0
0.0.0.0                         Discard    34 RT-ifl 0
10.102.1/24                     Resolve   569 RT-ifl 70 xe-1/0/0.0 ifl 70
10.102.1.0      10.102.1.0       Recv      567 RT-ifl 70 xe-1/0/0.0 ifl 70
10.102.1.1     10.102.1.1       Local     568 RT-ifl 0
10.102.1.254                    Hold      602 RT-ifl 70 xe-1/0/0.0 ifl 70
10.102.1.255                    Bcast     566 RT-ifl 70 xe-1/0/0.0 ifl 70
10.102.2/24                     Resolve   585 RT-ifl 71 xe-1/0/1.0 ifl 71
10.102.2.0     10.102.2.0       Recv      583 RT-ifl 71 xe-1/0/1.0 ifl 71
-- truncated --
```

As you can see in the actual data plane, the default route is not used. Now for our final example of this, we will install a default route in the data plane and you can see the difference. The point to note here is that it is perfectly fine, although somewhat illogical, to utilize the fxp0 in the same routing instance as transit traffic. Once the new default route was used, it took over for all of the traffic of the other default route.

```
root@srx3600n0> show route

inet.0: 16 destinations, 16 routes (16 active, 0 holddown, 0 hidden)
+ = Active Route, - = Last Active, * = Both

0.0.0.0/0          *[Static/5] 1w2d 00:03:49
                      to 172.19.100.1 via fxp0.0
                    > to 10.102.1.254 via xe-1/0/0.0
10.102.1.0/24      *[Direct/0] 1w2d 00:03:04
                    > via xe-1/0/0.0
10.102.1.1/32      *[Local/0] 5w1d 23:22:15
```

```
                    Local via xe-1/0/0.0
10.102.2.0/24      *[Direct/0] 1w2d 00:03:03
                    > via xe-1/0/1.0
10.102.2.1/32      *[Local/0] 5w1d 23:22:15
                      Local via xe-1/0/1.0
10.102.3.0/24      *[Direct/0] 1w2d 00:03:04
                    > via xe-1/0/0.0
-- truncated ---

root@srx3600n0> show route forwarding-table
Routing table: default.inet
Internet:
Destination        Type RtRef Next hop        Type Index NhRef Netif
default            user     2 10.102.1.254    hold   602     6 xe-1/0/0.0
default            perm     0                 rjct    36     1
0.0.0.0/32         perm     0                 dscd    34     1
10.102.1.0/24      intf     0                 rslv   569     1 xe-1/0/0.0
10.102.1.0/32      dest     0 10.102.1.0      recv   567     1 xe-1/0/0.0
10.102.1.1/32      intf     0 10.102.1.1      locl   568     2
10.102.1.1/32      dest     0 10.102.1.1      locl   568     2
10.102.1.254/32    dest     0 10.102.1.254    hold   602     6 xe-1/0/0.0
10.102.1.255/32    dest     0 10.102.1.255    bcst   566     1 xe-1/0/0.0
-- truncated ---

[flowd]FPC3.PIC0(vty)# show route ip

IPv4 Route Table 0, default.0, 0x0:
Destination    NH IP Addr  Type     NH ID Interface
------------   ----------- -------- ----- ---------
default                    Hold       602 RT-ifl 0 xe-1/0/0.0 ifl 70
0.0.0.0                    Discard     34 RT-ifl 0
10.102.1/24                Resolve    569 RT-ifl 70 xe-1/0/0.0 ifl 70
-- truncated ---
```

Best practice is to reduce the number of routes to the minimum for the fxp0 interface. There are some other use cases specific to dealing with chassis cluster, and those cases are discussed in Chapter 7. Another option that an administrator will use is to leave the fxp0 interface in the master routing instance and place all traffic interfaces in their own instance. This is reviewed later in this chapter.

The biggest challenge is that some services require the use of the master routing table to utilize their service, specifically with logging being the biggest issue, which is discussed later in this chapter. Since the release of the SRX, Juniper has been moving the majority of its services into any other routing instances, but due to the nature of how Junos shares its code with other platforms (e.g., MX or EX), a few services remain in the master VR. Throughout the book, these specific problems are highlighted in their respective sections.

Virtual Interfaces

Before we start to review the more interesting interface configurations, there are some interfaces that were displayed before that might be a bit confusing. As shown in the following display, there are many interfaces that are shown but they do not physically exist in the system. These interfaces are known as *virtual interfaces*. They are used for specific use cases. In Junos, for traffic to be processed, it typically needs to ingress an interface. Once the traffic is sent through an interface, it will then be acted on by specific policies, configurations, or both. Because of this, there are some virtual interfaces that exist to solve some specific problems. The most commonly used interfaces are shown in Table 4-2.

Table 4-2. Interface media types

Name	Media type
`st0`	Secure tunnel interface (IPsec VPNs)
`ip`	IP in IP tunneling (6in4 tunneling)
`gr`	Generic router encapsulation
`ppd`	Protocol independent multicast
`pimd`	PIM decapsulation
`pime`	PIM encapsulation
`lte`	Logical tunnel interface
`lo0`	Loopback interface

Overall, these interfaces are only important when you need them for a specific application. Otherwise, I suggest ignoring these interfaces. Throughout the book, these interfaces are discussed when needed, but otherwise they are unused.

Logical Interfaces

When an interface is configured for use on the network, it must always be configured with what is known as a *unit*. A unit is a logical entity that is applied to an interface. A physical interface must have at least 1 unit, but it can have as many as 16,000, depending on the need. Although this seems strange at first, it is actually extremely advantageous when configuring your device. It gives the administrator a sense of flexibility in how the device is configured. It also allows the simple migration of units between interfaces.

To communicate with other hosts and pass traffic through the device, protocols must be configured. Junos supports numerous protocols for network communication and several can be configured per unit. The most common protocol that is used is IPv4. This is the current standard on the Internet and in most networks. IPv6 is growing in popularity, and because of this, Junos has support for it as well. When configuring an interface, a protocol is called a *family*. This is because a protocol is often a family of protocols; an example is IP, as IP uses ICMP, TCP, and UDP for messaging purposes. Table 4-3 lists some of the most commonly supported families.

Table 4-3. Interface family types

Family	Description
inet	IPv4 protocol
inet6	IPv6 protocol
iso	ISO protocol used for IS-IS
ethernet-switching	Used for Layer 2 Ethernet switching

As stated, IPv4 is the most common protocol in use today, but IPv6 is up and coming. Here is an example of what an interface with both IPv4 and IPv6 would look like.

```
root@SRXEdge# show interfaces vlan
unit 0 {
    family inet {
        address 10.0.1.2/24;
    }
    family inet6 {
        address 2005:A704:C163::1/64;
    }
}

[edit]
root@SRXEdge# show interfaces vlan | display set
set interfaces vlan unit 0 family inet address 10.0.1.2/24
set interfaces vlan unit 0 family inet6 address 2005:A704:C163::1/64

[edit]
root@SRXEdge#
```

As seen here, configuring an IP address is fairly straightforward. To do so, you must first specify the unit, then the family, then the address that you would like applied. The command words unit, family, and address are used when specifying the configuration. These words are in bold in the preceding example.

Most administrators typically only utilize unit 0. The number doesn't particularly matter. The best practice is to use zero unless you are defining a VLAN tag to that unit. If a tag is defined, then chose a unit number that matches the tag number. The one thing that you do not want to do is randomly choose unit numbers on each interface. Keep some sort of theme or organization to the unit number. Doing so will make it much easier for the next person who has to look at the configuration.

When using units, there are some command-line tricks that you need to be aware of. It is possible to identify a unit using two methods. Both are displayed here.

```
[edit]
root@SRXEdge# set interfaces vlan unit 0
```

```
[edit]
root@SRXEdge# set interfaces vlan.0
```

In this example, using the word unit or the optional period joining the interface name and the unit number specified the unit configuration. The majority of the time the period is used, as it saves three characters of typing and it is also how interfaces are displayed in the operational configuration. The best practice is to use the period; when you keep typing interface configurations, you will be happy that you saved those three characters.

Although there is a lot that you can configure on a unit, the specific configurations are discussed in their appropriate sections and chapters. For now, you should be able to configure an IP address, which is what is required.

Switching Configuration

On the branch SRX Series (see Chapter 1), most Ethernet interfaces support the ability to do switching. The switching capabilities in the branch SRX Series are inherited from Juniper Networks' EX Series Ethernet Switches, so the functionality and configuration are nearly identical.

The most common configuration type is an *access port*. An access port is a port that does not accept VLAN tagged packets, but rather tags the packets internally to the switch. It will also allow the packet to exit as a tagged packet on a trunk port. (A VLAN must be assigned to an interface even if the traffic will never exit the device as a packet tagged with the VLAN. In cases such as these, the actual VLAN tag used is irrelevant.)

```
[edit interfaces ge-0/0/2.0]
root@JunosBook# set family ethernet-switching

[edit interfaces ge-0/0/2.0]
root@JunosBook# set family ethernet-switching port-mode access

[edit interfaces ge-0/0/2.0]
root@JunosBook# show
unit 0 {
    family ethernet-switching {
        port-mode access;
        vlan {
            members 100;
        }
    }
}

[edit interfaces ge-0/0/2.0]
root@JunosBook#
```

Here, `ethernet-switching` was added as a family (remember that a family represents a protocol suite, and in this case it represents switching). The port was set to `access` mode, which internally tags the packet after it enters the port. It is tagged with VLAN 100, as that is what is configured under the `vlan` stanza. An access port can only have a single VLAN configured. When configuring a VLAN, it can be specified with the tag number or a configured VLAN name. We discuss VLAN configuration later in this section.

Most of the branch SRX Series devices have several ports that you can configure for switching. In some cases, up to 24 sequential ports can be used for switching. Instead of having to configure all of the ports by hand, it's possible to use the `interface range` command. This configuration allows you to select several ports and then apply the same commands across all of the interfaces.

```
[edit interfaces]
root@JunosBook# show
interface-range interfaces-trust {
    member ge-0/0/1;
    member fe-0/0/2;
    member fe-0/0/3;
    member fe-0/0/4;
    member fe-0/0/5;
    member fe-0/0/7;
    unit 0 {
        family ethernet-switching {
            vlan {
                port-mode access;
                members 100;
            }
        }
    }
}
```

An interface range must be given a unique name, and then one or more interfaces can be added as members of the range. At this point, any configuration option that can normally be added to an interface can be added here. Because of this, the use of interface ranges is not just limited to switching. For example, unit 0 was created with Ethernet switching and VLAN 100. On commit, all interfaces have the same configuration applied to them.

Up to this point, all VLANs have been used with just a number tag. It is also possible to create VLANs and give them a name that allows for easier management and identification in the configuration. You can use the VLAN name instead of the tag name anywhere in the configuration.

```
[edit vlans]
root@JunosBook# show
vlan-trust {
    vlan-id 100;
    interface {
        fe-0/0/6.0;
    }
```

```
        l3-interface vlan.0;
    }

    [edit vlans]
    root@JunosBook#
```

Each VLAN is given a custom name. This name must be unique and must not overlap with any other existing VLAN name. You also must assign a VLAN ID to the VLAN. You can configure several other options under a VLAN, the most common of which concern the direct configuration of interfaces. Previously, when Ethernet switching was configured on each interface, a VLAN had to be configured. In this configuration example, the VLAN can be configured from one central location directly under the VLAN. Either option is valid; the usage is based on personal preference.

The other common option is the use of a VLAN interface. A VLAN interface allows for the termination of traffic that can then be routed out another interface on the device. The VLAN interface is accessible from any port that is a member of that VLAN. The interface is configured just like any other interface type.

```
[edit]
root@JunosBook# edit interfaces

[edit interfaces]
root@JunosBook# set vlan.0 family inet address 1.2.3.4/24

[edit interfaces]
root@JunosBook# edit interfaces

[edit interfaces]
root@JunosBook# show vlan
unit 0 {
    family inet {
        address 1.2.3.4/24;
    }
}

[edit interfaces]
root@JunosBook#
```

A *trunk port* is a port that has two or more VLANs configured on it, and traffic entering a trunk port must be tagged with a VLAN tag. A trunk port is typically used when connecting the SRX to another switch.

```
[edit]
root@JunosBook# edit interfaces

[edit interfaces]
root@JunosBook# set ge-0/0/2.0 family ethernet-switching port-mode trunk

[edit interfaces]
root@JunosBook# set ge-0/0/2.0 family ethernet-switching vlan members 200
```

```
[edit interfaces]
root@JunosBook# show ge-0/0/2.0
family ethernet-switching {
    port-mode trunk;
    vlan {
        members [ 100 200 ];
    }
}

[edit interfaces]
root@JunosBook#
```

As you can see, the configuration here is very similar to an access port. The differences are minor, as the port mode is configured as a trunk and multiple VLAN members are added to the port. Traffic entering the port must be tagged and must match the VLANs configured on the port.

Aggregate Interfaces

On most SRX platforms, it is possible to configure aggregate Ethernet interfaces. These interfaces are special, as they allow the addition of multiple Ethernet ports to the same logical interface. The most common use case for this is as a redundant Ethernet interface (reth). This is a special type of interface that is used in high availability clusters. This is covered fully in Chapter 7. However, another interface that is used in standalone devices is the ae interface.

Configuring an ae interface is easy. The biggest challenge is that it needs to be connected to either another aggregate interface or to a special switch. These interfaces are used when you want to offer additional bandwidth to an interface beyond what it can handle as a single interface.

To configure an aggregate interface, you must first activate these interfaces by specifying how many aggregate interfaces you want active. An example of this is shown here.

```
[edit]
root@SRXEdge# set chassis aggregated-devices ethernet device-count 2

root@SRXEdge# show | compare
[edit]
+  chassis {
+      aggregated-devices {
+          ethernet {
+              device-count 2;
+          }
+      }
+  }
```

To see how the command was applied, we issued `show | compare`. This shows the changes made to the configuration. As can be seen in the previous example, the aggregated devices are specified under the chassis hierarchy. Think about this as if we are inserting a virtual card into the chassis. Once this configuration is committed, you will be able to see the interfaces.

```
[edit]
root@SRXEdge# run show interfaces terse | match ae
ae0                      up    down
ae1                      up    down

[edit]
root@SRXEdge#
```

To show the interfaces from configuration mode, we issued `run`. This says "run this operational command from configuration mode." It is very convenient, as you need to check your work. We then took the output of the interfaces command and passed it to match, looking specifically for the string *ae*. This interface type is known as aggregate Ethernet. The ae interface can represent any type of Ethernet interface so the media does not matter. You cannot mix media types when aggregating interfaces on the SRX; they must be the same type.

Now you must add in which interfaces will be members of the aggregate device. This is done under the physical interfaces themselves under the ether-options, which relates to some of the advanced physical characteristics of the interfaces.

```
[edit]
root@SRXEdge# set interfaces fe-0/0/6 fastether-options 802.3ad ae0

[edit]
root@SRXEdge# set interfaces fe-0/0/7 fastether-options 802.3ad ae0

[edit]
root@SRXEdge# show | compare
[edit interfaces]
+   fe-0/0/6 {
+       fastether-options {
+           802.3ad ae0;
+       }
+   }
+   fe-0/0/7 {
+       fastether-options {
+           802.3ad ae0;
+       }
+   }
```

As can be seen in the previous code example, the parent they belong to was specified under the 802.3ad hierarchy. The number 802.3ad represents the IEEE standard for aggregate interfaces. Feel free to look it up if you would like to know more about the specification. Now that the child links are configured, we can specify an IP address on our newly created aggregate interface.

```
[edit]
root@SRXEdge# set interfaces ae0.0 family inet6 address 2002:1234::1/64

[edit]
root@SRXEdge# show | compare
[edit interfaces]
+   fe-0/0/6 {
+       fastether-options {
+           802.3ad ae0;
+       }
+   }
+   fe-0/0/7 {
+       fastether-options {
+           802.3ad ae0;
+       }
+   }
+   ae0 {
+       unit 0 {
+           family inet {
+               address 2.3.4.5/24;
+           }
+           family inet6 {
+               address 2002:1234::1/64;
+           }
+       }
+   }
[edit]
root@SRXEdge# commit
commit complete

[edit]
root@SRXEdge# run show interfaces ae0 terse
Interface         Admin Link Proto     Local                      Remote
ae0               up    up
ae0.0             up    up   inet      2.3.4.5/24
                             inet6     2002:1234::1/64
                                       fe80::2e6b:f5ff:fe02:82c0/64
[edit]
root@SRXEdge#
```

As we can see, once committed, the ae0.0 interface shows up as any other interface would be displayed.

LACP protocol

Although bundled links are fantastic, as they give you additional bandwidth, they are quite dumb. By default, aggregate interfaces do not negotiate to the other side of the physical link. They just assume that the other side of the link is up and that everything will be fine. As we all know, this is never the case in a network. To help with this, a protocol can be configured over the links called Link Aggregation Control Protocol (LACP). At the time of the writing of this book, LACP is only supported in Level 3 mode and not in Level 2 or transparent mode. Please check the Juniper support site for the latest updates and notes.

LACP offers a few important features, the first being link detection. LACP can detect that not only the link is up, but that the other side is active. There might be a Layer 1 switch (a switch that handles physical cabling connectivity) in between the two devices that has an error, or the other device might have some sort of issue. Second, LACP confirms that the other side can correctly handle the aggregate interfaces. The best practice is to use LACP when available. In an LACP configuration, one side should be configured as passive and the other as active. This sets the SRX to passively receive LACP messages. For the branch SRX, due to the small CPUs in the device, it is suggested to set the mode to *slow*.

```
[edit interfaces ae0 aggregated-ether-options]
root@SRXEdge# set minimum-links 1

[edit interfaces ae0 aggregated-ether-options lacp]
root@SRXEdge# set periodic slow

[edit interfaces ae0 aggregated-ether-options lacp]
root@SRXEdge# set passive

[edit interfaces ae0 aggregated-ether-options]
root@SRXEdge# show
minimum-links 1;
lacp {
    passive;
    periodic slow;
    link-protection;
}
```

Once configured, it is fairly easy to check the status of your LACP links. 187

```
root@SRXEdge> show lacp interfaces
Aggregated interface: ae0
 LACP state:      Role Exp Def Dist  Col  Syn  Aggr Timeout  Activity
   fe-0/0/6      Actor  No  No  Yes  Yes  Yes   Yes    Slow    Active
   fe-0/0/6    Partner  No  No  Yes  Yes  Yes   Yes    Slow    Passive
   fe-0/0/7      Actor  No  No  Yes  Yes  Yes   Yes    Slow    Active
   ge-0/0/7    Partner  No  No  Yes  Yes  Yes   Yes    Slow    Passive
 LACP protocol:   Receive State  Transmit State         Mux State
   fe-0/0/6             Current   Slow periodic Collecting distributing
   fe-0/0/7             Current   Slow periodic Collecting distributing

root@EX2200-C1>
```

Transparent Interfaces

By default, an SRX operates in what is known as routing or Layer 3 mode. This means that the device forwards packets based on their destination IP address. This is how the majority of SRX devices are deployed. However, there are times when implementing a firewall in this mode is not possible. An example would be if the network routing configuration were unable to be altered. This could be due to lack of IP addresses or the need to keep security implemented as a separate domain.

Whatever the reason might be, the SRX offers a feature called transparent mode. Transparent mode forwards packets based on their destination MAC address rather than their IP. However, the device still allows the user to block or allow hosts based on the same IP-based policies that are available in the routing mode. For complete information on how to utilize transparent mode, please see Chapter 6.

Configuring transparent mode interfaces is one step in the transparent mode configuration process. To do so is actually quite similar to how we configured an interface with an IP address. To enable a transparent mode interface, we would use the family *bridge* as opposed to family inet or inet6. We also need to specify a VLAN ID that binds the interface into a Layer 2 bridge domain. Think of this as placing the interface into a specific broadcast domain. Doing so limits the scope of which hosts can see each other.

```
root# show interfaces
fe-0/0/2 {
    unit 0 {
        family bridge {
            interface-mode access;
            vlan-id 10;
        }
    }
}

[edit]
root# show interfaces | display set
set interfaces fe-0/0/2 unit 0 family bridge interface-mode access
set interfaces fe-0/0/2 unit 0 family bridge vlan-id 10

[edit]
root#
```

If you are initially configuring transparent mode, a reboot is required after the configuration is committed. This will load the appropriate image on the data plane to forward based on MAC addresses as opposed to IP.

```
root# commit check
warning: Interfaces are changed from route mode to transparent mode. Please
reboot the device or all nodes in the HA cluster!
configuration check succeeds
```

Zones

A zone is a logical construct that is applied to an interface and is used as a building block for security policies on the SRX Series Services Gateways and the Juniper Networks

J Series Services Routers. The concept of the zone originated on the ScreenOS platform from NetScreen Technologies. When creating a security policy, the idea is to allow traffic from a source to go to a destination. The zone adds another dimension to that by allowing for the concept of a source zone and a destination zone. This was very different from all of the existing firewall products of the time. The division of a security policy base into multiple smaller policy sets, or contexts, enhanced performance and simplified management.

Security Zones

Creating a security zone is simple, as the minimum requirement is just a name. In the past, on NetScreen products, there was a concept of having prenamed zones called *Trust*, *Untrust*, and *DMZ*. These zone names were always left in place because the original ScreenOS devices actually used these as the interface names. Juniper has moved away from having the default names, and now allows users to name the zones whatever they want. Security zones are located under the `security zones` stanza.

```
[edit security zones]
root@SRX210-A# show
security-zone SuperZone {
    interfaces {
        ge-0/0/0.0;
    }
}

[edit security zones]
root@SRX210-A#
```

Security zones offer little to no value without the addition of interfaces. In the example shown here, the ge-0/0/0.0 interface is added to the new zone named `SuperZone`. The zone is now ready to be used in various security policies.

At least one interface must be bound in a zone to be able to use it to create security policies. Multiple interfaces can be added to a zone as well, and this might be helpful, depending on the goal of the network design. An interface can only be a member of one zone at a time. Logical interfaces are added to a zone, so it's possible to have multiple logical interfaces that are members of the same physical interface be members of multiple zones.

Functional Zones

Functional zones are a logical entity that is applied to the interface to enable it to have a special function. Interfaces that are a member of a functional zone cannot be used in a security zone. On the SRX, the only functional zone available at the time this book was written was the *management zone*. Adding an interface into the management zone allows the interface to be used for out-of-band management, a helpful tool for devices such as the branch SRX Series devices, which do not have a dedicated interface for management.

```
[edit security zones]
root@JunosBook# set functional-zone management interfaces fe-0/0/6.0

[edit security zones]
root@JunosBook# edit functional-zone management

[edit security zones functional-zone management]
root@JunosBook# show
interfaces {
    fe-0/0/6.0;
}
host-inbound-traffic {
    system-services {
        all;
    }
}

[edit security zones functional-zone management]
root@JunosBook#
```

Adding an interface to a functional zone is the same as using a security zone. A new element shown in this configuration is `host inbound traffic`. The `host inbound traffic` stanza can be configured under any zone, and it allows for the acceptance of two different types of traffic to the SRX itself. If the host inbound traffic is not configured, traffic will not be accepted. This is different from creating a security policy, as a security policy is only for transit traffic and not for traffic terminating on the device.

```
root@JunosBook# set host-inbound-traffic system-services ?
Possible completions:
  all                  All system services
  any-service          Enable services on entire port range
  dns                  DNS and DNS-proxy service
  finger               Finger service
  ftp                  FTP
  http                 Web management service using HTTP
  https                Web management service using HTTP secured by SSL
  ident-reset          Send back TCP RST to IDENT request for port 113
  ike                  Internet Key Exchange
  lsping               Label Switched Path ping service
  netconf              NETCONF service
  ntp                  Network Time Protocol service
  ping                 Internet Control Message Protocol echo requests
  reverse-ssh          Reverse SSH service
  reverse-telnet       Reverse telnet service
  rlogin               Rlogin service
  rpm                  Real-time performance monitoring
  rsh                  Rsh service
  sip                  Enable Session Initiation Protocol service
  snmp                 Simple Network Management Protocol service
```

```
  snmp-trap             Simple Network Management Protocol traps
  ssh                   SSH service
  telnet                Telnet service
  tftp                  TFTP
  traceroute            Traceroute service
  xnm-clear-text        JUNOScript API for unencrypted traffic over TCP
  xnm-ssl               JUNOScript API service over SSL
[edit security zones functional-zone management]
root@JunosBook# set host-inbound-traffic protocols ?
Possible completions:
  all                   All protocols
  bfd                   Bidirectional Forwarding Detection
  bgp                   Border Gateway Protocol
  dvmrp                 Distance Vector Multicast Routing Protocol
  igmp                  Internet Group Management Protocol
  ldp                   Label Distribution Protocol
  msdp                  Multicast Source Discovery Protocol
  ndp                   Enable Network Discovery Protocol
  nhrp                  Next Hop Resolution Protocol
  ospf                  Open Shortest Path First
  ospf3                 Open Shortest Path First version 3
  pgm                   Pragmatic General Multicast
  pim                   Protocol Independent Multicast
  rip                   Routing Information Protocol
  ripng                 Routing Information Protocol next generation
  router-discovery      Router Discovery
  rsvp                  Resource Reservation Protocol
  sap                   Session Announcement Protocol
  vrrp                  Virtual Router Redundancy Protocol
[edit security zones functional-zone management]
root@JunosBook# set host-inbound-traffic protocols
```

The first type of host inbound traffic is called *system services*. System services traffic is related to any service that is used for management on the SRX. This includes SSH, Telnet, and DNS. The other type of host inbound traffic is *protocols*. These are routing protocols or other protocols that are used for communicating with other network devices. Each individual service can be turned on, or all of them can be turned on using the `all` flag.

Given that an SRX is most often deployed as a security device, it's best practice to reduce the total number of host inbound protocols.

Host inbound traffic can also be enabled on a per-interface basis. This is a good idea when multiple interfaces are in a zone. Also, some protocols such as DHCP can only be enabled on a single interface and not on a per-zone basis. DHCP will not be allowed unless specifically enabled under the interface.

```
root@host# set interfaces fe-0/0/6.0 host-inbound-traffic system-services dhcp

[edit security zones functional-zone management]
root@JunosBook# show
interfaces {
    fe-0/0/6.0 {
        host-inbound-traffic {
            system-services {
                dhcp;
            }
        }
    }
}
host-inbound-traffic {
    system-services {
        all;
    }
}

[edit security zones functional-zone management]
root@JunosBook#
```

Basic Protocols

Routing protocol support and stability are key features of the Junos OS. The SRX, being a member of the Junos family, supports most of the protocols that are supported on the highest end routers. In practice, however, most customers do not use these features on the SRX. Because of this, we are only skimming the surface of what is possible on Junos. Books can easily be dedicated to just advanced routing policies without even covering the protocols. There are several other books that go over many of these routing features in the Juniper Networks Technical Library books (*http://juni.pr/162L7CW*) published by O'Reilly Media, and because of this they are not covered in great depth here. Where applicable, the use of the protocols is discussed in their various sections.

With that said, there are some routing fundamentals that are important to understand. In Junos, any method that can place a route in the routing table is considered a protocol. This includes static routing. Although it might seem strange to think of static routes as being protocols in Junos, they are considered as such. When configuring routing policies, a construct similar to firewall policies but applicable to route manipulation, static routes are referred to as protocol static.

Static Routing

Static routes are routes that are statically defined and are not manipulated by external protocols. The only way a static route can disappear is if the associated interface has disappeared. Other than that, once a static route is configured, it isn't going anywhere. Most commonly in an SRX, only static routing is used. One of the biggest reasons is to lower the scope of potential attack against the device. Keen administrators are always worried about the potential to exploit a key system. Juniper Networks spends a good deal of time hardening its routing services, but even a window with metal bars on it is still a window that can draw attention. Later in this section, we review more about best practices on when to use dynamic routing.

Configuring a static route is simple. It requires knowing what network you want to route to and what the next hop would be. The following are a few examples of static routes. The options that are variables are bolded. How to correctly select these items will be discussed next.

```
[edit routing-options]
root@SRXEdge# show
rib inet6.0 {
    static {
        route ::/0 next-hop 2004:4170:1c04:634::1;
    }
}
static {
    route 0.0.0.0/0 next-hop 59.12.52.174;
}

[edit routing-options]
root@SRXEdge# show | display set
set routing-options rib inet6.0 static route ::/0 next-hop 2004:4170:1c04:634::1
set routing-options static route 0.0.0.0/0 next-hop 59.12.52.174

[edit routing-options]
root@SRXEdge#
```

Static routes are added into the `routing-options` hierarchy. As shown by the previous set commands, first we specify that the route is static then we use the keywords `route` and `next-hop` to specify the two options. For `route`, we assign the prefix that we want to assign as the destination. For `next-hop`, we simply specify where the prefix will be sent. This is a bit more verbose than some devices, but Junos is designed for extensibility that leads to more detailed commands. In our example, we saw that the next hop was specified as an IP address. In some cases, such as an IPsec VPN, you can also specify an interface as the next hop. The best practice is to utilize an IP address, as that is most relatable to the next person that would need to read the configuration.

Configuring IPv6 routes is a bit different, as it includes one additional option to the command. For IPv6, not only do we need to specify the prefix and the next hop but we also need to specify the *rib* or routing information base. For IPv4 the static route, the *rib* does not need to be explicitly specified. But what exactly is a rib? A rib is nothing more than the formal term for a routing table or a collection of routes. Each protocol has at least one rib, but they could potentially have more if needed. Other protocols such as multiprotocol label switching also have their own rib.

When Junos was originally built, it only contained support for IPv4, and hence the static routing command is a bit focused on that protocol. Because Junos is designed to maintain backward compatibility for the configuration, there are some commands that might seem out of place, but that is due to the fact the command is quite old. As you can imagine, static routes would need to be Junos 1.0 supported features.

The naming convention when specifying a rib is *family.rib number*. Rib numbering always starts at zero. For IPv6, *inet6* is specified as the family. For comparison, IPv4 would be represented as just *inet*. For the majority of deployments, only a single routing table is needed per routing instance, but there are some cases where an extremely complex routing design is needed. Junos is happy to accommodate both the simple and complex use cases. Some designs that are currently deployed use thousands of routing instances and a dozen or more tables per instance.

There are many options that are available when configuring a static route. The following are the standard options. The specific configuration items that might be of interest to an administrator are shown in bold and are discussed next.

```
[edit routing-options]
root@SRXEdge# set static route 0/0 ?
Possible completions:
  active               Remove inactive route from forwarding table
+ apply-groups         Groups from which to inherit configuration data
+ apply-groups-except  Don't inherit configuration data from these groups
> as-path              Autonomous system path
  backup-pe-group      Multicast source redundancy group
> bfd-liveness-detection  Bidirectional Forwarding Detection (BFD) options
> color                Color (preference) value
> color2               Color (preference) value 2
+ community            BGP community identifier
  discard              Drop packets to destination; send no ICMP unreachables
  install              Install route into forwarding table
> lsp-next-hop         LSP next hop
> metric               Metric value
> metric2              Metric value 2
> metric3              Metric value 3
> metric4              Metric value 4
+ next-hop             Next hop to destination
  next-table           Next hop to another table
  no-install           Don't install route into forwarding table
  no-readvertise       Don't mark route as eligible to be readvertised
  no-resolve           Don't allow resolution of indirectly connected next hops
  no-retain            Don't always keep route in forwarding table
> p2mp-lsp-next-hop    Point-to-multipoint LSP next hop
  passive              Retain inactive route in forwarding table
> preference           Preference value
> preference2          Preference value 2
> qualified-next-hop   Next hop with qualifiers
  readvertise          Mark route as eligible to be readvertised
  receive              Install a receive route for the destination
```

```
    reject                  Drop packets to destination; send ICMP unreachables
    resolve                 Allow resolution of indirectly connected next hops
    retain                  Always keep route in forwarding table
  > static-lsp-next-hop  Static LSP next hop
  > tag                     Tag string
  > tag2                    Tag string 2
[edit routing-options]
root@SRXEdge#
```

For static routing, next-hop is the most commonly used option. However, there are a few other options that are helpful when dealing with static routing. The first two would be both *metric* and *preference*. Metric and preference are used in selecting which route is active. The routing process is a decision tree for which path should be selected to send the traffic out. Preferences are applied to each routing protocol, and then metrics are applied to routes within that protocol. Think of a preference as "How much do I trust the information provided by this protocol?" Table 4-4 shows the various default protocol preferences. The lower the preference value, the more trusted the route is.

Table 4-4. Routing protocol preferences

Preference	Protocol
0	Direct connection
1	NAT Proxy-ARP routes
4	System routes
5	Static routes and Static LSPs
7	RSVP-signaled LSPs
9	LDP-signaled LSPs
10	OSPF internal route
15	IS-IS Level 1 internal route
18	IS-IS Level 2 internal route
30	Redirects
40	Kernel
50	SNMP
55	Router Discovery
100	RIP
100	RIPng (RIP for IPv6)
105	PIM
110	DVMRP
130	Aggregate
150	OSPF AS external routes
160	IS-IS Level 1 external route
165	IS-IS Level 1 external route

Preference	Protocol
170	BGP
175	MSDP

As you can see, there are many different routing protocols that can be used on Junos. The protocol preferences for directly connected routes, system routes, and static routes are the lowest (lower being better in selection, with an example shown in Figure 4-1) as they are the most trusted. A directly connected route is automatically created for any configured interfaces. This way, the router can determine how to access which networks it is already a part of. It has the lowest or best preference as it is connected to the device and it does not need to go through a separate hop. Next up are proxy-arp routes and system routes. These are directly added by Junos and are not configured directly by the administrator. The last route preference to discuss is back to static routes, which is set at a preference of five. The majority of the remaining routes are from various dynamic routing protocols. If need be, on a static route, it is possible to set the preference. This is typically not needed, but it is available if you choose to do so.

When we looked at ribs, we saw that it was possible to create more than one routing table. With this, we can also point a route to continue being resolved at the next table. This will force Junos to look at another table for resolution. When Junos does a route lookup, it does it in one single pass. This pass might involve looking at multiple tables to determine where to send the packet, but it will continue to follow the links until it gets to the final destination. In the next section, we review routing instances and how this comes into play there.

Finally, options that are commonly used are the *reject* and *discard* options. These options are used to drop the packet as opposed to forwarding them. They both accomplish the same goal, but reject is used to notify the host sending the packet with an ICMP message that the packet has been dropped. Discard will silently discard the packet, and it will not notify the origin router. If you are looking to drop packets, this is a fairly efficient method. The best practice would be to use the discard method on an SRX. This will prevent an attacker from trying to launch timing attacks to get the device to overload itself by sending ICMP rejects. Although that scenario is unlikely, the Internet can be a dirty place, and lowering the scope of what can be done against you is ideal.

When troubleshooting routing, it is fairly easy to see what would happen to a particular packet. Using the operational command `show route <destination>`, you can specify what the destination host or network is and Junos will tell you what route it is choosing.

```
root@SRXEdge> show route 1.2.3.4

inet.0: 22 destinations, 22 routes (22 active, 0 holddown, 0 hidden)
+ = Active Route, - = Last Active, * = Both

0.0.0.0/0          *[Static/5] 1d 18:02:57
```

```
                        > to 52.85.92.14 via fe-0/0/0.0

root@SRXEdge> show route 10.0.2.10

inet.0: 22 destinations, 22 routes (22 active, 0 holddown, 0 hidden)
+ = Active Route, - = Last Active, * = Both

10.0.2.0/24        *[OSPF/10] 1d 18:03:51, metric 2
                    > to 10.0.1.254 via vlan.0

root@SRXEdge>
```

Here we checked two different routes. First, we looked at the destination 1.2.3.4, which was resolved, the default route of 0.0.0.0/0. Second, we looked at an internal network host, 10.0.2.10, that was found at another upstream routing device via Open Shortest Path First (OSPF). Even in complex scenarios where Junos uses dozens of routing tables, this command will show you what will happen. When showing the route table, Junos will print some metrics, such as how many destinations are available, the total number of routes, and how many are active. It will also tag which route is active. Let's take a look at this in more detail.

```
root@SRXEdge> show route

inet.0: 22 destinations, 22 routes (22 active, 0 holddown, 0 hidden)
+ = Active Route, - = Last Active, * = Both

0.0.0.0/0          *[Static/5] 1d 18:08:58
                    > to 70.96.53.14 via fe-0/0/0.0
10.0.1.0/24        *[Direct/0] 1d 18:08:58
                    > via vlan.0
10.0.1.2/32        *[Local/0] 3d 17:14:26
                      Local via vlan.0
10.0.2.0/24        *[OSPF/10] 1d 18:08:50, metric 2
                    > to 10.0.1.254 via vlan.0
```

At the top of the output, we can see some basic statistics about the routing table. The other important elements to look at on a route are the identifier for what route is active. The *, +, and – characters show this. The last active route is shown by either * or +. The * shows that the route is both active and was the last active route. The previously active route is shown with the –. When there is more than one route to the same destination, they will be shown as follows, with the active route marker showing which route is used.

```
{primary:node0}
root@SRX-HA-0> show route table traffic.inet.0

traffic.inet.0: 8 destinations, 9 routes (8 active, 0 holddown, 0 hidden)
+ = Active Route, - = Last Active, * = Both

0.0.0.0/0          *[Static/5] 00:23:39
                    > to 10.0.1.2 via reth0.0
```

```
                    [OSPF/150] 1d 18:36:14, metric 0, tag 0
                    > to 10.0.1.2 via reth0.0
```

Additional information on each route and why the route was selected can be seen via the *detail* flag. This is helpful if you aren't sure why a route was chosen.

```
root@SRX-HA-0> show route table traffic.inet.0 detail

traffic.inet.0: 8 destinations, 9 routes (8 active, 0 holddown, 0 hidden)
0.0.0.0/0 (2 entries, 1 announced)
        *Static Preference: 5
                Next hop type: Router, Next hop index: 652
                Address: 0x15d0b0c
                Next-hop reference count: 5
                Next hop: 10.0.1.2 via reth0.0, selected
                State: <Active Int Ext>
                Age: 26:20
                Task: RT
                Announcement bits (2): 0-KRT 2-Resolve tree 1
                AS path: I
         OSPF   Preference: 150
                Next hop type: Router, Next hop index: 652
                Address: 0x15d0b0c
                Next-hop reference count: 5
                Next hop: 10.0.1.2 via reth0.0, selected
                State: <Int Ext>
                Inactive reason: Route Preference
                Age: 1d 18:38:55        Metric: 0       Tag: 0
                Task: traffic-OSPF
                AS path: I
```

Finally, to close out this topic, Figure 4-1 is a simple reference chart that you can use to help determine why a route was chosen.

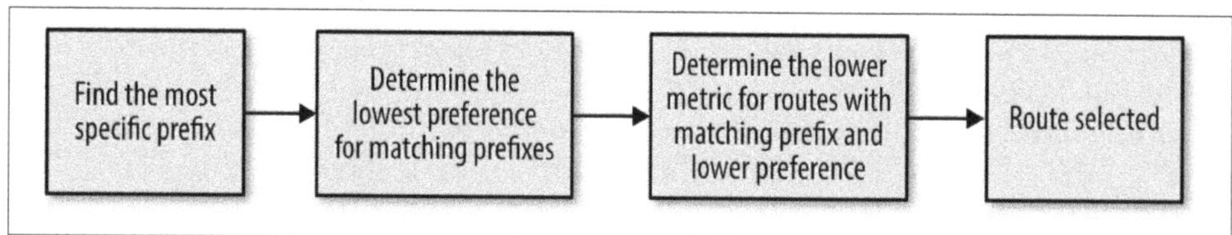

Figure 4-1. Route decision process

Dynamic Routing Protocols

SRX devices support a significant amount of dynamic routing protocols. This is uncharacteristic of a security device. However, the SRX inherits them from the Junos OS and its other sibling devices, such as the MX and M Series devices. This allows the SRX to be deployed in locations where other firewall products might not be able to interoperate with the surrounding networking devices. The following is an example of the routing protocol support that is offered on some SRX devices.

```
{primary:node0}[edit protocols]
root@SRX-HA-0# set ?
Possible completions:
+ apply-groups         Groups from which to inherit configuration data
+ apply-groups-except  Don't inherit configuration data from these groups
> bfd                  Bidirectional Forwarding Detection (BFD) options
> bgp                  BGP options
> connections          Circuit cross-connect configuration
> dot1x                802.1X options
> dvmrp                DVMRP options
> esis                 End system-intermediate system options
> gvrp                 GVRP configuration
> iccp                 ICCP options
> igmp                 IGMP options
> isis                 IS-IS options
> l2-learning          Layer 2 forwarding configuration
> l2circuit            Configuration for Layer 2 circuits over MPLS
> l2iw                 Configuration for Layer 2 interworking
> lacp                 Link Aggregation Control Protocol configuration
> ldp                  LDP options
> lldp                 Link Layer Detection Protocol
> lldp-med             LLDP Media Endpoint Discovery
> mld                  MLD options
> mpls                 Multiprotocol Label Switching options
> msdp                 MSDP configuration
> mstp                 Multiple Spanning Tree Protocol options
> neighbor-discovery   IPv6 neighbor discovery
> oam                  Operation, Administration, and Management configuration
> ospf                 OSPF configuration
> ospf3                OSPFv3 configuration
> pgm                  PGM options
> pim                  PIM configuration
> ppp                  Configure PPP process
> pppoe                Configure PPPoE process
> protection-group     Protection group
> r2cp                 Radio-to-Router Control Protocol configuration
> rip                  RIP options
> ripng                RIPng options
> router-advertisement  IPv6 router advertisement options
> router-discovery     ICMP router discovery options
> rstp                 Rapid Spanning Tree Protocol options
> rsvp                 RSVP options
> sap                  Session Advertisement Protocol options
> stp                  Spanning Tree Protocol options
> vrrp                 VRRP options
{primary:node0}[edit protocols]
root@SRX-HA-0#
```

In the preceding output, the most commonly used protocols are shown in bold. Many routing protocols, such as OSPF or RIP, were originally designed with only IPv4 in mind. To be able to utilize IPv6, some protocols were modified and released as new versions. Examples of this are RIPng (IPv6 RIP) and OSPFv3. The routing protocol IS-IS has made something of a comeback in the last five years.

IS-IS natively supports IPv4 and IPv6. It is also very friendly when utilizing MPLS VPNs, as it is able to share additional information about MPLS through the protocol. The other benefit of IS-IS is that it does not run over IP. IS-IS operates using the ISO Connectionless Network Protocol (CNLS). In a security setting, this can be advantageous because few people understand this protocol or even have access to it. If an attacker is unable to talk to your device, then he will be unable to attack it. IS-IS is very similar in design to OSPF as both protocols are link-state based.

As discussed several times in this chapter, the goal of this book is to focus on the security aspects of the SRX, and because of this, we have chosen to point you to other Junos books or the Junos documentation when you need to use dynamic routing.

Spanning Tree

Because a switched network is completely flat and the paths to devices are determined by the learning of MAC addresses on switch ports, as a switch learns MAC addresses, it creates a tree or path for which MAC address can be found on which ports. The following is an example of looking at the MAC table on an SRX. This feature is only supported on the branch SRX. Transparent mode, which is supported on both branch and the data center SRX, will forward the spanning tree protocol but not participate in it.

```
root@SRXEdge> show ethernet-switching table
Ethernet-switching table: 13 entries, 11 learned, 0 persistent entries
  VLAN              MAC address       Type         Age Interfaces
  Vlan10            *                 Flood          - All-members
  Vlan10            00:0c:29:9d:b3:86 Learn          0 fe-0/0/3.0
  Vlan10            00:10:db:ff:10:00 Learn          0 fe-0/0/3.0
  Vlan10            00:18:7d:1f:71:4a Learn          0 fe-0/0/3.0
  Vlan10            00:18:7d:24:4a:aa Learn          0 fe-0/0/3.0
  Vlan10            2c:6b:f5:02:82:88 Static         - Router
  Vlan10            58:6d:8f:2e:c2:ee Learn          0 fe-0/0/1.0
  Vlan10            5c:59:48:30:fc:96 Learn          0 fe-0/0/1.0
  Vlan10            78:e7:d1:f1:e3:24 Learn          0 fe-0/0/3.0
  Vlan10            78:fe:3d:e6:c1:81 Learn          0 fe-0/0/3.0
  Vlan10            78:fe:3d:e6:c6:01 Learn          0 fe-0/0/3.0
  Vlan10            7c:6d:62:d3:a7:5e Learn          0 fe-0/0/1.0
  Vlan10            e0:cb:4e:97:67:a7 Learn          0 fe-0/0/3.0

root@SRXEdge>
```

This command was run from operational mode and it shows the location for all of the MAC addresses that it knows about. So what happens if a switch learns the location of a MAC on two different ports? This enters your network into a world of pain, as you now have a Layer 2 loop. A loop means that the switches will continuously forward packets in a loop (see Figure 4-2). In a routed network, this behavior would be stopped with the decrementing of the TTL on a packet. In a Layer 2 network, the packets would loop infinitely.

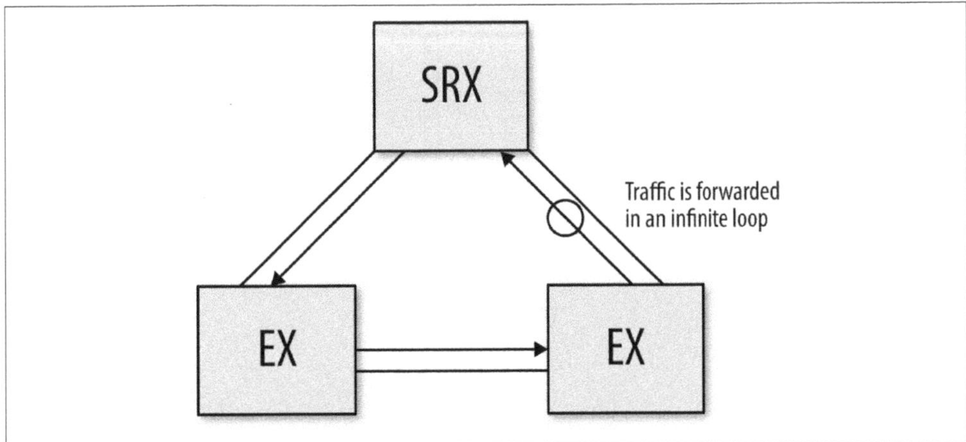

Figure 4-2. Switching loop example

To solve this problem, the spanning tree protocol was invented. Spanning tree sends small messages out from its ports to calculate the topology of the switched network (see Figure 4-3). These messages are called Bridge Protocol Data Units (BDPUs). The switches work together to calculate a single path throughout the network to ensure there are no loops. It is essential to use a loop mitigation technology when using switching on an SRX. Spanning tree is the most popular in use today, but there are a few new ideas coming up the ranks to try and remove spanning tree. Spanning tree can be painful in large networks as miscalculations or misconfigurations can lead to headaches.

There are several different types of spanning tree implementations. The most commonly used on a branch SRX device is called Multiple Spanning Tree Protocol (MSTP). This protocol uses a few different technologies to enhance the original spanning tree protocol. First, it implements the same capabilities of Rapid Spanning Tree Protocol (RSTP). RSTP offers several new port roles to speed up the convergence following a link failure. RSTP and MSTP are compatible with each other. MSTP also brings another important feature to the table: it allows the creation of a spanning tree per VLAN groups. This means that if you are utilizing many different VLANs, it can provide a tree for each group of VLANs. Figure 4-4 is an example of an MSTP topology.

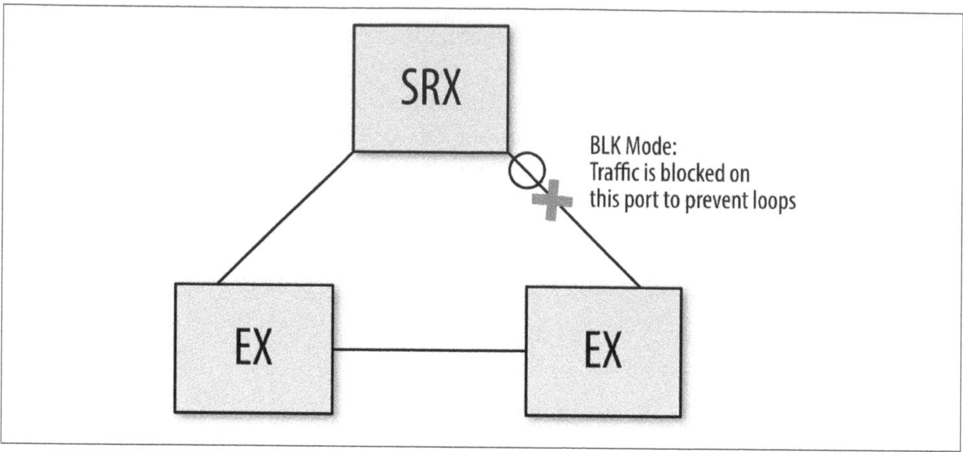

Figure 4-3. Spanning tree stops loops

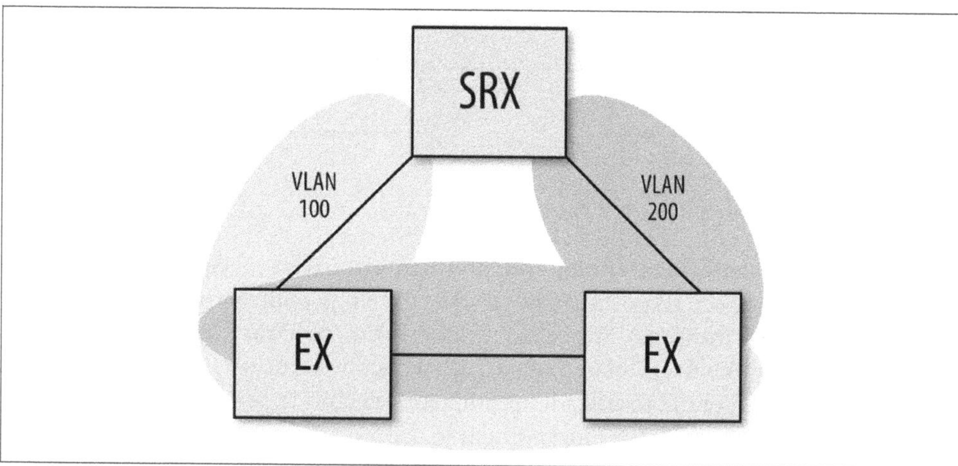

Figure 4-4. MSTP topology

The basics of enabling MSTP are simple, but mastering all of the various options can be quite detailed. As this book is focused on security, we only focus on what is needed to get you up and running. Later you will find more information about MSTP and other spanning tree configurations.

```
root@SRXEdge# show
interface fe-0/0/1.0 {
    edge;
}
interface fe-0/0/2.0 {
    edge;
```

```
}
interface fe-0/0/3.0 {
    edge;
}
interface fe-0/0/4.0 {
    edge;
}
interface fe-0/0/5.0 {
    edge;
}
interface fe-0/0/6.0 {
    edge;
}
interface fe-0/0/7.0 {
    edge;
}

[edit protocols mstp]
root@SRXEdge# show | display set
set protocols mstp interface fe-0/0/1.0 edge
set protocols mstp interface fe-0/0/2.0 edge
set protocols mstp interface fe-0/0/3.0 edge
set protocols mstp interface fe-0/0/4.0 edge
set protocols mstp interface fe-0/0/5.0 edge
set protocols mstp interface fe-0/0/6.0 edge
set protocols mstp interface fe-0/0/7.0 edge

[edit protocols mstp]
root@SRXEdge#
```

This configuration specifies the interfaces on which to enable MSTP and in which mode to operate. These are configured as an edge port, as no other bridges or switches are attached. If another switch is connected, it will be able to detect it. Alternatively, ports can be configured in point-to-point mode or shared mode if you will be connecting these ports to other switches. Point-to-point specifies that the port is connected to another switch, and shared specifies that the port is on a shared switch port.

To see the status of ports, you can use the *spanning-tree* operational commands to identify the ports' statuses. This will show you which ports are in forwarding mode or if they are being blocked (BLK) in the event that a potential loop is detected.

```
root@SRXEdge> show spanning-tree interface

Spanning tree interface parameters for instance 0

Interface    Port ID    Designated   Designated         Port    State  Role
                         port ID      bridge ID          Cost
fe-0/0/1.0    128:514    128:514  32768.2c6bf5028288  200000  FWD    DESG
fe-0/0/3.0    128:516    128:516  32768.2c6bf5028288  200000  FWD    DESG

root@SRXEdge>
```

Here is another example of a spanning tree output shown from an EX-2200-C switch. These two devices are connected together in the same topology.

```
root@EX2200-C1> show spanning-tree interface

Spanning tree interface parameters for instance 0

Interface    Port ID    Designated  Designated         Port    State  Role
                         port ID     bridge ID          Cost
ae0.0           128:1      128:1  32768.78fe3de6c181   10000  FWD    DESG
ge-0/0/0.0    128:513    128:516  32768.2c6bf5028288  200000  FWD    ROOT
ge-0/0/1.0    128:514    128:514  32768.78fe3de6c181   20000  FWD    DESG
ge-0/0/2.0    128:515    128:515  32768.78fe3de6c181   20000  FWD    DESG
ge-0/0/5.0    128:518    128:518  32768.78fe3de6c181   20000  FWD    DESG
ge-0/0/6.0    128:519    128:519  32768.78fe3de6c181  200000  FWD    DESG
ge-0/0/8.0    128:521    128:521  32768.78fe3de6c181  200000  FWD    DESG
ge-0/0/9.0    128:522    128:522  32768.78fe3de6c181  200000  FWD    DESG
ge-0/0/10.0   128:523    128:523  32768.78fe3de6c181  200000  FWD    DESG
ge-0/0/11.0   128:524    128:524  32768.78fe3de6c181  200000  FWD    DESG

root@EX2200-C1>
```

The SRX shares the same infrastructure of switching as the EX switch product line. Because of this, the branch SRX devices share a rich set of switching features that are beyond the scope of this book. If you want to learn more details about switching configuration options, see the book *Junos Enterprise Switching* by Harry Reynolds and Doug Marschke (O'Reilly).

Routing Instances

A routing instance in Junos is a collection of routing tables. Routing instances are also known as VRFs in Cisco's parlance. They are used to give you additional segregation over routing designs. As we discussed earlier regarding the fxp0 interface, there can be different uses for routing instances. A best practice is to leave the fxp0 interface in the default instance (also called the master instance in some documentation) and then place the remaining traffic passing interfaces into their own routing instance. This will provide completely separate routing domains. You can even have routes that overlap in separate routing instances. Figure 4-5 provides a logical example of what this best practice would look like.

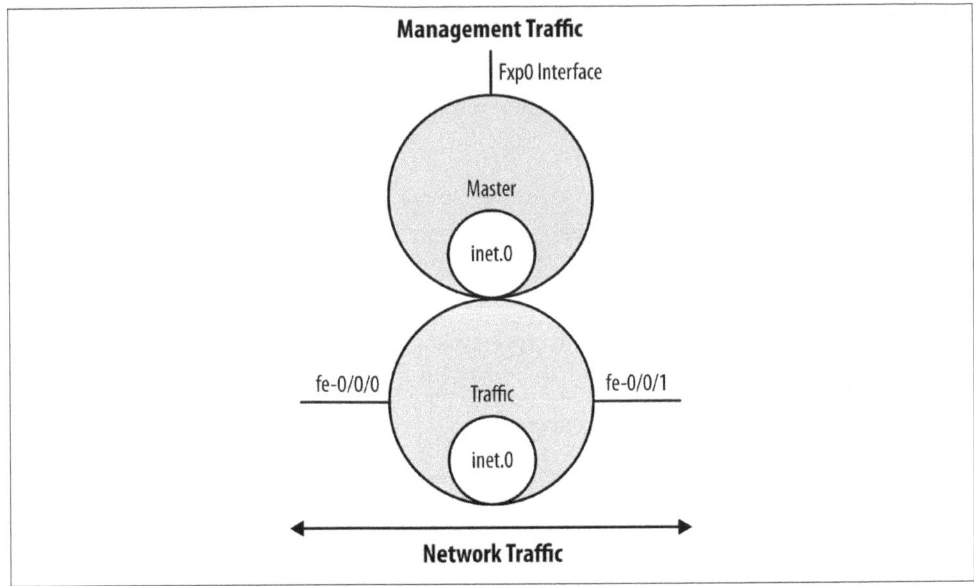

Figure 4-5. Logical example showing best practice

In many simple deployments, one default routing instance is used. However, it is becoming more common to utilize multiple routing instances. Besides separating the fxp0 from your data traffic, it also allows a simple form of network virtualization on the device. This is different from the administrative separation, which can be achieved using the logical system feature that is covered in its own chapter. In any network design, it is best to keep your design simple, as it will reduce the chances of error and potential security risks.

Routing Instance Types

A routing instance can offer a collection of various capabilities. In this chapter, the focus is on using the instance type of virtual router. A virtual router instance provides both routing tables and forwarding tables. In Junos, a VRF routing instance type is used for MPLS VPNs and it contains other routing tables for it. If you are not using MPLS-based VPNs, then the virtual router type is what you should utilize. Another type of domain that is discussed later in the book is the use of bridge domains. On an SRX, this is used in transparent mode designs where forwarding is done based on MAC addresses instead of routing by IP address.

Junos does support several other routing instance types, but these are intentionally left out of this book due to its focus on security rather than solely on networking features.

Configuring Routing Instances

Using routing instances is very easy. There are two steps to activating a routing instance. First, you would create the instance, give it a name, and then specify the instance type.

```
[edit routing-instances]
root@SRXEdge# show
traffic {
    instance-type virtual-router;
}

root@SRXEdge# show | display set
set routing-instances traffic instance-type virtual-router

[edit routing-instances]
root@SRXEdge# run show route instance
Instance             Type
         Primary RIB                          Active/holddown/hidden
master               forwarding
         inet.0                               22/0/0
         inet6.0                              10/0/0

__juniper_private1__ forwarding
         __juniper_private1__.inet.0          7/0/0

__juniper_private2__ forwarding
         __juniper_private2__.inet.0          0/0/1

__master.anon__      forwarding

traffic              virtual-router

[edit routing-instances]
root@SRXEdge#s
```

Now the routing instance is created, it has a name, and it exists, but it doesn't serve a lot of purpose. To make the routing instance useful, you need to add interfaces. Once interfaces are added, then the routing instance becomes active.

```
primary:node1}[edit]
root@SRX-HA-1# show routing-instances
traffic {
    instance-type virtual-router;
    interface reth0.0;
    interface reth1.0;
}

{primary:node1}[edit]
root@SRX-HA-1# run show route instance
Instance             Type
         Primary RIB                               Active/holddown/hidden
master               forwarding
```

```
        inet.0                                        5/0/0

__juniper_private1__ forwarding
        __juniper_private1__.inet.0                   9/0/0

__juniper_private2__ forwarding
        __juniper_private2__.inet.0                   0/0/1

__master.anon__      forwarding

traffic              virtual-router
        traffic.inet.0                                8/0/0
        traffic.inet6.0                               9/0/0

{primary:node1}[edit]
root@SRX-HA-1# run show route

inet.0: 5 destinations, 6 routes (5 active, 0 holddown, 0 hidden)
+ = Active Route, - = Last Active, * = Both

0.0.0.0/0          *[Static/5] 1w4d 20:50:28
                    > to 10.0.1.2 via fxp0.0
10.0.1.0/24        *[Direct/0] 1w4d 20:50:30
                    > via fxp0.0
                    [Direct/0] 1w4d 20:50:30
                    > via fxp0.0
10.0.1.252/32      *[Local/0] 1w4d 20:50:30
                      Local via fxp0.0
10.0.1.253/32      *[Local/0] 1w4d 20:50:30
                      Local via fxp0.0
10.0.2.0/24        *[Static/5] 1w4d 20:50:28
                      to table traffic.inet.0

traffic.inet.0: 8 destinations, 8 routes (8 active, 0 holddown, 0 hidden)
+ = Active Route, - = Last Active, * = Both

0.0.0.0/0          *[OSPF/150] 1w4d 13:05:41, metric 0, tag 0
                    > to 10.0.1.2 via reth0.0
10.0.1.0/24        *[Direct/0] 1w4d 20:50:01
                    > via reth0.0
10.0.1.245/32      *[Static/1] 1w4d 20:50:25
                      Discard
10.0.1.250/32      *[Static/1] 1w4d 20:50:25
                      Discard
10.0.1.254/32      *[Local/0] 1w4d 20:50:30
                      Local via reth0.0
10.0.2.0/24        *[Direct/0] 1w4d 20:49:56
                    > via reth1.0
10.0.2.1/32        *[Local/0] 1w4d 20:50:30
                      Local via reth1.0
224.0.0.5/32       *[OSPF/10] 1w4d 20:50:32, metric 1
                      MultiRecv
```

```
traffic.inet6.0: 9 destinations, 10 routes (9 active, 0 holddown, 0 hidden)
+ = Active Route, - = Last Active, * = Both

::/0               *[OSPF3/150] 1w4d 13:05:44, metric 0, tag 0
                    > to fe80::2e6b:f5ff:fe02:8288 via reth0.0
2001:4910:8163::/55 *[Direct/0] 1w4d 20:50:01
                    > via reth0.0
2001:4910:8163::2/128
                   *[Local/0] 1w4d 20:50:29
                      Local via reth0.0
2001:4910:8163:200::/55
                   *[Direct/0] 1w4d 20:49:56
                    > via reth1.0
2001:4910:8163:200::1/128
                   *[Local/0] 1w4d 20:50:29
                      Local via reth1.0
fe80::/64          *[Direct/0] 1w4d 20:50:01
                    > via reth0.0
                    [Direct/0] 1w4d 20:49:56
                    > via reth1.0
fe80::210:dbff:feff:1000/128
                   *[Local/0] 1w4d 20:50:29
                      Local via reth0.0
fe80::210:dbff:feff:1001/128
                   *[Local/0] 1w4d 20:50:29
                      Local via reth1.0
ff02::5/128        *[OSPF3/10] 1w4d 20:50:32, metric 1
                      MultiRecv

{primary:node1}[edit]
root@SRX-HA-1#
```

In this example, we can see that there are now routes in the routing instance traffic. We also can see that there are two separate tables. One table is for inet or IPv4 and the other for inet6 or IPv6. There are two separate tables, one for each protocol, but they are both separate and contained within the same routing instance. This means that IPv4 packets will not get routed from the IPv6 routing table. Figure 4-6 shows how this table is logically laid out.

Routing instances are a powerful feature in Junos. They allow the creation of potentially thousands of separate routing domains on a single device. In large-scale deployments, we have seen customers use a thousand or more instances. This provides clear separation for instances where you want to have multiple customers on the same device but you do not want them to be able to see each other. For the purposes of this book, we are keeping the topologies relatively simple and to what we see for an average deployment.

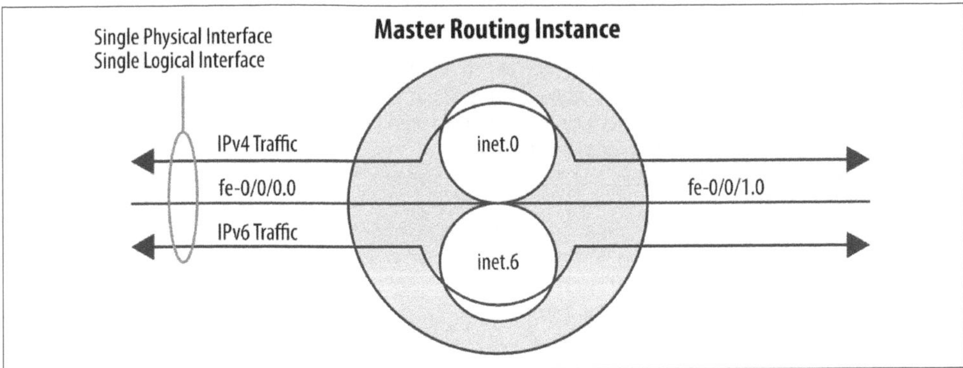

Figure 4-6. Routing instance example

Flow Mode and Packet Mode

On an SRX, the default mode of operation is to process traffic in what is called flow mode. This mode treats all traffic statefully or it monitors the state of all communications. This is very typical for modern firewalls. In the past, there were several types of firewalls: packet based, proxy, and stateful. Because of their effective handling of traffic and their reasonable price/performance ratio, stateful firewalls are the most commonly deployed. As the stateful firewall evolved, it began to bring in features from the other firewall types. An example of this is SSL inspection. The SRX is capable of acting as a proxy to decrypt SSL traffic. In this case, the SRX has both stateful and proxy-based properties. Also as the next-generation firewall market continues to evolve, there is an inclusion of using IPS technologies within firewalling. Application Firewall (AppFW) uses IPS-like inspection to determine what the protocol is beyond the traditional port number. By using a combination of techniques, firewalls today are able to provide a huge amount of performance with deeper traffic inspection.

On the branch SRX product lines, any SRX with a three-digit product number, such as 100 or 650, is able to operate in what is also known as packet mode. In this mode of operation, the SRX is able to inspect packets individually and not as part of a flow. The reason for this is to allow the SRX to operate more as a traditional router for some specific services. Routers and switches almost always operate in packet mode. The SRX is able to provide some services such as MPLS, IPv6 inspection bypass, and IP encapsulation, that require the administrator to process this traffic in packet mode.

There are a few different ways to utilize packet mode based on the use case. The first thing to look at is the security forwarding options. Under this stanza, packet mode can be enabled for protocols device wide, meaning that any traffic matching this protocol family will be processed in the specified mode. Alternatively, it is possible to enable packet mode selectively using firewall filters.

```
[edit security forwarding-options]
root@SRXEdge# set ?
Possible completions:
+ apply-groups         Groups from which to inherit configuration data
+ apply-groups-except  Don't inherit configuration data from these groups
> family               Security forwarding-options for family
[edit security forwarding-options]
root@SRXEdge# set family ?
Possible completions:
+ apply-groups         Groups from which to inherit configuration data
+ apply-groups-except  Don't inherit configuration data from these groups
> inet6                Family IPv6
> iso                  Family ISO
> mpls                 Family MPLS
[edit security forwarding-options]
root@SRXEdge# set family
```

Depending on the family, there are one or more options available. For this section, we focus on the inet6 or IPv6 family.

```
ot@SRXEdge# set mode ?
Possible completions:
  drop                 Disable forwarding
  flow-based           Enable flow-based forwarding
  packet-based         Enable packet-based forwarding
[edit security forwarding-options family inet6]
root@SRXEdge#
```

For inet6, there are three options available: drop, flow-based, or packet-based. Enabling drop will drop any IPv6 traffic without the need for an explicit firewall policy. Choose one of the other two options if you would like to enable flow-based processing or packet-based processing of IPv6. The best practice, if you will be using IPv6, is to enable flow-based processing. Packet-based processing can be enabled via firewall filters selectively, and it is suggested that you use only selective processing. You would want to selectively enable packet processing in the event you wanted to do 6in4 IPv6 tunneling. Changing this option will require a reboot. It is best to configure this before production or schedule a downtime event to change the option.

```
[edit security forwarding-options]
root@SRXEdge# show
family {
    inet6 {
        mode flow-based;
    }
}

[edit security forwarding-options]
root@SRXEdge# show | display set
set security forwarding-options family inet6 mode flow-based
```

```
[edit security forwarding-options]
root@SRXEdge#
```

Enabling selective IPv6 is fairly simple. Next, we present an example of how you would configure a firewall filter to allow IPv6 for 6in4 tunneling. The first step is to configure a firewall filter, which is a stateless inspection of traffic. It allows you to apply rules on a per-packet basis instead of flow based. The firewall stanza is a legacy naming option, as it was present since the origins of Junos. This makes it seem a bit confusing, as the SRX is a firewall and one would expect to configure the firewall stanza. To retain backward compatibility, however, Juniper Networks chose to leave the stanza as is and place the SRX's configuration under the security stanza.

To configure this filter, you should specify the IP address you will be terminating your 6in4 tunnel to. This will ensure that this traffic is only processed in packet mode. The following is our example configuration.

```
root@SRXEdge# show
filter Allow-v6 {
    term 1 {
        from {
            source-address {
                72.52.104.74/32;
            }
            protocol 41;
        }
        then packet-mode;
    }
    term 2 {
        from {
            destination-address {
                72.52.104.74/32;
            }
            protocol 41;
        }
        then packet-mode;
    }
    term 3 {
        then accept;
    }
}

[edit firewall]
root@SRXEdge# show | display set
set firewall filter Allow-v6 term 1 from source-address 72.52.104.74/32
set firewall filter Allow-v6 term 1 from protocol 41
set firewall filter Allow-v6 term 1 then packet-mode
set firewall filter Allow-v6 term 2 from destination-address 72.52.104.74/32
set firewall filter Allow-v6 term 2 from protocol 41
set firewall filter Allow-v6 term 2 then packet-mode
set firewall filter Allow-v6 term 3 then accept
```

```
[edit firewall]
root@SRXEdge#
```

In this example, we configured a firewall filter named *Allow-v6* and added three terms to the filter. Consider each term as a rule and the filter as a policy. Terms are evaluated in the order in which they are inserted into the policy. For simplicity, we named the terms as ordered integers, but you could easily name them any word. Being descriptive on your terms is critical, as it is kind of like inline documentation. For this policy, we specify that traffic that is sourced or destined to the IP 72.52.104.74, and the traffic is also if IP protocol 41. The action is to process this via stateless packet mode. This allows the traffic to bypass the flow engine and be processed as individual packets. Specifying protocol 41 means that the packets have an IP protocol number of 41. This protocol is defined as IPv6 encapsulation and is defined in both RFC 2473 and 3056. Finally, we add in a term of `then accept`. This term does not specify a "from" stanza, meaning that all other traffic not matched by the filter will be accepted and processed as flow-based traffic.

A firewall filter must be specifically applied to the interfaces that you wish to enforce it. This is easy to do. The two items that you must know are which interface to which you wish to apply the filter and in which direction you want to apply it. For this filter, we need to apply it on both the ingress and egress traffic.

```
[edit interfaces fe-0/0/0]
root@SRXEdge# show
unit 0 {
    family inet {
        filter {
            input Allow-v6;
            output Allow-v6;
        }
        address 52.74.55.232/24;
    }
}

[edit interfaces fe-0/0/0]
root@SRXEdge# show | display set
set interfaces fe-0/0/0 unit 0 family inet filter input Allow-v6
set interfaces fe-0/0/0 unit 0 family inet filter output Allow-v6
set interfaces fe-0/0/0 unit 0 family inet address 52.74.55.232/24

[edit interfaces fe-0/0/0]
root@SRXEdge#
```

When committing a firewall filter, best practice is to use commit confirmed. It is possible to forget the explicit accept and block yourself out of the device. Having an automated rollback will simplify the recovery of management to SRX in the event that you made a mistake in the configuration of your filter.

Sample Deployment

For our sample deployment, we are going to take a look at the configuration of the South Branch SRX100 device from our sample topology, shown in Figure 4-7. This simple configuration will allow us to demonstrate what we learned in a real-world deployment. The sample deployment will show the networking configurations including security zones. Below is the configuration in its entirety.

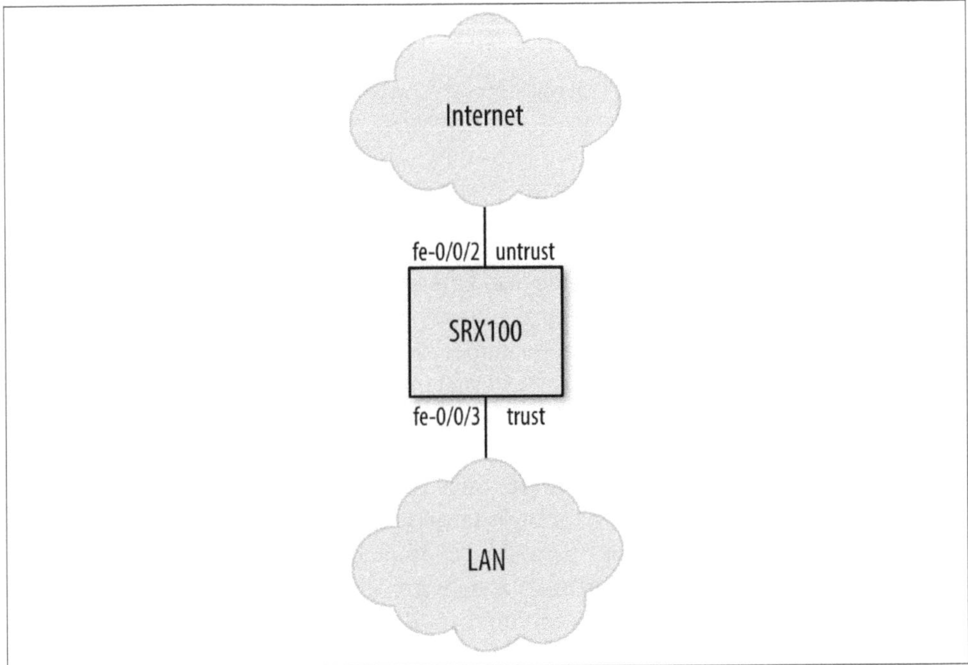

Figure 4-7. South Branch SRX100 sample topology

The first step is to configure the security zones. This does not have to be done first, but by doing it first we will know which interfaces we want to configure.

```
[edit]
root@SouthBranch# show security zones
security-zone untrust {
    interfaces {
        fe-0/0/2.0;
    }
}
security-zone trust {
    interfaces {
        fe-0/0/3.0 {
            host-inbound-traffic {
                system-services {
```

```
                    ssh;
                    ping;
                }
            }
        }
    }
}

[edit]
root@SouthBranch# show security zones | display set
set security zones security-zone untrust interfaces fe-0/0/2.0
set security zones security-zone trust interfaces fe-0/0/3.0 host-inbound-
traffic system-services ssh
set security zones security-zone trust interfaces fe-0/0/3.0 host-inbound-
traffic system-services ping

[edit]
root@SouthBranch#
```

We enabled ping, web management, and SSH inbound on the trust zone. This allows local administrators to manage the device. Externally, the fe-0/0/2.0 interface will not respond to any IP traffic. It will keep the device in stealth mode and prevent it from being detected in a ping scan. The zone names can be whatever you desire. We kept to using untrust as the zone name for the external interface and trust as the internal zone because it comes from the SRX's ScreenOS legacy. Back in the early days of ScreenOS, the interfaces were actually called trust and untrust. This led to these names being the default zone names on ScreenOS devices once unique interface naming was created. Because of this, it is very common for these terms to still be used today in zone naming. What follows is the output of the operational command `show security zones` depicting our configuration. The "junos-host" zone is predefined on the SRX. It can be used in the creation of policies to allow inbound traffic. We elected to use the traditional method of configuring allowed services directly on the zone as this chapter is focused on networking configurations.

```
root@SouthBranch> show security zones

Security zone: trust
  Send reset for non-SYN session TCP packets: Off
  Policy configurable: Yes
  Interfaces bound: 1
  Interfaces:
    fe-0/0/3.0

Security zone: untrust
  Send reset for non-SYN session TCP packets: Off
  Policy configurable: Yes
  Interfaces bound: 1
  Interfaces:
    fe-0/0/2.0
```

```
Security zone: junos-host
  Send reset for non-SYN session TCP packets: Off
  Policy configurable: Yes
  Interfaces bound: 0
  Interfaces:

root@SouthBranch>
```

Next, we need to configure the IP addressing for these defined interfaces. The following is an example of this configuration:

```
root@SouthBranch> show configuration interfaces
fe-0/0/2 {
    unit 0 {
        family inet {
            address 198.18.3.254/24;
        }
    }
}
fe-0/0/3 {
    unit 0 {
        family inet {
            address 192.168.3.1/24;
        }
    }
}

root@SouthBranch> show configuration interfaces | display set
set interfaces fe-0/0/2 unit 0 family inet address 198.18.3.254/24
set interfaces fe-0/0/3 unit 0 family inet address 192.168.3.1/24

root@SouthBranch>
```

For the example, we simply defined one IPv4 address for each interface. We then can check that this was correctly configured from the command `show interfaces terse`. Using the terse option will minimize the output, as all we want to verify is that the IP addresses are configured on the interfaces.

```
root@SouthBranch> show interfaces terse
Interface        Admin Link Proto    Local                 Remote
fe-0/0/0         up    down
gr-0/0/0         up    up
ip-0/0/0         up    up
lt-0/0/0         up    up
mt-0/0/0         up    up
sp-0/0/0         up    up
sp-0/0/0.0       up    up   inet
sp-0/0/0.16383   up    up   inet     10.0.0.1            --> 10.0.0.16
                                     10.0.0.6            --> 0/0
                                     128.0.0.1           --> 128.0.1.16
                                     128.0.0.6           --> 0/0
fe-0/0/1         up    down
fe-0/0/2         up    up
```

```
fe-0/0/2.0        up    up    inet     198.18.3.254/24
fe-0/0/3          up    up
fe-0/0/3.0        up    up    inet     192.168.3.1/24
fe-0/0/4          up    down
fe-0/0/5          up    down
fe-0/0/6          up    down
fe-0/0/7          up    down
gre               up    up
ipip              up    up
irb               up    up
lo0               up    up
lo0.16384         up    up    inet     127.0.0.1           --> 0/0
lo0.16385         up    up    inet     10.0.0.1            --> 0/0
                                       10.0.0.16           --> 0/0
                                       128.0.0.1           --> 0/0
                                       128.0.0.4           --> 0/0
                                       128.0.1.16          --> 0/0
lo0.32768         up    up
lsi               up    up
mtun              up    up
pimd              up    up
pime              up    up
pp0               up    up
ppd0              up    up
ppe0              up    up
st0               up    up
tap               up    up
vlan              up    up

root@SouthBranch>
```

The last element needed is the static route that can point us out to the Internet. This will allow us to talk with the other devices in the topology and the rest of the Internet.

```
root@SouthBranch> show configuration routing-options
static {
    route 0.0.0.0/0 next-hop 198.18.3.1;
}

root@SouthBranch> show configuration routing-options | display set
set routing-options static route 0.0.0.0/0 next-hop 198.18.3.1

root@SouthBranch>
```

Adding the static route is simple and it only takes one command. Finally, for our sample deployment, we will validate that the route is correctly configured.

```
root@SouthBranch> show route

inet.0: 5 destinations, 5 routes (5 active, 0 holddown, 0 hidden)
+ = Active Route, - = Last Active, * = Both

0.0.0.0/0          *[Static/5] 00:00:05
```

```
                        > to 198.18.3.1 via fe-0/0/2.0
192.168.3.0/24         *[Direct/0] 00:00:05
                        > via fe-0/0/3.0
192.168.3.1/32         *[Local/0] 00:08:44
                          Local via fe-0/0/3.0
198.18.3.0/24          *[Direct/0] 00:00:05
                        > via fe-0/0/2.0
198.18.3.254/32        *[Local/0] 00:08:44
                          Local via fe-0/0/2.0

root@SouthBranch>
```

Our configured default route is shown in bold text. The remaining routes come from two built-in sources, one being the directly connected networks as defined by being a type Direct route. The other route displayed is called a local route. This route means that the address is defined on that specified logical interface.

Summary

This chapter covered the basic networking capabilities of an SRX. Because an SRX runs Junos, it contains more networking capabilities than the majority of security devices today. This is both a blessing and a curse. It is a blessing because it allows the administrator to control the transmission of traffic on an SRX in extremely powerful ways. At Juniper Networks, we are constantly amazed at how the SRX is deployed. The typical deployment uses just a few interfaces and a couple of routes. Some deployments can be much more complex, using dozens of protocols, thousands of routing instances, and hundreds of thousands of routes.

Because the typical deployment does not utilize the majority of these networking features, the book's focus has been shifted to the security side of the configuration. Throughout the chapter there are callouts specifying where to go to get the best descriptions of the more advanced networking features if you feel that they are needed in your deployment. It is best to consult with a Junos expert or send a query out on the J-Net community forums if you are unsure of how to best implement your SRX. The best practice is always to keep your design as simple as possible by using the minimal set of options that are needed to accomplish your goal. Designs that are needlessly complex can lead to difficult troubleshooting sessions or behavior that can be confusing to less advanced users. The rule of thumb is to only deploy what the average person on your operations staff can understand. Networking mistakes are often the cause of security breaches. Don't become a victim; keep your configuration as simple as possible.

Study Questions

Questions

1. What is an IFD?
2. What is the name of a physical management interface on an SRX?
3. What are virtual interfaces used for?
4. What is a logical interface?
5. State the two ways that a logical interface can be specified during its creation.
6. What protocol can be used to negotiate aggregate interfaces?
7. What identifier is used to bind a transparent interface to a bridge domain?
8. Zones are used in the creation of security policies on an SRX. What is the point of a zone?
9. There are many different types of routing instances. What is the one that is most commonly used on an SRX?
10. What is the best type of network design to use on an SRX?

Answers

1. An IFD represents a physical interface or interface device. This is often the term used in Junos documentation for a physical interface.
2. A physical management interface that is dedicated to the management of the device is called fxp0.
3. Virtual interfaces provide a logical construct that Junos can use to pass traffic which contains certain properties. Typically, these are used for encapsulation or decapsulation of traffic such as an IPsec VPN.
4. A logical interface is represented as a unit. It can also be called an IFL in Junos documentation. A unit is used for configuring any logical properties such as supported protocol families and protocol addresses.
5. The term unit can be used when specifying a logical interface during its creation or modification (*set interfaces fe-0/0/0 unit 0*). A period can also be used as a shortened form to define a logical interface (*set interfaces fe-0/0/0.0*).
6. The LACP protocol can be utilized to assist in the negotiation of aggregate interfaces to the remote device.
7. Specifying a VLAN ID will bind a transparent interface to a bridge domain.
8. A zone provides a logical construct to which an interface or interfaces can be bound. It simplifies both the policy creation and lookup process. Zones also can be used to specify the inbound traffic allowed into the SRX.

9. The routing instance type virtual router is the most commonly used instance on an SRX. It offers both routing tables and forwarding tables. It is similar to a Cisco VRF.
10. The best type of networking design is a simple design. A misconfigured network is often the cause of security breaches. A simple misconfiguration can lead to unauthorized network access.

CHAPTER 5
System Services

To best leverage the SRX platforms, you need to have a solid understanding of both the security concepts and components, but also of the platform itself. Junos provides a very rich set of features when it comes to system services. Properly configuring and operating the system services is often overlooked during the initial setup of the system. Although most of these topics are the same as other Junos platforms, such as the EX/M/MX/T Series, there are some different implications with the SRX because it is a security device, and some of the security and hardware components rely on these differently. In this chapter, we examine the various system services that you should be aware of on the platform and how to properly leverage them to get the best operational state.

System Services Operation on the SRX

Before we delve into how to configure the individual components in the Junos system services family, we will first have a quick discussion of how the system services operate in the SRX itself so that you have a good understanding of how the system functions operationally. With the proper background, you will have the tools you need to effectively configure and operate the SRX.

Figure 5-1 shows a high-level view of where system services live on the SRX. This is true for both the branch and the high-end SRX because there is a true separation of the control and data plane—even if it is just processor/memory separation on the branch SRX.

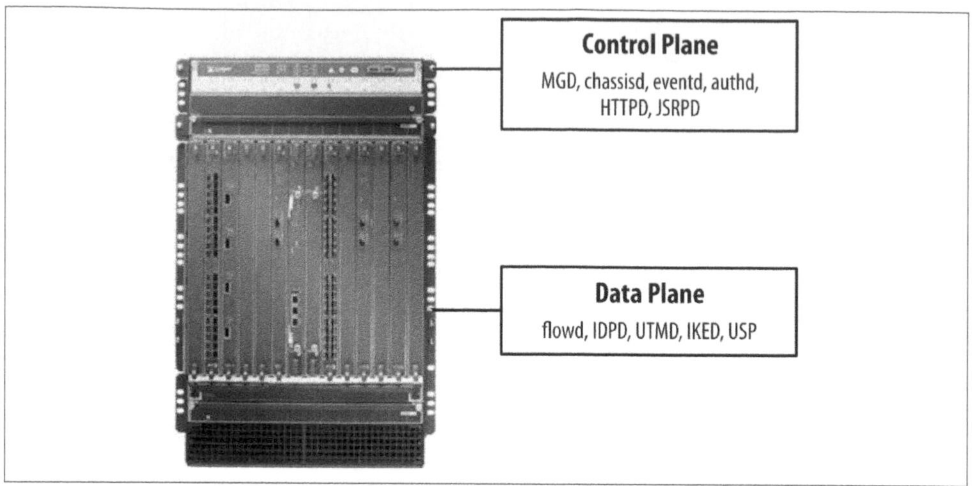

Figure 5-1. Control plane versus data plane services

System Services and the Control Plane

The control plane is responsible for operating most of the system services on the SRX. That is in large part due to the intended function of the control plane, which is to control the platform—rather than operating on the transit traffic itself. The control plane is responsible not only for acting as the interface for which you, the administrator, operate the device, but also for controlling the operation of the chassis, pushing the configuration to the data plane, and operating the daemons that provide functionality to the system. As you already know, the control plane operates the Junos OS, which is a FreeBSD variant. The OS only provides the very basic functionality that an OS provides. This includes process management, scheduling, resource control, and abstracting the hardware so that an array of software can operate on it. This software includes the daemons that provide the system services. Some of them you directly interface with, like MGD (our management daemon), whereas others operate behind the scenes and provide passive functions to the administrator. The good news is that from a configuration perspective, you, the administrator, do not have to be particularly concerned with the OS functions or the individual daemons themselves, Junos handles all of this for you. Instead, you influence the operation of these components based on how you configure the Junos configuration itself; Junos takes it from there.

There are several reasons why most system services operate from the control plane and not the data plane; the control plane is designed to provide a much richer set of features than the data plane. The data plane is intended simply to process traffic. It must be lean, and often it is completely distributed (e.g., on the SRX/M/MX/T/EX and others). The control plane has a bird's-eye view of the entire chassis and can act as the control point for underlying operations that must be performed on the data plane (e.g., pushing down routes to the forwarding table on all processors on the data plane).

Although the control plane can be thought of as the brains of the operation, processing input and pushing it down to all of the nodes on the data plane, as shown in Figure 5-2, the data plane itself must also have a mechanism to receive this data and act on it.

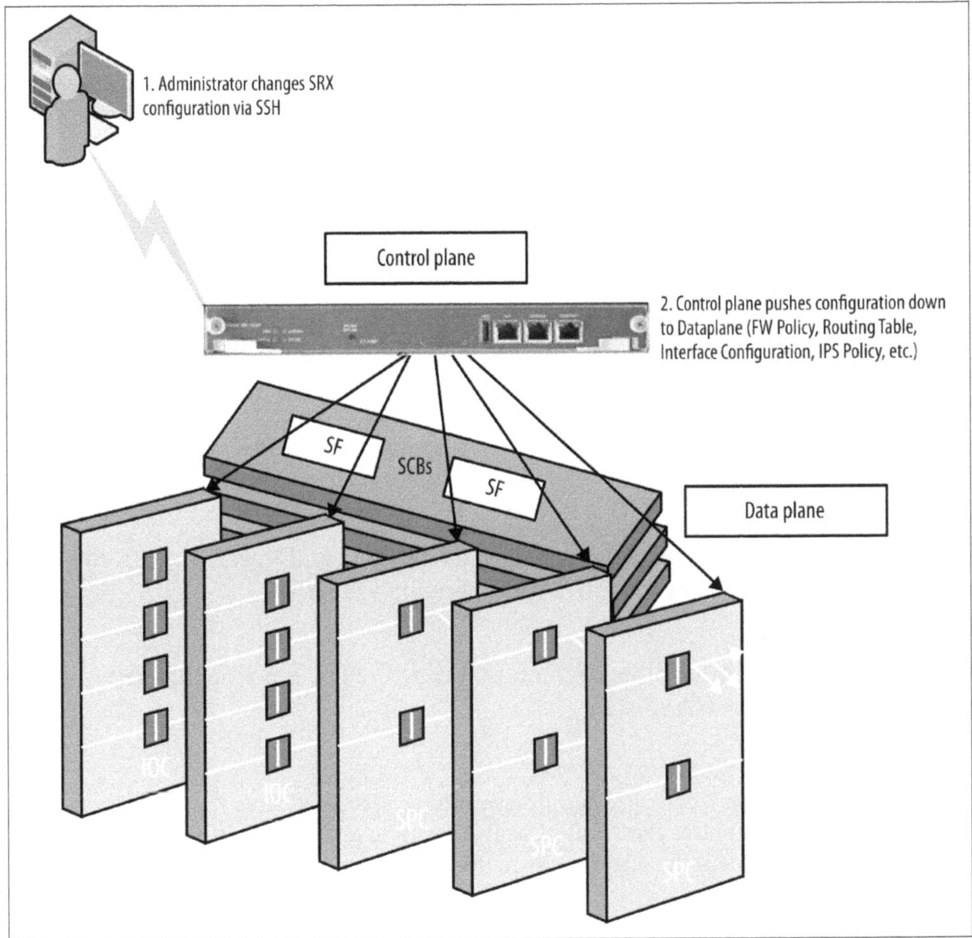

Figure 5-2. Control plane pushing configuration to data plane

Some system services do operate from the data plane, but typically they are specifically designed to operate functions on the data plane itself for maximum performance (e.g., Logging/JFlow as we'll see shortly).

System services that operate on the control plane

So we've alluded to the fact that most system services operate from the control plane, but we haven't specified which ones. It isn't necessary to understand where the services live to operate the platform, but it is certainly helpful to understand this concept.

Management Daemon (MGD)
: Provides the interface between the UI components and the backend configuration and is responsible for acting on the Junos configuration to the system itself.

Routing Protocol Daemon (RPD)
: All routing protocols including RIP, OSPF, IS-IS, BGP, PIM, IPv6 counterparts, and so on.

User interfaces
: Console, Telnet, SSH, J-Web, NetConf.

Filesystem interfaces
: FTP/SCP.

Syslogd
: Logging subsystem on the control plane, different than what is on the data plane. This generates the OS and application logs on the control plane.

Networking services
: DNS, DHCP, NTP, ICMP, ARP/ND, SNMP.

Chassisd
: Controls the hardware operations of the data plane and interfaces with the components to ensure they are active and operating properly.

JSRPD
: This is the high availability daemon that runs the HA functionality between two SRX chassis in an HA cluster.

This isn't a complete authoritative list of system services that operate on the control plane, but instead is meant to give you an idea of where functions of the platform are performed.

System Services and the Data Plane

We'd be remiss to say that there are no system services that function on the data plane—although truth be told, you are not likely to deal with them. Of course, there's little that you need to interface with on the control plane, more of just an understanding that they exist. On the data plane, the system services provide a different function, which is to directly act on traffic that is transiting the device. For instance, there is an Intrusion Detection and Prevention Daemon (IDPD) process that runs the IPS daemon on the control plane, but there it is responsible for signature downloads, policy compilation, pushing the policy to the data plane, and operational activities such as retrieving information from user-triggered commands, configuration changes, and automated system processes. IDPD also exists on the data plane (particularly in certain deployment modes like dedicated/inline tap modes) where it is responsible for not only interfacing with the IDPD process on the control plane to accept new configurations and provide statistics, but for directly processing the IPS-bound traffic itself. These two daemons are effectively different in function, acting as counterparts but sharing the same name.

IDPD was just one example; there are similar examples for IKED, PKID, and many other subsystems. The key is that control and data plane separation. The daemons running on the control plane operate to control the platform and provide operational instructions to the daemons running on the data plane, which operate directly on the traffic. Of course, there isn't strictly a 1:1 relation between control plane and data plane daemons, as lots of control plane subsystems cooperate with flowd on the data plane, which is the main data plane daemon, for instance.

Accounts for Administrative Users

Junos has a very robust infrastructure for administrative users on the SRX and other Junos devices. Not only does it support full local and remote authentication, but it also has perhaps the best role-based access control system in the industry. Junos has the ability not only to define read-only/read-write capabilities for the system, but you can actually restrict this down to configuration or operational stanzas and even down to the command level. Covering the complete set of capabilities for user authentication and RBAC in Junos is outside the scope of this book, but it is covered in other O'Reilly books like JUNOS Cookbook by Aviva Garrett (O'Reilly).

Configuring local users

Junos has two types of users: local and remote. For local users, you must define the user properties along with the login class information. The login class specifies what access they have on the device itself. There are several predefined classes, or you can create your own as we will do in the next example. In this example, we'll create the user Bob who is an operator and configure a plain-text password abc123.

```
root# set system login user Bob class ?
Possible completions:
  <class>               Login class
  operator              permissions [ clear network reset trace view ]
  read-only             permissions [ view ]
  super-user            permissions [ all ]
  unauthorized          permissions [ none ]

root# set system login user Bob class operator authentication ?
Possible completions:
```

```
+ apply-groups          Groups from which to inherit configuration data
+ apply-groups-except   Don't inherit configuration data from these groups
  encrypted-password    Encrypted password string
  load-key-file         File (URL) containing one or more ssh keys
  plain-text-password   Prompt for plain text password (autoencrypted)
> ssh-dsa               Secure shell (ssh) DSA public key string
> ssh-rsa               Secure shell (ssh) RSA public key string

 [edit]
root#  set  system  login  user  Bob  class  operator  authentication  plain-text-
password
New password:
Retype new password:

[edit]
root# show system login user Bob
class operator;
authentication {
    encrypted-password "$1$uLe/a9L4$tXkURwP1Z0YRwoQJA7Sfb/"; ## SECRET-DATA
}
```

As you can see from this example, there are four predefined classes, with the permissions listed to the right. In terms of local user authentication, you can use a password, an SSH key, or RSA/DSA SSH key, which is loaded by the terminal rather than by file. The encrypted password is useful if you're transferring a password from another system and don't know the real password but are loading it from the configuration.

Creating a login class

Login classes give you maximum control over permissions on the system for your administrators. You have complete control for what commands can be issued at an operational level as well as what can be viewed or configured within the configuration itself. You can explicitly define complete commands, but Junos also allows you to define them from a stanza perspective so you do not need to configure the complete commands to block everything underneath them.

In this example, we'll make a new class called Security Admin that will only allow users to use *show* and *clear* operational mode commands and only configure objects under "set security" and "set services" in the configuration, but it will allow them to view the entire configuration.

```
[edit]
root# set system login class "Security Admin" ?
Possible completions:
  access-end            End time for remote access (hh:mm)
  access-start          Start time for remote access (hh:mm)
  allow-commands        Regular expression for commands to allow explicitly
  allow-configuration   Regular expression for configure to allow explicitly
+ allow-configuration-regexps  Object path regular expressions to allow
+ allowed-days          Day(s) of week when access is allowed.
```

```
+ apply-groups         Groups from which to inherit configuration data
+ apply-groups-except  Don't inherit configuration data from these groups
  deny-commands        Regular expression for commands to deny explicitly
  deny-configuration   Regular expression for configure to deny explicitly
+ deny-configuration-regexps  Object path regular expressions to deny
  idle-timeout         Maximum idle time before logout (minutes)
  logical-system       Logical system associated with login
  login-alarms         Display system alarms when logging in
  login-script         Execute this login-script when logging in
  login-tip            Display tip when logging in
+ permissions          Set of permitted operation categories
  security-role        Common Criteria security role


[edit]
root# set system login class Security-Admin allow-commands "show|clear|config-
ure"

[edit]
root# set system login class Security-Admin ?
Possible completions:
  access-end           End time for remote access (hh:mm)
  access-start         Start time for remote access (hh:mm)
  allow-commands       Regular expression for commands to allow explicitly
  allow-configuration  Regular expression for configure to allow explicitly
+ allow-configuration-regexps  Object path regular expressions to allow
+ allowed-days         Day(s) of week when access is allowed.
+ apply-groups         Groups from which to inherit configuration data
+ apply-groups-except  Don't inherit configuration data from these groups
  deny-commands        Regular expression for commands to deny explicitly
  deny-configuration   Regular expression for configure to deny explicitly
+ deny-configuration-regexps  Object path regular expressions to deny
  idle-timeout         Maximum idle time before logout (minutes)
  logical-system       Logical system associated with login
  login-alarms         Display system alarms when logging in
  login-script         Execute this login-script when logging in
  login-tip            Display tip when logging in
+ permissions          Set of permitted operation categories
  security-role        Common Criteria security role

 [edit]
root# set system login class Security-Admin allow-configuration "security|serv-
ices"

[edit]
root# show system login class Security-Admin
allow-commands "show|clear|configure";
allow-configuration "security|services";
```

You can also opt to define what permissions you would like to assign rather than defining explicit regular expressions for operational/configuration mode with the Permissions fields.

```
[edit]
root# set system login class Security-Admin2 permissions ?
Possible completions:
  [                    Open a set of values
  access               Can view access configuration
  access-control       Can modify access configuration
  admin                Can view user accounts
  admin-control        Can modify user accounts
  all                  All permission bits turned on
  clear                Can clear learned network info
  configure            Can enter configuration mode
  control              Can modify any config
  field                Can use field debug commands
  firewall             Can view firewall configuration
  firewall-control     Can modify firewall configuration
  floppy               Can read and write the floppy
  flow-tap             Can view flow-tap configuration
  flow-tap-control     Can modify flow-tap configuration
  flow-tap-operation   Can tap flows
  idp-profiler-operation  Can Profiler data
  interface            Can view interface configuration
  interface-control    Can modify interface configuration
  maintenance          Can become the super-user
  network              Can access the network
  pgcp-session-mirroring  Can view pgcp session mirroring configuration
   pgcp-session-mirroring-control  Can modify pgcp session mirroring configura-
tion
  reset                Can reset/restart interfaces and daemons
  rollback             Can rollback to previous configurations
  routing              Can view routing configuration
  routing-control      Can modify routing configuration
  secret               Can view secret statements
  secret-control       Can modify secret statements
  security             Can view security configuration
  security-control     Can modify security configuration
  shell                Can start a local shell
  snmp                 Can view SNMP configuration
  snmp-control         Can modify SNMP configuration
  storage              Can view fibre channel storage protocol configuration
  storage-control      Can modify fibre channel storage protocol configuration
  system               Can view system configuration
  system-control       Can modify system configuration
  trace                Can view trace file settings
  trace-control        Can modify trace file settings
  view                 Can view current values and statistics
  view-configuration   Can view all configuration (not including secrets)
```

That description information is quite self-explanatory. A base option like "security" allows you to view the configuration, where the `<option>` control allows you to edit it as well.

Remote authentication

Junos supports remote authentication like RADIUS and Tacacs+ for administrative authentication. These days, RADIUS is a popular choice because most authentication systems that include two-factor authentication support it. Junos also allows you to gather the permissions and capabilities from the authentication system itself.

In this example, we configure a RADIUS Server at 192.168.1.250 with a port 1812 and a secret OnceUponAT1m3. We will try to authenticate users with RADIUS first, then a password if that fails. All users authenticated by RADIUS will have class super-user.

```
[edit]
root# set system radius-server 192.168.1.250 port 1812 secret OnceUponAT1m3

[edit]
root# set system authentication-order [radius password]

[edit]
root# set system login user remote class super-user

[edit]
root# set system login user Jim class operator


[edit]
root# show system radius-server
192.168.1.250 {
    port 1812;
    secret "$9$a0UH.AtOREyP5hyrlXxZUjkPQF3/pOIF3IcleW8"; ## SECRET-DATA
}

root# show system authentication-order
authentication-order [ radius password ];


[edit]
root# show system login user remote
class super-user;

[edit]
root# show system login user Jim
class operator;
```

Looking over the previous example, there are a few things to note. Mainly that there is a special user called "remote." This user is automatically authenticated by the external system and derives its class accordingly. You can define users manually to give them a special class (like Jim, who will be an operator). Because there is no password or other authentication defined, they cannot be authenticated locally. If there was a password defined, per our authentication order, we would authenticate the user via RADIUS first, and if we could not connect to the server, we'd fall back to a locally configured password.

There are plenty of other options for getting permissions served centrally from the RADIUS server. Juniper publishes its own Vendor-Specific Attributes for RADIUS (*http://juni.pr/11IZeYD*), which you can pass back to the system from RADIUS.

Accessing System Services: Control Plane Versus Data Plane

So we've discussed that the main system services that we interface exist on the control plane, for instance management and routing protocol subsystems. We know that Junos has an out-of-band management interface fxp0, which is a physical interface. Even on the branch, it's physical, although it doesn't necessarily have a dedicated interface that serves one purpose like that of the HE SRX and other M/MX/T platforms where fxp0 is located on the routing engine or on a specific port that's hardcoded to be fxp0. That brings up an interesting scenario in many deployments where you might have both fxp0 and transit data interfaces that you might want to access the device for management. If you connect directly to fxp0 on the control plane, you are going to bypass the data plane, so therefore the security components on the data plane will not be applied to inbound or outbound connections to and from fxp0. On the other hand, any inbound or outbound connections to the SRX on the data plane will be subjected to the controls of the data plane, such as firewall or IPS policies and other access controls applied to the data plane. That doesn't mean that you can't have connections destined to or from the control plane if they go in or out fxp0 rather than the data plane; it just means that you cannot control them via firewall policy.

To control connections to the control plane, we can apply stateless filters either directly to fxp0 or to lo0 if we want it to apply to any inbound connection coming from either the control plane or data plane to interact with the control plane. Typically, applying the filter to lo0 is the best approach because it can provide you with an additional layer of protection, rather than only applying it to fxp0.

Configuring a stateless firewall filter to control traffic on fxp0

In this example, we configure a stateless filter that we will apply to the fxp0 interface, which will allow only SSH connections from IP address 192.168.1.20 along with ICMP from any address. All other traffic (including routing protocols) will be dropped.

```
[edit]
root@srx3600n0# set firewall family inet filter Restrict-FXP0 term SSH-Inbound
from source-address 192.168.1.20

[edit]
root@srx3600n0# set firewall family inet filter Restrict-FXP0 term SSH-Inbound
from destination-port 22
```

```
[edit]
root@srx3600n0# set firewall family inet filter Restrict-FXP0 term SSH-Inbound
from protocol tcp

[edit]
root@srx3600n0# set firewall family inet filter Restrict-FXP0 term SSH-Inbound
then accept log

[edit]
root@srx3600n0# set firewall family inet filter Restrict-FXP0 term ICMP-Any
from protocol icmp

[edit]
root@srx3600n0# set firewall family inet filter Restrict-FXP0 term ICMP-Any
then accept

[edit]
root@srx3600n0# set firewall family inet filter Restrict-FXP0 term Deny-Else
then reject

[edit]
root@srx3600n0# set interfaces fxp0 unit 0 family inet filter input Restrict-
FXP0

[edit]
root@srx3600n0# show firewall
family inet {
    filter Restrict-FXP0 {
        term SSH-Inbound {
            from {
                source-address {
                    192.168.1.20/32;
                }
                protocol tcp;
                destination-port 22;
            }
            then {
                log;
                accept;
            }
        }
        term ICMP-Any {
            from {
                protocol icmp;
            }
            then accept;
        }
        term Deny-Else {
            then {
                reject;
            }
```

```
            }
        }
    }

    [edit]
    root@srx3600n0# show interfaces fxp0
    unit 0 {
        family inet {
            filter {
                input Restrict-FXP0;
            }
            address 192.168.1.49/24;
        }
    }
```

As we can see here, we have created a stateless firewall filter, which is different from a stateful security policy. This is a traditional access control list (ACL), which can be applied to either the control plane or the data plane, where security policies are applied to the data plane only and are stateful. Both stateless and stateful security policies can coexist on the data plane, where stateless policies are processed first. There is a great deal more configuration that can be discussed that is outside the scope of this book when it comes to stateless security policies. The goal here is to make you aware of stateless filters and how they can be applied to control fxp0 traffic.

Configuring a stateless firewall filter to control all inbound management traffic

In the previous example, we applied the firewall filter to the fxp0 interface only, meaning that the connection will be managed from fxp0 and not control connections that come into the data plane. Therefore, it is typically best to apply such filters to the loopback interface rather than to fxp0, so you can filter all connections whether they are terminated on fxp0 or a data plane interface. In this case, we would just apply the configuration to lo0 rather than fxp0. The difference here is that when applied to lo0, it will handle any traffic that is terminated to the device based on how the system services bind to interfaces internally.

```
[edit]
root@srx3600n0# set interfaces lo0 unit 0 family inet filter input Restrict-FXP0

[edit]
root@srx3600n0# show interfaces lo0
unit 0 {
    family inet {
        filter {
            input Restrict-FXP0;
        }
    }
}
```

In this example, we could have also placed this on a data plane interface like ge-0/0/0.0 if we wanted to restrict management traffic on only a single interface rather than on all.

Configuring a security policy to control data plane management traffic

With the data plane you have two options: you can either leverage stateless filters or, as of Junos 11.2r2+, you can also configure security policies to and from zone junos-host, including global policies. The junos-host zone is a special zone in which traffic either originates from (if in the from-zone field) or is destined to (if in the to-zone field) the SRX. There are several examples of controlling traffic with the full security policies on the data plane versus stateless filters, but as we mentioned, they will only take effect for traffic that enters on the data plane. If the traffic enters on the control plane, it will not be processed by the security policy, but you can still leverage the stateless firewall filters.

This example is covered at length in Chapter 8 alongside the security policies that handle transit traffic on the data plane.

Before you can access any services on the data plane, you *must* configure the system service to be active on that zone. Otherwise, the traffic will never be processed by the security policy and will be dropped at the interface level. We discuss how to do this in the next section. This is also covered in more detail in Chapter 8.

Zone-Based Service Control

The SRX has an additional layer of security when it comes to system services that operate on the SRX, which is the "host-inbound-traffic" feature that can be configured on a per-zone or per-interface basis within each individual security zone. By default, a security zone has all system services disabled, which means that it will not accept any inbound management or protocol requests on the control plane without explicitly enabling the service per interface or zone in the security zone stanzas. This is done to help improve the posture of the SRX as a security device and follows a method similar to ScreenOS, where you needed to enable the service on a per-zone basis. Of course, the SRX takes it a step further, allowing you to leverage much more granular control over the management through security policies and leveraging additional system services, such as IPS, that can run on top of the security policies.

As mentioned, you can enable individual system services (management) and protocols (routing protocols) on an interface-by-interface or on a zone-by-zone basis. To best explain this, let's look at an example.

Configuring system services and protocols per zone or interface

In this example, we configure two zones: trust and untrust. In the trust zone, there will be three interfaces: ge-0/0/0, ge-0/0/1.0, and ge-0/0/2.0. Allow all system services and protocols OSPF, BGP, and PIM on interface ge-0/0/0.0. Allow ping on all interfaces in the trust zone and DHCP on ge-0/0/2.0 On the untrust zone, only allow ping, traceroute, and VRRP on interface ge-0/0/4.0.

```
[edit]
root@srx3600n0# set security zones security-zone trust interfaces ge-0/0/0.0
host-inbound-traffic system-services all

[edit]
root@srx3600n0# set security zones security-zone trust interfaces ge-0/0/0.0
host-inbound-traffic protocols ospf

[edit]
root@srx3600n0# set security zones security-zone trust interfaces ge-0/0/0.0
host-inbound-traffic protocols bgp

[edit]
root@srx3600n0# set security zones security-zone trust interfaces ge-0/0/0.0
host-inbound-traffic protocols pim

[edit]
root@srx3600n0# set security zones security-zone trust interfaces ge-0/0/1.0

[edit]
root@srx3600n0# set security zones security-zone trust interfaces ge-0/0/2.0

[edit]
root@srx3600n0# set security zones security-zone trust host-inbound-traffic
system-services ping

[edit]
root@srx3600n0# set security zones security-zone trust interfaces ge-0/0/2.0
host-inbound-traffic system-services dhcp

[edit]
root@srx3600n0# set security zones security-zone untrust interfaces ge-0/0/4.0
host-inbound-traffic system-services ping

[edit]
root@srx3600n0# set security zones security-zone untrust interfaces ge-0/0/4.0
host-inbound-traffic system-services traceroute

[edit]
root@srx3600n0# set security zones security-zone untrust interfaces ge-0/0/4.0
host-inbound-traffic protocols vrrp
```

```
[edit]
root@srx3600n0# show security zones
security-zone trust {
    host-inbound-traffic {
        system-services {
            ping;
        }
    }
    interfaces {
        ge-0/0/0.0 {
            host-inbound-traffic {
                system-services {
                    all;
                }
                protocols {
                    ospf;
                    bgp;
                    pim;
                }
            }
        }
        ge-0/0/1.0;
        ge-0/0/2.0 {
            host-inbound-traffic {
                system-services {
                    dhcp;
                }
            }
        }
    }
}
security-zone untrust {
    interfaces {
        ge-0/0/4.0 {
            host-inbound-traffic {
                system-services {
                    ping;
                    traceroute;
                }
                protocols {
                    vrrp;
                }
            }
        }
    }
}
```

When you enable a service on an interface/zone, it is not changing how the system is listening for the service, but rather allowing that connection to come into the platform on the data plane (rather than using an implicit stateless firewall filter that blocks it on the data plane before it can reach the control plane). In other words, system services might be listening on all IP interfaces, but the data plane will prevent these services from being accessed by default by blocking them without explicitly allowing them with the configuration, as shown earlier. Additionally, there are other ways to limit access, including explicit stateless firewall filters, junos-host security policy rules (for the data plane only), and with some system services you can specify what interface it listens on, like J-Web.

Management Services

There are essentially four ways to manage the SRX (and other Junos platforms for that matter): CLI, web UI, Central Management (Junos Space/NSM), and via the Junos API NetConf. This section serves to show how you configure the individual management options we covered using the Junos CLI and the GUI management in earlier chapters. We also briefly discuss SNMP in this section, as it is a helpful mechanism to collect vital system information about the platform.

Command-Line Interfaces

There are essentially three CLI mechanisms to manage the SRX: the Console, Telnet, and SSH. Once you're logged in, they are the same, but accessing them requires different protocols. The console is enabled by default. There is nothing that you need to do to enable it; you need only connect a console cable to the SRX. Telnet and SSH are not on by default and must be configured. SSH is a much better mechanism to manage the SRX because it is encrypted. We don't recommend using Telnet unless it is an emergency or for open access like a public looking glass (not typically an SRX).

Configuring console options

There are a few options that you can leverage with the console port, including disabling it, securing the console when the cable is disconnected, root user control, and specifying the console type. In this example, we set the console to log out when the cable is disconnected and set the console to VT100.

```
root@srx3600n0# set system ports console ?
Possible completions:
+ apply-groups          Groups from which to inherit configuration data
+ apply-groups-except   Don't inherit configuration data from these groups
  disable               Disable console
  insecure              Disallow superuser access
```

```
    log-out-on-disconnect  Log out the console session when cable is unplugged
    type                   Terminal type
[edit]
root@srx3600n0# set system ports console log-out-on-disconnect type vt100

[edit]
root@srx3600n0# show system ports console
log-out-on-disconnect;
type vt100;
```

Configuring Telnet access

By default, Telnet is disabled. In this example, we configure Telnet on the SRX and set a limit of five concurrent Telnet connections. We only allow the connection through the fxp0 interface, so we won't enable it on the zone configuration.

```
[edit]
root@srx3600n0# set system services telnet ?
Possible completions:
  <[Enter]>            Execute this command
+ apply-groups         Groups from which to inherit configuration data
+ apply-groups-except  Don't inherit configuration data from these groups
  connection-limit     Maximum number of allowed connections (1..250)
  rate-limit           Maximum number of connections per minute (1..250)
  |                    Pipe through a command
[edit]
root@srx3600n0# set system services telnet connection-limit 5

[edit]
root@srx3600n0# show system services
telnet {
    connection-limit 5;
}
```

Configuring SSH access

SSH is the preferred remote access mechanism for the SRX. It is authenticated and encrypted, so your connection is secure. Additionally, you can run SCP over SSH to transfer files without any special configuration. You can use popular SSH clients like Putty, OpenSSH, and SecureCRT to access a system using SSH. In this example, let's configure SSH to be active on the SRX on both the control plane and on the trust interface ge-0/0/0.0. Disable root login via SSH, use only version 2, and restrict SSH to only five connections.

```
[edit]
root@srx3600n0# set system services ssh ?
Possible completions:
  <[Enter]>            Execute this command
+ apply-groups         Groups from which to inherit configuration data
+ apply-groups-except  Don't inherit configuration data from these groups
+ ciphers              Specify the ciphers allowed for protocol version 2
```

```
  client-alive-count-max  Threshold of missing client-alive responses that trig-
gers a disconnect (1..255)
  client-alive-interval  Frequency of client-alive requests (0..65535 seconds)
  connection-limit      Maximum number of allowed connections (1..250)
> hostkey-algorithm     Specify permissible SSH host-key algorithms
+ key-exchange          Specify ssh key-exchange for Diffie-Hellman keys
+ macs                  Message Authentication Code algorithms allowed (SSHv2)
  max-sessions-per-connection  Maximum number of sessions per single SSH connec-
tion (1..65535)
  no-tcp-forwarding     Do not allow forwarding TCP connections via SSH
+ protocol-version      Specify SSH protocol versions supported
  rate-limit            Maximum number of connections per minute (1..250)
  root-login            Configure root access via SSH
  tcp-forwarding        Allow forwarding TCP connections via SSH
  |                     Pipe through a command
 [edit]
root@srx3600n0# set system services ssh root-login deny

root@srx3600n0# set system services ssh protocol-version v2

[edit]
root@srx3600n0# set system services ssh connection-limit 5

[edit]
root@srx3600n0# show system services ssh
root-login deny;
protocol-version v2;
connection-limit 5;

[edit]
root@srx3600n0# set security zones security-zone trust interfaces ge-0/0/0.0
host-inbound-traffic system-services ssh

[edit]
root@srx3600n0# show security zones
security-zone trust {
    interfaces {
        xe-1/0/0.0 {
        ge-0/0/0.0 {
            host-inbound-traffic {
                system-services {
                    ssh;
                }
            }
        }
    }
}
```

At the time of writing this book, there is not an officially supported way to change the port that Telnet/SSH listens on; they only can use the predefined ports 23 and 22, respectively. It's always a good idea to limit what machines can connect to your management services, and this might be a decent mechanism to do so. One option, if you need to have the system service listen on a nonstandard port on the data plane, is to leverage destination NAT to do an inbound port translation, but typically going to this length isn't needed.

Additionally, you can upload the SSH public keys of your trusted clients so that you don't need to use password authentication. This is also helpful if you are doing automated processing like NetConf or batch processing. To do this, you can load the keys manually with the key text, specify a location to upload the keys from, or manually type the key string. In this example, we've uploaded a trusted public key to the SRX in */var/tmp* called ssh.pubkey, then we'll use the import process to add it.

```
[edit]
root@srx3600n0# set security ssh-known-hosts load-key-file /var/tmp/ssh.pubkey
Import SSH host keys from trusted source /var/tmp/ssh.pubkey ? [yes,no] (no) yes
```

Although it is out of the scope of this chapter, you can also refer to configuring users in this book and in the Junos documentation for extensive support for user creation, permissions, authentication, and more when it comes to management sessions. This impacts both the CLI and the web UI.

Web Management on the SRX

By default, the web interface is disabled on the SRX for security reasons, but you can easily enable it with a few simple commands. You have the option to enable the web interface for both HTTP and HTTPS, including what logical interface to restrict it to and what port it should listen on. Because the web interface can be used for Dynamic VPN, you can specify which URL should be used rather than just using the base URL. Let's look at an example where we enable HTTP on fxp0 port 80 and HTTPS on port 4430 on all interfaces. HTTPS should use the system-generated certificate. To keep the web management engine operating lean, allow no more than two concurrent users with a 60-minute logout.

```
[edit]
root@srx3600n0# set system services web-management session idle-timeout 60
session-limit 2

[edit]
root@srx3600n0# set system services web-management http interface fxp0
```

```
[edit]
root@srx3600n0# set system services web-management https port 4430 system-
generated-certificate

[edit]
root@srx3600n0# show system services web-management
http {
    port 80;
    interface fxp0.0;
}
https {
    port 4430;
    system-generated-certificate;
    interface fxp0.0;
}
session {
    idle-timeout 60;
    session-limit 2;
}
```

Enabling NetConf over SSH

NetConf over SSH is used to allow automated control over the SRX using the NetConf XML RPC. This is not only the mechanism to operate remote Junos Script, but also how systems like Junos Space communicate with the SRX. Here we enable NetConf on port 2200 with a maximum of five connections.

```
[edit]
root@srx3600n0# set system services netconf ssh ?
Possible completions:
  <[Enter]>            Execute this command
+ apply-groups         Groups from which to inherit configuration data
+ apply-groups-except  Don't inherit configuration data from these groups
  connection-limit     Maximum number of allowed connections (1..250)
  port                 Service port number (1..65535)
  rate-limit           Maximum number of connections per minute (1..250)
  |                    Pipe through a command
[edit]
root@srx3600n0# set system services netconf ssh port 2200 connection-limit 5

[edit]
root@srx3600n0# show system services netconf
ssh {
    connection-limit 5;
    port 2200;
}
```

A thorough discussion of Junos Script is outside the scope of this book because it can fill a book all on its own. There is an excellent Day One book on Junos Script, available for download for free (*http://juni.pr/15N5vH4*) from Juniper.

SNMP Management

Junos has one of the most extensive SNMP engines available for networking platforms. SNMP versions 1, 2c, and 3 are supported, including very extensive support for filtering requests and views, SNMP traps, automation over SNMP, and much more. SNMP is a powerful component to leverage not only for routing and switching platforms, but also for security. The SRX has finite storage facilities, so capturing long-term data for historical purposes is not a good option on the SRX. Instead, you can leverage third-party SNMP solutions that can poll, manipulate, and store SNMP data. There are both free solutions like MRTG, Nagios/Groundwork, and Cacti, as well as a wealth of commercial options like Solar Winds, Groundwork (commercial versions), OpenView, E-Health, and many others. They can provide much more functionality with reporting and alerting as well.

Configuring SNMP Management

Let's take a look at configuring an SNMP example for the SRX so we can monitor it with a solution like Cacti. For simplicity, we'll just demonstrate using SNMP v2c, which only leverages the community string for authentication. SNMP v2 is not encrypted so it is not the most secure solution, but it is fast to deploy. SNMP v3 is recommended for security, especially if the traffic is going over nonmanagement networks or is being used to alter the configuration. The configuration for SNMPv3 is much more extensive and requires a bunch of different concepts that are outside the scope of this book. In this example, we'll restrict SNMP to the fxp0 interface with client 192.168.1.50. The client should have read-only rights on Community SNMP-Community-2c.

```
[edit]
root@srx3600n0# set snmp ?
Possible completions:
+ apply-groups         Groups from which to inherit configuration data
+ apply-groups-except  Don't inherit configuration data from these groups
> client-list          Client list
> community            Configure a community string
  contact              Contact information for administrator
  description          System description
> engine-id            SNMPv3 engine ID
   filter-duplicates     Filter requests with duplicate source address/port and
request ID
> filter-interfaces    List of interfaces that needs to be filtered
> health-monitor       Health monitoring configuration
```

```
+ interface              Restrict SNMP requests to interfaces
  location               Physical location of system
  logical-system-trap-filter  Allow only logical-system specific traps
  name                   System name override
> nonvolatile            Configure the handling of nonvolatile SNMP Set requests
> proxy                  SNMP proxy configuration
> rmon                   Remote Monitoring configuration
> routing-instance-access  SNMP routing-instance options
> traceoptions           Trace options for SNMP
> trap-group             Configure traps and notifications
> trap-options           SNMP trap options
> v3                     SNMPv3 configuration information
> view                   Define MIB views
 [edit]
root@srx3600n0# set snmp interface fxp0 community SNMP-Community-2c clients
192.168.1.50/32

[edit]
root@srx3600n0# set snmp community SNMP-Community-2c authorization read-only

root@srx3600n0# show snmp
interface fxp0.0;
community SNMP-Community-2c {
    authorization read-only;
    clients {
        192.168.1.50/32;
    }
}
```

By default, Junos SNMP is v1/2c compatible, but you need to explicitly define if you want to use SNMP v3 with the appropriate configuration.

Configuring SNMP Traps

SNMP traps provide an efficient way to signal when certain conditions are reached on the device. To configure an SNMP trap, you need to define both what to trigger the trap on and where to send it with the appropriate community string. There are mechanisms to further limit SNMP traps, define traps based on changing values (Remote Monitor, or RMON), and many more—however, due to brevity and the advanced nature of the SNMP system, those are outside of the scope of this book. There is extensive information about using SNMP traps on Junos in the *JUNOS Cookbook* and in the documentation.

For this example, we'll limit the type of traps that are sent to just Chassis, Chassis-Cluster, Configuration, and Startup rather than sending all SNMP traps. Send the traps using community Desired-Traps to server 192.168.1.200. Ensure that the traps appear to come from the fxp0 interface regardless of the routing. For this example, fxp0 has an IP address of 192.168.2.50.

```
[edit]
root@srx3600n0#  set  snmp  trap-group  Desired-Traps  version  v2  targets
192.168.1.200

[edit]
root@srx3600n0# set snmp trap-group Desired-Traps categories ?
Possible completions:
+ apply-groups         Groups from which to inherit configuration data
+ apply-groups-except  Don't inherit configuration data from these groups
  authentication       Authentication failures
  chassis              Chassis or environment notifications
  chassis-cluster      Clustering notifications
  configuration        Configuration notifications
  link                 Link up-down transitions
> otn-alarms           OTN alarm trap subcategories
  remote-operations    Remote operations
  rmon-alarm           RMON rising and falling alarms
  routing              Routing protocol notifications
  services             Services notifications
> sonet-alarms         SONET alarm trap subcategories
  startup              System warm and cold starts
  vrrp-events          VRRP notifications
[edit]
root@srx3600n0# set snmp trap-group Desired-Traps categories chassis

[edit]
root@srx3600n0# set snmp trap-group Desired-Traps categories chassis-cluster

[edit]
root@srx3600n0# set snmp trap-group Desired-Traps categories configuration

[edit]
root@srx3600n0# set snmp trap-group Desired-Traps categories startup

[edit]
root@srx3600n0# set snmp trap-options source-address 192.168.2.50

[edit]
root@srx3600n0# show snmp
trap-options {
    source-address 192.168.2.50;
trap-group Desired-Traps {
    version v2;
    categories {
        chassis;
        startup;
        configuration;
        chassis-cluster;
    }
```

```
        targets {
            192.168.1.200;
        }
    }
```

SNMP in High Availability Chassis Clusters

When using high availability chassis clusters, you should ideally be using fxp0 interfaces on each node of the cluster as a best practice. Although this isn't strictly required, it allows you to manage each device independently. In the case of SNMP, if you manage it through the reth interface or fxp0 using master-only configuration, then you will only get the active control plane in the cluster, so you might miss out on stats for the standby control plane (remember, even in active/active, one control plane is active and one is passive; more discussion on this can be found in Chapter 7). If you can use fxp0 on both members of the cluster, then you will be able to poll both devices independently.

Junos SNMP MIB

If you are familiar with SNMP (or even if this was your first time), you'll be wondering what SNMP values you should be monitoring for when it comes to SNMP polling (since we covered how to send SNMP traps earlier). The good news is that Juniper publishes their SNMP MIB to define what Object Identifier (OID) values can be used to poll for specific information. The bad news is that it is truly massive. Most SNMP platforms are aware of the standard enterprise MIB for pulling standard values, but there are all sorts of custom objects that you might be interested in as an administrator for the SRX. The Junos MIB is published with the Junos software for each release of Junos because it can change when new OIDs are added; just look at the download location. In terms of what MIBs you should be monitoring, Table 5-1 lists some that are of interest.

Table 5-1. MIBs that should be monitored

Feature	MIB title
Firewall Filters	`jnxFirewallsTable` `jnxFirewallCounterTable`

NAT	`jnxJsNatNotifications`
	`jnxJsNatObjects`
	`jnxJsNatTrapVars`
	`jnxJsNatMIB`

Security Policies	`jnxJsSecPolicyMIB`
	`jnxJsPolicyStatsTable` (*http://www.juniper.net/techpubs/en_US/junos12.1/topics/reference/general/jnxjspolicystatstable-nm-mib.html*)
	`jnxJsPolicyNotifications`
	`jnxJsPolicyObjects`
	`jnxJsPolicyTrapVars`

Feature	MIB title
Screens	jnxJsScreenMIB
IPsec	jnxIpSecFlowMonMIB jnxIkeTunnelTable jnxIPSecTunnelTable jnxIPSecSaTable
IPS	jnxJsIdpMIB jnxJsIdpAttackTable
UTM	jnxJsAntiVirus
Authentication	jnxUserAAAMibRoot jnxJsAuth
SPU Monitoring	jnxJsSPUMonitoringMIB
High Availability	jnxJsChassisCluster jnxJsChassisClusterSwitchover jnxJsChClusterIntfTrap
Interface/Security Stats	jnxJsIfMonEntry ifTable jnxJsIfMonTable
Configuration Management	jnxCfgMgmt
License MIB	jnxLicenseInstallTable

The list in Table 5-1 is not complete, and in reality you will need to actually view the MIB objects themselves in a MIB browser to provide the full detailed description for each object that is part of the MIB. The good news is that you can download all the MIBs for each SRX release under the documentation for each SRX release. Then, load up the MIB into a MIB browser like iReasoning or OID's MIB Browser. Commercial SNMP monitoring tools typically also have mechanisms to import MIBs and select what values to pull.

One nifty trick is that you don't actually need to use a separate MIB browser to view the actual values on the SRX; you can just use the `show snmp mib walk <OID>` command to crawl the MIB structure and pull all values under it. Here we can see the output of looking at an SRX3600 with seven SPCs in slots 3–9. You can see the CPU, Memory, Session, Max Session, and CP Session values.

```
root@srx3600n0> show snmp mib walk jnxJsSPUMonitoringMIB
jnxJsSPUMonitoringFPCIndex.3 = 3
jnxJsSPUMonitoringFPCIndex.4 = 4
jnxJsSPUMonitoringFPCIndex.5 = 5
jnxJsSPUMonitoringFPCIndex.6 = 6
jnxJsSPUMonitoringFPCIndex.7 = 7
jnxJsSPUMonitoringFPCIndex.8 = 8
jnxJsSPUMonitoringFPCIndex.9 = 9
jnxJsSPUMonitoringSPUIndex.3 = 0
```

```
jnxJsSPUMonitoringSPUIndex.4 = 0
jnxJsSPUMonitoringSPUIndex.5 = 0
jnxJsSPUMonitoringSPUIndex.6 = 0
jnxJsSPUMonitoringSPUIndex.7 = 0
jnxJsSPUMonitoringSPUIndex.8 = 0
jnxJsSPUMonitoringSPUIndex.9 = 0
jnxJsSPUMonitoringCPUUsage.3 = 0
jnxJsSPUMonitoringCPUUsage.4 = 0
jnxJsSPUMonitoringCPUUsage.5 = 0
jnxJsSPUMonitoringCPUUsage.6 = 0
jnxJsSPUMonitoringCPUUsage.7 = 0
jnxJsSPUMonitoringCPUUsage.8 = 0
jnxJsSPUMonitoringCPUUsage.9 = 0
jnxJsSPUMonitoringMemoryUsage.3 = 69
jnxJsSPUMonitoringMemoryUsage.4 = 68
jnxJsSPUMonitoringMemoryUsage.5 = 68
jnxJsSPUMonitoringMemoryUsage.6 = 68
jnxJsSPUMonitoringMemoryUsage.7 = 68
jnxJsSPUMonitoringMemoryUsage.8 = 69
jnxJsSPUMonitoringMemoryUsage.9 = 69
jnxJsSPUMonitoringCurrentFlowSession.3 = 0
jnxJsSPUMonitoringCurrentFlowSession.4 = 0
jnxJsSPUMonitoringCurrentFlowSession.5 = 0
jnxJsSPUMonitoringCurrentFlowSession.6 = 0
jnxJsSPUMonitoringCurrentFlowSession.7 = 0
jnxJsSPUMonitoringCurrentFlowSession.8 = 0
jnxJsSPUMonitoringCurrentFlowSession.9 = 0
jnxJsSPUMonitoringMaxFlowSession.3 = 131072
jnxJsSPUMonitoringMaxFlowSession.4 = 262144
jnxJsSPUMonitoringMaxFlowSession.5 = 262144
jnxJsSPUMonitoringMaxFlowSession.6 = 262144
jnxJsSPUMonitoringMaxFlowSession.7 = 262144
jnxJsSPUMonitoringMaxFlowSession.8 = 262144
jnxJsSPUMonitoringMaxFlowSession.9 = 262144
jnxJsSPUMonitoringCurrentCPSession.3 = 0
jnxJsSPUMonitoringCurrentCPSession.4 = 0
jnxJsSPUMonitoringCurrentCPSession.5 = 0
jnxJsSPUMonitoringCurrentCPSession.6 = 0
jnxJsSPUMonitoringCurrentCPSession.7 = 0
jnxJsSPUMonitoringCurrentCPSession.8 = 0
jnxJsSPUMonitoringCurrentCPSession.9 = 0
jnxJsSPUMonitoringMaxCPSession.3 = 2359296
jnxJsSPUMonitoringMaxCPSession.4 = 0
jnxJsSPUMonitoringMaxCPSession.5 = 0
jnxJsSPUMonitoringMaxCPSession.6 = 0
jnxJsSPUMonitoringMaxCPSession.7 = 0
jnxJsSPUMonitoringMaxCPSession.8 = 0
jnxJsSPUMonitoringMaxCPSession.9 = 0
jnxJsSPUMonitoringNodeIndex.3 = 0
jnxJsSPUMonitoringNodeIndex.4 = 0
jnxJsSPUMonitoringNodeIndex.5 = 0
jnxJsSPUMonitoringNodeIndex.6 = 0
```

```
jnxJsSPUMonitoringNodeIndex.7 = 0
jnxJsSPUMonitoringNodeIndex.8 = 0
jnxJsSPUMonitoringNodeIndex.9 = 0
jnxJsSPUMonitoringNodeDescr.3 = single
jnxJsSPUMonitoringNodeDescr.4 = single
jnxJsSPUMonitoringNodeDescr.5 = single
jnxJsSPUMonitoringNodeDescr.6 = single
jnxJsSPUMonitoringNodeDescr.7 = single
jnxJsSPUMonitoringNodeDescr.8 = single
jnxJsSPUMonitoringNodeDescr.9 = single
jnxJsSPUMonitoringCurrentTotalSession.0 = 0
jnxJsSPUMonitoringMaxTotalSession.0 = 1703936
jnxJsClusterMonitoringNodeIndex.0 = 0
jnxJsClusterMonitoringNodeDescr.0 = single
jnxJsNodeCurrentTotalSession.0 = 0
jnxJsNodeMaxTotalSession.0 = 1703936
jnxJsNodeSessionCreationPerSecond.0 = 0
```

Networking Services

The SRX is a very powerful platform that can not only offer services to manage itself, but also provide functionality on the network itself. The SRX itself will use services like Network Time Protocol (NTP), DNS, and possibly DHCP, but it can also leverage those to provide these services on the data plane. In this section, we discuss the configuration for primary system services that the SRX operates.

Network Time Protocol

The importance of using NTP on the SRX cannot be overstated! It's always a best practice to leverage proper timekeeping on any computer system, but for the SRX it is even more important. For starters, without proper timekeeping, the clocks will drift, making your security logs and platform events out of sync with the actual time, in turn making troubleshooting more difficult. Next, when using some time-based features like schedulers, not having NTP properly sync the time will mean that you might have security policies activated at incorrect times. Finally, on the HE SRX, the SPUs have to use NTP to get updates on the SPUs in the data plane. Without this, it can cause issues with features like IPsec and others. To make life simple, use NTP!

Manually configuring SRX time

When you are getting the system set up initially, it can be helpful to manually set the date and time, especially when the SRX isn't fully on the network. The time will be kept even when power is off using the lithium battery on the control plane (assuming it doesn't fail), but it is still a good idea to run NTP to prevent clock drift.

```
root@srx3600n0> set date 201212151855.25
Sat Dec 15 18:55:25 UTC 2012
```

It's important to note that we are running this command in operational mode, not configuration mode, as this isn't entered into the configuration.

Configuring the SRX as an NTP client

In this example, we configure the SRX to get its time from an NTP server at IP address 192.168.1.20. We also trigger the NTP client to initiate a request manually.

```
[edit]
root@srx3600n0# set system ntp server 192.168.1.20

[edit]
root@srx3600n0# show system ntp
server 192.168.1.20;


[edit]
root@srx3600n0#commit

root@srx3600n0> set date ntp
 9 Dec 23:50:15 ntpdate[21105]: step time server 192.168.1.20 offset -0.000055
sec
```

As you can see, there isn't too much to the NTP Client configuration. There are some additional options to specify what version of NTP to use, what the source address is (to override the loopback interface/preferred interface address), and also to use authentication if you have that configured on your NTP server. You can trigger a manual NTP clock sync was we did previously. If you don't specify anything beyond "set date ntp" in operational mode, then it will sync from the first NTP server; otherwise, you can specify what server to sync from.

You might also notice that there is another option called "peer" rather than server in the NTP configuration. The difference is that the server option instructs the SRX to accept the time from the NTP server, whereas the peer statement instructs the SRX to do a symmetric time sync between it and the NTP server (which must also be configured for this).

Configuring the SRX as an NTP server

The SRX itself can act as a time server to clients on the network. Besides configuring the SRX to operate the NTP server and specify the parameters, you also need to make sure that the SRX is configured to allow inbound system services. This includes the following:

1. Enabling the system server per interface/zone.

2. Configuring a security policy (if using global/junos-host policies).
3. Configuring firewall filters to permit it (if using firewall filters on data plane interface/loopback interfaces).

For the SRX, there are two NTP modes: one is to broadcast the NTP traffic on each interface on which it is active and the other is to operate on demand. You merely need to leverage the broadcast option to do broadcast. So let's configure the SRX to get its time from NTP server 192.168.1.20 and to serve it on interface ge-0/0/0.0 in the trust zone.

```
[edit]
root@srx3600n0# set system ntp server 192.168.1.20

[edit]
root@srx3600n0# show system ntp
server 192.168.1.20;

[edit]
root@srx3600n0# set security zones security-zone trust interfaces ge-0/0/0.0
host-inbound-traffic system-services ntp

[edit]
root@srx3600n0# show security zones security-zone trust
interfaces {
    ge-0/0/0.0 {
        host-inbound-traffic {
            system-services {
                ntp;
            }
        }
    }
}
```

Wait a minute: what's the difference here between configuring the SRX as a client as opposed to a server, besides the fact that in the server mode, we're enabling the SRX to accept inbound connections for NTP on the ge-0/0/0.0 trust interface? The answer is that the SRX will implicitly act as a time server if you have configured it to get an upstream time source. You still need to configure the SRX to accept the inbound traffic on the respective interface or zone for the host-inbound traffic and, optionally, security policy and firewall filters if you are using them to filter inbound traffic to the device.

Domain Name System

We all know the benefits of leveraging DNS in our daily browsing lives. Without it, we'd be forced to memorize IP addresses for every server we want to access, it would be much harder to multiplex different web applications to the same server, and a lot of high availability would be limited without being able to serve up new addresses. When it comes to the SRX, it can act as a client for DNS, which is important so it can access resources by name. The SRX can also act as a DNS Proxy (or server) so that internal machines do not need to reference external servers directly. When acting as a DNS proxy, it can also be configured to rewrite certain requests if the DNS application layer gateway (ALG) is enabled.

Configuring the SRX as a DNS client

Using DNS is not a strict requirement to operate the SRX, but it makes it much easier than entering static name entries. Let's configure the SRX to get its DNS updates from server 192.168.1.20, but also make a static mapping for an internal host that doesn't have a DNS entry in the server; map ICMPServer.company.local to 192.168.1.30.

```
[edit]
root@srx3600n0# set system name-server 192.168.1.20

[edit]
root@srx3600n0# show system name-server
192.168.1.20;

[edit]
root@srx3600n0# set system static-host-mapping ICMPServer.company.local inet
192.168.1.30

[edit]
root@srx3600n0# show system static-host-mapping
ICMPServer.company.local inet 192.168.1.30;
```

As you can see, there is very little to configure when it comes to DNS as a client on the SRX; simply specify the nameserver and that's all. You can also specify more than one server if you wish. We also showed how to configure static-host mappings if you have an entry that must be hardcoded.

Configuring the SRX as a proxy server

The SRX can also be configured as a proxy server for internal clients. Let's configure an example that forwards DNS requests that are not known to public server 4.2.2.2, sets a max TTL of 600 seconds for any entry regardless of what TTL the server provides, and allows clients on interface ge-0/0/0.0 to query the SRX.

```
[edit]
root@srx3600n0# set system services dns forwarders 4.2.2.2

[edit]
root@srx3600n0# set system services dns max-cache-ttl 600

[edit]
root@srx3600n0# set security zones security-zone trust interfaces ge-0/0/0.0
host-inbound-traffic system-services dns

[edit]
```

```
root@srx3600n0# show system services dns
max-cache-ttl 600;
forwarders {
    4.2.2.2;
}

[edit]
root@srx3600n0# show security zones security-zone trust
interfaces {
    ge-0/0/0.0 {
        host-inbound-traffic {
            system-services {
                dns;
            }
        }
    }
}
```

Dynamic Host Configuration Protocol

The SRX supports DHCP both as a server to distribute IP address information to hosts on the connected subnet and as a DHCP client itself to receive an address from a server. There are truly far too many DHCP configurations to discuss in a single book. The Junos DHCP implementation is quite extensive and offers all sorts of capabilities to define custom DHCP options. In this section, we focus on the three most common DHCP configurations: the SRX as a DHCP server, the SRX as a DHCP client (most common on the branch SRX), and the SRX as a DHCP relay.

Configuring the SRX as a DHCP server

When it comes to defining a DHCP server, you need to define at least the subnet on which the server will be active (which will imply to the interface it should respond to DHCP requests) and the address range that should be served. Most commonly, you'll also define the gateway IP address, a DNS server, and the DHCP lease time, which is a good idea—particularly in a busy environment like a corporate environment or open access point where IP addresses can be used up quickly if not released when idle. In this example, we configure the SRX to serve up the IP addresses 172.16.1.2 through 172.16.1.253 on interface ge-0/0/1, which is in the Clients zone. The IP address of the clients interface is 172.16.1.1. Because this is on a corporate network, we set a four-hour lease time. Also, configure this pool to propagate the server configuration on interface ge-0/0/0.0, which we configure in the next example.

```
[edit]
root@srx3600n0# set system services dhcp pool 172.16.1.0/24 address-range low
172.16.1.2

[edit]
root@srx3600n0# set system services dhcp pool 172.16.1.0/24 address-range high
```

```
172.16.1.253

[edit]
root@srx3600n0# set system services dhcp pool 172.16.1.0/24 router 172.16.1.1

[edit]
root@srx3600n0# set system services dhcp pool 172.16.1.0/24 default-lease-time
14400

[edit]
root@srx3600n0# set system services dhcp pool 172.16.1.0/24 propagate-settings
ge-0/0/0.0

[edit]
root@srx3600n0# show system services dhcp
pool 172.16.1.0/24 {
    address-range low 172.16.1.2 high 172.16.1.253;
    default-lease-time 14400;
    router {
        172.16.1.1;
    }
    propagate-settings ge-0/0/0.0;
}

[edit]
root@srx3600n0# set interfaces ge-0/0/1 unit 0 family inet address 172.16.1.1/24

[edit]
root@srx3600n0# set security zones security-zone Clients interfaces ge-0/0/1
host-inbound-traffic system-services dhcp

[edit]
root@srx3600n0# show security zones security-zone Clients
interfaces {
    ge-0/0/1.0 {
        host-inbound-traffic {
            system-services {
                dhcp;
            }
        }
    }
}

[edit]
root@srx3600n0# show interfaces ge-0/0/1
unit 0 {
    family inet {
        address 172.16.1.1/24;
    }
}
```

Reviewing this example, we notice a few things. First, the DHCP server is defined under System Services. You see that you define DHCP on a subnet-by-subnet basis. The system infers what interface to use to respond to the DHCP requests based on the subnet being matched up to an interface subnet in the DHCP pool configuration. Within the DHCP pool, you must define the IP range to be handed out to clients. You can define addresses that should be excluded from the contiguous range, and you can also explicitly define IP-to-MAC address mapping for reserved addresses. Many fields and behaviors can be defined in the DHCP pool. In our example, we defined the most common options like the default gateway for the clients (router option), the nameservers that the clients should query (name-server), and a lease time. The SRX can even serve up custom DHCP options of your choosing!

The interesting thing, which is very easy to forget, is that when serving up DHCP on the SRX, you must enable DHCP on the zone configuration as an allowed system service. If not, the SRX will never send the DHCP query from the client up to the routing engine. This is very easy to overlook. Another thing that might not be overtly obvious is that the DHCP service is only configurable in the zone configuration under the interface host-inbound traffic configuration rather than at the zone level itself.

Configuring the SRX as a DHCP client

When the SRX is installed in a Customer Premise Equipment (CPE) use case, common in branch deployments, it often does not have a static predefined public IP address. The SRX does support not only serving up IP addresses, but also receiving them itself on an interface. Most often this is done on the Internet-facing interface.

In this example, we configure the ge-0/0/0 interface as a DHCP client to get an IP address from the upstream provider. Configure the DHCP client to update the DHCP server with the parameters received.

```
[edit]
root@srx3600n0# set interfaces ge-0/0/0 unit 0 family inet dhcp update-server

[edit]
root@srx3600n0# set security zones security-zone untrust interfaces ge-0/0/0.0
host-inbound-traffic system-services dhcp

[edit]
root@srx3600n0# show interfaces ge-0/0/0
unit 0 {
    family inet {
        dhcp {
            update-server;
        }
    }
}
```

```
[edit]
root@srx3600n0# show security zones security-zone untrust
interfaces {
    ge-0/0/0.0 {
        host-inbound-traffic {
            system-services {
                dhcp;
            }
        }
    }
}
```

In this example, we have defined the ge-0/0/0 interface to act as a DHCP client. The configuration is quite straightforward, as you can see. To add in the plug-and-play deployment of a CPE device, we update the server parameters with the upstream information (such as DNS servers) provided by the upstream provider server. Just like the DHCP server example, we must define the untrust zone to accept DHCP messages; otherwise, they will be blocked on the data plane itself.

Configuring the SRX as a DHCP relay server

DHCP is, by default, a broadcast protocol that is not ordinarily exchanged across Layer 3 boundaries. The issue here is that often you might want to have a central DHCP server that can control DHCP centrally rather than having every Layer 3 device be responsible for serving up DHCP addresses locally. Because DHCP is only provided at a Layer 3 boundary, each Layer 3 device must be able to accept the request and forward it on to the appropriate DHCP server. In this example, we configure the SRX to listen for DHCP requests on interface ge-0/0/3.0 in the Clients-2 zone and forward them to the server at IP address 10.1.0.2, which is off interface ge-0/0/4.0 in the Servers zone.

```
[edit]
root@srx3600n0# set forwarding-options helpers bootp interface ge-0/0/3.0 serv-
er 10.1.0.2

[edit]
root@srx3600n0#  set  security  zones  security-zone  Clients-2  interfaces
ge-0/0/3.0 host-inbound-traffic system-services dhcp

[edit]
root@srx3600n0# set security zones security-zone Servers interfaces ge-0/0/4.0
host-inbound-traffic system-services dhcp

[edit]
root@srx3600n0# show forwarding-options
helpers {
    bootp {
        interface {
            ge-0/0/3.0 {
                server 10.1.0.2;
```

```
            }
        }
    }
}

[edit]
root@srx3600n0# show security zones
security-zone Clients-2 {
    interfaces {
        ge-0/0/3.0 {
            host-inbound-traffic {
                system-services {
                    dhcp;
                }
            }
        }
    }
}
security-zone Servers {
    interfaces {
        ge-0/0/4.0 {
            host-inbound-traffic {
                system-services {
                    dhcp;
                }
            }
        }
    }
}
```

In this example, we see that the DHCP Server Relay configuration is primarily configured under the "set forwarding-options helpers" configuration. Here, you define the interface that the SRX should listen to for the inbound DHCP request along with the IP address of the DHCP server to which all requests should be forwarded. The interesting thing in this example is that we must configure DHCP in the security zone host-inbound traffic configuration for both the interface that the traffic is received on along with the interface that requests are forwarded to the server (even if not on the same local interface as the server); otherwise, the SRX will drop the requests.

SRX Logging and Flow Records

Proper logging is one of the most important things that is often overlooked when it comes to firewall management. The SRX collects a great deal of information when processing firewall sessions; however, due to restrictions of storing this real-time information, after the session is complete, the information will be deleted from the system tables—with the exception of counters, which are usually too high level to get specific information about individual sessions. Logging provides you a way to export this information to an external system for logging, reporting, security intelligence, forensics, and other traffic visibility functions. The SRX leverages three types of syslog formats for this function, along with JFlow record export. The SRX can log information sourced from both the control plane and data plane—including sending the information externally or storing it locally on the control plane. In this section, we explore both control plane and data plane logging, and how to export it.

Control Plane Versus Data Plane Logs

As we mentioned, you can log messages from both the control plan and the data plane. So what's the difference? Following the traditional Junos theme, the control plane logs have to do with events triggered by daemons on the control plane. This includes messages about the underlying hardware (chassisd), general-purpose messages (messages), and various protocol daemons like IDPD, appidd, and so on. Control plane logging is on by default to log locally, but you can override this with your own logfiles, syslog hosts, and criteria for different log messages. All logs are stored in the */var/log* directory on the control plane.

Data plane logs, on the other hand, are primarily those generated by components that process traffic on the data plane. These include the firewall logs (RT_LOG, which stands for Real-Time Log because it is not stored on the data plane) from the flowd process, IPS logs, UTM logs, and logs from other security components like Screens. Data plane logging is off by default and must be configured. Typically, it is recommended that you send logs off the SRX to a syslog host due to the large volume of logs that can be generated from the data plane, particularly on high-end SRX platforms like the 5800. In fact, it can take an entire infrastructure of syslog servers to handle the large volume of syslog messages that the high-end SRX can generate per second. For this reason, there are two different mechanisms that we can use to log messages to the control plane, as discussed in the next section.

Data plane logs: Event versus Stream mode

The data plane supports two different ways to log messages. The first is Event mode, in which all log messages are logged to the control plane through the internal SRX infrastructure that lets the data plane communicate with the control plane—you need only configure Event mode along with a few optional settings and the logs will flow to the control plane. The other mode, Stream mode, is preferred. This logs messages directly from the data plane to an external source. The benefit of this that the SRX can log at extremely high rates (into the hundreds of thousands of logs per second). This is especially important when dealing with the distributed architecture of the high-end SRX. Of course, this is true of other security platforms as well—it is simply a difficult proposition to store large volumes of logs for historical purposes, particularly in high-demand environments.

At the time of writing this book, the SRX can only log to the control plane (Event mode) or log out the data plane (Stream mode) at one time, so it is generally recommended to log out the data plane to an external syslog server.

Configuring control plane logging on the SRX

As we mentioned, control plane logs are enabled by default on the SRX and also allow you to configure your own logs to capture information as you see fit. In this example, we leverage three control plane logs.

First, we modify the default logfile *interactive-commands* to display only the commands that were logged, rather than showing their entire contents. Second, we log all security logs on the SRX of any severity to a file called *Severity* that will archive up to ten 1 million-byte files that can only be read by root. Finally, we log all control plane logs to our STRM server at host 192.168.1.100 port 514 using structured syslog.

```
[edit system syslog]
root@srx3600n0# set file interactive-commands match "command"

[edit system syslog]
root@srx3600n0# set file Security security any

[edit system syslog]
root@srx3600n0#  set  file  Security  archive  files  10  size  1000000  no-world-
readable

[edit system syslog]
root@srx3600n0# set host 192.168.1.100 port 514 any any

[edit system syslog]
root@srx3600n0# show
host 192.168.1.100 {
    any any;
    port 514;
}
file messages {
    any notice;
    authorization info;
}
file interactive-commands {
    interactive-commands any;
    match command;
}
```

```
file default-log-messages {
    any any;
       match "(requested 'commit' operation)|(copying configuration to juni-
per.save)|ifAdminStatus|(FRU power)|(FRU removal)|(FRU insertion)|(link UP)|(vc
add)|(vc             delete)|transitioned|Transferred|transfer-file|QFABRIC_NET-
WORK_NODE_GROUP|QFABRIC_SERVER_NODE_GROUP|QFABRIC_NODE|(license  add)|(license
delete)|(package -X update)|(package -X delete)|GRES|CFMD_CCM_DEFECT";
    structured-data;
}
file Security {
    security any;
    archive size 1000000 files 10 no-world-readable;
}

root@srx3600n0> show log ?
Possible completions:
  <[Enter]>             Execute this command
  <filename>            Name of log file
  __jsrpd_commit_check__  Size: 52, Last changed: Dec 11 02:02:32
  appid-log             Size: 97042, Last changed: Apr 12 2011
  appidd                Size: 0, Last changed: May 28 2010
  authd_libstats        Size: 0, Last changed: Jul 27 2011
  authd_profilelib      Size: 0, Last changed: Nov 01 2009
  authd_sdb.log         Size: 232, Last changed: Nov 03 2010
  authlib_jdhcpd_trace.log  Size: 0, Last changed: Jul 05 11:14:04
  bin_messages          Size: 7, Last changed: Nov 01 2011
  chassisd              Size: 2237124, Last changed: Dec 21 23:45:26
  chassisd.0.gz         Size: 194195, Last changed: Nov 26 18:29:18
  cosd                  Size: 2078339, Last changed: Dec 21 00:07:50
  cscript.log           Size: 387, Last changed: May 28 2010
  dcd                   Size: 542271, Last changed: Dec 21 00:13:31
  debug-idp.log         Size: 105748, Last changed: Jun 07 2011
  default-log-messages  Size: 720210, Last changed: Dec 21 00:13:31
  default-log-messages.0.gz  Size: 129653, Last changed: Nov 20 05:15:00
  default-log-messages.1.gz  Size: 128204, Last changed: Nov 11 02:45:00
  dfwc                  Size: 0, Last changed: Nov 01 2009
  dfwd                  Size: 208, Last changed: May 29 2010
  e2e_capture           Size: 9, Last changed: Dec 21 00:07:19
  e2e_events            Size: 779, Last changed: Dec 21 00:13:17
  eccd                  Size: 0, Last changed: Nov 01 2009
  escript.log           Size: 1680, Last changed: Apr 15 2011
  ext/                  Last changed: Nov 01 2009
  flowc/                Last changed: Nov 01 2009
  flowlog               Size: 0, Last changed: Nov 30 2010
  fwauthd_chk_only      Size: 297, Last changed: Dec 11 02:02:32
  ggsn/                 Last changed: Nov 01 2009
  gprsd_chk_only        Size: 1135, Last changed: Dec 11 02:02:31
  gprsinfo_log          Size: 1136, Last changed: Sep 06 2011
  gres-tp               Size: 562248, Last changed: Dec 21 00:07:50
  group_db.log          Size: 0, Last changed: Jun 12 2011
  hostname-cached       Size: 11552, Last changed: Dec 11 02:02:34
```

```
httpd.log             Size: 5634, Last changed: Dec 23 23:33:05
httpd.log.old         Size: 8630, Last changed: Dec 21 00:04:45
idpd                  Size: 97394, Last changed: Jul 26 2011
idpd.addver           Size: 185, Last changed: Dec 21 00:17:03
ifstraced             Size: 1803, Last changed: Dec 11 02:02:31
ike                   Size: 17285, Last changed: Sep 23 2011
install               Size: 967, Last changed: Dec 11 02:00:15
install.0.gz          Size: 541, Last changed: Nov 27 15:16:53
install.1.gz          Size: 543, Last changed: Nov 26 18:29:17
install.2.gz          Size: 819, Last changed: Nov 11 00:09:22
install.3.gz          Size: 905, Last changed: Nov 06 23:19:04
interactive-commands  Size: 458242, Last changed: Dec 23 23:54:32
interactive-commands.0.gz  Size: 70463, Last changed: Nov 27 17:30:00
inventory             Size: 833339, Last changed: Dec 21 00:13:31
jdhcpd_era_discover.log  Size: 594, Last changed: Jul 05 13:08:17
jdhcpd_era_discover.log.0  Size: 594, Last changed: Jul 05 11:14:25
jdhcpd_era_discover.log.1  Size: 0, Last changed: Jul 05 11:14:04
jdhcpd_era_solicit.log  Size: 593, Last changed: Jul 05 13:08:17
jdhcpd_era_solicit.log.0  Size: 593, Last changed: Jul 05 11:14:25
jdhcpd_era_solicit.log.1  Size: 0, Last changed: Jul 05 11:14:04
jdhcpd_profilelib     Size: 0, Last changed: Jul 05 11:14:04
jdhcpd_sdb.log        Size: 0, Last changed: Jul 05 11:14:04
jsrpd                 Size: 942785, Last changed: Dec 21 00:13:31
jsrpd_chk_only        Size: 43, Last changed: May 28 2010
kmd                   Size: 800700, Last changed: Dec 21 00:13:31
kmd.0.gz              Size: 37342, Last changed: Dec 16 16:08:37
license               Size: 240, Last changed: May 28 2010
license_subs_trace.log  Size: 242501, Last changed: Dec 21 00:07:50
lsys-cpu-utilization-log  Size: 0, Last changed: Oct 19 2011
mastership            Size: 279307, Last changed: Dec 21 00:07:18
messages              Size: 522982, Last changed: Dec 23 23:54:32
messages.0.gz         Size: 82394, Last changed: Dec 20 21:15:00
messages.1.gz         Size: 112586, Last changed: Dec 11 02:15:00
messages.2.gz         Size: 107409, Last changed: Nov 26 20:30:00
messages.3.gz         Size: 138088, Last changed: Nov 12 18:30:00
messages.4.gz         Size: 104667, Last changed: Nov 11 01:30:00
messages.5.gz         Size: 68982, Last changed: Nov 09 18:00:00
named                 Size: 0, Last changed: Oct 17 14:27:16
nsd_chk_only          Size: 39556, Last changed: Dec 20 18:59:45
nstraced_chk_only     Size: 736, Last changed: Dec 11 02:02:32
op-script.log         Size: 4789122, Last changed: Dec 23 19:27:54
pcre_db.log           Size: 0, Last changed: Jun 12 2011
pf                    Size: 17792, Last changed: Dec 11 02:02:28
pfed                  Size: 167586, Last changed: Dec 21 00:07:50
pfed_jdhcpd_trace.log  Size: 0, Last changed: Jul 05 11:14:04
pfed_trace.log        Size: 0, Last changed: Nov 01 2009
pgmd                  Size: 10471, Last changed: Dec 11 02:02:33
rexp_db.log           Size: 2630, Last changed: Apr 20 2012
rpc.log               Size: 1188687, Last changed: Oct 18 2011
rtlogd                Size: 755636, Last changed: Dec 21 00:07:12
sampled               Size: 5461, Last changed: May 28 2010
sdxd                  Size: 0, Last changed: Nov 01 2009
```

```
  secdb_db.log          Size: 7557, Last changed: Jul 06 20:42:25
  slbd                  Size: 1806553, Last changed: Dec 23 23:48:09
  slbd_chk_only         Size: 546, Last changed: Apr 04 2012
  slbd_opcmd            Size: 0, Last changed: Dec 21 00:07:47
  smartd.trace          Size: 71914, Last changed: Dec 23 20:11:28
  snapshot              Size: 1955, Last changed: May 20 2012
  test-file             Size: 0, Last changed: Apr 11 2011
  user                  Show recent user logins
  utmp                  Size: 0, Last changed: Nov 01 2009
  wtmp                  Size: 210028, Last changed: Dec 23 23:54:25
  wtmp.0.gz             Size: 3372, Last changed: Dec 06 22:19:26
  wtmp.1.gz             Size: 27, Last changed: Nov 06 22:49:46
  |                     Pipe through a command

root@srx3600n0> show log interactive-commands
Nov 27 17:32:05  srx3600n0 mgd[1952]: UI_CMDLINE_READ_LINE: User 'root', com-
mand 'show security idp attack table | no-more '
Nov 27 17:32:06  srx3600n0 mgd[1955]: UI_CMDLINE_READ_LINE: User 'root', com-
mand 'show security idp counters packet | no-more '
Nov 27 17:32:07  srx3600n0 mgd[1958]: UI_CMDLINE_READ_LINE: User 'root', com-
mand 'show security idp counters memory | no-more '
Nov 27 17:32:07  srx3600n0 mgd[1961]: UI_CMDLINE_READ_LINE: User 'root', com-
mand 'show security idp counters flow | no-more '
Nov 27 17:32:08  srx3600n0 mgd[1964]: UI_CMDLINE_READ_LINE: User 'root', com-
mand 'show security idp counters application-identification | no-more '
Nov 27 17:32:08  srx3600n0 mgd[1967]: UI_CMDLINE_READ_LINE: User 'root', com-
mand 'clear security idp counters packet '
Nov 27 17:32:09  srx3600n0 mgd[1970]: UI_CMDLINE_READ_LINE: User 'root', com-
mand 'clear security idp counters flow '
Nov 27 17:32:09  srx3600n0 mgd[1973]: UI_CMDLINE_READ_LINE: User 'root', com-
mand 'clear security idp counters application-identification '
Nov 27 17:32:10  srx3600n0 mgd[1976]: UI_CMDLINE_READ_LINE: User 'root', com-
mand 'clear security idp attack table '
Nov 27 17:32:11  srx3600n0 mgd[1979]: UI_CMDLINE_READ_LINE: User 'root', com-
mand 'clear security flow session '
```

As you can see from the preceding output, we have modified the predefined log *interactive-commands* to only log commands that are entered on the platform, along with defining a log called Security that logs any security-related events, and we defined the SRX to log all control plane messages to our STRM server at 192.168.1.100. You can view any logs by using the `show log` command followed by the name of the logfile in the */var/log* directory. The SRX will compress logs and append a chronological number as part of the archive process, and the `show log` command will automatically decompress these. You can also leverage the standard Junos output modifiers by using the `pipe` command following the `show log` command. For instance, we can view the contents of *interactive-commands*, which include clear, as follows:

```
root@srx3600n0> show log interactive-commands | ?
Possible completions:
  count                 Count occurrences
  display               Show additional kinds of information
```

```
    except                  Show only text that does not match a pattern
    find                    Search for first occurrence of pattern
    hold                    Hold text without exiting the --More-- prompt
    last                    Display end of output only
    match                   Show only text that matches a pattern
    no-more                 Don't paginate output
    request                 Make system-level requests
    resolve                 Resolve IP addresses
    save                    Save output text to file
    trim                    Trim specified number of columns from start of line

root@srx3600n0> show log interactive-commands | match clear
Nov 27 17:32:08   srx3600n0 mgd[1967]: UI_CMDLINE_READ_LINE: User 'root', com-
mand 'clear security idp counters packet '
Nov 27 17:32:09   srx3600n0 mgd[1970]: UI_CMDLINE_READ_LINE: User 'root', com-
mand 'clear security idp counters flow '
Nov 27 17:32:09   srx3600n0 mgd[1973]: UI_CMDLINE_READ_LINE: User 'root', com-
mand 'clear security idp counters application-identification '
Nov 27 17:32:10   srx3600n0 mgd[1976]: UI_CMDLINE_READ_LINE: User 'root', com-
mand 'clear security idp attack table '
Nov 27 17:32:11   srx3600n0 mgd[1979]: UI_CMDLINE_READ_LINE: User 'root', com-
mand 'clear security flow session '
Nov 27 17:32:35   srx3600n0 mgd[1982]: UI_CMDLINE_READ_LINE: User 'root', com-
mand 'clear services application-identification application-system-cache '
Nov 27 17:35:24   srx3600n0 mgd[2020]: UI_CMDLINE_READ_LINE: User 'root', com-
mand 'clear security idp counters packet '
Nov 27 17:35:25   srx3600n0 mgd[2023]: UI_CMDLINE_READ_LINE: User 'root', com-
mand 'clear security idp counters flow '
Nov 27 17:35:26   srx3600n0 mgd[2026]: UI_CMDLINE_READ_LINE: User 'root', com-
mand 'clear security idp counters application-identification '
Nov 27 17:35:26   srx3600n0 mgd[2029]: UI_CMDLINE_READ_LINE: User 'root', com-
mand 'clear security idp attack table '
```

Configuring Stream mode logging on the data plane

Stream mode is preferred for data plane logging on the SRX due to the architecture and massive rate of logs that can be produced. Configuring Stream mode is very simple: you simply define the stream properties, and define the IP address/port of the syslog collector along with the format of the logs. There are optional properties for source address, category (SRX Branch), and severity filters as well. In this example, we configure the data plane logs to send to the STRM server with structured syslog on IP address 192.168.1.100 port 514.

```
[edit]
root@srx3600n0# set security log mode stream source-address 192.168.1.1 format
sd-syslog stream STRM-192.168.1.100 host 192.168.1.100 port 514

[edit]
root@srx3600n0# show security log
mode stream;
format sd-syslog;
```

```
    source-address 192.168.1.1;
    stream STRM-192.168.1.100 {
        host {
            192.168.1.100;
            port 514;
        }
    }
```

Let's analyze this output. At the root level of "security log" we have defined the mode to be Stream. As we mentioned earlier, at the time of writing this book, the SRX can only be in either Stream mode (log out the data plane) or Event mode (log from the data plane to the control plane) at one time. There are four different log formats at the time of writing this book: standard syslog, structured syslog, Webtrends Log Format (WELF), and binary syslog. Here we have chosen to use structured syslog, which is by far the most common. By default, the SRX will assign the source address to whatever the egress interface is for the data plane logs, but for other reasons, you might want the source address to show up as something else on your syslog collector (e.g., the IP address of your loopback interface). Finally, we have defined our "stream" object, which is called STRM-192.168.1.100 (the name is arbitrary), along with the IP/port of the collector.

Syslog format types

Regarding the different types of syslog formats, the overall function and differences are as follows:

Standard
: Messages are sent exactly as generated in the system as an ASCII text string.

Structured
: Similar to standard syslog but each field is prepended with a label, such as `source-address=192.168.1.1`; standard syslog would just list the IP address itself, 192.168.1.1, and not prepend the label. Structured is best leveraged, particularly when using third-party syslog servers that might not know which field applies to which value. By leveraging the label of structured syslog, a third-party product can receive the information without any special configuration and parse it. Like standard syslog, it is ASCII based, although it does use more bytes than standard syslog due to labeling each field.

Binary
: Binary syslog is a relatively new feature that is the best of both worlds of structured and standard syslog, but at a reduced byte count. As we mentioned, standard syslog and structured syslog are in ASCII format as text, which means that they are not efficient when it comes to log volume, particularly at high speed. Binary is a predefined log format defined by a log dictionary (provided by Juniper on the download site per version) that defines exactly which bit fields stand for which value so the SRX does not need to use any labels, but can leverage binary versus ASCII,

resulting in dramatically smaller logs. For instance, if we were to represent an IP address in 8-bit ASCII, the IP address field for `source-address=192.168.1.1` would be 11 bytes in standard syslog (ASCII for the IP address 192.168.1.1.), 26 bytes for structured (due to the 11 bytes of the IP address + the 15-byte label), or 4 bytes for binary because it would list out the IP address directly in binary bit notation and would not need to use any label, as each bit of the message maps to a predefined field as defined by the dictionary file, which must be installed on the syslog collector. This format is promising, but does require support for binary logging which isn't supported by all third-party platforms.

WELF
Similar to structured but provides a specific ASCII format for exchanging logs. This is best leveraged with Webtrends reporting servers.

Configuring Event mode logging to the control plane

When dealing with smaller SRX deployments or in environments without a syslog server, you can use Event mode logging to log all data plane logs to the control plane through an internal channel rather than out the data plane. This is known as Event mode logging. As we mentioned, you can only log in Stream or Event mode at one time on the SRX. In this example, we log all data plane logs to the control plane, along with making a few custom logfiles to catch any firewall and IPS logs in their own file. To ensure that we don't overwhelm the control plane, we limit this to 100 logs a second (note that this number is arbitrary; the SRX supports up to 1,500 logs per second today, just for the sake of example).

```
root@srx3600n0# set system syslog file IPS any any

[edit]
root@srx3600n0# set system syslog file IPS match "IDP_ATTACK_LOG_EVENT"

[edit]
root@srx3600n0# set system syslog file FW any any

[edit]
root@srx3600n0# set system syslog file FW match "RT_FLOW"


[edit]
root@srx3600n0# show system syslog
file IPS {
    any any;
    match IDP_ATTACK_LOG_EVENT;
}
file FW {
    any any;
    match RT_FLOW;
}
```

```
[edit]
root@srx3600n0# show security log
mode event;
event-rate 100;
```

In this example, we defined mode Event and then defined two new logfiles on the control plane that will match text for our respective security facilities. We can then use the `show log IPS` or `show log FW` commands to view the contents of these files, including other pipe facilities and the monitor start/stop command to tail the files.

If you are logging in Event mode to the control plane, you can still send data plane logs to a syslog server, you just have to use the standard control plane syslog facilities to do so. For instance, you would configure logging in Event mode as shown in the previous example, then under the `set system syslog` stanza you can define a host to send logs to. This can be all logs (including control plane logs) or you could write filters to only send specific logs to specific hosts or files locally. Although this isn't the best option when it comes to performance, if your logging rates are not high, it can provide an alternative to logging all data plane logs out the data plane.

There is one other important item to note: unless you are configuring Event mode logging and sending the logs out the control plane as we just described, if you want to log both the control plane logs and the data plane logs to external syslog servers, this does require the two configurations, one under `set system syslog` for the control plane logs and one under `set security log` for the data plane logs, even if they go to the same destination. Because this causes the separation of the control plane and data plane, there is just a bit more complexity.

Tips for Viewing Syslog Messages

Feeling lost in determining what logs you want to capture or how they are formatted? The good news is that Juniper documents these in the System Log Reference available with each version of Junos as well as on the system itself. For instance, let's say you want to learn more about the log format for IPS attack logs, but you are not sure where they exist or how they are formatted. We can use the `help` command to determine this formation.

```
root@srx3600n0> help syslog IDP?
Possible completions:
  <syslog-tag>         System log tag or regular expression
  IDP_APPDDOS_APP_ATTACK_EVENT  LOG_PFE,IDP: DDOS attack on application
  IDP_APPDDOS_APP_ATTACK_EVENT_LS  LOG_PFE,IDP: DDOS attack on application
   IDP_APPDDOS_APP_STATE_EVENT  LOG_PFE,IDP: DDOS application state transition
event
```

```
  IDP_APPDDOS_APP_STATE_EVENT_LS  LOG_PFE,IDP: DDOS application state transi-
tion event
  IDP_ATTACK_LOG_EVENT_LS  LOG_PFE,IDP attack log
  IDP_COMMIT_COMPLETED  LOG_AUTH,IDP policy commit completed
  IDP_COMMIT_FAILED    LOG_AUTH,IDP commit exited with failure
  IDP_DAEMON_INIT_FAILED  LOG_AUTH,Failed to initialize IDP daemon
  IDP_IGNORED_IPV6_ADDRESSES  LOG_AUTH,IDP ingnores IPv6 addresses
  IDP_INTERNAL_ERROR   LOG_AUTH,IDP daemon encountered an internal error.
  IDP_POLICY_COMPILATION_FAILED  LOG_AUTH,IDP policy compilation failed
  IDP_POLICY_LOAD_FAILED  LOG_AUTH,Failed to load an IDP policy
  IDP_POLICY_LOAD_SUCCEEDED  LOG_AUTH,IDP policy loaded successfully
  IDP_POLICY_UNLOAD_FAILED  LOG_AUTH,Failed to unload an IDP policy
  IDP_POLICY_UNLOAD_SUCCEEDED  LOG_AUTH,IDP policy unloaded successfully
  IDP_SCHEDULEDUPDATE_START_FAILED  LOG_AUTH,Failed to start scheduled update
  IDP_SCHEDULED_UPDATE_STARTED  LOG_AUTH,Scheduled update has started
  IDP_SECURITY_INSTALL_RESULT  LOG_AUTH,IDP security package install result
  IDP_SESSION_LOG_EVENT  LOG_PFE,IDP session event log
  IDP_SESSION_LOG_EVENT_LS  LOG_PFE,IDP session event log
  IDP_SIGNATURE_LICENSE_EXPIRED  LOG_AUTH,IDP signature update license key has
expired
root@srx3600n0> help syslog IDP_ATTACK_LOG_EVENT_LS
Name:          IDP_ATTACK_LOG_EVENT_LS
Message:       Lsys <logical-system-name>: IDP: At <epoch-time>, <message-type>
Attack  log  <<source-address>/<source-port>-><destination-address>/<destination-
port>> for <protocol-name> protocol and service
                <service-name> application <application-name> by rule <rule-
name>  of  rulebase  <rulebase-name>  in  policy  <policy-name>.  attack:
repeat=<repeat-count>, action=<action>,
               threat-severity=<threat-severity>, name=<attack-name>, NAT <<nat-
source-address>:<nat-source-port>-><nat-destination-address>:<nat-destination-
port>>, time-elapsed=<elapsed-time>,
                          inbytes=<inbound-bytes>,  outbytes=<outbound-bytes>,
inpackets=<inbound-packets>, outpackets=<outbound-packets>,
                intf:<source-zone-name>:<source-interface-name>-><destination-
zone-name>:<destination-interface-name>,  packet-log-id:  <packet-log-id>  and
misc-message <message>
Help:          IDP attack log
Description:   IDP Attack log generated for attack
Type:          Event: This message reports an event, not an error
Severity:      info
Facility:      LOG_PFE
```

Here we can see all of the different types of logs, and if you drill into the logs, you can see the message format, which provides the template for the log messages that will be sent, along with some meta information about the log type that can be helpful. This is not at all limited to IDP; you can do this for any standard log message that Junos generates (meaning debug messages are typically not covered here).

JFlow on the SRX

The SRX platform supports exporting flow records in the JFlow format to an external flow collector like the STRM. JFlow provides sampled packets that can be analyzed by the flow collector. Although the traffic is sampled rather than sending every packet, it can still provide a great deal of visibility to the flow collector, and very advanced systems like STRM and Arbor Peakflow provide network intelligence based on the behaviors (and changes in behavior) seen in the network platform.

In this example, we configure JFlow to sample 1 in every 100 packets, up to 500 packets per second on interface xe-0/1/0. This will be exported to our STRM at 192.168.1.50 on UDP port 2055 (the standard JFlow port) using JFlow version 8.

```
[edit]
root@srx3600n0# set interfaces xe-0/1/0 unit 0 family inet sampling input

[edit]
root@srx3600n0# set interfaces xe-0/1/0 unit 0 family inet sampling output

[edit]
root@srx3600n0#  set  interfaces  xe-0/1/0  unit  0  family  inet  address
192.168.2.1/24

 [edit]
root@srx3600n0# set forwarding-options sampling input ?
Possible completions:
+ apply-groups         Groups from which to inherit configuration data
+ apply-groups-except  Don't inherit configuration data from these groups
  max-packets-per-second  Threshold of samples per second before dropping
  maximum-packet-length  Maximum length of the sampled packet (0..9192 bytes)
  rate                 Ratio of packets to be sampled (1 out of N) (1..65535)
  run-length           Number of samples after initial trigger (0..20)

[edit]
root@srx3600n0# set forwarding-options sampling input rate 100

[edit]
root@srx3600n0# set forwarding-options sampling input max-packets-per-second 500

[edit]
root@srx3600n0# set forwarding-options sampling family inet output flow-server
192.168.1.50 ?
Possible completions:
  <[Enter]>            Execute this command
> aggregation            Aggregations to perform for exported flows (version 8
only)
+ apply-groups         Groups from which to inherit configuration data
+ apply-groups-except  Don't inherit configuration data from these groups
  autonomous-system-type  Type of autonomous system number to export
  local-dump           Dump cflowd records to log file before exporting
  no-local-dump        Don't dump cflowd records to log file before exporting
```

```
  port                  UDP port number on host collecting cflowd packets
  source-address        Source IPv4 address for cflowd packets
  version               Format of exported cflowd aggregates
  |                     Pipe through a command

[edit]
root@srx3600n0# set forwarding-options sampling family inet output flow-server
192.168.1.50 version ?
Possible completions:
  5                     Export cflowd aggregates in version 5 format
  500                   Export cflowd aggregates in ASN 500 format
  8                     Export cflowd aggregates in version 8 format

[edit]
root@srx3600n0# set forwarding-options sampling family inet output flow-server
192.168.1.50 version 8 port 2055


[edit]
root@srx3600n0# show interfaces xe-0/1/0
unit 0 {
    family inet {
        sampling {
            input;
            output;
        }
        address 192.168.2.1/24;
    }
}
[edit]
root@srx3600n0# show forwarding-options sampling
input {
    rate 100;
    max-packets-per-second 500;
}
family inet {
    output {
        flow-server 192.168.1.50 {
            port 2055;
            version 8;
        }
    }
}
```

Let's break down this example a bit, as there are a lot of different configuration elements that are possible here. First, you need to enable flow sampling at an interface level. You can do so holistically, as we have, by enabling sampling in the input or output direction of the interface (ingress or egress, respectively, per interface). This will not distinguish any packets. If you want to selectively choose which packets to sample, that can be done with stateless firewall filters with the sample action.

Next, you need to define how many packets should be logged, and this is a very important detail. There are a few different options here, the first being the rate. This is calculated as 1:X where X is the rate that you define. If you selected a rate of 1 (1:1), then it would log every packet. This is a very bad idea! Ideally you should be sampling something much higher. The exact number depends on the needs of your flow collector, the amount of traffic passing through the device, and what you're trying to accomplish. There are specialized platforms like Niksun if you need true line speed packet capture. The purpose of JFlow is to sample packets to give an approximation of network behavior rather than sample every packet. Next, to ensure that the system does not get overwhelmed (because a sample rate of even 1:100 can be high at, say, 10 Gbps, which would be 100 Mbps of sampled packets), you can define a maximum sampled PPS rate. Although we did not do it in this example, you can define the maximum packet size to sample (e.g., don't sample jumbo frames by limiting the maximum packet size to 1,514 bytes) or to define how many packets to log for a flow before stopping.

Finally, you must define what you want to do with the collected packets. You can actually log them locally, log them both locally and to a server, or log them to just a server. Additionally, the SRX supports performing some aggregation. In most cases, you typically want to export the logs to a flow collection server like the STRM. You must define what the IP address and port is, and you can also define what version of JFlow to use [see NetFlow Wiki (*http://en.wikipedia.org/wiki/NetFlow*) for more detail on the differences]. You can also define what source address the packets should be marked with, whether to log the information locally, and whether to tag the AS number in the data (if BGP is used).

At the time of writing this book, the high-end SRX supports versions 5 and 8, and the branch SRX supports 5, 8, and 9. Keep posted with the release notes for changes in supported versions and feature support.

Best Practices

This chapter covers a wide range of topics for system services, so we will list a few of the best practices when it comes to configuring system services on the SRX.

- It is really important to keep proper time on the SRX. The best way to do this is to leverage NTP. This is especially important on the high-end SRX, which relies on NTP to sync the individual SPCs to ensure a common clock, but is important for many other features and is generally a best practice.
- Logging is a critical feature for any security administrator to perform. On the SRX, there are two logging systems: one on the control plane and one on the data plane. Both should be configured to log to an external system like an STRM, Security Intelligence, or third-party syslog receiver so that logs can be retained for historical

purposes. Although the SRX can log both control plane and data plane logs locally to the control plane, this is not a best practice as it has more performance impact and the SRX is not designed to store information long term at high logging rates.

- We discussed management services on the SRX. In most cases, it is ideal to support encrypted communication like SSH and HTTPS over Telnet and HTTP for security purposes. Additionally, it is always best to leverage fxp0 for out-of-band management wherever possible rather than in-band management on the data plane. There are a few reasons for this. First, if the data plane becomes unavailable due to a network incident or DoS attack, the control plane will still likely be available. Next, it allows you to configure a much more restrictive configuration on the data plane in terms of management, including disabling management services entirely.
- SNMP is a very powerful tool for network administrators to glean important operational information from the SRX both from a polling and also from a trap perspective. There are numerous examples of both open source and commercial SNMP tools that can be leveraged to provide an advanced network infrastructure monitoring solution. Just be sure to lock SNMP down by only listening on interfaces like fxp0, using unusual community strings and access lists—and even SNMPv3 for encryption and authentication.
- SNMP can seem like a large and complex feature to operate, but the good news is that there are some good ways to narrow down the scope of OIDs that you would like to monitor. Juniper documents all of the SNMP OID values, and additionally, you can leverage both the "enterprise" common values along with an SNMP MIB browser to parse through the SNMP MIB in an efficient manner. Additionally, you can leverage the built-in SNMP walk capabilities on the SRX to view the values locally.
- JFlow allows you to sample packets and send them to an external JFlow collector. There is plenty of information that can be gleaned from sampled packets, particularly with a powerful network analysis tool like STRM. In conjunction with other tools like AppTrack and IPS, JFlow can provide a great deal of visibility into network activity and behaviors, particularly at a holistic level.
- When using DHCP, you can leverage it as a client, server, and relay. In terms of best practices, you should only use DHCP where it is necessary, and not on every interface. DHCP should not be enabled when not in use at the security zone level.
- Don't forget about the Help facility in operational mode, which not only contains the documentation for each feature, but also allows you to search syslog messages and other suggestions for features so you need to look no further than the CLI to get help!

Troubleshooting and Operation

In this chapter, we covered several different system services features on the SRX. There are a few helpful systems that you can leverage when it comes to troubleshooting and operations on the SRX:

Viewing the System Connection Table

When troubleshooting to determine why a system isn't available, it can be helpful to view what connections the system is listening for, along with what connections are active on the system (bidirectional). This is exactly what the `show system connections` command does. You can also use the |output modifier to restrict what output you are looking for. The following is an abridged list of connections on an SRX.

```
root@srx3600n0> show system connections
Active Internet connections (including servers)
Proto Recv-Q Send-Q  Local Address       Foreign Address       (state)
tcp4       0     52  172.19.100.49.22    172.23.4.189.54012    ESTABLISHED
tcp4       0      0  *.38                *.*                  LISTEN
tcp4       0      0  *.9000              *.*                  LISTEN
tcp4       0      0  *.33064             *.*                  LISTEN
tcp4       0      0  *.33040             *.*                  LISTEN
tcp4       0      0  *.6156              *.*                  LISTEN
tcp46      0      0  *.443               *.*                  LISTEN
tcp46      0      0  *.80                *.*                  LISTEN
tcp4       0      0  *.23                *.*                  LISTEN
tcp4       0      0  *.22                *.*                  LISTEN
tcp4       0      0  *.21                *.*                  LISTEN
tcp4       0      0  *.79                *.*                  LISTEN
tcp4       0      0  *.514               *.*                  LISTEN
tcp4       0      0  *.513               *.*                  LISTEN
tcp4       0      0  *.6234              *.*                  LISTEN
udp46      0      0  *.514               *.*
udp4       0      0  *.514               *.*
udp46      0      0  *.4500              *.*
udp4       0      0  *.4500              *.*
udp46      0      0  *.500               *.*
udp4       0      0  *.500               *.*
udp46      0      0  *.161               *.*
udp4       0      0  *.161               *.*
udp4       0      0  *.123               *.*
```

Viewing the Services/Counters on the Interface

It is useful to check service counters at the interface level to see if packets are getting filtered, particularly if there are any firewall filters or other service limiting features enabled:

```
root@srx3600n0> show interfaces xe-1/0/0 extensive
Physical interface: xe-1/0/0, Enabled, Physical link is Up
```

```
  Interface index: 148, SNMP ifIndex: 548, Generation: 166
  Description: EX4500 port xe-0/0/32
  Link-level type: Ethernet, MTU: 1514, LAN-PHY mode, Speed: 10Gbps, Loopback:
None, Source filtering: Disabled, Flow control: Enabled
  Device flags   : Present Running
  Interface flags: SNMP-Traps Internal: 0x0
  Link flags     : None
  CoS queues     : 8 supported, 4 maximum usable queues
  Schedulers     : 0
  Hold-times     : Up 0 ms, Down 0 ms
  Current address: 00:21:59:8b:40:90, Hardware address: 00:21:59:8b:40:90
  Last flapped   : 2012-12-24 14:41:08 UTC (1w6d 04:29 ago)
  Statistics last cleared: Never
  Traffic statistics:
   Input  bytes  :         176878109672                    0 bps
   Output bytes  :         102563098568                    0 bps
   Input  packets:            263787865                    0 pps
   Output packets:            151357662                    0 pps
   IPv6 transit statistics:
    Input  bytes  :              389338
    Output bytes  :                   0
    Input  packets:                 462
    Output packets:                   0
  Dropped traffic statistics due to STP State:
   Input  bytes  :                    0
   Output bytes  :                    0
   Input  packets:                    0
   Output packets:                    0
  Input errors:
    Errors: 0, Drops: 0, Framing errors: 0, Runts: 0, Policed discards: 0, L3
incompletes: 0, L2 channel errors: 0, L2 mismatch timeouts: 0, FIFO errors: 0,
Resource errors: 0
  Output errors:
    Carrier transitions: 1, Errors: 0, Drops: 0, Collisions: 0, Aged packets:
0, FIFO errors: 0, HS link CRC errors: 0, MTU errors: 0, Resource errors: 0
  Egress queues: 8 supported, 4 in use
  Queue counters:   Queued packets  Transmitted packets  Dropped packets
    0 best-effort        149062906            149062906                0
    1 expedited-fo               0                    0                0
    2 assured-forw               0                    0                0
    3 network-cont         2294745              2294745                0
  Queue number:         Mapped forwarding classes
    0                     best-effort
    1                     expedited-forwarding
    2                     assured-forwarding
    3                     network-control
  Active alarms  : None
  Active defects : None
  PCS statistics                      Seconds
    Bit errors                             0
    Errored blocks                         0
  MAC statistics:                      Receive         Transmit
```

```
    Total octets                   177933310938      103181618095
    Total packets                     263788085         151357662
    Unicast packets                   263559764         151033796
    Broadcast packets                     22721             79840
    Multicast packets                     50167            244026
    CRC/Align errors                          0                 0
    FIFO errors                               0                 0
    MAC control frames                        0                 0
    MAC pause frames                          0                 0
    Oversized frames                          0
    Jabber frames                             0
    Fragment frames                           0
    VLAN tagged frames                        0
    Code violations                           0
  Filter statistics:
    Input packet count                263788085
    Input packet rejects                    177
    Input DA rejects                          0
    Input SA rejects                          0
    Output packet count                                 151357662
    Output packet pad count                                     0
    Output packet error count                                   0
    CAM destination filters: 0, CAM source filters: 0
  Packet Forwarding Engine configuration:
    Destination slot: 1
  CoS information:
    Direction : Output
    CoS transmit queue  Bandwidth        Buffer Priority   Limit
                            %               bps    %           usec
    0 best-effort          95      9500000000     95              0        low
none
    3 network-control       5       500000000      5              0        low
none
  Interface transmit statistics: Disabled

  Logical interface xe-1/0/0.0 (Index 70) (SNMP ifIndex 570) (Generation 138)
    Flags: SNMP-Traps 0x0 Encapsulation: ENET2
    Traffic statistics:
     Input  bytes  :        176878109672
     Output bytes  :        102399875752
     Input  packets:           263787865
     Output packets:           149451823
     IPv6 transit statistics:
      Input  bytes  :             389338
      Output bytes  :                  0
      Input  packets:                462
      Output packets:                  0
    Local statistics:
     Input  bytes  :            15273660
     Output bytes  :            23415666
     Input  packets:               66227
     Output packets:              317127
```

```
    Transit statistics:
     Input  bytes  :                   0                    0 bps
     Output bytes  :                   0                    0 bps
     Input  packets:                   0                    0 pps
     Output packets:                   0                    0 pps
     IPv6 transit statistics:
      Input  bytes  :                  0
      Output bytes  :                  0
      Input  packets:                  0
      Output packets:                  0
    Security: Zone: trust
     Allowed host-inbound traffic : bootp bfd bgp dns dvmrp igmp ldp msdp nhrp
ospf ospf3 pgm pim rip ripng router-discovery rsvp sap vrrp dhcp finger ftp
tftp ident-reset http https ike netconf ping
     reverse-telnet reverse-ssh rlogin rpm rsh snmp snmp-trap ssh telnet tracer-
oute xnm-clear-text xnm-ssl lsping ntp sip dhcpv6 r2cp
    Flow Statistics :
    Flow Input statistics :
      Self packets :                     21752
      ICMP packets :                     63516667
      VPN packets :                      0
      Multicast packets :                0
      Bytes permitted by policy :        127187179409
      Connections established :          75034327
    Flow Output statistics:
      Multicast packets :                0
      Bytes permitted by policy :        95604936318
    Flow error statistics (Packets dropped due to):
      Address spoofing:                  0
      Authentication failed:             0
      Incoming NAT errors:               0
      Invalid zone received packet:      0
      Multiple user authentications:     0
      Multiple incoming NAT:             0
      No parent for a gate:              0
      No one interested in self packets: 0
      No minor session:                  0
      No more sessions:                  0
      No NAT gate:                       0
      No route present:                  9950
      No SA for incoming SPI:            0
      No tunnel found:                   0
      No session for a gate:             0
      No zone or NULL zone binding       0
      Policy denied:                     0
      Security association not active:   0
      TCP sequence number out of window: 260192
      Syn-attack protection:             0
      User authentication errors:        0
    Protocol inet, MTU: 1500, Generation: 163, Route table: 0
      Flags: Sendbcast-pkt-to-re
      Addresses, Flags: Is-Preferred Is-Primary
```

```
        Destination: 10.102.1/24, Local: 10.102.1.1, Broadcast: 10.102.1.255,
Generation: 160
    Input Filters: Inbound-QoS
    Output Filters: Outbound-QoS
      Addresses, Flags: Is-Preferred
        Destination: 10.102.3/24, Local: 10.102.3.1, Broadcast: 10.102.3.255,
Generation: 162
    Protocol inet6, MTU: 1500, Generation: 164, Route table: 0
      Flags: Is-Primary
      Addresses, Flags: Is-Default Is-Preferred Is-Primary
        Destination: 2001::/120, Local: 2001::1
    Generation: 164
      Addresses, Flags: Is-Preferred
        Destination: fe80::/64, Local: fe80::221:59ff:fe8b:4090
    Protocol multiservice, MTU: Unlimited, Generation: 166
    Generation: 165, Route table: 0
      Policer: Input: __default_arp_policer__
```

Don't forget to check the lo0 interface when it comes to firewall filters, as that can be a reason why system services might be filtered along with being filtered at the interface level, at the security zone host-inbound-traffic level, and the security policy junos-host level. We cover the junos-host level in Chapter 8.

Also, if you configure the "count" action when configuring stateless firewall filters, you can view how many hits are being tagged by the SRX for that rule with the command `show firewall counter <counter-name> filter <filter-name>`.

Checking NTP Status

When running NTP, it is often helpful to check the status of the service along with what associations it currently has as a client, server, or peer. You can do so with two commands: `show ntp status` and `show ntp associations`.

```
root@srx3600n0> show ntp status
status=0664 leap_none, sync_ntp, 6 events, event_peer/strat_chg,
version="ntpd 4.2.0-a Wed Nov 28 19:09:38 UTC 2012 (1)",
processor="powerpc", system="JUNOS11.4R6.5", leap=00, stratum=4,
precision=-18, rootdelay=185.795, rootdispersion=98.477, peer=19068,
refid=172.19.100.91,
reftime=d4944965.94c948f8  Sun, Jan  6 2013 19:05:09.581, poll=9,
clock=d4944e60.6e12d8ed  Sun, Jan  6 2013 19:26:24.429, state=4,
offset=-0.965, frequency=-0.618, jitter=0.627, stability=0.013
```

```
root@srx3600n0> show ntp associations
     remote           refid      st t when poll reach   delay   offset  jitter
==============================================================================
*172.19.100.91   178.78.255.254   3 -  255  512  377    0.187   -0.965   0.739
```

Checking SNMP Status

SNMP has numerous tools that can be used to view the status and operation. We already covered the `show snmp mib walk` command earlier in the chapter. Another helpful command is to check the SNMP statistics, which include a lot of useful information about the number of messages sent and received and other conditions that might have occurred.

```
root@srx3600n0> show snmp statistics
SNMP statistics:
  Input:
    Packets: 0, Bad versions: 0, Bad community names: 0,
    Bad community uses: 0, ASN parse errors: 0,
    Too bigs: 0, No such names: 0, Bad values: 0,
    Read onlys: 0, General errors: 0,
    Total request varbinds: 0, Total set varbinds: 0,
    Get requests: 0, Get nexts: 0, Set requests: 0,
    Get responses: 0, Traps: 0,
    Silent drops: 0, Proxy drops: 0, Commit pending drops: 0,
    Throttle drops: 0, Duplicate request drops: 0
  V3 Input:
    Unknown security models: 0, Invalid messages: 0
    Unknown pdu handlers: 0, Unavailable contexts: 0
    Unknown contexts: 0, Unsupported security levels: 0
    Not in time windows: 0, Unknown user names: 0
    Unknown engine ids: 0, Wrong digests: 0, Decryption errors: 0
  Output:
    Packets: 5126, Too bigs: 0, No such names: 0,
    Bad values: 0, General errors: 0,
    Get requests: 0, Get nexts: 0, Set requests: 0,
    Get responses: 0, Traps: 5126
```

DHCP Operational Mode Commands

There are several different relevant items that you can leverage when it comes to operating DHCP. A big part of this has to do with the fact that you can leverage DHCP as a client, server, and relay. Most of these commands are available under the `show system services dhcp` operational mode commands. You can check for items like the client to IP binding, any conflicts seen, stats as a DHCP client and relay server, pool configuration, and very helpful stats about the DHCP messages sent and received on the system.

```
{primary:node0}
root@SRX100HM> show system services dhcp ?
Possible completions:
```

```
  binding                 Show DHCP client binding information
  client                  Show DHCP client information
  conflict                Show DHCP address conflict
  global                  Show DHCP global scope information
  pool                    Show DHCP address pool information
  relay-statistics        Show DHCP relay statistics information
  statistics              Show DHCP statistics
{primary:node0}
root@SRX100HM> show system services dhcp binding
node0:
--------------------------------------------------------------
IP address       Hardware address   Type     Lease expires at
192.168.1.100  00:11:39:00:43:91  static   never

{primary:node0}
root@SRX100HM> show system services dhcp client
Logical Interface name          ge-0/0/1.0
        Hardware address         00:21:59:8b:40:01
        Client status            Active
        Address obtained         1.1.1.1
        Update server            disabled

{primary:node0}
root@SRX100HM> show system services dhcp pool
node0:
-----------------------------------------------------------------
Pool name           Low address      High address     Excluded addresses
192.168.1.0/24    192.168.1.100  192.168.1.200

{primary:node0}
root@SRX100HM> show system services dhcp statistics
node0:
-----------------------------------------------------------------
Packets dropped:
    Total                       3

Messages received:
    BOOTREQUEST                 0
    DHCPDECLINE                 0
    DHCPDISCOVER                5
    DHCPINFORM                  0
    DHCPRELEASE                 1
    DHCPREQUEST                 15

Messages sent:
    BOOTREPLY                   0
    DHCPOFFER                   15
    DHCPACK                     14
    DHCPNAK                     1
```

Viewing Security Logs Locally

If you are logging security event logs locally on the SRX, you can view them in J-Web and the CLI by leveraging the `show security log` command along with the appropriate modifier. The SRX provides a great number of options when it comes to filtering these logs down. Of course, doing this externally on a platform like the STRM is much better for historical purposes and long-term approaches, whereas doing it locally can be helpful for small deployments and simple troubleshooting.

```
{primary:node0}
root@SRX100HM> show security log ?
Possible completions:
  <[Enter]>            Execute this command
  ascending            Sort in ascending order
  descending           Sort in descending order
  destination-address  Destination address and optional prefix length
  destination-port     Destination port
  detail               Show detail alarm information
  event-id             Event ID filter
  failure              Event was a failure
  file                 Show security logs in binary format
  interface-name       Name of interface
  newer-than           Events newer than filter (YYYY-MM-DD.HH:MM:SS)
  older-than           Events older than filter (YYYY-MM-DD.HH:MM:SS)
  policy-name          Policy name filter
  process              Process that generated the event
  protocol             Protocol filter
  severity             Severity of the event
  sort-by              Sort by selected field
  source-address       Source address and optional prefix length
  source-port          Source port
  success              Event was successful
  username             Username filter
  |                    Pipe through a command
```

Checking for Core Dumps

When something goes wrong on the platform, the first thing that can be checked is whether there are any core dumps. For instance, if your IPS sigpack download were to fail, you might see a core dump from IDPD. If the data plane were to crash, there could be a flowd or chassisd core dump. Although you yourself cannot troubleshoot these, they can be given to the Juniper Networks Technical Assistance Center (JTAC) for analysis. Still, if you see a core dump, it can give some hints, including the potential need to restart a service.

```
root@srx3600n0> show system core-dumps
-rw-r--r--  1 root  wheel  1048630488 Dec 20 20:56 /var/crash/core-CPP0.core.0
-rw-rw----    1  nobody  wheel  264597650  Dec  24  14:37  /var/tmp/flowd_xlr-
SPC8_PIC0.core.0.gz
/var/tmp/pics/*core*: No such file or directory
```

```
/var/crash/kernel.*: No such file or directory
/tftpboot/corefiles/*core*: No such file or directory
total 2
```

This command is helpful because it checks all locations in which core dumps can be generated, along with running it on both members if running in HA. Here we can see that there were two different types of core dumps on December 20 and December 24. Although we don't know exactly what the cause was, JTAC can usually get to the bottom of these.

Restarting Platform Daemons

From time to time you might run into a scenario where you need to restart a service for one reason or another. The good news is that you don't need to restart the entire platform in most cases; you can just restart individual services with the `restart <service>` command. In this example, we restart the IPS policy, which will trigger a policy recompile and have the system push the policy to the data plane. We will run the `show system processes extensive | match idpd` command to check and see the process number before and after we do the restart.

```
root@srx3600n0> show system processes extensive | match idpd
 1184 root        1  96    0 32200K 20328K select  15:14  0.00% idpd

root@srx3600n0> restart idp-policy
IDP policy daemon started, pid 28506

root@srx3600n0> show system processes extensive | match idpd
28506 root        1 132    0   108M 77132K RUN      0:04 76.30% idpd

root@srx3600n0> restart ?
Possible completions:
  application-identification  Application-identification process
  application-security  Application security daemon
  audit-process        Audit process
  chassis-control      Chassis control process
  class-of-service     Class-of-service process
  database-replication  Database Replication process
  datapath-trace-service  DATAPATH Trace process
  dhcp                 Dynamic Host Configuration Protocol process
  dhcp-service         Dynamic Host Configuration Protocol process
  disk-monitoring      Disk monitoring process
  dynamic-flow-capture  Dynamic flow capture service
  ethernet-connectivity-fault-management  Connectivity fault management process
  event-processing     Event processing process
  fipsd                FIPS daemon
  firewall             Firewall process
  firewall-authentication-service  Firewall authentication daemon
  general-authentication-service  General authentication process
  gprs-process         gprs daemon
  gracefully           Gracefully restart the process
```

```
idp-policy           IDP policy daemon
immediately          Immediately restart (SIGKILL) the process
interface-control    Interface control process
ipmi                 Intelligent platform management interface daemon
ipsec-key-management  IPSec Key Management daemon
jsrp-service         Juniper Stateful Redundancy Protocol Daemon
kernel-replication   Kernel replication process
l2-learning          Layer 2 address flooding and learning process
l2cpd-service        Layer 2 Control Protocol process
lacp                 Link Aggregation Control Protocol process
license-service      Feature license management process
logical-system-service  Logical System Daemon
mib-process          Management Information Base II process
mountd-service       Service for NFS mounts requests
named-service        DNS server process
network-security     Network security daemon
network-security-trace  Network security trace daemon
nfsd-service         Remote NFS server
ntpd-service         Network Time Protocol Service
pgm                  Pragmatic General Multicast process
pic-services-logging  PIC services logging process
pki-service          PKI service daemon
profilerd            Profiler Daemon
remote-operations    Remote operations process
routing              Routing protocol process
sampling             Traffic sampling control process
secure-neighbor-discovery  Secure Neighbor Discovery Protocol process
security-log         Security Log Daemon
service-deployment   Service Deployment Client
simple-mail-client-service  Simple Mail Transfer Protocol Client process
snmp                 Simple Network Management Protocol process
soft                 Soft reset (SIGHUP) the process
statistics-service   Packet Forwarding Engine statistics management process
subscriber-management  Subscriber management process
subscriber-management-helper  Subscriber management helper process
tunnel-oamd          Tunnel OAM process
uac-service          Unified access control daemon
vrrp                 Virtual Router Redundancy Protocol process
web-management       Web management process
```

Troubleshooting Individual Daemons

Most system daemons have the ability to be debugged beyond the normal stats and show commands by leveraging traceoptions. Because there are so many different daemons and the traceoptions vary from subsystem to subsystem, we are not going to cover them extensively, but we want to point out that you might be able to leverage the traceoptions if need be. Typically, it is a better idea to just contact JTAC if you are unsure of what you're doing, but if you are confident, you might be able to troubleshoot a simple issue yourself by activating a traceoption and viewing the output.

Most system traceoptions are done on a feature-by-feature basis. You need to activate the traceoption, define what file to log to, define what flags you want to activate, and then commit the configuration for the trace to take effect. You can then view the output in the logfile you specified, followed by deactivating, deleting, or rolling back your configuration so that the traceoptions is no longer active. It is typically best to only use traceoptions for the precise time that they are needed. This ensures that additional system resources aren't consumed unnecessarily. The following are a few examples of enabling system traceoptions.

```
[edit]
root@srx3600n0# set snmp traceoptions ?
Possible completions:
+ apply-groups         Groups from which to inherit configuration data
+ apply-groups-except  Don't inherit configuration data from these groups
> file                 Trace file information
> flag                 Tracing parameters
  no-remote-trace      Disable remote tracing

[edit]
root@srx3600n0# set system services dhcp traceoptions ?
Possible completions:
+ apply-groups         Groups from which to inherit configuration data
+ apply-groups-except  Don't inherit configuration data from these groups
> file                 Trace file information
> flag                 Area of DHCP server process to enable debugging output
  level                Level of debugging output
  no-remote-trace      Disable remote tracing

[edit]
root@srx3600n0# set security log traceoptions ?
Possible completions:
+ apply-groups         Groups from which to inherit configuration data
+ apply-groups-except  Don't inherit configuration data from these groups
> file                 Trace file information
> flag                 List of things to include in trace
  no-remote-trace      Disable remote tracing
```

Summary

The SRX is a very powerful platform and we could spend an entire book covering all of the different system services and their configuration options. Instead we choose to focus on the most common ones with the most important configuration values so you can get a system up and running properly. Regardless of how the SRX is deployed, whether it be for a service provider environment or in a branch perimeter deployment on an SRX100, the SRX can offer a great deal of functionality via the system services that have been born and bred from the Internet core. Although not the most obvious topic to focus on when configuring the SRX, properly configuring the system services can alleviate a lot of heartache later and maximize the functionality of your deployment.

Study Questions

Questions

1. How do you manually set the system time on the SRX?
2. What are the different NTP modes the SRX supports?
3. What are the three DHCP modes that the SRX supports and what do they do?
4. What is unique about DHCP from a security zone configuration perspective on the SRX?
5. Explain the difference between control plane and data plane logging on the SRX.
6. What is JFlow?
7. What is the difference between an SNMP query and an SNMP trap?
8. What is the best interface to use for network management on the SRX?
9. How can you view the format of system log messages locally on the SRX without having to refer to online manuals?
10. What formats can you use to send syslog messages on the control plane and data plane to syslog collectors?

Answers

1. You can manually set the system time by using the operational mode command `set date` because this is a real-time parameter rather than a configuration mode element.
2. The SRX can provide NTP client, server, and peer functionality. As a client it receives its configuration from an NTP server, as a server it provides NTP functionality to clients that request it or receive it via broadcast configuration, and as a peer the SRX and NTP peer sync each other's time.
3. The SRX can act as a DHCP client, server, and relay. As a client, it receives its DHCP configuration from an upstream DHCP server; as a server, it distributes the DHCP information to clients; and as a relay, it takes local DHCP broadcast requests and forwards them on to the DHCP server, which exists on a different Layer 3 segment.
4. DHCP is the only service that can be configured only under an interface in the host-inbound traffic configuration within a security zone configuration rather than at the zone level.
5. Control plane logging on the SRX is for messages that are generated on the control plane. They can be stored to files or sent out via syslog to external hosts. Typically these are generated by control plane daemons and are logged to */var/log* under the respective files for that daemon or traceoption configuration. Data plane logs are generated based on traffic that passes through the SRX such

as firewall logs, IPS logs, UTM logs, and so on. These can be sent directly out the data plane or logged up to the control plane where they can either be stored locally or sent to a syslog server. Logging data plane logs out the data plane directly is typically the best option from a performance perspective to ensure that the control plane isn't overwhelmed by the rate of data plane messages.

6. JFlow is similar to Cisco's NetFlow and provides the ability to sample packets to an external flow collector, which can receive them and analyze them accordingly. JFlow is an excellent tool for network analysis at a higher level to identify trends and network behaviors.
7. An SNMP query is polled from an SNMP collector to a system like the SRX. It specifies an index value known as an OID to retrieve and respond back to the query agent. An SNMP trap, on the other hand, is generated on the SRX and sent to an SNMP collector. Typically, this contains information about a system event or condition defined by the network administrator.
8. Typically, fxp0, which is the out-of-band control plane interface, is the best interface to use on the SRX, if possible. This is because it does not need to rely on the data plane availability and can be put on its own private network for ideal out-of-band management versus the transit traffic on the network.
9. You can leverage the operational mode `help syslog` command to view the log messages, formats, and examples for each subsystem. Additionally, the help function contains other documentation information that can be valuable to operators on the SRX and in Junos in general.
10. The SRX control plane supports both unstructured (standard) and structured syslog, whereas the data plane supports sending messages in unstructured (standard), structured, binary, and WELF format.

CHAPTER 6

Transparent Mode

There are two common challenges to deploying traditional Layer 3 network firewalls into a network. The first challenge is that you typically must change the IP routing to support the new firewall into the network, which can be a particularly difficult task, especially when dealing with readdressing segments. The other challenge with traditional firewalls is that they are very weak routers, at least in terms of dynamic routing protocol support, not to mention the fact that the security teams, which managed the firewalls, are typically separate from the teams that managed the routing infrastructure.

Because the SRX runs Junos, you're already equipped with the best routing platform there is, so routing support isn't an issue for the SRX, even though it is for many competitive firewalls and the previous generation of ScreenOS devices.

Transparent mode essentially allows the SRX to act as a Layer 2 bridge with the added security functionality of being a stateful firewall, as well as providing additional services such as IPS and AppSecure.

Transparent Mode Overview

Fundamentally, transparent mode is very similar to Layer 3 routed mode on the SRX platform. Although there are some limitations that are discussed later in this chapter that you should be aware of when balancing the decision to deploy transparent mode, this is a feature that certainly has its place in contemporary networking. First this chapter reviews the reasons for deployment, how the technology functions, and the different components and concepts to be aware of when deploying transparent mode. After this review, actual configuration examples are shown through a case study.

When to Use Transparent Mode

You should consider using transparent mode because certain networking scenarios are not ideal for a Layer 3 implementation of a firewall. The good news is that transparent mode can be a viable alternative for administrators who want to avoid deployment dilemmas that Layer 3 implementations can cause. In this section, we review common scenarios where transparent mode can provide significant value.

Segmenting a Layer 2 domain

Sometimes day-to-day operations require that a firewall be placed where it did not exist before, a common example being for compliance with security standards such as PCI, HIPAA, SOX, and other international security standards. For instance, these standards might require that firewalling is present between a web server farm and a database server farm existing in a DMZ. Although integrating a Layer 3 firewall might be an option, it would require you to make IP address changes on at least one set of the devices. This can be easier than it sounds, especially if you have lots of hooks accessing the applications by IP address and if the applications cannot easily change their IP address. In this situation, you can simply implement a transparent mode firewall between the web and server farms, without having to change any IP addresses or make any changes on the application side. At the same time, you can now enforce security between these different segments.

Figure 6-1 shows a before and after view of how a transparent mode SRX can be inserted into a network to provide security.

As you can see, if the firewall is in Layer 3 mode, it can't separate hosts on the same Layer 2 domain because of where it is logically placed. If you wanted to insert a Layer 3 firewall, you could, but you would need to re-IP-address your network to accommodate the changes. Transparent mode firewalls, on the other hand, do not segment your network from a Layer 3 perspective, and therefore they can sit between hosts on the same Layer 2 network to protect them from other hosts on the same Layer 2 network, along with enforcing security against remote attacks.

Complex routing environments

Traditional firewalls typically did not make good routers, both from a routing capacity perspective and from a feature perspective. Now that Juniper offers a firewall that is on Junos, there is a very complete routing infrastructure on the firewall itself, so this might not be as big a concern as it is with other products. Nevertheless, some environments might feel more comfortable with firewalls only performing security functions, and leaving routing up to other devices. In these environments, firewalls can sit between routers transparently and simply inspect the traffic and forward it like a Layer 2 switch.

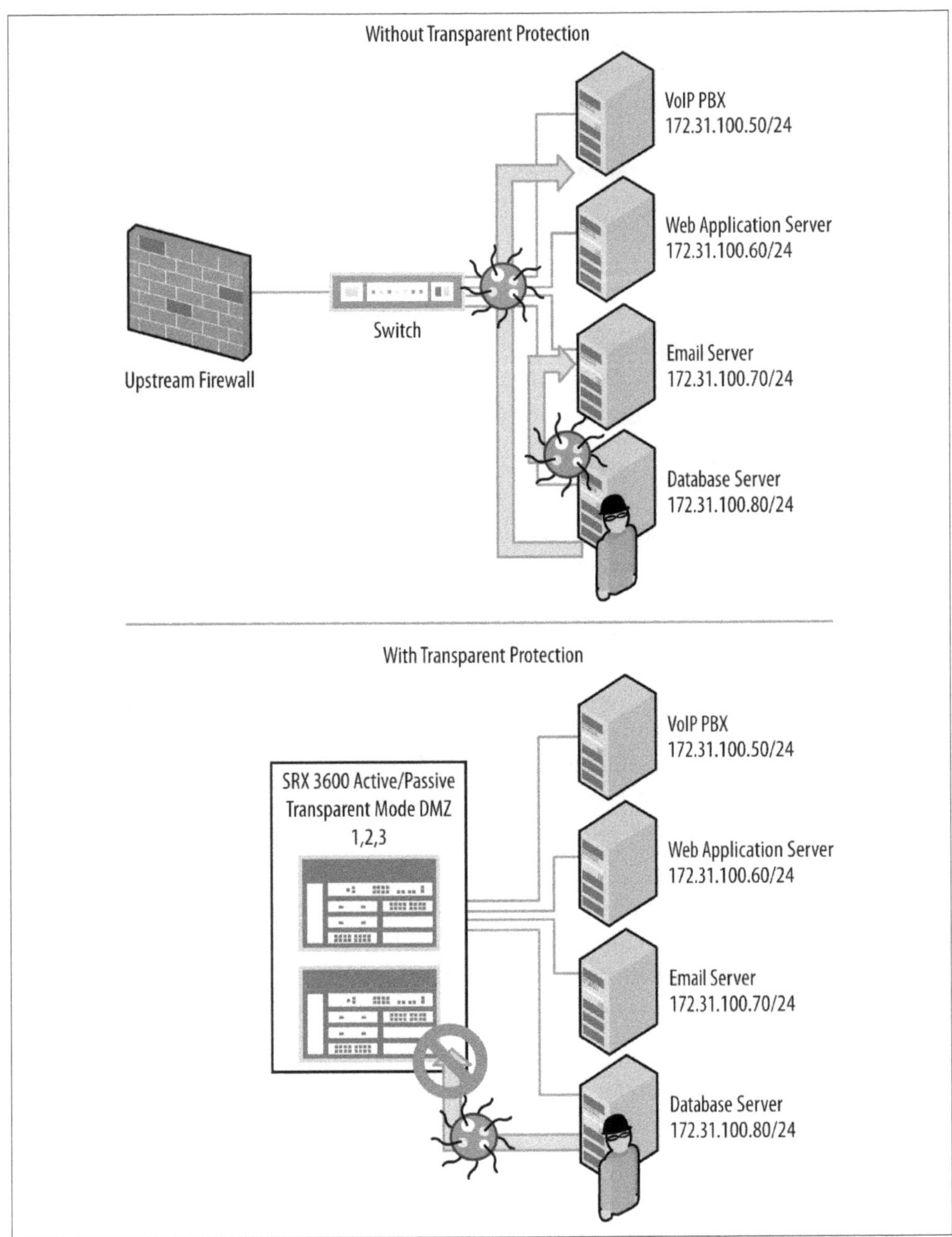

Figure 6-1. Segmenting a Layer 2 domain

Separation of duties

In some environments, separate teams manage the routing, switching, firewalling, and IPS services, or some combination of these roles. In these environments, having routing on the firewalls might mean separate teams have to be involved, which might not be ideal. Although there is no technical reason for using transparent mode in this scenario, other factors such as logistical and political issues can make transparent mode more ideal.

Existing transparent mode infrastructure

Sometimes an existing transparent mode firewall infrastructure is in place that must be upgraded. In these scenarios, swapping out the existing transparent mode firewalls with new transparent mode firewalls is the easiest transition, as switching from Layer 2 to Layer 3 would result in changes that need to occur with the Layer 3 infrastructure.

MAC Address Learning

An SRX in transparent mode acts like a switch with regard to how it forwards traffic. As you know, a true Layer 2 switch does not forward based on IP addresses, but rather based on the destination MAC addresses of the frames it receives. To forward to a destination, the SRX must learn where the MAC addresses "live" on the network. To do this, the SRX learns on which ports MAC addresses are located based on the source MAC address that is learned on that particular port. These entries are cached into a bridging table on the SRX and are used for packet forwarding, including policy lookup, as we discuss in the section "Transparent Mode Flow Process" on page 248 later in this chapter. If the SRX does not know on which port in the VLAN the destination MAC address can be reached, it performs one of two actions depending on the configuration:

Flood the frame
: By default, the SRX simply floods the packet out all interfaces in the same VLAN except the port on which the packet arrived. This is how a switch normally functions when it doesn't know the destination MAC address.

ARP with traceroute
: In some cases, customers might not wish to flood any packets out for security reasons, so Junos offers you an alternative to flooding the traffic, which is to send an Address Resolution Protocol (ARP) and optionally an ICMP packet with a TTL of 1, while queuing the packet. If no destination responds, the original packet is dropped.

Transparent Mode and Bridge Loops, Spanning Tree Protocol

One thing you must be aware of when working with transparent mode firewalls is that if you do not properly configure a transparent mode firewall, you might trigger a *bridge loop*. If you are connecting the SRX directly to routed interfaces on peer devices, this should not be an issue, but if you are connecting the SRX to switch interfaces, you need to give some thought to your design. Because at the time of this writing the SRX does not actively participate in Spanning Tree Protocol (STP) itself, it does forward the BPDUs and the STP messages. Additionally, you might need to tweak your spanning tree configuration to properly forward traffic to the active SRX node. If you do not do this, traffic might not pass through the SRX, or failovers between nodes might not function properly. These different configurations are examined throughout this chapter.

Transparent Mode Limitations

There are some limitations when it comes to transparent mode on the SRX, particularly in contrast to ScreenOS. You should be aware of the following limitations before configuring transparent mode:

Virtual private network support
: At the time of this writing, VPN termination on Integrated Routing and Bridging (IRB) interfaces is not supported in transparent mode. This termination is supported on VLAN interfaces in ScreenOS, but it is not yet supported on the SRX in transparent mode. This feature will likely be supported in the future.

Mixed mode Layer 2/Layer 3 support
: At the time of this writing, you can only configure Layer 2 or Layer 3, but not both simultaneously. This was never supported on ScreenOS, however, and is likely to be supported in the near future on SRX.

Network Address Translation
: At the time of this writing, NAT is not supported in transparent mode. Policy NAT is supported in ScreenOS starting with version 6.1, but this is not yet supported in the SRX for transparent mode.

Virtual router support
: At the time of this writing, you cannot place IRB interfaces into different virtual routers; they must remain in the master `inet.0` routing table.

Q-in-Q tunneling
: Q-in-Q tunneling is not supported on the high-end SRX (either in Layer 3 or in Layer 2) at the time of this writing.

Changing modes
: To change from Layer 3 to Layer 2 mode (or vice versa) you must reboot the chassis.

Limitations per release
: Because there are many variations of platforms and releases, it would be too extensive to compile into a book. The best option is to refer to the pathfinder tool (*http://pathfinder.juniper.net*), which documents up-to-date releases with what

features are supported. This requires a customer portal login. In pathfinder, you will want to use the feature explorer to review feature limitations for transparent mode as well as any other feature support that is listed here.

Transparent Mode Components

There are several components of transparent mode, some common to Layer 3 and some specific to transparent mode itself. This section examines the different components of transparent mode; configuration examples follow later in the chapter. These components are also the building blocks of the case study at the end of the chapter.

Interfaces, family bridge, and bridge domains in transparent mode

Transparent mode ushers in a few new concepts concerning interfaces and forwarding. Transparent mode follows the same interface model as standard Layer 3 interfaces, with the use of physical interface properties, followed by logical interface configuration. The main differences that exist are as follows:

Family bridge
: Rather than using family Inet, Inet6, ISO, and so on, because there is no explicit IP address configuration, we will use the family bridge, which is the same as what the MX Series uses for its platform.

Interface addressing
: In transparent mode, there is no IP address assigned to a logical interface. The SRX functions as a switch and not as a router. Traffic is switched toward the SRX by listening for MAC addresses and determining that they live on the other side of the SRX. The interfaces do have MAC addresses, but the source and destination MAC addresses of transit traffic will never be of the SRX's interfaces themselves. A concept of IRB interfaces allows you to send management traffic to the SRX, but other than that, the traffic will not be addressed to the SRX itself.

Bridge domains
: These are the Layer 2 equivalent of virtual routers in Layer 3 mode. Essentially, bridge domains allow you to separate the Layer 2 traffic, including spanning tree domains, and other forwarding options. We will cover bridge domains and how they influence transparent mode in the section "Configuring Integrated Routing and Bridging" on page 257 later in this chapter.

Interface Modes in Transparent Mode

In transparent mode, there are two different modes in which you can place an interface: access mode and trunk mode. If you have any experience with the EX Series or MX Series platforms, the SRX follows the same convention here, although, unlike the EX

Series platform (and like the MX Series platform), the SRX uses the family bridge convention.

Access mode
: Access mode is the default mode for family bridge interfaces. In access mode, the interface only has a single unit that uses a single VLAN member, which can be configured for the interface. Traffic arriving on the interface is classified with the VLAN, which is configured. The term *access mode* comes from the fact that most end systems that access the network on these types of interfaces are configured on a switch. For the SRX, however, access mode simply means there is only a single VLAN configured on the interface.

Trunk mode
: The SRX supports the ability to terminate multiple VLANs on a single interface through the use of 802.1q trunking. To accommodate this, you will need to configure an interface in trunk mode, which uses VLAN tagging to differentiate VLANs for the purposes of separation and classification of traffic. You can use a native VLAN, which is untagged, or you can use an interface with all tagged VLANs. When using trunk mode, you can configure multiple units (logical interfaces), each having one or more VLAN members present on it.

You cannot mix both access mode units and trunk mode units on a single interface, and, if you are using access mode, you can only have a single unit present. Just like Layer 3 mode, you can put different logical interface units into different zones, and you can put different VLANs into different bridge domains (similar to how you can put different logical interface units into different virtual routers in Layer 3 mode).

Bridge Domains

As mentioned earlier in this chapter, bridge domains are used to logically separate traffic on the SRX. In reality, they are very similar to VLANs in terms of how the traffic is processed in the system; however, the bridge domain allows Junos to abstract the VLANs and their associated tags from the actual traffic processing. Typically, most implementations require that you configure a separate bridge domain for each VLAN, although this isn't a strict requirement; you can bridge multiple VLANs together if you wish.

Within a bridge domain, you can configure either a single or multiple VLANs to be part of the same bridge domain; however, you can only configure an IRB interface in a bridge domain if you are using a single VLAN for the bridge domain.

IRB Interfaces

As mentioned, the standard logical interfaces on the SRX do not support IP addresses when the SRX is configured in transparent mode; however, the SRX does support a special type of interface called an *IRB interface*. You can think of an IRB interface as a VLAN interface from Junos' switching capabilities. IRB interfaces are virtual interfaces that allow you to configure IP addressing on the interface so that even in transparent mode you can communicate with the SRX on data plane interfaces. Of course, even in transparent mode you can manage the device through the fxp0 interface, which does have full management capabilities. The purpose of IRB interfaces is to allow you to manage a transparent mode device on the data plane by making an addressable interface. The IRB interface cannot route traffic itself; rather, you can use it to accept inbound management connections, including pings, SSH, Telnet, and HTTP, and you can make outbound connections on the IRB interface to other devices.

In transparent mode, you cannot put IRB interfaces into different virtual routing instances, because different virtual routers are not supported.

Transparent Mode Zones

For those of you who have a rich experience working with ScreenOS, there is a slight difference with the way security zones are defined in Junos. Unlike ScreenOS, where you were required to prepend a Layer 2 security zone name with `L2-<name>`, in Junos there is no requirement for any special naming convention. Security zones are associated with Layer 2 by the interfaces that are in them, and therefore the system is smart enough to know it is a Layer 2 zone without any special naming requirements. So, in reality, there are no differences between Layer 2 and Layer 3 security zones from a configuration perspective. Just like Layer 3 security zones, you place the logical interfaces (e.g., ge-0/0/4.20) into the security zones, so the SRX can support not only access mode interfaces but also 802.1q VLANs that are bound to a specific unit on a trunk link. One exception is that IRB interfaces themselves are not placed within security zones, but the surrounding Layer 2 interfaces are, so you can still filter out traffic for them. We cover this in more detail in the configuration examples later in this chapter.

Transparent Mode Security Policy

Security policies in transparent mode are almost identical to those in Layer 3, with the only exception being that VPN is not supported in transparent mode, so therefore policy-based VPNs would not be supported within the security policies.

For those of you who do not have experience with ScreenOS, the Layer 2 security policies in Junos are pretty straightforward. In transparent mode, the security policy is no different from a Layer 3 policy. The transparent mode policy is still composed of filtering based on from-to-zones, source addresses, destination addresses, and applications (source port, destination port, and protocol). However, one thing to keep in mind is that, unlike ScreenOS, intrazone blocking is always enforced (for both Layer 2 and Layer 3 modes), so you always need a security policy, even for traffic coming from and going to the same zone (e.g., from Trust to Trust). Also note that in transparent mode, you cannot filter on Layer 2 components (again, we cover this later in this chapter).

Transparent Mode Specific Options

Transparent mode supports the following flow configurations that are not supported in Layer 3:

Block all non-IP packets
: If the SRX sees non-IP packets (or packets that are not involved with IP, such as ARP, Internet Group Management Protocol [IGMP], or DHCP, for example), the SRX will silently drop them. This includes broadcast and multicast traffic.

Bypass all non-IP unicast traffic
: This option permits non-IP unicast traffic to be sent through the box. Note that this does not include IPv6, which is dropped if you attempt to forward it through the SRX. If you do need to forward IPv6 through the SRX, the recommendation is to use GRE tunneling on the routers.

No packet flooding
: By default, the SRX floods all packets with an unknown destination MAC address out all interfaces in the same VLAN on which the packet arrived, except the source interface. This is the standard behavior for bridging and switching devices when they do not know on which port the destination MAC address can be reached. Some administrators would like to avoid this behavior if the destination MAC address is not known and have the SRX ARP for the destination MAC address. There are two options for this: ARP and send an ICMP traceroute, or just simply ARP.

QoS in Transparent Mode

The SRX supports the ability to perform Quality of Service (QoS) in transparent mode. Transparent mode QoS allows you to perform classification and rewriting based on 802.1p values, along with being able to do standard shaping and priority processing based on these QoS values. Note that transparent mode does not support classification or rewriting based on IP precedence or Differentiated Services Code Point (DSCP) values, only on the Layer 2 802.1p values. So if you need to classify based on IP precedence or DSCP, you should do it upstream or downstream and copy the equivalent values into the 802.1p field so that the SRX can apply the appropriate QoS in transparent mode. The section "Configuring Transparent Mode QoS" on page 265 later in this chapter takes a deep look at this functionality.

VLAN Rewriting

Many network engineers consider VLAN rewriting (also known as VLAN retagging) as the NAT of Layer 2 VLAN tags when in Layer 2 mode. In some networks, VLAN rewriting is used to ensure that "clean" traffic that might be on the same VLAN has passed through a firewall; to do this, we can use different VLAN tags on different sides of the firewall. In other cases, there might be a handoff between different network boundaries (e.g., between a customer and an ISP), so to keep things simple on the customer end, VLAN rewriting can be used to ensure that there is no VLAN overlap. In Layer 3 mode, networks can be segmented simply by routing the traffic between VLANs (including performing other services such as firewalling and IPS); however, in Layer 2 mode, a device does not perform any of the routing transforms to route traffic between Layer 3 networks. When you want to transform the VLAN on one side of the firewall in transparent mode, you would want to use VLAN rewriting. Essentially, VLAN rewriting simply defines how the VLANs are translated by mapping VLANs on a one-to-one ratio. For instance, in Figure 6-2, we are mapping VLAN 20 to VLAN 80. We cover this concept later in the configuration example section.

Only tagged traffic on VLANs can be translated. This means the traffic on the native VLAN cannot be translated because there is no tag. You would need to make sure the surrounding networking devices tagged this native VLAN on their end, for you to translate the VLAN on the SRX.

High Availability with Transparent Mode

The SRX supports the ability to operate an SRX chassis cluster in transparent mode. Chassis clustering in transparent mode operates very similarly to Layer 3 mode, but with the same differences as standalone Layer 3 compared to standalone Layer 2.

When operating in transparent mode HA clusters, you need to be especially aware of bridge loops and how transparent mode triggers traffic failovers. In Layer 3 mode, the SRX will send Gratuitous ARPs (GARPs) out the new active reth interface member after a failover to signal to the surrounding switches that the SRX's MAC address has moved to a new interface (that of the new active reth member). In transparent mode, there is no active MAC address or IP address on which to terminate the traffic, so no GARPs can be sent. Instead, the SRX flaps the old active interfaces up and down to trigger an STP recalculation. If STP is not properly configured on the surrounding switches (if applicable), it can lead to traffic not failing over or other disruptions. Note that in active/passive mode, only one SRX in the cluster has its data plane active at a time (just like in active/passive Layer 3 mode). In Layer 2 active/active mode, an individual redundancy group is only active on a single SRX data plane at a time, but both SRX data planes can have different redundancy groups active on them, just like Layer 3 active/active. Of

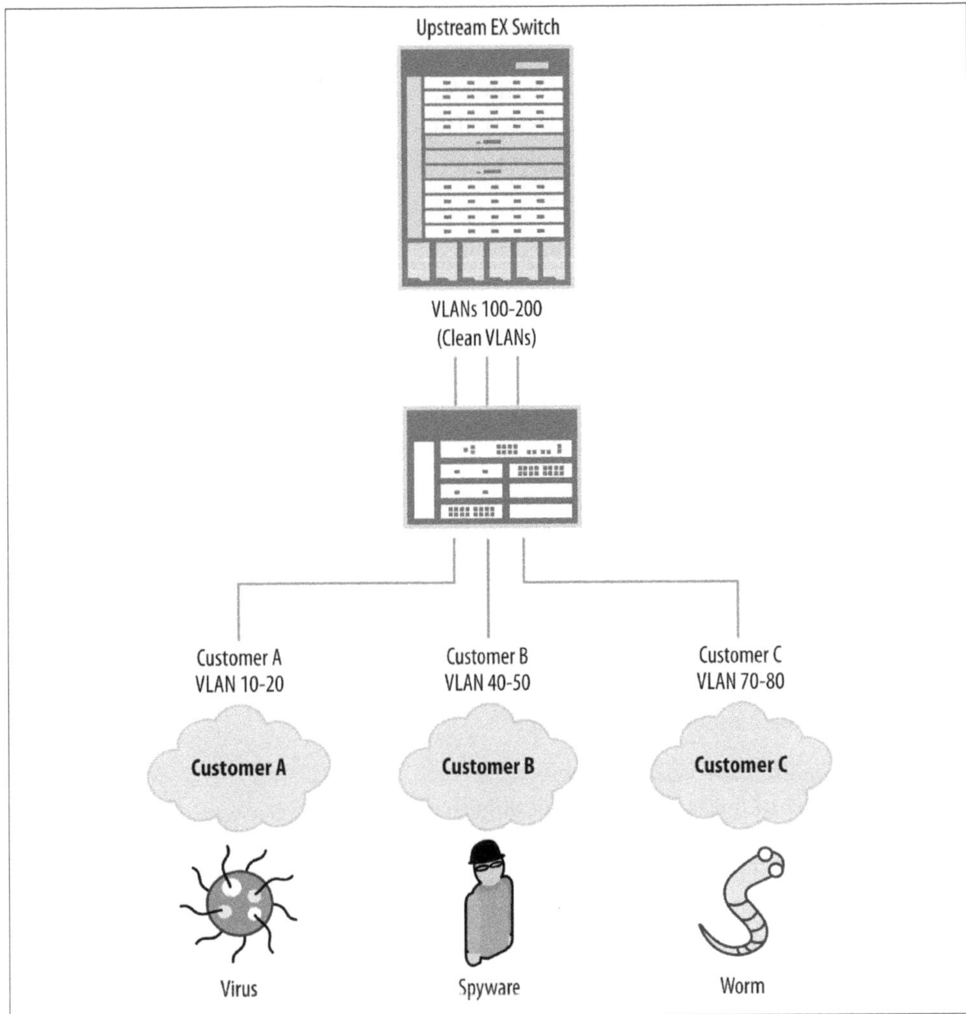

Figure 6-2. VLAN rewriting

course, you can't have an individual redundancy group active on both cluster members at the same time, as this would cause a bridge loop. The case study later in this chapter includes an example of using transparent mode in HA. In addition, the next section details where to use STP and what version of STP you should be using, and Chapter 7 discusses chassis clustering in great detail.

Spanning Tree Protocol in transparent mode Layer 2 deployments

When Layer 3 devices surround the SRX cluster in transparent mode, there really isn't much of a concern for spanning tree. However, in many cases, Layer 2 switching will be deployed surrounding the SRX transparent mode cluster. In these cases, although the SRX will not forward traffic that it receives on an interface that is not active for its redundancy group, it will forward the BPDUs, and therefore the switches will view this as a network loop. Disabling STP is generally a bad idea in a production network because if someone makes a mistake, it can trigger a bridge loop because STP is disabled. At the same time, using standard STP can be less than ideal because of failover timings (up to 50 seconds after a topology change).

It doesn't really matter if you are using active/passive or active/active. The concerns are going to be the same.

Here are some guidelines for what you should use for the transparent mode switching architecture:

Transparent mode without VLAN trunking
: If you are not using VLAN trunking on your transparent mode reth interfaces, you can simply use RSTP, which will provide much better failover times and reliability than standard STP.

Multiple Spanning Tree Protocol (MSTP)
: MSTP is actually preferable to RSTP, although in the case of no VLAN trunking, it shouldn't make much of a difference.

Transparent mode with VLAN trunking
: If VLAN trunking is used, it is possible that a bridge loop might occur within an individual VLAN, but not on the entire trunk itself. RSTP does not provide any way to prevent bridge loops within VLANs on a trunk unless the entire link has a loop on the native VLAN. Instead, you can use MSTP, which enables you to provide separate instances of STP. This gives you the same benefits of RSTP in terms of redundancy, but with the ability to separate STP domains similar to PVST+.

You can use Cisco proprietary protocols such as PVST+ and RPVST, but there really isn't much of a point with the standardized implementations of STP that exist.

Transparent Mode Flow Process

The transparent mode flow process is very similar to that of the routed Layer 3 mode flow processing. Essentially, the differences between Layer 2 and Layer 3 are in the forwarding process, and at the same time, there are some features that are not supported in transparent mode. There is no difference in the packet flow in terms of the flow between the Network Processing Unit, control point, and Services Processing Unit (SPU) on the high-end SRXs; all of this occurs in the same fashion. However, the actual process within the SPU varies slightly. The branch devices do not use NPUs, CPs, or SPUs, so the portions that do not apply to the branch SRXs will be noted.

Figure 6-3 shows the transparent mode packet flow.

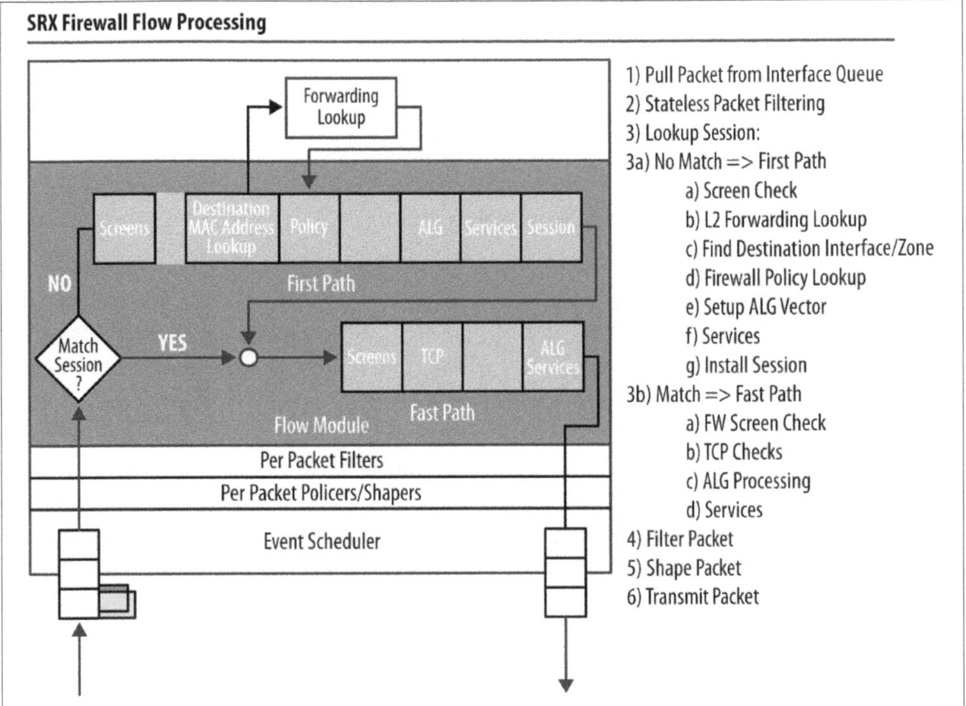

Figure 6-3. Packet flow diagram

Slow-path SPU packet processing

Slow-path packet processing consists of the following steps:

1. The initial packet is forwarded from the NPU to the CP and then from the CP to the SPU, which the CP selects to process the flow (data center SRX only).
2. The policing, stateless filtering, and screens can be performed on the SPU (although this can also occur elsewhere). Most of the screens are performed on the NPU, but a few screens are performed on the SPU. These screens are typically related to processing session limits (in conjunction with the CP, which knows about the session numbers of all source and destination IP addresses being processed on the box; data center SRX only). On the branch devices, these functions are all performed within the single data plane processor.

3. The SPU will determine if it knows about the session or not. If the session is known, it will fast-path the session, but in the case of a new session, additional processing must be performed (data center SRX only).
4. Transparent mode differs from Layer 3 routed mode because not only is there no IP address on its interfaces, but also it does not perform forwarding based on a routing lookup, but rather based on a bridging lookup, as both network segments are within the same Layer 3 domain. Two scenarios occur during packet processing:
   a. If the destination MAC address is known, it is "learned," similar to how a bridge or switch would normally function by simply listening for packets and examining the source MAC address. When a new source MAC address is learned, it is added to the bridging table. If the destination MAC address for the packet that the SRX is forwarding is known, it determines the egress interface (and therefore the egress zone) based on the bridging lookup.
   b. If the destination MAC address is unknown, the SRX must try to determine what port the destination MAC address lives on (even if only two interfaces are present). By default, the SRX simply floods the packet out all interfaces in the same VLAN, except for the port on which the packet arrived. This is how a switch normally functions when it doesn't know the destination MAC address. In some cases, customers might not wish to flood any packets out for security reasons. For this reason, Junos offers you an alternative to flooding the traffic, which is to send an ARP, and optionally a traceroute, while queuing the packet. If no destination responds, the original packet is dropped. You can configure how the platform responds to unknown destination MAC addresses in the flow configuration, configured later in this chapter.
5. Step 4 determined what destination interface to forward the traffic out of, and therefore the destination zone is known. The source zone is known as soon as the packet arrives, because the system knows what interface it arrived on, and therefore what the source zone is. With the knowledge of the source and destination zones in hand, the SRX can then do a policy lookup in the from-to- zone context. The SRX performs a policy lookup in the specific from-to-zone context to match traffic on the source IP, destination IP, and application (source/destination ports and protocol).
6. If ALGs are configured, such as FTP, the SRX must examine any control traffic that is matched to an ALG. An example of this would be port 21 for FTP, although custom ports can also be used by the ALG, which is configured in a custom application object. For ALG control traffic, the SRX must do several things. First, it must perform packet reassembly if fragmentation is used, along with TCP reassembly if the application message spans multiple TCP packets. Then the ALG determines if any additional data sessions need to be opened on the SRX.

7. After the ALG stage is processed (if present), the SRX performs additional services, such as IPS, if configuration is present.
8. The last stage of packet processing before forwarding the initial packet is to install the session. In the case of the high-end SRX, the session will be installed on the ingress/egress NPUs along with the CP and, of course, the session table of the SPU processing the traffic itself (data center SRX only). On the branch SRX, the data plane will simply forward the packet from the data plane CPU out the correct interface.
9. The packet is sent to the egress NPU where it will be forwarded out the egress interface (data center SRX only).

Fast-path SPU packet processing

In Figure 6-3, you can see fast-path processing by following the flowchart and taking the Match Session "Yes" track. The fast-path packet process consists of the following steps:

1. An inbound packet is received by an interface and sent to the NPU, which provides processing for that interface. The NPU performs a session lookup and determines that it knows the session and the SPU processing it. The NPU then forwards the packet directly to the SPU that owns the session (data center SRX only).
2. Policing, stateless filtering, and screens are performed. Technically, the screens that are applied after the initial packet setup are all on the NPU on the high-end SRX platforms. On the branch SRX, these functions are applied directly by the data plane CPU.
3. The SPU or branch data plane CPU determines if it knows about the session already, which in this case it does. The session entry will provide cached instructions on how to process the packet so that the SRX does not have to do any forwarding or policy checks, as these have already been determined in the first packet processing. Note that if the egress interface that the session is tied to fails, the SRX will attempt to find a new forwarding path for the destination MAC address, if possible. It either floods the packet or sends an ARP, and optionally a traceroute, depending on your configuration.
4. If ALGs are configured, such as FTP, the SRX must examine any control traffic that is matched to an ALG. An example of this would be port 21 for FTP, although custom ports can also be used by the ALG, which are configured as custom application objects. For ALG control traffic, the SRX must do several things. First, it must perform packet reassembly if fragmentation is used, along with TCP reassembly if the application message spans multiple TCP packets. The ALG then determines if any additional data sessions need to be opened on the SRX.

5. After the ALG stage is processed (if present), the SRX performs additional services such as IPS, if configuration is present.
6. The packet is sent to the egress NPU where it is forwarded out the egress interface (data center SRX only). The branch device's data plane CPU directly forwards the traffic out the correct egress interface.

Session teardown

All sessions must come to an end at some point. A session could be terminated for several different reasons:

TCP
: A FIN or RESET is sent.

Session timeout
: Sessions that do not have any traffic after the defined idle timeout for that service will be cleared as a *session ageout*.

ALG
: An ALG can terminate a session based on the control traffic. This could terminate the control portion, data portion, or both of the session.

Other
: There are other reasons why a session might be cleared out, such as an IPS closing a session due to an attack being detected. Changes to policies or policy schedules can also trigger a session to close.

After a session has been closed, the SPU signals to the ingress/egress NPUs, the CP, and, if in an HA chassis cluster, its peer SPU that the session has closed.

Configuring Transparent Mode

Now that you have learned the various components of transparent mode, you can evaluate the configuration of the SRX in transparent mode. This section covers examples of the different concepts of transparent mode in the same order in which they were introduced in the preceding section.

Configuring Transparent Mode Basics

This example creates four interfaces. Two of the interfaces are going to be in access mode and two are going to be in trunk mode. Additionally, there are six different VLANs and six different bridge domains.

The interfaces and VLANs are as follows:

- ge-0/0/1 will be in access mode, with VLAN 10 as its VLAN for unit 0.

- ge-0/0/2 will be in access mode, with VLAN 20 as its VLAN for unit 0.
- ge-0/0/3 will be in trunk mode, with VLAN 10 on unit 10, VLAN 30 on unit 30, and VLAN 40 on unit 40.
- ge-0/0/4 will be in trunk mode, with VLAN 20 on unit 10, VLAN 50 on unit 50, and VLAN 60 on unit 60.

The six bridge domains are each called `L2-VLAN-XX` where *XX* is the VLAN number. The bridge domains logically separate the traffic for the different VLANs.

```
{secondary:node0}[edit]
root@SRX3400-1# edit interfaces ge-0/0/1 unit 0 family bridge

{secondary:node0}[edit interfaces ge-0/0/1 unit 0 family bridge]
root@SRX3400-1# set interface-mode access vlan-id 10

{secondary:node0}[edit interfaces ge-0/0/1 unit 0 family bridge]
root@SRX3400-1# up 3

{secondary:node0}[edit interfaces]
root@SRX3400-1# edit ge-0/0/2 unit 0 family bridge

{secondary:node0}[edit interfaces ge-0/0/2 unit 0 family bridge]
root@SRX3400-1# set interface-mode access vlan-id 20

{secondary:node0}[edit interfaces ge-0/0/2 unit 0 family bridge]
root@SRX3400-1# up 3

{secondary:node0}[edit interfaces]
root@SRX3400-1# edit ge-0/0/3

{secondary:node0}[edit interfaces ge-0/0/3]
root@SRX3400-1# set unit 10 family bridge interface-mode trunk vlan-id-list 10

{secondary:node0}[edit interfaces ge-0/0/3]
root@SRX3400-1# set unit 30 family bridge interface-mode trunk vlan-id-list 30

{secondary:node0}[edit interfaces ge-0/0/3]
root@SRX3400-1# set unit 40 family bridge interface-mode trunk vlan-id-list 40

{secondary:node0}[edit interfaces ge-0/0/3]
root@SRX3400-1# set vlan-tagging

{secondary:node0}[edit interfaces ge-0/0/3]
root@SRX3400-1# up

{secondary:node0}[edit interfaces]
root@SRX3400-1# edit ge-0/0/4

{secondary:node0}[edit interfaces ge-0/0/4]
root@SRX3400-1# set unit 20 family bridge interface-mode trunk vlan-id-list 20
```

```
{secondary:node0}[edit interfaces ge-0/0/4]
root@SRX3400-1# set unit 50 family bridge interface-mode trunk vlan-id-list 50

{secondary:node0}[edit interfaces ge-0/0/4]
root@SRX3400-1# set unit 60 family bridge interface-mode trunk vlan-id-list 60

{secondary:node0}[edit interfaces ge-0/0/3]
root@SRX3400-1# set vlan-tagging

{secondary:node0}[edit interfaces ge-0/0/4]
root@SRX3400-1# up

{secondary:node0}[edit interfaces]
root@SRX3400-1# show
ge-0/0/1 {
    unit 0 {
        family bridge {
            interface-mode access;
            vlan-id 10;
        }
    }
}
ge-0/0/2 {
    unit 0 {
        family bridge {
            interface-mode access;
            vlan-id 20;
        }
    }
}
ge-0/0/3 {
    vlan-tagging;
    unit 10 {
        family bridge {
            interface-mode trunk;
            vlan-id-list 10;
        }
    }
    unit 30 {
        family bridge {
            interface-mode trunk;
            vlan-id-list 30;
        }
    }
    unit 40 {
        family bridge {
            interface-mode trunk;
            vlan-id-list 40;
        }
    }
}
```

```
ge-0/0/4 {
    vlan-tagging;
    unit 20 {
        family bridge {
            interface-mode trunk;
            vlan-id-list 20;
        }
    }
    unit 50 {
        family bridge {
            interface-mode trunk;
            vlan-id-list 50;
        }
    }
    unit 60 {
        family bridge {
            interface-mode trunk;
            vlan-id-list 60;
        }
    }
}

{secondary:node0}[edit interfaces]
root@SRX3400-1# up

{secondary:node0}[edit]
root@SRX3400-1# set bridge-domains L2-VLAN-10 domain-type bridge vlan-id 10

{secondary:node0}[edit]
root@SRX3400-1# set bridge-domains L2-VLAN-20 domain-type bridge vlan-id 20

{secondary:node0}[edit]
root@SRX3400-1# set bridge-domains L2-VLAN-30 domain-type bridge vlan-id 30

{secondary:node0}[edit]
root@SRX3400-1# set bridge-domains L2-VLAN-40 domain-type bridge vlan-id 40

{secondary:node0}[edit]
root@SRX3400-1# set bridge-domains L2-VLAN-50 domain-type bridge vlan-id 50

{secondary:node0}[edit]
root@SRX3400-1# set bridge-domains L2-VLAN-60 domain-type bridge vlan-id 60

{secondary:node0}[edit]
root@SRX3400-1# show bridge-domains
L2-VLAN-10 {
    domain-type bridge;
    vlan-id 10;
}
L2-VLAN-20 {
    domain-type bridge;
    vlan-id 20;
```

```
    }
    L2-VLAN-30 {
        domain-type bridge;
        vlan-id 30;
    }
    L2-VLAN-40 {
        domain-type bridge;
        vlan-id 40;
    }
    L2-VLAN-50 {
        domain-type bridge;
        vlan-id 50;
    }
    L2-VLAN-60 {
        domain-type bridge;
        vlan-id 60;
    }
```

Before you can switch from Layer 3 to Layer 2, you must reboot the firewalls in the cluster. This is required whenever switching from Layer 3 to Layer 2 modes.

```
{secondary:node0}[edit]
root@SRX3400-1# commit and-quit
warning: Interfaces are changed from route mode to transparent mode. Please
reboot the device or all nodes in the HA cluster!
node0:
configuration check succeeds
node1:
warning: Interfaces are changed from route mode to transparent mode. Please
reboot the device or all nodes in the HA cluster!
commit complete
node0:
commit complete

{primary:node0}
root@SRX3400-1> request system reboot

{secondary:node2}
root@SRX3400-2> request system reboot
```

You might be asking yourself, why is `vlan-id` used for the access mode interfaces and `vlan-id-list` for the trunk mode interfaces? This is because access mode interfaces can only have a single VLAN ID (which is untagged). With trunk mode interfaces, you can have multiple units, each with different VLANs, or you can tie a group of VLANs to a single trunk mode logical interface. These will be bridged separately (if they are part of different bridge domains), but it essentially allows you to take a shortcut with defining the interfaces themselves.

One important thing to note from this example is that for the trunk interfaces with this configuration, any untagged packets are dropped (or packets tagged for VLANs that you are not looking for). If you would like to accept untagged packets, you would want to use the following code:

```
{secondary:node0}[edit interfaces ge-0/0/3]
root@SRX3400-1# set native-vlan-id 5
```

Traditional Switching

Plain Layer 2 switching is covered in Chapter 4. For complete and through coverage of the Junos switching capabilities, please refer to *Junos Enterprise Switching*.

Configuring Integrated Routing and Bridging

Transparent mode does not use Layer 3 IP addresses on its interfaces; therefore, there is no way to communicate with it directly or to send traffic from the transparent mode interfaces directly. To solve this issue, the SRX supports IRB interfaces, so you can send traffic from the SRX as well as manage the SRX on these interfaces. IRB interfaces are not required in transparent mode, but they are required if you want to send traffic out the data plane or receive traffic directed at the SRX on the data plane in transparent mode. In this example, the SRX is configured to send syslog messages out the IRB.0 interface in transparent mode, along with allowing inbound management via SSH and ping. To do this, configure the following:

- Configure the IRB.0 interface in VLAN 60, with an IP address of 192.168.60.1/24.
- Route traffic to syslog server 192.16.15.20 via next-hop 192.168.60.254.
- Allow inbound SSH and pings for the IRB.0 interface.

```
{primary:node0}[edit]
root@SRX3400-1# set interfaces irb unit 0 family inet address 192.168.60.1/24


{primary:node0}[edit]
root@SRX3400-1# show interfaces irb
unit 0 {
    family inet {
        address 192.168.60.1/24;
    }
}

{primary:node0}[edit]
root@SRX3400-1#  set  routing-options  static  route  192.168.15.20  next-
hop192.168.60.254

{primary:node0}[edit]
root@SRX3400-1# show routing-options
static {
    route 192.168.15.20/32 next-hop 192.168.60.254;
}
```

```
{primary:node0}[edit]
root@SRX3400-1# set bridge-domains L2-VLAN-60 routing-interface irb.0

{primary:node0}[edit]
root@SRX3400-1# show bridge-domains L2-VLAN-60
domain-type bridge;
vlan-id 60;
routing-interface irb.0;

{primary:node0}[edit]
root@SRX3400-1# set system services ssh


{primary:node0}[edit]
root@SRX3400-1# show system services
ssh;

{primary:node0}[edit]
root@SRX3400-1# edit firewall family inet filter Services term Inbound

{primary:node0}[edit firewall family inet filter Services term Inbound]
root@SRX3400-1# set Inbound from protocol tcp


{primary:node0}[edit firewall family inet filter Services term Inbound]
root@SRX3400-1# set from destination-port 22

{primary:node0}[edit firewall family inet filter Services term Inbound]
root@SRX3400-1# set then accept

{primary:node0}[edit firewall family inet filter Services term Inbound]
root@SRX3400-1# up

{primary:node0}[edit firewall family inet filter Services]
root@SRX3400-1# edit term ICMP

{primary:node0}[edit firewall family inet filter Services term ICMP]
root@SRX3400-1# set from protocol icmp icmp-type echo-request

{primary:node0}[edit firewall family inet filter Services term ICMP]
root@SRX3400-1# set then accept

{primary:node0}[edit firewall family inet filter Services term ICMP]
root@SRX3400-1# up


{primary:node0}[edit firewall family inet filter Services]
root@SRX3400-1# show
term Inbound {
    from {
        protocol tcp;
```

```
            destination-port 22;
        }
        then accept;
    }
    term ICMP {
        from {
            protocol icmp;
            icmp-type echo-request;
        }
        then accept;
    }

{primary:node0}[edit]
root@SRX3400-1# set interfaces irb unit 0 family inet filter input Services


{primary:node0}[edit]
root@SRX3400-1# show interfaces irb
unit 0 {
    family inet {
        filter {
            input Services;
        }
        address 192.168.60.1/24;
    }
}
```

If you want to restrict what services to listen on for the IRB interface, you should limit the system services allowed on the surrounding interfaces in the zones the VLANs are in and use standard Junos firewall filters to limit what services are listened for on the IRB interfaces.

Configuring Transparent Mode Security Zones

Now that you have seen the interfaces and placed them into their respective bridge domains, let's add them into security zones on the SRX. As mentioned earlier in the chapter, the Layer 2 security zones don't have any special properties to them, and the configuration is just like Layer 3. In this example, the interfaces that were created two examples ago are configured as follows:

- Place interface ge-0/0/1.0 into the trust zone.
- Place interface ge-0/0/2.0 into the untrust zone.
- Place interfaces ge-0/0/3.40, ge-0/0/4.20, and ge-0/0/4.60 into the trust zone.
- Place interfaces ge-0/0/3.10, ge-0/0/3.30, and ge-0/04.50 into the untrust zone.

- Enable ping and SSH for all interfaces in the trust zone; only allow ping for interfaces in the untrust zone.

```
{primary:node0}[edit]
root@SRX3400-1# edit security zones security-zone trust

{primary:node0}[edit security zones security-zone trust]
root@SRX3400-1# show
host-inbound-traffic {
    system-services {
        ping;
        ssh;
    }
}
interfaces {
    ge-0/0/1.0;
    ge-0/0/3.40;
    ge-0/0/4.20;
    ge-0/0/4.60;
}


{primary:node0}[edit security zones security-zone trust]
root@SRX3400-1# up

{primary:node0}[edit security zones]
root@SRX3400-1# edit security-zone untrust

{primary:node0}[edit security zones security-zone untrust]
root@SRX3400-1# set interfaces ge-0/0/2.0

{primary:node0}[edit security zones security-zone untrust]
root@SRX3400-1# set interfaces ge-0/0/3.10

{primary:node0}[edit security zones security-zone untrust]
root@SRX3400-1# set interfaces ge-0/0/3.30

{primary:node0}[edit security zones security-zone untrust]
root@SRX3400-1# set interfaces ge-0/0/4.50

{primary:node0}[edit security zones security-zone untrust]
root@SRX3400-1# set host-inbound-traffic system-services ping

{primary:node0}[edit security zones security-zone untrust]
root@SRX3400-1# show
host-inbound-traffic {
    system-services {
        ping;
    }
}
interfaces {
    ge-0/0/2.0;
```

```
        ge-0/0/3.10;
        ge-0/0/3.30;
        ge-0/0/4.50;
    }
```

Configuring Transparent Mode Security Policies

305 Now that the separate logical Layer 2 interfaces have been created and assigned to security zones, let's create security policies to dictate what traffic is or isn't allowed to pass through the device between the various zones.

In this example, the following properties are configured:

- Create a rule from trust to untrust that allows any HTTP, HTTPS, SMTP, and FTP traffic to go from the three trust networks 172.31.20.0/24, 172.31.40.0/24, and 172.31.60.0/24 to the three untrust networks 172.31.10.0/24, 172.31.30.0/24, and 172.31.50.0/24.
- Create a rule that allows only UDP-DNS and PING to return from the three untrust networks to the three trust networks.
- Log all policies on session close.
- Set the default policy to Deny-All (it should be set as this by default).

```
{primary:node0}[edit]
root@SRX3400-1#   set   security   address-book   address   172.31.20.0/24
172.31.20.0/24

{primary:node0}[edit]
root@SRX3400-1#   set   security   address-book   address   172.31.40.0/24
172.31.40.0/24

{primary:node0}[edit]
root@SRX3400-1#   set   security   address-book   address   172.31.60.0/24
172.31.60.0/24

{primary:node0}[edit]
root@SRX3400-1#   set   security   address-book   address   172.31.10.0/24
172.31.10.0/24

{primary:node0}[edit]
root@SRX3400-1#   set   security   address-book   address   172.31.30.0/24
172.31.30.0/24

{primary:node0}[edit]
root@SRX3400-1#   set   security   address-book   address   172.31.50.0/24
172.31.50.0/24

{primary:node0}[edit]
root@SRX3400-1# show security zones
```

```
    security-zone untrust {
        host-inbound-traffic {
            system-services {
                ping;
            }
        }
        interfaces {
            ge-0/0/2.0;
            ge-0/0/3.10;
            ge-0/0/3.30;
            ge-0/0/4.50;
        }
    }
    security-zone trust {
        host-inbound-traffic {
            system-services {
                ping;
                ssh;
            }
            protocols {
                all;
            }
        }
        interfaces {
            ge-0/0/1.0;
            ge-0/0/3.40;
            ge-0/0/4.20;
            ge-0/0/4.60;
        }
    }


{primary:node0}[edit]
root@SRX3400-1# edit security policies from-zone trust to-zone untrust poli
cyAllow-Traffic

{primary:node0}[edit security policies from-zone trust to-zone untrust policy
Allow-Traffic]
root@SRX3400-1#   set   match   source-address   [   172.31.20.0/24
172.31.40.0/24172.31.60.0/24 ]

{primary:node0}[edit security policies from-zone trust to-zone untrust policy
Allow-Traffic]
root@SRX3400-1#   set   match   destination-address   [   172.31.10.0/24
172.31.30.0/24172.31.50.0/24 ]

{primary:node0}[edit security policies from-zone trust to-zone untrust policy
Allow-Traffic]
root@SRX3400-1#  set  match  application  [  junos-http  junos-https  junos-
smtpjunos-ftp ]

{primary:node0}[edit security policies from-zone trust to-zone untrust policy
```

```
Allow-Traffic]
root@SRX3400-1# set then permit

{primary:node0}[edit security policies from-zone trust to-zone untrust policy
Allow-Traffic]
root@SRX3400-1# set then log session-close

{primary:node0}[edit security policies from-zone trust to-zone untrust policy
Allow-Traffic]
root@SRX3400-1# up 2

{primary:node0}[edit security policies]
root@SRX3400-1# edit from-zone untrust to-zone trust policy Allow-Inbound

{primary:node0}[edit security policies from-zone untrust to-zone trust policy
Allow-Inbound]
root@SRX3400-1#    set    match    source-address    [    172.31.10.0/24
172.31.30.0/24172.31.50.0/24 ]

{primary:node0}[edit security policies from-zone untrust to-zone trust policy
Allow-Inbound]
root@SRX3400-1#    set    match    destination-address    [    172.31.20.0/24
172.31.40.0/24172.31.60.0/24 ]

{primary:node0}[edit security policies from-zone untrust to-zone trust policy
Allow-Inbound]
root@SRX3400-1# set match application [ junos-dns-udp junos-ping ]

{primary:node0}[edit security policies from-zone untrust to-zone trust policy
Allow-Inbound]
root@SRX3400-1# set then permit

{primary:node0}[edit security policies from-zone untrust to-zone trust policy
Allow-Inbound]
root@SRX3400-1# set then log session-close

{primary:node0}[edit security policies from-zone untrust to-zone trust policy
Allow-Inbound]
root@SRX3400-1# up 2

{primary:node0}[edit security policies]
root@SRX3400-1# set default-policy deny-all


{primary:node0}[edit security policies]
root@SRX3400-1# show
from-zone trust to-zone untrust {
    policy Allow-Traffic {
        match {
            source-address [ 172.31.20.0/24 172.31.40.0/24 172.31.60.0/24 ];
                        destination-address  [  172.31.10.0/24  172.31.30.0/24
172.31.50.0/24 ];
```

```
                application [ junos-http junos-https junos-smtp junos-ftp ];
            }
            then {
                permit;
                log {
                    session-close;
                }
            }
        }
    }
    from-zone untrust to-zone trust {
        policy Allow-Inbound {
            match {
                source-address [ 172.31.10.0/24 172.31.30.0/24 172.31.50.0/24 ];
                            destination-address  [  172.31.20.0/24  172.31.40.0/24
    172.31.60.0/24 ];
                application [ junos-dns-udp junos-ping ];
            }
            then {
                permit;
                log {
                    session-close;
                }
            }
        }
    }
    default-policy {
        deny-all;
    }
```

Configuring Bridging Options

309 Several bridging options can be configured on the SRX to manipulate how it processes packets and performs learning operations in transparent mode. Typically, you won't need to alter the configuration of these options, but just in case, this section demonstrates how to do exactly that.

In this example, the following configurations are performed:

- Your network has some legacy applications that require IPX, DECNET, AppleTalk, and Banyan VINES. Because the SRX does not support these protocols, configure the firewall to just bypass them from the firewall for processing.
- Your security posture is strict in terms of information leakage, so configure the SRX not to flood any packets with an unknown MAC address.

```
{primary:node0}[edit]
root@SRX3400-1# edit security flow bridge

{primary:node0}[edit security flow bridge]
root@SRX3400-1# set bypass-non-ip-unicast
```

```
{primary:node0}[edit security flow bridge]
root@SRX3400-1# set no-packet-flooding

{primary:node0}[edit security flow bridge]
root@SRX3400-1# show
bypass-non-ip-unicast;
no-packet-flooding;
```

Restricting BPDUs to VLANs

In an effort to provide more deployment flexibility, Juniper added the ability to restrict BPDUs to only the VLANs on which they originate. As stated, the default behavior is to receive and then flood BPDUs out all active ports on the SRX. To activate this new behavior, only one command is required to be entered and then committed.

```
[edit]
root@srx3600n0# set security flow bridge bpdu-vlan-flooding

[edit]
root@srx3600n0# show security flow
bridge {
    bpdu-vlan-flooding;
}

[edit]
root@srx3600n0 # commit and-quit
```

Configuring Transparent Mode QoS

QoS in transparent mode is essentially the same as Layer 3 mode, with the primary exceptions of how the classification is performed and how the rewriting can be performed (802.1p bits only).

- Classify traffic matching the 802.1p bits 011 to the Expedited Forwarding Class (low loss priority) and 802.1p bits 111 to the Assured Forwarding Class (high loss priority) on interfaces reth0 and reth1.
- On reth0 and reth1, rewrite the outgoing 802.1p bits from 011 to 000 and 111 to 101, respectively.

```
[edit]
root@SRX3600-1# edit class-of-service classifiers ieee-802.1 011

[edit class-of-service classifiers ieee-802.1 011]
root@SRX3600-1# set forwarding-class expedited-forwarding loss-priority low
code-points 011

[edit class-of-service classifiers ieee-802.1 011]
root@SRX3600-1# up 1
```

```
[edit class-of-service classifiers]
root@SRX3600-1# edit ieee-802.1 111

[edit class-of-service classifiers ieee-802.1 111]
root@SRX3600-1# set forwarding-class assured-forwarding loss-priority high
code-points 111

[edit class-of-service classifiers ieee-802.1 111]
root@SRX3600-1# up 2

[edit class-of-service]
root@SRX3600-1# edit rewrite-rules

[edit class-of-service rewrite-rules]
root@SRX3600-1# edit ieee-802.1 011

[edit class-of-service rewrite-rules ieee-802.1 011]
root@SRX3600-1# set forwarding-class expedited-forwarding loss-priority low
code-point 000

[edit class-of-service rewrite-rules ieee-802.1 011]
root@SRX3600-1# up

[edit class-of-service rewrite-rules]
root@SRX3600-1# edit ieee-802.1 111

[edit class-of-service rewrite-rules ieee-802.1 111]
root@SRX3600-1# set forwarding-class assured-forwarding loss-priority high
code-point 101

[edit class-of-service rewrite-rules ieee-802.1 111]
root@SRX3600-1# up 2

[edit class-of-service]
root@SRX3600-1# set interfaces reth0 unit 0 classifiers ieee-802.1 011

[edit class-of-service]
root@SRX3600-1# set interfaces reth0 unit 0 rewrite-rules ieee-802.1 011

[edit class-of-service]
root@SRX3600-1# set interfaces reth1 unit 0 classifiers ieee-802.1 111

[edit class-of-service]
root@SRX3600-1# set interfaces reth1 unit 0 rewrite-rules ieee-802.1 111

[edit class-of-service]
root@SRX3600-1# show
classifiers {
    ieee-802.1 011 {
        forwarding-class expedited-forwarding {
            loss-priority low code-points 011;
```

```
            }
        }
        ieee-802.1 111 {
            forwarding-class assured-forwarding {
                loss-priority high code-points 111;
            }
        }
    }
    interfaces {
        reth0 {
            unit 0 {
                classifiers {
                    ieee-802.1 011;
                }
                rewrite-rules {
                    ieee-802.1 011;
                }
            }
        }
        reth1 {
            unit 0 {
                classifiers {
                    ieee-802.1 111;
                }
                rewrite-rules {
                    ieee-802.1 111;
                }
            }
        }
    }
    rewrite-rules {
        ieee-802.1 011 {
            forwarding-class expedited-forwarding {
                loss-priority low code-point 000;
            }
        }
        ieee-802.1 111 {
            forwarding-class assured-forwarding {
                loss-priority high code-point 101;
            }
        }
    }
```

Configuring VLAN Rewriting

Earlier in this chapter, we mentioned that you can use VLAN rewriting to rewrite one VLAN to another on an interface. This example does exactly that, with the following configuration:

- On interface ge-0/0/3, configure VLAN retagging to translate VLAN 100 to VLAN 10. Use unit 10 for this translation.

- On interface ge-0/0/4, configure VLAN retagging to translate VLAN 200 to VLAN 20. Use unit 20 for this translation.

```
{primary:node0}[edit]
root@SRX3400-1# edit interfaces ge-0/0/3

{primary:node0}[edit interfaces ge-0/0/3]
root@SRX3400-1# set unit 10 family bridge vlan-rewrite translate 100 10

{primary:node0}[edit interfaces ge-0/0/3]
root@SRX3400-1# show
vlan-tagging;
unit 10 {
    family bridge {
        interface-mode trunk;
        vlan-id-list 10;
        vlan-rewrite {
            translate 100 10;
        }
    }
}
unit 30 {
    family bridge {
        interface-mode trunk;
        vlan-id-list 30;
    }
}
unit 40 {
    family bridge {
        interface-mode trunk;
        vlan-id-list 40;
    }
}

{primary:node0}[edit interfaces ge-0/0/3]
root@SRX3400-1# up

{primary:node0}[edit interfaces]
root@SRX3400-1# edit ge-0/0/4

{primary:node0}[edit interfaces ge-0/0/4]
root@SRX3400-1# set unit 20 family bridge vlan-rewrite translate 200 20

{primary:node0}[edit interfaces ge-0/0/4]
root@SRX3400-1# show
vlan-tagging;
unit 20 {
    family bridge {
        interface-mode trunk;
        vlan-id-list 20;
        vlan-rewrite {
            translate 200 20;
```

```
            }
        }
    }
    unit 50 {
        family bridge {
            interface-mode trunk;
            vlan-id-list 50;
        }
    }
    unit 60 {
        family bridge {
            interface-mode trunk;
            vlan-id-list 60;
        }
    }
```

As you can see here, you need to configure `vlan-rewrite` under a logical unit that is configured as a trunk link. In the case of ge-0/0/3, traffic that arrives inbound, tagged with VLAN 100, is translated on ingress to VLAN 10 and processed accordingly. When traffic on VLAN 10 is leaving the SRX on that interface, it is reverse-translated on egress to VLAN 100. The same is true for ge-0/0/4 translating from VLAN 200 to 20 and vice versa. The main command that empowers this is the `set interfaces <interface> unit <unit> family bridge interface-mode trunk translate <incoming-vlan> <translated-vlan>` command. In addition, you must define the VLANs that are present on the unit using the `vlan-id-list` command.

Troubleshooting and Operation

Troubleshooting issues in transparent mode are almost identical to troubleshooting Layer 3, with a few exceptions that are the focus here. First, this section lists some of the useful commands in Layer 2 that you should be aware of, and then we will work our way through a step-by-step troubleshooting plan. Additional troubleshooting methodologies can be found in Chapter 8.

The next few commands are unique to transparent mode. We cover the rest of the steps in the section "Transparent Mode Troubleshooting Steps" on page 272 later in this chapter.

The show bridge domain Command

The `show bridge domain` command lists all of the active bridge domains on the device, along with the associated VLANs and interfaces for those domains. If you are experiencing an issue where traffic isn't flowing, you should check this first to make sure you have the correct interface, VLAN, and bridge domain configuration.

```
root@SRX3400-1> show bridge domain

Routing instance     Bridge domain       VLAN ID     Interfaces
default-switch       L2-VLAN-10          10
```

```
                                                          ge-0/0/1.0
                                                          ge-0/0/3.10
default-switch        L2-VLAN-20           20
                                                          ge-0/0/2.0
                                                          ge-0/0/4.20
default-switch        L2-VLAN-30           30
                                                          ge-0/0/3.30
default-switch        L2-VLAN-40           40
                                                          ge-0/0/3.40
default-switch        L2-VLAN-50           50
                                                          ge-0/0/4.50
default-switch        L2-VLAN-60           60
                                                          ge-0/0/4.60
```

The show bridge mac-table Command

The `show bridge mac-table` command is important for looking at the bridge MAC learning table. If you do not see the MAC addresses for the hosts in the correct bridge domain on the correct interface of this output, either the SRX is not seeing the MAC addresses at all (check the surrounding networking devices) or you're seeing them on the wrong interface or bridge domain (which might require some configuration changes).

```
{primary:node0}
root@SRX3400-1> show bridge mac-table

MAC flags (S -static MAC, D -dynamic MAC,
           SE -Statistics enabled, NM -Non configured MAC)

Routing instance : default-switch
 Bridging domain : L2-VLAN-20, VLAN : 20
   MAC                   MAC      Logical
   address               flags    interface
   00:1f:12:31:d3:21     D        ge-0/0/2.0
   00:1f:12:f4:ef:1c     D        ge-0/0/2.0
```

The show l2-learning global-information Command

This command lists the global configuration for the SRX bridge domains.

```
{primary:node0}
root@SRX3400-1> show l2-learning global-information
Global Configuration:

MAC aging interval     : 300
MAC learning           : Enabled
MAC statistics         : Disabled
MAC limit Count        : 131071
MAC limit hit          : Disabled
MAC packet action drop: Disabled
```

```
LE  aging time          : 1200
LE  BD aging time       : 1200
```

The show l2-learning global-mac-count Command

You might also want to check how many MAC addresses your system currently knows about, to ensure that the table is not full. At the time of this writing, the SRX supports 64,000 MAC address entries in the table.

```
{primary:node0}
root@SRX3400-1> show l2-learning global-mac-count
2 dynamic and static MAC addresses learned globally
```

The show l2-learning interface Command

Although the SRX doesn't support STP natively at the time of this writing, it will forward the BPDUs to ensure that there are no bridge loops. Additionally, there might be reasons why an interface is forwarding or VLANs within an interface are not forwarding, such as the physical interface being down, as shown in this example:

```
{primary:node0}
root@SRX3400-1> show l2-learning interface
Routing Instance Name : default-switch
Logical Interface flags (DL -disable learning, AD -packet action drop,
                         LH - MAC limit hit, DN - Interface Down )
Logical             BD          MAC         STP           Logical
Interface           Name        Limit       State         Interface flags
ge-0/0/1.0                      131071
                    L2-VLA..    131071      Forwarding
Routing Instance Name : default-switch
Logical Interface flags (DL -disable learning, AD -packet action drop,
                         LH - MAC limit hit, DN - Interface Down )
Logical             BD          MAC         STP           Logical
Interface           Name        Limit       State         Interface flags
ge-0/0/3.30                     131071
                    L2-VLA..    131071      Discarding
Routing Instance Name : default-switch
Logical Interface flags (DL -disable learning, AD -packet action drop,
                         LH - MAC limit hit, DN - Interface Down )
Logical             BD          MAC         STP           Logical
Interface           Name        Limit       State         Interface flags
ge-0/0/3.40                     131071
                    L2-VLA..    131071      Discarding
Routing Instance Name : default-switch
Logical Interface flags (DL -disable learning, AD -packet action drop,
                         LH - MAC limit hit, DN - Interface Down )
Logical             BD          MAC         STP           Logical
Interface           Name        Limit       State         Interface flags
ge-0/0/4.20                     131071
                    L2-VLA..    131071      Discarding
Routing Instance Name : default-switch
```

```
Logical Interface flags (DL -disable learning, AD -packet action drop,
                         LH - MAC limit hit, DN - Interface Down )
Logical             BD          MAC         STP            Logical
Interface           Name        Limit       State          Interface flags
ge-0/0/2.0                      131071
                    L2-VLA..    131071      Forwarding
Routing Instance Name : default-switch
Logical Interface flags (DL -disable learning, AD -packet action drop,
                         LH - MAC limit hit, DN - Interface Down )
Logical             BD          MAC         STP            Logical
Interface           Name        Limit       State          Interface flags
ge-0/0/4.50                     131071
                    L2-VLA..    131071      Discarding
Routing Instance Name : default-switch
Logical Interface flags (DL -disable learning, AD -packet action drop,
                         LH - MAC limit hit, DN - Interface Down )
Logical             BD          MAC         STP            Logical
Interface           Name        Limit       State          Interface flags
ge-0/0/4.60                     131071
                    L2-VLA..    131071      Discarding
Routing Instance Name : default-switch
Logical Interface flags (DL -disable learning, AD -packet action drop,
                         LH - MAC limit hit, DN - Interface Down )
Logical             BD          MAC         STP            Logical
Interface           Name        Limit       State          Interface flags
ge-0/0/3.10                     131071
                    L2-VLA..    131071      Discarding
```

Transparent Mode Troubleshooting Steps

Here are some recommended sequential troubleshooting steps for working in transparent mode.

1. Check the spanning tree.

   An issue with the spanning tree is the most common issue when traffic is not flowing through the SRX properly, as surrounding networking gear with spanning tree enabled could put the data interfaces into a blocking state. This is not an issue with the SRX itself, but you will need to run the respective commands on the surrounding networking gear to determine if any of the interfaces that are connected to the SRX are in the blocking state. In the Juniper Networks EX Series Ethernet Switches, you would do this in Junos with the `show spanning-tree interface` command to look for interfaces in the `BLK` state. On the MX Series, you would look in Junos with the `show l2-learning interface` command.

Checking the spanning tree is particularly important when dealing with HA clusters, as the interfaces could be in the blocking state for one member and not the other. You should test failover to ensure it works properly.

2. Check to see if MAC addresses are being learned.

   The absence of MAC addresses in the SRX bridging table certainly indicates that there is an issue, along with MAC addresses not appearing on the correct VLANs or interfaces. On the SRX, you can use the `show bridge mac-table` command.

3. Check the configuration.

   The first common issue that occurs with transparent mode is often a configuration mistake, including the wrong VLAN IDs or incorrect bridge domains. You must check the configuration on the surrounding networking devices along with the SRX. On the SRX, you would want to start by looking at the `show bridge domain` command to make sure the VLAN configuration is properly mapped to the correct domains. You might also want to review the configuration of the surrounding devices.

4. Check that the native VLANs are properly configured.

   On both the SRX and the surrounding networking devices, you must make sure the correct native VLANs are used (if any), or else there could be an issue with interpreting the traffic. The same is true for properly matching the correct traffic to the correct VLAN. If you do not have the correct mappings, there will be issues. Note that the units do not technically need to match between the two devices, but making sure the correct tags and the correct classification are used is essential.

5. Check that sessions are being established.

   If the traffic appears to be arriving on the SRX on the correct interfaces and VLANs, you should check to make sure the sessions are being established and matched to the correct rule. You can do this initially by just looking at the session table using the `show security flow session <modifiers>` command along with running the standard flow tracing operations. For instance, you can enable the `basic-datapath` debug and send the output to the file *L2Debug*. Additionally, you should configure a packet filter based around the traffic you are looking for to ensure that you don't match unnecessary traffic. Make sure to turn the debugging off after the issue has been resolved to ensure that performance isn't impacted.

   ```
   {primary:node0}[edit]
   root@SRX3400-1# edit security flow traceoptions

   {primary:node0}[edit security flow traceoptions]
   root@SRX3400-1# set flag basic-datapath
   ```

```
{primary:node0}[edit security flow traceoptions]
root@SRX3400-1# set file L2Debug

{primary:node0}[edit security flow traceoptions]
root@SRX3400-1# set packet-filter MatchTraffic interface ge-0/0/1.0 source-
prefix
 172.31.0.0/16 destination-prefix 192.168.1.1

{primary:node0}[edit security flow traceoptions]
root@SRX3400-1# show
file L2Debug;
flag basic-datapath;
packet-filter MatchTraffic {
    source-prefix 172.31.0.0/16;
    destination-prefix 192.168.1.1/32;
    interface ge-0/0/1.0;
}
```

6. Examine the debug output.

   From your debugs, you should be able to determine that the traffic is entering and exiting the correct interfaces, along with being matched by the correct security policy. If this isn't happening, the output in the debug should provide you with hints about what you need to change to resolve the issue.

7. Check if you are using any unsupported features or running into a known issue.

   Remember that some SRX features are not yet supported in transparent mode. We covered them at the beginning of this chapter, and you might check with the Juniper documentation for actual timing of these features. For known issues, you should check the release notes of the version you are running, along with any subsequent releases for issues that have been resolved in case it sounds like a bug. If you are using these features, that could be causing the issue. Check with the JTAC if you suspect this.

8. Troubleshoot the surrounding networking equipment.

   If the SRX appears to be processing the traffic properly and the traffic appears to be entering and exiting the SRX, you should access the neighboring devices to make sure the traffic is actually reaching them and that they are processing the traffic correctly. The methodology you would follow on the other devices depends on the device, but if you can, do an end-to-end packet trace to try to determine where things are breaking down. That is definitely useful when all other steps seem to yield no information.

9. Check the Juniper Knowledge Base.

   The Juniper Knowledge Base (*http://kb.juniper.net/*) might have additional information for troubleshooting these issues, along with potential major known issues.

10. Call JTAC.

If all else fails, and you have gathered all of the data from your troubleshooting steps, you should call JTAC for additional assistance in troubleshooting the issue. Having information such as network diagrams, packet captures, and access to the devices is very helpful for finding a speedy resolution (see Chapter 8 for a series of commands to run output that JTAC might want or need to see).

Sample Deployments

Now that you have covered all of the concepts related to transparent mode, let's bring it all together and provide a full configuration example, along with the use of chassis clustering to achieve an HA solution.

There really isn't much difference between clustering a transparent mode pair and clustering a Layer 3 mode pair from a configuration or concept perspective—you just need to be aware of the surrounding networking configuration to accommodate transparent mode.

This case study performs the following configuration according to this book's network diagram (see Figure 6-4):

1. Create a chassis cluster with the two SRX3600s that protect the DMZ. Configure all of the properties of the HA cluster as you see fit (except the interfaces as described shortly). Use ge-0/0/9 and ge-13/0/9 for the data links.
2. Support trunk link reth0, which will serve as the backbone link. Reth0 will have two tagged VLANs, one for VLAN 100 and another that allows VLAN 30 inbound, but translates it to VLAN 1. Reth0 will be composed of the physical interfaces ge-0/0/0 and ge-13/0/0.
3. There will be four other reth interfaces that connect into a switch before connecting to the end servers. These will all use the access mode interfaces. Reth1 will belong to the VoIP PBX zone and will be composed of ge-0/0/1 and ge-13/0/1. Reth2 will be in the WebApp zone and will be composed of ge-0/0/2 and ge-13/0/2. Reth3 will be in the Email-Server zone and will be composed of ge-0/0/3 and ge-13/0/3. Finally, reth4 will be in the Database zone and will be composed of ge-0/0/4 and ge-13/0/4. All of these interfaces will be in VLAN 30.
    - Create the respective bridge domains.
    - Create an IRB.30 interface with an IP address of 172.31.30.254/24.
4. For your policies, create the following:
    - Allow Dept-A and Dept-B to talk to the PBX via Real Time Streaming Protocol (RTSP) and vice versa.

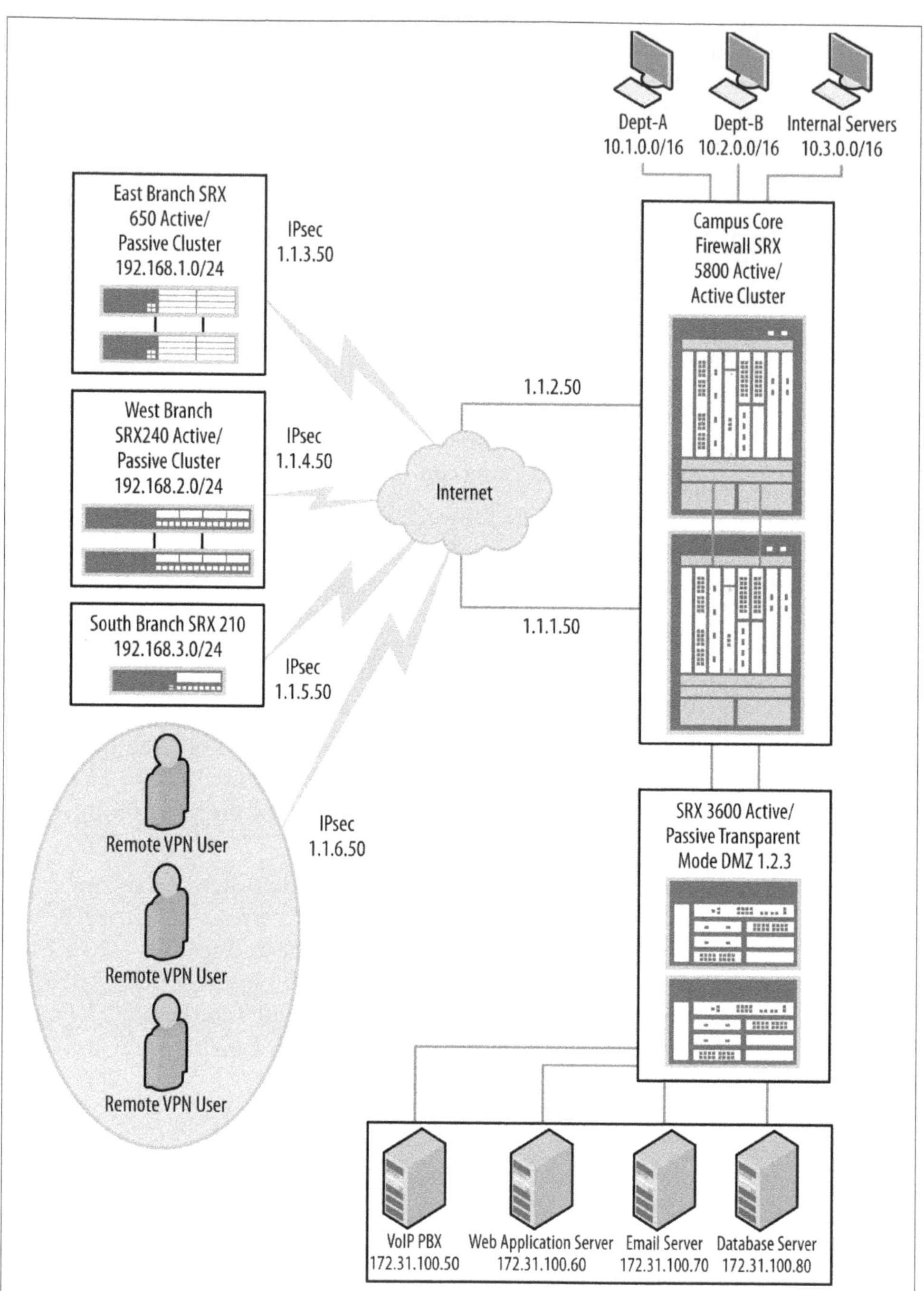

Figure 6-4. Sample deployment network diagram

- Allow inbound HTTP and HTTPS to the web server from any IP coming from the backbone.
- Allow the web server to query the database with SQL.
- Allow SMTP connections into the email server and from the email server out, along with DNS.

Set the chassis cluster IDs and node configuration, and reboot as follows:

```
root@SRX3400-1> set chassis cluster cluster-id 1 node 0 reboot
root@SRX3400-2> set chassis cluster cluster-id 1 node 1 reboot
```

This is an operational mode command. Also, because this is using SRX3600s, you don't need to configure any control ports.

Configure the data links.

```
{primary:node0}[edit]
root@SRX3400-1# set interfaces fab0 fabric-options member-interfaces ge-0/0/9

{primary:node0}[edit]
root@SRX3400-1# set interfaces fab1 fabric-options member-interfaces ge-13/0/9
```

Configure the node-specific properties.

```
{primary:node0}[edit]
root@SRX3400-1# set groups node0
{primary:node0}[edit]
root@SRX3400-1# set groups node1
{primary:node0}[edit]
root@SRX3400-1# set groups node0 system host-name SRX3600-1

{primary:node0}[edit]
root@SRX3400-1# set groups node0 interfaces fxp0 unit 0 family inet ad
dress10.3.5.1/24

{primary:node0}[edit]
root@SRX3400-1# set groups node0 system backup-router 10.3.5.254 destina
tion0.0.0.0/0

{primary:node0}[edit]
root@SRX3400-1# set groups node1 system host-name SRX3600-2

{primary:node0}[edit]
root@SRX3400-1# set groups node1 interfaces fxp0 unit 0 family inet ad
dress10.3.5.2/24

{primary:node0}[edit]
```

```
root@SRX3400-1# set groups node1 system backup-router 10.3.5.254 destina
tion0.0.0.0/0

{primary:node0}[edit]
root@SRX3400-1# set apply-groups ${node}
```

Configure the reth count and redundancy groups.

```
{primary:node0}[edit]
root@SRX3400-1# set chassis cluster reth-count 5

{primary:node0}[edit]
root@SRX3400-1# set chassis cluster redundancy-group 0 node 0 priority 129

{primary:node0}[edit]
root@SRX3400-1# set chassis cluster redundancy-group 0 node 1 priority 128

{primary:node0}[edit]
root@SRX3400-1# set chassis cluster redundancy-group 1 node 0 priority 129

{primary:node0}[edit]
root@SRX3400-1# set chassis cluster redundancy-group 1 node 1 priority 128
```

Configure the reth and IRB interfaces.

```
{primary:node0}[edit]
root@SRX3400-1# set interfaces ge-0/0/0 gigether-options redundant-parent reth0

{primary:node0}[edit]
root@SRX3400-1# set interfaces ge-13/0/0 gigether-options redundant-parent reth0

{primary:node0}[edit]
root@SRX3400-1# set interfaces ge-0/0/1 gigether-options redundant-parent reth1

{primary:node0}[edit]
root@SRX3400-1# set interfaces ge-13/0/1 gigether-options redundant-parent reth1

{primary:node0}[edit]
root@SRX3400-1# set interfaces ge-0/0/2 gigether-options redundant-parent reth2

{primary:node0}[edit]
root@SRX3400-1# set interfaces ge-13/0/2 gigether-options redundant-parent reth2

{primary:node0}[edit]
root@SRX3400-1# set interfaces ge-0/0/3 gigether-options redundant-parent reth3

{primary:node0}[edit]
root@SRX3400-1# set interfaces ge-13/0/3 gigether-options redundant-parent reth3

{primary:node0}[edit]
root@SRX3400-1# set interfaces ge-0/0/4 gigether-options redundant-parent reth4

{primary:node0}[edit]
root@SRX3400-1# set interfaces ge-13/0/4 gigether-options redundant-parent reth4
```

```
{primary:node0}[edit]
root@SRX3400-1# set interfaces reth0 redundant-ether-options redundancy-group 1

{primary:node0}[edit]
root@SRX3400-1# set interfaces reth1 redundant-ether-options redundancy-group 1

{primary:node0}[edit]
root@SRX3400-1# set interfaces reth2 redundant-ether-options redundancy-group 1

{primary:node0}[edit]
root@SRX3400-1# set interfaces reth3 redundant-ether-options redundancy-group 1

{primary:node0}[edit]
root@SRX3400-1# set interfaces reth4 redundant-ether-options redundancy-group 1

{primary:node0}[edit]
root@SRX3400-1# set interfaces reth0 vlan-tagging

{primary:node0}[edit]
root@SRX3400-1# set interfaces reth0 unit 100 family bridge interface-mode
trunkvlan-id-list 100

{primary:node0}[edit]
root@SRX3400-1# set interfaces reth0 unit 30 family bridge interface-mode trunk

{primary:node0}[edit]
root@SRX3400-1# set interfaces reth0 unit 30 family bridge vlan-rewrite trans
late30 1

{primary:node0}[edit]
root@SRX3400-1# set interfaces reth1 unit 0 family bridge interface-mode ac
cessvlan-id 100

{primary:node0}[edit]
root@SRX3400-1# set interfaces reth2 unit 0 family bridge interface-mode ac
cessvlan-id 100

{primary:node0}[edit]
root@SRX3400-1# set interfaces reth3 unit 0 family bridge interface-mode ac
cessvlan-id 100

{primary:node0}[edit]
root@SRX3400-1# set interfaces reth4 unit 0 family bridge interface-mode ac
cessvlan-id 100

{primary:node0}[edit]
root@SRX3400-1# set interfaces irb unit 100 family inet address
172.31.100.254/24
```

Configure the bridge domains.

```
{primary:node0}[edit]
root@SRX3400-1# set bridge-domains VLAN1 domain-type bridge vlan-id 1

{primary:node0}[edit]
root@SRX3400-1# set bridge-domains VLAN100 domain-type bridge vlan-id
100routing-interface irb.100
```

Configure security zones and address objects.

```
{primary:node0}[edit]
root@SRX3400-1# set security zones security-zones Backbone interfaces reth0.100

{primary:node0}[edit]
root@SRX3400-1# set security zones security-zones Backbone interfaces reth0.30

{primary:node0}[edit]
root@SRX3400-1# set security zones security-zones VoIP interfaces reth1

{primary:node0}[edit]
root@SRX3400-1# set security zones security-zones WebApp interfaces reth2

{primary:node0}[edit]
root@SRX3400-1# set security zones security-zones Email-Server interfaces reth3

{primary:node0}[edit]
root@SRX3400-1# set security zones security-zones Database interfaces reth4

{primary:node0}[edit]
root@SRX3400-1# set security zones security-zones Backbone address-book ad
dressDept-A 10.1.0.0/16

{primary:node0}[edit]
root@SRX3400-1# set security zones security-zones Backbone address-book ad
dressDept-B 10.2.0.0/16

{primary:node0}[edit]
root@SRX3400-1# set security zones security-zones VoIP address-book address
VoIP-PBX 172.31.100.50/32

{primary:node0}[edit]
root@SRX3400-1# set security zones security-zones WebApp address-book addressWe-
bApp 172.31.100.60/32

{primary:node0}[edit]
root@SRX3400-1# set security zones security-zones Email-Server address-bookad-
dress WebApp 172.31.100.70/32

{primary:node0}[edit]
root@SRX3400-1# set security zones security-zones Database address-book ad
dress172.31.100.80/32
```

Configure the security policies.

```
{primary:node0}[edit security policies]
root@SRX3400-1# set from-zone Backbone to-zone VoIP policy Allow-RTSP
matchsource-address [ Dept-A Dept-B ] destination-address VoIP-PBX application
junos-rtsp

{primary:node0}[edit security policies]
root@SRX3400-1# set from-zone Backbone to-zone VoIP policy Allow-RTSP then per
mit

{primary:node0}[edit security policies]
root@SRX3400-1# set from-zone VoIP to-zone Backbone policy Allow-RTSP-Out
matchsource-address VoIP-PBX destination-address [ Dept-A Dept-B ] application
junos-rtsp

{primary:node0}[edit security policies]
root@SRX3400-1# set from-zone Backbone to-zone VoIP policy Allow-RTSP-Out
thenpermit

{primary:node0}[edit security policies]
root@SRX3400-1# set from-zone Backbone to-zone WebApp policy Allow-Inbound-
Webmatch source-address any destination-address WebApp application [ junos-
httpjunos-https ]

{primary:node0}[edit security policies]
root@SRX3400-1# set from-zone Backbone to-zone WebApp policy Allow-Inbound-
Webthen permit

{primary:node0}[edit security policies]
root@SRX3400-1# set from-zone WebApp to-zone Database policy Allow-Web-
Queriesmatch source-address WebApp destination-address Database
application[ junos-sql ]

{primary:node0}[edit security policies]
root@SRX3400-1# set from-zone WebApp to-zone Database policy Allow-Web-
Queriesthen permit

{primary:node0}[edit security policies]
root@SRX3400-1# set from-zone Backbone to-zone Email-Server policy Allow-Emails-
Inbound match source-address any destination-address Email-Server application
[ junos-smtp ]

{primary:node0}[edit security policies]
root@SRX3400-1# set from-zone Backbone to-zone Email-Server policy Allow-Emails-
Inbound then permit

{primary:node0}[edit security policies]
root@SRX3400-1# set from-zone Email-Server to-zone Backbone policy Allow-Emails-
Outbound match source-address Email-Server destination-address any application
[ junos-smtp junos-dns-udp ]

{primary:node0}[edit security policies]
root@SRX3400-1# set from-zone Email-Server to-zone Backbone policy Allow-Emails-
```

```
Outbound then permit

{primary:node0}[edit security policies]
root@SRX3400-1# set default-policy deny-all
```

Summary

Transparent mode is a very powerful feature that can dramatically ease the deployment of a firewall while providing advanced support for securing your network. Most of the configuration relating to transparent mode is just like standard Layer 3 routed mode, but there are a few new concepts that you need to be aware of regarding the actual interface and VLAN configurations.

Although transparent mode is typically quite easy to deploy, you do need to be aware of the potential for bridge loops, along with the fact that spanning tree might cause links to go into the blocking state, and therefore not pass traffic properly.

In this chapter, we discussed many tools on the SRX and surrounding devices that can help you to determine the cause of an issue so that you can take appropriate steps to resolve it.

Finally, there are a few limitations of transparent mode at the time of this writing that you need to be aware of. As time goes on, Juniper will continue to strive to eliminate these limitations and achieve full-feature parity, so monitor the Junos release notes to determine what new features and support have arrived in the latest release. After all, Juniper comes out with new software every three months, so things can be developed quite quickly for the SRX.

Study Questions

Questions

1. Why is transparent mode a popular deployment model for firewall deployments?
2. What is the name of the family used on interfaces in transparent mode?
3. How can a device in transparent mode communicate with other devices on the network if the interfaces do not have any Layer 3 addressing?
4. What is the difference between interfaces in access mode and trunk mode?
5. What is the default method for resolving an unknown MAC address when the SRX has received a packet with an unknown MAC address and needs to forward it?
6. If you have non-IP traffic on your network, how can you have the SRX forward it?
7. With what fields can the SRX perform QoS for transit traffic?

8. What is the purpose of VLAN rewriting?
9. What is the most common issue in transparent mode that prevents traffic from flowing properly through the SRX?
10. How does the SRX inform surrounding networking equipment to recalculate spanning tree in the event of a failure?

Answers

1. Transparent mode allows easy deployment of a firewall because the underlying network structure does not need to change from a Layer 3 perspective, thus making it easy to deploy a firewall in transparent mode. Additionally, because the device does not have to perform any routing, this makes it ideal when being inserted into complex routing topologies, although this isn't so much of an issue with the SRX because the SRX supports Junos.
2. The family bridge is the family used on the interface in transparent mode.
3. In transparent mode, you can use IRB interfaces within VLANs to provide a virtual Layer 3 interface that can send and receive traffic, although it cannot route transit traffic itself at the time of this writing.
4. Access mode interfaces provide a single untagged interface on which traffic can arrive. Access mode interfaces do allow the interface to classify any traffic being received on them as being from a particular VLAN; however, the traffic itself is not tagged. Trunk interfaces allow the interface to accept traffic from multiple VLANs, which are distinguished by different tags (a tag or range of tags can be allowed by a particular bridge domain) along with the ability to support a native VLAN that has no tag, but all untagged traffic will be classified as being part of this VLAN on the system.
5. The default method of resolution is to forward the packet out all interfaces in the same VLAN except the one on which it was received. Alternatively, you can configure the SRX to ARP for the destination on behalf of the client, along with sending an ICMP with a TTL of 1 to determine the interface on which the destination MAC address lives.
6. You will need to enable the `set security flow bridge bypass-non-ip-unicast` command to allow all non-IP traffic (except IPv6, which currently will be dropped unless tunneled) through the SRX.
7. The SRX can perform classification and rewriting with the 802.1p bits that are present in 802.1q frames. You cannot use IP precedence or DSCP bits for classification on the SRX in transparent mode; you can only do so in Layer 3 mode.
8. VLAN rewriting, also known as VLAN retagging, allows the SRX to swap the incoming or outgoing VLAN tag with another that the system will use for internal processing. This is useful when you want to translate the VLAN tags on the SRX without using routing to transform the packets.

9. A misconfigured spanning tree can result in surrounding network equipment thinking there is a loop in the network, and therefore putting interfaces in blocking mode that otherwise shouldn't be. This can also impact the failover between chassis cluster members.
10. The SRX will flap the interfaces for the respective secondary redundancy groups that are failing over so that the switches will recalculate spanning tree in favor of the new primary node for the respective redundancy groups.

CHAPTER 7
High Availability

Information availability is a daily part of modern society. People make phone calls, read the news, stream songs, check sports scores, and watch television all over the Internet or on their local provider's network. At any given time, at any given location, almost any bit of information can be made available over the Internet. Today, and in the near future, it's expected that there should be no interruptions to the access of this flow of information. Failure to provide all of the world's information at any user's fingertips at any time, day or night, will create great wrath on whomever's network is in the way. Welcome to the twenty-first century.

The average user of Internet services is unable to comprehend why the information she desires is not available. All that user knows is that it isn't, and that is no longer acceptable. Consumers clamor for compensation and complain to all available outlets. Business users call the help desk and demand explanations while escalating their lost connection to all levels. Revenue is lost and the world looks bleak. Information must always be *highly* available, not just available.

The most likely location of a failure somewhere in the network is typically between the client device and the server. This chapter is dedicated to training network administrators on how to ensure that their SRX is not the device that brings down the network. Firewalls are placed in the most critical locations in the network, and when problems occur, trust us, users notice.

A router handles each packet as its own entity. It does not process traffic as though the packets had a relationship to each other. The packet could be attempting to start a new connection, end a connection, or have all sorts of strange data inside. A router simply looks at the Layer 3 header and passes the packet on. Because of this, packets can come in any order and leave the router in any way. If the router only sees one packet out of an entire connection and never sees another, it doesn't matter. If one router failed, another router can easily pick up all of the traffic utilizing dynamic routing. Designing for high availability (HA) with stateful firewalls is different because of their stateful nature.

Stateful firewalls need to see the creation and teardown of the communication between two devices. All of the packets in the middle of this communication need to be seen as well. If some of the packets are missed, the firewall will start dropping them as it misses changes in the state of communications. Once stateful firewalls came into the picture, the nature of HA changed. The state of traffic must be preserved between redundant firewalls. If one firewall fails, the one attempting to take over for it must have knowledge of all of the traffic that is passing through it. All established connections will be dropped if the new firewall does not have knowledge of these sessions. This creates the challenge of ensuring that state synchronization can occur between the two devices. If not, the whole reason for having redundancy in the firewalls is lost.

Understanding High Availability in the SRX

The design of the SRX is extremely robust regardless of the model or platform. It has a complete OS and many underlying processors and subsystems. Depending on the platform, it could have dozens of processors. Because of this, the SRX implements HA in a radically different way than most firewalls. Common features such as configuration and session synchronization are still in the product, but how the two chassis interact is different.

Chassis Cluster

An SRX HA cluster implements a concept called *chassis cluster*. A chassis cluster takes the two SRX devices and represents them as a single device. The interfaces are numbered in such a way that they are counted starting at the first chassis and then ending on the second chassis. Figure 7-1 shows a chassis cluster. On the left chassis, the FPC starts counting as normal; on the second chassis, the FPCs are counted as though they were part of the first chassis.

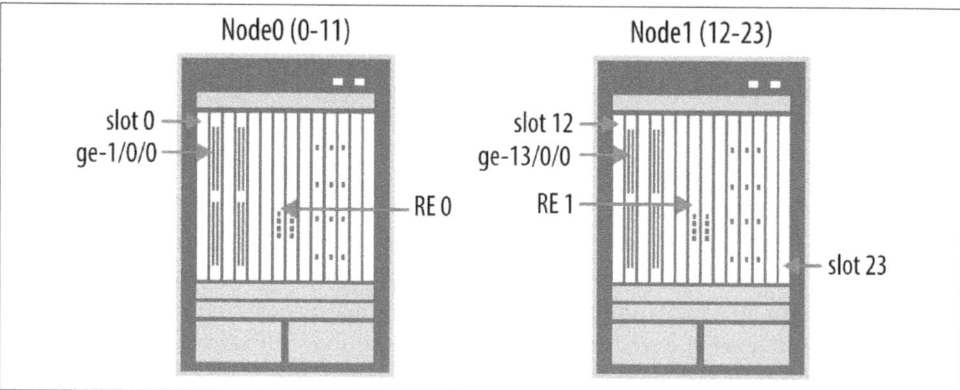

Figure 7-1. Chassis cluster FPC numbering

> ### FPCs, PICs, and Ports, Oh My!
>
> Junos-based devices use a specific naming convention for their interfaces and interface devices. An FPC is a flexible PIC concentrator. The FPC is the device that holds the PICs. The FPC connects into the fabric of the chassis. The PIC contains network processors and typically one or more ports. A port could be a WAN interface or one or more Ethernet interfaces.
>
> Interfaces are numbered in the following format: media-FPC/PIC/PORT. The media represents the type of media. This could be fast Ethernet (fe), 10 gigabit Ethernet (xe), or a T1 (t1). The FPC/PIC/PORT represents the physical location in the chassis. The FPC number is the FPC's number. FPC counting starts at zero. An FPC can contain one or more PICs. Similar to FPCs, the PICs are numbered from zero and then counted up from there. Finally, ports are counted from zero and upward from there.

In Chapter 2, we discussed the concept of the route engine. In an SRX cluster, each SRX has one active RE. When the cluster is created, the two REs work together to provide redundancy. This is similar to the Juniper M Series, T Series, and MX Series routing platforms that support dual REs. The Junos OS is currently limited to supporting two REs per device. Because of this, the SRX cluster can only have one RE per chassis. When the chassis are combined and act as a single chassis, the devices reach the two-RE limit.

Multiple REs in a single SRX are only supported to provide dual control links. They do not provide any other services.

The chassis cluster concept, although new to the SRX, is not new to Juniper Networks. The SRX utilizes the code infrastructure from the TX Matrix products. The TX Matrix is a multichassis router that is considered one of the largest routers in the world. Only the largest service providers and cloud networks utilize the product. Because of its robust design and reliable infrastructure, it's great to think that the code from such a product sits inside every SRX. When the SRX was designed, the engineers at Juniper looked at the current available options and saw that the TX Matrix provided the infrastructure they needed. This is a great example of how using the Junos OS across multiple platforms benefits all products.

To run a device in clustering mode, there are a set of specific requirements. For the SRX1400, SRX3000, and SRX5000 lines, the devices must have an identical number of SPCs and the SPCs must be in identical locations. The SRXs, however, can have any number of interface cards and they do not have to be in the same slots. Best practice suggests, though, that you deploy interfaces in the same FPCs or PIC slots, as this will make it easier to troubleshoot in the long run.

For most network administrators, this concept of a single logical chassis is very different from traditional HA firewall deployment. To provide some comparison, in ScreenOS, for example, the two devices were treated independently of each other. The configuration, as well as network traffic state, was synchronized between the devices, but each device had its own set of interfaces.

On the branch SRX Series products, Ethernet switching as of Junos 11.1 is supported when the devices are in chassis cluster mode. You will also need to allocate an additional interface to provide switching redundancy. This is covered later in the chapter.

The Control Plane

As discussed throughout this book, the SRX has a separated control plane and data plane. Depending on the SRX platform architecture, the separation varies from being separate processes running on separate cores to completely physically differentiated subsystems. For the purposes of this discussion, however, it's enough to know that the control and data planes are separated.

The control plane is used in HA to synchronize the kernel state between the two REs. It also provides a path between the two devices to send hello messages between them. On the RE, a process or daemon runs, called *jsrpd*. This stands for *Junos stateful redundancy protocol daemon*. This daemon is responsible for sending the messages and doing failovers between the two devices. Another kernel, *ksyncd*, is used for synchronizing the kernel state between the two devices. All of this occurs over the control plane link.

The control plane is always in an *active/backup* state. This means only one RE can be the master over the cluster's configuration and state. This ensures that there is only one ultimate truth over the state of the cluster. If the primary RE fails, the secondary takes over for it. Creating an active/active control plane makes synchronization more difficult because many checks would need to be put in place to validate which RE is right.

The two devices' control planes talk to each other over a control link. This link is reserved for control plane communication. It is critical that the link maintain its integrity to allow for communication between the two devices.

The Data Plane

The data plane's responsibility in the SRX is to pass data and processes based on the administrator's configuration. All session and service states are maintained on the data plane. The REs, control plane, or both are not responsible for maintaining state (the RE simply requests data and statistics from the data plane and returns them to the administrator).

The data plane has a few responsibilities when it comes to HA implementation. First and foremost is state synchronization. The state of sessions and services is shared between the two devices. Sessions are the state of the current set of traffic that is going through the SRX, and services are other items such as the VPN, IPS, and ALGs.

On the branch SRX Series, synchronization happens between the flowd daemon running on the data plane. The SRX Series for the branch, as discussed in Chapter 1, runs a single multicore processor with a single multithreaded flowd process. The data center SRX distributed architecture state synchronization is handled in a similar fashion. Figure 7-2 shows a detailed example.

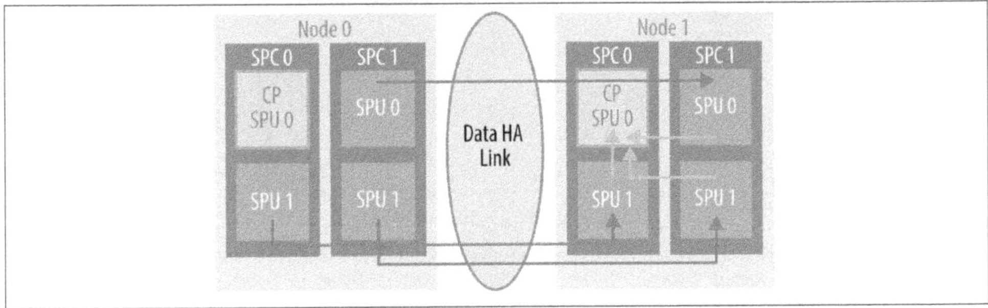

Figure 7-2. Data center SRX state synchronization

In Figure 7-2, two SRX data center platforms are shown. Node 0 is shown on the left and node 1 is on the right. Each device is depicted with two SPCs. SPC 0 is the SPC that contains the CP SPU and a second flow SPU. In SPC 1, both SPUs are flow SPUs. Both SRX data center platforms are required to have the same number and location of SPCs and NPCs. This is required because the SPUs talk to their peer SPU in the same FPC and PIC location. As seen in the back of Figure 7-2, the flow SPU in FPC 0 on node 0 sends a message to node 1 on FPC 0 in PIC 1. This is the session synchronization message. Once the SPU on node 1 validates and creates the session, it sends a message to its local CP. As stated in Chapter 1, the CP processors are responsible for maintaining the state for all of the exiting sessions on the SRX. The secondary device now has all of the necessary information to handle the traffic in the event of a failover.

Information is synchronized in what is known as a real-time object (RTO). This RTO contains the necessary information to synchronize the data to the other node. The remote side does not send an acknowledgment of the RTO because doing so would slow down the session creation process, and frankly, an acknowledgment is rarely needed. There are many different RTO message types. New ones can be added based on the creation of new features on the SRX. The most commonly used message types are the ones for session creation and session closure.

334 The second task the SRX needs to handle is forwarding traffic between the two devices. This is also known as *data path* or *Z path forwarding*. Figure 7-3 illustrates this. Under most configuration deployments, Z path forwarding is not necessary. However, in specific designs, this operation might be very common. (The details are further explored in the section "Deployment Concepts" on page 294 later in this chapter.) In the event that traffic is received by a node, the node will always forward the traffic to a node on which the traffic will egress.

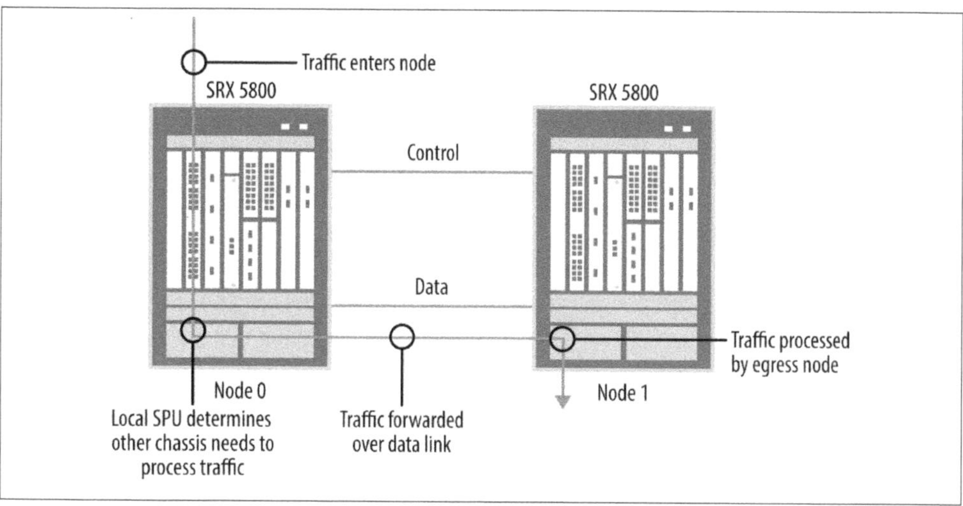

Figure 7-3. Data path or Z path forwarding

The last task for the data link is to send jsrpd messages between the two devices. The jsrpd daemon passes messages over the data plane to validate that it is operating correctly. These are similar to the messages that are sent over the control link, except that they go through the data plane. By sending these additional messages over the data plane, the RE ensures that the data plane is up and capable of passing traffic. On the branch SRX Series devices, the message exits the control plane, passes through flowd and over the data link, and then to the second device. The second device receives the packet, flowd, and passes the packet to the control plane and on to jsrpd. Depending on the platform, the rate for the messages will vary.

All of these data plane messages pass over the data link. The data link is also known as the *fabric link*, depending on the context of the discussion. The size of the link varies based on the requirements. These requirements consist of the amount of data forwarding between devices and the number of new connections per second:

- On the SRX100, SRX110, SRX210, and SRX220, a 100 MB Ethernet link is acceptable for the data link.
- For the SRX550, SRX650, and SRX240, it's suggested that you use a 1 GB link.
- On the data center SRXs, a 1 GB link is acceptable unless data forwarding is going to occur.
- Even on an SRX5000 Series with a maximum of 380,000 new CPS, a 1 GB link can sustain the RTOs throughput.
- If data forwarding is in the design, a 10 GB link is suggested.

Getting Started with High Availability

This chapter started with the concept of the chassis cluster because it's the fundamental concept for the entire chapter. There are several important aspects to the chassis cluster; some concern how the cluster is configured, and others are simply key to the fault tolerance the chassis cluster provides. In this section, we explore the deeper concepts of the chassis cluster.

Cluster ID

Each cluster must share a unique identifier among all of its members. This identifier is used in a few different ways, but most important it is used when two devices are communicating with each other. Fifteen cluster IDs are available for use when creating a cluster. The cluster ID is also used when determining MAC addresses for the redundant Ethernet interfaces.

Node ID

The node ID is the unique identifier for a device within a cluster. There are two node IDs: 0 and 1. The node with an ID of 0 is considered the base node. The node ID does not give the device any sort of priority over its mastership, only in interface ordering. Node 0 is the first node for the interface numbering in the chassis cluster. The second node, node 1, is the second and last node in the cluster.

Redundancy Groups

In an HA cluster, the goal is the ability to fail over resources in case something goes wrong. A *redundancy group* is a collection of resources that need to fail over between the two devices. Only one node at a time can be responsible for a redundancy group; however, a single node can be the primary node for any number of redundancy groups.

Two different items are placed in a redundancy group: the control plane and the interfaces. The default redundancy group is group 0. Redundancy group 0 represents the control plane. The node that is the master over redundancy group 0 has the active RE. The active RE is responsible for controlling the data plane and pushing new configurations. It is considered the *ultimate truth* in matters regarding what is happening on the device.

The data plane components for redundancy groups exist in numbers 1 and greater. The different SRX platforms support different numbers of redundancy groups. A data plane redundancy group contains one or more redundant Ethernet interfaces. Each member in the cluster has a physical interface bound into a reth. The active node's physical interface will be active and the backup node's interface will be passive and will not pass traffic. It is easier to think of this as a binary switch. Only one of the members of the reth is active at any given time. The section "Deployment Concepts" on page 294 later in this chapter details the use of data plane redundancy groups.

Interfaces

A network device doesn't help a network without participating in traffic processing. An SRX has two different interface types that it can use to process traffic. The first is the reth. A reth is a Junos aggregate Ethernet interface and it has special properties compared to a traditional aggregate Ethernet interface. The reth allows the administrator to add one or more child links per chassis. Figure 7-4 shows an example of this where node 0 is represented on the left and node 1 is represented on the right.

In Figure 7-4, node 0 has interface xe-0/0/0 as a child link of reth0 and node 1 has interface xe-12/0/0. The interface reth0 is a member of redundancy group 1. The node, in this case node 0, has its link active. Node 1's link is in an up state but it does not accept or pass traffic. After a failover between nodes, the newly active node sends out GARPs. Both nodes share the same MAC address on the reth. The surrounding switches will learn the new port that has the reth MAC address. The hosts are still sending their data to the same MAC, so they do not have to relearn anything.

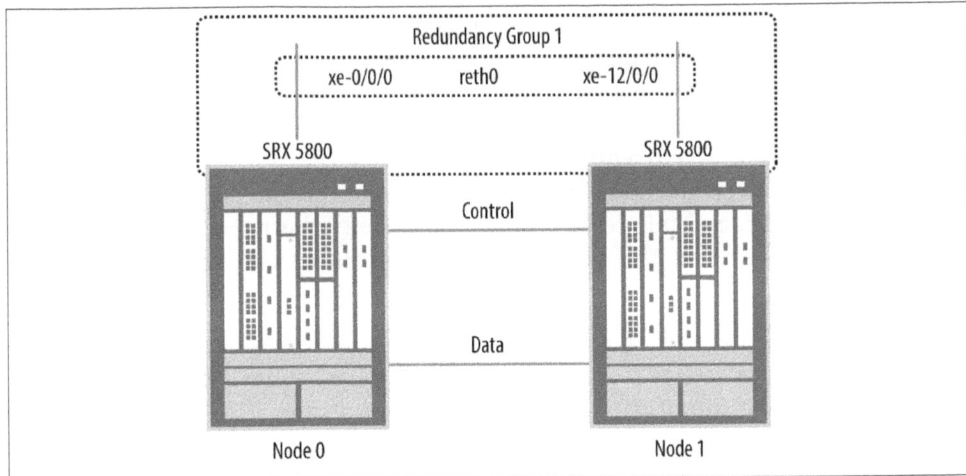

Figure 7-4. Reth example

The MAC address for the reth is based on a combination of the cluster ID and the reth number. Figure 7-5 shows the algorithm that determines the MAC address. In Figure 7-5, there are two types of fields: the hex field represents one bit by using a hexadecimal representation of a byte using two base-16 digits; the bit field represents a number in binary with eight bits.

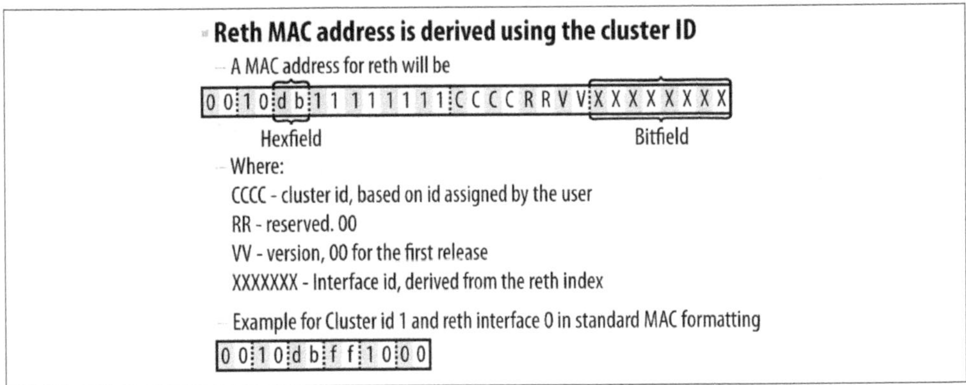

Figure 7-5. Reth MAC address

The first four of the six bytes are fixed. They do not change between cluster deployments. The last two bytes vary based on the cluster ID and the reth index. In Figure 7-5, *CCCC* represents the cluster ID in binary. With four bits, the maximum number is 15, which is the same number of cluster IDs supported. Next, the *RR* represents a reserved field for future expansion. It is currently set to 0 for both bits. The *VV* represents the version of the chassis cluster, which today is set at 0 for both of the bits. Last is the field filled with *XXXXXXXXX*, and this represents the redundant Ethernet index ID. Based on Figure 7-5, it's easy to see that collision of MAC addresses between clusters can be avoided.

When configured in a chassis cluster, the SRX is also able to support local interfaces. A local interface is an interface that is configured local to a specific node. This method of configuration on an interface is the same method of configuration on a standalone device. The significance of a local interface in an SRX cluster is that it does not have a backup interface on the other chassis, meaning that it is part of neither a reth nor a redundancy group. If this interface were to fail, its IP address would not fail over to the other node. Although this feature might seem perplexing at first, it actually provides a lot of value in complex network topologies, and it is further explored later in this chapter.

Deployment Concepts

It's time to apply all these concepts to actual deployment scenarios. For HA clusters, there is a lot of terminology for the mode of actually deploying devices, and this section attempts to give administrators a clear idea of what methods of deployment are available to them.

Earlier in this chapter we discussed control plane redundancy, whereby the control plane is deployed in an active/passive fashion. One RE is active for controlling the cluster, and the second RE is passive. The secondary RE performs some basic maintenance for the local chassis and synchronizes the configuration as well as checks that the other chassis is alive.

In this section, we discuss what can be done with the redundancy groups on the data plane. The configuration on the data plane determines in which mode the SRXs are operating. The SRX doesn't have an idea of being forced into a specific mode of HA, but operates in that mode based on the configuration. There are three basic modes of operation and one creative alternative:

- Active/passive
- Active/active
- Mixed mode
- The six pack

Active/passive

In the active/passive mode, the first SRX data plane is actively passing traffic while the second SRX data plane is sitting in a passive setting not passing traffic. On a fault condition, of course, the passive data plane will take over and begin passing traffic. To accomplish this, the SRX uses one data plane redundancy group and one or more redundant Ethernet interfaces. Figure 7-6 illustrates an example of this active/passive process.

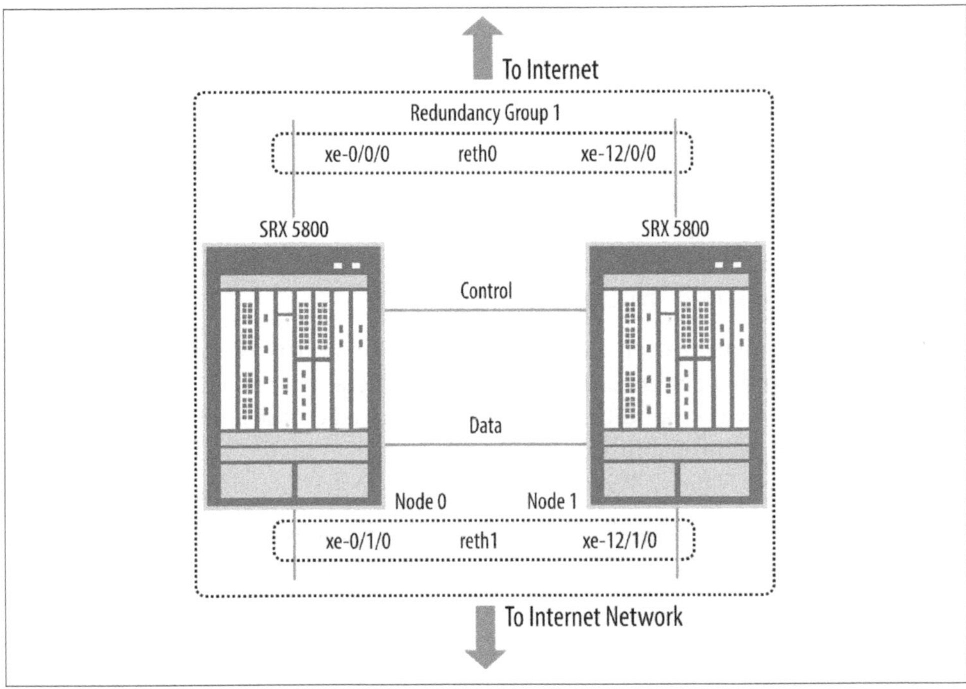

Figure 7-6. Active/passive cluster

As shown in Figure 7-6, node 0, on the left, is currently active and node 1 is passive. In this example, there are two reth interfaces: reth0 and reth1. Reth0 goes toward the Internet and reth1 goes toward the internal network. Because node 0 is currently active, it is passing all of the traffic between the Internet and the internal network. Node 1's data plane is (patiently) waiting for any issue to arise so that it can take over and continue to pass traffic. The interfaces on node 1 that are in the reth0 and reth1 groups are physically up but are unable to pass traffic. Because node 0 is currently active, it synchronizes any new sessions that are created to node 1. When node 1 needs to take over for node 0, it will have the same session information locally.

Active/active

In an active/active deployment, both SRXs are simultaneously passing traffic. Although it sounds difficult, the concept is simple—active/active is merely active/passive but done twice. In this case, each member of the cluster is active for its own redundancy group and the other device is passive for the redundancy group. In the event of a failure, the remaining node will take over for the traffic for the failed device. Synchronization happens between both nodes. Sessions for both redundancy groups are available on both nodes.

So, this question remains: what does this type of deployment mean for the administrator? The biggest advantage is that passing traffic over the backup node ensures that the backup data plane is ready and correctly functioning. Nothing is worse than having an HA cluster running for months and then, during the moment of truth, a failure occurs, and the second node is in a degraded state and no one discovered this ahead of time. A good example of avoiding this is to have one of the redundancy groups passing a majority of the traffic while the other redundancy group is used to pass only a single health check. This is a great design because the second device is verified and the administrator doesn't have to troubleshoot load-sharing scenarios.

Active/active deployments can also be used to share load between the two hosts. The only downside to this design is that it might be difficult to troubleshoot flows going through the two devices, but ultimately that varies based on the administrator and the environment, and it's probably better to have the option available in the administrator's tool chest than not. Figure 7-7 shows an example of an active/active cluster.

Figure 7-7 shows an active/active cluster as simply two active/passive configurations. Building from Figure 7-6, the example starts with the same configuration as before. The clusters had a single redundancy group 1 and two reths, reth0 and reth1, with node 0 being the designated primary. In this example, a second redundancy group is added, redundancy group 2, and two additional reths are added to accommodate it. Reth2 is on the Internet-facing side of the firewalls and reth3 is toward the internal network. This redundancy group, however, has node 1 as the primary, so traffic that is localized to redundancy group 2 is only sent through node 1 unless a failure occurs.

Mixed mode

Mixed mode, perhaps the most interesting HA configuration, builds on the concepts already demonstrated but expands to include local interfaces. As we discussed earlier, a local interface is an interface that has configurations local to the node for which it is attached. The other node is not required to have a backup to this interface as in the case of a reth.

This option has significance in two specific use cases.

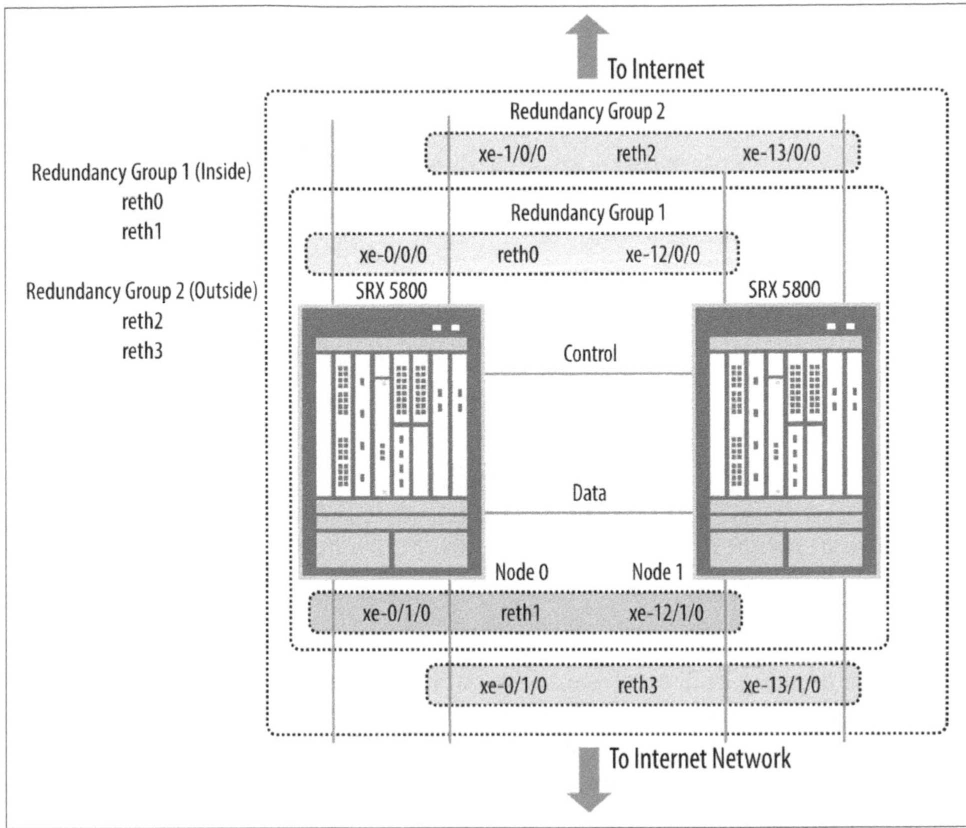

Figure 7-7. Active/active cluster

The first use case is WAN interfaces. For this use case, there are two SRX210s, each with a T1 interface and a single reth to present back to the LAN, as depicted in Figure 7-8. Node 0 on the left has a T1 to provider A and node 1 on the right has a T1 to provider B. Each node has a single interface connected to the LAN switch. These two interfaces are bound together as reth0. The reth0 interface provides a redundant, reliable gateway to present to clients. Because of the way a T1 works, it is not possible to have a common Layer 2 domain between the two T1 interfaces, so each T1 is its own local interface to the local node.

Traffic can enter or exit either T1 interface, and it is always directed out to the correct interface. In the case shown in Figure 7-8, that would be reth0, as it is the only other interface configured. The benefit of this design is that the two T1s provide redundancy and increased capacity, and sessions between the two interfaces are synchronized. It's great when you are using T1 interfaces as connections to a remote VPN site.

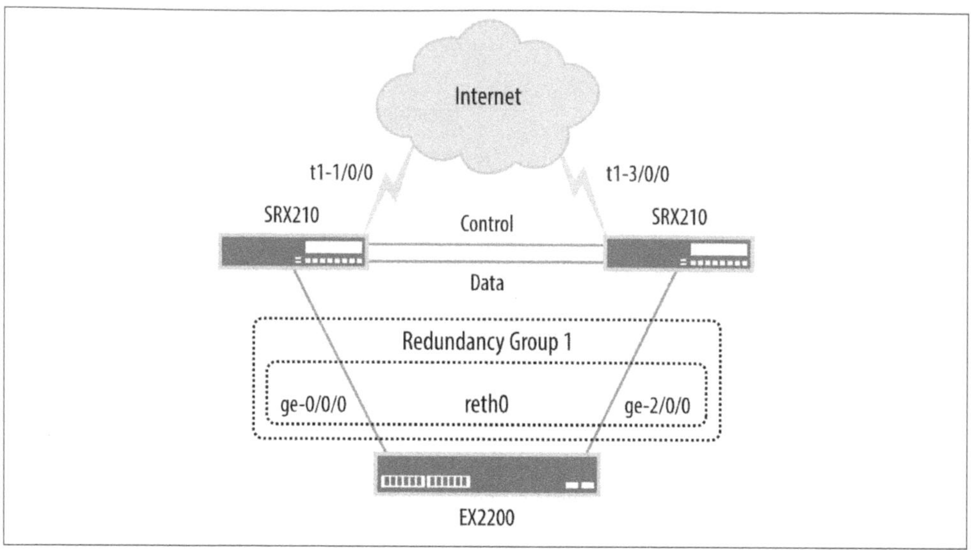

Figure 7-8. Mixed mode with WAN interfaces

A second great use case for mixed mode is with data centers using a dynamic routing integration design. The design is similar to our previous example, but in this case all of the interfaces are Ethernet. The two SRXs each have two interfaces connected into two different M120 routers, all of which can be seen in Figure 7-9. Having two links each going to two different routers provides a better level of redundancy in case links or routers fail. The OSPF routing protocol is enabled between the SRXs and the upstream routers, allowing for simplified failover between the links and ensuring that the four devices can determine the best path to the upstream networks. If a link fails, OSPF recalculates and determines the next best path.

You can see in Figure 7-9 that the southbound interfaces connect into two EX8200 core switches. These switches provide a common Layer 2 domain between the southbound interfaces, which allows for the creation of reth0 (similar to the rest of the designs seen in this chapter).

Six pack

It's possible to forgo redundant Ethernet interfaces altogether and use only local interfaces. This is similar to the data center mixed mode design, except it takes the idea one step further and uses local interfaces for both the north- and southbound connections. A common name for this design is *six pack*. It uses four routers and two firewalls and is shown in Figure 7-10.

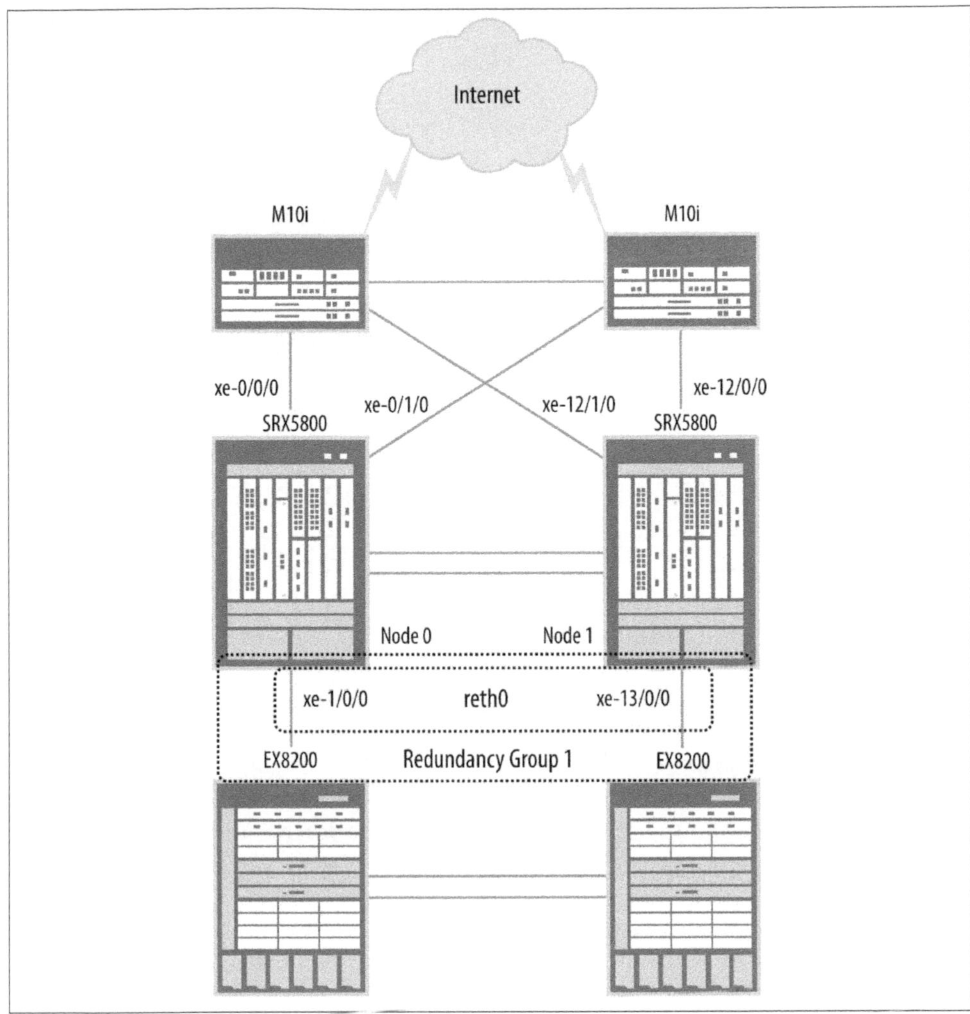

Figure 7-9. Data center mixed mode design

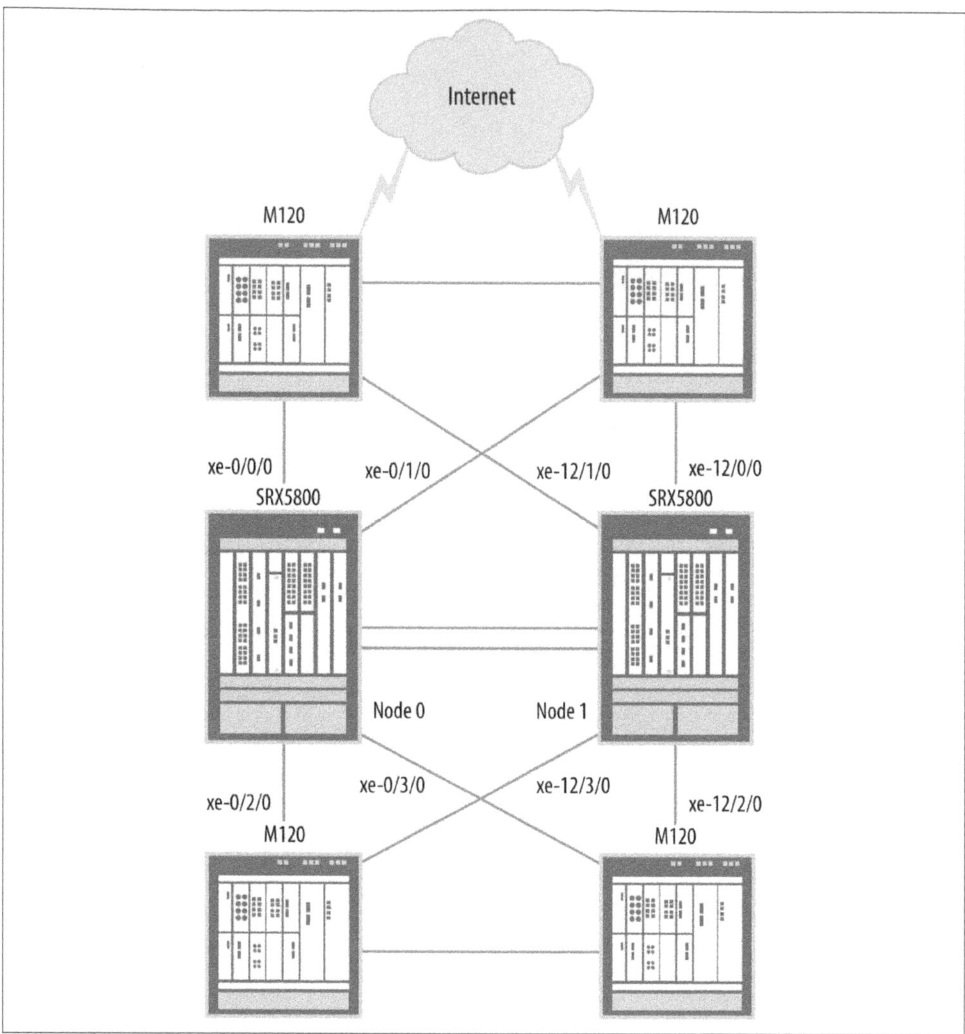

Figure 7-10. Six pack HA design

Much like the mixed mode design, the two northbound routers in Figure 7-10 are connected to the SRXs with two links. Each router has a connection to each SRX. On the southbound routers, the same design is replicated. This allows for a fully meshed, active/active, and truly HA network to exist. In this case, the SRXs are acting more like how a traditional router would be deployed. OSPF is used for the design to direct traffic through the SRXs, and it's even possible to use equal cost multipath routing to do balancing for upstream hosts.

The six pack design shows just how flexible the SRXs can be to meet the needs of nearly any environment. These deployments can even be done in either the traditional Layer 3 routing mode or Layer 2 transparent mode.

Preparing Devices for Deployment

Understanding how a chassis cluster works is half the battle in attaining acceptable HA levels. The rest concerns configuring a cluster.

To be fair, the configuration is actually quite easy—it's just a few steps to get the cluster up and running. Setting it up correctly is the key to a stable implementation, and needless to say, rushing through some important steps can cause serious pain later on. We therefore suggest that you start with fresh configurations, if possible, even if this means clustering the devices starting with a minimal configuration and then adding on from there.

If there is an existing configuration, set it aside and then create the cluster. After the cluster is running happily, then migrate the configuration back on.

Differences from Standalone

When an administrator enters configuration mode on a standalone SRX, all of the active users who log in to the device can see the configuration and edit it. When each user's changes can be seen by the other users on the device, it's called a *shared configuration*. Once chassis clustering is enabled, the devices must be configured in what is called *configure private*, or *private*, mode, which allows each administrator to see only her own configuration changes. This imposes several restrictions on the end administrator while using configure private mode.

The first notable restriction is that all configuration commits must be done from the root, or top, of the configuration hierarchy. Second, the option to do `commit confirmed` is no longer allowed, which, as you know, allows for a rollback to the previous configuration if things go wrong. Both are very nice features that are not available when in clustering mode. The reason these are disabled is simple: stability.

A lot of communication is going on between the two SRXs when they are in a clustered mode, so when committing a change, it is best to minimize the chances of differences between the two devices' local configurations at the time of the commit. If each node had a user modifying the configuration at the same time, this would add an unneeded level of complexity to ensure that the configurations are synchronized. Because of this, private mode is required while making configuration changes.

Activating Juniper Services Redundancy Protocol

The first step in creating a cluster is to place the device into cluster mode. By default, the SRX does not run the jsrpd daemon, so this must be triggered. To enable the jsrpd daemon and turn the device into an eligible chassis cluster member, a few special bits must be set in the Non Volatile Random Access Memory (NVRAM) on the device, triggering the SRX, on boot, to enable jsrpd and enter chassis cluster mode.

These settings are permanent until they are otherwise removed. An initial reboot is required after setting the cluster ID to get the jsrpd daemon to start. The daemon will start every time the bits are seen in the NVRAM.

It takes a single command, and it takes effect only on reboot. Although it is unfortunate that a reboot is required, it is required only once. You must run the command from operational mode and as a user with superuser privileges.

```
root@SRX210-H> set chassis cluster cluster-id 1 node 0 reboot
Successfully enabled chassis cluster. Going to reboot now

root@SRX210-H>
*** FINAL System shutdown message from root@SRX210-H ***
System going down IMMEDIATELY
```

For this command to work, we needed to choose the cluster ID and the node ID. For most implementations, cluster ID 1 is perfectly acceptable, as we discussed earlier. The node ID is easy, too: for the first node that is being set up, use node 0, and for the second node, use node 1. There isn't a specific preference between the two. Being node 0 or node 1 doesn't provide any special benefit; it's only a unique identifier for the device.

Once the device comes back up, it's easy to notice the changes. Right above the shell prompt is a new line:

```
{primary:node0} #<----new to the the prompt
root>
```

This line gives the administrator two important pieces of information. The part to the left of the colon is the current status of the cluster control plane in relevance to the cluster, and it will define which state the RE is in.

This only shows the control plane status. This *does not* show which device has the active data plane. This is a common mistake for those using the SRX. That message should be on its own page all by itself, as it's that important to remember.

There are several different options for control plane status, as listed in Table 7-1. On boot, the device enters the hold state. During this state, the control plane is preparing itself to enter the cluster. Next the device enters the secondary state when the RE checks to see if there is already a primary RE in the cluster. If not, it then transitions to the primary state.

Table 7-1. Control plane states

State	Meaning
Hold	This is the initial state on boot. The RE is preparing to join the cluster.
Secondary	The RE is in backup state and is ready to take over for the primary.
Primary	The RE is the controller for the cluster.
Ineligible	Something has occurred that makes the RE no longer eligible to be part of the cluster.
Disabled	The RE is no longer eligible to enter the cluster. It must be rebooted to rejoin the cluster.
Unknown	A critical failure has occurred. The device is unable to determine its current state. It must be rebooted to attempt to reenter the cluster.
Lost	Communication with the other node is lost. A node cannot be in a lost state; this is only listed under the `show chassis cluster status` command when the other device was never detected.
Secondary-hold	A device enters secondary-hold when it is identified as a secondary but the configured hold-down timer has not yet expired. In the event of a critical failure, the redundancy group can still fail over.

After the primary states are three states that occur only when something goes wrong. *Ineligible* occurs when something happens that invalidates the member from the cluster. From there, the device enters the *disabled* state after a period of time while being ineligible. The last state, *unknown*, can occur only if some disastrous, unexpected event occurs.

Once the system is up, and in either the final primary or secondary state, there are a few steps you can take to validate that the chassis cluster is indeed up and running. First, check that the jsrpd daemon is up and running. If the new cluster status message is above the prompt, it's pretty certain that the daemon is running.

```
{primary:node0}
root> show system processes | match jsrpd
  863  ??  S       0:00.24 /usr/sbin/jsrpd -N

{primary:node0}
root> show chassis cluster status
Cluster ID: 1
Node                    Priority          Status   Preempt   Manual failover

Redundancy group: 0 , Failover count: 1
    node0                      1          primary       no        no
    node1                      0          lost          n/a       n/a

{primary:node0}
root>
```

The greatest friend of anyone using the chassis cluster is the `show chassis cluster status` command. It is the most common command for looking at the current status of the cluster and it is full of information. The first bit of information is the cluster ID, the one that was initially configured and will likely stay that way until cleared. Next is information regarding all of the redundancy groups that are configured; the first one in our case is redundancy group 0. This represents the control plane only and has no relevance on who is actively passing traffic.

Under each redundancy group, each node is listed along with its priorities, status, preempt status, and whether the device is in manual failover. By default, redundancy group 0 is created without user intervention. Each device is given a default priority of 1. Because of this, the first node that becomes primary will be primary until a failure occurs. Next, the status is listed. The last two columns are preempt and manual failover. Preempt is the ability to configure the device with the higher priority to preempt the device with the lower priority. The manual failover column will state if the node was manually failed over to by the administrator.

Managing Cluster Members

Most Junos devices have a special interface named fxp0 that is used to manage the SRXs. It is typically connected to the RE, although some devices, such as the SRX100 and SRX200 Series, do not have a dedicated port for fxp0 because the devices are designed to provide the maximum number of ports for branch devices. However, when SRX devices are configured in a cluster, the secondary node cannot be directly managed unless it has either a local interface or the fxp0 port. To ease management of the SRX100 and SRX200 Series, the fe-0/0/6 port automatically becomes the fxp0 port. In the section "Node-Specific Information" on page 316 later in this chapter, we discuss how to configure this port.

The fxp0 interface exists on the majority of Junos devices. This is due to the devices' service-provider-like design. Fxp0 allows for secure out-of-band management, enabling administrators to access the device no matter what is happening on the network. Because of this, many of the capabilities and management services often operate best through the fxp0 port. Tools such as NSM and Junos Space operate best when talking to an fxp0 port. Also, updates for IDP and UTM will work best through this interface. After 12.1, this is no longer the case, and you are freed from this limitation.

Managing branch devices that are remote can often be a challenge. It might not be possible to directly connect to the backup node. This is especially an issue when using a management tool such as NSM or Junos Space. Luckily, Juniper created a way to tunnel a management connection to the secondary node through the first. This mode is called "cluster-master" mode.

This mode requires a single command to activate.

```
{secondary:node1}[edit]
root@SRX-HA-1# set chassis cluster network-management cluster-master

{secondary:node1}[edit]
root@SRX-HA-1# edit chassis cluster

{secondary:node1}[edit chassis cluster]
root@SRX-HA-1# show
reth-count 2;
heartbeat-threshold 3;
network-management {
    cluster-master;
}
redundancy-group 0 {
    node 0 priority 254;
    node 1 priority 1;
}
redundancy-group 1 {
    node 0 priority 254;
    node 1 priority 1;
}

{secondary:node1}[edit chassis cluster]
root@SRX-HA-1#
```

Configuring the Control Ports

Now that the devices are up and running, it's time to get the two devices talking. There are two communication paths for the devices to talk over; the first leads to the second. The control port is the first, and by configuring the control port it's possible to get the devices communicating early on. Then, once the devices are in a cluster, the configuration is automatically synchronized for a consistent second method. This can cut the administrator's work in half as both devices need to be configured only once.

Different platforms have different requirements for configuring the control port. Table 7-2 lists each platform and the control port location. Because each platform has different subsystems under the hood, so to speak, there are different ways to configure the control port. The only device that requires manual configuration is the SRX5000. Some devices also support dual or redundant control ports.

Table 7-2. Control ports by platform

Device	Control port	Description	Dual support?
SRX100, SRX110, and SRX210	fe-0/0/7	Dedicated as a control port upon enabling clustering	No
SRX220	ge-0/0/7	Dedicated as a control port upon enabling clustering	No
SRX240 and SRX650	ge-0/0/1	Dedicated as a control port upon enabling clustering	No

Device	Control port	Description	Dual support?
SRX1400	ge-0/0/10 and optionally ge-0/0/11	Dedicated as a control port upon enabling clustering	Yes
SRX3000	Both located on the SFB	No user configuration required	Yes
SRX5000	Located on the SPC	Manual configuration required	Yes

When connecting control ports, you connect the control port from each device to the other device. It is not recommended that you join two primary devices together—it's best to reboot the secondary and then connect the control port. On reboot, the two devices will begin to communicate.

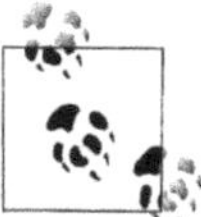

For all of the SRX devices, except the SRX5000, you can do this right after the initial cluster configuration. For the SRX5000 Series, two reboots are required.

The SRX5000 Series control ports are located on the SPC, because when Juniper was creating the SRX5000, the SPC was the only part that was created from scratch and the remaining parts were taken from the MX Series. Ultimately, locating the control ports on the SPC removes the control ports from other components while adding some additional resiliency. The SPC and its underlying traffic processing are physically separate from the control ports even though they are located on the same card. The SRX5000 must use fiber SFPs to connect the two chassis.

Enabling Dual Control Links

The data center SRX is designed with many hardware components. Because of this, it requires additional hardware to enable dual control links. Inside each chassis there are two physically separate Ethernet control networks. By default, only one of the two networks is up and operational. This network is enabled by the RE in each chassis.

To enable the secondary network that will allow for the use of dual control links, an additional piece of hardware is needed. On the SRX5000 Series, a second RE is needed. This RE is only used to enable the secondary control network and then turns off. On the SRX3000 Series, an SRX clustering module (SCM) is used. It serves a similar function, but it is a different part than a standard RE. An RE on the SRX3000 also contains the component that controls all of the line cards. This part is removed on the SCM.

Two physically separate control networks are used to provide complete redundancy. Although it would be possible to use two links between the chassis and use a protocol such as STP to prevent Layer 2 loops, no one would want such a critical feature relying on spanning tree.

The SRX1400 series has the SCM component built into the RE, so to offer two control links no additional hardware is required.

To configure the control ports on the SRX5000, the administrator first needs to determine which ports she wants to configure based on which FPC the control port is located within. Next, the administrator must identify the port number (either port 0 or port 1).

```
{primary:node0}[edit chassis cluster]
root@SRX5800A# set control-ports fpc 1 port 0
root@SRX5800A# set control-ports fpc 2 port 1
root@SRX5800A# show
control-link-recovery;
control-ports {
    fpc 1 port 0;
    fpc 2 port 1;
}
root@SRX5800A# commit
```

There is logic in how the control ports should be configured on the SRX5000s. The control ports can be on the same FPC, but ideally, the SRX should not be configured that way. If possible, do not place the control port on the same card as the CP or central point processor because the CP is used as a hop for the data link. If the FPC with the CP fails, and the control link is on it and it's a single control link, the SRX cluster can go into *split brain* or *dual mastership*. Because of this, separating the two is recommended. So, if an administrator is going to utilize dual control links, it's recommended that she place each control link on separate SPCs and the CP on a third SPC. This would require at least three SPCs, but this is the recommendation for the ultimate in HA.

Once the control links are up and running, and the secondary node is rebooted and up and running, it's time to check that the cluster is communicating. Again, we go back to the `show chassis cluster status` command.

```
{primary:node0}
root> show chassis cluster status
Cluster ID: 1
Node                 Priority      Status     Preempt  Manual failover

Redundancy group: 0 , Failover count: 1
    node0                    1             primary        no        no
    node1                    1             secondary      no        no

{primary:node0}
root>
```

Both devices should be able to see each other, as shown here, with one device being primary and the other secondary.

Next, because there are two devices, it's possible to check communications between the two, this time using the `show chassis cluster statistics` command.

```
{primary:node0}
root> show chassis cluster control-plane statistics
Control link statistics:
    Control link 0:
        Heartbeat packets sent: 217
        Heartbeat packets received: 21
        Heartbeat packet errors: 0
Fabric link statistics:
    Probes sent: 4286
    Probes received: 0
    Probe errors: 0
```

At this point in the cluster creation, you should see only heartbeat messages on the control link, such as under the statistic `Heartbeat packets received:`. In the preceding output, 21 packets have been received. Typically, the number of heartbeat packets sent and received will not match, as one device started before the other and did not receive messages for a period of time. But once the sent and received numbers consistently match, everything on the control plane should be in order.

The SRX1400, SRX3000, and the SRX5000 are able to use two control links that are provided for redundancy only. In the event that one of the control links on the device fails, the second is utilized. But to use the second control link, an additional component is needed. The SRX3000 uses a component called the SCM, which is used to activate and control the secondary control link. On the SRX5000, a standard RE can be used. The RE needs to have Junos 10.0 or later loaded to operate the control link. Both the SCM and the secondary RE are loaded into the second RE port on the platform. These modules do not act as an RE or backup to the RE, but rather are used only for the backup control link.

These components must be placed into the chassis while it is powered off. On boot, the secondary link will be up and functional.

A quick look at the output of the `show chassis cluster control-plane statistics` command shows the second control link working.

```
root > show chassis cluster control-plane statistics
Control link statistics:
    Control link 0:
        Heartbeat packets sent: 1114
        Heartbeat packets received: 217
        Heartbeat packet errors: 0
    Control link 1:
        Heartbeat packets sent: 1114
        Heartbeat packets received: 217
        Heartbeat packet errors: 0
Fabric link statistics:
```

```
Probes sent: 1575937
Probes received: 1575224
Probe errors: 0
```

A final configuration option needs to be configured for the control link, and that is control link recovery. Control link recovery allows for automated recovery of the secondary chassis in the event that the control link fails. If the single or both control links fail, then the secondary device will go into the disabled state.

On the data center SRXs, a feature called *unified in-service software upgrade* (ISSU) can be used. This method is a graceful upgrade method that allows for the SRXs to upgrade without losing sessions or traffic.

The process might take some time to complete because the kernel on the two devices must synchronize and the software must be updated. It is suggested that you have all of the redundancy groups on a single member in the cluster. The process is similar to the other, except the upgrade only needs to be run on one SRX.

```
{primary:node0}
root@SRX5800-1> request system software in-service-upgradejunos-
srx5000-12.1X44.10-domestic.tgz reboot
```

The command will upgrade each node and reboot them as needed. No further commands are required.

There is one last option that the unified ISSU process can use: the `no-old-master-upgrade` command, which leaves the master in a nonupgraded state. This ensures that there is a working box should the software upgrade fail. After successful completion of the upgrade, the old master is manually upgraded, as shown here.

```
{primary:node0}
root@SRX5800-1> request system software in-service-upgradejunos-
srx5000-12.1X44.D10-domestic.tgz no-old-master-upgrade

##next on the old master

{primary:node0}
root@SRX5800-1> request system software add junos-srx5000-12.1X44D10-
domestic.tgz

{primary:node0}
root@SRX5800-1> request chassis cluster in-service-upgrade abort

{primary:node0}
root@SRX5800-1> request system reboot
```

If things do go wrong and both nodes are unable to complete the upgrade in the unified ISSU process, the upgraded node needs to be rolled back. This is simple. First, you must abort the unified ISSU process, then roll back the software on that node, and then reboot the system.

```
{primary:node0}
root@SRX5800-1> request chassis cluster in-service-upgrade abort
Exiting in-service-upgrade window

{primary:node0}
root@SRX5800-1> request system software rollback

{primary:node0}
root@SRX5800-1> request system reboot
```

To recover, the device must be rebooted. The risk is that the device might not be able to see the primary on reboot, so if that occurs, dual mastership or split brain will result. The better option is to enable control link recovery. It only takes a single command to enable, as shown in the next example.

```
{primary:node0}[edit chassis cluster]
root# set control-link-recovery

{primary:node0}[edit chassis cluster]
root# show
control-link-recovery;
```

Once control link recovery is enabled, a user can manually reconnect the control link. After the control link has been up for about 30 seconds and the SRXs have determined that the link is healthy, the secondary node will reboot. After recovering from the reboot, the cluster will be up and synchronized and ready to operate. Although a reboot seems harsh for such a recovery, it is the best way to ensure that the backup node is up and completely operational.

Configuring the Fabric Links

The second half of the chassis cluster communication equation is the fabric connection. Unlike the control link, the fabric link provides several functions and a great deal of value to the cluster, the most important being *session synchronization*. Without session synchronization, there would be little value to an SRX cluster. A second feature of the fabric link is the ability to forward traffic between the two chassis. The egress chassis is responsible for processing the traffic, so traffic is forwarded to the other cluster member only if the egress interface is on that chassis.

Each node in the chassis needs its own fabric interface configured. The interfaces should be directly connected to each other. Creating the fabric link between the two chassis requires the creation of a special interface called the *fab* interface. The fab interface is a special version of the aggregate Ethernet interface that allows for the binding of one or more interfaces into a special bundle. Interfaces are added to the fab interface with node 0's fabric interface, called fab0, and node 1's fabric interface, called fab1. Set the interface this way.

```
{primary:node0}[edit interfaces]
root# set fab0 fabric-options member-interfaces fe-0/0/4

{primary:node0}[edit interfaces]
root# set fab1 fabric-options member-interfaces fe-2/0/4

{primary:node0}[edit]
root# show interfaces
fab0 {
    fabric-options {
        member-interfaces {
            fe-0/0/4;
        }
    }
}
fab1 {
    fabric-options {
        member-interfaces {
            fe-2/0/4;
        }
    }
}

{primary:node0}[edit]
root# run show interfaces terse
Interface               Admin Link Proto    Local                 Remote
ge-0/0/0                up    down
ge-0/0/1                up    down
fe-0/0/2                up    down
fe-0/0/3                up    down
fe-0/0/4                up    up
fe-0/0/4.0              up    up   aenet    --> fab0.0
fe-0/0/5                up    up
fe-0/0/6                up    up
fe-0/0/7                up    up
ge-2/0/0                up    down
ge-2/0/1                up    down
fe-2/0/2                up    down
fe-2/0/3                up    down
fe-2/0/4                up    up
fe-2/0/4.0              up    up   aenet    --> fab1.0
fe-2/0/5                up    up
fe-2/0/6                up    up
fe-2/0/7                up    up
fab0                    up    up
fab0.0                  up    up   inet     30.17.0.200/24
fab1                    up    up
fab1.0                  up    up   inet     30.18.0.200/24
fxp0                    up    up
fxp0.0                  up    up   inet     10.0.1.210/24
fxp1                    up    up
fxp1.0                  up    up   inet     129.16.0.1/2
```

```
                                        tnp      0x1100001
fxp2                        up    up
gre                         up    up
ipip                        up    up
lo0                         up    up
lo0.16384                   up    up   inet    127.0.0.1          --> 0/0
lo0.16385                   up    up   inet    10.0.0.1           --> 0/0
                                               10.0.0.16          --> 0/0
                                               128.0.0.1          --> 0/0
                                               128.0.1.16         --> 0/0
                                       inet6   fe80::224:dcff:fed4:e000
lo0.32768                   up    up
lsi                         up    up
mtun                        up    up
pimd                        up    up
pime                        up    up
pp0                         up    up
st0                         up    up
tap                         up    up
vlan                        up    down
{primary:node0}[edit]
root#
```

As shown in the preceding output, interfaces fe-0/0/4 and fe-2/0/4 are members of an `aenet` bundle. Interface fe-0/0/4 is a member of fab0.0, and fe-2/0/4 is a member of fab1.0. If you look closely at fab0.0 and at fab1.0, each is given an internal IP address. The address is used for internal communication and does not need to be configured by the administrator.

You should verify that the two SRXs are talking over the fabric link. The send and receive statistics should be increasing.

```
{primary:node0}[edit interfaces]
root# set fab0 fabric-options member-interfaces fe-0/0/4

{primary:node0}[edit interfaces]
root# set fab1 fabric-options member-interfaces fe-2/0/4

{primary:node0}[edit]
root# show interfaces
fab0 {
    fabric-options {
        member-interfaces {
            fe-0/0/4;
        }
    }
}
```

When the SRX needs to forward traffic across the data plane, it encapsulates the entire packet and then forwards it over the link. The fabric link is automatically configured using jumbo frames, or frames that are larger than the standard 1,514-byte frame.

Juniper supports up to a 9,192-byte frame. The difficulty here is that the SRX cannot take a maximum size frame and then encapsulate it because it would be far too large to push over the fabric link, and the SRX is not able to fragment the packet. Therefore, it's best to set the maximum transmission unit (MTU) on the SRX interfaces to less than 8,900 to ensure that the packets are able to pass over the fabric link.

If you're using an active/passive cluster, this should not be an issue.

As of Junos 12.1X44, all SRX platforms are able to use redundant fabric link ports, unlike control link redundancy, which is restricted to the data center SRXs only. Adding a second link is identical to creating the first link and it also requires a second link to be physically cabled between the two chassis. For some platforms, such as the SRX100 or SRX210, that might seem excessive because adding a second fabric link would mean half of the ports on the chassis would be taken up by links for HA: one control link, two fabric links, and a management link. Only three are required, but the fourth is optional.

There are good reasons to add a redundant fabric link on the smaller SRX devices. The first is that there is an important level of redundancy on the critical links between the SRXs, and it helps to prevent split brain, a critical requirement especially in a remote branch location. (We discuss dealing with split brain further in the sections "Fault Monitoring" on page 333 and "Troubleshooting and Operation" on page 349.)

To configure the second fabric link utilize the following commands:

```
{primary:node0}[edit interfaces]
root# set fab0 fabric-options member-interfaces fe-0/0/5

{primary:node0}[edit interfaces]
root# set fab1 fabric-options member-interfaces fe-2/0/5

{primary:node0}[edit]
root# show interfaces
fab0 {
    fabric-options {
        member-interfaces {
            fe-0/0/4;
           fe-0/0/5;
        }
    }
}
fab1 {
    fabric-options {
        member-interfaces {
            fe-2/0/4;
            fe-2/0/5;
```

```
        }
    }
}
{primary:node0}
root> show interfaces terse
Interface               Admin Link Proto    Local           Remote
ge-0/0/0                up    down
ge-0/0/1                up    down
fe-0/0/2                up    down
fe-0/0/3                up    down
fe-0/0/4                up    up
fe-0/0/4.0              up    up   aenet    --> fab0.0
fe-0/0/5                up    up
fe-0/0/5.0              up    up   aenet    --> fab0.0
fe-0/0/6                up    up
fe-0/0/7                up    up
ge-2/0/0                up    down
ge-2/0/1                up    down
fe-2/0/2                up    down
fe-2/0/3                up    down
fe-2/0/4                up    up
fe-2/0/4.0              up    up   aenet    --> fab1.0
fe-2/0/5                up    up
fe-2/0/5.0              up    up   aenet    --> fab1.0
fe-2/0/6                up    up
fe-2/0/7                up    up
fab0                    up    up
fab0.0                  up    up   inet     30.17.0.200/24
fab1                    up    up
fab1.0                  up    up   inet     30.18.0.200/24
fxp0                    up    up
fxp0.0                  up    up   inet     10.0.1.210/24
fxp1                    up    up
fxp1.0                  up    up   inet     129.16.0.1/2
                                   tnp      0x1100001
fxp2                    up    up
gre                     up    up
ipip                    up    up
lo0                     up    up
lo0.16384               up    up   inet     127.0.0.1         --> 0/0
lo0.16385               up    up   inet     10.0.0.1          --> 0/0
                                            10.0.0.16         --> 0/0
                                            128.0.0.1         --> 0/0
                                            128.0.1.16        --> 0/0
                                   inet6    fe80::224:dc0f:fcd4:e000
lo0.32768               up    up
lsi                     up    up
mtun                    up    up
pimd                    up    up
pime                    up    up
pp0                     up    up
ppd0                    up    up
```

```
ppe0                    up     up
st0                     up     up
tap                     up     up
vlan                    up     down

{primary:node0}
root>
```

In this output's configuration, each fabric link has a second member interface added to it. So, fe-0/0/5 is added to fab0, and fe-2/0/5 is added to fab1. Because a fab link is like an aggregate Ethernet interface, the configuration also looks similar. Note that packets will only pass over one fab link at a time, as the second fab link is only used as a backup.

Configuring the Switching Fabric Interface

The branch series of devices has the ability to perform local switching. However, once you enter chassis cluster mode, what do you do when you still need to provide local switching? The branch SRX devices now have the ability to share a single switching domain across two devices. This is excellent for small branches that need to offer switching to hosts without even needing to add standalone switches. There are a few things to take into consideration before you enable switching in your cluster.

First, to enable switching in a cluster, you need to dedicate one interface on each SRX to connect to the other cluster member. This allows a dedicated path to connect between the two switches. On some of the smaller SRXs this will eat up another valuable port. This is why the feature is only supported on the SRX240 and up; it makes more sense to enable this configuration. For the SRX550 or the SRX650 that have G-PIMs, you need to create a switch fabric interface between each G-PIM that you want to bridge switching between. Also Q-in-Q features are not supported in chassis cluster due to hardware limitations.

```
{primary:node1}[edit]
root@SRX-650# set interfaces swfab0 fabric-options member-interfaces ge-2/0/5

{primary:node1}[edit]
root@SRX-650# set interfaces swfab0 fabric-options member-interfaces ge-11/0/5

{primary:node1}[edit]
root@SRX-650# show interfaces
-- snip --
swfab0 {
    fabric-options {
        member-interfaces {
            ge-2/0/5;
        }
    }
}
swfab1 {
    fabric-options {
```

```
            member-interfaces {
                ge-11/0/5;
            }
        }
    }

{primary:node1}[edit]
root@SRX-650# run show chassis cluster ethernet-switching statistics

Switch fabric link statistics:
    Probe state : UP
    Probes sent: 1866
    Probes received: 1871
    Probe recv errors: 0
    Probe send errors: 0
```

Node-Specific Information

A chassis cluster HA configuration takes two devices and makes them look as though they are one. However, the administrator might still want some elements to be unique between the cluster members, such as the hostname and the IP address on fxp0, which are typically unique per device. No matter what unique configuration is required or desired, it's possible to achieve it by using Junos *groups*. Groups provide the ability to create a configuration and apply it anywhere inside the configuration hierarchy. It's an extremely powerful feature, and here we use it to create a group for each node.

Each group is named after the node it is applied to, and it's a special naming that the SRX looks for. After commit, only the group that matches the local node name is applied, as shown in the following configuration:

```
{primary:node0}[edit groups]
root# show
node0 {
    system {
        host-name SRX210-A;
    }
    interfaces {
        fxp0 {
            unit 0 {
                family inet {
                    address 10.0.1.210/24;
                }
            }
        }
    }
}
node1 {
    system {
        host-name SRX210-B;
    }
    interfaces {
```

```
            fxp0 {
                unit 0 {
                    family inet {
                        address 10.0.1.211/24;
                    }
                }
            }
        }
    }

{primary:node0}[edit groups]
root#
```

In this configuration example, there are two groups, created under the `groups` hierarchy, which is at the top of the configuration tree. The `node0` group has its hostname set as `SRX210-A`, and `node1` has its hostname set as `SRX210-B`. To apply the groups, the administrator needs to use the `apply-groups` command at the root of the configuration. When the configuration is committed to the device, Junos will see the command and merge the correct group to match the node name.

```
{primary:node0}[edit]
root# set apply-groups "${node}"

{primary:node0}[edit]
root# show apply-groups
## Last changed: 2010-03-31 14:25:09 UTC
apply-groups "${node}";

{primary:node0}[edit]
root#

root# show interfaces | display inheritance
fab0 {
    fabric-options {
        member-interfaces {
            fe-0/0/4;
            fe-0/0/5;
        }
    }
}
fab1 {
    fabric-options {
        member-interfaces {
            fe-2/0/4;
            fe-2/0/5;
        }
    }
}
##
## 'fxp0' was inherited from group 'node0'
##
fxp0 {
```

```
        ##
        ## '0' was inherited from group 'node0'
        ##
        unit 0 {
            ##
            ## 'inet' was inherited from group 'node0'
            ##
            family inet {
                ##
                ## '10.0.1.210/24' was inherited from group 'node0'
                ##
                address 10.0.1.210/24;
            }
        }
    }

    {primary:node0}[edit]
    root#
```

To apply the configurations to the correct node, a special command was used: the `set apply-groups "${node}"` command. The variable `"${node}"` is interpreted as the local node name. Next in the output example is the `show | display inheritance` command, which shows the components of the configuration that are inherited from the group—the component that is inherited has three lines above it that all begin with `##`, with the second line specifying from which group the value is inherited.

As discussed, the fxp0 management port can be configured like a standard interface providing a management IP address for each device, but it's also possible to provide a shared IP address between each device so that when connecting to the IP it is redirected back to the primary RE. This way, the administrator does not have to figure out which is the master RE before connecting to it. The administrator can connect to what is called the *master-only* IP.

To do so, a tag is added to the end of the command when configuring the IP address, which is configured in the main configuration and not in the groups (because the tag is applied to both devices, there is no need to place it in the groups).

```
{primary:node0}[edit]
root# set interfaces fxp0.0 family inet address 10.0.1.212/24 master-only

{primary:node0}[edit]
root# show interfaces fxp0
unit 0 {
    family inet {
        address 10.0.1.212/24 {
            master-only;
        }
    }
}
```

```
{primary:node0}
root@SRX210-A> show interfaces fxp0 terse
Interface               Admin Link Proto    Local                 Remote
fxp0                    up    up
fxp0.0                  up    up   inet     10.0.1.210/24
                                            10.0.1.212/24

{primary:node0}
root@SRX210-A>
```

Configuring Heartbeat Timers

The SRX sends heartbeat messages on both the control and data links to ensure that the links are up and running. Although the device itself could look to see if the link is up or down, that is not enough to validate it. Heartbeat messages provide three layers of validation: link, daemon, and internal paths.

The message requires the two jsrpd daemons to successfully communicate, ensuring that the other daemon isn't in a state of disarray and validating the internal paths between the two daemons, including the physical link and the underlying subsystems. For the data link, the packets are even sent through the data plane, validating that the flow daemons are communicating properly.

Each platform has default heartbeat timers that are appropriate for that device. The reason for the differences is due to the ability of the kernel to guarantee the time to the jsrpd daemon. Generally, the larger the device, the larger the processor on the RE; the larger the processor, the faster it can process tasks; and the faster the device can process tasks, the quicker it can move on to the next task.

This begs the question of how fast an administrator needs a device to fail over. Of course, the world would like zero downtime and guaranteed reliability for every service, but the answer is as fast as a device can fail over in a reasonable amount of time while maintaining stability.

Table 7-3 lists the various configuration options for heartbeat timers based on the SRX platform. The branch platforms use a higher timer because they use slower processors to ensure stability at the branch. Although a faster failover might be desired, stability is the most important goal. If the device fails over but is lost in the process, it is of no use.

Table 7-3. Control plane heartbeats

Platform	Control plane timer min (ms)	Control plane timer max (ms)	Missed heartbeat threshold min (sec)	Missed heartbeat threshold max (sec)	Min missing peer detection time (sec)
SRX100	1,000	2,000	3	8	3
SRX110	1,000	2,000	3	8	3
SRX210	1,000	2,000	3	8	3
SRX220	1,000	2,000	3	8	3
SRX240	1,000	2,000	3	8	3
SRX550	1,000	2,000	3	8	3
SRX650	1,000	2,000	3	8	3
SRX1400	1,000	2,000	3	8	3
SRX3400	1,000	2,000	3	8	3
SRX3600	1,000	2,000	3	8	3
SRX5600	1,000	2,000	3	8	3
SRX5800	1,000	2,000	3	8	3

The SRXs have a default failover detection time of three seconds, and these platforms can be easily modified. There are two options to set: threshold and interval. Increasing the failover time is needed in many networks. Surrounding STP convergence might have high timers, and to match the failover times you might need to increase your failover detection times.

```
{primary:node0}[edit chassis cluster]
root@SRX210-A# set heartbeat-interval 2000

{primary:node0}[edit chassis cluster]
root@SRX210-A# set heartbeat-threshold 8

{primary:node0}[edit chassis cluster]
root@SRX210-A# show control-link-recovery;
heartbeat-interval 2000;
heartbeat-threshold 8;

{primary:node0}[edit chassis cluster]
root@SRX210-A#
```

Redundancy Groups

Redundancy groups are the core of the failover mechanism for the SRX and they are used for both the control and data planes. On any SRX cluster there can be at least 1 redundancy group at a minimum, and up to 128 at a maximum (including redundancy group 0). How many you deploy, of course, varies by platform and deployment scenario.

A redundancy group is a collection of objects, and it represents which node is the owner of the objects. The objects are either interfaces or the control plane. Whichever node is the primary owner for the redundancy group is the owner of the items in the redundancy group. On ScreenOS firewalls this was called a *VSD* (virtual security device). When a cluster is created, redundancy group 0 is also created by default. No additional configuration is required to make it work.

Each node is given a priority within a redundancy group. The higher-priority device is given mastership over the redundancy group. This depends on a few options, and one of them, by default, is that a node with a higher priority will not preempt the device with the lower priority. The result is that if a lower-priority node were to have ownership of a redundancy group and then a node with the higher-priority were to come online, it would not give ownership to the higher-priority device. To enable this, the preempt option would need to be enabled, and the device with the higher priority would take ownership of the redundancy group when it was healthy to do so. Most organizations do not use this option—they want to manually move the redundancy group back to the node after the failover is investigated.

Creating a redundancy group is the same for the control or data plane, with the only difference seen when configuring the interfaces. Let's create an example with redundancy group 0. Remember that this is not required, but doing so helps to create the redundancy group and set the node priorities, because if the node priorities are not set they default to 1.

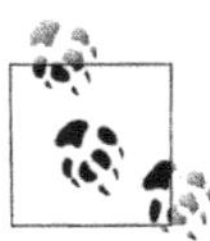

Most organizations use node 0 as the higher-priority device. It's best when configuring the cluster to keep the configuration logical. When troubleshooting in the middle of the night, it's great to know that node 0 should be the higher-priority node and that it is the same across the whole organization.

Let's create the redundancy group:

```
Default:
root@SRX210-A> show chassis cluster status
Cluster ID: 1
Node                  Priority        Status    Preempt  Manual failover

Redundancy group: 0 , Failover count: 1
    node0                   1              primary        no         no
    node1                   1          secondary      no        no

{primary:node0}
root@SRX210-A>

{primary:node0}[edit chassis cluster]
root@SRX210-A# set redundancy-group 0 node 0 priority 254
```

```
{primary:node0}[edit chassis cluster]
root@SRX210-A# set redundancy-group 0 node 1 priority 1

{primary:node0}[edit chassis cluster]
root@SRX210-A# show redundancy-group 0
node 0 priority 254;
node 1 priority 1;

root@SRX210-A> show chassis cluster status
Cluster ID: 1
Node                    Priority       Status     Preempt  Manual failover

Redundancy group: 0 , Failover count: 1
    node0                       254         primary        no       no
    node1                       1           secondary      no       no

{primary:node0}
root@SRX210-A>
```

Now let's create redundancy group 1. The most common firewall deployment for the SRX is a Layer 3-routed active/passive deployment. This means the firewalls are configured as a router and that one device is active and the other is passive. To accomplish this, a single data plane redundancy group is created. It uses the same commands as used to create redundancy group 0 except for the name `redundancy-group 1`.

```
{primary:node0}[edit chassis cluster]
root@SRX210-A# set redundancy-group 1 node 0 priority 254

{primary:node0}[edit chassis cluster]
root@SRX210-A# set redundancy-group 1 node 1 priority 1

{primary:node0}[edit chassis cluster]
root@SRX210-A# set chassis cluster reth-count 2

{primary:node0}[edit chassis cluster]
root@SRX210-A# show
control-link-recovery;
reth-count 2;
heartbeat-interval 2000;
heartbeat-threshold 8;
redundancy-group 0 {
    node 0 priority 254;
    node 1 priority 1;
}
redundancy-group 1 {
    node 0 priority 254;
    node 1 priority 1;
}

{primary:node0}[edit chassis cluster]
root@SRX210-A#
```

```
{primary:node0}
root@SRX210-A> show chassis cluster status
Cluster ID: 1
Node                    Priority       Status     Preempt  Manual failover

Redundancy group: 0 , Failover count: 1
    node0                     254          primary        no         no
    node1                     1            secondary      no         no

Redundancy group: 1 , Failover count: 1
    node0                     254          primary        no         no
    node1                     1            secondary      no         no

{primary:node0}
root@SRX210-A>
```

To keep things consistent, redundancy group 1 also gives node 0 a priority of 254 and node 1 a priority of 1. To be able to commit the configuration, at least one reth has to be enabled (it's shown here but is further discussed in the next section). After commit, the new redundancy group can be seen in the cluster status. It looks exactly like redundancy group 0 and contains the same properties.

When creating an active/active configuration and utilizing redundant Ethernet interfaces, the SRX needs to have at least two redundancy groups. Each node in the cluster will have an active redundancy group on it. You configure this redundancy group in the same way as you did the other redundancy group, except that the other node will be configured with a higher priority. In this case, node 1 will have priority 254 and node 0 will have priority 1.

```
{primary:node0}[edit chassis cluster]
root@SRX210-A# set redundancy-group 2 node 0 priority 1

{primary:node0}[edit chassis cluster]
root@SRX210-A# set redundancy-group 2 node 1 priority 254

{primary:node0}[edit chassis cluster]
root@SRX210-A# show
control-link-recovery;
reth-count 2;
heartbeat-interval 2000;
heartbeat-threshold 8;
redundancy-group 0 {
    node 0 priority 254;
    node 1 priority 1;
}
redundancy-group 1 {
    node 0 priority 254;
    node 1 priority 1;
}
redundancy-group 2 {
    node 0 priority 1;
```

```
    node 1 priority 254;
}

{primary:node0}[edit chassis cluster]
root@SRX210-A#

{primary:node0}
root@SRX210-A> show chassis cluster status
Cluster ID: 1
Node                    Priority      Status     Preempt  Manual failover

Redundancy group: 0 , Failover count: 1
    node0                      254          primary         no         no
    node1                      1            secondary       no         no

Redundancy group: 1 , Failover count: 1
    node0                      254          primary         no         no
    node1                      1            secondary       no         no

Redundancy group: 2 , Failover count: 0
    node0                      1            secondary       no         no
    node1                      254          primary         no         no

{primary:node0}
root@SRX210-A>
```

Now, three redundancy groups are listed. The newest redundancy group, redundancy group 2, has node 1 as its primary and node 0 as its secondary. In this case, all of the traffic for redundancy group 2 will be flowing through node 1, and redundancy group 1's traffic will be flowing through node 0. In the event of a failover each node has a mirrored state table of the peer device so it is possible for either node to take over all redundancy groups.

It's important to plan for the possibility that a single device might have to handle all of the traffic for all of the redundancy groups. If you don't plan for this, the single device can be overwhelmed.

Each redundancy group needs a minimum of one reth in it to operate. Because of this, the total number of redundancy groups is tied to the total number of reths per platform, plus one for redundancy group 0. Table 7-4 lists the number of supported redundancy groups per SRX platform.

Table 7-4. Redundancy groups per platform

Platform	Redundancy groups
SRX100	9
SRX110	9

Platform	Redundancy groups
SRX210	9
SRX220	9
SRX240	25
SRX550	69
SRX650	69
SRX1400	128
SRX3400	128
SRX3600	128
SRX5600	128
SRX5800	128

As previously discussed, it's possible to have the node with the higher priority preemptively take over the redundancy group. By default, the administrator would need to manually fail over the redundancy group to the other node. Configuring a preempt only requires a single command under the redundancy group as shown here, but redundancy groups also have a default hold-down timer, or the time that the redundancy group must wait until it can preempt. On redundancy group 1 and greater, it is set to one second. On redundancy group 0, it is set to 300 seconds or 5 minutes to prevent instability on the control plane.

```
{primary:node0}[edit chassis cluster]
root@SRX210-A# set redundancy-group 1 preempt

{primary:node0}[edit chassis cluster]
root@SRX210-A# show
control-link-recovery;
reth-count 2;
heartbeat-interval 2000;
heartbeat-threshold 8;
redundancy-group 0 {
    node 0 priority 254;
    node 1 priority 1;
}
redundancy-group 1 {
    node 0 priority 254;
    node 1 priority 1;
    preempt;
}

{primary:node0}[edit chassis cluster]
root@SRX210-A#

{primary:node0}
root@SRX210-A> show chassis cluster status
Cluster ID: 1
```

```
Node                     Priority          Status     Preempt  Manual failover

Redundancy group: 0 , Failover count: 1
    node0                      254         primary       no         no
    node1                      1           secondary     no         no

Redundancy group: 1 , Failover count: 1
    node0                      254         primary       yes        no
    node1                      1           secondary     yes        no

{primary:node0}
root@SRX210-A>
```

A hold-down timer can be set to prevent unnecessary failovers in a chassis cluster, used in conjunction with preempt as the number of seconds to wait until the redundancy group can fail over. As previously mentioned, default hold-down timers are configured: for redundancy group 1, it's 1 second; for redundancy group, 0 it's 300 seconds. You can customize the timer and set it between 0 and 1,800 seconds, but best practice suggests to never set redundancy group 0 to less than 300 seconds to prevent instability on the control plane.

It's best to set a safe number for the redundancy groups to ensure that the network is ready for the failover, and in the event of a hard failure on the other node, the redundancy group will fail over as fast as possible.

```
{primary:node0}[edit chassis cluster]
root@SRX210-A# set redundancy-group 1 hold-down-interval 5

{primary:node0}[edit chassis cluster]
root@SRX210-A# show
control-link-recovery;
reth-count 2;
heartbeat-interval 2000;
heartbeat-threshold 8;
redundancy-group 0 {
    node 0 priority 254;
    node 1 priority 1;
}
redundancy-group 1 {
    node 0 priority 254;
    node 1 priority 1;
    preempt;
    hold-down-interval 5;
}

{primary:node0}[edit chassis cluster]
root@SRX210-A#
```

Integrating the Cluster into Your Network

Once the SRXs are talking with each other and their configurations are correctly syncing, it is time to integrate the devices into your network. Waiting to configure the network after enabling the cluster is the best practice to follow. Not only does it save time but it reduces the amount of configuration steps needed as the configuration is shared across both devices. To use a cluster in your network, you need to create a special interface called a reth (often pronounced like *wreath*) interface. This interface is used as a shared interface between the devices. Although there are other more advanced methods to add a cluster into a network, the suggested design is to use an active/active cluster.

Configuring Interfaces

A firewall without interfaces is like a car without tires—it's just not going to get you very far. In the case of chassis clusters, there are two different options: the reth, and the local interface. A reth is a special type of interface that integrates the features of an aggregate Ethernet interface together with redundancy groups.

Before redundant Ethernet interfaces are created, the total number of interfaces in the chassis must be specified. This is required because the reth is effectively an aggregate Ethernet interface, and an interface needs to be provisioned before it can work.

It is suggested that you only provision the total number of interfaces that are required to conserve resources.

Let's set the number of interfaces in the chassis and then move on to create redundancy groups 1+ and configure the interfaces.

```
{primary:node0}[edit chassis cluster]
root@SRX210-A# set reth-count 2

{primary:node0}[edit chassis cluster]
root@SRX210-A# show
control-link-recovery;
reth-count 2;
redundancy-group 0 {
    node 0 priority 254;
    node 1 priority 1;
}
redundancy-group 1 {
    node 0 priority 254;
    node 1 priority 1;
}
```

```
{primary:node0}[edit chassis cluster]
root@SRX210-A#

{primary:node0}
root@SRX210-A> show interfaces terse | match reth
reth0                   up    up
reth1                   up    up
```

Each SRX platform has a maximum number of reths that it can support, as listed in Table 7-5.

Table 7-5. Reth count per platform

Platform	Redundant Ethernet interfaces
SRX100	8
SRX110	8
SRX210	8
SRX220	8
SRX240	24
SRX550	58
SRX650	68
SRX1400	128
SRX3400	128
SRX3600	128
SRX5600	128
SRX5800	128

Now let's create a reth. When using a reth, each member of the cluster has one or more local interfaces that participate in the reth.

```
{primary:node0}[edit interfaces]
root@SRX210-A# set fe-0/0/2 fastether-options redundant-parent reth0

{primary:node0}[edit interfaces]
root@SRX210-A# set fe-2/0/2 fastether-options redundant-parent reth0

{primary:node0}[edit interfaces]
root@SRX210-A# set reth0.0 family inet address 172.16.0.1/24

{primary:node0}[edit]
root@SRX210-A# set interfaces reth0 redundant-ether-options redundancy-group 1

{primary:node0}[edit interfaces]
root@SRX210-A# show
fe-0/0/2 {
    fastether-options {
        redundant-parent reth0;
    }
```

```
    }
    fe-2/0/2 {
        fastether-options {
            redundant-parent reth0;
        }
    }
    fab0 {
        fabric-options {
            member-interfaces {
                fe-0/0/4;
                fe-0/0/5;
            }
        }
    }
    fab1 {
        fabric-options {
            member-interfaces {
                fe-2/0/4;
                fe-2/0/5;
            }
        }
    }
    fxp0 {
        unit 0 {
            family inet {
                address 10.0.1.212/24 {
                    master-only;
                }
            }
        }
    }
    reth0 {
        redundant-ether-options {
            redundancy-group 1;
        }
        unit 0 {
            family inet {
                address 172.16.0.1/24;
            }
        }
    }

{primary:node0}[edit]
root@SRX210-A#
```

In this configuration example, interfaces fe-0/0/2 and fe-2/0/2 have reth0 specified as their parent. Then the reth0 interface is specified as a member of redundancy group 1, and finally the interface is given an IP address. From here the interface can be configured with a zone so that it can be used in security policies for passing network traffic.

After commit, there are two places to validate that the interface is functioning properly, as shown in the following output. First, the user can look at the interface listing to show the child links and also the reth itself. Second, under the chassis cluster status, Junos shows if the interface is up or not. The reason to use the second method of validation is that although the child links might be physically up, the redundancy groups might have a problem, and the interface could be down as far as jsrpd is concerned (we discussed this in the section "Cluster ID" on page 291 in this chapter).

```
{primary:node0}
root@SRX210-A> show interfaces terse | match reth0
fe-0/0/2.0              up    up   aenet    --> reth0.0
fe-2/0/2.0              up    up   aenet    --> reth0.0
reth0                   up    up
reth0.0                 up    up   inet     172.16.0.1/24

{primary:node0}
root@SRX210-A> show chassis cluster interfaces
Control link 0 name: fxp1

Redundant-ethernet Information:
    Name         Status      Redundancy-group
    reth0        Up          1
    reth1        Down        Not configured

{primary:node0}
root@SRX210-A>
```

With the data center SRX firewalls, it's possible to utilize multiple child links per node in the cluster, meaning that each node can have up to eight links configured together for its reth interface. The requirement for this to work is that both nodes must have the same number of links on each chassis. It works exactly like a traditional reth where only one chassis will have its links active, and the secondary node's links are still waiting until a failover occurs. Configuring this is similar to what was done before; the noted difference is that additional interfaces are made child members of the reth.

```
{primary:node0}[edit interfaces
root@SRX5800-1# set xe-6/2/0 gigether-options redundant-parent reth0

{primary:node0}[edit interfaces]
root@SRX5800-1# set xe-6/3/0 gigether-options redundant-parent reth1

{primary:node0}[edit interfaces]
root@SRX5800-1# set xe-18/2/0 gigether-options redundant-parent reth0

{primary:node0}[edit interfaces]
root@SRX5800-1# set xe-18/3/0 gigether-options redundant-parent reth1

{primary:node0}[edit interfaces]
root@SRX5800-1# show interfaces
xe-6/0/0 {
    gigether-options {
        redundant-parent reth0;
    }
```

```
}
xe-6/1/0 {
    gigether-options {
        redundant-parent reth1;
    }
}
xe-6/2/0 {
    gigether-options {
        redundant-parent reth0;
    }
}
xe-6/3/0 {
    gigether-options {
        redundant-parent reth1;
    }
}
xe-18/0/0 {
    gigether-options {
        redundant-parent reth0;
    }
}
xe-18/1/0 {
    gigether-options {
        redundant-parent reth1;
    }
}
xe-18/2/0 {
    gigether-options {
        redundant-parent reth0;
    }
}
xe-18/3/0 {
    gigether-options {
        redundant-parent reth1;
    }
}
reth0 {
    redundant-ether-options {
        redundancy-group 1;
    }
    unit 0 {
        family inet {
            address 1.0.0.1/16;
        }
    }
}
reth1 {
    redundant-ether-options {
        redundancy-group 1;
    }
    unit 0 {
        family inet {
```

```
                address 2.0.0.1/16;
            }
        }
    }

{primary:node0}[edit]
root@SRX5800-1#

{primary:node0}
root@SRX5800-1> show interfaces terse | match reth
xe-6/0/0.0              up    up   aenet    --> reth0.0
xe-6/1/0.0              up    up   aenet    --> reth1.0
xe-6/2/0.0              up    down aenet    --> reth0.0
xe-6/3/0.0              up    down aenet    --> reth1.0
xe-18/0/0.0             up    up   aenet    --> reth0.0
xe-18/1/0.0             up    up   aenet    --> reth1.0
xe-18/2/0.0             up    up   aenet    --> reth0.0
xe-18/3/0.0             up    up   aenet    --> reth1.0
reth0                   up    up
reth0.0                 up    up   inet     1.0.0.1/16
reth1                   up    up
reth1.0                 up    up   inet     2.0.0.1/16

{primary:node0}
root@SRX5800-1> show chassis cluster interfaces
Control link 0 name: em0
Control link 1 name: em1

Redundant-ethernet Information:
    Name         Status      Redundancy-group
    reth0        Up          1
    reth1        Up          1

{primary:node0}
root@SRX5800-1>
```

As seen here, the configuration is identical except that additional interfaces are added as members of the reth. As far as the switch it is connected to, the interface is considered an *aggregate Ethernet*, *link agg group*, or *EtherChannel* depending on the vendor. It's also possible to use LACP as well.

When a failover occurs to the secondary node, the node must announce to the world that it is now owner of the MAC address associated with the reth interface (because the reth's MAC is shared between nodes). It does this using GARPs, ARPs that are broadcast but not specifically requested. Once a GARP is sent, the local switch will be able to update its MAC table to map which port the MAC address is associated with. By default, the SRX sends four GARPs per reth on a failover. These are sent from the control plane and out through the data plane. To modify the number of GARPs sent, this must be configured on a per-redundancy-group basis. Use the `set gratuitous-arp-count` command and a parameter between 1 and 16.

```
{primary:node0}[edit chassis cluster redundancy-group 1]
root@SRX210-A# set gratuitous-arp-count 5

{primary:node0}[edit chassis cluster redundancy-group 1]
root@SRX210-A# show
node 0 priority 254;
node 1 priority 1;
gratuitous-arp-count 5;

{primary:node0}[edit]
root@SRX210-A#
```

One last item to mention is the use of local interfaces. A local interface is not bound or configured to a redundancy group; it's exactly what the name means: a local interface. It is configured like any traditional type of interface on a Junos device and is used in an active/active scenario. It does not have a backup interface on the second device.

Fault Monitoring

"In the event of a failure, your seat cushion may be used as a flotation device." If your plane were to crash and you were given notice, you would take the appropriate action to prevent disaster. When working with a chassis cluster, an administrator wants to see the smoke before the fire. That is what happens when an administrator configures monitoring options in the chassis cluster. The administrator is looking to see if the plane is going down so that she can take evasive action before it's too late. By default, the SRX monitors for various internal failures such as hardware and software issues. But what if other events occur, such as interfaces failing or upstream gateways going away? If the administrator wants to take action based on these events, she must configure the SRX to take action.

The SRX monitoring options are configured on a per-redundancy-group basis, meaning that if specific items were to fail, that redundancy group can fail over to the other chassis. In complex topologies, this gives the administrator extremely flexible options on what to fail over and when. Two integrated features can be used to monitor the redundancy groups: interface monitoring and IP monitoring.

And there are two situations the SRXs can be in when a failure occurs. The first is that the SRXs are communicating and the two nodes in the cluster are both functional. If this is the case, and a failure occurs, the failover between the two nodes will be extremely fast because the two nodes can quickly transfer responsibility for passing traffic between them. The second scenario is when the two nodes lose communication. This could be caused by a loss of power or other factors. In this case, all heartbeats between the chassis must be missed before the secondary node can take over for the primary, taking anywhere from 3 to 16 seconds, depending on the platform.

In this section, each failure scenario is outlined so that the administrator can gain a complete understanding of what to expect if or when a failure occurs.

Interface Monitoring

Interface monitoring monitors the physical status of an interface. It checks to see if the interface is in an up or down state. When one or more monitored interfaces fail, the redundancy group fails over to the other node in the cluster.

The determining factor is when a specific weight is met, and in this case it is 255. The weight of 255 is the redundancy group threshold that is shared between interface monitoring and IP monitoring. Once enough interfaces have failed to meet this weight, the failover for the redundancy group occurs. In most situations, interface monitoring is configured in such a way that if one interface were to fail, the entire redundancy group would fail over. However, it could be configured that two interfaces need to fail. In this first configuration, only one interface needs to fail to initiate a failover.

```
{primary:node0}[edit chassis cluster redundancy-group 1]
root@SRX210-A# set interface-monitor fe-0/0/2 weight 255

{primary:node0}[edit chassis cluster redundancy-group 1]
root@SRX210-A# set interface-monitor fe-2/0/2 weight 255

{primary:node0}[edit chassis cluster redundancy-group 1]
root@SRX210-A# show
node 0 priority 254;
node 1 priority 1;
interface-monitor {
    fe-0/0/2 weight 255;
    fe-2/0/2 weight 255;
}

{primary:node0}[edit chassis cluster redundancy-group 1]
root@SRX210-A#
root@SRX210-A> show chassis cluster interfaces
Control link 0 name: fxp1

Redundant-ethernet Information:
    Name         Status       Redundancy-group
    reth0        Up           1
    reth1        Down         Not configured

Interface Monitoring:
    Interface           Weight     Status      Redundancy-group
    fe-2/0/2            255        Up          1
    fe-0/0/2            255        Up          1

{primary:node0}
root@SRX210-A>
```

In this example, interfaces fe-0/0/2 and fe-2/0/2 are configured with a weight of 255. In the event that either interface fails, the redundancy group will fail over.

In the next example, the interface has failed. Node 0 immediately becomes secondary and its priority becomes zero for redundancy group 1. This means it will only be used as a last resort for the primary of redundancy group 1. After restoring the cables, everything becomes normal again.

```
{primary:node0}
root@SRX210-A> show chassis cluster interfaces
Control link 0 name: fxp1

Redundant-ethernet Information:
    Name         Status      Redundancy-group
    reth0        Up          1
    reth1        Down        Not configured

Interface Monitoring:
    Interface          Weight    Status    Redundancy-group
    fe-2/0/2           255       Up        1
    fe-0/0/2           255       Down      1

{primary:node0}
root@SRX210-A> show chassis cluster status
Cluster ID: 1
Node                   Priority          Status    Preempt  Manual failover

Redundancy group: 0 , Failover count: 1
    node0                    254         primary        no       no
    node1                    1           secondary      no       no

Redundancy group: 1 , Failover count: 2
    node0                    0           secondary      no       no
    node1                    1           primary        no       no

{primary:node0}
root@SRX210-A>
```

In this example:

```
{primary:node0}[edit]
root@SRX210-A# set interfaces fe-0/0/3 fastether-options redundant-parent reth1

{primary:node0}[edit]
root@SRX210-A# set interfaces fe-2/0/3 fastether-options redundant-parent reth1

{primary:node0}[edit]
root@SRX210-A# set interfaces reth0 redundant-ether-options redundancy-group 1

{primary:node0}[edit]
root@SRX210-A# set interfaces reth1 redundant-ether-options redundancy-group 1
```

```
{primary:node0}[edit]
root@SRX210-A# set interfaces reth1.0 family inet address 172.17.0.1/24

{primary:node0}[edit]
root@SRX210-A# show interfaces ## Truncated to only show these interfaces
fe-0/0/3 {
    fastether-options {
        redundant-parent reth1;
    }
}
fe-2/0/3 {
    fastether-options {
        redundant-parent reth1;
    }
}
reth1 {
    redundant-ether-options {
        redundancy-group 1;
    }
    unit 0 {
        family inet {
            address 172.17.0.1/24;
        }
    }
}

{primary:node0}[edit chassis cluster redundancy-group 1]
root@SRX210-A# set interface-monitor fe-0/0/2 weight 128

{primary:node0}[edit chassis cluster redundancy-group 1]
root@SRX210-A# set interface-monitor fe-2/0/2 weight 128

{primary:node0}[edit chassis cluster redundancy-group 1]
root@SRX210-A# show
node 0 priority 254;
node 1 priority 1;
interface-monitor {
    fe-0/0/2 weight 128;
    fe-2/0/2 weight 128;
}

{primary:node0}[edit chassis cluster redundancy-group 1]
root@SRX210-A#

{primary:node0}
root@SRX210-A> show chassis cluster interfaces
Control link 0 name: fxp1

Redundant-ethernet Information:
    Name          Status       Redundancy-group
    reth0         Up           1
    reth1         Up           1
```

```
Interface Monitoring:
    Interface          Weight    Status    Redundancy-group
    fe-2/0/2           128       Up        1
    fe-0/0/2           128       Up        1

{primary:node0}
root@SRX210-A>
```

Both interfaces are needed to trigger a failover. The next sequence shows where node 0 will lose one interface from each of its reths. This causes a failover to occur on node 1.

```
{primary:node0}[edit]
root@SRX210-A# show chassis cluster redundancy-group 1
node 0 priority 254;
node 1 priority 1;
interface-monitor {
    fe-0/0/2 weight 128;
    fe-0/0/3 weight 128;
}

{primary:node0}[edit]
root@SRX210-A#

{primary:node0}
root@SRX210-A> show chassis cluster status
Cluster ID: 1
Node                  Priority      Status     Preempt  Manual failover

Redundancy group: 0 , Failover count: 1
    node0                   254          primary        no       no
    node1                   1            secondary      no       no

Redundancy group: 1 , Failover count: 3
    node0                   254          primary        no       no
    node1                   1            secondary      no       no

{primary:node0}
root@SRX210-A> show chassis cluster interfaces
Control link 0 name: fxp1

Redundant-ethernet Information:
    Name         Status       Redundancy-group
    reth0        Up           1
    reth1        Up           1

Interface Monitoring:
    Interface          Weight    Status    Redundancy-group
    fe-0/0/3           128       Up        1
    fe-0/0/2           128       Up        1

{primary:node0}
root@SRX210-A>
```

```
{primary:node0}
root@SRX210-A> show chassis cluster interfaces
Control link 0 name: fxp1

Redundant-ethernet Information:
    Name         Status      Redundancy-group
    reth0        Up          1
    reth1        Up          1

Interface Monitoring:
    Interface          Weight     Status     Redundancy-group
    fe-0/0/3           128        Down       1
    fe-0/0/2           128        Down       1

{primary:node0}
root@SRX210-A> show chassis cluster status
Cluster ID: 1
Node                  Priority       Status     Preempt  Manual failover

Redundancy group: 0 , Failover count: 1
    node0                   254          primary        no       no
    node1                   1            secondary      no       no

Redundancy group: 1 , Failover count: 4
    node0                   0            secondary      no       no
    node1                   1            primary        no       no

{primary:node0}
root@SRX210-A>
```

Here it required both interfaces to go down to fail over to the other node.

Only physical interfaces can be monitored. The reths themselves can't be monitored.

Interface monitoring should be done on nonzero redundancy groups and not on the control plane, because best practice urges you to only allow the control plane to fail over in the event of a hard failure.

IP Monitoring

IP monitoring allows for the monitoring of upstream gateways. When using IP monitoring, the ping probe validates the entire end-to-end path from the SRX to the remote node and back. The feature is typically used to monitor its next hop gateway, ensuring the gateway is ready to accept packets from the SRX. This is key, as the SRX's link to its local switch could be working but the upstream devices might not.

IP monitoring is configured per redundancy group and has some similarities to interface monitoring. It also uses weights, and when the weights add up to exceed the redundancy group weight, a failover is triggered. But with IP monitoring, the SRX is monitoring remote gateways, not interfaces.

In each redundancy group there are four global options that affect all of the hosts that are to be monitored:

- The first option is the global weight. This is the weight that is subtracted from the redundancy group weight for all of the hosts being monitored.
- The second option is the global threshold. This is the number that needs to be met or exceeded by all of the cumulative weights of the monitored IPs to trigger a failover.
- The last two options are the retry attempts for the ping. The first is the retry count, which is the number of times to retry between failures. The minimum setting is five retries.
- The last is the retry interval, and this value specifies the number of seconds between replies. The default retry time is one second.

Here the configuration options can be seen using the help prompt.

```
root@SRX5800-1# set redundancy-group 1 ip-monitoring ?
Possible completions:
+ apply-groups         Groups from which to inherit configuration data
+ apply-groups-except  Don't inherit configuration data from these groups
> family               Define protocol family
  global-threshold     Define global threshold for IP monitoring (0..255)
  global-weight        Define global weight for IP monitoring (0..255)
  retry-count          Number of retries needed to declare reachablity failure
(5..15)
  retry-interval       Define the time interval in seconds between retries.
(1..30)
{primary:node0}[edit chassis cluster]
root@SRX5800-1#
```

These IP monitoring options can be overwhelming, but they are designed to give the user more flexibility. The redundancy group can be configured to fail over if one or more of the monitored IPs fail or if a combination of the monitored IPs and interfaces fail.

In the next example, two monitored IPs are going to be configured. Both of them need to fail to trigger a redundancy group failure. The SRX will use routing to resolve which interface should be used to ping the remote host (you could also go across virtual routers as of Junos 10.1 and later).

```
{primary:node0}[edit chassis cluster redundancy-group 1]
root@SRX5800-1# set ip-monitoring family inet 1.2.3.4 weight 128

{primary:node0}[edit chassis cluster redundancy-group 1]
root@SRX5800-1# set ip-monitoring family inet 1.3.4.5 weight 128
```

```
{primary:node0}[edit chassis cluster redundancy-group 1]
root@SRX5800-1# show
node 0 priority 200;
node 1 priority 100;
ip-monitoring {
    global-weight 255;
    global-threshold 255;
    family {
        inet {
            1.2.3.4 weight 128;
            1.3.4.5 weight 128;
        }
    }
}

{primary:node0}[edit chassis cluster redundancy-group 1]
root@SRX5800-1#


{primary:node0}[edit chassis cluster redundancy-group 1]
root@SRX5800-1# run show chassis cluster ip-monitoring status
node0:
--------------------------------------------------------------------------

Redundancy group: 1

IP address     Status        Failure count  Reason
1.3.4.5        unreachable     1            redundancy-group state unknown
1.2.3.4        unreachable     1            redundancy-group state unknown

node1:
---------------------------------------------------------------------

Redundancy group: 1

IP address     Status        Failure count  Reason
1.3.4.5        unreachable     1            redundancy-group state unknown
1.2.3.4        unreachable     1            redundancy-group state unknown

{primary:node0}[edit chassis cluster redundancy-group 1]
root@SRX5800-1# run show chassis cluster status
Cluster ID: 1
Node                    Priority          Status     Preempt  Manual failover

Redundancy group: 0 , Failover count: 1
    node0                     200         primary        no       no
    node1                     100         secondary      no       no

Redundancy group: 1 , Failover count: 1
    node0                     0           primary        no       no
    node1                     0           secondary      no       no
```

```
{primary:node0}[edit chassis cluster redundancy-group 1]
root@SRX5800-1#
```

After you have studied that, the next example uses a combination of both IP monitoring and interface monitoring, and it shows how the combined weight of the two will trigger a failover.

```
{primary:node0}[edit chassis cluster redundancy-group 1]
root@SRX5800-1# show
node 0 priority 200;
node 1 priority 100;
interface-monitor {
    xe-6/1/0 weight 255;
}
ip-monitoring {
    global-weight 255;
    global-threshold 255;
    family {
        inet {
            1.2.3.4 weight 128;
        }
    }
}

{primary:node0}[edit]
root@SRX5800-1# run show chassis cluster status
Cluster ID: 1
Node                  Priority          Status    Preempt  Manual failover

Redundancy group: 0 , Failover count: 1
    node0                   200         primary        no       no
    node1                   100         secondary      no       no

Redundancy group: 1 , Failover count: 2
    node0                   200         secondary      no       no
    node1                   100         primary        no       no

{primary:node0}[edit]
root@SRX5800-1# run show chassis cluster ip-monitoring status
node0:
------------------------------------------------------------------

Redundancy group: 1

IP address  Status      Failure count  Reason
1.2.3.4     unreachable  1             redundancy-group state unknown

node1:
-------------------------------------------------------------------

Redundancy group: 1
```

```
IP address  Status      Failure count  Reason
1.2.3.4     unreachable  1             redundancy-group state unknown

{primary:node0}[edit]
root@SRX5800-1# run show chassis cluster interfaces ?
Possible completions:
  <[Enter]>            Execute this command
  |                    Pipe through a command
{primary:node0}[edit]
root@SRX5800-1# run show chassis cluster interfaces
Control link 0 name: em0
Control link 1 name: em1

Redundant-ethernet Information:
    Name         Status      Redundancy-group
    reth0        Up          1
    reth1        Up          1
    reth2        Down        1
    reth3        Up          1

Interface Monitoring:
    Interface          Weight    Status    Redundancy-group
    xe-6/1/0           128       Up        1

{primary:node0}[edit]
root@SRX5800-1#
```

Here the ping for IP monitoring is sourced from the reth's active device, with the IP address configured on the specified interface. Optionally, it's possible to configure a secondary IP to trigger the ping to come from the configured secondary IP address and from the backup interface, allowing the administrator to check the backup path coming from the secondary node. This would ensure that before a failover occurs, the backup path is working. Let's configure this option. It only takes one additional step per monitored IP.

```
{primary:node0}[edit chassis cluster redundancy-group 1]
root@SRX5800-1# set ip-monitoring family inet 1.2.3.4 weight 255interface
reth0.0 secondary-ip-address 1.0.0.10

{primary:node0}[edit chassis cluster redundancy-group 1]
root@SRX5800-1# show
node 0 priority 200;
node 1 priority 100;
ip-monitoring {
    global-weight 255;
    global-threshold 255;
    family {
        inet {
            1.2.3.4 {
                weight 255;
                interface reth0.0 secondary-ip-address 1.0.0.10;
```

```
            }
        }
    }
}

{primary:node0}[edit]
root@SRX5800-1# run show chassis cluster ip-monitoring status
node0:
--------------------------------------------------------------------------

Redundancy group: 1

IP address                 Status        Failure count  Reason
1.2.3.4                    unreachable     0            no route to host

node1:
--------------------------------------------------------------------------

Redundancy group: 1

IP address                 Status        Failure count  Reason
1.2.3.4                    unreachable     0            no route to host

{primary:node0}[edit]
root@SRX5800-1#
```

The SRX5000 Series products can create up to 64 monitored IPs and the SRX3000 Series can create 32. The ping is generated from the second SPU on the system, which is the first non-CP SPU, and because of that, it is not limited to scheduling or processing restrictions found on the RE. The branch devices operate slightly differently. The best practice is to minimize the total number of monitored hosts to two on the branch devices. The more devices that you add, the more difficult it could be to ensure the device has the processing to monitor the remote nodes.

Hardware Monitoring

On the SRX, there is a daemon running called *chassisd*. This process is designed to run and control the system hardware, and it is also used to monitor for faults. If the chassisd determines that the system has experienced specific faults, it will trigger a failover to the other node. Depending on the SRX platform, various components can fail before a complete failover is triggered.

The majority of the branch platforms are not component-based. This means the entire system consists of a single board, and if anything were to go wrong on the main board, generally the complete system would fail. The branch SRX devices also have interface cards, and if the cards fail, the local interfaces are lost. Interface monitoring can be used to detect if the interface has failed.

The data center devices are a different story. These devices have many different boards and system components, and because of this, the failover scenarios can get fairly complex. Both Juniper Networks and customers thoroughly test the reliability of the devices, and each component is failed in a matrix of testing scenarios to ensure that failovers are correctly covered.

Route engine

The RE is the local brain of a chassis. Its job is to maintain control over the local cards in the chassis. It ensures that all of them are up and running and it allows the administrator to manage the device. If the RE fails, it can no longer control the local chassis, and if that RE was the primary for the cluster, the secondary engineer will pause until enough heartbeats are missed that it assumes mastership.

During this period, the local chassis will continue to forward (the data plane without an RE will continue to run for up to three minutes), but as soon as the other RE contacts the SPUs, they will no longer process traffic. By this time, the secondary data plane will have taken over for the traffic.

In the event that the secondary RE fails, that chassis immediately becomes lost. After the heartbeat threshold is passed, the primary RE will assume the other chassis has failed, and any active traffic running on the chassis in redundancy groups will fail over to the remaining node. Traffic that used local interfaces must use another protocol, such as OSPF, to fail over to the other node.

Switch control board

The switch control board is a component that is unique to the SRX5000 Series. This component contains three important systems: the switch fabric, the control plane network, and the carrier slot for the RE. It's a fairly complex component, as it effectively connects everything in the device. The SRX5600 requires one SCB and can have a second for redundancy. The SRX5800 requires two SCBs and can have a third for redundancy.

If an SCB fails in the SRX5600, it will fail over to the second SCB. Its redundancy, however, causes a brief blip in traffic and then things start moving along. The second SCB also requires the use of a local RE, the same simple RE that is used to bring up dual control links. The second RE is needed to activate the local control plane switching chip on the second SCB—if this was not in place, the RE would be unable to talk to the rest of the chassis.

The SRX5800's behavior is different because, by default, it has two SCBs. These are required to provide full throughput to the entire chassis, and if one were to fail, the throughput would be halved until a new SCB is brought online. The same conditions as the SRX5600 also apply here. If the SCB containing the RE were to fail, a secondary RE would need to be in the second SCB to provide the backup control network for the RE to communicate. If the SCB that does not contain the primary RE fails, the maximum throughput of the chassis is cut in half. This means all of the paths in the box are halved. If a third SCB is installed, it will take over for either of the failed SCBs. It cannot provide a redundant control link as it is not able to contain an RE, and when the switchover happens to the third SCB, it will briefly interrupt traffic as the switchover occurs.

Now, all of this should pose a question to the careful reader: if the RE is contained in an SCB and the SCB fails, will this affect the RE? The answer depends on the type of failure. If the fabric chips fail, the RE will be fine, as the SCB simply extends the connections from the back plane into the RE. The engineers put the RE in the SCB to conserve slots in the chassis and reserve them for traffic processing cards. It is possible for an SCB to fail in such a way that it will disable the engineer; it's unlikely, but possible.

Switch fabric board

The SFB is a component unique to the SRX3000 Series platform. It contains the switch fabric, the primary control plane switch, the secondary control plane switch, an interface card, and the control ports. If this component were to fail, the chassis would effectively be lost. The SFB's individual components can fail as well, causing various levels of device degradation. In the end, once the integrity of the card is lost, the services residing in that chassis will fail over to the remaining node.

Services Processing Card/Next Generation Services Processing Card

The SPC contains one, two, or up to four SPUs, depending on the model of the SRX. Each SPU is monitored directly by the SRX's local RE chassisd process. If any SPU fails, several events will immediately occur. The RE will reset all of the cards on the data plane, including interfaces and NPCs. Such an SPU failure causes the chassis monitoring threshold to hit 255. This causes all of the data plane services to fail over to the secondary chassis. Messages relating to SPUs failing can be seen in the jsrpd logs. The entire data plane is reset because it is easier to ensure that everything is up and running after a clean restart, rather than having to validate many individual subsystems. Each subsystem is validated after a clean restart of the chassis.

Network Processing Card

A separate NPC is unique to the SRX3000 Series (these items are located on the interface cards on the SRX5000). They were separated out to lower the component costs and to lower the overall cost of the chassis. The SRX3000 has static bindings to each interface. So if an NPC were to fail, the interface bound to it would effectively be lost, as it would not have access to the switching fabric. The chassis will be able to detect this by using simple health checks; alternatively, IP monitoring can be used to validate the next hop. This message would be sent from the SPC and then through the NPC. Because the NPC has failed, the messages will not make it out of the chassis. At this point, IP monitoring triggers a failover to the other node. The NPC failure ultimately triggers a failover to the remaining node in the chassis, and the chassis with the failure restarts all of the cards. If the NPC with the failure is unable to restart, the interfaces are mapped to new NPCs, assuming there are some remaining. Although the device can run in a degraded state, it's best to leave all of the traffic on the good node and replace the failed component.

Interface card

The SRX data center devices have both types of interface cards, often referred to as input/output cards. However, there are stark differences between the two. The IOCs on the SRX3000 contain a switching chip (used to connect multiple interfaces to a single bus) and a Field Programmable Gate Array (FPGA) to connect into the fabric. The IOCs on the SRX5000s contain two or more sets of NPUs, fabric connect chips, and physical interfaces. If an SRX5000 Series interface card fails and it does not contain a monitored interface, or the only fabric link, the SRX will rely on the administrator to use interface monitoring or IP monitoring to detect a failure. The same is true with the SRX3000 Series platforms. On the SRX5000 Series, it is also possible to hot-swap interfaces to replace the card, whereas the SRX3000 requires that the chassis be powered off to replace a card.

Control link

The control link is a critical component in the system. It allows the two brains, the REs, to talk to each other. If the control link physically goes down and the fabric link is up, the secondary RE immediately goes into ineligible state. Eventually, it will go into disabled state. Once it becomes ineligible, the only way to recover the secondary node is to reboot the device. If control link recovery is enabled, the device will reboot itself after one minute of successful communications. (Using control link recovery is the best option in this scenario, as it allows the device to reboot when it knows communications are working correctly.) The important item here is that for this scenario to work, at least one fabric link must still be up. With the fabric link still remaining, the primary RE knows that the secondary is still alive but a problem has occurred.

The secondary node goes into disabled state to prevent split brain (the state when two devices both think they are master). If this occurs, effectively two nodes are fighting to be the primary node for the cluster. They will use GARPs to try to take over and process the traffic on the network, typically causing an outage. This is a good reason you should use dual control links and data links when possible.

Data link

The data link uses jsrpd heartbeat messages to validate that the path is up and is actively working. This is similar to the control link. However, the data link is more forgiving. It can take up to 120 seconds for the data link to detect that it is down. This is because it's possible for the data link to get completely full of RTOs, or data forwarding messages, hence the data link is more forgiving in missing messages from the other node. However, after the required amount of time has passed, the secondary node will become disabled just like the control link. There isn't an automatic reboot like the control link—the secondary node must be manually rebooted to recover it.

To increase stability of the SRXs, the data link is no longer monitored. This was changed to allow administrators to move the data link cables around without impacting the cluster.

Control link and data link failure

Rarely do both the fabric and data links go down at the same time, meaning within the same second. But we all know this can occur for all sorts of reasons, from hardware failures to a machete-wielding utility helper chopping up cables in the data center. It's a common request and test that Juniper Networks receives, so it's best that we cover it rather than leave administrators wondering.

If the control link and the data link were to fail at the same time, the worst possible scenario would occur, split brain, leaving the cluster members thinking the other node has failed, which effectively causes an outage. There are several ways to prevent this.

It is possible to use dual fabric links on the branch SRX Series devices. Even if a control link and a fabric link were to fail, the last remaining control link would prevent split brain from occurring. So, generally speaking, split brain will not occur on the branch platforms.

For the data center platforms, utilizing dual control links and dual fabric links will provide the same level of split brain prevention, with one point to note. On the SRX5000 Series, the control port is on the SPC, and the SPC containing the CP is a part of the data path. So, if the administrator were to configure the control link, and the CP is on the same SPC and it failed, split brain would occur. The CP is always located on the SPU in the lowest numbered FPC and PIC slot.

You can use the `show chassis fpc pic-status` command to identify the location of the FPC.

The best practice is to place the control port on any SPC other than the one containing the CP. If redundant control links are required, it's best to place them on two separate SPCs. This would mean that on an SRX5000 Series, three SPCs—one containing the CP and the other two each containing a control link—would be used for the best level of redundancy. The same goes for the fabric link. Placing each redundant fabric link on a separate SPC would be the best practice for availability. Although this might seem like overkill, if ultimate availability is required, this is the suggested deployment.

Although it does look like the CP is a single point of failure, that isn't true. If the CP fails, the data plane will be reset. As soon as the SPCs receive power, the control links will come up rapidly, allowing the cluster to continue control plane communications and preventing split brain.

Power supplies

It's obvious that if the device's sole source of power fails, the device shuts off. This will cause the remaining node to perform Dead Peer Detection (DPD) to determine if the other node is alive. DPD is done with jsrpd heartbeats. If the remaining node is the primary device for the control and data planes, it continues to forward traffic as is. It notes that the other node is down because it cannot communicate with it. If the remaining node was secondary, it will wait until all of the heartbeats are missed before it determines that the node has failed. Once the heartbeats have been passed, it assumes mastership of the node.

For devices with redundant power supplies, the remaining power supply will power the chassis and it will continue to operate. This is applicable to the SRX650 and the SRX3400. The SRX3600 has up to four power supplies, and it requires at least two to operate. The other two are used for redundancy. So, in the best availability deployment, four should be deployed.

The SRX5000 Series devices each have up to four power supplies. At a suggested minimum, three should be used. Depending on the total number of cards running in the chassis, a single power supply can be used. If the total draw from the installed components exceeds the available power, all of the cards will be turned off. The RE will continue attempting to start the cards until the power is available. It's always best to deploy the SRXs with the highest amount of available power supply to ensure availability.

Software Monitoring

The SRX is set up to monitor the software that is running, and this is true for both the control and data planes. The SRX attempts to detect a failure within the system as soon as it happens, and if and when it can detect a failure within the system, it must react accordingly. The SRX platform has some fairly complex internals, but it is built to protect against failures. So if the RE has a process that fails, it can restart it, and the failure is logged for additional troubleshooting.

The branch's data plane consists of a core flowd process. The RE is in constant communication to watch if it is acting correctly. In the event that the flowd process crashes or hangs up, the control plane quickly fails over to the other node. This will happen in less than the time it would take to detect a dead node. In any failure case where the two nodes are still in communication, the failover time is quite fast. These cases include IP monitoring, manual failover, and interface monitoring.

On the data center SRX's data plane, each SPU has both control and data software running on it. The RE talks directly to each SPU's control software for status updates and for configuration changes. Because of this, the RE will know if the data plane fails. If the flowd processes crash on the data plane (there is one per SPU), the entire data plane will be hard-reset, which means all of the line cards will be reset. This is done to ensure that the control plane is completely up to an acceptable running standard. To do this, the data plane is failed over to the secondary node.

Preserving the Control Plane

If a device is set up to rapidly fail over, it's possible that it could be jumping the gun and attempting a failover for no reason. When it's time to move between two firewalls, it's best to ensure that the time is correct for the failover. There are methods in dynamic routing to do extremely fast failover using a protocol called *bidirectional forwarding detection* (BFD). This protocol is used in conjunction with a routing protocol such as OSPF. It can provide 50-ms failovers. That is extremely fast but provides little threat to the network. In this case, BFD is rerouting around a link or device failure typically in a stateless manner. Because it's done stateless, there is little threat to the traffic.

When a stateful firewall does a failover, there is much more in play than simply rerouting traffic. The new device needs to accept all of the traffic and match up the packets with the existing sessions that are synchronized to the second node. Also, the primary device needs to relinquish control of the traffic. On the data plane, it's a fairly stable process to fail over and fail back between nodes. In fact, this can be done rapidly and nearly continuously without much worry. It's best to let the control plane fail over only in the event of a failure, as there simply isn't a need to fail over the control plane unless a critical event occurs.

The biggest reason for any concern is that the control plane talks to the various daemons on the other chassis and on the data plane. If rapid failover were to occur, it's possible to destabilize the control plane. This is not a rule, it's an exception, just as the owner of a car isn't going to jam the car into reverse on the highway. Often, administrators want to test the limits of the SRX and drop them off shelves and whatnot, so it's fair to call this out as a warning before it's tested in production.

Troubleshooting and Operation

From time to time things can go wrong. You can be driving along in your car and a tire can blow out; sometimes a firewall can crash. Nothing that is made by humans is precluded from undergoing an unseen failure. Because of this, the administrator must be prepared to deal with the worst possible scenarios. In this section, we discuss various methods that show the administrator how to troubleshoot a chassis cluster gone awry.

First Steps

There are a few commands to use when trying to look into an issue. The administrator needs to first identify the cluster status and determine if it is communicating.

The `show chassis cluster status` command, although simple in nature, shows the administrator the status of the cluster. It shows who is the primary member for each redundancy group and the status of those nodes, and it will give insight into who should be passing traffic in the network. Here's a sample:

```
{primary:node1}
root@SRX210-B> show chassis cluster status
Cluster ID: 1
Node                 Priority           Status     Preempt  Manual failover

Redundancy group: 0 , Failover count: 1
    node0                  254          secondary       no         no
    node1                  1            primary         no         no

Redundancy group: 1 , Failover count: 2
    node0                  254          primary         no         no
    node1                  1            secondary       no         no

{primary:node1}
root@SRX210-B>
```

You should have seen this many times in this chapter, as it is used frequently. Things to look for here are that both nodes show as up; both have a priority greater than zero; both have a status of either primary, secondary, or secondary-hold; and one and only one node is primary for each redundancy group. Generally, if those conditions are met, things in the cluster should be looking okay. If not, and for some reason one of the nodes does not show up in this output, communication to the other node has been lost. The administrator should then connect to the other node and verify that it can communicate.

To validate that the two nodes can communicate, the show `chassis cluster control-plane statistics` command is used, showing the messages that are being sent between the two members. The send and receive numbers should be incrementing between the two nodes. If they are not, something might be wrong with both the control and fabric links. Here is an example with the statistics in bold:

```
{primary:node0}
root@SRX210-A> show chassis cluster control-plane statistics
Control link statistics:
    Control link 0:
        Heartbeat packets sent: 124
        Heartbeat packets received: 95
        Heartbeat packet errors: 0
Fabric link statistics:
    Probes sent: 122
    Probes received: 56
```

```
        Probe errors: 0

{primary:node0}
root@SRX210-A>
```

Again, this command should be familiar as it has been used in this chapter. If these (boldface) numbers are not increasing, check the fabric and control plane interfaces. The fabric interfaces method is the same across all SRX products.

Next let's check the fabric links. It's important to verify that the fabric link and the child links show they are in an up state.

```
{primary:node0}
root@SRX210-A> show interfaces terse
Interface               Admin Link Proto    Local                Remote
--snip--
fe-0/0/4.0              up    up   aenet    --> fab0.0
fe-0/0/5                up    up
fe-0/0/5.0              up    up   aenet    --> fab0.0
--snip--
fe-2/0/4.0              up    up   aenet    --> fab1.0
fe-2/0/5                up    up
fe-2/0/5.0              up    up   aenet    --> fab1.0
--snip--
fab0                    up    up
fab0.0                  up    up   inet     30.17.0.200/24
fab1                    up    up
fab1.0                  up    up   inet     30.18.0.200/24
--snip--
{primary:node0}
root@SRX210-A>
```

If any of the child links of the fabric link, `fabX`, show in a down state, this would show the interface that is physically down on the node. This must be restored to enable communications.

The control link is the most critical to verify, and it varies per SRX platform type. On the branch devices, the interface that is configured as the control link must be checked. This is specified in Table 7-2's control ports by platform. The procedure would be the same as any physical interface. Here an example from an SRX210 was used, and it shows that the specified interfaces are up.

```
{primary:node0}
root@SRX210-A> show interfaces terse
Interface               Admin Link Proto    Local                Remote
--snip--
fe-0/0/7                up    up
--snip--
fe-2/0/7                up    up
--snip--
```

```
{primary:node0}
root@SRX210-A>
```

On the data center SRXs, there is no direct way to check the state of the control ports; because the ports are dedicated off of switches inside the SRX and they are not typical interfaces, it's not possible to check them. It is possible, however, to check the switch that is on the SCB to ensure that packets are being received from that card. Generally, though, if the port is up and configured correctly, there should be no reason why it won't communicate. But checking the internal switch should show that packets are passing from the SPC to the RE. There will also be other communications coming from the card as well, but this at least provides insight into the communication. To check, the node and FPC that has the control link must be known. In the following command, the specified port coincides with the FPC number of the SPC with the control port.

```
{primary:node0}
root@SRX5800-1> show chassis ethernet-switch statistics 1 node 0
node0:
--------------------------------------------------------------------------
Displaying port statistics for switch 0
Statistics for port 1 connected to device FPC1:
  TX Packets 64 Octets         7636786
  TX Packets 65-127 Octets     989668
  TX Packets 128-255 Octets    37108
  TX Packets 256-511 Octets    35685
  TX Packets 512-1023 Octets   233238
  TX Packets 1024-1518 Octets  374077
  TX Packets 1519-2047 Octets  0
  TX Packets 2048-4095 Octets  0
  TX Packets 4096-9216 Octets  0
  TX 1519-1522 Good Vlan frms  0
  TX Octets                    9306562
  TX Multicast Packets         24723
  TX Broadcast Packets         219029
  TX Single Collision frames   0
  TX Mult. Collision frames    0
  TX Late Collisions           0
  TX Excessive Collisions      0
  TX Collision frames          0
  TX PAUSEMAC Ctrl Frames      0
  TX MAC ctrl frames           0
  TX Frame deferred Xmns       0
  TX Frame excessive deferl    0
  TX Oversize Packets          0
  TX Jabbers                   0
  TX FCS Error Counter         0
  TX Fragment Counter          0
  TX Byte Counter              1335951885
  RX Packets 64 Octets         6672950
  RX Packets 65-127 Octets     2226967
  RX Packets 128-255 Octets    39459
  RX Packets 256-511 Octets    34332
```

```
    RX Packets 512-1023 Octets  523505
    RX Packets 1024-1518 Octets  51945
    RX Packets 1519-2047 Octets  0
    RX Packets 2048-4095 Octets  0
    RX Packets 4096-9216 Octets  0
    RX Octets                   9549158
    RX Multicast Packets        24674
    RX Broadcast Packets        364537
    RX FCS Errors               0
    RX Align Errors             0
    RX Fragments                0
    RX Symbol errors            0
    RX Unsupported opcodes      0
    RX Out of Range Length      0
    RX False Carrier Errors     0
    RX Undersize Packets        0
    RX Oversize Packets         0
    RX Jabbers                  0
    RX 1519-1522 Good Vlan frms 0
    RX MTU Exceed Counter       0
    RX Control Frame Counter    0
    RX Pause Frame Counter      0
    RX Byte Counter             999614473

  {primary:node0}
  root@SRX5800-1>
```

The output looks like standard port statistics from a switch. Looking in here will validate that packets are coming from the SPC. Because the SRX3000 has its control ports on the SFB, and there is nothing to configure for the control ports, there is little to look at on the interface. It is best to focus on the result from the `show chassis cluster control-plane statistics` command.

If checking the interfaces yields mixed results where they seem to be up but they are not passing traffic, it's possible to reboot the node in the degraded state. The risk here is that the node could come up in split brain. Because that is a possibility, it's best to disable its interfaces, or physically disable all of them except the control or data link. The ports can even be disabled on the switch to which they are connected. This way, on boot, if the node determines it is master, it will not interrupt traffic. A correctly operating node using the minimal control port and fabric port configuration should be able to communicate to its peer. If, after a reboot, it still cannot communicate to the other node, it's best to verify the configuration and cabling. Finally, the box or cluster interfaces might be bad.

Checking Interfaces

Interfaces are required to pass traffic through the SRX, and for the SRX to be effective in its job, it needs to have interfaces up and able to pass traffic. The SRX can use both local and redundant Ethernet interfaces, and for our purposes here, both have similar methods of troubleshooting.

To troubleshoot an interface, first check to see if the interface is physically up. Use the `show interfaces terse` command to quickly see all of the interfaces in both chassis.

```
{primary:node0}
root@SRX210-A> show interfaces terse
Interface               Admin Link Proto    Local                 Remote
ge-0/0/0                up    down
ge-0/0/1                up    down
fe-0/0/2                up    up
```

This should be familiar if you've been reading through this chapter, and certainly throughout the book. The other item to check is the status of the reth within a redundancy group to see if the interface is up or down inside the reth. It's possible that the reth could be physically up but logically down (in the event that there was an issue on the data plane). To check the status of a reth interface, use the `show chassis cluster interfaces` command.

```
root@SRX210-A> show chassis cluster interfaces
Control link 0 name: fxp1
Redundant-ethernet Information:
    Name         Status      Redundancy-group
    reth0        Up          1
    reth1        Up          1

Interface Monitoring:
    Interface          Weight     Status     Redundancy-group
    fe-0/0/2           255        Up         1
    fe-2/0/2           255        Up         1

{primary:node0}
root@SRX210-A>
```

If the interfaces are physically up but the redundant interfaces show that they are in a down state, it's time to look at the data plane.

Verifying the Data Plane

The data plane on the SRX passes and processes the traffic. Because it is an independent component from the RE, it could be down while the administrator is still in the RE. There are a few things to check on the SRX to validate the data plane.

Because the data plane is very different between the branch SRX platform and the data center platform, there will be some variance between the commands.

Verifying the FPCs and PICs is the first step, and this shows the status of the underlying hardware that needs to be up to process the data traffic. On the branch SRX, the data plane is a single multithreaded process, however, so running the `show chassis fpc pic-status` command shows the status of the data plane.

```
root@SRX210-A> show chassis fpc pic-status
node0:
--------------------------------------------------------------------------
Slot 0   Online       FPC
  PIC 0  Online       2x GE, 6x FE, 1x 3G

node1:
--------------------------------------------------------------------------
Slot 0   Online       FPC
  PIC 0  Online       2x GE, 6x FE, 1x 3G

{primary:node0}
root@SRX210-A>
```

As you can see, this output is from an SRX210, but the command will list the status of the data plane on each SRX. Here it shows a single FPC and a single PIC. Although the output does not mention anything about flowd or the data plane, the output shows that the SRX is up and ready to pass traffic.

Now let's show node 1 with a failed data plane.

```
{primary:node0}
root@SRX210-A> show chassis fpc pic-status
node0:
--------------------------------------------------------------------------
Slot 0   Online       FPC
  PIC 0  Online       2x GE, 6x FE, 1x 3G

node1:
--------------------------------------------------------------------------
Slot 0   Offline      FPC

{primary:node0}
root@SRX210-A>
```

Here, node 1's data plane went offline, caused by the loss of the flowd process. Another event that can be seen is that redundancy groups 1 and greater will have their priority as zero (to be discussed in the next section).

The output of the `pic status` command should correlate with the hardware that is in the chassis, which can be seen in the output of `show chassis hardware`.

```
{primary:node0}
root@SRX210-A> show chassis hardware
node0:
--------------------------------------------------------------------------
Hardware inventory:
```

```
Item              Version  Part number  Serial number  Description
Chassis                                 AD2609AA0497   SRX210h
Routing Engine    REV 28   750-021779   AAAH2307       RE-SRX210-HIGHMEM
FPC 0                                                  FPC
  PIC 0                                                2x GE, 6x FE, 1x 3G
Power Supply 0

node1:
--------------------------------------------------------------------------
Hardware inventory:
Item              Version  Part number  Serial number  Description
Chassis                                 AD2909AA0346   SRX210h
Routing Engine    REV 28   750-021779   AAAH4743       RE-SRX210-HIGHMEM
FPC 0                                                  FPC
  PIC 0                                                2x GE, 6x FE, 1x 3G
Power Supply 0

{primary:node0}
root@SRX210-A>
```

Here the command shows the hardware in PIC 0, which is the same as shown in the `pic status` command. This command is more useful on the data center platform because on the data center SRX, it's a little more complex, as there are typically many different processors.

For example, here's the PIC status of an SRX5800:

```
{primary:node0}
root@SRX5800-1> show chassis fpc pic-status
node0:
--------------------------------------------------------------------------
Slot 0   Online       SRX5k SPC
  PIC 0  Online       SPU Cp
  PIC 1  Online       SPU Flow
Slot 1   Online       SRX5k SPC
  PIC 0  Online       SPU Flow
  PIC 1  Online       SPU Flow
Slot 3   Online       SRX5k SPC
  PIC 0  Online       SPU Flow
  PIC 1  Online       SPU Flow
Slot 6   Online       SRX5k DPC 4X 10GE
  PIC 0  Online       1x 10GE(LAN/WAN) RichQ
  PIC 1  Online       1x 10GE(LAN/WAN) RichQ
  PIC 2  Online       1x 10GE(LAN/WAN) RichQ
  PIC 3  Online       1x 10GE(LAN/WAN) RichQ
Slot 11  Online       SRX5k DPC 40x 1GE
  PIC 0  Online       10x 1GE RichQ
  PIC 1  Online       10x 1GE RichQ
  PIC 2  Online       10x 1GE RichQ
  PIC 3  Online       10x 1GE RichQ

node1:
```

```
----------------------------------------------------------------------
Slot 0   Online       SRX5k SPC
  PIC 0  Online       SPU Cp
  PIC 1  Online       SPU Flow
Slot 1   Online       SRX5k  SPC
  PIC 0  Online       SPU Flow
  PIC 1  Online       SPU Flow
Slot 3   Online       SRX5k SPC
  PIC 0  Online       SPU Flow
  PIC 1  Online       SPU Flow
Slot 6   Online       SRX5k DPC 4X 10GE
  PIC 0  Online       1x 10GE(LAN/WAN) RichQ
  PIC 1  Online       1x 10GE(LAN/WAN) RichQ
  PIC 2  Online       1x 10GE(LAN/WAN) RichQ
  PIC 3  Online       1x 10GE(LAN/WAN) RichQ
Slot 11  Online       SRX5k DPC 40x 1GE
  PIC 0  Online       10x 1GE RichQ
  PIC 1  Online       10x 1GE RichQ
  PIC 2  Online       10x 1GE RichQ
  PIC 3  Online       10x 1GE RichQ

{primary:node0}
root@SRX5800-1>
```

Here the command shows the SPCs that are online, which SPU is the CP, and the interface cards. A correctly operating device should have all of its SPCs online, and unless they are disabled, the interfaces should be online. Cards that have not booted yet will be offline or present. In a data center SRX, it can take up to five minutes for the data plane to completely start up. As the cards come online, the following messages will be sent to the command prompts. These messages should only come up once during the process and then they will be logged to the messages file.

```
{primary:node0}
root@SRX5800-1>
Message from syslogd@SRX5800-1 at Mar 13 22:01:48  ...
SRX5800-1 node0.fpc1.pic0 SCHED: Thread 4 (Module Init) ran for 1806 ms without
yielding

Message from syslogd@SRX5800-1 at Mar 13 22:01:49  ...
SRX5800-1 node0.fpc1.pic1 SCHED: Thread 4 (Module Init) ran for 1825 ms without
yielding


{primary:node0}
root@SRX5800-1>
```

If these messages are coming up on the CLI, the SPUs are constantly restarting and should identify a problem, perhaps because not enough power is being sent to the data plane and the SPUs are restarting.

Let's show the hardware that should match up to the output of the `show chassis cluster fpc pic-status` command in the previous example. This will show all of the FPCs that are SPCs, and the administrator should be able to match up which PICs should be online and active.

```
{primary:node0}
root@SRX5800-1> show chassis hardware
node0:
--------------------------------------------------------------------------
Hardware inventory:
Item             Version  Part number  Serial number  Description
Chassis                                JN112A0AEAGA   SRX 5800
Midplane         REV 01   710-024803   TR8821         SRX 5800 Backplane
FPM Board        REV 01   710-024632   WX3786         Front Panel Display
PDM              Rev 03   740-013110   QCS12365066    Power Distribution Module
PEM 0            Rev 01   740-023514   QCS1233E066    PS 1.7kW; 200-240VAC in
PEM 1            Rev 01   740-023514   QCS1233E02V    PS 1.7kW; 200-240VAC in
PEM 2            Rev 01   740-023514   QCS1233E02E    PS 1.7kW; 200-240VAC in
Routing Engine 0 REV 03   740-023530   9009007746     RE-S-1300
CB 0             REV 03   710-024802   WX5793         SRX5k SCB
CB 1             REV 03   710-024802   WV8373         SRX5k SCB
FPC 0            REV 12   750-023996   XS7597         SRX5k SPC
  CPU            REV 03   710-024633   XS6648         SRX5k DPC PMB
  PIC 0                   BUILTIN      BUILTIN        SPU Cp
  PIC 1                   BUILTIN      BUILTIN        SPU Flow
FPC 1            REV 08   750-023996   XA7212         SRX5k SPC
  CPU            REV 02   710-024633   WZ0740         SRX5k DPC PMB
  PIC 0                   BUILTIN      BUILTIN        SPU Flow
  PIC 1                   BUILTIN      BUILTIN        SPU Flow
FPC 3            REV 12   750-023996   XS7625         SRX5k SPC
  CPU            REV 03   710-024633   XS6820         SRX5k DPC PMB
  PIC 0                   BUILTIN      BUILTIN        SPU Flow
  PIC 1                   BUILTIN      BUILTIN        SPU Flow
FPC 6            REV 17   750-020751   WY2754         SRX5k DPC 4X 10GE
  CPU            REV 02   710-024633   WY3706         SRX5k DPC PMB
  PIC 0                   BUILTIN      BUILTIN        1x 10GE(LAN/WAN) RichQ
    Xcvr 0       REV 02   740-011571   C831XJ039      XFP-10G-SR
  PIC 1                   BUILTIN      BUILTIN        1x 10GE(LAN/WAN) RichQ
    Xcvr 0       REV 01   740-011571   C744XJ021      XFP-10G-SR
  PIC 2                   BUILTIN      BUILTIN        1x 10GE(LAN/WAN) RichQ
  PIC 3                   BUILTIN      BUILTIN        1x 10GE(LAN/WAN) RichQ
FPC 11           REV 14   750-020235   WY8697         SRX5k DPC 40x 1GE
  CPU            REV 02   710-024633   WY3743         SRX5k DPC PMB
  PIC 0                   BUILTIN      BUILTIN        10x 1GE RichQ
--snip--
  PIC 1                   BUILTIN      BUILTIN        10x 1GE RichQ
--snip--
  PIC 2                   BUILTIN      BUILTIN        10x 1GE RichQ
--snip--
  PIC 3                   BUILTIN      BUILTIN        10x 1GE RichQ
    Xcvr 0       REV 01   740-013111   8280380        SFP-T
--snip--
```

```
Fan Tray 0       REV 05   740-014971   TP8104         Fan Tray
Fan Tray 1       REV 05   740-014971   TP8089         Fan Tray

{primary:node0}
root@SRX5800-1>
```

Core Dumps

A core dump occurs when things have gone wrong and a process crashes. The memory for the process is then dumped to local storage. If something goes wrong and a process crashes on the SRX, the core dump is stored to several different directories on the local RE. Here's an example of how to find core dumps:

```
{primary:node0}
root@SRX5800-1> show system core-dumps
node0:
--------------------------------------------------------------------------
/var/crash/*core*: No such file or directory
/var/tmp/*core*: No such file or directory
/var/crash/kernel.*: No such file or directory
/tftpboot/corefiles/*core*: No such file or directory

node1:
--------------------------------------------------------------------------
/var/crash/*core*: No such file or directory
-rw-rw----  1 root  wheel   104611 Feb 26 22:22 /var/tmp/csh.core.0.gz
-rw-rw----  1 root  wheel   108254 Feb 26 23:11 /var/tmp/csh.core.1.gz
-rw-rw----  1 root  wheel   107730 Feb 26 23:11 /var/tmp/csh.core.2.gz
/var/crash/kernel.*: No such file or directory
/tftpboot/corefiles/*core*: No such file or directory
total 3

{primary:node0}
root@SRX5800-1>
```

If core dumps are found, there isn't much for the users to troubleshoot. Although sometimes core dumps from CSH or a C shell can occur when a user uses Ctrl-C to terminate a program, these generally can be ignored. However, if a core dump for flowd or other processes exists, it should be reported to JTAC, as it might be an indicator of a more complex problem.

The Dreaded Priority Zero

For most administrators, the following output is a disaster:

```
{primary:node0}
root@SRX210-A> show chassis cluster status
Cluster ID: 1
Node                    Priority      Status    Preempt  Manual failover

Redundancy group: 0 , Failover count: 1
```

```
    node0                   254     primary         no          no
    node1                   1       secondary       no          no

Redundancy group: 1 , Failover count: 1
    node0                   254     primary         no          no
    node1                   0       secondary       no          no

{primary:node0}
root@SRX210-A>
```

Seeing a priority of zero tends to leave administrators in a state of confusion, but the simple reason this occurs could be a problem on the data plane. Determining the problem can be difficult. Although some of the troubleshooting steps we already discussed can be helpful, you might try another. Everything that happens with jsrpd is logged to the file *jsrpd*, in the directory */var/log*. You can view the file by using the `show log jsrpd` command. The contents of the file vary, based on the events that occur with jsrpd, but the file is typically quite readable.

There are some specific items to check for. The first is coldsync, which is the initial synchronization between the kernels on the two REs. A failed coldsync will cause the priority to be set to zero. If there is a problem and coldsync cannot complete, the coldsync monitoring weight will be set to 255. If it completes, it is set to zero. Here's an example of a coldsync log:

```
{primary:node0}
root@SRX210-A> show log jsrpd | match coldsync

Apr 11 08:44:14 coldsync is completed for all the PFEs. cs monitoring weight
is set to ZERO
Apr 11 13:09:38 coldsync status message received from PFE: 0, status: 0x1
Apr 11 13:09:38 duplicate coldsync completed message from PFE: 0 ignored
Apr 11 13:09:38 coldsync is completed for all the PFEs. cs monitoring weight
is set to ZERO
Apr 11 13:11:20 coldsync status message received from PFE: 0, status: 0x1
Apr 11 13:11:20 duplicate coldsync completed message from PFE: 0 ignored
Apr 11 13:11:20 coldsync is completed for all the PFEs. cs monitoring weight
is set to ZERO
Apr 11 13:19:05 coldsync status message received from PFE: 0, status: 0x1
Apr 11 13:19:05 duplicate coldsync completed message from PFE: 0 ignored
Apr 11 13:19:05 coldsync is completed for all the PFEs. cs monitoring weight
is set to ZERO
```

If coldsync fails, it's possible to do two things. First, on either device, issue a `commit full` command, which will resend the complete configuration to the data and control planes (this might impact traffic as it reapplies all of the policies). The other option is to reboot the secondary node and attempt the coldsync process again. (As a last resort, read the next section.)

In the logfile, the history of interfaces going up and down, node mastership, and other events are kept. Most of the events are quite obvious to administrators and should provide a road map to what happened on the device.

Additional information can be gathered by turning on the traceoptions; just be aware that a lot of additional processing can be required based on the type of traceoptions you enable. If all events are enabled, it will spike the chassis process to 100 percent utilization.

Do not enable traceoptions for more than a few minutes!

There have been countless times where administrators have left traceoptions enabled for all events, and all sorts of trouble has occurred, from service outages to crashing devices, if traceoptions stays active for a long enough period of time.

When All Else Fails

The SRX is a complex and feature-rich product, and Junos provides all sorts of configuration knobs that are not available on other products, all of it engineered with an appreciation that uptime is critical to any organization.

If the SRX is going to be deployed in a complex environment, the administrator should become familiar with the product before deployment. The administrator's knowledge and understanding of the product is the first line of defense for ensuring that the product is going to work in the environment. The more critical the environment, the more detailed an administrator should be in her testing and knowledge about the product. Before deployment, some administrators spend months learning and staging the SRX. Although that might seem like an excessive amount for you and your network needs, it's a fact that the most prepared administrators have the fewest issues. It's one of the reasons we wrote this book, and hopefully, you've read this far into it.

There are other sources for studying and analyzing the SRX. For instance, the J-Net community (*http://forums.juniper.net/*) allows users and product experts to communicate, sharing solutions and issues about Juniper products. It's also a really great set of resources to learn from what other users are doing. Another great resource is the juniper-nsp mailing list. This mailing list has been around for many years and the SRX has become a popular topic (*http://bit.ly/13AdnHO*).

You might also look at a new and budding series of free Day One booklets (*http://www.juniper.net/dayone*) from Juniper Networks that cover the SRX product line.

But truly, when all else fails, it's a good idea to contact JTAC (*http://juni.pr/Y2y66g*)for support. When contacting JTAC, it's important to provide the correct information. If you share the correct data with JTAC, they can quickly get to the root of the problem.

First, collect the output from the command `request support information`. The output can be quite large. If possible, save it locally to the RE, then transfer it off the box by using `request support information | save SupportInfo.txt`, and then use the following sequence of commands to copy off the file:

```
{primary:node0}
root@SRX5800-1>   copy   file   SupportInfo.txt   ftp://tester:password@myftpserv-
er.com:/

OR

{primary:node0}
root@SRX5800-1> copy file SupportInfo.txt scp://172.19.100.50:
root@172.19.100.50's password:
SupportInfo.txt
100% 7882      7.7KB/s   00:00

{primary:node0}
root@SRX5800-1>
```

JTAC might also request the contents of the */var/log* directory. If possible, when opening a case, have the support information file, the */var/log* contents, any core dumps, and a simple topology diagram readily available. By providing this, you will solve half the problem for JTAC in getting to the root of the issue. If some event occurs and it's not reflected in the logs, there isn't much JTAC can do. Be sure to document the event and share what was observed in the network. JTAC can take it from there and work with you to resolve the issue.

Manual Failover

Although the SRX has control over which node is in charge of each redundancy group, sometimes the administrator needs to fail over a redundancy group—say, for maintenance or troubleshooting purposes. No matter the reason, it's possible to manually fail over any of the redundancy groups. By executing a manual failover, the SRX will place the new master node with a priority of 255 (you can't configure this priority as it is only used for a manual failover).

The only event that can take over a manual failover is a hard failure, such as the device failing. When using a manual failover, it's best to unset the manual failover flag so that the SRX can manage it from there.

In this example, redundancy group 1 is failed over between the two chassis and then reset to the default state.

```
{primary:node0}
root@SRX210-A> show chassis cluster status
```

```
Cluster ID: 1
Node                Priority          Status    Preempt  Manual failover

Redundancy group: 0 , Failover count: 1
    node0               254         primary        no       no
    node1               1           secondary      no       no

Redundancy group: 1 , Failover count: 5
    node0               254         primary        no       no
    node1               1           secondary      no       no

{primary:node0}
root@SRX210-A> request chassis cluster failover redundancy-group 1 node 1
node1:
--------------------------------------------------------------------------

Initiated manual failover for redundancy group 1

{primary:node0}
root@SRX210-A> show chassis cluster status
Cluster ID: 1
Node                Priority          Status    Preempt  Manual failover

Redundancy group: 0 , Failover count: 1
    node0               254         primary        no       no
    node1               1           secondary      no       no

Redundancy group: 1 , Failover count: 6
    node0               254         secondary      no       yes
    node1               255         primary        no       yes

{primary:node0}
root@SRX210-A> request chassis cluster failover reset redundancy-group 1
node0:
--------------------------------------------------------------------------
No reset required for redundancy group 1.

node1:
--------------------------------------------------------------------------
Successfully reset manual failover for redundancy group 1

{primary:node0}
root@SRX210-A> request chassis cluster failover redundancy-group 1 node 0
node0:
--------------------------------------------------------------------------
Initiated manual failover for redundancy group 1

root@SRX210-A> show chassis cluster status
Cluster ID: 1
Node                Priority          Status    Preempt  Manual failover

Redundancy group: 0 , Failover count: 1
```

```
    node0                254          primary         no        no
    node1                1            secondary       no        no

Redundancy group: 1 , Failover count: 7
    node0                255          primary         no        yes
    node1                1            secondary       no        yes

{primary:node0}
root@SRX210-A> request chassis cluster failover reset redundancy-group 1
node0:
--------------------------------------------------------------------------
Successfully reset manual failover for redundancy group 1

node1:
--------------------------------------------------------------------------
No reset required for redundancy group 1.

{primary:node0}
root@SRX210-A>
```

Here redundancy group 1 is failed over to node 1. Then, as you can see, the priority is set to 255 and the manual failover flag is set. Once this flag is set, another manual failover cannot occur until it is cleared. Next, the failover is reset for redundancy group 1, using the `request chassis cluster failover reset redundancy group 1` command, allowing the redundancy group to be failed over again. Next, the redundancy group is failed over back to the original node and the manual failover is reset. If a hold-down timer was configured, the manual failover cannot go over the hold-down timer, meaning that a manual failover cannot occur until the hold-down timer has passed.

It is also possible to do this for the control plane. However, it's best to not rapidly fail over the control plane, and best practice recommends that you use a 300-second hold-down timer to prevent excessive flapping of the control plane (which was discussed in the section "Preserving the Control Plane" on page 349 earlier in this chapter).

Now, in this manual failover example, redundancy group 0 is failed over and then the hold-down timer prevents a manual failover.

```
{primary:node0}
root@SRX210-A> show configuration chassis cluster
control-link-recovery;
reth-count 2;
heartbeat-interval 2000;
heartbeat-threshold 8;
redundancy-group 0 {
    node 0 priority 254;
    node 1 priority 1;
    hold-down-interval 300;
}
redundancy-group 1 {
    node 0 priority 254;
    node 1 priority 1;
```

```
    interface-monitor {
        fe-2/0/2 weight 255;
        fe-0/0/2 weight 255;
    }
}

{primary:node0}
root@SRX210-A> show chassis cluster status
Cluster ID: 1
Node                Priority           Status     Preempt  Manual failover

Redundancy group: 0 , Failover count: 1
    node0               254           primary        no        no
    node1               1             secondary      no        no

Redundancy group: 1 , Failover count: 7
    node0               254           primary        no        no
    node1               1             secondary      no        no

{primary:node0}
root@SRX210-A> request chassis cluster failover redundancy-group 0 node 1
node1:
--------------------------------------------------------------------------
Initiated manual failover for redundancy group 0

{primary:node0}
root@SRX210-A> show chassis cluster status
Cluster ID: 1
Node                Priority           Status     Preempt  Manual failover

Redundancy group: 0 , Failover count: 2
    node0               254           secondary-hold no        yes
    node1               255           primary        no        yes

Redundancy group: 1 , Failover count: 7
    node0               254           primary        no        no
    node1               1             secondary      no        no

{secondary-hold:node0}
root@SRX210-A> request chassis cluster failover reset redundancy-group 0
node0:
--------------------------------------------------------------------------
No reset required for redundancy group 0.

node1:
--------------------------------------------------------------------------
Successfully reset manual failover for redundancy group 0

{secondary-hold:node0}
root@SRX210-A> request chassis cluster failover redundancy-group 0 node 0
node0:
--------------------------------------------------------------------------
```

```
Manual failover is not permitted as redundancy-group 0 on node0 is in secondary-
hold state.

{secondary-hold:node0}
root@SRX210-A> show chassis cluster status
Cluster ID: 1
Node                Priority          Status    Preempt  Manual failover

Redundancy group: 0 , Failover count: 2
    node0                254          secondary-hold no       no
    node1                1            primary        no       no

Redundancy group: 1 , Failover count: 7
    node0                254          primary        no       no
    node1                1            secondary      no       no

{secondary-hold:node0}
root@SRX210-A>
```

Here redundancy group 0 is failed over from node 0 to node 1. This is just as before. It creates the priority on the new primary as 255 and sets the manual failover to `yes`. However, now node 0 shows `secondary-hold` as its status, indicating that it is in secondary mode but is also on a hold-down timer. When the timer expires, it will show `secondary`. In the event of a critical failure to the primary device, the `secondary-hold` unit can still take over. Finally, an attempt to manually fail over the node is made, and it's not possible to fail over because the node is on a hold-down timer.

Sample Deployments

The most common chassis cluster deployment on an SRX is active/passive. This type of deployment has many benefits that outweigh its drawbacks. An active/passive deployment offers resiliency in the event of a failover and is fairly easy to operate. The downside is that the backup box lays dormant until it is needed to step in for the primary device. The risk is that the backup device could run into an issue while waiting for its turn. If this occurs, your network will go down. So when running an SRX active/passive cluster, you should routinely fail the devices over to ensure both devices are operational.

For our sample deployment, we show a typical SRX100 branch deployment. Figure 7-11 shows our example topology.

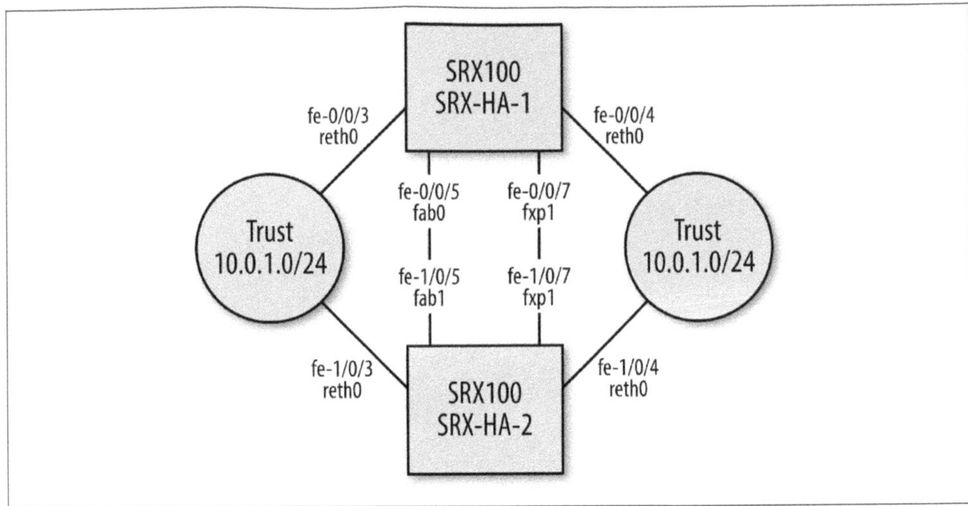

Figure 7-11. SRX100 sample HA deployment

In this deployment, we have two subnets: Trust and Untrust. The Untrust subnet is 10.0.2.0/24 and the Trust subnet is 10.0.1.0/24. We will implement one reth interface for each subnet. We will also utilize fxp0 interfaces for management. This is how our interfaces are configured:

```
{secondary:node1}[edit]
root@SRX-HA-1# show interfaces | display inheritance
fe-0/0/3 {
    fastether-options {
        redundant-parent reth0;
    }
}
fe-0/0/4 {
    fastether-options {
        redundant-parent reth1;
    }
}
fe-1/0/3 {
    fastether-options {
        redundant-parent reth0;
    }
}
fe-1/0/4 {
    fastether-options {
        redundant-parent reth1;
    }
}
fab0 {
    fabric-options {
        member-interfaces {
```

```
                fe-0/0/5;
            }
        }
    }
    fab1 {
        fabric-options {
            member-interfaces {
                fe-1/0/5;
            }
        }
    }
    fxp0 {
        unit 0 {
            family inet {
                address 10.0.1.253/24 {
                    master-only;
                }
                ##
                ## '10.0.1.252/24' was inherited from group 'node1'
                ##
                address 10.0.1.252/24;
            }
        }
    }
    reth0 {
        redundant-ether-options {
            redundancy-group 1;
        }
        unit 0 {
            family inet {
                address 10.0.1.254/24;
            }
            family inet6 {
                address 2001:4270:8163::2/55;
            }
        }
    }
    reth1 {
        redundant-ether-options {
            redundancy-group 1;
        }
        unit 0 {
            family inet {
                address 10.0.2.1/24;
            }
            family inet6 {
                address 2001:4720:8163:200::1/55;
            }
        }
    }
```

From this output, we can only see one fxp0 interface. This is because we are on the secondary node. Using `show interfaces | display inheritance`, we can see that the fxp0 interface is being imported into the configuration from node groups. Next you can see our node group configuration. This gives each host a unique hostname and management IP.

```
{secondary:node1}[edit]
root@SRX-HA-1# show groups
node0 {
    system {
        host-name SRX-HA-0;
        backup-router 10.0.1.2 destination 0.0.0.0/0;
    }
    interfaces {
        fxp0 {
            unit 0 {
                family inet {
                    address 10.0.1.251/24;
                }
            }
        }
    }
}
node1 {
    system {
        host-name SRX-HA-1;
        backup-router 10.0.1.2 destination 0.0.0.0/0;
    }
    interfaces {
        fxp0 {
            unit 0 {
                family inet {
                    address 10.0.1.252/24;
                }
            }
        }
    }
}
```

We can check to see that the devices are correctly working through the standard chassis cluster status commands.

```
{secondary:node1}
root@SRX-HA-1> show chassis cluster status
Cluster ID: 1
Node                  Priority          Status    Preempt  Manual failover

Redundancy group: 0 , Failover count: 0
    node0                   254         primary        no       no
    node1                   1           secondary      no       no

Redundancy group: 1 , Failover count: 0
```

```
    node0                     254         primary      no        no
    node1                     1           secondary    no        no

{secondary:node1}
root@SRX-HA-1> show chassis cluster interfaces
Control link status: Up

Control interfaces:
    Index   Interface        Status
    0       fxp1             Up

Fabric link status: Up

Fabric interfaces:
    Name    Child-interface    Status
    fab0    fe-0/0/5           Up
    fab0
    fab1    fe-1/0/5           Up
    fab1

Redundant-ethernet Information:
    Name         Status      Redundancy-group
    reth0        Up          1
    reth1        Up          1

{secondary:node1}
root@SRX-HA-1>
```

Summary

Because the SRX will be placed in a mission-critical location in the network, it is extremely important to ensure that it is up and functional. Firewalls are placed in between the untrusted and trusted locations within a network. If the firewall fails, there is nothing left to bring the two networks together, causing a major outage. As you saw in this chapter, the SRX has a robust HA architecture that can survive the worst of tragedies.

The biggest benefit to the SRX HA design is the flexibility it gives to the end user. The ability to use redundancy groups and mix and match them with local interfaces is very powerful. It allows you to overcome the traditional limitations of a redundant firewall configuration and explore new design scenarios. At first, the new paradigm of mixing redundant interfaces, redundancy groups, and local interfaces is overwhelming. Hopefully, this chapter will allow you to think more freely and move away from past firewall limitations.

Study Questions

Questions

1. What is the purpose of the control link?
2. What are the three types of communication that pass over the fabric link?
3. Can configuration groups be used for any other tasks on a Junos device? Be specific.
4. What feature needs to be enabled when using dynamic routing?
5. What are the two most important commands when troubleshooting an SRX cluster?
6. From what Juniper product did the SRX get part of its HA code infrastructure?
7. Which platform supports the automatic upgrade of the secondary node?
8. Are acknowledgments sent for session synchronization messages?
9. What is a redundancy group?
10. Why is the control port so important?

Answers

1. The control link is used for the two REs to talk to each other. The kernels synchronize state between each other, the REs talk to the data plane on the other node, and jsrpd communicates. The jsrpd daemon sends heartbeat messages to validate that the other side is up and running.
2. Heartbeats are sent by the jsrpd daemon to ensure that the remote node is up and healthy. The heartbeats pass through the data planes of both devices and back to the other side. This validates the entire path end to end, making sure it is able to pass traffic. In the event that traffic needs to be forwarded between the two nodes, it is done over the data link. Last but not least, the data link is used to synchronize RTO messages between the two chassis. RTOs are used in the maintenance of the state between the two devices. This includes session creation and session closing messages.
3. Node-specific information is configured using Junos groups. This was one of the fundamental features that was created in Junos. Junos groups can also be thought of as configuration templates or snippets. They can be used to do such things as enabling logging on all firewall policies and configuring specific snippets of information. Using Junos groups where it makes sense simplifies the administration of the SRX and makes reading the configuration easier.

4. When using dynamic routing, the graceful restart feature should be enabled. It allows the data plane to keep dynamic routes active if the control plane fails over. It also allows for other routers that surround the SRX to assist it during a control plane failover.
5. The two most important commands are `show chassis cluster status` and `show chassis cluster statistics`. This will allow for the current state of the cluster and the current status of communication between the two nodes. Anyone who is administering a cluster will use these two commands the most.
6. The SRX used code from the TX Series products. The TX Series are some of the largest and most scalable routing products in the world.
7. The data center SRXs support unified in-service software upgrades. This feature allows for an automatic upgrade of the backup node without impacting network availability.
8. Session synchronization messages are not acknowledged. This would take additional time and resources away from the processors by forcing the processing of an additional message.
9. A redundancy group is a logical collection of objects. It can contain either the control plane (redundancy group 0 only) or interfaces (redundancy group 1+).
10. The control port provides critical communication between the two REs. If this link is lost, the two REs cannot synchronize the state of the kernels. Because of this, if the control link goes down, the secondary node will go into a disabled state.

CHAPTER 8
Security Policies

Security policies are at the core of applying the security mechanisms of the SRX. This makes logical sense because of the granular, flexible nature of the firewall rulebase. Up until this point, we have had various discussions about the platform-level support of the SRX, but now, as we enter the second half of the book, we focus in on the actual application of security features.

In this chapter, we begin by quickly reviewing the packet flow of the SRX, followed by a discussion of the related security policy components, and an in-depth discussion of the SRX policy configuration itself. We explore some additional security policy features like the Level 7 security features and ALGs. We conclude this chapter with some hands-on discussions of best practices, troubleshooting and device operations, and sample deployments. By the end of this chapter, you should be a pro at not only configuring security policies, but also properly designing an effective security policy in your network.

Packet Flow

Earlier in the book we reviewed the packet flow of an SRX, but it is helpful to briefly discuss it here as a refresher (or if you're just reading this chapter out of the book by itself).

Figure 8-1 gives us a visual representation of the security policy. When it comes to security policy enforcement on the SRX, this is entirely handled on the data plane of the SRX, unlike ScreenOS, which would do at least the policy lookup on the control plane. Completely leveraging the data plane for the processing of security policies protects the SRX from succumbing to DoS attacks that could leave the management engine unavailable.

From a firewall policy enforcement perspective, it is important to understand that firewall policy lookup only happens once per session (with one slight exception to that), which is on the initial packet arriving for that flow. Every time a packet arrives, we check to see if it is part of a known session. If it is not part of an existing session, then we put it through the full slow path lookup, which includes performing NAT, route/switching lookups, and the firewall security policy in addition to the standard processing of screens, Level 3 or Level 4 enforcement checks, and ALG/services. Because this only needs to happen once, the performance is usually quite good.

For sessions that already match a known session, we don't need to go through the entire lookup process. We simply match the session criteria to an existing session in the firewall session table, which gives us instructions on how to process existing flows (see Figure 8-1), including what firewall policy they are based on, NAT translation instructions, ALG and other Level 7 services, and so on.

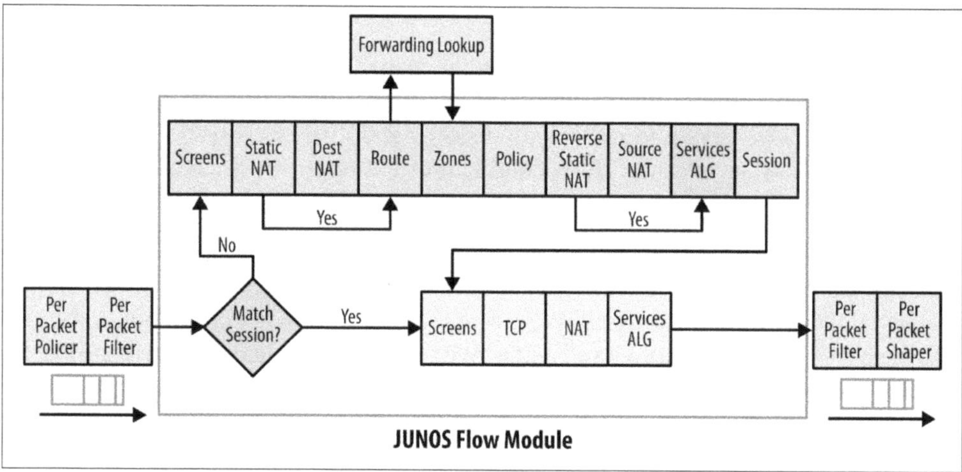

Figure 8-1. Junos SRX packet flow

So you might be wondering what exactly makes up session criteria? There are a few things, so let's look at the output of a session table entry.

```
Session ID: 936, Status: Normal, State: Active
Flag: 0x8100000
Policy name: GOutbound/12
Source NAT pool: Host-Outbound, Application: junos-https/58
Dynamic application: junos:AIM,
Application firewall rule-set: Allowed-Outbound, Rule: 1
Maximum timeout: 1800, Current timeout: 1624
Session State: Valid
Start time: 64145, Duration: 1922656
   In: 192.168.1.30/1454 --> 64.12.165.69/443;tcp,
    Interface: reth1.0,
    Session token: 0x5007, Flag: 0x621
    Route: 0x6353c2, Gateway: 192.168.1.30, Tunnel: 0
```

```
    Port sequence: 0, FIN sequence: 0,
    FIN state: 0,
    Pkts: 10888, Bytes: 545020
   Out: 64.12.165.69/443 --> 173.169.214.17/55484;tcp,
    Interface: reth0.0,
    Session token: 0x4006, Flag: 0x620
    Route: 0x627bc2, Gateway: 173.169.214.17, Tunnel: 0
    Port sequence: 0, FIN sequence: 0,
    FIN state: 0,
    Pkts: 10888, Bytes: 436945
```

From the output shown here, there are a number of values that we see in an individual session. These tell most of the story from a match criteria point of view.

- Source Interface (Reth1.0)
- Source IP Address (192.168.1.30)
- Destination IP Address (64.12.165.69)
- Source Port (1454)
- Destination Port (443)
- Protocol (TCP)

There is certainly additional information, such as the session ID (0x936), the NAT translation, route, outbound interfaces, and packet and byte counters. If you look closely, you can see that the SRX contains two parts of the session, the In and the Out "wings" as they are known. This allows the firewall to match the packets for both the ingress and egress interfaces, including with NAT transforms.

When it comes to the initial policy lookup, the SRX takes the following criteria into account to determine what policy to select (in no particular order). This is known as the nine-tuple. In the past, prior to Logical Systems (LSYS) and User Identity as part of UserFW, this was known as the *seven-tuple*.

1. Source zone (based on ingress logical interface)
2. Destination zone (based on the route/switching lookup to determine the egress interface)
3. Source IP address
4. Destination IP address (after static and destination NAT transform, so the security policy must match the translated destination IP address)
5. Source port
6. Destination port (after the destination NAT transformation so the security policy must match the translated destination port in the packet)
7. Logical system (if applicable, based on the ingress interface)

8. User identity (in Junos 12.1 and higher; see Chapter 12 for more details)
9. Protocol (what Level 3/Level 4 protocol)

It is important to note here that the destination/destination-static NAT takes place on the ingress before the policy lookup as we see in Figure 8-1, so your firewall policy has to take this into account to ensure that you're matching the right parameters. Source/source-static NAT, on the other hand, is performed after the policy lookup, so you do not need to take it into account in the security policy configuration.

Security Policy Criteria and Precedence

Before we dive into the actual security policies themselves, we need to familiarize (or refamiliarize in some cases) ourselves with the various components that make up security policies. Typically, you will want to have these defined before configuring the security policies, or at least before you commit the configuration. The following are components of the security policies and their descriptions:

Zones
: Each security policy will have two zones, a source and destination (or from/to) zone, with the exception of the global zone, which encompasses both the source and destination.

Address objects
: These are objects that either directly or indirectly refer to IP addresses or are groups of address objects. These can be applied to both the source and destination fields of the security policy. There are a few different types of address objects, which we explore shortly.

Application objects
: In ScreenOS these were known as service objects. For the purpose of this book, we refer to them with the same convention that is used in Junos, which is application objects. These refer to Level 3/Level 4 application objects, and not those of Level 7 or dynamic application objects that are used in the AppSecure policies. Application objects can include the Level 3/Level 4 protocol, along with port information for UDP/TCP, and type info for ICMP.

User objects
: These are for the UserFW feature, which will explore in Chapter 12. They are visible in Junos 12.1 and newer, so if you are running an older version of Junos they won't be applicable.

Scheduler objects
: These define a time period for the policy to be active. This is useful if you want to apply different policies based on time of day or day of week, such as policies enforced during business hours.

Action profiles

The preceding objects primarily have to do with match criteria, but once a policy is matched, you need to decide what to do with it. If the action is to permit the traffic (from a security policy perspective), then additional processing can be done on the session to which it is matched. There are numerous types of action profiles including UTM, AppSecure, SSL Proxy, and a handful of others that we overview in this chapter and explore in greater depth in their respective chapters.

Security Policy Precedence

When it comes to a policy match, it is important to understand how the firewall evaluates security policies. Juniper calls a security policy context the policy that is within the same from-to-zone pair, for instance all policies within from-zone trust to-zone untrust are in the same context. In terms of context precedence, the SRX follows the following order:

1. Match intrazone policies: Evaluate the initial packet in an unknown session to determine if the source and destination zones are the same (e.g., from-zone trust to-zone trust). This would happen if both the ingress and egress interfaces are in the same zone. This context match has the highest precedence and will be matched first if it exists.
2. Match interzone policies: If the session does not match an intrazone context or policy, then the next thing to evaluate is if it matches a from-zone and to-zone context such as from-zone trust to-zone untrust. If the context matches, then the policies within the context will be evaluated for a match. Interzone policies will only be evaluated if there is no matching intrazone policy match, and happen before a global policy match.
3. Global policies: If there is no policy match for intrazone or interzone policies, then the next policy that would be matched would be global policies. This matches any zone context so to speak, but has the same match criteria for the policies as any other firewall policy (e.g., source address, destination address, application, user object, and so on). It is the last policy set to be evaluated after intrazone and interzone policies.
4. Default action: This is the action that should be taken if there is no match on intrazone, interzone, or global policies.

For those of you migrating from ScreenOS, note that in ScreenOS interfaces in the same zone were permitted by default (intrazone blocking was off by default). With the SRX, intrazone blocking is always on, so you need to explicitly permit the traffic to communicate intrazone.

Top to Bottom Policy Evaluation

It is important to understand that the policy evaluation in the rulebase will be evaluated from the top of the rulebase down to the bottom. The first policy to match the criteria of the policy will be matched. This means that the firewall rules are terminal. All criteria must match the rule for it to considered a match; there are no partial matches. If no policy is matched, the firewall will evaluate the next context or default match in the same order that we just discussed: intrazone, then interzone, then global, and finally default.

Let's look at the following sample policy, which includes intrazone, interzone, global, and a default match.

```
{primary:node0}[edit]
root@SRX550-Node0# show security policies
from-zone trust to-zone untrust {
    policy Block-FTP {
        match {
            source-address any;
            destination-address any;
            application junos-ftp;
        }
        then {
            deny;
            log {
                session-init;
            }
        }
    }
    policy Allow-Any {
        match {
            source-address any;
            destination-address any;
            application any;
        }
        then {
            permit;
            log {
                session-close;
            }
        }
    }
}
from-zone trust to-zone trust {
    policy Intra-zone {
        match {
            source-address any;
            destination-address any;
            application any;
        }
        then {
            permit;
```

```
            }
        }
    }
    global {
        policy deny-all-log {
            match {
                source-address any;
                destination-address any;
                application any;
            }
            then {
                deny;
                log {
                    session-init;
                }
            }
        }
    }
    default-policy {
        deny-all;
    }
```

You should be able to determine which policy is which. The policy called intrazone is an intrazone policy not merely because of its name, but because both the from- and to-zones are the same ("trust" in this case.) If the ingress and egress interface are both in the trust zone, we will match this policy. Next is the trust to untrust context, which has two rules. The first blocks FTP if it matches from any IP address while any other service is permitted. Order is important here because if the Allow-Any rule was first, we would never match the Block-FTP rule because of top-down precedence. Of course, this context will only be evaluated if the ingress and egress interfaces are in the trust and untrust zones, respectively. Let's say that both interfaces are in the untrust zone; then we won't match the intrazone or interzone policies because of the context match failure. Instead, they would match the global policy called deny-all-log.

In this example, there is no possibility of matching the "default-policy" action, which is deny all. This is because the match criteria for the global policy deny-all-log is any source, any destination, or any application, which essentially means everything. So why have a global policy if we could just do this with the default action? The answer is because with the default policy you can only permit or deny, but you can't reject or log the traffic. It's a good idea to configure the default policy just as a catchall in case you make a mistake but also leverage the global policy as your catchall. Of course, if you have catchall rules in your firewall contexts (like Allow-Any for the trust to untrust context), then as long as there is a context match (e.g., the from-zone is trust and the to-zone is untrust), you won't evaluate further than that context.

Global policies are supported in Junos 11.2r2 and 11.4+. If you are running an earlier version, only intrazone, interzone, and default actions are supported.

Security Policy Components in Depth

Now that we have overviewed the different components of the security policies, let's dig into the individual elements and explore how they are configured and applied. In this section, we begin with the match criteria of security policies, which include the zones, address objects, and application objects. This is followed by a detailed look at the action components of the security policies.

Match Criteria

Before we can take any action on the traffic with our security policies, we need to identify how the traffic is matched. The match criteria do exactly what they state: they match traffic that falls within the range of the parameters defined. In a way, you can think of the match criteria as a filter set to match the values in that range.

When working with match criteria, remember that the SRX is stateful, so it isn't a strict static access list like those of older routing platforms where you might need to define both directions (depending on how it is defined). The SRX security policy only defines the initial packet parameters as the match criteria, and will automatically allow the return traffic for the session by installing a reverse "wing" as we will see later.

Security zones

As we mentioned earlier, the security zones allow us to define the origin and destination of the traffic passing through the SRX. The source zone (from-zone) defines the interface (or collection of interfaces that fall within that source zone), and the destination zone (to-zone) defines the egress interface (or pools of interfaces) for the traffic. Whereas the source interface is known when the traffic arrives on the SRX, the egress interface is not known until the policy lookup time when the SRX will either do a routing lookup (in Level 3 mode) or a switching lookup (in Level 2 mode).

One interface per zone versus multiple interfaces per zone. We've alluded to the fact that you can have one or more interfaces per zone. As you recall from Chapter 3, zones essentially define a security grouping of interfaces that you want to be classified with the same security level. You can still separate them with intrazone security policies, of course. One other reason to have multiple interfaces in the same zone is for traffic failover. Let's say you have traffic arriving on ge-0/0/0 and leaving on interface ge-0/0/1, as shown in

Figure 8-2. Then the interface ge-0/0/1 goes down, triggering a route failover to interface ge-0/0/2. As long as those interfaces are in the same zone, the traffic will be failed over to the other interface due to the route change. If the route were to point to an interface in a different zone, the traffic would be dropped because the interfaces aren't in the same zone. This is true for both ingress and egress traffic.

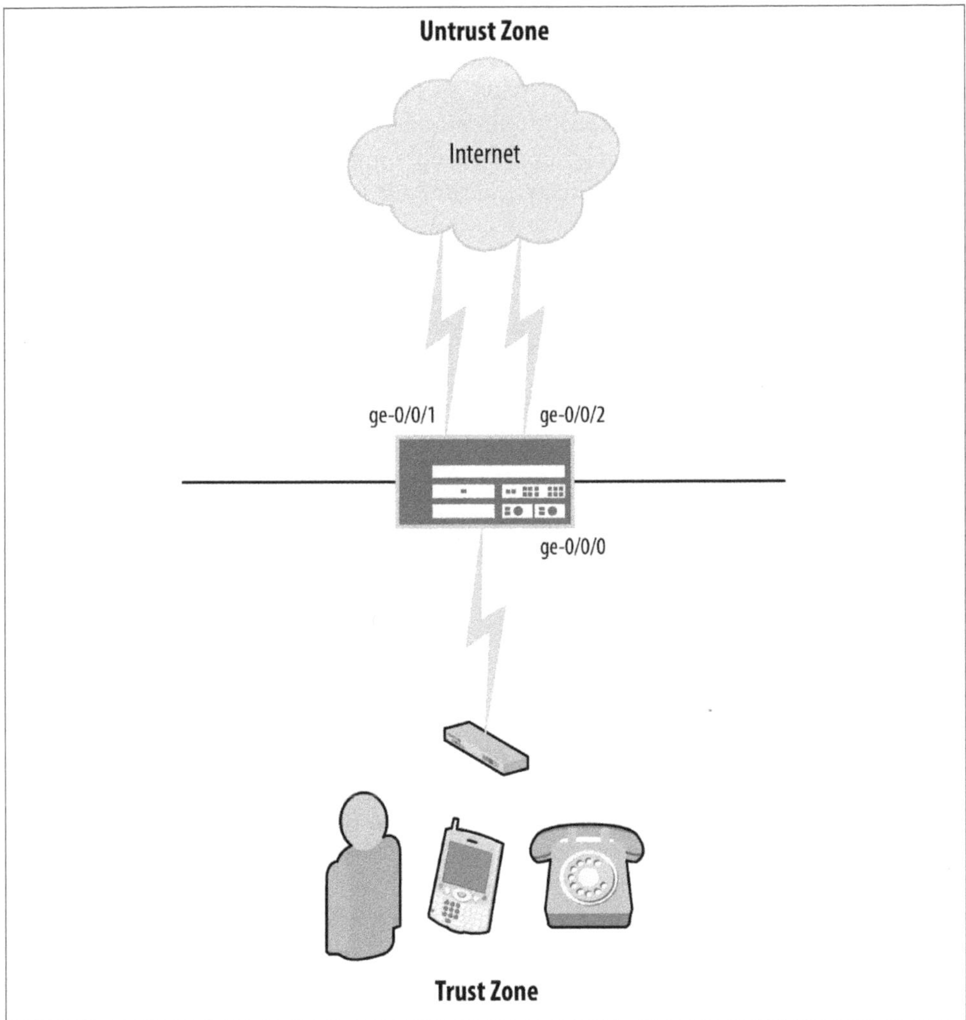

Figure 8-2. Policy failover

Remember that when we say interfaces we are really referring to logical interfaces, so you can have different logical interfaces on the same physical interfaces in different zones. For instance, ge-0/0/0.0 could be in zone trust, and ge-0/0/0.100 could be in zone untrust. These can also span the physical boundaries, so ge-0/0/0.0 could be in trust along with xe-0/1/0.0.

Configuring security zones. Just as a refresher, or for those who didn't read Chapter 3, configuring the security zones is really quite simple. In this example, we configure two security zones, trust and untrust, for use in our upcoming examples. Security zone trust will have interface reth0.0, and security zone untrust will contain reth1.0.

```
{primary:node0}[edit]
root@SRX550-Node0# set security zones security-zone trust interfaces reth0.0

{primary:node0}[edit]
root@SRX550-Node0# set security zones security-zone untrust interfaces reth1.0

{primary:node0}[edit]
root@SRX550-Node0# show security zones
security-zone trust {
    interfaces {
        reth0.0;
    }
}
security-zone untrust {
    interfaces {
        reth1.0;
    }
}
```

In this example, we aren't yet defining which interface is going to be the source or destination zone; that will be defined by our security policy context, as we showed earlier. The important thing to take in here is that we need to define the security zone as a classifier of the interface so that we can apply it to the security policies later on. This is different from some other competitive platforms that might have a flat rulebase (e.g., CheckPoint) and rely on the IP addresses to define direction. The direction of the traffic is inherently defined by the rulebase from-to-zones—with the exception of an intrazone or global policy. This is because the intrazone policy has the same source and destination zones so direction doesn't matter as long as it's within that context, and global is from any zone to any zone so it is zone agnostic, so to speak.

Address books

An address book is essentially a high-level container for the address objects that exist within it. By default, starting in Junos 11.2, there is a default address book called global.

Other address books can be created and attached to individual zones. Prior to Junos 11.2, you had to define addresses under the zone configuration. This was less than ideal because you might have objects that need to be defined in duplicate zones, and also they couldn't be used in other policies like NAT and IPS. We focus on defining the new model, because many of you will be doing new deployments or will be moving to post-11.2 releases if you haven't already.

From our perspective, it is best to just define objects in the global zone rather than applying them to individual zones. This is because you can reuse the objects rather than having to define them for each zone. On the other hand, if you are most security conscious, then defining them per zone has the slight advantage of not using them in security zones for which they weren't intended. This is more of a corner case, however, because you still need to define the security policies to permit the traffic anyway.

In this example, we just show how addresses are added to the global address book, along with how to attach an address book called "trust" to zone trust.

```
{primary:node0}[edit]
root@SRX550-Node0# set security address-book global address Internal-Clients
1.1.1.0/24

{primary:node0}[edit]
root@SRX550-Node0# set security address-book global address Trust-Clients
2.1.1.0/24


{primary:node0}[edit]
root@SRX550-Node0# set security address-book trust attach zone trust

{primary:node0}[edit]
root@SRX550-Node0# show security address-book
global {
    address Internal-Clients 1.1.1.0/24;
}
trust {
    address Trust-Clients 2.1.1.0/24
    attach {
        zone trust;
    }
}
```

Address objects

Address objects are used to map an IP address to an object that can be used elsewhere in the device configuration, rather than strictly defining IP prefixes. This is much easier to deal with, particularly when you can tie a mnemonic name to the objects that will better classify what the IP object represents. This is useful for the same reason we have DNS: human-readable names are much easier for humans to remember than a series of numbers. Behind the scenes, the SRX doesn't care at all about the object name but rather the IP address information it represents. Of course, you can always just make the object name the same as the IP address, or better yet, include a mnemonic name and the IP prefix information, which is the best of both worlds.

There are several different types of Address objects that you can leverage in the SRX policies, each of which we discuss in turn.

You can only specify one type per object at a time, so you can't have an object that is, say, both a wildcard and an IP prefix object at the same time. You can, however, define multiple objects and put them into a group.

IP prefix address objects. IP prefix objects are the simplest form of address objects that you can define, and the most traditional. Put simply, they define an IP prefix, as the name suggests. This means the IP network and netmask is given in the form X.X.X.X/YY where X is the IP address prefix and Y is the netmask in the shorthand notation. In the previous example for Internal-Clients, this was written as 1.1.1.0/24. Of course, IPv6 address prefixes are also supported using the standard IPv6 conventions (including the :: shorthand) and the shorthand netmask notation; for example, 2001::6:1/120.

Configuring IP prefix address objects. In this example, we configure an IP prefix object that will be tied to the global address book for the public DNS server 8.8.8.8, which is a Google Public DNS server. Google also has a public IPv6 DNS server 2001:4860:4860::8888 that we will add as well. Finally, we also attach a description to the object to specify that it is a public DNS server.

```
{primary:node0}[edit]
root@SRX550-Node0# set security address-book global address Public-DNS descrip-
tion "Public DNS Server" 8.8.8.8/32

root@SRX550-Node0# set security address-book global address IPv6-Public-DNS de-
scription "Public IPv6 DNS Server" 2001:4860:4860::8.8.8.8/128


{primary:node0}[edit]
root@SRX550-Node0# show security address-book
global {
    address Public-DNS {
        description "Public DNS Server";
        8.8.8.8/32;
```

```
        }
        address IPv6-Public-DNS {
            description "Public IPv6 DNS Server";
            2001:4860:4860::8.8.8.8/128;
        }

}
```

DNS address objects. Sometimes you have an object that might change its IP address from time to time, rather than setting a fixed IP address using the IP prefix option. The DNS address object type allows you to do exactly this. There are a few things that you should know about this.

- DNS objects require you to have a DNS server configured that the SRX can query. The queries will be sent from the INET.0 routing instance by default, but you can manipulate them to go through other interfaces or instances with routing.
- DNS objects can accept up to 32 IP addresses per DNS object at the time of writing this book.
- IPv4 and IPv6 are supported.
- The SRX honors the TTLs of the DNS objects that are defined by the DNS server. When the TTL expires, the SRX will requery the DNS server. If the response is different from the last values, the SRX will update the policy accordingly.
- All DNS queries are done in advance (at commit/ttl expire) rather than in real time for performance reasons. If an IP address changes, then the SRX will update on the next TTL expiration.
- If no DNS server is reachable or the host is unknown, the object will be left blank so you won't be able to do any match with it.

Configuring DNS address objects. In this example, we configure the SRX to query an internal DNS server 192.168.0.50, and we create an object for www.juniper.net (*http://www.juniper.net*) and attach it to the global address book.

```
{primary:node0}[edit]
root@SRX550-Node0# set system name-server 192.168.0.50

root@SRX550-Node0# show system name-server
192.168.0.50;

{primary:node0}[edit]
root@SRX550-Node0# set security address-book global address www.juniper.net dns-
name www.juniper.net

{primary:node0}[edit]
root@SRX550-Node0# show security address-book
global {
```

```
    address www.juniper.net {
        dns-name www.juniper.net;
    }
}
```

You might have noticed that you can also specify an IP prefix object as a DNS name. So what's the difference? If you specify an IP prefix object as a DNS name, the SRX will resolve the name and will put it in the configuration as the IP address, meaning that it will not change in the future like a true DNS object. If you want the SRX to continuously resolve the DNS to IP mapping then you need to explicitly specify that it should use the DNS-Name as we did in this previous example.

```
## As IP Object ##
{primary:node0}[edit]
root@SRX550-Node0# set security address-book global address serv-
ices.netscreen.com services.netscreen.com

{primary:node0}[edit]
root@SRX550-Node0# show security address-book
global {
    address services.netscreen.com 207.17.137.227/32;
}

## As DNS Object ##
{primary:node0}[edit]
root@SRX550-Node0# set security address-book global address serv-
ices.netscreen.com dns-name services.netscreen.com

{primary:node0}[edit]
root@SRX550-Node0# show security address-book
global {
    address services.netscreen.com {
        dns-name services.netscreen.com;
    }
}
```

IP range objects. IP range objects were added in the Junos 12.1X45 release, allowing you to define a contiguous range of IP addresses. This is helpful when you need to define a range of IP addresses that doesn't fit neatly with an IP prefix boundary without over- or underextending the access. At the time of writing this book, this feature is only supported by IPv4 and not IPv6. Essentially, you define the bottom and top IP addresses in the contiguous range, and it will create an object that is inclusive of the bottom and top IP addresses. For instance, if you defined an IP range object as 192.168.1.1 through 192.168.1.4, it would include 192.168.1.1, 192.168.1.2, 192.168.1.3, and 192.168.1.4.

Configuring IP range objects. In this example, we configure an IP range object called DHCP-Addresses-192.168.1.50-100 that includes IP addresses 192.168.1.50 through

192.168.1.100. We place it in the global address book and give it the description DHCP Client Range.

```
{primary:node0}[edit]
root@SRX550-Node0#   set   security   address-book   global   address   DHCP-
Addresses-192.168.1.50-100  description  "DHCP  Client  Range"  range-address
192.168.1.50 to 192.168.1.100

{primary:node0}[edit]
root@SRX550-Node0# show security address-book
global {
    address DHCP-Addresses-192.168.1.50-100 {
        description "DHCP Client Range";
        range-address 192.168.1.50 {
            to {
                192.168.1.100;
            }
        }
    }
}
```

Wildcard address objects. Traditional IP address objects are useful when defining an IP host or IP prefix that you want to match in a policy. There are, however, some limitations with IP prefix-based matches. First, the subnet mask has to be contiguous, meaning that it starts as all 1s, and once a 0 bit is used, the rest of the values must be 0s. For instance

- Valid IP subnet (/24)
  - 11111111.11111111.11111111.00000000
- Invalid IP subnet, valid wildcard mask
  - 11111110.11111111.11111111.00000000

In this example, the first is a valid subnet mask because there are contiguous 1s followed by contiguous 0s. The second example is invalid because the last bit of the first octet is a 0, which is in between 1s. This is valid for a wildcard mask, though, and it would mean that we don't care what that bit is. It does not have to be a match when comparing an IP address to the wildcard address or mask.

So why would you want to use this? Two scenarios can come up. First, you're a totally old-school IOS administrator, and you still want to use wildcard matching in your devices like you did with old IOS access lists. More common, however, is that sometimes you can structure some really efficient security policies if your network follows a certain standard addressing scheme.

For instance, let's say you operate a large retail environment with thousands of stores connected via a hub and spoke VPN. At every store the components have the same IP address with a different subnet. For example, the stores have their own class C in the

10.50.x.0/24 range. At each store the cash register is 10.50.x.100. You could make a wildcard mask that would be 10.50.0.100/255.255.0.255, which would match .100 for any subnet in the 10.50.x range.

Unlike Cisco IOS, the Junos wildcard match does not require that you use inverse notation, but the same notation as subnet masks—it's just that the contiguous restriction is relaxed. Second, at the time of writing this book, only IPv4 is supported for wildcard addresses, not IPv6.

With the preceding example, you could use this single address object in a policy at the head end, along with the branch networks to represent any cash register.

Configuring wildcard address objects. Let's configure the example that we just discussed in the preceding section as a wildcard address for an object called Cash-Registers.

```
{primary:node0}[edit]
{primary:node0}[edit]
root@SRX550-Node0# set security address-book global address Cash-Registers de-
scription "All Corporate Cash Registers Wildcard Object" wildcard-address
10.50.0.100/255.255.0.255

{primary:node0}[edit]
root@SRX550-Node0# show security address-book
global {
    address Cash-Registers {
        description "All Corporate Cash Registers Wildcard Object";
        wildcard-address 10.50.0.100/255.255.0.255;
    }
}
```

Address sets. Now that we have explored creating the various types of individual address objects, you might find it useful to group these together for ease of use within other firewall frameworks such as security policies. Quite often in organizations there will be common requirements for similar types of access across different rules, so leveraging groups (particularly when it's more than a few objects) is quite advantageous. In Junos, groups are known as sets; it is the same concept, just a different name.

You can have any number of different types of objects within a set (e.g., host, network, dns, wildcard, etc.) and even other groups (in Junos 11.2 and newer) within a group.

Configuring address sets. Address sets are very simple objects: you simply define them, specify which address or other address sets you would like to add, optionally define a description, and you're good to go. The address set can then be used in place of individual address objects in a policy. In this example, we define two sets: one called Active-Directory with two objects (DC1: 192.168.1.1/32 and DC2: 192.168.4.1/32), and we include another address set in the Active Directory set called Exchange, which has one object called Mail1: 192.168.5.1/32.

```
[edit]
root@srx3600n0# edit security address-book global

[edit security address-book global]
root@srx3600n0# set address-set Active-Directory address DC1

[edit security address-book global]
root@srx3600n0# set address-set Active-Directory address DC2

 [edit security address-book global]
root@srx3600n0# set address-set Active-Directory description "Active Directory
Domain Controllers"

 [edit security address-book global]
root@srx3600n0# set address DC1 192.168.1.1/32

[edit security address-book global]
root@srx3600n0# set address DC2 192.168.4.1/32

[edit security address-book global]
root@srx3600n0# set address Mail1 192.168.5.1/32

[edit security address-book global]
root@srx3600n0# set address-set Exchange address Mail1

[edit security address-book global]
root@srx3600n0# set address-set Exchange description "Exchange Servers"

[edit security address-book global]
root@srx3600n0# set address-set Active-Directory address-set Exchange

[edit security address-book global]
root@srx3600n0# show
address DC1 192.168.1.1/32;
address DC2 192.168.4.1/32;
address Mail1 192.168.5.1/32;
address-set Active-Directory {
    description "Active Directory Domain Controllers";
    address DC1;
    address DC2;
    address-set Exchange;
}
address-set Exchange {
    description "Exchange Servers";
    address Mail1;
}
```

Application objects

Similar to address objects, application objects allow you to specify objects to be used in the match criteria of security policies. For those of you who are coming from the world of ScreenOS, application objects are the same as service objects in ScreenOS; they are Layer 3 or Layer 4 objects for ports or protocols, rather than Layer 7 application objects that are dynamically determined by Application Identification (known as dynamic applications). These objects do not match any patterns using regex, unlike their Layer 7 counterparts, which we explore in Chapter 12.

The SRX does come with a list of prepopulated address objects so you don't necessarily need to define your own unless it is truly a custom service.

For some unknown reason, at the time of writing this book, there is still no official command to view the predefined application objects in Junos —but there is a trick to do this, which can also be used to view other Junos default configurations. The junos-defaults group is a hidden group, but if you just type it out, you can specify any modifier after it. In this case, it is `applications`, as we are at the base Junos Config level, but you could do `security` or `security idp` after it if you wanted for the same effect. The full output of this table is too long to list here, but you can check it out on your own system.

```
root@srx3600n0> show configuration groups junos-defaults applications
#
# File Transfer Protocol
#
application junos-ftp {
    application-protocol ftp;
    protocol tcp;
    destination-port 21;
}
#
# Trivial File Transfer Protocol
#
application junos-tftp {
    application-protocol tftp;
    protocol udp;
    destination-port 69;
}
#
# Real Time Streaming Protocol
#
application junos-rtsp {
    application-protocol rtsp;
    protocol tcp;
    destination-port 554;
}
```

```
#
# Network Basic Input Output System  - networking protocol used on
# Windows networks   session service port
#
application junos-netbios-session {
    protocol tcp;
    destination-port 139;
}
application junos-smb-session {
    protocol tcp;
    destination-port 445;
}
```

Application objects allow you to set numerous attributes to help define what the match criteria for this object should be. Let's take a look at each attribute here:

```
[edit]
root@srx3600n0# set applications application Custom440 ?
Possible completions:
  application-protocol  Application protocol type
+ apply-groups         Groups from which to inherit configuration data
+ apply-groups-except  Don't inherit configuration data from these groups
  description          Text description of application
  destination-port     Match TCP/UDP destination port
  do-not-translate-A-query-to-AAAA-query  Knob to control the translation of A
query to AAAA query
   do-not-translate-AAAA-query-to-A-query  Knob to control the translation of
AAAA query to A query
  ether-type           Match ether type
  icmp-code            Match ICMP message code
  icmp-type            Match ICMP message type
  icmp6-code           Match ICMP6 message code
  icmp6-type           Match ICMP6 message type
  inactivity-timeout   Application-specific inactivity timeout (seconds)
  protocol             Match IP protocol type
  rpc-program-number   Match range of RPC program numbers
  source-port          Match TCP/UDP source port
> term                 Define individual application protocols
  uuid                 Match universal unique identifier for DCE RPC objects
```

Application protocol
: This is used if you would like to monitor (or not monitor) an application on this port or protocol using an ALG. For instance, if you wanted to have the FTP Control session on port 10021, or maybe you didn't want to listen for DNS on port 53, you could specify a custom application object and either specify the ALG you would like to use or ignore to disable it. Then you would use this object in the firewall policy accordingly.

Description
: Simply that: give this a description!

Destination port
: Defines what destination port should be used to match this object. Can be for TCP or UDP.

Do not translate A to AAAA query
: The SRX can automatically translate between IPv4 and IPv6 DNS objects, but this knob tells the SRX not to do this.

Do not translate AAAA to A query
: This is the opposite of the previous object, which is not to translate IPv6 into IPv4 objects.

Ether-type
: This is useful for matching Level 2 objects in the policy, but not usually required.

ICMP-code
: If you're matching the ICMP protocol, you can further filter down to individual ICMP codes rather than ICMP as a whole (IPv4).

ICMP-type
: In addition to ICMP codes, you can filter by types (IPv4).

There is a full list of ICMP code/types available from IANA (*http://bit.ly/14lZ5OY*).

ICMP6-code
: If matching ICMPv6, there are different codes than V4, so there is a different object if matching IPv6.

ICMP6-type
: If matching ICMPv6, there are different types than V4, so there is a different object if matching IPv6.

Inactivity timeout
: Also known as the idle timeout that should be applied to this application object. By default, TCP has a 30-minute idle timeout, and UDP has a 60-second idle timeout. Known IP protocols have a 30-minute timeout, whereas unknown ones have a 60-second timeout. Setting the inactivity timeout is very useful, particularly if you are concerned about applications either timing out or remaining idle for too long and filling up the session table.

Inactivity timeouts are only used when a session is idle, but not if it is closed by some other mechanism. For instance, if a TCP session is closed by a TCP FIN or Reset sequence, the SRX won't wait for the idle timeout to kick in, and the session will be immediately closed. Other examples of closing a session would be as follows:

ALGs
: For instance, the DNS ALG will close the session when the DNS reply arrives in response to a query, rather than wait the normal 60 seconds for UDP.

Layer 7 components
: Services like IDP, AppSecure, UTM, and other objects can request a session to be closed—for instance, if an attack is seen and the setting is to close the session.

Manual session clear
: If the SRX administrator issues the `clear security flow session` command and the sessions are manually closed.

High availability
: If in an HA cluster, the other node can inform the SRX to clear the session.

Remember, the inactivity timeout is only used when the session is truly idle (no traffic is sent or received); as long as traffic is being sent and received, the idle timeout will be reset. It is only when there is no traffic seen that the idle timeout starts to decrease until it goes to 0 and the session is closed.

Protocol
: The protocol field refers to what IP protocol number you might be using for this value. For instance, you might specify TCP, UDP, or something else. If you only specified a destination port (e.g., 53) but no protocol, then the application would match either TCP or UDP for that destination port. Besides the known protocols shown here, you can also specify any other protocol number of your choosing 0–255.

```
root@srx3600n0# set applications application Custom440 protocol ?
Possible completions:
  <number>             Numeric protocol value (0 .. 255)
  ah                   IP Security authentication header
  egp                  Exterior gateway protocol
  esp                  IPSec Encapsulating Security Payload
  gre                  Generic routing encapsulation
  icmp                 Internet Control Message Protocol
  icmp6                Internet Control Message Protocol Version 6
  igmp                 Internet Group Management Protocol
```

```
ipip                    IP in IP
ospf                    Open Shortest Path First
pim                     Protocol Independent Multicast
rsvp                    Resource Reservation Protocol
sctp                    Stream Control Transmission Protocol
tcp                     Transmission Control Protocol
udp                     User Datagram Protocol
```

RPC-Program-Number
: This attribute is set if you want to specify a specific RPC program number if you are using the RPC ALG.

Source port
: This parameter allows you to specify the source port to match for an application for UDP and TCP. Beware: usually you want to specify the destination port rather than the source port for most protocols, as the source port is randomly selected by the client machine OS. There are some scenarios where the source port might be fixed, and in these cases it could be ideal to use the source port parameter, but it is not common, particularly with contemporary applications.

Term
: If you are familiar with creating firewall filters and policy statements, you will be familiar with using terms in your policies. Term allows you to specify multiple criteria within a single object. For instance, let's say you want to select multiple different ports for an application that can communicate over a set of different ports. You can use terms to specify multiple criteria rather than specifying multiple application objects and then putting them together in a set. You'll see how to do this in our example coming up.

UUID
: This is useful when using an RPC protocol to narrow down which UUIDs apply to the application rather than allowing any communication to go through.

Application sets. Just like address objects, you can define sets of applications or even other nested application sets so that you can provide for a cleaner policy rather than having to reference multiple application objects in the policy. You can use both predefined and custom-defined application objects. This is especially handy if you need to reuse these objects in multiple locations in the security policy.

Configuring applications and application sets. In this example, we create three custom applications: one for Remote Desktop on TCP port 3389: one for FTP on TCP port 10021 with the FTP ALG enabled; and one for a Custom DNS on UDP port 53 and UDP port 5353, with an inactivity timeout of four seconds, with the ALG disabled. All three of these custom applications will be grouped in an application set called Custom-App-Group.

```
[edit]
root@srx3600n0# set applications application Remote-Desktop protocol tcp
destination-port 3389

root@srx3600n0# set applications application Custom-FTP application-protocol
ftp protocol tcp destination-port 10021

[edit]
root@srx3600n0# set applications application Custom-DNS inactivity-timeout 4
term 1 protocol udp destination-port 53

[edit]
root@srx3600n0# set applications application Custom-DNS application-protocol ig-
nore term 2 protocol udp destination-port 5353

root@srx3600n0# set applications application-set Custom-App-Group application
Custom-DNS

[edit]
root@srx3600n0# set applications application-set Custom-App-Group application
Custom-FTP

 [edit]
root@srx3600n0# set applications application-set Custom-App-Group application
Remote-Desktop

[edit]
root@srx3600n0# show applications
application Remote-Desktop {
    protocol tcp;
    destination-port 3389;
}
application Custom-FTP {
    application-protocol ftp;
    protocol tcp;
    destination-port 10021;
}
application Custom-DNS {
    application-protocol ignore;
    inactivity-timeout 4;
    term 1 protocol udp destination-port 53;
    term 2 protocol udp destination-port 5353;
}
application-set Custom-App-Group {
    application Custom-DNS;
    application Custom-FTP;
    application Remote-Desktop;
}
```

Source-Identity. Starting in Junos 12.1, we can support an additional field in the SRX called Source-Identity, which serves as match criteria to identify a user tied to a source

IP address. This is in addition to the other criteria of From-To-Zone, Source IP, Destination IP, and Application. We cover Source-Identity in depth in Chapter 12.

Negated source and destination objects

Starting in Junos 12.1X45, the SRX supports the ability to define objects to be excluded from firewall rules for source or destination address match criteria. Prior to 12.1X45, you could accomplish the same functionality, but it would take two rules: a specific rule with the exempted objects to be matched with a permit or deny action, then a second rule matching everything else with the opposite action. Negated Address support allows you to simplify your ruleset. Note that it is not supported for applications, just source and destination addresses.

```
[edit]
root# set security policies from-zone trust to-zone untrust policy Negate
match ?
Possible completions:
  <[Enter]>            Execute this command
+ application          Port-based application
+ apply-groups         Groups from which to inherit configuration data
+ apply-groups-except  Don't inherit configuration data from these groups
+ destination-address  Match destination address
  destination-address-excluded  Exclude destination addresses
+ source-address       Match source address
  source-address-excluded  Exclude source addresses
+ source-identity      Match source identity
  |                    Pipe through a command
```

The `source-address-excluded` and `destination-address-excluded` are just attributes. When they are on, all addresses for the source, destination, or both will be excluded. It cannot be done on an individual object basis within the firewall rule itself, but can be applied to only source addresses, only destination addresses, or both.

Schedulers

Although not an explicit part of the match criteria, policy schedulers allow you to define when the policy is active, and thus are an implicit match criterion. They are useful for defining day-of-week and time-of-day criteria to determine when the policy will be active. For instance, you might want to define security policies that open or close access based on business hours. This can be both for permit and deny policies, but also for other Level 7 services like AppSecure (especially AppFW/AppQoS) and UTM (particularly URL Filtering). Often organizations use these to increase productivity by only allowing external web browsing during lunch and nonbusiness hours, or only permitting business partners to connect at certain times in conjunction with contracts.

You can define multiple schedulers that can be defined in the system and applied to different policies, but only one scheduler can be active per policy.

When a scheduler is inactive, you can think of that policy as not existing. Similar to how the deactivate statement works, the policy lookup engine will bypass these policies.

For existing sessions, you can either choose to use Policy Rematch (which will re-evaluate sessions when a policy change occurs) or by default it will continue to take the original action of the original policy lookup.

In terms of scheduler components, they are very simple and contain the following parameters:

Day of week
: Each individual weekday can be defined individually, along with the option to select all days.

Time of days
: For each day, you can define what time you want the policies to be active. This is done on a day-by-day basis unless you select daily, in which case it is applied evenly to all days.

Start date
: You can define when you want this schedule to take effect from a year/month/day/time perspective if you want to stage changes for a future date.

At the time of writing this book, you cannot define which weeks, months, or years you want the policy to be active, just on a day-of-week basis. Days of the week are the most common use case, but you could leverage Junos Scripts or Security Design to schedule policies to take place in a completely custom fashion if so desired.

Configuring schedulers. Now that we've looked at schedulers, we actually configure them in an example. Here we configure three different schedulers to examine the different options:

- Configure a scheduler called Business-Hours that is active Monday through Friday from 9 a.m. to 5 p.m. Apply this scheduler to a security policy called Allowed-Business-Hours.

- Configure a scheduler called All-Day-Friday that is active all day long on Friday and is applied to a policy called All-Day-Friday-Policy.
- Configure a scheduler called B2B-Contract that activates a policy on January 1, 2013, at 8 a.m. and is active until December 31, 2013, at 11:59 p.m. This policy should be active between 5 p.m. and 7 p.m. on Sundays, which is applied to a policy called B2B-Policy.
- Configure the SRX to reevaluate the security policies when the schedulers change status.
- Configure the SRX to get its time from NTP Server 192.168.50.50.

It is very important that you have a reliable time source that the SRX can leverage when using schedulers, both for the SRX and the other devices connecting through it. If the SRX and the clients and servers have vastly differing clocks, this could result in unexpected results such as unintentional denial of access. This is not a concern that is specific to schedulers; there are plenty of reasons to have accurate time throughout your infrastructure. This just adds to the list.

```
[edit]
root@srx3600n0# set schedulers scheduler Business-Hours daily start-time 09:00
stop-time 17:00

 [edit]
root@srx3600n0# set schedulers scheduler Business-Hours saturday exclude

[edit]
root@srx3600n0# set schedulers scheduler Business-Hours sunday exclude

[edit]
root@srx3600n0# set security policies from-zone Trust to-zone Untrust policy
Allowed-Business-Hours scheduler-name Business-Hours

[edit]
root@srx3600n0# set schedulers scheduler All-Day-Friday friday all-day

[edit]
root@srx3600n0# set schedulers scheduler B2B-Contract sunday start-time 17:00
stop-time 19:00

root@srx3600n0# set security policies from-zone Trust to-zone Untrust policy
B2B-Policy scheduler-name B2B-Contract

from-zone Trust to-zone Untrust {
    policy Allowed-Business-Hours {
        scheduler-name Business-Hours;
```

```
    }
    policy All-Day-Friday-Policy {
        scheduler-name All-Day-Friday;
    }
    policy B2B-Policy {
        scheduler-name B2B-Contract;
    }
}
policy-rematch;

[edit]
root@srx3600n0# show system ntp
server 192.168.50.50;
```

This security policy is technically incomplete because we haven't defined the full match/then criteria, but for this example we are just highlighting the scheduler configuration. A complete example is shown in the section "Sample Deployment" on page 442 later in this chapter.

Action Criteria

Now that we have covered the components that lead to matching actual firewall sessions, we next discuss the action criteria. Action criteria define the action the firewall should perform with the session once it's been matched by the policy engine.

The action criteria available in security policies are broken down into the following areas:

Primary actions
: These are the main actions that define how the traffic will be processed. Only one of these options can be configured in a single security policy rule, and one action must be configured or an error will be thrown at commit time.

  Deny
  : The deny action instructs the firewall to silently drop all packets for the session. The firewall will not send any active control messages like TCP Resets or ICMP Unreachable messages when this option is enabled. Most often, the deny action is useful for hiding assets from untrusted resources. The lack of response makes identifying destinations in the packet much more difficult. Typically, scanners like NMAP and Nessus will try to scan and look at what responses are received, including to anomalous packets. The deny action provides them no response to work with and also causes the scan to take much longer, particularly if they are trying to be stealthy with longer timeouts.

  Reject
  : When the reject action is configured, the SRX will send a TCP Reset if the protocol is TCP and an ICMP reset if it is UDP, ICMP, or any other IP protocol.

This option is most useful when facing trusted resources so that the applications don't spend unnecessary time waiting for timeouts and instead get the active message. Typically, reject isn't recommended in segments that face untrusted resources because it gives attackers a bit more to key off of, but this isn't a major concern, just a best practice to use deny in those cases.

Permit
: Traffic is permitted at the Level 3/Level 4 level according to the security policy. That isn't to say that the traffic couldn't be blocked at some later point in the session by stateful firewall, ALG, UTM, IPS, and other services, but just based on the initial policy lookup the packet is permitted. We explore this option in greater detail in the next section.

Secondary actions
: These are parallel actions taken with the primary action. They are optional and independent of the primary action. Either one can be configured in any combination, as they are mutually exclusive.

Count
: This action performs an internal counting function of the bytes transmitted in this policy. You can also set alarms based on thresholds per second or minute on a policy-by-policy basis. The count option is useful if you don't have an external syslog server to monitor traffic consumption or if you are particularly interested in certain FW rules and the traffic behavior in them.

Log
: Logging is a very important option to configure in most cases. By default, the SRX will not log on any firewall rule passing through the device. This means that while a session is active you can view it in the session table, but after the session has ended there will not be a trace of it. Logging instructs the system to generate a log for the session. Logs can be generated on session initialization or on session close. The session-init logs are good for Deny/Reject policies when the traffic is immediately closed, or when you want to be notified when a session is opened, such as for troubleshooting purposes. Session Close is the ideal option when permitting traffic. Unlike Session Init, the close has a lot more information, such as the bytes or packets sent and received, the reason for closing the session, and Level 7 session information. Because this information is not known when the session is established, it can only be reported when the session is closed. The only downside to using session-close logs is that you only know about the session (from a logging perspective) when the session closes. This is normally fine, but if you are trying to troubleshoot, you might want to use Session Init as well. That's right, you can configure both options. The main reason for not doing both is primarily the fact that you'll be getting twice as many logs, but if that's not a concern, then it's fine.

Permit options

In the last section, we alluded to a number of options being available under the permit stanza, and we explore them in this section. The options available include launching Layer 7 services like AppSecure, UTM, IPS, SSL Proxy, Unified Access Control, Firewall Authentication, Policy-Based IPsec VPNs, TCP options, and destination NAT options. That sounds like a lot, and in a way it is. One question you might have is why we only have these options enabled under the permit stanzas rather than for deny and reject. The reason is simple: if the initial packet is blocked by policy (and thus the entire session) then there is really no reason to process the traffic further with other services, so those options don't apply in the case of deny and reject.

We examine all of the available UTM, IPS, AppSecure, and IPsec options at length in their respective chapters, but we cover the other policy-based options in this chapter.

There are some differences in the "then" actions between the high-end SRX and the branch SRX. For instance, at the time of writing this book, SSL Proxy and AppQoS are not available on the branch SRX, and UTM is not available on the high-end SRX. Some options, like services offload, are only available on the HE SRX and aren't likely to be ported to the branch based on platform architecture.

```
**************************
From an SRX 3600 on 12.1R1
**************************
[edit]
root@srx3600n0# set security policies from-zone trust to-zone untrust policy 2
then permit ?
Possible completions:
  <[Enter]>            Execute this command
> application-services  Application Services
+ apply-groups         Groups from which to inherit configuration data
+ apply-groups-except  Don't inherit configuration data from these groups
> destination-address  Enable destination address translation
> firewall-authentication  Enable authentication for this policy if permit or
tunnel
  services-offload     Enable services offloading
> tcp-options          Transmission Control Protocol session configuration
> tunnel               Tunnel packets
  |                    Pipe through a command
[edit]
root@srx3600n0# set security policies from-zone trust to-zone untrust policy 2
then permit application-services ?
Possible completions:
> application-firewall  Application firewall services
> application-traffic-control  Application traffic control services
+ apply-groups         Groups from which to inherit configuration data
+ apply-groups-except  Don't inherit configuration data from these groups
```

```
  gprs-gtp-profile     Specify GPRS Tunneling Protocol profile name
  gprs-sctp-profile    Specify GPRS stream control protocol profile name
  idp                  Intrusion detection and prevention
> ssl-proxy            SSL proxy services
> uac-policy           Enable unified access control enforcement of policy

************************
From an SRX100 on 12.1R1
************************
{primary:node0}[edit]
root@SRX100HM# set security policies from-zone trust to-zone untrust policy 2
then permit ?
Possible completions:
  <[Enter]>            Execute this command
> application-services  Application Services
+ apply-groups         Groups from which to inherit configuration data
+ apply-groups-except  Don't inherit configuration data from these groups
> destination-address  Enable destination address translation
> firewall-authentication  Enable authentication for this policy if permit or
tunnel
> tcp-options          Transmission Control Protocol session configuration
> tunnel               Tunnel packets
  |                    Pipe through a command
{primary:node0}[edit]
root@SRX100HM# set security policies from-zone trust to-zone untrust policy 2
then permit application-services ?
Possible completions:
> application-firewall  Application firewall services
+ apply-groups         Groups from which to inherit configuration data
+ apply-groups-except  Don't inherit configuration data from these groups
  gprs-gtp-profile     Specify GPRS Tunneling Protocol profile name
  gprs-sctp-profile    Specify GPRS stream control protocol profile name
  idp                  Intrusion detection and prevention
  redirect-wx          Set WX redirection
  reverse-redirect-wx  Set WX reverse redirection
> uac-policy           Enable unified access control enforcement of policy
  utm-policy           Specify utm policy name
```

Configuring security policies

Now that we have examined the various options that are used to compose a security policy, let's dig in and explore some different examples. After all, hands-on learning is much more effective than just studying the theory! In this example, we are going to configure five different policies with options as follows:

1. Policy from-zone trust to-zone untrust called Allow-Web that permits traffic from 192.168.1.0/24 to any destination on HTTP and HTTPS. Log traffic on this policy.
2. Policy from-zone trust to-zone untrust called NTP-DNS that permits traffic from any source in trust to time.nist.gov and 4.2.2.2 on NTP/DNS (udp) ports. Log this traffic.

3. All intrazone traffic from trust to trust should be permitted, but logged.
4. Allow inbound traffic from untrust to dmz called Email-Inbound, which allows SMTP traffic from any source to the DMZ email server 172.16.100.50.
5. Create a global rule to drop all traffic with logging.
6. Configure policy rematch.
7. Just for thoroughness, configure the policy engine to drop all unmatched traffic by default (note that this won't take effect with the global policy, but we'll just configure it anyway).

```
[edit]
root@srx3600n0# edit security policies from-zone trust to-zone untrust

[edit security policies from-zone trust to-zone untrust]
root@srx3600n0# set policy Allow-Web match source-address 192.168.1.0/24
destination-address any application [junos-http junos-https]

[edit security policies from-zone trust to-zone untrust]
root@srx3600n0# set policy Allow-Web then permit

[edit security policies from-zone trust to-zone untrust]
root@srx3600n0# set policy Allow-Web then log session-close

[edit security policies from-zone trust to-zone untrust]
root@srx3600n0# set policy NTP-DNS match source-address any destination-
address [time.nist.gov 4.2.2.2] application [junos-dns-udp junos-ntp]

[edit security policies from-zone trust to-zone untrust]
root@srx3600n0# set policy NTP-DNS then permit

[edit security policies from-zone trust to-zone untrust]
root@srx3600n0# set policy NTP-DNS then log session-close

[edit security policies from-zone trust to-zone untrust]
root@srx3600n0# up

[edit security policies]
root@srx3600n0# set from-zone trust to-zone trust policy Allow-All match
source-address any destination-address any application any

[edit security policies]
root@srx3600n0# set from-zone trust to-zone trust policy Allow-All then permit

[edit security policies]
root@srx3600n0# set from-zone trust to-zone trust policy Allow-All then log
session-close

[edit security policies]
root@srx3600n0# set from-zone untrust to-zone dmz policy Email-Inbound match
source-address any destination-address 172.16.100.50 application junos-smtp
```

```
[edit security policies]
root@srx3600n0# set from-zone untrust to-zone dmz policy Email-Inbound then
permit

[edit security policies]
root@srx3600n0# set from-zone untrust to-zone dmz policy Email-Inbound then
log session-close

[edit security policies]
root@srx3600n0# set global policy Deny-All-Log match source-address any
destination-address any application any

root@srx3600n0# set global policy Deny-All-Log then deny

[edit security policies]
root@srx3600n0# set global policy Deny-All-Log then log session-init

root@srx3600n0# set policy-rematch

[edit security policies]
root@srx3600n0# set default-policy deny-all

[edit security]
root@srx3600n0# show policies
from-zone trust to-zone untrust {
    policy Allow-Web {
        match {
            source-address 192.168.1.0/24;
            destination-address any;
            application [ junos-http junos-https ];
        }
        then {
            permit;
            log {
                session-close;
            }
        }
    }
    policy NTP-DNS {
        match {
            source-address any;
            destination-address [ time.nist.gov 4.2.2.2 ];
            application [ junos-dns-udp junos-ntp ];
        }
        then {
            permit;
            log {
                session-close;
            }
        }
    }
```

```
}
from-zone trust to-zone trust {
    policy Allow-All {
        match {
            source-address any;
            destination-address any;
            application any;
        }
        then {
            permit;
            log {
                session-close;
            }
        }
    }
}
from-zone untrust to-zone dmz {
    policy Email-Inbound {
        match {
            source-address any;
            destination-address 172.16.100.50;
            application junos-smtp;
        }
        then {
            permit;
            log {
                session-close;
            }
        }
    }
}
global {
    policy Deny-All-Log {
        match {
            source-address any;
            destination-address any;
            application any;
        }
        then {
            deny;
            log {
                session-init;
            }
        }
    }
}
default-policy {
    deny-all;
}
policy-rematch;
```

```
[edit security]
root@srx3600n0# show address-book
global {
    address 192.168.1.0/24 192.168.1.0/24;
    address 4.2.2.2 4.2.2.2/32;
    address 172.16.100.50 172.16.100.50/32;
    address time.nist.gov {
        dns-name time.nist.gov;
    }
}
```

If you haven't noticed already, when you create a security policy rule it automatically places the rule at the bottom of the security policy context (e.g., trust to untrust) rather than at the top. The reason for this is because it stands the least likelihood of causing issues if you forget to specify where to put it. When using the CLI, you can use the `insert` command to move the policy statement in the policy set. If using J-Web or SD, you have options in the GUI to reorder the rule placement.

```
[edit]
root@srx3600n0# show security policies from-zone untrust to-zone trust
from-zone untrust to-zone trust {
    policy 3 {
        match {
            source-address any;
            destination-address any;
            application any;
        }
        then {
            permit {
                application-services {
                    idp;
                    ssl-proxy {
                        profile-name CA;
                    }
                }
            }
        }
    }
    policy 2 {
        match {
            source-address any;
            destination-address any;
            application any;
        }
        then {
            permit {
                application-services {
                    idp;
```

```
                }
            }
            log {
                session-close;
            }
        }
    }
}
default-policy {
    permit-all;
}

[edit]
root@srx3600n0# insert security policies from-zone untrust to-zone trust policy
2 before policy 3

[edit]
root@srx3600n0# show security policies from-zone untrust to-zone trust
policy 2 {
    match {
        source-address any;
        destination-address any;
        application any;
    }
    then {
        permit {
            application-services {
                idp;
            }
        }
        log {
            session-close;
        }
    }
}
policy 3 {
    match {
        source-address any;
        destination-address any;
        application any;
    }
    then {
        permit {
            application-services {
                idp;
                ssl-proxy {
                    profile-name CA;
                }
            }
        }
    }
}
```

Host security policies

There is one other type of security policy that was added in the Junos 11.2 time frame, which is to evaluate security policies for traffic originated from or terminated on the SRX itself. Prior to this feature being added, you could configure stateless firewall filters and apply them to the loopback interface or other transit interfaces, but this had its shortcomings. First, it was another place you had to look to evaluate access control. Second, firewall filters do not share the same address object and application object components, and they can't be used with advanced actions like IPS. Heeding customer feedback, Juniper added the ability to configure security policies based on a new zone type called junos-host. If you want to control traffic from the SRX to an external destination, then you would leverage junos-host as the from-zone (and whatever pertinent zone the traffic will egress). If you want to define what traffic should be permitted to the firewall, then you would define firewall rules with junos-host as the destination zone.

This feature only applies to traffic arriving or leaving on the data plane. If the traffic is terminated or generated on fxp0 of the control plane, this security won't be enforced.

Configuring a policy to restrict inbound or outbound management requests. The concepts here are really no different than with other security policies, except by default the SRX will not filter traffic in these rules if they are not present. Let's try an example: we will filter inbound connections so that SSH and HTTP are only permitted from the untrust zone from host 192.168.1.0/24 on the firewall itself. Let's also restrict the firewall from any outbound connections to the untrust zone for security purposes.

```
[edit]
root@srx3600n0# set security policies from-zone untrust to-zone junos-host poli-
cy Allow-Management match source-address 192.168.1.0/24 destination-address
172.16.1.1 application [junos-ssh junos-http]

[edit]
root@srx3600n0# ...security policies from-zone untrust to-zone junos-host poli-
cy Allow-Management then permit

[edit]
root@srx3600n0# set security policies from-zone untrust to-zone junos-host poli-
cy Allow-Management then log session-close

[edit]
root@srx3600n0# set security policies from-zone untrust to-zone junos-host poli-
cy Deny-All-Else match source-address any destination-address any application
any
```

```
[edit]
root@srx3600n0# set security policies from-zone untrust to-zone junos-host poli-
cy Deny-All-Else then deny

[edit]
root@srx3600n0# set security policies from-zone untrust to-zone junos-host poli-
cy Deny-All-Else then log session-init

[edit]
root@srx3600n0# set security policies from-zone junos-host to-zone untrust poli-
cy Deny-All match source-address any destination-address any application any

[edit]
root@srx3600n0# set security policies from-zone junos-host to-zone untrust poli-
cy Deny-All then deny

[edit]
root@srx3600n0# set security policies from-zone junos-host to-zone untrust poli-
cy Deny-All then log session-init
```

```
from-zone untrust to-zone junos-host {
    policy Allow-Management {
        match {
            source-address 192.168.1.0/24;
            destination-address 172.16.1.1;
            application [ junos-ssh junos-http ];
        }
        then {
            permit;
            log {
                session-close;
            }
        }
    }
    policy Deny-All-Else {
        match {
            source-address any;
            destination-address any;
            application any;
        }
        then {
            deny;
            log {
                session-init;
            }
        }
    }
}
from-zone junos-host to-zone untrust {
    policy Deny-All {
```

```
            match {
                source-address any;
                destination-address any;
                application any;
            }
            then {
                deny;
                log {
                    session-init;
                }
            }
        }
    }
    [edit]
    root@srx3600n0# set security zones security-zone untrust host-inbound-traffic
    system-services ssh

    [edit]
    root@srx3600n0# set security zones security-zone untrust host-inbound-traffic
    system-services http

    [edit]
    root@srx3600n0# show security zones security-zone untrust
    host-inbound-traffic {
        system-services {
            ssh;
            http;
        }
    }
    interfaces {
        xe-1/0/1.0;
    }
```

You can also leverage the global security policies as a catchall here. Be sure that you allow the system service to listen on the ingress interface or else the system won't activate the service on that interface (thus your policy will work but there won't be any listener for the daemon on that interface). Also, as mentioned before, this only works for data plane connections, and not for those on fxp0. If you want to filter connections on fxp0, you will need to use traditional firewall filters and apply them to the lo0 interface.

Application Layer Gateways

We'd be remiss to not discuss ALGs in this chapter, as they very much have to do with security policies. Although many contemporary applications have shifted away from relying on multiple TCP/IP sessions per application session with another host, particularly to avoid using dynamic sessions and reverse connections from server to client, there are still many applications both legacy and modern that rely on this type of functionality. A prime example is FTP. Although there are many modes of FTP, the traditional active mode relies on a connection from the client to server on destination port 21, and the server makes a reverse connection back to the client on port 20. At the time that FTP was designed, access control (and stateful firewalls for that matter) were not as prevalent as they are today, nor were all of the security threats. Without an ALG to make this type of behavior work properly, you would have to create both a firewall rule to allow traffic outbound on port 21 and also inbound on port 20. This becomes an issue particularly if you are using NAT and if you can't restrict down the server IPs. Other applications like FTP passive might have a standard control port like 21 from client to server, and the server provides the client with a dynamic port on which to make a second connection to the server, rather than having the server connect back to the client as in active mode. The issue here is that if you have a solid firewall policy, you won't let some arbitrary dynamic connection outbound on an anomalous port. Again, we need something that can dynamically handle this, as shown in Figure 8-3.

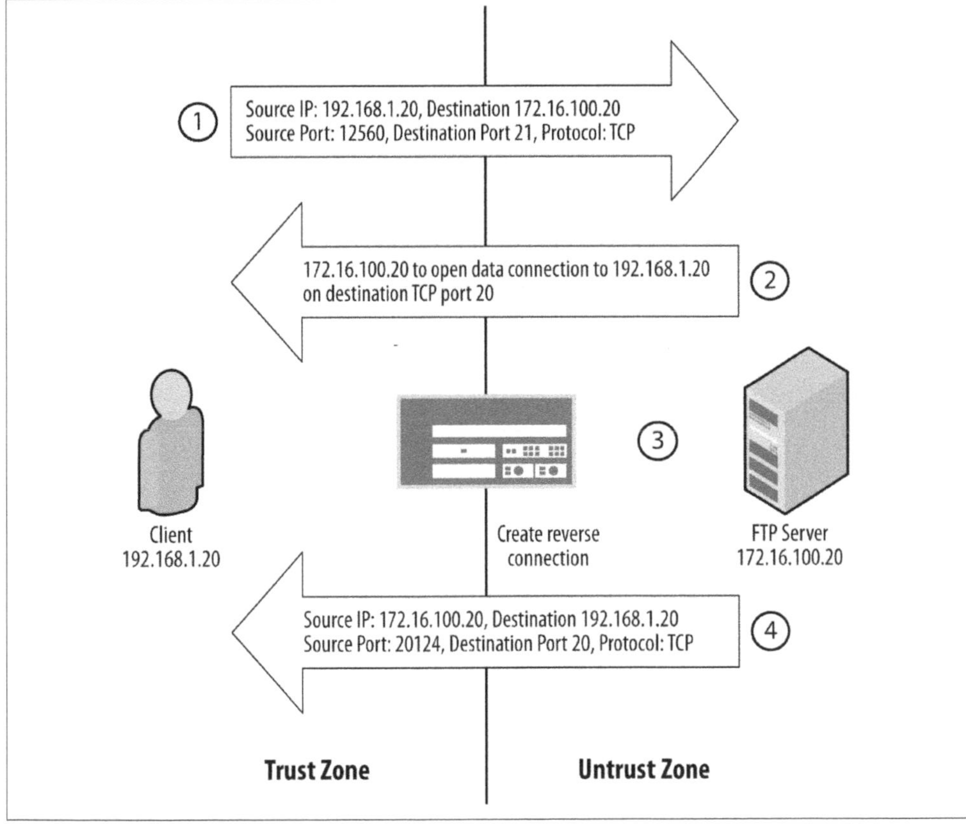

Figure 8-3. FTP ALG flowchart

Many real-time voice and video protocols like SIP, H.323, RTSP, MGCP, and others have similar behaviors, along with data-driven protocols like RPC (MSRPC and SunRPC).

The solution to this problem is not to configure a wide open security policy (which probably wouldn't work in scenarios with NAT anyway), but rather to leverage ALGs that can automate the process of dynamically opening "pinhole" sessions for you based on the application negotiation.

To explain this in more detail, an ALG works as follows:

1. A client makes a connection to a server on a control channel. This can be a well-known port or you can define a custom application with an ALG enabled in it as we did in the application configuration section. This traffic must be permitted by firewall policy.
2. The ALG inspects the connection and parses the information at Layer 7 to identify what port or protocol the auxiliary session will be required for.
3. The ALG creates a pinhole session in the firewall for the auxiliary dynamic session that is negotiated between the client and server. This session does not require an explicit policy in the security rulebase, and is derived based on the real-time traffic between the client and server.
4. Once the session is completed (e.g., TCP FIN/RST or application response such as a DNS reply or timeout), the auxiliary session and the control session will be cleared from the firewall session table.

It looks like the following in the session table. You can use the `resource-manager` qualifier to look for any sessions that are using ALGs, or you could also look it up by destination port. You can see when an ALG is active by the resource information.

```
{primary:node0}
root@SRX100HM> show security flow session resource-manager
node0:
--------------------------------------------------------------------------

Session ID: 7804, Policy name: General-Outbound/14, State: Active, Timeout:
1762, Valid
Resource information : FTP ALG, 20, 0
  In: 192.168.1.30/2634 --> 207.17.137.56/21;tcp, If: reth1.0, Pkts: 11, Bytes:
526
    Out: 207.17.137.56/21  --> 172.16.1.20/35732;tcp, If: reth0.0, Pkts: 10,
Bytes: 623
Total sessions: 1
```

We can look for the pinhole sessions or "gates" that are dynamically opened from the ALG.

```
{primary:node0}
root@SRX100HM> show security flow gate
```

```
node0:
--------------------------------------------------------------------------

Hole: 207.17.137.56-207.17.137.56/0-0->172.16.1.20-172.16.1.20/20-20
  Translated: 207.17.137.56/0->192.168.1.30/0
  Protocol: tcp
  Application: FTP ALG
  Age: 65534 seconds
  Flags: 0x0020
  Zone: Danger
  Reference count: 3
  Resource: 6-13-8

Valid gates: 1
Pending gates: 0
Invalidated gates: 0
Gates in other states: 0
Total gates: 1
```

The following ALGs are available on the firewall platforms at the time of writing this book. Note that some are disabled by default.

```
root@srx3600n0> show security alg status
ALG Status :
  DNS       : Enabled
  FTP       : Enabled
  H323      : Disabled
  MGCP      : Disabled
  MSRPC     : Enabled
  PPTP      : Enabled
  RSH       : Enabled
  RTSP      : Disabled
  SCCP      : Disabled
  SIP       : Disabled
  SQL       : Enabled
  SUNRPC    : Enabled
  TALK      : Enabled
  TFTP      : Enabled
  IKE-ESP   : Disabled
```

Enabling an ALG example

Let's enable the SIP ALG, which is disabled by default on the system. To do this we simply need to activate it in the security ALG stanza. Note that different ALGs have a variety of options, but digging into the various ALGs is outside the scope of this book, as they are not typically needed and are considered an advanced feature that you would perform with a strong understanding of the application or with the direction of JTAC.

```
[edit]
root@srx3600n0# set security alg sip

[edit]
```

```
root@srx3600n0# set security alg sip ?
Possible completions:
  <[Enter]>            Execute this command
> application-screen   Configure application screens
+ apply-groups         Groups from which to inherit configuration data
+ apply-groups-except  Don't inherit configuration data from these groups
  c-timeout            Set C timeout (3..10 minutes)
  disable              Disable SIP ALG
> dscp-rewrite         DSCP code rewrite
  inactive-media-timeout  Set inactive media timeout (10..2550 seconds)
  maximum-call-duration  Set maximum call duration (3..720 minutes)
  retain-hold-resource  Retain SDP resources during call hold
  t1-interval          Set T1 interval (500..5000 milliseconds)
  t4-interval          Set T4 interval (5..10 seconds)
> traceoptions         SIP ALG trace options
  |
```

Remember that you can create custom Layer 3/Layer 4 application objects under `set applications application`, with which you can both enable or disable the ALGs for certain objects and reference them in policies if need be. An example would be if you wanted to run an ALG on a nonstandard port like FTP control channel on 10021 or disable an ALG like DNS so that it doesn't automatically close the session when the response is received but instead waits for the UDP timeout.

ALGs also have the ability to control application behaviors, as we saw in the SIP ALG. Some ALGs like DNS do not open auxiliary sessions but operate to manipulate data like DNS Proxy, or to close sessions quickly like when a DNS response is heard. The options vary among ALGs. Other behaviors can also be controlled through Level 7 services like IPS.

Best Practices

Configuring security policies is really the easy part of implementing the SRX as an effective enforcement point in a network. The part that makes this more of an art than a science is specifically how you craft the rules and order, and how they interact with the traffic. There are several best practices that can be employed when defining an effective firewall policy.

Least privilege
: This means that your firewall rules should be as tight as possible in terms of match criteria and permitting traffic. Only traffic that is permitted by organizational policy should be permitted; all other traffic should be denied. This is true not only for inbound security policies from the Internet to internal resources, but also from internal resource to other internal resources and outbound to the Internet. It takes

more effort to design this than a policy that merely allows out traffic outbound, but this is the first fundamental step to ensuring that you have an effective security policy. A least privilege security policy cannot guarantee that threats cannot affect your network, but it can help to minimize your attack surface, which makes other controls more effective and the work of an attacker that much more difficult.

Segment logically
: The SRX is a zone-based firewall, which means that you can place different interfaces into different zones. The SRX can only enforce traffic that crosses it, which means that you must properly design your network so that different resources are placed in a manner where the firewall can enforce controls (e.g., in different zones, or at least different interfaces on the firewall because you can still control traffic with an intrazone policy). Products like the UAC allow you to extend the security control to the access layer.

Most specific firewall rules first
: Typically, it is best to place the most explicit firewall rules at the top of the rulebase for any given context because we match traffic starting at the top of the rulebase, going down with the first match. If you place a less specific rule at the top, it is more likely to shadow the less specific rules lower down in the rulebase.

Use address and application sets where possible
: Address and application sets make administration of the firewall policies much simpler. First, they allow you to group large sets of objects so that you can reference them as a single object in the security policy. Second, changes to the group membership will automatically be updated into the security rules. The more rules you can reference to these groups, the simpler it is to make changes. Because most organizations have logical objects that can be grouped, these containers make perfect sense for the security policies.

Explicit drop rules
: Placing an any-any-any drop rule at the bottom of each security zone context (e.g., trust to untrust) along with the global policy is considered a best practice to ensure that undesired traffic is not leaked through the security policy. This doesn't replace the need to properly define your firewall rules, but it does provide a simple catchall mechanism to capture unclassified traffic. Ideally, you should log this traffic.

To log or not to log
: Logging on all firewall policies is highly recommended for most environments. This gives you an audit trail of network activity both for troubleshooting and diagnosis. Because it's difficult to retroactively collect this information, it is best to log and leverage a log collector like STRM, Splunk, Syslog-NG, or another application to manage the logs. The main reason you might not want to log on a policy rule would be the volume of logs it might generate. This is common in service provider environments where CPS are in the hundreds of thousands per second. For most other

environments, it's advisable (if not also required by organizational policy, laws, and regulations) to log firewall rules, both deny and permit.

Log on Session Close versus Log on Session Init
: Unless you are troubleshooting, it is typically best to use Log on Session Close instead of Log on Session Init when permitting traffic because it will include a great deal more information about the session that is useful for historical purposes. Log on Session Init is good for situations where you might have long-lived sessions and you are trying to do some troubleshooting or if you are dropping the traffic, because they will only be logged on session init.

Use NTP
: Proper clock synchronization is key for many aspects of the security functionality. If the clock is wrong, not only will your log and troubleshooting information be incorrect, but security objects like schedulers will also have unintended impacts. NTP is a simple way to ensure that this won't occur.

Leverage ALGs
: Use ALGs to open specific auxiliary sessions rather than wide open security policies. Data ALGs are enabled by default, but VoIP/Video ALGs are disabled by default.

Troubleshooting and Operation

Because security policies are the cornerstone of traffic processing on the SRX, it is imperative to have a solid understanding of their operation. There is a lot of data that can be gleaned from the various operational and troubleshooting facilities in security and flow processing, and we examine the most pertinent ones here.

Viewing Security Policies

Besides leveraging the configuration itself, you can view the security policies with the `show security policies` command. There are numerous parameters that you can use to filter the output returned. It is often helpful to view the firewall rules both before and after you create a rule to make sure that its creation and placement are correct. Here we show the various options to view the security policy along with the difference between the default output and the detailed output.

```
root@srx3600n0> show security policies ?
Possible completions:
  <[Enter]>            Execute this command
  application-firewall  Show the information of application-firewall
  count                Number of policies to show (1..65535)
  detail               Show the detailed information
  from-zone              Show the policy information matching the given source
zone
```

```
  global                Show the policy information of global policies
  hit-count             Show the hit count of policies
  logical-system        Logical-system name
   policy-name            Show the policy information matching the given policy
name
  root-logical-system  Root logical-system (default)
  start                 Show the policies from a given position (1..65535)
   to-zone               Show the policy information matching the given destina-
tion zone
   zone-context           Show the count of policies in each context (from-zone
and to-zone)
  |                     Pipe through a command

root@srx3600n0> show security policies
Default policy: permit-all
From zone: trust, To zone: untrust
  Policy: 1, State: enabled, Index: 4, Scope Policy: 0, Sequence number: 1
    Source addresses: any
    Destination addresses: any
    Applications: any
    Source identities: any
    Action: permit, application services, log
From zone: untrust, To zone: trust
  Policy: 3, State: enabled, Index: 5, Scope Policy: 0, Sequence number: 1
    Source addresses: any
    Destination addresses: any
    Applications: any
    Action: permit, application services
  Policy: 2, State: enabled, Index: 6, Scope Policy: 0, Sequence number: 2
    Source addresses: any
    Destination addresses: any
    Applications: any
    Action: permit, application services

root@srx3600n0> show security policies detail
Default policy: permit-all
Policy: 1, action-type: permit, State: enabled, Index: 4, Scope Policy: 0
  Policy Type: Configured
  Sequence number: 1
  From zone: trust, To zone: untrust
  Source addresses:
    any-ipv4(global): 0.0.0.0/0
    any-ipv6(global): ::/0
  Destination addresses:
    any-ipv4(global): 0.0.0.0/0
    any-ipv6(global): ::/0
  Application: any
    IP protocol: 0, ALG: 0, Inactivity timeout: 0
      Source port range: [0-0]
      Destination port range: [0-0]
  Source identities:
```

```
      any
    Per policy TCP Options: SYN check: No, SEQ check: No
    Intrusion Detection and Prevention: enabled
    Unified Access Control: disabled
    Session log: at-close
  Policy: 3, action-type: permit, State: enabled, Index: 5, Scope Policy: 0
    Policy Type: Configured
    Sequence number: 1
    From zone: untrust, To zone: trust
    Source addresses:
      any-ipv4(global): 0.0.0.0/0
      any-ipv6(global): ::/0
    Destination addresses:
      any-ipv4(global): 0.0.0.0/0
      any-ipv6(global): ::/0
    Application: any
      IP protocol: 0, ALG: 0, Inactivity timeout: 0
        Source port range: [0-0]
        Destination port range: [0-0]
    Per policy TCP Options: SYN check: No, SEQ check: No
    Intrusion Detection and Prevention: enabled
    Unified Access Control: disabled
    SSL Proxy Profile Name: CA
  Policy: 2, action-type: permit, State: enabled, Index: 6, Scope Policy: 0
    Policy Type: Configured
    Sequence number: 2
    From zone: untrust, To zone: trust
    Source addresses:
      any-ipv4(global): 0.0.0.0/0
      any-ipv6(global): ::/0
    Destination addresses:
      any-ipv4(global): 0.0.0.0/0
      any-ipv6(global): ::/0
    Application: any
      IP protocol: 0, ALG: 0, Inactivity timeout: 0
        Source port range: [0-0]
        Destination port range: [0-0]
    Per policy TCP Options: SYN check: No, SEQ check: No
    Intrusion Detection and Prevention: enabled
    Unified Access Control: disabled
```

Security policy tools

Besides looking at the security policy itself in the configuration or with the operational mode commands, there are some useful tools in the SRX that allow you to gain some additional information about the firewall rule usage along with the ability to determine what traffic will match which rules in the device. Here we look at both of these.

```
Hit Count:


root@srx3600n0> show security policies hit-count ?
```

```
Possible completions:
  <[Enter]>            Execute this command
  ascending            Ascending order
  descending           Descending order
  from-zone            Show the policy hit-count matching the given source zone
  greater-than         Minimum hit-count  (0..4294967295)
  less-than            Maximum hit-count  (0..4294967295)
  logical-system       Logical-system name
  root-logical-system  Root logical-system (default)
  to-zone               Show the policy hit-count matching the given destination
zone
  |                    Pipe through a command
root@srx3600n0> show security policies hit-count
Logical system: root-logical-system
 Index   From zone        To zone           Name           Policy count
 1       trust            untrust           1              137398256
 2       untrust          trust             3              366305
 3       untrust          trust             2              0

Number of policy: 3


Match Policies

root@srx3600n0> show security match-policies source-ip 1.1.1.1 destination-ip
2.2.2.2 from-zone trust to-zone untrust destination-port 21 protocol tcp root-
logical-system source-port 5000
Policy: 1, action-type: permit, State: enabled, Index: 4
0
  Policy Type: Configured
  Sequence number: 1
  From zone: trust, To zone: untrust
  Source addresses:
    any-ipv4(global): 0.0.0.0/0
    any-ipv6(global): ::/0
  Destination addresses:
    any-ipv4(global): 0.0.0.0/0
    any-ipv6(global): ::/0
  Application: any
    IP protocol: 0, ALG: 0, Inactivity timeout: 0
      Source port range: [0-0]
      Destination port range: [0-0]
  Source identities:
    any
  Per policy TCP Options: SYN check: No, SEQ check: No
  Intrusion Detection and Prevention: enabled
  Unified Access Control: disabled
  Session log: at-close
```

The Hit Count output is especially useful when you are operating with a very large policy set and you want to view which rules are being highly utilized and which ones might not be used at all. Particularly when you see rules that don't have any hits, you might want to do some investigating to determine if they are being shadowed by another policy and thus are not active. The match policy allows you to take the flow criteria that would be evaluated for a session and see how they would be matched in the security policy. This is very telling and makes it much easier for an administrator to manage the device without having to manually generate traffic, which can be difficult to do, particularly for certain scenarios where you don't control the resources. Do keep in mind that this command is a bit cumbersome in that you must specify all of the criteria, including source port and so forth. Because this is going to simulate a policy lookup, you cannot define IP prefixes or port ranges, but rather the atomic criteria that would normally be in a session.

Viewing the Firewall Session Table

One of the most powerful troubleshooting tools at your disposal is the contents of the session table. The session table in its entirety would probably result in information overload, but Junos has some excellent facilities to filter the contents of the session table down to individual sessions along with different criteria. We start by viewing the available criteria that you can choose from to filter the table, followed by the terse (default) output of this command and the extensive output of the command.

```
root@srx3600n0> show security flow session ?
Possible completions:
  <[Enter]>            Execute this command
  application          Application protocol name
  application-firewall  Show application-firewall sessions
  application-firewall-rule-set  Show application-firewall session by rule-set
  application-traffic-control  Show application-traffic-control sessions
   application-traffic-control-rule-set   Show application-traffic-control ses-
sion by rule-set
  brief                Show brief output (default)
  destination-port     Destination port (1..65535)
  destination-prefix   Destination IP prefix or address
  dynamic-application  Dynamic application name
  dynamic-application-group  Dynamic application group name
  encrypted            Show encrypted traffic
  extensive            Show detailed output
  family               Protocol family
  idp                  IDP sessions
  interface            Name of incoming or outgoing interface
  logical-system       Logical-system name
  nat                  Sessions with network address translation
  protocol             IP protocol number
  resource-manager     Sessions with resource manager
  root-logical-system  Root logical-system (default)
  services-offload     Services-offload sessions
  session-identifier   Show session with specified session identifier
  source-port          Source port (1..65535)
  source-prefix        Source IP prefix or address
  summary              Show output summary
```

```
  tunnel               Tunnel sessions
  |                    Pipe through a command

root@srx3600n0> show security flow session
Flow Sessions on FPC3 PIC0:

Session ID: 60000167, Policy name: 1/4, Timeout: 1800, Valid
   In: 10.102.1.87/48308 --> 10.102.2.186/80;tcp, If: xe-1/0/0.0, Pkts: 6,
Bytes: 548
   Out: 10.102.2.186/80 --> 10.102.1.87/48308;tcp, If: xe-1/0/1.0, Pkts: 5,
Bytes: 4448

Session ID: 60000414, Policy name: 1/4, Timeout: 1800, Valid
   In: 10.102.1.148/8191 --> 10.102.2.160/80;tcp, If: xe-1/0/0.0, Pkts: 297,
Bytes: 15684
   Out: 10.102.2.160/80 --> 10.102.1.148/8191;tcp, If: xe-1/0/1.0, Pkts: 302,
Bytes: 443622

root@srx3600n0> show security flow session extensive
Flow Sessions on FPC3 PIC0:

Session ID: 60000014, Status: Normal
Flag: 0x80000042
Policy name: 1/4
Source NAT pool: Null, Application: junos-dns-udp/16
Dynamic application: junos:DNS,
Application traffic control rule-set: INVALID, Rule: INVALID
Maximum timeout: 2, Current timeout: 2
Session State: Valid
Start time: 698343, Duration: 0
   In: 10.102.1.69/47144 --> 10.102.2.106/53;udp,
    Interface: xe-1/0/0.0,
    Session token: 0x6, Flag: 0x2621
    Route: 0xa40010, Gateway: 10.102.1.69, Tunnel: 0
    Port sequence: 0, FIN sequence: 0,
    FIN state: 0,
    Pkts: 1, Bytes: 72
   Out: 10.102.2.106/53 --> 10.102.1.69/47144;udp,
    Interface: xe-1/0/1.0,
    Session token: 0x7, Flag: 0x2620
    Route: 0x1be0010, Gateway: 10.102.2.106, Tunnel: 0
    Port sequence: 0, FIN sequence: 0,
    FIN state: 0,
    Pkts: 1, Bytes: 88

Session ID: 60000024, Status: Normal
Flag: 0x42
Policy name: 1/4
Source NAT pool: Null
Dynamic application: junos:RPC,
Application traffic control rule-set: INVALID, Rule: INVALID
Maximum timeout: 60, Current timeout: 54
```

```
Session State: Valid
Start time: 698338, Duration: 5
   In: 10.102.1.162/46036 --> 10.102.2.33/63413;udp,
    Interface: xe-1/0/0.0,
    Session token: 0x6, Flag: 0x2621
    Route: 0x450010, Gateway: 10.102.1.162, Tunnel: 0
    Port sequence: 0, FIN sequence: 0,
    FIN state: 0,
    Pkts: 2, Bytes: 268
   Out: 10.102.2.33/63413 --> 10.102.1.162/46036;udp,
    Interface: xe-1/0/1.0,
    Session token: 0x7, Flag: 0x2620
    Route: 0x1030010, Gateway: 10.102.2.33, Tunnel: 0
    Port sequence: 0, FIN sequence: 0,
    FIN state: 0,
    Pkts: 2, Bytes: 152

root@srx3600n0> show security flow session summary
Flow Sessions on FPC3 PIC0:
Unicast-sessions: 3365
Multicast-sessions: 0
Services-offload-sessions: 0
Failed-sessions: 0
Sessions-in-use: 4724
  Valid sessions: 3334
  Pending sessions: 0
  Invalidated sessions: 1390
  Sessions in other states: 0
Maximum-sessions: 131072

Flow Sessions on FPC4 PIC0:
Unicast-sessions: 11286
Multicast-sessions: 0
Services-offload-sessions: 0
Failed-sessions: 1376487
Sessions-in-use: 13053
  Valid sessions: 11739
  Pending sessions: 3
  Invalidated sessions: 1311
  Sessions in other states: 0
Maximum-sessions: 262144

Flow Sessions on FPC5 PIC0:
Unicast-sessions: 12132
Multicast-sessions: 0
Services-offload-sessions: 0
Failed-sessions: 736153
Sessions-in-use: 14059
  Valid sessions: 12141
  Pending sessions: 0
  Invalidated sessions: 1918
  Sessions in other states: 0
```

```
Maximum-sessions: 262144

Flow Sessions on FPC6 PIC0:
Unicast-sessions: 12559
Multicast-sessions: 0
Services-offload-sessions: 0
Failed-sessions: 1084150
Sessions-in-use: 14522
  Valid sessions: 12487
  Pending sessions: 1
  Invalidated sessions: 2034
  Sessions in other states: 0
Maximum-sessions: 262144
```

As you can see, Junos offers a very extensive set of options when it comes to filtering the session table. You can filter on just about any session property. If you just need an overview, you can use the `show security flow session` command with modifiers to dump the matching sessions. This is good if you just need basic information about the sessions like the Flow info (including NAT translations), policy match, timeout, and the packets and bytes that are sent in both directions. You can also issue the extensive modifier after `show security flow session` and any optional filters to get the full details of the individual session. Finally, we showed session summary information. Note that this was done on a high-end SRX, so you can see the breakout of the session table on each of the SPUs. This includes open sessions, those that are pending termination (invalidated sessions), pending sessions (those that are being created), and counters on failed counters and the maximum number of firewall sessions per SPU.

Let's look at the output of one of the preceding sessions and dissect what each field stands for.

```
root@srx3600n0> show security flow session
Flow Sessions on FPC3 PIC0:

Session ID: 60000167, Policy name: 1/4, Timeout: 1800, Valid
   In: 10.102.1.87/48308 --> 207.102.2.186/80;tcp, If: xe-1/0/0.0, Pkts: 6,
Bytes: 548
  Out: 207.102.2.186/80 --> 173.167.229.50/59201;tcp, If: xe-1/0/1.0, Pkts: 5,
Bytes: 4448
```

The following output indicates that this session has the unique ID of 60000167 on the platform. It matches Policy name 1, and the timeout is 1,800 seconds. While a session is actively transmitting data, you will see the maximum timeout for that service. In this case, TCP is 30 minutes or 1,800 seconds. Valid indicates the state of that session. Other states can be pending (creation), invalid (terminated, waiting for garbage cleanup), and backup (HA).

We also see there is an IN and an OUT portion of this session. These refer to the two wings of the session, or in this case, the traffic that arrives on the firewall from client to server, and the return traffic from server to client. We see different IP addresses here because we are using source NAT for this session, so the traffic arrives from source 10.102.1.87 source port 48308 to destination 207.102.2.186 on destination port 80. The traffic arrives on interface xe-1/0/0.0. At the time of polling this command, we have seen 6 packets/528 bytes of data in this direction.

The OUT direction indicates the return of the traffic. We notice that now the server is the source and there is a different IP address in the destination because we are performing source NAT on the traffic, and the session table shows the wings exactly as they are installed on the device for how the SRX should handle the traffic as it arrives. The destination port of the OUT direction is also different from the original source port, which means that we must also be doing port overloading in the source NAT. We also see that the traffic arrives on the device on port xe-1/0/1.0 and has seen 5 packets/4,448 bytes in the server-to-client direction.

Different NAT scenarios will look different in the session table; for instance, with destination NAT you would see the translated source in the OUT direction, and if you do both source and destination NAT, both criteria would be translated in the return direction. The firewall leverages the translated data in the OUT direction because it needs to be able to perform a fast lookup when the return traffic arrives on the device. That way, we only need to do the NAT policy lookup once, then the transform instructions are attached to the firewall session behind the scenes so that we can perform fast path processing from that point on.

Sample firewall logs

Although looking at counters and session tables is useful when the traffic is live on the device, they don't give you a good audit capability, particularly after the session has closed. When it comes to firewall logs, there are three different types that we're interested in: deny logs, and session init and close logs for permitted traffic. There are three different types of data plane logs today on the SRX: standard syslog, structured syslog, and binary syslog. All three essentially contain the same information but in different formats. In this example, we dissect structured syslog (which includes the field headers) for each event.

Session close:

```
<14>1 2012-11-19T02:40:08.985 SRX210-HoneyNet RT_FLOW - RT_FLOW_SESSION_CLOSE
[junos@2636.1.1.1.2.36 reason="timeout" source-address="64.40.9.8" source-
port="51697" destination-address="172.16.42.204" destination-port="53" service-
name="junos-dns-udp" nat-source-address="64.40.9.8" nat-source-port="51697" nat-
destination-address="172.16.42.204" nat-destination-port="53" src-nat-rule-
name="None" dst-nat-rule-name="None" protocol-id="17" policy-name="Allow-
Internet" source-zone-name="LAN" destination-zone-name="HoneyNet" session-
id-32="23211" packets-from-client="1" bytes-from-client="64" packets-from-
server="1" bytes-from-server="3863" elapsed-time="2" application="junos:DNS"
nested-application="UNKNOWN" username="N/A" roles="N/A" packet-incoming-
interface="ge-0/0/0.0" encrypted="UNKNOWN"]
```

We won't go through every single field in this session because there are a lot, but we do cover the main ones. We can see this log was generated on an SRX called SRX210-HoneyNET. The source address was 64.40.9.8 and the destination was 172.16.42.204 with a destination port of 53, so we can assume the traffic was DNS. Because there was no NAT configured, we don't see any source or destination NAT rules, but if it was configured, we would see the name accordingly. The source zone of the traffic is LAN and the destination is Honeynet using the firewall policy Allow-Internet. Additionally, information about the bytes and packets sent and received is included. The elapsed time is the amount of time the session was active. The Application field is the Level 7 application, which is junos:DNS. There is no nested application here. If we were using the UserFW feature, then we would have a username and role here. We can see the traffic originated on interface ge-0/0/0.0. Encrypted refers to traffic like SSL that can be decrypted, so the answer here is really no. You can also see that the session was closed due to a timeout, which means that the ALG was likely disabled, otherwise we would have seen a message about the ALG closing the session. When TCP is used, we usually see TCP FIN or TCP RST, although there can be plenty of other reasons a session might be closed, including Layer 7 features like IPS, UTM, manually cleared by the administrator, HA, and others.

If you're wondering, RT stands for real time in the logs, which is the name of the subsystem that handles the logging on the data plane. It is called real time because it isn't saved to disk or memory (at least not on the data plane; it can be sent to the control plane).

Session init (Create):

```
<14>1 2012-11-19T03:02:24.173 SRX210-HoneyNet RT_FLOW - RT_FLOW_SESSION_CREATE
[junos@2636.1.1.1.2.36    source-address="98.109.158.154"    source-port="1329"
destination-address="172.16.42.205" destination-port="139" service-name="junos-
smb" nat-source-address="98.109.158.154" nat-source-port="1329" nat-destination-
address="172.16.42.205" nat-destination-port="139" src-nat-rule-name="None" dst-
nat-rule-name="None" protocol-id="6" policy-name="Allow-Internet" source-zone-
name="LAN"      destination-zone-name="HoneyNet"      session-id-32="30171"
username="N/A"    roles="N/A"    packet-incoming-interface="ge-0/0/0.0"    applica-
tion="UNKNOWN" nested-application="UNKNOWN" encrypted="UNKNOWN"]
```

When you have the session-init option enabled to log traffic that is permitted, the output of the syslog will look like what we just saw. Unlike the deny traffic that follows, we do see information about the NAT rules and session info, in addition to the basic flow and policy info. We don't have all of the same data that are available in the session-close log because this can only be gleaned at the end of the session.

Session deny:

```
<14>1 2012-11-19T02:55:08.975 SRX210-HoneyNet RT_FLOW - RT_FLOW_SESSION_DENY
[junos@2636.1.1.1.2.36 source-address="192.168.4.30" source-port="3690"
destination-address="172.16.42.20" destination-port="55" service-name="None"
protocol-id="6" icmp-type="0" policy-name="Block-Internal-Else" source-zone-
name="LAN" destination-zone-name="HoneyNet" application="UNKNOWN" nested-
application="UNKNOWN" username="N/A" roles="N/A" packet-incoming-
interface="ge-0/0/0.0" encrypted="UNKNOWN" reason="policy deny"]
```

It's easy to see that this session was denied by the reason field "`policy deny`" along with the fact that the log is called RT_FLOW_SESSION_DENY. Just like the preceding output, the fields are pretty much the same, but because no traffic is allowed to flow in this output, there are no data-like bytes and packets sent and received. Because the traffic is blocked at the firewall level, there isn't information about the NAT rules or session information like we see in the session-init for permitted traffic.

At the time of writing this book, you MUST use the session-init option on deny/rejected traffic to log it. Session-close will only work for permitted traffic; if you aren't seeing denied traffic in your log system, that's probably why.

Of course all of this information is in the raw text of the syslog messages. Syslog collection platforms like STRM, Security Insight, Splunk, Arcsight, and others can do a much better job of representing the data. When using external log collectors, it is usually best to use structured syslog unless they natively understand the messages (or have the binary dictionary); otherwise the logs might just be a flat text string.

Monitoring Interface Counters

There are a number of interface counters that are very helpful when it comes to troubleshooting. If you use the `extensive` parameter with the `show interfaces` operational mode command, you will get both the traditional information that you would see in other platforms and some very helpful information that is pertinent to the SRX as a security platform, most notably the flow error statistics on a per-interface basis (logged on the ingress interface). Most of these errors are self-explanatory. You can clear the stats with `clear interface statistics` or specify an interface to clear if you are troubleshooting and you want to watch how fast these counters are increasing. The error statistics can represent issues with processing traffic, as well as potential attacks from malicious parties, so it's not necessarily unlikely to see these counters present. You can further leverage flow traces to get more information about individual sessions—this is just a very quick sanity check.

```
root@srx3600n0> show interfaces xe-1/0/0.0 extensive
  Logical interface xe-1/0/0.0 (Index 70) (SNMP ifIndex 570) (Generation 135)
    Flags: SNMP-Traps 0x0 Encapsulation: ENET2
    Traffic statistics:
```

```
    Input  bytes  :          554090633312
    Output bytes  :          568304820836
    Input  packets:            3068138050
    Output packets:            1214983255
    IPv6 transit statistics:
     Input  bytes  :                     0
     Output bytes  :                     0
     Input  packets:                     0
     Output packets:                     0
   Local statistics:
    Input  bytes  :              21417726
    Output bytes  :              15835172
    Input  packets:                244984
    Output packets:                218750
   Transit statistics:
    Input  bytes  :                     0                     0 bps
    Output bytes  :                     0                     0 bps
    Input  packets:                     0                     0 pps
    Output packets:                     0                     0 pps
    IPv6 transit statistics:
     Input  bytes  :                    0
     Output bytes  :                    0
     Input  packets:                    0
     Output packets:                    0
   Security: Zone: trust
    Allowed host-inbound traffic : bootp bfd bgp dns dvmrp igmp ldp msdp nhrp
ospf pgm pim rip router-discovery rsvp sap vrrp dhcp finger ftp tftp ident-
reset http https ike netconf ping reverse-telnet
    reverse-ssh rlogin rpm rsh snmp snmp-trap ssh telnet traceroute xnm-clear-
text xnm-ssl lsping ntp sip r2cp
   Flow Statistics :
   Flow Input statistics :
     Self packets :                     14325
     ICMP packets :                     6
     VPN packets :                      0
     Multicast packets :                0
     Bytes permitted by policy :        274623218636
     Connections established :          110601667
   Flow Output statistics:
     Multicast packets :                0
     Bytes permitted by policy :        501476506302
   Flow error statistics (Packets dropped due to):
     Address spoofing:                  0
     Authentication failed:             0
     Incoming NAT errors:               0
     Invalid zone received packet:      0
     Multiple user authentications:     0
     Multiple incoming NAT:             0
     No parent for a gate:              0
     No one interested in self packets: 0
     No minor session:                  0
     No more sessions:                  2061160
```

```
        No NAT gate:                      0
        No route present:                 40
        No SA for incoming SPI:           0
        No tunnel found:                  0
        No session for a gate:            0
        No zone or NULL zone binding      0
        Policy denied:                    0
        Security association not active:  0
        TCP sequence number out of window: 1037145
        Syn-attack protection:            0
        User authentication errors:       0
      Protocol inet, MTU: 1500, Generation: 154, Route table: 0
        Flags: Sendbcast-pkt-to-re
        Addresses, Flags: Is-Preferred Is-Primary
           Destination: 10.102.1/24, Local: 10.102.1.1, Broadcast: 10.102.1.255,
Generation: 140
        Addresses, Flags: Is-Preferred
           Destination: 10.102.3/24, Local: 10.102.3.1, Broadcast: 10.102.3.255,
Generation: 142
      Protocol inet6, MTU: 1500, Generation: 155, Route table: 0
        Flags: Is-Primary
        Addresses, Flags: Is-Default Is-Preferred Is-Primary
          Destination: 2001::/120, Local: 2001::1
      Generation: 144
        Addresses, Flags: Is-Preferred
          Destination: fe80::/64, Local: fe80::221:59ff:fe8b:4090
      Protocol multiservice, MTU: Unlimited, Generation: 146
      Generation: 156, Route table: 0
        Flags: Is-Primary
        Policer: Input: __default_arp_policer__
```

Performing a Flow Trace

When the first lines of troubleshooting steps like checking the firewall logs, security policy sanity check, and counters fail, it can be useful to leverage the power of packet flow traces (or flow debugs). The SRX has the ability to dump a log of all of the decisions the SRX makes on a packet or flow to help provide guidance on what is occurring during the packet forwarding. At the time of writing this book, the flow debug is configured in the actual configuration itself rather than in operational mode, but you do have the ability to dump the debug to logfiles (including all of the standard Junos log functionality, like off-box storage, archiving, file size definitions, etc.). The following is an overview of how to configure the flow debug. Essentially, it is broken up into a few steps:

1. Define what events you would like to log: Basic-Datapath, Packet-Drops, or All.
2. Specify where you would like this information to be logged. The logfile will be stored in */var/log* on the SRX. You can optionally define the various file parameters mentioned earlier and others.

3. Define a packet filter (this is very important). Without a packet filter, the SRX will log debugs on all packets, which not only affects performance, but also will generate way too much information for you to parse without losing some sanity. The packet filter has the standard tuple information that you'd expect: Source/Destination Prefix, Source/Destination Port, Protocol, and Interface. Note that you can only define one of each parameter per filter, but you can assign multiple active filters to the debug.
4. Commit the configuration for it take effect.
5. Generate traffic and review the logfile.
6. Disable to delete the flow trace.

```
{primary:node0}[edit]
root@SRX100HM# set security flow traceoptions ?
Possible completions:
+ apply-groups         Groups from which to inherit configuration data
+ apply-groups-except  Don't inherit configuration data from these groups
> file                 Trace file information
> flag                 Events and other information to include in trace output
  no-remote-trace      Disable remote tracing
> packet-filter        Flow packet debug filters
   rate-limit                Limit the incoming rate of trace messages
(0..4294967295)
{primary:node0}[edit]
root@SRX100HM# set security flow traceoptions flag ?
Possible completions:
  all                  All events
  basic-datapath       Basic packet flow
  packet-drops         Packet drops
{primary:node0}[edit]
root@SRX100HM# set security flow traceoptions flag basic-datapath

{primary:node0}[edit]
root@SRX100HM# set security flow traceoptions file FlowTrace

{primary:node0}[edit]
root@SRX100HM# set security flow traceoptions packet-filter ?
Possible completions:
  <filter-name>        Name of the filter
{primary:node0}[edit]
root@SRX100HM# set security flow traceoptions packet-filter 1 ?
Possible completions:
+ apply-groups         Groups from which to inherit configuration data
+ apply-groups-except  Don't inherit configuration data from these groups
  destination-port     Match TCP/UDP destination port
  destination-prefix   Destination IP address prefix
  interface            Logical interface
  protocol             Match IP protocol type
  source-port          Match TCP/UDP source port
  source-prefix        Source IP address prefix
```

```
{primary:node0}[edit]
root@SRX100HM# set security flow traceoptions packet-filter 1 destination-
port 21

{primary:node0}[edit]
root@SRX100HM# show security flow traceoptions
file FlowTrace;
flag basic-datapath;
packet-filter 1 {
    destination-port 21;
}

{primary:node0}[edit]
root@SRX100HM# commit
node0:
commit complete
node1:
commit complete

{primary:node0}[edit]
root@SRX100HM# run show log FlowTrace

Nov    19    18:19:59    18:19:58.868688:CID-1:RT:<192.168.4.30/2460-
>207.17.137.56/21;6> matched filter 1:

Nov 19 18:19:59 18:19:58.868688:CID-1:RT:packet [48] ipid = 27864, @0x4232701a

Nov  19  18:19:59  18:19:58.868688:CID-1:RT:----  flow_process_pkt:  (thd  1):
flow_ctxt type 15, common flag 0x0, mbuf 0x42326e00, rtbl_idx = 5

Nov 19 18:19:59 18:19:58.868688:CID-1:RT: sysstats_inc_InCnts

Nov 19 18:19:59 18:19:58.868688:CID-1:RT: flow process pak fast ifl 71 in_ifp
reth1.0

Nov   19   18:19:59   18:19:58.868688:CID-1:RT:      reth1.0:192.168.4.30/2460-
>207.17.137.56/21, tcp, flag 2 syn

Nov  19  18:19:59  18:19:58.868688:CID-1:RT:  find  flow:  table  0x4cbeec78,  hash
4532(0xffff), sa 192.168.4.30, da 207.17.137.56, sp 2460, dp 21, proto 6, tok
20487

Nov  19  18:19:59  18:19:58.868688:CID-1:RT:   no  session  found,  start  first
path. in_tunnel - 0x0, from_cp_flag - 0

Nov 19 18:19:59 18:19:58.868688:CID-1:RT:  flow_first_create_session

Nov   19   18:19:59   18:19:58.868688:CID-1:RT:     flow_first_in_dst_nat:  in
<reth1.0>, out <N/A> dst_adr 207.17.137.56, sp 2460, dp 21

Nov  19  18:19:59  18:19:58.868688:CID-1:RT:  chose  interface  reth1.0  as  incom-
ing nat if.
```

```
Nov 19 18:19:59 18:19:58.868688:CID-1:RT:flow_first_rule_dst_xlate: DST no-xlate: 0.0.0.0(0) to 207.17.137.56(21)

Nov 19 18:19:59 18:19:58.868688:CID-1:RT:flow_first_routing: vr_id 5, call flow_route_lookup(): src_ip 192.168.4.30, x_dst_ip 207.17.137.56, in ifp reth1.0, out ifp N/A sp 2460, dp 21, ip_proto 6, tos 0

Nov 19 18:19:59 18:19:58.868688:CID-1:RT:Doing DESTINATION addr route-lookup

Nov 19 18:19:59 18:19:58.868688:CID-1:RT:  routed (x_dst_ip 207.17.137.56) from LAN (reth1.0 in 1) to reth0.0, Next-hop: 172.16.200.14

Nov 19 18:19:59 18:19:58.868688:CID-1:RT:  policy search from zone LAN-> zone Danger (0x0,0x99c0015,0x15)

Nov 19 18:19:59 18:19:58.868688:CID-1:RT:  policy has app_id 1

Nov 19 18:19:59 18:19:58.868688:CID-1:RT:  policy has timeout 900

Nov 19 18:19:59 18:19:58.868688:CID-1:RT:  app 1, timeout 1800s, curr ageout 20s

Nov 19 18:19:59 18:19:58.868688:CID-1:RT:flow_first_src_xlate:  nat_src_xlated: False, nat_src_xlate_failed: False

Nov 19 18:19:59 18:19:58.868688:CID-1:RT:flow_first_src_xlate: src nat returns status: 1, rule/pool id: 1/32772, pst_nat: False.

Nov 19 18:19:59 18:19:58.868688:CID-1:RT:  dip id = 4/1, 192.168.4.30/2460->172.16.200.7/50088 protocol 6

Nov 19 18:19:59 18:19:58.868688:CID-1:RT:  choose interface reth0.0 as outgoing phy if

Nov 19 18:19:59 18:19:58.868688:CID-1:RT:is_loop_pak: No loop: on ifp: reth0.0, addr: 207.17.137.56, rtt_idx:4

Nov 19 18:19:59 18:19:58.868688:CID-1:RT:  check nsrp pak fwd: in_tun=0x0, VSD 1 for out ifp reth0.0

Nov 19 18:19:59 18:19:58.868688:CID-1:RT:  vsd 1 is active

Nov 19 18:19:59 18:19:58.868688:CID-1:RT:-jsf : Alloc sess plugin info for session 390842026058
```

Here we can see lots of details: the packet is a new session not currently known. We perform a route lookup, determine the egress interface is reth0.0, and then do a policy lookup that matches policy 1. We see the timeout is 1,800 seconds, which is the default TCP timeout; and the current ageout is set to 20 seconds because this is the first packet in the TCP session, and the default initial TCP timeout is 20 seconds until the handshake has been completed. We also see that there is source NAT occurring here and that it is applied to Pool ID 1, no persistent NAT, the transform is defined, and the packet is sent to the physical interface to be sent out. Subsequent packets in an existing session will have much less information because they will match existing sessions and many of the lookups only need to happen on the first packet.

```
Nov       19       18:19:59       18:19:58.873415:CID-1:RT:<192.168.4.30/2460-
>207.17.137.56/21;6> matched filter 1:

Nov 19 18:19:59 18:19:58.873415:CID-1:RT:packet [44] ipid = 29333, @0x4392c8c0

Nov  19  18:19:59  18:19:58.873415:CID-1:RT:----  flow_process_pkt:  (thd  1):
flow_ctxt type 28, common flag 0x800, mbuf 0x4392c680, rtbl_idx = 0

Nov 19 18:19:59 18:19:58.873415:CID-1:RT: in_ifp <LAN:reth1.0>

Nov 19 18:19:59 18:19:58.873415:CID-1:RT:setting rtt to:0x4ccc1458 based on VR
ID:5 carried over in flow ctxt,  proto 2(ipv4)

Nov  19  18:19:59  18:19:58.873415:CID-1:RT:flow_process_pkt_exception:  setting
rtt in lpak to 0x4ccc1458

Nov  19  18:19:59  18:19:58.873415:CID-1:RT:  jsf  reinj:  ctxt  flag  0  sess
390842026058 src pid 25 reinj flag 6

Nov 19 18:19:59 18:19:58.873415:CID-1:RT:  flow session id 2122

Nov 19 18:19:59 18:19:58.873415:CID-1:RT: vector bits 0x94a2 vector 0x4ac0df20

Nov 19 18:19:59 18:19:58.873415:CID-1:RT:  vsd 1 is active

Nov 19 18:19:59 18:19:58.873415:CID-1:RT:****jsf svc chain: sess id 2122, dir
1. No more plugins

Nov 19 18:19:59 18:19:58.873415:CID-1:RT: tcp strict 3way handshake check: tcp
flag 0x2, datalen=0

Nov 19 18:19:59 18:19:58.873415:CID-1:RT:  tcp flags 0x2, flag 0x2

Nov  19  18:19:59  18:19:58.873415:CID-1:RT:    Got  syn,  192.168.4.30(2460)-
>207.17.137.56(21), nspflag 0x1621, 0x620

Nov 19 18:19:59 18:19:58.873415:CID-1:RT:flow_xlate_pak

Nov  19  18:19:59  18:19:58.873415:CID-1:RT:   post  addr  xlation:  172.16.200.7-
>207.17.137.56.

Nov  19  18:19:59  18:19:58.873415:CID-1:RT:   post  addr  xlation:  172.16.200.7-
>207.17.137.56.

Nov  19  18:19:59  18:19:58.873415:CID-1:RT:skip  pre-frag:  is_tunnel_if-  0,
is_if_mtu_configured- 0
```

```
Nov 19 18:19:59 18:19:58.873415:CID-1:RT:flow_dscp_vector: natp 0x4fdec978 dscp
0x0

Nov 19 18:19:59 18:19:58.873415:CID-1:RT: sysstats_inc_OutCnts

Nov 19 18:19:59 18:19:58.873415:CID-1:RT:mbuf 0x4392c680, exit nh 0x861bc2

Nov  19  18:19:59  18:19:58.873415:CID-1:RT:flow_process_pkt_exception:  Freeing
lpak 0x4cc6d630 associated with mbuf 0x4392c680

Nov 19 18:19:59 18:19:58.873415:CID-1:RT: ----- flow_process_pkt rc 0x0 (fp rc
0)
```

Let's take a quick look at one more example in which the traffic is denied so we are familiar with how that looks as well. I've changed my flow debug to look at port 2121, which is denied by policy, then generated the traffic.

```
{primary:node0}[edit]
root@SRX100HM# set security flow traceoptions packet-filter 1 destination-port
2121

{primary:node0}[edit]
root@SRX100HM# show security flow traceoptions
file FlowTrace;
flag basic-datapath;
packet-filter 1 {
    destination-port 2121;
}

{primary:node0}[edit]
root@SRX100HM# commit
node0:
configuration check succeeds
node1:
commit complete
node0:
commit complete
Exiting configuration mode

{primary:node0}[edit]
root@SRX100HM# run clear log FlowTrace

{primary:node0}[edit]
root@SRX100HM# run show log FlowTrace
Nov 19 18:36:09 SRX100HM clear-log[89025]: logfile cleared

Nov        19        18:36:22        18:36:21.1135406:CID-1:RT:<192.168.4.30/2604-
>207.17.137.56/2121;6> matched filter 1:

Nov 19 18:36:22 18:36:21.1135406:CID-1:RT:packet [48] ipid = 3357, @0x423c551a
```

```
Nov  19  18:36:22  18:36:21.1135406:CID-1:RT:----  flow_process_pkt:  (thd  1):
flow_ctxt type 15, common flag 0x0, mbuf 0x423c5300, rtbl_idx = 5

Nov 19 18:36:22 18:36:21.1135406:CID-1:RT: sysstats_inc_InCnts

Nov 19 18:36:22 18:36:21.1135406:CID-1:RT: flow process pak fast ifl 71 in_ifp
reth1.0

Nov   19   18:36:22   18:36:21.1135406:CID-1:RT:      reth1.0:192.168.4.30/2604-
>207.17.137.56/2121, tcp, flag 2 syn

Nov 19 18:36:22 18:36:21.1135406:CID-1:RT: find flow: table 0x4cbeec78, hash
55216(0xffff), sa 192.168.4.30, da 207.17.137.56, sp 2604, dp 2121, proto 6,
tok 20487

Nov 19 18:36:22 18:36:21.1135406:CID-1:RT:  no session found, start first path.
in_tunnel - 0x0, from_cp_flag - 0

Nov 19 18:36:22 18:36:21.1135406:CID-1:RT:  flow_first_create_session

Nov  19  18:36:22  18:36:21.1135406:CID-1:RT:     flow_first_in_dst_nat:  in
<reth1.0>, out <N/A> dst_adr 207.17.137.56, sp 2604, dp 2121

Nov 19 18:36:22 18:36:21.1135406:CID-1:RT:  chose interface reth1.0 as incoming
nat if.

Nov  19  18:36:22  18:36:21.1135406:CID-1:RT:flow_first_rule_dst_xlate:  DST  no-
xlate: 0.0.0.0(0) to 207.17.137.56(2121)

Nov  19  18:36:22  18:36:21.1135406:CID-1:RT:flow_first_routing:  vr_id  5,  call
flow_route_lookup():  src_ip  192.168.4.30,  x_dst_ip  207.17.137.56,  in  ifp
reth1.0, out ifp N/A sp 2604, dp 2121, ip_proto 6, tos 0

Nov 19 18:36:22 18:36:21.1135406:CID-1:RT:Doing DESTINATION addr route-lookup

Nov  19  18:36:22  18:36:21.1135406:CID-1:RT:   routed  (x_dst_ip  207.17.137.56)
from LAN (reth1.0 in 1) to reth0.0, Next-hop: 172.16.200.14

Nov 19 18:36:22 18:36:21.1135406:CID-1:RT:  policy search from zone LAN-> zone
Danger (0x0,0xa2c0849,0x849)

Nov 19 18:36:22 18:36:21.1135406:CID-1:RT:  app 0, timeout 1800s, curr ageout
20s

Nov 19 18:36:22 18:36:21.1135406:CID-1:RT:  packet dropped, denied by policy

Nov 19 18:36:22 18:36:21.1135406:CID-1:RT:  packet dropped,  policy deny.

Nov 19 18:36:22 18:36:21.1135406:CID-1:RT:  flow find session returns error.

Nov 19 18:36:22 18:36:21.1135406:CID-1:RT: ----- flow_process_pkt rc 0x7 (fp rc
-1)
```

As we see in the preceding output, we get the initial packet, perform destination NAT checks followed by a route lookup to determine the egress interface, and then we can determine the egress or to-zone. In this case, the context is "from LAN to Danger" and the security policy lookup matches a deny rule, thus the packet is dropped.

Enabling a flow trace should not impact the forwarding performance of the platform as long as you define specific filters. If there is no filter defined for the traffic, the SRX will process it normally. However, if the session matches the packet filter in the flow traceoption, then the SRX will record the detailed output. Ideally, this should only be done for the first few packets that are received by the SRX, not a high-speed data transfer! As long as this is honored, then the process should have a negligible impact.

The full details of a debug are admittedly a bit esoteric and verbose. Juniper has expressed interest in improving their troubleshooting facilities, so definitely stay tuned to the release notes, forums, and KBs for up-to-the-minute information on what might have changed.

At the time of writing this book, Juniper is also beta testing a new feature called monitor flow that does not require you to make a configuration change. Please monitor the current release notes for more information on this feature's release.

Performing a Packet Capture on SRX Branch

Due to the architectural differences of the high-end and branch SRX, there are two different ways to do packet captures depending on which platform you are using. For the branch, because it is a central CPU-based platform, there is a single method to collect the data. The high-end SRX has a truly granular mechanism for collecting the packet capture at multiple different locations in the platform due to the distributed nature of the architecture. You can even collect packet captures (PCAPs) at different locations in the processing path on the data plane!

Let's start with the branch SRX debug. The tasks involved include the following:

1. Enable the packet capture in the forwarding-options configuration.
2. Define the file to log this to.
3. Define the maximum bytes per packet to log (snaplength).
4. Define the firewall filter that defines the packets that you would like to match and sample.

5. Apply the firewall filter to an interface.
6. Commit.

For instance, let's log any packets that are destined to port 21 on destination IP 207.17.137.56 (*ftp.juniper.net*). Apply this to the reth0.0 interface

```
{primary:node0}[edit]
root@SRX100HM# set forwarding-options packet-capture file filename FTP

{primary:node0}[edit]
root@SRX100HM# set forwarding-options packet-capture maximum-capture-size 1500

{primary:node0}[edit]
root@SRX100HM#  set  firewall  filter  FTP  term  1  from  destination-address
207.17.137.56/32

{primary:node0}[edit]
root@SRX100HM# set firewall filter FTP term 1 from protocol tcp

root@SRX100HM# set firewall filter FTP term 1 from destination-port 21

{primary:node0}[edit]
root@SRX100HM# set firewall filter FTP term 1 then accept sample

root@SRX100HM# set firewall filter FTP term default then accept

{primary:node0}[edit]
root@SRX100HM# set interfaces reth1.0 family inet filter input FTP

{primary:node0}[edit]
root@SRX100HM# set interfaces reth1.0 family inet filter output FTP

{primary:node0}[edit]
root@SRX100HM# show interfaces reth1.0
family inet {
    primary;
    filter {
        input FTP;
        output FTP;
    }
    address 192.168.4.1/24;
}

{primary:node0}[edit]
root@SRX100HM# show forwarding-options
packet-capture {
    file filename FTP size 10000000;
    maximum-capture-size 1500;
}

{primary:node0}[edit]
```

```
root@SRX100HM# show firewall filter FTP
term 1 {
    from {
        destination-address {
            207.17.137.56/32;
        }
        protocol tcp;
        destination-port 21;
    }
    then {
        sample;
        accept;
    }
}
term default {
    then accept;
}

{primary:node0}[edit]
root@SRX100HM# commit
node0:
configuration check succeeds
node1:
commit complete
node0:
commit complete

{primary:node0}[edit]
root@SRX100HM# exit
Exiting configuration mode
```

Don't forget to set the default accept rule or else you will deny the traffic that doesn't match the filter by default! Also, the packet filter is stateless, so you might need to define both directions of the traffic (depending on how you craft your filter), including the reverse direction. When it comes to applying the filter, you need to ensure that the firewall filter matches the packet as it arrives on the firewall (pre-NAT) if you are capturing on the ingress interface, or post-NAT if capturing on the egress interface.

Regarding HA, at the time of writing this book, the SRX will create two packet capture filters, one with the ingress and one with the egress packet capture when using the capture on reth interfaces.

```
{primary:node0}
root@SRX100HM> file list /cf/var/tmp

/cf/var/tmp:
FTP.reth1
```

```
cleanup-pkgs.log
eedebug_bin_file
gksdchk.log
gres-tp/
idp_license_info
install/
kmdchk.log
krt_gencfg_filter.txt
pics/
rtsdb/
sampled.pkts
sec-download/
spu_kmd_init
usb/
vi.recover/

{primary:node0}
root@SRX100HM> start shell
root@SRX100HM% tcpdump -r /cf/var/tmp/FTP.reth1

19:01:47.102785    In  IP  192.168.4.30.2825  >  colo-ftp2.juniper.net.ftp:  S
1610170857:1610170857(0) win 65535 <mss 1460,nop,nop,sackOK>
19:01:47.167478   In  IP  192.168.4.30.2825  >  colo-ftp2.juniper.net.ftp:  .  ack
3940080389 win 65535
19:01:47.167575   In IP 192.168.4.30.2825 > colo-ftp2.juniper.net.ftp: . ack 21
win 65515
```

As you can see from this output, the SRX will log this file named *<filename>.<interface-name>* into the */var/tmp* directory. You can either grab this PCAP off of the SRX using FTP/SCP and load it onto your favorite PCAP viewer on your desktop, or you can even leverage TCPDUMP on the box and read it directly as just shown.

Performing a Packet Capture on the High-End SRX

The high-end SRX platforms leverage a different mechanism for collecting PCAPs on the data plane, as the architecture is different, so you have some additional options for the packet capture. On the high-end SRX, the name of this feature is End to End Data-path Debug because there are multiple components that play a role in the processing of a packet from ingress to egress. To aid in troubleshooting, Juniper has provided the ability to collect the PCAPs at different locations in the data plane.

The following tasks must be performed to enable end-to-end debug:

1. Define the capture file.
2. Define the maximum capture size per packet (snaplen).
3. Define the Action profile (which specifies what to do with the matched packets).
4. Define the packet filter.

5. Commit the configuration.
6. Enable Datapath Debug at the operational-mode level.
7. Capture traffic.
8. Disable Datapath Debug at the operational-mode level.
9. Convert PCAP (for export) or view locally.

This probably sounds like a lot, but it only takes a few steps. The key is to be sure to set solid packet filters that define what traffic to capture so you don't capture all traffic, and also to choose the right location to capture the PCAP. Just like the branch packet capture function, the high end allows you to define multiple packet filters, and the filters match the packets as defined. In terms of the location, you can see that you can capture the packets at many different locations in the processing path, but typically you can use NP-Ingress if you want to see what is arriving on the SRX before firewall processing, and if you need to compare what's coming in versus out, you can define NP-Egress as well. The other options are helpful, but are geared more for JTAC and developers than administrators.

There are other options besides capturing the full packet, but for our purposes, we'll just focus on the packet-capture or packet-dump option.

```
[edit]
root@srx3600n0# set security datapath-debug action-profile Capture ?
Possible completions:
+ apply-groups         Groups from which to inherit configuration data
+ apply-groups-except  Don't inherit configuration data from these groups
> event
> module
  preserve-trace-order  Preserve trace order (has performance overhead)
  record-pic-history   Record the PIC(s) in which the packet has been processed
[edit]
root@srx3600n0# set security datapath-debug action-profile Capture event ?
Possible completions:
  jexec                JExec
  lbt                  Load-Balance-Thread
  lt-enter             LT(Logical Tunnel) enter
  lt-leave             LT(Logical Tunnel) leave
  mac-egress           A2/A10 IOC Mac(broadcom) egress
  mac-ingress          A2/A10 IOC Mac(broadcom) ingress
  np-egress            NP egress
  np-ingress           NP ingress
  pot                  Packet-Order-Thread
[edit]
root@srx3600n0# set security datapath-debug action-profile Capture module ?
Possible completions:
  flow                 Flow module
```

```
[edit]
root@srx3600n0# set security datapath-debug action-profile Capture event np-
ingress ?
Possible completions:
+ apply-groups         Groups from which to inherit configuration data
+ apply-groups-except  Don't inherit configuration data from these groups
  count                Count action
  packet-dump          Packet dump action
  packet-summary       Packet summary action
  trace                Trace action
[edit]
root@srx3600n0# set security datapath-debug action-profile Capture event np-
ingress packet-dump

[edit]
root@srx3600n0# set security datapath-debug packet-filter 1 destination-port 21
action-profile Capture

[edit]
root@srx3600n0# show security datapath-debug
capture-file PCAP;
maximum-capture-size 10000;
action-profile {
    Capture {
        event np-ingress {
            packet-dump;
        }
    }
}
packet-filter 1 {
    action-profile Capture;
    destination-port 21;
}

[edit]
root@srx3600n0# commit and-quit
commit complete
Exiting configuration mode

root@srx3600n0> request security datapath-debug st
                                                 ^
syntax error, expecting <command>.
root@srx3600n0> request security datapath-debug ?
Possible completions:
  capture
root@srx3600n0> request security datapath-debug capture st
                                                         ^
'st' is ambiguous.
Possible completions:
  start                Start datapath debug packet capture
  stop                 Stop datapath debug packet capture
```

```
root@srx3600n0> request security datapath-debug capture start
datapath-debug capture started on file PCAP

###Generate Traffic###

root@srx3600n0> request security datapath-debug capture stop
datapath-debug capture succesfully stopped, use show security datapath-debug
capture to view

root@srx3600n0> show security datapath-debug capture
Packet 1: (C0/F11:np-ingress)
00 21 59 8b 40 90 02 1a c5 01 00 49 08 00 45 00
00 38 21 dd 40 00 20 06 20 07 0a 66 01 49 0a 66
02 c8 97 9f 00 15 e1 39 26 a6 00 00 00 00 90 02
16 a0 03 9a 00 00 02 04 05 b4 01 01 08 0a 1f 41
6d 23 00 00 00 00
Packet 2: (C0/F11:np-ingress)
00 21 59 8b 40 90 02 1a c5 01 00 49 08 00 45 00
00 28 21 3f 40 00 20 06 20 b5 0a 66 01 49 0a 66
02 c8 97 9f 00 15 e1 39 26 a7 63 86 8a 6f 50 10
16 a0 f2 cc 00 00 00 00 00 00 00 00
Packet 3: (C0/F11:np-ingress)
00 21 59 8b 40 90 02 1a c5 01 00 49 08 00 45 00
00 28 21 38 40 00 20 06 20 bc 0a 66 01 49 0a 66
02 c8 97 9f 00 15 e1 39 26 a7 63 86 8a 7c 50 10
1c 54 ed 0b 00 00 00 00 00 00 00 00
```

This is something, but not exactly human readable. Let's convert it to something we and PCAP viewers like Wireshark/TCP Dump can understand.

```
root@srx3600n0% e2einfo -Ccapture -Snormalize -I PCAP -F output.pcap
sucessfully convert 1491 packets
root@srx3600n0% tcpdump -r PCAP -c 5
Reverse lookup for 10.102.1.73 failed (check DNS reachability).
Other reverse lookup failures will not be reported.
Use <no-resolve> to avoid reverse lookups on IP addresses.

02:13:28.340303   C0/F11   event:1(np-ingress)   IP   10.102.1.73.38815   >
10.102.2.200.ftp: S 3778619046:3778619046(0) win 5792 <mss 1460,nop,nop,time-
stamp 524381475 0>
02:13:28.359050   C0/F11   event:1(np-ingress)   IP   10.102.1.73.38815   >
10.102.2.200.ftp: . ack 1669761647 win 5792
02:13:28.359999   C0/F11   event:1(np-ingress)   IP   10.102.1.73.38815   >
10.102.2.200.ftp: . ack 14 win 7252
02:13:28.360370   C0/F11   event:1(np-ingress)   IP   10.102.1.73.38815   >
10.102.2.200.ftp: P 0:16(16) ack 14 win 7252
02:13:28.361917   C0/F11   event:1(np-ingress)   IP   10.102.1.73.38815   >
10.102.2.200.ftp: . ack 51 win 8712
root@srx3600n0% tcpdump -r output.pcap -c 5
Reverse lookup for 10.102.1.73 failed (check DNS reachability).
Other reverse lookup failures will not be reported.
Use <no-resolve> to avoid reverse lookups on IP addresses.
```

```
02:13:28.340303     IP     10.102.1.73.38815     >     10.102.2.200.ftp:     S
3778619046:3778619046(0) win 5792 <mss 1460,nop,nop,timestamp 524381475 0>
02:13:28.359050 IP 10.102.1.73.38815 > 10.102.2.200.ftp: . ack 1669761647 win
5792
02:13:28.359999 IP 10.102.1.73.38815 > 10.102.2.200.ftp: . ack 14 win 7252
02:13:28.360370 IP 10.102.1.73.38815 > 10.102.2.200.ftp: P 0:16(16) ack 14 win
7252
02:13:28.361917 IP 10.102.1.73.38815 > 10.102.2.200.ftp: . ack 51 win 8712
```

In this output, we use the e2e configure tool to convert the original capture PCAP to output.pcap. The syntax is `e2einfo -Ccapture -Snormalize -I <end-to-end-debug-pcap> -F <standard pcap>`. Although TCP dump does a decent job of parsing the original PCAP (we can see the metadata about the np-ingress info in the header) most other programs like Wireshark will scoff at the capture as corrupted. Once the capture is converted, you can retrieve it from the SRX and export it to your host machine with FTP/SCP for better viewing.

Sample Deployment

Now that we have covered so many concepts in this chapter, let's leverage an example that examines the key concepts we have discussed in this chapter. The example is configured as follows:

- Configure an intrazone policy for the "trust" zone that permits ICMP between hosts but blocks any other communication between hosts in the trust zone that crosses the firewall.
- Configure a security policy from "trust" to "untrust" called HTTP-Business-Hours that only allows HTTP on TCP port 80 and 8000 out to the Internet between 9 a.m. and 5 p.m. Monday through Friday. All internal hosts from the subnet 192.168.1.0/24 should be allowed to talk to the Internet. Log this traffic in a way that collects the most information about the traffic being sent.
- Configure the firewall to actively terminate any other traffic in the trust to untrust zone rather than silently drop it.
- Enable the SIP ALG and configure it for UDP port 5061, which is a port that some VoIP solutions use rather than 5060. This service should have a timeout of five times the normal timeout of UDP.
- Create a policy called Internal-VoIP that allows the internal users in the subnet 192.168.1.0/24 of the trust to connect on the new custom SIP application to destination voip.company.local. The firewall should be able to dynamically change the IP address of this object if it changes in the internal infrastructure without having to reconfigure the SRX. The VoIP server is in the zone Internal-Servers.

- Create a policy from zone Branch-Office to zone Internal-Servers that allows any cash registers at IP address 10.x.100.50 to talk to servers 172.16.100.50-100. Make an application set for this policy that includes HTTP, ICMP, FTP, and SSH.
- Create a policy that allows only host 192.168.1.100 from the trust zone to connect to the SRX via SSH. Log these connections.
- Finally, create a global policy that silently drops and logs any other traffic.

```
[edit]
root@srx3600n0# set security zones security-zone trust

[edit]
root@srx3600n0# set security zones security-zone untrust

[edit]
root@srx3600n0# set security policies from-zone trust to-zone trust policy
Allow-ICMP match source-address any destination-address any application junos-
icmp-all

[edit]
root@srx3600n0# set security policies from-zone trust to-zone trust policy
Allow-ICMP then permit

root@srx3600n0# set security policy from-zone trust to-zone trust policy
Block-All-Else match source-address any destination-address any application
any

[edit]
root@srx3600n0# set security policies from-zone trust to-zone trust policy
Block-All-Else then deny

[edit]
root@srx3600n0# set applications application Custom-HTTP-8000 protocol tcp
destination-port 8000

[edit]
root@srx3600n0# set security address-book global address 192.168.1.0/24
192.168.1.0/24

[edit]
root@srx3600n0# set schedulers scheduler Business-Hours daily start-time
09:00:00 stop-time 17:00:00

[edit]
root@srx3600n0# set schedulers scheduler Business-Hours saturday exclude

[edit]
root@srx3600n0# set schedulers scheduler Business-Hours sunday exclude

[edit]
root@srx3600n0# set security policies from-zone trust to-zone untrust policy
```

```
HTTP-Business-Hours match source-address 192.168.1.0/24 destination-address
any application [junos-http Custom-HTTP-8000]

[edit]
root@srx3600n0# set security policies from-zone trust to-zone untrust policy
HTTP-Business-Hours then permit

[edit]
root@srx3600n0# set security policies from-zone trust to-zone untrust policy
HTTP-Business-Hours then log session-close

[edit]
root@srx3600n0# set security policies from-zone trust to-zone untrust policy
HTTP-Business-Hours scheduler-name Business-Hours

[edit]
root@srx3600n0# set security policeis from-zone trust to-zone untrust policy
Reject-All-Else match source-address any destination-address any application
any

[edit]
root@srx3600n0# set security policies from-zone trust to-zone untrust policy
Reject-All-Else then reject

[edit]
root@srx3600n0# set applications application Custom-SIP-5061 protocol udp
destination-port 5061 application-protocol sip inactivity-timeout 300

[edit]
root@srx3600n0# set security policies from-zone trust to-zone Internal-
Servers policy Internal-VoIP match source-address 192.168.1.0/24 destination-
address voip.company.local application Custom-SIP-5061

[edit]
root@srx3600n0# set security policies from-zone trust to-zone Internal-
Servers policy Internal-VoIP then permit

[edit]
root@srx3600n0# set security zones security-zone Branch-Office

[edit]
root@srx3600n0# set security address-book global address Cash-Registers
wildcard-address 10.0.100.50/255.0.255.255

[edit]
root@srx3600n0# set security address-book global address Servers range-
address 172.16.100.50 to 172.16.100.100

[edit]
root@srx3600n0# set applications application-set Cash-Register-Apps applica-
tion junos-http
```

```
[edit]
root@srx3600n0# set applications application-set Cash-Register-Apps applica-
tion junos-icmp-all

[edit]
root@srx3600n0# set applications application-set Cash-Register-Apps applica-
tion junos-ftp

[edit]
root@srx3600n0# set applications application-set Cash-Register-Apps applica-
tion junos-ssh

[edit]
root@srx3600n0# set security policies from-zone Branch-Office to-zone
Internal-Servers policy Cash-Register match source-address Cash-Registers
destination-address Servers application Cash-Register-Apps

[edit]
root@srx3600n0# set security policies from-zone Branch-Office to-zone
Internal-Servers policy Cash-Register then permit

[edit]
root@srx3600n0# set security policies from-zone trust to-zone junos-host poli-
cy Allow-SSH match source-address 192.168.1.100 destination-address any appli-
cation junos-ssh

[edit]
root@srx3600n0# set security policies from-zone trust to-zone junos-host poli-
cy Allow-SSH then permit

[edit]
root@srx3600n0# set security policies from-zone trust to-zone junos-host poli-
cy Allow-SSH then log session-close

[edit]
root@srx3600n0# set security policies global policy Drop-All match source-
address any destination-address any application any

[edit]
root@srx3600n0# set security policies global policy Drop-All then deny

[edit]
root@srx3600n0# set security policies global policy Drop-All then log session-
init

[edit]
root@srx3600n0# show security policies
from-zone trust to-zone trust {
    policy Allow-ICMP {
        match {
            source-address any;
            destination-address any;
```

```
                application junos-icmp-all ;
            }
            then {
                permit;
            }
        }
        policy Block-All-Else {
            match {
                source-address any;
                destination-address any;
                application any;
            }
            then {
                deny;
            }
        }
    }
    from-zone trust to-zone untrust {
        policy HTTP-Business-Hours {
            match {
                source-address 192.168.1.0/24;
                destination-address any;
                application [ junos-http Custom-HTTP-8000 ];
            }
            then {
                permit;
                log {
                    session-close;
                }
            }
            scheduler-name Business-Hours;
        }
        policy Reject-All-Else {
            match {
                source-address any;
                destination-address any;
                application any;
            }
            then {
                reject;
            }
        }
    }
    from-zone trust to-zone Internal-Servers {
        policy Internal-VoIP {
            match {
                source-address 192.168.1.0/24;
                destination-address voip.company.local;
                application Custom-SIP-5061;
            }
            then {
                permit;
```

```
        }
    }
}
from-zone Branch-Office to-zone Internal-Servers {
    policy Cash-Register {
        match {
            source-address Cash-Registers;
            destination-address Servers;
            application Cash-Register-Apps;
        }
        then {
            permit;
        }
    }
}
from-zone trust to-zone junos-host {
    policy Allow-SSH {
        match {
            source-address 192.168.1.100;
            destination-address any;
            application junos-ssh;
        }
        then {
            permit;
            log {
                session-close;
            }
        }
    }
}
global {
    policy Drop-All {
        match {
            source-address any;
            destination-address any;
            application any;
        }
        then {
            deny;
            log {
                session-init;
            }
        }
    }
}


[edit]
root@srx3600n0# show security address-book
global {
    address 192.168.1.0/24 192.168.1.0/24;
    address voip.company.local {
```

```
            dns-name voip.company.local;
        }
        address Cash-Registers {
            wildcard-address 10.0.100.50/255.0.255.255;
        }
        address Servers {
            range-address 172.16.100.50 {
                to {
                    172.16.100.100;
                }
            }
        }
    }

[edit]
root@srx3600n0# show applications
application Custom-HTTP-8000 {
    protocol tcp;
    destination-port 8000;
}
application Custom-SIP-5061 {
    application-protocol sip;
    protocol udp;
    destination-port 5061;
    inactivity-timeout 300;
}
application-set Cash-Register-Apps {
    application junos-http;
    application junos-ftp;
    application junos-ssh;
    application junos-icmp-all;
}

[edit]
root@srx3600n0# show security zones
security-zone trust;
security-zone untrust;
security-zone Internal-Servers;
security-zone Branch-Office;

[edit]
root@srx3600n0# show schedulers
scheduler Business-Hours {
    daily {
        start-time 09:00:00 stop-time 17:00:00;
    }
    sunday exclude;
    saturday exclude;
}
```

Summary

In this chapter, we covered the security policy components of the SRX. Security policies provide a centralized pivot point for processing of traffic on the SRX. They define how traffic should be matched, along with how it will be processed. There are a lot of options when it comes to processing traffic, many of which we discussed here and some that are discussed in later chapters, like UTM, IPS, and AppSecure. By not only learning how security policies function, but also how to properly leverage them for administrative purposes, you can create powerful security policies that are easy to maintain, reduce your attack surface, and provide visibility for your infrastructure. Without a good understanding of how security policies function, you will not be able to effectively enforce other security controls in the platform. We will constantly reference the security policies throughout the other chapters in this book, so this chapter is not only effective as an educational tool but also as a reference!

Study Questions

Questions

1. What type of firewall inspection does the SRX perform and how does it logically separate network segments?
2. What is a security policy context?
3. What are the three types of security policy contexts and in which order are they evaluated?
4. How does the firewall determine the source and destination (from and to) zones?
5. In what order are the rules in a security policy context evaluated?
6. How are network segments classified by zones?
7. Is intrazone traffic permitted by default?
8. What parameters make up the match criteria for a security rule?
9. True or False: You need to define a reverse policy to allow the return traffic from server to client to flow properly.
10. What is the difference between a regular address object and a wildcard address object?
11. What is the difference between an address object that uses the “dns-name” attribute and one that just specifies the name in the fully qualified domain name (FQDN) format?
12. What type of objects can be part of an address or application set?
13. At what layers does the application object operate?

14. What is an ALG and how does it function?
15. What is policy rematch?
16. What are the main actions that a firewall can take on the traffic and which option allows you to leverage further processing options?
17. What is the difference between Log and Count?
18. What is the difference between session init and session close?
19. What are the default timeouts for TCP, UDP, and other protocols?
20. What is the difference between configuring a policy for IPv4 and IPv6?
21. When creating a new firewall rule in the CLI, where in the rulebase is the rule placed by default?

Answers

1. The SRX is a stateful firewall that leverages security zones to logically separate network segments.
2. A security policy context is a pair of security zones that define the direction traffic will take. Traffic arrives on the source zone and leaves the destination zone (e.g., trust to untrust). All security policies in this context follow in that traffic direction.
3. Intrazone, interzone, and global. They are evaluated in that order.
4. The source (from) zone is determined by which interface the traffic arrives on in the firewall, whereas the destination (to) zone is determined by either a routing lookup in Layer 3 or a switching lookup in Layer 2 transparent mode to determine what the egress interface is. Once the egress interface is known, the system knows what the egress zone is, and thus the security policy context in which to match a firewall rule.
5. The rules within a context are evaluated from top to bottom, looking for the most specific match. Once a match is found, no more rules are evaluated.
6. Network segments are classified by zones by placing interfaces into zones. Technically this is at the IFL level (subinterface) so you can have an untagged interface in a zone or individual VLANs in separate zones.
7. No, unlike ScreenOS, intrazone traffic requires a security policy to be permitted.
8. From-To-Zone, Source Address, Destination Address, and Application. Starting in Junos 12.1, Source-Identity is also on this list. Schedulers are not technically under the match criteria but in their own way are a match criteria based on time and day.
9. False. The firewall will automatically allow return traffic for a given session back to the client. You do not need to define a return rule.

10. A standard address entry follows the standard variable length subnet mask notation with both an address prefix and a subnet mask. The subnet mask bits must be contiguous. A wildcard address object specifies an address prefix but rather than a contiguous mask, the bits in the wildcard mask do not need to be contiguous. This is useful for making address objects that follow some convention like all Odd/Even objects or all objects with a specific IP address in the last octet. For instance, if you have retail environments where every cash register and printer uses the .10 address in a subnet, 192.168.x.10/255.255.0.255. The wildcard mask in this case would match the first, second, and fourth octets, but not the third. You don't have to do this on octet boundaries; any bit combination is acceptable.
11. When you use the `dns-name` attribute, that triggers the SRX to dynamically resolve the hostname at policy commit time, boot time, and every time the TTL expires or the cache list is purged. If you specify the address object by name without the `dns-name` attribute, then the firewall will immediately resolve the name and put the IP address into the configuration at commit time, but it will not be automatically resolved after that point.
12. Address sets can have any address object type or other address sets in them (e.g., address, DNS name, wildcard, range, and other address sets), whereas application sets can have any application objects and other application object sets.
13. Application objects primarily operate at Layer 3 and Layer 4 (technically they can be used to specify ALGs, which in a way operate at Layer 7). These are different than dynamic application objects (covered in Chapter 12), which truly operate at Layer 7 and match patterns and application behaviors in the protocol stream.
14. An ALG is an application layer gateway. It is used to monitor the control channels of applications and determine if auxiliary firewall sessions called pinholes must be opened. They operate at Layer 7. Some ALGs are also used to permit or deny application behaviors within the traffic stream.
15. Policy rematch instructs the firewall to reevaluate firewall policies for existing sessions when changes are made to the security rulebase. Essentially, the firewall rules will be reevaluated as if they were at the beginning of the session.
16. The three primary options for actions in the security policy are permit, deny, and reject. Permit allows the traffic, deny silently drops the traffic, and reject drops the traffic but sends a TCP reset for TCP and a ICMP message if it is non-TCP. Only permit allows you to configure other processing options, because if the traffic is dropped, there is no point in performing additional actions.
17. Both log and count are optional actions that can be taken regardless of which action is selected (permit, deny, reject). Log triggers a syslog message to be

generated, whereas count tracks the data throughput for the given firewall rule on which it is configured.

18. Session init triggers a log message when the session is created (ideal for troubleshooting or deny/reject sessions), whereas session close triggers a log message when the session closes. The session-close option has a lot more information than session init because additional information about the traffic is only available at session close (duration, bytes sent or received, application type, reason for close, and others), whereas session init can only define the state of the connection when the traffic is established.

19. By default, TCP has a 30-minute idle timeout, UDP has a 60-second idle timeout, known IP traffic has a 30-minute idle timeout, and unknown has a 60-second idle timeout. Idle means that there is no traffic passing through the device for the session; if the timeout is reached, the session will be cleared. A session can be closed by TCP Reset/FIN, ALG, Level 7 service like IPS/AppSecure/UTM, manually cleared, or by other system events, along with aging out from the idle timeout.

20. There is not any difference between IPv4 and IPv6 objects in security policies; they can be referenced independently or concurrently in security policies. There are some limitations with IPv6 when it comes to address objects like range and wildcard support, but within policies you can use them side by side with IPv4 and IPv6. It is important to point out that at the time of writing this book, an address object can only have one time, either IPv4 or IPv6, but not both. This also goes for "any" objects.

21. The rule is placed at the bottom of the security policy context (e.g., trust to untrust; it will be the bottom rule until you move it).

CHAPTER 9

Network Address Translation

Network Address Translation (NAT) is a fascinating and storied technology in computer networks. Perhaps more than any other network technology, NAT has found itself in the corner of many different use cases. Originally developed to extend the life of the IPv4 protocol after the exhaustion of the 4 billion public IP addresses (because an IPv4 address has 32 bits, and thus there are 2^{32} available addresses). From its original purpose it gained wide popularity as a security technology to hide IP addresses and prevent inbound network connections, and now has seen many other uses. Today, it is being used extensively by service providers for carrier-grade NAT, by network administrators worldwide for IPv4 to IPv6 translation, and even on virtual machine hosts. Who would have seen a single physical computer needing to leverage NAT 15 years ago? Although it certainly isn't the sexiest technology discussed in this book, it is necessary in most contemporary networks and can provide other benefits to provide a transparent network experience to users on their networks.

In this chapter, we focus on the core NAT technologies offered by the SRX. We start with a discussion of how NAT is processed on the SRX, with a thorough look at how it is implemented and configured from an administrative perspective. We delve into each of the different core NAT technologies supported on the SRX, including source, static, and destination NAT. We also examine IPv6 with NAT, including IPv4 to IPv6 NAT translations so that you can adapt to the exhaustion of available IPv4 addresses and a smooth translation to IPv6.

The Need for NAT

For those of you who are not extensively familiar with NAT, it is primarily used for a few functions. First, it was originally developed to extend the life of IPv4 by creating private address ranges that could be hidden behind the public address ranges on the Internet. In that way, fewer public IP addresses are needed for each individual and organization connecting to the Internet. The private addresses are not unique, and are not valid on the Internet, so they must be translated to public IP addresses before they can be routed on the Internet. It's similar to having a telephone private branch exchange (PBX) with internal extensions versus public phone numbers. Inside the network you can just dial the extensions and connect directly with other members of the internal network, but someone from the outside cannot dial those extensions directly without the PBX handling them based on a publically routable phone number. Likewise, you need to have the PBX handle the routing of your phone call to outbound destinations or else you won't be able to communicate with entities outside of your network.

Besides using NAT for extending the IP address ranges of IPv4, some network engineers took it a step further and intentionally leveraged NAT to hide the true IP addresses of their internal infrastructure so that it was much more difficult for attackers to connect directly to the addresses.

NAT can also be used for other utility functions like redirecting traffic from one IP port to another (even if not using public–private address ranges), and with IPv6 you can use it to translate between IPv4 and IPv6.

Finally, NAT can be used in some large-carrier ISP environments to further extend customer access when IP addresses are in short supply or when they are migrating from one range to another.

NAT as a Security Component?

Some network security engineers feel that NAT is truly a security component. In our opinion, that is a bit of a fallacy. It is true that NAT provides another layer of configuration that an attacker would have to hop through, but it's nothing that a properly configured security policy couldn't also do. The problem with using NAT as a security vector is that attackers have largely shifted their tactics with contemporary attacks. For instance, NAT doesn't help you with services that need to be available on the Internet; it merely translates the traffic from the public to the private addresses (both malicious attacks and legitimate traffic). Although it does hide the internal source address of the public host, if attackers can compromise that host, they will be able to glean information about the internal network architecture anyway. And, of course, NAT isn't going to help much with data exfiltration attacks like SQL injection or other data leakage.

With regard to protecting internal clients with NAT, attackers have found an enormous attack surface on the client machines of the network. New applications that try to provide a better user experience along with common applications installed on most user machines (Flash, Adobe PDF, Java, ActiveX, MS Office, etc.) have become a very reliable exploitation base. The attackers use various mechanisms to lure clients to malicious sites where they can exploit them. These methods include phishing and spear fishing, hijacking legitimate sites, leveraging forums, and drive-by downloads. Thus the client comes to the server and NAT cannot offer protection.

So what's the moral of this section? Use NAT as a networking tool for multiplexing IP addresses onto your network without requiring a public IP address per host, use it to translate between private–public ranges, and use it to translate between protocols (e.g., IPv4 to IPv6). Although it will give you some implicit security benefits, these are not anything that you're not able to get with other mechanisms. Don't cut yourself short thinking that NAT will solve your security challenges. You will need to go much deeper with other services like UTM and IPS (along with other network and host-based protections) to provide in-depth security.

Junos NAT Fundamentals

In the early design phase of developing the SRX platform, it was clear that although ScreenOS had been wildly successful as a platform, its NAT capabilities left something to be desired. There was very little that you couldn't do with ScreenOS NAT, but that didn't mean that you might not have to jump through some hoops. ScreenOS primarily relied on two forms of NAT: interface-based NAT (Mapped IP 1:1, Destination IP 1:Many, and Virtual IP Many:1) and NAT directly referenced in the security policy rule itself. There were plenty of differences between these two models, with overlaps in functionality, many caveats to each approach, and the loss of some flexibility because the NAT was either tied to an interface or to a specific security policy rule. Although this often worked fine for simple use cases, it became much more difficult when it came to advanced NAT, where you would need granular rules. Additionally, there were many scenarios that required you to configure NAT on loopback interfaces, create pseudo-routes, and group NAT objects together to achieve the desired functionality. In addition, it could be more difficult to troubleshoot due to the fact that NAT could be placed in so many locations (does the dreaded trust interface NAT come to mind?).

The good news is that with the shortcomings of ScreenOS in mind, we set out to design a far superior model in Junos that leverages the best of simplicity, granularity, and flexibility in a new policy-based NAT approach. The Junos model varies from ScreenOS (see Table 9-1) in that it takes a policy-like approach to NAT, where NAT has its own rulebases with match and action criteria similar to firewall policies. NAT itself is abstracted from the security policies and other components like interfaces, although it can take in the properties of these rulesets to function. In Junos 11.2r2 and newer releases, we can also leverage address objects themselves in the NAT policies for a simpler user experience.

Table 9-1. ScreenOS versus Junos NAT

Feature	ScreenOS	SRX
One to one NAT	Mapped IP (MIP) at interface level	Static NAT via NAT Policy
Source NAT (many to one)	Dynamic IP (DIP) at interface level Interface NAT (NAT vs. route mode per interface) Dynamic IP via Security Policy	Source NAT via NAT Policy

Feature	ScreenOS	SRX
Destination NAT (many to one)	Virtual IP (VIP) at interface level Virtual IP in the Security Policy	Destination NAT via NAT Policy
Proxy-ARP	Implicitly enabled when using MIP/DIP/VIP Configurable entries per interface/IP address	Configurable per interface/IP address

Throughout this chapter when describing the different forms of NAT with examples, we might refer to internal/external and private/public mapping. It's important to understand that these are purely topical; you can use any of these technologies in different scenarios (e.g., translating one public IP address to another, or using source NAT to translate one private IP address to another). In the broader discussions (outside of the specific examples) we're just referring to the most familiar uses of these technologies for the sake of discussion.

Junos NAT Types

Before we get too far into the discussion of how NAT works and how to configure and operate it, let's talk about what the three different types of Junos NAT are, and when you would use them.

- Static NAT is a 1:1 bidirectional NAT that maps one IP address to another. For instance, in the trust zone the IP address might be 1.1.1.1, but when it goes out the untrust zone, it will be mapped to 2.2.2.2. Because this NAT is bidirectional, if the traffic comes in the reverse direction, it will be mapped from 2.2.2.2 to 1.1.1.1, security policy permitting. This means that you don't need to manually create a reverse NAT entry for this mapping (as you'll see later). The main use case for this type of NAT is when you have a host on which you want to perform NAT and you want both inbound access to this host and outbound access to come from the same IP address. Often it is used in DMZ scenarios where you have enough IP addresses present that you don't want to overload the public IP addresses, or if you want to simply hide the internal addressing scheme without overloading or multiplexing of the IP addresses for simplicity.
- Source NAT is a many:1 NAT that can map many IP addresses to one or more addresses, but not in a 1:1 fashion like static NAT. This NAT is dynamically allocated in real time based on the available IP addresses and ports in the pool. Unlike static NAT, there is no reverse entry so to speak (well, there is one exception with full cone NAT, but that is outside the scope of this book). For instance, you might want to hide all hosts in the trust zone in the subnet 192.168.1.0/24 behind a public IP address 2.2.2.3 when they connect out to the Internet. Hosts on the Internet cannot make a new connection back to the hosts because it is not a bidirectional form of NAT like static NAT. The typical use case for source NAT is to hide clients within

a network behind one or more IP addresses when they browse out to the Internet. Because public IP addresses (particularly with IPv4) are at a premium, especially these days now that all ranges have been allocated since 2012, source NAT is a technology used in almost all networks. Everything from home broadband routers to mobile ISPs leverage source NAT to multiplex multiple hosts behind shared IP addresses. Some administrators also feel that NAT is a security mechanism. Although there is some truth to this, it is more of a side effect than the true purpose of NAT, and attackers have found numerous ways around NAT as a security mechanism. Source NAT can also be used to connect to trading partners when you use internal IP addresses to hide overlap, or to simplify routing and security on both sides.

- Destination NAT is a 1: many form of NAT that allows you to map a single IP address to multiple IP addresses. For instance, inbound connections to IP address 2.2.2.4 in the untrust zone could be mapped to internal machines at 1.1.1.2, 1.1.1.3, 1.1.1.4, and 1.1.1.5. The mechanism to determine which internal host to map them to would be based on the port number in the destination IP address of the connection. For instance, if a packet arrives on 2.2.2.4 with destination port 25 (2.2.2.4:25), it will go to 1.1.1.2, 2.2.2.4:80 to 1.1.1.3, 2.2.2.4:443 to 1.1.1.4, and 2.2.2.4:10000 to 1.1.1.5. The main use case for this is when you are limited in the public IP addresses that you have but you need to make multiple services available on the Internet. If you don't have enough public IP addresses to map 1:1 using static NAT, then you would need to use destination NAT. Destination NAT maps a table based on the destination IP address and destination port. This will translate the IP address to the internal address, and optionally you can also translate the destination port as well. Occasionally it is also used when there is IP address overlap (e.g., with a trading partner over a private IP network) where you might need to translate both the source and the destination IP addresses but you do not have enough IP addresses for 1:1 NAT.

We'll explore more examples throughout this chapter, so a basic understanding of what each of the three types does is a great place to be at this point.

IPv6 was introduced to the SRX starting in Junos 10.2. NAT first became available in the Junos 11.2 releases for NAT 66, and then in 12.1 for NAT translation between IPv4 and IPv6. We'll assume you're running Junos 12.1 or newer code in this chapter for maximum feature support.

NAT Precedence in the Junos Event Chain

As we have referenced many times before in this book, the Junos packet flow is critical to understand when it comes to NAT implementation in the SRX, particularly for the policy lookup when the first packet arrives. When the initial packet arrives, the SRX will actually perform static NAT and destination NAT before it does the routing lookup or policy lookup, as we can see in Figure 9-1. This is because we are a zone-based firewall and we need to determine the security zone context. We know what the from-zone is based on the fact that we know what interface (and thus zone) the traffic arrived on, but to determine the egress interface (and thus the to-zone), we need to do a route lookup. If NAT is performed on the destination address of the packet (e.g., from the Internet inbound to an internal machine with a private address), we will need to perform NAT on the destination first to get the internal address, so that we can perform the route lookup. Technically you can do destination-based NAT to translate the destination IP address for any location; it doesn't have to be an internal resource, but that's definitely the most common use case.

At this point, you might be wondering what the difference is between static and destination NAT. Hold on to that thought, but for now just mentally note that they occur before the route lookup and that static NAT has precedence over destination NAT.

So now we've performed a transform on the destination address of the packet if there is a static or destination NAT rule configured that says to do so. What next? As mentioned, we perform a route lookup to determine the egress interface, and thus the egress zone. Now we can actually look for the matching security policy to determine how to process this traffic further.

Looking at Figure 9-1, we see that after the policy lookup we then perform the reverse static NAT and then source NAT (more to come on what both of these mean shortly). Why don't we put the reverse static NAT and source NAT before the security policy, you might ask? The answer is simple: performance. We need to do the destination NAT so we can determine the egress interface and thus the egress zone for the security policy, but we don't need to determine the source NAT at that stage. Instead we can defer that decision until after the policy lookup so that we don't waste cycles doing another lookup if we're just going to drop the traffic anyway. We'll see more about the interesting implications that this has on the traffic later in this chapter.

Now that the NAT transforms and policy lookups are complete, we perform any Layer 7 services and install the session into the firewall table. When the next packet arrives for this session, we match the session, so we don't have to do all of these lookups again. Instead, we fast path the traffic. We see that screens (packet based) and TCP (sanity checks like sequence/state) are performed, followed by NAT, where NAT refers to the transforms, so we don't need to do another policy lookup after the initial policy lookup.

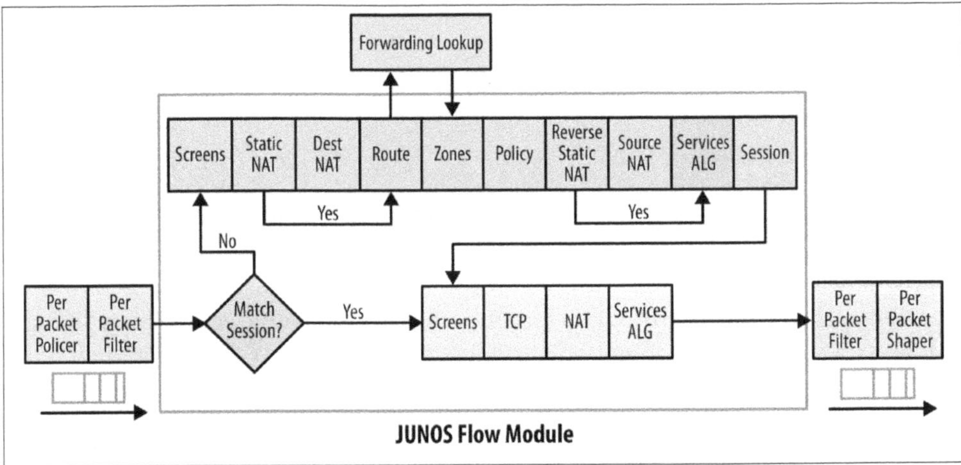

Figure 9-1. Junos packet flow

At the time of writing this book, Junos NAT is only supported in Layer 3 mode, not in transparent mode.

NAT type precedence

The important takeaway from Figure 9-1 when it comes to NAT is that you can only have one type of NAT for both source and destination. Static NAT is bidirectional so it applies to both the source and destination IP or ports, whereas source or destination NAT is unidirectional, for its respective type of NAT. Static NAT always takes precedence over destination or source NAT if an entry is present. If there is no entry found for static NAT, then the destination NAT rulebase will be examined. The same is true for static NAT on the Source fields; if there is an entry, it will take precedence over source NAT. The NAT that is performed on the Source and Destination fields are mutually exclusive. It can be summarized as follows:

1. Static NAT transform on destination address if matching static NAT rule is present.
2. If no static NAT entry is matched for the destination address, then check for a match in the destination NAT ruleset and perform the transform if an entry is found.
3. Static NAT transform on source address if matching static NAT rule is present.
4. If no static NAT entry is matched for the source address, then check for a match in the source NAT ruleset and perform the transform if an entry is found.

The following would be valid examples:

- Static NAT
- Source NAT only
- Destination NAT only
- Source and destination NAT

In the scenario when you have static + source NAT or static + destination NAT, the static entry would always take precedence over the source or destination NAT if there is an overlapping entry. This is because if there is a static NAT for the destination or source, we will bypass the respective lookup for the destination or source NAT. The system will still let you configure this example; it will just be shadowed. We're going to go much deeper into NAT examples throughout this chapter, so don't worry if you don't entirely follow the differences here, just make sure that you understand that there is precedence and which NAT takes precedence.

Junos NAT Components

Now that we have a fundamental understanding of the packet flow on the SRX when it comes to Junos NAT, we can have a more in-depth discussion of how you as the administrator can actually accomplish NAT on the SRX. To do so, we cover the different NAT components including rulesets, rules, match criteria, pools, interfaces, and proxy-arp from a high level, then dig into how this pertains to each type of NAT: static, source, and destination.

Rulesets

The first component of NAT that we discuss is rulesets. Rulesets are to NAT as security contexts are to security policies (e.g., trust to untrust). NAT rulesets define a context that contains NAT rules with match and action criteria. The main difference with rulesets in NAT versus contexts in security policies, is that in security policies the contexts have a source zone and destination zone, one each per context, and it can only be a zone (e.g., trust to untrust). With NAT, you have a bit more granular control. You can not only define a zone ruleset based on zones, but also based on interfaces or routing instance. The NAT ruleset acts as the context for which the firewall should select which table of rules should be evaluated. In a way, it is a match criterion for the traffic, but its purpose is twofold. First, it creates a nice administrative separation for the administrator to group rules that should be evaluated together, and second, it helps performance by splitting up the rules into logical groups so that rather than evaluating every potential NAT rule for that given type, we can evaluate only the ones that match the traffic direction.

In fact, unlike security contexts where you can only have one from- and to-zone per context, with NAT rules you can have multiple interfaces, zones, or routing instances per context—although you cannot mix two types, so you could for instance, have both interfaces xe-1/0/0 and xe-1/0/1, or zones trust and untrust, but not interface xe-1/0/0 and zone trust in a single ruleset. This might sound a bit confusing at first, but we'll provide some examples shortly to solidify your understanding.

Static NAT rulesets

Static NAT rulesets are evaluated before the routing lookup, so therefore you can only match on the from (source) interface, zone, or routing instance for the context. For instance, when the packet arrives and it is a member of a new session in Figure 9-1, we know what interface it arrived on, and because that interface is tied to both a zone and a routing instance, we thus know what the source context will be for that packet. We then do a lookup in these rulesets to find a matching rule.

Note that because static NAT is 1:1, meaning it is bidirectional (in fact the only NAT that is truly bidirectional), the SRX will automatically create a reverse mapping for translations in the opposite direction. Of course, you still need to have a security policy that permits the traffic, it's just that the reverse transform is automatic.

Destination NAT rulesets

Destination NAT rulesets, like static rulesets, are evaluated before the routing lookup, so they only leverage the from (source) interface, zone, or routing instance for the context. The main difference here is that this rule is only from inbound sessions to translate the destination address. Traffic initiated in the opposite direction will not be matched to this rule. Notice how we say that this is for traffic that is initiated; this is because we always handle the transforms for both directions of a flow, but the SRX does not automatically create a reverse mapping for NAT in the opposite direction like it does with static NAT.

Source NAT rulesets

Source NAT rulesets are evaluated after the routing/policy lookup, so the SRX knows not only the source interface, zone, or routing instance, but also the destination interface, zone, or routing instance. Thus both items are taken into account when determining which source NAT ruleset to use to find the specific match rule.

NAT ruleset precedence

Earlier we mentioned that you can have multiple NAT rulesets within each NAT type (static, source, and destination) and also you can have different criteria for the context, either interface, zone, or routing instance. Although you can have multiple criteria such as two different zones or interfaces (logical OR) you can only have one context type per ruleset. That said, you can have contexts made of one or more interfaces, zones, or routing instances for each NAT type. So how does the SRX determine which ruleset to select? The precedence is in this order:

1. Match context by interface
2. Match context by zone
3. Match context by routing instance

NAT ruleset precedence example. Let's take a look at matching precedence. We omit the actual rules themselves and just use static NAT for simplicity for this precedence example. We'll dive into the rules and each of the NAT types shortly.

Let's say that we are looking for rules within the following four contexts. Assuming that interfaces xe-1/0/0 and xe-1/0/1 are in the trust zone and the trust routing instance, we'd first try to find a rule in ruleset 1 because it's interface based and the most specific ruleset, then we would search 2 for a match, then 3, and then ruleset 4, until we found a match. If no match was found, no NAT would be performed. If we had another interface xe-1/0/2 that was in the untrust routing instance, then we'd only check ruleset 5 and skip the others. As mentioned, the order looks for a matching rule (which we get into shortly) and then performs the action. Like the security policy, the rules are terminal; if we find a match, we don't search any further. If no match is found, NAT will not be performed for that type.

```
[edit security nat static]
root@srx3600n0# show
rule-set 1 {
    from interface xe-1/0/0.0;
}
rule-set 2 {
    from interface [ xe-1/0/0.0 xe-1/0/1.0 ];
}
rule-set 3 {
    from zone trust;
}
rule-set 4 {
    from routing-instance trust;
}
rule-set 5 {
    From routing-instance untrust;
}

[edit]
root@srx3600n0# show security zones
security-zone trust {
    interfaces {
        xe-1/0/0.0;
        xe-1/0/1.0;
    }
```

```
}
security-zone untrust {
    interfaces {
        xe-1/0/2.0;
    }
}

[edit]
root@srx3600n0# show routing-instances
trust {
    instance-type virtual-router;
    interface xe-1/0/0.0;
    interface xe-1/0/1.0;
}
untrust {
    instance-type virtual-router;
    interface xe-1/0/2.0;
}
```

NAT Interfaces, Pools, and Mapping Objects

When you configure a NAT rule to define the transform that should happen when the match criteria is met, you must specify how the session should be modified. To do this, we rely on three different types of objects to simplify configuration and also allow easy reuse of common configuration elements. Here we are not referring to the match criteria (which can be IP prefixes or address objects), but rather the transform objects.

Static NAT transforms

When you are using static NAT, there are three types of mapping objects that you can use to define the transform.

IP prefix
: This is a standard `<ip-address/subnet-mask>` combination. It is supported for both IPv4 and IPv6.

Prefix-name
: This is also known as an address object from the address book. This allows you to use a predefined object like you would in the security policy rather than having to specify the prefix again. This can be used for both IPv4 and IPv6.

Inet
: This is used when you want to convert IPv4 to IPv6 (and vice versa) and is based on stripping the first 96 bits off the IPv6 address (128 bits) to leave the last 32 (the number of bits for an IPv4 address.) For instance, if you had an IPv6 /96 prefix of 2001::/96 and an IP network of 192.168.1.0/24, then it would map to 2001::192.168.1.0 → 192.168.1.0 with masks up to 32 bits of the IPv4 address. Note

that the translation is automatic; you just need to make sure that you have properly defined the IPv4 and IPv6 networks. We'll examine this further with an example.

Source NAT transforms

Interfaces. When using source NAT, you can specify that the source addresses of the sessions matching the NAT rule should be translated to appear as the interface IP address of the egress interface itself. This is only applicable for source NAT, and not for static or destination NAT. Typically, this option is used when you are limited in the number of public IP addresses that you have available so you cannot use a pool of multiple IP addresses, or if you want to hide all of the matching traffic behind a specific IP rather than break out into a pool. As mentioned, in this case, the IP address will be the same as the egress interface.

Interfaces can be used both as the primary form of NAT as well as a backup option when NAT pools are exhausted. Interfaces force you to leverage NAT overloading where multiple internal IP addresses are mapped to a single public IP address. This has to be done with overloading because we are multiplexing more than one internal IP address to a single external IP address, so we can't map 1:1.

Pools. There are two types of source NAT pools: standard pools and overflow pools. The main difference is that the standard pools will be used primarily until they are exhausted, and overflow pools are used after that point to prevent connectivity issues. With source NAT, you can use different types of mapping, including dynamically allocated 1:1 source NAT where each internal host gets a public IP address (different than static because you don't hardcode the mappings, they are allocated at runtime) as well as overloaded scenarios where hosts get mapped to public IP addresses that are shared by leveraging port overloading.

Earlier versions of Junos only allowed you to define source NAT pools with more than one IP address, but this restriction has been lifted in the modern code so you can now define source pools with just one IP address or more.

Destination NAT pools

Destination NAT also leverages pools to perform the NAT transform, although it uses these exclusively. The pool defines what the destination should be translated to and, optionally, if the destination port should be translated as well.

NAT Rules

After the NAT ruleset context is matched for a given type, then the rules within the ruleset are evaluated for a match. Just like security policy rules, the NAT rules are evaluated from top to bottom in the ruleset for a match. If a match is found, it is a terminal match, meaning that we will not evaluate any other NAT rules, but perform the action dictated in that rule. If no matches are found in the ruleset, other less specific NAT rulesets will be evaluated for each type, as we discussed in the last section regarding NAT ruleset precedence. If no other NAT rulesets or rules match, then no NAT will occur on this traffic.

NAT and Security Policies

Earlier we discussed the fact that NAT can affect the match criteria of the security policy, and now that we have had a discussion of the NAT components and how they work, we can dig into the actual implications. We recall that static NAT for the destination IP address and destination NAT (both for the destination IP address and optionally the application port) happen before the security policy lookup, with the static NAT on the source address and source NAT happening after the policy lookup.

What does this mean in terms of the match criteria that you should use in your security policies when using NAT? The following rules summarize the strategy:

1. When transforming the destination IP address, the translated IP address should be used in the security policy as the match criteria, not the original address that is in the packet when it arrives on the device. This is because the IP address will be translated before the SRX does the policy lookup.
2. When transforming the source IP address using either static NAT or source NAT, because this transform happens after the policy lookup, you should use the original or untranslated IP address in your security policy.

When using Juniper IPS, your rulesets should always use the translated IP addresses in the match criteria of the policy. This is because the IPS maintains its own security policy, but this lookup happens at the end of the processing chain after both destination and source NAT occur, so the IPS will always see the translated IP addresses.

We demonstrate the concepts that we have discussed here in the next section with a security policy for each example with the NAT transformation for completeness.

Proxy-ARP and Proxy-NDP

We need to cover one final concept before we dive into the actual configuration of NAT: Proxy-ARP and Proxy-NDP (Neighbor Discovery Protocol, the equivalent for IPv6). Proxy-ARP and Proxy-NDP are required for IPv4 and IPv6, respectively, when you are performing NAT and using a public range that is local to the subnet of the egress interface rather than a routed subnet. For instance, in Figure 9-2, the subnet 198.18.6.0/24 and 2001::198:18:6:0/120 are shared between the MX480 Internet router and the SRX3600 firewall. If the SRX is going to leverage addresses from these ranges as public IP addresses in their NAT pool, they must leverage Proxy-ARP and Proxy-NDP for this to function properly.

In this case, where the SRX is using IP addresses in the shard range, it must respond to ARP/NDP requests on behalf of the IP addresses for which it is proxying. Without the proxy ARP/NDP the neighboring router will not know what MAC address maps to the respective IP address. That is unless the ARP entry is statically coded on the router, but that is not a good idea, as entries can change, as can the router, so it's best to use Proxy-ARP/NDP on the firewall itself.

Proxy-ARP/NDP simply informs the interface to which it is applied to respond to incoming ARP/NDP requests for IP addresses with its own interface MAC address so that the peer device will forward traffic destined to the NAT addresses to the firewall, which will handle the traffic and translation from there.

Configuring Proxy-ARP/NDP

Taking Figure 9-2, let's configure Proxy-ARP/NDP on the ge-0/0/0 interface of the SRX to respond to any inbound requests for the NAT ranges with its own MAC address for both IPv4 and IPv6. In terms of the configuration, you can either define individual addresses to perform Proxy-ARP/NDP, or in this example, because we have contiguous ranges, we can use the "low address to high address" format. You can have multiple IPs or ranges per interface; the main requirement is that the ARP/NDP range must be within the subnet range of the interface, and it must not include the interface IP address itself. You do not have to specify the MAC address of the interface, as the SRX will automatically handle that.

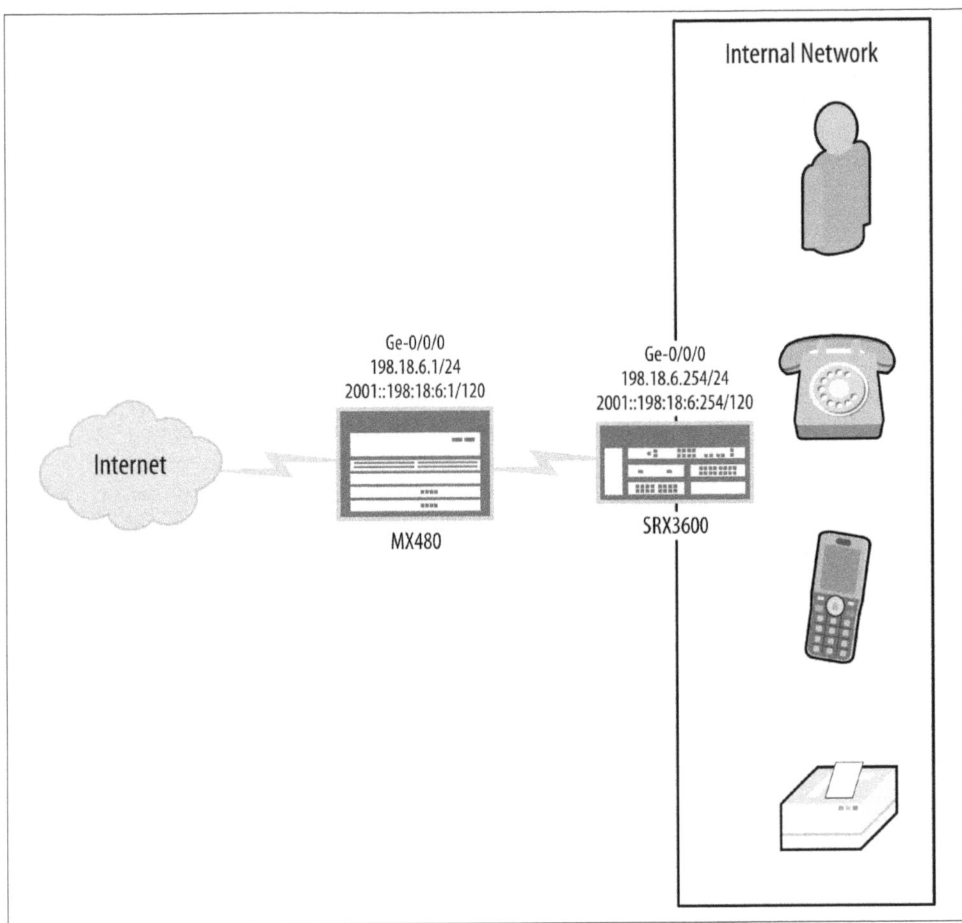

Figure 9-2. Proxy-ARP/Proxy-NDP example

```
[edit]
root@srx3600n0# set security nat proxy-arp interface ge-0/0/0 address
198.18.6.2 to 198.18.6.253

[edit]
root@srx3600n0# set security nat proxy-ndp interface ge-0/0/0 address
2001::198:18:6:2 to 2001::198:18:6:253

[edit]
root@srx3600n0# show security nat proxy-arp
interface ge-0/0/0.0 {
    address {
        198.18.6.2/32 to 198.18.6.253/32;
    }
}
```

```
[edit]
root@srx3600n0# show security nat proxy-ndp
interface ge-0/0/0.0 {
    address {
        2001::198:18:6:2/128 to 2001::198:18:6:253;
    }
}
```

If you're moving from ScreenOS, you might be wondering why you never had to define a Proxy-ARP/NDP statement there but you do in Junos. The reason was that in Junos you would configure the MIP/VIP/DIP on the interface itself, and the ScreenOS device would automatically resolve the IP/MAC mapping and perform Proxy-ARP on your behalf. Although this was handled in ScreenOS, there were plenty of shortcomings in using NAT tied to interfaces. So when we moved to Junos and went with the policy-based approach, we got a far superior model, though you do have to manually add the proxy-arp/ndp statements.

When you don't need Proxy-ARP/NDP. Proxy-ARP/NDP, got it right? Whenever you use a subnet range for any type of NAT that doesn't include the interface itself, you need to define proxy-arp/NAT. What about when you don't need to use it? There are two main scenarios:

1. You are using interface-based NAT (so the SRX will respond to the ARP request automatically because it owns the IP address already).
2. When you are using a subnet for NAT that is not tied to the shared network between the firewall and the upstream router.

Figure 9-3 exemplifies precisely when you don't need to use NAT. If we are doing source NAT or destination NAT on interface 198.18.6.2 / 2001::198:18:6:2, then the SRX will handle the proxy ARP automatically with no special configuration needed. With the NAT range 198.18.7.0/24/2001::198:18:7:0/120 that is handled by the SRX3600, it is not in the local subnet that is shared between the MX 480 and the SRX 3600 (198.18.6.0/30 / 2001::198:18:6:0/126), so the MX will not ARP for the traffic. However, although you don't need any Proxy-ARP/NDP configuration because it is not in the same subnet, you do need to make sure that the MX has a route for 198.18.7.0/24 and 2001::198:18:7:0/120 pointing to the SRX's ge-0/0/0 interface (198.18.6.2 and 2001::198:18:6:2) or else the traffic will never arrive on the SRX. This is an important point because often you might not control the upstream device, so you need to make sure your service provider adds this route or you won't see the traffic!

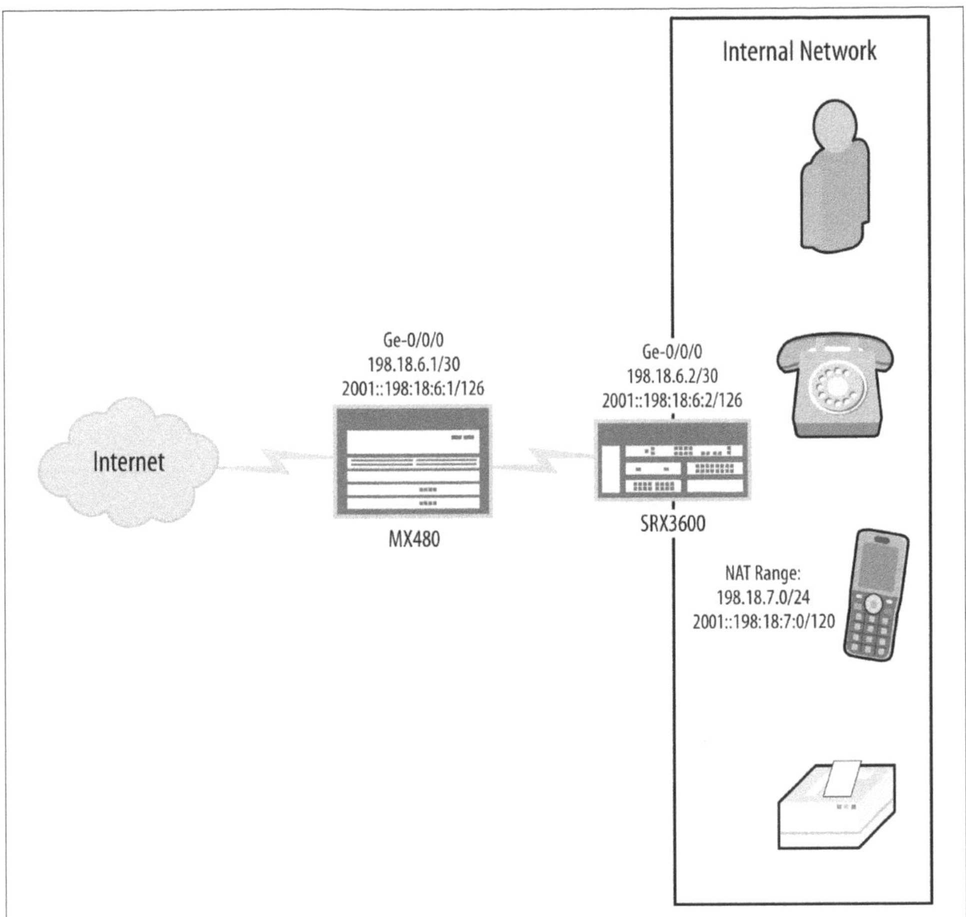

Figure 9-3. NAT network diagram

Junos NAT in Practice

Now that we have discussed the fundamentals and the components of NAT, we put it all together and work through examples of applying NAT in actual configurations so that we can solidify your understanding of these concepts in practical hands-on applications that you are likely to come across yourself in your operation of the SRX platform. We start with static NAT and examine the different deployment options for these features, and we follow that up with source and, finally, destination NAT. By the end of this section, you should have a good understanding of how these technologies are applied. We discuss both IPv4 and IPv6 NAT for each NAT type. Figure 9-4 serves as a model for the NAT configuration in this section.

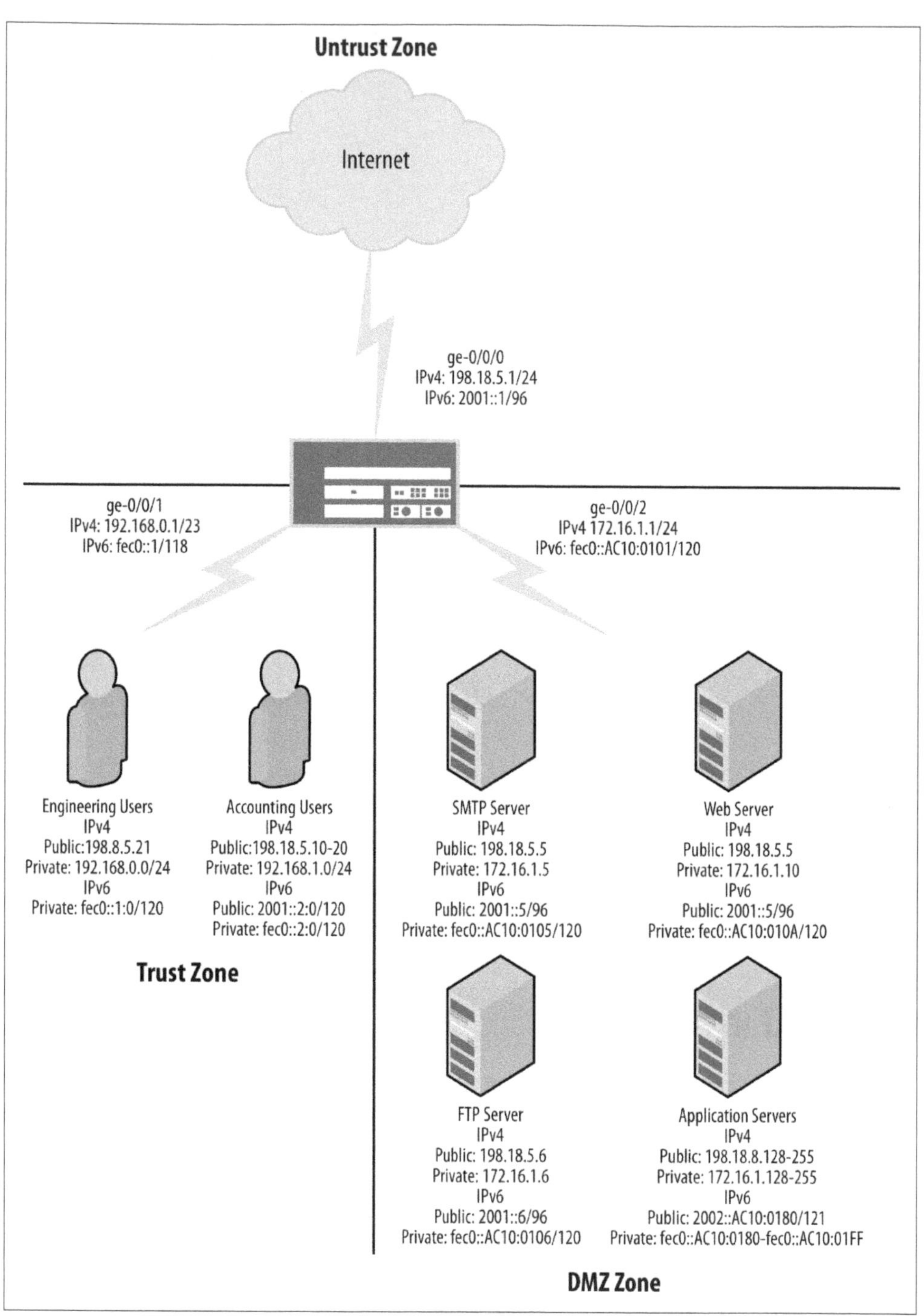

Untrust Zone
Internet
ge-0/0/0
IPv4: 198.18.5.1/24
IPv6: 2001::1/96
ge-0/0/1
IPv4: 192.168.0.1/23
IPv6: fec0::1/118
ge-0/0/2
IPv4 172.16.1.1/24
IPv6: fec0::AC10:0101/120
Engineering Users
IPv4
Public:198.8.5.21
Private: 192.168.0.0/24
IPv6
Private: fec0::1:0/120
Accounting Users
IPv4
Public:198.18.5.10-20
Private: 192.168.1.0/24
IPv6
Public: 2001::2:0/120
Private: fec0::2:0/120
Trust Zone
SMTP Server
IPv4
Public: 198.18.5.5
Private: 172.16.1.5
IPv6
Public: 2001::5/96
Private: fec0::AC10:0105/120
Web Server
IPv4
Public: 198.18.5.5
Private: 172.16.1.10
IPv6
Public: 2001::5/96
Private: fec0::AC10:010A/120
FTP Server
IPv4
Public: 198.18.5.6
Private: 172.16.1.6
IPv6
Public: 2001::6/96
Private: fec0::AC10:0106/120
Application Servers
IPv4
Public: 198.18.8.128-255
Private: 172.16.1.128-255
IPv6
Public: 2002::AC10:0180/121
Private: fec0::AC10:0180-fec0::AC10:01FF
DMZ Zone

Figure 9-4. NAT example topology

Static NAT

We start our first set of examples taking a look at static NAT because it has the simplest functionality, being 1:1 in nature. We examine both IPv4 and IPv6 in the two examples in this section. We can see that the FTP server and the application servers will be using 1:1 NAT based on the nature of the public and private mappings.

Static NAT one-to-one mapping

For the first example, we configure NAT for our FTP server, which is the simple 1:1 static NAT. We configure both IPv4 and IPv6 for this example. We configure both the NAT and the security policy statement from untrust to DMZ to permit FTP traffic to this server.

```
[edit]
root@srx3600n0# set interfaces ge-0/0/0 unit 0 family inet address 198.18.5.1/24

[edit]
root@srx3600n0# set interfaces ge-0/0/0 unit 0 family inet6 address 2001::1/96

[edit]
root@srx3600n0# set interfaces ge-0/0/2 unit 0 family inet address 172.16.1.1/24

[edit]
root@srx3600n0#  set  interfaces  ge-0/0/2  unit  0  family  inet6  address
fec0::AC10:0101/120

[edit]
root@srx3600n0# set security forwarding-options family inet6 mode flow-based

[edit]
root@srx3600n0# set security zones security-zone untrust interfaces ge-0/0/0

[edit]
root@srx3600n0# set security zones security-zone dmz interfaces ge-0/0/2

[edit]
root@srx3600n0# set security nat proxy-arp interface ge-0/0/0 address 198.18.5.6

[edit]
root@srx3600n0# set security nat proxy-ndp interface ge-0/0/0 address 2001::6

[edit]
root@srx3600n0#   set   security   address-book   global   address   FTP-Server-
v4-172.16.1.6/32 172.16.1.6/32

[edit]
root@srx3600n0#   set   security   address-book   global   address   FTP-Server-v6-
fec0::AC10:0106/120 fec0::AC10:0106/120
```

```
[edit]
root@srx3600n0# set security nat static rule-set Static-NAT rule FTP-v4 match
destination-address 198.18.5.6

[edit]
root@srx3600n0# set security nat static rule-set Static-NAT rule FTP-v4 then
static-nat prefix-name FTP-Server-v4-172.16.1.6/32

[edit]
root@srx3600n0# set security nat static rule-set Static-NAT rule FTP-v6 match
destination-address 2001::6

[edit]
root@srx3600n0# set security nat static rule-set Static-NAT rule FTP-v6 then
static-nat prefix-name FTP-Server-v6-fec0::AC10:0106/120

[edit]
root@srx3600n0# set security policies from-zone untrust to-zone dmz policy FTP-
Inbound match source-address any destination-address [FTP-Server-
v4-172.16.1.6/32 FTP-Server-v6-fec0::AC10:0106/120] application junos-ftp

[edit]
root@srx3600n0# set security policies from-zone untrust to-zone dmz policy FTP-
Inbound then permit

[edit]
root@srx3600n0# set security policies from-zone untrust to-zone dmz policy FTP-
Inbound then log session-close

[edit]
root@srx3600n0# show interfaces
ge-0/0/0 {
    unit 0 {
        family inet {
            address 198.18.5.1/24;
        }
        family inet6 {
            address 2001::1/96;
        }
    }
}
ge-0/0/2 {
    unit 0 {
        family inet {
            address 172.16.1.1/24;
        }
        family inet6 {
            address fec0::AC10:0101/120;
        }
    }
}
```

```
[edit]
root@srx3600n0# show security zones
security-zone untrust {
    interfaces {
        ge-0/0/0.0;
    }
}
security-zone dmz {
    interfaces {
        ge-0/0/2.0;
    }
}

[edit]
root@srx3600n0# show security nat
static {
    rule-set Static-NAT {
        from zone untrust;
        rule FTP-v4 {
            match {
                destination-address 198.18.5.6/32;
            }
            then {
                static-nat {
                    prefix-name {
                        FTP-Server-v4-172.16.1.6/32;
                    }
                }
            }
        }
        rule FTP-v6 {
            match {
                destination-address 2001::6/128;
            }
            then {
                static-nat {
                    prefix-name {
                        FTP-Server-v6-fec0::AC10:0106/120;
                    }
                }
            }
        }
    }
}
proxy-arp {
    interface ge-0/0/0.0 {
        address {
            198.18.5.6/32;
        }
    }
}
```

```
proxy-ndp {
    interface ge-0/0/0.0 {
        address {
            2001::6/128;
        }
    }
}

[edit]
root@srx3600n0# show security forwarding-options
family {
    inet6 {
        mode flow-based;
    }
}

[edit]
root@srx3600n0# show security policies from-zone untrust to-zone dmz
policy FTP-Inbound {
    match {
        source-address any;
            destination-address [ FTP-Server-v4-172.16.1.6/32 FTP-Server-v6-
fec0::AC10:0106/120 ];
        application junos-ftp;
    }
    then {
        permit;
        log {
            session-close;
        }
    }
}
```

Let's dissect this example a bit for some clarity. First, we just went through the fundamental tasks of defining the interface and zone configurations. Note that because we are using IPv6 we also have to make sure that it is configured under `set security forwarding-options inet6`. Note that this requires a reboot to take place, so typically you'll want to do this ahead of time for the proper configuration parsing. Next, we defined some address objects for this configuration because we'll need to use them in the security policy. What should be noted here is that we used the internal addresses rather than the external. Back to our earlier theory, because we translate the destination IP address first, we need to use the internal address in our security policy or else the traffic won't be properly matched.

Because we are using public IP addresses that are in the shared subnet between our firewall and the upstream device on the ge-0/0/0 interface, we need to make sure that we configure both a Proxy-ARP and a Proxy-NDP entry on the SRX so that it will properly respond to those requests.

Next we define a static NAT ruleset from zone untrust. This will handle the translation bidirectionally (from untrust to dmz and dmz to untrust). In the rules themselves we opted to use the IP prefix as the match object and the address book object as the transform. We could have done it the other way around or used address objects or prefixes for both, just to demonstrate some flexibility. The match criteria for this example would have been the public IPv4/IPv6 addresses, and the action criteria would be translated addresses used in the DMZ.

Finally, we define the security rule that allows FTP to be accessed from the untrust network in the DMZ. As mentioned before, because the security policy lookup is done after the destination address transform, we use the internal address objects in the policy.

Static NAT many-to-many mapping

Another static NAT scenario that can occur is when you have a wide number of addresses that you want to translate between. Assuming that the IP addresses are contiguous on both sides (e.g. 192.168.1.1 → 10.0.0.1 ... 192.168.1.254 → 10.0.0.254) then you can leverage a major shortcut for NAT processing, a per-prefix translation. In this example, we perform NAT for our application servers. There will be three options: one where we do a simple NAT transform for both IPv4 and IPv6 ranges (NAT44, NAT66), the second option for IPv6 (NAT64) using a static mapping, and the third option using NAT Port Translation (NATPT) to automatically translate the IPv6 address to an IPv4 address by stripping off the leading /96 bits of the IPv6 address.

For the next three examples, we are doing network-to-network translations to show a wide variety of examples, but they can also be used for host-to-host translations as well.

Option 1: NAT44/NAT66. Configure NAT44 and NAT66 mapping to translate application servers for both ranges to their respective range of the same protocol. Allow HTTP inbound to these servers, and allow the servers to connect outbound on HTTPS.

```
[edit]
root@srx3600n0# set interfaces ge-0/0/0 unit 0 family inet address 198.18.5.1/24

[edit]
root@srx3600n0# set interfaces ge-0/0/0 unit 0 family inet6 address 2001::1/96

[edit]
root@srx3600n0# set interfaces ge-0/0/2 unit 0 family inet address 172.16.1.1/24

[edit]
root@srx3600n0#  set  interfaces  ge-0/0/2  unit  0  family  inet6  address
fec0::AC10:0101/120
```

```
[edit]
root@srx3600n0# set security forwarding-options family inet6 mode flow-based

[edit]
root@srx3600n0# set security zones security-zone untrust interfaces ge-0/0/0

[edit]
root@srx3600n0# set security zones security-zone dmz interfaces ge-0/0/2

[edit]
root@srx3600n0# set security address-book global address Application-Servers-v4-
Public-198.18.8.128/25 198.18.8.128/25

[edit]
root@srx3600n0# set security address-book global address Application-Servers-v6-
Public-2002::AC10:0180/121 2002::AC10:0180/121

[edit]
root@srx3600n0# set security address-book global address Application-Servers-v4-
Public-198.18.8.128/25 198.18.8.128/25

[edit]
root@srx3600n0# set security address-book global address Application-Servers-v6-
Public-2002::AC10:0180/21 2002::AC10:0180/121

[edit]
root@srx3600n0# set security address-book global address Application-Servers-v4-
Private-172.16.1.128/25 172.16.1.128/25

[edit]
root@srx3600n0# set security address-book global address Application-Servers-v6-
Private-fec0::AC10:0180/121 fec0::AC10:0180/121

[edit]
root@srx3600n0# set security nat static rule-set Application-Servers from inter-
face ge-0/0/0

[edit]
root@srx3600n0# set security nat static rule-set Application-Servers rule
AppServer-v4 match destination-address-name Application-Servers-v4-
Public-198.18.8.128/25

[edit]
root@srx3600n0# set security nat static rule-set Application-Servers rule
AppServer-v4 then static-nat prefix-name Application-Servers-v4-
Private-172.16.1.128/25

[edit]
root@srx3600n0# set security nat static rule-set Application-Servers rule
AppServer-v6 match destination-address-name Application-Servers-v6-
Public-2002::AC10:0180/121
```

```
[edit]
root@srx3600n0# set security nat static rule-set Application-Servers rule
AppServer-v6 then static-nat prefix-name Application-Servers-v6-Private-
fec0::AC10:0180/121

[edit]
root@srx3600n0# set security policies from-zone untrust to-zone dmz policy
Inbound-HTTP match source-address any destination-address [Application-Servers-
v4-Private-172.16.1.128/25 Application-Servers-v6-Private-fec0::AC10:0180/121 ]
application junos-http

[edit]
root@srx3600n0# set security policies from-zone untrust to-zone dmz policy
Inbound-HTTP then permit

[edit]
root@srx3600n0# set security policies from-zone untrust to-zone dmz policy
Inbound-HTTP then log session-close

[edit]
root@srx3600n0# set security policies from-zone dmz to-zone untrust policy
Outbound-HTTPS match source-address [Application-Servers-v4-
Private-172.16.1.128/25 Application-Servers-v6-Private-fec0::AC10:0180/121 ]
destination-address any application junos-https

[edit]
root@srx3600n0# set security policies from-zone dmz to-zone untrust policy
Outbound-HTTPS then permit

[edit]
root@srx3600n0# set security policies from-zone dmz to-zone untrust policy
Outbound-HTTPS then log session-close

[edit]
root@srx3600n0# show interfaces
ge-0/0/0 {
    unit 0 {
        family inet {
            address 198.18.5.1/24;
        }
        family inet6 {
            address 2001::1/96;
        }
    }
}
ge-0/0/2 {
    unit 0 {
        family inet {
            address 172.16.1.1/24;
        }
        family inet6 {
            address fec0::AC10:0101/120;
```

```
        }
    }
}

[edit]
root@srx3600n0# show security zones
security-zone untrust {
    interfaces {
        ge-0/0/0.0;
    }
}
security-zone dmz {
    interfaces {
        ge-0/0/2.0;
    }
}

[edit]
root@srx3600n0# show security forwarding-options
family {
    inet6 {
        mode flow-based;
    }
}

[edit]
root@srx3600n0# show security address-book
global {
    address Application-Servers-v4-Public-198.18.8.128/25 198.18.8.128/25;
                address    Application-Servers-v6-Public-2002::AC10:0180/121
2002::AC10:0180/121;
    address Application-Servers-v4-Private-172.16.1.128/25 172.16.1.128/25;
                address    Application-Servers-v6-Private-fec0::AC10:0180/121
fec0::ac10:0180/121;
}

[edit]
root@srx3600n0# show security nat
static {
    rule-set Application-Servers {
        from interface ge-0/0/0.0;
        rule AppServer-v4 {
            match {
                                destination-address-name  Application-Servers-v4-
Public-198.18.8.128/25;
            }
            then {
                static-nat {
                    prefix-name {
                        Application-Servers-v4-Private-172.16.1.128/25;
                    }
                }
```

```
            }
        }
        rule AppServer-v6 {
            match {
                                        destination-address-name  Application-Servers-v6-
Public-2002::AC10:0180/121;
            }
            then {
                static-nat {
                    prefix-name {
                        Application-Servers-v6-Private-fec0::AC10:0180/121;
                    }
                }
            }
        }
    }
}

[edit]
root@srx3600n0# show security policies from-zone untrust to-zone dmz
policy Inbound-HTTP {
    match {
        source-address any;
           destination-address  [  Application-Servers-v4-Private-172.16.1.128/25
Application-Servers-v6-Private-fec0::AC10:0180/121 ];
        application junos-http;
    }
    then {
        permit;
        log {
            session-close;
        }
    }
}

[edit]
root@srx3600n0# show security policies from-zone dmz to-zone untrust
policy Outbound-HTTPS {
    match {
               source-address  [  Application-Servers-v4-Private-172.16.1.128/25
Application-Servers-v6-Private-fec0::AC10:0180/121 ];
        destination-address any;
        application junos-https;
    }
    then {
        permit;
        log {
            session-close;
        }
    }
}
```

Let's break down this example a little bit. First, because the public ranges 2002::AC10:0180/121 and 198.18.8.128/25 are not in the same range as the ge-0/0/0 interface, we did not have to use proxy-arp/ndp. What isn't shown is that whatever the upstream router is, it would need to route both subnets to the SRX via 198.18.5.1 and 2001::1 for IPv4/IPv6, respectively.

Next, just to show some contrast in our NAT rulebase, we used the interface context (ge-0/0/0) rather than a zone or routing instance. We discussed the merits of using one or another earlier in the chapter. In this case, either would have worked, but if you had multiple interfaces in the untrust zone, you might want to use specific NAT for specific interfaces, and that is how it could be done. Next, we used an address book entry for both the IPv4 and IPv6 entries, just to show that this could be done rather than using the prefix for one or another as we did in the last example. As you noticed, we transitioned the entire subnets from one to another, rather than doing a 1:1 translation for each address separately.

Finally, in this example we show the applications not only being accessed from untrust to dmz, but in the reverse direction as well. This is where understanding of Figure 9-1 is important. Because the destination NAT transform happens first on the Inbound-HTTP rule, we use the internal addresses in the destination field for that rule. Conversely, because the source NAT transform happens after the policy lookup in the Outbound-HTTPS rule, we also use the internal private addresses there as well rather than matching the public.

Option 2: NAT46 Static mapping. In this example, we are going to perform NAT46 for our application servers where we translate the inbound NAT from the public IPv4 to IPv6 on the internal network and vice versa, using the same example of allowing HTTP inbound and HTTPS outbound. This option is useful when you want to refer to your servers publically with IPv4, but perhaps you want to use IPv6 internally. Assume that the interface, zone, and IPv6 flow configuration has already been completed, as shown in the previous example.

We could also do the opposite in this example referring to IPv6 publically and IPv4 privately. The main difference is your match and action criteria in the NAT policy (you would use the IPv6 object as the match, IPv4 as the action). You would also have to use the internal private range in your security policy, so it would be the IPv4 object as the destination in the Inbound-HTTP policy and the IPv4 object as the source in the Outbound-HTTPS policy—once again due to the order of operations with the policy lookup.

```
[edit]
root@srx3600n0# set security nat static rule-set NAT46 from zone untrust

[edit]
root@srx3600n0# set security nat static rule-set NAT46 rule Application-Server
match destination-address 198.18.8.128/25

root@srx3600n0# set security nat static rule-set NAT46 rule Application-Server
then static-nat prefix fec0::ac10:0180/121

[edit]
root@srx3600n0# set security address-book global address Application-Servers-v6-
Private-fec0::ac10:0180/121 fec0::ac10:0180/121

[edit]
root@srx3600n0# set security policies from-zone untrust to-zone dmz policy
Inbound-HTTP match source-address any destination-address Application-Servers-
v6-Private-fec0::ac10:0180/121 application junos-http

root@srx3600n0# set security policies from-zone untrust to-zone dmz policy
Inbound-HTTP then permit

[edit]
root@srx3600n0# set security policies from-zone untrust to-zone dmz policy
Inbound-HTTP then log session-close

[edit]
root@srx3600n0# set security policies from-zone dmz to-zone untrust policy
Outbound-HTTPS match source-address Application-Servers-v6-Private-
fec0::ac10:0180/121 destination-address any application junos-https

[edit]
root@srx3600n0# set security policies from-zone dmz to-zone untrust policy
Outbound-HTTPS then permit

[edit]
root@srx3600n0# set security policies from-zone dmz to-zone untrust policy
Outbound-HTTPS then log session-close

[edit]
root@srx3600n0# show security nat
static {
    rule-set NAT46 {
        from zone untrust;
        rule Application-Server {
            match {
                destination-address 198.18.8.128/25;
            }
            then {
                static-nat {
                    prefix {
                        fec0::ac10:0180/121;
```

```
                    }
                }
            }
        }
    }
}

[edit]
root@srx3600n0# show security policies from-zone dmz to-zone untrust
policy Outbound-HTTPS {
    match {
        source-address Application-Servers-v6-Private-fec0::ac10:0180/121;
        destination-address any;
        application junos-https;
    }
    then {
        permit;
        log {
            session-close;
        }
    }
}

[edit]
root@srx3600n0# show security policies from-zone untrust to-zone dmz
policy Inbound-HTTP {
    match {
        source-address any;
                           destination-address   [Application-Servers-v6-Private-
fec0::ac10:0180/121 ];
        application junos-http;
    }
    then {
        permit;
        log {
            session-close;
        }
    }
}

[edit]
root@srx3600n0# show security address-book
global {
               address   Application-Servers-v6-Private-fec0::ac10:0180/121
fec0::ac10:0180/121;
}
```

Reviewing this configuration, the main thing that stands out is that we translated a destination IP subnet from 198.18.8.128/25 to a completely different protocol and destination fec0::ac10:0180/121 and this was not for a 1:1 translation but for a whole subnet (although the config would have been the same for a 1:1, just different subnet boundaries). We can see that the Junos Security NAT policy allows us to easily interchange which protocol is used without any specific identifiers. In this example, we just used the direct prefix rather than the address objects, but we could have done it either way. Again no proxy-arp config is needed because 198.18.8.128 is outside of the 198.18.5.0/24 subnet on the ge-0/0/0 interface. You would need to make sure that there was a route present on the upstream router to route this traffic to the SRX, though.

Option 3: NAT 64 automatic translation. In this example, we have external hosts communicate with our application servers via the IPv6 range 2002::AC10:0180/121, but the servers will only use their internal IPv4 addresses. We do it in a way that allows us to implicitly translate the IPv6 NAT to IPv4 without having to specify a custom mapping. Create a security policy that permits HTTP traffic inbound while allowing the servers to communicate out via HTTPS. We assume the interface, zone, IPv6 Flow config is already complete per previous examples.

```
[edit]
root@srx3600n0# set security nat static rule-set NAT64 from zone untrust

[edit]
root@srx3600n0# set security nat static rule-set NAT64 rule AppServer match
destination-address 2002::AC10:0180/121

root@srx3600n0# set security nat static rule-set NAT64 rule AppServer then
static-nat inet

[edit]
root@srx3600n0# set security address-book global address Application-Servers-v4-
Private-172.16.1.128/25 172.16.1.128/25

[edit]
root@srx3600n0# set security policies from-zone untrust to-zone dmz policy
Inbound-HTTP match source-address any destination-address Application-Servers-
v4-Private-172.16.1.128/25 application junos-http

[edit]
root@srx3600n0# set security policies from-zone untrust to-zone dmz policy
Inbound-HTTP then permit

[edit]
root@srx3600n0# set security policies from-zone untrust to-zone dmz policy
Inbound-HTTP then log session-close

[edit]
root@srx3600n0# set security policies from-zone dmz to-zone untrust policy
Outbound-HTTPS        match        source-address        Application-Servers-v4-
Private-172.16.1.128/25 destination-address any application junos-https

[edit]
root@srx3600n0# set security policies from-zone dmz to-zone untrust policy
Outbound-HTTPS then permit
```

```
[edit]
root@srx3600n0# set security policies from-zone dmz to-zone untrust policy
Outbound-HTTPS then log session-close

[edit]
root@srx3600n0# show security nat
static {
    rule-set NAT64 {
        from zone untrust;
        rule AppServer {
            match {
                destination-address 2002::AC10:0180/121;
            }
            then {
                static-nat {
                    inet;
                }
            }
        }
    }
}

[edit]
root@srx3600n0# show security address-book
global {
    address Application-Servers-v4-Private-172.16.1.128/25 172.16.1.128/25;
}

[edit]
root@srx3600n0# show security policies from-zone untrust to-zone dmz
policy Inbound-HTTP {
    match {
        source-address any;
        destination-address Application-Servers-v4-Private-172.16.1.128/25;
        application junos-http;
    }
    then {
        permit;
        log {
            session-close;
        }
    }
}

[edit]
root@srx3600n0# show security policies from-zone dmz to-zone untrust
policy Outbound-HTTPS {
    match {
        source-address Application-Servers-v4-Private-172.16.1.128/25;
        destination-address any;
        application junos-https;
    }
```

```
        then {
            permit;
            log {
                session-close;
            }
        }
    }
```

The interesting thing about this example is that we are not explicitly defining what we should translate the 2002::AC10:0180/121 network to, but rather just defining `inet`. As we discussed earlier, this means to automatically translate the IPv6 address to IPv4. To do this we strip off the first 96 most significant bits from the 128-bit IPv6 address. In this case, it would be 2002:0000:0000:0000:0000:0000, leaving behind C612:0880, which is hex for the IP address 172.16.1.128/25! If your network architecture properly can map the public to private ranges based on the last 32 bits of the public IPv6 address, then you can use this NAT as a shortcut. With IPv6 this is pretty easy because most organizations are getting such large subnets assigned to them. If not, then you can always use the standard static NAT mapping to accomplish this.

As of 12.1X45, Juniper has added the ability to match not only on Destination Address and Destination Port, but also Source Address and Source Port for the match criteria. This just provides some additional granularity that might be required in environments where you want to differentiate the application of static NAT based on the Source Address, Source Port, or both, in addition to the Destination Address and optionally Destination Port

Source NAT

Although static NAT allows you to define bidirectional NAT translations, it is not ideal in all scenarios. First, you might not have the IP address ranges (particularly on the public side) to support every internal host. Second, you might not want to have a static mapping, but instead want something dynamic, whether with giving hosts a dynamic 1:1 mapping or overloading multiple private hosts to the same public address. Of course, you also might want to simplify routing with trading partners and thus hide behind an interface address. For all of these reasons, you might need to leverage source NAT. In this section, we look at a few examples of leveraging source NAT:

1. Source NAT with interfaces (overloading)
2. Source NAT with pools and interfaces (both overloading and no overloading example)

For each example we assume Figure 9-4, and we demonstrate it with both IPv4 and IPv6 to demonstrate how these can interact.

Source NAT with interfaces

In this example, we translate the hosts in the engineering department to get the public IP address of ge-0/0/0 on the firewall for both IPv4 and IPv6 when they go from trust to untrust. We allow any service outbound for this example, but we do not allow reverse connections.

```
[edit]
root@srx3600n0# set interfaces ge-0/0/0 unit 0 family inet address 198.18.5.1/24

[edit]
root@srx3600n0# set interfaces ge-0/0/0 unit 0 family inet6 address 2001::1/96

[edit]
root@srx3600n0# set security zones security-zone untrust interfaces ge-0/0/0

[edit]
root@srx3600n0# set interfaces ge-0/0/1 unit 0 family inet address
192.168.0.1/23

[edit]
root@srx3600n0# set interfaces ge-0/0/1 unit 0 family inet6 address fec0::1/118

[edit]
root@srx3600n0# set security zones security-zone trust interfaces ge-0/0/1

[edit]
root@srx3600n0# set security address-book global address
Engineering-192.168.0.0/24 192.168.0.0/24

[edit]
root@srx3600n0# set security address-book global address Engineering-v6-
fec0::1:0/120 fec0::1:0/120

[edit]
root@srx3600n0# set security nat source rule-set Trust-Untrust from zone trust

[edit]
root@srx3600n0# set security nat source rule-set Trust-Untrust to zone untrust

[edit]
root@srx3600n0# set security nat source rule-set Trust-Untrust rule Engineering-
v4 match source-address-name Engineering-192.168.0.0/24

[edit]
root@srx3600n0# set security nat source rule-set Trust-Untrust rule Engineering-
v4 then source-nat interface

[edit]
root@srx3600n0# set security nat source rule-set Trust-Untrust rule Engineering-
v6 match source-address fec0::1:0/120
```

```
[edit]
root@srx3600n0# set security nat source rule-set Trust-Untrust rule Engineering-
v6 then source-nat interface

[edit]
root@srx3600n0# set security forwarding-options family inet6 mode flow-based

[edit]
root@srx3600n0# set security policies from-zone trust to-zone untrust policy
Engineering-Outbound  match  source-address  [Engineering-192.168.0.0/24
Engineering-v6-fec0::1:0/120 ] destination-address any application any

[edit]
root@srx3600n0# set security policies from-zone trust to-zone untrust policy
Engineering-Outbound then permit

[edit]
root@srx3600n0# set security policies from-zone trust to-zone untrust policy
Engineering-Outbound then log session-close

[edit]
root@srx3600n0# set security forwarding-options family inet6 mode flow-based

root@srx3600n0# show security forwarding-options
family {
    inet6 {
        mode flow-based;
    }
}

[edit]
root@srx3600n0# show security nat
source {
    rule-set Trust-Untrust {
        from zone trust;
        to zone untrust;
        rule Engineering-v4 {
            match {
                source-address-name Engineering-192.168.0.0/24;
            }
            then {
                source-nat {
                    interface;
                }
            }
        }
        rule Engineering-v6 {
            match {
                source-address-name Engineering-v6-fec0::1:0/120;
            }
            then {
                source-nat {
```

```
                    interface;
                }
            }
        }
    }
}

[edit]
root@srx3600n0# show security policies from-zone trust to-zone untrust
policy Engineering-Outbound {
    match {
                source-address  [  Engineering-192.168.0.0/24  Engineering-v6-
fec0::1:0/120 ];
        destination-address any;
        application any;
    }
    then {
        permit;
        log {
            session-close;
        }
    }
}

[edit]
root@srx3600n0# show security address-book
global {
    address Engineering-192.168.0.0/24 192.168.0.0/24;
    address Engineering-v6-fec0::1:0/120 fec0::1:0/120;
}

[edit]
root@srx3600n0# show security zones
security-zone trust {
    interfaces {
        ge-0/0/1.0;
    }
}
security-zone untrust {
    interfaces {
        ge-0/0/0.0;
    }
}

[edit]
root@srx3600n0# show interfaces
ge-0/0/0 {
    unit 0 {
        family inet {
            address 198.18.5.1/24;
        }
        family inet6 {
```

```
                address 2001::1/96;
            }
        }
    }
    ge-0/0/1 {
        unit 0 {
            family inet {
                address 192.168.0.1/23;
            }
            family inet6 {
                address fec0::1/118;
            }
        }
    }
```

Breaking down this example a bit, we configured two different NAT translations for our static NAT: one for IPv4 and one for IPv6. Because we're using interface-based NAT, the SRX will maintain the same protocol (e.g., NAT44/NAT66). If you want to convert between the two, you must use pools to do this properly. For the source NAT itself, we used the context from-zone trust to-zone untrust, although we could have done from interface ge-0/0/1 to interface ge-0/0/0 or even a combination of interfaces and zones if desired. In the match criteria itself, we only specified the source addresses here, although you can also specify the destination, port, and protocol information as well if you so desired to have a more specific match. For simple outbound rules, just specifying the source address is usually fine, although sometimes you might want to control the translation based on where the traffic is going (e.g., present a different source IP based on the destination or port). Because we are translating to the IP address of the interface, we don't need to worry about using Proxy-ARP/NDP in this example.

Source NAT with pools and interfaces

In the last example, we simply translated all outbound connections to the interface address itself. This is useful for small networks where you will not hit the maximum number of connections per IP address or if you don't need to allocate a single IP address per host. In this example, we do the following using Figure 9-4 as a model:

1. Translate engineering users from 192.168.0.0/24 to 198.8.5.21 for IPv4 and IPv6.
2. Translate accounting IPv4 from 192.168.1.0/24 to the 198.18.5.10-20 range, and use the engineering public IP as an overflow if the public accounting range is exhausted.
3. Translate the accounting IPv6 from fec0::2:0/120 to 2001::2:0/120, and if the pool runs out of IP addresses, configure it to overflow to the egress interface.
4. Allow HTTP and SMTP from trust to untrust for accounting, and HTTP and FTP for engineering from trust to untrust.

```
[edit]
root@srx3600n0# set interfaces ge-0/0/0 unit 0 family inet address 198.18.5.1/24

[edit]
root@srx3600n0# set interfaces ge-0/0/0 unit 0 family inet6 address 2001::1/96

[edit]
root@srx3600n0# set security zones security-zone untrust interfaces ge-0/0/0

[edit]
root@srx3600n0#  set  interfaces  ge-0/0/1  unit  0  family  inet  address
192.168.0.1/23

[edit]
root@srx3600n0# set interfaces ge-0/0/1 unit 0 family inet6 address fec0::1/118

[edit]
root@srx3600n0# set security zones security-zone trust interfaces ge-0/0/1

[edit]
root@srx3600n0#  set  security  address-book  global  address  Engineering-Private-
v4-192.168.0.0/24 192.168.0.0/24

[edit]
root@srx3600n0#  set  security  address-book  global  address  Engineering--Private-
v6-fec0::1:0/120 fec0::1:0/120

[edit]
root@srx3600n0#  set  security  address-book  global  address  Accounting-Private-v6-
fec0::2:0/120 fec0::2:0/120

[edit]
root@srx3600n0#  set  security  address-book  global  address  Accounting-Private-
v4-192.168.1.0/24 192.168.1.0/24

[edit]
root@srx3600n0# set security forwarding-options family inet6 mode flow-based

[edit]
root@srx3600n0#  set  security  nat  proxy-arp  interface  ge-0/0/0  address
198.18.5.10 to 198.18.5.21

[edit]
root@srx3600n0#  set  security  nat  proxy-ndp  interface  ge-0/0/0  address
2001::2:0/120

[edit]
root@srx3600n0# set security nat source pool Engineering-v4 address 198.18.5.21

[edit]
root@srx3600n0# set security nat source rule-set Trust-Untrust from zone trust
```

```
[edit]
root@srx3600n0# set security nat source rule-set Trust-Untrust to zone untrust

[edit]
root@srx3600n0# set security nat source rule-set Trust-Untrust rule Engineering
match source-address-name Engineering-Private-v4-192.168.0.0/24

[edit]
root@srx3600n0# set security nat source rule-set Trust-Untrust rule Engineering
match source-address-name Engineering-Private-v6-fec0::1:0/120

[edit]
root@srx3600n0# set security nat source rule-set Trust-Untrust rule Engineering
then source-nat pool Engineering-v4

[edit]
root@srx3600n0# set security nat source pool Accounting-v4 address 198.18.5.10
to 198.18.5.20

[edit]
root@srx3600n0# set security nat source pool Accounting-v4 port no-translation

[edit]
root@srx3600n0#  set  security  nat  source  pool  Accounting-v4  overflow-pool
Engineering-v4

[edit]
root@srx3600n0# set security nat source pool Accounting-v6 address 2001::2:0/120

[edit]
root@srx3600n0# set security nat source pool Accounting-v6 port no-translation

[edit]
root@srx3600n0# set security nat source pool Accounting-v6 overflow-pool inter-
face

[edit]
root@srx3600n0# set security nat source rule-set Trust-Untrust rule Accounting-
v4 match source-address-name Accounting-Private-v4-192.168.1.0/24

[edit]
root@srx3600n0# set security nat source rule-set Trust-Untrust rule Accounting-
v4 then source-nat pool Accounting-v4

[edit]
root@srx3600n0# set security nat source rule-set Trust-Untrust rule Accounting-
v6 match source-address-name Accounting-Private-v6-fec0::2:0/120

[edit]
root@srx3600n0# set security nat source rule-set Trust-Untrust rule Accounting-
v6 then source-nat pool Accounting-v6
```

```
[edit]
root@srx3600n0# set security policies from-zone trust to-zone untrust policy
Engineering-Outbound      match      source-address      [Engineering-Private-
v4-192.168.0.0/24  Engineering-Private-v6-fec0::1:0/120  ] destination-address
any application [junos-http junos-ftp]

[edit]
root@srx3600n0# set security policies from-zone trust to-zone untrust policy
Engineering-Outbound then permit

[edit]
root@srx3600n0# set security policies from-zone trust to-zone untrust policy
Engineering-Outbound then log session-close

[edit]
root@srx3600n0# set security policies from-zone trust to-zone untrust policy
Accounting-Outbound   match   source-address   [Accounting-v4-192.168.1.0/24
Accounting-Private-v6-fec0::2:0/120] destination-address any application [junos-
http junos-smtp]

[edit]
root@srx3600n0# set security policies from-zone trust to-zone untrust policy
Accounting-Outbound then permit

[edit]
root@srx3600n0# set security policies from-zone trust to-zone untrust policy
Accounting-Outbound then log session-close

[edit]
root@srx3600n0# show security address-book
global {
    address Engineering-Private-v4-192.168.0.0/24 192.168.0.0/24;
    address Engineering-Private-v6-fec0::1:0/120 fec0::1:0/120;
    address Accounting-Private-v6-fec0::2:0/120 fec0::2:0/120;
    address Accounting-Private-v4-192.168.1.0/24 192.168.1.0/24;
}


root@srx3600n0# show security forwarding-options
family {
    inet6 {
        mode flow-based;
    }
}


[edit]
root@srx3600n0# show security nat
source {
    pool Engineering-v4 {
        address {
            198.18.5.21/32;
```

```
        }
    }
    pool Accounting-v4 {
        address {
            198.18.5.10/32 to 198.18.5.20/32;
        }
        port no-translation;
        overflow-pool Engineering-v4;
    }
    pool Accounting-v6 {
        address {
            2001::2:0/120;
        }
        port no-translation;
        overflow-pool interface;
    }
    rule-set Trust-Untrust {
        from zone trust;
        to zone untrust;
        rule Engineering {
            match {
                    source-address-name [ Engineering-Private-v4-192.168.0.0/24
Engineering-Private-v6-fec0::1:0/120 ];
            }
            then {
                source-nat {
                    pool {
                        Engineering-v4;
                    }
                }
            }
        }
        rule Accounting-v4 {
            match {
                source-address-name Accounting-Private-v4-192.168.1.0/24;
            }
            then {
                source-nat {
                    pool {
                        Accounting-v4;
                    }
                }
            }
        }
        rule Accounting-v6 {
            match {
                source-address-name Accounting-Private-v6-fec0::2:0/120;
            }
            then {
                source-nat {
                    pool {
                        Accounting-v6;
```

```
                    }
                }
            }
        }
    }
}
proxy-arp {
    interface ge-0/0/0.0 {
        address {
            198.18.5.10/32 to 198.18.5.21/32;
        }
    }
}
proxy-ndp {
    interface ge-0/0/0.0 {
        address {
            2001::2:0/120;
        }
    }
}


[edit]
root@srx3600n0# show security policies from-zone trust to-zone untrust
policy Engineering-Outbound {
    match {
            source-address [ Engineering-Private-v4-192.168.0.0/24 Engineering-
Private-v6-fec0::1:0/120 ];
        destination-address any;
        application [ junos-http junos-ftp ];
    }
    then {
        permit;
        log {
            session-close;
        }
    }
}
policy Accounting-Outbound {
    match {
             source-address [ Accounting-Private-v4-192.168.1.0/24 Accounting-
Private-v6-fec0::2:0/120 ];
        destination-address any;
        application [ junos-http junos-smtp ];
    }
    then {
        permit;
        log {
            session-close;
        }
    }
}
```

```
[edit]
root@srx3600n0# show security zones
security-zone trust {
    interfaces {
        ge-0/0/1.0;
    }
}
security-zone untrust {
    interfaces {
        ge-0/0/0.0;
    }
}

[edit]
root@srx3600n0# show interfaces
ge-0/0/0 {
    unit 0 {
        family inet {
            address 198.18.5.1/24;
        }
        family inet6 {
            address 2001::1/96;
        }
    }
}
ge-0/0/1 {
    unit 0 {
        family inet {
            address 192.168.0.1/23;
        }
        family inet6 {
            address fec0::1/118;
        }
    }
}
```

There's a lot more going on in this example than first meets the eye. We need to set up the NAT infrastructure. Because we are translating to pools within the egress subnet, we need to leverage proxy-arp/ndp. Next, we have to set up our pools for both accounting and engineering, IPv4 and IPv6 including the overflows. There isn't any major difference between IPv4 and IPv6 in terms of the configuration here. We define our pool IP addresses, but also no port translation and overflow configs. No port translation instructs the SRX to allocate IP addresses to internal hosts for as long as those hosts have sessions open, without overloading the public IP addresses. In the event that there are no more IP addresses available in the pool, then we can fall back to an overflow pool or interface as we did in this example. This allows you to prevent a network outage scenario if you run out of IP addresses in the pool. Again, each IP is tied to a source for as long as that source has persistent sessions open (by default.) Note that all pools will leverage overloading by default; you have to manually disable it as we did with the accounting-v4 and accounting-v6 pools.

Our source NAT policy follows the configuration of the instructions. We have an engineering rule that matches both IPv4 and IPv6 engineering and translates them to the IPv4 engineering-v4 pool using overloading. The accounting rules are slightly different. We assign a separate IPv4 and IPv6 NAT translation depending on the original addresses (IPv4 and IPv6, respectively). Finally, we have our security policy configuration, which allows the respective traffic outbound based on the origin (accounting versus engineering).

Other SRX source NAT configuration options

You might have noticed a few other options if you were poking around the source NAT configuration throughout these examples. There are more options when it comes to source NAT, but these are often more advanced options that are used in service provider or very large enterprise environments in specific cases. We discuss them here so that you are aware of them should you have a need to leverage these advanced behaviors.

- Address persistence: You can enable address persistence from a high level in the source NAT configuration. This instructs the SRX to hold source IP mappings between the internal and external mappings rather than relinquish them after all existing sessions close. This might be a useful option under certain circumstances where this information does not change; otherwise, persistent NAT might be a better option.
- Address-shifting: This is a legacy option that came out of the ScreenOS days. It allows you to define a source range mapped to a destination range based on an address shift, for instance, map 10.1.1.1/25 to 1.1.1.128/25 where the mapping is not 1:1 from an octet perspective.
- Persistent NAT: This is a very powerful form of NAT that is common for service providers. The main issue with source NAT for service providers is that it is difficult to allow hosts to be dynamically assigned but also function with some applications, including those that need to allow reverse inbound connections back in. Persistent NAT allows you to dynamically assign a public source IP, assign a timeout (rather than strictly being persistent or terminating after no more connections are active), and define three different types of inbound access policies: allow any connections in from any hosts after the source connects outbound, allow any inbound connections from a host that the internal host has connected to, or let the host that an internal source has connected to make a reverse connection on the same port. You can define persistent NAT per NAT pool so this can be applied in a very granular fashion. In modern networks, persistent NAT is usually a better choice than using the address persistence option.

- Port randomization: By default, source port randomization is enabled for security purposes to make it more difficult for attackers to guess source ports for potential spoofing attacks like DNS poisoning. Some legacy applications might have an issue with this, so you can disable it. Note that this is only for pool-based NAT and not for interface-based NAT.
- Pool default source port range: Normally this is between 1024 and 63487, but you can restrict this to a smaller range if there is a need for it. This is not a common option, but some use cases (e.g., VoIP) might require it.

When using High Availability and Source NAT with Port overloading, by default each IP address can use 32k ports out of the 65k (1024 are reserved). This is because the SRX is in active/active HA mode by default, and 32k ports are reserved for each node. If you want to be able to use all 64k ports, then you must configure the SRX using a hidden command to set it to active/passive mode:

```
{primary:node1}[edit]
root@SRX100HM# run show chassis cluster information
node0:
--------------------------------------------------------------------------
Redundancy mode:
    Configured mode: active-active
    Operational mode: active-active

Redundancy group: 0, Threshold: 255, Monitoring failures: none
    Events:
        Apr  5 15:46:56.258 : hold->secondary, reason: Hold timer expired

Redundancy group: 1, Threshold: 255, Monitoring failures: none
    Events:
        Apr  5 15:46:56.277 : hold->secondary, reason: Hold timer expired


{primary:node1}[edit]
root@SRX100HM# set chassis cluster redundancy-mode active-backup

{primary:node1}[edit]
root@SRX100HM# show chassis cluster
control-link-recovery;
redundancy-mode active-backup;
reth-count 2;
redundancy-group 0 {
    node 0 priority 100;
    node 1 priority 99;
}
redundancy-group 1 {
```

```
        node 0 priority 100;
        node 1 priority 99;
        interface-monitor {
            fe-0/0/1 weight 255;
            fe-0/0/2 weight 255;
            fe-1/0/1 weight 255;
            fe-1/0/2 weight 255;
        }
    }
```

Destination NAT

Destination NAT fulfills two primary use cases. First, it is essential when you want to make services available on the Internet when you do not have the necessary IP address space, and it also allows you to translate the IP or port from one range to another. Sometimes this is helpful when an application is configured a certain way and you don't want to or can't modify it, but instead want to make the transform in the NAT policy. Let's look at an example that will allow us to fulfill both scenarios.

Configuration destination NAT

Let's configure an example using Figure 9-4 that performs the following options:

1. Leverage the public IP address 198.18.5.5/2001::5 for both the SMTP and HTTP servers in the DMZ, but allow inbound connections on port 25 to go to the SMTP server and inbound connections on port 80 to go to the HTTP server for IPv4 and IPv6, respectively.
2. Translate any inbound connections to port 8080 to port 443 on the HTTP server to the IPv4 address for both IPv4 and IPv6 because the server is only listening on port 443 for IPv4 and not IPv6.

```
[edit]
root@srx3600n0# set interfaces ge-0/0/0 unit 0 family inet address
198.18.5.1/24

[edit]
root@srx3600n0# set interfaces ge-0/0/0 unit 0 family inet6 address 2001::1/96

[edit]
root@srx3600n0# set security zones security-zone untrust interfaces ge-0/0/0

[edit]
root@srx3600n0# set interfaces ge-0/0/2 unit 0 family inet address
172.16.1.1/24

[edit]
root@srx3600n0# set interfaces ge-0/0/2 unit 0 family inet6 address
fec0::ac10:0101/120
```

```
[edit]
root@srx3600n0# set security zones security-zone dmz interfaces ge-0/0/2

[edit]
root@srx3600n0# set security forwarding-options family inet6 mode flow-based

[edit]
root@srx3600n0# set security nat destination pool SMTP-Server-v4 address
172.16.1.5

[edit]
root@srx3600n0# set security nat destination pool SMTP-Server-v6 address
fec0::ac10:0105

[edit]
root@srx3600n0# set security nat destination pool Web-Server-v4 address
172.16.1.10

[edit]
root@srx3600n0# set security nat destination pool Web-Server-v6 address
fec0::ac10:010a

[edit]
root@srx3600n0# set security nat destination pool Web-Server-8080 address
172.16.1.10 port 443

[edit]
root@srx3600n0# set security nat destination rule-set Inbound-NAT from zone
untrust

[edit]
root@srx3600n0# set security nat destination rule-set Inbound-NAT rule SMTP-
Server-V4 match destination-address 198.18.5.5

[edit]
root@srx3600n0# set security nat destination rule-set Inbound-NAT rule SMTP-
Server-V4 match destination-port 25

[edit]
root@srx3600n0# set security nat destination rule-set Inbound-NAT rule SMTP-
Server-V4 match protocol tcp

[edit]
root@srx3600n0# set security nat destination rule-set Inbound-NAT rule SMTP-
Server-V4 then destination-nat pool SMTP-Server-v4

[edit]
root@srx3600n0# set security nat destination rule-set Inbound-NAT rule SMTP-
Server-V6 match destination-address 2001::5
```

```
[edit]
root@srx3600n0# set security nat destination rule-set Inbound-NAT rule SMTP-
Server-V6 match destination-port 25

root@srx3600n0# set security nat destination rule-set Inbound-NAT rule SMTP-
Server-V6 match protocol tcp

root@srx3600n0# set security nat destination rule-set Inbound-NAT rule SMTP-
Server-V6 then destination-nat pool SMTP-Server-v6

[edit]
root@srx3600n0# set security nat destination rule-set Inbound-NAT rule Web-
Server-V4 match destination-address 198.18.5.5

[edit]
root@srx3600n0# set security nat destination rule-set Inbound-NAT rule Web-
Server-V4 match destination-port 80

[edit]
root@srx3600n0# set security nat destination rule-set Inbound-NAT rule Web-
Server-V4 match protocol tcp

[edit]
root@srx3600n0# set security nat destination rule-set Inbound-NAT rule Web-
Server-V4 then destination-nat pool Web-Server-v4

[edit]
root@srx3600n0# set security nat destination rule-set Inbound-NAT rule Web-
Server-V6 match destination-address 2001::5

[edit]
root@srx3600n0# set security nat destination rule-set Inbound-NAT rule Web-
Server-V6 match destination-port 80

[edit]
root@srx3600n0# set security nat destination rule-set Inbound-NAT rule Web-
Server-V6 match protocol tcp

[edit]
root@srx3600n0# set security nat destination rule-set Inbound-NAT rule Web-
Server-V6 then destination-nat pool Web-Server-v6

[edit]
root@srx3600n0# set security nat destination rule-set Inbound-NAT rule Web-
Server-8080-v6 match destination-address 2001::5

[edit]
root@srx3600n0# set security nat destination rule-set Inbound-NAT rule Web-
Server-8080-v6 match destination-port 8080

[edit]
```

```
root@srx3600n0# set security nat destination rule-set Inbound-NAT rule Web-
Server-8080-v6 match protocol tcp

[edit]
root@srx3600n0# set security nat destination rule-set Inbound-NAT rule Web-
Server-8080-v6 then destination-nat pool Web-Server-8080

[edit]
root@srx3600n0# set security nat destination rule-set Inbound-NAT rule Web-
Server-8080-v4 match destination-address 198.18.5.5

[edit]
root@srx3600n0# set security nat destination rule-set Inbound-NAT rule Web-
Server-8080-v4 match destination-port 8080

[edit]
root@srx3600n0# set security nat destination rule-set Inbound-NAT rule Web-
Server-8080-v4 match protocol tcp

[edit]
root@srx3600n0# set security nat destination rule-set Inbound-NAT rule Web-
Server-8080-v4 then destination-nat pool Web-Server-8080

[edit]
root@srx3600n0#  set  security  nat  proxy-arp  interface  ge-0/0/0  address
198.18.5.5

[edit]
root@srx3600n0# set security nat proxy-ndp interface ge-0/0/0 address 2001::5

[edit]
root@srx3600n0# set security policies from-zone untrust to-zone dmz policy
SMTP-Server match source-address any destination-address [SMTP-Server-Private-
v4-172.16.1.5/32  SMTP-Server-Private-v6-fec0::ac10:0105/128]  application
junos-smtp

[edit]
root@srx3600n0# set security policies from-zone untrust to-zone dmz policy
SMTP-Server then permit

[edit]
root@srx3600n0# set security policies from-zone untrust to-zone dmz policy
SMTP-Server then log session-close

[edit]
root@srx3600n0# set security policies from-zone untrust to-zone dmz policy
Web-Server match source-address any destination-address [Web-Server-Private-
v4-172.16.1.10/32  Web-Server-Private-v6-fec0::ac10:010a/128  ]  application
junos-http

[edit]
root@srx3600n0# set security policies from-zone untrust to-zone dmz policy
```

```
Web-Server then permit

[edit]
root@srx3600n0# set security policies from-zone untrust to-zone dmz policy
Web-Server then log session-close

[edit]
root@srx3600n0# set security policies from-zone untrust to-zone dmz policy
Web-Server match source-address any destination-address Web-Server-Private-
v4-172.16.1.10/32 application junos-https

[edit]
root@srx3600n0# set security policies from-zone untrust to-zone dmz policy
Web-Server-8080 then permit

[edit]
root@srx3600n0# set security policies from-zone untrust to-zone dmz policy
Web-Server-8080 then log session-close

[edit]
root@srx3600n0# show security policies
from-zone untrust to-zone dmz {
    policy SMTP-Server {
        match {
            source-address any;
              destination-address [ SMTP-Server-Private-v4-172.16.1.5/32 SMTP-
Server-Private-v6-fec0::ac10:0105/128 ];
            application junos-smtp;
        }
        then {
            permit;
            log {
                session-close;
            }
        }
    }
    policy Web-Server {
        match {
            source-address any;
               destination-address [ Web-Server-Private-v4-172.16.1.10/32 Web-
Server-Private-v6-fec0::ac10:010a/128 ];
            application junos-http;
        }
        then {
            permit;
            log {
                session-close;
            }
        }
    }
    policy Web-Server-8080 {
        match {
```

```
                source-address any;
                destination-address Web-Server-Private-v4-172.16.1.10/32;
                application junos-https;
            }
            then {
                permit;
                log {
                    session-close;
                }
            }
        }
    }

[edit]
root@srx3600n0# show security nat
destination {
    pool SMTP-Server-v4 {
        address 172.16.1.5/32;
    }
    pool SMTP-Server-v6 {
        address fec0::ac10:0105/128;
    }
    pool Web-Server-v4 {
        address 172.16.1.10/32;
    }
    pool Web-Server-v6 {
        address fec0::ac10:010a/128;
    }
    pool Web-Server-8080 {
        address 172.16.1.10/32 port 443;
    }
    rule-set Inbound-NAT {
        from zone untrust;
        rule SMTP-Server-V4 {
            match {
                destination-address 198.18.5.5/32;
                destination-port 25;
                protocol tcp;
            }
            then {
                destination-nat pool SMTP-Server-v4;
            }
        }
        rule SMTP-Server-V6 {
            match {
                destination-address 2001::5/128;
                destination-port 25;
                protocol tcp;
            }
            then {
                destination-nat pool SMTP-Server-v6;
            }
```

```
            }
            rule Web-Server-V4 {
                match {
                    destination-address 198.18.5.5/32;
                    destination-port 80;
                    protocol tcp;
                }
                then {
                    destination-nat pool Web-Server-v4;
                }
            }
            rule Web-Server-V6 {
                match {
                    destination-address 2001::5/128;
                    destination-port 80;
                    protocol tcp;
                }
                then {
                    destination-nat pool Web-Server-v6;
                }
            }
            rule Web-Server-8080-v6 {
                match {
                    destination-address 2001::5/128;
                    destination-port 8080;
                    protocol tcp;
                }
                then {
                    destination-nat pool Web-Server-8080;
                }
            }
            rule Web-Server-8080-v4 {
                match {
                    destination-address 198.18.5.5/32;
                    destination-port 8080;
                    protocol tcp;
                }
                then {
                    destination-nat pool Web-Server-8080;
                }
            }
        }
    }
    proxy-arp {
        interface ge-0/0/0.0 {
            address {
                198.18.5.5/32;
            }
        }
    }
    proxy-ndp {
        interface ge-0/0/0.0 {
```

```
            address {
                2001::5/128;
            }
        }
    }

    root@srx3600n0# show security forwarding-options
    family {
        inet6 {
            mode flow-based;
        }
    }


    [edit]
    root@srx3600n0# show security zones
    security-zone dmz {
        interfaces {
            ge-0/0/2.0;
        }
    }
    security-zone untrust {
        interfaces {
            ge-0/0/0.0;
        }
    }
    [edit]
    root@srx3600n0# show interfaces
    ge-0/0/0 {
        unit 0 {
            family inet {
                address 198.18.5.1/24;
            }
            family inet6 {
                address 2001::1/96;
            }
        }
    }
    ge-0/0/2 {
        unit 0 {
            family inet {
                address 172.16.1.1/24;
            }
            family inet6 {
                address fec0::ac10:0101/120;
            }
        }
    }
```

This example goes over a few different scenarios in Figure 9-4 for the inbound NAT for the web and SMTP server. Because these share the same address publically, we can't use static NAT—and for the port translation from 8080 to 443 we must use destination NAT to accomplish this. Destination NAT requires that we have pools defined (even if just for one address or port combination). Because we're doing this for both IPv4 and IPv6, we must have a pool for each, plus one to do the mapping for the web server to port 443 on 172.16.1.10. After that point, we craft the NAT policy, for which we used the untrust zone as the from context, although we could have used the interface as well. For the match criteria, we are primarily concerned with where the traffic is going, so we match on the destination address, port, or protocol for both IPv4 and IPv6, and then translate it with the correct pool.

The trickier part is the integration with the firewall policy. Because destination NAT happens before the policy lookup (including the port transform), we need to make sure that we properly account for this in our rules. We know that the destination address needs to map to the translated address, but in our third example we also transform the inbound ports from 8080 to 443. We had to reference the translated port (junos-https) to properly match the traffic.

Combination Source and Destination NAT

In one interesting scenario, you might want to have a host be accessible on the Internet by one address, but have it be translated to another address when it initiates connections out to the Internet. You cannot properly use static NAT in this scenario because it forms a 1:1 bidirectional mapping that also takes precedence over source or destination NAT. Instead we must leverage both source and destination NAT. Using our web server in Figure 9-4, we will have it accept inbound connections on 198.18.5.5 and 2001::5 on port 80, but when it makes a connection back out to the Internet, it should come from the egress interface ge-0/0/0 (198.18.5.1/2001::1).

```
[edit]
root@srx3600n0# set interfaces ge-0/0/0 unit 0 family inet address 198.18.5.1/24

[edit]
root@srx3600n0# set interfaces ge-0/0/0 unit 0 family inet6 address 2001::1/96

[edit]
root@srx3600n0# set security zones security-zone untrust interfaces ge-0/0/0

[edit]
root@srx3600n0# set interfaces ge-0/0/2 unit 0 family inet address 172.16.1.1/24

[edit]
root@srx3600n0#  set  interfaces  ge-0/0/2  unit  0  family  inet6  address
fec0::ac10:0101/120

[edit]
root@srx3600n0# set security zones security-zone dmz interfaces ge-0/0/2

[edit]
root@srx3600n0# set security forwarding-options family inet6 mode flow-based
```

```
[edit]
root@srx3600n0# set security nat destination pool Web-Server-v4 address
172.16.1.10

[edit]
root@srx3600n0# set security nat destination pool Web-Server-v6 address
fec0::ac10:010a

[edit]
root@srx3600n0# set security nat destination rule-set Inbound-NAT from zone un-
trust

[edit]
root@srx3600n0# set security nat destination rule-set Inbound-NAT rule Web-
Server-V4 match destination-address 198.18.5.5

[edit]
root@srx3600n0# set security nat destination rule-set Inbound-NAT rule Web-
Server-V4 match destination-port 80

[edit]
root@srx3600n0# set security nat destination rule-set Inbound-NAT rule Web-
Server-V4 match protocol tcp

[edit]
root@srx3600n0# set security nat destination rule-set Inbound-NAT rule Web-
Server-V4 then destination-nat pool Web-Server-v4

[edit]
root@srx3600n0# set security nat destination rule-set Inbound-NAT rule Web-
Server-V6 match destination-address 2001::5

[edit]
root@srx3600n0# set security nat destination rule-set Inbound-NAT rule Web-
Server-V6 match destination-port 80

[edit]
root@srx3600n0# set security nat destination rule-set Inbound-NAT rule Web-
Server-V6 match protocol tcp

[edit]
root@srx3600n0# set security nat destination rule-set Inbound-NAT rule Web-
Server-V6 then destination-nat pool Web-Server-v6

[edit]
root@srx3600n0# set security nat source rule-set Trust-Untrust from zone trust

[edit]
root@srx3600n0# set security nat source rule-set Trust-Untrust to zone untrust
```

```
[edit]
root@srx3600n0# set security nat source rule-set Trust-Untrust rule WebServer-
Outbound match source-address-name [Web-Server-Private-v4-172.16.1.10/32 Web-
Server-Private-fec0::ac10:010a/128]

[edit]
root@srx3600n0# ...ust rule WebServerOutbound then source-nat interface


[edit]
root@srx3600n0# set security policies from-zone untrust to-zone dmz policy Web-
Server match source-address any destination-address [Web-Server-Private-
v4-172.16.1.10/32 Web-Server-Private-v6-fec0::ac10:010a/128 ] application junos-
http

[edit]
root@srx3600n0# set security policies from-zone untrust to-zone dmz policy Web-
Server then permit

[edit]
root@srx3600n0# set security policies from-zone untrust to-zone dmz policy Web-
Server then log session-close


[edit]
root@srx3600n0# set security policeis from-zone trust to-zone untrust policy
WebServerOutbound match source-address [ Web-Server-Private-v4-172.16.1.10/32
Web-Server-Private-v6-fec0::ac10:010a/128 ] destination-address any application
any

[edit]
root@srx3600n0# set security policies from-zone trust to-zone untrust policy
WebServerOutbound then permit

[edit]
root@srx3600n0# set security policies from-zone trust to-zone untrust policy
WebServerOutbound then log session-close

[edit]
root@srx3600n0# show security policies
from-zone untrust to-zone dmz {
    policy Web-Server {
        match {
            source-address any;
                destination-address [ Web-Server-Private-v4-172.16.1.10/32 Web-
Server-Private-v6-fec0::ac10:010a/128 ];
            application junos-http;
        }
        then {
            permit;
            log {
                session-close;
```

```
            }
        }
    }
}
from-zone trust to-zone untrust {
   policy WebServerOutbound {
        match {
               source-address [ Web-Server-Private-v4-172.16.1.10/32 Web-Server-
Private-v6-fec0::ac10:010a/128 ];
            destination-address any;
            application any;
        }
        then {
            permit;
            log {
                session-close;
            }
        }
    }
}
[edit]
root@srx3600n0# show security nat
destination {
    pool Web-Server-v4 {
        address 172.16.1.10/32;
    }
    pool Web-Server-v6 {
        address fec0::ac10:010a/128;
    }
    rule-set Inbound-NAT {
        from zone untrust;
        rule Web-Server-V4 {
            match {
                destination-address 198.18.5.5/32;
                destination-port 80;
                protocol tcp;
            }
            then {
                destination-nat pool Web-Server-v4;
            }
        }
        rule Web-Server-V6 {
            match {
                destination-address 2001::5/128;
                destination-port 80;
                protocol tcp;
            }
            then {
                destination-nat pool Web-Server-v6;
            }
        }
    }
```

```
}
proxy-arp {
    interface ge-0/0/0.0 {
        address {
            198.18.5.5/32;
        }
    }
}
proxy-ndp {
    interface ge-0/0/0.0 {
        address {
            2001::5/128;
        }
    }
}

root@srx3600n0# show security forwarding-options
family {
    inet6 {
        mode flow-based;
    }
}


[edit]
root@srx3600n0# show security zones
security-zone dmz {
    interfaces {
        ge-0/0/2.0;
    }
}
security-zone untrust {
    interfaces {
        ge-0/0/0.0;
    }
}
[edit]
root@srx3600n0# show interfaces
ge-0/0/0 {
    unit 0 {
        family inet {
            address 198.18.5.1/24;
        }
        family inet6 {
            address 2001::1/96;
        }
    }
}
ge-0/0/2 {
    unit 0 {
        family inet {
            address 172.16.1.1/24;
```

```
            }
            family inet6 {
                address fec0::ac10:0101/120;
            }
        }
    }
```

In many ways this example is a hybrid of the source and destination NAT, but with a unified example showing both coexisting to provide both inbound and outbound Internet connectivity to the web server with a customized access behavior. This scenario isn't that uncommon because even when you use destination NAT to handle inbound NAT, typically these servers need to be able to connect out to the Internet, and because destination NAT is only a one-way transform, you will likely need to provide them with a publically available address. Alternatively, in this example we could have used a source NAT pool rather than the egress interface, but the methodology is essentially the same.

No-NAT with Source or Destination NAT

One final option that is available when configuring source and destination NAT is to specify rules to not perform NAT. The idea behind this is that sometimes you do not want or need to perform NAT. Because the rulebase is evaluated from top to bottom and is terminal, you can easily define the match criteria and exempt a rule from a NAT transform. As mentioned earlier, this is only available for source and destination NAT and not static NAT, due to the fact that static NAT is hardcoded and bidirectional without advanced match criteria, so it's not likely you'll need it for NAT.

Let's take a look at simple example here using Figure 9-5 as a model. For this example, we configure the following:

- All FTP servers in the DMZ are listening on port 21, so to prevent scanning attempts, all other ports and addresses should be NAT'd to the HoneyPot server for recording the behavior.
- FTP server 1 and 2 have public IP addresses that they should use going out to the Internet, but the HoneyPot server and all future servers in the DMZ will have private addresses and will need to be NAT'd to the egress interface when they go out to the Internet for updates so they are publically routable.

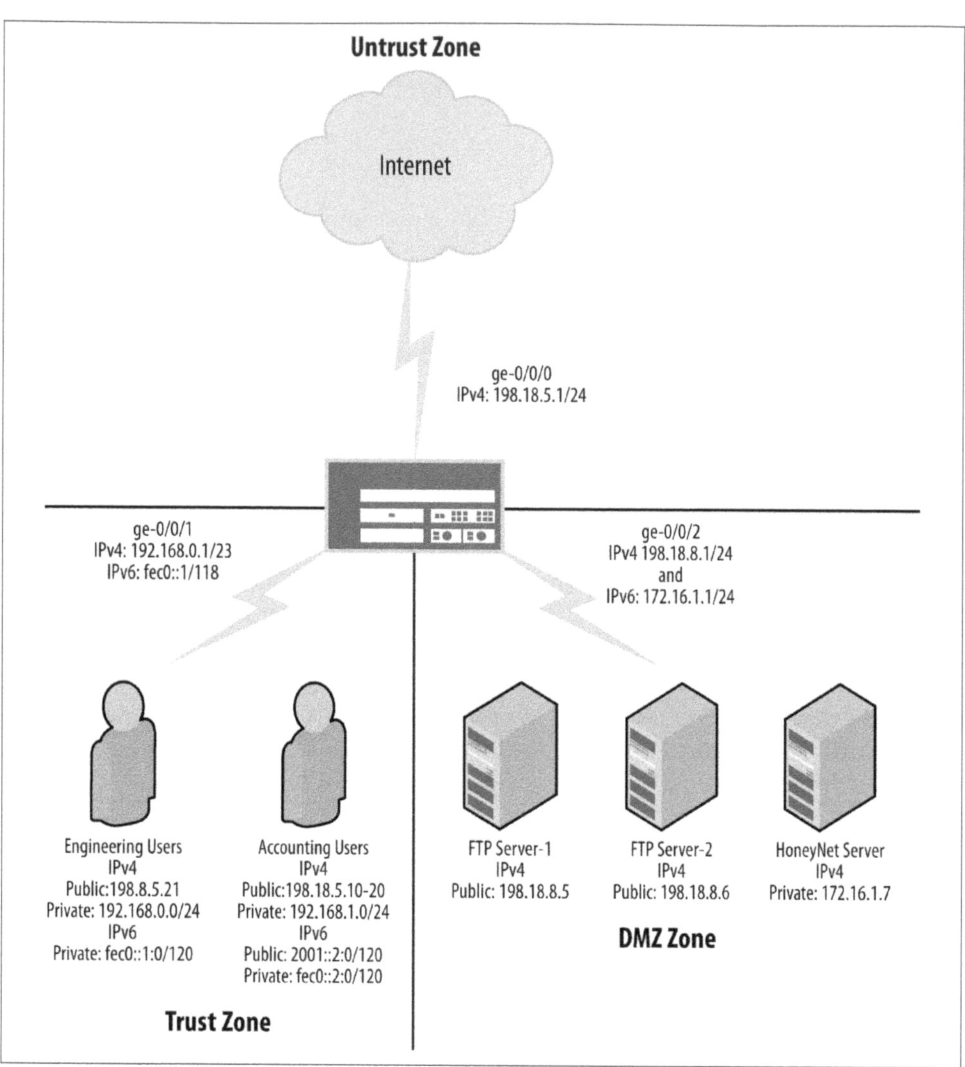

Figure 9-5. No-NAT example

```
[edit]
root@srx3600n0# set interfaces ge-0/0/2 unit 0 family inet address 198.18.8.1/24

[edit]
root@srx3600n0# set interfaces ge-0/0/2 unit 0 family inet address 172.16.1.1/24

[edit]
root@srx3600n0# set interfaces ge-0/0/0 unit 0 family inet address 198.18.5.1/24

[edit]
root@srx3600n0# set security zones security-zone untrust interfaces ge-0/0/0
```

```
[edit]
root@srx3600n0# set security zones security-zone dmz interfaces ge-0/0/2

root@srx3600n0#    set    security    address-book    global    address    FTP-
Server-1-198.18.8.5/32 198.18.8.5/32

[edit]
root@srx3600n0#    set    security    address-book    global    address    FTP-
Server-2-198.18.8.6/32 198.18.8.6/32

[edit]
root@srx3600n0#   set   security   address-book   global   address   HoneyNet-
Server-172.16.1.7/32 172.16.1.7/32

[edit]
root@srx3600n0# set security nat destination pool HoneyNet address 172.16.1.7

[edit]
root@srx3600n0# set security nat destination rule-set Inbound from zone untrust

[edit]
root@srx3600n0# set security nat destination rule-set Inbound rule FTP-1 match
destination-address-name FTP-Server-1-198.18.8.5/32

[edit]
root@srx3600n0# set security nat destination rule-set Inbound rule FTP-1 match
destination-port 21

[edit]
root@srx3600n0# set security nat destination rule-set Inbound rule FTP-1 match
protocol tcp

[edit]
root@srx3600n0# set security nat destination rule-set Inbound rule FTP-1 then
destination-nat off

[edit]
root@srx3600n0# set security nat destination rule-set Inbound rule FTP-1 match
destination-address-name FTP-Server-2-198.18.8.6/32

[edit]
root@srx3600n0# set security nat destination rule-set Inbound rule FTP-2 match
destination-address-name FTP-Server-2-198.18.8.6/32

[edit]
root@srx3600n0# set security nat destination rule-set Inbound rule FTP-1 match
destination-address-name FTP-Server-1-198.18.8.5/32

[edit]
root@srx3600n0# set security nat destination rule-set Inbound rule FTP-2 match
destination-port 21
```

```
[edit]
root@srx3600n0# set security nat destination rule-set Inbound rule FTP-2 match
protocol tcp

[edit]
root@srx3600n0# set security nat destination rule-set Inbound rule FTP-2 then
destination-nat off

[edit]
root@srx3600n0# set security nat destination rule-set Inbound rule All-Else
match destination-address 0/0

[edit]
root@srx3600n0# set security nat destination rule-set Inbound rule All-Else
then destination-nat pool HoneyNet

[edit]
root@srx3600n0# set security nat source rule-set DMZ-Out from zone dmz

[edit]
root@srx3600n0# set security nat source rule-set DMZ-Out to zone untrust

[edit]
root@srx3600n0# set security nat source rule-set DMZ-Out rule FTP-Out match
source-address-name [FTP-Server-1-198.18.8.5/32 FTP-Server-2-198.18.8.6/32]

[edit]
root@srx3600n0# set security nat source rule-set DMZ-Out rule FTP-Out then
source-nat off

[edit]
root@srx3600n0# set security nat source rule-set DMZ-Out rule Else match source-
address 0/0

[edit]
root@srx3600n0# set security nat source rule-set DMZ-Out rule Else then source-
nat interface

[edit]
root@srx3600n0#set security policies from-zone untrust to-zone dmz policy
Inbound-Permit match source-address any destination-address any application any

[edit]
root@srx3600n0#set security policies from-zone untrust to-zone dmz policy
Inbound-Permit then permit

[edit]
root@srx3600n0#set security policies from-zone untrust to-zone dmz policy
Inbound-Permit then log session-close

[edit]
```

```
root@srx3600n0#set security policies from-zone dmz to-zone untrust policy
Outbound-Permit match source-address any destination-address any application any

[edit]
root@srx3600n0#set security policies from-zone dmz to-zone untrust policy
Outbound-Permit then permit

[edit]
root@srx3600n0#set security policies from-zone dmz to-zone untrust policy
Outbound-Permit then log session-close

[edit]
root@srx3600n0# show security nat
source {
    rule-set DMZ-Out {
        from zone dmz;
        to zone untrust;
        rule FTP-Out {
            match {
                          source-address-name [ FTP-Server-1-198.18.8.5/32 FTP-
Server-2-198.18.8.6/32 ];
            }
            then {
                source-nat {
                    off;
                }
            }
        }
        rule Else {
            match {
                source-address 0.0.0.0/0;
            }
            then {
                source-nat {
                    interface;
                }
            }
        }
    }
}
destination {
    pool HoneyNet {
        address 172.16.1.7/32;
    }
    rule-set Inbound {
        from zone untrust;
        rule FTP-1 {
            match {
                destination-address-name FTP-Server-1-198.18.8.5/32;
                destination-port 21;
                protocol tcp;
            }
```

```
            then {
                destination-nat off;
            }
        }
        rule FTP-2 {
            match {
                destination-address-name FTP-Server-2-198.18.8.6/32;
                destination-port 21;
                protocol tcp;
            }
            then {
                destination-nat off;
            }
        }
        rule All-Else {
            match {
                destination-address 0.0.0.0/0;
            }
            then {
                destination-nat pool HoneyNet;
            }
        }
    }
}

[edit]
root@srx3600n0# show security policies
from-zone dmz to-zone untrust {
    policy Outbound-Permit {
        match {
            source-address any;
            destination-address any;
            application any;
        }
        then {
            permit;
            log {
                session-close;
            }
        }
    }
}
from-zone untrust to-zone dmz {
    policy Inbound-Permit {
        match {
            source-address any;
            destination-address any;
            application any;
        }
        then {
            permit;
            log {
```

```
                    session-close;
                }
            }
        }
    }

    [edit]
    root@srx3600n0# show interfaces
    ge-0/0/0 {
        unit 0 {
            family inet {
                address 198.18.5.1/24;
            }
        }
    }
    ge-0/0/2 {
        unit 0 {
            family inet {
                address 198.18.8.1/24;
                address 172.16.1.1/24;
            }
        }
    }


    [edit]
    root@srx3600n0# show security zones
    security-zone untrust {
         interfaces {
             ge-0/0/0.0;
        }
    }
    security-zone dmz {
        interfaces {
            ge-0/0/2.0;
        }
    }
```

As you can see from the NAT rulebase, we have identified traffic that must be translated and other traffic that should not be translated. Some of the examples are a bit contrived for the sake of example, but overriding NAT isn't that uncommon depending on the architecture of your network and use cases. It is far more common with some competitive platforms like CheckPoint that have a flat rulebase that cannot distinguish contexts and therefore you have to load no-NAT rules at the top. Using no-NAT rules definitely requires a good understanding of the order of precedence and ruleset evaluation. Because the rules at the top are evaluated first, and they are terminal, having them more specific is most ideal, just like placing the most specific security policies at the top of the firewall rulebase.

Best Practices

- Just like security policies, NAT is best leveraged when your network is properly segmented to provide differing levels of security and logical separation. This phase is important not only as a physical boundary between interfaces separating segments, but also in how you address your network. Ideally, resources being accessed from the Internet should be in a separate security zone like a DMZ. You should not have Internet resources directly connecting to clients, and you should not make your core internal infrastructure available on the Internet.
- Define both how internal resources should access external resources and how external resources should access those inside of your network. Based on the needs of your network, you can determine what NAT will be required. Source NAT is usually needed, but whether or not you need static or destination NAT depends on the available public address ranges and what type of access you need to provide. Static NAT provides the most flexibility, but it isn't always possible if you don't have 1:1 public:private IP addresses, so you might need to resort to source and destination NAT.
- NAT is not a security mechanism! Although NAT does have some implicit security functions, it is not in and of itself a security mechanism; modern attackers have found ways to bypass both NAT and inbound access to resources via the firewall rules. NAT can provide an additional layer of obfuscation, but it is not enough to stop modern attacks. A properly tuned security policy will provide all of the same protection as NAT and more. NAT should primarily be used for its networking function and not as a security function.
- Architect contiguous NAT ranges where possible. This will allow you to better classify access and reduce the number of rules and objects that you will need to define. For instance, if you have a contiguous range for static NAT you might be able to get away with one statement for a whole /24 rather than 254 separate statements.
- With regard to NAT ruleset contexts, it is often best to be as specific as possible when creating a context if you are creating a large NAT ruleset with hundreds of rules. If your ruleset is going to be smaller, you can rely simply on the zone or even possibly the routing instance level. You can also structure your NAT rulebase to provide different NAT criteria based on the specific nature of the context match (Interface → Zone → Routing Instance).
- Within a NAT context, make sure to place the most specific NAT rules first, and define the necessary criteria for the match. If criteria are needed to properly identify the matches, you should define them rather than omit them to avoid unintended consequences. For example, if you need to match on not only a destination IP address but a port and protocol, don't leave out the port and protocol.

- Sometimes it is best to leverage no-NAT rules for source and destination NAT rather than not matching criteria for the rulesets. For instance, if you have a specific rule that should be a no-NAT rule, put it at the top of the ruleset as a no-NAT rule, rather than not matching all of the match + NAT statements, as you are more likely to have a mistake.
- If possible, it is usually best to have upstream routers route traffic to you rather than leveraging the same subnet as the upstream router for NAT addresses. This is because you will have to rely on Proxy-ARP/NDP and this can be a messy business. Besides the configuration, you cannot control the upstream router, so if there is a MAC address change, you might not be able to trigger a failover without waiting for the entry to expire. If you can leverage routing, then you merely need to make sure the upstream infrastructure points the subnet to your firewall. This does have design implications with the subnet configuration between you and the upstream network, but it is often best to keep that to a /30 while putting the network addresses behind the firewall.
- Use address objects where possible. By using address objects rather than specifying the IP prefix, you will likely cut down on potential human errors when entering the configuration because you can use the same object for the network along with the NAT ruleset.
- When using address pools, make sure that you properly scope the size of the address pool to match up with the number of hosts and sessions that are required to support in your environment (plus extra scale for the future). You have to be especially careful if you are not using address translation because you can only have one private host active per public IP in the NAT pool at any time. With the overflow pool, then, it will likely last for much longer because you get to multiplex hosts and sessions on demand per NAT IP or port, so there are far fewer unused network ports and IPs in the pool.
- Ideally, you should also leverage overflow pools or interfaces to ensure that if you do use all of the IPs or ports in the main pool, your hosts won't be left without an Internet connection due to lack of available public NAT elements.
- Be sure to remember how NAT interacts with the security policies. If you don't properly configure your security policies, then you will properly NAT the traffic but you won't match the appropriate security policy. Static (destination) NAT then destination NAT occur (with static NAT taking precedence) before the security policy lookup, so you need to use the translated IP or port info in your security policy. Reverse static (source) NAT and source NAT happen after the security policy lookup, so you should use the original source addresses in the security policies.

Troubleshooting and Operation

Now that we have gone into great detail with the concepts and examples of NAT in the SRX, let's take a look at some useful tools at your disposal to aid the deployment, operation, and troubleshooting of NAT.

NAT Rule and Usage Counters

Let's take a look at a few of the NAT tools that we can look at when troubleshooting NAT in the form of NAT counters and rule views. To start, you can look at interface NAT with the port information available there with the `show security nat interface-nat-ports` command. The following additional commands are available:

- Source

  `show security nat source summary`
  : Shows the high-level rulebase configuration and information in a more user-friendly format than reading the configuration directly.

  `show security nat source rule`
  : Provides an in-depth look at the source NAT rule configuration including hit counts.

  `show security nat source pool`
  : Provides information about the pool configuration for source NAT pools including hit counts.

- Static

  `show security nat static rule`
  : Provides details about the static NAT rulebase configuration.

- Destination

  `show security nat destination summary`
  : Shows the high-level rulebase configuration and information in a more user-friendly format than reading the configuration directly.

  `show security nat destination rule`
  : Provides an in-depth look at the destination NAT rule configuration including hit counts.

  `show security nat destination pool`
  : Provides information about the pool configuration for destination NAT pools including hit counts.

```
root@SRX100HM> show security nat interface-nat-ports
node0:
--------------------------------------------------------------
Pool   Total  Single ports  Single ports  Twin ports  Twin ports
```

```
index  ports     allocated      available  allocated    available
    0  64510             0          63486          0         1024
    1  64510             0          63486          0         1024
    2  64510             0          63486          0         1024
    3  64510             0          63486          0         1024
    4  64510             0          63486          0         1024
    5  64510             0          63486          0         1024
    6  64510             0          63486          0         1024
    7  64510             0          63486          0         1024


{primary:node0}
root@SRX100HM> show security nat source summary
node0:
--------------------------------------------------------------------------
Total port number usage for port translation pool: 64512
Maximum port number for port translation pool: 16777216
Total pools: 1
Pool            Address              Routing           PAT  Total
Name            Range                Instance               Address
Host-Outbound   172.16.40.7-172.16.40.7 default         yes  1

Total rules: 3
Rule name       Ruleset   From         To           Action
1               Inet-IF    LAN          Danger        Host-Outbound
NoDNSNAT        Self       junos-host   Danger        off
2               Self       junos-host   Danger        Host-Outbound

{primary:node0}
root@SRX100HM> show security nat source rule all
node0:
--------------------------------------------------------------------------
Total rules: 3
Total referenced IPv4/IPv6 ip-prefixes: 3/0

source NAT rule: 1                    Rule-set: Inet-IF
  Rule-Id                     : 1
  Rule position               : 1
  From zone                   : LAN
  To zone                     : Danger
  Match
    Source addresses          : Any               - 255.255.255.255
    Destination port          : 0                 - 0
  Action                        : Host-Outbound
    Persistent NAT type         : N/A
    Persistent NAT mapping type : address-port-mapping
    Inactivity timeout          : 0
    Max session number          : 0
  Translation hits            : 1341902

source NAT rule: NoDNSNAT             Rule-set: Self
  Rule-Id                     : 2
```

```
  Rule position              : 2
  From zone                  : junos-host
  To zone                    : Danger
  Match
    Source addresses         : 172.16.40.0    - 172.16.40.15
    Destination port         : 53               - 53
    IP protocol              : udp
  Action                        : off
    Persistent NAT type         : N/A
    Persistent NAT mapping type : address-port-mapping
    Inactivity timeout          : 0
    Max session number          : 0
  Translation hits           : 8

source NAT rule: 2                     Rule-set: Self
  Rule-Id                    : 3
  Rule position              : 3
  From zone                  : junos-host
  To zone                    : Danger
  Match
    Source addresses         : Any              - 255.255.255.255
    Destination port         : 0                - 0
  Action                        : Host-Outbound
    Persistent NAT type         : N/A
    Persistent NAT mapping type : address-port-mapping
    Inactivity timeout          : 0
    Max session number          : 0
  Translation hits           : 101165

{primary:node0}
root@SRX100HM> show security nat source pool all
node0:
--------------------------------------------------------------
Total pools: 1

Pool name           : Host-Outbound
Pool id             : 4
Routing instance    : default
Host address base   : 0.0.0.0
Port                : [1024, 63487]
port overloading    : 1
Total addresses     : 1
Translation hits    : 1443081
Address range                        Single Ports   Twin Ports
      172.16.40.7 - 172.16.40.7      45             0


root@SRX100HM> show security nat static rule    all
node0:
--------------------------------------------------------------
Total static-nat rules: 5
Total referenced IPv4/IPv6 ip-prefixes: 10/0
```

```
Static NAT rule: 1                    Rule-set: Danger
  Rule-Id                    : 1
  Rule position              : 1
  From zone                  : Danger
  Destination addresses      : 172.16.40.2
  Host addresses             : 172.16.42.220
  Netmask                    : 32
  Host routing-instance      : LAN
  Translation hits           : 23106

Static NAT rule: 2                    Rule-set: Danger
  Rule-Id                    : 2
  Rule position              : 2
  From zone                  : Danger
  Destination addresses      : 172.16.40.3
  Host addresses             : 172.16.42.230
  Netmask                    : 32
  Host routing-instance      : LAN
  Translation hits           : 3033

Static NAT rule: 3                    Rule-set: Danger
  Rule-Id                    : 3
  Rule position              : 3
  From zone                  : Danger
  Destination addresses      : 172.16.40.4
  Host addresses             : 172.16.42.204
  Netmask                    : 32
  Host routing-instance      : LAN
  Translation hits           : 1491764

Static NAT rule: 4                    Rule-set: Danger
  Rule-Id                    : 4
  Rule position              : 4
  From zone                  : Danger
  Destination addresses      : 172.16.40.5
  Host addresses             : 172.16.42.205
  Netmask                    : 32
  Host routing-instance      : LAN
  Translation hits           : 17123

Static NAT rule: 5                    Rule-set: Danger
  Rule-Id                    : 5
  Rule position              : 5
  From zone                  : Danger
  Destination addresses      : 172.16.40.6
  Host addresses             : 172.16.42.238
  Netmask                    : 32
  Host routing-instance      : LAN
  Translation hits           : 2493
```

```
{primary:node0}
root@SRX100HM> show security nat destination    pool all
node0:
--------------------------------------------------------------------------
Total destination-nat pools: 4

Pool name       : 99
Pool id         : 1
Routing instance: LAN
Total address   : 1
Translation hits: 278
Address range                          Port
 192.168.1.99 - 192.168.1.99        0

Pool name       : 65
Pool id         : 2
Routing instance: LAN
Total address   : 1
Translation hits: 1153
Address range                          Port
 192.168.1.65 - 192.168.1.65        0

Pool name       : 46
Pool id         : 3
Routing instance: LAN
Total address   : 1
Translation hits: 334
Address range                          Port
 192.168.1.46 - 192.168.1.46        0

Pool name       : 45
Pool id         : 4
Routing instance: LAN
Total address   : 1
Translation hits: 11491
Address range                          Port
 192.168.1.45 - 192.168.1.45        0

{primary:node0}
root@SRX100HM> show security nat destination pool all    rule all
node0:
--------------------------------------------------------------------------
Total destination-nat rules: 5
Total referenced IPv4/IPv6 ip-prefixes: 5/0

Destination NAT rule: 1                      Rule-set: VIP
  Rule-Id                      : 1
  Rule position                : 1
  From zone                    : Danger
    Destination addresses      : 172.16.40.13  - 172.16.40.13

  Destination port             : 23
```

```
  Action                      : 99
  Translation hits            : 278

Destination NAT rule: 2                    Rule-set: VIP
  Rule-Id                     : 2
  Rule position               : 2
  From zone                   : Danger
    Destination addresses     : 172.16.40.13  - 172.16.40.13

  Destination port            : 25
  Action                      : 65
  Translation hits            : 1153

Destination NAT rule: 3                    Rule-set: VIP
  Rule-Id                     : 3
  Rule position               : 3
  From zone                   : Danger
    Destination addresses     : 172.16.40.13  - 172.16.40.13

  Destination port            : 80
  Action                      : 46
  Translation hits            : 334

Destination NAT rule: 4                    Rule-set: VIP
  Rule-Id                     : 4
  Rule position               : 4
  From zone                   : Danger
    Destination addresses     : 172.16.40.13  - 172.16.40.13

  Destination port            : 443
  Action                      : 45
  Translation hits            : 3009

Destination NAT rule: 5                    Rule-set: VIP
  Rule-Id                     : 5
  Rule position               : 5
  From zone                   : Danger
    Destination addresses     : 172.16.40.13  - 172.16.40.13

  Destination port            : 4500
  Action                      : 45
  Translation hits            : 8482

{primary:node0}
root@SRX100HM> show security nat destination rule all      summary
node0:
------------------------------------------------------------------
Total pools: 4
Pool name     Address                        Routing       Port  Total
              Range                          Instance            Address
99            192.168.1.99 - 192.168.1.99    LAN           0     1
65            192.168.1.65 - 192.168.1.65    LAN           0     1
```

```
46          192.168.1.46 - 192.168.1.46    LAN          0     1
45          192.168.1.45 - 192.168.1.45    LAN          0     1

Total rules: 5
Rule name              Ruleset         From              Action
1                      VIP              Danger             99
2                      VIP              Danger             65
3                      VIP              Danger             46
4                      VIP              Danger             45
5                      VIP              Danger             45
```

Viewing the Session Table

As we discussed earlier in this chapter and in Chapter 8, you can check the output of the session table including the extensive information for detailed translation information (how the packet arrives on or leaves the platform). This is definitely valuable information that can be a starting point to catch any obvious issues before doing a full flow debug.

```
{primary:node0}
root@SRX100HM> show security flow session interface reth0.0
node0:
--------------------------------------------------------------------------

Session ID: 1, Policy name: N/A, State: Active, Timeout: N/A, Valid
   In: 99.182.0.14/31201  --> 172.16.40.13/60915;esp,  If:  reth0.0,  Pkts:  0,
Bytes: 0

Session ID: 2, Policy name: N/A, State: Active, Timeout: N/A, Valid
  In: 99.182.0.14/0 --> 172.16.40.13/0;esp, If: reth0.0, Pkts: 0, Bytes: 0

Session ID: 12, Policy name: General-Outbound/14, State: Active, Timeout: 1722,
Valid
  In: 192.168.1.30/4532 --> 74.125.226.47/80;tcp, If: reth1.0, Pkts: 4, Bytes:
658
  Out: 74.125.226.47/80 --> 172.16.40.7/45460;tcp, If: reth0.0, Pkts: 3, Bytes:
343

Session  ID:  164,  Policy  name:  General-Outbound/14,  State:  Active,  Timeout:
1764, Valid
  In: 192.168.1.30/4277 --> 64.12.24.29/443;tcp, If: reth1.0, Pkts: 767, Bytes:
51014
   Out:  64.12.24.29/443  -->  172.16.40.7/60549;tcp,  If:  reth0.0,  Pkts:  847,
Bytes: 194757

Session  ID:  452,  Policy  name:  HoneyNet-Inbound/8,  State:  Active,  Timeout:  2,
Valid
  In: 31.132.2.146/25345 --> 172.16.40.4/53;udp, If: reth0.0, Pkts: 1, Bytes: 64
   Out:  172.16.42.204/53  -->  31.132.2.146/25345;udp,  If:  reth1.0,  Pkts:  1,
Bytes: 3891
```

```
Session ID: 660, Policy name: General-Outbound/14, State: Active, Timeout:
1718, Valid
  In: 192.168.1.30/4517 --> 74.125.225.75/80;tcp, If: reth1.0, Pkts: 9, Bytes:
703
   Out: 74.125.225.75/80 --> 172.16.40.7/57358;tcp, If: reth0.0, Pkts: 11,
Bytes: 12020

Session ID: 682, Policy name: self-traffic-policy/1, State: Active, Timeout:
1778, Valid
  In: 192.168.1.234/52772 --> 208.87.234.140/80;tcp, If: .local..0, Pkts: 16,
Bytes: 2195
   Out: 208.87.234.140/80 --> 172.16.40.7/45991;tcp, If: reth0.0, Pkts: 12,
Bytes: 2732

Session ID: 1406, Policy name: General-Outbound/14, State: Active, Timeout:
1718, Valid
  In: 192.168.1.30/4513 --> 74.125.225.75/80;tcp, If: reth1.0, Pkts: 9, Bytes:
1038
   Out: 74.125.225.75/80 --> 172.16.40.7/63263;tcp, If: reth0.0, Pkts: 11,
Bytes: 12251

{primary:node0}
root@SRX100HM> show security flow session interface reth0.0 extensive
node0:

Session ID: 164, Status: Normal, State: Active
Flag: 0x8100000
Policy name: General-Outbound/14
Source NAT pool: Host-Outbound, Application: junos-https/58
Dynamic application: junos:SSL,
Maximum timeout: 1800, Current timeout: 1632
Session State: Valid
Start time: 3621298, Duration: 105795
   In: 192.168.1.30/4277 --> 64.12.24.29/443;tcp,
    Interface: reth1.0,
    Session token: 0x5007, Flag: 0x621
    Route: 0x71f3c2, Gateway: 192.168.1.30, Tunnel: 0
    Port sequence: 0, FIN sequence: 0,
    FIN state: 0,
    Pkts: 767, Bytes: 51014
   Out: 64.12.24.29/443 --> 172.16.40.7/60549;tcp,
    Interface: reth0.0,
    Session token: 0x4006, Flag: 0x620
    Route: 0x861bc2, Gateway: 172.16.40.14, Tunnel: 0
    Port sequence: 0, FIN sequence: 0,
    FIN state: 0,
    Pkts: 847, Bytes: 194757

Session ID: 243, Status: Normal, State: Active
Flag: 0x8c100000
Policy name: HoneyNet-Inbound/8
Source NAT pool: Null, Application: junos-dns-udp/16
```

```
Dynamic application: junos:DNS, Dynamic nested application: INCONCLUSIVE
Maximum timeout: 2, Current timeout: 2
Session State: Valid
Start time: 3727091, Duration: 2
   In: 37.247.99.67/49542 --> 172.16.40.4/53;udp,
    Interface: reth0.0,
    Session token: 0x4006, Flag: 0x621
    Route: 0x861bc2, Gateway: 172.16.40.14, Tunnel: 0
    Port sequence: 0, FIN sequence: 0,
    FIN state: 0,
    Pkts: 1, Bytes: 64
   Out: 172.16.42.204/53 --> 37.247.99.67/49542;udp,
    Interface: reth1.0,
    Session token: 0x5007, Flag: 0x620
    Route: 0x867bc2, Gateway: 192.168.1.24, Tunnel: 0
    Port sequence: 0, FIN sequence: 0,
    FIN state: 0,
    Pkts: 1, Bytes: 3891

Session ID: 945, Status: Normal, State: Active
Flag: 0x8c100000
Policy name: HoneyNet-Inbound/8
Source NAT pool: Null, Application: junos-dns-udp/16
Dynamic application: junos:DNS, Dynamic nested application: INCONCLUSIVE
Maximum timeout: 2, Current timeout: 2
Session State: Valid
Start time: 3727093, Duration: 0
   In: 37.247.99.67/57562 --> 172.16.40.4/53;udp,
    Interface: reth0.0,
    Session token: 0x4006, Flag: 0x621
    Route: 0x861bc2, Gateway: 172.16.40.14, Tunnel: 0
    Port sequence: 0, FIN sequence: 0,
    FIN state: 0,
    Pkts: 1, Bytes: 64
   Out: 172.16.42.204/53 --> 37.247.99.67/57562;udp,
    Interface: reth1.0,
    Session token: 0x5007, Flag: 0x620
    Route: 0x867bc2, Gateway: 192.168.1.24, Tunnel: 0
    Port sequence: 0, FIN sequence: 0,
    FIN state: 0,
    Pkts: 1, Bytes: 3891


Session ID: 2027, Status: Normal, State: Active
Flag: 0x8c100000
Policy name: HoneyNet-Inbound/8
Source NAT pool: Null, Application: junos-dns-udp/16
Dynamic application: junos:DNS, Dynamic nested application: INCONCLUSIVE
Maximum timeout: 2, Current timeout: 2
Session State: Valid
Start time: 3727093, Duration: 0
   In: 31.132.2.146/25345 --> 172.16.40.4/53;udp,
```

```
    Interface: reth0.0,
    Session token: 0x4006, Flag: 0x621
    Route: 0x861bc2, Gateway: 172.16.40.14, Tunnel: 0
    Port sequence: 0, FIN sequence: 0,
    FIN state: 0,
    Pkts: 1, Bytes: 64
   Out: 172.16.42.204/53 --> 31.132.2.146/25345;udp,
    Interface: reth1.0,
    Session token: 0x5007, Flag: 0x620
    Route: 0x867bc2, Gateway: 192.168.1.24, Tunnel: 0
    Port sequence: 0, FIN sequence: 0,
    FIN state: 0,
    Pkts: 1, Bytes: 3891

Session ID: 2186, Status: Normal, State: Active
Flag: 0x8100000
Policy name: self-traffic-policy/1
Source NAT pool: Host-Outbound, Application: junos-http/6
Dynamic application: junos:HTTP, Dynamic nested application: junos:UNKNOWN
Maximum timeout: 1800, Current timeout: 1774
Session State: Valid
Start time: 3727006, Duration: 87
   In: 192.168.1.234/57320 --> 208.87.234.140/80;tcp,
    Interface: .local..0,
    Session token: 0x2, Flag: 0x631
    Route: 0xfffb0006, Gateway: 192.168.1.234, Tunnel: 0
    Port sequence: 0, FIN sequence: 0,
    FIN state: 0,
    Pkts: 8, Bytes: 935
   Out: 208.87.234.140/80 --> 172.16.40.7/34719;tcp,
    Interface: reth0.0,
    Session token: 0x4006, Flag: 0x620
    Route: 0x861bc2, Gateway: 172.16.40.14, Tunnel: 0
    Port sequence: 0, FIN sequence: 0,
    FIN state: 0,
    Pkts: 5, Bytes: 534

Session ID: 3048, Status: Normal, State: Active
Flag: 0x8c100000
Policy name: HoneyNet-Inbound/8
Source NAT pool: Null, Application: junos-dns-udp/16
Dynamic application: junos:DNS, Dynamic nested application: INCONCLUSIVE
Maximum timeout: 2, Current timeout: 2
Session State: Valid
Start time: 3727092, Duration: 1
   In: 37.247.99.67/46102 --> 172.16.40.4/53;udp,
    Interface: reth0.0,
    Session token: 0x4006, Flag: 0x621
    Route: 0x861bc2, Gateway: 172.16.40.14, Tunnel: 0
    Port sequence: 0, FIN sequence: 0,
    FIN state: 0,
    Pkts: 1, Bytes: 64
```

```
    Out: 172.16.42.204/53 --> 37.247.99.67/46102;udp,
     Interface: reth1.0,
     Session token: 0x5007, Flag: 0x620
     Route: 0x867bc2, Gateway: 192.168.1.24, Tunnel: 0
     Port sequence: 0, FIN sequence: 0,
     FIN state: 0,
     Pkts: 1, Bytes: 3891

Session ID: 3233, Status: Normal, State: Active
Flag: 0xc100000
Policy name: SSL-Inbound/4
Source NAT pool: Null, Application: junos-https/58
Dynamic application: junos:SSL,
Maximum timeout: 1800, Current timeout: 1800
Session State: Valid
Start time: 3726004, Duration: 1089
   In: 66.129.232.2/48272 --> 172.16.40.13/443;tcp,
    Interface: reth0.0,
    Session token: 0x4006, Flag: 0x621
    Route: 0x861bc2, Gateway: 172.16.40.14, Tunnel: 0
    Port sequence: 0, FIN sequence: 0,
    FIN state: 0,
    Pkts: 7735, Bytes: 438290
   Out: 192.168.1.45/443 --> 66.129.232.2/48272;tcp,
    Interface: reth1.0,
    Session token: 0x5007, Flag: 0x620
    Route: 0x86dbc2, Gateway: 192.168.1.45, Tunnel: 0
    Port sequence: 0, FIN sequence: 0,
    FIN state: 0,
    Pkts: 13866, Bytes: 13819678
```

View NAT Errors

Each interface tracks its own NAT error information, which can be helpful when troubleshooting issues (particularly when running out of resources). You can view this on an interface-by-interface basis. In particular, are the NAT counters incrementing? If so, you might want to run a flow debug to determine why this is occurring.

```
{primary:node0}
root@SRX100HM> show interfaces reth0.0 extensive
  Logical interface reth0.0 (Index 69) (SNMP ifIndex 531) (Generation 134)
    Flags: SNMP-Traps 0x0 Encapsulation: ENET2
    Statistics        Packets        pps         Bytes          bps
    Bundle:
        Input :      37583250         19   18085283733        18304
        Output:      51125926         71   36049681531       455928
    Link:
      fe-1/0/1.0
        Input :             0          0             0            0
        Output:             0          0             0            0
      fe-0/0/1.0
        Input :      37583250         19   18085283733        18304
```

```
    Output:       51116766          71   36048862455         455928
  Marker Statistics:    Marker Rx    Resp Tx   Unknown Rx   Illegal Rx
    fe-1/0/1.0                  0          0            0            0
    fe-0/0/1.0                  0          0            0            0
  Security: Zone: Danger
  Allowed host-inbound traffic : ike ping
  Flow Statistics :
  Flow Input statistics :
    Self packets :                     879427
    ICMP packets :                     937609
    VPN packets :                      10363870
    Multicast packets :                0
    Bytes permitted by policy :        14791682432
    Connections established :          1561865
  Flow Output statistics:
    Multicast packets :                0
    Bytes permitted by policy :        33694905891
  Flow error statistics (Packets dropped due to):
    Address spoofing:                  0
    Authentication failed:             0
    Incoming NAT errors:               0
    Invalid zone received packet:      0
    Multiple user authentications:     0
    Multiple incoming NAT:             0
    No parent for a gate:              0
    No one interested in self packets: 0
    No minor session:                  0
    No more sessions:                  0
    No NAT gate:                       0
    No route present:                  57029
    No SA for incoming SPI:            230
    No tunnel found:                   0
    No session for a gate:             0
    No zone or NULL zone binding       0
    Policy denied:                     278
    Security association not active:   240039
    TCP sequence number out of window: 38
    Syn-attack protection:             11
    User authentication errors:        0
  Protocol inet, MTU: 1500, Generation: 148, Route table: 4
    Flags: Sendbcast-pkt-to-re, Is-Primary
    Input Filters: Inbound-QoS
    Addresses, Flags: Is-Default Is-Preferred Is-Primary
        Destination: 172.16.40.0/28, Local: 172.16.40.13, Broadcast:
172.16.40.15, Generation: 145
```

View Firewall Logs with NAT

The firewall logs themselves provide historical information about the type of NAT translation that is occurring. The logs (both init and close) provide not only the original and translated information (source and destination IP or port), but also the NAT rules that are matched for this traffic. This lookup only occurs at the beginning of the session and cannot change midsession. What follows is an example of destination NAT, as we can see that there is no source or destination NAT rule present, but we are translating the destination from 172.16.42.204 to 172.18.42.204. At the time of writing this book, Junos doesn't specify a static NAT rule, but you can see if a source or destination NAT rule is configured, and you can also determine how the traffic is being transformed by comparing the original information to the NAT output later in the log.

Session Close:

```
<14>1 2012-11-19T02:40:08.985 SRX210-HoneyNet RT_FLOW - RT_FLOW_SESSION_CLOSE
[junos@2636.1.1.1.2.36 reason="timeout" source-address="64.40.9.8" source-
port="51697" destination-address="172.16.42.204" destination-port="53" service-
name="junos-dns-udp" nat-source-address="64.40.9.8" nat-source-port="51697" nat-
destination-address="172.18.42.204" nat-destination-port="53" src-nat-rule-
name="None" dst-nat-rule-name="None" protocol-id="17" policy-name="Allow-
Internet" source-zone-name="LAN" destination-zone-name="HoneyNet" session-
id-32="23211" packets-from-client="1" bytes-from-client="64" packets-from-
server="1" bytes-from-server="3863" elapsed-time="2" application="junos:DNS"
nested-application="UNKNOWN" username="N/A" roles="N/A" packet-incoming-
interface="ge-0/0/0.0" encrypted="UNKNOWN"]
```

Session Init (Create):

```
<14>1 2012-11-19T03:02:24.173 SRX210-HoneyNet RT_FLOW - RT_FLOW_SESSION_CREATE
[junos@2636.1.1.1.2.36 source-address="98.109.158.154" source-port="1329"
destination-address="172.16.42.205" destination-port="139" service-name="junos-
smb" nat-source-address="98.109.158.154" nat-source-port="1329" nat-destination-
address="172.16.42.205" nat-destination-port="139" src-nat-rule-name="None" dst-
nat-rule-name="None" protocol-id="6" policy-name="Allow-Internet" source-zone-
name="LAN" destination-zone-name="HoneyNet" session-id-32="30171"
username="N/A" roles="N/A" packet-incoming-interface="ge-0/0/0.0" applica-
tion="UNKNOWN" nested-application="UNKNOWN" encrypted="UNKNOWN"]
```

Flow Debugging with NAT

In this section, we take a quick look at three excerpts from a flow debug on source, destination, and static NAT. This is the same process as enabling the flow debug in Chapter 8. The main thing to remember when configuring NAT is that when you're using the packet filters they match the traffic as it arrives on the device, so the packet filters should match the original traffic before NAT translation.

Source NAT

In Example 9-1, we can see that we are using source NAT. There are a few statements that call that out. The first specifies that Src NAT is active and identifies the pool index. PST_NAT stands for persistent NAT, which is off. Then we see the second boldface statement, which identifies what the transform is (original → transformed). DIP ID is a legacy term from the ScreenOS days where this operation was called source translation to a Dynamic IP pool. You'll also notice that the NAT action is taking effect after the security policy lookup, as we pointed out several times throughout this chapter.

Example 9-1. Source NAT example

```
{primary:node0}
root@SRX100HM> show log FlowTrace
Dec 1 21:49:11 SRX100HM clear-log[20146]: logfile cleared
Dec  1 21:49:15  21:49:15.591147:CID-1:RT:<192.168.1.30/2537->184.85.87.148/80;6>
matched filter 1:

Dec  1 21:49:15 21:49:15.591147:CID-1:RT:packet [48] ipid = 2314, @0x423a9b1a

Dec  1 21:49:15 21:49:15.591147:CID-1:RT:---- flow_process_pkt: (thd 1): flow_ctxt
type 15, common flag 0x0, mbuf 0x423a9900, rtbl_idx = 5

Dec  1 21:49:15 21:49:15.591147:CID-1:RT: sysstats_inc_InCnts

Dec  1 21:49:15  21:49:15.591147:CID-1:RT:  flow process  pak  fast  ifl  71  in_ifp
reth1.0

Dec     1    21:49:15    21:49:15.591147:CID-1:RT:       reth1.0:192.168.1.30/2537-
>184.85.87.148/80, tcp, flag 2 syn

Dec   1  21:49:15  21:49:15.591147:CID-1:RT:  find  flow:  table  0x4cbeec78,  hash
25339(0xffff), sa 192.168.1.30, da 184.85.87.148, sp 2537, dp 80, proto 6, tok 20487

Dec  1  21:49:15  21:49:15.591147:CID-1:RT:   no  session  found,  start  first  path.
in_tunnel - 0x0, from_cp_flag - 0

Dec  1 21:49:15 21:49:15.591147:CID-1:RT:  flow_first_create_session

Dec  1 21:49:15 21:49:15.591147:CID-1:RT:  flow_first_in_dst_nat: in <reth1.0>, out
<N/A> dst_adr 184.85.87.148, sp 2537, dp 80

Dec  1 21:49:15 21:49:15.591147:CID-1:RT:  chose interface reth1.0 as incoming nat
if.

Dec  1 21:49:15 21:49:15.591147:CID-1:RT:flow_first_rule_dst_xlate: DST  no-xlate:
0.0.0.0(0) to 184.85.87.148(80)

Dec   1  21:49:15  21:49:15.591147:CID-1:RT:flow_first_routing:  vr_id  5,  call
flow_route_lookup(): src_ip 192.168.1.30, x_dst_ip 184.85.87.148, in ifp reth1.0,
out ifp N/A sp 2537, dp 80, ip_proto 6, tos 0

Dec  1 21:49:15 21:49:15.591147:CID-1:RT:Doing DESTINATION addr route-lookup

Dec  1 21:49:15 21:49:15.591147:CID-1:RT:  routed (x_dst_ip 184.85.87.148) from LAN
(reth1.0 in 1) to reth0.0, Next-hop: 172.16.40.14

Dec  1 21:49:15 21:49:15.591147:CID-1:RT:  policy search from zone LAN-> zone Dan-
ger (0x0,0x9e90050,0x50)
```

```
Dec  1 21:49:15 21:49:15.591147:CID-1:RT:  policy has timeout 900

Dec  1 21:49:15 21:49:15.591147:CID-1:RT:  app 6, timeout 1800s, curr ageout 20s
```

```
Dec  1 21:49:15 21:49:15.591147:CID-1:RT:flow_first_src_xlate: src nat returns sta-
tus: 1, rule/pool id: 1/32772, pst_nat: False.

Dec  1 21:49:15 21:49:15.591147:CID-1:RT:  dip id = 4/1, 192.168.1.30/2537-
>172.16.40.7/39174 protocol 6
```

```
Dec  1 21:49:15 21:49:15.591147:CID-1:RT:  choose interface reth0.0 as outgoing phy
if

Dec  1 21:49:15 21:49:15.591147:CID-1:RT:is_loop_pak: No loop: on ifp: reth0.0,
addr: 184.85.87.148, rtt_idx:4

Dec  1 21:49:15 21:49:15.591147:CID-1:RT:  check nsrp pak fwd: in_tun=0x0, VSD 1
for out ifp reth0.0

Dec  1 21:49:15 21:49:15.591147:CID-1:RT:  vsd 1 is active

Dec  1 21:49:15 21:49:15.591147:CID-1:RT:-jsf : Alloc sess plugin info for session
98784258070
```

Destination NAT

In Example 9-2, we are using destination NAT to translate the inbound traffic to an internal server. As we know, this lookup happens before the security policy lookup—which we intentionally show because this traffic is denied by policy. You can see how the NAT transform is happening in the boldface text where both the DST XLATE fields show the original → transform rules as well as the route lookup that occurs after it.

Example 9-2. Destination NAT example

```
Dec  1 22:06:55 22:06:54.1015362:CID-1:RT:<66.129.232.2/60970->172.16.40.13/23;6>
matched filter 1:

Dec  1 22:06:55 22:06:54.1015362:CID-1:RT:packet [52] ipid = 1079, @0x4236b89a

Dec  1 22:06:55 22:06:54.1015362:CID-1:RT:---- flow_process_pkt: (thd 1): flow_ctxt
type 15, common flag 0x0, mbuf 0x4236b680, rtbl_idx = 4

Dec  1 22:06:55 22:06:54.1015362:CID-1:RT: sysstats_inc_InCnts

Dec  1 22:06:55 22:06:54.1015362:CID-1:RT: flow process pak fast ifl 69 in_ifp
reth0.0

Dec  1 22:06:55 22:06:54.1015362:CID-1:RT:  reth0.0:66.129.232.2/60970-
>172.16.40.13/23, tcp, flag 2 syn
```

```
Dec  1 22:06:55 22:06:54.1015362:CID-1:RT: find flow: table 0x4cbeec78, hash
33768(0xffff), sa 66.129.232.2, da 172.16.40.13, sp 60970, dp 23, proto 6, tok 16390

Dec  1 22:06:55 22:06:54.1015362:CID-1:RT:  no session found, start first path.
in_tunnel - 0x0, from_cp_flag - 0

Dec  1 22:06:55 22:06:54.1015362:CID-1:RT:check self-traffic on reth0.0, in_tunnel
0x0

Dec  1 22:06:55 22:06:54.1015362:CID-1:RT:retcode: 0x1301

Dec  1 22:06:55 22:06:54.1015362:CID-1:RT:pak_for_self : proto 6, dst port 23, ac-
tion 0x0

Dec  1 22:06:55 22:06:54.1015362:CID-1:RT:  flow_first_create_session

Dec  1 22:06:55 22:06:54.1015362:CID-1:RT:  flow_first_in_dst_nat: in <reth0.0>,
out <N/A> dst_adr 172.16.40.13, sp 60970, dp 23

Dec  1 22:06:55 22:06:54.1015362:CID-1:RT:  chose interface reth0.0 as incoming nat
if.

Dec  1 22:06:55 22:06:54.1015362:CID-1:RT:flow_first_rule_dst_xlate: DST xlate:
172.16.40.13(23) to 192.168.1.99(23), rule/pool id 1/32769.

Dec  1 22:06:55 22:06:54.1015362:CID-1:RT:flow_first_routing: vr_id 5, call
flow_route_lookup(): src_ip 66.129.232.2, x_dst_ip 192.168.1.99, in ifp reth0.0,
out ifp N/A sp 60970, dp 23, ip_proto 6, tos 20

Dec  1 22:06:55 22:06:54.1015362:CID-1:RT:Doing DESTINATION addr route-lookup

Dec  1 22:06:55 22:06:54.1015362:CID-1:RT:  routed (x_dst_ip 192.168.1.99) from Dan-
ger (reth0.0 in 1) to reth1.0, Next-hop: 192.168.1.99

Dec  1 22:06:55 22:06:54.1015362:CID-1:RT:  policy search from zone Danger-> zone
LAN (0x110,0xee2a0017,0x17)

Dec  1 22:06:55 22:06:54.1015362:CID-1:RT:  app 10, timeout 1800s, curr ageout 20s

Dec  1 22:06:55 22:06:54.1015362:CID-1:RT: Error : get sess plugin info 0x4fe5d970

Dec  1 22:06:55 22:06:54.1015362:CID-1:RT: Error : get sess plugin info 0x4fe5d970

Dec  1 22:06:55 22:06:54.1015362:CID-1:RT:  packet dropped, denied by policy

Dec  1 22:06:55 22:06:54.1015362:CID-1:RT:  packet dropped,  policy deny.
```

Static NAT

In Example 9-3, we are using static NAT. Although the debug doesn't explicitly call this out, there are a few clues. First, in the first boldface rule we can see that there is no reference to the port as there is in the destination NAT example (23). Second, there is no port transform occurring (although this is not a requirement of destination NAT), which static NAT cannot do. Also remember that static NAT will occur before destination NAT when you're doing a debug with NAT.

Example 9-3. Static NAT example

```
Dec  1 22:14:27  22:14:26.1488828:CID-1:RT:<66.129.232.2/58887->172.16.40.5/22;6>
matched filter 1:

Dec 1 22:14:27 22:14:26.1488828:CID-1:RT:packet [52] ipid = 2523, @0x422b551a

Dec 1 22:14:27 22:14:26.1488828:CID-1:RT:---- flow_process_pkt: (thd 1): flow_ctxt
type 15, common flag 0x0, mbuf 0x422b5300, rtbl_idx = 4

Dec 1 22:14:27 22:14:26.1488828:CID-1:RT: sysstats_inc_InCnts

Dec  1 22:14:27 22:14:26.1488828:CID-1:RT: flow process pak fast ifl 69 in_ifp
reth0.0

Dec    1   22:14:27   22:14:26.1488828:CID-1:RT:      reth0.0:66.129.232.2/58887-
>172.16.40.5/22, tcp, flag 2 syn

Dec  1 22:14:27  22:14:26.1488828:CID-1:RT: find flow: table 0x4cbeec78, hash
20615(0xffff), sa 66.129.232.2, da 172.16.40.5, sp 58887, dp 22, proto 6, tok 16390

Dec  1 22:14:27 22:14:26.1488828:CID-1:RT:  no session found, start first path.
in_tunnel - 0x0, from_cp_flag - 0

Dec 1 22:14:27 22:14:26.1488828:CID-1:RT:  flow_first_create_session

Dec  1 22:14:27 22:14:26.1488828:CID-1:RT:  flow_first_in_dst_nat: in <reth0.0>,
out <N/A> dst_adr 172.16.40.5, sp 58887, dp 22

Dec 1 22:14:27 22:14:26.1488828:CID-1:RT:  chose interface reth0.0 as incoming nat
if.

Dec    1   22:14:27   22:14:26.1488828:CID-1:RT:flow_first_rule_dst_xlate:   packet
66.129.232.2->172.16.40.5 nsp2 0.0.0.0->172.16.42.205.

Dec    1   22:14:27   22:14:26.1488828:CID-1:RT:flow_first_routing:  vr_id  5,  call
flow_route_lookup(): src_ip 66.129.232.2, x_dst_ip 172.16.42.205, in ifp reth0.0,
out ifp N/A sp 58887, dp 22, ip_proto 6, tos 20

Dec 1 22:14:27 22:14:26.1488828:CID-1:RT:Doing DESTINATION addr route-lookup

Dec  1 22:14:27 22:14:26.1488828:CID-1:RT:  routed (x_dst_ip 172.16.42.205) from
Danger (reth0.0 in 1) to reth1.0, Next-hop: 192.168.1.24

Dec  1 22:14:27 22:14:26.1488828:CID-1:RT:  policy search from zone Danger-> zone
LAN (0x114,0xe6070016,0x16)

Dec 1 22:14:27 22:14:26.1488828:CID-1:RT:  app 22, timeout 1800s, curr ageout 20s
```

```
Dec   1 22:14:27  22:14:26.1488828:CID-1:RT:flow_first_src_xlate:   nat_src_xlated:
False, nat_src_xlate_failed: False

Dec  1 22:14:27 22:14:26.1488828:CID-1:RT:flow_first_src_xlate: src nat returns sta-
tus: 0, rule/pool id: 0/0, pst_nat: False.

Dec   1  22:14:27  22:14:26.1488828:CID-1:RT:   dip  id  =  0/0,  66.129.232.2/58887-
>66.129.232.2/58887 protocol 0

Dec   1 22:14:27  22:14:26.1488828:CID-1:RT:  choose  interface reth1.0 as  outgoing
phy if

Dec   1 22:14:27  22:14:26.1488828:CID-1:RT:is_loop_pak: No  loop: on ifp: reth1.0,
addr: 172.16.42.205, rtt_idx:5

Dec   1 22:14:27 22:14:26.1488828:CID-1:RT:  check nsrp pak fwd: in_tun=0x0, VSD 1
for out ifp reth1.0

Dec  1 22:14:27 22:14:26.1488828:CID-1:RT:  vsd 1 is active

Dec  1 22:14:27 22:14:26.1488828:CID-1:RT:-jsf : Alloc sess plugin info for session
90194318307
```

Also, remember that static NAT can also transform the source if it matches the bidirectional (implicit) reverse rule. It will look similar to source NAT except it won't do any port translation or reference a pool, as shown in the following output, where we perform reverse static NAT.

```
Dec    1  22:28:30  22:28:30.749281:CID-1:RT:<192.168.1.55/40093->4.2.2.2/80;6>
matched filter 1:

Dec  1 22:28:30 22:28:30.749281:CID-1:RT:packet [60] ipid = 11363, @0x422e9e9a

Dec    1  22:28:30  22:28:30.749281:CID-1:RT:----  flow_process_pkt:  (thd  1):
flow_ctxt type 15, common flag 0x0, mbuf 0x422e9c80, rtbl_idx = 5

Dec  1 22:28:30 22:28:30.749281:CID-1:RT: sysstats_inc_InCnts

Dec   1 22:28:30 22:28:30.749281:CID-1:RT: flow process pak fast ifl 71 in_ifp
reth1.0

Dec     1   22:28:30   22:28:30.749281:CID-1:RT:      reth1.0:192.168.1.55/40093-
>4.2.2.2/80, tcp, flag 2 syn

Dec   1 22:28:30  22:28:30.749281:CID-1:RT: find  flow: table 0x4cbeec78, hash
5142(0xffff), sa 192.168.1.55, da 4.2.2.2, sp 40093, dp 80, proto 6, tok 20487

Dec  1 22:28:30 22:28:30.749281:CID-1:RT:  no session found, start first path.
in_tunnel - 0x0, from_cp_flag - 0

Dec  1 22:28:30 22:28:30.749281:CID-1:RT:  flow_first_create_session
```

```
Dec  1 22:28:30 22:28:30.749281:CID-1:RT:  flow_first_in_dst_nat: in <reth1.0>,
out <N/A> dst_adr 4.2.2.2, sp 40093, dp 80

Dec  1 22:28:30 22:28:30.749281:CID-1:RT:  chose interface reth1.0 as incoming
nat if.

Dec  1 22:28:30 22:28:30.749281:CID-1:RT:flow_first_rule_dst_xlate: DST no-
xlate: 0.0.0.0(0) to 4.2.2.2(80)

Dec  1 22:28:30 22:28:30.749281:CID-1:RT:flow_first_routing: vr_id 5, call
flow_route_lookup(): src_ip 192.168.1.55, x_dst_ip 4.2.2.2, in ifp reth1.0, out
ifp N/A sp 40093, dp 80, ip_proto 6, tos 10

Dec  1 22:28:30 22:28:30.749281:CID-1:RT:Doing DESTINATION addr route-lookup

Dec  1 22:28:30 22:28:30.749281:CID-1:RT:  routed (x_dst_ip 4.2.2.2) from LAN
(reth1.0 in 1) to reth0.0, Next-hop: 172.16.40.14

Dec  1 22:28:30 22:28:30.749281:CID-1:RT:  policy search from zone LAN-> zone
Danger (0x0,0x9c9d0050,0x50)

Dec  1 22:28:30 22:28:30.749281:CID-1:RT:  policy has timeout 900

Dec  1 22:28:30 22:28:30.749281:CID-1:RT:  app 6, timeout 1800s, curr ageout 20s

Dec  1 22:28:30 22:28:30.749281:CID-1:RT:  found reversed mip 172.16.40.9 for
192.168.1.55 (on reth0.0)

Dec  1 22:28:30 22:28:30.749281:CID-1:RT:flow_first_src_xlate:  nat_src_xlated:
True, nat_src_xlate_failed: False

Dec  1 22:28:30 22:28:30.749281:CID-1:RT:flow_first_src_xlate: hip xlate:
192.168.1.55->172.16.40.9 at reth0.0 (vs. reth0.0)

Dec  1 22:28:30 22:28:30.749281:CID-1:RT:  dip id = 0/0, 192.168.1.55/40093-
>172.16.40.9/40093 protocol 0

Dec  1 22:28:30 22:28:30.749281:CID-1:RT:  choose interface reth0.0 as outgoing
phy if

Dec  1 22:28:30 22:28:30.749281:CID-1:RT:is_loop_pak: No loop: on ifp: reth0.0,
addr: 4.2.2.2, rtt_idx:4

Dec  1 22:28:30 22:28:30.749281:CID-1:RT:  check nsrp pak fwd: in_tun=0x0, VSD
1 for out ifp reth0.0

Dec  1 22:28:30 22:28:30.749281:CID-1:RT:  vsd 1 is active

Dec  1 22:28:30 22:28:30.749281:CID-1:RT:-jsf : Alloc sess plugin info for ses-
sion 107374185892
```

The key to identifying that this is not source NAT is the reverse MIP statement and the source NAT HIP statement. Mapped IP (MIP) is the same transform as ScreenOS (although there are differences in how it is implemented as we mentioned, but this is just a legacy statement). Also note that there is no DIP pool used. This translation would have used a source NAT rule, but because static NAT takes precedence over source and destination NAT, it was selected in this instance.

Of course, you could also see a combination of these types, such as source and destination NAT, which essentially just shows both source and destination operations taking place.

Sample Deployment

Throughout this chapter we provided several examples (including a holistic network example for both IPv4 and IPv6 for each type of NAT), so please refer to the examples in this chapter as this chapter's sample deployments.

Summary

The original intention of NAT was to extend the lifeline of IPv4, but it has found a wide range of new uses in modern networks. NAT is likely to be a part of networks into the future as we migrate to IPv6 and nonroutable internal networks that must be translated to reach the Internet or access trading partners. Throughout this chapter we discussed the different NAT techniques available and how to implement them with best practices in mind for your network. By properly leveraging NAT in your SRX, you are less likely to run into configuration and support issues, and you can make the most efficient use of your available IP address space. NAT is more than likely to exist in our networks long into the future after IPv6 is deployed and the original need for NAT is nullified.

Study Questions

Questions

1. Describe the three main NAT technologies supported on the SRX.
2. What does it mean that static NAT is bidirectional? Are the other NATs only translated in one direction of a flow?
3. What is the order of precedence when it comes to NAT in the flow lookup policy?
4. What happens if no NAT rule is matched during the policy lookup phase?
5. What is a NAT context, and what options are available for the three different types of NAT rulesets?
6. How are rule matches found when doing a NAT lookup?

7. What are Proxy-ARP and Proxy-NDP and when are they needed?
8. What translation options do you have for each type of NAT?
9. What source, destination, and application should you use in your security policy when using static, source, and destination NAT (discuss them separately)?
10. What is the best practice for crafting the rules in a NAT ruleset?
11. Why would you use no-NAT rules in your NAT policy, and which NAT types support them?

Answers

1. The three NAT types are static, source, and destination. Static NAT is used for 1:1 bidirectional address translation. Source NAT translates the source address and ports for traffic leaving the firewall from one range to another. You can use this to both perform NAT where each internal IP gets its own IP address or you can overload the sources to individual interface IPs or pools of IP addresses. Finally, destination is used to translate the destination address or port of an inbound connection on the SRX. This is often used when you are limited with IP address space and want to multiplex multiple internal hosts to the same public IP address based on service.
2. Because the SRX is a stateful firewall, it handles translating the two directions of the flows for a given session regardless of what type is used. What we mean by bidirectional for static NAT is that the translation will happen for both initiated directions of traffic without having to configure a reverse rule. Source NAT and destination NAT only occur in one direction, and you would have to configure a reverse mapping if you wanted such a translation to happen (and it couldn't be to the same address most likely). For instance, if you have a host in the DMZ, and you set up a static NAT rule from the untrust zone to perform the 1:1 NAT in the DMZ, the SRX will handle the NAT from untrust to DMZ and from DMZ to untrust (firewall rule permitting). Source NAT, on the other hand, might be set up from trust to untrust—but it will only happen for sessions initiated in that direction, not from untrust to trust. In the case of destination NAT, if you have a translation from untrust to DMZ, it only happens in that one direction, and you would need to configure source NAT to NAT the traffic from DMZ to untrust.
3. Before the security policy lookup, static NAT (destination address) is processed first. If there is no static NAT rule matched, then destination NAT will be examined for the destination address or port translation. Next comes the security policy lookup, followed by a lookup in the reverse static NAT rulebase. If there is no rule match there, then the source NAT rulebase will be examined to see if there is a match and then a transform.
4. The traffic will not be transformed by NAT.

5. A NAT context defines the high-level directionality match criteria for the NAT ruleset. You can match on one or more interfaces, zones, or routing instances (although only one type per context). The order of precedence is interfaces, then zones, then routing instances from highest to lowest priority match. Static NAT uses only "from" in its context, destination NAT uses only "from" in its context, and source NAT uses both "from" and "to" in its context.
6. For the respective NAT type (static, destination, source), first the NAT engine will try to match an actual context. If no match is found, no NAT will occur for that type. If a match occurs, NAT will start with the most specific NAT type (interface, then zone, then routing instance). Next, from the top down in the NAT ruleset for the first matched context, the NAT policy will attempt to match the packet to the same criteria defined in the rule. If a match occurs, that action will be taken. If no match occurs in that ruleset, the SRX will try to match it to another ruleset context and rule, or if none are available no NAT will occur for the traffic.
7. Proxy-ARP and its IPv6 relative Proxy-NDP allow the SRX to respond to an ARP request on behalf of the virtual destination's IP address (which the SRX hosts) with its own MAC address to the peer device will properly forward the traffic to the SRX. This must be manually configured, and is required when you are using virtual IP addresses in the egress subnet shared between the SRX and the upstream device (because it hosts ARP for a MAC address on their local subnet). You do not need to use Proxy-ARP or Proxy-NDP if the upstream device is routing the traffic for that subnet to you, or if you are terminating NAT on the interface itself, in which case the SRX will respond to queries for MAC addresses that it owns.
8. Each type of NAT supports both IPv4 and IPv6 NAT, including translating IPv4 to IPv6 and vice versa. For static NAT, you can translate one address to another, or entire contiguous ranges from one network to another. Destination NAT allows you to translate matched traffic by altering the destination address and port. You can do this to one address or multiple addresses in a pool. Source NAT has the most options (some of which were only topically discussed in this book). You can translate source addresses to both interfaces and pools. When using source NAT, you can define whether to use port translation (overloading), and you can also use advanced options like persistent NAT and address shifting and control how addresses are allocated from the pool.
9. For static NAT, your source address should be the original (untranslated) IP address, but the destination should be the translated IP address in the security policy (static NAT comes before the policy lookup, static NAT comes after the security policy). For source NAT, you should always use the original untranslated IP addresses in your security policy because the source NAT happens after the policy lookup. For destination NAT, you should use the translated addresses

or ports in your security policy because it happens before the security policy lookup.

10. It is best to have the most specific NAT rule matches at the top of the ruleset with the less specific matches below so that you avoid shadowing wherever possible. This is the same as with the security policies.
11. Source and destination NAT support no-NAT as an option when you make a match. This is useful if you want to exclude certain conditions from being processed by NAT. Particularly with source NAT where you might have a catchall at the bottom of the rulebase, you might want to not match on any rule that might trigger NAT, so use this rule first and specify no-Nat for your action.

CHAPTER 10
IPsec VPN

The SRX product suite combines the robust IP Security virtual private network (IPsec VPN) features from ScreenOS into the legendary networking platform of Junos. IPsec VPNs have become a central component of modern computer networks for securing the data between different sites and remote users. As more critical applications and sensitive information have been transferred into electronic format, the demand to secure this information has grown. IPsec VPNs are sometimes confused with Layer 2 or Layer 3 VPNs, which do not actually encrypt the data, but rather tunnel the traffic that flows through the VPNs; however, IPsec VPNs are VPNs that provide encryption and authentication to secure traffic.

There are two high-level uses for IPsec VPNs: to secure data between two or more computer networks and to secure data between a remote user and a computer network. This chapter details the technologies behind both site-to-site and remote access VPNs and how these technologies are implemented on the SRX. There has also been a great deal of development when it comes to new IPsec features since *Junos Security*, so we examine some of these new features and how they can improve the functionality that the SRX has to offer when it comes to IPsec. After a thorough discussion of the technology and the implementation of the IPsec VPNs on the SRX, we examine verification and troubleshooting features and conclude with some case studies to provide you with a few real-world implementation examples.

VPN Architecture Overview

VPNs not only secure communication between two devices, but they also create a virtual channel that data can traverse. In this section, we examine two primary VPN architectures: site-to-site and remote access. Although the underlying technologies are essentially the same, the manner in which the VPNs interconnect varies between the different models.

Site-to-Site IPsec VPNs

Site-to-site IPsec VPNs connect two sites together to allow for secure communication between those sites, as shown in Figure 10-1. Site-to-site VPNs are most often deployed to secure data between sites in an organization, or between an organization and a partner organization. Site-to-site VPNs are more common over the Internet than across private networks; however, many organizations are encrypting data between sites on private networks to secure the communication. Internet site-to-site VPNs also offer a cost and availability benefit over private site-to-site links, making them a good choice for securing data, especially when performance is not a major concern. The Internet site-to-site VPNs can also serve as a backup link to private links, in the event the private link should fail. There are a couple of variations of site-to-site VPNs besides the direct site-to-site architecture; these include hub and spoke, full mesh, and multipoint VPNs.

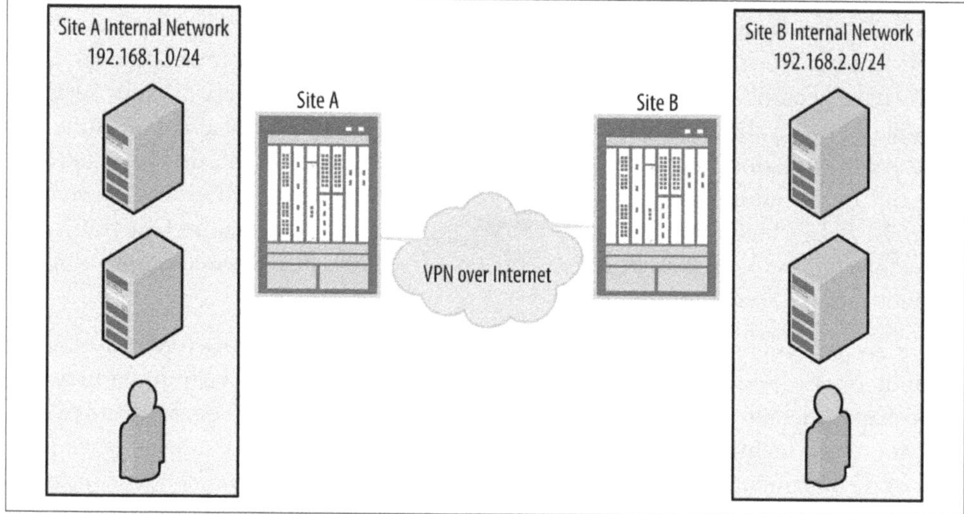

Figure 10-1. Sample site-to-site VPN

Hub and Spoke IPsec VPNs

Many enterprise networks have one or more large offices with multiple branch offices. In some cases, branch offices need to access resources in all other branches; in other cases, they might only need to access resources in the central sites. In the latter case, hub and spoke VPN networks provide a simple method of accomplishing this goal, as illustrated in Figure 10-2. Each remote site connects into the central site, but they do not connect into each other directly; rather, they connect through the central site, hence the hub and spoke moniker.

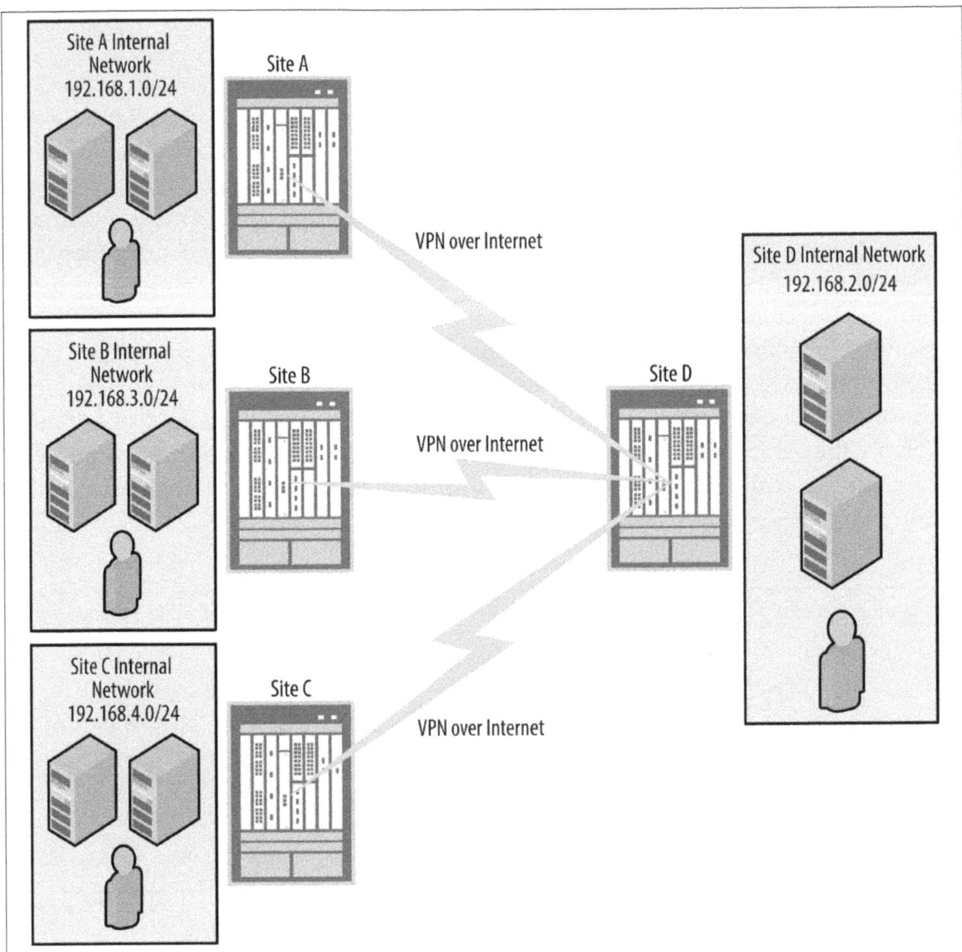

Figure 10-2. Sample hub and spoke VPN

From a management perspective, hub and spoke networks are straightforward to administer because all spokes connect to the hub. They are easy to scale because there is a minimum amount of state that must be maintained. (Only *N* VPNs must be maintained, where *N* is the number of VPNs, or remote sites; full mesh VPNs, which we will discuss next, require $N(N - 1)/2$ VPNs. This means that with 10 remote sites, only 10 VPNs would need to be maintained in a hub and spoke network, whereas 25 would need to be maintained in a full mesh network.) Finally, it is much easier to secure hub and spoke networks, as well as provide services for each connected network, because the security and services can be administered centrally at the hub rather than occurring at all of the spokes (this, as you can imagine, equates to cost savings).

Full Mesh VPNs

Although hub and spoke VPNs might be commonplace because of their simplicity, there are a few factors that could make this model undesirable for your particular network. First, all traffic must go from the spoke to the hub and then to the other spoke when trying to send traffic between spokes. This can result in a lag in performance and can cause latency issues, as the hub site must process all of the traffic. This is a common issue in modern networks that run real-time applications such as VoIP and video conferencing, which are sensitive to bandwidth and latency issues and generally work better when the sites can communicate directly with each other. Therefore, full mesh is most typically implemented for connecting remote offices within an organization (and is not so common between separate organizations) because it allows each site to communicate directly with all other sites, as shown in Figure 10-3. The disadvantages of full mesh VPNs are the complexity of implementation (because all sites must be interconnected), the inability to scale, and the management overhead associated with maintaining all of the VPNs.

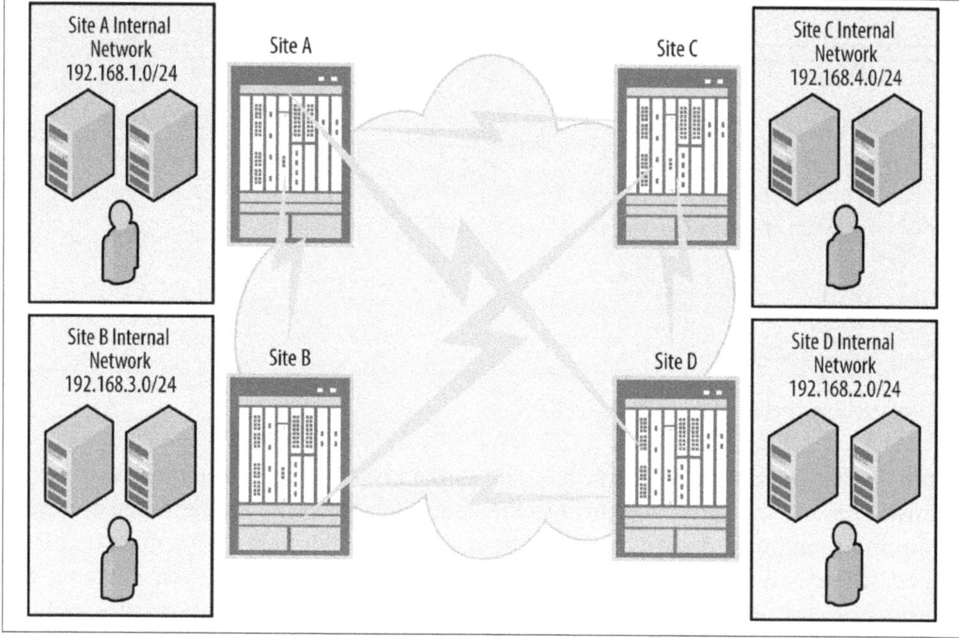

Figure 10-3. Sample full mesh VPN

Partial Mesh VPNs

Partial mesh VPNs are a hybrid of hub and spoke and full mesh, and they attempt to combine the advantages of each model, as depicted in Figure 10-4. In partial mesh VPNs, some spokes also have direct connections between each other to improve bandwidth and latency without constricting the hub site. Suffice it to say that multipoint VPNs do have some different mechanisms to establish themselves dynamically; they are typically implemented to connect remote offices with the hub, and in some cases with each other, within an organization.

The obvious advantage of partial mesh VPNs is that the remote offices still connect to the hub but also can connect to each other. This is common in environments with some real-time applications that might need to connect to each other for performance reasons. When a VPN must be established between spokes, the spokes negotiate the connections dynamically and shut the VPNs down after the communication has ceased.

As of Junos 12.1X44, the SRX supports AutoVPN, which allows the SRX to make automatic hub and spoke connections, perfect for the hub and spoke model. At the time of writing this book, the automatic spoke-to-spoke functionality is still in development, but you can look at deploying such VPNs leveraging Junos Space Security Design to establish the remote VPNs.

Remote Access VPNs

Site-to-site VPNs commonly connect sites together, and another form of IPsec VPN allows a remote user to connect to a true site for remote access. The underlying technologies of site-to-site and remote access IPsec VPNs are essentially the same; the main difference is that a site-to-site VPN is typically terminated between two VPN gateways, such as two SRX platforms. There is no requirement for software on any of the end systems. In fact, the end systems do not have to be aware that there is a VPN at all; the VPN is completely transparent to the end systems, the applications, and the users. The problem is that site-to-site VPNs are not always possible to implement because of the additional hardware requirement. To help alleviate this requirement, and empower remote users to be able to access corporate resources, remote access VPNs are used to provide this functionality.

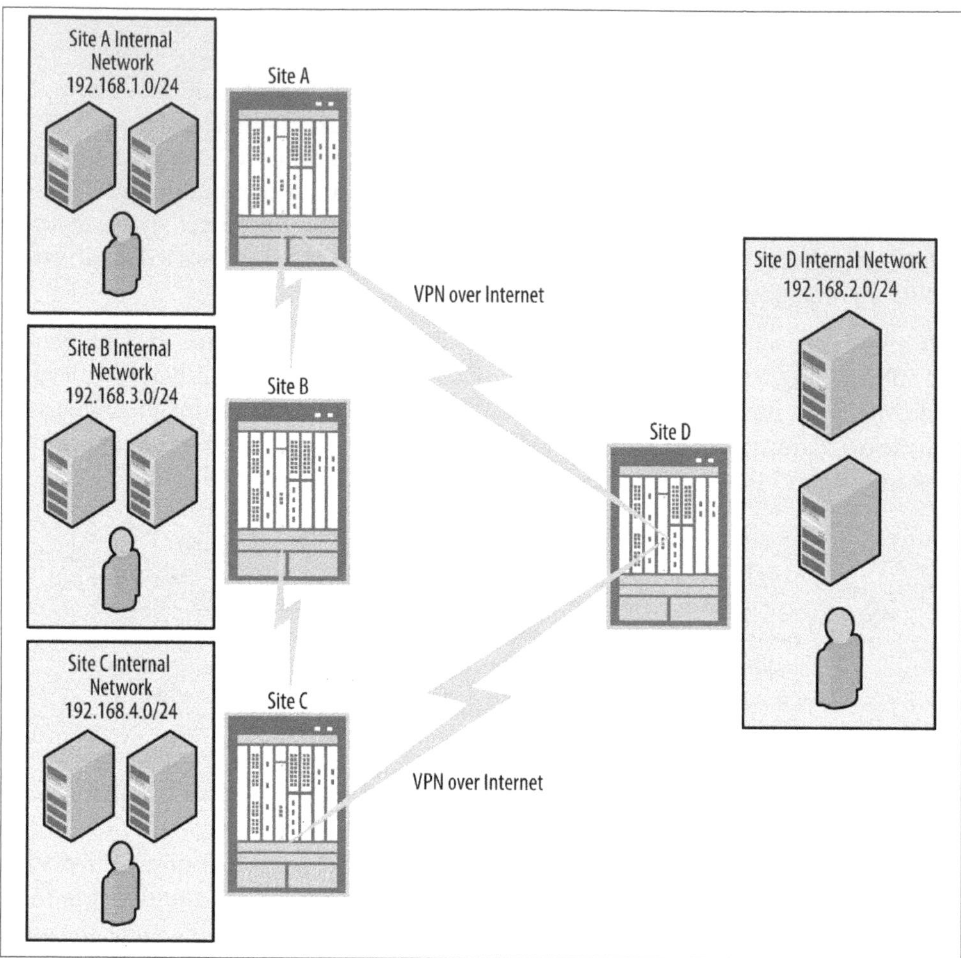

Figure 10-4. Sample multipoint VPN

Remote access VPNs are created by running software on the end systems that will establish a VPN to the central site VPN gateway such as an SRX, as shown in Figure 10-5.

Remote access VPNs are commonly available in two forms: IPsec VPNs and SSL VPNs. Although the functionality is essentially transparent to the user, there are differences between IPsec VPNs and SSL VPNs.

IPsec VPNs
: IPsec VPNs use underlying Layer 3 encryption to establish secure VPNs between a host and VPN gateway. The user traffic might or might not be tunneled, and IPsec processing is optimized for processing network traffic. IPsec VPNs also are considered to have the strongest security of any kind of remote access.

SSL VPNs
: SSL VPNs are widely deployed for their simplicity, in part because they often utilize the Secure Sockets Layer of a web browser (although SSL VPNs can also use separate applications to process this traffic as well). SSL VPNs (including the Juniper Networks Secure Access SSL VPN Gateway) gained popularity because of their interoperability with end systems and their ability to function within most networks.

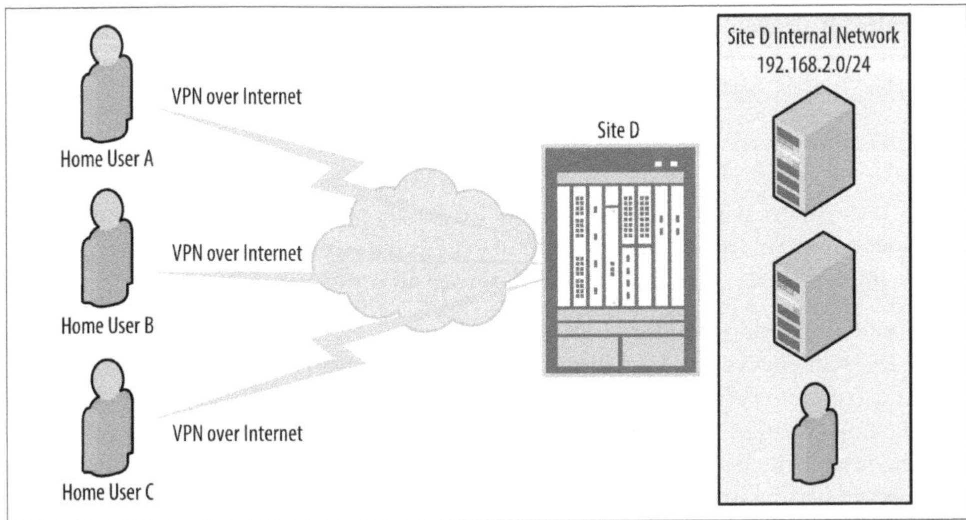

Figure 10-5. Sample remote access VPN

Branch SRX devices support both the Dynamic VPN and the Pulse client, but they only support termination via IPsec today for performance reasons. If you truly need to use SSL as a protocol over IPsec, then it is best to look at the Juniper Secure Access platforms (including the VMWare version), which can provide this functionality at the time of writing this book.

IPsec VPN Concepts Overview

IPsec VPNs come in many different flavors and support a multitude of configuration options to adapt to the needs of various networks while securing the data that travel in the VPN. This adaptive variation, and the fact that IPsec VPNs are popularly deployed, demand that we take a little time to demystify these options and provide you with some insight into how the different features can be used.

IPsec Encryption Algorithms

Encryption serves VPNs by obfuscating unencrypted traffic into a form that only the two sides of the VPN can understand. The SRX supports the use of the following standards-based encryption algorithms for this purpose. (For the sake of brevity, we have condensed our explanation of how the different encryption algorithms actually function, and instead we examine the strength and performance impact.)

Data Encryption Standard (DES)
: DES was one of the first widely deployed encryption algorithms for IPsec. It is lightweight in terms of processing power; thus, this algorithm is more susceptible to brute force attacks because there is not as large of a key space to encrypt the traffic. It's largely been replaced with the newer encryption algorithms of 3DES and AES. Best security practices tend for DES not to be used unless security is not a concern and only basic encryption is desired.

Triple Data Encryption Standard (3DES)
: 3DES is a more powerful version of DES and subjects the data to additional rounds of encryption, making it more difficult to identify clear-text traffic. Although 3DES does require more processing power than DES, it is considered to be a safe algorithm to implement for data that is of medium sensitivity.

Advanced Encryption Standard (AES)
: AES is an encryption algorithm developed by the National Institute of Standards and Technology (NIST) to provide secure and efficient encryption for very sensitive data. AES comes in different key bit lengths, most commonly 128, 256, and 384—the longer the key length, the more secure the data. Note also that the longer the key length, the more processing power is required to encrypt the data. AES should be used to encrypt the most sensitive traffic.

IPsec Authentication Algorithms

IPsec authentication, also known as *hashing*, protects the authenticity of the source of the encryption traffic. Without authentication, the two VPN endpoints would be unable to ensure that the traffic arrived unmodified, or even that it came from its original source. IPsec authentication performs this task by using a hashing algorithm. A hashing algorithm essentially calculates a special value based on the data it hashes. Even a change of a single bit of data results in a completely different hash result. Also, a hash algorithm is meant to be nonreversible, so if an attacker had the result of the hash algorithm, it would still be difficult for him to determine the original contents. Although there is a possibility that two or more data sets could produce the same hash result, this is very unlikely, and even if there is a collision whereby two values create the same hash, it is unlikely that the two data sets would be interchangeable in clear-text form.

The SRX supports three different hash algorithms to provide IPsec authentication:

Message-Digest Algorithm 5
MD5 is a widely deployed hash algorithm that consists of a 128-bit hash space. Although acceptable as a hashing algorithm, it is not recommended for the most sensitive applications.

Secure Hash Algorithm 1
SHA-1 is an improvement over MD5, using a more robust algorithm with a larger key space (168-bit) to provide more security over MD5. SHA-1 is recommended for sensitive data that need more powerful security than MD5. SHA-1 is slowly being replaced with the new SHA-2 algorithm, although deployment of SHA-2, at the time of this writing, is not common.

Secure Hash Algorithm 2
SHA-2 is a very powerful secure hash algorithm which is supported on the SRX. It uses a larger key space than both MD5 and SHA-1 to provide maximum security (now 256- and 384-bit key lengths) and has some modifications to help maximize performance and security.

IKE Version 1 Overview

IPsec can establish a VPN in one of two ways: via the Internet Key Exchange protocol or via manual key exchange. Manual key exchange is exactly that: both sides exchange the keys in some manual fashion (e.g., phone or email), and once everything is configured, the VPN can be established. IKE is a more involved process that negotiates the VPN between both VPN endpoints. It should be strongly noted that using IKE to negotiate VPNs between two endpoints is much more common and much more secure than manual key exchange. IKE allows both sides to renegotiate VPNs on the fly so that the encryption keys are constantly changing, making it more difficult for an eavesdropper to compromise the security of the network. Manual keys do not change (or at least not automatically), so if the keys are somehow determined, administrative intervention must take place to change the keys.

Two versions of the IKE standard are available: IKE version 1 and IKE version 2, not to be confused with the different phases of IKE negotiation.

Further, IKE negotiation takes place in two phases, known as Phase 1 and Phase 2. The purpose of Phase 1 is to authenticate the identities of both sides of the VPN and to establish a secure communication channel between both sides for further negotiation. In Phase 2, the remainder of the VPN negotiation process completes, and the encryption keys are exchanged to be used to secure the data that traverses the VPN.

Let's drill down just a little into Phase 1 and Phase 2 of IKE version 1 negotiations just to ensure that you understand the process. Numerous options could be implemented, and those options are examined further next.

Phase 1 IKE negotiation modes

IPsec VPNs can use two different modes when negotiating the IKE in Phase 1. The two modes of negotiation of Phase 1 are called Main mode and Aggressive mode. Only one mode is used for negotiation of Phase 1 of the VPN tunnel, and the mode must be configured the same on both sides of the tunnel; otherwise, Phase 1 is not able to complete.

Main mode. When building site-to-site VPNs, Main mode is the most common and secure way to establish the VPN because it provides additional security during the setup phase of the VPN tunnel and requires that six messages be exchanged during the negotiation. The advantage in security of Main mode over Aggressive mode is that the IKE identities are encrypted and cannot be determined by eavesdroppers. Main mode does require additional processing and it is typically used when the IP address of the client is not fixed or known in advance.

The following sequence of message exchange occurs during Main mode:

1. Initiator proposes the encryption and authentication algorithms to be used to establish the VPN.
2. Responder must accept the proposal and provide the other VPN gateway with a proposal of the encryption and authentication algorithm.
3. Initiator starts the Diffie-Hellman key exchange process by presenting a generated public key, along with a pseudorandom number.
4. Responder responds to the initiator with its public key as part of the Diffie-Hellman key exchange. After this message, both parties communicate via an encrypted channel.
5. Initiator sends the responder its IKE identity to authenticate itself.
6. Responder sends the initiator its IKE identity. Message 6 completes Phase 1 of the IKE negotiation.

Aggressive mode. Aggressive mode is an alternative to Main mode IPsec negotiation and it is most common when building VPNs from client workstations to VPN gateways, where the client's IP address is neither known in advance nor fixed. Aggressive mode requires half of the messages that Main mode does when establishing Phase 1, but it does so at the cost of disclosing the IKE identities in clear text; thus, it is a little aggressive in its security negotiations.

Aggressive mode uses the following sequence of messages:

1. Initiator proposes the encryption and authentication algorithms to be used, begins the Diffie-Hellman key exchange, and sends its IKE identity and pseudorandom number.
2. Responder must accept the proposal, and will provide the initiator with a pseudorandom number and the IKE identity of the responder. The responder will have also authenticated the initiator in this stage.
3. Initiator authenticates the responder and confirms the exchange. At this point, both parties have established a secure channel for negotiating the IPsec VPN in Phase 2 and Phase 1 is now complete.

During these initial Phase 1 IKE negotiations, a secure channel must be established between the two VPN peers; however, a question might arise: how do you form a secure communication channel that can be negotiated over an insecure network? The answer is to use the Diffie-Hellman key exchange method. The intimate details of this exchange are beyond the scope of this book and are not necessary to understand VPN configuration. Suffice it to say that essentially, the Diffie-Hellman key exchange uses public key encryption whereby each party shares each other's public keys while retaining the private keys. They then encrypt the authentication parameter (e.g., password) and send it to the other peer, which decrypts it with their private key. This happens in both directions. If both peers cannot successfully authenticate the other peer, Phase 1 cannot be established.

Diffie-Hellman *groups* refer to the size of the key length used for negotiating the VPN. There are several different groups, not all of which are supported by all vendors. When setting up a VPN with another party, the Diffie-Hellman groups must match on both peers; otherwise, the VPN connection will not establish, and error messages should detail the failure. The larger the key length, the stronger it is considered to be, because there are more possibilities for bit combinations. For instance, a 1-bit key would have two values, 0 and 1. A 2-bit key would have four values, 0, 1, 2, and 3, which in binary is 00, 01, 10, and 11. Therefore, the larger the key, the more possibilities for different keys and the more difficult it is to guess the correct key used for encryption. Consider these three groups and their escalating strength:

Group 1: 768-bit strength
Group 2: 1,024-bit strength
Group 5: 1,536-bit strength

Starting in Junos 12.1X45 as part of the Suite B support, the SRX supports these additional Diffie-Hellman groups, which are considerably stronger than groups 1, 2, and 5: 14, 19, 20, and 24.

Phase 2 IKE negotiation modes

IKE Phase 2 is responsible for generating the encryption keys used to encrypt the data traffic within the VPN. Just like in Phase 1, messages are exchanged between the two VPN gateways, and there are some similarities. Unlike Phase 1, however, there is only one negotiation mode, called Quick mode. In Quick mode, the following events always occur during Phase 2:

1. The encryption and authentication algorithms to be used to encrypt the data traffic are negotiated.
2. The method to be used to encrypt the data traffic is negotiated: either Encapsulating Security Payload or Authentication Header (AH).
3. Proxy IDs that identify the traffic to be encrypted are negotiated.
4. Phase 2 optional processing, including Perfect Forward Secrecy (PFS), is negotiated.

Additional processing might optionally take place either in Phase 2 or between Phase 1 and Phase 2. XAuth is an authentication mechanism that is commonly used for remote client IPsec VPNs, and it takes place between Phase 1 and Phase 2. We cover XAuth later in this chapter.

Perfect Forward Secrecy. PFS renegotiates Phase 1 before proceeding to negotiate Phase 2. The purpose of PFS is because in Phase 1, the exchange of keys and other encryption components can present a risk, particularly in Aggressive mode, where IKE identities are sent in the clear.

PFS mitigates those concerns by renegotiating Phase 1 in the same secure channel that Phase 1 previously built. The new Phase 1 channel is used to renegotiate Phase 2. In terms of properties, PFS essentially allows the user to suggest a different Diffie-Hellman group; however, the encryption and authentication algorithms are the same as the ones used for the original Phase 1 negotiation.

Quick mode. The only mode of negotiating Phase 2 in IPsec, known as Quick mode, exchanges three messages:

Encryption and authentication algorithms
: The encryption and authentication algorithms that are used as part of the IPsec VPN.

Proxy IDs
: The proxy IDs that identify what traffic is part of the VPN.

Mode and encapsulation
: The VPN protocol and mode the VPN uses (ESP/AH and Tunnel/Transport).

There are some additional parameters that can be configured as part of Phase 2, and they might or might not be negotiated as part of the Quick mode process.

Proxy ID negotiation. A proxy ID is a mechanism for identifying the traffic carried within the VPN, and it contains two components: the local and remote IP prefix, and the service. Within IKE version 1, only a single prefix can be defined per local and remote IP value, along with a single service.

Strictly speaking, the proxy IDs do not really need to match the traffic at all, but both parties must match what they are negotiating in the VPN. Proxy IDs have long been considered a nuisance when configuring VPNs because they are not really needed, and in large part because different vendors have determined the proxy IDs differently. There is an exception to this that was supported in ScreenOS (multiple proxy IDs), but this isn't supported today in the SRX.

The issue is that the proxy IDs are defined within the IKE RFC, which strictly defines how they are formatted and what they contain. However, the RFC doesn't exactly state how the proxy IDs should be derived, and therefore vendors have interpreted this differently. Ultimately, this has caused interoperability issues when trying to establish VPN tunnels, so be advised that some tuning might be required.

IKE Version 2

IKE version 2 is the successor to the IKEv1 method. There are some challenges with the IKEv1 protocol, particularly when it comes to interoperability, in large part because it evolved over a long period of time with so many different parties. There is a plethora of different RFCs that make up aspects of IKEv1, and anyone who has done large-scale VPN concentrator projects with multiple vendors can speak of the horrors of getting these implementations up and running properly.

There is not technically Phase 1 and Phase 2 of IKEv2 like there is for IKEv1, but rather there are four exchanges (in a request/response format) that occur to negotiate an IPsec tunnel with IKEv2. In reality, only the first two are necessary, and the second two can happen to extend the IPsec relationship.

IKE-SA-INIT
: This exchange negotiates the security attributes that will be used to establish the IPsec tunnel. This includes exchanging the protocols/parameters used, NONCE values, and Diffie-Hellman groups.

IKE-AUTH
: Each peer establishes or authenticates their identities. At this stage, the IPsec tunnel is established.

CREATE_CHILD_SA
: This allows the peers to create additional security associations between each other, similar to how multiple proxy IDs function in IKEv1.

INFORMATIONAL
: Allows the peers to perform some housekeeping functions, including peer liveliness detection, removing SA relationships, and reporting error messages.

It's important to understand that IKEv2 just defines the method by which the IPsec tunnels are negotiated; it doesn't directly impact the type of encryption or authentication that is used to secure the actual transit traffic itself. In fact, from a configuration perspective on the SRX, there are virtually no differences between configuring an IKEv1 versus IKEv2 tunnel other than the explicit configuration of the IKE version that is defined in the gateway configuration.

IKEv1 versus IKEv2

So what are some of the challenges with IKEv1 that spurred the introduction of IKEv2? As we mentioned, there are many RFCs for IKEv1-related functionality like NAT-T, DPD, route-based VPNs, certificate support, proxy ID support, and a lack of any ability to extend IKEv1 without crafting entire new mechanisms. In addition, IKEv2 has a much more streamlined negotiation process that is much less prone to DoS attacks, which are well known in IKE negotiations. For instance, an attacker can attack an IKEv1 gateway by spoofing the first IKE packet and consuming resources on the IKE gateway without IKE having a good way to validate that the incoming message is authentic. IKEv2 builds in a cookie negotiation similar in ways to a SYN Cookie to ensure that the peer is a valid peer before wasting resources on the negotiation until the host is validated. Also, there are some ambiguous aspects of IKEv1 that different vendors have implemented differently and this has led to incompatibility issues.

Additionally, in many cases with IKEv1, negotiations would fail because of a lack of exact match. IKEv2 goes a long way to support flexibility in the negotiations to allow gateways to propose certain attributes or values. IKEv2 can also be much more proactive and require much less state than IKEv1 to be maintained.

So why not always use IKEv2? If you can, it's certainly not a bad thing. IKEv2 hasn't seen quite as widespread of a deployment as IKEv1, including for IPv6, so you might be limited to falling back to IKEv1 unless you control all of the IPsec hosts or can mandate IKEv2 support. IKEv2 is also preferred in large environments with numerous spoke sites because it is faster to negotiate than IKEv1, although the actual encryption itself doesn't become any easier; just the setup phases occur with less overhead on the peers.

The full implementation details of IKEv1 and IKEv2 can be viewed in their respective RFCs online (IKEv1 has several, but primarily 2407, 2408, and 2409; IKEv2 is RFC 4306).

IPsec VPN Protocol

Two different VPN protocols can be used for IPsec VPNs, regardless of what IKE parameters are used to establish the VPN. The two protocols are ESP and AH.

ESP
: This performs encryption and authentication on the traffic within the VPN, thus protecting the confidentiality of the traffic within the VPN. It also authenticates the data within the VPN, ensuring that it has not been modified and that it originated from the correct source.

AH
: This protocol does not encrypt the traffic within the VPN, but simply authenticates the traffic to ensure that it came from the correct source and has not been modified.

ESP is much more widely deployed than AH, because typically, organizations want to ensure that data originated from the correct location and that it wasn't modified (they might also want to ensure that the data is confidential). Because additional effort is not required to configure the encryption on the VPN gateway, most network administrators or organizations simply encrypt and authenticate. Note that additional processing must take place to perform both the encryption and the authentication, so ESP might not perform as well as AH, but the security benefits of ESP far outweigh any performance impact it might have.

IPsec VPN Mode

In addition to the choice of VPN protocol, there are two different *modes* that determine how the traffic is exchanged in the VPN.

Tunnel mode
: Tunnel mode encapsulates the original IP packet within another packet in the VPN tunnel. This is most commonly used when hosts within separate private networks want to communicate over a public network. Both VPN gateways establish the VPN tunnel to each other, and all traffic between the two gateways appears to be from the two gateways, with the original packet embedded within the exterior IPsec packet. Note that whether the original packet is encrypted depends on whether ESP or AH mode has been selected. ESP encapsulates, encrypts, and authenticates the original Layer 3 through Layer 7 IP traffic, whereas AH only encapsulates and authenticates the original Layer 3 through Layer 7 IP traffic.

Transport mode

Transport mode does not encapsulate the original packet in a new packet, like Tunnel mode does; rather, it sends the packet directly between the two hosts that have established the IPsec tunnel. Depending on whether ESP or AH mode is used, the data is either encrypted and authenticated, or just authenticated. This includes encryption and authentication for Layer 4 through Layer 7 in ESP mode, or just authentication for AH for Layer 4 through Layer 7 of the original IP packet.

Tunnel mode is the most common VPN mode on the Internet because it easily allows entire networks (particularly those with private address space) to communicate over public IP networks. Transport mode is primarily used when encrypting traffic between two hosts to secure communication where IP address overlap is not an issue (e.g., between a host and a server on a private network). Today, the SRX only supports Tunnel mode and does not support Transport mode.

IPsec Manual Keys

In certain situations, IKE negotiations are not preferable. Although an individual IKE negotiation might not require too many resources to establish, setting up hundreds or thousands of VPNs per second can be very difficult due to the key generation that must take place for each VPN. Another non-IKE-preferred scenario is when an organization does not want the keys to expire.

Manual keys aren't that popular these days except in very narrow situations, so they are outside the scope of this book, but are supported by the SRX.

IPv6 and IPsec on the SRX

At the time of writing this book, IPv6 support for IPsec on the SRX is still a bit lacking, even compared to the legacy ScreenOS platforms. This has largely been due to a slower than expected transition of features from ScreenOS to Junos, so IPv6 was delayed while other mission-critical IPv4 features were implemented. The good news is that this is all changing, and quickly. In fact, at the time of writing this book, the first major phase of IPv6 support for IPsec is in beta testing (well, technically, IPv6 IPsec support does already exist on the branch SRX for policy-based VPNs, but it's a very narrow use case). Moving forward, you should start to see the widespread implementation of these features, so keep current on the release notes.

The good news when it comes to IPv6 versus IPv4 in IPsec is that they are nearly identical from an implementation standpoint. For the most part, it's simply a matter of plugging in an IPv6 address for an IPv4 address and you should be good to go, so all of the concepts that we are covering here still apply.

IKE Negotiations

Now that you know a little more about how the VPN negotiation takes place, let's drill down into a detailed discussion and break down the individual components of Phase 1 IKE negotiation.

IKE Authentication

A few pages back you learned about Phase 1 IKE negotiations for IKEv1 and IKE_INIT_SA for IKEv2. These negotiations only provide the ability to establish a secure channel over which two parties can communicate—you still need to define how they should authenticate each other. This is where IKE authentication is used to ensure that the other party is authorized to establish the VPN.

IKE authentication comes in two forms: preshared key (password) and certificate authentication.

Preshared key authentication

The most common way to establish a VPN connection is to use preshared keys, which is essentially a password that is the same for both parties. This password must be exchanged in advance in some out-of-band mechanism, such as over the phone, via a verbal exchange, or via less secure mechanisms, even email. The parties then authenticate each other by encrypting the preshared key with the peer's public key, which was obtained in the Diffie-Hellman exchange.

Preshared keys are commonly deployed for site-to-site IPsec VPNs, either within a single organization or between different organizations. Preshared key authentication is popular because the keys do not require the overhead of certificates, and many administrators are much more familiar with passwords than they are with certificates. To ensure that preshared keys are used in the most secure fashion, a preshared key must consist of at least 8 characters (12 or more is recommended) using a combination of letters, numbers, and nonalphanumeric characters, along with different cases for the letters (i.e., the preshared key should not use a dictionary word). An example of a complex password is *H7bK1Mc2$#cNa*.

When using nonalphanumeric characters, make sure they are not special characters which could be mistaken by some OSs. A common example is the question mark (?), which can typically trigger a CLI to think the user is requesting context-sensitive help. Although most OSs support the use of a control sequence, some do not, so you might want to avoid using a control sequence if you are unsure whether the peer supports it.

Certificate authentication

Certificate-based authentication is considered more secure than preshared key authentication because the certificate key cannot be compromised easily (as can a weak preshared key). Certificates are also far more ideal in larger scale environments with numerous peer sites that should not all share a preshared key. In addition, optional mechanisms can be used within certificate authentication to ensure that a certificate is still valid. Finally, certificates are not easily vulnerable to visual eavesdropping, like a preshared key might be, although certificates can still be compromised if access to the filesystem on which they are stored is obtained.

Certificates are composed of a public and private key, and can be "signed" by a master certificate known as a *certificate authority* (CA). In this way, certificates can be checked to see if they are signed with a CA that is trusted. Certificates can also be revoked should they be compromised, or if they expire (as certificates are generated with an expiration date, although there is no standard time frame for generated certificates).

The many aspects of certificate-based authentication could fill an entire book, so all the intricate details of this form of authentication are not covered here. For the purposes of this chapter, we expect you to have a working understanding of Public Key Infrastructure (PKI), including certificates, CAs, and the technologies that deliver these capabilities. Later in this chapter we discuss the configuration specifics on the SRX to get you working with this technology.

IKE Identities

You can think of the IKE identity as the username that is associated with the authentication method (preshared key or certificate). Although that isn't exactly the purpose of this feature, IKE identity performs a similar functionality.

The SRX platform supports a few different types of IKE identities, and you can use them to verify the identity (along with other attributes such as the preshared key or certificate) of the remote party.

IP address
: The most common form of IKE identity for site-to-site VPNs is the IP address. Typically, this is automatically derived from the configuration of a peer gateway, by using the IP address. IP addresses are not commonly used for remote access VPNs because the client IP address is typically not static, but there is nothing technically wrong with using an IP address for the client IKE identity. This can be either an IPv4 or IPv6 address.

Hostname
: The hostname, or fully qualified domain name, is essentially a string that identifies the end system. This does not strictly have to match the actual FQDN of the end system; however, this is recommended for ease of management.

User FQDN
: A user FQDN (UFQDN) is also known as a *user-at-hostname*. It is a simple string that follows the same format as an email address: *user@company.com*. Note that

this doesn't have to match the user's actual hostname; however, it is recommended that you use the same email address as the user's actual email address for ease of management.

Distinguished name
: The distinguished name (DN) is the full name that is used in certificates to identify a unique user in a certificate. An example of a DN is "CN=user, DC=company, DC=com," the ASN.1 encoding standard.

IKE-ID
: This supports either a shared or group IKE ID that can be used among many different peers. These are common when using Auto-VPN and Remote Access scenarios.

When using site-to-site VPNs, the most common type of IKE identity is the IP address, assuming that the host has a static IP address. If the host does not have a static IP address, a hostname can be used. When a dial-up remote access client (rather than a gateway) is used, a UFQDN is the most common IKE identity. If certificates are used, the DN or a subset of the name can be used to identify the users of an organization or a unit of the organization.

Flow Processing and IPsec VPNs

It is important to understand where IPsec processing of traffic happens in the traffic processing chain. When a session is created on the SRX (as discussed in Chapter 8), we perform all of the flow processing steps, which includes services at the end of the processing chain. If a flow is destined for a VPN (whether it is route- or policy-based) the traffic will be sent into the VPN as one of the last steps in the processing chain (just before actually sending the traffic out of the physical media itself). Placing the VPN at the end of the processing chain allows other services to take place on the plain-text traffic (e.g., UTM, IPS, NAT, ALG, etc.) and the reverse operation can happen after the traffic is decrypted, returning from another IPsec peer. If the VPN is not already established when the traffic is destined for a VPN peer, the SRX will queue the traffic while it establishes the VPN and then will send it out as soon as the VPN is established—or drop it if the VPN cannot be established. Just like clear-text traffic, VPN-bound traffic is fully flow-aware (and is enforced by flow processing). The IPsec tunnel is just an abstraction layer on top of the standard flow processing itself.

SRX VPN Types

Two types of VPNs can be configured on the SRX—policy-based VPNs and route-based VPNs—and their underlying IPsec functionality is essentially the same in terms of traffic being encrypted. It's the implementation that's different and that can be used to leverage administrative functionality.

Not all vendors provide both policy- and route-based VPNs. However, there are no compatibility issues with running a policy-based VPN to a route-based VPN. There is one exception: when running dynamic routing protocols such as Routing Information Protocol (RIP), OSPF, IS-IS, or PIM on the VPN, only route-based VPNs can be used.

Policy-Based VPNs

Policy-based VPNs utilize the power of a firewall security policy to define what traffic should be passed through a VPN. Policy-based VPNs allow traffic to be directed to a VPN on a policy-by-policy basis, including the ability to match traffic based on the source IP, destination IP, application, and respective to- and from-zones. When using policy-based VPNs, the action of "Tunnel" is used, which implies that the traffic is permitted along with defining the VPN to be used in that policy. Additional policy processing such as application services (IPS, URL filtering, antivirus, logging, etc.) can be used in policy-based VPNs.

When using policy-based VPNs, the proxy IDs are derived from the firewall policy that is used. The policy's source address maps to the proxy ID's local ID, the destination address maps to the remote ID, and the service maps to the application for traffic that is destined for the tunnel (to be encrypted; e.g., Trust to Untrust). In the case where traffic is arriving encrypted from the VPN (to be decrypted; e.g., Untrust to Trust) the proxy ID source address will be the remote ID, the destination address is the local ID, and the service is the application.

Determining the Proxy IDs on Policy-Based VPNs

When address object sets, or multicelled source or destination addresses, are used, the respective IDs will be negotiated as 0.0.0.0/0. In the case of service, when either an application set or multicelled applications are used, the service will be negotiated as Any. Although the same proxy ID can be used multiple times on the platform, it can only be defined once per VPN endpoint. For instance, if three different VPNs negotiate the proxy IDs as Local: 0.0.0.0/0, Remote 0.0.0.0/0, and Service Any, that is fine; however, the same VPN can only have this once. If it is defined multiple times for a single VPN, the SRX will issue a commit error due to the overlapping proxy IDs. Proxy IDs can be manually hardcoded by the administrator for the VPN rather than being derived automatically from the policies. The main thing to take away is how the proxy IDs can be derived, as the proxy IDs must match on both sides for VPN negotiation to be successful.

With policy-based VPNs, you can override the proxy IDs that are derived from the policy by defining them (like you would with route-based VPNs) in the Phase 2 configuration. We discuss the configuration for defining the proxy IDs later in this chapter.

Policy-based VPNs are primarily used for simple site-to-site VPNs and for remote access VPNs. For more advanced needs, route-based VPNs should be considered.

Route-Based VPNs

The alternative to policy-based VPNs is route-based VPNs. Route-based VPNs use a virtual interface known as a *secure tunnel interface* (st0 interface) in which all traffic routed into the interface will be sent into a VPN. The traffic is directed into the interface just like any other traffic decision through the use of routing, hence the term *route-based VPN*. Route-based VPNs still have a secure policy applied to them; however, the security policy does not use the action of Tunnel, but rather the action of Permit. The routing decision causes the traffic to be sent into the VPN. The interesting part of route-based VPNs is that they can be used to leverage advanced features such as use of dynamic routing protocols. Dynamic routing protocols allow easier administration and the ability to fail traffic over to different links. Note that dynamic routing is not required for route-based VPNs; static routes will work just fine as well.

The negotiation of proxy IDs for route-based VPNs is relatively simple. Because they must be manually defined for each VPN, they are not derived from a policy or other source. Just like policy-based VPNs, only a single proxy ID combination can be used per VPN; however, proxy IDs from different VPNs can overlap.

The st0 interface must be configured within a security zone just like any other logical interface. Versions older than 11.1 had limitations of what VR the IPsec VPN could be terminated in, and what VR the st0 interface could be placed in, but these are no longer limitations with contemporary versions of Junos.

Numbered versus unnumbered st0 interfaces

In a point-to-point VPN configuration, the st0 interface can function similarly to a Point-to-Point Protocol (PPP) interface in that it doesn't have to be numbered (configured with an IP address) because there are only two hosts on the communication channel (the IPsec VPN). If you use an unnumbered interface, you will essentially borrow the IP address of another interface rather than using an explicit IP address for the interface itself. Typically, it is a good idea to just configure IP addresses on the interface rather than using unnumbered interfaces. You can always use private IP addressing within the IPsec VPN because, as the name implies, it is private. Not only is it encrypted, but also the actual network within the IPsec tunnel is not impacted by the IP addressing of the network it is running over.

Point-to-point versus point-to-multipoint VPNs

Route-based VPNs offer two different types of architectures: point-to-point and point-to-multipoint. Point-to-point VPNs map a single VPN to a single logical interface unit, so the SRX connects directly to a single peer VPN gateway on the interface. Point-to-multipoint VPNs allow the device to connect to multiple peer gateways on a single logical interface.

An important design consideration to make when building a VPN infrastructure is when to use point-to-point and when to use point-to-multipoint. Point-to-point VPNs are an obvious design decision when only a single peer needs to be connected; when multiple peers need to be connected, point-to-multipoint should be considered.

Point-to-multipoint also has the advantage of conserving IP subnets along with the number of logical interfaces that are used. For example, in the case of point-to-point VPNs, an IP subnet and logical interface must be used for each VPN. When only a few VPNs are used, the consumption of IP subnets and logical interfaces might not be much of a concern. However, when thousands of VPNs are used, platform limits could occur with point-to-point VPNs.

On the other hand, point-to-point VPNs have the advantage of being able to define each logical interface to a separate zone, whereas point-to-multipoint VPNs are all part of the same zone. Note that even when point-to-multipoint is used, each VPN can still be segmented by security policies, as intrazone blocking is hardcoded into each zone.

Typically, when connecting to other trading partners that are not part of your organization, point-to-point rather than point-to-multipoint VPNs should be used.

Special point-to-multipoint attributes

It is important to understand that point-to-multipoint VPNs require additional configuration to be supported. First, on the hub's st0 interface, you must also specify that it is a multipoint interface, as shown in the following output:

```
[edit]
root@SRX5800-1# show interfaces st0
unit 0 {
    multipoint;
    family inet {
        address 192.168.100.5/24;
    }
}
```

Also, if you are using auto Next-Hop Tunnel Binding (NHTB), no additional configuration is required; if your peer device doesn't support auto NHTB, you must manually specify these entries, as shown in the following output. If you do not specify this information, your point-to-multipoint VPN will not be able to properly establish and route traffic accordingly.

```
[edit]
root@SRX5800-1# show interfaces st0
```

```
unit 0 {
   multipoint;
   family inet {
      next-hop-tunnel 192.168.100.1 ipsec-vpn East-Branch;
      next-hop-tunnel 192.168.100.2 ipsec-vpn West-Branch;
      next-hop-tunnel 192.168.100.3 ipsec-vpn South-Branch;
      address 192.168.100.5/24;
    }
}
```

Point-to-multipoint NHTB

Point-to-multipoint VPNs allow you to bind multiple VPNs to a single interface on the hub. For this to work properly, the SRX must know not only which VPN to send the traffic into on the st0 interface to which it is bound, but also which next-hop will be used for routing that traffic on the interface. To accomplish this, the SRX uses a mechanism called an NHTB table on the interface to map all of this information.

On the SRX, if you are going to another SRX or ScreenOS device and you are using static routing, the SRX can automatically exchange the next-hop tunnel information with the peer as part of the optional vendor attribute exchanges in Phase 2 (also known as auto NHTB). If you are not using an SRX or ScreenOS device, and the peer doesn't support these attributes (it should just ignore them), you will need to manually enter the table mappings to show what the next-hop should be (also known as manual NHTB). Alternatively, if you are using a dynamic routing protocol (e.g., RIP, OSPF, or BGP), you will not need to make a manual mapping entry because the SRX can build the table automatically from the routing updates matching the next-hop to the tunnel it came out of.

Which should you use: Policy- or route-based VPN?

This is an obvious question that probably came up as you read through the last section. In general, route-based VPNs are the way to go because they have better feature support with the SRX, including NAT and enhanced Level 7 support. Policy-based VPNs should only be used in some dial-up VPN scenarios (which have largely been alleviated with Junos 12.1X45+) and for some vendor compatibility purposes. If you don't have an explicit reason to use policy-based VPNs, we suggest that you default to route-based VPNs.

Other SRX VPN Components

There are several other VPN components of the SRX platform, many of which are optional enhancements, although some happen automatically and can be altered manually if desired. It is important to have a thorough understanding of the individual features before enabling them, because enabling the features incorrectly could lead to undesirable effects. Knowledge is power, especially with a powerful device such as the SRX.

Dead Peer Detection

One particular issue that IKE does not account for is sudden failure of the VPN peer during communication. Because the VPN gateway is not typically initiating traffic (except in the case of dynamic routing protocols), it typically doesn't notice if or when the VPN has failed, at least not until the IPsec keys expire and the VPN needs to be renegotiated.

To help improve the detection of such failures, the standards-based feature DPD can be implemented. DPD essentially sends a UDP message at defined intervals, and if messages are not responded to, the peer is considered to be down. Using DPD, a gateway can perform some alternative action such as defaulting to another VPN whenever a failure is detected.

DPD is primarily used with VPNs where dynamic routing is not used (e.g., OSPF), because dynamic routing protocols can both detect a failure and default over to another path without the need for DPD.

VPN Monitoring

One issue with DPD is that it doesn't necessarily mean the underlying VPN is up and running, just that the peer is up and responding. VPN monitoring is not an IPsec standard feature, but it utilizes ICMP to determine if the VPN is up. VPN monitoring allows the SRX to send ICMP traffic either to the peer gateway or to another destination on the other end of the tunnel (e.g., a server), along with specifying the source IP address of the ICMP traffic. If the ICMP traffic fails, the VPN is considered down.

An SRX VPN monitoring option, called Optimized, sends only the ICMP traffic through the tunnel when there is an absence of user traffic. If user traffic is traversing the tunnel, the SRX assumes it to be up and does not send the ICMP messages. If the traffic ceases, the SRX starts sending the ICMP messages until user traffic begins again.

Even though VPN monitoring is not an IPsec standard feature like DPD, it can be used with other vendors' devices and does not require the VPN peer gateway. You can think of VPN monitoring as Track IP specifically designed for VPNs.

XAuth

XAuth is an SRX feature that allows extensible authentication to IPsec VPN negotiation. XAuth actually takes place between Phase 1 and Phase 2 processing, and is a standards-based feature. Typically, XAuth is used with client remote access VPNs to provide further authentication, such as authentication to a corporate directory service such as Active Directory, which IKE does not allow. However, it can also be used for advanced IPsec authentication between two gateways, such as Zero Touch Hub/Spoke style deployments. XAuth is used in addition to the authentication that takes place in IKE Phase 1.

NAT Traversal

One issue with terminating IPsec remote access clients on VPN gateways in contemporary networks is that often the users are located behind a device that performs source NAT. When performing source NAT on IPsec traffic, a device can modify the source address and UDP port in the packet and therefore make the hash (which was calculated on the original packet) invalid. To help resolve this common scenario, *NAT Traversal* (NAT-T) was created.

NAT-T encapsulates the original ESP or AH traffic in an additional UDP packet. When the VPN gateway receives the UDP traffic, it will simply decapsulate the ESP or AH packet from the UDP layer.

NAT-T also uses UDP port 4500 (by default) rather than the standard UDP port 500 (which is only used for IKE negotiations, not ESP or AH), because the VPN gateway might try to process the traffic as IKE rather than as actual data traffic that is to be processed. NAT-T works with either ESP or AH and with either Tunnel or Transport mode.

On the SRX, NAT-T support is enabled by default and must be explicitly disabled on a VPN-by-VPN basis. It's recommended that you enable NAT-T whenever remote access VPNs are deployed.

The SRX has greatly extended the NAT-T support starting with Junos 11.4r4+. In the past, there used to be many aspects of NAT-T that weren't supported depending on where the peer was set up and how it was connecting to the SRX. If you are using NAT-T, it is best to use Junos 11.4r4+ for maximum interoperability.

Anti-Replay Protection

One liability of IPsec VPNs is that an attacker can capture valid packets and replay them into the network to try to confuse the VPN gateway or remote host. Although the attacker cannot determine the contents of the IPsec message, he might be able to cause a DoS attack by injecting the traffic.

IPsec protects against this method of attack by using a sequence of numbers that are built into the IPsec packet—the system does not accept a packet for which it has already seen the same sequence number. Each sequence number is unique and is not based on the original data packet itself, but is maintained by the gateway; even in the case of TCP retransmissions, the sequence number is different. If the remote gateway sees a packet with a duplicate sequence number, it is considered to be *replayed*.

If Anti-Replay protection is enabled, and a duplicate is seen, the packet is dropped and a log message is generated. If Anti-Replay protection is not enabled, the traffic is processed (decrypted), although other security features such as stateful firewall, ALGs, and IDP might drop the decrypted packet later in the processing chain.

Anti-Replay protection can be enabled independently on each side of the VPN. Because the IPsec messages always contain the sequence number, the option for Anti-Replay is essentially whether or not the VPN gateway monitors the connection to determine the existence of a replayed packet.

Fragmentation

Data networks enforce maximum sizes for frames and packets. Originally, on multiaccess networks that shared a collision domain (e.g., systems connected by an Ethernet hub), use of data sizes that were too large greatly increased the likelihood of collisions, so limits were placed on packet size to optimize packet processing.

Collisions weren't the only issue with regulating frame size, because when packets were too large, small packets could be delayed for processing behind larger packets, and systems couldn't be optimized for efficient packet processing.

> ### Maximum Transmission Unit (MTU) and Maximum Segment Size (MSS)
>
> MTU can refer to the size of a Layer 2 frame or the size of a Layer 3 packet (depending on the vendor). Juniper refers to the MTU as the complete Layer 2 frame, including the header. Standard Ethernet uses an MTU of 1,500 bytes of Layer 3 (including the IP header, Layer 4 header, and data), along with the 14-byte Ethernet header, for a total of 1,514 bytes. The IP header takes up 20 bytes, and the Layer 4 header (either TCP or UDP) will take up 20 bytes. This means that with a 1,514-byte Layer 2 MTU, and 54 bytes of Layer 2 through Layer 4 headers, there can be 1,460 bytes of user data. Note that different media can employ different MTU sizes; for example, the SRX can support Ethernet jumbo frames of up to 9,192 bytes.

Fragmentation comes into play when a packet is sent that is too large to meet the constraints of the underlying transmission medium's MTU. When a network device receives a packet that is too large to be transmitted on the egress transmission medium, it has a choice of either fragmenting the packet (chopping the packet into smaller messages) or dropping the packet.

It is common to employ fragmentation in VPN processing because there is additional overhead in the messages sent over the VPN, including the ESP or AH header, and in Tunnel mode the original packet is encapsulated in another IP packet. Furthermore, in remote access VPNs with NAT-T, the packet is encapsulated yet again in a UDP packet. So, when a gateway receives the original packet, if it is 1,500 bytes, all of the additional overhead of the IPsec headers will make it too big to be sent over a standard 1,514-byte Ethernet network. In this case, the gateway must fragment the packet or drop it.

When configuring an SRX VPN, it is important to be cognizant of the underlying MTU and the MSS that is derived from the MTU (MTU – Layer 4 header overhead = MSS).

There is also an option for processing the *Don't Fragment* (`DF`) bit in IP messages—the bit can be ignored, set, or cleared when processing the original packet.

Differentiated Services Code Point

Differentiated Services Code Point is an eight-bit field in an IP header that helps to classify the packet from a QoS perspective so that network devices can properly provide the appropriate precedence when processing the packet. DSCP bits don't force the network devices to provide a certain level of service, but they can be leveraged to do so.

The SRX automatically copies the DSCP bits from the original packet to the IPsec packet so that the network devices between the two VPN gateways can provide the appropriate processing on the encrypted traffic.

IKEv1 Key Lifetimes

Keys are generated in both Phase 1 and Phase 2 IPsec. The keys in Phase 1 are generated to create a secure channel for the Phase 2 keys to be negotiated. The Phase 2 keys are the keys that are used to negotiate the user traffic. In both Phase 1 and Phase 2, the keys are considered active for a certain period of time, known as the *key lifetime*. Phase 1 is always negotiated as a period of time, but Phase 2 can be either a period of time or a certain amount of data that is transmitted in kilobytes. Key lifetimes are important because the longer that keys are active, the more potential there is for compromised security. That isn't to say that IPsec is insecure—quite the opposite; however, the longer the same keys are used, the more potential there is to determine what those keys are and decrypt the content that is transmitted. Again, when properly configured, this is not a major concern, but something to keep in mind when selecting key lifetime.

Each phase allows the ability to configure the key lifetime for that individual phase. The shorter the lifetime, the more often the keys are renegotiated. Although renegotiating often provides some security advantage, it can be costly from a performance perspective on the VPN gateways when operating on a large scale. IKEv2 doesn't require key lifetimes to be set, as the peers can alter the state of the VPNs at any time.

IPsec does not have any official default timers for IPsec key negotiation but uses default key lifetimes (if not explicitly defined) of 86,400 seconds for Phase 1 and 3,600 seconds for Phase 2. This means Phase 2 times out before the Phase 1 key lifetime, which is an ideal event because only the keys in Phase 2 are used to encrypt the actual data, whereas the Phase 1 keys are only used to create a secure channel to negotiate the Phase 2 keys.

It's important to understand that different vendors' devices might choose different key lifetimes, and that sometimes a mismatch in key lifetimes could cause VPN establishment issues and even stability issues, so it's important to match the values wherever possible.

Network Time Protocol

Network Time Protocol is not a strict requirement for IPsec VPNs, but there is good cause for enabling it. First, the obvious need is to have the time properly synchronized for many reasons related to management (timestamps, schedulers, etc.), so this is just a best practice in general. But also, for IPsec with certificates, it is especially important because certificates are dependent on accurate time to ensure that they have not expired. If the time is not synchronized, this could make the SRX think the certificate has expired (or has been generated for a future time) when in reality it hasn't. Finally, the less obvious reason pertains to the high-end SRX. The high-end SRX is a distributed processing system with SPUs that operate independently. This also means they might not maintain the same time, and this can create some issues, particularly with VPNs and retrieving information from the SPUs. To ensure no issues, you should always enable NTP on the platform to ensure that the SPUs are synchronized (because the route engine will sync the time down to the SPUs when NTP is enabled).

Certificate Validation

One of the strengths of certificate-based IPsec authentication is that the certificate can be revoked should it be compromised in any way, in addition to the SRX being able to validate the certificate itself to ensure that it has been signed by the correct CA certificate. By default, if you only upload the CA certificate to the SRX, the SRX can only determine whether the proposed certificate is signed by the CA certificate; it cannot determine whether the certificate had been revoked or is on hold. A certificate on hold is not permanently revoked, but in this state it cannot be used for authentication. To determine if the certificate has been revoked, the SRX must poll the CA itself to determine which certificates have been revoked. Typically, there are two ways to do this: via certificate revocation lists (CRLs) or via Online Certificate Status Protocol (OCSP).

CRL

With this method, the SRX will poll the CA for a list of all of the serial numbers of the revoked or on-hold certificates. Typically, this is done either manually or on a periodic basis. When the SRX needs to validate a certificate, it will then check to make sure the certificate is signed by the CA, and if that succeeds, it will check the CRL to see if it includes the proposed certificate's serial number. If the serial number is not on the CRL, the certificate will be considered valid; if it is on the CRL, the certificate will be considered revoked and the authentication will fail. Also note that a certificate that is expiring will not be on the CRL, although it will be considered invalid if it has expired. Furthermore, the CRL itself has a lifetime that can be used to ensure that the CRL is not valid after a long period of time.

At the time of this writing, the SRX supports CRL collection via HTTP or Lightweight Directory Access Protocol (LDAP). If configured to use CRL checking, the SRX will try to download the CRL that is specified in the CA certificate itself, and if that fails, the SRX will follow the configuration, which specifies the CRL path.

OCSP

OSCP is currently in beta at the time of writing this book. It is primarily used to authenticate X.509 certificates similar to CRL checking, but is slightly different in a few ways. First, it doesn't need to download the entire CRL (which is good when the CRL grows very large), but instead queries the OCSP server to determine if an individual certificate is valid, revoked, or on hold. Next, OCSP can query for certificate status in real time, on an as-needed basis. This also helps to ensure that certificates have not expired between CRL polling periods. Finally, OCSP can cache individual certificate authentication responses rather than having to poll for each certificate every time (within a timeout; e.g., 10 minutes).

Simple Certificate Enrollment Protocol

When using large-scale certificate deployments, the simple task of deploying and managing certificates can become a nightmare very quickly. To help alleviate the management needs of large-scale certificate environments, the SRX supports the use of Simple Certificate Enrollment Protocol (SCEP). SCEP is used on SRX devices to reach out to the CA for certificate-related management tasks. These include initial certificate enrollment (get the initial client certificate on the SRX), client certificate renewal, CA certificate renewal, and the ability to get new certificates before the old ones expire. The CA is typically software that runs on a server such as Microsoft Certificate Authority or INSTA-CA; other CAs are maintained by certificate signing organizations. When using SCEP, the SRX simply acts as a client to update its own certificates and CA certificates; it is not used to authenticate other certificates in the way that CRL or OCSP checking is.

Group VPN

Starting in version 10.2, the branch SRX Series devices support a VPN technology called Group VPN (also known by the Cisco implementation GETVPN), based on RFC 3547. Group VPN is intended to solve the issue of large-scale IPsec implementations that connect branch locations to central hub sites in a scalable and automated fashion over a private network such as MPLS/VPLS. The Juniper Group VPN solution is largely compatible with the Cisco GETVPN solution, because they are based on the same RFC. Covering Group VPN is outside the scope of this book (in part because thorough coverage of the feature is enough to fill a book in itself) but there are AppNotes and other available materials that cover this content.

Dynamic VPN

Dynamic VPN is a feature that is specific to branch SRX Series devices that allows client systems to create remote access VPNs that are terminated on the branch SRX Series gateways. Essentially, this provides a streamlined way to provision and connect users to an SRX over the Internet or other private network. The client that is installed on the user machine is downloaded from the SRX gateway's web interface and is automatically installed. Then, when the user wishes to connect to the SRX, he simply does so by logging in to the SRX's Dynamic VPN web interface, which triggers the VPN session on the user's PC. The administrator does not need to provision any software or configuration, as this is automatically installed on the user's system. Additionally, if upgrades to the client are required, this is automatically performed without the need for administrative intervention.

It is important to understand a few things when it comes to Dynamic VPNs. The following limitations exist at the time of this writing:

- To use the Dynamic VPN feature, you must purchase and install licenses for the clients. This isn't a limitation on the number of clients, but rather the number of clients that can connect at the same time. See the datasheets for more information on platform-specific limits.
- The Dynamic VPN client can only use IPsec to create a secure connection to the SRX. SSL support may come at a later point in time.
- Only Windows is supported by Dynamic VPN at the time of writing this book. The SRX can also provide the Junos Pulse package for the clients, and it is likely that it will be extended for other OSs in the near future, so stay posted to the release notes.

Selecting the Appropriate VPN Configuration

The previous sections of this chapter gave you a lot of information—some generalized, some SRX-specific. It's time to make use of that information and provide you with some real-world guidance on how to select the appropriate properties for your SRX VPN configuration.

As you've come to realize by now, there are many different VPN configuration options. However, deciding which options to select is quite easy once you understand them. Here we'll detail 12 key configuration options with recommendations and tips on when and where you might use them.

AutoKey IKE versus manual keys
: The first decision you should make when determining how to deploy your VPNs is whether IKE will be used to negotiate the VPN keys or whether to use manual keys. For just about every scenario, AutoKey IKE should be used over manual key encryption because AutoKey IKE is dynamic and renegotiates the keys used rather than using the same key indefinitely. The only exception to this rule is if security isn't much of a concern, due to the impact that AutoKey negotiation would put on your system. Although individual IKE negotiation might not put much load on the system, negotiating lots of VPN tunnels simultaneously can be very computationally intensive, making manual keys preferable.

IKEv1 versus IKEv2
: We discussed the benefits of IKEv2 compared with IKEv1 earlier in the chapter. If both gateways support IKEv2 without any issues, then this would probably be the preferred version to select.

ESP versus AH

ESP is the most widely deployed VPN protocol because it not only performs authentication, but also provides security by encrypting the data. Although encrypting the data is a computationally intensive process, it typically can be offloaded by using some hardware acceleration. Therefore, unless there is a specific reason to only provide authentication, ESP should be used to provide both encryption and authentication.

Main mode versus Aggressive mode (IKEv1 only)

The rule of thumb when it comes to Main mode versus Aggressive mode is that if both nodes have a static IP address (or an address that can be resolved via DNS), Main mode should be used. However, if a gateway or host has a dynamic IP address, typically Aggressive mode should be used for the best interoperability (although depending on the implementation of the VPN gateways, Main mode might be able to be used).

Diffie-Hellman group number

Diffie-Hellman key exchange is used to negotiate Phase 1 and PFS aspects of IPsec. The larger the key, the more difficult it will be to compromise the security of the negotiation, but the more computationally intensive the negotiation will be. Typically, Diffie-Hellman Group 2 is considered secure at the time of this writing, although larger key lengths (e.g., Group 5, 14, etc.) are more secure, but might be unnecessary. Remember that Diffie-Hellman is used to negotiate the secure channel to negotiate the Phase 2 keys, but does not actually encrypt the data itself.

Preshared keys versus certificate authentication

As previously discussed, you can authenticate IPsec peers in two ways: via preshared keys and via certificates. Preshared keys are easier to deploy, and are the most common form of authentication. Certificates are a very powerful form of authentication, as you can scale them to large implementations and you can revoke certificates and authenticate certificates dynamically. Certificates do have a certain amount of overhead when it comes to generation, signing, checking status, and renewing, however, and therefore they are most commonly used for large implementations. When just using simple site-to-site VPNs, or VPNs between other organizations, preshared keys are easier to use. If you are deploying site-to-site or client VPNs within an organization on the scale of several hundred or several thousand, certificates should be examined, as they provide some scaling advantages.

If you are using certificates, you also need to determine what format or algorithm will be used to authenticate them. In the past, only DSA and RSA certificates were supported, but now with Suite B support the SRX also supports ECDSA certificates.

IKE identity

IKE identity is commonly overlooked as a major component of a VPN; however, it is important to select the appropriate IKE identity. The IKE identity essentially acts as the username for the IKE authentication in a roundabout way. Typically, when both sides of a site-to-site VPN have static IP addresses, the IKE identity is the IP address for both nodes. When a single node is using a dynamic IP address, that node typically uses the `Hostname` attribute, which can be a simple name to identify the peer. But when a user is connecting to a gateway, that user should use the UFQDN. It is important to make sure both sides can properly authenticate the other peer with the method that the other side is expecting, as a mismatch or improper IKE identity causes failure.

Configure remote identity when you do not know the remote peer's IP address. Configure local identity if you do not have a static IP address (e.g., your gateway uses DHCP).

VPN encryption algorithm
: When selecting the VPN encryption algorithm, the important things to remember are the sensitivity of the data within the VPN, the amount of data sent over the VPN in terms of throughput, and whether the algorithm that is used will be accelerated by hardware. DES is largely considered to be an obsolete encryption algorithm by today's standards because the key space is only 56 bits and it can be broken with modern computers in a few months' time. 3DES and AES are widely considered to be much better algorithms and are secure against attacks with modern computer hardware. If the data is extremely sensitive and needs to be protected against attacks under extremely powerful computing power, both now and in the future, you should use an algorithm such as AES-256.

VPN authentication algorithm
: The VPN authentication algorithm is used to create a hash of the traffic to ensure that it has not been modified or forged. Two hash algorithms are implemented in the SRX at the time of this writing: MD5 and SHA-1. SHA-1 is considered to be a stronger hash algorithm than MD5, and because both are implemented in hardware, it is recommended that you use SHA-1 rather than MD5, although MD5 isn't necessarily an obsolete algorithm. The SRX now supports stronger authentication algorithms like SHA-256 and SHA-384.

Perfect Forward Secrecy
: PFS is a mechanism used to renegotiate the Phase 1 keys over an established Phase 1 channel. It is primarily meant to help provide additional security to Aggressive mode authentication where the IKE identities are negotiated in clear text, but it can also be used to renegotiate Phase 1 for additional security. It is recommended that you use PFS when using Aggressive mode, or in the most sensitive of security environments, and it is very important to choose the correct preshared key (if you're

using preshared keys) along with the proper encryption and authentication algorithms.

Policy-based VPNs versus route-based VPNs
: Policy-based VPNs are common when configuring simple site-to-site VPNs or remote access VPNs, especially when interoperating with VPN products from other vendors. When only a few VPNs are needed, or if the VPNs are simple, it might make sense to use policy-based VPNs because they are easier to set up and have fewer components (from a configuration perspective) than route-based VPNs. When you're setting up a VPN infrastructure with a large number of remote access tunnels, or when multicast or dynamic routing protocols are used, you should use route-based VPNs. In general, route-based VPNs are more powerful than policy-based VPNs, so they are generally preferred over policy-based VPNs, but simple implementations can still use policy-based VPNs.

Predefined proposal sets versus custom proposal sets
: To help ease configuration, the SRX has predefined proposal sets for both Phase 1 and Phase 2 IKE negotiations. You can choose to use these predefined sets or create your own. It is really just a matter of preference. There are three predefined proposals: basic, standard, and compatible. Typically, it is best to just define your own, as it takes the guesswork out of configuring the VPNs, especially if you are establishing a VPN to another vendor (which might not use the same terminology). Additionally, if you use predefined sets, you might have to go through several proposals with the peer before finding a match (which would leave a log trail as well), so it is best to just configure identical proposals as the peer.

IPsec VPN Configuration

Now that we have broken down the individual components of IPsec VPNs, let's examine how to put these features into practice on the SRX with the configuration of a hub and spoke VPN.

Because certain aspects of VPNs can only have single attributes (e.g., preshared key or certificates, but not both), we cover some configuration elements that do not apply to our actual VPN infrastructure. Figure 10-6 shows a network diagram of the IPsec VPN infrastructure that is being implemented. We cover the various configuration elements in the order in which they should be configured, because certain elements reference other aspects of the configuration.

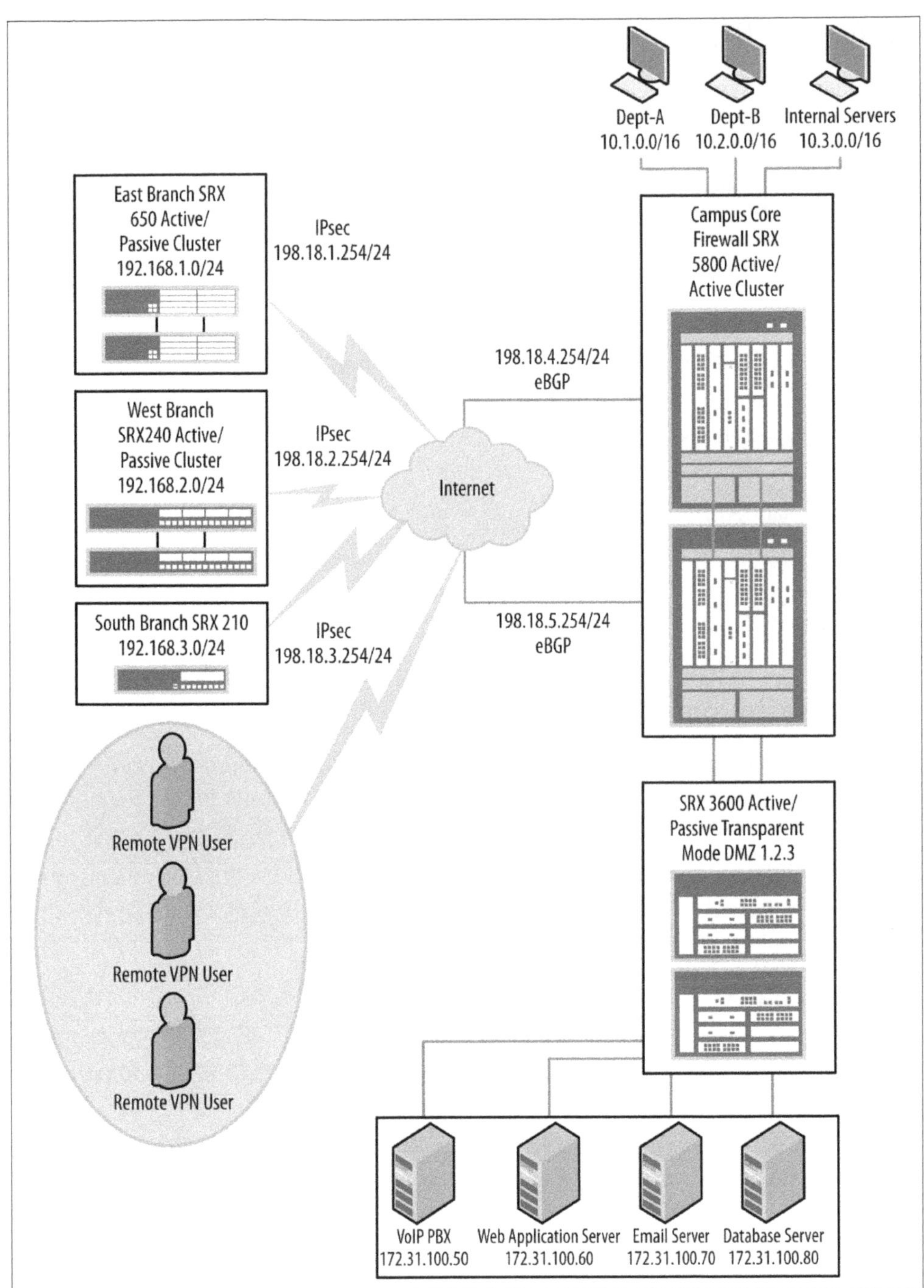

Figure 10-6. IPsec VPN infrastructure

Configuring NTP

Although we covered NTP configuration earlier in the book, it is a very important function of VPN, so we will reiterate how to configure it here. The following configuration assumes that you already have network connectivity and routing set up (you can also use domain names as your NTP servers, as long as you have DNS configured; also, note that the SRX will resolve the name and place it into the final configuration).

```
[edit]
root@SRX3600-1# set system name-server 4.2.2.2

[edit]
root@SRX3600-1# set system ntp server pool.ntp.org

[edit]
root@SRX3600-1# show system
host-name SRX3600-1;
domain-name jnpr.net;
name-server {
    4.2.2.2;
}
ntp {
    server 74.207.249.60;
}
```

Certificate Preconfiguration Tasks

When configuring your SRX for certificate authentication for Phase 1, you need to do several things before you can use certificate authentication to its fullest advantage (if you are using preshared keys only, this section does not apply).

In this example, we do the following to prepare our SRX for certificate authentication. Not all of these are strictly required, but to cover all of the common scenarios we include them in a single example.

- Generate a locally generated certificate called IPSEC.
- Create a CA profile called CAPROFILE. The CA profile should be configured to use CRL checking and to download the CRL from *http://172.31.100.50* every two hours. The name of the CA server identifier is CASERVER.
- Configure SCEP to enroll a certificate to an SCEP server. SCEP should also be configured to automatically grab the CA certificate, reenroll the certificate before it expires, and download the new CA certificate before it expires. The SRX should retry every 3,600 seconds to download a new certificate.
- Use HTTP-based CRL checking to ensure that certificates proposed by the client are valid certificates that have not been revoked. This should be polled every two hours for an updated CRL.

```
root@SRX3600-1> request security pki generate-key-pair certificate-id IPSEC
Generated key pair IPSEC, key size 1024 bits

root@SRX3600-1> edit

[edit]
root@SRX3600-1# edit security pki ca-profile CAPROFILE

[edit security pki ca-profile CAPROFILE]
root@SRX3600-1#  set  ca-identity  CASERVER  revocation-check  crl  refresh-
interval 2
url http://172.31.100.50

[edit security pki ca-profile CAPROFILE]
root@SRX3600-1# set enrollment retry-interval 3600

[edit security pki ca-profile CAPROFILE]
root@SRX3600-1# up

[edit security pki]
root@SRX3600-1#  set  auto-re-enrollment  certificate-id  CAPROFILE  ca-profile-
name
qqq challenge-password aaa re-enroll-trigger-time-percentage 10
re-generate-keypair

[edit security pki ca-profile CAPROFILE]
root@SRX3600-1# run request pki ca-certificate enroll ca-profile CAPROFILE

Fingerprint:
75:1b:2f:a7:95:bc:2e:3b:54:d0:71:ae:86:42:09:e2:cc:75:34:d1 (sha1)
C1:4d:cc:fc:8f:10:d2:04:e9:80:09:68:4c:01:bd:42 (md5)
Do you want to load the above CA certificate ? [yes,no]
## Enroll the Local Certificate to Microsoft SCEP Server##

[edit security pki ca-profile CAPROFILE]
root@SRX3600-1#   set   enrollment   url   http://172.31.100.50/certsrv/mscep/
mscep.dll

[edit security pki ca-profile CAPROFILE]
root@SRX3600-1# run request security pki local-certificate enroll ca-profile
CAPROFILE
certificate-id qqq challenge-password aaa domain-name my.company.com
email qqq@company.com ip-address 10.10.10.10 subject DC=company,
CN=SRX, OU=IT, O=my, L=sunnyvale, ST=california, C=us
```

At the time of writing this book, only the Microsoft CA is fully qualified as a CA Server for functionalities like SCEP, but Juniper is working on extending this support including for other server types and OSCP. Stay tuned to the release notes and the documentation for a full set of CAs supported in the future.

Phase 1 IKE Configuration

Let's begin with the Phase 1 configuration, which has several different configuration elements—some optional, some required—for proper IPsec establishment. The important thing to remember as part of the Phase 1 configuration is that Phase 1 is not actually used to encrypt the data within the VPN, but rather to establish the secure channel to negotiate the Phase 2 keys that will be used to establish the IPsec VPN.

One great thing about configuring VPNs in the SRX compared to ScreenOS is that the configuration is not immediately applied and can be altered without removing all instances of the configuration to edit elements. This means that as long as you don't commit the configuration, these settings can be made in any particular order—an enormous advantage over ScreenOS and many other vendors' products. Another major advantage is that Junos separates the Phase 1 elements into three areas: proposal, policy, and gateway. This is advantageous when multiple gateways use the same policy, proposals, or both, and allows for template-like functionality for VPNs.

Our Phase 1 IKE configuration follows this process:

1. Configure the elements of the Phase 1 proposal, which defines the encryption and authentication policies.
2. Define the Phase 1 mode, preshared key or certificate, and proposal.
3. Configure the actual Phase 1 gateway properties.

Configuring Phase 1 proposals

The Phase 1 proposal provides the framework for the encryption and authentication parameters that are used in policy and gateway functionality. All Phase 1 proposals are configured under the `[security ike proposal <proposal-name>]` level in the configuration hierarchy. In our example, we configure the following elements (they can be configured in any order within the Phase 1 proposal):

Authentication method
: The authentication method defines whether preshared keys or certificates are used for Phase 1 authentication. Note that the `rsa-signatures` attribute signifies certificates using RSA key generation. This step does not refer to the authentication algorithm of Phase 1, but rather to how Phase 1 peers can authenticate each other.

Diffie-Hellman group
: The Diffie-Hellman group defines which group or key length will be used for the Phase 1 keys. The larger the key, the more secure it is, but also the more computationally complex it is to establish.

Encryption algorithm
: The encryption algorithm determines which algorithm will be used to encrypt the data within the Phase 1 secure channel. The SRX supports DES, 3DES, AES-128, AES-192, and AES-256, which are the most powerful (in that order) and the most demanding, although hardware acceleration makes this less of a concern. (Note that CBC stands for Cipher Block Chaining and it has to do with the fact that these algorithms are using block encryption rather than stream encryption, but it is not a detail that you need to be concerned with.)

Authentication parameter
: The authentication parameter defines what authentication algorithm is used to ensure that data have been received from the correct VPN peer and that they haven't been modified.

Key lifetimes
: Key lifetimes determine how long the VPN keys are active until they expire, and then the VPN Keys must be renegotiated when Phase 1 needs to be renegotiated.

Configuration for Remote-Office1 proposal with preshared keys. Configure the following properties for the Remote-Office-PSK proposal:

- Preshared key authentication
- Diffie-Hellman Group 2
- 3DES-CBC encryption algorithm
- SHA-1 authentication algorithm
- Key lifetime of 86,400 seconds

```
[edit]
root@SRX5800#edit security ike proposal Remote-Office-PSK

[edit security ike proposal Remote-Office-PSK]
root@SRX5800#set authentication-method pre-shared-keys

[edit security ike proposal Remote-Office-PSK]
root@SRX5800#set dh-group group2

[edit security ike proposal Remote-Office-PSK]
root@SRX5800#encryption-algorithm 3des-cbc

[edit security ike proposal Remote-Office-PSK]
root@SRX5800#set authentication algorithm sha1

[edit security ike proposal Remote-Office-PSK]
root@SRX5800#set lifetime-seconds 86400

[edit security ike proposal Remote-Office-PSK]
```

```
root@SRX5800# show
authentication-method pre-shared-keys;
dh-group group2;
authentication-algorithm sha1;
encryption-algorithm 3des-cbc;
lifetime-seconds 86400;

[edit security ike proposal Remote-Office-PSK]
root@SRX5800#top commit
```

Configuration for Remote-Office1 proposal with certificates. Alternatively, configure the following properties for the Remote-Office-Cert proposal:

- Certificate authentication
- Diffie-Hellman Group 2
- 3DES-CBC encryption algorithm
- SHA-1 authentication algorithm
- Key lifetime of 86,400 seconds

```
[edit]
root@SRX5800#edit security ike proposal Remote-Office-Cert

[edit security ike proposal Remote-Office-Cert]
root@SRX5800#set authentication-method certificates

[edit security ike proposal Remote-Office-Cert]
root@SRX5800#set dh-group group2

[edit security ike proposal Remote-Office-Cert]
root@SRX5800#encryption-algorithm 3des-cbc

[edit security ike proposal Remote-Office-Cert]
root@SRX5800#set authentication algorithm sha1

[edit security ike proposal Remote-Office-Cert]
root@SRX5800#set lifetime-seconds 86400

[edit security ike proposal Remote-Office-Cert]
root@SRX5800# show
authentication-method certificates;
dh-group group2;
authentication-algorithm sha1;
encryption-algorithm 3des-cbc;
lifetime-seconds 86400;

[edit security ike proposal Remote-Office-Cert]
root@SRX5800#top commit
```

Configuring IKEv1 Phase 1 policies

Phase 1 policies define the actual criteria of the VPN tunnel as well as which proposals can be used as part of the Phase 1 negotiation. Note that Junos supports up to four Phase 1 proposals in a single policy. Basically, if the peer initiates the VPN, the SRX will allow any of the listed proposals. If the SRX is initiating the VPN, it will try the different proposals in the order in which they are listed until either a proposal is accepted by the peer or negotiations fail. Keep in mind that for Phase 1, preshared keys or certificates can be used with any combination of the parameters and proposals, but they are exclusive in that only one method can be used, not both.

Configuring Phase 1 mode
: Main mode or Aggressive mode should be selected, depending on the configuration of the tunnel.

Configuring preshared keys
: Preshared keys are used for each peer to authenticate each other during Phase 1. Preshared keys can be entered as either a clear-text string (ASCII text) or hexadecimal text. This must be specified when entering the preshared key. Typically, ASCII text will be used to specify the password, because it can support human-readable strings, whereas hexadecimal is 0–9, a–f text.

Configuring certificates
: Certificates can be used as an alternative to preshared keys because they offer more dynamic support for strong authentication than preshared keys. You need to specify a few parameters, including the local certificate to use, the trusted CA with which to authenticate the peer certificate (it must be loaded on the SRX), and the peer certificate type that defines the peer's certificate format.

Configuring the local certificate
: This is the certificate to be presented to the IPsec peer.

Configuring the trusted CA
: This is used to authenticate the peer's certificate.

Configuring the peer certificate type
: The SRX supports negotiation with either PKCS7 or X.509 signature encoding. A peer certificate type must be defined for the certificates that are being negotiated. The type of certificate depends on which encoding process the certificate is generated with and must be negotiated with the peer gateway.

Configuring proposals
: A proposal or set of proposals must be chosen for the IKE policy to define which encryption or authentication algorithms are used when negotiating the peer IPsec VPN. Up to four proposals can be selected, although only a single proposal is required. There are also some predefined proposals that can be used.

Configuring IKEv1 Phase 1 IKE policy with preshared key, Main mode. Configure the Remote-Office-Static Phase 1 IKE policy using the following values:

- IKE Phase 1 Main mode
- A preshared key of $up3r$ecReT
- The Remote-Office-PSK proposal

```
[edit]
root@SRX5800#edit security ike policy Remote-Office-Static

[edit security ike policy Remote-Office-Static]
root@SRX5800#set mode main

[edit security ike policy Remote-Office-Static]
root@SRX5800#set pre-shared-key ascii-text $up3r$ecReT

[edit security ike policy Remote-Office-Static]
root@SRX5800#set proposals Remote-Office-PSK

[edit security ike policy Remote-Office-Static]
root@SRX5800#show
mode main;
proposals Remote-Office-PSK;
pre-shared-key ascii-text "$9$JTUHq5Tz9tO5QhSlex7bsYgoGiHm5zns2Q3";
## SECRET-DATA

[edit security ike policy Remote-Office-Static]
root@SRX5800#top commit
```

Configuring IKEv1 Phase 1 IKE policy with preshared key, Aggressive mode. Configure the Remote-Office-Dynamic Phase 1 IKE policy for gateways with dynamic IP addresses using the following values:

- IKE Phase 1 Aggressive mode
- A preshared key of $up3r$ecReT
- The Remote-Office1 proposal

```
[edit]
root@SRX5800#edit security ike policy Remote-Office-Dynamic

[edit security ike policy Remote-Office-Dynamic]
root@SRX5800#set mode aggressive

[edit security ike policy Remote-Office-Dynamic]
root@SRX5800#set pre-shared-key ascii-text $up3r$ecReT

[edit security ike policy Remote-Office-Dynamic]
```

```
root@SRX5800#set proposals Remote-Office-PSK

[edit security ike policy Remote-Office-Dynamic]
root@SRX5800#show
mode aggressive;
proposals Remote-Office-PSK;
pre-shared-key ascii-text "$9$JTUHq5Tz9tO5QhSlex7bsYgoGiHm5zns2Q3";
## SECRET-DATA
```

Configuring IKEv1 Phase 1 IKE policy with certificates. For this example, we create a Phase 1 IKE policy using certificates that builds on our previous work creating a local certificate and setting up the CA profile:

- Create an IKE policy called Remote-Office-Static-Cert that uses certificate authentication rather than preshared key authentication.
- This policy should use Main mode for the Phase 1 IKE mode.
- You should trust any valid certificate signed by a CA that you have configured to trust.
- Use the local-certificate IPSEC that we generated earlier for authentication to your peer. This certificate should be in the PKCS7 format.
- Use Remote-Office1 for the proposal.

```
[edit]
root@SRX5800#edit security ike policy Remote-Office-Static-Cert

[edit security ike policy Remote-Office-Static-Cert]
root@SRX5800#set mode main

[edit security ike policy Remote-Office-Static-Cert]
root@SRX5800#set certificate local-certificate IPSEC

[edit security ike policy Remote-Office-Static-Cert]
root@SRX5800#set certificate trusted-ca use-all

[edit security ike policy Remote-Office-Static-Cert]
root@SRX5800#set certificate peer-certificate-type pkcs7

[edit security ike policy Remote-Office-Static-Cert]
root@SRX5800#set Office1 proposals Remote-Office1

[edit security ike policy Remote-Office-Static-Cert]
root@SRX5800# show
mode main;
proposals Remote-Office1;
certificate {
    local-certificate IPSEC;
    trusted-ca use-all;
    peer-certificate-type pkcs7;
```

```
}

root@SRX5800#top commit
```

Configuring IKEv1 Phase 1 gateways

The last aspect of Phase 1 that must be configured is the actual gateway itself. The gateway identifies the remote peer the IPsec VPN peers with and defines the appropriate parameters for that IPsec VPN. As we discussed earlier in this chapter, there are two types of gateways: those with static IP addresses and those with dynamic IP addresses (including remote clients).

The SRX allows you to define multiple gateways with the same policies, which is a feature that can greatly simplify configuration, particularly if multiple gateways have the same proposal and policy. Here we cover the aspects of configuring both static and dynamic IP gateways and the various properties for IPsec VPN gateways.

Configuring remote gateways with a static IP address
: The optimal setup for two VPN gateways is to have both of them use static IP addresses. This simplifies the Phase 1 setup between the two gateways, as well as potential troubleshooting because the IP address of the gateway is always known.

In addition to the primary IP address defined in the gateway definition, up to four backup gateways can also be defined should the primary gateway fail.

Configuring remote gateways with a dynamic IP address
: When the remote IPsec gateway does not have a static IP address, but rather is assigned via DHCP, or is perhaps a gateway that moves between different locations, dynamic IKE identities are used rather than configuring a fixed IP address. A few properties might have to be defined as part of this configuration:

  Configuring local identities
  : Local identities are required when a device is using a dynamic IP address to identify itself to the other gateway. This can be a DN, an FQDN, an IP address, or a UFQDN. Typically, for site-to-site VPNs, the FQDN or hostname is used to define the local identity and the DN is used for certificate-based authentication. UFQDN is typically used for remote client VPNs.

  Configuring remote identities
  : Remote identities are required when the remote party does not have a static IP address and therefore must use a dynamic IKE identity. The identity types are the same for the remote identities as they are for the local identities.

Configuring the external interface
: The external interface is the interface on which the SRX terminates the IPsec VPN. The interface that the traffic terminates on must match the interface defined for that gateway or Phase 1 negotiations will fail. This is often overlooked in the configuration and is a source of confusion when experiencing issues establishing the VPN. Note that the interface must also include the IPsec unit number; if it is not defined, it is set as unit 0, but if the unit is not correct, establishment issues will occur. Note that prior to version 10.4, termination of IPsec VPNs on non-inet.0 VRs is not supported.

Configuring interfaces and zones to allow IKE traffic
: On top of configuring the external interface on which the IPsec VPN is terminated, you must also make sure that IKE traffic is allowed on the interface or zone on the SRX; otherwise, the SRX will drop the traffic before the IKE daemon can process it. This is a security precaution to prevent DoS attacks against IKE gateways on interfaces that shouldn't be allowed to accept the IKE traffic. Additionally, further restrictions can be made through the use of interface access lists that can prevent IKE traffic based on stateless firewall filters, so it is important to make sure such filters are not interfering with the traffic.

Configuring IKE policy
: The IPsec VPN gateway must define the IKE policy previously configured. The IKE policy defines the preshared key or certificates used, along with the other properties of the IPsec tunnel such as the encryption and authentication algorithms. The name of the IKE policy does not have to match the name of the gateway, but this is often done for simplicity. Also, IKE policies can be reused by other gateways, assuming that the properties are the same.

Configuring NAT-T
: NAT-T is required when the remote IPsec gateway or client is behind a device performing NAT. By default, NAT-T is enabled on the SRX, so it must be explicitly disabled to turn it off on a gateway-by-gateway basis.

Configuring NAT keepalives
: NAT keepalives (also known as *session keepalives*) might be required when the remote client or gateway is behind a device performing NAT. The NAT device maintains a table that maps the translations of each session (including that of the IPsec VPN session). The sessions and their corresponding translations typically time out after a certain period of time if no traffic is received (known as an *idle timeout*). If the VPN is expected to have large periods of inactivity during which the session and translation might time out, NAT keepalives should be enabled to generate "artificial" traffic to keep the session active on the NAT device.

Configuring DPD
: DPD allows the two gateways to determine if the peer gateway is up and responding to the DPD messages that are negotiated during IPsec establishment.

Configuring an IKEv1 gateway with static IP address and DPD. Configure the Remote-Office1 IKE gateway with the following parameters:

- IP address of 198.18.1.254.
- External interface of ge-0/0/0.0.
- Accept inbound IKE traffic on host ge-0/0/0.0 in the untrust zone.
- Remote-Office1 IKE policy.
- Enable DPD with an interval of every 10 seconds and a threshold of 3.
- Don't have DPD always send keepalives; only send them in the absence of traffic.

```
[edit]
root@SRX5800#edit security ike gateway Remote-Office1

[edit security ike gateway Remote-Office1]
root@SRX5800#set address 198.18.1.254

[edit security ike gateway Remote-Office1]
root@SRX5800#set external-interface ge-0/0/0.0

[edit security ike gateway Remote-Office1]
root@SRX5800#set ike-policy Remote-Office1

[edit security ike gateway Remote-Office1]
root@SRX5800#set dead-peer-detection interval 10

[edit security ike gateway Remote-Office1]
root@SRX5800#set dead-peer-detection threshold 3

[edit security ike gateway Remote-Office1]
root@SRX5800# show
ike-policy Remote-Office1;
address 198.18.1.254;
dead-peer-detection {
    interval 10;
    threshold 3;
}
external-interface ge-0/0/0.0;

[edit security ike gateway Remote-Office1]
root@SRX5800#top edit security zones security-zone untrust
interfaces ge-0/0/0.0 host-inbound-traffic system-services

[edit security zones security-zone untrust interfaces ge-0/0/0.0
host-inbound-traffic system-services]
```

```
root@SRX5800#set ike

[edit security zones security-zone untrust interfaces ge-0/0/0.0
host-inbound-traffic system-services]
root@SRX5800#show
ike;

[edit security zones security-zone untrust interfaces ge-0/0/0.0
host-inbound-traffic system-services]
root@SRX5800#top commit
```

Configuring dynamic gateways and remote access clients

Some properties of IKE Phase 1 apply only to remote clients connecting to the SRX. These are primarily centered on XAuth and IKE IDs.

Configuring XAuth
: XAuth negotiation technically takes place between Phase 1 and Phase 2 of the VPN establishment, but is herewith discussed as part of the Phase 1 negotiation. The SRX only supports authenticating clients with XAuth and not authenticating itself to another XAuth-capable peer. Also, the SRX must use RADIUS to authenticate remote users, and cannot use local XAuth users like ScreenOS can (at the time of this writing). A few things must be configured as part of the XAuth configuration, including the XAuth access profile, the XAuth RADIUS server configuration, and the XAuth configuration within IKE. Also, when configuring remote users, an IKE gateway must be configured to define the IKE identity of the user.

Configuring IKE connection sharing
: IKE connection sharing allows an administrator to define a single IKE gateway object that allows multiple users to connect to it with the same properties. This is most commonly performed when using multiple remote clients that are also using XAuth to authenticate; however, this is not a requirement. It is primarily used as a matter of convenience for administrators so that they don't have to configure multiple gateways as well as remote clients with separate configuration files, but rather can use a single remote configuration and single gateway configuration. This is known as a shared-IKE ID.

Configuring an IKE gateway with a dynamic IP address. Configure the Remote-Office3 gateway that uses a dynamic IP address with the following properties:

- Remote-Office-Dynamic IKE policy
- Remote-Office3.company.com used as identity of Remote-Office3
- External interface of ge-0/0/0.0
- IKE processing enabled on interface ge-0/0/0.0

```
[edit]
root@SRX5800#edit security ike gateway Remote-Office3

[edit security ike gateway Remote-Office3]
root@SRX5800#set dynamic hostname Remote-Office3.company.com

[edit security ike gateway Remote-Office3]
root@SRX5800#set external-interface ge-0/0/0.0

set security zones security-zone untrust interfaces ge-0/0/0.0
host-inbound-traffic system-services ike

[edit security ike gateway Remote-Office3]
root@SRX5800#set ike-policy Remote-Office-Dynamic

[edit security ike gateway Remote-Office3
root@5800# show
ike-policy Remote-Office-Dynamic;
dynamic hostname Remote-Office3.company.com;
external-interface ge-0/0/0.0;

[edit security ike gateway Remote-Office3]
root@SRX5800#top edit security zones security-zone untrust interfaces
ge-0/0/0.0 host-inbound-traffic system-services

[edit security zones security-zone untrust interfaces ge-0/0/0.0
host-inbound-traffic system-services]
root@SRX5800#set ike

[edit security zones security-zone untrust interfaces ge-0/0/0.0
host-inbound-traffic system-services]
root@SRX5800#show
ike;

[edit security zones security-zone untrust interfaces ge-0/0/0.0
host-inbound-traffic system-services]
root@SRX5800#top commit
```

Configuring an IKEv1 remote access client. Configure the following properties for a remote client connection:

- The remote client's identity should be a shared IKE ID type, with up to 25 simultaneous connections.
- The user should use the UFQDN *Remote-Client@company.com*.
- The VPNs should be terminated on the ge-0/0/0.0 interface and ensure that IKE traffic can be processed on this interface.
- The Remote-Office-Dynamic IKE policy should be selected.

- XAuth will be used for this connection with an access profile of Remote-Client, via RADIUS server 10.3.1.50, with a secret of RadiU$Secr3+.

```
[edit]
root@SRX5800# edit security ike gateway Remote-Client

[edit security ike gateway Remote-Client]
root@SRX5800# set dynamic user-at-hostname Remote-Client@company.com

[edit security ike gateway Remote-Client]
root@SRX5800# set external-interface ge-0/0/0.0

[edit security ike gateway Remote-Client]
root@SRX5800# set ike-policy Remote-Office-Dynamic

[edit security ike gateway Remote-Client]
root@SRX5800# set xauth access-profile Remote-Client

[edit security ike gateway Remote-Client]
root@SRX5800# set dynamic connection-limit 25

[edit security ike gateway Remote-Client]
root@SRX5800# set Dynamic dynamic ike-user-type shared-ike-id

[edit security ike gateway Remote-Client
root@SRX5800# show
ike-policy Remote-Office-Dynamic;
dynamic {
    user-at-hostname Remote-Client@company.com;
    connections-limit 25;
    ike-user-type shared-ike-id;
}
local-identity hostname HQ.company.com;
external-interface ge-0/0/0.0;
xauth access-profile Remote-Client;

[edit security ike gateway Remote-Client]
root@SRX5800#top edit security zones security-zone untrust interfaces
ge-0/0/0.0 host-inbound-traffic system-services

[edit security zones security-zone untrust interfaces ge-0/0/0.0
host-inbound-traffic system-services
root@SRX5800#set ike

[edit security zones security-zone untrust interfaces ge-0/0/0.0
host-inbound-traffic system-services
root@SRX5800#show
ike;

[edit security zones security-zone untrust interfaces ge-0/0/0.0
host-inbound-traffic system-services
root@SRX5800# top edit access profile Remote-Client
```

```
[edit access profile Remote-Client]
root@SRX5800# set authentication-order radius

[edit access profile Remote-Client]
root@SRX5800# set radius-server 10.3.1.50 secret RaDiU$Secr3+

[edit access profile Remote-Client]
root@SRX5800# show
authentication-order radius;
radius-server {
        10.3.1.50 secret "$9$PTn9AtOEhyQFrKvWXxjik.PQn6AuBE/9Ec";
## SECRET-DATA
    }

[edit access profile Remote-Client]
root@SRX5800#top commit
```

Phase 2 IKE Configuration

Phase 2 IKE configuration requires several parameters to be defined for the IPsec VPN to be established. Phase 2 primarily deals with securing the data traffic located within the IPsec VPN tunnel. This communication takes place on top of the secure communication channel formed in Phase 1.

In this section, we cover the following regarding Phase 2 configuration: Phase 2 proposal, Phase 2 policy, and common VPN components.

Configuring IKEv1 Phase 2 proposals

Phase 2 IKE proposals are similar to Phase 1 IKE proposals in that encryption and authentication algorithms are selected, along with key lifetimes. As mentioned before, the purpose of the Phase 2 encryption and authentication algorithms differs from that of Phase 1 encryption and authentication algorithms, but the actual components of the proposals are essentially the same. It is important to note that the names of the proposals, policies, and VPNs do not have to match those of the Phase 1 policies used, as they will be referenced accordingly, but name matching is often done for simplicity of management.

Configuring the encryption algorithm
: The encryption algorithm defines which encryption algorithm is used to encrypt the data within the IPsec VPN. This is only applicable when using ESP, as AH does not encrypt the actual content of the VPN.

Configuring the authentication algorithm
: The authentication algorithm is used to ensure that the data have arrived from the correct source and have not been modified.

Configuring the IPsec protocol
: ESP or AH must be selected for determining the type of VPN. ESP provides both encryption and authentication, whereas AH provides only authentication.

Configuring the key lifetimes
: Key lifetimes for Phase 2 can be configured in seconds or as kilobytes. If the goal is to ensure that Phase 2 keys are active for only a certain period of time, seconds is the appropriate choice; if the goal is to keep keys active until a certain amount of data has been sent (based on VPN usage), kilobytes is preferred. If you do not specify the value, by default 3,600 seconds (or one hour) will be used for the Phase 2 key lifetime.

Configuring an IKEv1 Phase 2 proposal for remote offices and client connections. Configure the following properties for the Remote-Office Phase 2 proposal that will be used for all remote offices and client connections:

- Use AES-256 for the encryption algorithm.
- Use SHA-1 for the authentication algorithm.
- Use ESP as the IPsec protocol.
- Set a lifetime of one hour for the Phase 2 keys.

```
[edit]
root@SRX5800# edit security ipsec proposal Remote-Office-Client

[edit security ipsec proposal Remote-Office-Client]
root@SRX5800# set encryption-algorithm aes-256-cbc

[edit security ipsec proposal Remote-Office-Client]
root@SRX5800# set authentication-algorithm hmac-sha1-96

[edit security ipsec proposal Remote-Office-Client]
root@SRX5800# set protocol esp

[edit security ipsec proposal Remote-Office-Client]
root@SRX5800# set lifetime-seconds 3600

[edit security ipsec proposal Remote-Office-Client]
root@SRX5800# show
protocol esp;
authentication-algorithm hmac-sha1-96;
encryption-algorithm aes-256-cbc;
lifetime-seconds 3600;

[edit security ipsec proposal Remote-Office-Client]
root@SRX5800#top commit
```

Configuring Phase 2 IPsec policy

The Phase 2 IPsec policy defines how the VPN is established. A few properties are defined in the IPsec policy, including which proposals are to be used, as well as whether PFS is to be used on the VPN.

Configuring the IPsec proposals
: Up to four proposals can be negotiated for the IPsec tunnel, although only one is used for the actual IPsec traffic encryption and authentication. Essentially, the initiator tries to negotiate each IPsec tunnel until a proposal is accepted by the peer or there are no other IPsec proposals left to negotiate.

Configuring PFS
: If PFS is to be used, it is configured in the IPsec policy, and actually takes effect after Phase 1 but before Phase 2 is negotiated. As part of the configuration, the Diffie-Hellman group must be defined to be negotiated for the PFS. It does not have to match the Diffie-Hellman group negotiated in Phase 1.

Configuring an IPsec policy defining the Phase 2 proposal. You must configure an IPsec policy that defines which Phase 2 proposal will be selected and if PSK will be used for the VPN, if applicable. Configure the Remote-Office-Client Phase 2 IPsec policy, which will be used for all remote office and client connections with the following properties:

- Use the Remote-Office-Client proposal.
- Use PFS with Diffie-Hellman Group 5 for additional security.

```
[edit]
root@SRX5800# edit security ipsec policy Remote-Office-Client

[edit security ipsec policy Remote-Office-Client]
root@SRX5800# set proposals Remote-Office-Client

[edit security ipsec policy Remote-Office-Client]
root@SRX5800# set perfect-forward-secrecy keys group5

[edit security ipsec policy Remote-Office-Client]
root@SRX5800# show
perfect-forward-secrecy {
    keys group5;
}
proposals Remote-Office-Client;

[edit security ipsec policy Remote-Office-Client]
root@SRX5800#top commit
```

Configuring common IPsec VPN components

Now that the IPsec proposal and the policy have been configured, the VPN object can be completed with the final configuration of Phase 2. This information includes the proxy IDs, the IPsec policy, the tunnel binding (if route-based VPNs are used), and other properties of the VPN tunnel including replay detection, fragmentation, and VPN monitoring. We begin with the VPN configuration components that are common to both policy-based and route-based VPNs, and then cover the components specific to policy- and route-based VPNs, respectively. Some of the components covered in this section are optional and are noted as such.

Configuring the IPsec VPN gateway
: The IPsec VPN gateway must be configured in Phase 2. This references the IKE VPN gateway object configured in Phase 1.

Configuring the IPsec policy
: The IPsec policy defines the proposal and PFS configuration for the VPN.

Configuring VPN establishment
: The VPN can be established immediately when the configuration is applied (and subsequently whenever the VPN expires), or it can be established on-traffic when there is user data traffic. By default, VPNs are established on-traffic.

Configuring fragmentation
: Fragmentation might be required on VPN traffic because of the overhead associated with IPsec VPNs (either ESP/AH overhead or overhead associated with Tunnel mode) and the underlying MTU of the physical data links. A few options can be selected for the fragmentation. You can alternatively clear the `DF` bit, set the `DF` bit, and copy the `DF` bit. If fragmentation is required but the `DF` bit is set (and honored by the SRX), that traffic will be dropped.

Configuring Anti-Replay detection
: By default, Anti-Replay detection is enabled. It essentially consists of checking the sequence numbers and enforcing the check, rather than just ignoring the sequence numbers. Anti-Replay detection can be disabled manually if desired on a VPN-by-VPN basis.

Configuring VPN monitoring
: VPN monitoring is a proprietary method of ensuring that the VPN is actually established (which goes beyond the VPN gateway availability of DPD to actually ensure that the VPN itself is up). A few parameters must be configured as part of VPN monitoring, including what device to ping, what source interface is used, and whether the traffic is optimized. The optimized setting omits sending the pings when user data is present.

Configuring a common site-to-site VPN component. Configure a VPN called East-Branch, which will serve as the site-to-site VPN for the East Branch to Campus site.

- Use an IKE gateway called East-Branch.
- Use an IPsec policy called `Remote-Office-Client`.
- Establish the VPNs immediately and automatically rekey.
- Disable Anti-Replay detection.
- Always clear the `DF` bit.
- Monitor the VPN by pinging the IP address 192.168.1.50 using a method in which the pings are only sent in the absence of traffic every three seconds with a failure threshold of three.

```
[edit]
root@SRX5800# edit security ipsec vpn East-Branch

[edit security ipsec vpn East-Branch]
root@SRX5800# set ike gateway East-Branch

[edit security ipsec vpn East-Branch]
root@SRX5800# set ike ipsec-policy Remote-Office-Client

[edit security ipsec vpn East-Branch]
root@SRX5800# set establish-tunnels immediately

[edit security ipsec vpn East-Branch]
root@SRX5800# set df-bit clear

[edit security ipsec vpn East-Branch]
root@SRX5800# set ike no-anti-replay

[edit security ipsec vpn East-Branch]
root@SRX5800# set vpn-monitor optimized source-interface st0.0
destination-ip 192.168.1.50

[edit security ipsec vpn East-Branch]
root@SRX5800# show
df-bit clear;
vpn-monitor {
    optimized;
    destination-ip 192.168.1.50;
}
ike {
    gateway East-Branch;
    no-anti-replay;
}
ipsec-policy Remote-Office-Client;
```

```
[edit security ipsec vpn East-Branch]
root@SRX5800# up

[edit security ipsec]
root@SRX5800# set vpn-monitor-options inverval 3 threshold 3


[edit security ipsec]
root@SRX5800# show
vpn-monitor-options {
    interval 3;
    threshold 3;
}

[edit security ipsec]
root@SRX5800#top commit
```

IKEv1 Versus IKEv2 Configuration

Before we wrap up route-based VPNs, let's take a look at how IKEv2 VPNs are configured on the SRX. First, only route-based VPNs are supported today, so that excludes policy-based VPNs. But how does the SRX know whether or not to use IKEv1 or IKEv2 for negotiation?

Simple: it is defined in the gateway configuration. In fact, a gateway configuration can only be IKEv1 or IKEv2. You cannot configure the VPN to fall back to IKEv1 from IKEv2 or upgrade to IKEv2 if available, so you'll need to sort this out in advance. The configuration is really quite simple and is done under the gateway configuration as follows:

```
[edit]
root@srx3600n0# set security ike gateway V2-Gateway version ?
Possible completions:
  v1-only              The connection must be initiated using IKE version 1
  v2-only              The connection must be initiated using IKE version 2
[edit]
root@srx3600n0# set security ike gateway V2-Gateway version v2-only
```

The default configuration is v1-only, so if you want to use v2, you need to explicitly define this to be the case.

Configuring policy-based VPNs

The main thing that needs to be configured as part of policy-based VPNs is the tunnel action of the appropriate security policy rule. One thing that is often forgotten when it comes to configuring policy-based VPNs is that a route might still be needed to force the traffic to go to the correct destination zone. This is not special to the VPN configuration, as it also applies to standard traffic to determine the egress interface and egress zone.

Configuring a policy-based VPN for the East Branch to the Central site VPN. In this example, we configure a policy-based VPN for the East Branch to the Central site VPN. Use the following properties for creating this policy-based VPN:

- Allow any HTTP traffic to or from the 10.0.0.0/8 network to 192.168.1.0/24 for the East-Branch VPN created in the previous steps.
- Log the connections on session close.

```
[edit]
root@SRX5800# set security zones security-zones trust address-book
address 10.0.0.0/8 10.0.0.0/8

[edit]
root@SRX5800# show security zones security-zone trust address-book
address 10.0.0.0/8 10.0.0.0/8


[edit]
root@SRX5800# set security zones security-zones untrust address-book
address 192.168.1.0/24 192.168.1.0/24

[edit]
root@SRX5800# show security zones security-zone untrust address-book
address 192.168.1.0/24 192.168.1.0/24

[edit]
root@SRX5800# edit security policies from-zone trust to-zone untrust policy
East-Branch-Outbound

[edit security policies from-zone trust to-zone untrust policy
East-Branch-Outbound]
root@SRX5800# set match source-address 10.0.0.0/8 destination-address
192.168.1.0/24 application junos-http

[edit security policies from-zone trust to-zone untrust policy
East-Branch-Outbound]
root@SRX5800# set then permit tunnel ipsec-vpn East-Branch pair-policy
East-Branch-Inbound

[edit security policies from-zone trust to-zone untrust policy
East-Branch-Outbound]
root@SRX5800# set then log session-close

[edit security policies from-zone trust to-zone untrust policy
East-Branch-Outbound]
root@SRX5800# show
match {
        source-address 10.0.0.0/8;
        destination-address 192.168.1.0/24;
        application junos-http;
```

```
        }
 then {
        permit {
               tunnel {
                 ipsec-vpn East-Branch;
                 pair-policy East-Branch-Inbound;
                }
         }
            log {
                session-close;
            }
 }

[edit security policies from-zone trust to-zone untrust policy
East-Branch-Outbound]
root@SRX5800#top edit security policies from-zone untrust to-zone
trust policy East-Branch-Inbound

[edit security policies from-zone trust to-zone untrust policy
East-Branch-Inbound]
root@SRX5800# show
match {
        source-address 192.168.1.0/24;
        destination-address 10.0.0.0/8;
        application junos-http;
        }
 then {
        permit {
               tunnel {
                 ipsec-vpn East-Branch;
                 pair-policy East-Branch-Outbound;
                }
         }
            log {
                session-close;
            }
 }

[edit security policies from-zone trust to-zone untrust policy
East-Branch-Inbound]
root@SRX5800#top commit
```

Configuring route-based VPNs

Route-based VPNs require a few extra components over policy-based VPNs, as outlined here:

Configuring secure tunnel interfaces
: Secure tunnel interfaces are virtual interfaces that place all of the traffic that arrives in them into VPNs that are bound to the tunnel interface. They are required for route-based VPNs, where the traffic destined to the VPN is routed into the secure

tunnel interface. It is important to understand that just like standard logical interfaces, the units can be in different zones from each other, so they can be separate.

Configuring interface binding
: Once the st0.*x* interface has been created, the VPN must be bound to the appropriate secure tunnel interface. This is done within the Phase 2 configuration.

Configuring proxy IDs
: Proxy IDs must be configured for route-based VPNs because they cannot be derived from anything like policy-based VPNs can. Policy-based VPNs can also be overwritten by defining the proxy IDs manually. At the time of this writing, only a single proxy ID can be defined per VPN on the SRX.

Configuring routing
: The SRX must know how to reach the destination networks. This can be done through the use of static routing or dynamic routing. In this example configuration, static routing is used.

Although route-based VPNs do not require a policy with the Tunnel action, security policies to allow the traffic are still required. The policy is a regular policy, with the standard Permit action. The following syntax shows the Then action of the policy, followed by a complete example of a match policy:

```
[edit]
root@SRX5800# set interfaces st0 unit 0 family inet address 192.168.100.1/24

root@SRX5800# show interfaces st0
unit 0 {
    family inet {
        address 192.168.100.1/24;
    }
}

[edit]
root@SRX5800# edit security ipsec vpn East-Branch

[edit security ipsec vpn East-Branch]
root@SRX5800# set bind-interface st0.0

[edit security ipsec vpn East-Branch]
root@SRX5800# set ike proxy-identity local 10.0.0.0/8 remote 192.168.1.0/24
service junos-http

[edit security ipsec vpn East-Branch]
root@SRX5800# set ike gateway East-Branch

[edit security ipsec vpn East-Branch]
root@SRX5800# set ipsec-policy Remote-Office-Client
```

```
[edit security ipsec vpn East-Branch]
root@SRX5800# show
bind-interface st0.0;
ike {
    gateway East-Branch;
    proxy-identity {
        local 10.0.0.0/8;
        remote 192.168.1.0/24;
        service junos-http;
    }
    ipsec-policy Remote-Office-Client;
}

[edit security ipsec vpn East-Branch]
root@SRX5800# top


[edit]
root@SRX5800# set routing-options static route 192.168.1.0/24
next-hop 192.168.100.254

[edit]
root@SRX5800# show routing-options static route 192.168.1.0/24
next-hop 192.168.100.254

[edit]
root@SRX5800# set security zones security-zones trust address-book
address 10.0.0.0/8 10.0.0.0/8

[edit]
root@SRX5800# show security zones security-zone trust address-book
address 10.0.0.0/8 10.0.0.0/8

[edit]
root@SRX5800# set security zones security-zones untrust address-book
address 192.168.1.0/24 192.168.1.0/24[edit]
root@SRX5800# show security zones security-zone untrust address-book
address 192.168.1.0/24 192.168.1.0/24

[edit]
root@SRX5800# edit security policies from-zone trust to-zone untrust policy
East-Branch-Outbound

[edit security policies from-zone trust to-zone untrust policy
East-Branch-Outbound]
root@SRX5800# set match source-address 10.0.0.0/8 destination-address
192.168.1.0/24 application junos-http

[edit security policies from-zone trust to-zone untrust policy
East-Branch-Outbound]
root@SRX5800# set then permit
```

```
[edit security policies from-zone trust to-zone untrust policy
East-Branch-Outbound]
root@SRX5800# set then log session-close

[edit security policies from-zone trust to-zone untrust policy
East-Branch-Outbound]
root@SRX5800# show
match {
        source-address 10.0.0.0/8;
        destination-address 192.168.1.0/24;
        application junos-http;
        }
 then {
        permit
        log {
                session-close;
            }
  }

[edit security policies from-zone trust to-zone untrust policy
East-Branch-Outbound]
root@SRX5800#top edit security policies from-zone untrust to-zone trust policy
East-Branch-Inbound

[edit security policies from-zone untrust to-zone trust policy
East-Branch-Inbound]
root@SRX5800# set match source-address 192.168.1.0/24 destination-address
192.168.1.0/24 application junos-http

[edit security policies from-zone untrust to-zone trust policy
East-Branch-Inbound]
root@SRX5800# set then permit

[edit security policies from-zone untrust to-zone trust policy
East-Branch-Inbound]
root@SRX5800# set then log session-close


[edit security policies from-zone untrust to-zone trust policy
East-Branch-Inbound]
root@SRX5800# show
match {
        source-address 192.168.1.0/24;
        destination-address 10.0.0.0/8;
        application junos-http;
        }
 then {
        permit
        log {
                session-close;
            }
  }
```

```
[edit security policies from-zone untrust to-zone trust policy
East-Branch-Inbound]
root@SRX5800#top commit
```

IPsec and SRX HA

When it comes to HA, there are a few pertinent items to discuss with IPsec on the SRX.

IPsec termination in HA

When using HA, terminating IPsec tunnels is a bit more complex because there is technically more than one place on the SRX that the IPsec tunnel can be terminated (particularly with active/active HA infrastructure). It is possible to terminate a VPN on a local interface, a reth interface, or, as of Junos 12.1X44, a loopback interface. Typically, you should not terminate a VPN on a local interface when using HA, and in fact this isn't supported for active/active HA clusters. In terms of whether or not to terminate on a reth interface or loopback interface in the case of 12.1X44+, that just depends on how your SRX connects to the network. If you only have one upstream/downstream path, then it makes sense to terminate the VPN simply on the reth interface that faces the peer because the reth interface will automatically handle the failover between different nodes. You'd want to use a loopback interface rather than a reth interface if you have multiple upstream/downstream connections (e.g., multihomed Internet connections) and you don't want to terminate multiple VPNs on your device, one for each segment (which would rely on dynamic routing to fail over between VPNs). In this case, you simply terminate the VPN to the loopback interface, so regardless of what the underlying routing dictates for reaching the peer, the endpoints will remain the same.

ISSU for VPN

ISSU is a feature that today is supported on the high-end SRX. As of Junos 12.1X44, the high-end SRX supports ISSU with IPsec configurations. This means that you can perform a hitless upgrade where the secondary device will be upgraded first, then once it is upgraded and back up and in the cluster, the primary will fail over to the upgraded device including all VPNs. Then the original primary will upgrade itself. This all happens with only a single command to be issued that will upgrade the entire cluster.

At the time of writing this book, the branch SRX only supports partial ISSU support in that it does not statefully fail over firewall sessions, but rather fails over the devices and upgrades them with the use of a single command. The expansion of ISSU and synchronization of the feature sets between the branch and high-end SRX will likely come very soon so stay posted to the release notes.

Dynamic VPN

In this example, we demonstrate how to leverage the built-in Dynamic VPN client on the branch SRX Series devices to connect remote clients to the corporate network.

Phase 1 proposal
: Create a proposal called Dynamic-VPN that uses 3DES-SHA1, preshared keys, Diffie-Hellman Group 2, and a lifetime of four hours, and set a description.

Phase 1 policy
: Create a policy called Dynamic-VPN-Policy that uses aggressive mode, the preshared key DialUp4123, and the Dynamic-VPN proposal, and set a description.

Phase 1 gateway
: Create an IKE gateway called Dynamic-VPN-Gateway. You will use the XAuth parameters that we defined earlier in the chapter for our XAuth profile called XAuth. Limit the number of connections to five using a shared IKE ID of *dynvpn@company.com*. This VPN should be terminated on interface ge-0/0/0.0 using the IKE policy Dynamic-VPN-Policy. Ensure that the ge-0/0/0.0 interface allows inbound IKE and HTTP/HTTPS connections so that the user can access the web interface and make sure VPNs can establish properly.

Phase 2 proposal
: Create a proposal called Dynamic-VPN using AES256-SHA1 with ESP as the IPsec protocol, set the lifetime to 3,600 seconds, and provide a description for the proposal.

Phase 2 policy
: Create a policy called Dynamic-VPN-Policy that uses the Dynamic-VPN Phase 2 proposal with PDF Diffie-Hellman Group 2.

Phase 2 VPN
: Create a Phase 2 VPN called Dynamic-VPN that uses Dynamic-VPN-Gateway as the gateway and Dynamic-VPN-Policy as the Phase 2 policy.

Dynamic VPN client configuration
: Create a Dynamic VPN client configuration called Dynamic-VPN-Clients that uses the Dynamic-VPN configuration we defined for user `dynvpn`. This profile should allow users to access the resource 10.0.0.0/8 behind the firewall when they are connected. Use the XAuth profile XAuth, and also force the client to upgrade if an upgrade to the client is necessary on login.

Local certificate
: Finally, generate a local certificate that can be used to host HTTPS on the web server on the ge-0/0/0.0 interface. This is needed so that we can allow users to log in securely. You must also ensure that the ge-0/0/0.0 interface allows the HTTPS connection inbound.

```
[edit]
root@SRX210# edit security ike proposal Dynamic-VPN

[edit security ike proposal Dynamic-VPN]
root@SRX210# set authentication-method pre-shared-keys dh-group group2
authentication-algorithm sha1 encryption algorithm 3des-cbc lifetime-seconds
12000 description "Dynamic VPN Proposal"

[edit security ike proposal Dynamic-VPN]
root@SRX210# show
description "Dynamic VPN Proposal";
authentication-method pre-shared-keys;
dh-group group2;
authentication-algorithm sha1;
encryption-algorithm 3des-cbc;
lifetime-seconds 12000;

[edit security ike proposal Dynamic-VPN]
root@SRX210#up

[edit security ike]
root@SRX210# edit policy Dynamic-VPN-Policy

[edit security ike policy Dynamic-VPN-Policy]
root@SRX210# set mode aggressive description "Dynamic-VPN IKE Policy" proposals
Dynamic-VPN pre-shared-key ascii-text DialUp4123

[edit security ike policy Dynamic-VPN-Policy]
root@SRX210# show
mode aggressive;
description "Dynamic-VPN IKE Policy";
proposals Dynamic-VPN;
pre-shared-key ascii-text "$9$K8zvWXY2aZGi7-.f5T9CM8LxVw24aUik"; ## SECRET-DATA

[edit security ike policy Dynamic-VPN-Policy]
root@SRX210# up

[edit security ike]
root@SRX210# edit gateway Dynamic-VPN-Gateway

[edit security ike gateway Dynamic-VPN-Gateway]
root@SRX210# set external-interface ge-0/0/0.0 ike-policy Dynamic-VPN-Policy
xauth access-profile XAuth

[edit security ike gateway Dynamic-VPN-Gateway]
root@SRX210# set dynamic connection-limit 5 user-at-hostname dynvpn@company.com
ike-user-type shared-ike-id

[edit security ike gateway Dynamic-VPN-Gateway]
root@SRX210# show
ike-policy Dynamic-VPN-Policy;
dynamic {
```

```
    user-at-hostname "dynvpn@company.com";
    connections-limit 5;
    ike-user-type shared-ike-id;
}
external-interface ge-0/0/0;
xauth access-profile XAuth;

[edit security ike gateway Dynamic-VPN-Gateway]
root@SRX210# top

[edit]
root@SRX210# show access-profile
XAuth;

[edit]
root@SRX210# show access profile XAuth
authentication-order radius;
radius-server {
    192.168.224.60 {
        port 1812;
        secret "$9$pf5hB1hrev7dbgoJDk.zFIEclMX"; ## SECRET-DATA
        source-address 192.168.224.3;
    }
}

[edit]
root@SRX210# show security zones security-zone trust
interfaces {
    ge-0/0/0.0 {
        host-inbound-traffic {
            system-services {
                http;
                https;
                ping;
                ike;
            }
            protocols {
                ospf;
            }
        }
    }
}

[edit]
root@SRX210# edit security ipsec proposal Dynamic-VPN

[edit security ipsec proposal Dynamic-VPN]
root@SRX210# set description "Dynamic VPN Proposal" authentication-algorithm
hmac-sha1-96 encryption-algorithm aes-256-cbc lifetime-seconds 3600 protocol esp

[edit security ipsec proposal Dynamic-VPN]
root@SRX210# show
```

```
description "Dynamic VPN Proposal";
protocol esp;
authentication-algorithm hmac-sha1-96;
encryption-algorithm aes-256-cbc;
lifetime-seconds 3600;

[edit security ipsec proposal Dynamic-VPN]
root@SRX210# up

[edit security ipsec]
root@SRX210# edit policy Dynamic-VPN-Policy

[edit security ipsec policy Dynamic-VPN-Policy]
root@SRX210# set description "Dynamic VPN Phase 2 Policy" proposals Dynamic-VPN
perfect-forward-secrecy keys group2

[edit security ipsec policy Dynamic-VPN-Policy]
root@SRX210# show
description "Dynamic VPN Phase 2 Policy";
perfect-forward-secrecy {
    keys group2;
}
proposals Dynamic-VPN;

[edit security ipsec policy Dynamic-VPN-Policy]
root@SRX210 up

[edit security ipsec]
root@SRX210# edit vpn Dynamic-VPN

[edit security ipsec vpn Dynamic-VPN]
root@SRX210# set ike gateway Dynamic-VPN-Gateway ipsec-policy Dynamic-VPN-Policy

[edit security ipsec vpn Dynamic-VPN]
root@SRX210# show
ike {
    gateway Dynamic-VPN-Gateway;
    ipsec-policy Dynamic-VPN-Policy;
}

[edit security ipsec vpn Dynamic-VPN]
root@SRX210# up 2

[edit security]
root@SRX210# edit dynamic-vpn

[edit security dynamic-vpn
root@SRX210# set clients Dynamic-VPN-Clients remote-protected-resources
10.0.0.0/8

[edit security dynamic-vpn]
root@SRX210# set clients Dynamic-VPN-Clients user dynvpn
```

```
[edit security dynamic-vpn]
root@SRX210# set clients Dynamic-VPN-Clients ipsec-vpn Dynamic-VPN

[edit security dynamic-vpn]
root@SRX210# set force-upgrade

[edit security dynamic-vpn]
root@SRX210# set access-profile XAuth

[edit security dynamic-vpn]
root@SRX210# show
force-upgrade;
access-profile XAuth;
clients {
    Dynamic-VPN-Clients {
        remote-protected-resources {
            10.0.0.0/8;
        }
        ipsec-vpn Dynamic-VPN;
        user {
            dynvpn;
        }
    }
}

[edit security dynamic-vpn]
root@SRX210# top

[edit]
root@SRX210# run request security pki generate-key-pair certificate-id HTTPS
Generated key pair HTTPS, key size 1024 bits

[edit]
root@SRX210# set system services web-management https
system-generated-certificate interface ge-0/0/0.0

[edit]
root@SRX210# show system services web-management
https {
    system-generated-certificate;
    interface ge-0/0/0.0;
}
```

Best Practices

There are plenty of best practices when it comes to operating IPsec VPNs on the SRX. We review some of the more notable ones here for your convenience.

1. You should always use NTP when managing the SRX, but this is particularly true for devices running IPsec VPNs, the high-end SRX platforms, and HA clusters.

Running NTP will help to keep the clocks in sync across all of the components in the system and ensure that log messages and system state timing are accurate.

2. It's typically a best practice to use route-based VPNs on the SRX unless you have a special vendor interoperability scenario or legacy support for dial-up VPNs where you might be better off running policy-based VPNs. Going forward, both of these will likely change as Juniper looks to introduce Multi-Proxy-ID and enhancements to the remote access products, so keep current with the release notes.
3. In almost all cases, you will want to use IKE over manual key encryption. It is far more secure and easier to set up. The only scenarios where you would want manual key is if the other peer didn't support IKE; you wanted the keys to never expire, perhaps in a proof-of-concept scenario; or you were trying to do something evasive by skipping IKE and just encrypting traffic (something that an evasive application might do).
4. Regarding choosing between IKEv1 and IKEv2, IKE v2 is definitely a better protocol. From a configuration perspective, it's trivial to configure a VPN to use IKEv2 instead of IKEv1 (or allow it to use either). The main question is whether the other peer accepts it.
5. If using IKEv1, Main mode is a better choice when you have an established identity for the peer such as a site-to-site VPN. Although there are six messages rather than three, it keeps the identity information in the clear. If you are dealing with dial-up users, Aggressive mode might be your only option. IKEv2 doesn't support the concept of Main versus Aggressive mode.
6. When deciding whether to use preshared keys or certificates, typical guidance is that if you only have a handful of sites, particularly if they are run by third-party peers, preshared keys are best because they are easy to exchange and don't have the overhead of certificates + signing + loading CAs, CRL, OSCP, and so on. On the other hand, if you are doing a large deployment either with numerous remote hub and spoke sites or with numerous remote access users, then certificates are likely the way to go. Certificates are unique to each site and user, however they can be independently authenticated, easily generated, revoked on demand, and not act as a single point of failure (e.g., 100 users using the same preshared keys).
7. It is typically a best practice to use ESP as your IPsec protocol rather than AH. The difference is that ESP actually encrypts the data rather than just putting a signed header that authenticates the data has not been altered. Most organizations want the additional security of encrypting the traffic itself. AH might make more sense when the intention isn't at all to keep the data secret, just to ensure that the data is authentic and has not been altered. Needless to say, these use cases are few and far between, so you'll likely be working with ESP in all of your implementations.
8. Transport versus Tunnel mode is an easy one. The SRX doesn't currently support Transport mode (which merely leverages the original packets and puts another

header on for ESP or AH to secure the communication). Only Tunnel mode is supported at the time of writing this book. Tunnel mode encapsulates the original packet into a new packet between the two gateways. This is so popular because often you can't have internal hosts communicating together due to private IP ranges as discussed in Transport mode.

9. For environments that want additional security insurance around their VPN setup and don't have a major concern for the number of new tunnels per second, it's a good idea to use PFS to provide another layer of negotiation to ensure that keys aren't compromised.

10. In terms of choosing the DH group, encryption strength, and authentication algorithm, there are a few factors. You can obviously select the most powerful encryption and authentication algorithms and the highest bit lengths, but this might not be ideal because they are extremely computationally intensive, and in some cases the hardware encryption engines can't support them so they are done in hardware. The other factor is to determine what protocols your other peers support because they might not support the latest and greatest. Juniper also provides predefined proposal sets that can help to make this process easier if you are unsure. The Standard protocol sets seem adequate, whereas the Suite B are more advanced.

11. It is a best practice to run Dynamic VPN on a different interface than the web management interface (e.g., reserve web managed to only fxp0 but allow Dynamic VPN to take place on other interfaces as well). This is much more secure and provides some additional flexibility for control. If you can't distinguish the interfaces for management, you should at least use different URLs for management versus Dynamic VPNs, leverage access lists if possible, and use different nonstandard ports.

12. If you are dealing with a hub and spoke site and all of the spokes can share the same virtual router and zone (e.g., they all are considered to be in the security framework, there is no overlapping routing information), it can be advantageous to run them off of a point-to-multiple interface rather than making them all point-to-point. It is much easier from an administrative perspective on the hub side to do this, particularly when you are leveraging a dynamic routing protocol.

13. It is best practice to leverage VPN monitoring on mission-critical sites because VPN monitoring can make active checks to see if the VPN is still up and running on both sides rather than just relying on the gateways responding to messages like DPD. VPN monitoring and DPD do have scale limits when dealing with thousands of VPNs, however.

14. Perform CRL checks when using certificates because it allows you to ensure not only that the certificate is valid, but also that it is not revoked. In the future, when the SRX supports OCSP, that will be an even more preferred method, which can

provide real-time status checking, whereas CRL is only updated periodically (which is still very effective).

15. If you are dealing with a large-scale VPN infrastructure with hundreds or thousands of sites, it is a good idea to run SCEP to ensure that when the endpoint's certificate expires, it can dynamically get a new cert.
16. When selecting the IKE identity, there are different strategies that can be used depending on the type of connection. For instance, for a standard site-to-site with static IP addresses, the IP address is usually good enough. For site-to-site where the spoke uses dynamic IP addresses, you can use an FQDN for a user@hostname with shared IKE if you have multiple users sharing the same IKE identity. Finally, if you are using an Auto-VPN or larger scale certificate-based model, you would leverage DN and Group-IKE-ID to support limiting the appropriate certificates. Auto-VPN is outside of the scope of this book, but it's a good thing to keep in mind for future support.
17. It is typically a best practice to use numbered st0 interfaces rather than unnumbered interfaces because they offer much more interoperability and feature support, particularly for NAT and routing.

Troubleshooting and Operation

Once the configuration of the VPN is complete and committed, you should take some additional steps to ensure that the VPN is operational. You can also use these steps whenever there appears to be an issue with VPN establishment or connectivity. This section details the useful commands that can help provide information on the status of VPNs, as well as troubleshooting steps and available facilities that can provide advanced diagnostics for resolving VPN issues.

Useful VPN Commands

The SRX has several useful commands when it comes to determining the state of VPNs, including commands that identify specific aspects of VPNs.

show security ike security-associations

The `show security ike security-associations` command shows any VPNs that have passed Phase 1 and have an active IKE security association for Phase 1.

This command is important because if IKE fails to complete Phase 1, it can't proceed to Phase 2. (An exception is that if the IKE Phase 1 lifetime expires before the Phase 2 lifetime expires, there might not be a listing for the IKE security association, although there will be one for Phase 2. However, when the Phase 2 security association expires, the Phase 1 IKE security association will need to be renegotiated first.)

The following output shows an actively established Phase 1 security association, first without the `detail` argument and then with the `detail` argument. There are lots of useful reasons for using the `detail` command to show the properties of the tunnel itself. It's often most useful to define the peer gateway before the detail to only show a specific gateway's status. When troubleshooting VPN establishment, you must first verify that Phase 1 is completed successfully before moving on to Phase 2, and this command helps provide that information.

```
 {primary:node1}
root@SRX100HM> show security ike active-peer
node1:
--------------------------------------------------------------------------
Remote Address        Port      Peer IKE-ID          XAUTH username     Assigned
IP
99.18.0.11                           500      99.18.0.11

{primary:node1}
root@SRX100HM> show security ike security-associations detail
node1:
--------------------------------------------------------------------------
IKE peer 99.18.0.11, Index 13000261, Gateway Name: SFLD
  Role: Initiator, State: UP
  Initiator cookie: 4af4dbc0477fa2eb, Responder cookie: a9698c65f2417867
  Exchange type: Main, Authentication method: Pre-shared-keys
  Local: 173.167.1.14:500, Remote: 99.18.0.11:500
  Lifetime: Expires in 81973 seconds
  Peer ike-id: 99.18.0.11
  Xauth assigned IP: 0.0.0.0
  Algorithms:
   Authentication        : hmac-sha1-96
   Encryption            : aes128-cbc
   Pseudo random function: hmac-sha1
   Diffie-Hellman group  : DH-group-2
  Traffic statistics:
   Input  bytes  :                1268
   Output bytes  :                2340
   Input  packets:                   7
   Output packets:                  10
  Flags: IKE SA is created
  IPSec security associations: 2 created, 1 deleted
  Phase 2 negotiations in progress: 0

    Negotiation type: Quick mode, Role: Initiator, Message ID: 0
    Local: 173.167.1.14:500, Remote: 99.18.0.11:500
    Local identity: 173.167.224.13
    Remote identity: 99.182.0.14
    Flags: IKE SA is created
```

show security ipsec security-associations

Once Phase 1 has been established, you might need to determine whether Phase 2 has been successfully completed. A very useful command is the `show security ipsec security-associations` command. It will show the established Phase 2 security associations and applicable properties. The `detail` command provides much more information regarding the state of the VPN.

```
{primary:node1}
root@SRX100HM> show security ipsec security-associations
node1:
--------------------------------------------------------------------------
  Total active tunnels: 1
  ID     Algorithm       SPI      Life:sec/kb  Mon lsys Port  Gateway
  <131073 ESP:aes-128/sha1 56068996 792/ unlim -   root 500   99.182.0.14
  >131073 ESP:aes-128/sha1 31ac37d 792/ unlim  -   root 500   99.182.0.14
  <131073 ESP:aes-128/sha1 aac3e068 795/ unlim -   root 500   99.182.0.14
  >131073 ESP:aes-128/sha1 31ac37e 795/ unlim  -   root 500   99.182.0.14

{primary:node1}
root@SRX100HM> show security ipsec security-associations detail
node1:
--------------------------------------------------------------------------
  ID: 131073 Virtual-system: root, VPN Name: Southfield
  Local Gateway: 173.167.224.13, Remote Gateway: 99.182.0.14
  Local Identity: ipv4_subnet(any:0,[0..7]=0.0.0.0/0)
  Remote Identity: ipv4_subnet(any:0,[0..7]=0.0.0.0/0)
  Version: IKEv1
    DF-bit: copy
    Bind-interface: st0.0

  Port: 500, Nego#: 467, Fail#: 0, Def-Del#: 0 Flag: 600a29
  Tunnel Down Reason: Lifetime expired
    Direction: inbound, SPI: 56068996, AUX-SPI: 0
                              , VPN Monitoring: -
    Hard lifetime: Expires in 784 seconds
    Lifesize Remaining:  Unlimited
    Soft lifetime: Expires in 202 seconds
    Mode: Tunnel(0 0), Type: dynamic, State: installed
    Protocol: ESP, Authentication: hmac-sha1-96, Encryption: aes-cbc (128 bits)
    Anti-replay service: counter-based enabled, Replay window size: 64

    Direction: outbound, SPI: 31ac37d, AUX-SPI: 0
                              , VPN Monitoring: -
    Hard lifetime: Expires in 784 seconds
    Lifesize Remaining:  Unlimited
    Soft lifetime: Expires in 202 seconds
    Mode: Tunnel(0 0), Type: dynamic, State: installed
    Protocol: ESP, Authentication: hmac-sha1-96, Encryption: aes-cbc (128 bits)
    Anti-replay service: counter-based enabled, Replay window size: 64

    Direction: inbound, SPI: aac3e068, AUX-SPI: 0
```

```
                          , VPN Monitoring: -
  Hard lifetime: Expires in 787 seconds
  Lifesize Remaining:  Unlimited
  Soft lifetime: Expires in 176 seconds
  Mode: Tunnel(0 0), Type: dynamic, State: installed
  Protocol: ESP, Authentication: hmac-sha1-96, Encryption: aes-cbc (128 bits)
  Anti-replay service: counter-based enabled, Replay window size: 64

  Direction: outbound, SPI: 31ac37e, AUX-SPI: 0
                          , VPN Monitoring: -
  Hard lifetime: Expires in 787 seconds
  Lifesize Remaining:  Unlimited
  Soft lifetime: Expires in 176 seconds
  Mode: Tunnel(0 0), Type: dynamic, State: installed
  Protocol: ESP, Authentication: hmac-sha1-96, Encryption: aes-cbc (128 bits)
  Anti-replay service: counter-based enabled, Replay window size: 64
```

show security ipsec inactive-tunnels

This command shows you any tunnels that aren't active. Especially when you are dealing with a large VPN infrastructure, it can be more important to view the tunnels that are not up and running to determine if there is an issue rather than trying to search for every tunnel that should be up and running. That's exactly what this command does.

```
{primary:node1}
root@SRX100HM> show security ipsec inactive-tunnels
node1:
--------------------------------------------------------------------------
  Total inactive tunnels: 1
  Total inactive tunnels with establish immediately: 0
  ID     Port  Nego#  Fail#  Flag      Gateway          Tunnel Down Reason
  131073 500   469    0      600a29    99.182.0.14      Cleared via CLI
```

show security ipsec statistics

It's always useful to gather high-level information regarding how the platform is processing security information, including issues with encryption and decryption. The command show `security ipsec statistics` provides such useful information, including the number of encrypted and decrypted ESP and AH packets, as well as the different types of failures. You can check this command multiple times when trying to determine if the number of failures and errors is increasing.

```
 {primary:node1}
root@SRX100HM> show security ipsec statistics
node0:
--------------------------------------------------------------------------

ESP Statistics:
  Encrypted bytes:              0
  Decrypted bytes:              0
  Encrypted packets:            0
```

```
  Decrypted packets:             0
AH Statistics:
  Input bytes:                   0
  Output bytes:                  0
  Input packets:                 0
  Output packets:                0
Errors:
  AH authentication failures: 0, Replay errors: 0
  ESP authentication failures: 0, ESP decryption failures: 0
  Bad headers: 0, Bad trailers: 0

node1:
--------------------------------------------------------------------------

ESP Statistics:
  Encrypted bytes:        1739394688
  Decrypted bytes:        2837890889
  Encrypted packets:         7337056
  Decrypted packets:         9923867
AH Statistics:
  Input bytes:                   0
  Output bytes:                  0
  Input packets:                 0
  Output packets:                0
Errors:
  AH authentication failures: 0, Replay errors: 0
  ESP authentication failures: 0, ESP decryption failures: 0
  Bad headers: 0, Bad trailers: 0
```

You can clear the information with the `clear security ipsec statistics` command.

Checking interface statistics

It can be helpful to check the interface statistics of the interface where the VPN is terminating because there can be some very good information there. In this example, we look at the reth0.0 interface.

```
{primary:node1}
root@SRX100HM> show interfaces reth0.0 extensive
  Logical interface reth0.0 (Index 69) (SNMP ifIndex 531) (Generation 134)
    Flags: SNMP-Traps 0x0 Encapsulation: ENET2
    Statistics        Packets        pps         Bytes          bps
    Bundle:
        Input :      59888370         49   18111686816        68000
        Output:     167667336        106  196744917958       939632
    Link:
      fe-1/0/1.0
        Input :      59888370         49   18111686816        68000
```

```
    Output:     167667336        106  196744917958       939632
  fe-0/0/1.0
    Input :             0          0            0            0
    Output:             0          0            0            0
Marker Statistics:   Marker Rx     Resp Tx   Unknown Rx   Illegal Rx
  fe-1/0/1.0                 0           0            0            0
  fe-0/0/1.0                 0           0            0            0
Security: Zone: Danger
Allowed host-inbound traffic : ike ping
Flow Statistics :
Flow Input statistics :
  Self packets :                     742416
  ICMP packets :                     255719
  VPN packets :                      9926999
  Multicast packets :                0
  Bytes permitted by policy :        14558953261
  Connections established :          13929614
Flow Output statistics:
  Multicast packets :                0
  Bytes permitted by policy :        140828777920
Flow error statistics (Packets dropped due to):
  Address spoofing:                  0
  Authentication failed:             0
  Incoming NAT errors:               0
  Invalid zone received packet:      0
  Multiple user authentications:     0
  Multiple incoming NAT:             0
  No parent for a gate:              0
  No one interested in self packets: 0
  No minor session:                  0
  No more sessions:                  0
  No NAT gate:                       0
  No route present:                  74280
  No SA for incoming SPI:            117
  No tunnel found:                   0
  No session for a gate:             0
  No zone or NULL zone binding       0
  Policy denied:                     237
  Security association not active:   12480
  TCP sequence number out of window: 24
  Syn-attack protection:             0
  User authentication errors:        0
Protocol inet, MTU: 1500, Generation: 148, Route table: 4
  Flags: Sendbcast-pkt-to-re, Is-Primary
  Input Filters: Inbound-QoS
  Addresses, Flags: Is-Default Is-Preferred Is-Primary
         Destination: 173.167.224.0/28, Local: 173.167.224.13, Broadcast:
173.167.224.15, Generation: 145
```

You can see in the preceding output there are some useful counters that are tracked on the interface-by-interface basis. These self-explanatory counters can help you identify a potential issue with IPsec setup.

VPN Tracing and Debugging

When the information contained within the output of the show commands is not enough to determine the root cause of VPN negotiation failures, more detailed information is required to determine where the message breakdown occurs. The SRX offers detailed breakdowns of the debugging of VPN establishment, even down to the individual IPsec messages that are sent and received by the SRX. Let's cover the individual troubleshooting steps that you can use to help troubleshoot a VPN issue. Then we discuss how to perform tracing and, finally, what to look for in the output.

```
{primary:node1}
root@SRX100HM> request security ike debug-enable local 173.167.224.13 remote
99.182.0.14 level 15

{primary:node1}
root@SRX100HM> show log kmd
Feb 17 18:55:20 SRX100HM clear-log[53078]: logfile cleared

{primary:node1}
root@SRX100HM> clear security ike security-associations

{primary:node1}
root@SRX100HM> show log kmd
Feb 17 18:55:20 SRX100HM clear-log[53078]: logfile cleared
[Feb 17 18:59:57][173.167.224.13 <-> 99.182.0.14]  iked_ha_check_ike_sa_active-
ness_by_rg_id:RG 1 is active on this chassiss
[Feb 17 18:59:57][173.167.224.13 <-> 99.182.0.14]  iked_ha_check_ike_sa_active-
ness_by_rg_id:RG 1 is active on this chassiss
[Feb 17 18:59:57][173.167.224.13 <-> 99.182.0.14]  Initiate IKE P1 SA 13000278
delete. curr ref count 1, del flags 0x2
[Feb 17 18:59:57][173.167.224.13 <-> 99.182.0.14]  iked_pm_ike_sa_delete_noti-
fy_done_cb: For p1 sa index 13000278, ref cnt 1, status: Error ok
[Feb 17 18:59:57][173.167.224.13 <-> 99.182.0.14]  ssh_set_debug_gw_info:
ssh_set_debug_gw_info: set gw debug info - local 173.167.224.13 remote
99.182.0.14
[Feb 17 18:59:57][173.167.224.13 <-> 99.182.0.14]  ike_expire_callback: Start,
expire SA = { e749e216 6d85b041 - 720b8a27 af119af8}, nego = -1
[Feb 17 18:59:57][173.167.224.13 <-> 99.182.0.14]  iked_ha_check_ike_sa_active-
ness_by_rg_id:RG 1 is active on this chassiss
[Feb 17 18:59:57][173.167.224.13 <-> 99.182.0.14]  ike_alloc_negotiation:
Start, SA = { e749e216 6d85b041 - 720b8a27 af119af8}
[Feb 17 18:59:57][173.167.224.13 <-> 99.182.0.14]  ike_alloc_negotiation: Found
slot 1, max 2
[Feb 17 18:59:57][173.167.224.13 <-> 99.182.0.14]  ike_init_info_exchange: New
informational negotiation message_id = a524ef42 initialized using slot 1
[Feb 17 18:59:57][173.167.224.13 <-> 99.182.0.14]  ike_init_info_exchange: Cre-
ated random message id = a524ef42
[Feb 17 18:59:57][173.167.224.13 <-> 99.182.0.14]  ike_init_info_exchange:
Phase 1 done, use HASH and N or D payload
[Feb 17 18:59:57][173.167.224.13 <-> 99.182.0.14]  ike_encode_packet: Start, SA
= { 0xe749e216 6d85b041 - 720b8a27 af119af8 } / a524ef42, nego = 1
```

```
[Feb 17 18:59:57][173.167.224.13 <-> 99.182.0.14]  ike_encode_packet: Payload length = 24
[Feb 17 18:59:57][173.167.224.13 <-> 99.182.0.14]  ike_encode_packet: Payload length = 28
[Feb 17 18:59:57][173.167.224.13 <-> 99.182.0.14]  ike_encode_packet: Packet length = 92
[Feb 17 18:59:57][173.167.224.13 <-> 99.182.0.14]  ike_encode_packet: Calling finalizing function for payload[0].type = 8
[Feb 17 18:59:57][173.167.224.13 <-> 99.182.0.14]  ike_encode_packet: Encrypting packet
[Feb 17 18:59:57][173.167.224.13 <-> 99.182.0.14]  ike_encode_packet: Final length = 92
[Feb 17 18:59:57][173.167.224.13 <-> 99.182.0.14]  ike_expire_callback: Sending notification to 99.182.0.14:500
[Feb 17 18:59:57][173.167.224.13 <-> 99.182.0.14]  ike_send_packet: Start, send SA = { e749e216 6d85b041 - 720b8a27 af119af8}, nego = 1, dst = 99.182.0.14:500, routing table id = 4
[Feb 17 18:59:57][173.167.224.13 <-> 99.182.0.14]  ike_free_packet: Start
[Feb 17 18:59:57][173.167.224.13 <-> 99.182.0.14]  ike_delete_negotiation: Start, SA = { e749e216 6d85b041 - 720b8a27 af119af8}, nego = 1
[Feb 17 18:59:57][173.167.224.13 <-> 99.182.0.14]  ike_free_negotiation_info: Start, nego = 1
[Feb 17 18:59:57][173.167.224.13 <-> 99.182.0.14]  ike_free_negotiation: Start, nego = 1
[Feb 17 18:59:57][173.167.224.13 <-> 99.182.0.14]  ikev2_fb_phase_ii_sa_freed: Phase-II free Entered
[Feb 17 18:59:57][173.167.224.13 <-> 99.182.0.14]  ssh_set_debug_gw_info: ssh_set_debug_gw_info: set gw debug info - local 173.167.224.13 remote 99.182.0.14
[Feb 17 18:59:57][173.167.224.13 <-> 99.182.0.14]  ike_remove_callback: Start, delete SA = { e749e216 6d85b041 - 720b8a27 af119af8}, nego = -1
[Feb 17 18:59:57][173.167.224.13 <-> 99.182.0.14]  ike_delete_negotiation: Start, SA = { e749e216 6d85b041 - 720b8a27 af119af8}, nego = -1
[Feb 17 18:59:57][173.167.224.13 <-> 99.182.0.14]  ssh_ike_tunnel_table_entry_delete: Deleting tunnel_id: 0 from IKE tunnel table
[Feb 17 18:59:57][173.167.224.13 <-> 99.182.0.14]  ssh_ike_tunnel_table_entry_delete: The tunnel id: 0 doesn't exist in IKE tunnel table
[Feb 17 18:59:57][173.167.224.13 <-> 99.182.0.14]  ike_sa_delete: Start, SA = { e749e216 6d85b041 - 720b8a27 af119af8 }
[Feb 17 18:59:57][173.167.224.13 <-> 99.182.0.14]  ike_free_negotiation_qm: Start, nego = 0
[Feb 17 18:59:57][173.167.224.13 <-> 99.182.0.14]  ike_free_negotiation: Start, nego = 0
[Feb 17 18:59:57][173.167.224.13 <-> 99.182.0.14]  ike_free_packet: Start
[Feb 17 18:59:57][173.167.224.13 <-> 99.182.0.14]  ike_free_packet: Start
[Feb 17 18:59:57][173.167.224.13 <-> 99.182.0.14]  ike_free_packet: Start
[Feb 17 18:59:57][173.167.224.13 <-> 99.182.0.14]  ikev2_fb_qm_sa_freed: QM free Entered
[Feb 17 18:59:57][173.167.224.13 <-> 99.182.0.14]  ike_free_id_payload: Start, id type = 4
[Feb 17 18:59:57][173.167.224.13 <-> 99.182.0.14]  ike_free_id_payload: Start, id type = 4
```

```
[Feb 17 18:59:57][173.167.224.13 <-> 99.182.0.14]  ike_free_id_payload: Start,
id type = 4
[Feb 17 18:59:57][173.167.224.13 <-> 99.182.0.14]  ike_free_id_payload: Start,
id type = 4
[Feb 17 18:59:57][173.167.224.13 <-> 99.182.0.14]  ike_free_negotiation_isakmp:
Start, nego = -1
[Feb 17 18:59:57][173.167.224.13 <-> 99.182.0.14]  ike_free_negotiation: Start,
nego = -1
[Feb 17 18:59:57][173.167.224.13 <-> 99.182.0.14]  ikev2_fb_isakmp_sa_freed: Re-
ceived notification from the ISAKMP library that the IKE SA dfe400 is freed
[Feb 17 18:59:57][173.167.224.13 <-> 99.182.0.14]  ikev2_fb_isakmp_sa_freed:
FB; Calling v2 policy function ike_sa_delete
[Feb 17 18:59:57][173.167.224.13 <-> 99.182.0.14]  IKE SA delete called for p1
sa 13000278 (ref cnt 1) local:173.167.224.13, remote:99.182.0.14, IKEv1
[Feb 17 18:59:57][173.167.224.13 <-> 99.182.0.14]  P1 SA 13000278 stop timer.
timer duration 30, reason 0.
[Feb 17 18:59:57][173.167.224.13 <-> 99.182.0.14]  iked_ha_check_ike_sa_active-
ness_by_rg_id:RG 1 is active on this chassiss
[Feb 17 18:59:57][173.167.224.13 <-> 99.182.0.14]  iked_del_ha_blob: Error de-
leting blob with type = phase1 mod, tunnel id 0.  Error: No such file or direc-
tory
[Feb 17 18:59:57][173.167.224.13 <-> 99.182.0.14]  Deleted the blob requested
[Feb 17 18:59:57][173.167.224.13 <-> 99.182.0.14]  Freeing reference to P1 SA
13000278 to ref count 0
[Feb 17 18:59:57][173.167.224.13 <-> 99.182.0.14]  iked_pm_p1_sa_destroy:  p1
sa 13000278 (ref cnt 0), waiting_for_del 0x0
[Feb 17 18:59:57][173.167.224.13 <-> 99.182.0.14]  iked_peer_remove_p1sa_entry:
Remove p1 sa 13000278 from peer entry 0xdeb400
[Feb 17 18:59:57][173.167.224.13 <-> 99.182.0.14]  Deleting p1 sa (13000278)
node from IKE p1 SA P-tree
[Feb 17 18:59:57][173.167.224.13 <-> 99.182.0.14]  ikev2_udp_window_uninit:
Freeing transmission windows for SA dfe400
[Feb 17 18:59:57][173.167.224.13 <-> 99.182.0.14]  ike_free_id_payload: Start,
id type = 1
[Feb 17 18:59:57][173.167.224.13 <-> 99.182.0.14]  ike_free_id_payload: Start,
id type = 1
[Feb 17 18:59:57][173.167.224.13 <-> 99.182.0.14]  ike_free_sa: Start
```

It's not possible to review every message that is discussed here, but the key is that by running this debug, if you are familiar with the general nomenclature of the SRX debug information, it should provide you with a very good breakdown of what's happening step by step and any potential errors that you might see along the way. This can be used in conjunction with the VPN troubleshooting process, discussed next.

VPN troubleshooting process

Follow these steps when troubleshooting a VPN issue:

1. Verify that the peer gateway is reachable. If there is an issue with routing to the remote gateway, or if a device is limiting access (e.g., IKE traffic, ESP/AH traffic, NAT-T tunneled traffic), VPN establishment will fail. Basic tests could include ping

and traceroute (assuming that these services are available on the remote device) to ensure that routing is functioning properly and there are no ISP issues. The following services should not be blocked by any device between the SRX and the remote peer.

   a. UDP port 500 (default port for IKE negotiation). If this is blocked, IKE negotiation will fail, with messages on the initiating gateway indicating that the connection limit has been reached. On the responder device, there will be no messages at all because the IKE traffic will not have reached the gateway.
   b. IP Protocol 50 (ESP) if using ESP. If this is blocked, IKE negotiation might complete successfully, but VPN traffic will not be able to communicate when using ESP.
   c. IP Protocol 51 (AH) if using AH. If this is blocked, IKE negotiation might complete successfully, but VPN traffic will not be able to communicate when using AH.
   d. UDP port 4500 (default port for NAT-T). If this is blocked, IKE negotiation might complete successfully, but VPN traffic will not be able to communicate when using NAT-T.

2. Check the access lists and zone settings. On the SRX, if an access list is enabled on the external interface terminating the VPN or the lo0 interface that blocks any of the services mentioned in Step 1, the VPN will not be able to establish. Additionally, the SRX requires IKE to be enabled on the interface, or in the zone of the external interface as a host-inbound-traffic system service (it can be at the zone or interface level, with the interface level overriding the zone level). Make sure this is enabled; otherwise, the VPN will fail to establish.
3. Check whether hostnames are used for the gateway. You can optionally define the gateway address as a DNS address rather than an IP address. In this case, DNS must be enabled and functioning properly to be able to identify the remote gateway. Configuring multiple DNS servers often helps in case of a DNS server failure.
4. Check whether the VPN is terminating on the correct interface. In Phase 1 of the VPN, you must define on which interface the VPN will terminate. If the VPN is trying to terminate on a different interface (even if the logical unit is wrong), the VPN will fail to establish.
5. Check whether both nodes are trying to use the same IKE version.
6. Check whether the Phase 1 modes match on both gateways. Both gateways must use the same Phase 1 mode, either Main mode or Aggressive mode. If the modes don't match, the VPN establishment will fail.
7. Check whether the Phase 1 proposals match. The Phase 1 proposals must match on both VPN gateways. If they do not match, negotiations will fail. The SRX supports up to four proposals, so if the first proposal negotiation fails, it will try the

other proposals if available, but if there are no matches the negotiations will fail in Phase 1. Check the proper combination of certificate versus PSK, encryption and authentication algorithms, along with the proper Diffie-Hellman groups.

8. Check whether the IKE identities are configured correctly. As mentioned, there are a few different types of IKE identities, namely IP address, FQDN, and UFQDN. You can define the local identity (to be presented to the peer) and the peer identity (to be presented by the peer). The local and peer must match on the respective systems or else Phase 1 will fail.

9. Check whether the Phase 1 authentication is properly configured. There are two types of Phase 1 authentication: preshared keys and certificates. In the case of preshared keys, the preshared keys must match on both VPN gateways for the VPN to complete Phase 1. In the case of certificates, the certificate presented must be signed by a trusted CA (configured to work for the VPN). Next, if certificate revocation checking is enabled, the certificate must not be revoked for the authentication to pass.

10. If XAuth is used, check whether authentication is succeeding. XAuth occurs between Phase 1 and Phase 2 of the VPN establishment process. At the time of this writing, XAuth is only supported for authentication of RADIUS users and not local users on the firewall. If XAuth authentication does not succeed, authentication will fail before Phase 2.

11. Check whether PFS is configured. If PFS is configured, it must be configured on both gateways. Additionally, the same Diffie-Hellman groups must be used between the peers for PFS. Note that the Diffie-Hellman groups do not need to be the same as what is used in Phase 1; however, both peers must use the same group in the PFS configuration.

12. Check whether Phase 2 proposals match. Just like Phase 1, the Phase 2 proposals must match on both ends (including encryption and authentication algorithms). If they don't match, Phase 2 negotiations will fail. Up to four proposals may be defined and will be negotiated in order of definition if the previous proposal fails, but if no proposal matches, the Phase 2 proposals will fail.

13. Check whether the proxy IDs match. This is probably the most common reason for VPN negotiations to fail, especially when trying to establish VPNs between different vendors. Proxy IDs can be manually defined in the Phase 2 IPsec VPN configuration, or they can be derived from the respective policies that are used for the VPN in the case of policy-based VPNs. Doing a trace will show whether the VPN is failing due to proxy ID mismatch, but this is something to be aware of.

14. Check whether the key lifetimes match. This isn't an explicitly required parameter, but sometimes this could matter with other vendors' implementations of IPsec VPNs, so it is best to set the VPNs to support the same key lifetimes to ensure proper interoperability.

15. If policy-based VPNs are enabled, check whether the correct policy is being matched. With policy-based VPNs, the traffic should match the correct policy. If it is not matching the correct policy, this might be a result of the incorrect policy configuration, or a routing issue or misconfiguration. Remember that even in the case of policy-based VPNs, the SRX must know what the egress interface and, thus, the egress zone is to match the correct from-to-zone pair. It doesn't matter whether static or dynamic routing is used; the routing must be properly configured. Doing a simple flow trace will identify whether the traffic is being matched to the correct policy along with the correct routing information. Also, make sure the policy is configured to tunnel the traffic to the correct VPN.
16. If route-based VPNs are configured, check whether proper routing and security policies are configured. With a route-based VPN, you still need to define the correct security policy to permit the traffic. If the traffic is not being permitted by policy, it cannot enter the VPN. You can determine this by doing a flow debug to enable logging on the policies to ensure that the traffic is being permitted. Additionally, with route-based VPNs, the appropriate routing must be configured to route the traffic into the correct tunnel interface. Both static and dynamic routing can be used, but in the case of dynamic routing, you must make sure the applicable protocols are enabled on the tunnel interface (from the protocol configuration, along with the host-inbound-traffic protocol configuration).
17. If route-based VPNs are configured, check whether the VPN is bound to the correct interface. Route-based VPNs must be bound to the correct interface. If they are bound to the wrong interface, VPN negotiation might establish, but the traffic will not go through the right VPN.
18. Check whether NAT is occurring between the two VPN gateways. If so, NAT-T must be enabled (primarily for remote access VPNs and not site-to-site VPNs) because the ESP/AH packets will be modified, which will invalidate the hash for integrity checking.
19. If all else fails, check the release notes to see if there are any known issues for the release of Junos you are running, and check the Knowledge Base. If you still cannot find an answer, contact JTAC for additional assistance in troubleshooting.

Configuring and analyzing VPN tracing

Troubleshooting IPsec has come a long way since the last edition of the *Junos Security* book. You still can set up VPN tracing under the IKE/IPsec traceoptions and have them log to the box, but that's not the best way to go about things. One challenge of that solution was that it did not work well when you had numerous VPNs because the output was far too verbose, particularly across all of the sites. Instead Juniper has developed a targeted VPN debugging facility where you specify the local and remote IP addresses and enable the debug accordingly. The benefit of this model is that you can hone in on the specific VPN that you want to debug, and it works for both site-to-site and remote VPNs.

Sample Deployments

Although there are truly limitless combinations of VPN configurations that we could discuss, most often VPN configurations will be quite similar. This section discusses the two main types of VPNs: a site-to-site VPN (with multiple remote sites) and a VPN that connects a remote IPsec client.

Site-to-Site VPN

The goal of this case study is to establish site-to-site VPNs between the Campus Core and the three remote offices (East, West, and South Branches). The following properties should be present for this configuration, as shown in Figure 10-7:

- VPNs should use Main mode in a point-to-multipoint configuration.
- OSPF should be used as a dynamic routing protocol for this example on the tunnel interfaces, with all st0 interfaces in Area 0. Because this isn't true broadcast, define neighbors in the configuration.
- The architecture will be hub and spoke (utilizing point-to-multipoint VPNs).
- The st0 interface should be in the VPN zone. Use the following IP addressing for the st0 interfaces on the Campus Core and the remote offices:
  - Campus Core: 192.168.100.5/24
  - East Branch: 192.168.100.1/24
  - West Branch: 192.168.100.2/24
  - South Branch: 192.168.100.3/24
- Only the respective networks for each side should be allowed through the VPN, with any service allowed between the networks.
- The Phase 1 proposal should use 3DES SHA-1 with preshared keys. The key will be 8aifMhau%% using Diffie-Hellman Group 2.
- Phase 2 of the VPN should use AES128-SHA1 as the proposal, and no PFS.
- Branch VPN gateways should use 198.18.5.254 as the primary VPN connection and 198.18.4.254 as the backup.
- Ensure that IKE can be terminated on the external interfaces in the untrust zone.
- IKEv2 should be used for the West and South Branch, and use only IKEv1 on the East Branch.

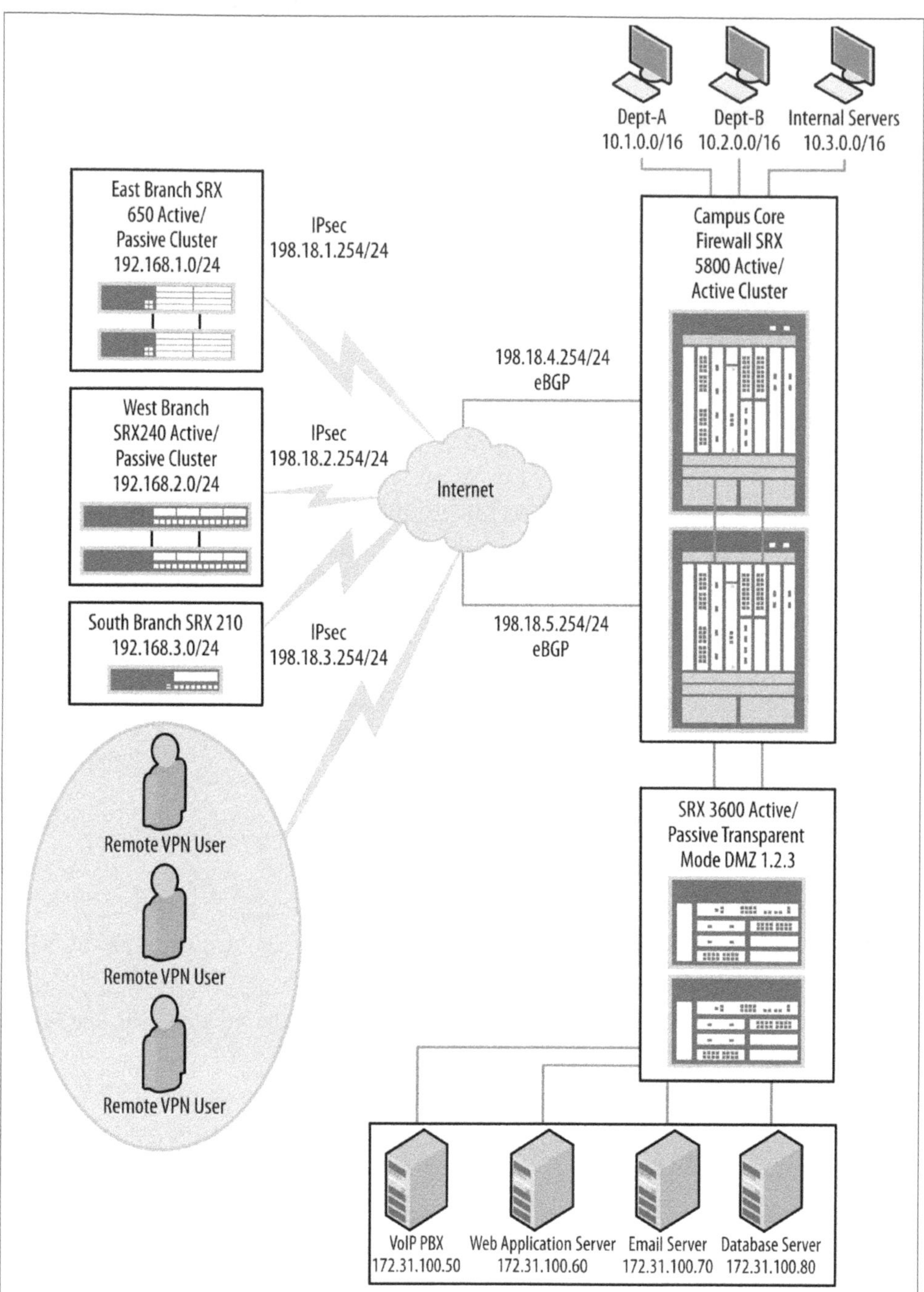

Figure 10-7. Case study network diagram

- For the proxy ID, just use local-id 0.0.0.0/0, remote-id 0.0.0.0, and service Any to simplify the IKE configuration to the respective gateways, and demonstrate that proxy IDs only impact negotiation by making sure both sides match, but not what traffic can pass through the VPN.

```
/*This Phase 1 Proposal is Applied to Campus and Remote Offices*/
[edit security ike proposal Remote-Office-PSK]
root@SRX5800# show
authentication-method pre-shared-keys;
dh-group group2;
authentication-algorithm sha1;
encryption-algorithm 3des-cbc;
/*This Phase 1 Policy is Applied to Campus and East Branch*/
[edit security ike policy Remote-Office-Static]
root@SRX5800#show
mode main;
proposals Remote-Office-PSK;
pre-shared-key  ascii-text  "$9$hA7cvWLX-VwgEc7dVsJZUjHqT3AtuREc";  ##  SECRET-
DATA

/*This Policy is Applied to South and West Branches*/
[edit security ike policy Remote-Office-Static]
root@SRX5800#show
proposals Remote-Office-PSK;
pre-shared-key  ascii-text  "$9$hA7cvWLX-VwgEc7dVsJZUjHqT3AtuREc";  ##  SECRET-
DATA


/*Getway Configuration on the Campus Core SRX*/
[edit security ike gateway Eastbranch-Remote-Office]
root@SRX5800# show
ike-policy Remote-Office-Static;
address 198.18.1.254;
dead-peer-detection {
    interval 10;
    threshold 3;
}
no-nat-traversal;
external-interface ge-0/0/0.0;
version v1-only

[edit security ike gateway Westbranch-Remote-Office]
root@SRX5800# show
ike-policy Remote-Office-Static;
address 198.18.2.254;
dead-peer-detection {
    interval 10;
    threshold 3;
}
no-nat-traversal;
external-interface ge-0/0/0.0;
```

```
version v2-only

[edit security ike gateway Southbranch-Remote-Office]
root@SRX5800# show
ike-policy Remote-Office-Static;
address 198.18.3.254;
dead-peer-detection {
    interval 10;
    threshold 3;
}
no-nat-traversal;
external-interface ge-0/0/0.0;
version v2-only

/*Gateway Configuration on the South and West Offices*/
[edit security ike gateway Eastbranch-Remote-Office]
root@SRX650# show
ike-policy Remote-Office-Static;
address [ 198.18.5.254 198.18.4.254 ];
dead-peer-detection {
    interval 10;
    threshold 3;
}
no-nat-traversal;
external-interface ge-0/0/0.0;
version v2-only

/*Gateway Configuration on the East Offices*/
[edit security ike gateway Eastbranch-Remote-Office]
root@SRX650# show
ike-policy Remote-Office-Static;
address [ 198.18.5.254 198.18.4.254 ];
dead-peer-detection {
    interval 10;
    threshold 3;
}
no-nat-traversal;
external-interface ge-0/0/0.0;
version v2-only



/*This Zone Configuration is applied to Campus and Remote Offices*/
[edit   security   zones   security-zone   untrust   host-inbound-traffic   system-
services]
root@SRX5800#show
ike;
/*Phase 2 Proposal is applied to Campus and Remote Offices*/
[edit security ipsec proposal Remote-Offices]
root@SRX5800# show
protocol esp;
authentication-algorithm hmac-sha1-96;
```

```
encryption-algorithm aes-128-cbc;
/*Phase 2 Proposal is applied to Campus and Remote Offices*/
[edit security ipsec policy Remote-Offices]
root@SRX5800# show
proposals Remote-Offices
/*Phase 2 VPN Configuration for Campus Core*/
[edit security ipsec vpn East-Branch]
root@SRX5800# show
bind-interface st0.0;
ike {
    gateway East-Branch;
    proxy-identity {
        local 0.0.0.0/0;
        remote 0.0.0.0/0;
        service any;
    }
    ipsec-policy Remote-Offices;
}

[edit security ipsec vpn West-Branch]
root@SRX5800# show
bind-interface st0.0;
ike {
    gateway West-Branch;
    proxy-identity {
        local 0.0.0.0/0;
        remote 0.0.0.0/0;
        service any;
    }
    ipsec-policy Remote-Offices;
}

[edit security ipsec vpn South-Branch]
root@SRX5800# show
bind-interface st0.0;
ike {
    gateway South-Branch;
    proxy-identity {
        local 0.0.0.0/0;
        remote 0.0.0.0/0;
        service any;
    }
    ipsec-policy Remote-Offices;
}
/*Phase 2 VPN Configuration for Remote Gateways*/
[edit security ipsec vpn Campus-Core]
root@SRX650# show
bind-interface st0.0;
ike {
    gateway Campus-Core;
    proxy-identity {
        local 0.0.0.0/0;
```

```
            remote 0.0.0.0/0;
            service any;
        }
        ipsec-policy Remote-Offices;
    }


/*ST0 Configuration for Campus Core*/
[edit interfaces st0]
root@SRX5800#
unit 0 {
    multpoint;
    family inet {
        address 192.168.100.5/24;
    }
}
/*ST0 Configuration for East-Branch*/
[edit interfaces st0]
root@SRX650#
unit 0 {
    family inet {
        address 192.168.100.1/24;
    }
}
/*ST0 Configuration for West-Branch*/
[edit interfaces st0]
root@SRX240#
unit 0 {
    family inet {
        address 192.168.100.2/24;
    }
}
/*ST0 Configuration for South-Branch*/
[edit interfaces st0]
root@SRX210#
unit 0 {
    family inet {
        address 192.168.100.3/24;
    }
}
/*ST0 Zone Configuration for Campus Core and Remote Offices*/
[edit security zones security-zones vpn]
root@SRX5800#show
interfaces {
        st0.0 {
            host-inbound-traffic {
                system-services {
                    ike;
                }
                protocols {
                    ospf;
                }
```

```
}
/*OSPF Protocol Configuration for Campus Core*/
[edit protocols]
root@SRX5800#show
ospf {
    area 0.0.0.0 {
        interface st0.0 {
            neighbor 192.168.100.1;
           neighbor 192.168.100.2;
           neighbor 192.168.100.3;
        interface-type p2mp;
        dynamic-neighbor
        }
    }
}
/*OSPF Protocol Configuration for Remote Offices*/
[edit protocols]
root@SRX5800#show
ospf {
    area 0.0.0.0 {
        interface st0.0 {
            neighbor 192.168.100.5;
          dynamic-neighbor;
        }
    }
}
/*Security Policies for Route-Based VPN Campus Core*/


[edit]
root@SRX5800# show security zones security-zone trust address-book
address 10.0.0.0/8 10.0.0.0/8;


[edit]
root@SRX5800# show security zones security-zone vpn address-book
address 192.168.1.0/24 192.168.1.0/24;
address 192.168.2.0/24 192.168.2.0/24;
address 192.168.3.0/24 192.168.3.0/24;



[edit security policies from-zone trust to-zone vpn policy Remote-Offices]
root@SRX5800# show
match {
        source-address 10.0.0.0/8;
        destination-address [ 192.168.1.0/24 192.168.2.0/24 192.168.3.0/24 ];
        application any;
        }
 then {
        permit
        log {
```

```
                session-close;
            }
   }

[edit security policies from-zone vpn to-zone trust policy Remote-Offices]
root@SRX5800# show
match {
        source-address [ 192.168.1.0/24 192.168.2.0/24 192.168.3.0/24 ];
        destination-address 10.0.0.0/8;
        application any;
        }
 then {
        permit
        log {
                session-close;
            }
   }
/*Security Policies for Route-Based VPN East-Branch Core*/


[edit]
root@SRX650# show security zones security-zone vpn address-book
address 10.0.0.0/8 10.0.0.0/8;
address 192.168.2.0/24 192.168.2.0/24;
address 192.168.3.0/24 192.168.3.0/24;



[edit]
root@SRX650# show security zones security-zone trust address-book
address 192.168.1.0/24 192.168.1.0/24;



[edit security policies from-zone trust to-zone vpn policy Remote-Offices]
root@SRX650# show
match {
        source-address 192.168.1.0/24;
        destination-address [10.0.0.0/8 192.168.2.0/24 192.168.3.0/24 ];
        application any;
        }
 then {
        permit
        log {
                session-close;
            }
   }

[edit security policies from-zone vpn to-zone trust policy Remote-Offices]
root@SRX650# show
match {
        source-address [ 10.0.0.0/8 192.168.2.0/24 192.168.3.0/24 ];
```

```
        destination-address 192.168.1.0/24;
        application any;
        }
 then {
        permit
        log {
                session-close;
            }
  }
```

/*Security Policies for Route-Based VPN West-Branch Core*/

```
[edit]
root@SRX240# show security zones security-zone vpn address-book
address 10.0.0.0/8 10.0.0.0/8;
address 192.168.1.0/24 192.168.1.0/24;
address 192.168.3.0/24 192.168.3.0/24;
```

```
[edit]
root@SRX240# show security zones security-zone trust address-book
address 192.168.2.0/24 192.168.2.0/24;
```

```
[edit security policies from-zone trust to-zone vpn policy Remote-Offices]
root@SRX240# show
match {
        source-address 192.168.2.0/24;
        destination-address [10.0.0.0/8 192.168.1.0/24 192.168.3.0/24 ];
        application any;
        }
 then {
        permit
        log {
                session-close;
            }
  }

[edit security policies from-zone vpn to-zone trust policy Remote-Offices]
root@SRX240# show
match {
        source-address [ 10.0.0.0/8 192.168.1.0/24 192.168.3.0/24 ];
        destination-address 192.168.2.0/24;
        application any;
        }
 then {
        permit
        log {
                session-close;
            }
```

```
  }
/*Security Policies for Route-Based VPN South-Branch Core*/


[edit]
root@SRX210# show security zones security-zone vpn address-book
address 10.0.0.0/8 10.0.0.0/8;
address 192.168.1.0/24 192.168.1.0/24;
address 192.168.2.0/24 192.168.2.0/24;



[edit]
root@SRX210# show security zones security-zone trust address-book
address 192.168.3.0/24 192.168.3.0/24;



[edit security policies from-zone trust to-zone vpn policy Remote-Offices]
root@SRX210# show
match {
        source-address 192.168.3.0/24;
        destination-address [10.0.0.0/8 192.168.1.0/24 192.168.2.0/24 ];
        application any;
        }
 then {
        permit
        log {
                session-close;
            }
  }

[edit security policies from-zone vpn to-zone trust policy Remote-Offices]
root@SRX210# show
match {
        source-address [ 10.0.0.0/8 192.168.1.0/24 192.168.2.0/24 ];
        destination-address 192.168.3.0/24;
        application any;
        }
 then {
        permit
        log {
                session-close;
            }
  }
```

Remote Access VPN

The goal of this case study is to configure an IPsec client VPN on the SRX. The configurations will largely be the same as in the preceding case study, except where noted. The configuration should be set up as follows:

- Phase 1 should use Aggressive mode, and PFS (Diffie-Hellman Group2) should be used to secure the VPN, terminated on the ge-0/0/0 Untrust interface.
- For the standard-based IPsec client, use an IKE identity of *ipsecike@company.com*. No specific client software will be examined here; however, any standards-based client implementation should interoperate with this example.
- Phase 1 should use 3DES-MD5 for the proposal with Diffie-Hellman Group 2.
- Use the preshared key 71hajfy44.
- Phase 2 should use AES128-SHA1 with ESP Tunnel mode for the proposal.
- Use a policy-based VPN for this configuration to allow the clients access to the Campus Core networks (10.0.0.0/8).

```
/* IPSec Remote Client*/
[edit security ike proposal Remote-Client]
root@SRX5800# show
authentication-method pre-shared-keys;
dh-group group2;
authentication-algorithm md5;
encryption-algorithm 3des-cbc;

[edit security ike policy Remote-Client]
root@SRX5800#show
mode aggressive;
proposals Remote-Office-PSK;
pre-shared-key ascii-text "$9$VWYJGDikqmTX74ZDif5revM7-s24"; ## SECRET-DATA

[edit security ike gateway Remote-Client]
root@SRX5800# show
ike-policy Remote-Client;
dynamic {
    user-at-hostname ipsecike@company.com;
}
external-interface ge-0/0/0.0;

[edit security ipsec proposal Remote-Client]
root@SRX5800# show
protocol esp;
authentication-algorithm hmac-sha1-96;
encryption-algorithm aes-128-cbc;

[edit security ipsec policy Remote-Client]
root@SRX5800# show
perfect-forward-secrecy {
    keys group2;
}
proposals Remote-Client;

[edit security ipsec vpn Remote-Client]
root@SRX5800# show
```

```
ike {
    gateway Remote-Client;
}
ipsec-policy Remote-Client;

[edit security zones security-zones trust address-book]
root@SRX5800# show
address 10.0.0.0/8 10.0.0.0/8;

[edit security policies from-zone untrust to-zone trust policy Remote-Client]
root@SRX5800# show
match {
        source-address any;
        destination-address 10.0.0.0/8;
        application any;
        }
 then {
        permit {
               tunnel {
                 ipsec-vpn Remote-Client;
                 }
         }
            log {
                session-close;
            }
  }

[edit security zones security-zone untrust host-inbound-traffic system-services]
root@SRX5800#show
ike;
```

IPsec Caveats on SRX

We've discussed a few caveats with IPsec in this chapter, and we want to summarize them in a single section. It's important to understand that Juniper is working on closing the gaps in many of these caveats, so regularly check the release notes for the latest and greatest.

- IPsec is not supported when the SRX is in Transparent mode.
- Transport mode is not supported for IPsec; use Tunnel mode instead.
- When terminating an IPsec VPN with LSYS, the VPN must be terminated in the root LSYS but the st0 interface can be placed within a child LSYS.
- Policy-based VPNs are targeted to very simple use cases without complex routing and NAT use cases. It is best to use route-based VPNs for anything but the simplest of scenarios.

- Remote access VPNs are limited to IKEv1 and don't support bidirectional traffic today.
- Before Junos 11.1, there were challenges with terminating VPNs in non-inet.0 VRs including where st0 was placed, but this has largely been resolved in more modern versions.
- Terminating VPNs on local interfaces in active/active HA is not supported.
- NAT-T had several limitations prior to 11.4R4 with the different modes that were supported. If you are having issues when using NAT-T, you might want to be on Junos 11.4r4+ to support the newer modes for better interoperability.
- IPv6 for IPsec Phase 1 is currently in beta testing at the time of writing this book. The features and functionality will be coming to Junos, but we can't give an exact readout at the moment. Work with your Juniper account team to get a roadmap, and—even better—get involved with beta testing!

Summary

IPsec VPNs have been a core tenet of network security and stateful firewalls for well over a decade. Their importance cannot be overstated, even in a constantly evolving era of new applications, virtualization, cloudy technologies, Software Defined Networking (SDN), and globalization. IPsec VPNs will definitely play an increasingly important role going forward. Writing a single chapter about IPsec is a very difficult task to undertake, as there are entire books written just explaining how the concepts themselves function, let alone the actual vendor implementation. In addition, the SRX is an extensive platform when it comes to IPsec and is greatly extending the capabilities of IPsec going forward, extending the GroupVPN, AutoVPN, IPv6, and other large-scale tunneling support. It's definitely a very exciting time to be a part of the SRX development team when it comes to IPsec!

In this chapter, we covered a wide variety of the most common IPsec technologies that most network administrators are likely to interact with when building site-to-site and remote access VPNs. We couldn't cover some of the more advanced esoteric technologies in this book due to space and scope, but to leverage any of those technologies you'll need to have mastered these technologies first, not to mention the troubleshooting and operation components that can be leveraged for both mechanisms. If you have a solid understanding of the concepts in this chapter, you should be able to deploy the several primary IPsec functions in most real-world scenarios and have no problem with the IPsec section of the JNCIE-Sec certification!

Study Questions

Questions

1. What are the differences between IKEv1 and IKEv2?
2. What is the purpose of IKEv1 Phase 1 in IPsec negotiations?
3. With IKEv1, what is the difference between Main and Aggressive modes, and in which phase of negotiations do they occur?
4. Why would Aggressive mode be necessary instead of Main mode?
5. How many Phase 1 and Phase 2 proposals can be configured on the SRX, and how are they evaluated?
6. What is PFS and what purpose does it serve?
7. What are the advantages and disadvantages of policy-based VPNs versus route-based VPNs?
8. What is the difference between point-to-point and point-to-multipoint VPNs?
9. What is the difference between numbered and unnumbered st0 interfaces?
10. What is the difference between DPD and VPN monitoring?
11. What is NAT-T and when must it be used?
12. What are the advantages and disadvantages of certificate authentication versus preshared key authentication?
13. What is a proxy ID, how is it used in IPsec negotiations, and why is it a common cause of VPN establishment issues?
14. What are the two settings that define how VPN tunnels should be triggered for setup?
15. What must you configure at the zone level before IPsec tunnels can be established on the SRX?
16. What is the difference between a CRL, OSCP, and SCEP when it comes to certificate authentication?
17. What does DH stand for, and how is it used by IPsec technologies?
18. How does the SRX handle DSCP bits of original packets for the tunneled traffic? What about `DF` bits?
19. Can third-party IPsec clients be used to connect to the SRX for remote access?

Answers

1. IKEv2 is the successor to IKEv1. IKEv1 is split into two different phases, with Phase 1 operating in Main or Aggressive mode, and Phase 2 supporting Quick mode. IKEv1 was developed over three core RFCs with several extraneous RFCs that describe different extensions and aspects of IKEv1. There are some

ambiguous elements to IKEv1 that have led to different vendors implementing IKE differently and led to interoperability issues. IKEv2 is a greatly simplified protocol that operates in a request/response format, offers more flexibility and options during negotiation, and provides better details as to acceptable parameters in the event that negotiation fails.

2. IKEv1 Phase 1 is used to create a secure channel to negotiate the Phase 2 encryption keys that will be used to secure the traffic.
3. Both Main and Aggressive modes occur in Phase 1 of IPsec negotiations. The difference is that Main mode negotiates the Phase 1 security with a six-message exchange with the IKE identities encrypted, whereas Aggressive mode negotiates them in a three-message exchange with the IKE identities in clear text. IKEv2 only supports one method of negotiation and doesn't have a different mode. It is somewhat of a hybrid between Main and Aggressive mode of IKEv1.
4. Aggressive mode is necessary when the IP address of the remote peer is dynamic and another mechanism such as dynamic DNS is not used to help identify the host.
5. The SRX supports up to four Phase 1 and four Phase 2 IPsec proposals per gateway. They are evaluated in order from first to last, until a proposal can be matched with the peer, or negotiations fail because a proposal cannot be chosen.
6. PFS stands for Perfect Forward Secrecy. This is an optional configuration option that can be used to trigger a renegotiation of Phase 1 keys after Phase 1 has been completed. This is most often performed when using Aggressive mode for Phase 1 authentication.
7. Policy-based VPNs are good for simple VPNs without any needs for NAT, advanced Level 7 features, or complex routing. Route-based VPNs are more powerful, with the ability to not only control traffic, but also interact with dynamic routing protocols, provide automatic failover, and integrate more generally into the network architecture.
8. Point-to-point VPNs map a single VPN to a single st0 interface, whereas point-to-multipoint VPNs map multiple VPNs to a single st0 interface on the hub site. Each spoke still views its connection as a point-to-point connection. All VPNs' st0 interfaces will be in the same zone subnet when it comes to the hub site using point to multipoint.
9. A numbered st0 interface means that it has an IP address on it, whereas an unnumbered st0 interface (which is only supported for point-to-point connections) will not have an IP address on it. Typically, it is best to use numbered interfaces for better routing and NAT support when it comes to point-to-point networks, but you can use unnumbered interfaces in very simple use cases.

10. DPD stands for Dead Peer Detection. This is a standard IKE capability to detect if the peer gateway is up by sending IKE pings. It is negotiated in Phase 1. VPN monitoring is not a standard IKE component, but rather relies on sending peers from the gateway through the IPsec tunnel to determine if it is up. It is a more reliable mechanism because it allows one to take into account not only whether the peer is up, but also whether the VPN is up. VPN monitoring and DPD results can then be used by the SRX to consider the VPN up or down, and make alternative arrangements if available to send the traffic over another VPN.

11. NAT-T is a technique for encapsulating IPsec traffic in UDP traffic so that it can pass through a NAT device (most commonly used for remote clients that are behind a NAT gateway). This is required because NAT can alter fields that will then make the authentication invalid. By encapsulating the IPsec traffic in a UDP packet, the UDP packet is NATed, and then, when it arrives at the gateway, the UDP headers are stripped off and the IPsec traffic is processed as normal.

12. Preshared keys are simple to implement, with little overhead. They are best used for site-to-site VPNs where only a few VPNs are used, or for remote access VPNs when there are only a few clients. The disadvantage of preshared key VPNs is that they don't scale easily without compromising security (by using the same key). Certificates have the ability to dynamically update a certificate's status, along with the ability to provide a unique certificate to each client. More overhead is associated with certificate authentication because it requires a CA to be generated, also called certificate generation (revocation and expiry). Other mechanisms such as CRL and OCSP can be used to ensure the validity of a certificate.

13. Proxy IDs are negotiated in Phase 2/IKE-Auth and are meant to provide information about the type of traffic that will be carried over the VPN. In reality, proxy IDs do not enforce any real control over the actual traffic that passes over the VPN; however, they must match to establish the VPNs. Proxy IDs are a common source of issues when establishing IPsec VPNs, particularly when establishing them between different vendors, because the IKEv1 standard did not specify exactly how the proxy IDs should be derived, and therefore different vendors derive them differently. This means the proxy IDs might not match, and therefore will require tuning for proper configuration.

14. You must enable IKE under the host-inbound-traffic configuration fields before IPsec VPNs are allowed to be established on the SRX. Additionally, if you are using any stateless ACL or security policies for traffic coming from or to the junos-host zone, you need to make sure that IKE and ESP/AH are permitted, otherwise negotiations will fail.

15. There are two settings that define how the SRX should establish traffic, on-traffic and immediately. On-traffic will establish the VPN only when there is traffic to be tunneled through the SRX, while immediately will trigger the SRX to always keep the IPsec tunnel up.
16. CRLs are generated by the CA that signs them. It includes a list of all of the certificates that have been revoked or are on hold. The lists are usually updated in real time, but are downloaded at an interval so it is possible for a certificate to be revoked with an older CRL file saying that it is still valid. OCSP allows for on-demand checking of certificate status rather than checking CRLs that might have outdated information. OSCP essentially acts as a request/response protocol. SCEP has nothing to do with certificate validation but instead is used to renew certificates dynamically. If you are supporting a large IPsec infrastructure with hundreds of devices, you need an automated way to renew and reenroll certificates, and SCEP supports doing just that by reenrolling and typically getting new certificates from the CA when a certificate is going to expire.
17. DH stands for Diffie-Hellman and refers to a method to securely establish a two-way encrypted channel for exchanging the symmetric keys that will ultimately encrypt the traffic.
18. The SRX will automatically copy the DSCP bits of the original traffic to the ESP/AH header so that other devices will get the same processing by up/downstream devices. `DF` stands for Don't Fragment. By default, the SRX will honor the same behavior of the packets, but you can set it to copy, clear, or set the bits to the IPsec header.
19. Yes, third-party IPsec clients can be used to provide remote access to the SRX as long as they support the same standards-based implementations that the SRX supports. It is important to note, however, that JTAC cannot assist in troubleshooting client-side issues for third-party software, only on the SRX side. Clients like Shrew and NCP have been tested in the past and shown to work well in most cases.

CHAPTER 11
Screens and Flow Options

Screen technology is one of the most powerful yet extremely misunderstood features that is part of the SRX, and it has been around since the NetScreen days. As an engineer who has seen countless deployments, many implementations of Screens are not properly tuned or understood by customers. With all of the advanced Layer 7 threats present in modern-day networking, it is very easy to overlook Layer 3 and Layer 4 threats. The truth is that although the main source of Internet threats has shifted to Layer 7 over the past decade, Layer 3 and 4 threats are still every bit as pertinent and potent, especially if you do not have adequate defenses against them.

At this point you might be asking yourself, what exactly are Screens? A Screen is a Layer 3 or Layer 4 IPS setting that can be used to detect and block various anomalies and set certain thresholds for activities at those layers. They are effective at blocking such Layer 3 and Layer 4 DoS attacks that are still perpetrated every day with great effectiveness. Examining the headlines over the last few years regarding well-known hacking, political, cybercrime, and military organizations, you will discover numerous instances of Layer 3 and Layer 4 DoS attacks that are extremely effective, in addition to those that take place at Layer 7.

In this chapter, we are going to dissect the Screen technology piece by piece. We explore how the different Screens function, where they are implemented, how they should be deployed, and how to effectively tune them for maximum effectiveness.

Additionally, we explore some of the flow configuration options supported by the SRX that often complement the many Screens to not only enforce network behaviors, but also prevent some DoS vectors. By the end of this chapter, you should have a high degree of confidence in deploying Screens and flow options properly so that they can be effective before a DoS attack, rather than learning this information in hindsight (as is often the case with many organizations).

A Brief Review of Denial-of-Service Attacks

Before examining the Screen technology at length, it is important to review the challenge that this technology solves to gain a proper understanding of how to apply it. Most security specialists are quite familiar with the concept of a DoS attack at a high level, particularly with all of the notoriety given to many modern attacks against well-known institutions in the last few years. Still, there is a bit more analysis that must be done when considering Screens. For the purpose of this chapter, we break up DoS attacks into two categories: exploit based and flood based.

Exploit-Based DoS

An exploit-based DoS attack (see Figure 11-1) is one that exploits a particular software vulnerability to create a system or service outage. The outage could cause the service to become completely unavailable or just unavailable during the attack itself. Typically, exploit-based attacks are not high-volume attacks, but rather cause the system to become unstable in one form or another due to a vulnerability. It's important to remember that not all vulnerabilities lead to a compromise of the victim system giving the attacker control; it all depends on the nature of the vulnerability and several other factors about the vulnerable code to determine if one can actually compromise the system. Often one might find a vulnerability that cannot (feasibly) be compromised to give the attacker control, but could still make the system unstable by overwriting some memory with random data and causing a segmentation fault or some other unpredictable execution. We consider these to be exploit-based DoS attacks because they attack a specific vulnerability. Exploit-based attacks are not the primary focus of Screens, as this is something that is much more effectively covered by IPS and is discussed in Chapter 13.

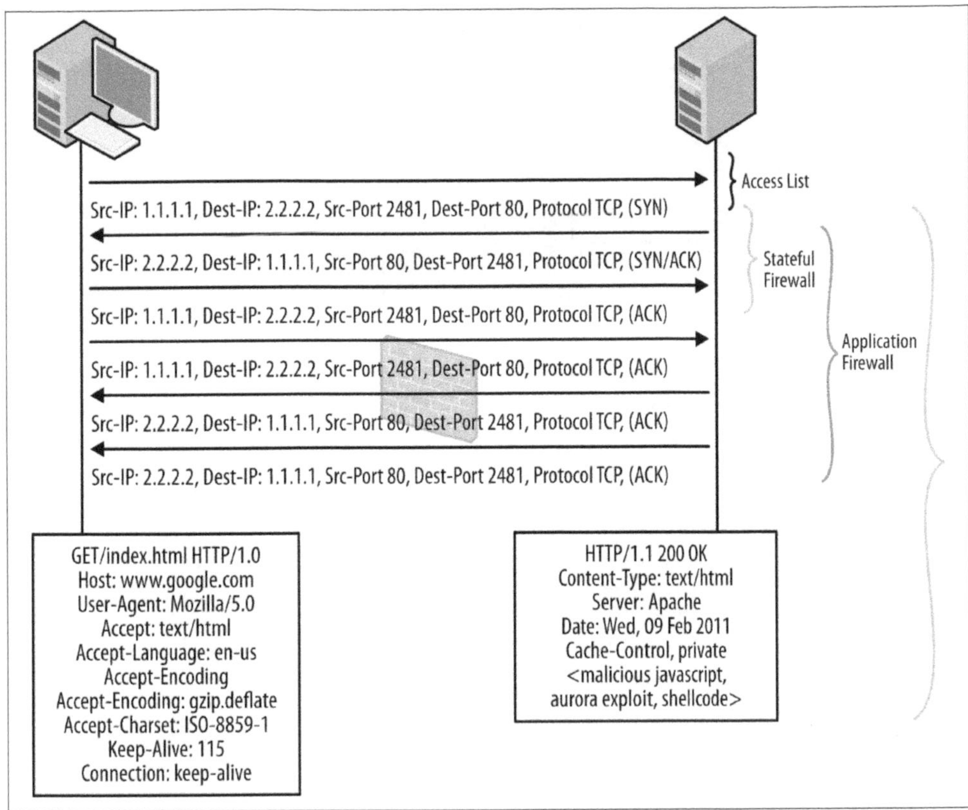

Figure 11-1. Exploit-based DoS attack

Flood-Based DoS

A flood-based DoS attack is very different from an exploit-based DoS attack in virtually every way, as shown in Figure 11-2. Unlike the exploit-based DoS attack, which exploits a vulnerability in the victim system, a flood-based DoS attack overwhelms the victim system with legitimate traffic—although at an anomalous rate—leaving the victim system unavailable. Sometimes the effects of the attack will only be felt while the attack is underway, but other instances will leave the system overwhelmed and cause it to crash completely, requiring manual intervention to restart it. In fact, many security and application engineers will likely have stories of such attacks (or misconfigurations like a bridge loop) not only bringing a system offline, but actually corrupting the filesystem or applications.

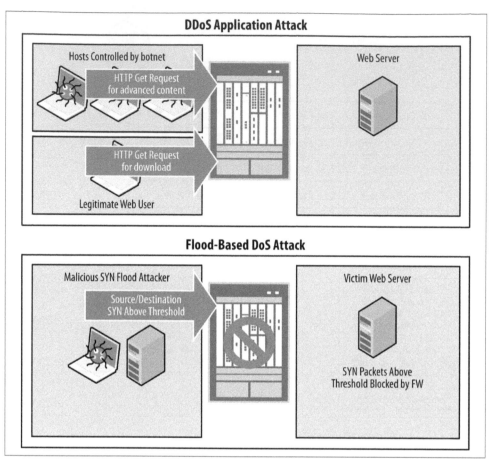

Figure 11-2. Flood-based DoS attack

Flood-based DoS attacks can take many forms, which we discuss in this chapter. Some of the common attacks would include SYN floods, UDP floods, ICMP floods, and IP packet floods, which serve to overwhelm the victim system. Often, without adequate protection, not only can the end systems be victimized, but so can the intermediate networking devices, especially those that operate at Layer 4 and above. It is therefore very important to keep this in mind for virtually every firewall deployment.

> There is technically a hybrid of a flood + exploit DoS attack, which exploits a vulnerability that consumes more CPU cycles than a standard operation, but in and of itself won't cause a DoS scenario. Instead, this attack must be flooded over multiple sessions to create a cumulative effect. Some examples of this type of attack include CVE-2011-3192 against Apache and CVE-2011-1473 against OpenSSL.

DoS Versus DDoS

If you're somewhat unfamiliar with this category of attacks, it is helpful to classify what a DoS versus a DDoS attack is. A DoS is a denial-of-service attack in general, but it does not specify the magnitude of sources. A distributed denial-of-service attack is coordinated by a large number of sources (hundreds, thousands, or even millions). Typically, these attacks are launched by an individual or organization that controls the attacking hosts through a botnet. This attack produces a coordinated effect that is much more difficult to deflect than an attack from an individual hacker, which can be surgically blocked from a source IP address perspective. For the purposes of this chapter, DoS and DDoS can be used relatively interchangeably, and Screens are just as effective for protecting against DDoS as they are DoS to the limits of the platform.

Screen functionality is primarily for Layer 3 and Layer 4 DoS/DDoS protection, but do not provide DDoS protection at Layer 7. Although Screens are still a critical technology to deploy even if concerned with L7-based DDoS attacks, to provide complete coverage Screens should be used in conjunction with a Layer 7 anti-DDoS technology. In 2013, Juniper acquired Webscreen Technologies and their appliance/VM-based DDoS solution. This has been rebranded as Junos DDoS Secure. This solution should definitely be examined to provide protection against Layer 7 DDoS attacks.

Screen Theory and Examples

Now that we've examined some of the threats that lead to the need for a Layer 3 and Layer 4 DoS solution, let's dive deeper into the threats, technologies, and examples. For this section, we are going to explore several facets of Screens, so it is helpful to break them down into digestible segments for each type of attack. We explore each type of attack and how Screens can be applied.

With the emergence of IPv6 in modern networks, it is only logical that these same attacks can be perpetrated on IPv6 as well as IPv4. The good news is that the SRX provides protection for both IPv4 and IPv6 with Screens. There are a few exceptions with the IP packet Screens which only apply to IPv4, including the Security Option and Loose/Strict Route Options which don't apply to IPv6. But for the most part, Screens provides similar capabilities for IPv6 by default when IPv6 processing is enabled.

How Screens Fit into the Packet Flow

So far, we have discussed in general what Screens do, but we haven't explained why they are so effective at protecting both end systems along with the firewall itself. Screens are so effective because they are lightweight, and more important, they are processed as early in the flow chain as possible. This means that before we start going through the effort of setting up a session or fully examining the packet for protocol state, we apply the Screens, so that packets can be dropped as early in the process as possible. Figure 11-3 shows where the Screens are applied. Note that the packet-based Screens are always applied regardless of whether the session is established, whereas other Screens are only applied at session inception. We explain how this works on a Screen-by-Screen basis later in this chapter.

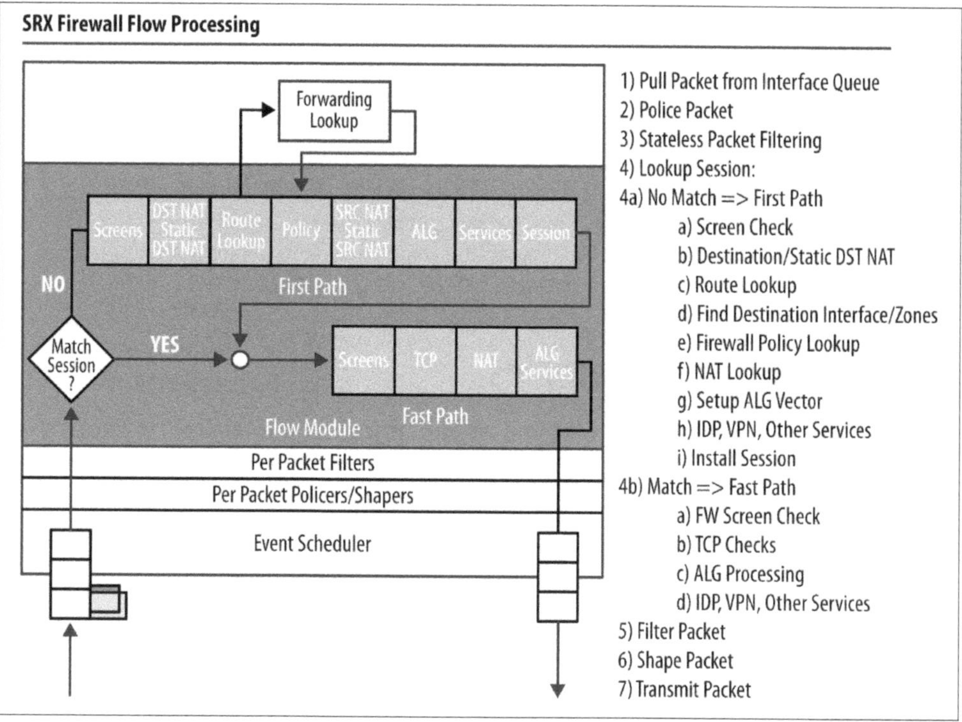

Figure 11-3. Packet flow

Screen Processing only happens on the ingress interface

It is very important to understand that Screens are only applied when the packet arrives on the SRX, not at any other point in the packet flow. This is because we want to deny an offense as soon as it arrives on the SRX rather than process the packet only to drop it later for some violation. It's important to remember that Screens are only processed on the ingress, so when you consider where to enable a Screen, it should always be on the zone on which the packet arrives. Screens don't have a concept of from- and to-zones; they are processed on a zone-by-zone basis when they arrive on an interface, as shown in Figure 11-4.

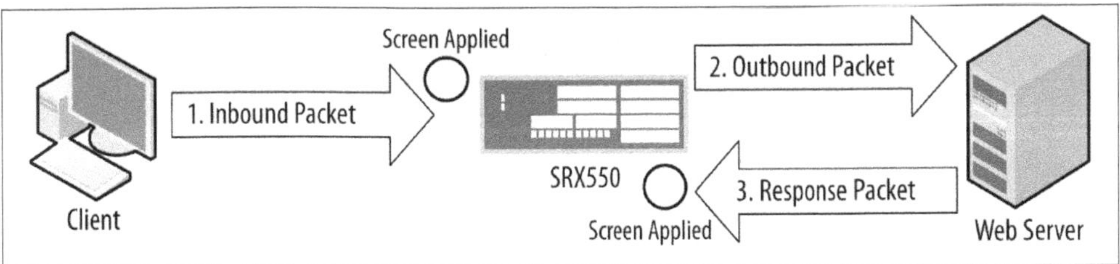

Figure 11-4. Screens processing on an ingress interface

At the time of writing this book, the SRX does not support applying Screens to tunnel interfaces, only to IFL interfaces like ge-0/0/0.0. This might change in the future, so check the current release notes and documentation for the current status.

Screens in Hardware and Software

Another factor that makes Screens so effective is that on the high-end SRX platforms, most of them are done in hardware on the NPU, so that the platform can essentially process the Screens at line rate. All of the packet-based Screens along with the flood-based Screens are handled in the NPUs. The only Screens that are not done in the NPU are those that require some additional state tracking across the entire box. For instance, IP Session Limits, TCP/UDP Sweep, and Port Scan Screens must be done in a combination of the CP and SPU because not all packets flow through a single NPU or SPU (unless that is the only NPU or SPU in the platform). The CP has a master list of the sessions and is aware of the sessions that exist on the platform, so it can effectively determine whether the limits have been violated. It is important to note that even in this case, these Screens are performed well after the initial packet and flood-based Screens are performed to better protect the platform.

The branch SRX always processes Screens in software in the central processor, but they are all done on the data plane and not on the control plane, so the platform should still be able to remain available in the face of a DoS attack (particularly if you are using fxp0 for out-of-band management rather than an in-band revenue interface). Screens are quite effective for the branch SRX, but if you are truly concerned about massive DoS attacks, you should really consider an SRX high-end platform.

As mentioned, all Screens and other data processing is done on the data plane and not on the control plane. This means that the platform should still remain available for management even in the event that it comes under a massive attack that reaches the limits of the platform.

It's a best practice to not leave flow debugs or packet captures enabled when not in a specific troubleshooting case, as these messages are sent to the RE, so it can affect performance and result in availability issues if you were under a DoS attack.

Screen Profiles

Before we dive into the plethora of Screens and the various options for configuring them, it is important to understand how Screens are applied and enforced on the SRX. In the SRX, Screens are essentially configured as profiles that are applied at the zone level; that is, Screens can be applied on a zone-by-zone basis to provide the firewall administrator with the ability to define different thresholds and limits on a zone-by-zone basis. This is very important, because often, an administrator will want to configure different limits on the external-facing zone, where DoS threats are the most likely, rather than the internal segments where more control of users is possible. That isn't to say you shouldn't configure Screens on an internal zone, because we know that even the resources of an organization can become infected with malware that could participate in a DoS attack toward the Internet or consume unnecessary resources. The point is that you have the ability to apply different thresholds for the different zones to complement the varying security posture of each segment that connects to the firewall.

Packet versus threshold Screens

Screens can be broken down into two different types: packet-based Screens and threshold-based Screens. Packet-based Screens are evaluated on a packet-by-packet basis in a stateless fashion. For instance, the SYN-FIN Screen checks each packet to see if the TCP packet has both the SYN and FIN bits set, which is clearly illegal. This is done on a packet-by-packet basis without regard to other factors.

Threshold-based Screens, on the other hand, are applied in a semistateful fashion. The SRX must track the threshold on some basis within each zone (e.g., per source IP), and once the configured threshold is reached, an action will be taken. For instance, the SYN Flood Screen allows the administrator to define how many SYN packets can be sent from or to a source or destination. Any SYN packets below the threshold will be passed, but once the threshold is reached, any packets violating the limit will be dropped. Don't worry about remembering the specific Screens here, as we will be covering each one in depth later in the chapter.

Applying Screen profiles to single and multiple zones

You can think of a Screen profile as an independent profile that can be applied to one or more zones. When a zone consists of multiple interfaces, a Screen is tracked at the zone level, with each interface contributing to the threshold-based Screens that can be triggered. On the other hand, when you have a Screen profile that is applied to multiple zones, each zone will be treated and tracked separately, so the profile is only the same from a configuration perspective.

Just remember, when SRX configurations are applied to a zone, they affect the member interfaces collectively, but they are tracked separately from other zones just like any other zone-based setting.

Configuring a Screen profile

Screen profiles are defined under the `Security Screen` stanzas as a profile, which is then applied at the zone level as discussed. This example configures a Screen called `Internet-Screen` and will apply it to the Internet zone:

```
root@SRX550-Node0# set security screen ids-option SRX Internet-Screen descrip-
tion "Screen Applied to the Internet Zone"
{primary:node0}[edit]
root@SRX550-Node0# set security zones security-zone Internet screen Internet-
Screen
{primary:node0}[edit]
root@SRX550-Node0# show security screen
ids-option Internet-Screen {
    description "Screen Applied to the Internet Zone";
}

{primary:node0}[edit]
root@SRX550-Node0# show security zones
security-zone Internet {
    screen Internet-Screen;
}
```

Screen profiles only have one option (besides the description), which is `alarm-without-drop`. This setting means that a log or alarm will be triggered for the event, but no action will be taken. This is a simple switch to turn Screen enforcement on and off on a per Screen profile basis. It is useful when doing initial deployments to ensure that you are not going to cause any adverse impacts to the network.

Among your fellow engineers, no doubt there are some battle stories about how some third party decided to write their own TCP/IP stack or behave in some anomalous fashion that simulates a suspicious behavior that such protections can break. Sometimes it helps to do a brief trial with Screens enabled before turning on enforcement to ensure there won't be any adverse effects or that they can be investigated before taking action.

DoS Attacks with IP Protocols

In this section, we examine the plethora of IP protocol attacks that the SRX can defend against. Although many of these attacks are packet anomalies that might not be able to actually crash any modern OS, their presence on the network still should be viewed with suspicion. Additionally, although well-known modern OSs are not typically vulnerable to issues with the packet anomalies, the great expansion of mobile, tablet, and network-capable peripheral devices could well make them vulnerable. In the case of the mobile and tablet world, many OSs have not stood the test of time; network peripheral devices especially run very stripped-down OSs that are unlikely to have been fuzzed or pen tested with security analysis tools.

Bad IP Option Screen

Both IPv4 and IPv6 support a dynamic field called the IP Options field. This field contains a Type/Length/Value tuple that can be of variable length. The Bad Option Screen will drop any packets that are malformed due to incorrect IP options in the IP header.

A thorough discussion of IP options can be viewed at the IANA website for IPv4 (*http://bit.ly/ZSqwJ0*) and IPv6 (*http://bit.ly/Zq1lBb*).

Screen Type: Per-Packet

Screen Processing Location: NPU for high-end SRX, Forwarding Engine branch SRX

Configuring Bad IP Option Screen. The Bad IP Option Screen is very easy to configure as it is either on or off; there are no other options or considerations for enabling this Screen.

```
{primary:node0}[edit security screen]
root@SRX550-Node0# set ids-option Internet-Screen ip bad-option

{primary:node0}[edit security screen]
root@SRX550-Node0# show
ids-option Internet-Screen {
    ip {
```

```
            bad-option;
        }
    }
```

Block Frag Screen

IP fragments are packets that have been divided from an original packet when the MTU of the link between a client and server can't support the packet size somewhere along the path. The MTU for Ethernet is 1,514 (including the Level 2 header) meaning that the IP packet can be 1,500 bytes long. Sometimes when you are further encapsulating the packet in protocols like IPsec, GRE, PPPoE, and others that must still transmit over the same link MTU of 1,514, the packets might have to be split up. There are other cases when fragmentation can be used that are entirely legitimate.

In some cases, though, packet fragmentation can be used as an offensive technique both from a DoS perspective and also for evading Layer 7 devices, which might not properly parse the fragmented packets, especially when they come out of order or overlap. Packet fragmentation might be perfectly acceptable, but if there is no reason why packets should be fragmented, you can use this Screen to block them entirely when they arrive on the firewall.

Also remember that for IPv6, fragments are supported on routers; however, unlike IPv4, an IPv6 router will not do any fragmentation itself. It will drop any packet that is too large to send on the upstream/downstream media. Instead, IPv6 relies on a Path MTU ICMPv6 message to ensure that no fragmentation will need to happen elsewhere on the data path. The reason for this is because it can be taxing for routers to have to fragment the packets and, ideally, this shouldn't be the router's responsibility. This doesn't mean that you need to enable the Block Frag Option in IPv6, but it is important to remember as the firewall will drop IPv6 packets that need to be fragmented, regardless of whether the Block Frag Screen is enabled or not.

Screen Type: Per Packet

Screen Processing Location: NPU for high-end SRX, Forwarding Engine branch SRX

Configuring Block Frag Screen. Configuring the Block Frag Screen is very easy, as it requires no additional options, just to be enabled for the Screen profile.

```
{primary:node0}[edit security screen]
root@SRX550-Node0# set ids-option Internet-Screen ip block-frag

{primary:node0}[edit security screen]
root@SRX550-Node0# show
ids-option Internet-Screen {
    ip {
        block-frag;
    }
}
```

Route Option Screens

Another set of IP option Screens are those of the IP Route Option family. There are four Route Option Screens that you can configure blocking on independently:

Record Route Option
: This option is to trigger the router to insert its IP address into the IP option field to inform the endpoint of the routers along this path. This can be used for recon purposes by an attacker.

Loose Source Route Option
: Source routing allows the source to define the path a packet should take. Loose source routing means that certain routes must be taken, but it is not necessarily the entire path. An attacker can use this to define the way a packet should traverse a network, potentially bypassing segments and transit devices. Normally, an attacker shouldn't control the path. Source routing is not typical for modern networks.

Strict Source Route Option
: This route option defines the explicit path a packet should take through a network to reach the endpoint. Like the Loose Source Route Option, it is not a common option that should be enabled in modern networks.

Source Route Option
: This blocks any route option that is source route in nature, including loose and strict options.

Screen Type: Per Packet

Screen Processing Location: NPU for high-end SRX, Forwarding Engine branch SRX

Configuring Route Option Screens. Configuring Route Option Screens is simple; as they are either enabled or disabled, there are no threshold or other considerations. For this example, we enable all four Route Option Screens.

```
{primary:node0}[edit security screen]
root@SRX550-Node0# set ids-option Internet-Screen ip record-route-option

{primary:node0}[edit security screen]
root@SRX550-Node0# set ids-option Internet-Screen ip loose-source-route-option

{primary:node0}[edit security screen]
root@SRX550-Node0# set ids-option Internet-Screen ip source-route-option

root@SRX550-Node0# set ids-option Internet-Screen ip strict-source-route-option

{primary:node0}[edit security screen]
root@SRX550-Node0# show
ids-option Internet-Screen {
    ip {
        record-route-option;
```

```
            source-route-option;
            loose-source-route-option;
            strict-source-route-option;
        }
    }
```

IP Security Option Screen

The IP Security Option is largely deprecated and probably will never be seen on any modern network for legitimate uses. Originally, it was an RFC developed by the US Department of Defense (791, 1038). It was never really implemented and is considered obsolete. It is best to block any packets that have this option enabled.

Screen Type: Per Packet

Screen Processing Location: NPU for high-end SRX, Forwarding Engine branch SRX

Configuring the IP Security Option Screen. There is nothing special about this Screen's configuration. It is either enabled or disabled on a Screen on a profile-by-profile basis.

```
{primary:node0}[edit security screen]
root@SRX550-Node0# set ids-option Internet-Screen ip security-option

{primary:node0}[edit security screen]
root@SRX550-Node0# show
ids-option Internet-Screen {
    ip {
        security-option;
    }
}
```

IP Spoofing Screen

IP spoofing attacks have been well known and understood in the routing world for a long time. Essentially, the attacker impersonates a victim source address when transmitting packets to a destination, so that the destination believes the packet came from the victim rather than the attacker. These types of attacks were much more effective before the days of stateful firewalls where stateless access lists (especially those that weren't well crafted) could be bypassed with such techniques. Although these techniques are much more difficult with a stateful firewall, particularly with a well-crafted rulebase of least privilege, they are still possible when source packets fall within the source address ranges of the rule (particularly when using Any as a source address).

The IP Spoofing Screen will cross-reference the source IP address of packets that arrive on the platform with that of a Unicast Reverse Path Forwarding (uRPF) lookup, to ensure that the firewall would route packets back to that source based on the same interface as it originated. The IP Spoofing Screen also works when multiple active routes are available for a source, such as when using equal cost multiple path routing. The only requirement is that the routes must be active. The SRX performs a loose RPF check as part of the IP Spoofing Screen at the time of writing this book.

For more information on uRPF checks, see Wikipedia's entry on reverse path forwarding (*http://bit.ly/ZAOvRt*).

Screen Type: Per Flow

Screen Processing Location: SPU for high-end SRX during session create, Forwarding Engine branch SRX

Configuring the IP Spoofing Screen. Configuring the IP Spoofing Screen is simple, as all of the intelligence with the Screen is handled by the system by looking at the routing table.

```
{primary:node0}[edit security screen]
root@SRX550-Node0# set Internet-Screen ip security-option spoofing

{primary:node0}[edit security screen]
root@SRX550-Node0# show
ids-option Internet-Screen {
    ip {
        spoofing;
    }
}
```

IP Stream Option Screen

The IP Stream Option is an obsolete option for linking an IPv4 packet to a stream (also called a flow or session). This option is not commonly used, and therefore there isn't much of a reason to use it in modern networking. Packets containing it can therefore be dropped, as they are likely malicious.

Screen Type: Per Packet

Screen Processing Location: NPU for high-end SRX, Forwarding Engine branch SRX

Configuring the IP Stream Option Screen. Configuring the IP Stream Option is straightforward, as it is either on or off per Screen profile. No additional values or settings must be configured.

```
{primary:node0}[edit security screen]
root@SRX550-Node0# set ids-option Internet-Screen ip stream-option

{primary:node0}[edit security screen]
root@SRX550-Node0# show
ids-option Internet-Screen {
    ip {
```

```
            stream-option;
        }
    }
```

IP Tear Drop Screen

The IP Tear Drop attack is a very nasty technique to crash a remote system (both end systems as well as transit systems like routers, firewalls, etc.) Essentially, this attack leverages IP fragmentation where overlapping fragments are used to create confusion when the packets are attempted to be reassembled. Most modern OSs can protect against this type of attack, but it could still be problematic for legacy systems or some newer peripheral devices. Because this is a common evasion technique (along with a DoS attack) there is no reason why this should be present in the network. It indicates malicious activity at worst and a very poorly coded IP stack at best, so it should always be blocked.

If you have the Block Frag Screen enabled, this Screen won't be required because all fragments will be blocked.

The SRX leverages a Fragment Processing engine in the SPU that will ensure that fragments are complete and ordered before passing them to an end system. The SRX will also do reassembly when Level 7 services like IPS are enabled, or if the Force IP Reassemble flow option is enabled.

Screen Type: Per Flow

Screen Processing Location: SPU for high-end SRX Fragment Processing engine, Forwarding Engine branch SRX Fragment Processing engine

Configuring the IP Tear Drop Screen. The IP Tear Drop Attack Screen, like many of the other IP Fragment Screens, is very simple to enable with no configurable options.

```
{primary:node0}[edit security screen]
root@SRX550-Node0# set ids-option Internet-Screen ip tear-drop

{primary:node0}[edit security screen]
root@SRX550-Node0# show
ids-option Internet-Screen {
    ip {
        tear-drop;
    }
}
```

IP Timestamp Option Screen

The IP Timestamp Option is a Screen that can be used to identify the time the packet was sent in the originating host. This isn't inherently malicious, but if a vulnerability exists on the destination host with regard to this option, it could be possible to create a DoS attack or worse. Therefore if this option isn't required, it is best to follow the strategy of least privilege and disable it.

Screen Type: Per Packet

Screen Processing Location: NPU for high-end SRX, Forwarding Engine branch SRX

Configuring the IP Timestamp Option Screen. The IP Timestamp Option Screen is very straightforward to configure, as shown here:

```
{primary:node0}[edit security screen]
root@SRX550-Node0# set ids-option Internet-Screen ip timestamp-option

{primary:node0}[edit security screen]
root@SRX550-Node0# show
ids-option Internet-Screen {
    ip {
        timestamp-option;
    }
}
```

Unknown IP Protocol Screen

For the most part, there are very few IPv4 protocols used on modern networks. You are most familiar with TCP (Protocol 6), UDP (Protocol 17), and ICMP (Protocol 1), along with others like ESP, AH, GRE, IPIP, and a few others. There are 256 potential IP protocols in all (the IP protocol field is eight bits long), although most of them are either unused or obsolete. In most cases, if you see some traffic on such unknown IP protocols, it is likely malicious activity and should be blocked. The Unknown IP Protocol Screen does just this.

For a full list of IP protocol numbers, see the IANA website (*http://bit.ly/13AeabJ*).

Screen Type: Per Packet

Screen Processing Location: NPU for high-end SRX, Forwarding Engine branch SRX

Configuring the Unknown IP Protocol Screen. The powerful Unknown IP Protocol Screen is simple and effective. You might not need it if you have a very strict security policy, as the FW rulebase can filter these filters, but it is especially useful if you have rules with Any as the application.

```
{primary:node0}[edit security screen]
root@SRX550-Node0# show
ids-option Internet-Screen {
    ip {
        unknown-protocol;
    }
}
```

DoS Attacks with ICMP

ICMP is a fundamental protocol to Internet functionality. Not only is it a utility function to check liveliness, informing hosts of network parameters and paths, but it also functions as a powerful reconnaissance tool for attackers. In typical networks (particularly at the Internet edge) there should only be a few types of ICMP messages that you would legitimately receive. Additionally, the volume of those messages shouldn't be excessive.

ICMP messages have also been used to tunnel data, perpetuate DoS attacks, and glean valuable diagnostic information for attackers, so they aren't quite as harmless as they seem on the surface. There are certainly much more serious threats to a network than ICMP, but anomalous ICMP behavior would certainly warrant some further investigation, as it might be part of a more serious attack.

In this section, we review the different ICMP Screens that the SRX has to offer, how they function, and how they are implemented.

ICMP Flood Screen

An ICMP flood attack can be a particularly vicious attack that can affect not only the end systems, but also transit devices along the path. ICMP is a protocol that might or might not be processed in ASICs due to some complex logic that needs to take place. This feature was originally introduced in ScreenOS because ICMP messages had to be processed in the CPU of the ASIC-based ScreenOS platforms. Junos only needs to process IP packets addressed to the firewall itself in the ASIC (and only if the FW is listening for ICMP on that port and doesn't have an access list configured to block it). Still, ICMP is powerful because it is usually permitted to traverse the network and it can be easily spoofed.

The ICMP Flood Screen works on a very simple premise, which is that you configure the threshold that should be applied to the ICMP Screen in how many ICMP messages per second can be received to a destination server before the threshold is reached. Note that this is tracked on a server-by-server basis for the zone, although you do not need to explicitly configure what IP addresses or servers are used, just the threshold.

Screen Type: Per Packet, Threshold

Screen Processing Location: NPU for high-end SRX, Forwarding Engine branch SRX

Configuring the ICMP Flood Screen. As mentioned, for the ICMP Flood Screen you need only define the maximum number of ICMP packets (regardless of type) that should be received per destination server per second. Usually this number shouldn't be too high, especially if it is not a commonly monitored server by external resources. In determining the threshold, you should identify the baseline number of ICMP messages that is acceptable for normal day-to-day operation and set that as the threshold. Any messages in excess of that limit will take the action for the Screen profile (drop/log or log only). In this example, we use a threshold of 100 ICMP packets per second per host.

```
{primary:node0}[edit security screen]
root@SRX550-Node0# set ids-option Internet-Screen icmp flood threshold 100

{primary:node0}[edit security screen]
root@SRX550-Node0# show
ids-option Internet-Screen {
    icmp {
        flood threshold 100;
    }
}
```

ICMP Fragment Screen

ICMP packets should not ordinarily be fragmented in a network, as they are usually small in nature, but this is a technique that the ICMP protocol supports. In most cases, such packets will not have a legitimate use and will be anomalous in nature. This Screen is recommended for most scenarios unless there is a truly a need to support large ICMP packets.

ICMP fragments will be superseded by the Block IP Fragment Screen, although it won't hurt to have it enabled.

Screen Type: Per Packet

Screen Processing Location: NPU for high-end SRX, Forwarding Engine branch SRX

Configuring the ICMP Fragment Screen. The ICMP Fragment Screen is very easy to configure as it's either enabled or disabled per profile, and no additional parameters are required.

```
{primary:node0}[edit security screen]
root@SRX550-Node0# set ids-option Internet-Screen icmp fragment
```

```
{primary:node0}[edit security screen]
root@SRX550-Node0# show
ids-option Internet-Screen {
    icmp {
        fragment;
    }
}
```

ICMP IP Sweep Screen

Although the ICMP Flood Screen protects you against a volume-based attack against end hosts with ICMP, an attacker can still use ICMP to map a network. In modern networks with many devices with power-saving features, IP sweeps can be disruptive, as they can wake up devices unnecessarily. The ICMP Sweep Screen allows you to set a threshold for how many ICMP messages you can receive within a range from a given source IP address. Because this Screen has to keep track of ICMP packets crossing session and host boundaries, we must process this in conjunction with the CP and the SPU, because the SPU/NPUs don't have full visibility to all hosts per platform.

Screen Type: Per Packet, Threshold

Screen Processing Location: CP/SPU for high-end SRX, Forwarding Engine branch SRX

Configuring the ICMP IP Sweep Screen. The ICMP IP Sweep Screen only has one parameter, which is to define how many tens of ICMP packets you can receive per source address as defined in a microsecond (μs) threshold. So for instance, in this example, we will define that you should not receive more than 10 ICMP packets per 3,000 microseconds or 3 milliseconds across any hosts protected by the Screen.

```
{primary:node0}[edit security screen]
root@SRX550-Node0# ...-Screen icmp ip-sweep threshold 3000

{primary:node0}[edit security screen]
root@SRX550-Node0# show
ids-option Internet-Screen {
    icmp {
        ip-sweep threshold 3000;
    }
}
```

ICMP Large Packet Screen

Under normal circumstances, ICMP packets should usually be quite small, with the exception of trying to troubleshoot certain link-size-related issues or determining MTU with ICMP. The problem with large ICMP packets is that they can be used for DoS purposes, but they can also be used for application tunneling. Unless there is a specific need to permit large ICMP packets, they should probably be denied. The ICMP Large

Packet Screen blocks ICMP packets larger than 1,024 bytes. This value isn't configurable today, so you can also use stateless firewall filters if you want more granularity here.

Screen Type: Per Packet

Screen Processing Location: NPU for high-end SRX, Forwarding Engine branch SRX

Configuring the ICMP Large Packet Screen. The ICMP Large Packet Screen is a simple Screen that is only enabled or disabled. As discussed, no threshold or packet-size-based configurations are required.

```
{primary:node0}[edit security screen]
root@SRX550-Node0# set ids-option Internet-Screen icmp large

{primary:node0}[edit security screen]
root@SRX550-Node0# show
ids-option Internet-Screen {
    icmp {
        large;
    }
}
```

ICMP Ping of Death Screen

The ICMP Ping of Death attack is an old yet very powerful attack from the mid-1990s that leveraged both fragmentation and a maximum packet size of 65,536 bytes, which is permitted by IP. By sending such packets, it triggered all sorts of vulnerabilities in well-known OSs. This bug has long since been fixed in modern OSs, but such behavior is very suspicious and should be blocked from modern networks. Note that if the Block IP Fragment Screen is enabled, it will supersede this Screen.

Screen Type: Per Reassembled Packet

Screen Processing Location: SPU for high-end SRX, Forwarding Engine branch SRX

For more information, see the Wikipedia entry on Ping of Death (*http://bit.ly/120VZJo*).

Configuring the ICMP Ping of Death Screen. To configure the ICMP Ping of Death Screen, you just need to enable the Screen for the zone you would like to enforce.

```
{primary:node0}[edit security screen]
root@SRX550-Node0# set ids-option Internet-Screen icmp ping-death

{primary:node0}[edit security screen]
root@SRX550-Node0# show
ids-option Internet-Screen {
```

```
        icmp {
            ping-death;
        }
    }
```

DoS Attacks with UDP

UDP is a connectionless transport protocol used for lightweight networking functions such as DNS, NTP, and multicast, as well as real-time traffic like VoIP and video. Although the attack surface with UDP is much smaller than IP, ICMP, and TCP, there are still DoS attacks that are possible with this protocol, and you can use it for port scanning. In this brief section, we examine how the UDP Flood and UDP Sweep Screens function and how they are implemented.

UDP Flood Screen

Much like the ICMP Flood Screen, the UDP Flood Screen is used to detect when too many UDP packets are being sent to a destination in the configured zone. A flood of UDP packets can easily overwhelm a destination, and because UDP packets aren't connection oriented like TCP, they can be spoofed and flooded without the need to fully establish a session.

Screen Type: Per Packet, Threshold

Screen Processing Location: NPU for high-end SRX, Forwarding Engine branch SRX

Configuring the UDP Flood Screen. The UDP Flood Screen only has one parameter, which is to define the threshold at which packets should be dropped. Note that this is the destination threshold, because the source can be trivially spoofed. This limit is tracked on a host-by-host basis for each zone to which the Screen is applied. In this example, we set the threshold to be 1000 UDP packets per second to a destination.

```
{primary:node0}[edit security screen]
root@SRX550-Node0# set ids-option Internet-Screen udp flood threshold 1000

{primary:node0}[edit security screen]
root@SRX550-Node0# show
ids-option Internet-Screen {
    udp {
        flood threshold 1000;
    }
}
```

UDP Sweep Screen

Similar to the IP sweep protection, the UDP Sweep Screen is useful for identifying scan attempts leveraging UDP to identify if the end systems in a host are up and what UDP services they might be listening on.

Screen Type: Per Packet, Threshold

Screen Processing Location: CP/SPU for high-end SRX, Forwarding Engine branch SRX

Configuring the UDP Sweep Screen. To configure the UDP Sweep Screen, you simply need to define the time in microseconds per 10 UDP packets. In this example, we specify the threshold of 1,000 microseconds (e.g., 1 ms per 10 packets)

```
{primary:node0}[edit security screen]
root@SRX550-Node0# set ids-option Internet-Screen udp udp-sweep threshold 1000

{primary:node0}[edit security screen]
root@SRX550-Node0# show
ids-option Internet-Screen {
    udp {
        udp-sweep threshold 1000;
    }
}
```

DoS Attacks with TCP

IP, ICMP, and UDP are all potential DoS vectors, but TCP is the Level 4 protocol that most applications run on today, and thus is likely to be what most attackers will try to exploit. Being connection oriented, supporting various options, and with odd behaviors buried deep within the RFCs, it's no wonder that TCP is a popular attack vector. New research about attacks (mostly academic in nature) continues to surface even now. In this section, we cover the various Screens that the SRX supports for protection against TCP-based threats. We follow this section with an examination of some flow-based options that also are pertinent to TCP and flow processing on the SRX.

FIN-No-ACK Screen

Typically, when a FIN is sent to signal the end of the connection, there should be an ACK flag set to acknowledge the receipt of the previous packet. Some scanning tools use this technique to try to enumerate what hosts might be listening depending on the response. Because this is an invalid option, it should typically be dropped.

Screen Type: Per Packet

Screen Processing Location: NPU for high-end SRX, Forwarding Engine branch SRX

Configuring the FIN-No-ACK Screen. Configuring the TCP FIN-No-ACK Screen is straightforward. It is either enabled or disabled per Screen profile as shown here.

```
{primary:node0}[edit security screen]
root@SRX550-Node0# set ids-option Internet-Screen tcp fin-no-ack
```

```
{primary:node0}[edit security screen]
root@SRX550-Node0# show
ids-option Internet-Screen {
    tcp {
        fin-no-ack;
    }
}
```

LAND Attack Screen

The LAND attack is a well-known attack that impacted several old OSs in the 1990s. It was done by setting the same IP address as the source and destination and using a TCP packet with a SYN. This caused an overflow that would crash the system. Of course, a packet should never be sent from or to the same IP address on a network segment, so these types of packets should be considered malicious in nature.

Screen Type: Per Packet

Screen Processing Location: NPU for high-end SRX, Forwarding Engine branch SRX

Configuring the LAND Attack Screen. The LAND Attack Screen is quite simple to configure as it is a per-packet Screen with no configurable options other than being enabled or disabled.

```
{primary:node0}[edit security screen]
root@SRX550-Node0# set ids-option Internet-Screen tcp land

{primary:node0}[edit security screen]
root@SRX550-Node0# show
ids-option Internet-Screen {
    tcp {
        land;
    }
}
```

TCP Port Scan Screen

The TCP Port Scan Screen is used to detect port scans across a particular host. It differs from the TCP Sweep Screen, which identifies packets being sent across hosts (horizontal scan) versus across ports on a single host to identify what services are available (vertical scan). Typically, they should both be leveraged together to protect against recon attacks.

Screen Type: Per Packet, Threshold

Screen Processing Location: CP/SPU for high-end SRX, Forwarding Engine branch SRX

Configuring the TCP Port Scan Screen. The TCP Port Scan Screen only has one parameter to configure, which is what the threshold in microseconds should be between a count of 10 scan packets before you consider the packets to be in violation. For instance, in this example we configure a threshold of 5,000 microseconds (5 milliseconds) in which 10 SYN scan packets can be sent to a host before we would consider additional SYN packets to be in violation of this Screen.

```
{primary:node0}[edit security screen]
root@SRX550-Node0# set ids-option Internet-Screen tcp port-scan threshold 1000

{primary:node0}[edit security screen]
root@SRX550-Node0# show
ids-option Internet-Screen {
    tcp {
        port-scan threshold 1000;
    }
}
```

SYN-ACK-ACK Proxy Screen

The SRX can act as a proxy for authentication sessions such as those for transparent authentication of users with Telnet/FTP/HTTP/HTTPS and possibly others in the future. Because we respond on behalf of the server to authenticate the user (acting as a TCP Proxy), there is a vulnerability that could exist if an attacker opened a large number of open sessions without completing them, just as would be the case with normal end systems. The SYN-ACK-ACK Proxy Screen is used to protect the SRX against such attacks by limiting the number of unauthenticated connections that can be opened and not completed.

Screen Type: Per Connection, Threshold

Screen Processing Location: CP/SPU for high-end SRX, Forwarding Engine branch SRX

Configuring the SYN-ACK-ACK-Proxy Screen. To configure the SYN-ACK-ACK Proxy Screen, you need only define the threshold of how many half-open sessions can be opened by a source host at a time. In this example, we'll configure a limit of five to limit a source host to only be able to have five half-open sessions at a time.

```
{primary:node0}[edit security screen]
root@SRX550-Node0# set ids-option Internet-Screen tcp syn-ack-ack-proxy thresh-
old 100

{primary:node0}[edit security screen]
root@SRX550-Node0# show
ids-option Internet-Screen {
    tcp {
        syn-ack-ack-proxy threshold 5;
    }
}
```

SYN-FIN Screen

TCP packets can only have certain TCP flag combinations to be considered valid. Having both the SYN and FIN flags set in the same TCP header is considered invalid because it would signal both the beginning and end of a connection. There is no legitimate use for this, and if you see this combination it is likely malicious and should be dropped.

Screen Type: Per Packet

Screen Processing Location: NPU for high-end SRX, Forwarding Engine branch SRX

Configuring the SYN-FIN Screen. The SYN-FIN Screen is very simple to configure, as it is either enabled or disabled per Screen. We enable it in this example.

```
{primary:node0}[edit security screen]
root@SRX550-Node0# set ids-option Internet-Screen tcp syn-fin

{primary:node0}[edit security screen]
root@SRX550-Node0# show
ids-option Internet-Screen {
    tcp {
        syn-fin;
    }
}
```

SYN flood/spoofing attacks

SYN flood attack protection is perhaps the most advanced set Screen protection in the SRX arsenal. There are numerous examples of SYN attack tools like juno.c (no relation to Junos), and this attack is still perpetuated today because it is very potent, particularly on platforms that don't have hardware-based protections or aren't configured properly. A SYN attack is very simple, yet defending against it is much more complex. As part of this Screen there are a few different components that we examine:

- The SYN flood rate limiting
- Alarm thresholds
- Attack thresholds
- Spoof protection (SYN Cookie / SYN Proxy)

SYN flood rate limiting. Simple SYN rate limiting can be accomplished by configuring the source and destination SYN flood limits in the SYN Flood Screen. This works just like the UDP/ICMP Flood Screens, which function by rate limiting the number of SYN packets per second on both a source IP and a destination IP basis. This helps protect the platform from a massive SYN flood by dropping the SYNs early in the data path. So why do we need anything else? The challenge is that if we merely rate limit the Screens, we could also drop legitimate traffic as well. Still, we should set a rate limit for the maximum number of SYN packets for a source or destination that we want to process, to help protect the platform.

SYN Flood:

Screen Type: Per Packet

Screen Processing Location: NPU for high-end SRX, Forwarding Engine branch SRX

Configuring SYN Flood Rate Limiting. For this example, we set a rate limit of 100 source SYNs per second that a host can send and 1,000 that a destination can receive. Remember that the source IP address of the SYNs can be spoofed, but TCP has a mechanism to help protect us against this, which we explore next.

```
{primary:node0}[edit security screen]
root@SRX550-Node0#  set  ids-option  Internet-Screen  tcp  syn-flood  source-
threshold 100 destination-threshold 1000

{primary:node0}[edit security screen]
root@SRX550-Node0# show
ids-option Internet-Screen {
    tcp {
        syn-flood {
            source-threshold 100;
            destination-threshold 1000;
        }
    }
}
```

SYN Spoofing Protection Modes. As we indicated, the SRX has two SYN spoofing capabilities that allow us to validate that the SYN packets aren't spoofed. This is different from UDP/IP/ICMP, which is why we do not provide a source threshold, as this could be trivially spoofed. With TCP, we have the option to use SYN Cookies and SYN Proxy to protect end systems and the SRX itself from spoofing attacks.

SYN Cookies (see Figure 11-5) work by responding to a client's initial SYN with a SYN/ACK on behalf of the server. Instead of just setting a standard sequence number, the SRX will encode a sequence number based on a hash of the connection information tuple, plus a pseudorandom "magic" number known only to the SRX platform. At this point, the SRX won't record any state of the connection, in case the SYN is spoofed. Instead, it will send the SYN/ACK back toward the client. If it was spoofed, the client will either drop the SYN or send a reset, but won't process the packet. If the client is real, it will respond with its ACK using the sequence number provided by the server. If the sequence number doesn't match what is expected, then the SRX will not process the connection. Essentially, this ensures that the client is real and not spoofed (assuming that the attacker isn't in the same path) so that a host can't do a massive spoofed SYN flood, and at the same time we can validate that the client is real. After the client has completed the three-way handshake, then the SRX will open the connection to the destination server. Of course, because the SRX uses a custom sequence number, it needs to rewrite the sequence numbers bidirectionally on the fly so that this operation is transparent to both the client and the server.

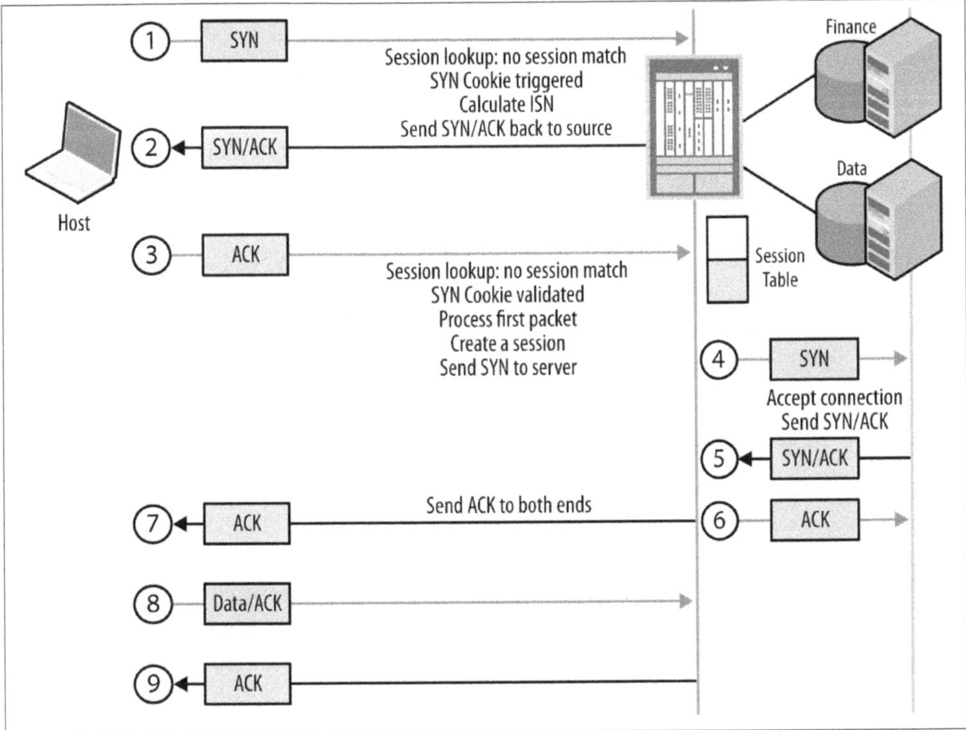

Figure 11-5. SYN Cookie

As for SYN Proxy, this feature also responds to the client's SYN with a SYN/ACK and waits for the client to complete the handshake before establishing the TCP connection with the server. It will not start the connection until the handshake has completed.

The main difference between these two techniques is that SYN Cookie leverages the calculated sequence number in its SYN/ACK and doesn't record any state until the three-way handshake is completed, whereas the SYN Proxy will not use a special TCP sequence number and will hold the state for the initial TCP timeout. Unless you have some special reason not to use SYN Cookie, it is recommended that you use it instead of SYN Proxy because it is lighter weight in the case of an attack.

There are three components of SYN Cookie/SYN Proxy that you should be aware of: the alarm threshold, the attack threshold, and the timeout. It functions as follows:

1. While the rate of incoming SYN packets for the Screen is below the alarm threshold, no action will be taken. Once it goes above the alarm threshold, a log will be generated indicating that the threshold has been reached, but no action will be taken.
2. When the SYNs go over the attack threshold, the SRX will go from normal TCP processing to implementing either SYN Cookie or SYN Proxy based on your configuration.
3. The SYN Cookie/SYN Proxy application will continue until the SYN rate has fallen below the attack threshold plus the timeout that you have defined.
4. If at any time the SYN packets go above the SYN source or destination flood threshold (tracked per host), the system will drop those packets. In a way this operates independently.
5. Optionally, in Junos 12.1 there is a whitelist object for SYN Flood Screen that can exempt hosts from SYN flood processing if you have certain needs for an individual server.

SYN Cookie/Proxy:

Screen Type: Per Packet

Screen Processing Location: CP/SPU for high-end SRX, Forwarding Engine branch SRX

Configuring SYN Cookie/Proxy Protection. In addition to the protection that you configured for SYN floods in the previous example, add SYN Cookie protection to your Screen with an alarm threshold of 1,000 SYNs per second, attack threshold of 1,500 SYNs per second, and a timeout of 30 seconds after the attack has subsided.

```
{primary:node0}[edit security screen]
root@SRX550-Node0# set ids-option Internet-Screen tcp syn-flood alarm-threshold
1000

{primary:node0}[edit security screen]
root@SRX550-Node0#  set  ids-option  Internet-Screen  tcp  syn-flood  attack-
threshold 1500

{primary:node0}[edit security screen]
root@SRX550-Node0# set ids-option Internet-Screen tcp syn-flood timeout 30

{primary:node0}[edit security screen]
root@SRX550-Node0# top

{primary:node0}[edit]
root@SRX550-Node0# set security flow syn-flood-protection-mode syn-cookie

{primary:node0}[edit]
root@SRX550-Node0# show security screen
```

```
ids-option Internet-Screen {
    tcp {
        syn-flood {
            alarm-threshold 1000;
            attack-threshold 1500;
            source-threshold 100;
            destination-threshold 1000;
            timeout 30;
        }
    }
}

{primary:node0}[edit]
root@SRX550-Node0# show security flow
syn-flood-protection-mode syn-cookie;
```

SYN-Frag Screen

Another anomalous type of behavior with TCP is to fragment the packets so small that the TCP header can't be fully viewed. In particular, this technique can be leveraged with SYN packets because it will cause the system to hold resources waiting for the other fragment, along with possibly preparing to set up the new connection. This can be leveraged to attack a firewall's resources along with those of an end system. This behavior is highly suspicious and shouldn't be seen legitimately in networks, so it should be blocked.

Screen Type: Per Packet

Screen Processing Location: NPU for high-end SRX, Forwarding Engine branch SRX

Configuring the SYN-Frag Screen. To configure the SYN-Frag Screen, it need only be enabled on the Screen profile. Remember that if you already block IP fragments with the Block IP Fragment Screen, this will supersede this Screen.

```
{primary:node0}[edit security screen]
root@SRX550-Node0# set ids-option Internet-Screen tcp syn-frag

{primary:node0}[edit security screen]
root@SRX550-Node0# show
ids-option Internet-Screen {
    tcp {
        syn-frag;
    }
}
```

TCP No Flags Screen

According to RFC 791, all TCP packets must have some flags set, as a TCP packet without flags set is invalid. Such packets should never be seen with legitimate traffic and likely signify that there is some malicious activity occurring, such as network scanning. Such packets should always be dropped.

Screen Type: Per Packet

Screen Processing Location: NPU for high-end SRX, Forwarding Engine branch SRX

Configuring the TCP No Flags Screen. Configuring the TCP No Flags Screen is quite simple as it is either on or off; there are no thresholds or other values that need to be configured.

```
{primary:node0}[edit security screen]
root@SRX550-Node0# set ids-option Internet-Screen tcp tcp-no-flag

{primary:node0}[edit security screen]
root@SRX550-Node0# show
ids-option Internet-Screen {
    tcp {
        tcp-no-flag;
    }
}
```

TCP Sweep Screen

Similar to the UDP and ICMP Sweep Screens, the TCP Sweep Screen is used to detect sweeps across different hosts on a network known as a horizontal scan (rather than a port scan, which is a vertical scan.) This behavior usually indicates a network reconnaissance scan being used to map your network, so typically this behavior should be blocked by the Screen to prevent an attacker from identifying important characteristics of your network.

Screen Type: Per Packet, Threshold

Screen Processing Location: CP/SPU for high-end SRX, Forwarding Engine branch SRX

Configuring the TCP Sweep Screen. For the TCP Sweep Screen, you need only configure the threshold of how many scan packets must be received before triggering the Screen. The threshold is how many microseconds to wait between seeing 10 scan packets. The lower the threshold, the faster this would kick in. In this example, we use 2,000 microseconds as our threshold, or 2 milliseconds.

```
{primary:node0}[edit security screen]
root@SRX550-Node0# set ids-option Internet-Screen tcp tcp-sweep threshold 2000

{primary:node0}[edit security screen]
root@SRX550-Node0# show
ids-option Internet-Screen {
    tcp {
        tcp-sweep threshold 2000;
```

```
    }
}
```

WinNuke Screen

WinNuke is a legacy Windows attack from the 1990s. With a single packet, this caused a Windows machine to blue screen. The TCP packet was sent to NetBIOS port 139 with the Urgent flag set, which resulted in the system instability. Although this attack is unlikely to impact modern OSs, it might still be worth enabling as it likely signifies malicious activity.

Screen Type: Per Packet

Screen Processing Location: NPU for high-end SRX, Forwarding Engine branch SRX

More information about WinNuke is available at Wikipedia's WinNuke entry (*http://bit.ly/11qyqut*).

Configuring the WinNuke Screen. The WinNuke Screen is simple to configure, as it is either on or off. You cannot configure the ports or flags for this Screen, nor their thresholds.

```
{primary:node0}[edit security screen]
root@SRX550-Node0# set ids-option Internet-Screen tcp winnuke

{primary:node0}[edit security screen]
root@SRX550-Node0# show
ids-option Internet-Screen {
    tcp {
        winnuke;
    }
}
```

Session Limit Screens

There are two session limit Screens at the time of writing this book: the Source-IP Session Limit and the Destination-IP Session Limit. Session limit Screens are important to consider deploying; without them, an attack could potentially create a DoS attack by consuming a large number of sessions so that the session table on the FW or on the end host is consumed, even if they are not sending a high volume of traffic. Such attacks have been seen with Slowloris and TCP SockStress. Although they are slightly different in nature, they both seek to consume sessions on the system by holding open connections.

For more information on the Slowloris attack, see Wikipedia's Slowloris entry (*http://bit.ly/ZAOT2x*).

For more information on TCP SockStress, an excellent write-up can be found at Wikipedia's SockStress entry (*http://bit.ly/Y2yRMF*).

In other cases, misconfigured or compromised devices can also result in massive session consumption. All of these vectors could be mitigated by Session Limit Screens. Although they might not be the ultimate solution, they are very effective with using other Screens and settings to limit the impact of such session attacks.

Source IP Session Limit Screen

Limiting the number of sessions an individual source IP address can establish is a critically important control to limit different DoS attacks, particularly those that are not individual spoofed packets (which can be better handled with other components). To effectively configure this Screen, it is ideal to have a baseline of how many sessions you would expect an individual IP address to legitimately have. Because we can configure Screens with different profiles on a zone-by-zone basis, it is ideal to identify these limits based on the source of the traffic. For instance, an external resource accessing the DMZ web server likely has a different number of sessions than an internal user going out to the Internet.

There isn't any perfect way to define how many sessions an individual source should have, but an easy way is to enable this Screen with the Alarm Without Drop Screen and start with a low number and go up until you reach a level you think is legitimate and doesn't fire on normal activity—or you can start high and go lower. You can also count sessions in the flow table to get an idea of how many sessions per host. For instance, you could use `show security flow session source-prefix 192.168.2.50/32 summary` to get a count per host or per subnet. Of course, not all hosts are going to be equal, but it gives you a place to start.

When dealing with Screens on the Internet, you should also consider the fact that some hosts might be behind NAT devices, so be sure to give yourself a bit of extra room for this Screen.

Screen Type: Per Session

Screen Processing Location: CP/SPU for high-end SRX, Forwarding Engine branch SRX

Configuring the Source IP Session Limit Screen. Once you've identified the threshold that you want to configure, the Source IP Session Limit Screen is quite easy to implement: you merely define the value. In this example, we set a limit of 50 sessions per source IP address.

```
{primary:node0}[edit security screen]
root@SRX550-Node0# set ids-option Internet-Screen limit-session source-ip-based
50

{primary:node0}[edit security screen]
root@SRX550-Node0# show
ids-option Internet-Screen {
    limit-session {
        source-ip-based 50;
    }
}
```

Destination IP Session Limit Screen

The opposite of the Source IP Session Limit Screen is the Destination IP Session Limit Screen. Although not quite as powerful as the Source IP Session Limit Screen at limiting DoS attacks, this Screen is still effective, especially at protecting DMZ resources. For instance, you can use this Screen at the Internet-facing zone to limit how many sessions can go to your DMZ servers to prevent them from being overwhelmed by a session flood. Of course, this Screen should ideally be used in conjunction with the Source IP Session Limit Screen because it could result in a DoS for legitimate users if a source or group of sources can hit the destination limit. Additionally, this can be used to limit how many sessions internal users can access for individual external resources. This can be good to try to detect certain anomalous activity. Again, this Screen is best used in conjunction with the Source IP Limit Screen.

Screen Type: Per Session

Screen Processing Location: CP/SPU for high-end SRX, Forwarding Engine branch SRX

Configuring the Destination IP Session Limit Screen. The configuration for the Destination IP Session Limit Screen is identical to the configuration of the Source IP address. The same methods can be used to establish baselines for the Screen thresholds in your environment. For this example, we assume that we are protecting inbound sessions on a DMZ server farm that can handle up to 10,000 sessions per host.

```
{primary:node0}[edit security screen]
root@SRX550-Node0# set ids-option Internet-Screen limit-session destination-ip-
based 10000

{primary:node0}[edit security screen]
root@SRX550-Node0# show
ids-option Internet-Screen {
    limit-session {
        destination-ip-based 10000;
    }
}
```

SRX Flow Options

The flow options on the SRX are often overlooked by administrators when setting up the SRX. Although they are a slightly more advanced topic, it is really important to understand them, particularly because their configuration can impact the function of the firewall. Juniper does try to set the default values to be as secure as possible, but it can cause issues in some environments, so it's good to review these different options to ensure that they meet the needs of your network.

In this section, we do not cover all of the flow options, but instead cover those that are most pertinent to Screens, which include the Aging and TCP-Session Options. There are some ancillary flow options outside the scope of this chapter, including TCP MSS, IP Reassembly, and a few others, but the Aging and TCP-Session Screens can impact DoS attacks, which is the focus of this chapter.

Unless otherwise specified, flow options are applied globally to the platform.

Aggressive session aging

A very commonly overlooked feature to prevent both intentional DoS attacks and outages caused by some other consumption of the session table is aggressive session aging. Essentially, this feature allows you to set a low and high threshold (watermark) for the platform session table consumption before it kicks into high gear and starts aggressively aging old idle sessions. In many deployments, due to complex application needs, administrators change the default timeouts of such applications from the system-defined defaults (30 minutes for TCP, 60 seconds for UDP and ICMP; IP protocols vary) to something much higher. For TCP, if the session is closed gracefully, we will end it immediately. For other protocols like UDP, IP, and ICMP, we can only close them using ALGs (e.g., for DNS); otherwise they will remain open until the session goes idle for the prescribed timeout. Under normal circumstances you might never approach the limits of your session table for your given platform—but this isn't always the case, especially in a DoS attack or other misconfiguration.

Aggressive session aging is triggered when the percentage consumption of the session table goes above the high watermark. Then, instead of following the default idle timeout, the platform uses the new early-ageout timeout that is set for the flow. Of course, this only applies for sessions that are idle, not for sessions that are actively transmitting. You can think of it as an override of the default idle timeout when the high watermark condition is met. The aggressive session aging process will complete once the number of sessions goes below the low watermark you set. For instance, let's say your platform supports 1 million firewall sessions and you set the high watermark as 80 percent and the low watermark as 60 percent, with an early ageout of three seconds. When the number of sessions goes above 800,000, the early ageout will kick in for any sessions that are idle for more than three seconds. This will continue until the session table dips below 600,000 sessions, when the normal session idle timeouts will resume (until you go back above 80 percent again).

At this point, you should also recognize the importance of leveraging the IP Session Limit Screens that we discussed in the last section, as they complement this feature very nicely by preventing an individual from consuming too many sessions.

Aggressive session aging has been in the branch platforms since its inception in Junos 9.5, but was only recently added to the high-end SRX in Junos 11.4 and beyond.

Configuring the aggressive session ageout flow option. To configure aggressive session aging, you merely need to determine your low and high watermarks as defined by percentage, and the early ageout you would like to apply to sessions during the aggressive session aging process. Because the values are applied as a percentage, you don't need to concern yourself with knowing the exact session capacities of your platform, although you can always determine it in the datasheets. It's also important to note that with new code optimizations and the shift to 64-bit or additional memory, these limits might be further increased, so rather than post them here, you should view the latest datasheets to make sure you have an accurate understanding. You can also determine the max session count and consumption for your platform with the `show security monitoring fpc <x>` command if you have an SRX handy. Here we show this value for both an SRX550 and an SRX3600.

```
root@SRX550-Node0> show security monitoring fpc 0
node0:
--------------------------------------------------------------------------
FPC 0
  PIC 0
    CPU utilization      :    7 %
    Memory utilization   :   67 %
    Current flow session :    23785 ←Current Session Consumption
    Max flow session     : 409600   ←Maximum Sessions (with IPv6 enabled)
Session Creation Per Second (for last 96 seconds on average):    0

root@srx3600n0> show security monitoring fpc 3
FPC 3
  PIC 0
    CPU utilization      :    5 %
    Memory utilization   :   70 %
    Current flow session : 127322    ←Current Utilizaiton for this SPU
    Max flow session     : 131072
```

```
    Current CP session   : 1477271 ←Currrent Utilization for this platform
    Max CP session       : 2359296 <-Max # of sessions per platform
Session Creation Per Second (for last 96 seconds on average): 6025
```

For this example, we configure the aggressive session aging Screen to activate at 80 percent and set an early ageout of three seconds. The session aging will terminate when the session utilization falls below 60 percent.

```
{primary:node0}[edit security flow]
root@SRX550-Node0# set aging high-watermark 80 low-watermark 60 early-ageout 3

{primary:node0}[edit security flow]
root@SRX550-Node0# show
aging {
    early-ageout 3;
    low-watermark 60;
    high-watermark 80;
}
```

TCP sequence checks

By default, the SRX enforces checks to ensure that packets arriving on the SRX for a session fall within the TCP window of the session. This prevents hijacking attacks against existing sessions by external attackers. The SRX monitors the TCP window as it progresses during the communication and ensures that TCP packets that arrive on the firewall fall within the window; otherwise they are dropped.

A very detailed discussion of TCP and especially TCP windowing is available in *TCP/IP* by Craig Hunt (O'Reilly).

TCP sequence checks should normally be on for security purposes. Sometimes if the traffic is asymmetric (meaning that the SRX can only see one side of the flow), the TCP sequence check must be disabled.

Configuring TCP sequence checks. TCP sequence checks are enabled by default at the global platform level, or also on an FW rule-by-rule basis. If they are configured on a rule-by-rule basis, you must disable the TCP sequence check globally and then enable it per FW rule. Because they are enabled by default, the only global configuration option is to disable them (see Examples 11-1 and 11-2).

Example 11-1. Disabling TCP sequence checks globally

```
{primary:node0}[edit security flow]
root@SRX550-Node0# set tcp-session no-sequence-check

{primary:node0}[edit security flow]
```

```
root@SRX550-Node0# show
tcp-session {
    no-sequence-check;
}
```

Example 11-2. Configuring TCP sequence checks per FW rule

```
{primary:node0}[edit security flow]
root@SRX550-Node0# set tcp-session no-sequence-check

{primary:node0}[edit security flow]
root@SRX550-Node0# show
tcp-session {
    no-sequence-check;
}

root@SRX550-Node0# set security policies from-zone trust to-zone untrust policy 1
match source-address any destination-address any application any

{primary:node0}[edit]
root@SRX550-Node0# set security policies from-zone trust to-zone untrust policy 1
then permit tcp-options sequence-check-required

{primary:node0}[edit]
root@SRX550-Node0# set security policies from-zone trust to-zone untrust policy 1
then log session-close


{primary:node0}[edit]
root@SRX550-Node0# show security policies
from-zone trust to-zone untrust {
    policy 1 {
        match {
            source-address any;
            destination-address any;
            application any;
        }
        then {
            permit {
                tcp-options {
                    sequence-check-required;
                }
            }
            log {
                session-close;
            }
        }
    }
}
```

In this example, we disabled the TCP sequence check globally and enabled the TCP sequence check per FW rule.

Configuring TCP sequence checks for RST packets

To prevent an attacker from sending a TCP reset flood with the desire to close sessions, you can also enforce the checking of the TCP Reset packets to ensure that they are in sequence as well.

```
{primary:node0}[edit security flow]
root@SRX550-Node0# set tcp-session rst-sequence-check

{primary:node0}[edit security flow]
root@SRX550-Node0# show
tcp-session {
    rst-sequence-check;
}
```

TCP SYN checks

By default, the SRX will check any new inbound TCP session to ensure that it is statefully established with a SYN first by the client. In some cases, you might need to disable the SYN checking because of asymmetric traffic flows. Asymmetric traffic through a firewall greatly reduces its effectiveness (particularly with Layer 7 security) and is not advisable. If you must disable SYN checks, that can either be done globally or enabled on a per FW rule basis as shown here.

```
{primary:node0}[edit security flow]
root@SRX550-Node0# set tcp-session no-syn-check

{primary:node0}[edit security flow]
root@SRX550-Node0# show
tcp-session {
    no-syn-check;
}

root@SRX550-Node0# set security policies from-zone trust to-zone untrust policy
1 match source-address any destination-address any application any

{primary:node0}[edit]
root@SRX550-Node0# set security policies from-zone trust to-zone untrust policy
1 then permit tcp-options syn-check-required

{primary:node0}[edit]
root@SRX550-Node0# set security policies from-zone trust to-zone untrust policy
1 then log session-close


{primary:node0}[edit]
root@SRX550-Node0# show security policies
from-zone trust to-zone untrust {
    policy 1 {
        match {
            source-address any;
            destination-address any;
```

```
                application any;
            }
            then {
                permit {
                    tcp-options {
                        syn-check-required;
                    }
                }
                log {
                    session-close;
                }
            }
        }
    }
```

Strict SYN checks. By default, the SYN check only ensures that the first packet sent from client to server is a SYN packet. However, you can ensure that the handshake is a true three-way handshake with the client sending the SYN, the server responding with the SYN/ACK, and then the client responding with an ACK using the strict SYN check. This can be used to ensure that no other anomalous negotiation takes place, including the TCP split handshake, where the client sends a SYN, followed by the server sending a SYN back to the client, the client sending the SYN/ACK, and the server sending the SYN. This is part of the TCP RFC 791 that most people don't know. Although it isn't an issue for the SRX firewall (we don't mistake which direction the flow is going and who is the client and server), it can be for other firewalls, and especially for Layer 7 devices that might get this confused (UTM, IPS, load balancers, etc.). Again, this is not a problem for Juniper equipment, but it usually a good idea to enable it.

Configuring the strict SYN check.

```
{primary:node0}[edit security flow]
root@SRX550-Node0# set tcp-session strict-syn-check

{primary:node0}[edit]
root@SRX550-Node0# show
tcp-session {
    strict-syn-check;
}
```

SYN checks in tunnels

The SRX supports disabling TCP SYN checks for tunneled traffic separate from the global clear-text values. This can be useful when you have asymmetric routing with IPsec tunnels or for IPsec session failover. Although it isn't ideal to disable the SYN checks for tunneled traffic, a tunnel is not quite as unsolicited as normal traffic can be from the Internet, so there is a bit more confidence in the traffic arriving.

```
{primary:node0}[edit security flow]
root@SRX550-Node0# set tcp-session no-syn-check-in-tunnel
```

```
{primary:node0}[edit security flow]
root@SRX550-Node0# show
tcp-session {
    no-syn-check-in-tunnel;
}
```

TCP state timeouts

Besides the standard application timeouts that can be configured on an application-by-application basis, you can also apply a special timeout for TCP sessions in the initial state and time wait states.

The TCP initial timeout is the timeout that is imposed after the SYN has been seen but before the session is fully established. This is to prevent a full TCP session with a default of 30 minutes from being established on the firewall without the client/server fully establishing the session. By default, the value is 20 seconds at the time of writing this book.

This does not apply if SYN checking is disabled, in which case the session will be established immediately.

The TCP wait state timeout is used to keep a session in memory in the "CLOSED" state after it has been terminated by a FIN/RESET. The purpose of this is to ensure that old delayed packets that might be received after the session has been closed can be properly handled and won't end up as part of a new TCP session. You have two options: you can either use the default two-second timeout, or you can instruct the firewall to use the default ageout for that application. We recommend just using the default option unless you have an explicit need to change it.

Configuring the TCP initial session timeout and TCP time wait timeout. In this example, we configure the TCP initial session timeout for a value of 25 seconds, and the TCP time wait timeout will be 3 seconds.

```
{primary:node0}[edit security flow]
root@SRX550-Node0# set tcp-session time-wait-state session-timeout 3

{primary:node0}[edit security flow]
root@SRX550-Node0# set tcp-session tcp-initial-timeout 25

{primary:node0}[edit security flow]
root@SRX550-Node0# show
tcp-session {
    tcp-initial-timeout 25;
    time-wait-state {
        session-timeout 3;
```

```
        }
    }
```

Best Practices

With so many options discussed in this chapter, it is easy to get lost when it comes to what you should actually configure in real deployments. Here's a bit of guidance when looking at deploying Screens and flow options.

1. First, gain an understanding of the firewall and the segments to which it connects. You need to have an understanding of traffic volumes and expected behaviors in the network.
2. Remember that you can always initially deploy Screens with the Alarm Without Drop Setting per Screen Profile. This allows you to test the waters so to speak when it comes to deploying Screens to ensure that your thresholds are properly set, and that some of the packet anomaly signatures are not firing on broken applications.
3. If you do not have an idea of what your thresholds are, you can examine various output commands on the SRX, along with using a sliding scale for the Screen threshold configuration to determine what thresholds you want to set.
4. Don't forget to enable Screens on network segments that you control, not just the Internet segments. You will likely want to use a separate Screen profile for different segments as the acceptable threshold limits and anomaly Screens might be different. Additionally, you might want to enable alarm without drop on internal segments if you don't want the Screens to be enforced, although it is best to turn this off once you have a handle on the configuration.
5. It is a very good idea to set up both flood-based Screens and session limit Screens, particularly on the Internet-facing segments or segments that your organizations don't control. Some of the packet anomalies might be harmless to modern OSs, but the flood-based attacks are perpetual and not only affect the end systems, but can impact the firewalls as well.
6. Just like standard firewall policy rules, you should leverage the concept of least privilege with Screens as well. This means that if it isn't explicitly needed on the network for accepted behavior, it should be denied by Screens.
7. Don't forget to examine the flow options that can be configured to assist in preventing certain DoS attacks and other network outages.
8. Although we didn't cover stateless filters and ingress policers in this chapter, they can also complement Screens, along with a solid firewall policy, IPS, and AppDDoS protection.
9. Finally, if at all possible, you should always leave SYN checking and TCP sequence checking on. Although it might not always be possible due to network architecture,

disabling these features can expose end systems to potential TCP attack vectors. If you must disable them, you might want to consider using per FW rule SYN/SEQ checks to provide some point security.

Troubleshooting and Operation

Operating Screens can be greatly simplified by keeping a few resources in mind. In this section, we examine a few Screen and flow options that will aid in the operation of the features.

Viewing Screen Profile Settings

You can easily view the configuration of a Screen profile from the configuration mode using the `show security screen ids-option <Screen>` command.

```
{primary:node0}
root@SRX100HM> show security screen ids-option Screen
node0:
------------------------------------------------------------------
Screen object status:

Name                                          Value
  ICMP flood threshold                        200
  UDP flood threshold                         1000
  TCP winnuke                                 enabled
  TCP port scan threshold                     1000
  ICMP address sweep threshold                2000
  TCP sweep threshold                         1000
  UDP sweep threshold                         1000
  IP tear drop                                enabled
  TCP SYN flood attack threshold              100
  TCP SYN flood alarm threshold               50
  TCP SYN flood source threshold              100
  TCP SYN flood destination threshold         100
  TCP SYN flood timeout                       30
  IP spoofing                                 enabled
  ICMP ping of death                          enabled
  IP source route option                      enabled
  TCP land attack                             enabled
  TCP SYN fragment                            enabled
  TCP no flag                                 enabled
  IP unknown protocol                         enabled
  IP bad options                              enabled
  IP record route option                      enabled
  IP timestamp option                         enabled
  IP security option                          enabled
  IP loose source route option                enabled
  IP strict source route option               enabled
  IP stream option                            enabled
```

```
ICMP fragmentation                              enabled
ICMP large packet                               enabled
TCP SYN FIN                                     enabled
TCP FIN no ACK                                  enabled
Session source limit threshold                  500
Session destination limit threshold             500
Alarm without drop                              enabled
```

Viewing the Screen Attack Statistics

During operation, you might want to get information on how often the Screens are firing on the platform. You can do this by viewing the output of the `show security screen statistics interface|zone <interface|zone>` command, which is either per interface or per zone.

```
{primary:node0}
root@SRX100HM> show security screen statistics zone untrust
node0:
--------------------------------------------------------------
Screen statistics:

IDS attack type                                 Statistics
  ICMP flood                                    255
  UDP flood                                     10241
  TCP winnuke                                   0
  TCP port scan                                 0
  ICMP address sweep                            73
  TCP sweep                                     0
  UDP sweep                                     0
  IP tear drop                                  0
  TCP SYN flood                                 0
  IP spoofing                                   8991
  ICMP ping of death                            0
  IP source route option                        0
  TCP land attack                               0
  TCP SYN fragment                              0
  TCP no flag                                   431
  IP unknown protocol                           28
  IP bad options                                0
  IP record route option                        0
  IP timestamp option                           0
  IP security option                            0
  IP loose source route option                  0
  IP strict source route option                 0
  IP stream option                              0
  ICMP fragment                                 0
  ICMP large packet                             0
  TCP SYN FIN                                   0
  TCP FIN no ACK                                0
  Source session limit                          5432
  TCP SYN-ACK-ACK proxy                         0
```

```
    IP block fragment                          0
    Destination session limit                  15
```

Viewing Flow Exceptions

In addition to the various Screen stats that you might be interested in viewing, there are numerous options per interface that might be of interest. As you can see next, the output of the interface stats includes not only information about bytes and packets transmitted and QoS information, but also a great deal of very valuable flow exception information. These counters can be indicative of suspicious activity on the network as well.

```
{primary:node0}
root@SRX100HM> show interfaces reth0 extensive
Physical interface: reth0, Enabled, Physical link is Up
  Interface index: 128, SNMP ifIndex: 527, Generation: 157
   Link-level type: Ethernet, MTU: 1514, Speed: 100mbps, BPDU Error: None, MAC-
REWRITE Error: None, Loopback: Disabled, Source filtering: Disabled, Flow con-
trol: Disabled,
  Minimum links needed: 1, Minimum bandwidth needed: 0
  Device flags   : Present Running
  Interface flags: SNMP-Traps Internal: 0x0
  Current address: 00:10:db:ff:20:10, Hardware address: 00:10:db:ff:20:10
  Last flapped   : 2012-08-16 14:19:04 EDT (1w1d 21:07 ago)
  Statistics last cleared: Never
  Traffic statistics:
   Input  bytes  :          13475873486               10512 bps
   Output bytes  :          25926029274                9608 bps
   Input  packets:             22960010                   9 pps
   Output packets:             33791779                   9 pps
  Dropped traffic statistics due to STP State:
   Input  bytes  :                    0
   Output bytes  :                    0
   Input  packets:                    0
   Output packets:                    0
  Input errors:
     Errors: 0, Drops: 0, Framing errors: 0, Runts: 0, Giants: 0, Policed dis-
cards: 0, Resource errors: 0
  Output errors:
     Carrier transitions: 0, Errors: 0, Drops: 0, MTU errors: 0, Resource er-
rors: 0
  Ingress queues: 8 supported, 4 in use
  Queue counters:       Queued packets  Transmitted packets  Dropped packets
    0 best-effort                    0                    0                0
    1 expedited-fo                   0                    0                0
    2 assured-forw                   0                    0                0
    3 network-cont                   0                    0                0
  Egress queues: 8 supported, 4 in use
  Queue counters:       Queued packets  Transmitted packets  Dropped packets
    0 best-effort             33840462             33840462                0
    1 expedited-fo                   0                    0                0
    2 assured-forw                   0                    0                0
```

```
  3 network-cont                 307                   307                  0
Queue number:          Mapped forwarding classes
  0                    best-effort
  1                    expedited-forwarding
  2                    assured-forwarding
  3                    network-control

Logical interface reth0.0 (Index 70) (SNMP ifIndex 531) (Generation 156)
  Flags: SNMP-Traps 0x0 Encapsulation: ENET2
  Statistics        Packets        pps         Bytes          bps
  Bundle:
      Input :      22960010          9   13475873486        10512
      Output:      33791779          9   25902216474         9608
  Link:
    fe-1/0/1.0
      Input :           169          0         24604            0
      Output:             0          0             0            0
    fe-0/0/1.0
      Input :      22959841          9   13475848882        10512
      Output:      33791779          9   25902216474         9608
  Marker Statistics:   Marker Rx   Resp Tx   Unknown Rx   Illegal Rx
    fe-1/0/1.0                 0         0            0            0
    fe-0/0/1.0                 0         0            0            0
  Security: Zone: Untrust
  Allowed host-inbound traffic : ike ping
  Flow Statistics :
  Flow Input statistics :
    Self packets :                     384590
    ICMP packets :                     258667
    VPN packets :                      4221134
    Multicast packets :                0
    Bytes permitted by policy :        11951135993
    Connections established :          26276
  Flow Output statistics:
    Multicast packets :                0
    Bytes permitted by policy :        24882784274
  Flow error statistics (Packets dropped due to):
    Address spoofing:                  0
    Authentication failed:             0
    Incoming NAT errors:               0
    Invalid zone received packet:      0
    Multiple user authentications:     0
    Multiple incoming NAT:             0
    No parent for a gate:              0
    No one interested in self packets: 135
    No minor session:                  0
    No more sessions:                  0
    No NAT gate:                       0
    No route present:                  46566
    No SA for incoming SPI:            2890
    No tunnel found:                   0
    No session for a gate:             0
```

```
      No zone or NULL zone binding      0
      Policy denied:                    37
      Security association not active:   1440
      TCP sequence number out of window: 3
      Syn-attack protection:            0
      User authentication errors:       0
    Protocol inet, MTU: 1500, Generation: 180, Route table: 4
      Flags: Sendbcast-pkt-to-re, Is-Primary
      Input Filters: Inbound-QoS
      Addresses, Flags: Is-Default Is-Preferred Is-Primary
        Destination: 192.168.1.1/24, Local: 192.168.1.1, Broadcast:
192.168.1.1, Generation: 170
```

Sample Deployment

For this sample deployment, we configure two Screen profiles that will be applied on our SRX5800 Internet edge firewalls. The first Screen profile will be called Internet-Screen and will be applied to the Internet zone, and the second Screen profile will be called Internal-Screen and will be applied to the LAN (Dept-A, Dept-B, and Internal-Servers) and DMZ zones. The goal is to ensure that we have a solid Screen profile to protect internal resources from inbound Internet attacks, while also flagging (but not disrupting) any suspicious internal activity for further investigation. The profiles will be set up as follows:

Internet-Screen

- Enforce all actions with packet drops.
- Deny all packet-based anomalies for TCP, UDP, IP, and ICMP, but allow for IP fragments.
- Limit individual source IPs on the Internet to only 100 sessions per host, and only allow each DMZ server to accept 25,000 sessions. There is no policy to allow inbound traffic directly from the Internet to the internal network so this Screen won't impact the internal zone.
- To prevent scanning, ensure that the minimum value is set between IP, TCP, UDP, and TCP port scan sweeps.
- To prevent flooding, only allow each host to send 100 SYNs per second, and receive no more than 1,000 SYNs, 1,000 UDP, and 300 ICMP packets per second.
- Set a timeout of 30 seconds on the SYN attacks, with an alarm threshold of 750 SYNs per second, and when SYN packets hit 2,000 per second initiate SYN Cookies.

Internal-Screens (Dept-A, Dept-B, Internal Servers Zones)

- Log all violations but no packet drops.
- Look for all packet-based anomalies except IP fragmentation.

- Internal sources with more than 300 sessions should be flagged.
- Look for suspicious port scan activity by setting a violation for more than 10 packets per 5,000 microseconds for TCP, UDP, and IP/ICMP.
- Any host that sends more than 200 SYNs per second, 2,000 UDP packets, or 100 ICMP packets should be flagged.

Flow Options

- Ensure strict SYN checks are enabled.
- If the session table goes above 80 percent utilization, initiate an early ageout of two seconds until the platform goes below 65 percent.

Configuration for Screen and Flow Option Sample Deployment

This configuration would look as follows:

```
root@SRX5800> show configuration security screen
ids-option Internet-Screen {
    icmp {
        ip-sweep threshold 1000;
        fragment;
        large;
        flood threshold 300;
        ping-death;
    }
    ip {
        bad-option;
        record-route-option;
        timestamp-option;
        security-option;
        stream-option;
        spoofing;
        source-route-option;
        loose-source-route-option;
        strict-source-route-option;
        unknown-protocol;
        tear-drop;
    }
    tcp {
        syn-fin;
        fin-no-ack;
        tcp-no-flag;
        syn-frag;
        port-scan threshold 1000;
        syn-flood {
            alarm-threshold 750;
            attack-threshold 2000;
            source-threshold 50;
            destination-threshold 1000;
```

```
                timeout 30;
            }
            land;
            winnuke;
            tcp-sweep threshold 1000;
        }
        udp {
            flood threshold 1000;
            udp-sweep threshold 1000;
        }
        limit-session {
            source-ip-based 100;
            destination-ip-based 25000;
        }
    }


    ids-option Internal-Screen {
        alarm-without-drop;
        icmp {
            ip-sweep threshold 5000;
            fragment;
            large;
            flood threshold 100;
            ping-death;
        }
        ip {
            bad-option;
            record-route-option;
            timestamp-option;
            security-option;
            stream-option;
            spoofing;
            source-route-option;
            loose-source-route-option;
            strict-source-route-option;
            unknown-protocol;
            tear-drop;
        }
        tcp {
            syn-fin;
            fin-no-ack;
            tcp-no-flag;
            syn-frag;
            port-scan threshold 5000;
            syn-flood {
                source-threshold 200;
            }
            land;
            winnuke;
            tcp-sweep threshold 5000;
        }
```

```
    udp {
        flood threshold 2000;
        udp-sweep threshold 5000;
    }
    limit-session {
        source-ip-based 300;
    }
}

root@SRX5800> show configuration security flow
syn-flood-protection-mode syn-cookie;
aging {
    early-ageout 2;
    low-watermark 66;
    high-watermark 80;
}
tcp-session {
    strict-syn-check;
}

root@SRX5800> show configuration security zones
security-zone Internet {
    screen Internet-Screen;
    interfaces {
        reth0.0 {
}
security-zone Dept-A {
    screen Internal-Screen;
    interfaces {
        reth1.0 {
}
security-zone Dept-B {
    screen Internal-Screen;
    interfaces {
        reth1.1 {
}
security-zone Internal-Servers {
    screen Internal-Screen;
    interfaces {
        reth1.2 {
}

security-zone DMZ {
    screen Internal-Screen;
    interfaces {
        reth2.0 {
}
```

Summary

The importance of deploying Screens cannot be overstated in modern networks. Most administrators might think that Level 3 and Level 4 attacks are ancient history, but many of them are perpetual and are just as effective today as they were at their inception—there's just better protection against these attacks today. Screens and flow options are the missing piece to this puzzle that is often overlooked in deployments. In this chapter, we not only explored how they function, but also how the attacks they prevent against work, and how they can be leveraged to protect both your end systems and the SRX itself. With this information, you can ensure that you are adequately protected against such attacks so you can focus your efforts on the much more challenging ones such as those at Layer 7.

Study Questions

Questions

1. At what OSI layers do the SRX Screens function?
2. How are Screens applied to the SRX?
3. What option is available to only log the Screen attack detection?
4. What are the two types of Screens that the SRX leverages?
5. What flow option is available to change the idle timeout of sessions when the firewall's session table becomes heavily utilized?
6. What's the difference between SYN checks and strict SYN checks?
7. What are the two methods that the SRX can use to validate that SYN packets are not spoofed?
8. Where can TCP sequence and SYN checks be configured?
9. What type of RPF check does the IP Spoofing Screen use?
10. How does the SRX perform a TCP sequence check?
11. Where are Screens processed in the packet flow? On the ingress side (arriving on the SRX) or on the egress side (leaving the SRX)?
12. If traffic arrives on the Internet zone destined for the DMZ, and you want to apply a Screen to protect the DMZ, would you apply it to the Internet zone or the DMZ?

Answers

1. Layers 3 and 4 of the OSI model.
2. Screens are configured as profiles that can be applied at the zone level on a zone-by-zone basis.

3. The Alarm Without Drop action is available per Screen profile and can be used only to log when an attack is detected with Screens rather than to enforce the blocking.
4. The SRX has both flood- and anomaly-based Screens. The flood Screens leverage a threshold, whereas the anomaly Screens are processed per packet.
5. The aggressive session aging feature can be used to set a new ageout timeout when the high session watermark is surpassed.
6. SYN checks only check that the first packet in the session is a SYN (no other flags) packet, whereas the strict SYN check enforces that the client sends a SYN, followed by the SYN/ACK from the server and the ACK from the client.
7. SYN Cookies and SYN Proxy can be used to validate that the sender is not spoofing the SYN packet by establishing the session on the firewall first before doing so on the end system.
8. TCP SYN and SEQ checks can be configured both at the global level and on a per FW rule basis.
9. The IP Spoofing Screen uses a Loose Reverse Path Forwarding lookup to determine IP spoofing.
10. The SRX checks to ensure that the TCP packet's sequence number is within the current TCP window range of the flow. If it is not, it will drop the packet.
11. Screens are processed on the ingress side when packets arrive, regardless of which side is the client or server.
12. You would place this on the Internet side. If you applied it to the DMZ side, it would only be applied when packets are sent from the DMZ to the Internet.

CHAPTER 12
AppSecure Basics

Digging up any computer networking reference material from the 1990s and early 2000s will surely emphasize that application servers listen on "well-known" ports for communication, including the infamous HTTP on TCP port 80. Although many of these conventions are still honored today, we must recognize several facts that have changed since the earlier days of the Internet. First—and this has always been the truth—no application *must* listen on a particular port or protocol. The only thing that must be true is that the client and server are speaking the same application layer protocol on the expected ports or protocols, and that all transit networking equipment must understand how to forward packets between the client and the server. Over time, web browsers gained popularity and became ubiquitous for virtually any network-capable device. At the same time, server-side technology for HTTP became much more powerful with both open source and commercial tools for not only the web servers themselves, but a plethora of server-side technologies that could bring a dynamic user experience that was once only possible with full client applications. This, coupled with the fact that most computer network administrators allowed only certain ports out of their network (chiefly TCP port 80 for HTTP), gave web technologies even more popularity as communication protocols.

During this time, both nefarious and undesirable parties took notice of the shift in access control and adjusted their applications accordingly. More and more legitimate (although perhaps undesirable) applications shifted to use HTTP as a new transport, or at least communicate over TCP port 80, and other parties that traditionally designed their applications to run over nonstandard ports changed their tune to also leverage TCP port 80, or perhaps other well-known ports that they spoofed to appear as a legitimate application.

For these reasons, simply leveraging a stateful firewall rulebase is not enough to adequately control application access on your network (particularly when dealing with unknown third parties on the Internet). The good news is that in addition to other mechanisms already provided in the SRX, the AppSecure feature set can further assist in not only controlling malicious behavior, but controlling what applications are allowed to communicate over the network itself.

AppSecure Component Overview

Now that we know that traditional Layer 3/Layer 4 stateful firewall policies alone might not be enough to control contemporary application behavior on modern networks, we can explore some proven solutions to empower the administrator to be able to achieve such goals. AppSecure is a suite of components composed of Application Identification at the core, followed by AppTrack, AppFW, AppQoS, AppDDoS, and IPS. There are also the auxiliary components SSL Proxy, User Role Firewall, and UTM. In this chapter, we focus on AI, AppTrack, AppFW, AppQoS, User Role Firewall, and SSL Proxy. IPS and UTM are covered in their own respective chapters, and AppDDoS is outside the scope of this book.

We'll start with a high-level description of what each component does, and then follow that with an in-depth examination of those features in action.

Application Identification

AppSecure is the name of a product suite that was born from Application Identification (AI) technology. This technology is not new at all, and in fact has been a part of Juniper's portfolio of products since the IDP standalone devices in 2007, and has been in the SRX as part of IPS since the first version 9.2. AI technology essentially leverages the same components used in the IPS engine but for a defined purpose, which is to identify applications rather than malicious intrusive attacks. In fact, originally it was part of the IPS engine itself, but was abstracted from the IPS engine in version 10.2 and placed in the flow module so that other components can leverage the results of the AI process. AI can identify applications by several different mechanisms, including signature based, heuristic based, and statically defined regardless of the application port or protocol that is used to transmit the application.

AI is only the beginning of the process chain. The beauty of AppSecure is that the AI information is distributed among other modules in the processing chain, as shown in Figure 12-1. These other components can perform various tasks on the traffic based on the result of the AI process and the configuration of each module. We cover what each module does later in this chapter.

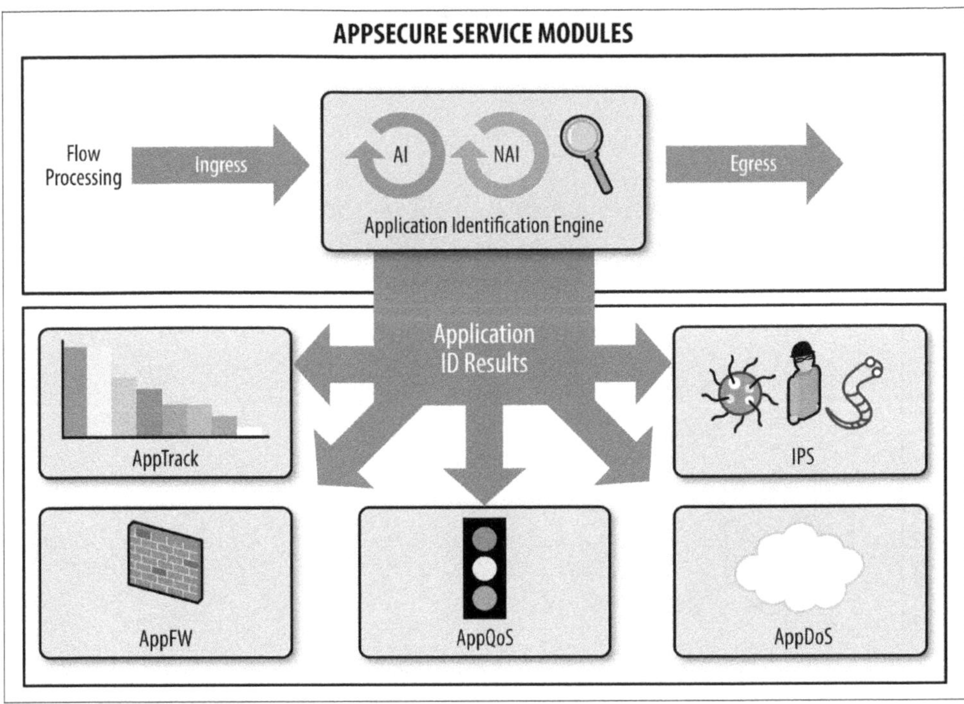

Figure 12-1. AppSecure service models

Application Tracking

AppTrack was the first AppSecure feature, added back in version 10.2. It is essentially a logging and reporting tool that can be used to share information for application visibility. After AI identifies the application, AppTrack not only keeps statistics on the box for application usage, but also it sends log messages via syslog providing application activity update messages (see Figure 12-2). Because these are sent by syslog, they can be consumed by both Juniper products like the STRM and third-party devices.

AppTrack log information is also contained in firewall logs so long as another AI component is enabled like AppFW or AppQoS. Typically, this is best leveraged by itself if you are not running another AppSecure component but want to still collect this information.

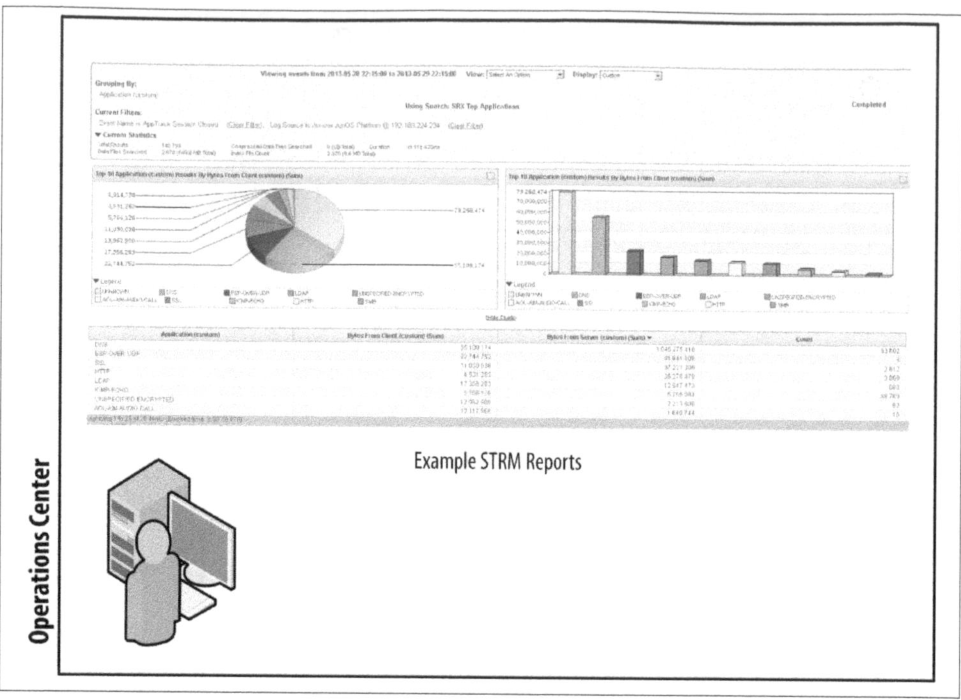

Figure 12-2. Example STRM reports

Application Firewall

Application Firewall (AppFW) refers to the ability to take the results from the AI engine and leverage them to make an informed decision to permit, deny/reject, or redirect the traffic, as shown in Figure 12-3. AppFW sits on top of the existing stateful firewall engine that makes decisions based on the standard seven-tuple (from-/to-zone, source/destination IP address, source/destination port, and protocol). This allows you to still enforce traditional firewall controls on the traffic while layering AppFW to enforce that the application conforms not only to the well-known port information, but to what is actually being transmitted between the client and the server. As we'll see later, AppFW provides an auxiliary rulebase that is tied to each firewall rule for maximum granularity with the ability to leverage the standard match criteria of the firewall rule, plus the application identity. You can permit, deny, and reject applications, along with a special redirect feature for HTTP and HTTPS. The redirect action provides a better user experience; rather than explicitly blocking the application, the user can be redirected to an SRX or externally hosted URL. We explore AppFW in much more detail later.

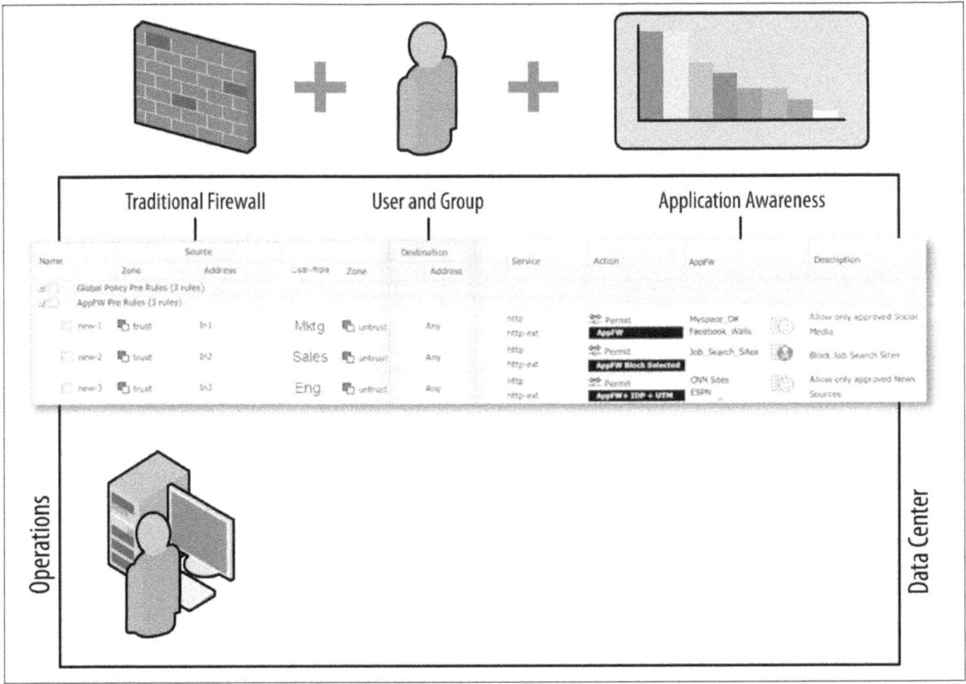

Figure 12-3. AppFW

Application Quality of Service

Sometimes permitting or denying traffic in and of itself is not granular enough for real-world scenarios. For instance, you might have traffic that you don't want to explicitly block, but at the same time, you don't want to give it free reign on your network. Often such examples include applications that impact productivity (e.g., online games) or consume large amounts of bandwidth such as peer-to-peer apps or streaming video. Alternatively, you might also have applications that you want to provide a higher QoS ranking that will prioritize the traffic over other applications.

AppQoS allows you to do this by providing the ability to invoke AppQoS on top of the firewall rulebase (similar to how AppFW is instantiated). AppQoS provides the ability to prioritize, rate limit, DSCP rewrite, set loss priority, and queue traffic, as shown in Figure 12-4. It leverages the underlying Junos QoS engine (and hardware on the high-end SRX) but also provides the granularity of the stateful firewall rulebase (including User Role Firewall and Dynamic Application identified by AppID) to match and enforce QoS at the application layer. We examine this feature in much more depth later in the chapter.

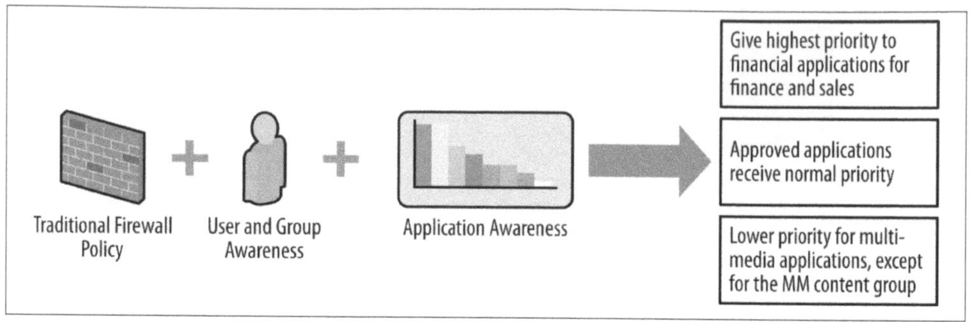

Figure 12-4. AppQoS

User Role Firewalling

Over time we've seen computers develop from mainframes to desktops to laptops to ubiquitous mobile and tablet devices. Because the devices themselves have become so portable, this also means that they are not staying in the same place on computer networks, and may move around a computer network numerous times in a single day. The mobility of computing devices means that leveraging traditional firewall techniques based on source addresses has become much more difficult to effectively enforce. This is particularly true when you must deliver a varying network experience for different users based on their identity rather than their IP address. Enter User Role Firewalling, which provides a foolproof mechanism to authenticate users against a backend Active Directory database, local database, or external identity feed, as shown in Figure 12-5. Once the identity information is determined, it can be used in the security policy to provide differentiated services based on the user's identity rather than strictly on the standard seven-tuple. This even includes the ability to apply differing application firewall, QoS, UTM, IPS, and other services based on user identity.

User Role Firewalling was added starting in Junos 12.1. In this chapter, we examine how it works and how to leverage it with other security components.

SSL Forward Proxy

With the advancement of HTTP as a protocol used to deliver applications and communication, it was only a natural progression that the technology that secured it, Secure Sockets Layer (SSL), would become even more prevalent. At the same time, attackers have shifted their attacks from client-to-server to server-to-client as firewalls have secured inbound connections. Evasive applications and malicious attackers have also taken note and sought to use SSL to encrypt communications to bypass traditional security mechanisms like IPS. To help protect against evasive applications tunneling over SSL or malicious threats over SSL against your clients, you can leverage SSL Forward Proxy to crack open the SSL session between the client and server to inspect it with AppSecure and IPS technologies, as shown in Figure 12-6.

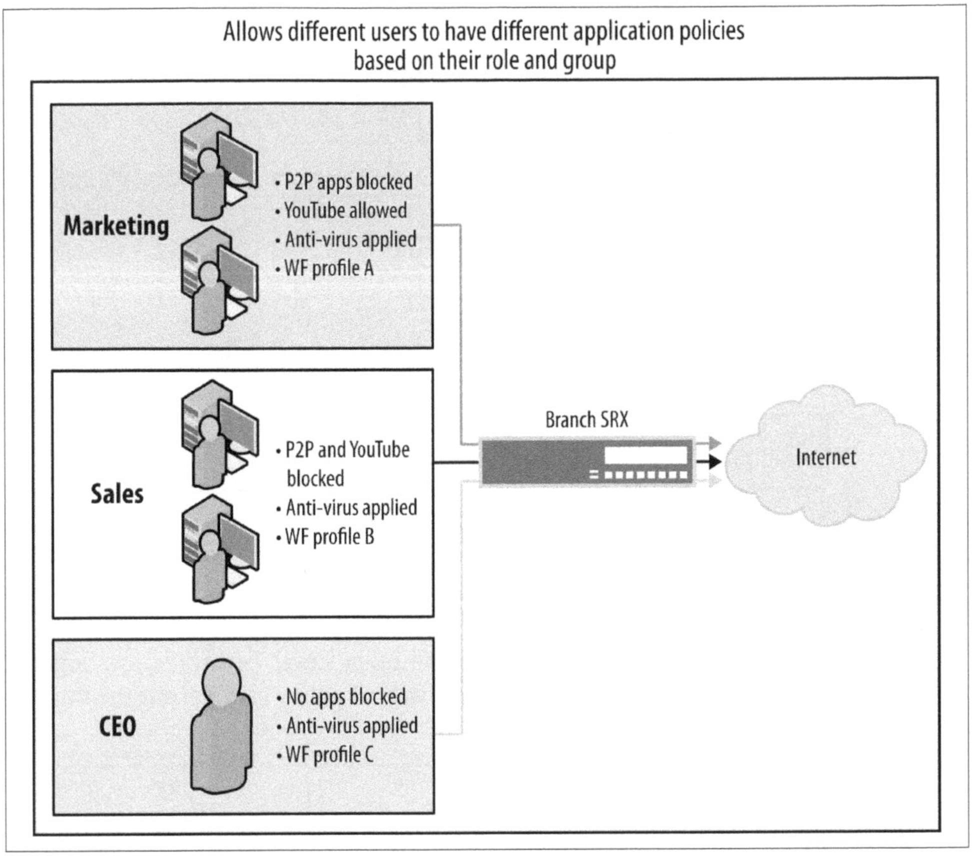

Figure 12-5. Role firewalling

> The high-end SRX also supports SSL Reverse Proxy for IPS, which allows you to protect your SSL-enabled web servers against client-to-server attacks from malicious clients. This functions by loading the SSL private key onto the SRX and is different from SSL Forward Proxy, which functions to protect your clients against threats from web servers that you do not control. SSL Reverse Proxy is outside the scope of this book but is covered in documentation and in *Junos Security* (O'Reilly).

AI Processing Architecture

Now that we've discussed some of the features that leverage the AppSecure technology, let's get a deeper understanding of how AI works and feeds the application identity to other components. Looking at our familiar Figure 12-7, AI sits in the services

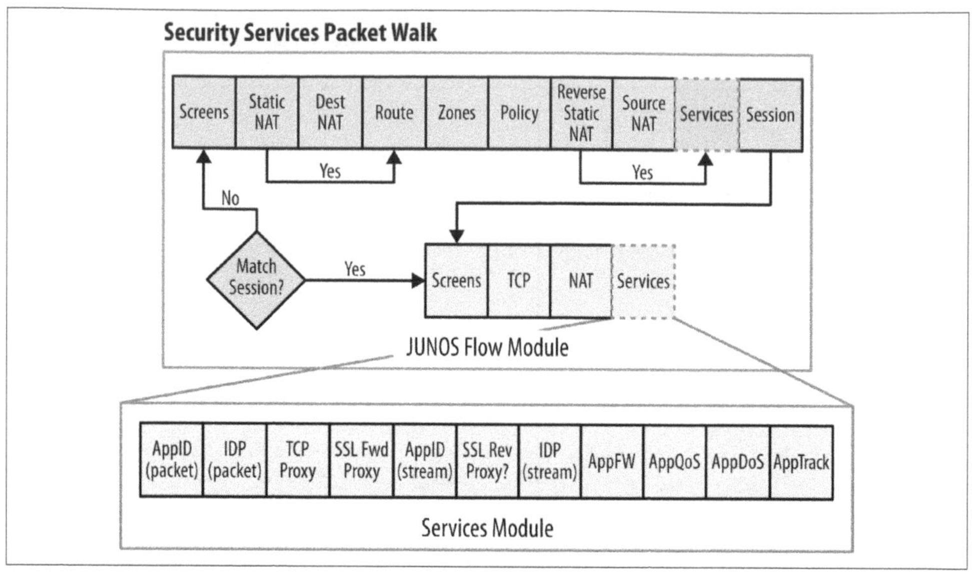

Figure 12-6. SSL Forward Proxy

component of the firewall flow engine—as do all other Level 7 features, although AI starts to occur with session setup assuming the firewall policy is to permit the traffic.

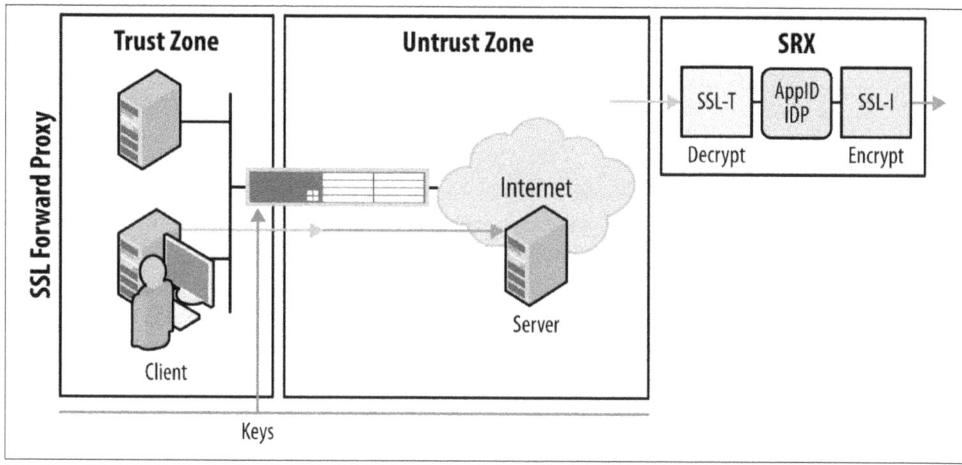

Figure 12-7. Firewall processing architecture

Once the AI module is invoked (on firewall permit), then the AI process will begin. We'll talk a little more about how this works in some detail later, but assume for now that this process is invoked and returns a result. This result in and of itself does not do anything to the traffic; however, the result is delivered to other modules like AppFW, Application Quality of Service (AppQoS), Application DDoS (AppDoS), IDP (aka IPS), and the AppTrack module. These modules can take some action on the traffic that will affect its forwarding and reporting.

It's important to understand the fundamental importance of the firewall rulebase in this process. If the result of the firewall policy lookup is a deny, then AI will never take place because it will be dropped on the first ingress packet before the AI engine is ever invoked. This differs from some competitive platforms that might still allow traffic to be permitted until an application is identified, even if the firewall action is to be denied—resulting in an information leak!

How Application Identification identifies applications

So we know that AppSecure is a suite of features that relies on AI to identify the applications communicating within firewall sessions, and that these results are shared among other components that can perform some action on the traffic; let's talk about how the AI process actually identifies the applications themselves. There are essentially five different mechanisms that AI can use to identify traffic at the time of writing this book.

- Signature-based pattern match.
- Heuristic engine match.
- Predictive session matching.
- Application system cache.
- Level 3/Level 4 application entries.

Additionally, just like IPS, to ensure that the AI process is not vulnerable to network evasions, the firewall flow engine helps with packet serialization and reassembly before a match is made for identification purposes.

What's important to note is that the SRX need not take port numbers or even protocol into account when identifying applications with signature-based or heuristic pattern match (cached and manually defined are not really applicable to this statement because they are not really detection mechanisms but rather predetermined results). Rather than just relying on the fact that HTTP's well-known port is TCP port 80 to identify the result. The AppID performed by the SRX will actually dig into the traffic stream itself to determine what the identity of the traffic is based on well-known patterns and behaviors of these applications.

Signature-based pattern matching

As we alluded to earlier, signature-based pattern matching is one of the most common mechanisms to identify applications, particularly those that are not evasive. Signature-based matching leverages the same pattern-matching technology that is used by the IPS engine to match attacks, but it has been repurposed (particularly from a UI perspective) to be leveraged by the AI engine. AI primarily uses Deterministic Finite Automaton (DFA) technology for pattern matching. The details of this mechanism, shown in Figure 12-8, are beyond the scope of this book, but you can think of it as a state machine that matches patterns based on evaluating different pattern-matching states at each bit of the traffic stream compared to match criteria. When a match occurs, a result can be determined.

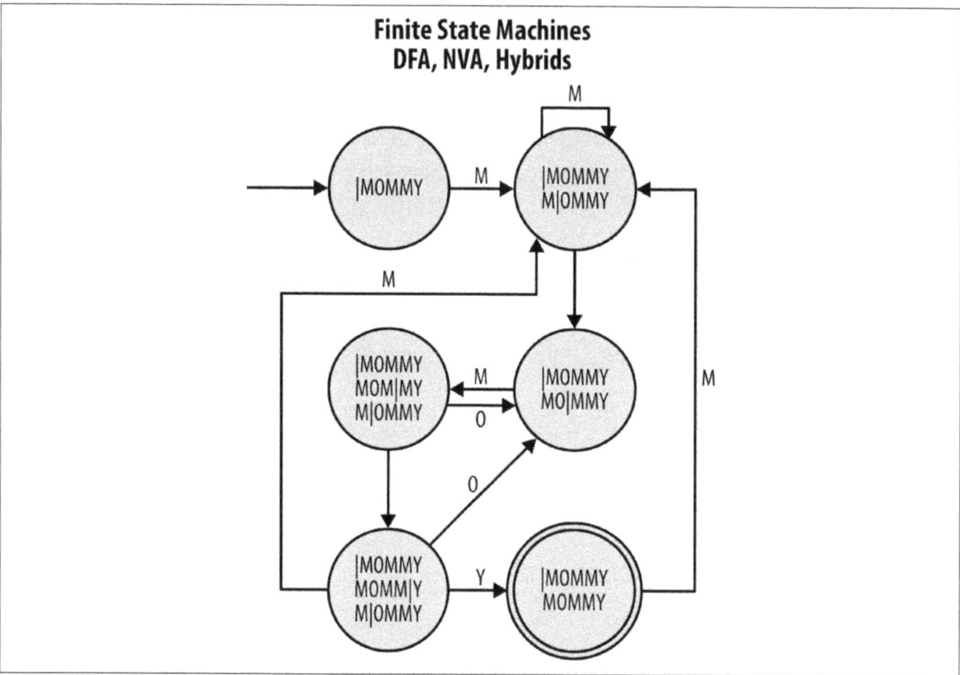

Figure 12-8. Pattern matching with finite state machines

All of Juniper's AI objects are fully open and can be viewed on the SRX—a really nice feature that most competitive platforms do not provide with closed source signatures. The benefit here is that you can not only view the signatures yourself, but also leverage them to create new signatures of your own.

Let's look at an example that shows the content of the HTTP object.

```
root@srx3600n0> show services application-identification application detail ju-
nos:HTTP
Application Name: junos:HTTP
Application type: HTTP
Description: This signature detects HyperText Transfer Protocol (HTTP), which
is a protocol used by the World Wide Web. It defines how messages are formatted
and transmitted and what actions Web servers
                and browsers should take in response to various commands. HTTP
usually runs on TCP port 80.
Application ID: 64
Disabled: No
Number of Parent Group(s): 1
Application Groups:
    junos:web
Application Tags:
    characteristic        : Can Leak Information
    characteristic        : Supports File Transfer
    characteristic        : Prone to Misuse
    characteristic        : Known Vulnerabilities
    characteristic        : Carrier of Malware
    characteristic        : Capable of Tunneling
    risk                  : 5
    category              : Web
Port Mapping:
    Default ports: TCP/80,3128,8000,8080
Signature:
    Port range: TCP/0-65535
    Client-to-server
         DFA Pattern: (\[OPTIONS|HEAD|GET|POST|PUT|B?DELETE|TRACE|SEARCH|B?PROP-
FIND|PROPPATCH|MKCOL|B?COPY|B?MOVE|LOCK|UNLOCK|CHECKOUT|CHECKIN|UNCHECKOUT|
VERSION-CONTROL|CONTINUE|REPORT|UPDATE|MKWORKSPACE|LABEL|MERGE|BASELINE-CONTROL|
MKACTIVITY|CMD|RPC_CONNECT|PATCH|UNLINK|POLL|CONNECT|BPROPPATCH|(UN)?SUBSCRIBE|
RPC_IN_DATA|INDEX|REVLOG|CCM_POST|RPC_OUT_DATA|INVOKE|BITS_POST|SMS_POST|B?PROP-
PATCH|NOTIFY|X-MS-ENUMATTS|DESCRIBE\])[\s\x07\x0b\x1b].+

        Regex Pattern: None
    Server-to-client
         DFA Pattern: (.*HTTP/1\.[01]\s|.?.?\u[\x3C]!\[DOCTYPE\]\u|.?.?\u[\x3C]\
[HTML\]\u|.?.?\u[\x3C]\?\[xml\]\u|\[Content-type\]: ).*
        Regex Pattern: None
    Minimum data client-to-server: 8
    Minimum data server-to-client: 8
    Order: 186
```

Looking at the output of the AI object, we can see a few things. First, there is a lot of detail around descriptions and characteristics of the signature, but most important we can see how the application is being detected. The port range shows that we're looking for this on any port 0-65535. There is a default port setting, but that's only used when AI is disabled for services like IPS that normally rely on it. A very important feature that the SRX has is that we match patterns on both client to server and server to client. If you match patterns only on one direction, it could not only be more prone to false positives, but also could be prone to evasions. There are specific patterns that are matched in the client-to-server and in the server-to-client portions of the communication. If we don't match both directions, we do not have a match.

There is also a regex field, but this refers to PCRE regex rather than the standard Juniper Regex engine. Most signatures just use the Juniper Regex rather than both engines (more performing impacting).

Nested application signatures. Identifying traditional applications like FTP, SSH, SMTP, and others can be useful, but sometimes when you have applications like HTTP act as their own transport layer, stopping at just identifying the application is not useful. Instead we can opt to look deeper into the application stream to identify not only what the base application is, but what application runs on top of it. For instance, in this example, we show the application object for Google.

```
root@srx3600n0> show services application-identification application detail ju-
nos:GOOGLE
Application Name: junos:GOOGLE
Application type: GOOGLE
Description: This signature detects traffic to Google.com.
Application ID: 987
Disabled: No
Number of Parent Group(s): 1
Application Groups:
    junos:web:portal
Application Tags:
    characteristic          : Loss of Productivity
    characteristic          : Bandwidth Consumer
    risk                    : 2
    subcategory             : Portal
    category                : Web
Signature NestedApplication:GOOGLE
    Layer-7 Protocol: HTTP
    Chain Order: Yes
    Maximum Transactions: 15
    Order: 33459
    Member(s): 1
        Member 0
            Context: http-header-host
            Pattern: (.*\.)?google\.com
            Direction: CTS
```

Here we can see that this is a nested application. The base Layer 7 Protocol is HTTP, meaning that the engine must first identify HTTP as an application, then it will look deeper. In this case, it looks at the header host to determine if it is a well-known Google host. HTTP is not the only application that supports nested apps today; there are 11 others, although HTTP is by far the most commonly used protocol when it comes to nested applications.

Keeping honest applications honest. The important thing to note is that AI is not perfect, and is primarily meant to keep honest applications honest; it is not a security panacea. The best security is a layered approach, not a single mechanism (despite hype from other vendors). For instance, in the last example, technically, if a server would accept it's IP address as the hostname rather than a DNS name (or the name could be spoofed), then it would be possible to get AppID to detect it as another application (although it can vary between applications based on how the match is performed). It is particularly difficult to identify applications when both the client and the server are colluding. Other mechanisms such as IPS, URL filtering, AV, and other mechanisms can further help to ensure that even if a service acts evasively that the behavior can be detected as such and flagged. For this same reason, just because you have an IPS engine, you shouldn't merely disable your entire stateful firewall policy; IPS is not perfect at detecting attacks. Security mechanisms are all about mitigating risk, so it's best to deploy AppSecure with this in mind, and use it as another layer to filter out undesirable applications and to identify behaviors that you might want to block, in conjunction with other traditional mechanisms.

Heuristic-based detection

Another mechanism that the SRX can use to identify evasive applications that do not provide any obvious patterns to match is by leveraging heuristics. Heuristics allow the SRX to look at the traffic in an analytical fashion to detect what application is running. For instance, the SRX supports detecting unknown encrypted applications. If the AI engine cannot detect the application as being another protocol, it can then examine the byte stream to determine if it is encrypted by measuring the randomness of the payload bytes. Any application stream that is encrypted (or compressed) will exhibit a highly randomized byte stream. Again, this isn't looking for any specific pattern, but looking at the behavior of the traffic. Heuristic-based detection is very similar to the protocol anomalies in the IPS engine, in that it is not something for which we can publish the signatures, because it is code that's built into the IPS engine itself.

Heuristics is a very powerful mechanism that will likely become even more and more important going into the future as applications become more and more evasive to avoid traditional pattern-matching techniques. Of course, we also have an application named "junos:UNKNOWN," which means that a pattern match was not possible, so it is also possible to catch any others with this and perform an action accordingly.

Predictive session identification

Sometimes the SRX can identify that a future session will be based on other sessions or activity. For instance, with ALGs (assuming they are enabled) the SRX can identify that the data (auxiliary) session will be based on the control session that negotiates the port or protocol between the client and server dynamically. This is supported for any ALG supported on the SRX. Additionally, using the heuristic engine, the SRX can identify applications based on other information exchanged. For instance, the SRX can look at the distributed hash tables exchanged by peer-to-peer (P2P) applications to determine what servers are super nodes or other server infrastructure for P2P apps, which often change frequently. This ability is called predictive session identification, another mechanism that can be used to identify applications. This won't appear as a signature with a pattern per se, but will be used to identify application objects that can be used in enforcement control of other components like AppFW and AppQoS.

Application system cache

Application caching is a technique that can be used so that the engine does not have to go through the effort of processing the session with AI each and every time that the traffic is sent through the box. Essentially, application caching (enabled by default) will do a lookup on the first pass of processing traffic to determine if it already knows the identity of the application. This is based on the server IP address, server port, Layer 3/ Layer 4 protocol, and LSYS (if used). If the system can identify what the application is, it will make an entry for it so that this isn't required next time (with a default timeout of 60 minutes).

```
{primary:node0}
root@SRX100HM> show services application-identification application-system-cache
node0:
-----------------------------------------
Application System Cache Configurations:
  application-cache: on
  nested-application-cache: on
  cache-unknown-result: on
  cache-entry-timeout: 3600 seconds
pic: 0/0
Logical system name: 0
IP address: 173.255.241.134                Port: 53     Protocol: UDP
Application: DNS                           Encrypted: No

Logical system name: 0
IP address: 172.16.42.205                  Port: 445    Protocol: TCP
Application: SMB                           Encrypted: No

Logical system name: 0
IP address: 192.168.222.50                 Port: 1096   Protocol: TCP
Application: MSRPC                         Encrypted: No

Logical system name: 0
IP address: 68.169.198.3                   Port: 80     Protocol: TCP
Application: HTTP                          Encrypted: No

Logical system name: 0
IP address: 192.168.222.35                 Port: 80     Protocol: TCP
Application: HTTP                          Encrypted: No
```

```
Logical system name: 0
IP address: 172.16.42.204                 Port: 445    Protocol: TCP
Application: SMB                          Encrypted: No

Logical system name: 0
IP address: 64.208.138.126                Port: 80     Protocol: TCP
Application: HTTP                         Encrypted: No
```

We can see from this example that a table is maintained that has a breakdown of each server, destination port, and protocol. This helps to improve performance for AI to near firewall performance when in use, assuming a decent number of cache hits. If a cache hit does occur, the AI engine does not need to inspect the traffic, although other functions will still occur like IPS, AppFW, UTM, and so on.

The benefit to using cache is performance, and the disadvantage is that if a client and server are colluding they might be able to evade the AI engine if they change the session between each round. Running IPS can help to better detect this behavior with the use of anomaly detection, or you can also disable the AI cache so that AI examines the traffic every time.

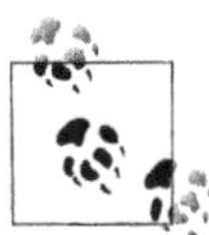

Of the mechanisms just listed, you can create your own custom signatures and Layer 3/Layer 4 objects, along with influencing if application caching is enabled, and what ALGs and heuristic mechanisms are enabled for AI—although you can't create your own heuristics or predictive session identification techniques because these are coded into the AI engine itself.

As we showed in Figure 12-2, once the AI engine has produced a match (or unknown), it will publish this application to other components internally that are "interested" in the result. There is nothing that you as the administrator need to do make this data exchange occur, assuming that you haven't altered any default options (as you can technically disable AI for services like IPS).

Deploying AppSecure

In this section, we discuss how to deploy the different components of AppSecure. We also take a deeper look at each feature so that you have a solid background on how to deploy them. We start with the basics of getting AppSecure up and running, and then break into each feature itself with detailed examples and use cases for each scenario.

AppSecure Licensing

Just like IPS, you don't technically need a license to run AppSecure, but you will need to load your own AI signatures. This can be useful as a utility function if you have a specific need to detect a particular application. For most users, licensing will be the route to go when it comes to AppSecure. Essentially, the license gets you the Juniper application feed, which can be downloaded for updates from the Juniper live server. Typically, AI objects are discovered and updated on a daily basis with exports shipped at least once a week (to allow for thorough QA testing). The license SKUs vary slightly between the branch SRX and the high-end SRX at the time of writing this book. The branch SRX has licenses for AI + IPS, along with bundle licenses that include other components like UTM as well. Licenses are offered in one-, three-, and five-year terms and are tied to a serial number. On the high-end SRX Series, you can license AI + IPS, but there are no other bundles at this time.

Just like other licenses, if running in HA, you must license both nodes in the cluster. If you do not, on failover, the secondary device will not have an active policy.

Regarding license expiration, Juniper has a 30-day grace period on expired licensing. After that, AppSecure will continue to run but will not be able to update its objects. Installing and checking licensing is just like any other feature, such as IPS or UTM. You would use the `request system license add` command (with either the `terminal` attribute to pull the license from the CLI or specify the filename to retrieve the license from a file either on a local or remote system) along with the `show system license` command to view the licenses loaded and their status. Note that these commands are node specific, so you need to run them on the specific node on which you want to retrieve the information.

Downloading and Installing Application Identification Sigpacks

There are two ways that you can download and install the AI sigpacks: either by leveraging the AI framework or using the IPS framework. The difference is that IPS relies on AI to function, so it will automatically pull down both AI + IPS sigpacks. Alternatively, you can also leverage the AI framework to download and install just the AI sigpacks.

Downloading/Installing via IPS

```
{primary:node0}
root@SRX100HM> request security idp security-package download
node0:
--------------------------------------------------------------------------
Will be processed in async mode. Check the status using the status checking CLI
```

```
root@SRX100HM> request security idp security-package download status
node0:
--------------------------------------------------------------------------
Done;Successfully    downloaded    from(https://services.netscreen.com/cgi-bin/
index.cgi)
and synchronized to backup.
Version info:2223(Wed Jan  9 19:12:58 2013 UTC, Detector=12.6.160121210)

{primary:node0}
root@SRX100HM> request security idp security-package install
node0:
--------------------------------------------------------------------------
Will be processed in async mode. Check the status using the status checking CLI

node1:
--------------------------------------------------------------------------
Will be processed in async mode. Check the status using the status checking CLI

{primary:node0}
root@SRX100HM> request security idp security-package install status
node0:
--------------------------------------------------------------------------
Done;Attack DB update : successful - [UpdateNumber=2222,ExportDate=Mon Jan  7
23:39:10 2013 UTC,Detector=12.6.140121210]
     Updating control-plane with new detector : successful
     Updating data-plane with new attack or detector : sucessful

node1:
--------------------------------------------------------------------------
Done;Attack DB update : successful - [UpdateNumber=2222,ExportDate=Mon Jan  7
23:39:10 2013 UTC,Detector=12.6.140121210]
     Updating control-plane with new detector : successful
     Updating data-plane with new attack or detector : sucessful
```

Prior to Junos 11.4, applications were installed into the Junos configuration itself. Now the applications are installed into a database so they don't clog up the configuration or get in the way of the commit process.

Also, starting in Junos 12.1, the SRX will automatically synchronize the IPS and AI packages to the secondary member when in an HA cluster. Prior to 12.1, you had to have fxp0 active on both devices and able to reach the Internet. If you did not, then only the active control plane would get the update while the secondary would not. Now with 12.1 regardless of whether you are using fxp0 on both nodes or just leveraging the data plane to get the updates rather than directly out the control plane, the primary SRX will download the package and synchronize it to the secondary node. Installation is still the same process.

Downloading/Installing via AI

```
root@srx3600n0> request services application-identification download
Please use command "request services application-identification download sta-
tus" to check status

root@srx3600n0> request services application-identification download status
Downloading application package 2223 succeed.

root@srx3600n0> request services application-identification install
Please use command "request services application-identification install status"
to check status

root@srx3600n0> request services application-identification install status
Install application package 2223 succeed
```

Controlling application caching

Application caching is a feature that allows you to improve performance by caching the results of application detection for a given server IP, protocol, or protocol combination so that in the future the SRX won't need to run AppID again until the session ages out (one hour by default). Application caching poses the traditional performance versus security dilemma. For the most security-sensitive environments, it's best to disable this so that AppID runs every time (along with running other services like IPS, UTM, and others). Although the potential for application cache attacks is not very common, it is technically possible if the client and server are both colluding (e.g., with a very intentionally evasive application). There aren't many common examples of this on the Internet, but we never know how things could change in the future. Running other services (particularly IPS) on top of AppID really solidifies the threat vector because noncompliant applications will more than likely light up the protocol anomaly engine like a Christmas tree.

There are a few options that you have when working with application caching:

- Disable application caching entirely: Application caching is enabled by default, but you can disable it entirely.
- Disabling application caching for nested applications: The SRX will not cache the results of nested applications like Facebook, so that AppID will need to run on any application that is nested, but still caches base applications.
- You can alter the cache timeout so that application ID entries are stored for a shorter period of time.

In this example, we alter the default settings on two different devices. On the SRX100 we disable application caching entirely, whereas on our SRX3600 we disable the caching of nested applications and change the default cache time to 10 minutes.

```
[edit]
root@SRX100# set services application-identification no-application-system-cache

[edit]
root@SRX100# show services application-identification
no-application-system-cache;

[edit]
root@srx3600n0#  set  services  application-identification  nested-application-
settings no-application-system-cache

 [edit]
root@srx3600n0#  set  services  application-identification  application-system-
cache-timeout 600

[edit]
root@srx3600n0# show services application-identification
nested-application-settings {
    no-application-system-cache;
}
application-system-cache-timeout 600;
```

Enabling application identification heuristics. The SRX can leverage both signature-based pattern matching and heuristic-based application matching. At the time of writing this book, heuristic-based pattern matching is disabled by default, but it can be enabled quite simply. The heuristic engine will allow you to detect applications by other mechanisms that are contained within the AppID engine itself. For instance, the SRX can detect the presence of encrypted applications that are not standard such as ESP, SSL, SSH, and so on. You can then use this result in your AppFW ruleset or other AppSecure features to control the "Unspecified-Encrypted" application. More features will likely be added in the future, so definitely keep updated on the release notes.

```
[edit]
root@srx3600n0# set services application-identification enable-heuristics

[edit]
root@srx3600n0# show services application-identification
enable-heuristics;
```

AppID Signature Operations

Although you do not necessarily need to do any of these defined actions, it is very helpful to have a working knowledge of the AppID operations in this section. We discuss enabling and disabling applications, application groups, and creating your own applications or application groups. It is important to understand that starting in Junos 11.4, predefined AppID objects are no longer stored in the Junos configuration, but in a separate database. This is for performance optimization purposes, but it also means that you will need to leverage some other facilities to work with the configuration.

Enabling and disabling applications and application groups

Although it isn't common, you might find yourself in a position where you need to turn off certain AppID objects or groups (or perhaps you turned some off in the past and you need to turn them back on). With Junos 12.1X44+, you can also override applications using Layer 3/Layer 4 applications if you have a false positive, which we show you how to do in this section. Let's say, though, that you have a signature that is misfiring on applications broadly. You can disable the signature or group as follows:

```
root@srx3600n0> show services application-identification application summary
Application(s): 233
Nested Application(s): 872
  Applications                                  Disabled         ID      Order
  junos:TWITTER-SSL                              No               1287    33694
  junos:EBAY-CLASSIFIEDS                         No               1286    33693
  junos:MYSPACE-SSL                              No               1285    33692
  junos:DROPBOX-CLEAR                            No               1284    33689
  junos:IPERNITY                                 No               1282    33680
  junos:PLAXO                                    No               1281    33681
  junos:PROJECTPLACE                             No               1280    33685
  junos:MICROSOFT-LIVE-SERVICES                  No               1279    33686
  junos:CLARIZEN-SSL                             No               1278    33688
  junos:CLARIZEN                                 No               1277    33687
  junos:ZORPIA                                   No               1276    33678
  junos:PINTEREST                                No               1275    33679
  junos:GATHER                                   No               1274    33676
  junos:GAIAONLINE                               No               1273    33675
  junos:FEDGEWING                                No               1272    33677

root@srx3600n0> show services application-identification group summary
Application Group(s): 82
Application Groups                                        Disabled  ID
  junos:web:social-networking:business                     No         84
  junos:web:infrastructure:encryption                      No         83
  junos:web:remote-access:tunneling                        No         82
  junos:web:infrastructure:mobile                          No         81
  junos:web:infrastructure:software-update                 No         80
  junos:web:infrastructure:database                        No         79
  junos:web:infrastructure                                 No         78
  junos:web:gaming:protocols                               No         77
  junos:web:p2p:file-sharing                               No         76
  junos:web:p2p                                            No         75
  junos:web:multimedia:audio-streaming                     No         74
  junos:web:social-networking:linkedin                     No         73
  junos:web:messaging:mail                                 No         72
  junos:web:multimedia:adult                               No         71
  junos:web:remote-access:interactive-desktop              No         70
  junos:web:remote-access                                  No         69

root@srx3600n0> request services application-identification application disable
junos:TWITTER-SSL
Please wait while we are re-compiling signatures ...
```

```
Please wait while we are re-compiling signatures ...
Please wait while we are re-compiling signatures ...
Disable application junos:TWITTER-SSL succeed.

root@srx3600n0> show services application-identification application summary
Application(s): 233
Nested Application(s): 872
  Applications                          Disabled        ID      Order
  junos:TWITTER-SSL                      Yes             1287    33694
  junos:EBAY-CLASSIFIEDS                 No              1286    33693
  junos:MYSPACE-SSL                      No              1285    33692
  junos:DROPBOX-CLEAR                    No              1284    33689
  junos:IPERNITY                         No              1282    33680
  junos:PLAXO                            No              1281    33681
  junos:PROJECTPLACE                     No              1280    33685
  junos:MICROSOFT-LIVE-SERVICES          No              1279    33686
  junos:CLARIZEN-SSL                     No              1278    33688


root@srx3600n0> request services application-identification group disable ju-
nos:messaging
Disable application group junos:messaging succeed.

root@srx3600n0> request services application-identification group enable ju-
nos:messaging
Enable application group junos:messaging succeed.

root@srx3600n0> request services application-identification application enable
junos:TWITTER-SSL
Please wait while we are re-compiling signatures ...
Please wait while we are re-compiling signatures ...
Enable application junos:TWITTER-SSL succeed.
```

In that example, we first viewed a summary of the application status along with the group status (both outputs were trimmed for brevity, but you can run these on your system). Then we disabled a signature and group and reenabled them just for an example. This is how you would disable a signature or group or reenable signatures if need be. By default, all applications and groups in the export are active (a different concept than how it is run in IPS, where you need to explicitly enable objects). There is also a copy function as part of the request command that allows you to copy the signature into a custom signature so you can modify it, as you can't modify any predefined signatures—although you can copy it to a new one, modify it, and disable the predefined one. Also note that the action of enabling and disabling signatures survives reboots and application package updates, so you must manually undo it.

We already showed how to view the contents of application objects in the preceding section, but you can also view the contents of application groups with the following command (which can be used recursively to dig deeper into the group until only members remain):

```
root@srx3600n0>   show   services   application-identification   group   detail   ju-
nos:web:multimedia
Group Name: junos:web:multimedia
Group ID: 60
Description: N/A
Disabled: No
Number of Applications: 0
Number of Sub-Groups: 4
Number of Parent-Groups: 1
Sub Groups:
    junos:web:multimedia:audio-streaming
    junos:web:multimedia:adult
    junos:web:multimedia:web-based
    junos:web:multimedia:video-streaming
Parent Groups:
    junos:web

root@srx3600n0>   show   services   application-identification   group   detail
junos:web:multimedia:web-based
Group Name: junos:web:multimedia:web-based
Group ID: 64
Description: N/A
Disabled: No
Number of Applications: 65
Number of Sub-Groups: 0
Number of Parent-Groups: 1
Applications:
    junos:NETFLIX
    junos:AAJTAK
    junos:STEREOMOOD
    junos:HULU
    junos:GROOVESHARK-STREAMING
    junos:BABELGUM
    junos:MOG
    junos:VIDEOSURF
    junos:DEEZER
    junos:WE7
    junos:VIMEO
    junos:HTTP-VIDEO
    junos:SOCIALTV
    junos:LAST-FM-STREAMING
    junos:JUSTIN-TV
    junos:PANDORA
    junos:BEEMP3
    junos:PDF
    junos:METACAFE
    junos:FREEETV
    junos:SILVERLIGHT
    junos:CRACKLE
    junos:IMGUR
    junos:NETFLIX-STREAM
    junos:TIDALTV
```

```
junos:TUDOU
junos:AOL-VIDEO
junos:LIVEFLASH
junos:JANGO
junos:MIXCLOUD
junos:YOUTUBE-COMMENT
junos:TAGOO
junos:ZAYCEV
junos:LIVE365
junos:YOUKU
junos:YUVUTU
junos:GOOGLE-VIDEOS
junos:BOXEE-TV
junos:YOUTUBE
junos:DAILYMOTION
junos:NETFLIX-PLAYER
junos:TED
junos:MTV-HD-VIDEO-STREAM
junos:SONGS-PK
junos:PPLIVE
junos:TWITVID
junos:NEWGROUNDS
junos:STARTV
junos:MOBILATORY-SEND-TO-PHONE
junos:YAHOO-DOUGA
junos:YOUTUBE-STREAM
junos:USTREAM
junos:TVUNETWORKS
```

Creating Layer 3/Layer 4 applications

In this example, we create a Layer 3/Layer 4 application that overrides the application name for the server 192.168.1.2 on TCP port 80 rather than using the standard AppID pattern matching. This is useful when you have a signature that is having false positive issues on a particular server, but is still valid more broadly on the system (e.g., when you have a poorly written application). Rather than disabling the signature entirely, you can make a Layer 3/Layer 4 signature that overrides this setting for the server only while leaving the signature intact. Then this object can be referenced in other AppSecure policies.

```
[edit]
root@srx3600n0#   set   services   application-identification   application
Override-192.168.1.2:TCP80 address-mapping Override destination ip 192.168.1.2
port-range tcp 80

[edit]
root@srx3600n0#   set   services   application-identification   application
Override-192.168.1.2:TCP80 address-mapping Override order 1500

[edit]
root@srx3600n0# show services application-identification
```

```
application Override-192.168.1.2:TCP80 {
    address-mapping Override {
        destination {
            ip 192.168.1.2/32;
            port-range {
                tcp 80;
            }
        }
        order 1500;
    }
}
```

In that example, we specified a new AppID object that is based on a particular destination IP address and protocol and port match. We also need to define the order when using multiple Layer 3/Layer 4 application signatures for the match. Note that you would also use the same base command to define custom applications with pattern regex, but that is a more advanced topic that is outside the scope of this book.

Creating custom application groups

The SRX allows you to define your own custom application group, which can be composed of predefined applications, as well as custom applications and groups. This group can then be referenced in the AppSecure policies just like any other Application object.

```
[edit]
root@srx3600n0# set services application-identification application-group Web-
and-Games application-groups junos:web

[edit]
root@srx3600n0# set services application-identification application-group Web-
and-Games application-groups junos:gaming


[edit]
root@srx3600n0# set services application-identification application-group Web-
and-Games applications junos:BITTORRENT-UDP

[edit]
root@srx3600n0# show services application-identification
application-group Web-and-Games {
    application-groups {
        junos:gaming;
        junos:web;
    }
    applications {
        junos:BITTORRENT-UDP;
    }
}
```

In that example, we created a new group called Web and Games that contains all applications in the Junos:web group, Junos:gaming group, and a standalone application junos:BITTORRENT-UDP, just for example.

Configuring and Deploying AppTrack

AppTrack is a useful feature to provide visibility into the applications that are traversing your network at the application layer rather than just the standard firewall log information. The first question you might have is this: do I need to deploy AppTrack? The answer is yes or no, depending on your scenario. Let's explore why you might need to leverage AppTrack.

- You want to collect Level 7 application information and you do not have another AppSecure feature enabled like AppFW, AppQoS, or IPS. If you have these other features configured in a zone context, it will enable AI for that zone and thus the information will be included in the firewall logs.
- You want additional application statistics to be tracked on box. At the time of writing this book, the SRX provides additional statistics on box if you are running AppTrack. These stats can still be collected on a third-party device if AppTrack isn't being used, however.
- You want to collect syslog information not only at the creation or close of a session, but also at defined intervals.

AppTrack generates log messages in addition to the standard firewall log messages that are generated by the stateful firewall process. The information provides some additional information such as dynamic application, nested application, and packets and bytes sent from client to server and server to client. For the most part, these messages are very similar to the firewall logs, especially after Junos 11.1.

```
<Application Create Log>

<14>1 2013-01-19T15:18:17.040 SRX100HM RT_FLOW - APPTRACK_SESSION_CREATE [ju-
nos@2636.1.1.1.2.41 source-address="192.168.224.30" source-port="3129"
destination-address="207.17.137.56" destination-port="21" service-name="junos-
ftp" application="UNKNOWN" nested-application="UNKNOWN" nat-source-
address="173.167.224.7" nat-source-port="14406" nat-destination-
address="207.17.137.56" nat-destination-port="21" src-nat-rule-name="1" dst-nat-
rule-name="None" protocol-id="6" policy-name="General-Outbound" source-zone-
name="LAN" destination-zone-name="Danger" session-id-32="5058" username="N/A"
roles="N/A" encrypted="N/A"]

<Application Update Log>

<14>1 2013-01-19T15:18:17.040 SRX100HM RT_FLOW - APPTRACK_SESSION_VOL_UPDATE
[junos@2636.1.1.1.2.41 source-address="192.168.224.30" source-port="3129"
destination-address="207.17.137.56" destination-port="21" service-name="junos-
```

```
ftp" application="UNKNOWN" nested-application="UNKNOWN" nat-source-
address="173.167.224.7" nat-source-port="14406" nat-destination-
address="207.17.137.56" nat-destination-port="21" src-nat-rule-name="1" dst-nat-
rule-name="None" protocol-id="6" policy-name="General-Outbound" source-zone-
name="LAN" destination-zone-name="Danger" session-id-32="5058" packets-from-
client="1" bytes-from-client="48" packets-from-server="0" bytes-from-server="0"
elapsed-time="0" username="N/A" roles="N/A" encrypted="N/A"]

<Application Close Log>

<14>1 2013-01-19T15:18:17.040 SRX100HM RT_FLOW - APPTRACK_SESSION_CLOSE [ju-
nos@2636.1.1.1.2.41 reason="application failure or action" source-
address="192.168.224.30" source-port="3129" destination-address="207.17.137.56"
destination-port="21" service-name="junos-ftp" application="FTP" nested-
application="UNKNOWN" nat-source-address="173.167.224.7" nat-source-
port="14406" nat-destination-address="207.17.137.56" nat-destination-port="21"
src-nat-rule-name="1" dst-nat-rule-name="None" protocol-id="6" policy-
name="General-Outbound" source-zone-name="LAN" destination-zone-name="Danger"
session-id-32="5058" packets-from-client="3" bytes-from-client="144" packets-
from-server="2" bytes-from-server="104" elapsed-time="1" username="N/A"
roles="N/A" encrypted="N/A"]
```

As you can see, the AppTrack logs nearly mirror the standard firewall logs, but they also provide the ability to log when a session is created, during the session at predefined intervals (update logs), and at the session close—whereas the firewall can only log at the session open and close. These logs are generated in syslog format so you can send them to any syslog device. Juniper's STRM platform has customized dashboards, log views, and reports prebuilt for AppTrack and other AppSecure functions, so it's always a good choice if you want a plug-and-play experience. Figures 12-9 and 12-10 show samples of the log views in STRM.

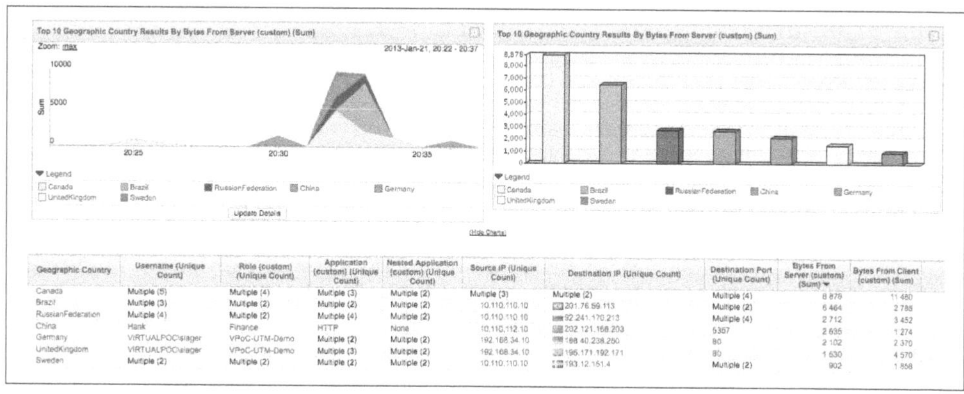

Figure 12-9. STRM AppTrack logging by application and country

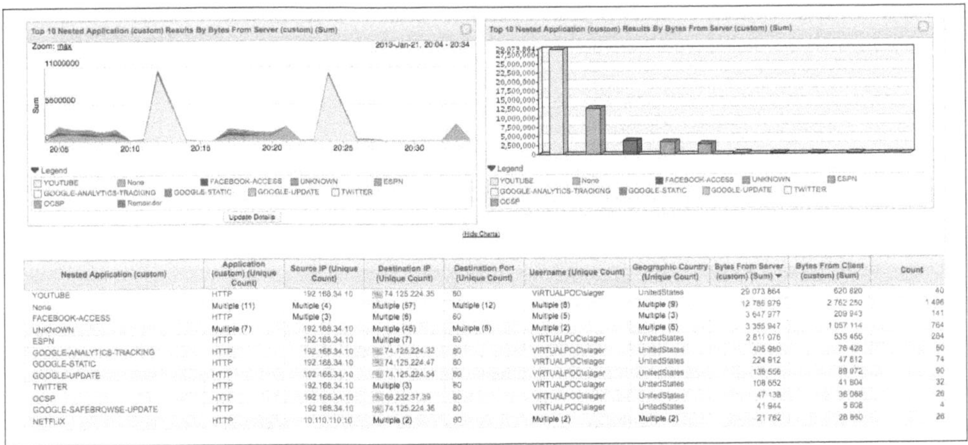

Nested Application (custom)	Application (custom) (Unique Count)	Source IP (Unique Count)	Destination IP (Unique Count)	Destination Port (Unique Count)	Username (Unique Count)	Geographic Country (Unique Count)	Bytes From Server (custom) (Sum)	Bytes From Client (custom) (Sum)	Count
YOUTUBE	HTTP	192.168.34.10	74.125.224.35	80	VIRTUALPOC\slager	UnitedStates	29 073 864	620 820	40
None	Multiple (11)	Multiple (4)	Multiple (57)	Multiple (12)	Multiple (8)	Multiple (9)	12 786 979	2 762 250	1 496
FACEBOOK-ACCESS	HTTP	Multiple (3)	Multiple (6)	80	Multiple (5)	Multiple (3)	3 647 977	209 943	141
UNKNOWN	Multiple (7)	192.168.34.10	Multiple (45)	Multiple (8)	Multiple (2)	Multiple (5)	3 355 947	1 057 114	764
ESPN	HTTP	192.168.34.10	Multiple (7)	80	VIRTUALPOC\slager	UnitedStates	2 811 076	535 456	284
GOOGLE-ANALYTICS-TRACKING	HTTP	192.168.34.10	74.125.224.32	80	VIRTUALPOC\slager	UnitedStates	405 980	76 428	50
GOOGLE-STATIC	HTTP	192.168.34.10	74.125.224.47	80	VIRTUALPOC\slager	UnitedStates	224 912	47 612	74
GOOGLE-UPDATE	HTTP	192.168.34.10	74.125.224.34	80	VIRTUALPOC\slager	UnitedStates	136 556	89 072	90
TWITTER	HTTP	192.168.34.10	Multiple (3)	80	VIRTUALPOC\slager	UnitedStates	108 652	41 804	32
OCSP	HTTP	192.168.34.10	68.232.37.39	80	VIRTUALPOC\slager	UnitedStates	47 138	36 088	26
GOOGLE-SAFEBROWSE-UPDATE	HTTP	192.168.34.10	74.125.224.36	80	VIRTUALPOC\slager	UnitedStates	41 944	5 808	4
NETFLIX	HTTP	10.110.110.10	Multiple (2)	80	Multiple (2)	Multiple (2)	21 762	28 860	26

Figure 12-10. STRM application usage

Additionally, AppTrack records some additional session statistics on the platform itself about applications seen sessions, bytes, and so on.

```
root@SRX3600> show services application-identification statistics applications

Last Reset: 2013-01-19 07:28:30 EST
                   Application      Sessions            Bytes  Encrypted
                    APPLE-PUSH             7            46492         No
                           BGP           276           341167         No
                      BUZZFEED             1             4775         No
                           DNS         10778          2429503         No
                       DROPBOX             2            16110         No
                   ENCODED-DNS         52041       1493293274         No
                   ESP-OVER-UDP           60             4960         No
               FACEBOOK-ACCESS             9            51360         No
           FACEBOOK-ACCESS-SSL           354          4906829         No
                         FLASH            32           126965         No
                           FTP             9         13581304         No
                        GOOGLE            15           779906         No
     GOOGLE-ANALYTICS-TRACKING             2          2175642         No
        GOOGLE-MOBILE-MAPS-APP             2           208041         No
         GOOGLE-SAFEBROWSE-SUB            59         19727033         No
      GOOGLE-SAFEBROWSE-UPDATE            57          5766450         No
                 GOOGLE-STATIC            32          1498515         No
                 GOOGLE-UPDATE            14          2347290         No
                          HTTP          2711        216440024         No
                    HTTP-VIDEO             1            57112         No
                        ITUNES             3            71617         No
                          KRB5             4             3544         No
                          LDAP           530          7393707         No
                      LINKEDIN             2            50315         No
            LIVE-SKYDRIVE-SSL             3           294613         No
              MICROSOFT-UPDATE             4            23185         No
```

```
        MSRPC         792         3368107         No
       NBNAME          40           43076         No
          NTP         205           45524         No
         OCSP           8           42636         No
 OUTLOOK-LIVE          21          172475         No
   PICASA-WEB         147         1935022         No
          RDP          15           45565         No
          SIP           9            3941         No
          SMB         416         2476519         No
         SMTP         181          368336         No
         SPDY         120          225731         No
          SSH         353          867939         No
          SSL         900       207951891        Yes
  STUMBLEUPON           2            6423         No
       SYSLOG        2512       157987112         No
       TEREDO           5             420         No
      TWITTER           7          131803         No
      YOUTUBE          14          126084         No
      unknown          16             492         No
```

You might be asking yourself why the SRX generates separate logs for AppTrack versus standard firewall, considering they are so similar? The answer is that AppTrack started in Junos 10.2, and the other features of AppSecure were not available at that point. Because the AppTrack feature used some internal application constructs, it generated its own logs so as to not interfere with the firewall logs. Now that the AppSecure suite is more fully integrated into the SRX infrastructure, it is likely that at some point in the future the logs and functionality will be merged into a single firewall log. Keep posted on the latest Junos release for more information. For now, AppTrack is useful if you want application visibility without deploying other AppSecure features, session update logs, or additional statistics.

Enabling AppTrack

Turning on AppTrack is very simple once you've licensed the box and downloaded signature packs (assuming you're not using your own custom applications). All you need to do is to enable AppTrack on a zone-by-zone basis. This will enable the AppTrack function for any traffic that traverses the zone, whether the zone is the source or destination zone. This provides some granularity when it comes to enabling AI. Once you have AppTrack enabled, the only other thing that you need to do is to make sure that you have data plane logging enabled, either to a syslog server or locally through the control plane. We discussed how to configure this at length in Chapter 5.

In this example, we enable AppTrack in the trust and untrust zone, along with a syslog server to send the logs to our STRM at 192.168.1.20.

```
[edit]
root@srx3600n0# set security zones security-zone trust application-tracking

[edit]
```

```
root@srx3600n0# set security zones security-zone untrust application-tracking

[edit]
root@srx3600n0# set security log mode stream format sd-syslog stream STRM host
192.168.1.20

[edit]
root@srx3600n0# show security zones
security-zone trust {
    interfaces {
        xe-1/0/0.0;
    }
    application-tracking;
}
security-zone untrust {
    interfaces {
        xe-1/0/1.0;
    }
    application-tracking;
}


[edit]
root@srx3600n0# show security log
mode stream;
format sd-syslog;
stream STRM {
    host {
        192.168.1.20;
    }
}
```

Configuring AppTrack options

In this example, we extend AppTrack from our last example to turn on logging when the session is first created, and set the update interval to every five minutes for long-lived sessions.

```
[edit]
root@srx3600n0# set security application-tracking first-update session-update-
interval 5

[edit]
root@srx3600n0# show security application-tracking
first-update;
session-update-interval 5;
```

Configuring and Deploying Application Firewall

If you seek to not only have the visibility of AppTrack but also the ability to enforce control on L7 traffic, then AppFW is what you should look to deploy. As we discussed earlier, AppFW is a module that sits on top of the existing firewall policy to extend its capability to enforce beyond the standard seven-tuple (eight if you consider the Source-Identity we discuss later in this chapter) to look at the L7 application as well. The key to properly deploying AppFW is to first ensure that you are building the AppFW policy on a solid security policy just as you have always done with the practice of least privilege. Although some competitors have touted AppFW as a the panacea for security, in our opinion it is just another layer of protection that should be stacked on top of your firewall policy to ensure the identity of the applications conform with the intentions of the security administrator. To do this, the SRX will leverage a separate AppFW policy. This policy or ruleset, to be specific, is very simple. It contains the ability to "match" applications or application groups, along with a "then" action that should be taken on that traffic. Additionally, there is a default action that is taken on the traffic in that rulebase that doesn't match any rule. Although only one AppFW ruleset can be applied to an individual firewall policy rule, you can specify different AppFW profiles for each firewall policy rule. Additionally, each ruleset can have multiple rules to match different applications.

Three types of Application Firewall rulesets

There are three types of AppFW rulesets: blacklist, whitelist, and hybrid. Actually, hybrid is a new feature starting in Junos 12.1X44. As we mentioned earlier, you can define match criteria for the rules in the ruleset and the action criteria, along with a default action. If you were using a blacklist approach, you would define the rules with actions of deny/reject/redirect and the default action as permit. If you were using the whitelist approach, you would define rules with the action of permit, and the default action would be deny/reject/redirect. The hybrid technique comes from the challenge of nested applications. For instance, let's say you wanted to define a rule that blocked Facebook, allowed all other HTTP-based web traffic, and denied all other applications. Prior to Junos 12.1X44 you could not do this, because you could not mix permit and deny in the rules; all of the rules had to be either permit or deny, with the default action the opposite. As of version 12.1X45, we added the ability to also leverage redirect as an action of the firewall ruleset for HTTP and HTTPS traffic to redirect to a local splash page, or send the results externally. Just like standard firewall rules, the AppFW ruleset is evaluated from top to bottom until a match is made or the default action is reached.

Let's take a look at setting up each one of these examples.

Configuring a blacklist application ruleset. In this example, we perform a very common scenario where we want to make sure that a certain application and application group are not allowed. Often this happens with HTTP when you want to allow HTTP as an application but you don't want to allow certain applications, like Facebook, to be sent. For this example, we allow HTTP as a Layer 4 application out to the Internet on TCP port 80, but we will ensure that Facebook Farmville or any known games are not allowed.

```
[edit]
root@srx3600n0# set security application-firewall rule-sets Facebook-Games rule
1 match dynamic-application junos:FACEBOOK-FARMVILLE

[edit]
root@srx3600n0# set security application-firewall rule-sets Facebook-Games rule
1 then deny

[edit]
root@srx3600n0# set security application-firewall rule-sets Facebook-Games rule
2 match dynamic-application-group junos:gaming

[edit]
root@srx3600n0# set security application-firewall rule-sets Facebook-Games rule
2 then deny

[edit]
root@srx3600n0# set security application-firewall rule-sets Facebook-Games
default-rule permit

[edit]
root@srx3600n0# set security policies from-zone trust to-zone untrust policy
Allowed-Outbound match source-address any destination-address any application
junos-http

root@srx3600n0# set security policies from-zone trust to-zone untrust policy
Allowed-Outbound then permit application-services application-firewall rule-set
Facebook-Games

[edit]
root@srx3600n0# set security policies from-zone trust to-zone untrust policy
Allowed-Outbound then log session-close

[edit]
root@srx3600n0# show security application-firewall rule-sets Facebook-Games
rule 1 {
    match {
        dynamic-application junos:FACEBOOK-FARMVILLE;
    }
    then {
        deny;
    }
}
rule 2 {
    match {
        dynamic-application-group junos:gaming;
    }
    then {
        deny;
    }
}
default-rule {
```

```
        permit;
    }

    [edit]
    root@srx3600n0# show security policies from-zone trust to-zone untrust policy
    Allowed-Outbound
    match {
        source-address any;
        destination-address any;
        application junos-http;
    }
    then {
        permit {
            application-services {
                application-firewall {
                    rule-set Facebook-Games;
                }
            }
        }
        log {
            session-close;
        }
    }
```

So we can see in that example that we first set up an AppFW ruleset that looks to block Facebook Farmville, followed by another rule that blocks any known games. Technically, we could have placed these in the same rule, but we separated them for a cleaner look. Any traffic that doesn't match those first two rules is then allowed. This AppFW ruleset is applied to our allowed-outbound rule. Of course, this only works when the traffic is permitted because otherwise the AppFW ruleset wouldn't ever be triggered if we dropped at a Layer 3/Layer 4 level. We also restricted the application match to only junos-http rather than making this any. Why? As we suggested, you shouldn't put all of your eggs in any one basket when it comes to security. Why open the attack surface to other ports when we can funnel everything outbound to just port 80 and inspect it to ensure that whatever is allowed through at Layer 3/Layer 4 is correct at the Layer 7 level? In your network you'll likely also specify source and destination addresses as you see fit.

Here it can be good to leverage the following show commands to see both group membership and individual application members:

```
root@srx3600n0# run show services application-identification application detail
junos:FACEBOOK-FARMVILLE
Application Name: junos:FACEBOOK-FARMVILLE
Application type: FACEBOOK-FARMVILLE
Description: This signature detects the Facebook embedded version of FarmVille.
FarmVille is a social game that allows the user to control a virtual farm and
share the farming experience with other users.
```

```
Application ID: 510
Disabled: No
Number of Parent Group(s): 1
Application Groups:
    junos:web:social-networking:facebook
Application Tags:
    characteristic        : Loss of Productivity
    risk                  : 1
    subcategory           : Social-Networking
    category              : Web
Signature NestedApplication:FACEBOOK-FARMVILLE
    Layer-7 Protocol: HTTP
    Chain Order: no
    Maximum Transactions: 1
    Order: 33048
    Member(s): 2
        Member 0
            Context: http-header-host
            Pattern: apps\.facebook\.com
            Direction: CTS
        Member 1
            Context: http-url-parsed
            Pattern: /onthefarm/.*
            Direction: CTS

 [edit]
root@srx3600n0# run show services application-identification group detail ju-
nos:gaming
Group Name: junos:gaming
Group ID: 3
Description: N/A
Disabled: No
Number of Applications: 0
Number of Sub-Groups: 2
Number of Parent-Groups: 1
Sub Groups:
    junos:gaming:web-based
    junos:gaming:protocols
```

Configuring a whitelist application ruleset. The opposite of explicitly blacklisting certain applications and allowing all others in a ruleset is the whitelist ruleset. The whitelist ruleset explicitly defines the applications that you want to allow while denying all others. The format is the same, but you use the inverse actions of the blacklist ruleset. For this example, we want to allow traffic out on TCP port 80, but we want to ensure that it is truly HTTP and not some other protocol like Skype that is masquerading on TCP port 80.

```
[edit]
root@srx3600n0# set security application-firewall rule-sets Allow-Web rule 1
match dynamic-application-group junos:web
```

```
[edit]
root@srx3600n0# set security application-firewall rule-sets Allow-Web rule 1
then permit

[edit]
root@srx3600n0# set security application-firewall rule-sets Allow-Web default-
rule deny

[edit]
root@srx3600n0# set security policies from-zone trust to-zone untrust policy
Allowed-Outbound match source-address any destination-address any application
junos-http

root@srx3600n0# set security policies from-zone trust to-zone untrust policy
Allowed-Outbound then permit application-services application-firewall rule-set
Allow-Web

[edit]
root@srx3600n0# set security policies from-zone trust to-zone untrust policy
Allowed-Outbound then log session-close

[edit]
root@srx3600n0# show security policies from-zone trust to-zone untrust policy
Allowed-Outbound
match {
    source-address any;
    destination-address any;
    application junos-http;
}
then {
    permit {
        application-services {
            application-firewall {
                rule-set Allow-Web;
            }
        }
    }
    log {
        session-close;
    }
}


[edit]
root@srx3600n0# show security application-firewall rule-sets Allow-Web
rule 1 {
    match {
        dynamic-application-group junos:web;
    }
    then {
        permit;
    }
```

```
    }
    default-rule {
        deny;
    }
```

Looking at the example, we see a few interesting things. First, our AppFW ruleset explicitly permits junos:web and denies all else, effectively enforcing that the traffic is web based or denied. The firewall rule is essentially the same as before except it is referencing a different ruleset. Why did we choose to do junos:web rather than junos:HTTP here? The reason is because of a unique ability for HTTP. Unlike other protocols like, say, FTP, SMTP, and DNS (among hundreds of other Level 7 base applications), HTTP can carry additional applications on it called nested apps. If we only defined junos:HTTP, we would only allow applications that we could detect to be HTTP but that we don't have a more specific match for, like junos:Facebook. By using the junos:web group, we're including all known web applications functioning over HTTP. This is the best option when you're looking to generally permit web versus a specific application. Again, this is unique to HTTP at this time. This is true for both blacklist, whitelist, and other apps.

Configuring a hybrid application ruleset. Starting in 12.1X44, we have the ability to define hybrid rulesets, which is useful when you are using nested applications in a complex fashion. As we mentioned, prior to 12.1X44, you could only have one action in your rules (permit or deny) with the default action the opposite. Now you can mix them. Let's look at a real-world example of how you would do this. In this example, we block any Facebook traffic, allow any other web traffic, and ensure that no applications are allowed to communicate over this rule, which allows traffic on TCP port 80. Silently drop any traffic going to Facebook, but the other nonweb traffic should be actively closed immediately.

```
[edit]
root@srx3600n0# set security application-firewall rule-sets Allow-Web-No-
Facebook rule 1 match dynamic-application-group junos:web:social-
networking:facebook

[edit]
root@srx3600n0# set security application-firewall rule-sets Allow-Web-No-
Facebook rule 1 then deny

[edit]
root@srx3600n0# set security application-firewall rule-sets Allow-Web-No-
Facebook rule 2 match dynamic-application-group junos:web

[edit]
root@srx3600n0# set security application-firewall rule-sets Allow-Web-No-
Facebook rule 2 then permit

[edit]
root@srx3600n0# set security application-firewall rule-sets Allow-Web-No-
Facebook default-rule reject
```

```
[edit]
root@srx3600n0# set security policies from-zone trust to-zone untrust policy
Allowed-Outbound match source-address any destination-address any application
junos-http

root@srx3600n0# set security policies from-zone trust to-zone untrust policy
Allowed-Outbound then permit application-services application-firewall rule-set
Allow-Web-No-Facebook

[edit]
root@srx3600n0# set security policies from-zone trust to-zone untrust policy
Allowed-Outbound then log session-close

[edit]
root@srx3600n0# show security policies from-zone trust to-zone untrust policy
Allowed-Outbound
match {
    source-address any;
    destination-address any;
    application junos-http;
}
then {
    permit {
        application-services {
            application-firewall {
                rule-set Allow-Web-No-Facebook;
            }
        }
    }
    log {
        session-close;
    }
}

[edit]
root@srx3600n0# show security application-firewall rule-sets Allow-Web-No-
Facebook
rule 1 {
    match {
        dynamic-application-group junos:web:social-networking:facebook;
    }
    then {
        deny;
    }
}
rule 2 {
    match {
        dynamic-application-group junos:web;
    }
    then {
        permit;
```

```
        }
    }
    default-rule {
        reject;
    }
```

This example shows a few things. First, we have the rule that matches any Facebook traffic (we used the group rather than individual Facebook applications), which we deny. That means that we silently drop the traffic. We have to place the rule before the second rule that allows all web traffic because order is important. If we had the allow all web traffic rule first, we'd never hit the rule that would block Facebook traffic. Finally, we have a default rule that rejects all traffic that isn't web to ensure that no other applications can be passed through this device. The difference between deny and reject is that the system will send a TCP reset to the client and server rather than just silently dropping the traffic. This is often better for clients because a silent drop will result in application timeouts and sometimes hanging until the OS times out the session rather than immediately reporting the connection loss. Just as before, this hybrid ruleset is applied to our firewall rule, which only permits traffic on the Layer 3/Layer 4 application HTTP.

One question that we often hear when discussing the hybrid approach is why use the hybrid approach instead of splitting this up into multiple firewall rules? The answer is that it depends. If you can key in on some specific attribute like source IP or destination IP, then you might be able to stick to blacklist and whitelist using multiple firewall rules. The issue is that often this functionality is needed when you have a single allow outbound-like rule that doesn't explicitly define the source and destination hosts, which is normally the case allowing traffic out to the Internet. In these cases where you can't separate the traffic into separate firewall rules, and you are dealing with nested apps, you might need to use the hybrid approach. This is usually not needed for base applications like FTP, SMTP, DNS, and so on because there is no such overlap in the application traffic like there is with nested apps.

When to use blacklist, whitelist, and hybrid rulesets. So the obvious question here is this: Is there some strategy that I should use when configuring these rulesets? Yes! You can use the following points as a guide:

1. If you want to allow specific applications while blocking anything else, the whitelist-based approach is best.
2. If you want to explicitly block specific applications but allow all others, then the blacklist approach is best.
3. If you are filtering on nested applications and you want to allow some through while blocking others, performing a broader action on all other traffic, then the hybrid approach is best.

From a security perspective, whitelisting is usually the best (particularly if you are specific on the applications you want to allow) because all anomalous and evasive applications will be blocked (unless they are masquerading as the applications you are allowing; in such cases IPS and other Level 7 UTM is helpful as well). Blacklisting is best if you want to prevent certain applications from functioning.

Configuring application redirect. Starting in Junos 12.1X45, you have an additional option that instead of merely silently dropping the traffic or sending a TCP reset (neither of which are particularly pleasant from a user experience perspective), you can redirect the user to either a local web page explaining the violation or to a third-party web server where the connection information is posted as a URL variable so the web server can generate a nice-looking web page with the information to inform the user of the violation.

```
[edit]
root@srx3600n0# set security application-firewall profile Redirect block-
message type custom-text content "YOUR APPLICATION IS BLOCKED DUE TO POLICY VIO-
LATION"

 [edit]
root@srx3600n0# set security application-firewall rule-sets Facebook-Games pro-
file Redirect

 [edit]
root@srx3600n0# set security application-firewall rule-sets Facebook-Games rule
1 then reject block-message

[edit]
root@srx3600n0# set security application-firewall profile Redirect-Server block-
message type custom-redirect-url content "http://blockpage.company.local/ ?
JNI_SRCIP=<src-ip>&JNI_SRCPORT=<src-port>&JNI_DSTIP=<dst-ip>&JNI_DSTPORT=<dst-
port>&JNI_USER=<username>&JNI_APPNAME=<appname>""

[edit]
root@srx3600n0# set security application-firewall rule-sets Allow-Web profile
Redirect-Server

[edit]
root@srx3600n0# set security application-firewall rule-sets Allow-Web default-
rule reject block-message

[edit]
root@srx3600n0# show security application-firewall
profile Redirect {
    block-message {
        type {
            custom-text {
                content "YOUR APPLICATION IS BLOCKED DUE TO POLICY VIOLATION";
            }
        }
```

```
    }
}
profile Redirect-Server {
    block-message {
        type {
            custom-redirect-url {
                        content  http://blockpage.company.local/  ?JNI_SRCIP=<src-
ip>&JNI_SRCPORT=<src-port>&JNI_DSTIP=<dst-ip>&JNI_DSTPORT=<dst-
port>&JNI_USER=<username>&JNI_APPNAME=<appname>";
            }
        }
    }
}
rule-sets Facebook-Games {
    rule 1 {
        match {
            dynamic-application junos:FACEBOOK-FARMVILLE;
        }
        then {
            reject {
                block-message;
            }
        }
    }
    rule 2 {
        match {
            dynamic-application-group junos:gaming;
        }
        then {
            deny;
        }
    }
    default-rule {
        permit;
    }
    profile Redirect;
}
rule-sets Allow-Web {
    rule 1 {
        match {
            dynamic-application-group junos:web;
        }
        then {
            permit;
        }
    }
    default-rule {
        reject {
            block-message;
        }
    }
```

```
        profile Redirect-Server;
    }
```

So, as you can see, there are two options that we can leverage for redirects when using either the deny or reject actions in any of the rules or the default rule. You can redirect locally, where you just redirect them to an internal page, or you can redirect to a third-party device. In this case, we redirect to *http://blockpage.company.local/* but we append a special URL string that passes variables: ?JNI_SRCIP=<src-ip>&JNI_SRCPORT=<src-port>&JNI_DSTIP=<dst-ip>&JNI_DSTPORT=<dst-port>&JNI_USER=<username>&JNI_APPNAME=<appname>. Essentially, this passes the information to the third-party web server so that the content can be displayed in a more elegant fashion, as the server can take the information in the URL and turn that into a custom page with the real parameters of the message.

Configuring and Deploying Application Quality of Service

Sometimes the pure action of dropping an application is not appropriate, but at the same time, you might want to have some sort of control of the traffic and not give it carte blanche access to the network from a traffic perspective. There are several common scenarios for this. For instance, many universities and ISPs might not be able to block traffic, but they also want to ensure that particular applications like P2P applications cannot completely saturate the network bandwidth either. Another major use case is in the enterprise, ensuring that traffic receives a certain priority of processing within the network. Of course, you could always handle this with the standard Junos QoS facilities, but these cannot function at the application level and operate at the packet level. AppQoS allows you to take the application identity information into account to jump to the next level with QoS.

AppQoS only takes place on the egress interface of the SRX and does not take place on the ingress. If you want to do ingress traffic processing, then you should use ingress policing. This is not application aware but can leverage stateless filters to define how it should be processed.

So we know that AppQoS leverages the application identity information determined from AppID, but how does it function? Very similar to AppFW, AppQoS uses a ruleset-based approach that is enabled on a per firewall rule basis. The ruleset contains rules that define match criteria, which is the application or application groups. AppQoS does not have a default-rule like AppFW, but you can leverage the concept of unknown or any application along with specific groups and applications. The actions of each rule include configuring any or all of the following:

- DSCP rewrite
- Forwarding class
- Logging when thresholds are met
- Loss priority
- Rate limiters (configurable in both client-to-server and server-to-client directions)

It's worthwhile to note that on the high-end SRX platforms, all of the QoS is done in the network processor for maximum capabilities and minimal impact on the system. Because this is done in a potentially distributed manner, if your traffic happens to egress multiple network processors, each network processor will handle the rate limiting and forwarding class separately so it is possible that more traffic could be sent than what is defined if not all of the traffic for an individual profile passes through multiple NPUs. However, you can usually engineer around this, and on the high-end SRX you're usually dealing with much larger circuits so this won't be a main concern.

The next logical question is what function and use case each of the items provides. Let's take a look.

DSCP rewrite

DSCP is a standard 6-bit field in the IP header that is well understood by networking equipment like routers, switches, firewalls and other devices. This field can be leveraged to make class of service, routing, and filtering decisions by upstream and downstream devices in the data path. The advantage of setting this on the SRX is that the SRX is application aware, whereas most of the routers and switches are not or would have to incur a major performance tax. The SRX could therefore be used to identify that the traffic is, say, VoIP, and rewrite the DSCP so that other devices in the network will give it low latency prioritized forwarding. On the other hand, you could change the bits for unknown or P2P traffic so that at your edge router it could give it the lowest service. This is particularly useful if you have multiple firewalls that do not sit directly on the edge but rather an edge router like an MX.

Forwarding class

Forwarding classes are a concept that is used to define how traffic is mapped to different hardware queues in the network processor (or in software on the branch SRX). These different queues are serviced by the engine in different ways, depending on the settings. Junos includes four default forwarding classes or queues: Best Effort, Expedited Forwarding, Assured Forwarding, and Network Control. Typically, you would put general traffic in Best Effort, higher priority traffic that needs better service in Expedited Forwarding, sensitive latency traffic into Assured Forwarding, and leave network protocol traffic for the Network Control queue. This allows you to better service traffic when bandwidth is in contention on the egress interface and decisions need to be made on which traffic to service first (queuing strategies).

Forwarding classes can be very complex and offer a lot of different tuning knobs that are outside the scope of this book. We recommend that you review the Class of Service Configuration guide if you're interested in deeper detail with custom forwarding classes. For the purposes of this book, we focus on leveraging the predefined forwarding classes.

Logging

This is a simple on–off setting that can be defined on a per-rule basis. When it is enabled and a QoS action is triggered, like exceeding a rate limit, a separate AppQoS log message will be generated (on the data plane via syslog), which informs that a QoS action was taken on the traffic.

Loss priority

Loss priority is a concept that is used to define if the traffic should be dropped when there is congestion. The SRX supports four different loss priorities, Low, Medium Low, Medium High, and High. Different loss priorities define at what level of queue saturation (in percentage) the probability of dropping traffic will be. By default, all of the loss priorities have the default drop priority, but you can set your own as well (in fact you will need to; otherwise, it won't have an effect until the interface is at 100 percent capacity which isn't of much use). This is because Juniper has no idea how individual customers will want their system to behave when the queue begins to fill so this makes sense and is considered an advanced feature.

Rate limiter

Rate limiters are really at the core of AppQoS and allow you to define a rate at which traffic will be permitted to flow out of the SRX. This allows you to specifically set caps on the traffic in both the client-to-server and the server-to-client directions. Setting a bidirectional limiter is very important because your circuit might have asymmetric data rates—very common in broadband environments. The rate limiter allows you to set the bandwidth limit as well as the burst size. The bandwidth limit is the base amount of bandwidth that you want to allow the traffic to be allowed to use, although the burst size is the amount of traffic that you will allow the traffic to use if there is room available.

Configuring an AppQoS example

We've examined what AppQoS looks like from a high level, but there's nothing better than looking at an example to see how it is actually leveraged. In this example, we configure AppQoS on a firewall rule called allowed outbound in a university environment where no traffic filtering can be performed, but traffic can be classified and rate limited based on type. We assume the following criteria:

- P2P traffic should be put into the Best Effort forwarding class, and should be rate limited to 100 Mbps in each direction. Log when a violation occurs.
- Multimedia traffic should be given Expedited Forwarding and limited to 200 Mbps in the download direction and 50 Mbps in the upload direction.
- Unknown applications should be put in the Best Effort forwarding class and be given 25 Mbps in both directions. Set the DSCP value to 000000, which upstream routers know should be given the lowest processing priority.
- Any other known application should be given 50 Mbps in both directions.

```
[edit]
root@srx3600n0# set class-of-service application-traffic-control rule-sets
AppQoS rule 1 match application-group junos:p2p

 [edit]
root@srx3600n0# set class-of-service application-traffic-control rule-sets
AppQoS rule 1 then forwarding-class best-effort log rate-limit client-to-
server 100Mbps server-to-client 100Mbps

[edit]
root@srx3600n0# set class-of-service application-traffic-control rule-sets
AppQoS rule 2 match application-group junos:multimedia

[edit]
root@srx3600n0# set class-of-service application-traffic-control rule-sets
AppQoS rule 2 then forwarding-class expedited-forwarding rate-limit client-to-
server 50Mbps server-to-client 200Mbps

 [edit]
root@srx3600n0# set class-of-service application-traffic-control rule-sets
AppQoS rule 3 match application-unknown

[edit]
root@srx3600n0# set class-of-service application-traffic-control rule-sets
AppQoS rule 3 then dscp-code-point 000000

[edit]
root@srx3600n0# set class-of-service application-traffic-control rule-sets
AppQoS rule 3 then forwarding-class best-effort rate-limit client-to-server
25Mbps server-to-client 25Mbps

[edit]
root@srx3600n0# set class-of-service application-traffic-control rule-sets
AppQoS rule 4 match application-known

[edit]
```

```
root@srx3600n0# set class-of-service application-traffic-control rule-sets
AppQoS rule 4 then rate-limit client-to-server 50Mbps server-to-client 50Mbps

[edit]
root@srx3600n0# set security policies from-zone trust to-zone untrust policy
Allowed-Outbound match source-address any destination-address any application
any

[edit]
root@srx3600n0# set security policies from-zone trust to-zone untrust policy
Allowed-Outbound then permit application-services application-traffic-control
rule-set AppQoS

[edit]
root@srx3600n0# set security policies from-zone trust to-zone untrust policy
Allowed-Outbound then log session-close

[edit]
root@srx3600n0# show class-of-service
application-traffic-control {
    rate-limiters HTTP {
        bandwidth-limit 5000;
    }
    rate-limiters P2P {
        bandwidth-limit 100000;
    }
    rate-limiters 100Mbps {
        bandwidth-limit 100000;
    }
    rate-limiters 200Mbps {
        bandwidth-limit 200000;
    }
    rate-limiters 50Mbps {
        bandwidth-limit 50000;
    }
    rate-limiters 25Mbps {
        bandwidth-limit 25000;
    }
    rule-sets AppQoS {
        rule 1 {
            match {
                application-group junos:p2p;
            }
            then {
                forwarding-class best-effort;
                rate-limit {
                    client-to-server 100Mbps;
                    server-to-client 100Mbps;
                }
                log;
            }
        }
```

```
        rule 2 {
            match {
                application-group junos:multimedia;
            }
            then {
                forwarding-class expedited-forwarding;
                rate-limit {
                    client-to-server 50Mbps;
                    server-to-client 200Mbps;
                }
            }
        }
        rule 3 {
            match {
                application-unknown;
            }
            then {
                dscp-code-point 000000;
                forwarding-class best-effort;
                rate-limit {
                    client-to-server 25Mbps;
                    server-to-client 25Mbps;
                }
            }
        }
        rule 4 {
            match {
                application-known;
            }
            then {
                rate-limit {
                    client-to-server 50Mbps;
                    server-to-client 50Mbps;
                }
            }
        }
    }
}

[edit]
root@srx3600n0# show security policies from-zone trust to-zone untrust policy
Allowed-Outbound
match {
    source-address any;
    destination-address any;
    application any ;
}
then {
    permit {
        application-services {
            application-traffic-control {
                rule-set AppQoS;
```

```
                }
            }
        }
        log {
            session-close;
        }
    }
```

So let's talk a bit about this example. The first thing that we had to do is to configure the AppQoS infrastructure, which in this case was rate limiters. If you were doing all sorts of advanced options like configuring custom forwarding classes, queues, schedulers, loss priority, and so on, then you would also want to do this first. Each of these values are configured under the `set class-of-service` stanzas, which is common to standard Junos QoS rather than in the security configuration. This is because these components are shared with the standard QoS facilities in Junos, although the application-traffic-control ruleset is unique to AppQoS today. Next you create an AppQoS ruleset that is similar to AppFW from the perspective that it matches applications and groups and then applies a QoS action. Finally, this ruleset is applied to a firewall rule if the action is permit. In this example, we only set the bandwidth limit without configuring a burst size, because the system can automatically generate one for us and that's fine for most cases. We had to define a rate limit for each bandwidth amount leveraged, in this case 25 Mbps, 50 Mbps, 100 Mbps, and 200 Mbps. The setting itself is in Kbps not Mbps (1 Mb is 1,000 Kb) and remember we're talking about bits not bytes (1 byte = 8 bits)—although the burst size is actually defined in bytes, which is no doubt a gotcha. By letting the system define it, you don't have to worry much about it.

For the rulesets, order is important. And like AppFW we try to leverage application groups wherever possible because they can encompass numerous applications of the same type and are automatically updated with new members when they are created. There are three constructs in AppQoS that are a bit unique to AppQoS versus AppFW, which are Application Any, Application Known, and Application Unknown. Basically, Application Any is any application known or unknown, Application Known is any application that is not Unknown (so we have a match for it in the AppID database), and Application Unknown is any application for which we do not have a match in the database. We leveraged these identities for the last two rules. Unknown apps in particular are often items that you would want to rate limit because they could be some sort of P2P or evasive application that could consume a lot of bandwidth (if you can't outright block them due to organizational policy).

When setting rate limiters, it is important to understand that these are applied to the rule as a whole so collectively all traffic that is processed by the rule will be counted toward the rate limit. At the time of writing this book, there is no per user or per flow rate limiting available in AppQoS. You can, however, break out firewall rules to provide better granularity for enforcing per user controls, but this probably isn't ideal at scale.

Configuring and Deploying User Role Firewall

Much has changed in the last 10 years in networking. We've shifted from legacy desktop PCs hard-wired into the network to laptops and now mobile devices that fit in our pockets. Users can be placed anywhere in the network, and they desire the same experience wherever they are. At the same time, as a network security administrator, you are tasked with the job of securing the network and providing this level of functionality. We feel that it is always best to segment users into separate VLANs with different security controls wherever possible through the use of end-to-end Network Access/Admission Control (NAC), such as the Juniper Unified Access Control system. The challenge with this system for the casual network administrator who wears many hats is that it can be a lot of work to do a full NAC deployment. For the environments that do have the resources to deploy this, it is a very powerful capability to be leveraged. For instance, you can fully authenticate and evaluate a host's security posture before it ever even gets an IP address on the network, and it can be segmented into the appropriate VLAN, too. When deploying full NAC is not an option, the User Role Firewall (UserFW) feature is a good option to provide identity services and control at the firewall level for enforcement. Even better, because the SRX uses the User Identity in the match criteria, this can be used to incorporate other Level 7 services including different AppFW, AppQoS, IPS, and UTM criteria.

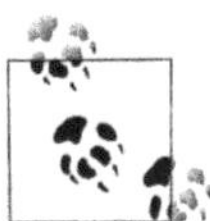

UserFW requires that you are running Junos 12.1+ on the SRX along with UAC 4.2+. Ideally, you will be running UAC 4.3+ because that has some additional tools for newer versions of Active Directory.

UserFW functionality overview

At the time of writing this book, the UserFW feature leverages both the SRX and the UAC solution that is available in a UAC, Juniper MAG Gateways, or VM appliance. In terms of functionality, this is how UserFW operates:

1. The SRX and UAC are configured to securely connect to each other, creating a control channel to exchange user-to-IP information.

2. A new firewall session arrives on the SRX. The SRX does the normal packet lookup to determine what should happen with the traffic. There is an additional match criteria field that defines the identity of the source IP from a user-to-IP mapping. As part of the firewall policy lookup, the SRX is responsible for determining if there is a known user-to-IP mapping for that source IP. If there is, the firewall will evaluate the policy as usual without any additional external intervention.
3. If there is no source-to-IP mapping for that source, the SRX will do a redirect to the UAC on the traffic (if configured to do so) to trigger authentication. This redirect works for HTTP or HTTPS traffic. If the traffic is not HTTP or HTTPS, it cannot be redirected, but the good news is that most modern OSs automatically send an HTTP message to the Internet to determine if they are behind a captive portal or not, so even if a web browser isn't open, you'll likely see a message to authenticate. This can also be done in an automated fashion using Windows Login scripts pushed out by Group Policy.
4. The redirected HTTP(S) traffic will arrive on the UAC. The UAC will attempt to trigger an SPNEGO authentication session with the browser. SPNEGO is a standards-based authentication mechanism in web browsers that instructs the user's machine to go out and get a Kerberos ticket from the domain controller and present it to the server. The server will then validate the user Kerberos ticket with Active Directory to ensure its validity.
    a. If the client browser doesn't support SPNEGO (most all of them do, but some need to be configured to do so; see the browser documentation for more information), then the UAC will fall back to captive portal authentication where the user will enter his domain credentials. If you have an advanced UAC license, then you can also leverage other authentication mechanisms like certificates so that the user doesn't need to manually authenticate with credentials.
5. Once the SPNEGO exchange has occurred, the client session will maintain an HTTPS AJAX session with the UAC that will send a heartbeat every five seconds to ensure that no other device could come in and steal the IP address of the user and gain that user's privileges if he were to log off.
6. The UAC will then send a message to the SRX that will include the user-to-IP mapping and the associated Roles for that user.
7. From now on, the SRX will have the user-to-IP mapping until the client's session ends so the policy lookup will be very fast and not require any user intervention. When the user closes his session, the UAC will remove the user-to-IP mapping from the SRX.

All of this might sound a little bit more complex than competitive solutions, and in truth it is; however, it is also more secure. Many competitive solutions merely place an agent on a domain controller in the hopes that the client will "log in" to the machine without cached credentials and the domain controller will know about it. In reality, we know that this doesn't always happen. Second, these solutions can't account for the fact that users log off (which Active Directory doesn't do a great job of tracking) nor that they might simply drop from the network—particularly on Wi-Fi. All of this opens them up to another user coming along and leveraging the IP address of the said client and gaining their privileges. This isn't possible with the SRX solution. The aforementioned competitive approach might be fine for environments that merely want a best effort security implementation, but for those that want deterministic security, the SRX and UAC solution is the way to go—and for even more powerful security, the full UAC NAC solution can offer end-to-end deterministic security.

Additionally, the SRX solution scales considerably better than the competitive solutions, with up to 50,000 concurrent users per platform on the high-end SRX at the time of writing this book (hopefully much higher in the future). It also functions well in domains with multiple domain controllers, trusts, and forests, something that other competitive solutions cannot boast, as they would need to install agents on every domain controller.

At the time of writing this book, Juniper is also in a beta phase of testing an Integrated UserFW product that doesn't require a secondary device or agent. Keep posted to the release notes for more information.

UserFW packaging and licensing

As we pointed out, the UserFW solution today does require the use of the UAC platform. The good news is that Juniper has packaged this in a way that it isn't cost or administratively prohibitive to deploy. First, on the SRX itself, there are no additional licensing or cost requirements; you simply need to be running Junos 12.1+. On the UAC, the MAG2600 starts at $1,500, with licensing for 25 role-based firewall users at $300, making this affordable for all but the smallest of SMB deployments. This can scale up to massive deployments with tens of thousands of users on the high-end SRX with full HA capabilities on both the SRX and the UAC platforms.

Deploying UserFW

The initial deployment of the UserFW feature is a little bit complex, but if you follow these steps, you should be able to get it up and running without issues. The good news is that once the UserFW setup is up and running, you should be able to operate it without much effort because the overhead is quite small. In terms of setting things up, the tasks break down into three areas:

- Configuring the SRX
- Configuring the UAC
- Miscellaneous tasks in your Active Directory environment

In the following sections, we look at what must be done in each of these three areas to ensure that your infrastructure is set up to run UserFW properly. We use Figure 12-11 as a model for our configuration, with clients in the trust zone, a server zone that houses our Active Directory infrastructure, and the Infranet controller, and resources that our users want to access on the Internet.

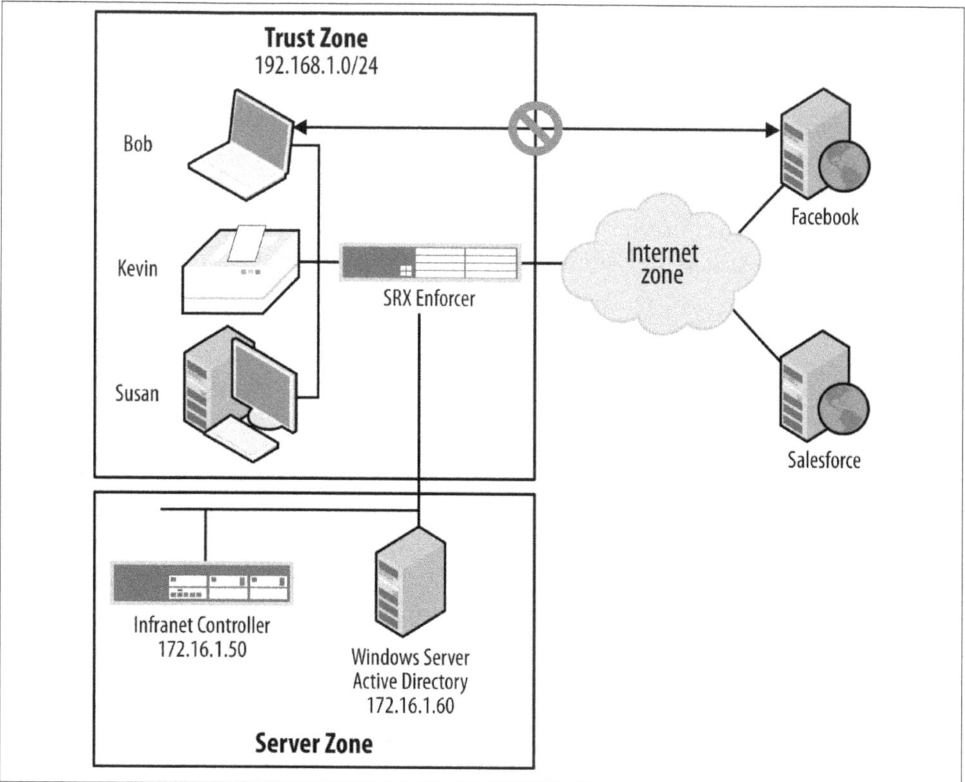

Figure 12-11. UserFW topology

Configuring the SRX for UserFW

There are a few required and some optional configuration elements that we discuss in this section to help prepare the SRX to act as a UserFW enforcer.

Required steps include the following:

1. Configure the SRX to UAC communication.
2. Ensure that DNS and NTP are enabled on the SRX.
3. Configure firewall rules to redirect clients to UAC.

4. Configure firewall rules leveraging Source-Identity to match users.

Optionally, depending on your deployment, you might want or need to do the following:

1. Create firewall rules to allow clients to communicate with the Infranet controller and Active Directory infrastructure (required in our example because clients and the IC/AD are in different zones; if they were all in the trust zone, it wouldn't be required).
2. Create rules to allow IC/AD infrastructure or other equipment to communicate out the firewall (required in this example, for AD to go to the Internet for DNS resolution).
3. Configure local entries for UserFW. This is useful if you want to bypass UAC authentication or if you are using NetConf as a user identity feed to pass user-to-IP mapping via some other channel.

Let's look at configuring this example with the required components just mentioned. Let's assume the following information:

- Clients are in the 192.168.1.0/24 Subnet in the trust zone.
- The Servers zone contains the Infranet controller and the Active Directory domain controller. The IC has an IP address of 172.16.1.50 and the domain controller is 172.16.1.60. The IC has a DNS name of ic.company.local.
- Kevin has a hardcoded IP address that we want to enter into the local database as 192.168.1.100. He is part of the Sales Team for the Sales role. He should be able to reach Salesforce.
- Bob is the CEO and should be able to access both Facebook and Salesforce.
- Susan is part of the Marketing role and should be able to reach Facebook to perform company-related marketing tasks.

Let's start by configuring the SRX to IC communication.

```
[edit]
root@srx3600n0# set services unified-access-control certificate-verification
warning timeout-action open

[edit]
root@srx3600n0# set services unified-access-control captive-portal IC-Redirect
redirect-traffic unauthenticated redirect-url "https://ic.company.local/"

[edit]
root@srx3600n0# set services unified-access-control infranet-controller ic.com-
pany.local address 172.16.1.50 interface ge-0/0/0 password onetimepassword

[edit]
root@srx3600n0# set system name-server 172.16.1.60
```

```
[edit]
root@srx3600n0# set system ntp server 172.16.1.60

[edit]
root@srx3600n0# show services unified-access-control
infranet-controller ic.company.local {
    address 172.16.1.50;
    interface ge-0/0/0.0;
    password "$9$T39peK8-dsWLs4aU.mz36/pBIRSeMXhS4ZjqQzhSrlK8"; ## SECRET-DATA
}
certificate-verification warning;
timeout-action open;
captive-portal IC-Redirect {
    redirect-traffic unauthenticated;
    redirect-url https://ic.company.local/;
}

[edit]
root@srx3600n0# show system ntp
server 172.16.1.60;

[edit]
root@srx3600n0# show system name-server
172.16.1.60;
```

If you want the IC to automatically redirect users to the original destination to which they were browsing, then you would define the redirect-url to "https://<ic.fqdn>/<sign-in page>?`target=%dest-url%&enforcer=%enforcer-id%&policy=%policy-id%`". Where the ic.fqdn is the hostname, the sign-in page is optional. The rest is information that will be passed from the SRX to the UAC via the redirect URL so that after successfully logging in, the UAC can redirect the client to the target destination.

There are a few things going on in the preceding example. First, we specify the high-level configuration parameters for the UAC communication. Because the IC and SRX communicate via an encrypted SSL channel, you need to upload trusted certificates and a CA to the SRX and IC. In this example, we're going to skip this and just configure the SRX to warn us if the certificate between the SRX and IC are not trusted (which it won't be). To make it trusted, you will need to install the public CA certificate on both the SRX and IC and generate a certificate for both separately and install them using the certificate for communication.

Next, we specified the captive portal configuration. This will be used in the firewall policy configuration to determine where the users should be redirected. This must be to the IC and is best in the FQDN format. If you are using a separate realm, you would also post it at the end of the URL as well. For this example, we assume the realm is just at the base URL for the IC. We specify that all unauthenticated traffic be sent to the IC, but this is really overridden at the firewall policy level.

Finally, we specified the IP address and password along with the optional source interface for the SRX to communicate with the IC from. The SRX will always contact the IC, so if there is any firewall filtering device between the SRX and the IC, you need to make sure that it allows communication between the two. The default port is TCP 11122 for the secure control channel communication. We did add DNS and NTP to resolve from the AD domain controller because we want to make sure time and name resolution are in sync with the domain.

Next let's look at configuring the security policy infrastructure.

```
[edit]
root@srx3600n0# set security policies from-zone trust to-zone servers policy
Clients-to-IC match source-address Clients-192.168.1.0/24 destination-address
IC-172.16.1.50/32 application [junos-http junos-https]

[edit]
root@srx3600n0# set security policies from-zone trust to-zone servers policy
Clients-to-IC then permit

[edit]
root@srx3600n0# set security policies from-zone trust to-zone servers policy
Clients-to-IC then log session-close

[edit]
root@srx3600n0# set security policies from-zone trust to-zone servers policy
Allow-AD  match  source-address  Clients-192.168.1.0/24  destination-address
AD-172.16.1.60/32 application any

[edit]
root@srx3600n0# set security policies from-zone trust to-zone servers policy
Allow-AD then permit

root@srx3600n0# set security policies from-zone trust to-zone servers policy
Allow-AD then log session-close

[edit]
root@srx3600n0# set security policies from-zone servers to-zone untrust policy
Allow-DNS-NTP match source-address AD-172.16.1.60/32 destination-address any ap-
plication [junos-dns-udp junos-ntp]

[edit]
root@srx3600n0# set security policies from-zone servers to-zone untrust policy
Allow-DNS-NTP then permit

[edit]
root@srx3600n0# set security policies from-zone servers to-zone untrust policy
Allow-DNS-NTP then log session-close
```

```
[edit]
root@srx3600n0# set security policies from-zone trust to-zone internet policy
Redirect-Unauthenticated match source-address Clients-192.168.1.0/24 source-
identity unauthenticated-user destination-address any application any

[edit]
root@srx3600n0# set security policies from-zone trust to-zone internet policy
Redirect-Unauthenticated then permit application-services uac-policy captive-
portal IC-Redirect

[edit]
root@srx3600n0# set security policies from-zone trust to-zone internet policy
Redirect-Unauthenticated then log session-close

[edit]
root@srx3600n0# set security policies from-zone trust to-zone internet policy
Facebook match source-address Clients-192.168.1.0/24 source-identity [CEO Mar-
keting] destination-address www.facebook.com application [junos-https]

[edit]
root@srx3600n0# set security policies from-zone trust to-zone internet policy
Facebook then permit

[edit]
root@srx3600n0# set security policies from-zone trust to-zone internet policy
Facebook then log session-close

[edit]
root@srx3600n0# set security policies from-zone trust to-zone internet policy
Salesforce match source-address Clients-192.168.1.0/24 source-identity [CEO
Sales] destination-address www.salesforce.com application [junos-https]

[edit]
root@srx3600n0# set security policies from-zone trust to-zone internet policy
Salesforce then permit

[edit]
root@srx3600n0# set security policies from-zone trust to-zone internet policy
Salesforce then log session-close

[edit]
root@srx3600n0# set security address-book global address Clients-192.168.1.0/24
192.168.1.0/24

[edit]
root@srx3600n0# set security address-book global address IC-172.16.1.50/32
172.16.1.50/32

[edit]
root@srx3600n0# set security address-book global address AD-172.16.1.60/32
172.16.1.60/32
```

```
[edit]
root@srx3600n0# set security address-book global address www.facebook.com dns-
name www.facebook.com

[edit]
root@srx3600n0# set security address-book global address www.salesforce.com dns-
name www.salesforce.com

[edit]
root@srx3600n0# run request security user-identification local-authentication-
table add user-name Kevin roles Sales ip-address 192.168.1.100

[edit]
root@srx3600n0# run show security user-identification local-authentication-
table all
Total entries: 5
Source IP       Username     Roles
192.168.1.100   kevin        sales

[edit]
root@srx3600n0# show security address-book
global {
    address Clients-192.168.1.0/24 192.168.1.0/24;
    address IC-172.16.1.50/32 172.16.1.50/32;
    address AD-172.16.1.60/32 172.16.1.60/32;
    address www.facebook.com {
        dns-name www.facebook.com;
    }
    address www.salesforce.com {
        dns-name www.salesforce.com;
    }
}

[edit]
root@srx3600n0# show security policies | no-more
from-zone trust to-zone servers {
    policy Clients-to-IC {
        match {
            source-address any;
            destination-address IC-172.16.1.50/32;
            application [ junos-http junos-https ];
        }
        then {
            permit;
            log {
                session-close;
            }
        }
    }
    policy Allow-AD {
        match {
```

```
                source-address any;
                destination-address AD-172.16.1.60/32;
                application any;
            }
            then {
                permit;
                log {
                    session-close;
                }
            }
        }
    }
    from-zone servers to-zone untrust {
        policy Allow-DNS-NTP {
            match {
                source-address AD-172.16.1.60/32;
                destination-address any;
                application [ junos-dns-udp junos-ntp ];
            }
            then {
                permit;
                log {
                    session-close;
                }
            }
        }
    }
    from-zone trust to-zone internet {
        policy Redirect-Unauthenticated {
            match {
                source-address Clients-192.168.1.0/24;
                destination-address any;
                application any;
                source-identity [ unauthenticated-user ];
            }
            then {
                permit {
                    application-services {
                        uac-policy {
                            captive-portal IC-Redirect;
                        }
                    }
                }
                log {
                    session-close;
                }
            }
        }
        policy Facebook {
            match {
                source-address Clients-192.168.1.0/24;
                destination-address www.facebook.com;
```

```
                application junos-https;
                source-identity [ CEO Marketing ];
            }
            then {
                permit;
                log {
                    session-close;
                }
            }
        }
        policy Salesforce {
            match {
                source-address Clients-192.168.1.0/24;
                destination-address www.salesforce.com;
                application junos-https;
                source-identity [ CEO Sales ];
            }
            then {
                permit;
                log {
                    session-close;
                }
            }
        }

    }
```

There are a few more things going on here. Let's review them. Here we are building out our UserFW policy infrastructure. As we mentioned at first, because the clients and the IC/AD infrastructure are in a different zone, you need to configure rules to allow them to communicate, hence the rules in the "trust to servers" policy context. If they were all in the same zone, like trust, this would not be necessary. However, we would still likely need to create some rules to allow the AD infrastructure to communicate with other areas of the network (like other AD servers) or to the Internet for things like NTP/DNS resolution, as we assume our domain controller is also our DNS server. That is what we have done in the `servers to internet` policy ruleset. Finally, and the most interesting part, we have set up our security policy infrastructure for our client access out to the Internet. This is where all of the magic really happens, because we can now leverage the "Source-Identity" field! Notice in this example, we do not reference the users by name, but instead by role. This is how the SRX is designed at the time of writing this book, but this will likely change in the future to be able to reference users and AD groups directly. We see how these are mapped in the IC to the domain groups later, and we can also see in this example, how Kevin is mapped locally to the Sales role by local mapping.

Finally, we configure the actual security policy infrastructure for the trust to Internet rules. At the top of this ruleset is the rule that matches any clients with Source-Identity unknown or unauthenticated, with an action of permit and to redirect to the IC. There are three special roles in the SRX: unknown, unauthenticated, and any. Unknown is a role that matches users when the IC communication is down so that you can still leverage fallback policies. Unauthenticated is any IP address that doesn't have an actively associated identity to it, and any is any user, known, unauthenticated, or unknown. In this example, we choose to use unauthenticated so that these users will be matched and redirected to the IC to have their identity validated. All of their HTTP and HTTPS sessions will be redirected to the IC until they authenticate. All other traffic will be dropped. Once users are authenticated, they will no longer match the unauthenticated user role, but instead will have a role like CEO, Marketing, or Sales and thus will match rules. As you can see, just like with standard firewall policies, rule ordering is very important. If you put the redirect in the wrong place, they might match a different rule (including one without user identity) first and might never be authenticated. Again, once you have the UserFW infrastructure in place, this is a very simple task from an administration perspective, but it does take a bit of extra work up front to get going.

It is important to understand that at the time of writing this book, the Source-Identity field refers to a role name that is either delivered from the IC or from the local database. In both the IC and local database, the user is mapped to a given role. In the future, this will likely change to allow you to reference the users directly. This is very important to understand not only when writing the firewall policy, but when you are creating roles, and especially in the role mapping section in the upcoming IC configuration steps, as you will soon see.

Configuring the IC

Now that we have configured the SRX, we'll look at the IC. Technically you can configure the IC first if you want. IC tasks would include the following:

1. Configure the SRX to IC communication.
2. Configure the authentication server.
3. Configure the realm, role, and sign-in policy.

For this example, we assume that you already have the IC up and running on the network, licensed with the User Role or Full User Access licenses, and that it has a certificate that your client devices in your domain trust so that they don't get warning messages when they get redirected. If you are new to the UAC solution and working with the IC, we suggest you review the Juniper Jump Start guides on the UAC solution for getting the box up and running, along with the appropriate information. Juniper also offers full courses on the UAC solution that are very worthwhile, particularly if you are thinking about extending this configuration to full end-to-end NAC in the future.

For this example, we are going to be working with the IC, not the SRX, so we handle the configuration format a little bit differently because the IC doesn't have a command line so to speak.

Configuring the SRX as an IC enforcer. Once you've set up the SRX configuration, the SRX will try to connect to the IC; however, the IC won't accept the connections until you complete this stage in the IC Admin interface.

1. Go to UAC, click Infranet Enforcer, then click Connections.
2. Click New Enforcer
3. In the new window, select the Enforcer Type as the Junos SRX.
4. Give a name to the connection, specify the shared password that you set on the SRX, and specify the serial numbers of the SRX (see "show chassis hardware" from the SRX CLI). We say numbers because you can do this in HA.
5. The location group should be left at No 802.1x, and you don't need to check the IDP module option.
6. Click Save Changes to complete this step.

Configuring the authentication server. This step is relatively simple in the IC. We're assuming that you already have the SRX up and running and configured, along with the IC setup and on the network. It is best to have the SRX communicate with the IC on the internal port. We also assume that you have added the licensing, and set up the proper DNS and NTP (where the DNS really should be a DNS server in your domain or capable of authenticating to the domain). We recommend using UAC 4.3+ so that you can use the new Active Directory mode that automatically resolves the AD structure. The legacy AD mode (configurable by the button at the bottom) works, too, but you have to manually specify the domain controllers and it isn't quite as resilient, so you should use the new mode wherever possible.

1. Add a new Authentication Server of type Active Directory under Authentication, Auth Servers, by selecting Active Directory/Windows NT and clicking New.
2. Specify a name in the IC to reference the IC.
3. Specify the NetBIOS domain name (in our example it's COMPANY) along with the full Kerberos Realm name, which in our example is COMPANY.LOCAL.
4. Specify the domain credentials for the IC service account. You can also use an account with domain admin rights, but it is a best practice to give a specific service account for the IC.
5. For the IC to work, it will need to join the domain, so you must specify where the machine should be created. By default, this is in the Computers container, but you

might want to do it elsewhere. You should also specify the name of the IC that will be in the domain. This name should be capable of being resolved internally and your certificate on the IC should match this name so clients don't get error messages.

6. The final step is to Enable SPNEGO and upload the Kerberos ticket file that you created in Active Directory.
7. Click Save Changes.

If all goes well, the Domain Status should turn green after a short period of time. If it doesn't work, you will likely see an error message. You can also check in the Event Log as well. Common mistakes include incorrect credentials or insufficient rights, incorrect domain name, incorrect DNS settings, and IC unable to contact the domain controller due to routing or firewall policies. If you need more explanation of these steps, the IC documentation goes into all of them, including getting the system up and running in great detail. There is also a guided setup wizard when you first log in to the system as an administrator.

Configuring realms, roles, and sign-in policies. For this section, we assume that you are somewhat familiar with the concepts of realms, roles, and sign-in policies on the IC.

1. Start by creating one or more roles. The role is a logical container for the user to role mapping. To create a new role, go to Users, select User Roles, and then select New-User-Role.
2. The only thing that you need to make sure is enabled in the role is under the Agentless tab. Enable Agentless Access for this role. Repeat for each different role for which you want to set up access.
3. Click Save Changes.
4. Next, you will want to make a new realm for authenticating the clients to your IC. Under Users, select User Realms, then select New User Realm.
5. Give the new realm a name, and specify the authentication and directory services. This should be the authentication server that you created in the previous example for both the authentication and directory services.
6. Click Save Changes. This would be done for the CEO, Marketing, and Sales roles.
7. Next you will want to create the role mapping rules within the realm. These define how the user will be mapped to what role. The IC automatically takes you to this screen.
8. You will need to create a new role.
9. There are a few paths that you can take in the next step, and it all depends on how you want to map the user. You can do it simply by listing the usernames that you want to be part of the role. That is simply done by listing the users in the Username

text box. For this example, we could simply do it based on username to map Kevin, Susan, and Bob to their respective roles. In many cases, you will want to map users based on Active Directory group membership. This is done by changing the Rule Based On drop-down menu setting to Group Membership, then clicking Update. You will see the page refresh, which will create a new button called Groups. If you haven't clicked this before, it will open a new window that can query Active Directory for group membership names. You can enter the name directly into that field or click Search and search for the name in Active Directory. Once you have identified the group that you want to select, click OK. You now select the Group names and move them from the Available groups list to the Selected groups list.

10. Next you will need to select the appropriate roles to be mapped to this rule by selecting the roles in the Available roles list and moving them into the Selected roles list. Typically, you will want to select the Stop processing checkbox unless you want users to fall under multiple roles. Click Save Changes to complete this step.

11. From Step 10 you've now mapped incoming users that are authenticated to a role that you created. You can repeat this stage for each new rule you want. Order is important for role mapping, as roles are mapped from top to bottom until a match is hit (if Stop processing is enabled for that role).

12. The final step is to make sure that the realm is part of the sign-in page that you've specified in the Redirect-URL on the SRX. By default, the only sign-in page that is created is the "/" sign-in page. For instance, if your server is called *https://ic.company.local/*, that would be the base page. You can create additional sign-in pages as well, but it's not required. For this example, we won't create a new sign-in page, but we must add our realm to the list of realms; preferably you will only have one realm on this page.

13. To select the realm in the sign-in page, go to Authentication, select Signing-In, and then click Sign-In Policies and select the user policy "*/".

14. By default, there will be a realm called Users in there, but you will be able to change this to the realm you created in Step 4. You should also change the Authentication Protocol Set to "Not Applicable" by clicking the 802.1x field, changing the value, and clicking the checkbox. Finally, click Save Changes.

If you just want to leverage a simple captive portal-based form of authentication rather than the transparent SPNEGO auth, you do not need to configure the Active Directory server, but instead you can rely on the local database on the IC. This makes for a simpler configuration and sometimes is ideal to use for testing to ensure that the platforms are up and talking correctly. There is nothing special about this configuration. It is the same as it would be with the standard Coordinated Threat Control configuration except the SRX can now leverage the Source-Identity in the policy itself.

As we mentioned earlier, in this example, you are defining a role and mapping users to that role. In the SRX Source-Identity field you will be referencing the role name, not the username, at least at the time of writing this book. This might change in the future, so check the release notes. That should complete the IC configuration necessary to get things up and running. There are numerous options and customizations that you can use to further extend the capabilities of the IC with the SRX, but they are outside the scope of this book. We suggest you check out the IC documentation or training courses for detailed information on all of the other available options if they appeal to you.

Miscellaneous Active Directory tasks

Now that we have the SRX and UAC fully up and running, the last set of tasks is to perform a few tasks in Active Directory. Again, you can do these before the SRX/IC steps if you would like. The exact steps to configure these will largely be outside the scope of this book because they have to do with Microsoft Active Directory tasks, but documentation is largely available online for completing these tasks in your environment. We focus on the how where necessary.

1. Set up a DNS entry for the IC in your company's DNS infrastructure. This is needed so that clients can resolve the ic.company.local (in this example).
2. Create an SSL certificate for your IC. Technically this doesn't need to be done in AD, but can be done by another CA like OpenSSL/OpenCA. The benefit of doing this in AD is that your clients will automatically trust the IC certificate. This certificate will need to be imported in the IC.
3. Create a Kerberos ticket with KTPass, which is imported into the IC so that the IC can speak directly with AD and validate the client's Kerberos tickets.

In this example, we focus on the third step as creating DNS entries and SSL certificates are well-known tasks in AD, but creating the Kerberos tickets is probably not. The good news is that you only need to do this once. This ticket should be created on the command line of one of your domain controllers with a domain administrator account. The `KTpass` command has the following syntax that we are concerned with:

```
Ktpass -out <kerberos-ticket-output-file> -mapuser <IC Service Account in AD> -
prin HTTP/<IC-FQDN>@<kerberos-realm> /pass <Service Account password>
```

Let's assume the following information and configure this command for real.

- We create a Kerberos file named *kbt-ticket*.
- Our user will be ICDomainAdmin.
- Our IC FQDN is ic.company.local.
- Our NetBIOS realm name is COMPANY.
- Our password is onetimepassword.

Then the output would look like this:

```
C:\Documents and Settings\Administrator>ktpass -out kbt-ticket -mapuser ICDomai-
nAdmin@company.local -princ HTTP/ic.company.local@COMPANY /pass onetimepassword
Targeting domain controller: dc.company.local
Successfully mapped HTTP/ic.company.local to ICDomainAdmin.
Output keytab to out:
Keytab version: 0x502
keysize 71 HTTP/ic.company.local@COMPANY ptype 0 (KRB5_NT_UNKNOWN) vno 1
ketype 0x17 (RC4-HMAC) keylength 16 (0xd2b330d2301b3bb5c18f5c0394089938)
```

We then take the keyfile and upload it into the IC in our Active Directory server by following these steps:

1. Authentication → Auth Servers → <Active Directory Auth Server>
2. Under Advanced Options → SPNEGO, click Browse to upload your Kerberos keyfile.
3. You should receive a success message and no errors when uploading the file.

Configuring and Deploying SSL Forward Proxy

The final component of AppSecure that we discuss in this chapter is SSL Forward Proxy. The high-end SRX supports two types of SSL inspection technology: SSL Forward Proxy (SSL FP) and SSL Reverse Proxy (SSL RP). SSL RP is used when you are looking to crack open the SSL traffic for a web server that you own so you can provide its private keys to the SRX. This feature is outside the scope of this book and is primarily intended to protect your web servers from malicious external clients. We are concerned with SSL FP, which is used to protect your clients from malicious external servers by leveraging the fact that SSL uses a trust relationship with certificates in which the clients trust any certificates that are signed by a trusted CA (and are not revoked), as shown in Figure 12-12. In this case, we install a CA certificate on the SRX, which must be delivered to clients so that they trust the CA certificate themselves. Each web browser and even the OS itself has a list of trusted CAs, although this list can be manipulated to add and

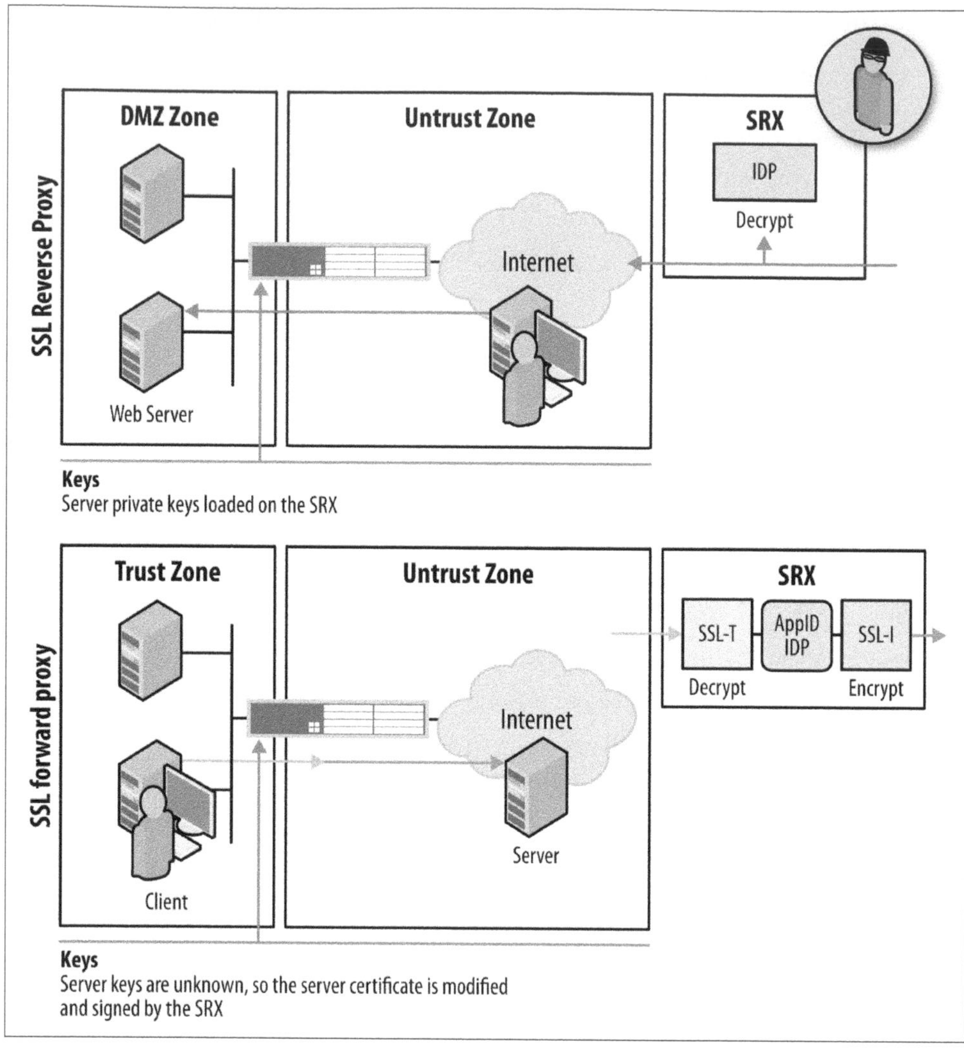

Figure 12-12. SSL Forward/Reverse Proxy

remove trusted CAs. This allows the SRX to "rewrite" target destination certificates on the fly so that the SRX makes an SSL session between the client and itself, with another SSL session between the SRX and the destination server. This allows the SRX to inspect the traffic and then perform additional actions on it.

At the time of writing this book, SSL FP on the branch SRX is in beta. Please check the release notes for the latest information on when it will be released. SSL RP is not planned for the branch SRX at this point due to the use case of leveraging it in data centers where an SRX1400 and higher is best leveraged.

When it comes to configuration, the following steps are required for configuring SSL FP:

1. Generate a CA certificate (can be done locally on the SRX or can be done on a separate CA like OpenSSL, Active Directory Certificate Services, etc., and imported to the SRX with both public and private keys).
2. Configure an SSL profile on the SRX.
3. Import any trusted CAs to the SRX (optional).
4. Distribute the public key to all of your clients as a trusted CA.
5. Configure SSL FP on a firewall rule-by-rule basis along with Level 7 features like AppFW/IPS.

Configuring SSL Forward Proxy on the SRX

SSL FP essentially supports two different ways to install the CA certificate that will be used to rewrite the traffic in the SSL Proxy example. You can either generate a self-signed certificate on the box or you can import a CA certificate (with private key) that was generated by some external source like OpenSSL or Microsoft Certificate Services.

Generating a self-signed certificate is usually fine for lab and Proof of Concept (PoC) testing because it is very quick to set up, but generally in real-world deployments you would opt for a certificate that was part of the greater certificate infrastructure that your clients would implicitly trust—otherwise you will need to manually import the CA certificates into all of your clients.

In this example, we show both ways of installing the CA certificate along with configuring an SSL profile in a firewall rule. We use an AppFW ruleset that is already configured from previous examples, along with IPS for this rule.

Creating a self-signed CA certificate.

```
root@srx3600n0> request security pki generate-key-pair certificate-id SELF-
SIGNED size 2048 type ?
Possible completions:
  dsa                  DSA encryption with SHA-1 hash
  rsa                  RSA encryption
root@srx3600n0> request security pki generate-key-pair certificate-id SELF-
SIGNED size 2048 type rsa
```

```
Generated key pair SELF-SIGNED, key size 2048 bits

root@srx3600n0> req  uest security pki local-certificate generate-self-signed
add-ca-constraint certificate-id SELF-SIGNED domain-name company.local email ad-
min@company.local ip-address 192.168.1.1 subject "DC=company, DC=local"
Self-signed certificate generated and loaded successfully

root@srx3600n0> show security pki local-certificate
Certificate identifier: SELF-SIGNED
  Issued to: (null), Issued by: DC = company, DC = local
  Validity:
    Not before: 02- 5-2013 01:41
    Not after: 02- 4-2018 01:41
  Public key algorithm: rsaEncryption(2048 bits)
```

So we can see that first we generate a key pair, then we locally sign that on our box. We can also check its output as well. When signing the certificate, you would provide your own information that would be present in the certificate so others can identify it.

Importing an external certificate assumes that you loaded the certificate onto the device via SCP or another mechanism.

```
root@srx3600n0> request security pki local-certificate load certificate-id Ex-
ternal filename ca.cer key ca.key passphrase onetimepassword
Local certificate External loaded successfully
```

Now that you have chosen one of those two routes, the rest of the configuration will be the same as follows.

```
[edit]
root@srx3600n0# set services ssl proxy profile SSL-FP root-ca SELF-SIGNED white-
list www.salesforce.com preferred-ciphers strong

 [edit]
root@srx3600n0# set services ssl proxy profile SSL-FP actions disable-session-
resumption renegotiation allow-secure

[edit]
root@srx3600n0# set security policies from-zone trust to-zone untrust policy
SSLFP match source-address Clients-192.168.1.0/24 destination-address any appli-
cation any

[edit]
root@srx3600n0# set security policies from-zone trust to-zone untrust policy
SSLFP then permit application-services idp application-firewall rule-set Allow-
Web-No-Facebook

[edit]
root@srx3600n0# set security policies from-zone trust to-zone untrust policy
SSLFP then permit application-services ssl-proxy profile-name SSL-FP

[edit]
root@srx3600n0# show services ssl
```

```
proxy {
    profile SSL-FP {
        preferred-ciphers strong;
        root-ca SELF-SIGNED;
        whitelist www.salesforce.com;
        actions {
            renegotiation allow-secure;
            disable-session-resumption;
        }
    }
}

[edit]
root@srx3600n0# show security policies from-zone trust to-zone untrust policy
SSLFP
match {
    source-address Clients-192.168.1.0/24;
    destination-address any;
    application any;
}
then {
    permit {
        application-services {
            idp;
            ssl-proxy {
                profile-name SSL-FP;
            }
            application-firewall {
                rule-set Allow-Web-No-Facebook;
            }
        }
    }
}
```

There's a lot going on here, but actually it's not as complex as it seems. First, remember that once you have the SSL profile set up, it's as simple as referencing it in a policy as we did for the policy SSL FP.

Starting with the SSL profile itself, we've already generated and uploaded our CA certificate (in this example, we just used the self-signed one, but there's no difference from the configuration perspective if it is self-signed or uploaded). We then create an SSL Proxy profile, which you will notice is under the `set services` stanza rather than `set security` because this is a service that might be able to be leveraged by other components in the future. In the SSL Proxy profile itself there is really only one required field that we need to configure: the `root-ca` field, which specifies the CA certificate that we just generated and uploaded to the SRX. The rest of the fields are optional but are worth mentioning.

Whitelist

The whitelist field allows you to specify an address object (either by IP or even better FQDN) that will allow the SRX to bypass SSL inspection for that host based on the certificate name presented from the server. The important thing to note is that you can enable SSL Proxy on a firewall rule-by-rule basis, so there are other ways to bypass this, but the whitelist is helpful if you have broader firewall rules where SSL FP is enabled and you want a simple mechanism to bypass it for certain sites.

Preferred Ciphers

This allows you to define the cipher that should be accepted on the SRX/Servers to ensure that a lower than acceptable SSL cipher strength cannot be used. You can also define your own with the custom cipher list.

Trusted-CA

This allows you to add your own list of CAs that the SRX platform should trust when it acts as the client to the server destination. You would need to upload these CA certificates to the SRX and then would reference them here. Note that this isn't required if you have ignore-server-authentication enabled.

Logging

We have some additional logging facilities that are helpful both for audit and for troubleshooting purposes that can be used to log connections and outcomes for the SSL Proxy.

Actions

There are a handful of additional options, or *actions* as they are called here, that are important to review.

Ignore-Server-Auth-Failure

This option is best left for PoC environments. Essentially, it disables the check to see if the certificate that the server is presenting to the SRX is trusted. Normally your client would do this task, but because the client is only terminating the SSL connection on the SRX where it always trusts the certificate, it falls on the SRX to determine if the certificate is trusted. If you do not have any trusted CAs installed or are testing this in a PoC environment, you can enable this for simplicity, but generally you would not want to enable this because it would remove the SRX's ability to validate trust, just that the certificate is indeed in the valid format. That means that although your session would be secured by SSL, anyone could spoof the server identity on the other side.

Disable Session Resumption

SSL supports a concept called session resumption. Because it's an expensive task to do an SSL handshake, session resumption allows the SRX to store the session information and restart an SSL session that was previously negotiated even though its original TCP connection was closed. Turning this on or off is up to you. It does take more resources to keep the session information around, so if you don't think there will be much in the way of resumed session, then this is a good option to disable, but if you think the sessions will be restarted often, then leave it on.

Renegotiation
: SSL supports a feature called Renegotiation that allows either the client or the server to generate new SSL keys for the existing SSL session. This is similar to how IKE will renegotiate Phase 1 and 2 session keys after a certain time period or amount of bytes exchanged. You might want to disable it because of some well-known DDoS attacks with tools like BEAST. You can also leverage the Allow-Secure, which follows RFC 5746 to provide additional protection.

Once we've defined the SSL profile, then we merely need to reference it in the desired firewall rules. In this case, we did so in the SSL FP firewall rule. The one thing that you'll notice is that we left the application as any. We could have restricted it down to TCP port 443 with junos-https, but the SRX can automatically detect an SSL session using AppID and will be able to inspect it regardless of the port on which it is operating.

Using the SSL Proxy by itself wouldn't do us too much good; we would still want to have additional services like AppFW or IPS enabled to provide inspection now that we've cracked open the SSL sessions.

Finally, as we mentioned earlier, you can define multiple profiles, so this provides you with the ability to do different SSL profiles on a firewall rule-by-rule basis if you want to provide different options for the SSL processing.

At the time of writing this book, there are a few feature gaps with SSL Proxy that are no doubt being addressed by Juniper, so stay tuned to the release notes as these will likely be addressed soon! The branch SRX doesn't yet support SSL FP, and the UTM feature set does not support SSL FP yet, but these gaps should be resolved along with the other gaps in the AppSecure suite. Moving forward, there is a strong emphasis on not introducing any new gaps, so we should be in much better shape as SRX customers.

AppFW with encrypted applications

There is a special use case that we want to consider when it comes to AppFW and SSL encrypted sessions. Prior to the Junos 12.1 release when SSL FP was introduced, the SRX had another way to detect SSL-enabled applications without leveraging SSL Proxy, similar to how many URL filters do it: we would look at the certificate exchange to check the certificate name compared to the FQDN for the site. Because most sites (e.g., Facebook) would use the FQDN in the SSL certificate, this is a fairly decent way to detect SSL apps without having to crack them open. We would create a separate AppID object for this such as FACEBOOK-ACCESS-SSL versus standard HTTP access of FACEBOOK-ACCESS. The challenge here is how to properly rectify this when you now have an option to detect Facebook as HTTP, SSL Enabled, or within SSL Forward Proxy. In this case, FACEBOOK-ACCESS-SSL would still be the same because it detects it without cracking open the session, but how would you be able to block FACEBOOK-ACCESS if it looked the same unencrypted versus SSL encrypted? Many customers might want to block an application regardless of how it is delivered, whereas others might want to block a specific method while allowing others (like blocking unencrypted forms but allowing encrypted ones). For this we have developed a special option within the AppFW ruleset that defines if you want to enforce if it's SSL encrypted, not, or either.

```
[edit security application-firewall rule-sets Block-Facebook]
root@srx3600n0# show
rule 1 {
    match {
        dynamic-application junos:FACEBOOK-ACCESS;
    }
    then {
        deny;
    }
}
default-rule {
    permit;
}

[edit security application-firewall rule-sets Block-Facebook]
root@srx3600n0# set rule 1 ?
Possible completions:
  <[Enter]>            Execute this command
+ apply-groups         Groups from which to inherit configuration data
+ apply-groups-except  Don't inherit configuration data from these groups
> match                Specify security rule  match-criteria
> then                 Specify rule action to take when packet match criteria
  |                    Pipe through a command
[edit security application-firewall rule-sets Block-Facebook]
root@srx3600n0# set rule 1 then ?
Possible completions:
  <[Enter]>            Execute this command
+ apply-groups         Groups from which to inherit configuration data
+ apply-groups-except  Don't inherit configuration data from these groups
  deny                 Deny packets
  permit               Permit packets
  reject               Reject packets
  |                    Pipe through a command
[edit security application-firewall rule-sets Block-Facebook]
root@srx3600n0# set rule 1 match ?
Possible completions:
  <[Enter]>            Execute this command
+ apply-groups         Groups from which to inherit configuration data
+ apply-groups-except  Don't inherit configuration data from these groups
```

```
+ dynamic-application  Dynamic application
+ dynamic-application-group  Dynamic application group
  ssl-encryption       Select SSL encryption rules
  |                    Pipe through a command
[edit security application-firewall rule-sets Block-Facebook]
root@srx3600n0# set rule 1 match ssl-encryption ?
Possible completions:
  any                  Encrypted and non-encrypted rule
  no                   Non-encrypted rule
  yes                  Encrypted rule
[edit security application-firewall rule-sets Block-Facebook]
root@srx3600n0# set rule 1 match ssl-encryption any

[edit security application-firewall rule-sets Block-Facebook]
root@srx3600n0# show
rule 1 {
    match {
        dynamic-application junos:FACEBOOK-ACCESS;
        ssl-encryption any;
    }
    then {
        deny;
    }
}
default-rule {
    permit;
}
```

Per this example, we will block FACEBOOK-ACCESS if we see it encrypted or not encrypted. If we chose No, then we'd block it only if it was unencrypted and not if it was encrypted with SSL FP. If the answer was Yes, then we'd only block it if it was encrypted.

SSL FP can also come in very handy for blocking evasive applications that tunnel over SSL. For instance, applications like TOR, Ultrasurf, Skype, and many others have capabilities to use SSL to tunnel their traffic. They do so in a highly evasive manner that typically uses preshared keys. SSL Proxy can help prevent this as an evasive channel because it will not allow SSL traffic through that it cannot inspect. Additionally, by filtering unknown applications you can successfully block anything the SRX engine cannot identify.

Best Practices

There are many features in the AppSecure suite of products, and certainly several ways in which they can be deployed. Let's look at some of the examples of how to best leverage each technology on a feature-by-feature basis.

Application Identification

- It is typically best to schedule automatic updates for AppID. If you are also deploying IPS, then the SRX will automatically get the signatures downloaded via IPS because IPS relies on AppID.
- If you are most concerned about performance, it is best to leave application caching enabled; however, if you are more concerned about security, it is best to disable caching to prevent potential attackers from colluding to trick the system.
- Starting in Junos 12.1X44, you can define your own Level 3/Level 4 applications. These are useful if you want to explicitly override what application a particular connection will have. This is most commonly done based on the server IP, protocol, and port rather than having to write your own custom applications with pattern regex support.

AppTrack

- AppTrack is enabled on a zone-by-zone basis. If it is enabled for either the source or destination zone on the traffic, it will be active.
- To minimize the performance impact, only enable AppTrack on the zones of interest, particularly in high-performance environments. Although AppTrack doesn't have a major impact on performance in most cases, it's good to keep your device operating as lean as possible if you are not interested in the information or if you have AppFW enabled.

AppFW

- It is best to use the AppFW ruleset in the blacklist format when you want to block specific applications but allow all others through. This is best when you know that you do not want a particular application, but just want to identify the others rather than block them.
- Whitelist AppFW rulesets are a very powerful security mechanism that leverages least privilege to allow only those applications that are explicitly allowed, while all others (including unknowns) are blocked. This is best if you know a specific set of applications you want to permit and block anything else.
- Hybrid AppFW rulesets are only needed when you are filtering using nested objects like HTTP Applications where you want to do one action on some and another action on others, while taking the same action as the top rule for the default rule (e.g., Block Facebook, Allow HTTP, Block All Else).

- It is imperative that even with AppFW you should still use the same best practices of least privilege in the firewall policy whenever possible to ensure that you are containing the attack surface of applications going out to the Internet. Whenever possible, you should not configure policies with Allow Any policies whenever possible.
- It is usually best to use predefined application groups when dealing with broad category applications like those of HTTP. This is because these lists are frequently updated with new members, which will automatically be applied in the policy. If you are dealing with base applications (e.g., SMTP, FTP, DNS, etc.) that aren't likely to change, then it is okay to use the objects directly, but if you are trying to capture, say, all social networking applications, it is best to use groups like junos:web:social-networking rather than defining every single app if you want to apply the same policy.
- Starting in Junos 12.1X44, you have the ability to define how you want to filter applications when they can be detected over HTTP or HTTPS using the encryption knob. Typically, you'll want to leave this as any if you are concerned with detecting or enforcing an action on the app regardless of its SSL encryption status. If you want to detect the app in an SSL encrypted channel, select Yes (assuming SSL FP is enabled), or No if you only want to detect the plain-text version.

AppQoS

- AppQoS is applied in largely a similar manner to AppFW. The primary use case is to leverage AppQoS to rate limit applications, but you can also use it for prioritizing traffic, rewriting QoS values, setting loss priority, and setting the forwarding class.
- If you want to leverage forwarding classes, prioritization, and queuing, you will most likely need to customize the existing classes and settings or create your own new ones.

UserFW

- It is best to still define the Source-IP fields when using UserFW to help restrict the potential ranges that the users can access on the network rather than leaving it wide open. This allows you to enforce different security capabilities if the user is accessing the network from different subnets within the same zone.
- It is a best practice to not have a NAT device between the client and the SRX when using UserFW because the SRX will not be able to limit the traffic to the originating host. This can be done, however, with the full-blown NAC software.

- Depending on where your AD and IC servers are, you might need to create permit rules that allow the users to reach the servers to authenticate.
- You should typically put your redirect rule toward the top of your rulebase with your resource access rules that specify the user roles below so that users will be forced to authenticate before they can match the rules below per user.
- If you want to allow access to certain resources in the event the communication with the IC fails, then you can use the unknown-user predefined role. This is different than the unauthenticated-user, which is when the IC communication is fully functional but there is no active user-to-IP mapping on the SRX.
- It is a best practice to leverage Active Directory to push out Group Policy scripts to trigger a background web browser session when using SPNEGO so that the user will automatically be authenticated to the network without having to open a browser manually. Juniper provides a sample script that can do this, which is available within the documentation.
- It is a best practice to use both DNS resolution for the IC hostname as well as a certificate that is signed by the AD certificate services so that there is an established trust relationship between the clients and the IC so there will be less error messages.
- It is a best practice to define a unique service account for the IC to use when connecting to the domain rather than having a shared service account with other devices. This is done from a security perspective and also for auditing purposes.
- It is a best practice to leverage local authentication if you have a scenario where the user is not going to change on the machine, the machine does not support SPNEGO authentication, and falling back to captive portal is undesirable.
- It is a best practice to leverage a common DNS and NTP system in the domain, typically that of AD. Synchronized timekeeping (especially with the SRX/IC) is critical for the functionality to work properly, as the underlying mechanisms like Kerberos rely on synchronized clocks.
- If you want to leverage external automation for passing user information to the SRX, you can do so with NetConf over SSH to pass user or role-to-IP mapping. You can then leverage this feed to add, change, or delete users from any external authentication feed.

SSL FP

- It is a best practice to use a CA that your organization controls to generate the CA signing certificate that is placed on the SRX. Typically, this will be Active Directory for enterprise customers or some other open source or commercial CA product. This approach is much better than leveraging a self-generated CA certificate except when you are doing a PoC.

- It is essential to make sure that your CA certificate that the SRX is using to resign the certificates is trusted by all clients whose sessions are inspected by SSL FP. This is critical because if your clients do not trust the SRX's certificate as a trusted CA certificate, then all certificates it generates will not be trusted by the clients and will result in error messages.
- It is best to not disable server certificate authentication unless testing in a PoC lab. This is because if you disable the server certificate check, the SRX cannot confirm whether or not the certificate is coming from a trusted source. Normally, this function is carried out by the client, but because the SRX is proxying the client connection, it falls on the SRX to validate this behavior. If the check is off, then the SRX is only ensuring the certificate is in the proper format and that the traffic is secured by SSL—but it can't validate if the server is coming from the proper identity or if the certificate has been revoked.
- It is generally a good idea to enforce requirements for stronger ciphers and not weak ciphers. You may also customize this list if you need to, but generally it shouldn't be required.
- You can disable session resumption and renegotiation if you don't want the SRX to support these behaviors. They are not terribly common for most environments, but some applications do leverage them. Turning them off will allow the SRX to save resources tracking and controlling these functions.
- You can add your own CA certificates to the list of trusted CAs that the SRX should trust. This should be done for internal sites that come from a custom CA, along with some public CA servers at your discretion. The SRX must trust the CA certificate (unless server authentication is disabled) so this should typically be enabled.
- You can enable the SSL Proxy on a firewall rule-by-rule basis. This allows you to be quite granular when it comes to enabling SSL Proxy (e.g., for which source-ip addresses, users, destination IP addresses, etc.). You can also leverage the whitelist feature in the SSL Proxy profile, which can whitelist certain sites based on FQDN in the certificate. This is good for keeping your firewall rulebase clean while whitelisting some of the servers.
- You can also leverage logging for SSL to provide messages and information for successful SSL transactions, failures, and other events related to SSL processing.

Troubleshooting and Operation

We've covered several different technologies in this chapter, so now's a good time to review some of the capabilities that you have at your disposal as an operator of the platform. We cover AppID, AppTrack, AppFW, AppQoS, UserFW, and SSL FP.

Operating Application Identification

There are not many tasks that you will need to cover when operating Application Identification, but they mainly include checking the signature package version, application statistics, and the engine settings.

Checking the AppID package

You have two options when checking the AppID package. If you are using AppID by itself, then use the `show services application-identification version` command. If you are running IPS as well, you can check the `show security idp security-package-version`.

```
root@srx3600n0> show services application-identification version
  Application package version: 2227


root@srx3600n0> show security idp security-package-version
  Attack database version:2227(Wed Jan 23 19:12:53 2013 UTC)
  Detector version :12.6.140121210
  Policy template version :N/A
```

These packages should typically be the same unless you updated the AppID independently of the IDP package. If you are running into issues with installing the AppID package itself, it can be a good idea to run the `request services application-identification uninstall` command, followed by the `request services application-identification download` and finally the `request services application-identification install` command. After Junos 11.4, it is very rare to have AppID itself fail to install now that the applications have been moved to their own database instance rather than being part of the Junos configuration.

Checking the AppID engine settings and cache

This operation is one and the same. You use the `show services application-identification application-system-cache` command. At the top, you see the engine setting followed by the application cache entries. You can clear the cache with the `clear services application-identification application-system-cache` command.

```
root@srx3600n0> show services application-identification application-system-
cache
Application System Cache Configurations:
  application-cache: on
  nested-application-cache: off
  cache-unknown-result: on
  cache-entry-timeout: 600 seconds
pic: 2/0
Logical system name: root-logical-system
IP address: 10.102.2.36                        Port: 48929  Protocol: TCP
Application: EDONKEY-TCP                       Encrypted: No
```

```
Logical system name: root-logical-system
IP address: 10.102.2.122                         Port: 43604  Protocol: TCP
Application: UNSPECIFIED-ENCRYPTED               Encrypted: Yes

Logical system name: root-logical-system
IP address: 10.102.2.72                          Port: 50365  Protocol: TCP
Application: SKYPE                               Encrypted: No

Logical system name: root-logical-system
IP address: 10.102.2.244                         Port: 5060   Protocol: UDP
Application: SIP                                 Encrypted: No
```

On the high-end SRX, the cache is built on a per-SPU basis, because it is more expensive to try to synchronize the cache between the different SPUs (especially with the NG-SPC where there could be up to 88 in an SRX5800 platform), so you will see the output on a per PIC basis.

Checking AppID counters

Sometimes it can be helpful to take a look at the counters when having operational or performance issues with AppID. There can be some self-explanatory information in the output.

```
root@srx3600n0> show services application-identification counter
pic: 2/0
  Counter type                                            Value
 AI cache hits                                                 63920
 AI cache hits by nested application                           0
 AI cache misses                                               49272
 AI matches                                                    13589
 AI uni-matches                                                0
 AI no-matches                                                 11630
 AI partial matches                                            11111
 AI no-partial matches                                         16154
 AI address based matches                                      0
 AI ICMP based matches                                         0
 AI IP protocol based matches                                  0
 Sessions that triggered Appid create session API              113192
 Sessions that do not incur signature match or decoding        43880
 Sessions that incur signature match or decoding               68715
 Client-to-server packets processed                            154218
 Server-to-client packets processed                            92944
 Client-to-server layer-7 bytes processed                      45026050
 Server-to-client layer-7 bytes processed                      35646345
 Terminal first data packets on both direction                 22623
 Unspecified encrypted sessions                                798
 Encrypted P2P sessions                                        0
```

One thing to call out here is the AI cache hits and misses. Because we disabled the Nested AppID cache, there are no hits there, but we do have base application hits. Misses means that we did not have a cache hit and had to do inspection. If you have a lot of misses (and the cache is enabled), it means that your traffic is highly variable. The AI matches means that we were able to match the application. Partial means that we matched individual patterns or a single direction but not both. The rest of the information provides data about bytes and sessions processed.

Checking application statistics

The SRX allows you to capture statistics locally on the SRX about application matches. At the time of writing this book, this is only enabled when you have AppTrack on for the respective zones, but check the release notes for potential changes in the future. These stats provide a very quick way to see the type of applications that you are matching in your environment. You can do this both from an application level and an application group level.

```
root@srx3600n0> show services application-identification statistics applications
Last Reset: 2013-02-10 16:58:35 UTC
                  Application      Sessions           Bytes    Encrypted
                   ACTIVESYNC             7          178571           No
                          AIM         35772       226465959           No
                   APPLEJUICE          6791         1328038           No
                         ARES          6919        18396477           No
                          BGP          5161         6046977           No
                   BITTORRENT        131942         8095152           No
               BITTORRENT-DHT          2708          430654           No
                  BITTRACKER          28028        43695052           No
                      CHARGEN          5250       226980076           No
                      DISCARD          5234         4100251           No
                          DNS        287945        47335266           No
                         DRDA          5262        29171426           No
                         EBAY          2623        44445540           No
                         ECHO          5414         7790964           No
                  EDONKEY-TCP          7872         4075097           No
                  ENCODED-DNS           314           46890           No
                       FINGER          5481         2927491           No
                          FTP         10651        35538633           No
                        GMAIL          7478        98487632           No
                     GNUTELLA          2742        13844306           No
                 GNUTELLA-URN          2741        65261900           No
                       GOOGLE          8810        44408708           No
                 GOOGLE-EARTH          2802        14751472           No
               GOOGLE-WEBCHAT            20           25415           No
                   GOOGLETALK            40          243520           No
                       GOPHER          5380         2896172           No
                      H225RAS          9236         3930742           No
                      H225SGN          2742         3683995           No
                         HTTP          3889         6389789          Yes
                         HTTP        100371      1035498048           No
```

```
        HTTP-AUDIO-CONTENT        5829     153265606         No
                HTTP-VIDEO        9915     249373068         No
                       ICA           4           440         No
                   ICA-TCP        1045     832631416         No
                     IDENT        5369       2703354         No
                    IEC104        2617       1413180         No
                      IMAP       12873      90780242         No
                       IRC       10141     948940888         No
                    JABBER        4347     380166729         No
                      KRB5       77536      21185825         No
                      LDAP        5536       8486227         No
                       LPR        8183      10536126         No
                      MAPI        2613       4446501         No
   MICROSOFT-LIVE-SERVICES        7762      28117770         No
        MICROSOFT-UPDATE          2659      18645790         No
                 MINECRAFT        3176      60556222         No
             MMS-OVER-HTTP        3521      11057295         No
                    MODBUS        2698       1524370         No
                       MSN       20587     292382563         No
                     MSRPC        7894       9245891         No
                     MYSQL        5955     120751897         No
            NETFLIX-PLAYER        5426     100469152         No
                       NFS        2594       9677987         No
                      NNTP        2676       5555376         No
                       NTP       15716       2336032         No
                PCANYWHERE        2636        110712         No
                      POP3       13457    8141896095         No
              POPO163-P2P        10920     154547955         No
                PORTMAPPER        8178       1803490         No

root@srx3600n0> show services application-identification statistics application-
groups
Last Reset: 2013-02-10 16:58:35 UTC
                  Application Group          Sessions          Kilo Bytes
                       junos:gaming              3178               56640
             junos:gaming:protocols              3178               56640
               junos:infrastructure            610438             2449716
junos:infrastructure:authentication              4017                1315
      junos:infrastructure:database             16384              190020
     junos:infrastructure:directory             16976                5536
    junos:infrastructure:encryption            119560               51553
junos:infrastructure:file-servers               35331             1838589
junos:infrastructure:file-sharing                5380                   0
        junos:infrastructure:legacy             15898              228438
        junos:infrastructure:mobile               513                 513
    junos:infrastructure:monitoring              5319                2609
    junos:infrastructure:networking            317319                9243
           junos:infrastructure:rpc             18672                6002
         junos:infrastructure:scada              5315                   0
          junos:infrastructure:voip             49754              115898
                    junos:messaging            127355            10085786
junos:messaging:instant-messaging               89602             2027110
```

```
                    junos:messaging:mail          37753          8058676
                        junos:multimedia           2614                0
              junos:multimedia:transport           2614                0
                               junos:p2p         158974            24725
                   junos:p2p:file-sharing         158974            24725
                     junos:remote-access          31741           957306
             junos:remote-access:command          12042            73500
 junos:remote-access:interactive-desktop          17092           881199
           junos:remote-access:tunneling           2607             2607
                               junos:web         195405          2203529
                   junos:web:applications          10564            35551
                   junos:web:file-sharing          28028            27799
                 junos:web:infrastructure           2666            16974
          junos:web:infrastructure:mobile              7              171
 junos:web:infrastructure:software-update           2659            16803
                     junos:web:messaging          11019           100226
 junos:web:messaging:instant-messaging               20               20
                junos:web:messaging:mail           7478            91825
                    junos:web:multimedia          24694           917247
 junos:web:multimedia:audio-streaming              5829           146691
       junos:web:multimedia:web-based            18865           770556
                           junos:web:p2p           2741            62158
              junos:web:p2p:file-sharing           2741            62158
                        junos:web:portal           8810            37992
                      junos:web:shopping           2623            41874
                              unassigned           2651                0
                                 unknown         250807         12064862
```

We also covered how to show which AppID signatures and groups are active in the SRX earlier in this chapter. That output can also be helpful for troubleshooting operations if you have altered the default behavior, which is all signatures enabled.

AppTrack

AppTrack is relatively simple from an operational perspective. You only need to enable it per zone. There is only one troubleshooting command at the time of writing this book, which is to view the update messages. The presence of any failed messages would mean there is some sort of an issue that you should raise with JTAC. The other part of troubleshooting involves checking the AppTrack configuration and the zone configuration to ensure it is enabled.

```
root@srx3600n0> show configuration security application-tracking
first-update;
session-update-interval 5;

root@srx3600n0> show security application-tracking counters
Application tracking counters:

    AppTrack counter type                                   Value
  Session create messages                                     3683662
  Session close messages                                      3587760
```

```
 Session volume updates                                    0
 Failed messages                                           0

root@srx3600n0> show configuration security zones
security-zone trust {
    interfaces {
        xe-1/0/0.0 {
            host-inbound-traffic {
                system-services {
                    all;
                }
                protocols {
                    all;
                }
            }
        }
    }
    application-tracking;
}
security-zone untrust {
    host-inbound-traffic {
        system-services {
            ssh;
            http;
        }
    }
    interfaces {
        xe-1/0/1.0 {
            host-inbound-traffic {
                system-services {
                    all;
                }
                protocols {
                    all;
                }
            }
        }
    }
    application-tracking;
}
```

Operating Application Firewall

AppFW is a pretty simple feature to operate once it is set up. The main thing that you will be looking at (besides the syslog information that it generates) is the counters on box which show the hits per rule. This helps you to understand how the traffic is behaving in your network.

```
root@srx3600n0> show security application-firewall rule-set all
Rule-set: Block-P2P
    Logical system: root-logical-system
    Rule: 1
```

```
        Dynamic Application Groups: junos:p2p:file-sharing, junos:p2p
        SSL-Encryption: any
        Action:deny
        Number of sessions matched: 147665
    Rule: 2
        Dynamic Applications: junos:FACEBOOK-CHAT
        SSL-Encryption: any
        Action:deny
        Number of sessions matched: 0
Default rule:permit
        Number of sessions matched: 923639
Number of sessions with appid pending: 21707
```

The preceding output would show a stat for every ruleset (you can specify the individual ruleset to view as well). The output is pretty self-explanatory in terms of the counters. The number of sessions with AppID pending refers to sessions that haven't completed the AppID phase so their traffic is still allowed to pass.

```
root@srx3600n0> show security application-firewall match-rule rule-set Block-
P2P dynamic-application junos:BITTORRENT-UDP
Logical system: root-logical-system
Non-SSL-Encrypted rules:
    Rule: 1
        Dynamic Application Groups: junos:p2p:file-sharing, junos:p2p
        SSL-Encryption: any
        Action: deny
SSL-Encrypted rules:
    Rule: 1
        Dynamic Application Groups: junos:p2p:file-sharing, junos:p2p
        SSL-Encryption: any
        Action: deny

root@srx3600n0> show security application-firewall shadow-rules rule-set Block-
P2P

Number of shadowed dynamic application: 0
```

The preceding two commands allow you to look and see how dynamic applications would be matched in your ruleset and if there are any shadow rules. This is very similar to the functionality available for the standard firewall policy.

Starting in Junos 12.1X45, the preceding output also contains a new field that defines number of sessions redirected if you have redirection enabled.

Typically, AppFW is pretty easy to troubleshoot because it just enforces the output of the dynamic application that is detected. Sometimes you can have an issue with properly detecting an application due to a false positive. In these cases you can open a JTAC ticket, or if you have a copy of the packet capture for the application, you can submit it via email to *applications@juniper.net* for the team to review.

Operating Application QoS

AppQoS is very simple to operate. Enabling logging within the AppQoS ruleset as we discussed earlier in the chapter is a good way to see externally what sessions are being enforced on. You can also check the AppQoS counters and statistics to get some simple information about the processing information. Additionally, you can further look at the system-level QoS information about the different queue matching and real-time processing.

```
root@srx3600n0> show class-of-service application-traffic-control counter
pic: 2/0
  Counter type                                                Value
 Sessions processed                                           108470
 Sessions marked                                              370
 Sessions honored                                             370
 Sessions rate limited                                        1293
 Client-to-server flows rate limited                          1293
 Server-to-client flows rate limited                          1293

root@srx3600n0>  show  class-of-service  application-traffic-control  statistics
rule
pic: 2/0
 Ruleset                       Rule               Hits
 Limit-HTTP                    1                  1293
 Limit-HTTP                    2                  370

root@srx3600n0>  show  class-of-service  application-traffic-control  statistics
rate-limiter
pic: 2/0
 Ruleset          Application          Client-to-server   Rate(kbps)    Server-to-
client   Rate(kbps)
  Limit-HTTP       junos:HTTP             HTTP                         5000
HTTP               5000

Traffic statistics:
   Input  bytes  :        147620775030                   0 bps
   Output bytes  :         41752053072                   0 bps
   Input  packets:           185832453                   0 pps
   Output packets:           165929731                   0 pps
   IPv6 transit statistics:
    Input  bytes  :                  0
    Output bytes  :                  0
    Input  packets:                  0
    Output packets:                  0
  Dropped traffic statistics due to STP State:
   Input  bytes  :                   0
   Output bytes  :                   0
   Input  packets:                   0
```

```
    Output packets:                     0
   Input errors:
     Errors: 0, Drops: 0, Framing errors: 0, Runts: 0, Policed discards: 0, L3
incompletes: 0, L2 channel errors: 0, L2 mismatch timeouts: 0, FIFO errors: 0,
Resource errors: 0
   Output errors:
     Carrier transitions: 1, Errors: 0, Drops: 0, Collisions: 0, Aged packets:
0, FIFO errors: 0, HS link CRC errors: 0, MTU errors: 0, Resource errors: 0
   Egress queues: 8 supported, 4 in use
   Queue counters:  Queued packets  Transmitted packets Dropped packets
     0 best-effort      164953301           164953301               0
     1 expedited-fo             0                   0               0
     2 assured-forw             0                   0               0
     3 network-cont        250528              250528               0
   Queue number:         Mapped forwarding classes
     0                   best-effort
     1                   expedited-forwarding
     2                   assured-forwarding
     3                   network-control

root@srx3600n0> show class-of-service
Forwarding class                        ID      Queue  Restricted queue  Fabric
priority  Policing priority    SPU priority
   best-effort              0        0     0     low      normal       low
   expedited-forwarding     1        1     1     low      normal       low
   assured-forwarding       2        2     2     low      normal       low
   network-control          3        3     3     low      normal       low
***Output Limited***
```

This output shows five different commands that are useful for checking the status of AppQoS. First, you can look at the overall stats on how many sessions have been processed, rate limited, rewritten, and honored. Honored means that the system honors its own DSCP rewrite value to apply it to an appropriate forwarding class. The next command shows how many hits we are getting on a per-rule basis on the SRX. This is very important when you are not getting the expected results because you might have some sort of rule shadowing. The next command shows what the rate limiters are in terms of how they are configured to limit bandwidth. Looking at the extensive interface output is very helpful to see what activity is happening on the interface itself, and finally, a treasure trove of information is available in the `show class-of-service` command. This command literally dumps the entire Junos QoS running information, so it was too large to include here, but it is very valuable when troubleshooting advanced issues.

Of course, the configuration itself is another critical place to check when running into issues. The following are key items to check:

1. Check that the AI database is properly installed.
2. Check to ensure that your traffic is matching the correct firewall rule and that that rule references the correct AppQoS ruleset.

3. Check the overall CoS configuration under `show class-of-service` in the configuration. This is particularly true if you have modified any of the default CoS parameters.
4. Check your AppQoS configuration under `show class-of-service application-traffic-control`.

Operating UserFW

UserFW can be a bit tricky to operate, particularly when you are getting it up and running initially. Usually it's a piece of cake to operate after the initial setup, but that can be challenging. The following is a useful checklist.

1. If you are using the IC to operate UserFW (rather than just using local authentication), first check that the SRX is connected to the IC. If it is not, check to see if the SRX can properly connect to the IC (port TCP 11122 by default.) It could potentially be an access list or host-outbound traffic policy, routing issue, or intermediate device not allowing the connection like a firewall between the SRX and IC. Also, you should be connecting to the internal port on the IC.
   a. If this isn't working, but you can telnet from the SRX to the IC, check to see if the SRX and the IC have the right certificate trust. You can also disable this check as we discussed in the chapter.
2. If the IC to SRX is functioning properly, you should see roles being populated in the SRX and, ideally, the user information if the users are able to authenticate to the IC.
3. Ensure that the user is properly being redirected to the IC. There are several facets of this important step. First, you must make sure that the client is able to communicate with the IC/AD infrastructure (so FW rules might be required depending on where these components are placed). Next, you need to make sure that the redirect rules for unauthenticated users are above the actual resource rules that you want to match the appropriate users to. Finally, you need to make sure that you have the appropriate source identity in the respective resource rules.
4. As a quick workaround, if IC authentication is not working to AD, you can have the users authenticate locally to the IC using system authentication. That should help you resolve if there is an issue authenticating to the domain itself but that two-way communication including Role/IP/User mapping is working properly.
5. If you are experiencing authentication issues with Active Directory there are a few things to make sure of:
   a. Make sure that you have a valid service account for the IC and that the Kerberos ticket is based on that account. You should be able to check and ensure that this

is working under the IC event log along with the AD domain controller security log, which will log invalid authentication and resource access attempts.

b. Make sure that you have DNS working properly. Typically, if you point the SRX/IC to the AD that is operating a DNS server, that is the easiest model. Additionally, make sure that the IC has an FQDN in the domain.

c. Make sure that the SRX and IC have the appropriate time sync.

d. Ensure that the Kerberos ticket you generated on the domain controller is correct and installed on the IC.

6. If all of these facets are working but your client can't authenticate to the IC, it could be a few things.

   a. First, make sure that the client trusts the IC certificate. If you generated and signed this in AD, this shouldn't be an issue.

   b. Make sure that the client is being redirected to the correct sign-in page with the correct realm.

   c. Make sure the client has SPNEGO enabled and that the IC is a trusted site. Even if SPNEGO doesn't work, you should still be able to authenticate manually with the user's credentials. If this works, then you know that AD authentication is working and that it is likely just a web browser issue with the configuration to focus on.

   d. If all else fails, contact JTAC.

Now that we've taken a high-level look at all of the different steps to evaluate when running into issues with UserFW, let's look at some useful commands.

```
root@SRX1400> show services unified-access-control status
Host           Address          Port   Interface     State
192.168.226.45 192.168.226.45  11123  fxp0.0        connected


root@SRX1400> show services unified-access-control roles
Name                                    Identifier
Sales                                   0000000001.000005.0
Engineering                             0000000001.000006.0
Accounting                              0000000001.000007.0
Total: 3

root@SRX1400> show services unified-access-control authentication-table detail
Identifier: 1
  Source IP: 192.168.1.127
  Username: bradmatic
  Age: 0
  Role identifier       Role name
    0000000001.000005.0 Sales
Total: 1
```

There are also troubleshooting facilities available on the IC itself. Primarily you will be interested in looking at the Event Log and User Access Logs in the Admin console Log/ Monitoring → Events → Log, along with the User Access log. If you are familiar with Policy Tracing, that can be a helpful process as well. JTAC can definitely help if you run into issues here as well, as there is a great deal more debug information available with advanced troubleshooting procedures on the IC.

Beyond the preceding output, your troubleshooting is primarily the same as standard firewall troubleshooting as discussed in Chapter 8. You want to make sure that you're properly matching rules. The `show security match-policies` command is very helpful for this operation because you can specify the source identity.

```
root@srx3600n0> show security match-policies ?
Possible completions:
  destination-ip       Match policy for the given destination IP
  destination-port     Match policy for the given destination port) (1..65535)
  from-zone            Match policy for the given source zone
  global               Match global policy
  logical-system       Logical-system name
  protocol             Match policy for the given protocol)
  result-count         Expected results count (optional) (1..16)
  root-logical-system  Root logical-system (default)
  source-identity      Match policy for the given roles (optional)
  source-ip            Match policy for the given source IP
  source-port          Match policy for the given source port) (1..65535)
  to-zone              Match policy for the given destination zone
```

Operating SSL Forward Proxy

The last section that we look at is operating the SSL Forward Proxy feature. In terms of troubleshooting the SSL FP feature, it is useful to check the following items:

1. Make sure that you have properly generated or installed the SSL CA certificate on the SRX. This certificate must be a trusted CA certificate on all of your clients or else they will see warning messages. Active Directory and other software delivery platforms can help with the distribution aspect of this.
2. Ensure that your SSL Proxy is properly configured. This includes referencing the correct certificate, with the appropriate proxy settings.
3. Check to ensure that the SRX has the trusted CA certificates installed, or else you need to have the ignore-server-authentication enabled (which can be good for troubleshooting but is not recommended for permanent operation).
4. Finally, ensure that you have SSL Proxy enabled on the correct FW rules, that the traffic is being matched by those rules, and that the proper SSL Proxy profile is referenced.

5. If you are still running into issues, you can enable logging and tracing to look for additional clues or contact JTAC. Once SSL Proxy is enabled, it is pretty easy to operate and shouldn't require much maintenance other than ensuring that your CA certificate on the SRX hasn't expired or been revoked.

In terms of statistics, there is only one command, but it is useful for checking the status of sessions. On the high-end SRX, it is outputted on a per-SPU basis.

```
root@srx3600n0> show services ssl proxy statistics
PIC:spu-4 fpc[2] pic[0] ------
        sessions matched                    3389
        sessions whitelisted                   0
        sessions bypassed:non-ssl              0
        sessions bypassed:mem overflow         0
        sessions created                    3389
        sessions ignored                      54
        sessions active                        0
        sessions dropped                       1
```

Matched sessions are those that are enforced with SSL Forward Proxy. Whitelisted are those that are explicitly whitelisted in the configuration. Bypass non-ssl and memory overflow indicate some sort of issue processing the sessions. Ignored can occur for different reasons; you will need to look deeper into the logs. Sessions active are the sessions that are currently being processed by SSL Proxy, and sessions dropped occur when the system can't process the sessions and drops them (typically if there is some error or performance limit reached).

Finally, there are some useful facilities when checking the certificate status on the box, along with certificate operations to familiarize yourself with.

```
root@srx3600n0> show security pki ?
Possible completions:
  ca-certificate       Show certificate-authority certificate information
  certificate-request  Show PKCS-10 certificate request information
  crl                  Show certificate revocation list information
  local-certificate    Show router certificate information
root@srx3600n0> show security pki local-certificate
Certificate identifier: SELF-SIGNED
  Issued to: (null), Issued by: DC = company, DC = local
  Validity:
    Not before: 02- 5-2013 01:41
    Not after: 02- 4-2018 01:41
  Public key algorithm: rsaEncryption(2048 bits)

Certificate identifier: CA-CERT
  Issued to: www.juniper.net, Issued by: CN = www.juniper.net
  Validity:
    Not before: 11- 2-2011 14:47
    Not after: 10-31-2016 14:47
  Public key algorithm: rsaEncryption(2048 bits)
```

```
root@srx3600n0> request security pki ?
Possible completions:
  ca-certificate       Perform operations on certificate-authority certificates
  crl                  Perform operations on certificate revocation list
  generate-certificate-request  Generate the certificate request in PKCS-10 for-
mat
  generate-key-pair    Generate RSA private and public key pair
  local-certificate
  verify-integrity-status  Check the integrity of PKI files (in CC mode)
```

Sample Deployments

For the sample deployment, we are going to perform an overall example that includes all of the features that we discussed in the chapter, including mixing features like UserFW with AppFW, AppQoS, SSL FP, and even for other Level 7 features like IPS/UTM. This allows you to maximize your flexibility as an administrator. In this example, shown in Figure 12-13, we configure the following:

1. Enable AppTrack on the Trust zone.
2. For users in the Sales role, create an AppFW policy that allows them to go to any web-based real estate and social networking applications. Leverage AppQoS to ensure that they can only use 10 Mbps upload and download for any social networking applications, but leave everything else as is. Also enable SSL FP, IPS, and session logging for this rule. You should restrict this rule to TCP ports 80 and 443.
3. For users in the Engineering role, only allow them to view social networking applications between 12 noon and 1 p.m. during their lunch break. During all other times they should only be able to view forum sites. Enable SSL FP, IPS, and session logging. You should restrict this rule to TCP ports 80 and 443.
4. Allow all other users to go to the Internet, but make sure that the UTM Profile called Protect Users is enabled, which uses the default Websense Enhanced and Sophos AV profiles (more on this in Chapter 14). Block any multimedia-based web applications with AppFW, but allow any other known web application, while blocking everything else over TCP port 80.
5. For this example, we assume that the IC and SSL FP are already configured per earlier examples in this chapter, so we focus on the security policy sections.

At the time of writing this book, UTM was in beta testing for the high-end SRX. Stay tuned to the release notes for more information on its GA availability.

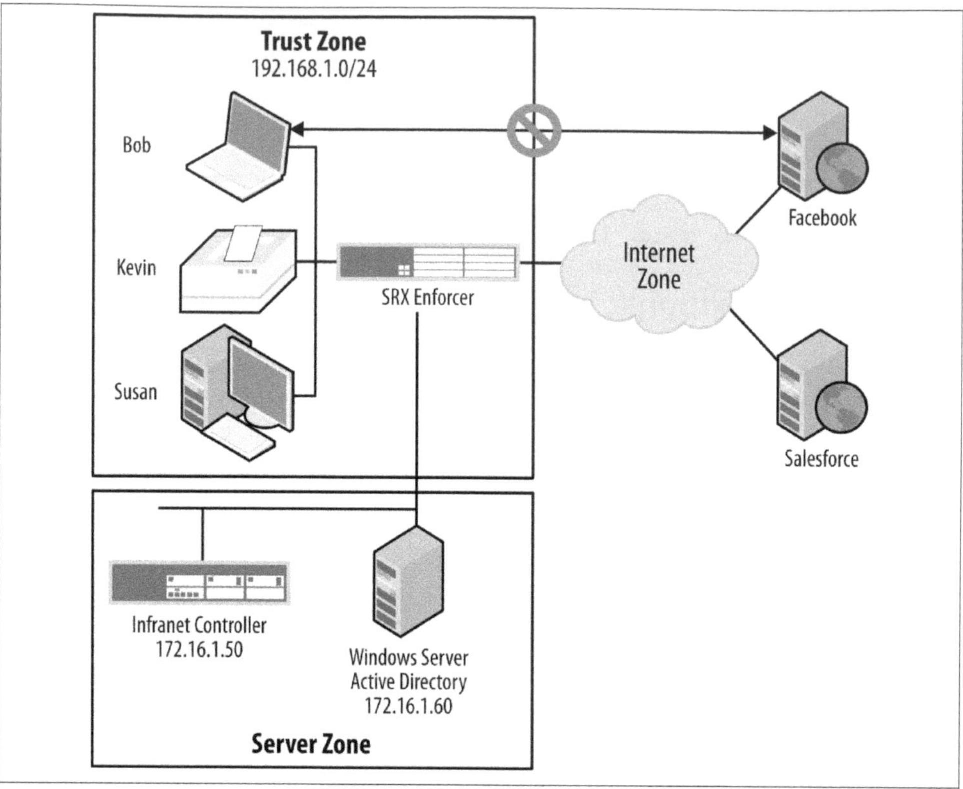

Figure 12-13. Sample deployment network diagram

```
[edit]
root@srx3600n0# set security zone security-zone Trust application-tracking

[edit]
root@srx3600n0# set security zones security-zone Internet

[edit]
root@srx3600n0# set security policies from-zone Trust to-zone Internet policy
Sales match source-address any source-identity Sales destination-address any ap-
plication [junos-http junos-https]

root@srx3600n0# set security policies from-zone Trust to-zone Internet policy
Sales then permit application-services application-traffic-control rule-set
10Mbps-Social-Networking

[edit]
root@srx3600n0# set security policies from-zone Trust to-zone Internet policy
Sales then permit application-services application-firewall rule-set Real-
Estate-Social-Networking
```

```
[edit]
root@srx3600n0# set security policies from-zone Trust to-zone Internet policy
Sales then permit application-services idp

root@srx3600n0# set security policies from-zone Trust to-zone Internet policy
Sales then permit application-services ssl-proxy profile-name SSL-FP

[edit]
root@srx3600n0# set security policies from-zone Trust to-zone Internet policy
Sales then log session-close

[edit]
root@srx3600n0# set security application-firewall rule-sets Real-Estate-Social-
Networking rule 1 match dynamic-application-group junos:web:real-estate

[edit]
root@srx3600n0# set security application-firewall rule-sets Real-Estate-Social-
Networking rule 1 match dynamic-application-group junos:web:social-networking

[edit]
root@srx3600n0# set security application-firewall rule-sets Real-Estate-Social-
Networking rule 1 then permit

root@srx3600n0# set security application-firewall rule-sets Real-Estate-Social-
Networking default-rule deny

 [edit]
root@srx3600n0# set class-of-service application-traffic-control rate-limiters
10Mbps bandwidth-limit 10000

 [edit]
root@srx3600n0#  set  class-of-service  application-traffic-control  rule-sets
10Mbps-Social-Networking  rule  1  match  application-group  junos:web:social-
networking

[edit]
 [edit]
root@srx3600n0#  set  class-of-service  application-traffic-control  rule-sets
10Mbps-Social-Networking rule 1 then rate-limit client-to-server 10Mbps

[edit]
root@srx3600n0#  set  class-of-service  application-traffic-control  rule-sets
10Mbps-Social-Networking rule 1 then rate-limit server-to-client 10Mbps


[edit]
root@srx3600n0# set security application-firewall rule-sets Social-Engineering
rule 1 match dynamic-application-group junos:web:social-networking

[edit]
root@srx3600n0# set security application-firewall rule-sets Social-Engineering
rule 1 then permit
```

```
[edit]
root@srx3600n0# set security application-firewall rule-sets Social-Engineering
default-rule deny

[edit]
root@srx3600n0# set security application-firewall rule-sets Forums rule 1 match
dynamic-application-group junos:web:forums

[edit]
root@srx3600n0# set security application-firewall rule-sets Forums rule 1 then
permit

[edit]
root@srx3600n0# set security application-firewall rule-sets Forums default-rule
deny

[edit]
root@srx3600n0# set schedulers scheduler Engineering daily start-time 12:00
stop-time 13:00

[edit]
root@srx3600n0# set security policies from-zone Trust to-zone Internet policy
Engineering-Lunch scheduler-name Engineering

[edit]
root@srx3600n0# set security policies from-zone Trust to-zone Internet policy
Engineering-Lunch match source-address any source-identity Engineering
destination-address any application [junos-http junos-https]

root@srx3600n0# set security policies from-zone Trust to-zone Internet policy
Engineering-Lunch then permit application-services application-firewall rule-
set Social-Engineering

[edit]
root@srx3600n0# set security policies from-zone Trust to-zone Internet policy
Engineering-Lunch then permit application-services idp

[edit]
root@srx3600n0# set security policies from-zone Trust to-zone Internet policy
Engineering-Lunch then permit application-services ssl-proxy profile-name SSL-FP

[edit]
root@srx3600n0# set security policies from-zone Trust to-zone Internet policy
Engineering-Lunch then log session-close


root@srx3600n0# set security policies from-zone Trust to-zone Internet policy
Engineering-Normal-Hours match source-address any source-identity Engineering
destination-address any application [junos-http junos-https]

root@srx3600n0# set security policies from-zone Trust to-zone Internet policy
```

```
Engineering-Normal-Hours then permit application-services application-firewall
rule-set Forums

[edit]
root@srx3600n0# set security policies from-zone Trust to-zone Internet policy
Engineering-Normal-Hours then permit application-services idp

[edit]
root@srx3600n0# set security policies from-zone Trust to-zone Internet policy
Engineering-Normal-Hours then permit application-services ssl-proxy profile-
name SSL-FP

[edit]
root@srx3600n0# set security policies from-zone Trust to-zone Internet policy
Engineering-Normal-Hours then log session-close

[edit]
root@srx3600n0# set security utm utm-policy "Protect Users" web-filtering http-
profile junos-wf-enhanced-default

[edit]
root@srx3600n0# set security utm utm-policy "Protect Users" anti-virus http-
profile junos-sophos-av-defaults


[edit]
root@srx3600n0# set security application-firewall rule-sets Other-Users rule 1
match dynamic-application-group junos:web:multimedia

[edit]
root@srx3600n0# set security application-firewall rule-sets Other-Users rule 1
then deny

[edit]
root@srx3600n0# set security application-firewall rule-sets Other-Users rule 2
match dynamic-application-group junos:web

[edit]
root@srx3600n0# set security application-firewall rule-sets Other-Users rule 2
then permit

root@srx3600n0# set security application-firewall rule-sets Other-Users default-
rule deny

[edit]
root@srx3600n0# set security policies from-zone Trust to-zone Internet policy
All-Other-Users match source-address any source-identity authenticated-user
destination-address any application junos-http

[edit]
root@srx3600n0# set security policies from-zone Trust to-zone Internet policy
All-Other-Users then permit application-services application-firewall rule-set
```

```
Other-Users

[edit]
root@srx3600n0# set security policies from-zone Trust to-zone Internet policy
All-Other-Users then permit application-services utm-policy "Protect Users"

[edit]
root@srx3600n0# set security policies from-zone Trust to-zone Internet policy
All-Other-Users then log session-close

[edit]
root@srx3600n0# show security policies from-zone Trust to-zone Internet
policy Sales {
    match {
        source-address any;
        destination-address any;
        application [ junos-http junos-https ];
        source-identity Sales;
    }
    then {
        permit {
            application-services {
                idp;
                ssl-proxy {
                    profile-name SSL-FP;
                }
                application-firewall {
                    rule-set Real-Estate-Social-Networking;
                }
                application-traffic-control {
                    rule-set 10Mbps-Social-Networking;
                }
            }
        }
        log {
            session-close;
        }
    }
}
policy Engineering-Lunch {
    match {
        source-address any;
        destination-address any;
        application [ junos-http junos-https ];
        source-identity Engineering;
    }
    then {
        permit {
            application-services {
                idp;
                ssl-proxy {
                    profile-name SSL-FP;
```

```
                }
                application-firewall {
                    rule-set Social-Engineering;
                }
            }
        }
        log {
            session-close;
        }
    }
    scheduler-name Engineering;
}
policy Engineering-Normal-Hours {
    match {
        source-address any;
        destination-address any;
        application [ junos-http junos-https ];
        source-identity Engineering;
    }
    then {
        permit {
            application-services {
                idp;
                ssl-proxy {
                    profile-name SSL-FP;
                }
                application-firewall {
                    rule-set Forums;
                }
            }
        }
        log {
            session-close;
        }
    }
}
policy All-Other-Users {
    match {
        source-address any;
        destination-address any;
        application junos-http;
        source-identity authenticated-user;
    }
    then {
        permit {
            application-services {
                utm-policy "Protect Users";
                application-firewall {
                    rule-set Other-Users;
                }
            }
        }
```

```
        log {
            session-close;
        }
    }
}

[edit]
root@srx3600n0# show security application-firewall
rule-sets Real-Estate-Social-Networking {
    rule 1 {
        match {
             dynamic-application-group [ junos:web:real-estate junos:web:social-
networking ];
        }
        then {
            permit;
        }
    }
    default-rule {
        deny;
    }
}
rule-sets Social-Engineering {
    rule 1 {
        match {
            dynamic-application-group junos:web:social-networking;
        }
        then {
            permit;
        }
    }
    default-rule {
        deny;
    }
}
rule-sets Forums {
    rule 1 {
        match {
            dynamic-application-group junos:web:forums;
        }
        then {
            permit;
        }
    }
    default-rule {
        deny;
    }
}
rule-sets Other-Users {
    rule 1 {
        match {
            dynamic-application-group junos:web:multimedia;
```

```
        }
        then {
            deny;
        }
    }
    rule 2 {
        match {
            dynamic-application-group junos:web;
        }
        then {
            permit;
        }
    }
    default-rule {
        deny;
    }
}

[edit]
root@srx3600n0# show security utm utm-policy "Protect Users"
anti-virus {
    http-profile junos-sophos-av-defaults;
}
web-filtering {
    http-profile junos-wf-enhanced-default;
}

[edit]
root@srx3600n0# show class-of-service application-traffic-control
rate-limiters 10Mbps {
    bandwidth-limit 10000;
}
rule-sets 10Mbps-Social-Networking {
    rule 1 {
        match {
            application-group junos:web:social-networking;
        }
        then {
            rate-limit {
                client-to-server 10Mbps;
                server-to-client 10Mbps;
            }
        }
    }
}
```

Summary

As computer networks have evolved, providing cutting-edge services and feature-rich applications, the underlying protocols that drive these improvements will also evolve. So, too, must our security capabilities on devices like firewalls to ensure that administrators can effectively secure their networks. The technologies offered as part of AppSecure are just a piece of the puzzle, but by no means should these be your only security mechanisms. AppSecure is just a building block that further strengthens the security controls that came before it, like stateful firewalling, IPS, and UTM. As time goes on, we'll definitely expect to see new and innovative features that are set to improve administrative controls and experience in the realm of application security. This is definitely a technology segment that you will want to stay updated on.

Study Questions

Questions

1. What do all of the components in AppSecure have in common?
2. Explain the functions of AppTrack, AppFW, AppQoS, UserFW, and SSL FP.
3. What does the Application Cache do? When is it best to have it on? When is it best to turn it off?
4. What options are available for AppTrack processing?
5. Where do you turn on AppTrack?
6. How is AppFW enforced in the SRX, and how are the AppFW rules evaluated?
7. What is the difference between whitelist, blacklist, and hybrid rulesets in AppFW?
8. What options are available when using AppFW and what do they do?
9. How is AppQoS enabled on the SRX, and what actions can it take on matched traffic?
10. What are the required and optional values available in the AppQoS rate limiters?
11. What are the roles and responsibilities of the components involved in UserFW?
12. How is the user-to-IP mapping leveraged in the SRX for security policies?
13. Explain how SSL Forward Proxy functions on the SRX.
14. What is the difference between SSL resumption and SSL renegotiation?
15. What is the difference between Application Identification with signatures and heuristics?

Answers

1. They all leverage AppID to provide application identity information to the different modules.
2. AppTrack is used to provide logging information via syslog and other on-box statistics around application usage. It not only captures the standard firewall information but also the Level 7 application as well. AppFW extends the logging and reporting side of AppTrack to be able to enforce an action on the traffic itself. This allows you to permit, deny, reject, or redirect traffic based on its application identity. AppQoS allows you to perform QoS on traffic based on its application identity. You can provide rate limiting, provide DSCP rewriting, set loss priority, and set the forwarding class (including priority queuing, guaranteeing bandwidth, and scheduling purposes). UserFW allows you to tie in user identity information to the firewall policies as match criteria. This further allows you to leverage the user identity information for other Level 7 services like AppFW, AppQoS, UTM, and IPS. Finally, SSL FP allows you to inspect outbound SSL Proxy connections from your internal clients to external resources on the Internet. You can leverage this for services like AppFW and IPS at the time of writing this book.
3. The application cache allows the SRX to record the results of previous AppID detection based on the server IP, protocol, and port, so that AppID doesn't need to run for future connections. It is on by default, and applications have a 60-minute timeout by default. If you are most concerned about network performance, it is best to leave it on; however, if you are more concerned about security, it is best to turn it off. Leveraging IPS will also help when it comes to AppID to ensure that evasive behaviors are not being employed to trick the system.
4. AppTrack allows you define whether or not to send a log on the AppTrack session creation, along with how often it should send application volume updates which can be useful to get a more real-time view of how data is being transmitted (especially important for long-lived sessions) rather than just logging at the end of the session.
5. AppTrack is enabled on a per zone basis under `set security zones security-zone <zone> application-tracking`.
6. AppFW can be configured on a firewall rule-by-rule basis for any rule that has an action of permit. Each rule allows you to define a single AppFW ruleset that should be enforced. Within the AppFW ruleset, rules are evaluated from top to bottom until an application match is hit or the default option is reached.
7. Whitelist, blacklist, and hybrid are just titles and aren't explicitly referenced in the configuration, but these are useful terms to describe what the AppFW ruleset is trying to accomplish. Whitelist is when you have one or more applications

or application groups that are matched at the top of the AppFW ruleset with an action of permit, and the default action is to deny any unmatched applications. Blacklists are the opposite: they try to match applications or application groups with an action of deny, reject, or redirect, and all other applications are matched to the default rule, which is permit. Finally, hybrid rulesets are those that use both deny and permit in the ruleset. These are sometimes necessary when you are filtering with nested applications in very specific manners.

8. AppFW supports permit, deny, reject, and redirect as actions. Permit is simply to allow the traffic, deny is a silent drop on the traffic, reject is a TCP RST on the traffic, and redirect can be used for HTTP and HTTPS traffic (when SSL Proxy is used) to redirect the traffic either internally on the SRX or to a third-party web server effectively blocking the traffic from being redirected to a final destination but providing a better user experience than a simple drop or reject.

9. AppQoS is deployed in a ruleset manner very similar to AppFW in that the rulesets are enabled on a per-firewall rule basis when the action is permit. Within the ruleset, applications are matched and then an action is defined. The actions can include rate limiting bandwidth to a maximum limit (configurable from both client to server and server to client) as a whole for the rule, setting the forwarding class, setting a DSCP value to rewrite the traffic, logging actions, and setting loss priority.

10. Besides setting the name of the rate limiter, there are only two values that are configurable. You must set the bandwidth limit that defines the maximum bandwidth cap available for the rate limiter to enforce (expressed in Kbps); setting the burst size is optional and expressed in bps (bytes per second). The system will automatically set this for you if you do not explicitly define it. The only time you would need to set this is if you want a larger burst size available if there is additional bandwidth.

11. There are essentially five components to UserFW (assuming you're not using local authentication): the client, the original destination server, the SRX, the Infranet Controller, and the Active Directory domain. When an unauthenticated client initiates traffic to a destination server through the SRX, the SRX will do a lookup to see if there is an active user-to-IP mapping for the client. Assuming there is no mapping, the SRX will do an HTTP redirect to redirect the HTTP session to the IC. The IC will attempt to authenticate the client via SPNEGO, which is a standards-based web authentication protocol. If the client supports it, it will retrieve a Kerberos ticket from the domain controller and present it to the IC which the IC will authenticate with the domain controller. If the client doesn't support (or isn't configured to support) SPNEGO, then the IC will fall back to captive portal to manually authenticate the client. Once the client is authenticated, they are allowed to continue on to the destination server. In the background, the client will maintain an HTTPS session with the IC that

will send an AJAX heartbeat every five seconds to ensure that the client maintains its presence on the network.

12. As of Junos 12.1, the SRX has a new field called Source-Identity that allows you to map a user role (locally generated or from the IC) in the policy as an additional match criteria just like source IP, destination IP, application, and so on. This then allows the policy to have user identity intelligence and this can be further leveraged by Level 7 rulebases like UTM, IPS, AppFW, AppQoS, and more.

13. SSL FP allows the SRX to inspect SSL traffic that is generated from internal clients to whom you can distribute a CA signing certificate. The SRX will intercept the traffic from both a TCP Proxy and SSL Proxy perspective to negotiate an SSL tunnel between the client and the SRX, and from the SRX to the destination server. This allows the SRX to inspect the contents with Level 7 functionality like AppFW and IPS. SSL FP is configured on a firewall rule-by-rule basis, allowing you to set SSL Proxy profiles on a per-rule basis. This is different than SSL RP, with which you are protecting your own web servers by placing their SSL private key on the SRX so the SRX can decrypt the secure communication and detect attacks from external clients to your web servers.

14. SSL session resumption allows a client and the SRX to start an SSL session with a previously established key negotiated in a previous SSL session (bypassing the need for the SSL establishment phase). SSL renegotiation is a feature that allows the client or the server to trigger a renegotiation of the SSL session key during an existing SSL session.

15. The SRX supports matching applications based on both patterns and heuristics. Most "honest" applications can be easily matched via signatures, but there are many evasive applications that intentionally do not follow a particularly obvious pattern. This is where the heuristics engine comes in. It can help to detect applications via traffic analysis. Although you can't code your own heuristic checks today, you can enable the predefined heuristic engine and then leverage the application identification results it generates for the purpose of AppSecure policy enforcement.

CHAPTER 13

Intrusion Prevention

Although stateful firewall technology is a powerful mechanism for controlling cyberthreats and preventing denials of service, controlling targeted exploitation requires deeper inspection and control of the application layer traffic itself. The SRX platform integrates the power of stateful firewalling, routing, NAT, and VPNs, along with the power of Juniper IDP technology, into a single unit. Make no mistake: this is true IPS, not a subset of inspection capabilities, and it's all done within integrated network purposed hardware so that additional types of components are not needed.

This chapter details the Juniper IPS functionality built into the SRX. It starts with an overview of IPS—what it does, why it's necessary, and how it compares to other technologies, including Juniper's legacy platforms. Then we look at how to configure, operate, tune, and troubleshoot the IPS on the SRX, and explore some of the features that have been introduced since the *Junos Security* series book was released. As with all the chapters in this book, questions at the end of the chapter should help those taking Juniper's security certification to prepare for their exam.

The Need for IPS

Despite what some flashy vendor advertisements and blogs might say, stateful firewalling is not dead, nor will it be anytime soon. Stateful firewalling provides a core layer of security to ensure that network traffic is restricted to only that which a policy dictates from the networking layer and the transport layer (Layers 3 and 4, respectively). It also goes a step further to ensure that the exchanges follow the exchanges that are expected in Layers 3 and 4.

This is a critical layer of network security; however, it should not be the only layer of network security you apply to protect a network infrastructure. The problem with stateful firewalling by itself is that it can go only so far to limit which source IP addresses can communicate to which destination IP addresses, and on which Layer 3 and Layer 4 protocols the communication can be exchanged (see Figure 13-1).

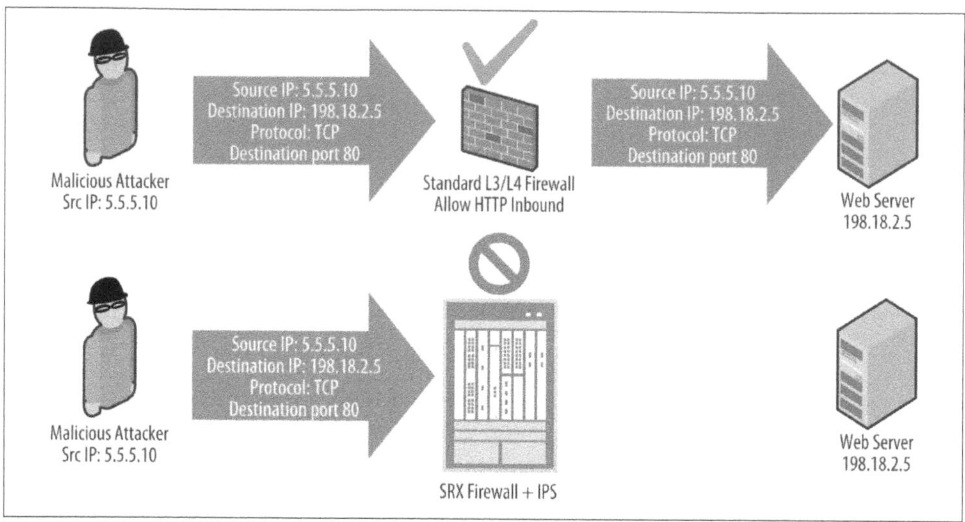

Figure 13-1. Firewall versus IPS

Stateful firewalling cannot actually limit what can be exchanged within the channels of permitted Layer 3 and Layer 4 communication. For instance, if your organization hosts a public web server to serve as the portal for the Internet (say, to get information about your company), assuming you're using standard ports and protocols, you would need to open a firewall rule that would allow any source IP address to be able to connect to the destination IP address of your web server on TCP port 80. From that perspective, the firewall would ensure that (barring no additional configuration to permit otherwise) only Internet connections to your web server on TCP port 80 would be allowed (no FTP, DNS, SMTP, SMB, etc.).

What About Application Firewalling in NGFW?

There has been a lot of splash over the last few years about the capabilities of application firewalling that has been introduced into firewalls. It is most certainly a very useful feature, and we offer it as a feature in the SRX itself. Juniper's approach, however, isn't to make your security policy revolve around the ability to identify applications. Just like we don't forsake firewalls even though we have IPS (which in a perfect world would remove the need for the access control that firewalls provide because we could just block the threats), we know that stateful firewalls are still a critical part of network infrastructures and probably will be for the foreseeable future. Application firewalling definitely plays an important role in controlling what applications can communicate over the network, but it does nothing to prevent attacks at Layers 3 through 7; it just controls what applications can communicate.

As shown in Figure 13-2, limiting access to only the essentials is very important both from a TCP/IP perspective and a Layer 7 perspective; however, the capabilities of stateful and application firewalling alone do little to control what is actually exchanged within these connections. You can make the analogy that IPS is to networking what airport screening checkpoints are to physical security (although we like to think that network-based IPS can do an even better job than airport security, and won't take your 3.5-ounce bottle of shampoo away either). In airport screening, not only are you inspected to determine where you are coming from and where you are going, but also your contents are searched via a combination of X-rays, metal detectors, chemical analysis, and sometimes airport security personnel. Although determining where you are coming from and where you are going might be important to security at some level, the items you carry with you are also extremely important to security. Computer networking is no different from physical airport security in the need to inspect and secure communications.

Luckily, although the task of security computer network communications is daunting, powerful tools within the SRX exist to make this task practical.

How Does IPS Work?

At a high level, IPS works by scrutinizing all of the bits contained within packets to look for both known and unknown attacks, as shown in Figure 13-3. Traditional firewalls primarily look only at Layers 3 and 4 when it comes to security, and ignore the actual contents of the payloads themselves. This makes for efficient processing, which can be accelerated in hardware, but it alone does not provide protection for traffic that is permitted by firewall policies.

So, why do we still need stateful or application firewalling at all if we can just use IPS to ensure that traffic is "scrubbed" to only permit desired traffic, regardless of where it comes from or what port it is on?

That's an excellent question, and one that some vendors claim the use of their IPS products will answer. The fact of the matter is that no security is perfect, and although in a perfect world using only IPS might be a valid solution, this is not a perfect world. By utilizing Level 3 through Level 7 firewalling as layers of security, you can weed out undesired traffic early in the process so that you don't have to use any more resources than are necessary for processing traffic that you know early on you don't want. It's important, because IPS is a very computationally expensive process that cannot be easily assisted through the use of ASIC-based inspection. By blocking traffic early on, you ensure that neither the IPS nor the destination servers have to process traffic unnecessarily. Resources are always going to be finite, and often expensive.

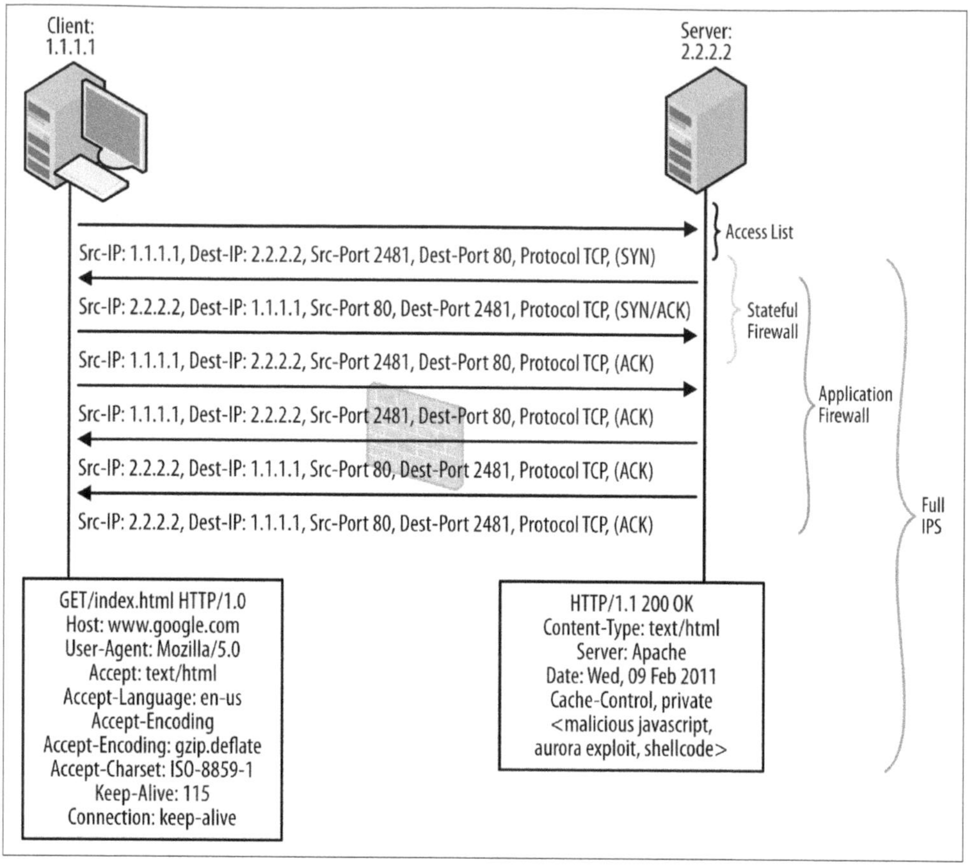

Figure 13-2. ACL versus FW versus AppFW versus IPS

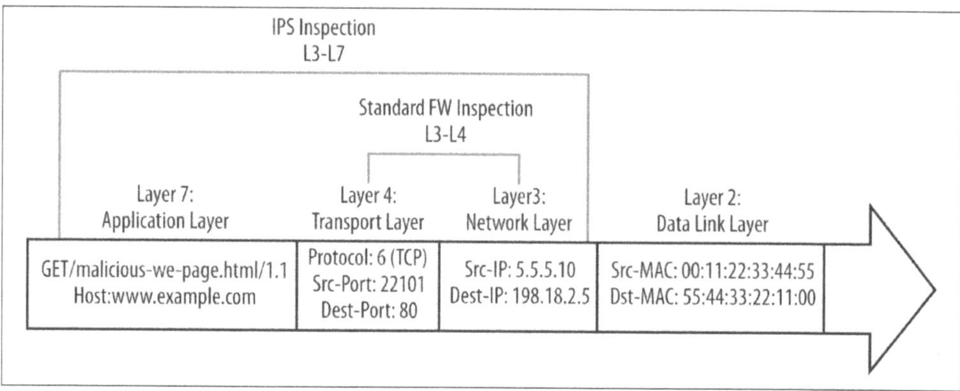

Figure 13-3. Firewall inspection of attack versus IPS

Eliminate processing of undesired traffic as early in the process as possible to ensure that no more resources than necessary are required.

Licensing

Licenses are required to download the Juniper attack objects and policy templates. If you are just using the IPS functionality and you want to only use your own attack objects, you can do so without the need for a license (although you will see a license warning).

At the time of writing this book, the IPS licenses are based on an annual subscription model, available in one-, three-, or five-year increments. The licenses can be purchased by themselves, or bundled with AppSecure and other UTM features. There is no variability in functionality with IPS. If you buy the license, you get the full capabilities.

Note that if the license expires, the ability to download attack object updates is prevented, but you will still be able to run IPS in its current state. Contact your Juniper reseller for information on getting licenses.

IPS and UTM

If you have IPS, do you still need UTM? The short answer to this question is "yes"; as mentioned previously, best practice dictates that IPS is not a substitute for antivirus or URL filtering, as they each fulfill a different need. IPS is primarily based on detecting attacks in network streams, and although it does some level of file level parsing, or can be used to block access to different websites, that's not its primary function. Instead we focus the IPS capabilities on looking for known and unknown exploits and anomalies in the traffic streams. Antivirus software is used both to identify known viruses in files exchanged over the network, along with providing a reputation feed for known malicious Uniform Resource Identifiers (URIs) where malware is being served, so that even if the specific virus isn't known, the system can still provide protection. URL filtering, on the other hand, also provides a layer of protection that can prevent you from going to other sites that might be malicious or affect productivity. Although the database does have an overlap in functionality as antivirus protection, it is never a bad idea to rely on two different types of detection.

Cyberthreats come in many different forms, but let's classify them as network-based or file-based protection.

Traditionally, IPS is primarily concerned with network-based threats and securing communication between different hosts, as shown in Figure 13-4. File-based protection is another story. Although files can certainly be exchanged over networks, they can also be exchanged through other mechanisms such as USB drives, CDs, DVDs, and sometimes secure communication channels such as IPsec VPNs that are not terminated on the IPS itself. This is true both for network-based antivirus servers and for IPS.

True security is best executed by providing layered security (see Figure 13-4); that is, using IPS for what it is best at, by securing communications between hosts, but on those hosts providing additional security through the use of host-based IPS and antivirus protection. Network-based antivirus software is an excellent perimeter tool as well, but just like IPS, it doesn't completely remove the need for host-based protection, because it is often difficult to inspect encrypted files and not all files might be exchanged over the network.

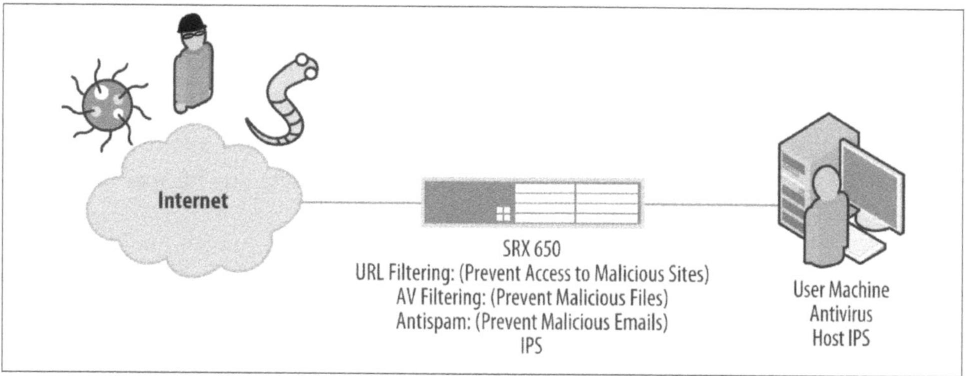

Figure 13-4. Layered security

Although the SRX does not focus on inspecting the contents of files, most contemporary threats try to spread themselves over the network, or "phone home" to command and control servers. Here the SRX can be used to not only identify these types of infection and control attempts, but also to actually block them and alert administrators to this activity (see Figure 13-5).

What Is the Difference Between Full IPS and Deep Inspection/IPS Lite?

Previous generations of Juniper firewalls such as the NetScreen and SSG Series (along with many other competitors) offer deep inspection or IPS lite functionality. This provides a limited subset of inspection capability by inspecting the traffic at Layer 7, but it is for only a handful of signatures. Deep inspection/IPS lite does not provide full inspection; therefore, it isn't really geared toward true security, and it has become more of a checkbox security feature that auditors tend to look for. If you are truly concerned about providing real security for your environment, full IPS should be a requirement. When evaluating solutions, it is important to determine exactly what level of IPS is

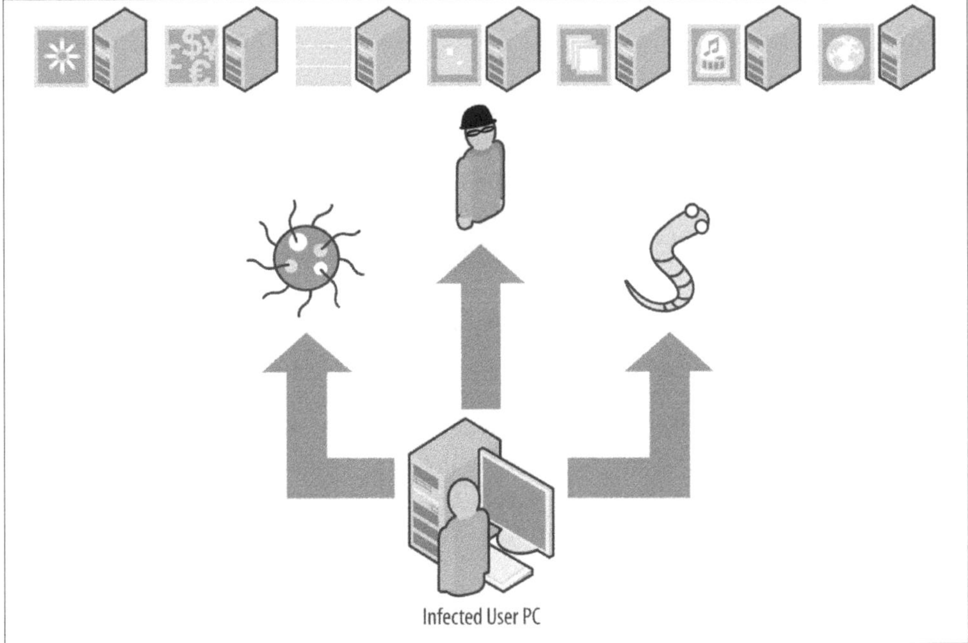

Figure 13-5. Infected host attempting to propagate

performed. On the SRX platforms (from the SRX100 to the SRX5800), IPS is a full-featured inspection technology that cuts no corners.

Is It IDP or IPS?

Many SRX administrators might be familiar with the previous generations of IPS products offered by Juniper Networks, including the standalone IDP appliance and the ISG with IDP security modules. In the past, these products referred to IPS functionality as IDP, which originated from OneSecure (developer of the first IPS [rather than IDS] platform). OneSecure was later acquired by NetScreen, which was acquired by Juniper.

To move more in line with industry-standard terms, Juniper Networks has begun to call its IDP *IPS*. You can still find a lot of references to IDP in the SRX configuration, but over the lifetime of this book, this will be migrated to IPS.

Juniper does not typically change CLI configuration statements without a formal process, so for the short and medium terms, you might notice that IDP is referenced rather than IPS. You can effectively refer to these terms equally.

False Positives and False Negatives in IPS

Some network administrators are wary of IPS because of the risk of *false positives*. A false positive is when something legitimate is detected as something malicious. If the administrator has configured protection against malicious attacks, it is likely that IPS might actually block legitimate traffic, which we all know can cause a few headaches. A *false negative* is when a real attack is deemed as legitimate traffic, and therefore is not detected. False negatives are as much a concern as false positives, although without an IPS in place, they would get through anyway.

False positives occur for several reasons, one of which might be that it isn't a false positive at all; that is, the IPS might detect the traffic accurately as it is instructed to do. Often, particularly in the case of protocol anomaly protection, if a vendor does not follow a standard implementation (e.g., an RFC or manufacturer spec) of a protocol, the IPS detects this as an attack, just like it is programmed to do. In other cases, a signature might be too broad in detection and could identify both malicious and legitimate traffic. Finally, false negatives might occur because the IPS isn't actually inspecting for such activity, the detection might be disabled, or the signatures might not detect particular iterations of an attack.

The good news is that the SRX goes to great lengths to minimize both false positives and false negatives, and this chapter details how the SRX does this through the use of intelligent application matching, protocol decoding, and context-based inspection. This chapter also discusses fine-tuning of the SRX so that you can minimize occurrences of false positives.

Management IPS Functionality on the SRX

Administrators familiar with prior generations of Juniper IPS products such as the standalone IDP appliance and the ISG with IDP security modules know that the Network and Security Manager (NSM) management platform was required to manage the IPS functionality on the IDP and ISG, respectively. The SRX is different in that it does not require the NSM for any IPS functionality at all, although the NSM can certainly manage the SRX IPS functionality. The SRX allows you to fully manage the SRX IPS via the CLI, and most functions are available via J-Web and Junos Space/Security Design. The STRM platform also has plenty of predefined log views, offenses, and reports for the Juniper IPS product, including the ability to collect PCAPs generated from SRX attacks. In the future, this will likely be added to the central management solution Security Insight as well.

You can view the contents of IPS attack objects online in the Juniper Security Portal including updates to the Attack Database at this link (*http://www.juniper.net/us/en/security/*).

Stages of a System Compromise

Understanding the stages of an attack is critical to being able to provide comprehensive security. Many security books go into great detail regarding the different stages of an attack, but for our purposes let's simplify them into four common stages or aspects of an attack. Note that not all stages are necessary for an attack, but they are common to most attacks.

Reconnaissance

The first phase of an attack typically identifies vulnerable hosts. Often, this includes port scanning, banner grabbing, and other techniques to get information to leak from the system regarding what platform it is and its respective software. Active reconnaissance is often the case when it comes to client-to-server-based attacks where the attacker actively targets a client directly. With most machines behind a firewall these days, the attackers cannot directly reach out to the clients. Instead they will employ other tactics like phishing emails, injecting malicious content into legitimate sites, and even DNS poisoning to set the stage for a client to go to a malicious site that they control (typically via HTTP) to attempt to compromise the client.

The SRX can help to protect against different types of sweeps and scans through the use of Screens, but also there are a large number of attack objects in the IPS that are associated with information leakage attempts. The SRX also provides a great number of known malicious attack objects that you can leverage to prevent such stages, including drive-by downloads from the server-to-client perspective. You can also use IP actions (discussed later in this chapter) to shun traffic from sources that are attempting such reconnaissance techniques.

Vulnerability exploitation

Once a vulnerable system is identified, the attacker tries to exploit the vulnerability in the system. There is a lot of confusion about this stage, because technically, the vulnerability exploitation does one of two things: it crashes the system or service (a DoS attack) or it changes the control of execution on the system. As part of the latter case, the attacker often injects code known as *shellcode*, which allows for further exploitation.

The SRX provides comprehensive protection of vulnerability exploitation with thousands of attack objects that protect against exploitation using both protocol anomaly and signature-based attack objects. These attack objects can protect against both attacks that cause a system or service to crash and attacks that try to compromise the system.

Shellcode execution

Assuming that the attack is meant to compromise the system rather than simply crash it, the attacker typically injects shellcode as part of the vulnerability exploitation stage. Shellcode is code that is executed in place of the regular application to further compromise the system. Examples of what shellcode can do include opening a backdoor on the system, creating outbound control connections, modifying the system by creating users or elevating access, and injecting malicious applications. Without the use of shellcode, the exploited system would not likely be compromised (controlled) even if the vulnerability was exploited.

Not only does the SRX detect and prevent the exploitation of vulnerabilities, but it can also detect shellcode, so even if it somehow missed the actual exploit, it would likely be able to detect the shellcode. Numerous shellcode attack signatures can be blocked in addition to the actual exploit itself.

Privilege escalation

Once an exploit has occurred and shellcode is executed, the shellcode is running in the context of the process that it compromised. If it is a system-level vulnerability, then privilege escalation is not usually necessary, but often this is not the case (e.g., compromising a web browser on a client machine). To gain broader control, another exploit must be used to compromise the local machine and escalate the privilege that the shellcode is running with. This stage of the attack is not detectable by the IPS because it doesn't occur over the network but is local to the compromised machine. This is where both proper patch management and host-based antimalware defenses can help to detect and protect against these types of escalations.

Infection attempts/phone-home traffic

Once a system is compromised, it typically tries to infect other machines, phone home to the control servers, or do both.

The SRX can detect these infection and phone-home techniques, depending on the nature of the infection method and the communication to the command and control system. The SRX can often detect attempts to infect other machines, with the ability to block those attempts and identify compromised machines. Additionally, the SRX might be able to identify command and control and phone-home traffic. Sometimes this traffic is encrypted, so the SRX might not be able to identify what the machine is controlled by, but the SRX can identify encrypted traffic streams (and block them if so desired).

As you can see, the SRX can do quite a lot to prevent attacks, minimize their impact, and identify and control the spread of machines that could be infected (e.g., a laptop that is infected in a foreign network). By implementing a *layered security approach*, the SRX can offer real security to the networks that it protects.

IPS Packet Processing on the SRX

To understand how IPS processing on the SRX works, you must first understand where IPS sits in the path of packet processing, what components are utilized for IPS processing, and the actual composition of the IPS functionality itself. Let's examine how SRX IPS fits into the big picture of your network security exactly in that order.

Packet processing path

We already discussed the packet flow on the SRX when it comes to session setup, steady state processing, and session close. Now let's focus in more depth on what happens to packet processing in terms of the IPS. It is important to remember that for the high-end SRX, a session is always anchored to a single SPU for the duration of its lifetime. The same holds true in the case of IPS. IPS is always going to be inspected on the same SPU as that of the firewall flow. Unlike previous generations of Juniper IDP platforms and many other vendors' products, the SRX does not require special hardware to perform its IPS processing. Instead, all IPS services are processed in the SPU itself. If additional IPS processing power is required, the administrator need only add additional SPUs.

In the case of the branch SRX Series, there is only one network processor where *all* processing is performed.

The SRX IPS functionality is tightly tied to its firewall functionality.

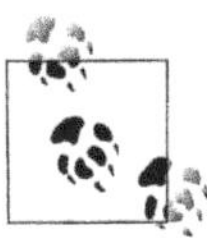

In the case of the branch SRX Series, if packet mode is used, that traffic cannot be inspected by the IPS engine. At the time of this writing, the high-end SRX does not support selective processing; it only supports flow mode.

Figure 13-6 illustrates a high-level flow chart of how packet processing operates in the SRX with regard to the different services. Note that IPS is one of the last things to be processed in the services chain. That means if the traffic is not permitted by a firewall policy (which must also reference it to be inspected by IPS), the traffic never hits the IPS engine. This is intentional, because you don't want to burden the IPS with inspecting traffic that is ultimately going to be dropped by some other mechanism anyway.

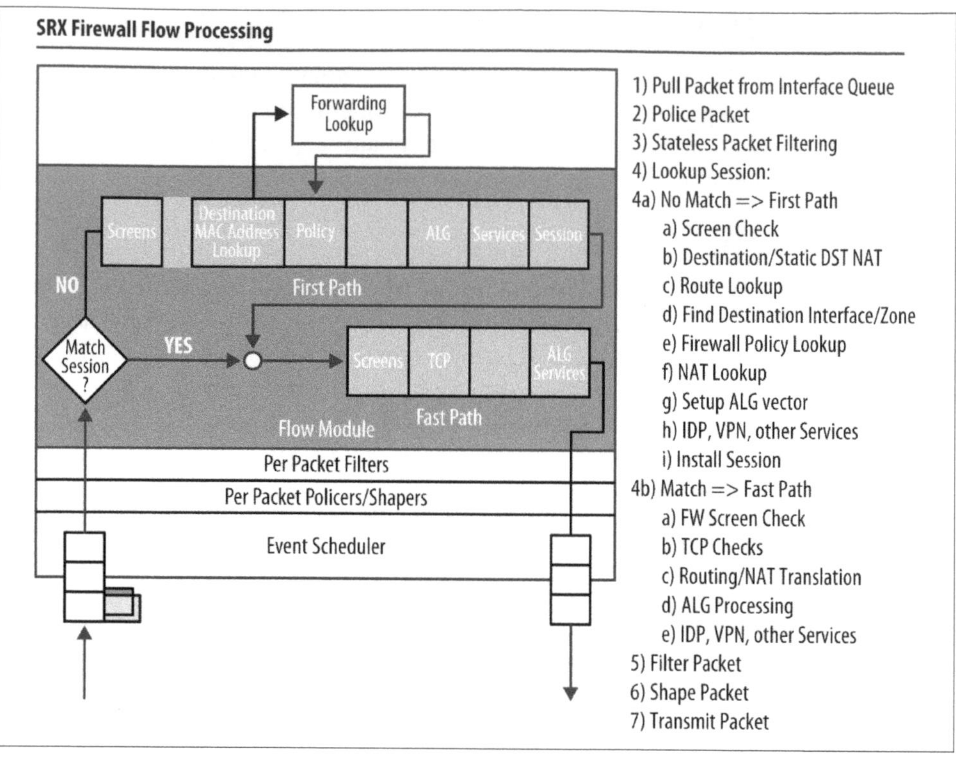

Figure 13-6. First path packet processing

One of the great things about the SRX IPS implementation is that it offers a great deal of granularity. Unlike many other vendors' implementations, the SRX allows you to enable IPS processing on a firewall rule-by-rule basis, rather than just turning on inspection across the board. This means traffic that is not marked by a firewall rule to be processed by IPS completely bypasses the IPS. Traffic that is marked for IPS processing is then handed off to the IPS engine.

In addition to referencing IPS processing on a firewall rule-by-rule basis, within the IPS rulebase you still have extremely granular rulebase control over how the IPS is enforced. We cover this in depth later in the chapter.

As mentioned, all IPS-bound traffic must be processed by the stateful firewall flow engine first (known as *flowd*). For now, suffice it to say that if the IPS engine needs to process traffic, the traffic will be handed off after the firewall has completed its processing (and only for permitted traffic). Within the IPS engine there are several stages of processing, as illustrated in Figure 13-7.

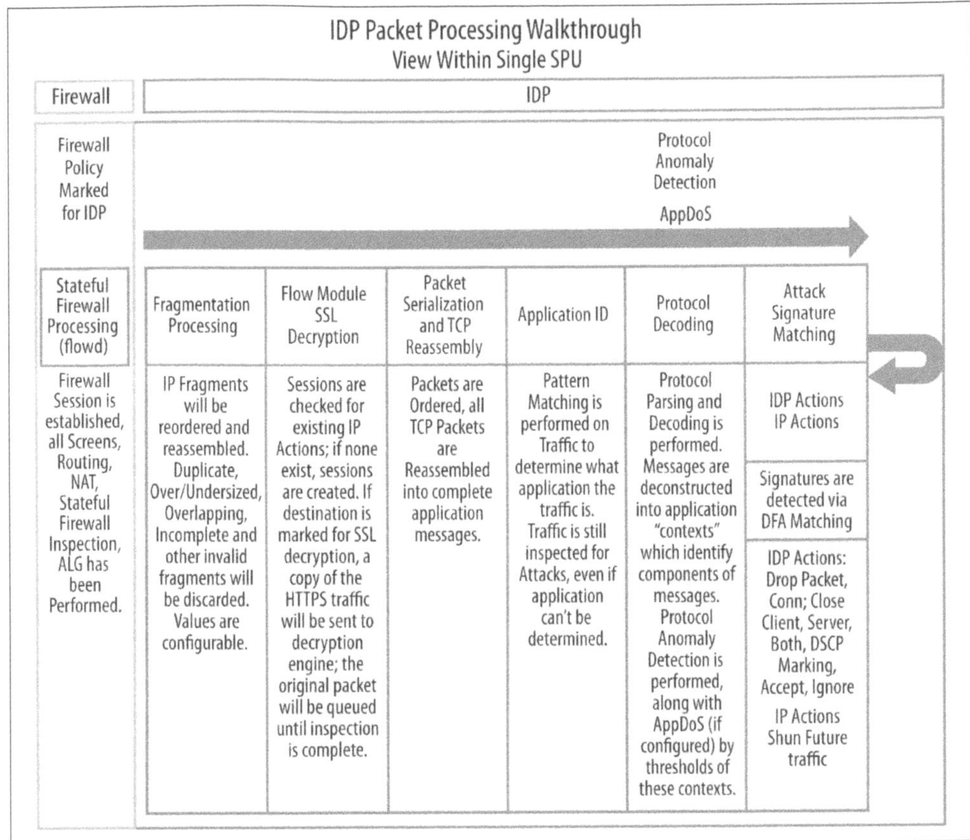
IDP Packet Processing Walkthrough
View Within Single SPU
Firewall
IDP
Firewall Policy Marked for IDP
Protocol Anomaly Detection
AppDoS
Stateful Firewall Processing (flowd)
Fragmentation Processing
Flow Module SSL Decryption
Packet Serialization and TCP Reassembly
Application ID
Protocol Decoding
Attack Signature Matching
Firewall Session is established, all Screens, Routing, NAT, Stateful Firewall Inspection, ALG has been Performed.
IP Fragments will be reordered and reassembled. Duplicate, Over/Undersized, Overlapping, Incomplete and other invalid fragments will be discarded. Values are configurable.
Sessions are checked for existing IP Actions; if none exist, sessions are created. If destination is marked for SSL decryption, a copy of the HTTPS traffic will be sent to decryption engine; the original packet will be queued until inspection is complete.
Packets are Ordered, all TCP Packets are Reassembled into complete application messages.
Pattern Matching is performed on Traffic to determine what application the traffic is. Traffic is still inspected for Attacks, even if application can't be determined.
Protocol Parsing and Decoding is performed. Messages are deconstructed into application "contexts" which identify components of messages. Protocol Anomaly Detection is performed, along with AppDoS (if configured) by thresholds of these contexts.
IDP Actions
IP Actions
Signatures are detected via DFA Matching
IDP Actions: Drop Packet, Conn; Close Client, Server, Both, DSCP Marking, Accept, Ignore
IP Actions Shun Future traffic

Figure 13-7. IPS processing flow chart

IPS processing on the SRX can be broken down into eight general stages of processing:

Stage 1: Fragmentation and serialization processing

The first thing that must happen before you can really get to the inspection is that the SRX must process fragmented traffic (if present). To ensure that common IDS evasion techniques using fragmentation are not effective, it rebuilds any fragmented traffic from a Layer 3 perspective. This stage also provides countermeasures against fragment-based attacks such as missing fragments, underlapping or overlapping fragments, duplicate fragments, and other fragment-based anomalies. Many of these values are also configurable in the IPS sensor configuration section, although defaults should suffice in most cases. Most of the fragmentation processing takes place in the flowd engine today outside of the anomaly inspection.

Stage 2: IPS flow setup
: After any Layer 3 fragments are processed, the SRX examines the traffic to see whether it has an existing session for it or if there is an existing session that might need some special processing. The IPS session table is different from the firewall session table, because additional IPS state related to the traffic is required.

Stage 3: SSL decryption (if applicable)
: If SSL decryption is configured, and traffic is destined to a web server that is configured to be decrypted, decryption happens in this phase. Note that SSL Reverse Proxy takes place after application identification if it detects the application as SSL.

Stage 4: Reassembly
: For accurate IPS processing, all messages must be processed in order, in a flow, and the messages must be reassembled if they span multiple packets. Without reassembly, an IPS engine can be easily evaded, which would result in lots of false positives. The SRX IPS engine ensures that before traffic is processed, it is ordered and reassembled in this stage of the processing.

Stage 5: Application identification
: The SRX has the ability to detect what application is running on any Layer 4 port. This is important because it allows the device to determine what traffic is running in a given flow regardless of whether it is running on a standard port. Even if the application cannot be identified, the SRX can still inspect it as a bytestream. This stage typically happens within the first couple of kilobytes of traffic, and the SRX uses both directions of the traffic to identify the application. If SSL Forward Proxy is enabled, it will take place after application identification has identified the traffic as SSL and proxy is enabled.

Starting with Junos 10.2+, the AppID module has been moved from IPS to flowd to provide support to all other components that wish to subscribe to its application identification data like AppFW, AppQoS, SSL Proxy, and so on.

Stage 6: Protocol decoding
: Once the application is identified (or is simply classified as a stream), the SRX decodes the application from a protocol level, a process known as *protocol decoding*. Protocol decoding allows the SRX to chop up the traffic into *contexts*, which are specific parts of different messages. Contexts are very important to IPS processing because they allow the SRX to look for attacks in the specific location where they actually occur, not just blindly by byte matching across all traffic that passes through the SRX. After all, you wouldn't want the SRX to block an email conversation between you and a peer discussing the latest exploit; you would only want the SRX to block the exploit in the precise location where it actually occurs. At the

time of this writing, the SRX supports almost 600 application contexts. Contexts are one of the ways that the SRX seeks to eliminate false positives. The protocol decoding stage is also where the SRX performs protocol anomaly protection. Anomaly protection is enabled just like any signature based on enabling an attack object that is of the protocol anomaly type.

Stage 7: Stateful signature detection
: The attack objects that rely on signatures (rather than anomaly detection) are processed in the stateful signature stage of the device's processing. These signatures are not blind pattern matches, but are highly accurate stateful signatures that not only match attacks within the contexts in which they occur, but also can be composed of multiple match criteria (using Boolean expressions between individual criteria). Typically, the attack signatures do not seek to detect a specific exploit, but rather protect against the vulnerability itself. This is important because attack exploits can vary, so writing signatures around a particular exploit is not a great tactic, but protecting against the actual vulnerability is much more powerful.

Stage 8: IDP and IP actions
: Once an attack object in the IPS policy is matched, the SRX can execute an action on that specific session, along with actions on future sessions. The ability to execute an action on that particular session is known as an *IDP action*. IDP actions can be one of the following: No-Action, Drop-Packet, Drop-Connection, Close-Client, Close-Server, Close-Client-and-Server, DSCP-Marking, Recommended, or Ignore. IP actions are actions that can be enforced on future sessions. These actions include IP-Close, IP-Block, and IP-Notify, which we cover in more depth later in the chapter.

Direction-specific detection

One theme in IPS processing that reoccurs throughout this chapter (and in other references) is the notion of client-to-server versus server-to-client traffic. There are typically two directions of traffic flow in modern client/server applications (with the exception of, say, multicast, which is primarily the multicast server sending to the clients). The client is always considered the device that initiates the connection (the source) and the server is the device that is accepting the connection (the destination). This is true even if the client is uploading data to the server.

This is important to know as an IPS administrator, and it's very important for creating custom attack objects. With that explanation, let's explore the significance of client-to-server versus server-to-client attacks:

Client-to-server attacks
: These are what most administrators think IPS does, which is to protect their server infrastructure from attacks generated by malicious clients to compromise or DoS a system. These attacks primarily work only when the client has access to the server, and firewalls can help mitigate access to unnecessary services on that server. IPS

can help to detect and prevent attacks that are generated on permitted services (such as a web server listening on HTTP, TCP port 80).

In this case, the attack is in the traffic generated from the client-to-server direction.

Server-to-client attacks
: Although attacking servers with client-to-server attacks allows attackers to pick their targets, most organizations use firewalls to limit inbound connections to only necessary systems wherever possible. As a result, attackers have changed their tactics, because they can't directly connect to the assets they are trying to compromise. Now, attackers make their victims come to them. There are many different ways to get a victim to come to the attacker (e.g., spam emails with malicious links, social networking, and other social engineering-based attempts). An example of this type of attack is when an attacker is running a web server that serves malicious HTML pages that exploit a JavaScript vulnerability in Internet Explorer, such as the Aurora exploit. Although the attacker might not always have control over which victims visit this malicious site, she typically doesn't have to worry about firewalls blocking this access because users are usually allowed to make connections outbound.

  In this case, the attack is in the traffic generated from the server-to-client direction.

SRX deployment options

Traditionally, there are a few different modes for deploying an IPS in the network. In the past, often an IPS was a device that sat transparently in the network, simply inspecting traffic as it passed through. Another option was that you could use *sniffer mode*, which passively listened for out-of-band attacks from the network traffic. This is typically accomplished via SPAN port or network tap. Rarely was an IPS deployed in routed mode, although some standalone IPS systems support that.

The SRX is a different story, because it is a full-featured router, firewall, and IPS device that can serve all of these needs.

One thing that is missing on the SRX at the time of writing this book is support for explicit sniffer mode. You can still accomplish sniffer mode with a bit of a workaround by mirroring traffic to an SRX and putting the interface on the SRX in promiscuous mode. We examine how to configure this later in the chapter.

Attack Object Types

Attack objects can be categorized into two different types: protocol anomaly and stateful signature-based attack objects. Both types of attack objects come bundled with the SRX signature updates and provide security against both known and unknown (zero-day) attacks.

Protocol anomaly attack objects
: These are predefined objects developed by the Juniper Security Team to detect activity that is outside the bounds of a protocol. Typically, the enforcement for what is considered acceptable behavior for protocols is based on an RFC specification or a manufacturer spec if there is no RFC. Protocol anomaly detection is built into the detector engine and is not based on any specific pattern. Administrators cannot create protocol anomaly objects, as this is code that is built into the detector engines; however, you can configure custom attack objects that utilize protocol anomaly objects as part of a compound attack object. If you determine there is a specific type of behavior protection that you need, you can email the Security Team (*signatures@juniper.net*) with descriptions and preferably PCAPs so they can examine if this can be covered by an anomaly.

Signature-based attack objects
: These are provided by the Juniper Security Team along with protocol anomaly attack objects, firmware, and detector engine updates. Signature-based attack objects are attack objects that actually match specific patterns through the use of a regular expression engine. The use of a regular expression engine provides the ability to match a range of patterns rather than a specific pattern. Additionally, a single attack object can be composed of multiple patterns that can be evaluated as a Boolean expression to make complex matches. As mentioned earlier in the chapter, signature-based attack objects are stateful signatures that match the attack object within the specific location in which it actually occurs in the attack itself (known as a context). You can create custom signature-based attack objects to use alongside predefined attack objects, as we discuss in the section "Custom attack objects and groups" on page 812 later in this chapter.

Application contexts

To aid in the accuracy and performance of IPS inspection, the SRX uses a concept called contexts to match an attack in the specific place where it occurs in the application protocol. This helps to ensure that performance is optimized by not searching for attacks where they would not occur, and it limits false positives. There could be many contexts within a single message. The SRX supports about 600 contexts at the time of this writing. Here is an example of an HTTP header message and the associated values and contexts (in bold, not found in the actual message) in that message:

```
GET /index.html Http1.1 http-get-url
Host: www.company.com http-header-host
Accept: image/gif, image/x-xbitmap, image/jpeg, image/pjpeg http-header-accept
Accept-Language: en http-header-accept-language
Accept-Encoding: gzip, deflate http-header-content-encoding
```

```
User-Agent: Mozilla/4.0 (compatible; MSIE 5.5; Windows NT 4.0)http-header-user-agent
```

Juniper maintains documentation that describes all of the different contexts and their associated function. You can find the documentation by searching the Juniper Support Knowledge Base.

Predefined attack objects and groups

Juniper provides predefined attack objects (both protocol anomaly and signatures) individually and in predefined groups to customers who have active licenses. The predefined attack objects cannot be edited for the most part; however, you can use these as a basis for creating custom attack objects. At the time of this writing, there are more than 9,000 predefined attack objects, and the number is growing every day as new threats emerge. Another feature of Juniper predefined attack objects is that customers can view the actual patterns that are used for signature-based attack objects. Many other vendors keep their signatures closed, which affects customers because they cannot view how the IPS is matching patterns (particularly with pattern matching). Juniper keeps only some signatures closed, if they are providing protection prior to when the vendor has a chance to patch the vulnerability, to ensure that the protection is not going to impact the community.

Custom attack objects and groups

In addition to the vast number of predefined attack objects that are provided as part of the IPS license, you also have a great deal of control over creating your own signature-based attack objects in the SRX. Additionally, you can create custom objects for application identification on the SRX so that you can identify not only custom attacks, but also custom applications. We covered this in greater detail in the section "Attack Object Types" on page 810.

Two types of custom attack groups can be configured in the SRX: static attack groups and dynamic attack groups. The primary difference is that static attack groups are exactly that: you must manually add or remove any attacks into this group. The only thing that will change is if an attack object itself is changed as part of an update, and then its contents will be updated; otherwise, the group does not change. Dynamic attack groups give you the ability to define filters that select which attacks are added into the attack group. The filters can be complex and can consist of multiple factors to identify attack objects to be selected for the dynamic attack group.

We discuss at length how to create custom attack groups (both static and dynamic), but custom attacks themselves are outside the scope of this book, as they are a more advanced topic that typically requires a good working knowledge of regular expressions. Custom attack examples and a custom attack configuration guide are available on the Juniper Knowledge Base.

Severities

Multiple severity levels are used to define the impact an attack can have on a system.

Critical
: Critical attacks are attacks that try to gain "root" level access to a system to crash the entire system. Critical attacks are also certain malicious evasion techniques that are clearly used for nefarious purposes.

Major
: Major attacks are attacks that try to gain "user" level access to a system to crash a particular service or application.

Minor
: Minor attacks are attacks that try to perform information leakage techniques, including those that exploit vulnerabilities to reveal information about the target.

Warning
: Warning attacks are attacks that are suspicious in nature, such as scans and other reconnaissance attempts. Juniper also might drop the severity of legacy attacks to Warning after they are no longer deemed a threat (e.g., Windows 3.1 and Windows 95 vulnerabilities).

Information
: Information attacks are not typically malicious activity, but rather can provide valuable information about activity on the network, such as applications that are running, potential vulnerable software, and best practice violations.

Signature performance impacts

A common question that many IPS administrators have concerns what impact different signatures have on the performance of their IPS (or in this case, the SRX). There is no simple answer to this question, in part because the impact that individual signatures have is not linear and based on the number of signatures, as some signatures have more of a performance impact than others. Generally speaking, the signatures that perform "context"-based matching are going to be the most efficient, as they only perform inspection based on specific locations of protocols; these would be followed by stream signatures, which inspect the entire stream up to a certain limit (e.g., 1 Kb). Signatures that inspect the entire stream for the duration of the session will generally have the worst performance. Juniper attempts to take the guesswork out of signature performance by classifying the signatures with the greatest impact on performance as being low-performing. These signatures are placed under the MISC category and also have a field called Performance. You can filter on the Performance values in dynamic attack groups, or just avoid the MISC signatures wherever possible.

It is important to understand that when you add signatures into the policy, regardless of whether you are permitting, blocking, or exempting them, you are performing inspection first and then determining what to do once an attack is found. For instance, the traffic is examined by the detector engine, and then it is examined again after a signature is matched based on what has been compiled into the policy. After a signature has been matched, the SRX will do a policy lookup to determine what the action should be for the respective traffic (based on the rulebase). This is the case regardless of the action or of whether it is exempted in the policy. The key takeaway is that by having a signature anywhere in the policy, you are going to take a performance hit for traffic matching that protocol. If you do not add an attack object into the policy, it will not be compiled into the policy, and therefore it won't impact performance. As mentioned earlier, attack objects don't all have the same performance impacts. Some signatures require more pattern matching than others, resulting in more computational cycles being spent on packet processing.

Understanding the performance impacts of the signatures is not meant to discourage you from deploying a sensible policy, but rather to empower you to understand how policies are impacted by their contents. When performance is the primary concern, you should craft your policy to only the essential attack objects that are necessary to inspect the traffic and provide adequate coverage. Rather than deploying a broad policy, you should create a policy that is very specific in the attack objects that are included. You can do this by using both static and dynamic attack object groups to select the signatures that should be added based on the components of the traffic itself. If your concerns are more focused on coverage rather than security, you can deploy a policy that has broader protection, but also signatures that are meant to provide protection or visibility for the traffic. As we progress through this chapter, we explore the mechanisms to configure and tune an effective policy for the SRX.

IPS Policy Components

A key feature that sets the SRX apart from other platforms that perform firewall and other services together is that the SRX provides extremely granular configuration and application of IPS inspection against processed traffic. The SRX offers exact control over what traffic is processed by the IPS engine, as well as within the IPS policy itself.

You should understand several components to create and apply effective security policies on the SRX, including rulebases, match criteria, actions, and packet logging. Let's cover the various components and how to apply them.

Rulebases

The IPS functionality in the SRX is composed of rulebases. Each rulebase consists of rules that define what traffic to match, and then what action to take on that traffic. At the time of this writing, three rulebases are part of the SRX IPS policy:

IPS rulebase
: The IPS rulebase defines what traffic should be inspected and what measures should be taken for traffic that matches the IPS attack objects defined in the policy. This is the traditional IPS rulebase used to define attacks and other applications that are enforced by the policy.

Application-DDoS rulebase
: The Application-DDoS rulebase is part of the AppDDoS suite that is only offered on the high-end SRX at the time of this writing. The Application-DDoS rulebase essentially defines the policy to be enforced to protect servers from application-level DoS attacks. AppDDoS is only supported on the high-end SRX and is outside the scope of this book.

Exempt rulebase
: The Exempt rulebase complements the IPS rulebase and provides a simple mechanism to override detected attacks. The Exempt rulebase provides a rulebase for a single location to bypass actions taken by the IPS engine in the IPS rulebase. Rather than having to make a complex IPS rulebase with these overrides, the Exempt rulebase provides a separate location to do this so that the IPS rulebase remains clean and focused on the attacks. Most often, the Exempt rulebase is used to ignore false positives or certain attack scenarios—traffic is first matched in the IPS rulebase, but then also examined in the Exempt rulebase, and if it matches a rule in the Exempt rulebase, it is permitted and nothing will be logged. We cover examples of this at length later in this chapter.

Match criteria

Each rule has match criteria to identify which traffic will have a particular action applied to it. There are several components of the match criteria, many of which are also present in the firewall policy. These criteria are not redundant, as the firewall policy identifies what traffic is to be sent to the IPS engine, and then the IPS engine applies IPS inspection based on the contents of that traffic. The following criteria are evaluated as part of the different rulebases:

From-zone
: Matches traffic based on the zone from which the traffic originates. This can be used to match traffic arriving on a particular logical interface, including per-VLAN matching.

To-zone
: Matches traffic based on which zone the traffic is going to as it leaves the SRX. The to-zone is determined by a route lookup, or in the case of transparent mode, by a bridge lookup to determine what the egress interface is, and therefore the egress zone.

Source address
: The source address defines the IP address of the client and is defined in the address book for the respective from-zone. It is important to remember that IPS processing happens after NAT transformations, so you must configure your source address to match the translated addresses. You can use individual source address objects, address sets, or any combination of object and group in this field.

Destination address
: The destination address defines the IP address of the server and is defined in the address book for the respective to-zone. It is important to remember that IPS processing happens after NAT transformations, so you must configure your destination address to match the translated address. You can use individual destination address objects, address sets, or any combination of object and group in this field.

Application
: The SRX IPS engine has the ability to match attacks on any port for the given Layer 4 protocol (TCP/UDP). By default, an attack is tied to a particular application (Layer 4 protocol) that might or might not have a specific list of ports on which the application will be detected. When the IPS is set to match the application default, it inspects the traffic for specific protocols on the ports they are listed for in the `application-id` object for that attack. You can override checking for applications on the default ports on a rule-by-rule basis.

Attacks
: The Attacks field defines what attacks to match as part of this rule. You can combine predefined and custom attacks within a single rule, along with using any combination of static or dynamic groups.

Then actions

On an IPS rule-by-rule basis, you can define what actions should be taken when the appropriate criteria are matched in the IPS engine. You can enforce two types of actions on the traffic: IPS actions and IP actions.

IPS actions perform an action on the offending traffic, whereas IP actions can take action on future sessions (e.g., preventing them). They are exclusive of each other, so you can configure one or the other, but it usually makes sense to configure IPS actions if you are using IP actions for a session. Additionally, you can configure logging and packet capture on a rule-by-rule basis.

The following lists define the IPS and IP actions available for the SRX. Note that these are available for the IPS rulebase, as the Exempt rulebase simply defines scenarios for which no action, logging, or attack counters should be triggered when an attack is matched.

IPS actions. The following IPS actions are available for the SRX:

No-Action
: No-Action means exactly what it says: no action will be taken on the session for this match. That isn't to say that another rule might not perform a drop or close on the traffic, because even when a rule matches, the IPS processing is not complete. So, you need to be aware of the fact that even with a No-Action defined, that doesn't mean other rules might not block this traffic.

Ignore-Connection
: Ignore-Connection means the traffic will be permitted, but also that the IPS engine will ignore the rest of the connection and will not process it at all. This is useful for identifying connections (e.g., custom applications) that you do not want to inspect. After a session has been marked Ignore-Connection, the IPS engine will not process it. It's important to keep that in mind, because an attack could be present later in the connection, but the IPS would not see it. If you only want to ignore a specific attack, but not ignore the rest of the connection, either put that attack in the Exempt rulebase (recommended) or configure the rule with No-Action.

Drop-Packet
: Drop-Packet will drop an individual offending packet, but not the rest of the session. Typically, you want to use the Drop-Connection action when malicious activity is detected on a flow, but in some cases, you might just want to prevent a particular activity that might be contained within a session (e.g., a file transfer) without dropping the entire session. Of course, this is highly dependent on the application's architecture, so when in doubt, either research the application or just use Drop-Connection. Drop-Packet might be useful for attacks that consist of only a single packet (e.g., SQL Slammer), but this isn't very common. Note that Drop-Packet will not have any impact in inline tap mode, as the original packet (not the copied one to the IPS engine) has already made it through the SRX and will be recorded as action DISMISS in the logs.

Drop-Connection
: Drop-Connection drops all packets (including the offending ones) of a connection, so essentially, if an attack is triggered, all packets of the session will be silently dropped. This is effective for all supported protocols. If inline tap mode is used, the original offending packet might make it through, but all future packets are dropped by the SRX. Drop-Connection is useful for silently dropping the connection without alerting the client or server that the session is being dropped.

Close-Client

If TCP is used as the protocol, the SRX can send a TCP Reset to the client (which will appear to be from the server, but is actually spoofed by the SRX) along with blocking all future packets in the flow. With the Close-Client option, the server will not be alerted that the session has been closed. This is useful when you want to protect a client from an attack from the server (e.g., an Internet Explorer exploit generated by the server). Because you are sending a TCP Reset, the web client won't just sit there and timeout, but will immediately inform the user that the connection was reset. If the Layer 4 protocol of the flow is not TCP, and the action is Close-Client, the action will effectively be Drop-Connection, as there will be no TCP Reset, but the traffic for the offending flow will still be silently dropped.

Close-Server

If TCP is used as the protocol, the SRX can send a TCP Reset to the server (which will appear to be from the client, but is actually spoofed by the SRX) along with blocking all future packets in the flow. With the Close-Server option, the client will not be alerted that the session has been closed. This is useful for protecting the server from client-based attacks such as resource utilization attacks against the server. By sending a reset, the server does not spend any more time holding the connection open and immediately closes the session out. If the Layer 4 protocol of the flow is not TCP, and the action is Close-Server, the action will effectively be Drop-Connection, as there will be no TCP Reset, but the traffic for the offending flow will still be silently dropped.

Close-Client-and-Server

If TCP is used as the protocol, the SRX can send a TCP Reset to both the client and the server. The resets are spoofed by the SRX and appear to be from the client (from the server's perspective) and from the server (from the client's perspective). Additionally, the SRX blocks all future packets in the connection. This is useful when you want to close the connections and inform both the client and the server so that they don't continue to retransmit packets or believe that the connection is still open when it really isn't (which can cause application issues). If the Layer 4 protocol of the flow is not TCP, and the action is Close-Client-Server, the action will effectively be Drop-Connection, as there will be no TCP Reset, but the traffic for the offending flow will still be silently dropped.

Mark-Diffserv

The SRX is capable of rewriting the DSCP bits of an IP header to a defined value within the IPS rulebase. This is useful if you want to use the IPS to identify applications such that upstream or downstream devices can perform QoS processing on the flows (e.g., on a router). At the time of this writing, the SRX does not honor the DSCP marking performed in the IPS engine because the classification phase of QoS on the SRX happens when traffic arrives, not after it has been processed by the IPS. DSCP marking is most useful for identifying actual applications from a Layer 7 perspective, which a standard router or switch would not be able to do. In the near future, and depending on when you are reading this, the SRX will be able to enforce its own DSCP policy along with shaping traffic based on the IPS policy.

Recommended
: Recommended uses the Whatever action and is defined within a predefined attack object (or within a custom attack object, whatever is configured by the administrator). Predefined attack objects come with a Recommended action set by the Juniper Security Team based on the nature of the attack and the suggested action to perform.

Notification actions. The following notification actions are available for the SRX:

Log attacks
: On a rule-by-rule basis, you can configure logging similar to how it is done on a rule-by-rule basis in a firewall policy. Additionally, the alert flag can be set to help security engineers identify significant events.

Severity
: The severity level can be configured on a rule-by-rule basis to signify events in the logs and to override the default severity levels defined within the attack objects.

Packet logging
: Packet logging is configured under the notification section of a rule and it is covered in detail in the next section.

Packet logging. The IPS packet logging feature is supported on the high-end SRX and is in beta for the SRX branch at the time of writing this book. The PCAPs are not stored locally, but rather are exported via DMI on the data plane to a PCAP receiver. Today, the STRM supports acting as a PCAP receiver that can integrate the IPS attack logs with the PCAP data for local viewing or for downloading for a packet viewing tool like Wireshark (see Figure 13-8).

The packet capture feature is flexible. You can configure it on an IPS rule-by-rule basis, and also define how many packets both before and after the attack should be included. You do need to exercise some caution when enabling packet captures. When packet captures are enabled, you can log packets both prior to and following the attack. To accommodate the capture before an attack functionality, the SRX must buffer packets in all flows prior so it does take some additional memory and processing cycles. Capturing packets after an attack is much more straightforward and has less of an impact. On top of that, if you are logging lots of attacks, you must also send the packet captures externally. For all of these reasons, packet logging should be strictly applied, and not applied across the board with all attacks. Besides the ability to apply packet captures on an IPS rule-by-rule basis, there are also a few parameters that you can configure.

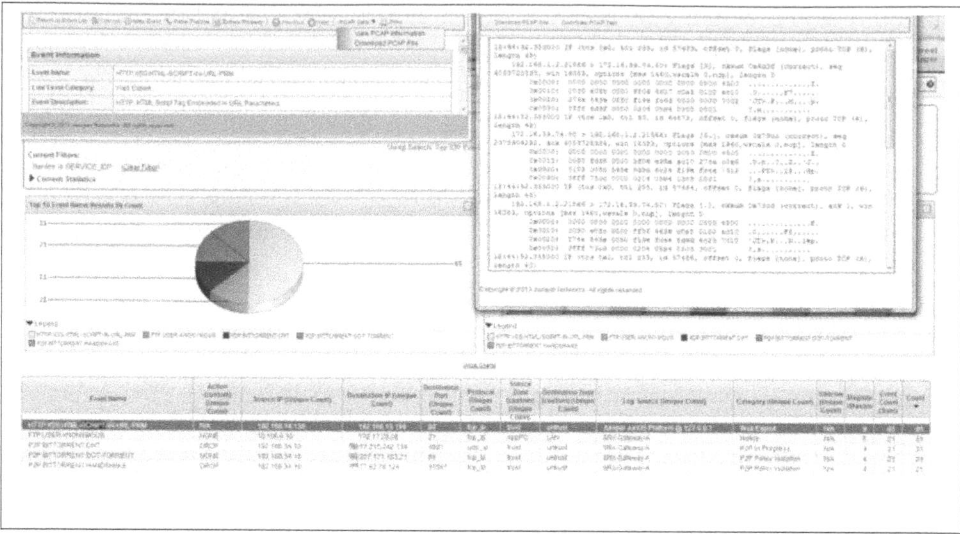

Figure 13-8. STRM PCAP capture/viewer/download

Host
: This is the host that receives the PCAP information. You also define the UDP port that will be used to send the data. This configuration is required.

Source-Address
: This is part of the configuration for sending the PCAP information to the logging host. This IP address is arbitrary, and you do not have to have it be the IP address of the SRX, but typically it's a best practice to do so.

Max Sessions
: You can configure a percentage value (1 percent to 100 percent) of sessions that are tracked with packet logs. This is an important way to limit how many sessions are processed for resource purposes.

Total-Memory
: You can define the percentage of memory that can be allocated to the packet capture feature.

Policy Configuration
: Within an IPS security policy, you can define how the packets should be logged on the SRX. Within the rule, you can define the following values (which should be used with care to ensure that memory is not overused for buffering and processing the packets):

Pre-Attack
: You can capture from 1 to 255 packets before an attack is triggered. This is accomplished by buffering all packets for the session up to the number of packets logged for the pre-attack limit for that particular rule.

Post-Attack
: You can log from 0 to 255 packets after an attack occurs. Note that if the attack triggers a drop or close connection, there might not be any more packets in the attack.

Post-Attack-Timeout
: When an attack is triggered, the SRX might not know how many packets will follow the attack (e.g., if you configure 20 packets to be logged after the attack, the SRX will not send the PCAP until it has all 20 packets). To ensure that the SRX does not hold on to the packets indefinitely, you configure a Post-Attack-Timeout to define how long the SRX should wait while holding on to the packets before sending them out.

Configuring packet logging in the STRM. To configure packet logging in the STRM, you need to be running a 2012 or later version of the STRM software. The configuration is quite simple in the STRM interface; you merely need to add the SRX device with packet capture enabled and respectively set this configuration on the SRX itself. Once the STRM is configured for the SRX, you can view the attack objects in log entries that contain it.

1. Go to the Admin tab, and in the Data Source section, click Log Sources.
2. Specify a name and IP address.
3. For the Log Source Type, select Juniper SRX.
4. For the Protocol, you must select PCAP Syslog Combination.
5. Specify the Log Source Identifier (can be an IP address).
6. Specify the port that the STRM should be listening for this traffic on.

On the SRX itself, you would configure the PCAP settings to point to the STRM under the IDP sensor configuration. For instance, if our STRM is listening on 192.168.1.20 on port 5000, and the SRX should send traffic from 192.168.1.1, then our configuration would look like this:

```
[edit]
root@srx3600n0#  set  security  idp  sensor-configuration  packet-log  host
192.168.1.20 port 5000

 [edit]
root@srx3600n0# set security idp sensor-configuration packet-log source-address
192.168.1.1
```

```
[edit]
root@srx3600n0# show security idp sensor-configuration
packet-log {
    source-address 192.168.1.1;
    host {
        192.168.1.20;
        port 5000;
    }
}
```

Then IPS PCAP is enabled on an IDP rule-by-rule basis in the action criteria.

```
[edit]
root@srx3600n0# set security idp idp-policy IDP rulebase-ips rule 1 then notifi-
cation packet-log ?
Possible completions:
  <[Enter]>            Execute this command
+ apply-groups         Groups from which to inherit configuration data
+ apply-groups-except  Don't inherit configuration data from these groups
  post-attack          No of packets to capture after attack (0..255)
   post-attack-timeout  Timeout (seconds) after attack before stopping packet
capture (0..1800)
  pre-attack           No of packets to capture before attack (1..255)
  |                    Pipe through a command
```

Figure 13-9 shows the STRM interface, which allows you to view and download the PCAPs collected from the SRX IPS function.

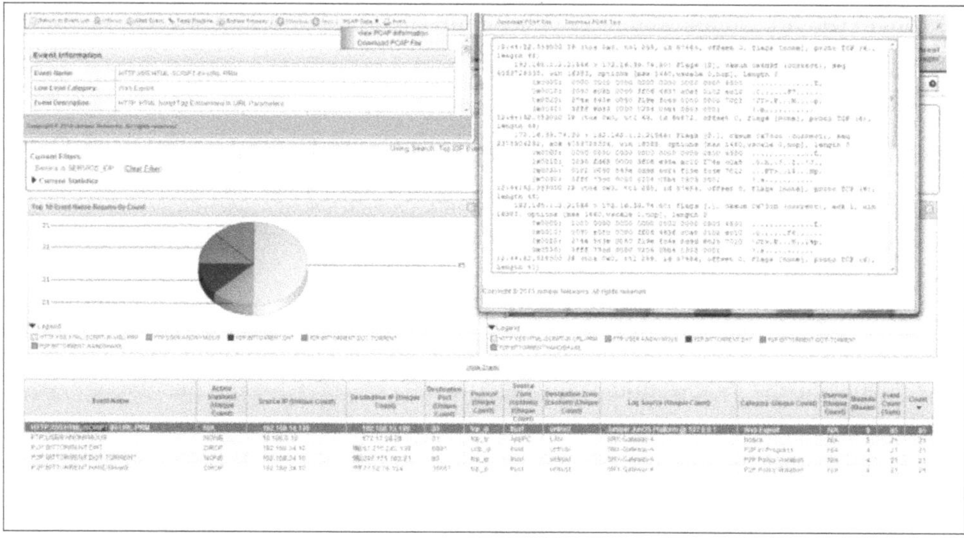

Figure 13-9. Viewing IPS PCAP data in the STRM

IP actions. The following IP actions are available for the SRX:

IP-Notify
: IP-Notify will simply generate a log when a connection is detected from a host that was previously identified for IP actions. This is useful if you don't want to block future connections that are identified by IP action, but you do want to identify any future connections made by that host based on the target or timeout.

IP-Block
: IP-Block allows you to silently block (drop) future connections made by hosts that were marked by IP-Block in a previous attack. This is tracked based on the target and timeout that are defined in the rule on which the attack was triggered.

IP-Close
: IP-Close is similar to IP-Block, except TCP Resets will be sent in addition to dropping all of the packets as part of that flow. This is tracked based on the target and timeout that are defined in the rule on which the attack was triggered. If the Layer 4 protocol is not TCP, a silent Drop-Connection will be applied.

Log/Log-Create
: The SRX allows you log when IP Actions take place or only when the IP Action has been triggered. This allows you the flexibility to get more visibility into attacks depending on your use case.

Refresh-Timeout
: The refresh timeout defines how the system should respond if additional sessions match the target parameters in the IP-Action table. Essentially, if you have this configured, it will continue to keep the IP Action active as long as the target is triggering new sessions to the SRX.

Targets and timeouts. Targets define which hosts have IP actions applied to them based on the information matched in the attack that triggered the IP action.

Destination-Address
: This performs the appropriate IP action on the destination address of the connection, so if IP-Block is the action, connections to the Destination-Address are blocked. This is good for blacklisting traffic to a botnet server, or other restricted destinations.

Service
: This performs the appropriate IP action on the source IP, destination IP, destination port, and protocol, so it's very selective in which connections are blocked. This is good if you want to prevent future connections from a source to a destination on a particular service (destination port and protocol, such as TCP port 80).

Source-Address

This matches future connections from a particular source address (regardless of which zone is used). This is useful if you want to protect a server from clients that attempt malicious activity. By using IP-Block or IP-Close with the Source-Address target, you can prevent future connections until the timeout expires.

Source-Zone

This is somewhat of a legacy feature, which will actually block the entire source zone at the time of this writing (that's right, we confirmed this with the developers). It originally came out of the ISG with IDP feature set. Typically, this won't be a desired action unless you are dealing with a very hostile source group of clients. Source-Zone-Address and Zone-Service are typically better choices.

Source-Zone-Address

This matches the target based on the Source Zone and Source Address. It is useful to use this rather than Source-Address Only if you might have IP overlap with different zones (e.g., when using different VRs for overlapping address space) or if the same IP might be coming through different source zones and you want to block the traffic in one scenario and not the other.

Zone-Service

This is similar to Service, but is also takes into account the Source-Zone in the event of IP overlaps.

The timeout defines how long the IP action is in effect for a given target—for instance, how long a connection will be blocked with IP-Block. You can configure this on a rule-by-rule basis in the IPS engine, so it's not a global configuration, but rather can be applied very granularly. If a timeout of 0 is configured, the timeout will not automatically expire, but rather will only be cleared via a manual clear of the IP action entry or a reboot.

Terminal Match

Terminal Match is somewhat of a legacy feature that arose from the earlier days of the standalone IDP to make it function similar to a firewall. By default, for IPS processing (both standalone IDP and SRX), even after a match is made for an attack, the rulebase continues to process that traffic to see if any other rules match. The IPS will always take the most stringent action (e.g., drop connection if a rule with Drop-Connection and No-Action is matched), but some customers might want to restrict this even further. By enabling Terminal Match, the IPS rulebase acts more like a firewall, in that once it finds a rule that matches the to-/from-zones, source IP, destination IP, and application, it will do whatever that rule says if the attack is detected; if not, it will not process that traffic any further. Generally, you should not use Terminal Match, especially with No-Action rules, because it can cause you to overlook potentially malicious traffic. Use this feature with caution unless you really know what you're doing.

Security Packages

Cyberthreats are dynamic in nature and require vigilance to provide up-to-date protection. To provide up-to-date security capabilities, attack updates are provided on a daily basis (if new signatures are required) and as emergencies if a zero-day threat is released.

The important thing to note is that a new attack object might not be required for new attacks, as the Juniper Security Team tries to create attack objects to protect against vulnerabilities and anomalous behavior rather than writing signatures against specific exploits (which could change very frequently). For instance, the Aurora Internet Explorer exploit that was discovered in December 2009 was already covered by the HTTP:STC:SCRIPT:FUNC-REASSIGN attack object (released August 2009, well ahead of the exploit), so customers were fully protected from this zero-day attack.

The security packages themselves are composed of several different components that are updated when a new version of the signature database and detector engines is available. You can either manually trigger the SRX to download the attack objects, or configure the SRX to automatically go and retrieve the updates. The following subsections describe the different components of Juniper security packages.

Attack database

The attack database contains all of the attack objects (both signature- and protocol anomaly-based) and is provided by the Juniper Security Team. New updates are typically posted daily, although sometimes there might not be a new exploit (which isn't already covered by existing signatures). When the attack database is downloaded, it contains the full attack database in a compressed form. If the attack database is downloaded directly to the SRX, it is stored in */var/db/idpd/sec-download* for staging. If it is downloaded from the NSM, it is stored in */var/db/idpd/nsm-download*. The */var/db/idpd/sec-repository* folder contains the attack, groups, applications, and detector engine files.

You can sign up for Technical Bulletins on the Juniper Support page (*http://kb.juniper.net/KB9890*) so that you receive email updates on the release of new detector engines and Junos firmware.

Attack object updates versus full updates

You can perform two types of updates for attack objects.

A standard update downloads the complete attack database to the SRX. You can automate this process so that it occurs at predefined intervals, or you can manually trigger it at your leisure.

Full updates include both the attack database and the latest detector engine. Typically, detector engine updates are released once per quarter, and attack databases are released daily (if there are updates to attack objects). Detector engine updates will provide bug fixes for the detector engine, new inspection capabilities, and new support for different application decoding.

Policy template updates are something that you must manually perform and are not included as part of the attack object updates.

Application objects

Application objects are used by the AppSecure features along with IPS. Per Chapter 12, you can either download these objects by themselves or as part of the IPS download package. Starting in Junos 11.4, the application objects are not stored in the SRX configuration file, but rather their own database similar to how the IPS stores its attack objects.

Detector engines

The detector engine is a module run by the IPS process on the SRX to execute protocol anomaly protection as well as signature-based pattern matching. Detector engine updates are released quarterly, and provide new protocol decoding capabilities, enhancements to protocol anomaly protection, and bug fixes. The detector engine is not installed by default with a signature update; rather, you must trigger a manual "full update" to download the detector engine and install it. The SRX allows for two detector engines to be installed concurrently when an update is applied so that all new sessions use the new detector engine, whereas the old sessions will still be processed by the previous detector engine. When all sessions from the old detector engine are closed, the original detector engine is removed. The installation of the new detector engine does not have any performance impact because of this graceful installation process. Just like the signature updates, you can sign up for notifications when new detector engines are available. The notifications also include release notes that detail all of the new features, addressed issues, and known limitations for that detector engine.

Policy templates

To assist administrators with new IPS installations, Juniper provides several different predefined policies that administrators can download and install. Although these are helpful to understand the basic mechanics of the IPS policies, every environment is going to be different, with different applications and different administrative goals. Best practice therefore recommends creating a customized policy for true enforcement.

The good news is that this chapter details how to deploy and tune an IPS policy effectively, minimizing false positives and providing real security. But in the meantime, you might want to take a look at the policy templates for examples. The policy templates are updated informally by the Juniper Security Team, so you need to check the version numbers for new policy templates.

Scheduling updates

Updates can be scheduled to automatically download and optionally install attack object updates, which include application object updates. When attack updates are scheduled, you can define the interval and schedule for when they should be downloaded, along with whether the SRX should install the new version. Of course, if you are using a central management system such as NSM or Junos Space, you can also trigger installations automatically from there.

Sensor Attributes

The SRX supports a wide range of tunable sensor settings when it comes to how the SRX functions. Most of these settings should generally not be modified without the guidance of JTAC or an expert-level implication of what the settings do; therefore, coverage of the sensor knobs (except for GZIP/Deflate) is outside the scope of this book.

SSL Inspection (Reverse Proxy)

The SRX supports two different types of SSL inspection: SSL Forward Proxy (discussed in Chapter 12), which can be used for IPS inspection as well, and the SSL Inspection (also known as SSL Reverse Proxy) feature, which is an IPS-only feature used to open SSL streams that are terminated on a web server that you control. In SSL Inspection, you would load your private key onto the SRX to allow it to decrypt the stream from the client to server. This feature is becoming less and less pertinent in most networks because customers who wish to run this often have a SSL load balancer that sits in front of their web server to offload the SSL processing. Therefore it is logical to place the SRX between the SSL load balancer and the web server for inspecting the traffic there. Also, at the time of writing this book, SSL Inspection in reverse proxy mode is only supported on the high-end SRX. Therefore covering the SSL Reverse Proxy feature is outside the scope of this book.

Custom Attack Groups

SRX IPS offers an extremely powerful feature that enables you to define your own groups (of both predefined and custom attack objects) along with your own custom attack objects. Although the casual IPS administrator might not need to define custom attack objects, the ability to customize attacks into groups is key to being able to make the administration of an IPS policy much easier to enforce.

Static attack groups

A static attack group is essentially a group to which you manually add attack objects and groups (both predefined and custom) that will not add members during attack updates. If attack objects are modified as part of an attack update, they are updated in the group; if they are deleted, they are removed from the group. No new attack objects are added to this group, however. Static groups are very useful if you want strict control over adding new attacks into attack groups during signature updates to ensure that you don't cause unexpected results with new attack objects. The only things you need to define for static groups are the members that are added to this group.

Dynamic attack groups

Dynamic attack groups provide administrators with a powerful ability to adjust to new threats when new attack objects are downloaded from Juniper. Whereas static attack groups allow you to create groups that don't automatically change with signature attack updates, dynamic attack groups do change. And they have very intelligent controls for defining what should be added or removed with attack updates. Dynamic attack groups use filters to define the attributes of attack objects that would select them to be implemented in the group. Additionally, you can override members in the groups to exclude them if need be.

You can use filter categories to select the attacks for the group. When you define multiple filters, they essentially form a logical AND between filters. For instance, if you define Category=HTTP and Severity=Critical, only attacks that are of that category and severity are present in this group. When new attacks are downloaded, if they fit this criteria they are added to the group. Here's more detail on filter fields you can dial:

Category
: Category defines the Juniper-defined categories for attacks. These are one of the most useful filters to define because they are the applications themselves, such as HTTP, FTP, DNS, and other types of attacks, such as spyware, viruses, Trojan horses, and worms.

Direction
: Direction defines the direction in which the attack takes place. There is a little more to this field than meets the eye. There are six possible values, along with the ability to define how they should be evaluated. The six values are the following:

Any
: Detect attacks that have a member with "Any" as the direction.

Client-to-Server
: Attack objects with members with the client-to-server direction.

Server-to-Client
: Attack objects with members with the server-to-client direction.

Exclude-Any
: Any attack objects that do not have members with "Any" as the direction.

Exclude-Client-to-Server
Any attack object that does not have members with client-to-server as the direction.

Exclude-Server-to-Client
Any attack object that does not have members with server-to-client as the direction.

The key here is that attack objects can have multiple members (known as complex attack objects). If you have an attack object with just one member, the direction is very simple: it's whatever direction the attack object specifies. But what about when you have an object with multiple members that have different directions (e.g., Member 1 is client-to-server and Member 2 is server-to-client)? In these cases, we support the use of an "Expression" that specifies if the SRX should apply AND logic or the default OR logic when it comes to selecting the direction for attacks. We'll explore this a bit more later in the chapter.

False-Positives
False-Positives is a field that is defined for each object indicating how frequently false positives are likely to occur with the individual object. Juniper defines these for predefined attack objects; you can configure this field in your custom attack objects.

Performance
Juniper tries to specify the attack object performance for the attack objects. This is not an exact science, and performance is typically holistic for the policy as a whole, rather than for an individual attack object. You can also specify this for custom attack objects and you can use this filter to only select the appropriate attacks based on performance impacts. The performance impact of signatures is as follows: 0 = Unknown, 1 = Fast, 5 = Normal, and 9 = Slow. You can use performance filtering in the dynamic attack groups to filter out slow-performing attack objects. Note that, generally, Juniper will put slow-performing attack objects under the MISC attack group.

Products
Juniper defines products to which the predefined attack objects apply—for instance, protecting against attacks on specific OSs, services, applications, and other software.

Recommended / No-Recommended
This filter is simply a field. If Recommended is selected, only attacks that are marked with the `Recommended` attribute are selected. Juniper defines the `Recommended` flag for attacks that are part of the recommended policy, and you can specify this flag for custom attacks as well. No-Recommended is the opposite of Recommended.

Service

Service defines the actual application protocol (e.g., HTTP, FTP, DNS, SMB, SMTP, etc.) to which the attack belongs. This is similar to some of the attacks defined under the category configuration.

Severity

You can use the Severity field (as we did earlier in this chapter) to define what traffic should be selected based on the severity defined for the attack object.

Type

This allows you to specify whether the attack is a signature-based attack object or an anomaly-based attack object.

At the time of writing this book, dynamic attack groups do not automatically include custom attack objects; however, you can manually add attack objects to static attack groups.

Configuring IPS Features on the SRX

If you have read this far, you've gone through a detailed explanation of just about every component of SRX IPS functionality. Now you can learn how to actually configure these different features within the SRX.

From here on out, you will learn the configuration of the individual elements and focus on common real-world implementations of these features. Let's get started.

Getting Started with IPS on the SRX

We should perform a few steps before we configure SRX IPS. Here is a list of things to do before configuring the SRX for IPS functionality:

1. Install the license. You must install an IDP license before you can download any attack objects. If you are using only custom attack objects, you don't need to install a license (earlier versions had a bug where they required it), but if you want to download Juniper predefined attack objects, you must have this license. Juniper provides you with the ability to download a 30-day trial license to permit this functionality for a brief period of time to evaluate the functionality. We covered license installation earlier in the book; all you need is the `request system license add` command either specifying a file, or copying and pasting it into the terminal.
2. Configure network access. Before you can download the attack objects, you must have network connectivity to either the Juniper download server or a local server from which the signatures can be downloaded. This typically requires network configuration (IP/Netmask, routing, and DNS) and permitted access to reach the

server. At the time of this writing, HTTP proxies are not supported, but you can configure a local web server from which to serve the files.

3. Download attack objects. Before deploying the IPS, you must first download the attack objects from which the policy will be compiled. Triggering a manual download does not configure the SRX to download them in the future, so you must configure automatic updates to download them.
4. Install attack objects. Once the download has been completed, you must install the attack updates before they are actually used in a policy. If you already have a policy configured, you do not need to recommit the policy—installing the updates adds them to the policy. The installation process compiles the attack objects that have been downloaded to a stage directory into the configured policy.
5. Download policy templates (optional). You can optionally download and install predefined IPS policies known as policy templates provided by Juniper to get started. After finishing this chapter, you should be able to configure your own policy, so you probably won't need policy templates.

Starting with Junos 12.1, the SRX will automatically push the signature package to the secondary member of the HA cluster. Prior to Junos 12.1, you had to use the fxp0 on both members of the cluster because both members had to download their own instance. With 12.1 and beyond, there is no explicit configuration; you will just see the SRX is downloading the package and pushing it to the secondary member during the download process.

Getting started example

Our first example shows the basic configuration and download of attack objects and how to install them prior to actually configuring a security policy. The steps in this example are as follows:

1. Check IPS status.
2. Download attack objects including sensor updates.
3. Install attack objects and sensor updates.
4. Download policy templates.
5. Install policy templates.

```
root@srx3600n0> show security idp security-package-version
  Attack database version:2229(Thu Feb 04 00:23:03 2013 UTC)
  Detector version :12.6.140121210
  Policy template version :N/A
```

```
root@srx3600n0> request security idp security-package download
Will be processed in async mode. Check the status using the status checking
CLI

root@srx3600n0> request security idp security-package download status
Done;Successfully    downloaded    from(https://services.netscreen.com/cgi-bin/
index.cgi).
Version info:2230(Mon Feb  4 19:40:12 2013 UTC, Detector=12.6.140121210)

root@srx3600n0> request security idp security-package install
Will be processed in async mode. Check the status using the status checking
CLI

root@srx3600n0> request security idp security-package install status
In progress:Installing AI ...

root@srx3600n0> request security idp security-package install status
In progress:performing DB update for an xml (SignatureUpdate.xml)

root@srx3600n0> request security idp security-package install status
Done;Attack DB update : successful - [UpdateNumber=2230,ExportDate=Mon Feb  4
19:40:12 2013 UTC,Detector=12.6.140121210]
     Updating control-plane with new detector : successful
     Updating data-plane with new attack or detector : sucessful
```

It's important to understand that compiling and applying an IPS policy can take some time, depending on the number of attack objects and the size of the policy. Starting with Junos 12.1, the SRX leverages a smarter compilation engine along with caching compiled information so that the compilation process takes much less time. The compilation process is conducted asynchronously, meaning that the SRX will start the process but it won't hold up your CLI, web, or SD session, but instead will allow you to check back later on the status.

Starting in Junos 12.1 in HA configurations, the SRX will produce a slightly different output because the download will be synchronized to the backup device rather than having each device perform the download.

```
{primary:node1}
root@SRX100HM> request security idp security-package download sta-
tus
node1:
--------------------------------------------------------------------------
Done;Successfully downloaded from(https://services.netscreen.com/
cgi-bin/index.cgi)
and synchronized to backup.
Version info:2233(Thu Feb 14 00:23:07 2013 UTC, Detec-
tor=12.6.160121210)
```

Configuring automatic updates

Although updating the SRX manually is a powerful way to inspect the new signatures before actually deploying them, it does require much more administrative dedication to keep signatures updated. You can configure the SRX to automatically update itself at an interval of your choosing to ensure that the SRX has up-to-date signatures without administrative intervention. This example demonstrates how to configure this functionality with the following objectives.

Enable automatic downloads to start May 7 at midnight, and attempt to download every 24 hours if there is an update. If the update stalls for more than five minutes, after a new version has been downloaded the SRX should install it.

```
{primary:node0}[edit]
root@SRX5800-1# edit security idp security-package

{primary:node0}[edit security idp security-package]
root@SRX5800-1# set install automatic start-time 05-07.00:00 interval 24 enable
```

Junos Space also offers another good option for graphically viewing and operating the download process (see Figure 13-10). You can download the attack objects locally to Space and then push them out to the firewalls (including firewalls that don't have Internet connections). You can also schedule updates for download and installation through Space along with seeing what contents of the attack download have changed.

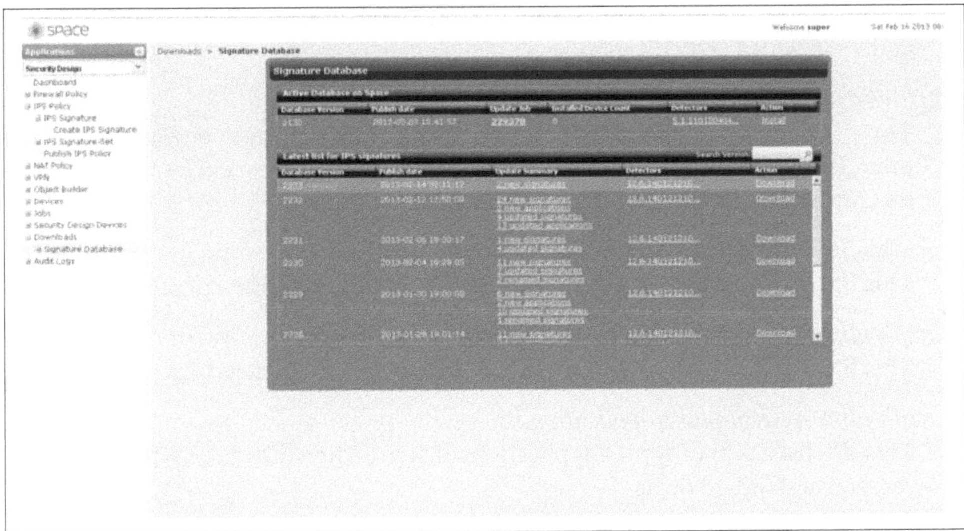

Figure 13-10. Junos Space and IPS signature downloads and updates

There is a procedure available on the Juniper Knowledge Base (*http://juni.pr/120WMtP*) that details how you can perform an offline update for Juniper IPS/Application Security data if your SRX cannot access the Internet and you don't have another solution like Space to serve the content locally to the SRX.

Useful IPS files

At the time of this writing, Juniper was still enhancing the CLI and J-Web to make them more usable for viewing predefined IPS objects (attacks, groups, applications, etc.). The exception is NSM, which has these laid out nicely in a table. Until then, all of the information is available on the SRX. You just need to know where to look.

You should download the attack signatures before viewing these files for the updated version.

/var/db/idpd/sec-download/SignatureUpdate.xml
: This file is the entire attack database. It details every attack, and for signature-based attack objects, it also provides the patterns used to match signatures. This file is the motherlode of the attack objects and provides you with the most information, but it's in XML format, so you will need to either load it into an XML browser or look at the file with a text editor.

/var/db/idpd/sec-download/groups.xml
: This file is the list of different predefined groups and the attack objects that fit into them. It's essentially a list of dynamic attack object groups that define the properties that attack objects should match to be part of the group.

/var/db/idpd/sec-repository/attack.list
: This file lists all attacks known by the SRX in their appropriate name format.

/var/db/idpd/sec-repository/attack-group.list
: This file lists all attack groups on the SRX based on their categories.

/var/db/idpd/sec-repository/application.list
: This file lists all the AppID applications that are known to the system and their respective standard ports.

Viewing IPS attack objects and group membership

At the time of writing this book, the best way to view the IPS attack objects is really through Security Design, which has a very nice interface for viewing the objects. On box you can leverage the `show security idp attack detail <attack-name>` command to view the contents of an individual attack, but it does not provide the complete information today. If you are working with an on-box implementation, it is really best to drop down to the shell to view this information. Additionally, you can view the object information on the Juniper Security Portal (*http://www.juniper.net/security*). Let's take a look at what you can do on box and in Junos Space.

```
root@srx3600n0> show security idp attack detail HTTP:XSS:NAGIOS-XI-ALERT-CLOUD
Display Name: HTTP: Nagios XI Alert Cloud Cross-Site Scripting
Severity: Major
Category: HTTP
Recommended: true
Recommended Action: Drop
Type: chain
False Positives: unknown
Service: HTTP
```

This command can be used to get a high-level output of the command. If you need more information like patterns and you are operating on box then you can drop down to the command line and view the output in the *SignatureUpdate.xml* file.

```
root@srx3600n0> file show /var/db/idpd/sec-download/SignatureUpdate.xml
/NAGIOS
        <Name>HTTP:XSS:NAGIOS-XI-ALERT-CLOUD</Name>
         <DisplayName>HTTP: Nagios XI Alert Cloud Cross-Site Scripting</Display-
Name>
        <Severity>Major</Severity>
        <Category>HTTP</Category>
        <Keywords>Alert Cloud Cross-Site Nagios Scripting XI</Keywords>
        <Recommended>true</Recommended>
        <RecommendedAction>Drop</RecommendedAction>
          <Description>This signature detects attempts to exploit a cross-site
scripting vulnerability in the Nagios XI Alert Cloud. An attacker can leverage
this issue to execute arbitrary script code in the
browser of an unsuspecting user in the context of the affected site</Descrip-
tion>
        <Tags>
          <Tag>
            <Name>severity</Name>
            <Value>Major</Value>
          </Tag>
          <Tag>
            <Name>itw</Name>
          </Tag>
          <Tag>
            <Name>category</Name>
            <Value>HTTP</Value>
          </Tag>
        </Tags>
        <Attacks>
          <Attack>
            <Type>chain</Type>
            <ExportID>1</ExportID>
```

```
            <FalsePositives>unknown</FalsePositives>
            <Performance>0</Performance>
            <Service>HTTP</Service>
            <Scope>transaction</Scope>
            <TimeBinding>
              <Scope>none</Scope>
              <Count>1</Count>
            </TimeBinding>
            <Order>no</Order>
            <Reset>no</Reset>
            <Hidden>false</Hidden>
            <Members>
              <Attack>
                <Member>m01</Member>
                <Type>Signature</Type>
                <Direction>CTS</Direction>
                <Flow>control</Flow>
                <Shellcode>no</Shellcode>
                <Context>http-url-parsed</Context>
                <Negate>false</Negate>
                  <Pattern><![CDATA[.*\[/nagiosxi/includes/components/alertcloud/
index\.php\]]]></Pattern>
                <Regex/>
              </Attack>
              <Attack>
                <Member>m02</Member>
                <Type>Signature</Type>
                <Direction>CTS</Direction>
                <Flow>control</Flow>
                <Shellcode>no</Shellcode>
                <Context>http-variable-parsed</Context>
                <Negate>false</Negate>
                <Pattern><![CDATA[.*=.*}.*]]></Pattern>
                <Regex/>
              </Attack>
            </Members>
            <Versions>
              <Version>idp-srx11.4</Version>
            </Versions>
          </Attack>
        </Attacks>
        <Direction>
          <Value>CTS</Value>
        </Direction>
        <FalsePositives>
          <Value>unknown</Value>
        </FalsePositives>
        <Performance>
          <Value>0</Value>
        </Performance>
        <Service>
          <Value>HTTP</Value>
```

```
        </Service>
        <Type>
          <Value>Signature</Value>
        </Type>
      </Entry>
      <Entry>
```

In terms of viewing the parameters that make up a group and the members of the group if you are doing this on device, your best bet is also to use the command line.

```
root@srx3600n0> file show /var/db/idpd/sec-download/groups.xml
/HTTP - Major
      <Name>HTTP - Major</Name>
      <Type>dynamic</Type>
      <Filters>
        <Filter>
          <Field>Category</Field>
          <Values>
            <Value>HTTP</Value>
          </Values>
        </Filter>
        <Filter>
          <Expression>And</Expression>
          <Field>Direction</Field>
          <Values>
            <Value>cts</Value>
            <Value>!stc</Value>
            <Value>!any</Value>
          </Values>
        </Filter>
        <Filter>
          <Field>Performance</Field>
          <Values>
            <Value>0</Value>
            <Value>1</Value>
            <Value>5</Value>
          </Values>
        </Filter>
        <Filter>
          <Field>Severity</Field>
          <Values>
            <Value>Major</Value>
          </Values>
        </Filter>
      </Filters>
    </Group>
    <Group>
```

In the preceding output, we can see the makeout of the HTTP – Major group. We can see the filters that are being applied, and what's important here is that we can use the same filters ourselves in our policy. The filters include the Severity=Major, Direction is "Client to Server" AND "Not Server to Client" AND "NOT Any" (which we explain in the dynamic group direction filter; this essentially means any attack object with members only in the client-to-server direction, none in the server-to-client direction, and none in the Any direction), and finally the Performance is anything that is 0/1/5, which corresponds to anything that isn't slow.

Finally, let's look at how to determine what members are resolved from dynamic and static groups. The easiest way is to look in the compiled policy itself. So, in this case, our Policy is called Recommended, and we want to see the contents of the Recommended-All Group.

```
root@srx3600n0>  show  configuration  security  idp  dynamic-attack-group
Recommended-All
filters {
    direction {
        values [ client-to-server exclude-any exclude-server-to-client ];
    }
    recommended;
}

root@srx3600n0> file show /var/db/idpd/sets/Recommended.set
/Recommended-All
        :Recommended-All (Recommended-All
                :type (group)
                :group (
                        :members (
                                : ("APP:ADOBE-CF-DIR-TRAV")
                                : ("APP:AGENTX-RECEIVE-INT-OF")
                                : ("APP:AGENTX-RECEIVE-OF")
                                : ("APP:AVAYA-CCRWEBCLIENT-RCE")
                                : ("APP:BULLETPROOF-FTP-BPS-BOF")
                                : ("APP:CA:ARCSRV:GWT-INFO-DISC")
                                : ("APP:CA:ARCSRV:RPC-TAPE-ENG")
                                : ("APP:CHKPOINT-FW-INFO-DISC")
                                : ("APP:CISCO:CNS-NETWORK-DOS")
                                : ("APP:CISCO:REGISTRAR-AUTH-BYPASS")
                                : ("APP:CITRIX:AG-CMD-INJ")
                                : ("APP:CITRIX:META-IMA-AUTH")
                                : ("APP:CITRIX:PROVISIONING-OPCODE")
                                : ("APP:CITRIX:PROVISIONINGSERV-)
##Output Abridged##
```

Figures 13-11 and 13-12 are screenshots of the Junos Space Security Design interface, which is a much better interface for navigating objects, group membership, and so forth if you have access to it.

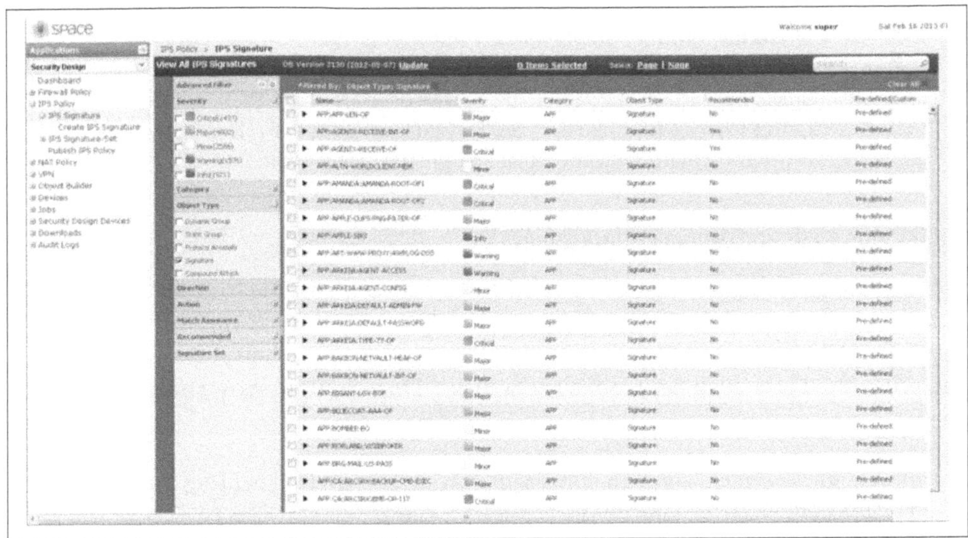

Figure 13-11. Viewing IPS attack objects in Junos Space

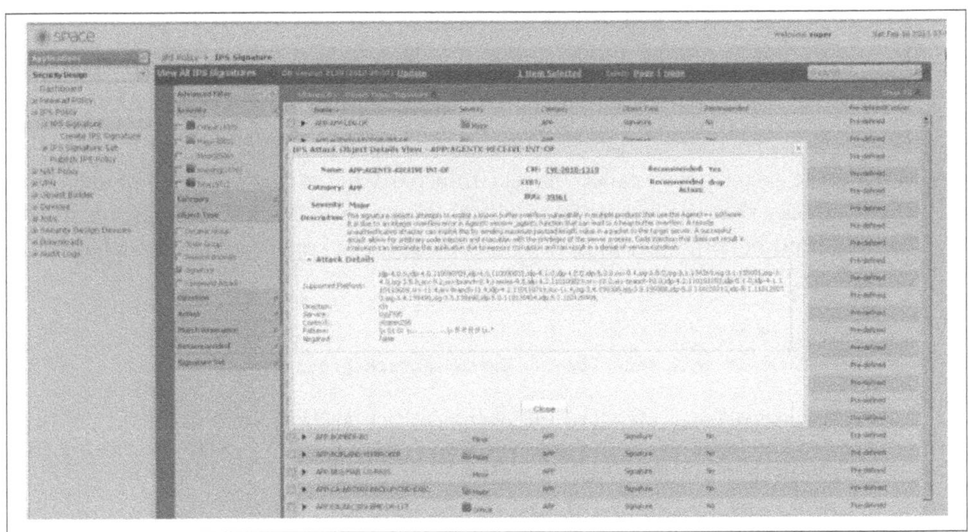

Figure 13-12. Viewing an individual attack object's contents in Junos Space

Hopefully, Juniper will be greatly improving the IPS object operation tasks in the future with better on-box support. Although the Junos Space operations are pretty strong, the on-box CLI/J-Web implementation leaves a bit to be desired. Stay current with the release notes for more information on the latest and greatest improvements.

Configuring static and dynamic attack groups

Unless you are going to use predefined attack groups, or the attack objects themselves, you should find yourself configuring static and dynamic attack groups prior to defining the policies. Defining these groups is quite simple, especially when you are familiar with the predefined attack object groups and attacks. This example shows how to configure the following groups:

- A static attack group named Aurora that includes the attacks HTTP:STC:SCRIPT:UNI-SHELLCODE and HTTP:STC:SCRIPT:FUNC-REASSIGN, which are two known attack objects that are triggered by the Aurora Internet Explorer exploit.
- A static attack group named Protect-FTP that contains the predefined attack groups FTP – Critical, FTP – Major, and FTP – Minor.
- A dynamic attack group called Malicious-Activity that contains all shellcode, worms, spyware, viruses, and Trojan horse signatures of severity Critical, Major, and Minor.
- A dynamic attack group called Protect-Internal-Clients that contains all server-to-client attacks that are of severity Critical, Major, and Minor. This group should contain members that are to defend clients, but it's okay if the members have CTS or ANY patterns as well.

```
{primary:node0}[edit]
root@SRX5800-1# edit security idp custom-attack-group Aurora

{primary:node0}[edit security idp custom-attack Aurora]
root@SRX5800-1#set        group-members        [        HTTP:STC:SCRIPT:UNI-
SHELLCODEHTTP:STC:SCRIPT:FUNC-REASSIGN ]

{primary:node0}[edit security idp custom-attack Aurora]
root@SRX5800-1# show
group-members [ HTTP:STC:SCRIPT:UNI-SHELLCODE HTTP:STC:SCRIPT:FUNC-REASSIGN ];

{primary:node0}[edit security idp custom-attack-group Aurora]
root@SRX5800-1# up

{primary:node0}[edit security idp]
root@SRX5800-1# edit custom-attack-group Protect-FTP
```

```
{primary:node0}[edit security idp custom-attack-group Protect-FTP]
root@SRX5800-1# set group-members [ "FTP - Critical" "FTP - Major""FTP - Mi
nor" ]

{primary:node0}[edit security idp custom-attack-group Protect-FTP]
root@SRX5800-1# show
group-members [ "FTP - Critical" "FTP - Major" "FTP - Minor" ];

{primary:node0}[edit security idp custom-attack-group Protect-FTP]
root@SRX5800-1# up

{primary:node0}[edit security idp]
root@SRX5800-1# edit dynamic-attack-group Malicious-Activity

{primary:node0}[edit security idp dynamic-attack-group Malicious-Activity]
root@SRX5800-1# set filters severity values [ critical major minor ]

{primary:node0}[edit security idp dynamic-attack-group Malicious-Activity]
root@SRX5800-1# set category values [ SHELLCODE VIRUS WORMS SPYWARE TROJAN]

{primary:node0}[edit security idp dynamic-attack-group Malicious-Activity]
root@SRX5800-1# show
filters {
  severity {
    values [ critical major minor ];
  }
  category {
    values [ SHELLCODE VIRUS WORMS SPYWARE TROJAN ];
  }
}

{primary:node0}[edit security idp dynamic-attack-group Malicious-Activity]
root@SRX5800-1# up

{primary:node0}[edit security idp]
root@SRX5800-1# edit dynamic-attack-group Protect-Internal-Clients

{primary:node0}[edit   security   idp   dynamic-attack-group   Protect-Internal-
Clients]
root@SRX5800-1# set filters direction values server-to-client

{primary:node0}[edit   security   idp   dynamic-attack-group   Protect-Internal-
Clients]
root@SRX5800-1# set filters severity values [ critical major minor ]

{primary:node0}[edit   security   idp   dynamic-attack-group   Protect-Internal-
Clients]
root@SRX5800-1# show
filters {
  direction {
    values server-to-client;
  }
```

```
    severity {
      values [ critical major minor ];
    }
  }

{primary:node0}[edit   security   idp   dynamic-attack-group   Protect-Internal-
Clients]
root@SRX5800-1# top

{primary:node0}[edit]
root@SRX5800-1# commit
node0:
configuration check succeeds
node1:
commit complete
node0:
commit complete
```

The one significant thing to note in this example is regarding the "direction" value of our Protect-Internal-Clients group. We defined this as server-to-client, but this will contain members with both server-to-client and client-to-server/any directions because we didn't leverage the AND logic to limit it to only server-to-client members.

Creating, activating, and referencing IPS

Before you can actually perform any inspection, you must define an IPS rulebase, apply it as the active IPS policy (at this time only one IPS policy can be active at a time), and reference this policy in the SRX security policy (firewall) rulebase. Although you could use a predefined policy template for your rulebase, you are going to create your own, because it's much more fun.

In this example, you will do the following:

- Create an IPS rulebase called Protect-Everything. You are going to be using the IPS rulebase. For all rules, you should match from Untrust to Trust, log events, and match any source, destination, or default application.
- The first rule should match any attack for the two static groups that you created, and silently drop their connections. Call this rule `Static-Groups`.
- For the two dynamic groups you created, you'll create a rule to match their connections and close both the client and the server, as well as silently drop traffic from future flows for 120 seconds. Call this rule `Dynamic-Groups`.
- You'll perform all of this from the Untrust to Trust direction for any traffic, and then log all of these events.

```
{primary:node0}[edit]
root@SRX5800-1# edit security idp idp-policy Protect-Everything rulebase-ips
```

```
{primary:node0}[edit security idp idp-policy Protect-Everything rulebase-ips]
root@SRX5800-1# set rule Static-Groups match from-zone untrust to-zone
trustsource-address any destination-address any application default attacks
custom-attack-groups [ Aurora Protect-FTP ]

{primary:node0}[edit security idp idp-policy Protect-Everything rulebase-ips]
root@SRX5800-1# set rule Static-Groups then action drop-connection

{primary:node0}[edit security idp idp-policy Protect-Everything rulebase-ips]
root@SRX5800-1# set rule Static-Groups then notification log-attacks

{primary:node0}[edit security idp idp-policy Protect-Everything rulebase-ips]
root@SRX5800-1# show
rule Static-Groups {
  match {
    from-zone untrust;
    source-address any;
    to-zone trust;
    destination-address any;
    application default;
    attacks {
      custom-attack-groups [ Aurora Protect-FTP ];
    }
  }
  then {
    action {
      drop-connection;
    }
    notification {
      log-attacks;
    }
  }
}

{primary:node0}[edit security idp idp-policy Protect-Everything rulebase-ips]
root@SRX5800-1# set rule Dynamic-Groups match from-zone untrust to-zone
trustsource-address any destination-address any application default attacks
dynamic-attack-groups [ Malicious-Activity Protect-Internal-Clients ]

{primary:node0}[edit security idp idp-policy Protect-Everything rulebase-ips]
root@SRX5800-1# set rule Dynamic-Groups then action close-client-and-server

{primary:node0}[edit security idp idp-policy Protect-Everything rulebase-ips]
root@SRX5800-1# set rule Dynamic-Groups then ip-action ip-block log target
source-address timeout 120

{primary:node0}[edit security idp idp-policy Protect-Everything rulebase-ips]
root@SRX5800-1# set rule Dynamic-Groups then notification log-attacks

{primary:node0}[edit security idp idp-policy Protect-Everything rulebase-ips]
root@SRX5800-1# show rule Dynamic-Groups
match {
```

```
    from-zone untrust;
    source-address any;
    to-zone trust;
    destination-address any;
    application default;
    attacks {
      dynamic-attack-groups [ Malicious-Activity Protect-Internal-Clients ];
    }
  }
  then {
    action {
      close-client-and-server;
    }
    ip-action {
      ip-block;
      target source-address;
      log;
      timeout 120;
    }
    notification {
      log-attacks;
    }
  }

{primary:node0}[edit security idp idp-policy Protect-Everything rulebase-ips]
root@SRX5800-1# up 2

{primary:node0}[edit security idp]
root@SRX5800-1# set active-policy Protect-Everything


{primary:node0}[edit security idp]
root@SRX5800-1# show active-policy
active-policy Protect-Everything;

{primary:node0}[edit security idp]
root@SRX5800-1# top

{primary:node0}[edit]
root@SRX5800-1# edit security policies from-zone untrust to-zone trust

{primary:node0}[edit security policies from-zone untrust to-zone trust]
root@SRX5800-1# set policy Inspect-IPS match source-address any destination-
address any application any

{primary:node0}[edit security policies from-zone untrust to-zone trust]
root@SRX5800-1# set policy Inspect-IPS then permit application-services idp

{primary:node0}[edit security policies from-zone untrust to-zone trust]
root@SRX5800-1# set policy Inspect-IPS then log session-close

{primary:node0}[edit security policies from-zone untrust to-zone trust]
```

```
root@SRX5800-1# show
policy Inspect-IPS {
  match {
    source-address any;
    destination-address any;
    application any;
  }
  then {
    permit {
      application-services {
        idp;
      }
    }
    log {
      session-close;
    }
  }
}

{primary:node0}[edit security policies from-zone untrust to-zone trust]
root@SRX5800-1# top

{primary:node0}[edit]
root@SRX5800-1# commit
node0:
configuration check succeeds
node1:
commit complete
node0:
commit complete
```

A lot is going on in this example. You have configured your IPS policy and rules, and configured the IPS to assign the active policy and associated firewall rules to send traffic to the IPS engine. Without these steps, the traffic would never be sent to the IPS. One important thing to note is that when you apply this in your environment, it might take some time to compile and apply the IPS policy. It all happens automatically, and no traffic will be disrupted. The best thing to do is to check the output of the `show security idp status` command to see if your active policy (in our case, `Protect-Everything`) has been applied and is active.

Exempt rulebase

Even with the best of intentions, you might find yourself in an IPS scenario where you have unexpectedly blocked legitimate traffic. For instance, if you are running protocol anomaly protection and you have mistaken some nonstandard application behavior that is not really malicious as an attack, it will be dropped according to your policy. To help make a clean IPS rulebase, with simple yet granular overrides, Juniper employs the Exempt rulebase to ensure that we can easily ignore certain scenarios, and at the same time not ignore inspection for the entire connection. In this example, you'll handle the following scenario.

After applying the IPS policy in the last example, some users are complaining that they are not able to access the web server. It turns out that their machines are infected with the FunWebProducts spyware, which adds a toolbar in Internet Explorer applications. It is more of a nuisance than actual malicious software, so you don't want to block your customers from accessing your web server at 172.31.100.60. Create an Exempt policy to not block this attack from the Internet to the 172.31.100.60 web server with the FunWebProducts attack object.

```
{primary:node0}[edit]
root@SRX5800-1# set security zones security-zone trust address-book address Web-
Server-172.31.100.60/32 172.31.100.60/32

{primary:node0}[edit security zones security-zone trust address-book]
root@SRX5800-1# show
address Web-Server-172.31.100.60/32 172.31.100.60/32;

{primary:node0}[edit]
root@SRX5800-1# edit security idp idp-policy Protect-Everything rulebase-exempt

{primary:node0}[edit security idp idp-policy Protect-Everything rulebase-exempt]
root@SRX5800-1# set rule FunWebProducts match from-zone untrust to-zone trust
source-address any destination-address Web-Server-172.31.100.60/32 attacks
predefined-attacks SPYWARE:BH:FUNWEBPRODUCTS

{primary:node0}[edit security idp idp-policy Protect-Everything rulebase-exempt]
root@SRX5800-1# show
rule FunWebProducts {
  match {
    from-zone untrust;
    source-address any;
    to-zone trust;
    destination-address Web-Server-172.31.100.60/32;
    attacks {
      predefined-attacks SPYWARE:BH:FUNWEBPRODUCTS;
    }
  }
}

{primary:node0}[edit security policies from-zone untrust to-zone trust]
root@SRX5800-1# top

{primary:node0}[edit]
root@SRX5800-1# commit
node0:
configuration check succeeds
node1:
commit complete
```

```
node0:
commit complete
```

Enabling GZIP/Deflate Decompression. There is one sensor knob that might be worth enabling, particularly if you are concerned with protecting internal resources: the GZIP/Deflate option for HTTP traffic. This can be an evasive channel that attackers can try to sneak server-to-client attacks through. You can enable it as shown here.

```
[edit]
root@srx3600n0# set security idp sensor-configuration detector protocol-name
http tunable-name sc_http_compress_inflating tunable-value 1

[edit]
root@srx3600n0# set security idp sensor-configuration detector protocol-name
http tunable-name sc_http_c2s_file_decode tunable-value 1

[edit]
root@srx3600n0# set security idp sensor-configuration detector protocol-name
http tunable-name sc_http_s2c_file_decode tunable-value 1

[edit]
root@srx3600n0# show security idp sensor-configuration
detector {
    protocol-name HTTP {
        tunable-name sc_http_compress_inflating {
            tunable-value 1;
        }
        tunable-name sc_http_c2s_file_decode {
            tunable-value 1;
        }
        tunable-name sc_http_s2c_file_decode {
            tunable-value 1;
        }
        tunable-name sc_http_html_parse_opt {
            tunable-value 1;
        }
        tunable-name sc_http_max_request_parameters {
            tunable-value 1000;
        }
        tunable-name sc_http_skip_contents_1 {
            tunable-value 1024;
        }
```

Deploying and Tuning IPS

Deploying IPS requires a slight learning curve. You could memorize every command and feature by heart and still have a rocky deployment. The challenge is that every environment is different, just like a fingerprint or DNA. There are different applications, different volumes of the applications, different policies on what is accepted activity, and different resources to protect, all of which can make for different goals for the IPS.

Although this book can't tell you exactly what your policy should be, it can certainly help you to build and deploy that policy.

First Steps to Deploying IPS

Before you get too caught up in the actual deployment, do a bit of legwork and map out the policy you want to deploy. Think of it as brainstorming for your IPS. You should identify the assets you want to protect, and identify the systems and applications and how they interact with others in your network. You might need to contact the application owners beforehand to identify this information. You should also determine your IPD protection goals. This would include the types of threats you want to prevent, and any other factors that might limit the scope of the deployment. (Often this involves management approval so that there aren't any surprises.)

Building the Policy

Once you have identified the assets and the goals of the IPS, and you have gotten all of the necessary approvals, you should be ready to build your IPS policy on the SRX. Remember that if you are using predefined attack objects, you must purchase and install the IPS license. You should then download and install the latest and greatest attack objects and detector engine using the full update. This ensures that you have all of the latest attack objects when writing your policy. With those prerequisite tasks taken care of, you should create your policy based on the skills you gained earlier in the chapter. If you want a decent place to start, you can download and install the policy templates, and then modify them to suit your needs. Don't apply the policy just yet, though.

Testing Your Policy

We would like to tell you to just deploy your IPS policy and let it go from there, but this is not the case for IPS (in our combined broad experience, with many competitor IPS systems, it is no different for them, either).

As mentioned, different environments with different applications make it difficult to make a one-size-fits-all policy with no adverse effects. The best thing that you can do is to test your policy before actually deploying it into production.

This can mean different things for different organizations. If you are a large organization that has lots of resources, you probably have a production lab in which you can replicate your production environment. You could place your SRX in that environment with the appropriate policy deployed and then see what happens. Because it is a lab, you can work out any of the kinks (e.g., false positives) there, without impacting production. Alternatively, you might be able to make a mirrored segment of the production segments on which you want to deploy the SRX using switchport mirroring (SPAN) or network taps so that even if the SRX has a false positive, it is on the mirrored segment rather than on the production segment.

On the other hand, many organizations don't have the luxury of full test labs. Fear not, because even in these environments you can still deploy with caution and confidence. The other option (which is a good idea to use even if you have the production lab) is to deploy the SRX, but not block anything in the IPS engine. You can do this by using the No-Action actions in the SRX IPS policy so that the SRX is not interfering with any traffic, but is still performing all of the inspection. In this configuration, you should have the SRX log the output to a syslog server such as the STRM so that you can evaluate the output and determine if any false positives are occurring, and if there is anything that should be tuned.

As part of the tuning process, you will likely be adding exceptions into the Exempt rulebase, tuning thresholds, and getting accustomed to the facilities that provide visibility into the SRX IPS and the actual traffic itself. Just like IPS policies, there is no standard length of time to perform this phase; however, typically you want to ensure that you have a good cycle of traffic. This means if you have certain applications that run only at certain times, you want to wait until they have been given a chance to run with IPS enabled to see if there are any adverse effects. If you are pressed for a single time frame, best practice says to let it run a month before enabling blocking (vary this to be shorter or longer depending on the environment), but any time frames can be worked with, as something is better than nothing.

By carefully performing this measured approach, you are going a long way toward ensuring the success of the SRX IPS deployment, and mitigating the risk of issues that might occur in production.

Leveraging sniffer mode for the deployment

You do have the option of deploying interfaces in sniffer mode rather than a full-blown inline mode (see Figure 13-13). You can do this as part of an initial deployment or on a more permanent basis. This configuration can be leveraged on an interface-by-interface basis so you don't need to choose all or nothing. Unfortunately, you do have to jump through a few hoops to pull off sniffer mode on the SRX today, at the time of writing this book. Essentially, you put the desired interface into sniffer mode, with that interface in its own VR zone so that you can manipulate the traffic to go back out of that interface. Because the traffic will be off a mirror port or network tap you will need to hardcode the route and static ARP of the next hop so the system doesn't try to resolve it. It will take a few steps, but once it's up and running you should be good to go.

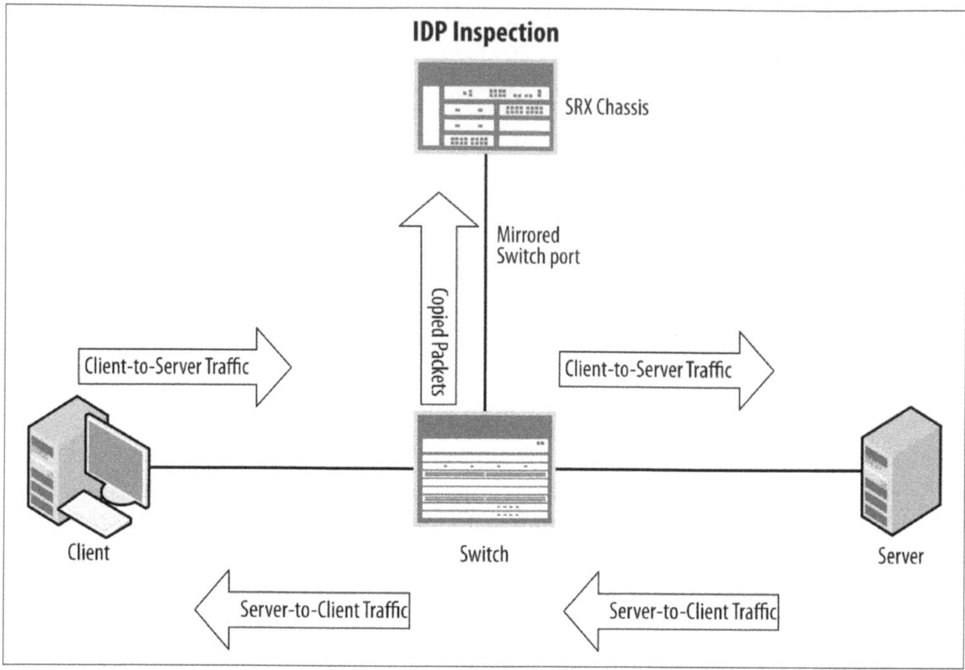

Figure 13-13. SRX sniffer mode

Let's configure an example where we put interface ge-0/0/0 into promiscuous mode in a VR called Sniffer, a Zone called Sniffer. Be sure to create a default route to next hop 192.168.1.254, which is on the same interface with a fake static ARP entry as well.

```
##Config Interface
[edit]
root@srx3600n0# set interfaces ge-0/0/0 promiscuous-mode

[edit]
root@srx3600n0#  set  interfaces  ge-0/0/0  unit  0  family  inet  address
192.168.1.1/24 arp 192.168.1.254 mac 00:00:01:01:01:01

##Config Custom VR
[edit]
root@srx3600n0# set routing-instances Sniffer instance-type virtual-router

[edit]
root@srx3600n0# set routing-instances Sniffer interface ge-0/0/0.0

[edit]
root@srx3600n0#  set  routing-instances  Sniffer  routing-options  static  route
0.0.0.0/0 next-hop 192.168.1.254

##Zone Config
[edit]
```

```
root@srx3600n0# set security zones security-zone Sniffer interfaces ge-0/0/0.0

##Define Policy

[edit]
root@srx3600n0# set security policies from-zone Sniffer to-zone Sniffer policy
1 match source-address any destination-address any application any

[edit]
root@srx3600n0# set security policies from-zone Sniffer to-zone Sniffer policy
1 then permit application-services idp

[edit]
root@srx3600n0# set security policies from-zone Sniffer to-zone Sniffer policy
1 then log session-close
```

Looking at this example, there are a few things that we need to call out. First, besides putting the physical interface in its own VR zone and creating the policy that references IPS, the interesting thing is the use of the static route that points back out the same interface. Of course, because the traffic is off a mirrored SPAN port, the traffic will never be received back on the real network, but this tricks the SRX into completing the data path processing by sending it back out. We need to also make a fake ARP entry because the SRX will not be able to resolve the next hop because this is a mirrored segment, and without the ARP entry the SRX will not be able to forward the traffic.

Technically, you can also accomplish this with Level 2 mode (without the need for promiscuous mode as that's for Level 3 mode only). In Level 2 mode, the SRX will forward the traffic similar to a switch so it doesn't care about the destination MAC or IP address of the packet so long as the switching table has a MAC address for the destination frame.

At the time of writing this book, the branch SRX does not support putting its interface in promiscuous in Layer 3 mode. Keep posted to the release notes to see if there is a change in this limitation. Another option when using a tap interface is to hardcode the MAC address for the interface the same as the upstream or downstream router so the SRX will listen for the packet. You can do this with multiple IP addresses on the same interface with multiple MAC addresses. It won't work well if the device is directly connected to a client segment, but if placed between two Level 3 devices, it should work fine. Just make sure that this is off of a network tap or mirrored switchport.

Actual Deployment

After you have completed your testing phase you are ready to deploy in an active blocking mode, unless your goal is just to keep it in an IDS state, in which case your work is finished.

If you did all of the legwork up front to build and tune the policy, typically the only thing to do here is to change the actions on the appropriate rules to the appropriate actions, rather than just taking no action. If all goes well, there really shouldn't be any surprises in this process. IPS is always going to be in somewhat of a state of evolution, because the threats themselves are always evolving, so it is not a set-and-forget technology as an unmanaged switch would be.

Day-to-Day IPS Management

Once you have completed the initial deployment, you (or your coworkers or external monitoring party) must still maintain the IPS and examine incidents. In terms of maintenance, it comes down to keeping the attack database on the SRX properly updated (not necessarily with the latest and greatest updates, but you should make sure you investigate updates and don't let them lapse too long) with detector engines and new features to help protect against new attacks.

Keeping the device updated can be automated. If you are concerned about new attacks being false positives, you should use static groups for the rules in which you block attacks, and only monitor new attacks with the `no-action` parameter so that you don't block new exploits without ensuring that it is safe to do so first. This means you have to manually add the new attack objects that you want to block into the static groups, but it provides the best balance of updated protection and stability.

The next thing you will likely do on a day-to-day basis is to monitor the IPS logs. Because you will probably see thousands of events per day (maybe more in large environments), you need a rational way to manage the alerts and to somehow investigate only the important ones. We recommend that you use reporting, such as that in the STRM, which can not only generate a report, but also allow you to drill down into that report (all the way to the offending logs themselves). This way, you will not go blind watching logs whiz by on the screen, but rather start from a high-level human-readable report that summarizes the pertinent events. Typically, you will have lots of different reports (e.g., worms, shellcode, server-to-client exploits, and more), but they will at least provide a good starting point. Then you can drill down where necessary to identify events that should be investigated in more detail.

Of course, simply logging and reporting all by itself probably does not provide everything you need. Generally, you are going to want to layer your implementation to provide different functionality for different events. For instance, some attacks you want to block when they occur, to protect the system's infrastructure, and other attacks you might not want to block, although you want to be notified when they occur. This can typically be accomplished with logging plus action on the syslog server to generate an email, or trap of some sort, to alert you that an event has occurred. (Be careful that you don't trigger a DoS yourself with too many alerts!) Next, you will have events that you don't want to block, and you don't need to be alerted right when they happen, but they are of interest (e.g., users running unauthorized games). This is where logging and reporting come in handy. You can review your logs at a later point to determine if further action is required.

Best Practices

Juniper's IPS has been around for more than 12 years at the time of writing this book, so plenty of features and enhancements have gone into its development and functionality. As a result, there are numerous capabilities that you have to deal with when working with the SRX. In this section, we review some of the best practices when it comes to managing the SRX IPS.

1. A good IPS deployment, whether it be with an SRX or some other competitive device, starts with clearly identifying the assets you wish to protect with IPS and the types of attacks you wish to protect them from (including by what vectors). For instance, what type of assets are you dealing with? Protecting servers? Clients? What services are they running?
2. When configuring an IPS policy, it is best to create an efficient policy rather than simply enabling All Attacks. Because Juniper has been developing IPS attacks for more than 12 years and seldom retires attack objects, enabling an all attacks policy (particularly when the device is in line with the traffic) can have performance effects if you aren't careful. Instead, you should look to craft an effective, efficient policy.
3. Be sure to follow the proper deployment methodology that we mentioned in this chapter. Rather than just putting the device in line with attacks in blocking mode, you should at least examine what type of baseline you are seeing in the network to ensure that turning on protect won't adversely affect the network with any potential false positives. This methodology is tried and true and can be used with other IPS products as well.
4. Only enable IPS on firewall policies that need it. The SRX allows you to leverage IPS on a firewall policy-by-policy basis so you don't need to turn it on device wide. This is good for keeping performance effects down on traffic that doesn't require it.
5. It is critical to leverage a layered security approach to network security and the same is true for leveraging the IPS. IPS serves a very critical need to protect your systems, but it shouldn't be relied on by itself. This means that you should still be leveraging a proper firewall policy, security features like Screens, UTM, and host-based protections like antivirus solutions, among others. No single technology is going to solve all of your problems, and any person or vendor who says otherwise is being disingenuous.
6. It is important to keep your IPS relatively up to date (if not completely up to date) when it comes to attack objects. Because new threats come out all the time, if you wait too long, your system might not be able to provide protection against the latest

and most critical threats. You can configure automatic attack object download along with installation at your own schedule. This is an ideal way to keep the box up to date if you don't have the time to review each new update.

7. Remember to leverage the *http://www.juniper.net/security* portal for attack information along with change logs and update information.

8. It is typically a best practice to not modify the IPS sensor configuration unless you have a solid understanding of the implications of the changes that you are making. This is because making changes can have impacts on the devices' capabilities and is not intended for folks who aren't experts.

9. It is a best practice to use static groups if you want to select a specific group of attack objects that you want to be part of a group. The membership won't change from attack object download to download, but members themselves can change if Juniper updates the signature. Dynamic groups are best to use if you have a broad requirement to select a group of attack objects based on characteristics rather than explicit attacks. Dynamic groups get updated when new attack objects are added, removed, or changed based on their tags and the filters you set in the policy.

10. It is best to not use the terminal option in policies unless you know what you are doing because it can potentially prevent you from inspecting traffic.

11. Remember that the No-Action option is preferred if you just want to continue to inspect the session, whereas the Ignore option is used to inform the IPS to stop inspection of a particular session. If you want to just prevent the IPS from taking action on an attack, you can simply use the Exempt rulebase.

12. It is a best practice to leave the "application" field in the IPS policy set to default so that the IPS will leverage AppID. If you change this field, then it can impact how the IPS will inspect traffic based on the Layer 3/Layer 4 service information. If this is your stated intention that's fine, but it's usually best to let AppID do the heavy lifting.

13. It is a best practice to not leave Packet Capture on if you can avoid it, especially with capture packets before the attack because the IPS will need to capture and store all packets for a period of time, having a performance impact. If you do want to leave this on at all times, do it with a bit of caution in your deployment to check and make sure that your device is not overwhelmed by it.

14. It is most certainly a best practice to review your devices' CPU and memory and to check to ensure that the security packages are being updated every so often. You can view the devices' CPU utilization via SNMP polling, through OpenNMS in Junos Space or other platforms like Cacti. See the MIB information that we discuss in Chapter 5 for more information. You can make this process quite painless via automation.

15. It is a best practice to have some cadence for reviewing security incidents. We're not suggesting that you watch logs being generated all day long, but instead leverage a combination of reporting and alerting to simplify this task. The STRM platform has an extensive predefined library of offenses that can trigger alerts (including via email), extensive predefined reports, and logview. That way you can be alerted when an important event happens, review security incidents as necessary, and leverage reporting to start with a high-level view that you can drill down into. You are not forced to use the Juniper STRM platform, however, because the SRX exports all of its information in syslog format (other than the PCAP, which is DMI, but that can be ported to other third-party platforms as well). The benefit of the STRM and in the future Security Insight is that they have this information predefined and customized for the SRX, but there's really nothing that stops you from using the solution that you are most comfortable with.

Troubleshooting and Operation

The SRX has a wealth of facilities that you can use to gain lots of information about IPS functionality and the security state of the inspection events for traffic that is passing through the SRX. So, in addition to the security events of the SRX, there are also troubleshooting facilities to look at in the IPS policy commit process. Additionally, Juniper has added a number of features since the 10.2 release to provide more IPS policy compilation and status information that can be very useful if you are running into any issues. In this section, we have broken down troubleshooting into several sections with examples of the commands, their output, and things to look for.

Checking IPS Status

First, it is important to make sure the SRX is up and running with an active IPS policy and that it is seeing traffic. If you don't see the information, the SRX is not inspecting traffic.

This first example shows the SRX without the IPS configured; the second example uses an active configuration. Note that on top of these steps, you can also add flow debugging to the list of things to examine. Although flow debugging won't get into the gory details of IPS debugging, it will give you a good idea of what is happening prior to IPS processing.

```
## Inactive IPS example, note Policy Name, No Detector Engine ##
root@SRX100HM> show security idp status
node0:
--------------------------------------------------------------------------
State of IDP: 2-default,    Up since: 1987-07-02 12:00:52 UTC (1179w6d 06:24
ago)
```

```
Packets/second: 0         Peak: 0 @ 1987-07-02 12:00:52 UTC
KBits/second : 0         Peak: 0 @ 1987-07-02 12:00:52 UTC
Latency (microseconds): [min: 0] [max: 0] [avg: 0]

Packet Statistics:
 [ICMP: 0] [TCP: 0] [UDP: 0] [Other: 0]

Flow Statistics:
 ICMP: [Current: 0] [Max: 0 @ 1987-07-02 12:00:52 UTC]
 TCP: [Current: 0] [Max: 0 @ 1987-07-02 12:00:52 UTC]
 UDP: [Current: 0] [Max: 0 @ 1987-07-02 12:00:52 UTC]
 Other: [Current: 0] [Max: 0 @ 1987-07-02 12:00:52 UTC]
Session Statistics:
 [ICMP: 0] [TCP: 0] [UDP: 0] [Other: 0]

Number of SSL Sessions : 0


 Policy Name : none

Forwarding process mode : maximizing sessions
## Active IPS policy, note detector engine and active stats ##

root@SRX100HM> show security idp status
node0:
--------------------------------------------------------------------------
State of IDP: Default,  Up since: 2013-02-05 18:42:49 EST (1w3d 01:17 ago)

Packets/second: 0              Peak: 0 @ 2013-02-05 18:42:49 EST
KBits/second  : 0              Peak: 0 @ 2013-02-05 18:42:49 EST
Latency (microseconds): [min: 0] [max: 0] [avg: 0]

Packet Statistics:
 [ICMP: 0] [TCP: 0] [UDP: 0] [Other: 0]

Flow Statistics:
  ICMP: [Current: 0] [Max: 0 @ 2013-02-05 18:42:49 EST]
  TCP: [Current: 0] [Max: 0 @ 2013-02-05 18:42:49 EST]
  UDP: [Current: 0] [Max: 0 @ 2013-02-05 18:42:49 EST]
  Other: [Current: 0] [Max: 0 @ 2013-02-05 18:42:49 EST]

Session Statistics:
 [ICMP: 0] [TCP: 0] [UDP: 0] [Other: 0]

  Policy Name : Recommended
  Running Detector Version : 12.6.160121210
```

This command is a very useful starting point because it lets you know if the engine is active and what policy is loaded, along with the detector engine version.

Checking Security Package Version

It is important to keep track of the active IPS security update version and the detector engine version. This is particularly important when running in HA to ensure that both devices are running the same version. It's easy to check by simply issuing the command shown here.

```
{primary:node1}
root@SRX100HM> show security idp security-package-version
node0:
--------------------------------------------------------------------------

  Attack database version:2233(Thu Feb 14 00:23:07 2013 UTC)
  Detector version :12.6.160121210
  Policy template version :N/A

node1:
--------------------------------------------------------------------------

  Attack database version:2233(Thu Feb 14 00:23:07 2013 UTC)
  Detector version :12.6.160121210
  Policy template version :N/A
```

Troubleshooting and Monitoring Security Package Installation

When downloading and installing a new security package, the output should look something like the output shown here. You can issue the status commands repeatedly to get the up-to-date status. Juniper chose to do this asynchronously because this process can take some time, and rather than holding up the command line, they allow you to check with the status option if you desire.

```
root@srx3600n0> request security idp security-package download
Will be processed in async mode. Check the status using the status checking CLI

root@srx3600n0> request security idp security-package download status
In progress:groups.xml.gz                                     100 % 76271 Bytes/
76271 Bytes

root@srx3600n0> request security idp security-package download status
Done;Successfully     downloaded     from(https://services.netscreen.com/cgi-bin/
index.cgi).
Version info:2233(Thu Feb 14 00:23:03 2013 UTC, Detector=12.6.140121210)

root@srx3600n0> request security idp security-package install
Will be processed in async mode. Check the status using the status checking CLI

root@srx3600n0> request security idp security-package install status
In progress:Installing AI ...

root@srx3600n0> request security idp security-package install status
Done;Attack DB update : successful - [UpdateNumber=2233,ExportDate=Thu Feb 14
```

```
00:23:03 2013 UTC,Detector=12.6.140121210]
     Updating control-plane with new detector : successful
     Updating data-plane with new attack or detector : successful
```

That output is roughly what you should be seeing when you go to download and install a new security package. If that isn't working for some reason, there are some things that you can check. You can enable flow traces on both the AppID installation and the IPS policy installation as follows, then check the logs that are generated for any obvious clues in the output of the trace. If the output doesn't give an obvious clue, then you might want to try clearing the download and cache files or contacting JTAC. There are far too many log entries in the trace to review, but usually you can tell if something is going dramatically wrong.

```
{primary:node1}
root@SRX100HM> show configuration services application-identification traceop-
tions
file AppID;
flag all;

{primary:node1}
root@SRX100HM> show configuration security idp traceoptions
file IDP-Commit;
flag all;
level all;

{edit]
root@SRX100HM# set security idp traceoptions flag ?
Possible completions:
  all                  All events
{primary:node1}[edit]
root@SRX100HM# set security idp traceoptions level ?
Possible completions:
  all                  Match all levels
  error                Match error conditions
  info                 Match informational messages
  notice               Match conditions that should be handled specially
  verbose              Match verbose messages
  warning              Match warning messages
```

You can use just the error level if you don't want all of the details in the output. If something is going wrong, there are usually a few culprits with the download and installation process.

- *Problem*

  You don't have proper DNS set up or network reachability to the update server services.netscreen.com.

  Solution

  Fix DNS/Routing/Access.

- *Problem*
  You have an IPS update in progress so the installation can't be completed.

  Solution
  Wait for the installation to be completed before installing the package.
- *Problem*
  Your disk drive is full!

  Solution
  Free up some space with `request system storage cleanup`.
- *Problem*
  The cache files are corrupted.

  Solution
  Clear the download and cache file and redownload.
- *Problem*
  There is a low memory condition on the data plane.

  Solution
  This can be a tough call. Usually it is best to contact JTAC if this is occurring.
- *Problem*
  You are running a really old version of Junos without all of the latest installation optimizations.

  Solution
  Ideally, you should be running 11.4r7 code or later because there have been a ton of enhancements that have gone into the newer code. Junos 12.1 has better support for HA and some new commands as well.

It is not an issue to leave traceoptions on at all times when it comes to these AppID and IPS settings, as they primarily deal with the download, installation, and compilation process and not real-time processing. For other features like flow traceoptions, you would not want to do that and instead only enable it selectively. There is usually not an issue with doing it here, however.

Clearing the download and cache files on the SRX

Starting in Junos 12.1, the SRX gives you support in the Junos command line to clear the download files and the cache files on the filesystem. Prior to this version, you would need to drop to the OS shell and simply remove the files. We show both methods here. With Junos 12.1+, there is support for deleting the download and cache files.

```
{primary:node1}
root@SRX100HM> request security idp storage-cleanup downloaded-files
node0:
--------------------------------------------------------------------------
Successfully deleted downloaded secdb files

node1:
--------------------------------------------------------------------------
Successfully deleted downloaded secdb files

{primary:node1}
root@SRX100HM> request security idp storage-cleanup cache-files
node0:
--------------------------------------------------------------------------
Successfully deleted cache files

node1:
--------------------------------------------------------------------------
Successfully deleted cache files
```

Prior to Junos 12.1, you could do this manually.

```
{primary:node1}
root@SRX100HM> start shell
root@SRX100HM% rm -rf /var/db/idpd/sec-download/*
root@SRX100HM% rm -rf /var/db/idpd/db/*
root@SRX100HM% cli
{primary:node1}
root@SRX100HM> restart idp-policy
IDP policy daemon started, pid 48044
```

Checking Policy Compilation Status

This is perhaps one of the most powerful commands that you can leverage when checking to see if a policy was generated successfully. This is good to run both when doing an installation of a security package and after you commit any changes to the IPS policy that result in policy compilation.

The policy installation and compilation roughly involves the following steps, which it is helpful to have a working understanding of:

1. Installing and compiling the AppID object
2. Compiling the IDP policy
3. Packaging the policy for loading
4. Loading the policy/detector to the data plane
5. Cleanup and completion

If you run the `show security idp policy-commit-status` command several times throughout the process, you will likely see different messages that explain what is happening with each step. You can also checkout the debug that we mentioned in the previous example for AppID and IPS to get more information about the play-by-play of the policy installation.

```
{primary:node1}
root@SRX100HM> show security idp policy-commit-status
node0:
--------------------------------------------------------------------------
  IDP  policy[/var/db/idpd/bins/Recommended.bin.gz.v]  and  detector[/var/db/idpd/
sec-repository/installed-detector/libidp-detector.so.tgz.v] loaded successfully.
 The loaded policy size is:19877540 Bytes

node1:
--------------------------------------------------------------------------
IDP  policy[/var/db/idpd/bins/Recommended.bin.gz.v]  and  detector[/var/db/idpd/
sec-repository/installed-detector/libidp-detector.so.tgz.v] loaded successfully.
 The loaded policy size is:19877540 Bytes
```

That output is what you should see when the process successfully completes. There are several different error messages that can occur here. Usually they are self-explanatory, but if not, please contact JTAC.

IPS Attack Table

Viewing the list of attacks detected will not give you the specifics of the attacks, so it's very useful to view the numbers to give you a better idea of your environment. You can also use modifiers to count or only match specific attacks, as shown here.

```
root@SRX5800-1> show security idp attack table
node0:
--------------------------------------------------------------------------
IDP attack statistics:

 Attack name                 #Hits
 TCP:OPTERR:NONSYN-MSS             9496
 TCP:AUDIT:S2C-OLD-ESTB             1923
 TCP:AUDIT:C2S-FUTURE-ACK            516
 HTTP:AUDIT:URL               120
 POP3:AUDIT:REQ-NESTED-REQUEST          83
 TCP:AUDIT:OPTIONS-UNNEGOT-TS           74
 POP3:AUDIT:REQ-INVALID-STATE           62
 IMAP:AUDIT:REQ-INVALID-STATE           56
 TCP:AUDIT:OLD-3WH-ACK            56
 TCP:AUDIT:S2C-FUTURE-ACK           40
 SMTP:AUDIT:REQ-NESTED-REQUEST          27
 APP:AI:PARTIAL-MATCH             19
 FTP:AUDIT:REQ-UNKNOWN-CMD           17
 PROTOCOLS:TRAFFIC:NOT-FTP           16
 HTTP:SQL:INJ:SQL-INJ-URL            15
 HTTP:SQL:INJ:CMD-CHAIN-1            14
 HTTP:SQL:INJ:CMD-IN-URL            14
 HTTP:SQL:INJ:CMD-CHAIN-2            10
 HTTP:REQERR:REQ-MALFORMED-URL          9
 HTTP:SQL:INJ:GENERIC             6
 HTTP:STC:SCRIPT:UNI-SHELLCODE          6
 CHAT:IRC:NICK              5
 HTTP:STC:ACTIVEX:UNCOMMON-AX           5
 CHAT:IRC:SRV-RESPONSE            4
 HTTP:STC:SCRIPT:UNICODE-SLED           4
 HTTP:EXT:METAFILE              3
 NNTP:AUDIT:NESTED-REQ            3
 HTTP:AUDIT:LENGTH-OVER-256           2
 HTTP:AUDIT:LENGTH-OVER-512           2
 HTTP:INFO:HTTPPOST-GETSTYLE          2
 HTTP:STC:STREAM:CONTENT-TYPE          2
 LPR:AUDIT:PORT               2
 POP3:EXT:DOT-WMF              2
```

```
 PROTOCOLS:PORT:FTP             2
 RTSP:EXPLOIT:INVALID-PORT         2
 VNC:SESSION                2
 CHAT:AUDIT:IRC-CMD             1
 CHAT:IRC:OVERFLOW:LINE           1
 FTP:CISCO-VPN-ACCESS            1
 FTP:OVERFLOW:LINE-TOO-LONG          1
 HTTP:AUDIT:LENGTH-OVER-1024         1
 HTTP:AUDIT:LENGTH-OVER-2048         1
 HTTP:AUDIT:LENGTH-OVER-4096         1


{primary:node0}
root@SRX5800-1> show security idp attack table | count
Count: 124 lines

{primary:node0}
root@SRX5800-1> show security idp attack table | match HTTP | match SQL
 HTTP:SQL:INJ:SQL-INJ-URL            15
 HTTP:SQL:INJ:CMD-CHAIN-1            14
 HTTP:SQL:INJ:CMD-IN-URL            14
 HTTP:SQL:INJ:CMD-CHAIN-2            10
 HTTP:SQL:INJ:GENERIC             6
```

IPS Counters

Several IPS counters are valuable to examine when determining the status of the IPS, the traffic that the IPS is processing, and the events that the IPS is taking. Several counters are worthwhile to examine, but we focus on the flow output in this example.

```
{primary:node0}
root@SRX5800-1> show security idp counters ?
Possible completions:
  application-identification  Show Application Identification counters
  dfa                  Show IDP DFA counters
  flow                 Show IDP Flow counters
  http-decoder         Show the HTTP decoder counters
  ips                  Show IPS counters
  log                  Show IDP Log counters
  packet               Show IDP Packet counters
  pdf-decoder          Show the PDF decoder counters
  policy-manager       Show IDP Policy counters
  tcp-reassembler      Show IDP Reassembler counters
{primary:node0}
root@SRX5800-1> show security idp counters flow node 0 | no-more
node0:
```

```
--------------------------------------------------------------------------
IDP counters:

 IDP counter type                            Value
 Fast-path packets                             53655
 Slow-path packets                             2289
 Session construction failed                        0
 Session limit reached                           0
 Memory limit reached                           0
 Not a new session                             0
 Invalide index at ageout                          0
 Packet logging                              0
 Busy packets                               0
 Busy packet Errors                            0
 Dropped queued packets (async mode)                    0
 Reinjected packets (async mode)                      0
 Policy cache hits                            802
 Policy cache misses                            1771
 Maximum flow hash collisions                       0
 Flow hash collisions                           0
 Gates added                                0
 Gate matches                               0
 Sessions deleted                             2052
 Sessions aged-out                            0
 Sessoins in-use while aged-out                      0
 TCP flows marked dead on RST/FIN                     1670
 Policy init failed                            0
 Number of Sessions exceeds high mark                   0
 Number of Sessions drops below low mark                  0
 Memory of Sessions exceeds high mark                   0
 Memory of Sessions drops below low mark                  0
 Sessions constructed                           2289
 SM Sessions ignored                            1890
 SM Sessions interested                          0
 SM Sessions not interested                         0
 SM Sessions interest error                         0
 Sessions destructed                           2138
 SM Session Create                            2289
 SM Packet Process                            0
 SM Session close                            0
 SM Client-to-server packets                        0
 SM Server-to-client packets                        0
 SM Client-to-server L7 bytes                       13395204
 SM Server-to-client L7 bytes                       25598889
```

IP Action Table

When a violation occurs, the administrator has the option to perform an action not only on that connection, but also on future connections depending on configuration. This is known as IP Action, and you can view the contents of this table, including using modifiers to select specific entries.

```
{primary:node0}
root@SRX5800-1>show security flow ip-action

Src-Addr  Src-Port  Dst-Addr  Proto/Dst-Port  Timeout(sec)
 16.0.80.0 0       0.0.0.0   0/0        598/600      0   close

 16.0.66.15 0       0.0.0.0   0/0        596/600      0   close

 16.0.74.17 0       0.0.0.0   0/0        595/600      0   close

 16.0.0.47 0       0.0.0.0   0/0        596/600      0   close

 16.0.80.56 0       0.0.0.0   0/0        596/600      0   close

 16.0.22.59 0       0.0.0.0   0/0        596/600      0   close

 16.0.78.76 0       0.0.0.0   0/0        598/600      0   close
```

From the output of the `show security flow ip-table` command you can determine if a host has been shunned (source, destination, protocol, destination port) and the timeout remaining in the maximum time. In this example, the shunned host shows a timeout of 600 seconds that counts down. The entries remain in the table until they timeout.

Sample Deployments

There is a lot to be said for putting the theory of IPS into action in a production network. The good news is that we will look at a few example policies that can be used to secure an enterprise network against internal and external threats. In this case study, we examine the ability to provide protection under three different scenarios:

DMZ network

In the DMZ, several servers must be protected against attacks by clients, including HTTP, HTTPS, FTP, SMTP, and DNS servers. For performance reasons, we only want to look at signatures that have members in the client-to-server direction. We also want to make sure these machines are not compromised and start to infect other machines in the network or the Internet at large with spyware, worms, Trojan horses, and viruses. The DMZ server can only talk outbound on HTTP and HTTPS for updates. All logs should be taken in this example. Assume that the DMZ zone uses the interface Reth4.

Internal clients

We want to protect internal clients against attacks from malicious servers in the wild. These hosts will only be allowed to communicate over HTTP, HTTPS, FTP, IM, and out to the Internet; all other services are restricted by the firewall policy itself. We also want to identify and block any hosts that are infected by spyware, worms, Trojan horses, or viruses for two hours, along with setting the `alert` flag in the logs. Assume that the Internal-Clients zone includes Dept-A and Dept-B with interfaces Reth2 and Reth3, respectively.

Internal servers

Clients are permitted to access a wide variety of services on the internal servers. Currently, your organization does not restrict services between internal clients and servers, but it does wish to provide additional security. At this time, management is hesitant to interfere with internal traffic, but they would like to provide visibility, so you should just log the attacks at this point. The internal servers are allowed to talk out to the Internet via HTTP and HTTPS for updates. Additionally, we want to identify any servers that might be infected by spyware, worms, Trojan horses, or viruses. Assume that the Internal-Servers zone uses interface Reth5.

For these examples, we leverage the power of dynamic groups. The most significant attacks will be located in the Critical, Major, and Minor severities. We will also use category, direction, and performance filters to ensure that our policy is as specific and lean as possible, while still providing serious coverage. Figure 13-14 shows an overview of the case study.

First, we define our network elements, their zones, and the firewall policy that will be used to pass the traffic to the IPS for inspection. We assume that the NAT has already been taken care of, as it will not change the objects in our policies.

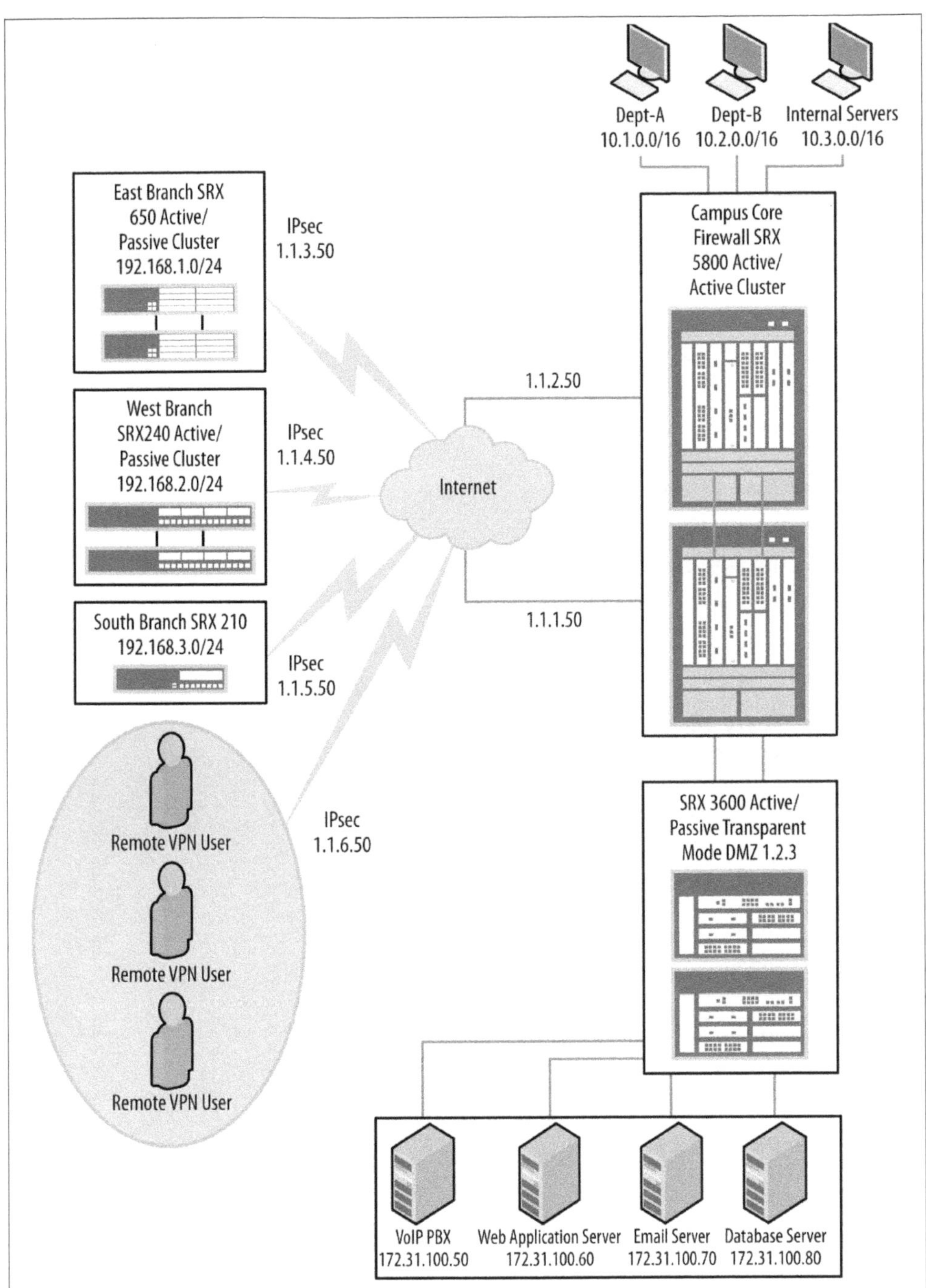

Figure 13-14. Case study overview

```
[edit]
root@SRX5800# set security address-book global address DMZ-
Server-172.31.100.0/24 172.31.100.0/24

[edit]
root@SRX5800# set security address-book global address-book address Dept-
A-10.1.0.0/16 10.1.0.0/16

[edit]
root@SRX5800# set security address-book global address Dept-B-10.2.0.0/16
10.2.0.0/16

[edit]
root@SRX5800# set security address-book global address Internal-
Servers-10.3.0.0/16 10.3.0.0/16


[edit]
root@SRX5800# edit security zones security-zone DMZ


[edit security zones security-zone DMZ]
root@SRX5800# set interfaces reth4

[edit security zones security-zone DMZ]
root@SRX5800# up

[edit security zones]
root@SRX5800# edit security-zone Dept-A



[edit security zones security-zone Dept-A]
root@SRX5800# set interfaces reth2

[edit security zones security-zone Dept-A]
root@SRX5800# up

[edit security zones]
root@SRX5800# edit security-zone Dept-B


[edit security zones security-zone Dept-B]
root@SRX5800# up

[edit security zones]
root@SRX5800# edit security-zone Internal-Servers


[edit security zones security-zone Internal-Servers]
root@SRX5800# set interfaces reth5
```

```
[edit security zones security-zone Internal-Servers]
root@SRX5800# up

[edit]
root@5800# show security address-book
    global {
        address DMZ-Server-172.31.100.0/24 172.31.100.0/24;
        address Dept-A-10.1.0.0/16 10.1.0.0/16;
        address Dept-B-10.2.0.0/16 10.2.0.0/16;
        address Internal-Servers-10.3.0.0/16 10.3.0.0/16;

    }


[edit security zones]
root@SRX5800# show
security-zone DMZ {

    interfaces {
        reth4.0;
    }
}
security-zone Dept-A {
    interfaces {
        reth2.0;
    }
}
security-zone Dept-B {
}
    interfaces {
        reth5.0;
    }
}

[edit security zones]
root@SRX5800# top

[edit]
root@SRX5800# set applications application-set DMZ-Services application
junos-http

[edit]
root@SRX5800# set applications application-set DMZ-Services application
junos-https

[edit]
root@SRX5800# set applications application-set DMZ-Services application
junos-ftp

[edit]
root@SRX5800# set applications application-set DMZ-Services application
junos-smtp
```

```
[edit]
root@SRX5800# set applications application-set DMZ-Services application
junos-dns-udp

[edit]
root@SRX5800# set applications application-set Allowed-Outbound application
junos-http

[edit]
root@SRX5800# set applications application-set Allowed-Outbound application
junos-https

[edit]
root@SRX5800# set applications application-set Allowed-Outbound application
junos-ftp

[edit]
root@SRX5800# set applications application-set Allowed-Outbound application
junos-aol

[edit]
root@SRX5800# set applications application-set Allowed-Outbound application
junos-ymsg

[edit]
root@SRX5800# show applications
application-set DMZ-Services {
    application junos-http;
    application junos-https;
    application junos-ftp;
    application junos-smtp;
    application junos-dns-udp;
}
application-set Allowed-Outbound {
    application junos-http;
    application junos-https;
    application junos-ftp;
    application junos-aol;
    application junos-ymsg;
}

[edit]
root@SRX5800# edit security policies from-zone Dept-A to-zone DMZ

[edit security policies from-zone Dept-A to-zone DMZ]
root@SRX5800# set policy Dept-A-to-DMZ match source-address Dept-A-10.1.0.0/16
destination-address DMZ-Server-172.31.100.0/24 application DMZ-Services

[edit security policies from-zone Dept-A to-zone DMZ]
root@SRX5800# set policy Dept-A-to-DMZ then permit application-services idp
```

```
[edit security policies from-zone Dept-A to-zone DMZ]
root@SRX5800# set policy Dept-A-to-DMZ then log session-close

[edit security policies from-zone Dept-A to-zone DMZ]
root@SRX5800# up

[edit security policies]
root@SRX5800# edit from-zone Dept-B to-zone DMZ

[edit security policies from-zone Dept-B to-zone DMZ]
root@SRX5800# set policy Dept-B-to-DMZ match source-address Dept-B-10.2.0.0/16
destination-address DMZ-Server-172.31.100.0/24 application DMZ-Services

[edit security policies from-zone Dept-B to-zone DMZ]
root@SRX5800# set policy Dept-B-to-DMZ then permit application-services idp

[edit security policies from-zone Dept-B to-zone DMZ]
root@SRX5800# set policy Dept-B-to-DMZ then log session-close

[edit security policies from-zone Dept-B to-zone DMZ]
root@SRX5800# up

[edit security policies]
root@SRX5800# edit from-zone Dept-A to-zone Internal-Servers

[edit security policies from-zone Dept-A to-zone Internal-Servers]
root@SRX5800# set policy Dept-A-to-Internal-Servers match source-address Dept-A-
10.1.0.0/16 destination-address Internal-Servers-10.3.0.0/16 application any

[edit security policies from-zone Dept-A to-zone Internal-Servers]
root@SRX5800# set policy Dept-A-to-Internal-Servers then permit application-
services idp

[edit security policies from-zone Dept-A to-zone Internal-Servers]
root@SRX5800# set policy Dept-A-to-Internal-Servers then log session-close

[edit security policies from-zone Dept-A to-zone Internal-Servers]
root@SRX5800# up

[edit security policies]
root@SRX5800# edit from-zone Dept-B to-zone Internal-Servers

[edit security policies from-zone Dept-B to-zone Internal-Servers]
root@SRX5800# set policy Dept-B-to-Internal-Servers match source-address Dept-B-
10.2.0.0/16 destination-address Internal-Servers-10.3.0.0/16 application any

[edit security policies from-zone Dept-B to-zone Internal-Servers]
root@SRX5800# set policy Dept-B-to-Internal-Servers then permit application-
services idp

[edit security policies from-zone Dept-B to-zone Internal-Servers]
root@SRX5800# set policy Dept-B-to-Internal-Servers then log session-close
```

```
[edit security policies from-zone Dept-B to-zone Internal-Servers]
root@SRX5800# up

[edit security policies]
root@SRX5800# edit from-zone untrust to-zone DMZ

[edit security policies from-zone untrust to-zone DMZ]
root@SRX5800# set policy untrust-to-DMZ match source-address any destination-
address DMZ-Server-172.31.100.0/24 application DMZ-Services

[edit security policies from-zone untrust to-zone DMZ]
root@SRX5800# set policy untrust-to-DMZ then permit application-services idp

[edit security policies from-zone untrust to-zone DMZ]
root@SRX5800# set policy untrust-to-DMZ then log session-close

[edit security policies from-zone untrust to-zone DMZ]
root@SRX5800# up

[edit security policies]
root@SRX5800# edit from-zone Dept-A to-zone untrust

[edit security policies from-zone Dept-A to-zone untrust]
root@SRX5800# set policy Dept-A-to-untrust match source-address
Dept-A-10.1.0.0/16 destination-address any application Allowed-Outbound

[edit security policies from-zone Dept-A to-zone untrust]
root@SRX5800# set policy Dept-A-to-untrust then permit application-services idp

[edit security policies from-zone Dept-A to-zone untrust]
root@SRX5800# set policy Dept-A-to-untrust then log session-close

[edit security policies from-zone Dept-A to-zone untrust]
root@SRX5800# up

[edit security policies]
root@SRX5800# edit from-zone Dept-B to-zone untrust

[edit security policies from-zone Dept-B to-zone untrust]
root@SRX5800# set policy Dept-B-to-untrust match source-address
Dept-B-10.2.0.0/16 destination-address any application Allowed-Outbound

[edit security policies from-zone Dept-B to-zone untrust]
root@SRX5800# set policy Dept-B-to-untrust then permit application-services idp

[edit security policies from-zone Dept-B to-zone untrust]
root@SRX5800# set policy Dept-B-to-untrust then log session-close

[edit security policies from-zone Dept-B to-zone untrust]
root@SRX5800# up
```

```
[edit security policies]
root@SRX5800# edit from-zone DMZ to-zone untrust

[edit security policies from-zone DMZ to-zone untrust]
root@SRX5800# set policy DMZ-to-untrust match source-address DMZ-Server-
172.31.100.0/24 destination-address any application [ junos-http junos-https ]

[edit security policies from-zone DMZ to-zone untrust]
root@SRX5800# set policy DMZ-to-untrust then permit application-services idp

[edit security policies from-zone DMZ to-zone untrust]
root@SRX5800# set policy DMZ-to-untrust then log session-close

[edit security policies from-zone DMZ to-zone untrust]
root@SRX5800# up

[edit security policies]
root@SRX5800# edit from-zone Internal-Servers to-zone untrust

[edit security policies from-zone Internal-Servers to-zone untrust]
root@SRX5800# set policy Internal-Servers-to-untrust match source-address
Internal-Servers-10.3.0.0/16 destination-address any application [ junos-http
junos-https ]

[edit security policies from-zone Internal-Servers to-zone untrust]
root@SRX5800# set policy Internal-Servers-to-untrust then permit application-
services idp

[edit security policies from-zone Internal-Servers to-zone untrust]
root@SRX5800# set policy Internal-Servers-to-untrust then log session-close

[edit security policies]
root@SRX5800# top

from-zone Dept-A to-zone DMZ {
    policy Dept-A-to-DMZ {
        match {
            source-address Dept-A-10.1.0.0/16;
            destination-address DMZ-Server-172.31.100.0/24;
            application DMZ-Services;
        }
        then {
            permit {
                application-services {
                    idp;
                }
            }
            log {
                session-close;
            }
        }
    }
```

```
}
from-zone Dept-B to-zone DMZ {
    policy Dept-B-to-DMZ {
        match {
            source-address Dept-B-10.2.0.0/16;
            destination-address DMZ-Server-172.31.100.0/24;
            application DMZ-Services;
        }
        then {
            permit {
                application-services {
                    idp;
                }
            }
            log {
                session-close;
            }
        }
    }
}
from-zone Dept-B to-zone Internal-Servers {
    policy Dept-B-to-Internal-Servers {
        match {
            source-address Dept-B-10.2.0.0/16;
            destination-address Internal-Servers-10.3.0.0/16;
            application any;
        }
        then {
            permit {
                application-services {
                    idp;
                }
            }
            log {
                session-close;
            }
        }
    }
}
from-zone Dept-A to-zone Internal-Servers {
    policy Dept-A-to-Internal-Servers {
        match {
            source-address Dept-A-10.1.0.0/16;
            destination-address Internal-Servers-10.3.0.0/16;
            application any;
        }
        then {
            permit {
                application-services {
                    idp;
                }
            }
```

```
                log {
                    session-close;
                }
            }
        }
    }
    from-zone untrust to-zone DMZ {
        policy untrust-to-DMZ {
            match {
                source-address any;
                destination-address DMZ-Server-172.31.100.0/24;
                application DMZ-Services;
            }
            then {
                permit {
                    application-services {
                        idp;
                    }
                }
                log {
                    session-close;
                }
            }
        }
    }
    from-zone Dept-A to-zone untrust {
        policy Dept-A-to-untrust {
            match {
                source-address Dept-A-10.1.0.0/16;
                destination-address any;
                application Allowed-Outbound;
            }
            then {
                permit {
                    application-services {
                        idp;
                    }
                }
                log {
                    session-close;
                }
            }
        }
    }
    from-zone Dept-B to-zone untrust {
        policy Dept-B-to-untrust {
            match {
                source-address Dept-B-10.2.0.0/16;
                destination-address any;
                application Allowed-Outbound;
            }
            then {
```

```
                permit {
                    application-services {
                        idp;
                    }
                }
                log {
                    session-close;
                }
            }
        }
    }
    from-zone DMZ to-zone untrust {
        policy DMZ-to-untrust {
            match {
                source-address DMZ-Server-172.31.100.0/24;
                destination-address any;
                application [ junos-http junos-https ];
            }
            then {
                permit {
                    application-services {
                        idp;
                    }
                }
                log {
                    session-close;
                }
            }
        }
    }
    from-zone Internal-Servers to-zone untrust {
        policy Internal-Servers-to-untrust {
            match {
                source-address Internal-Servers-10.3.0.0/16;
                destination-address any;
                application [ junos-http junos-https ];
            }
            then {
                permit {
                    application-services {
                        idp;
                    }
                }
                log {
                    session-close;
                }
            }
        }
    }
```

Next, we will create the dynamic group objects that will be used for the IPS policy to protect our infrastructure.

```
[edit]
root@SRX5800# edit security idp dynamic-attack-group Protect-DMZ
[edit security idp dynamic-attack-group Protect-DMZ]

[edit security idp dynamic-attack-group Protect-DMZ]
root@SRX5800# set filters category values [ HTTP SSL SMTP DNS SHELLCODE
WORM TROJAN ]

[edit security idp dynamic-attack-group Protect-DMZ]
root@SRX5800# set filters direction values [client-to-server exclude-server-to-
client exclude-any]

[edit security idp dynamic-attack-group Protect-DMZ]
root@SRX5800# set filters direction expression and

[edit security idp dynamic-attack-group Protect-DMZ]
root@SRX5800# set filters severity values [ critical major minor ]

[edit security idp dynamic-attack-group Protect-DMZ]
root@SRX5800# set filters performance values [ fast normal unknown ]


[edit security idp dynamic-attack-group Protect-DMZ]
root@SRX5800# up

[edit security idp]
root@SRX5800# edit dynamic-attack-group Protect-Clients

[edit security idp dynamic-attack-group Protect-Clients]
root@SRX5800# set filters severity values [ critical major minor ]

[edit security idp dynamic-attack-group Protect-Clients]
root@SRX5800# set filters performance values [ fast normal unknown ]

[edit security idp dynamic-attack-group Protect-Clients]
root@SRX5800# set filters direction values server-to-client

[edit security idp dynamic-attack-group Protect-Clients]
root@SRX5800# set filters category values [ HTTP SSL FTP CHAT SHELLCODE WORM
SPYWARE TROJAN VIRUS ]

[edit security idp dynamic-attack-group Protect-Clients]
root@SRX5800# up

[edit security idp]
root@SRX5800# edit dynamic-attack-group Detect-Infection

[edit security idp dynamic-attack-group Detect-Infection]
root@SRX5800# set filters performance values [ fast normal unknown ]

[edit security idp dynamic-attack-group Detect-Infection]
root@SRX5800# set filters direction values client-to-server
```

```
[edit security idp dynamic-attack-group Detect-Infection]
root@SRX5800# set filters severity values [ critical major minor ]

[edit security idp dynamic-attack-group Detect-Infection]
root@SRX5800# set filters category values [ WORM SPYWARE TROJAN VIRUS SHELL-
CODE ]

[edit security idp dynamic-attack-group Detect-Infection]
root@SRX5800# up

[edit security idp dynamic-attack-group Detect-Infection]
root@SRX5800# up

[edit security idp]
root@SRX5800# edit dynamic-attack-group Protect-Servers

[edit security idp dynamic-attack-group Protect-Servers]
root@SRX5800# set filters severity values [ critical major minor ]

[edit security idp dynamic-attack-group Protect-Servers]
root@SRX5800# set filters performance values [ fast normal unknown ]

[edit security idp dynamic-attack-group Protect-Servers]
root@SRX5800# set filters direction values client-to-server

[edit security idp dynamic-attack-group Protect-Servers]
root@SRX5800# up

[edit security idp dynamic-attack-group Protect-Servers]
root@SRX5800# show | find dynamic-attack-group
dynamic-attack-group Protect-DMZ {
    filters {
        direction {
            values client-to-server;
        }
        severity {
            values [ critical major minor ];
        }
        performance {
            values [ fast normal unknown ];
        }
        category {
            values [ HTTP SSL FTP SMTP DNS SHELLCODE WORM TROJAN ];
        }
    }
}
dynamic-attack-group Protect-Clients {
    filters {
        direction {
            values server-to-client;
        }
```

```
            severity {
                values [ critical major minor ];
            }
            performance {
                values [ fast normal unknown ];
            }
            category {
                values [ HTTP SSL FTP CHAT SHELLCODE WORM SPYWARE TROJAN VIRUS ];
            }
        }
    }
    dynamic-attack-group Detect-Infection {
        filters {
            direction {
                values client-to-server;
            }
            severity {
                values [ critical major minor ];
            }
            performance {
                values [ fast normal unknown ];
            }
            category {
                values [ WORM SPYWARE TROJAN VIRUS SHELLCODE ];
            }
        }
    }
    dynamic-attack-group Protect-Servers {
        filters {
            direction {
                values client-to-server;
            }
            severity {
                values [ critical major minor ];
            }
            performance {
                values [ fast normal unknown ];
            }
        }
    }
```

Now that we have defined all of the objects, firewall policy, and IPS attack groups, we will finally define the actual IPS policy to take everything into account in the objectives and put it into place.

```
[edit security idp]
root@SRX5800# edit idp-policy IDP rulebase-ips rule Protect-DMZ

[edit security idp idp-policy IDP rulebase-ips rule Protect-DMZ]
root@SRX5800# set match from-zone untrust to-zone DMZ source-address any
destination-address DMZ-Server-172.31.100.0/24 application default attacks
dynamic-attack-groups Protect-DMZ
```

```
[edit security idp idp-policy IDP rulebase-ips rule Protect-DMZ]
root@SRX5800# set then action drop-connection

[edit security idp idp-policy IDP rulebase-ips rule Protect-DMZ]
root@SRX5800# set then notification log-attacks

[edit security idp idp-policy IDP rulebase-ips rule Protect-DMZ]
root@SRX5800# up

[edit security idp idp-policy IDP rulebase-ips]
root@SRX5800# edit rule Protect-Clients-Dept-A

[edit security idp idp-policy IDP rulebase-ips rule Protect-Clients-Dept-A]
root@SRX5800# set match from-zone Dept-A to-zone untrust source-address Dept-A-
10.1.0.0/16 destination-address any application default attacks dynamic-attack-
groups [ Protect-Clients Detect-Infection ]

[edit security idp idp-policy IDP rulebase-ips rule Protect-Clients-Dept-A]
root@SRX5800# set then action drop-connection

[edit security idp idp-policy IDP rulebase-ips rule Protect-Clients-Dept-A]
root@SRX5800# set then notification log-attacks alert

[edit security idp idp-policy IDP rulebase-ips rule Protect-Clients-Dept-A]
root@SRX5800# set then ip-action ip-block target source-address timeout 7200 log

[edit security idp idp-policy IDP rulebase-ips rule Protect-Clients-Dept-A]
root@SRX5800# up

[edit security idp idp-policy IDP rulebase-ips]
root@SRX5800# edit rule Protect-Clients-Dept-B

[edit security idp idp-policy IDP rulebase-ips rule Protect-Clients-Dept-B]
root@SRX5800# set match from-zone Dept-B to-zone untrust source-address Dept-B-
10.2.0.0/16 destination-address any application default attacks dynamic-attack-
groups [ Protect-Clients Detect-Infection ]

[edit security idp idp-policy IDP rulebase-ips rule Protect-Clients-Dept-B]
root@SRX5800# set then action drop-connection

[edit security idp idp-policy IDP rulebase-ips rule Protect-Clients-Dept-B]
root@SRX5800# set then ip-action ip-block target source-address log timeout 7200

[edit security idp idp-policy IDP rulebase-ips rule Protect-Clients-Dept-B]
root@SRX5800# set then notification log-attacks alert

[edit security idp idp-policy IDP rulebase-ips rule Protect-Clients-Dept-B]
root@SRX5800# up

[edit security idp idp-policy IDP rulebase-ips rule Protect-Clients-Dept-B]
root@SRX5800# up
```

```
[edit security idp idp-policy IDP rulebase-ips]
root@SRX5800# edit rule Protect-DMZ-Outbound

[edit security idp idp-policy IDP rulebase-ips rule Protect-DMZ-Outbound]
root@SRX5800# set match from-zone DMZ to-zone untrust source-address DMZ-Server-
172.31.100.0/24 destination-address any application default attacks
dynamic-attack-groups [ Protect-Clients Detect-Infection ]

[edit security idp idp-policy IDP rulebase-ips rule Protect-DMZ-Outbound]
root@SRX5800# set then action drop-connection

[edit security idp idp-policy IDP rulebase-ips rule Protect-DMZ-Outbound]
root@SRX5800# set then ip-action ip-block target source-address log timeout 7200

[edit security idp idp-policy IDP rulebase-ips rule Protect-DMZ-Outbound]
root@SRX5800# set then notification log-attacks alert

[edit security idp idp-policy IDP rulebase-ips rule Protect-DMZ-Outbound]
root@SRX5800# up

[edit security idp idp-policy IDP rulebase-ips]
root@SRX5800# edit rule Protect-Servers-Outbound

[edit security idp idp-policy IDP rulebase-ips rule Protect-Servers-Outbound]
root@SRX5800# set match from-zone Internal-Servers to-zone untrust
source-address Internal-Servers-10.3.0.0/16 destination-address any application
default attacks dynamic-attack-groups [ Protect-Clients Detect-Infection ]

[edit security idp idp-policy IDP rulebase-ips rule Protect-Servers-Outbound]
root@SRX5800# set then action drop-connection

[edit security idp idp-policy IDP rulebase-ips rule Protect-Servers-Outbound]
root@SRX5800# set then ip-action ip-block target source-address log timeout 7200

[edit security idp idp-policy IDP rulebase-ips rule Protect-Servers-Outbound]
root@SRX5800# set then notification log-attacks alert

[edit security idp idp-policy IDP rulebase-ips rule Protect-Servers-Outbound]
root@SRX5800# up

[edit security idp idp-policy IDP rulebase-ips rule Protect-Servers-Outbound]
root@SRX5800# up

[edit security idp idp-policy IDP rulebase-ips]
root@SRX5800# edit rule Protect-Servers

[edit security idp idp-policy IDP rulebase-ips rule Protect-Servers]
root@SRX5800# set match from-zone any to-zone Internal-Servers source-address
any destination-address Internal-Servers-10.3.0.0/16 application default attacks
dynamic-attack-groups Protect-Servers
```

```
[edit security idp idp-policy IDP rulebase-ips rule Protect-Servers]
root@SRX5800# set then action no-action

[edit security idp idp-policy IDP rulebase-ips rule Protect-Servers]
root@SRX5800# set then notification log-attacks

[edit security idp idp-policy IDP rulebase-ips rule Protect-Servers]
root@SRX5800# up 3

[edit security idp]
root@SRX5800# set active-policy IDP

[edit security idp]
root@SRX5800# show idp-policy IDP
rulebase-ips {
    rule Custom {
        match {
            source-address any;
            destination-address any;
            attacks {
                custom-attacks [ Block-Facebook Compound-Attack ];
            }
        }
        then {
            action {
                drop-connection;
            }
        }
    }
    rule Protect-DMZ {
        match {
            from-zone untrust;
            source-address any;
            to-zone DMZ;
            destination-address [ edit security idp dynamic-attack-group Detect-
Infection DMZ-Server-172.31.100.0/24 ];
            application default;
            attacks {
                dynamic-attack-groups Protect-DMZ;
            }
        }
        then {
            action {
                drop-connection;
            }
            notification {
                log-attacks;
            }
        }
    }
    rule Protect-Clients-Dept-A {
        match {
```

```
            from-zone Dept-A;
            source-address Dept-A-10.1.0.0/16;
            to-zone untrust;
            destination-address any;
            application default;
            attacks {
                dynamic-attack-groups [ Protect-Clients Detect-Infection ];
            }
        }
        then {
            action {
                drop-connection;
            }
            ip-action {
                ip-block;
                target source-address;
                log;
                timeout 7200;
            }
            notification {
                log-attacks {
                    alert;
                }
            }
        }
    }
    rule Protect-Clients-Dept-B {
        match {
            from-zone Dept-B;
            source-address Dept-B-10.2.0.0/16;
            to-zone untrust;
            destination-address any;
            application default;
            attacks {
                dynamic-attack-groups [ Protect-Clients Detect-Infection ];
            }
        }
        then {
            action {
                drop-connection;
            }
            ip-action {
                ip-block;
                target source-address;
                log;
                timeout 7200;
            }
            notification {
                log-attacks {
                    alert;
                }
            }
```

```
        }
    }
    rule Protect-DMZ-Outbound {
        match {
            from-zone DMZ;
            source-address DMZ-Server-172.31.100.0/24;
            to-zone untrust;
            destination-address any;
            application default;
            attacks {
                dynamic-attack-groups [ Protect-Clients Detect-Infection ];
            }
        }
        then {
            action {
                drop-connection;
            }
            ip-action {
                ip-block;
                target source-address;
                log;
                timeout 7200;
            }
            notification {
                log-attacks {
                    alert;
                }
            }
        }
    }
    rule Protect-Servers-Outbound {
        match {
            from-zone Internal-Servers;
            source-address Internal-Servers-10.3.0.0/16;
            to-zone untrust;
            destination-address any;
            application default;
            attacks {
                dynamic-attack-groups [ Protect-Clients Detect-Infection ];
            }
        }
        then {
            action {
                drop-connection;
            }
            ip-action {
                ip-block;
                target source-address;
                log;
                timeout 7200;
            }
            notification {
```

```
                    log-attacks {
                        alert;
                    }
                }
            }
        }
        rule Protect-Servers {
            match {
                from-zone any;
                source-address any;
                to-zone Internal-Servers;
                destination-address Internal-Servers-10.3.0.0/16;
                application default;
                attacks {
                    dynamic-attack-groups Protect-Servers;
                }
            }
            then {
                action {
                    no-action;
                }
                notification {
                    log-attacks;
                }
            }
        }
    }

    [edit security idp]
    root@SRX5800# show active-policy
    active-policy IDP;

    [edit security idp]
    root@SRX5800# top

    [edit]
    root@SRX5800# commit
```

Summary

One of the key technologies that the SRX platform brings to the table when it comes to security is its IPS feature set. With a lineage of more than 12 years from the days of OneSecure, the Juniper IPS solution provides a full solution to inspect and protect against malicious threats that can traverse your network. There is no technology that acts as an overall panacea when it comes to security, but IPS is surely a layer of protection that you should strongly consider deploying in addition to other technologies that we have discussed throughout this book and in the industry at large. In this chapter, we covered the majority of the features in the IPS platform that an administrator is likely to leverage in day-to-day operations. We could easily fill an entire book with Juniper

SRX content all by itself, but if you have mastered the concepts in this chapter, then you should be able to get your IPS deployment up and running successfully, and maximize the impact that it can have on your security. IPS remains a key technology that Juniper is focusing on improving and integrating with new technologies going forward, so it should be very exciting to see where the future takes us and how IPS will remain a key contributor to securing our computer networks.

Study Questions

Questions

1. What is the difference between full IPS and deep inspection/IPS lite?
2. How are security updates handled when dealing with an HA cluster?
3. What types of exploits does IPS focus on preventing compared to technologies like antivirus protection and URL filtering?
4. What is the difference between signature-based attack objects and protocol anomaly detection?
5. Describe the key points and differences between an exploit, shellcode, privilege escalation, command and control, and further infection.
6. What is the difference between client-to-server and server-to-client attacks?
7. What is the difference between SSL Reverse Proxy and SSL Forward Proxy?
8. What is the difference between static and dynamic attack groups?
9. Can you create custom protocol anomaly objects?
10. Explain how Packet Capture works with IPS.
11. What does the terminal setting do in the IPS rulebase?
12. What is the difference between no-action, ignore, and exempting an attack?
13. What does setting the IPS application to default do compared to other services?
14. What is an IP action? How does it vary from a regular IPS action?
15. How is an IPS policy triggered for traffic passing through the firewall?
16. How many IPS policies can be active at a time?

Answers

1. Full IPS provides a much more complete inspection capability than deep inspection/IPS lite. This includes much more in the way of protocol inspection, decoding, application identification, and anomaly-based detection. Deep inspection is typically a small subset of IPS capabilities. The SRX only offers full IPS, including the full protocol parsing capabilities and anomaly protection, compared to legacy ScreenOS platforms and many competitive solutions.

2. Prior to Junos 12.1, you had to have both members enabled with fxp0 able to reach the Internet as they would independently contact the update server and download and install the database. Starting with 12.1, the primary device will download the package and synchronize it to the secondary device. There is no requirement for fxp0 connectivity (but it's still a good idea).
3. IPS is focused on detecting and protecting against network-based attacks and malicious activity. Although it can and does perform attack detection in files, and can prevent access to different resources similar to a URL filter, it is best to leverage an antivirus solution for virus protection and a URL filter for filtering policies as a best practice as they are more focused on their respective tasks.
4. Signature-based attack objects use detection based on stateful signatures and regular expressions, whereas protocol anomaly-based attack objects are coded into the detector engine to detect anomalous behavior, but this is not strictly a predefined regular expression pattern; rather, it is more intelligent detection.
5. An exploit is a piece of code that gains control over a victim machine, typically by assuming control over the execution of that program. Shellcode takes the attack a step further to perform some actions after the system execution has been commandeered. Privilege escalation is triggering another local exploit on the victim to raise the attacker's privileges from running in the context of the exploited process to something much greater. Command and control can be used to phone home to the attacker source for further instructions, and further infections can be used to pivot from the original victim to compromise other devices in the network.
6. Client-to-server attacks are attacks that are generated from the client, which is attacking the server of the connection. Server-to-client attacks are those in which the server attacks the client that made the connection to the server.
7. SSL Reverse Proxy (SSL Decryption/Inspection) is a feature supported only on the high-end SRX at the time of writing this book; the SRX will sit in front of an SSL-enabled web server and you will load the private SSL key of the web server on the SRX so that the SRX can crack open the SSL stream and inspect it for attacks. SSL Forward Proxy is used to protect your clients from external web servers by acting as a proxy that rewrites the SSL sessions between the client and the server (bidirectionally) to ensure that it can inspect the traffic and look for threats.
8. Static groups are groups that you add members into manually, and the groups' membership will not be changed during updates. Dynamic attack groups are specifically set up to define filters that define the criteria regarding which attack objects to add into the group.

9. You cannot define the protocol anomaly code itself, as that must be handled by the Juniper Security Team. However, you can create your own attack objects that are made up of protocol anomaly conditions.
10. Packet Capture is a feature that's supported in the IPS and can be triggered on an IPS rule-by-rule basis. It can capture not only the packets of the violating attack, but also packets before and after the attack. The packets are not stored on the device, but rather are sent via DMI to an external capture device like the Juniper STRM.
11. The terminal setting in an IPS rule informs the SRX to stop processing on that rule if the seven-tuple parameters match (just like a firewall). Normally the IPS will process the traffic and evaluate the entire policy in a nonterminal manner, taking the most restrictive action, but terminal informs the SRX to stop processing on that specific rule.
12. No-Action tells the SRX to keep processing the traffic but allows you to log the traffic (and will count it) if configured. Other actions can take place on the traffic. Ignore tells the IPS to stop processing the session and ignore the duration of the session. It will still be processed by the firewall and other Level 7 features. Exempt tells the SRX to silently ignore the specific attack without logging or counting it but continuing to inspect the rest of the connection for other attacks.
13. The application "default" in the IPS match criteria tells the SRX to use AppID to detect the application and use that for the attack inspection. Defining other applications will restrict what port or protocol range the IPS will look at for the attack.
14. A regular IPS action merely takes an action on the offending connection, but an IP action that can be triggered on a rule-by-rule basis specifies what should happen for future connections for the target. These actions can be to log, drop, or close future connections for different targets, which can include source IPs, destination IPs, combinations of the source, destination, zone, and service, and also to define some sort of timeout and refresh criteria when this happens.
15. You trigger IPS processing on a firewall rule-by-rule basis for traffic that is permitted at the firewall level. This traffic will be referred to the IPS engine for further inspection where it will be evaluated based on the active and defined IPS policy.
16. You can configure multiple IPS policies, but only one IPS policy can be active at a time. There is a slight variation when it comes to LSYS, but behind the scenes it is still only one policy.

CHAPTER 14

Unified Threat Management

Unified Threat Management (UTM) is an industry term that was coined to define Layer 7 protection against client-side threats. This does not include IPS (which also has protection against server-to-client attacks) but rather technologies such as network-based antivirus protection, URL filtering, antispam solutions, and content filtering. At this point, you might be asking yourself, if you have an IPS, why you need UTM? It's an excellent question, and one that many administrators confuse. IPS is primarily focused on network-based attacks on protocols, and is stream based, meaning that it processes traffic inline without modifying it as a stream. This works great from a performance perspective to detect attacks against services and applications. UTM, on the other hand, is meant more for protecting against files that are transmitted on top of the network streams. Although IPS might be more geared for detecting an overflow of the parser of the network stream, it isn't as well geared for detecting threats within files. That is, it certainly can detect such file-based attacks, but attackers can go to great lengths to encode, encrypt, and obfuscate files to perform some malicious action—and it is very difficult to detect these attacks in Stream mode.

If you think about it, network-based vulnerabilities have a very specific and fixed attack surface for the individual vulnerabilities, where, say, executables can be programmed to do virtually anything, both legitimate and malicious. To properly protect against such attacks you need a dedicated technology like antivirus software. We examine how this functions in this chapter.

Virus protection isn't the only feature that UTM provides. URL filtering is another powerful technology that can not only be used to prevent users from going to undesirable web content, but also as a mechanism to prevent them from going to known malicious sites. Again, you could use IPS to accomplish URL filtering, but particularly on a larger scale, it simply isn't geared to do so in an administrator-friendly manner. URL filtering, on the other hand, makes this process much easier, and has a large predefined database of URLs and categories to source for such reputations.

Antivirus protection and URL filtering are certainly the most commonly used UTM features, but the SRX also provides antispam solutions and content filtering features to protect clients against annoying and malicious spam. They also provide a mechanism for the administrator to do some lightweight data leak prevention. We explore these features in greater depth in this chapter.

As you can see, UTM is synonymous with protecting clients and enforcing organizational policy. In this chapter, we explore the various facets of UTM, how it functions, and how to properly deploy it in your network for maximum effectiveness.

Shifting Threats

As network administrators have gotten savvy about firewall placement and limiting inbound direct access to resources, along with the hardening of most common Internet-facing platforms like Apache, IIS, Exchange, and other platforms, attackers have shifted their attack strategies. Directly targeting and exploiting a specific victim on demand is the most ideal approach for attackers, but this has become much more difficult in modern networks. Both firewall infrastructure and DMZ best practices, along with these Internet-facing systems being stripped down and hardened, has made this much more difficult. Instead, attackers are taking advantage of a much more enticing target, the clients themselves. In many organizations, Internet-facing resources are somewhat quarantined in a DMZ, so even if they are compromised, it might be difficult to pivot and compromise other internal resources. On the other hand, many organizations leave their internal hosts with carte blanche access to internal resources. Additionally, as applications have shifted from being standalone clients, to network enabled, to web browser enabled, there has been a lot of effort to create a better user experience in these applications. Technologies such as Flash, Java, JavaScript, and ActiveX, as well as file-based attacks through PDF and Office documents have become a major source of exploits for malicious attackers.

For these reasons, attackers have shifted to target clients. Of course, you might think that it is harder to exploit because said attackers cannot be directly contacted, but it is actually easier than you think. There are numerous examples of such advanced attacks that leverage targeted emails, web links, drive-by downloads, and social engineering to ensnare either specific or broad targets for compromise. In fact, these methods are some of the most prevalent ways to compromise machines today. For the purpose of this chapter, we won't focus on a specific class of malware like viruses, worms, Trojans, or spyware. Malware is malware, and we discuss how to protect yourself against it with the SRX platform, and specifically UTM technologies.

UTM, IPS, or Both?

Before we go into an in-depth discussion of how UTM works and how to configure it, let's start with a brief overview of the applicable use cases for deploying UTM, and how it can be used in conjunction with other Layer 7 security technologies. Before delving into all of the details of how each technology works, let's take an overview of each technology and what issue it solves, followed by how services like AppSecure and IPS can interact with UTM to provide maximum security.

Antivirus

The antivirus component of UTM provides the ability to inspect files transmitted over several protocols to determine if the files exchanged are known malicious files, similar to how desktop antivirus software scans files for the same purpose. Of course, the antivirus protection integrated into the SRX is purely network based, so it can't provide enforcement for any files that aren't transmitted through the SRX. We offer both Kaspersky and Sophos engines in the SRX. You can only have one active at a time, but you can have different profiles active per engine. In addition to the file scanning, the Sophos engine also offers the ability to perform reputation analysis on URIs to determine if the location of the file is known to be malicious (more on this later).

Although antivirus is primarily viewed as a technology to protect clients, technically it can also be used for server-side inspection. For instance, if you run an SMTP, FTP, HTTP, IMAP, or POP3 server, antivirus can provide inspection for these as well—but typically this technology is used for protecting clients from threats on the Internet.

URL Filtering

URL filtering is strictly a client protection technology of UTM. It can be used for both providing policy enforcement, such as limiting access to what sites different users can access based on category and organizational policy, as well as to act as another layer of security by limiting access to potentially malicious sites. With the new Enhanced Web Filtering offered by Websense built into the SRX, we can also assign a reputation score to a site and base a decision on a score, similar to spam. This gives administrators a lot more flexibility, especially when it comes to using URL filtering as a security mechanism to limit exposure to potentially malicious sites.

Antispam

The antispam feature built into the SRX offers a lightweight antispam solution that can block spam based on source IP blacklists offered by Sophos. This isn't the most sophisticated form of antispam protection, but it does solve a simple use case that can be used to filter out well-known spam servers from forwarding spam into your email system.

Technically, this is a technology that operates on the server side, but if you think about it, it is geared toward protecting clients, even if indirectly.

Content Filtering

The content filtering functionality built into the SRX offers a simple mechanism to filter files from being transmitted across firewall boundaries. In the past, you would have to leverage either a standalone Data Leak Protection (DLP) solution or full-blown IPS with custom signatures to detect such communication. This is geared slightly more toward policy enforcement than it is for actual client-side security, but it can still be effective at enforcing some policies for exchanging different types of files. The content filtering solution shouldn't be considered to be a fully functioning DLP solution by any means. It is very lightweight, but it can simplify some of the operations from an administrative perspective and offer some quick fixes to limit certain data exchanges.

Antivirus + URL Filtering+ IPS?

So the question in your mind is probably why you need IPS if you have antivirus and URL filtering capabilities. Certainly, it depends. Remember that IPS is geared toward looking for exploits in network streams, both from a client-to-server perspective (client attacks the server) or from a server-to-client perspective (server is attacking the client). Antivirus is primarily interested in inspecting files, and these threats in the network stream (e.g., against an HTTP implementation) might not be bound within a file. Of course, with the new features like URI inspection with Sophos integration, the Sophos engine might be able to prevent you from accessing a malicious resource before the attacker has the opportunity to try to infect you.

URL filtering with the Enhanced Websense Filtering also offers some degree of overlap with antivirus when it comes to reputation filtering of URIs. It is never a bad idea to have two different databases for threat information. Of course, there can be performance concerns when it comes to running all of the technologies concurrently, and we go into more detail about the implementation and how to best leverage them later in this chapter. If performance is not a concern, these technologies can provide a nice overlap that can serve to protect your clients from Internet and network-based threats, and make it significantly more difficult for attackers to be successful.

URI versus URL? There is a difference, although many use them as one and the same. For a complete definition, Wikipedia has a nice write up at this link (*http://bit.ly/13AeF5z*).

I Have SRX Antivirus: Do I Need Desktop Antivirus?

The answer is a resounding yes. There are a few different reasons for this. First, not all potential malware threats might be transmitted over the network, or perhaps not always in band with the SRX. For instance, malware can be exchanged over USB devices and other portable media, or it could be exchanged internally through file shares and other media that might not pass through the SRX if it is placed at the perimeter. Another case might be for malware exchanged through encrypted protocols such as IPsec, or proprietary encryption that the SRX cannot inspect.

Another compelling reason for running desktop antivirus software is because it can dedicate a lot more resources toward inspecting traffic than a network-based device can, at least in real time. For instance, most desktop-based antivirus products have the ability to monitor the execution of an application and track the system calls and other behavioral activity. This simply isn't an easy task for a network-based antivirus product to perform. Additionally, many malware crimeware kits heavily obfuscate their programs, so searching for simple patterns can be very difficult to enforce because the malware can alter itself in subtle ways to try to evade these inspection techniques. Of course, the SRX relies on much more than simple pattern matching, but it cannot provide inline inspection with the same depth that a real-time system with execution analysis can. That's why new technologies like URI technologies are leveraged as another layer of protection, because it can offload the processing and leverage reputation to help make inspection decisions.

So if a network-based antivirus solution isn't as powerful as a desktop-based antivirus package, why should you even bother? The answer is because it's another layer, particularly if it's a different engine than what you are using on your desktops. Additionally, it can block threats at the perimeter, and it offers the ability to do some reputation analysis on the traffic as well, something that many desktop-based antivirus products do not do.

Not all Desktop AV products are created equal, as you might have experienced. They vary widely in effectiveness, stability, usability, central management, and so on. We are not seeking to endorse any anitvirus solutions in this book, but definitely have to do your research. There are third-party tests available like VB100, NSS Labs, and other independent analysis of various antivirus products and features available through your favorite search engine.

UTM Licensing

The UTM feature set all requires licenses with the exception of URL filtering with custom URLs only. This is because Juniper leverages third-party technology that is constantly updated to provide the most up-to-date inspection capabilities. Licenses can be purchased individually or as bundled licenses with other features like AppSecure/IPS. The licenses are term based and offered as per-year licenses.

If using an HA cluster, you must license each device in the cluster.

You can configure the features without the licenses, but they will not be active (or download their respective databases) until a valid license is installed. In terms of the licensing for the different features, you do need to purchase the specific solution license. For instance, there is a different antivirus license for Sophos, Kaspersky Full, and Kaspersky Lab, along with Websense or Websense Enhanced. You cannot purchase the Kaspersky engine and try to activate the Sophos feature set; they are specific to each feature.

Junos does offer a 30-day grace period after a license has expired before the functionality will no longer update.

Configuring Licensing

The UTM licenses are applied the same way that they are applied for other features. They must be done per chassis, using the `request system license add` command either adding the licenses from the terminal or loading the files to the SRX and installing them from the file.

```
{primary:node0}
root@SRX550-Node0> request system license add terminal
[Type ^D at a new line to end input,
 enter blank line between each license key]
JUNOS132562 aeaqea qmifgd embrgj aucmbq gi2qqb qcdo6o
            bpsna4 ukmsmc 6e7hxv vqapku laamzj zs534b
            wwmcqs l7nacd phmzv6 lblxol wwg62c ibqcwq
            ftq

add license succeded JUNOS132562

{primary:node0}
root@SRX550-Node0> show system license
License usage:
                          Licenses  Licenses Licenses Expiry
  Feature name                used installed   needed
  anti_spam_key_sbl             0         1         0 2013-09-01 00:00:00 UTC
  idp-sig                       0         1         0 2013-09-01 00:00:00 UTC
```

```
    dynamic-vpn                  0         2         0 permanent
    ax411-wlan-ap                0         2         0 permanent
    appid-sig                    0         1         0 2013-09-01 00:00:00 UTC
    av_key_sophos_engine         0         1         0 2013-09-01 00:00:00 UTC
    wf_key_websense_ewf          0         1         0 2013-09-01 00:00:00 UTC

  Licenses installed:
    License identifier: JUNOS132555
    License version: 2
    Valid for device: AL2012AA0011
    Features:
      av_key_sophos_engine - Anti Virus with Sophos Engine
        date-based, 2012-09-01 00:00:00 UTC - 2013-09-01 00:00:00 UTC

    License identifier: JUNOS132556
    License version: 2
    Valid for device: AL2012AA0011
    Features:
      wf_key_websense_ewf - Web Filtering EWF
        date-based, 2012-09-01 00:00:00 UTC - 2013-09-01 00:00:00 UTC

    License identifier: JUNOS132557
    License version: 2
    Valid for device: AL2012AA0011
    Features:
      anti_spam_key_sbl - Anti-Spam
        date-based, 2012-09-01 00:00:00 UTC - 2013-09-01 00:00:00 UTC

    License identifier: JUNOS132558
    License version: 2
    Valid for device: AL2012AA0011
    Features:
      idp-sig          - IDP Signature
        date-based, 2012-09-01 00:00:00 UTC - 2013-09-01 00:00:00 UTC

    License identifier: JUNOS132559
    License version: 2
    Valid for device: AL2012AA0011
    Features:
      appid-sig        - APPID Signature
        date-based, 2012-09-01 00:00:00 UTC - 2013-09-01 00:00:00 UTC
```

UTM Components

The UTM features implemented in the SRX follow similar concepts that apply across the different UTM technologies offered. There are feature profiles, custom objects, and UTM policies that can be configured in the SRX. We examine each one of these components, how they interact, and how they are leveraged in this section. We then delve into each UTM technology on a feature-by-feature basis.

From a high level, feature profiles specify how a feature is configured, and are applied to UTM policies, which then in turn are applied to firewall policies, as shown in Figure 14-1. Unlike IPS, which at the time of writing this book can only have one active policy at a time, UTM can have multiple active profiles. UTM profiles do not have their own seven-tuple rulebase like IPS does; it inherits the seven-tuple from the firewall rule in a sense. The power here comes especially with URL filtering, where you might want to have a separate configuration for different users or user groups. We examine how this functions in greater depth later in the chapter.

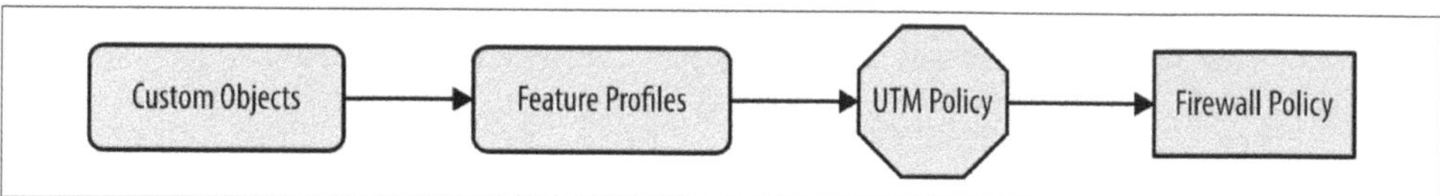

Figure 14-1. How UTM components are applied

Feature Profiles

Feature profiles specify how components of each should function. They are defined for each of the UTM technologies supported by the SRX. As mentioned, you are not limited to one single feature profile per platform. You can configure multiple feature profiles that can be applied through different UTM policies to firewall rules. Think of feature profiles as the actual rules and engine configuration for each feature. All UTM features share the fact that they have a feature profile, but each feature profile is different depending on the feature it supports, so we examine configuring feature profiles on a feature-by-feature basis.

Each UTM feature also has one or more predefined feature profiles that you can reference rather than having to create your own.

Custom Objects

Although the SRX supports predefined feature profiles that can handle most typical use cases, there are some cases where you might need to define your own objects, particularly for URL filtering, but also for antivirus and content filtering. This isn't quite as advanced as configuring IPS custom objects, which requires some knowledge of configuring regular expressions. Because custom objects can be configured in a feature-specific manner, we discuss implementing them on a feature-by-feature basis in the following sessions where applicable.

UTM Policies

UTM policies act as a logical container for the individual feature profiles. UTM profiles are then applied to specific traffic flows based on the classification of firewall rules in the security policy. This allows you to define separate UTM policies per firewall rule to differentiate the enforcement per firewall rule. You can only define one feature profile per feature (well, with a slight exception for antivirus, which can apply a feature profile per protocol) but you can combine the different UTM technologies per UTM policy, and even create different policies to be applied on a firewall rule-by-rule basis. Essentially, the firewall rulebase acts as the match criteria, and the UTM policy acts as action to be applied.

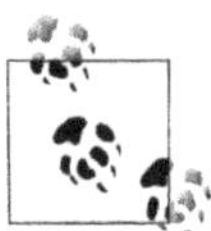

There are both predefined feature profiles and predefined UTM policies that can be leveraged in the system. In this chapter, we use only the predefined feature profiles for our UTM policies that are applied to the firewall rules rather than using the predefined UTM policies. The advantage here is that if using a predefined UTM policy, it is only for that one UTM technology (e.g., URL filtering or antivirus) and not both. By using the predefined feature profiles (which is a bulk of the config) you can mix and match the UTM technologies into a predefined UTM policy easily. If you only wanted to use one technology with the default option, you might be better off just referencing that predefined UTM policy from your firewall rule. You'll see how this is all done later in the chapter.

Application Proxy

To provide both advanced detection and also a better user experience, the UTM leverages a TCP application proxy for some of the components. This shouldn't require much consideration by the administrator, but it is important to understand that this technique is used. Application proxy allows the SRX to manipulate the traffic in certain ways. For instance, with antivirus it allows us to perform HTTP trickling to the client while the file is collected by the antivirus engine for inspection before fully transmitting it to the client. Additionally, it allows us to inject a redirect page for antivirus, URL filtering, and content filtering with HTTP when a threat or policy violation is detected. This allows for a better user experience than simply dropping a connection or sending a TCP Reset, which can result in strange application messages to the user. There are a few advanced options that can be configured to manipulate this, but it shouldn't be necessary for normal operation. We are bringing this to your attention because if you are troubleshooting an application issue for a protocol that antivirus supports, collecting PCAPs on client/server sides might yield some strange results if you weren't familiar with the fact that the SRX was leveraging this, although it should be entirely transparent to both users and applications.

Networking Requirements for UTM Features

Some of the UTM features either require Internet connections to get updates, or require Internet connections to function and perform lookups. For this to work, you need to have DNS, routing, and ideally NTP set up to be able to properly function. Of course, any upstream firewalls or access control must be opened up to allow the system to connect to the update servers. In each section we call out where this is required and what protocol is used.

Antivirus

The term UTM is somewhat synonymous with at least two technologies, antivirus and URL filtering, although the SRX offers more than just that. In this section, we examine the antivirus component of the SRX UTM offering, including how it functions, the various configuration and deployment options, and how it is applied.

Antivirus flavors in the SRX

The branch SRX Series offers three different types of antivirus engines at the time this book was written: Sophos, Kaspersky Full, and Kaspersky Express. The high-end SRX only supports Sophos antivirus. Why offer more than one solution, particularly from more than one vendor? Typically, customers will want to deploy a different antivirus system on their perimeter firewall than what they use on their internal hosts. Additionally, some customers have restrictions on purchasing security technologies from companies based in certain countries, so offering two vendors gives the customer the choice of which technology to deploy.

Sophos AV

Sophos AV was added to the branch SRX in the 11.1 release and is in beta for the high-end SRX at the time of writing this book. It offers two different inspection technologies to detect malware. First, it offers some traditional content inspection via hash checks and pattern matching that is common to most modern solutions. Second, it leverages a built-in reputation feed provided by Sophos that checks the requested resource URI to determine if it is a known source of malware. With the URI check, the firewall can actually block the user from downloading malware before the request even hits the server.

One important concept to understand with Sophos inspection is because there are millions of types of malware in the wild at any given time, along with billions (if not trillions) of potential URIs on the Internet, it is not feasible to load all of this information onto the SRX itself, particularly not the branch SRX. To keep the hardware requirements low while maximizing the inspection technology, the SRX leverages the Sophos cloud infrastructure to assist with the inspection. Assuming the default options are enabled, when a user requests access to a resource, the SRX will send an encoded message to the

Sophos cloud over DNS, which will have the resource information encoded in the DNS request. Sophos will then respond with an all-clear message or information about the suspected malware at that URI via a DNS reply. This process is displayed in Figure 14-2.

Assuming that the URI check does not yield any malware, the file transfer will continue. The SRX will keep track of the data as it's sent and continually hash chunks of it. These hashes will be sent to Sophos via encoded DNS requests, and Sophos can respond with a DNS reply that the file is a virus based on one or more chunks. Pattern matching for certain known malware can also occur in this process on the SRX itself.

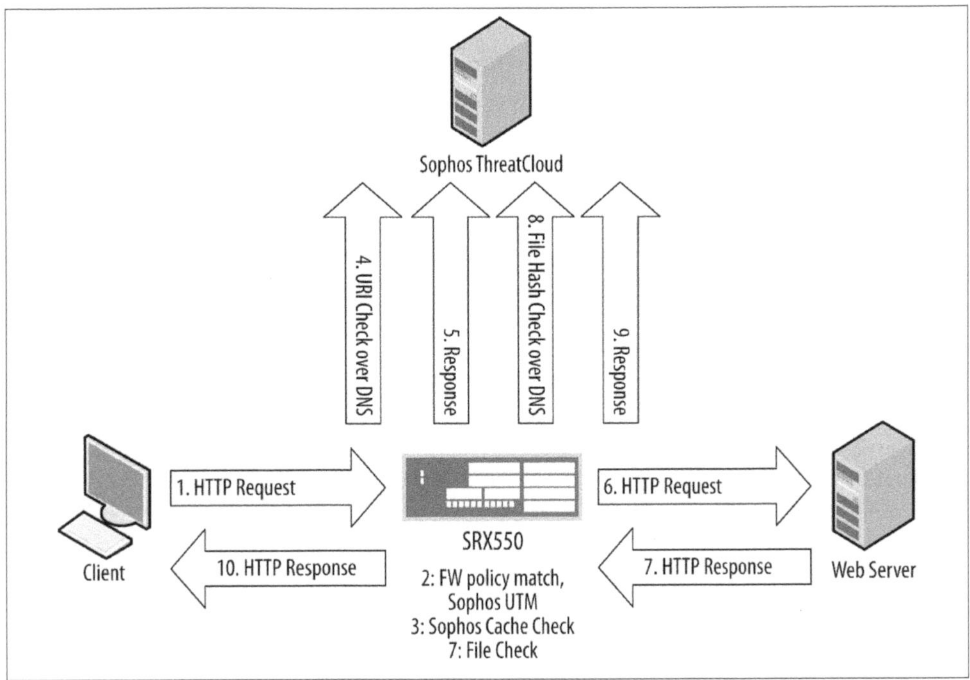

Figure 14-2. Sophos AV inspection diagram

This model allows a near unlimited malware database to be leveraged, while decreasing the cost of expensive pattern matching and execution analysis on the real-time traffic and provides much better security than most competitive AV platforms that load a limited database onto their devices. Additionally, with this solution, the SRX does not send any actual data payloads to the cloud, just the URI checks and the content hashes, so we don't have any latency hit or worries about forwarding actual private data through third parties. Of course, if you are leveraging the URI or content hash features, this does require that the SRX has access to the Sophos cloud via an Internet connection. You can run the Sophos feature without URI and content hash checks, but it won't be as effective.

The main challenge with malware detection with legacy antivirus technologies is that the actual malware can change rapidly, and often has mechanisms in it to alter itself on replication to avoid detection. Detecting these techniques with traditional malware engines is very difficult, particularly in network streams in real time. By leveraging the cloud to also provide some reputation analysis, the SRX can identify threats known to the Sophos database without trying to actually inspect the content and taking a large performance hit.

Implementing Sophos AV. In this section, we examine the various configuration options for enabling Sophos AV. We begin by looking at how to enable the default option, which doesn't require any additional configuration tuning, followed by some options that you may want to tweak.

Configuring Sophos with a default profile. In this example, we configure a UTM policy to use Sophos AV with the default profile configuration for both HTTP and FTP (download and upload). This UTM policy will be applied to an outbound firewall rule called Client-Outbound that will inspect any outbound traffic from the Internet-Client address-set to the Internet on TCP port 80 (HTTP) and TCP port 21/20 (FTP).

```
{primary:node0}[edit]
root@SRX550-Node0# edit security utm

{primary:node0}[edit security utm]
root@SRX550-Node0# set utm-policy Basic-UTM anti-virus http-profile junos-
sophos-av-defaults ftp upload-profile junos-sophos-av-default download-profile
junos-sophos-av-defaults

{primary:node0}[edit security utm]
root@SRX550-Node0# show
utm-policy Basic-UTM {
    anti-virus {
        http-profile junos-sophos-av-defaults;
        ftp {
            upload-profile junos-sophos-av-defaults;
            download-profile junos-sophos-av-defaults;
        }
    }
}


{primary:node0}[edit security utm]
root@SRX550-Node0# top

{primary:node0}[edit]
root@SRX550-Node0# edit security policies from zone trust to-zone untrust poli-
cy Client-Outbound
```

```
{primary:node0}[edit security policies from-zone trust to-zone untrust policy
Client-Outbound]
root@SRX550-Node0#  set  match  source-address  Internal-Clients  destination-
address any application [junos-http junos-ftp]

{primary:node0}[edit security policies from-zone trust to-zone untrust policy
Client-Outbound]
root@SRX550-Node0# set then permit application-services utm-policy Basic-UTM

{primary:node0}[edit security policies from-zone trust to-zone untrust policy
Client-Outbound]
root@SRX550-Node0# set then log session-close

{primary:node0}[edit security policies from-zone trust to-zone untrust policy
Client-Outbound]
root@SRX550-Node0# show
match {
    source-address Internal-Clients;
    destination-address any;
    application [ junos-http junos-ftp ];
}
then {
    permit {
        application-services {
            utm-policy Basic-UTM;
        }
    }
    log {
        session-close;
    }
}
```

As you can see from the preceding example, we are leveraging the predefined Sophos AV profile.

Default profile configuration. You can view the configuration of the default profiles next leveraging the hidden `show groups junos-defaults` command in configuration mode. This shows all hidden default configuration options that don't appear in the standard configuration with `show` commands.

```
{primary:node0}[edit]
root@SRX550-Node0# show groups junos-defaults security utm feature-profile anti-
virus

sophos-engine {
    pattern-update {
        url http://update.juniper-updates.net/SAV/;
        interval 1440;
    }
    profile junos-sophos-av-defaults {
```

```
        fallback-options {
            default log-and-permit;
            content-size log-and-permit;
            engine-not-ready log-and-permit;
            timeout log-and-permit;
            out-of-resources log-and-permit;
            too-many-requests log-and-permit;
        }
        scan-options {
            uri-check;
            content-size-limit 10000;
            timeout 180;
        }
        notification-options {
            virus-detection {
                type message;
                no-notify-mail-sender;
                custom-message "VIRUS WARNING";
            }
            fallback-block {
                type message;
                no-notify-mail-sender;
            }
        }
    }
```

Sophos AV feature profiles. For the most part, you will probably be able to leverage the standard Sophos AV profile when configuring antivirus, but your organizational security policies and user experience requirements might warrant a different configuration. In this section, we examine the various configuration options available for Sophos AV, then follow up with a bulk configuration of those options.

- Fallback options allows you to define the expected behavior when the engine cannot function as intended. There are several options and for each you can select whether you want to drop the session, permit the session and log it as bypass, or just permit the session bypassing AV.
  - The content size exceeds the size that the AV engine can handle.
  - The default is the action that should be taken when a condition is reached not specified by the other fallback settings.
  - Engine-not-ready occurs when the system is booting, if there is an issue with the engine (e.g., restarting), or if there is an issue contacting the update server to get a definition file when the system is not already running.
  - Out of resources can occur if there is not enough memory to process the session or if the maximum sessions for UTM are active.
  - Under a timeout, the engine cannot contact the Sophos cloud server when it is configured to do so.

- If there are too many outstanding requests, the engine cannot process them.

- Notification options are the options that can be used when a virus is detected or fallback is triggered for blocking or nonblocking.
  - Virus Detected: What should the SRX do if a virus is detected? This is for email. You can send a message to the sender, as well as altering the message or subject.
  - Fallback-Block: You can notify the sender and send an email to the administrator to let them know the message has been blocked.
  - Fallback-non-Block: You can notify the sender as well as the administrator that the message has been bypassed and not inspected.
- Scan-options are various options that can be configured when scanning content with Sophos, and this section allows you to define those.
  - Content Size Limit: You can define the maximum size of the inspected file before we would consider it to be too large per the Fallback-Options content size. This can be between 20 and 40,000 bytes (40 MB).
  - URI/NO-URL-Check: This option allows you to enable the URI check with Sophos rather than only relying on just payload inspection and not the reputation. Ideally, you should have this enabled so that you get much more security by leveraging reputation on top of just pattern matching.
  - Timeout: This is the timeout for how long it can inspect a file before considering it timed out.
  - Trickling allows the SRX to pass some traffic from the server to the client during inspection so that the client doesn't timeout the session while the antivirus engine reassembles the content being passed to it. There is a value from 0 to 600 seconds for how long the SRX should trickle a session before timing it out.
  - SXL Retry/Timeouts define what happens when the Sophos engine does not get a response from the Sophos server, how long the SRX should wait, and how many times it should retry before considering the connection down.
  - Pattern Update allows you to define a custom URL and frequency. Normally this is set once per day, which is fine, because as you know, the main part of the inspection occurs in real time in the cloud so more frequent updates aren't required. Normally you will not need to modify the URL unless specified by JTAC.

Configuring Sophos feature profile example. In this example, we configure a custom profile called Custom-Sophos-Profile, which alters the default content-size limits, and drops any session when the engine is out of resources or there are too many requests. This profile will then be applied to the UTM policy so that it will be active in our previous example.

```
{primary:node0}[edit]
root@SRX550-Node0# edit security utm feature-profile anti-virus sophos-engine
profile Custom-Sophos-Profile
root@SRX550-Node0# set fallback-options content-size block default log-and-
permit out-of-resources block too-many-requests block

{primary:node0}[edit security utm feature-profile anti-virus sophos-engine pro-
file Custom-Sophos-Profile]
root@SRX550-Node0# set scan-options content-size-limit 20000

{primary:node0}[edit security utm feature-profile anti-virus sophos-engine pro-
file Custom-Sophos-Profile]
root@SRX550-Node0# up 4

{primary:node0}[edit security utm]
root@SRX550-Node0# set utm-policy Basic-UTM anti-virus http-profile Custom-
Sophos-Profile ftp download-profile Custom-Sophos-Profile upload-profile Custom-
Sophos-Profile

{primary:node0}[edit security utm]
root@SRX550-Node0# show
feature-profile {
    anti-virus {
        sophos-engine {
            profile Custom-Sophos-Profile {
                fallback-options {
                    default log-and-permit;
                    content-size block;
                    out-of-resources block;
                    too-many-requests block;
                }
                scan-options {
                    content-size-limit 20000;
                }
            }
        }
    }
}
utm-policy Basic-UTM {
    anti-virus {
        http-profile Custom-Sophos-Profile;
        ftp {
            upload-profile Custom-Sophos-Profile;
            download-profile Custom-Sophos-Profile;
        }
    }
}
```

Kaspersky Full AV

Kaspersky Full AV has been offered on the SRX since Junos 9.6. It differs from Sophos because it relies entirely on built-in content inspection via pattern matching and some execution analysis and some file heuristics. Kaspersky doesn't need to access the Internet other than to get the pattern updates from Kaspersky. In this section, we demonstrate how Kaspersky functions, and the configuration options available for this mode. Kaspersky is essentially the same as Sophos for notification options and trickling, so we won't explore those items here, but instead focus on the fallback options and scan options, which have a few additional options that differ from Sophos.

- Fallback options define the action that should be taken (block, log and permit, or just permit) when a condition is met as defined here.
  - Content Size: Defines what action to take when the content size is too large to inspect as defined by the scan options.
  - Corrupt File: Defines what action to take when the file being transmitted is corrupted and cannot be inspected.
  - Decompress Layer: Kaspersky can decompress payloads such as ZIP files to inspect the contents within. This setting defines what happens when the number of compressed layers exceeds the defined supported number.
  - Default: What default action to take if a condition not specified by other fallback options occurs.
  - Engine Not Ready: What action to take if the engine is not ready to scan the traffic.
  - Out of Resources: This defines what action to take when the SRX doesn't have enough memory to inspect the payload.
  - Password File: What action to take when the file is password protected and cannot be inspected.
  - Timeout: Defines what happens when the scan timeout is reached.
  - Too Many Requests: What happens when the SRX has too many outstanding requests.
- Scan options define the antivirus scanner configuration and what values should be enforced for various limits (as defined by the fallback options).
  - Content Size Limit: Like the Sophos limit, this defines how large of a file to inspect, from 20 B to 40 MB.
  - Decompress Layer Limit: Allows the SRX to scan up to eight levels of compression.
  - No/Intelligent Prescreening: This is a feature that allows the SRX to use some heuristics to attempt to determine if the content is suspicious before requiring full inspection, which has a much greater performance impact.
  - Scan-Extension: Defines what file extensions should be inspected by the SRX. There is a default file list called junos-default-extension.

— Scan Mode: Allows you to define whether to always scan files or by the extension list only.

— Timeout: Defines the scanning timeout.

- Pattern update allows you to specify the URL, proxy settings (if applicable), and frequency information to download the new database.

Configuring Kaspersky with the default profile. In this example, we configure UTM to use Kaspersky as the antivirus engine using the default feature profile. This will be applied to the Basic-UTM policy that will be applied to the Client-Outbound firewall rule, which allows the UTM to inspect HTTP and FTP on ports TCP 80 and 21/20, respectively.

```
{primary:node0}[edit security utm]
root@SRX550-Node0# set utm-policy Basic-UTM anti-virus http-profile junos-av-defaults ftp download-profile junos-av-defaults upload-profile junos-av-defaults

{primary:node0}[edit security utm]
root@SRX550-Node0# show
utm-policy Basic-UTM {
    anti-virus {
        http-profile junos-av-defaults;
        ftp {
            upload-profile junos-av-defaults;
            download-profile junos-av-defaults;
        }
    }
}


{primary:node0}[edit security utm]
root@SRX550-Node0# top

{primary:node0}[edit]
root@SRX550-Node0# edit security policies from zone trust to-zone untrust poli-
cy Client-Outbound

{primary:node0}[edit security policies from-zone trust to-zone untrust policy
Client-Outbound]
root@SRX550-Node0# set match source-address Internal-Clients destination-
address any application [junos-http junos-ftp]

{primary:node0}[edit security policies from-zone trust to-zone untrust policy
Client-Outbound]
root@SRX550-Node0# set then permit application-services utm-policy Basic-UTM

{primary:node0}[edit security policies from-zone trust to-zone untrust policy
Client-Outbound]
root@SRX550-Node0# set then log session-close

{primary:node0}[edit security policies from-zone trust to-zone untrust policy
```

```
Client-Outbound]
root@SRX550-Node0# show
match {
    source-address Internal-Clients;
    destination-address any;
    application [ junos-http junos-ftp ];
}
then {
    permit {
        application-services {
            utm-policy Basic-UTM;
        }
    }
    log {
        session-close;
    }
}
```

Default Kaspersky profile configuration. For your reference, here is the default Kaspersky Full AV configuration.

```
{primary:node0}[edit]
root@SRX550-Node0# show groups junos-defaults security utm feature-profile anti-
virus
kaspersky-lab-engine {
    pattern-update {
        url http://update.juniper-updates.net/AV/SRX550/;
        interval 60;
    }
    profile junos-av-defaults {
        fallback-options {
            default log-and-permit;
            corrupt-file log-and-permit;
            password-file log-and-permit;
            decompress-layer log-and-permit;
            content-size log-and-permit;
            engine-not-ready log-and-permit;
            timeout log-and-permit;
            out-of-resources log-and-permit;
            too-many-requests log-and-permit;
        }
        scan-options {
            intelligent-prescreening;
            scan-mode all;
            content-size-limit 10000;
            timeout 180;
            decompress-layer-limit 2;
        }
        notification-options {
            virus-detection {
                type message;
                no-notify-mail-sender;
```

```
                custom-message "VIRUS WARNING";
            }
            fallback-block {
                type message;
                no-notify-mail-sender;
            }
        }
    }
}
```

Configuring Kaspersky AV scanning and fallback options. In this section, we configure the Kaspersky AV engine to drop antivirus files when the decompression limit is reached or corrupt or password-protected files are detected, but all other conditions should be permitted with logging. The decompression limit should be set to 2, scan all extensions, and content length to 20 MB.

```
{primary:node0}[edit]
root@SRX550-Node0# edit security utm feature-profile anti-virus kaspersky-lab-
engine profile Custom-Kaspersky-Profile

{primary:node0}[edit  security  utm  feature-profile  anti-virus  kaspersky-lab-
en-
gin
                                                        e profile Custom-Kaspersky-
Profile]
root@SRX550-Node0# set scan-options decompress-layer-limit 2 content-size-limit
20 scan-mode all

root@SRX550-Node0# set fallback-options default log-and-permit decompress-layer
block corrupt-file block password-file block

{primary:node0}[edit  security  utm  feature-profile  anti-virus  kaspersky-lab-
en-
gin
                                                        e profile Custom-Kaspersky-
Profile]
root@SRX550-Node0# show
fallback-options {
    default log-and-permit;
    corrupt-file block;
    password-file block;
    decompress-layer block;
}
scan-options {
    scan-mode all;
    content-size-limit 20;
    decompress-layer-limit 2;
}
```

Express AV

The SRX also offers a third scanning option called the Express AV engine. This is actually a version provided by Kaspersky that has a stripped-down function set to detect malware in a lightweight model. It isn't as good as the full Kaspersky or Sophos but is lighter from a performance perspective.

In this section, we just make a simple example of using the Express AV profile and apply it to our configuration profile as is for HTTP and FTP upload/download for our Client-Outbound rule. Express AV has the same profile options as Sophos AV, so you can reference that example for configuring the Sophos options.

```
 {primary:node0}[edit security utm]
root@SRX550-Node0# set utm-policy Basic-UTM anti-virus http-profile junos-eav-
defaults  ftp  download-profile  junos-eav-defaults  upload-profile  junos-eav-
defaults

{primary:node0}[edit security utm]
root@SRX550-Node0# show
utm-policy Basic-UTM {
    anti-virus {
        http-profile junos-eav-defaults;
        ftp {
            upload-profile junos-eav-defaults;
            download-profile junos-eav-defaults;
        }
    }
}

{primary:node0}[edit security utm]
root@SRX550-Node0# top

{primary:node0}[edit]
root@SRX550-Node0# edit security policies from zone trust to-zone untrust poli-
cy Client-Outbound

{primary:node0}[edit security policies from-zone trust to-zone untrust policy
Client-Outbound]
root@SRX550-Node0#  set  match  source-address  Internal-Clients  destination-
address any application [junos-http junos-ftp]

{primary:node0}[edit security policies from-zone trust to-zone untrust policy
Client-Outbound]
root@SRX550-Node0# set then permit application-services utm-policy Basic-UTM

{primary:node0}[edit security policies from-zone trust to-zone untrust policy
Client-Outbound]
root@SRX550-Node0# set then log session-close

{primary:node0}[edit security policies from-zone trust to-zone untrust policy
Client-Outbound]
root@SRX550-Node0# show
```

```
match {
    source-address Internal-Clients;
    destination-address any;
    application [ junos-http junos-ftp ];
}
then {
    permit {
        application-services {
            utm-policy Basic-UTM;
        }
    }
    log {
        session-close;
    }
}
```

Default Express AV profile. Here is a copy of the default express AV configuration for your reference if you are using this feature.

```
{primary:node0}[edit]
root@SRX550-Node0# show groups junos-defaults security utm feature-profile anti-
virus
juniper-express-engine {
    pattern-update {
        url http://update.juniper-updates.net/EAV/SRX550/;
        interval 1440;
    }
    profile junos-eav-defaults {
        fallback-options {
            default log-and-permit;
            content-size log-and-permit;
            engine-not-ready log-and-permit;
            timeout log-and-permit;
            out-of-resources log-and-permit;
            too-many-requests log-and-permit;
        }
        scan-options {
            intelligent-prescreening;
            content-size-limit 10000;
            timeout 180;
        }
        notification-options {
            virus-detection {
                type message;
                no-notify-mail-sender;
                custom-message "VIRUS WARNING";
            }
            fallback-block {
                type message;
                no-notify-mail-sender;
            }
        }
```

```
        }
    }
    }
```

Which AV to Choose?

Now that we've gone through all of the available AV options, you're probably asking yourself which one is right for you. We can't give the same answer for all cases, so here are some guidelines for and against each solution.

- Sophos
  - Pros: Very good detection, particularly with the URI checks. Medium in terms of performance impact of the three solutions, database is unlimited because it leverages the Sophos cloud. Can detect obfuscated malware.
  - Cons: Requires an active Internet connection to query Sophos cloud for URI checks, although this can be disabled.
  - Other: Based in the UK.
- Kaspersky Full
  - Pros: Full antivirus capabilities built in, ability to inspect compressed content, good detection capabilities for content loaded on device, doesn't require URI information to be sent, but does require Internet connection for downloads.
  - Cons: No reputation feed for URI, most impactful from a performance perspective, database limited by device memory, limited detection for obfuscated attacks if not known by patterns or heuristics.
  - Other: Based in Russia.
- Kaspersky Express AV
  - Pros: Lightest weight in terms of performance, doesn't require URI information to be sent, but does require Internet connection for downloads.
  - Cons: No reputation feed, pattern matching only, limited ability to detect any obfuscation or compressed malware
  - Other: Based in Russia.

URL Filtering

The URL filtering feature set in the SRX provides two desirable functions for network administrators. The first is obvious, which is to be able to control what web resources a user can access based on category or specific whitelists or blacklists, and the second is that it offers an additional layer of security by preventing users going to potentially malicious sites (if configured to do so). In this section, we examine the URL filtering feature set, the various flavors offered, and how they are implemented.

At the time of writing this book, URL filtering on the high-end SRX was in beta. The high-end SRX will only support Websense Enhanced URL filtering, which is the most effective. Alternatively, you can use filter-based forwarding to redirect traffic to other third-party servers.

URL filtering flavors

There are essentially four different flavors of URL filtering on the SRX.

Local
: Allows the administrator to define a custom whitelist or blacklist of URLs that are to be enforced by the SRX. This feature doesn't require a license because the administrator is responsible for defining his own list.

Websense Redirect
: This is useful when you have an existing Websense standalone server and you want the firewall to redirect the HTTP requests through the Websense server rather than out to the Internet for policy validation. There is a special protocol that the SRX understands that can redirect to the Websense server. It doesn't redirect all of the traffic, just the URL to which the Websense server will respond with the classification. This classification is then used to determine what action should be taken based on the URL filtering policy on the SRX. This feature does not require a license on the SRX, but does require that you have a standalone Websense server that is licensed with Websense accordingly.

Surfcontrol (Websense)
: This is called Surfcontrol because that was the original name before Websense purchased Surfcontrol. This option leverages the Websense cloud to send requests encoded in UDP port 9020 from the SRX to get the classification of the URL. This classification is then used to determine what action should be taken based on the URL filtering policy on the SRX.

Websense Enhanced
: This is a new feature as of Junos 11.4r1 that leverages the Websense cloud in a similar way as the older Surfcontrol option, but also offers additional categorization and a reputation-based feed that can identify malicious sites and provide a score that can be used to leverage policy. Finally, Websense Enhanced can also force well-known search engines like Google only to use Safe Searches, which won't return results for known malicious sites.

Just like antivirus, you can only have one URL filtering solution active at a time, not multiple types (although you can use custom URL blacklists and whitelists). You must apply the specific license for Surfcontrol or Websense Enhanced, including per cluster member.

Configuring the URL filtering with default profiles. You can leverage the default profiles in the device to simply activate the features without creating a full customized option. In this example, we show how to enable Websense Enhanced (although the same method is used for enabling any of the profiles). This profile is then applied to the Client-Outbound rule.

```
{primary:node0}[edit security utm]
root@SRX550-Node0# set utm-policy Basic-UTM web-filtering http-profile ?
Possible completions:
  <http-profile>       Web-filtering HTTP profile
    junos-wf-cpa-default   [security utm feature-profile web-filtering surf-
control-integrated profile]
    junos-wf-enhanced-default   [security utm feature-profile web-filtering
juniper-enhanced profile]
   junos-wf-local-default  [security utm feature-profile web-filtering juniper-
local profile]
    junos-wf-websense-default   [security utm feature-profile web-filtering
websense-redirect profile]
{primary:node0}[edit security utm]
root@SRX550-Node0# set utm-policy Basic-UTM web-filtering http-profile junos-wf-
enhanced-default

{primary:node0}[edit security utm]
root@SRX550-Node0# show
utm-policy Basic-UTM {
    web-filtering {
        http-profile junos-wf-enhanced-default;
    }
}

{primary:node0}[edit security utm]
root@SRX550-Node0# top

{primary:node0}[edit]
root@SRX550-Node0# edit security policies from zone trust to-zone untrust poli-
cy Client-Outbound

{primary:node0}[edit security policies from-zone trust to-zone untrust policy
Client-Outbound]
root@SRX550-Node0#  set  match  source-address  Internal-Clients  destination-
address any application [junos-http junos-ftp]

{primary:node0}[edit security policies from-zone trust to-zone untrust policy
Client-Outbound]
```

```
root@SRX550-Node0# set then permit application-services utm-policy Basic-UTM

{primary:node0}[edit security policies from-zone trust to-zone untrust policy
Client-Outbound]
root@SRX550-Node0# set then log session-close

{primary:node0}[edit security policies from-zone trust to-zone untrust policy
Client-Outbound]
root@SRX550-Node0# show
match {
    source-address Internal-Clients;
    destination-address any;
    application [ junos-http junos-ftp ];
}
then {
    permit {
        application-services {
            utm-policy Basic-UTM;
        }
    }
    log {
        session-close;
    }
}
```

Websense Enhanced filtering

Starting in Junos 11.4r1, the branch SRX supports the Websense Enhanced web filtering. The enhanced web filtering adds some additional technologies on top of the previous generation of Surfcontrol Web filtering. First, the category list is greatly expanded so it is more granular. Next, HTTPS is supported by the destination IP for lookups. Websense has integrated a reputation score for the website that is used to determine the risk of the site to deliver malware to clients. Finally, this also has the ability to turn on Safe Searching for search engines for HTTP searches (see Figure 14-3).

The Enhanced Web filtering functions in a similar way to the Surfcontrol Integrated in that it relies on the Websense Threatseeker cloud to perform the lookup and provide a response. The advantage here is that the device is not limited by the size of the available memory on the device, but instead can leverage the full Websense Threatseeker database which is updated in real time. Additionally, the full traffic does not need to be sent, just the header lookup. This feature also leverages a cache so that it does not need to perform a check every time the resource is looked up, but only if it is not in a blacklist or whitelist or in the cache. Most of the components for this feature are the same as the Surfcontrol Integrated, besides additional categories, Safe Search, and the reputation scores. Here is a breakdown of the features in the Websense Enhanced engine:

Cache
: The cache allows you to define how large the cache should be and how long to maintain entries in the cache before triggering another lookup.

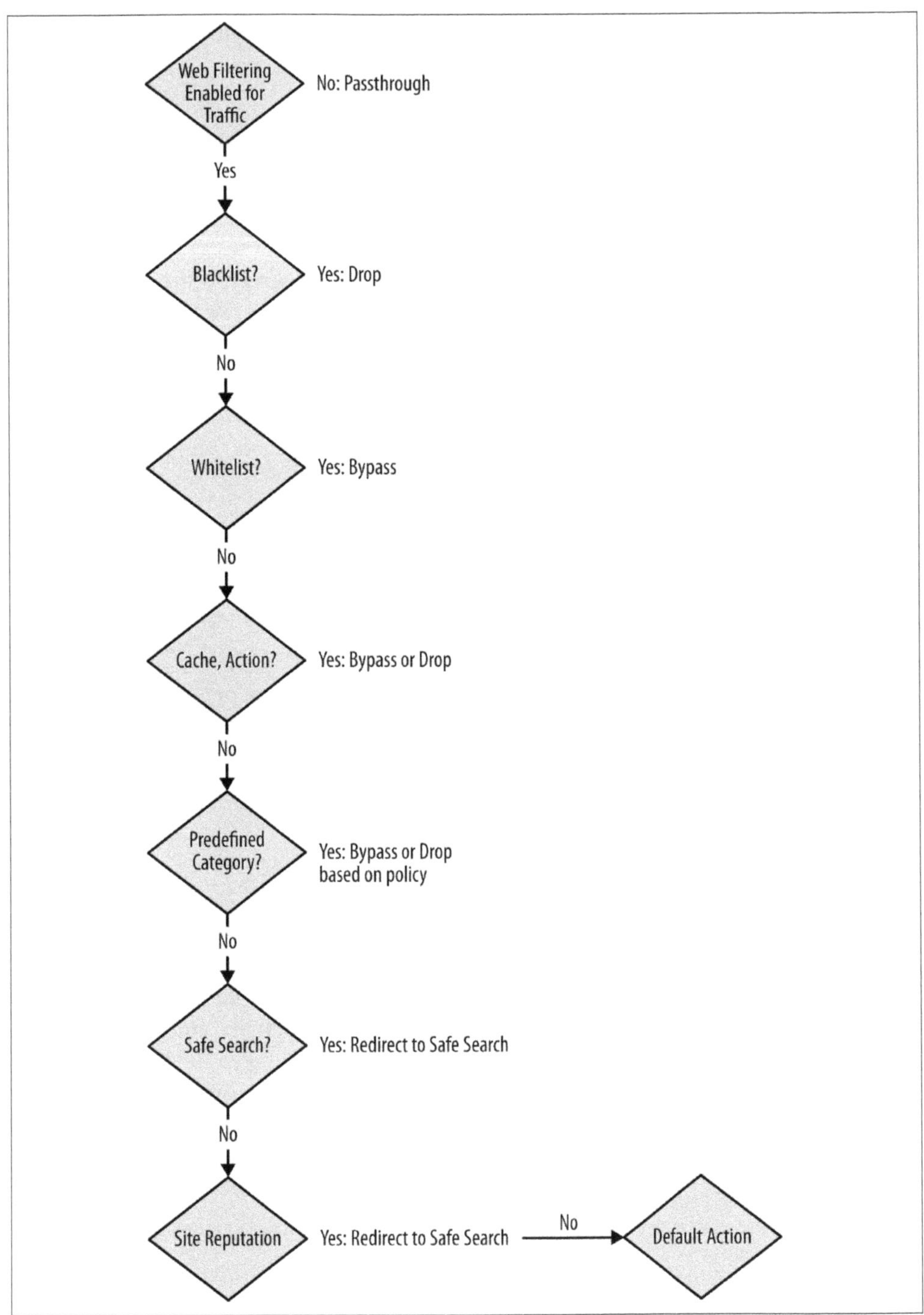

Figure 14-3. Websense Enhanced flowchart

Server

This allows you to define a different server to use in the Threatseeker cloud. In normal circumstances you will not need to use this option.

Profile

The profile defines the device configuration for this feature. There are several options that are available to configure, as shown here:

Block Message

This allows you to define an external URL to redirect users to when they are in violation of a policy rather than having them redirect to the internal UTM page on the SRX. The advantage here is that you are not restricted on what you can do on the external server, which gives you much better flexibility to provide a better user experience.

Category

This defines the category to action mapping (e.g., *Gambling* should be blocked).

Custom Block Message

Allows you to specify a custom block message to the clients.

Default

This is the action that should be taken when the URL doesn't have a category.

No-Safe-Search

Safe Search is on by default, and this turns it off for the profile.

Site Reputation Action

This provides a mapping between the site's reputation and the action (e.g., *Fairly-Safe* should be blocked).

Timeout

This is the value that should be applied to determine if the request to Websense has been timed out.

Fallback Settings

Provides the ability to define what action should be taken for any unknown condition (default), too many requests, server connectivity, and timeout values.

Configuring Websense Enhanced default profile. In this example, we simply enable the Juniper Websense Default Enhanced profile to our Basic-UTM profile, which is applied to the Client-Outbound firewall rule.

```
{primary:node0}[edit security utm]
root@SRX550-Node0# set utm-policy Basic-UTM web-filtering http-profile junos-wf-
enhanced-default

utm-policy Basic-UTM {
    web-filtering {
```

```
            http-profile junos-wf-enhanced-default;
        }
    }
    {primary:node0}[edit security utm]
    root@SRX550-Node0# top

    {primary:node0}[edit]
    root@SRX550-Node0# edit security policies from zone trust to-zone untrust poli-
    cy Client-Outbound

    {primary:node0}[edit security policies from-zone trust to-zone untrust policy
    Client-Outbound]
    root@SRX550-Node0#  set  match  source-address  Internal-Clients  destination-
    address any application [junos-http junos-ftp]

    {primary:node0}[edit security policies from-zone trust to-zone untrust policy
    Client-Outbound]
    root@SRX550-Node0# set then permit application-services utm-policy Basic-UTM

    {primary:node0}[edit security policies from-zone trust to-zone untrust policy
    Client-Outbound]
    root@SRX550-Node0# set then log session-close

    {primary:node0}[edit security policies from-zone trust to-zone untrust policy
    Client-Outbound]
    root@SRX550-Node0# show
    match {
        source-address Internal-Clients;
        destination-address any;
        application [ junos-http junos-ftp ];
    }
    then {
        permit {
            application-services {
                utm-policy Basic-UTM;
            }
        }
        log {
            session-close;
        }
    }
```

Default Websense Enhanced profile. This output is the default configuration for the Websense Enhanced predefined profile.

```
    {primary:node0}[edit]
    root@SRX550-Node0# show groups junos-defaults security utm web-filtering
            juniper-enhanced {
                server {
                    host rp.cloud.threatseeker.com;
                    port 80;
                }
```

```
profile junos-wf-enhanced-default {
    category {
        Enhanced_Adult_Material {
            action block;
        }
        Enhanced_Gambling {
            action block;
        }
        Enhanced_Games {
            action block;
        }
        Enhanced_Illegal_or_Questionable {
            action block;
        }
        Enhanced_Tasteless {
            action block;
        }
        Enhanced_Violence {
            action block;
        }
        Enhanced_Weapons {
            action block;
        }
        Enhanced_Militancy_and_Extremist {
            action block;
        }
        Enhanced_Racism_and_Hate {
            action block;
        }
        Enhanced_Advertisements {
            action block;
        }
        Enhanced_Nudity {
            action block;
        }
        Enhanced_Adult_Content {
            action block;
        }
        Enhanced_Sex {
            action block;
        }
        Enhanced_Hacking {
            action block;
        }
        Enhanced_Personals_and_Dating {
            action block;
        }
        Enhanced_Alcohol_and_Tobacco {
            action block;
        }
        Enhanced_Abused_Drugs {
            action block;
```

```
                        }
                        Enhanced_Marijuana {
                            action block;
                        }
                        Enhanced_Malicious_Web_Sites {
                            action block;
                        }
                        Enhanced_Spyware {
                            action block;
                        }
                        Enhanced_Phishing_and_Other_Frauds {
                            action block;
                        }
                        Enhanced_Keyloggers {
                            action block;
                        }
                        Enhanced_Emerging_Exploits {
                            action block;
                        }
                        Enhanced_Potentially_Damaging_Content {
                            action block;
                        }
                        Enhanced_Malicious_Embedded_Link {
                            action block;
                        }
                        Enhanced_Malicious_Embedded_iFrame {
                            action block;
                        }
                        Enhanced_Suspicious_Embedded_Link {
                            action block;
                        }
                    }
                    default log-and-permit;
                       custom-block-message "Juniper Web Filtering has been set to
block this site.";
                    fallback-settings {
                        default log-and-permit;
                        server-connectivity log-and-permit;
                        timeout log-and-permit;
                        too-many-requests log-and-permit;
                    }
                }
            }
        }
```

Configuring a custom Websense Enhanced profile. In this example, we create our own feature profile for the Websense Enhanced options to provide greater granularity for our profile. Our example is configured as follows:

- Create our own feature profile called Websense-Enhanced.

- It should have a cache timeout of 300 minutes.
- Block Enhanced_Tasteless and Enhanced_Political_Organizations.
- Set the default to permit and the timeout to four seconds.
- Configure very safe reputations as accepted, and all others to block.
- Block all fallback settings.

```
{primary:node0}[edit security utm]
root@SRX550-Node0# set feature-profile web-filtering juniper-enhanced profile
Websense-Enhanced category Enhanced_Tasteless action block

{primary:node0}[edit security utm]
root@SRX550-Node0#  set  feature-profile  Websense-Enhanced  site-reputation-
action fairly-safe block harmful block moderately-safe block suspicious block
very-safe permit

{primary:node0}[edit security utm]
root@SRX550-Node0# set profile Websense-Enhanced default permit timeout 4
fallback-settings default block server-connectivity block timeout block too-
many-requests block

{primary:node0}[edit security utm]
root@SRX550-Node0# set feature-profile web-filtering type juniper-enhanced


{primary:node0}[edit security utm]
root@SRX550-Node0# set feature-profile web-filtering juniper-enhanced cache
timeout 300

{primary:node0}[edit security utm]
root@SRX550-Node0#  set  utm-policy  Basic-UTM  web-filtering  http-profile
Websense-Enhanced

{primary:node0}[edit security utm]
root@SRX550-Node0# show
feature-profile {
    web-filtering {
        type juniper-enhanced;
        juniper-enhanced {
            cache {
                timeout 300;
            }
            profile Websense-Enhanced {
                category {
                    Enhanced_Political_Organizations {
                        action block;
                    }
                    Enhanced_Tasteless {
                        action block;
                    }
                }
```

```
                site-reputation-action {
                    very-safe permit;
                    moderately-safe block;
                    fairly-safe block;
                    suspicious block;
                    harmful block;
                }
                default permit;
                fallback-settings {
                    default block;
                    server-connectivity block;
                    timeout block;
                    too-many-requests block;
                }
                timeout 4;
            }
        }
    }
}
utm-policy Basic-UTM {
    web-filtering {
        http-profile Websense-Enhanced;
    }
}
```

Surfcontrol/Websense Integrated URL filtering

The Surfcontrol/Websense "Integrated" model URL filtering solution leverages the Surfcontrol/Websense cloud to perform the local lookups on the SRX. Because the URL database has entries in the billions, there is not a good way to store this entire database on the SRX itself, particularly on the branch SRX platforms, which are more limited with memory. Instead, the SRX performs a lookup by sending the request to the Websense cloud with the URL in the request and awaits an answer back on the categorization of the website. This categorization is then used in the policy lookup on the SRX itself to determine what action should be taken for that category. For this model, there is support for both predefined URL filtering profiles, as well as ones that you can define manually for each category to action mapping.

In this section, we discuss the various options for configuring Integrated Surfcontrol/ Websense and sample configurations. The following are components under the Surfcontrol/ Websense integrated feature profile:

Cache
: The SRX leverages a cache of URLs for some period of time so that the next time the resource is requested it doesn't need to go to the Surfcontrol/Websense server for a lookup. Under this option you can define how large the cache is, along with how long the timeout should be for a cached entry.

Server

This allows you to define a nondefault Surfcontrol server for this lookup. This is not usually necessary unless you're doing some sort of troubleshooting or beta testing. You would be instructed to connect to this specific server.

Profile

The profile defines the bulk of the engine configuration that you would be concerned with.

Categories

There are numerous categories, each of which can be associated with an action to permit or block the request. The default list was shown earlier in this chapter. Remember that there is a difference between the Surfcontrol and the Websense Enhanced list, so your categories will be specific to the feature you're using. If you are creating your own profiles, then you would need to define the categories and actions that should be taken.

Custom Block Message

This is the message that you want to appear for the user if they are blocked.

Default

This is the action that should be taken for an undefined URL that doesn't have an action.

Timeout

This is how long the SRX should wait before considering the Surfcontrol server to be unavailable.

Fallback options

The fallback options define what action should be taken when a defined condition occurs:

Default

What action to take on all undefined issues.

Timeout

What action to take if the request times out.

Server Connectivity

What action to take if the server connection is considered down (slightly different than timeout, which is for an individual request).

Too Many Requests

The action to take when SRX has too many requests queued up.

Configuring Surfcontrol Integrated with default profile. This example is very straightforward. We simply enable the Surfcontrol default profile with our Basic-UTM profile.

This leverages the default options, and is supported because we don't need to specify any server information because it is configured by default.

```
{primary:node0}[edit security utm]
root@SRX550-Node0# set utm-policy Basic-UTM web-filtering http-profile junos-wf-
cpa-default

{primary:node0}[edit security utm]
root@SRX550-Node0# show
utm-policy Basic-UTM {
    web-filtering {
        http-profile junos-wf-cpa-default;
    }
}

{primary:node0}[edit security utm]
root@SRX550-Node0# top

{primary:node0}[edit]
root@SRX550-Node0# edit security policies from zone trust to-zone untrust poli-
cy Client-Outbound

{primary:node0}[edit security policies from-zone trust to-zone untrust policy
Client-Outbound]
root@SRX550-Node0#  set  match  source-address  Internal-Clients  destination-
address any application [junos-http junos-ftp]

{primary:node0}[edit security policies from-zone trust to-zone untrust policy
Client-Outbound]
root@SRX550-Node0# set then permit application-services utm-policy Basic-UTM

{primary:node0}[edit security policies from-zone trust to-zone untrust policy
Client-Outbound]
root@SRX550-Node0# set then log session-close

{primary:node0}[edit security policies from-zone trust to-zone untrust policy
Client-Outbound]
root@SRX550-Node0# show
match {
    source-address Internal-Clients;
    destination-address any;
    application [ junos-http junos-ftp ];
}
then {
    permit {
        application-services {
            utm-policy Basic-UTM;
        }
    }
    log {
        session-close;
```

```
        }
    }
```

Default Surfcontrol/Websense profile configuration.

```
    {primary:node0}[edit]
    root@SRX550-Node0# show groups junos-defaults security utm web-filtering
    web-filtering {
            surf-control-integrated {
                server {
                    host cpa.surfcpa.com;
                    port 9020;
                }
                profile junos-wf-cpa-default {
                    category {
                        Adult_Sexually_Explicit {
                            action block;
                        }
                        Advertisements {
                            action block;
                        }
                        Arts_Entertainment {
                            action permit;
                        }
                        Chat {
                            action permit;
                        }
                        Computing_Internet {
                            action permit;
                        }
                        Criminal_Skills {
                            action block;
                        }
                        Drugs_Alcohol_Tobacco {
                            action block;
                        }
                        Education {
                            action permit;
                        }
                        Finance_Investment {
                            action permit;
                        }
                        Food_Drink {
                            action permit;
                        }
                        Gambling {
                            action block;
                        }
                        Games {
                            action block;
                        }
                        Glamour_Intimate_Apparel {
                            action permit;
```

```
}
Government_Politics {
    action permit;
}
Hacking {
    action block;
}
Hate_Speech {
    action block;
}
Health_Medicine {
    action permit;
}
Hobbies_Recreation {
    action permit;
}
Hosting_Sites {
    action permit;
}
Job_Search_Career_Development {
    action permit;
}
Kids_Sites {
    action permit;
}
Lifestyle_Culture {
    action permit;
}
Motor_Vehicles {
    action permit;
}
News {
    action permit;
}
Personals_Dating {
    action block;
}
Photo_Searches {
    action permit;
}
Real_Estate {
    action permit;
}
Reference {
    action permit;
}
Religion {
    action permit;
}
Remote_Proxies {
    action block;
}
```

```
                    Sex_Education {
                        action block;
                    }
                    Search_Engines {
                        action permit;
                    }
                    Shopping {
                        action permit;
                    }
                    Sports {
                        action permit;
                    }
                    Streaming_Media {
                        action permit;
                    }
                    Travel {
                        action permit;
                    }
                    Usenet_News {
                        action permit;
                    }
                    Violence {
                        action block;
                    }
                    Weapons {
                        action block;
                    }
                    Web_based_Email {
                        action permit;
                    }
                }
                default log-and-permit;
                    custom-block-message "Juniper Web Filtering has been set to
block this site.";
                fallback-settings {
                    default log-and-permit;
                    server-connectivity log-and-permit;
                    timeout log-and-permit;
                    too-many-requests log-and-permit;
                }
            }
        }
}
```

Configuring Surfcontrol/Websense Integrated options. In this example, we configure an example using some nondefault settings for Websense/Surfcontrol to alter the behavior of the URL filter as follows:

- Create a profile called Block-Hacking that blocks access to Adult Sexually Explicit and Remote proxies.

- The SRX should fail to open if it loses connection to the server or a request times out, but drop traffic when too many requests exist.
- Set the cache to 120-minute timeouts.
- Apply it to Basic-UTM policy.

```
{primary:node0}[edit security utm]
root@SRX550-Node0# set feature-profile web-filtering surf-control-integrated
profile Integrated-Websense category Audult_Sexually_Explicit action block

{primary:node0}[edit security utm]
root@SRX550-Node0# set feature-profile web-filtering surf-control-integrated
profile Integrated-Websense category Remote_Proxies action block

{primary:node0}[edit security utm]
root@SRX550-Node0#  set  feature-profile  web-filtering  type  surf-control-
integrated

root@SRX550-Node0# set feature-profile web-filtering surf-control-integrated
cache timeout 120

root@SRX550-Node0# set feature-profile web-filtering surf-control-integrated
profile Integrated-Websense default permit

{primary:node0}[edit security utm]
root@SRX550-Node0# set feature-profile web-filtering surf-control-integrated
profile Integrated-Websense fallback-settings default log-and-permit

{primary:node0}[edit security utm]
root@SRX550-Node0# set feature-profile web-filtering surf-control-integrated
profile Integrated-Websense fallback-settings too-many-requests block

{primary:node0}[edit security utm]
root@SRX550-Node0#  set  utm-policy  Basic-UTM  web-filtering  http-profile
Integrated-Websense

{primary:node0}[edit security utm]
root@SRX550-Node0# show
feature-profile {
    web-filtering {
        type surf-control-integrated;
        surf-control-integrated {
            cache {
                timeout 120;
            }
            profile Integrated-Websense {
                category {
                    Audult_Sexually_Explicit {
                        action block;
                    }
                    Remote_Proxies {
                        action block;
```

```
                    }
                }
                default permit;
                fallback-settings {
                    default log-and-permit;
                    too-many-requests block;
                }
            }
        }
    }
}
utm-policy Basic-UTM {
    web-filtering {
        http-profile Integrated-Websense;
    }
}
```

Websense Redirect

Websense Redirect is used if you have a standalone Websense server that you want to perform the URL check with rather than with some integrated form of URL authentication. The following configurations can be set on the SRX for configuring Websense Redirect. Note that you have to specify a server profile for Websense or at least the server attributes because the default profile won't know what server to send the traffic to.

Type
: This will always be set to Websense Redirect using this mode.

Profile
: This is the profile configuration for Websense Redirect.

  Account
  : The account name that is used on the server to authenticate the request.

  Custom Block Message
  : This is a block message that you can define on the SRX to display when the user is in violation of the policy.

  Server
  : Specifies the IP and port of the Websense server to contact.

  Sockets
  : There can be multiple connections to a single Websense standalone server if you have multiple firewalls doing redirects to it. Use a different socket number if this is the case (1-8).

  Timeout
  : How long to wait until you consider the request timed out.

Fallback settings

These are the fallback settings for the user traffic that are available if there is an issue with communicating with the Websense server:

Default

This is the default action that should be taken when a condition occurs that is not specified.

Server Connectivity

If there is an issue connecting to the Websense server, take this action.

Timeout

What action to take if the server doesn't respond to a request in a certain time period.

Too Many Requests

This is the action that should be taken if the FW has too many open requests.

Configuring Websense Redirect. In this example, we configure Websense Redirect to perform the following actions:

- Redirect to server 192.168.1.150 on port 9020, Socket 1.
- Use Account AC.
- Set the Custom Block Message to "Access is Restricted".
- Set the Fallback options to Default, server connectivity, and timeout to log and permit, too many requests to block.
- Apply this Websense Redirect profile to the Basic-UTM policy.

```
{primary:node0}[edit security utm]
root@SRX550-Node0# set feature-profile web-filtering websense-redirect pro-
file WS-Redirect account AC custom-block-message "Access is Restricted" serv-
er host 192.168.1.150 port 9020 socket 1


root@SRX550-Node0# set feature-profile web-filtering websense-redirect pro-
file WS-Redirect fallback-settings default log-and-permit server-connectivity
log-and-permit timeout log-and-permit too-many-requests block


{primary:node0}[edit security utm]
root@SRX550-Node0# set feature-profile web-filtering type websense-redirect

{primary:node0}[edit security utm]
root@SRX550-Node0# set utm-policy Basic-UTM web-filtering http-profile WS-
Redirect
```

```
{primary:node0}[edit security utm]
root@SRX550-Node0# show
feature-profile {
    web-filtering {
        websense-redirect {
            profile WS-Redirect {
                server {
                    host 192.168.1.150;
                    port 9020;
                }
                custom-block-message "Access is Restricted";
                fallback-settings {
                    default log-and-permit;
                    server-connectivity log-and-permit;
                    timeout log-and-permit;
                    too-many-requests block;
                }
                account AC;
            }
        }
    }
}


feature-profile {
    web-filtering {
        type websense-redirect;
        websense-redirect {
            profile WS-Redirect {
                server {
                    host 192.168.1.150;
                    port 9020;
                }
                custom-block-message "Access is Restricted";
                fallback-settings {
                    default log-and-permit;
                    server-connectivity log-and-permit;
                    timeout log-and-permit;
                    too-many-requests block;
                }
                account AC;
            }
        }
    }
}
utm-policy Basic-UTM {
    web-filtering {
        http-profile WS-Redirect;
    }
}
```

Default Websense Redirect profile. This output is the default configuration for the predefined Websense Redirect profile.

```
{primary:node0}[edit]
root@SRX550-Node0# show groups junos-defaults security utm web-filtering
        websense-redirect {
            profile junos-wf-websense-default {
                   custom-block-message "Juniper Web Filtering has been set to
block this site.";
                fallback-settings {
                    default log-and-permit;
                    server-connectivity log-and-permit;
                    timeout log-and-permit;
                    too-many-requests log-and-permit;
                }
            }
        }
```

Default local URL filtering profile. The default configuration for the predefined local URL profile is shown here.

```
{primary:node0}[edit]
root@SRX550-Node0# show groups junos-defaults security utm web-filtering
        juniper-local {
            profile junos-wf-local-default {
                   custom-block-message "Juniper Web Filtering has been set to
block this site.";
                fallback-settings {
                    default log-and-permit;
                    server-connectivity log-and-permit;
                    timeout log-and-permit;
                    too-many-requests log-and-permit;
                }
            }
    }
```

URL Custom URLs, blacklists, whitelists, and categories

To properly leverage Juniper Local filtering, you must define some blacklist and whitelist content that can be applied to the profile. You are only allowed to use one blacklist and one whitelist at a time, but it gives you enough flexibility to set up the system as you see fit. In this section, we examine creating the individual components which are to be leveraged for Local URL filtering, as shown in Figure 14-4.

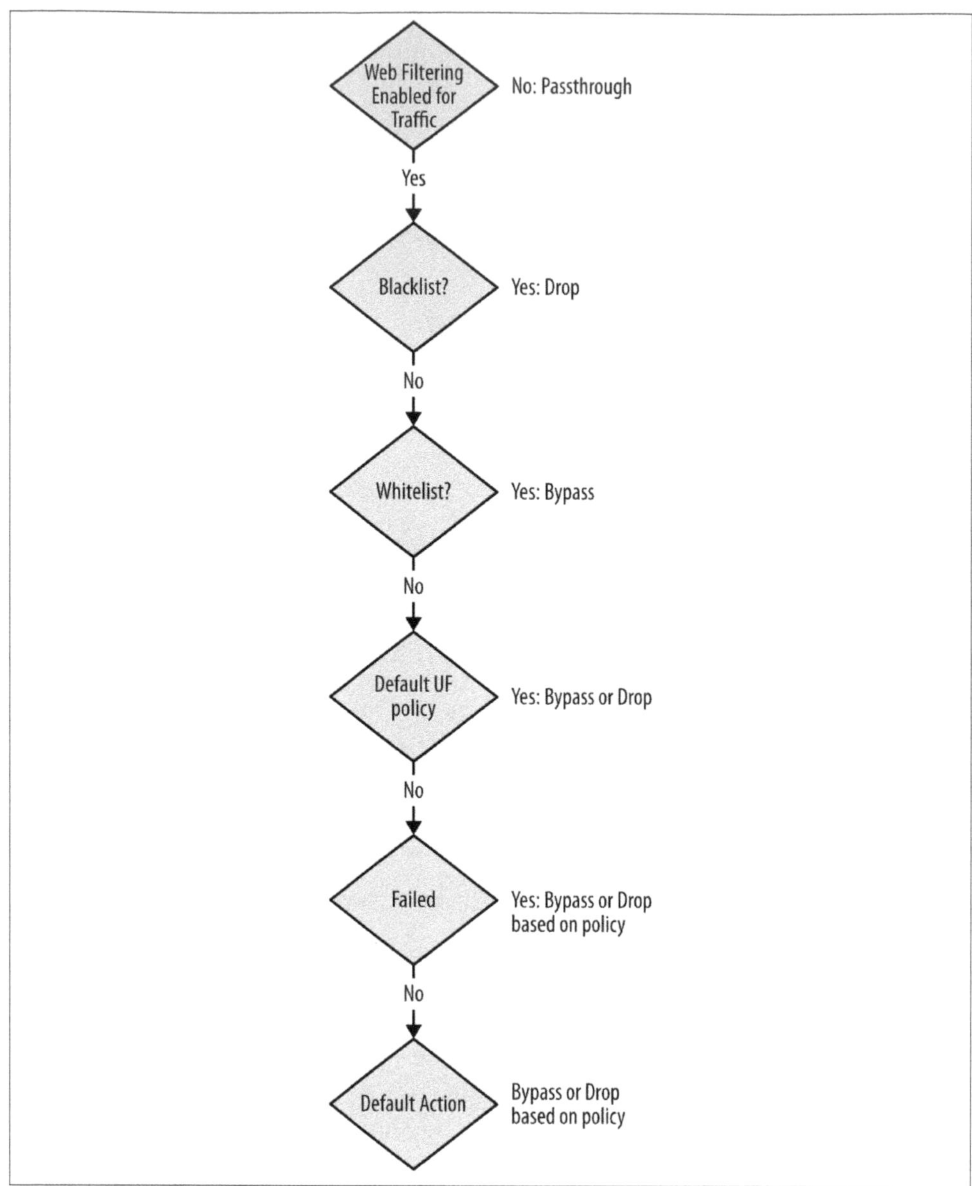

Figure 14-4. Local URL filtering flowchart

Custom URL patterns. Before you can create a category that is applied to a profile, you must define the URL pattern itself. Juniper allows you to use the * and ? regex wildcards. * means to match any characters before or after a character until the next specified value, and ? means to match 0 or one instance of any character. We show a few examples here.

1. Create a pattern that matches any subdomain for abc.com on HTTP.
2. Create a pattern that matches any top-layer domain suffix for www.abc (*http://www.abc*) on HTTP.
3. Create a pattern that matches an IP address 65.27.183.45 on HTTP.
4. Create a pattern that only looks for two-character top-layer domain names for www.abc (*http://www.abc*) on HTTP.

```
{primary:node0}[edit]
root@SRX550-Node0# edit security utm custom-objects


{primary:node0}[edit security utm custom-objects]
root@SRX550-Node0# set url-pattern Any-ABC-Domain value "http://*.abc.com"

{primary:node0}[edit security utm custom-objects]
root@SRX550-Node0# set url-pattern Any-ABC-Suffix value "http://www.abc.*"

{primary:node0}[edit security utm custom-objects]
root@SRX550-Node0# set url-pattern Specific-IP value "http://65.27.183.45"

{primary:node0}[edit security utm custom-objects]
root@SRX550-Node0# set url-pattern Two-TLD value "http://www.abc.??"

{primary:node0}[edit security utm custom-objects]
root@SRX550-Node0# show
url-pattern {
    Any-ABC-Domain {
        value http://*.abc.com;
    }
    Any-ABC-Suffix {
        value http://www.abc.*;
    }
    Specific-IP {
        value http://65.27.183.45;
    }
    Two-TLD {
        value "http://www.abc.??";
    }
}
```

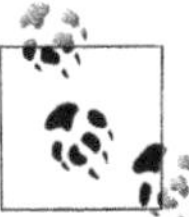

It is important to remember that the local URL feature does exactly what it says by matching the patterns in the host or URL field. If a user can talk to a URL via IP address, it could potentially bypass the engine, so be sure to specify by IP address as well if the server will accept the IP address as the header host field.

Custom URL category. Once you have defined a custom URL pattern, the next step is to specify a custom category for it. We make two categories, one called FQDN and one called IP-Address. The IP address example is in the IP-Address category, and the other three FQDN-based patterns will be in the FQDN category.

```
{primary:node0}[edit security utm custom-objects]
root@SRX550-Node0# set custom-url-category FQDN value [ Any-ABC-Domain Any-ABC-
Suffix Two-TLD ]

{primary:node0}[edit security utm custom-objects]
root@SRX550-Node0# set custom-url-category IP-Address value Specific-IP

{primary:node0}[edit security utm custom-objects]
root@SRX550-Node0# show
url-pattern {
    Any-ABC-Domain {
        value http://*.abc.com;
    }
    Any-ABC-Suffix {
        value http://www.abc.*;
    }
    Specific-IP {
        value http://65.27.183.45;
    }
    Two-TLD {
        value "http://www.abc.??";
    }
}
custom-url-category {
    FQDN {
        value [ Any-ABC-Domain Any-ABC-Suffix Two-TLD ];
    }
    IP-Address {
        value Specific-IP;
    }
}
```

URL filtering profiles

The default profiles can get you up and running quickly, but you might want to create your own profile and options. In this example, we apply the category to a whitelist, which is applied to the juniper-local profile.

```
{primary:node0}[edit security utm]
root@SRX550-Node0# set feature-profile web-filtering type juniper-local


{primary:node0}[edit security utm]
root@SRX550-Node0# set feature-profile web-filtering type juniper-local url-
whitelist Specific-IP
```

```
{primary:node0}[edit security utm]
root@SRX550-Node0# set feature-profile web-filtering type juniper-local url-
blacklist FQDN

{primary:node0}[edit security utm]
root@SRX550-Node0# show
custom-objects {
    url-pattern {
        Any-ABC-Domain {
            value http://*.abc.com;
        }
        Any-ABC-Suffix {
            value http://www.abc.*;
        }
        Specific-IP {
            value http://65.27.183.45;
        }
        Two-TLD {
            value "http://www.abc.??";
        }
    }
    custom-url-category {
        FQDN {
            value [ Any-ABC-Domain Any-ABC-Suffix Two-TLD ];
        }
        IP-Address {
            value Specific-IP;
        }
    }
}
feature-profile {
    web-filtering {
        url-whitelist FQDN;
        url-blacklist Specific-IP;
        type juniper-local;
    }
}
```

Juniper Local feature profile options. When defining your own local profile in the SRX, you have some options available to you based on the state of the internal engine. This section lists each of those options, what they signify, and an example of configuring them.

Custom Block Message
: Simple string message that can be displayed if the user is in violation of a page and is blocked rather than going to the original destination page.

Default
: This is the default action that should be taken on the traffic if it doesn't match a whitelist or blacklist.

Fallback Options

Either log and permit or block for each setting.

Default

Set a default action when the engine cannot complete the actions due to an undefined condition.

Too Many Requests

What to do when there are too many pending requests for the engine.

In this example, we configure the Junos-Local Feature profile to have a default action of permit for any undefined URL, and a fallback option of block when there are too many requests. Additionally, we will set a default block message of "Access to this Website is Restricted by Company Policy" for any block actions.

```
{primary:node0}[edit]
root@SRX550-Node0# edit security utm feature-profile web-filtering juniper-
local profile Juniper-Local

{primary:node0}[edit security utm feature-profile web-filtering juniper-local
profile Juniper-Local]
root@SRX550-Node0# set custom-block-message "Access to this Website is Restric-
ted by Company Policy"

{primary:node0}[edit security utm feature-profile web-filtering juniper-local
profile Juniper-Local]
root@SRX550-Node0# set default permit fallback-settings too-many-requests block

{primary:node0}[edit security utm feature-profile web-filtering juniper-local
profile Juniper-Local]

root@SRX550-Node0# show
default permit;
custom-block-message "Access to this Website is Restricted by Company Policy";
fallback-settings {
    too-many-requests block;
}
```

Putting it all together for Juniper Local web filtering. Now that we've examined each individual element of local web filtering, here is a final example with all of the above defined for a complete solution that is applied to a firewall rule.

```
{primary:node0}[edit security utm]
root@SRX550-Node0# show
custom-objects {
    url-pattern {
        Any-ABC-Domain {
            value http://*.abc.com;
        }
        Any-ABC-Suffix {
            value http://www.abc.*;
```

```
        }
        Specific-IP {
            value http://65.27.183.45;
        }
        Two-TLD {
            value "http://www.abc.??";
        }
    }
    custom-url-category {
        FQDN {
            value [ Any-ABC-Domain Any-ABC-Suffix Two-TLD ];
        }
        IP-Address {
            value Specific-IP;
        }
    }
}
feature-profile {
    web-filtering {
        url-whitelist FQDN;
        url-blacklist Specific-IP;
        type juniper-local;
        juniper-local {
            profile Juniper-Local {
                default permit;
                  custom-block-message "Access to this Website is Restricted by
Company Policy";
                fallback-settings {
                    default log-and-permit;
                    too-many-requests block;
                }
            }
        }
    }
}
utm-policy Basic-UTM {
    web-filtering {
        http-profile Juniper-Local;
    }
}

{primary:node0}[edit security policies from-zone trust to-zone untrust policy
Client-Outbound]
root@SRX550-Node0# show
match {
    source-address Internal-Clients;
    destination-address any;
    application [ junos-http junos-ftp ];
}
then {
    permit {
        application-services {
```

```
                utm-policy Basic-UTM;
            }
        }
        log {
            session-close;
        }
    }
```

Which URL filtering solution to choose?

Because there are four options for enabling web filtering, it can seem like it might be a tough call, but in this section we examine all of the options.

- Websense Enhanced
  - Pros: This is the most powerful integrated method in terms of detection and the integrated package. It has a granular list of URL categories, support for Google Safe Search, and a reputation engine. It also doesn't require any additional server components. This feature can also redirect users to a custom URL for block pages.
  - Cons: Requires an Internet connection to be able to contact the Threatseeker cloud to function. Requires Junos 11.4+, which is probably not a major issue going forward, but for some that are standardized on a legacy release it could be an issue.
- Websense/Surfcontrol Integrated
  - Pros: Supported from Junos 9.6, provides decent URL categorization and functionality. Still has a full URL list as the enhanced, just fewer categories.
  - Cons: It is not the most powerful URL filtering features. It doesn't support Safe Search or URL reputation, although you can use some categories for this. Requires an Internet connection to function by querying the cloud.
- Websense Redirect
  - Pros: Doesn't require an Internet connection, all queries are tracked locally. Can use the logging/reporting of a standalone Websense solution. Slightly lower latency because the server is onsite. You own the entire solution. Can be run from Junos 9.6.
  - Cons: Requires an expensive separate Websense server. Not as much functionality as directing the entire HTTP session through the Websense, but is equivalent to other integrated solutions.
- Juniper Local
  - Pros: Doesn't require a license. Good for defining your own blacklist or whitelist. Good if you only have a handful of URLs on which you want to enforce a policy.

— Cons: Not ideal for broad URL filtering support; only geared for specific URLs.

Antispam

The antispam technology that is built into the SRX offers a simple solution for filtering inbound spam on SMTP. In all candor, this is not the most powerful solution for blocking spam. It is only based on an IP reputation list offered from the cloud via Sophos. That being said, it can be much simpler to implement than a full-blown antispam solution and certainly less expensive. If this sounds like it meets your needs, then by all means use it, or even better you can use it in conjunction with a full solution.

Configuring the antispam solution is quite simple. It also leverages feature profiles like antivirus and URL filtering, although there are not as many options to configure, and only one solution. In this section, we examine configuring the default profile as well as a custom profile.

The antispam feature relies on DNS to get the IP blacklist information from the cloud. As of Junos 11.4, Juniper leverages Sophos for this functionality (formerly it was Symantec).

Configuration options for antispam

The following configuration options are available for configuring the antispam solution in the SRX.

Address Blacklist
: Defines a list of hosts that will be blocked by the antispam solution (regardless of the lookup result).

Address Whitelist
: Defines a list of hosts that will be permitted (regardless of the lookup result) in the antispam solution.

SBL
: This is the main part of the profile that defines what action should be taken.

  Custom Tag String:
  : This is a string that can be tagged in the header or the subject of the message if spam is detected (rather than dropping it). This can be used by a downstream antispam server or for rules in the client itself.

  No/SBL Default Server
  : Defines whether or not to use the default server for server blacklists, enabled by default.

Spam Action
: Defines what action should be taken if spam is detected. The options are block the message, tag the SMTP header, or tag the email subject line.

The following are the default configurations for antispam.

```
{primary:node0}[edit]
root@SRX100HM# show groups junos-defaults security utm feature-profile anti-spam
sbl {
    profile junos-as-defaults {
        sbl-default-server;
        spam-action block;
        custom-tag-string ***SPAM***;
    }
}
```

Configuring antispam with the default profile

The following example uses the default antispam profile and applies it to a rule from the Untrust to DMZ context called SMTP, which only allows SMTP to our email server called Email-Server.

```
{primary:node0}[edit security utm]
root@SRX550HM# set utm-policy MAIL anti-spam smtp-profile junos-as-defaults

{primary:node0}[edit]
root@SRX550HM# set security policies from-zone untrust to-zone DMZ policy Mail-
Inbound match source-address any destination-address SMTP-server application
junos-smtp

{primary:node0}[edit]
root@SRX550HM# set security policies from-zone untrust to-zone DMZ policy Mail-
Inbound then permit application-services utm-policy MAIL

{primary:node0}[edit]
root@SRX550HM#set security policies from-zone untrust to-zone DMZ policy Mail-
Inbound then log session-close

{primary:node0}[edit]
root@SRX550HM# show security policies from-zone untrust to-zone DMZ policy Mail-
Inbound
match {
    source-address any;
    destination-address SMTP-server;
    application junos-smtp;
}
then {
    permit {
        application-services {
            utm-policy MAIL;
            }
        }
```

```
    }
    log {
        session-close;
    }
}

primary:node0}[edit security utm]
root@SRX550HM# show utm-policy MAIL
anti-spam {
    smtp-profile junos-as-defaults;
}
```

Configuring a custom spam profile and policy

In this example, we configure a custom antispam profile that we apply to our firewall rule with the following configuration:

- Create a custom antispam profile called AS.
- The profile should apply a custom tag of SPAM Detected! to the subject line of any spam message that is detected but not block it.
- Apply this to the SMTP inbound rule for the email server.

```
{primary:node0}[edit]
root@SRX550HM# set feature-profile anti-spam sbl profile AS custom-tag-string
"Spam Detected!" spam-action tag-subject

{primary:node0}[edit security utm]
root@SRX550HM# set utm-policy MAIL anti-spam smtp-profile AS

{primary:node0}[edit]
root@SRX550HM# set security policies from-zone untrust to-zone DMZ policy
Mail-Inbound match source-address any destination-address SMTP-server applica-
tion junos-smtp

{primary:node0}[edit]
root@SRX550HM# set security policies from-zone untrust to-zone DMZ policy
Mail-Inbound then permit application-services utm-policy MAIL

{primary:node0}[edit]
root@SRX550HM#set security policies from-zone untrust to-zone DMZ policy Mail-
Inbound then log session-close

{primary:node0}[edit]
root@SRX550HM# show security policies from-zone untrust to-zone DMZ policy
Mail-Inbound
match {
    source-address any;
    destination-address SMTP-server;
    application junos-smtp;
}
```

```
then {
    permit {
        application-services {
            utm-policy MAIL;
            }
        }
    }
    log {
        session-close;
    }
}

{primary:node0}[edit security utm]
root@SRX550HM# show
feature-profile {
    anti-spam {
        sbl {
            profile AS {
                spam-action tag-subject;
                custom-tag-string "Spam Detected!";
            }
        }
    }
}
utm-policy MAIL {
    anti-spam {
        smtp-profile AS;
    }
}
```

Content Filtering

Content filtering is a very simple feature to provide some lightweight data leak prevention in the UTM feature set. This definitely isn't a full-blown DLP solution by any means. Most of the functionality can also be achieved using the IPS, but this is a much, much simpler approach from a configuration perspective. Content filtering is purely defined by you, the administrator, because the SRX has no way of knowing what activity to block or permit. This feature does not require any license (nor is there one) to function.

Content filtering provides the ability to whitelist or blacklist the following activity:

- Protocol Commands: You can either permit or block specific commands on a protocol-by-protocol basis. You simply define the command. Supported protocols are HTTP, IMAP, SMTP, FTP, and POP3.
- Content Types: The SRX can inspect files in HTTP, IMAP, SMTP, FTP, and POP3 and can block certain content types from being transmitted. These include ActiveX, Java applets, Windows executables, HTTP cookies, and ZIP files.

- Block Extensions: This is a list of file extensions that should be blocked over the supported protocols. Note that this is just per extension so it doesn't inspect the actual content.

If you want more in-depth filtering support than that offered by content filtering or you're using the high-end SRX, you can leverage IDP. This can not only block per extension or command, but works for virtually any protocol and it can inspect the actual content itself for content types.

Content filtering is applied in the same way that other UTM features are supported, although you must define the custom objects. Once custom objects are defined, they are applied to feature profiles that define the per profile activity, applying the feature profile to the UTM policy, and finally the UTM policy is applied to the firewall rule.

Configuring content filtering example

In this example, we configure content filtering to perform the following activity:

- Create a feature profile called Content-Filter, and apply it to a UTM policy called Content-Filter-Policy.
- Apply this UTM policy to the Client Outbound rule.
- Permit only GET HTTP commands.
- Block any EXE, ActiveX, and Java applets by inspecting the content to determine the file type.
- Block any extensions that have .js, .pdf, and .swf files.

```
{primary:node0}[edit security utm]
root@SRX550-Node0#  set  feature-profile  content-filtering  profile  Content-
Filtering permit-command "GET"

{primary:node0}[edit security utm]
root@SRX550-Node0#  set  feature-profile  content-filtering  profile  Content-
Filtering block-content-type activex exe java-applet

{primary:node0}[edit security utm]
root@SRX550-Node0#  set  feature-profile  content-filtering  profile  Content-
Filtering block-extension Extension-List

{primary:node0}[edit security utm]
root@SRX550-Node0# set custom-objects protocol-command GET value "GET"

{primary:node0}[edit security utm]
root@SRX550-Node0# set custom-objects filename-extension Extension-List value
[pdf swf js]
```

```
{primary:node0}[edit security utm]
root@SRX550-Node0# set utm-policy Content-Filter-Policy content-filtering
http-profile Content-Filtering


{primary:node0}[edit security utm]
root@SRX550-Node0# show
custom-objects {
    filename-extension {
        Extension-List {
            value [ pdf swf js ];
        }
    }
    protocol-command {
        GET {
            value GET;
        }
    }
}
feature-profile {
    content-filtering {
        profile Content-Filtering {
            permit-command GET;
            block-extension Extension-List;
            block-content-type {
                activex;
                java-applet;
                exe;
            }
        }
    }
}
utm-policy Content-Filter-Policy {
    content-filtering {
        http-profile Content-Filtering;
    }
}

{primary:node0}[edit security utm]
root@SRX550-Node0# top

{primary:node0}[edit]
root@SRX550-Node0# edit security policies from zone trust to-zone untrust pol-
icy Client-Outbound

{primary:node0}[edit security policies from-zone trust to-zone untrust policy
Client-Outbound]
root@SRX550-Node0# set match source-address Internal-Clients destination-
address any application junos-http

{primary:node0}[edit security policies from-zone trust to-zone untrust policy
```

```
Client-Outbound]
root@SRX550-Node0# set then permit application-services utm-policy Content-
Filter-Policy

{primary:node0}[edit security policies from-zone trust to-zone untrust policy
Client-Outbound]
root@SRX550-Node0# set then log session-close

{primary:node0}[edit security policies from-zone trust to-zone untrust policy
Client-Outbound]
root@SRX550-Node0# show
match {
    source-address Internal-Clients;
    destination-address any;
    application junos-http;
}
then {
    permit {
        application-services {
            utm-policy Content-Filter-Policy;
        }
    }
    log {
        session-close;
    }
}
```

Logging UTM Messages

The UTM feature set provides some very useful log messages on the SRX, which are enabled by default. You can both log them locally to the box (if Event mode logging is configured) or you can log them remotely to a syslog server. The log information can help you to get historical information, alerts, and reports. Because these messages are sent via syslog, there are no proprietary requirements on the syslog collector, so any solution that supports syslog will do. Of course, Juniper's STRM and Security Insight have predefined dashboards, log views, and reports that are tailored to the Juniper UTM solution, so it's more plug and play, but there is no strict requirement to use this technology if your organization wants to use another solution. To enable this, you simply need to enable syslog on the data plane just as you would for normal firewall and IPS logs.

Configuring syslog to send UTM to a remote server

Just to refresh, we configure the syslog server on the data plane to send the syslogs to a remote syslog server. In this example, our firewall sends syslog messages to a syslog server at IP address 192.168.2.50, with a source address 192.168.2.30 on UDP port 514.

```
{primary:node0}[edit security log]
root@SRX550-Node0# set mode stream format sd-syslog source-address 192.168.2.30
```

```
stream STRM category all host 192.168.2.50 port 514

{primary:node0}[edit security log]
root@SRX550-Node0# show
mode stream;
format sd-syslog;
source-address 192.168.2.30;
stream STRM {
    category all;
    host {
        192.168.2.50;
        port 514;
    }
}
```

If you only want to send UTM messages, you can define "category content-security" rather than "category all," which sends all messages to this syslog receiver.

Best Practices

We've covered a lot of ground in this chapter, so it can be easy to get lost in all of the details. Let's discuss a few best practices for each feature and overall for the UTM profiles.

1. Evaluate what your organization's needs are for UTM. Identify where the internal resources are and where the threats are. This will give you a good idea of where to apply the content filtering policies.
2. Determine which protocols are permitted to transit the network and what support there is for the UTM technologies on those protocols (HTTP, IMAP, POP3, SMTP, and FTP). Primarily you will be most concerned with HTTP.
3. In the case of URL filtering and antivirus, you need to determine which technology will best suit your needs. In both sections of this chapter we discuss the pros and cons of each technology, so you can leverage this to best select the technology that works for you.
4. When it comes to performance concerns, it can be an issue if you are leveraging multiple Level 7 technologies on top of each other like antivirus, URL filtering, and IPS, depending on the platform and traffic needs. The good news is that you can enable the profiles both for UTM and for IDP on a firewall rule-by-rule basis to limit the impacts and only apply the technologies where needed.
5. Juniper is making a lot of improvements to UTM functionality in its newer Junos code, so if you are using legacy code you might want to consider an upgrade to avoid these limitations. Check the release notes for each version to get more details on what new features are introduced and what issues have been fixed.

6. Particularly with initial deployments, you will want to keep an eye on the log messages generated and also the output of the `show security utm <feature> statistics|status` output. This will give you lot of great information about the current status of your system and what is occurring from a traffic and threat perspective. It can also be a good idea to monitor the performance and memory of your system with the `show security monitoring fpc <x>` and `show chassis routing-engine` commands to ensure that the CPU, SPU, and memory utilization isn't too high.

Troubleshooting and Operation

Now that we have discussed how the features work, let's also discuss how to troubleshoot and operate them. We break this down on a feature-by-feature basis.

UTM Engine

The UTM engine itself is not something that you need to explicitly configure. It is implicitly enabled, but if you are troubleshooting UTM, it can help to double-check that the system is running and that traffic is being inspected by the engine. The following two commands are useful for getting some high-level information. If you don't see that the service is running or no active sessions when you think they should, it could be the result of some misconfiguration or the engine not being active. Note that this is overall UTM sessions, not a specific feature, which we dig into shortly.

```
{primary:node0}
root@SRX100HM> show security utm status
node0:
--------------------------------------------------------
UTM service status: Running

node1:
--------------------------------------------------------
UTM service status: Running

{primary:node0}
root@SRX100HM> show security utm session
node0:
--------------------------------------------------------
 UTM session info:
 Maximum sessions:                  4000
 Total allocated sessions:          1239
 Total freed sessions:              1139
 Active sessions:                   57

node1:
--------------------------------------------------------
 UTM session info:
```

```
Maximum sessions:                  4000
Total allocated sessions:          1239
Total freed sessions:              1239
Active sessions:                   57
```

Also make sure that you have licenses for the features that you have enabled (if in a cluster, on both members). Not all UTM features require licenses, but without them, the configuration might apply but the engine won't run. A simple check of the output of the specific feature will give some hints that the engines aren't active due to licenses, but it's something that's easy to overlook. You can double-check the license status on a per-host basis with the `show system license` output to ensure the system is licensed and the license is active.

```
{primary:node0}
root@SRX550-Node0> show system license
License usage:
                             Licenses  Licenses Licenses Expiry
  Feature name                   used installed   needed
  anti_spam_key_sbl                 0         1        0 2013-09-01 00:00:00 UTC
  idp-sig                           0         1        0 2013-09-01 00:00:00 UTC
  dynamic-vpn                       0         2        0 permanent
  ax411-wlan-ap                     0         2        0 permanent
  appid-sig                         0         1        0 2013-09-01 00:00:00 UTC
  av_key_sophos_engine              0         1        0 2013-09-01 00:00:00 UTC
  wf_key_websense_ewf               0         1        0 2013-09-01 00:00:00 UTC

Licenses installed:
  License identifier: JUNOS132555
  License version: 2
  Valid for device: AL2012AA0011
  Features:
    av_key_sophos_engine - Anti Virus with Sophos Engine
      date-based, 2012-09-01 00:00:00 UTC - 2013-09-01 00:00:00 UTC

  License identifier: JUNOS132556
  License version: 2
  Valid for device: AL2012AA0011
  Features:
    wf_key_websense_ewf - Web Filtering EWF
      date-based, 2012-09-01 00:00:00 UTC - 2013-09-01 00:00:00 UTC

  License identifier: JUNOS132557
  License version: 2
  Valid for device: AL2012AA0011
  Features:
    anti_spam_key_sbl - Anti-Spam
      date-based, 2012-09-01 00:00:00 UTC - 2013-09-01 00:00:00 UTC

  License identifier: JUNOS132558
  License version: 2
  Valid for device: AL2012AA0011
```

```
Features:
  idp-sig          - IDP Signature
    date-based, 2012-09-01 00:00:00 UTC - 2013-09-01 00:00:00 UTC

License identifier: JUNOS132559
License version: 2
Valid for device: AL2012AA0011
Features:
  appid-sig        - APPID Signature
    date-based, 2012-09-01 00:00:00 UTC - 2013-09-01 00:00:00 UTC
```

If running this command on a cluster, you must run it on each cluster member. The same is true for adding licenses: they must be done on a per cluster member basis at the time of writing this book.

Antivirus

Although there are three different antivirus solutions available on the SRX, the troubleshooting and operation is relatively the same, particularly from the output commands. The two main commands you should start with are the `show security utm anti-virus status` and `show security anti-virus statistics` commands. These will show the status of the engine and some statistical information about the activity seen on the system, including inspected files, malware threats, and any engine failures. Note that the output for each AV solution will vary slightly because there are some different stats, but the commands are the same and quite self-explanatory.

```
{primary:node0}
root@SRX100HM> show security utm anti-virus statistics
node0:
--------------------------------------------------------------------------
 UTM Anti Virus statistics:
 MIME-whitelist passed:                0
 URL-whitelist passed:                 0
 Scan Request:

  Total            Clean          Threat-found     Fallback
     614              611                3               0

 Fallback:
                         Log-and-Permit    Block              Permit
 Engine not ready:           0                 0                  0
 Out of resources:           0                 0                  0
 Timeout:                    0                 0                  0
 Maximum content size:       0                 0                  0
 Too many requests:          0                 0                  0
 Others:                     0                 0                  0

node1:
```

```
------------------------------------------------------------------
 UTM Anti Virus statistics:
 MIME-whitelist passed:                0
 URL-whitelist passed:                 0
 Scan Request:

  Total            Clean          Threat-found     Fallback
      0                0               0               0

 Fallback:
                            Log-and-Permit    Block              Permit
 Engine not ready:              0                 0                   0
 Out of resources:              0                 0                   0
 Timeout:                       0                 0                   0
 Maximum content size:          0                 0                   0
 Too many requests:             0                 0                   0
 Others:                        0                 0                   0

{primary:node0}
root@SRX100HM> show security utm anti-virus status
node0:
------------------------------------------------------------------
 UTM anti-virus status:

    Anti-virus key expire date: 2012-11-13 19:00:00
    Update server: http://update.juniper-updates.net/SAV/
           Interval: 60 minutes
           Pattern update status: next update in 4 minutes
           Last result: already have latest database
    Anti-virus signature version: 1.02.0 (1.02)
    Scan engine type: sophos-engine
    Scan engine information: last action result: No error

node1:
------------------------------------------------------------------
 UTM anti-virus status:

    Anti-virus key expire date: 2012-11-13 19:00:00
    Update server: http://update.juniper-updates.net/SAV/
           Interval: 60 minutes
           Pattern update status: next update will be synchronized from primary
node
           Last result: already have latest database
    Anti-virus signature version: 1.02.0 (1.02)
    Scan engine type: sophos-engine
    Scan engine information: last action result: No error
```

Remember that for both pattern updates and also for Sophos URI checking, Internet connections must be available including DNS for hostname resolution. If you have upstream firewalls, they must permit the SRX to make the applicable connections to the cloud services (HTTP and DNS) to get updates. You will quickly find this out if you see errors in the preceding output like server connectivity timeouts and inability to download updates. Check both the networking on your SRX and also that the upstream system permits the traffic to pass through to the Internet.

You can also check to make sure that your system is properly updating with antivirus with the following request command:

```
{primary:node0}
root@SRX100HM> request security utm anti-virus sophos-engine pattern-update
node0:
--------------------------------------------------------------------------
Anti-virus update request results: av_mgr: pattern updater 2967 is started,
downloading from http://update.juniper-updates.net/SAV/.

node1:
--------------------------------------------------------------------------
Anti-virus update request results: av_mgr: updater exiting on secondary node
```

There are some additional traceoptions that you can enable on a UTM and feature-by-feature basis, but they are out of the scope of this chapter. Typically, if you need to enable them, it should be done with support from JTAC or via specific Knowledge Base articles on the Juniper Knowledge Base (*http://kb.juniper.net/*).

Testing antivirus

If you want to test that your antivirus is working properly, a very simple way is to just download the EICAR test virus, which is not a real virus, but one that the SRX and virtually all antivirus systems list as a test virus for the purpose of testing whether the engine is active or not. This is available on the Eicar.org website (*http://bit.ly/Ya6KO5*). Downloading it should trigger the antivirus engine to detect the EICAR virus if it is properly set up and applied to the firewall rule that your session is transmitting over.

URL Filtering

Similar to the antivirus feature, there are several different flavors of URL filtering, but luckily the methods of troubleshooting them are virtually the same. There two main commands that will be of interest after you have determined that the UTM service is active and URL filtering is licensed. These are `show security utm web-filtering statistics` and `show security utm web-filtering status`. These are shown here. There is a slight variation in the output depending on the solution you are using, but they are more or less the same and certainly intuitive.

```
{primary:node0}
root@SRX100HM> show security utm web-filtering statistics
node0:
--------------------------------------------------------------------------
 UTM web-filtering statistics:
    Total requests:                     529627
    white list hit:                     0
    Black list hit:                     0
```

```
    Queries to server:              181686
    Server reply permit:            144188
    Server reply block:             13
    Custom category permit:         0
    Custom category block:          0
    Site reputation permit:         37252
    Site reputation block:          63
    Cache hit permit:               347900
    Cache hit block:                22
    Safe-search redirect:           169
    Web-filtering sessions in total: 4000
    Web-filtering sessions in use:  0
    Fallback:                      log-and-permit          block
          Default                               1              0
          Timeout                               1              0
     Connectivity                               0              0
Too-many-requests                               0              0

node1:
--------------------------------------------------------------------
 UTM web-filtering statistics:
    Total requests:                 79
    white list hit:                 0
    Black list hit:                 0
    Queries to server:              71
    Server reply permit:            61
    Server reply block:             0
    Custom category permit:         0
    Custom category block:          0
    Site reputation permit:         6
    Site reputation block:          0
    Cache hit permit:               8
    Cache hit block:                0
    Safe-search redirect:           0
    Web-filtering sessions in total: 4000
    Web-filtering sessions in use:  50
    Fallback:                      log-and-permit          block
          Default                               0              0
          Timeout                               0              0
     Connectivity                               0              0
Too-many-requests                               0              0

{primary:node0}
root@SRX100HM> show security utm web-filtering status
node0:
-------------------------------------------------------------------
 UTM web-filtering status:
    Server status: Juniper Enhanced using Websense server UP

node1:
-------------------------------------------------------------------
```

```
UTM web-filtering status:
   Server status: Juniper Enhanced using Websense server DOWN
```

In the preceding implementation which is in HA, the secondary web service is down, but that's okay because all of the requests are handled by the active node. In the output, we get very detailed information about the actions that the feature has taken on traffic and any reported failures.

It is important to remember a few things when it comes to URL filtering troubleshooting. First, for both Websense/Surfcontrol and Websense Enhanced, it requires an Internet connection to function, so if the connection to the Surfcontrol or Websense server is down, you will likely get connectivity and timeout stat increases. You will need to have both DNS and also UDP 9020 for Surfcontrol, and HTTP for Websense Enhanced open. If you are running in Websense Redirect mode, the Websense server must be up and reachable. Local URL filtering shouldn't require any extra features other than DNS to resolve hostnames.

Websense site lookup tool

There is a test utility on the Junos command list called `test security utm web-filtering profile <profile> test-string <test-string>` but it is only geared for testing strings in the internal blacklist or whitelist. Websense does provide a site lookup tool on their website, but it requires you to log in. You can obtain a login from the Websense portal (*http://bit.ly/ZAPK3k*) and then use the tool for free to enter URLs and get the classification information.

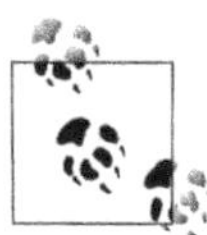

Testing a URL for the categorization and blocking action is pretty easy, as you can always set up a client to attempt to access a blocked resource and you should see it blocked on the client. You can also review the syslogs and stats for more information about what is being seen on the device. You also must make sure that the UTM profile with web filtering enabled is applied to the correct firewall rule to be triggered.

The traceoptions available for this feature is outside of the scope of this book,and shouldn't be required unless directed by JTAC.

Antispam

Troubleshooting antispam is usually pretty easy, as SMTP has the ability to queue messages rather than having to process them in real time as antivirus and URL filtering do. Also there is only one antispam solution available on the SRX. There are two primary commands that you will want to run on the SRX when troubleshooting antispam settings: `show security utm anti-spam status` and `show security utm anti-spam statistics`.

```
{primary:node0}
root@SRX100HM> show security utm anti-spam status
node0:
--------------------------------------------------------------------------
SBL Whitelist Server:
SBL Blacklist Server:
    msgsecurity.juniper.net

DNS Server:
    Primary  :          4.2.2.2, Src Interface: fe-0/0/1
    Secondary:          0.0.0.0, Src Interface: fe-0/0/2
    Ternary  :          0.0.0.0, Src Interface: fe-1/0/1

node1:
--------------------------------------------------------------------------
SBL Whitelist Server:
SBL Blacklist Server:
    msgsecurity.juniper.net

DNS Server:
    Primary  :          4.2.2.2, Src Interface: fe-0/0/1
    Secondary:          0.0.0.0, Src Interface: fe-0/0/2
    Ternary  :          0.0.0.0, Src Interface: fe-1/0/1

{primary:node0}
root@SRX100HM> show security utm anti-spam statistics
node0:
--------------------------------------------------------------------------
 UTM Anti Spam statistics:

Total connections:     1165
Denied connections:    0
Total greetings:       650
Denied greetings:      0
Total e-mail scanned:  592
White list hit:        0
Black list hit:        0
Spam total:            139
Spam tagged:           139
Spam dropped:          0
DNS errors:            0
Timeout errors:        0
Return errors:         0
Invalid parameter errors: 0

Statistics start time: 07/28/2012 21:06:27
Statistics for the last 10 days (permitted emails / spams):
day 1: 15/2
day 2: 14/1
day 3: 19/1
day 4: 28/0
day 5: 109/1
```

```
day 6: 25/2
day 7: 31/0
day 8: 28/4
day 9: 20/84
day 10: 11/25

node1:
--------------------------------------------------------------------------
 UTM Anti Spam statistics:

Total connections:      0
Denied connections:     0
Total greetings:        0
Denied greetings:       0
Total e-mail scanned:   0
White list hit:         0
Black list hit:         0
Spam total:             0
Spam tagged:            0
Spam dropped:           0
DNS errors:             0
Timeout errors:         0
Return errors:          0
Invalid parameter errors: 0

Statistics start time: 07/28/2012 21:05:45
```

As you can see from the preceding output, the SRX captures both stats about the spam detected, the action taken, and also some statistics about what is being done on the active system. For antispam to function properly, you need to ensure that DNS is allowed outbound and that the SRX performs the lookups for the IP reputation of the peer email server. This will inherit the same DNS information that is configured for the platform under `set system name-server`.

The traceoptions available for this feature are outside of the scope of this book and shouldn't be required unless directed by JTAC.

Content Filtering

The troubleshooting and operation of content filtering is quite straightforward, as this feature is entirely self-contained. You simply can check the `show security utm content-filtering statistics` command to get information about the number of hits for the different content types and actions taken.

```
{primary:node0}
root@SRX100HM> show security utm content-filtering statistics
node0:
--------------------------------------------------------------------------

 Content-filtering-statistic:          Blocked
```

```
    Base on command list:                4
    Base on mime list:                   0
    Base on extension list:              51
    ActiveX plugin:                      3
    Java applet:                         7
    EXE files:                           3
    ZIP files:                           0
    HTTP cookie:                         0

node1:
------------------------------------------------------------------

 Content-filtering-statistic:          Blocked
    Base on command list:                0
    Base on mime list:                   0
    Base on extension list:              0
    ActiveX plugin:                      0
    Java applet:                         0
    EXE files:                           0
    ZIP files:                           0
```

The traceoptions available for this feature is outside of the scope of this book and shouldn't be required unless directed by JTAC.

Sample Deployments

For this sample deployment, we are going to configure multiple UTM solutions to protect a sample solution as defined here. If you are proficient with the concepts discussed in this chapter, you should have no problem creating this same deployment in your own device.

- Antivirus
  - — Configure your own Sophos AV profile with the following properties:
    - — Max content size of 20 MB, engine timeout of 3 seconds, and trickling timeout of 10 seconds.
  - — Configure the SRX to always fail open and log in the case that the engine is not able to complete a request for any reason.
- URL filtering
  - — Enable Websense Enhanced URL filtering on the SRX with the following configuration:
    - — Cache timeout of two hours.
  - — Redirect any blocked users to the URL *http://192.168.1.70/blocked-request.html*, which is an internal web page that shows the company policy for browsing web resources.

- — Set the default option to permit any unknown URLs.
  - — Anything but very safe sites should be blocked.
  - — Block gambling and violence websites.
  - — If an issue occurs with the engine, be sure to fail open and log the request.
- Antispam
  - — Enable antispam with your own profile.
  - — Configure it to tag any detected spam with the subject "SPAM Detected".
- Create a Client-Outbound firewall rule that matches clients from the internal network 192.168.1.0/24 on the LAN zone going to any external resources on the Internet zone. This traffic should be inspected by your antivirus and URL filtering traffic. You should only allow HTTP outbound on this rule.
- Create another policy that allows SMTP traffic from the Internet into your SMTP server 2.2.2.50 in the DMZ. This traffic should be inspected by antivirus and antispam.

This solution could be configured as follows:

```
root@SRX550-Node0# show security utm
feature-profile {
    anti-virus {
        type sophos-engine;
        sophos-engine {
            profile Sophos {
                fallback-options {
                    default log-and-permit;
                    content-size log-and-permit;
                    engine-not-ready log-and-permit;
                    timeout log-and-permit;
                    out-of-resources log-and-permit;
                    too-many-requests log-and-permit;
                }
                scan-options {
                    content-size-limit 20000;
                    timeout 3;
                }
                trickling timeout 10;
            }
        }
    }
    web-filtering {
        type juniper-enhanced;
        juniper-enhanced {
            cache {
                timeout 120;
            }
            profile Websense {
```

```
                site-reputation-action {
                    very-safe permit;
                    moderately-safe block;
                    fairly-safe block;
                    suspicious block;
                    harmful block;
                }
                default permit;
                fallback-settings {
                    default log-and-permit;
                    server-connectivity log-and-permit;
                    timeout log-and-permit;
                    too-many-requests log-and-permit;
                }
                block-message {
                    type custom-redirect-url;
                    url http://192.168.1.70/blocked-request.html;
                }
            }
        }
    }
    anti-spam {
        sbl {
            profile AS {
                spam-action tag-subject;
                custom-tag-string "SPAM Detected";
            }
        }
    }
}
utm-policy Protect-Clients {
    anti-virus {
        http-profile Sophos;
    }
    web-filtering {
        http-profile Websense;
    }
}
utm-policy Email-Inspection {
    anti-virus {
        smtp-profile Sophos;
    }
    anti-spam {
        smtp-profile AS;
    }
}


{primary:node0}[edit]
root@SRX550-Node0# show security address-book
global {
    address Internal-Clients 1.1.1.0/24;
```

```
    address Internal-Clients-192.168.1.0/24 192.168.1.0/24;
    address SMTP-Server-2.2.2.50/32 2.2.2.50/32;
}

{primary:node0}[edit]
root@SRX550-Node0# show security policies
from-zone LAN to-zone Internet {
    policy Client-Outbound {
        match {
            source-address Internal-Clients-192.168.1.0/24;
            destination-address any;
            application junos-http;
        }
        then {
            permit {
                application-services {
                    utm-policy Protect-Clients;
                }
            }
            log {
                session-close;
            }
        }
    }
}
from-zone Internet to-zone DMZ {
    policy SMTP-Inbound {
        match {
            source-address any;
            destination-address SMTP-Server-2.2.2.50/32;
            application junos-smtp;
        }
        then {
            permit {
                application-services {
                    utm-policy Email-Inspection;
                }
            }
            log {
                session-close;
            }
        }
    }
}
```

Summary

In this chapter, we explored the far reaches of the UTM feature set implemented in the SRX. Each of the different UTM technologies along with the different flavors implemented were discussed, along with some guidance on selecting the correct implementation for your specific case. With this knowledge, you should be able to successfully deploy the SRX in your network, leveraging the UTM technologies to more effectively protect your client and server infrastructure from malware threats, along with controlling user activities to ensure that they are in compliance with your organizational policies. As malicious threats continue to evolve in the future, it will be essential to layer all of the protective defenses that you can possibly leverage to protect your resources and infrastructure. UTM on the perimeter and internal environment will certainly be a component of this overall defense in-depth approach.

Study Questions

Questions

1. What is the difference between antivirus and intrusion prevention on the SRX?
2. Which antivirus solution offered by the SRX can do URI reputation checking to determine if the resource being requested is potentially malicious?
3. Which protocols are supported by the Juniper antivirus and content filtering suites?
4. Order the three Juniper antivirus solutions from most to least expensive from a performance perspective.
5. What are the four different URL filtering techniques available on the SRX?
6. Which URL filtering solution supports site reputation scoring and enforcement?
7. What method does the SRX antispam feature leverage to detect spam messages?
8. True or False: You can have multiple antivirus or web filtering solution types enabled at the same time.
9. How are UTM policies applied to user traffic in the SRX configuration?
10. True or False: You can have different UTM policies applied to different traffic at the same time.
11. True or False: You need to apply UTM licenses to both nodes in an HA cluster.
12. True or False: You can use any antivirus technology as long as you license one of the antivirus solutions.
13. What are feature profiles and how are they implemented on the SRX?

14. Which flavor of URL filtering allows you to redirect users to a URL rather than the internal block page when a user tries to go to a blocked website?

Answers

1. Antivirus is geared toward detecting malware via transmitted files, whereas IPS is geared more toward detecting stream-based threats. Although it can detect some attacks in files and malicious payloads, it is not the strong suit of the technology, as it is stream-based versus the antivirus, which can act as a full TCP and application proxy.
2. The Sophos AV solution in the SRX supports this technique.
3. HTTP, SMTP, FTP, IMAP, and POP3 are supported.
4. Full Kaspersky, Sophos, ExpressAV.
5. Websense Enhanced, Surfcontrol/Websense Integrated, Websense Redirect, and Local.
6. Websense Enhanced.
7. The SRX antispam feature leverages an SMTP blacklist of known spamming servers.
8. False. You can have both antivirus and web filtering enabled concurrently, but only one type each can be used. For instance, you can run Sophos AV and Enhanced Web Filtering, but you can't run both Sophos AV and Kaspersky AV, or Enhanced Websense and Websense Redirect concurrently.
9. UTM policies are applied to firewall traffic on a firewall rule-by-rule basis.
10. True: The system allows you to have multiple UTM policies applied to different firewall rules at the same time.
11. True.
12. False.
13. Feature profiles define how an individual UTM feature should behave. They are specific to not only the UTM technology, but also the specific flavor of the solution (e.g., Sophos is different than Kaspersky). Each feature profile is applied to the UTM policies, and can be done on a protocol-by-protocol basis if that technology has multiple protocol support like AV and content filtering.
14. Websense Enhanced.

Index

Symbols

A

We'd like to hear your suggestions for improving our indexes. Send email to index@oreilly.com.

B

C

D

E

F

G

H

I

J

K

L

M

N

O

P

Q

R

S

T

U

V

W

X

Y

Z

About the Authors

Brad Woodberg is a product line engineer at Juniper Networks. He is JNCIE-M, JNCIE-SEC, JNCIS-FWV, JNCIS-SSL, JNCIA-IDP, JNCIA-EX, JNCIA-UAC, CCNP R&S and holds a bachelor's degree in computer engineering from Michigan State University. Before joining Juniper Networks, he spent four and a half years working at a Juniper reseller where he designed, deployed, supported, and managed computer networks worldwide with equipment from a variety of vendors. In addition to being a co-author of *Junos Security*, he is a coauthor of *Configuring Juniper Networks NetScreen and SSG Firewalls* and *Juniper Networks Secure SSL VPN*, both published by Syngress.

Rob Cameron is a director of product line engineering for the Security division at Juniper Networks. In his 10-plus-year career, he has held positions as a security reseller, service provider engineer, and security consultant. For the past five years, he has worked for Juniper Networks as a systems engineer, a data center architect, and a technical marketing engineer. He is the primary author of the books *Junos Security*, *Configuring NetScreen Firewalls* and *Configuring NetScreen and SSG Firewalls*, the last two both published by Syngress. He is also a contributing author of *Security Interviews Exposed* and *The Best Damn Firewall Book Period*, Second Edition (also published by Syngress), and has been a technical reviewer for any number of professional publications.

Colophon

The animal on the cover of *Juniper SRX Series* is the Spot-fin porcupinefish (*Diodon hystrix*). The porcupinefish is a close relative of the pufferfish family *Tetraodontidae*, which are commonly served as the Japanese delicacy Fugu. Like its famous relative, the porcupinefish secretes a poison thought to be tetradotoxin and can inflate itself to three times its normal size when threatened.

The porcupinefish has a short, round body and a mouth whose teeth are fused into two beak-like plates, making it easier for the porcupinefish to crush the shellfish it normally feeds on. It is grayish tan with black spots and is covered in small spines. It inhabits tropical areas in the Atlantic, Pacific, and Indian oceans. The porcupinefish begins its life floating in the open ocean, where it is often found near sargassum seaweed, along with thousands of sibling larvae. Young fish swim toward land and the adult fish spend the rest of their lives in shallow waters (3–20 meters below sea level). If eaten, the porcupinefish can sometimes escape by inflating itself in the throat of a predator.

The cover image is of unknown origin. The cover font is Adobe ITC Garamond. The text font is Adobe Minion Pro; the heading font is Adobe Myriad Condensed; and the code font is Dalton Maag's Ubuntu Mono.

Milton Keynes UK
Ingram Content Group UK Ltd.
UKHW050001041024
449168UK00007B/182